W9-CQK-847

LET'S GO

■ THE RESOURCE FOR THE INDEPENDENT TRAVELER

"The guides are aimed not only at young budget travelers but at the indepedent traveler; a sort of streetwise cookbook for traveling alone."

—The New York Times

"Unbeatable; good sight-seeing advice; up-to-date info on restaurants, hotels, and inns; a commitment to money-saving travel; and a wry style that brightens nearly every page."

—The Washington Post

"Lighthearted and sophisticated, informative and fun to read. [Let's Go] helps the novice traveler navigate like a knowledgeable old hand."

—Atlanta Journal-Constitution

"A world-wise traveling companion—always ready with friendly advice and helpful hints, all sprinkled with a bit of wit."

—The Philadelphia Inquirer

■ THE BEST TRAVEL BARGAINS IN YOUR PRICE RANGE

"All the dirt, dirt cheap."

—People

"Anything you need to know about budget traveling is detailed in this book."
—The Chicago Sun-Times

"Let's Go follows the creed that you don't have to toss your life's savings to the wind to travel—unless you want to."

—The Salt Lake Tribune

■ REAL ADVICE FOR REAL EXPERIENCES

er-packed bus and lunar-

LET'S GO PUBLICATIONS

TRAVEL GUIDES

Alaska & the Pacific Northwest 2003
Australia 2003
Austria & Switzerland 2003
Britain & Ireland 2003
California 2003
Central America 8th edition
Chile 1st edition **NEW TITLE**
China 4th edition
Costa Rica 1st edition **NEW TITLE**
Eastern Europe 2003
Egypt 2nd edition
Europe 2003
France 2003
Germany 2003
Greece 2003
Hawaii 2003 **NEW TITLE**
India & Nepal 7th edition
Ireland 2003
Israel 4th edition
Italy 2003
Mexico 19th edition
Middle East 4th edition
New Zealand 6th edition
Peru, Ecuador & Bolivia 3rd edition
South Africa 5th edition
Southeast Asia 8th edition
Southwest USA 2003

CITY GUIDES

Amsterdam 2003
Barcelona 2003
Boston 2003
London 2003
New York City 2003
Paris 2003
Rome 2003
San Francisco 2003
Washington, D.C. 2003

MAP GUIDES

Amsterdam
Berlin
Boston
Chicago
Dublin
Florence
Hong Kong
London
Los Angeles
Madrid
New Orleans
New York City
Paris
Prague

LET'S GO

CALIFORNIA
2003

NITIN SHAH EDITOR
ARIEL FOX ASSOCIATE EDITOR

RESEARCHER-WRITERS
SARA CLARK
ELIZA DICK
JAMES KEARNEY
KEVIN YIP

MATTHEW HARTZELL MAP EDITOR
HARRIETT GREEN MANAGING EDITOR
ANKUR GHOSH TYPESETTER

ST. MARTIN'S PRESS ✷ NEW YORK

Maps by David Lindroth copyright © 2003 by St. Martin's Press.

Distributed outside the USA and Canada by Macmillan.

ISBN: 0-312-30567-2

First edition
10 9 8 7 6 5 4 3 2 1

Let's Go: California is written by Let's Go Publications, 67 Mount Auburn Street, Cambridge, MA 02138, USA.

WHO WE ARE

A NEW LET'S GO FOR 2003

With a sleeker look and innovative new content, we have revamped the entire series to reflect more than ever the needs and interests of the independent traveler. Here are just some of the improvements you will notice when traveling with the new *Let's Go*.

MORE PRICE OPTIONS

Still the best resource for budget travelers, *Let's Go* recognizes that everyone needs the occassional indulgence. Our "Big Splurges" indicate establishments that are actually worth those extra pennies (pulas, pesos, or pounds), and price-level symbols (❶ ❷ ❸ ❹ ❺) allow you to quickly determine whether an accommodation or restaurant will break the bank. We may have diversified, but we'll never lose our budget focus—"Hidden Deals" reveal the best-kept travel secrets.

BEYOND THE TOURIST EXPERIENCE

Our Alternatives to Touism chapter offers ideas on immersing yourself in a new community through study, work, or volunteering.

AN INSIDER'S PERSPECTIVE

As always, every item is written and researched by our on-site writers. This year we have highlighted more viewpoints to help you gain an even more thorough understanding of the places you are visiting.

IN RECENT NEWS. *Let's Go* correspondents around the globe report back on current regional issues that may affect you as a traveler.

CONTRIBUTING WRITERS. Respected scholars and former *Let's Go* writers discuss topics on society and culture, going into greater depth than the usual guidebook summary.

THE LOCAL STORY. From the Parisian monk toting a cell phone to the Russian *babushka* confronting capitalism, *Let's Go* shares its revealing conversations with local personalities—a unique glimpse of what matters to real people.

FROM THE ROAD. Always helpful and sometimes downright hilarious, our researchers share useful insights on the typical (and atypical) travel experience.

SLIMMER SIZE

Don't be fooled by our new, smaller size. *Let's Go* is still packed with invaluable travel advice, but now it's easier to carry with a more compact design.

FORTY-THREE YEARS OF WISDOM

For over four decades *Let's Go* has provided the most up-to-date information on the hippest cafes, the most pristine beaches, and the best routes from border to border. It all started in 1960 when a few well-traveled students at Harvard University handed out a 20-page mimeographed pamphlet of their tips on budget travel to passengers on student charter flights to Europe. From humble beginnings, *Let's Go* has grown to cover six continents and *Let's Go: Europe* still reigns as the world's best-selling travel guide. This year we've beefed up our coverage of Latin America with *Let's Go: Costa Rica* and *Let's Go: Chile;* on the other side of the globe, we've added *Let's Go: Thailand* and *Let's Go: Hawaii.* Our new guides bring the total number of titles to 61, each infused with the spirit of adventure that travelers around the world have come to count on.

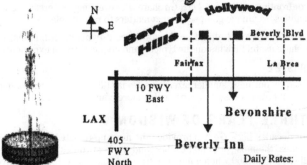

CONTENTS

HOW TO USE THIS BOOK

ORGANIZATION. The first three chapters of this book put you in a California state of mind. After that, the book takes travelers chapter-by-chapter from **San Francisco** and the **Bay Area** up Hwy. 1 to the **Far North.** From there, it's into the mountains of the **Sierra Nevada** and down through the **Central Valley** en route to the **Central Coast.** After that it's **Los Angeles, Around L.A.,** and down the ocean's edge to **San Diego** and **Baja California,** culminating in the **Desert.**

PRICE RANGES & RANKINGS. Our researchers list establishments in order of value from best to worst. Our absolute favorites are denoted by the Let's Go thumbs-up (🖑). Since the best value does not always mean the cheapest price, we have incorporated a system of price ranges in the guide. The table below lists how prices fall within each bracket.

CALIFORNIA	❶	❷	❸	❹	❺
ACCOMMODATIONS	$1-15	$16-30	$31-50	$51-80	$81+
FOOD	$1-5	$6-10	$11-15	$16-20	$21+

PHONE CODES & TELEPHONE NUMBERS. Area codes for each region appear opposite the name of the region and are denoted by the ☎ icon. Phone numbers in text are also preceded by the ☎ icon.

WHEN TO USE IT

TWO MONTHS BEFORE. The first chapter, **Discover California,** contains highlights of the region, including Suggested Itineraries (p. 6) that can help you plan your trip, whether you want to hop along the coastal cities, visit missions, or trek in the outdoors. The **Essentials** (p. 26) section contains practical information about traveling in California, including creating a budget, making reservations, renting a car, renewing a passport, keeping in touch, and more.

ONE MONTH BEFORE. Take care of insurance, and write down a list of emergency numbers and hotlines. Make a list of packing essentials (see **Packing,** p. 39) and shop for anything you are missing, like camping gear or weather-appropriate clothing. Read through the coverage and make sure you understand the logistics of your itinerary (mileage, catching trains and buses, etc.). Make any reservations for camping, hostels, hotels and B&Bs if necessary, along with any required bus, plane, boat or car reservations.

TWO WEEKS BEFORE. Leave an itinerary and a photocopy of important documents with someone at home. Take some time to peruse the **Life and Times** (see p. 8), which has info on history, culture, flora and fauna, recent political events, the entertainment industry, and more.

A NOTE TO OUR READERS The information for this book was gathered by *Let's Go* researchers from May through August of 2002. Each listing is based on one researcher's opinion, formed during his or her visit at a particular time. Those traveling at other times may have different experiences since prices, dates, hours, and conditions are always subject to change. You are urged to check the facts presented in this book beforehand to avoid inconvenience and surprises.

RESEARCHER-WRITERS

Sara Clark　　　　*Central Valley, Las Vegas, So. Calif., Baja Calif.*

Sara, a Bay Area native, set out for SoCal in her trusty station wagon, armed with her quick wit, discerning eye, and a bizarre warthog phobia. An avid rower, Sara braved the speed traps of Death Valley, the debauchery of Las Vegas, and the beaches of San Diego and Baja. And when her car got stuck in two feet of sand in the sizzling desert, Sara showed us the same tenacity that she displayed throughout her route, finding new ways to survive as a budget traveler.

Eliza Dick　　　　*North Coast, Bay Area, Central Coast*

Eliza explored the California Coast with tremendous energy and travel experience Down Under, in Europe, Africa, and the US. Eliza was always on the lookout for a new find, with great attention to places for travelers with special needs. Just as she racked up parking tickets in Santa Cruz, Eliza racked up scores of new listings so that readers will always know where to eat, sleep, surf, and where not to park.

James Kearney　　　　*Greater L.A. Area*

James applied his significant travel smarts, acquired through sojourns to Europe, Africa, and the US, to endure and thrive in the sprawling metropolis of Los Angeles. James somehow untangled the city's web of highways, hostels, and hot dog stands. And through his fantastic features and incisive interviews, James provided us with a window into the mind of the Angeleno.

Kevin Yip　　　　*Inland Empire, Sierra Nevada, Northern Interior*

Kevin, having held pretty much every job at Let's Go during his illustrious tenure, chose to head for California's golden hills this year. A one-time writer and editor of *Let's Go: USA*, former managing editor, and current web guru, Kevin swamped us with copious amounts of new hiking and camping coverage. His meticulous researching, extremely easygoing nature, and utter devotion to his craft made working with Kevin a downright pleasure.

Carleton Goold　　　　*Oregon, Klamath Falls, Lava Beds*
Shawn Snyder, Laura Spence, James Stillwell　　　　*San Francisco Bay Area*
Robert Cacace　　　　*Lake Tahoe, Nevada, Eastern Mojave, Grand Canyon*

Stephanie L. Smith was a researcher-writer for *Let's Go: California 1997* and *New Zealand 1998*. She worked as a freelancer for CitySearch Los Angeles and is now working in Hollywood as the features editor/writer for Channel One News online.

Matt Heid has researched for *Let's Go* in Alaska, the Yukon, Europe, and New Zealand. He is the author of *101 Hikes in Northern California* and *Camping & Backpacking the San Francisco Bay Area* (both available from Wilderness Press).

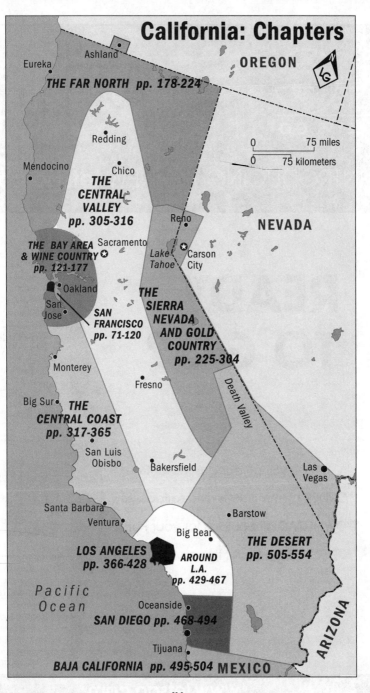

California: Chapters

OREGON

Eureka
Ashland

THE FAR NORTH pp. 178-224

Redding

0 — 75 miles
0 — 75 kilometers

Mendocino

Chico

THE CENTRAL VALLEY pp. 305-316

Reno

NEVADA

THE BAY AREA & WINE COUNTRY pp. 121-177

Sacramento

Lake Tahoe

Carson City

Oakland

San Jose

SAN FRANCISCO pp. 71-120

THE SIERRA NEVADA AND GOLD COUNTRY pp. 225-304

Monterey

Fresno

Death Valley

Big Sur

THE CENTRAL COAST pp. 317-365

San Luis Obisbo

Bakersfield

Las Vegas

Santa Barbara

Ventura

Barstow

Big Bear

THE DESERT pp. 505-554

LOS ANGELES pp. 366-428

AROUND L.A. pp. 429-467

Pacific Ocean

Oceanside

SAN DIEGO pp. 468-494

ARIZONA

Tijuana

BAJA CALIFORNIA pp. 495-504 MEXICO

ACKNOWLEDGMENTS

LET'S GO

CAL 2003 THANKS: Eliza, James, Kevin, and Sara, for living this book; the irrepressible Mapper Matt, for doing six times more than we could ask for; Harriett, for the sage wisdom and one-day turnaround; West B for jacking our Red Vines; and Wild Horses.

NITIN BLAMES: Ariel, without whom this book would be unalliterated and markedly less French. Harriett, for her level-headedness, and for the delightful awkward silences. Mapper Matt, for more than words can say. Chairman Dubbinwells, for horrific musical "taste" and an unfortunate penchant for hurling astronauts. Kuba the Krazy Kommie, Gov. Ewing, and Team USA, for the discourse and stupid catch-phrases. Nathaniel, Jesse, and Matt, for Mario Kart. California, divine inspiration of B-grade rock stars, hippie radicals, and all others who have touched it. Lastly, Mom, Dad, and Shefali, for everything, and then some.

ARIEL THANKS: Nitin, the "— man" (I mean boy), for trying to discern my funny looks; Harriet and Matt for dealing with us; Debbie for drinking tea and for not being some girl I didn't know when we moved in; Alex for being from Fresno; Colleen for lunching; Jane for "serious" discussions; Rach for shopping in Boston; Jeff for being the one who called; Chris for Long Island; Abi for the Taboo we never played; Subs, Fitz, Liz and Tony for knowing me before; Nathaniel for driving stick-shift; Chaiman DubbinWells; Eli and Kuba for politics; Team USA for the soap opera; Mom, Dad, and Elena for letting me go.

MATT THANKS: Those in my life who tolerated my love of maps from age 7. Ariel and Nitin, for scrutinizing eyes and bike rides. Nathaniel, Julie, and Harriett. And California, land of immense geographic diversity, and my home.

Editor
Nitin Shah
Associate Editor
Ariel Fox
Managing Editor
Harriett Green
Map Editor
Matthew Hartzell

Publishing Director
Matthew Gibson
Editor-in-Chief
Brian R. Walsh
Production Manager
C. Winslow Clayton
Cartography Manager
Julie Stephens
Design Manager
Amy Cain
Editorial Managers
Christopher Blazejewski,
Abigail Burger, D. Cody Dydek,
Harriett Green, Angela Mi Young Hur,
Marla Kaplan, Celeste Ng
Financial Manager
Noah Askin
Marketing & Publicity Managers
Michelle Bowman, Adam M. Grant
New Media Managers
Jesse Tov, Kevin Yip
Online Manager
Amélie Cherlin
Personnel Managers
Alex Leichtman, Owen Robinson
Production Associates
Caleb Epps, David Muehlke
Network Administrators
Steven Aponte, Eduardo Montoya
Design Associate
Juice Fong
Financial Assistant
Suzanne Siu
Office Coordinators
Alex Ewing, Adam Kline,
Efrat Kussel

Director of Advertising Sales
Erik Patton
Senior Advertising Associates
Patrick Donovan, Barbara Eghan,
Fernanda Winthrop
Advertising Artwork Editor
Leif Holtzman
Cover Photo Research
Laura Wyss

President
Bradley J. Olson
General Manager
Robert B. Rombauer
Assistant General Manager
Anne E. Chisholm

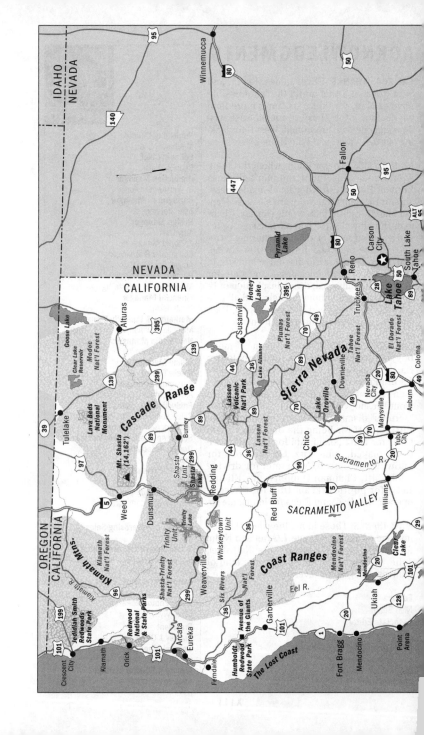

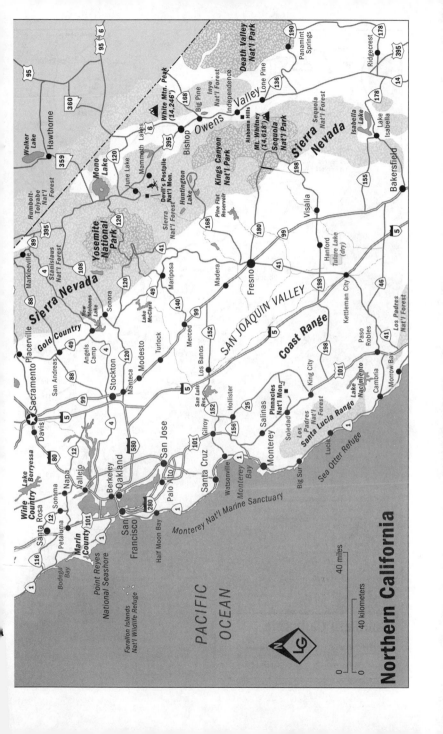

Northern California

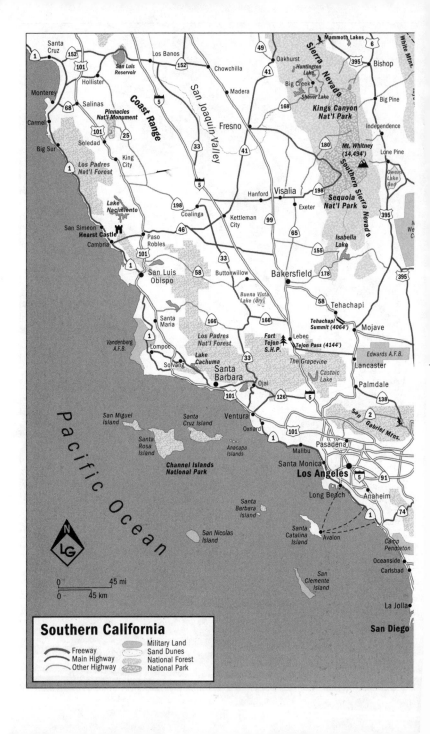

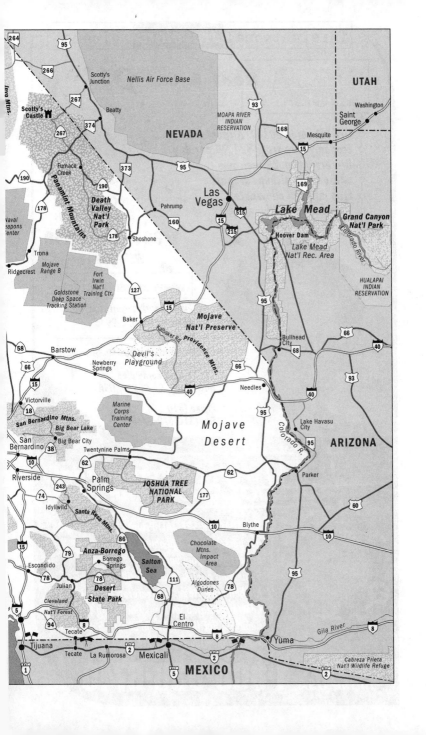

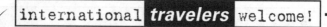

DISCOVER
CALIFORNIA

Freak Out!
 —Frank Zappa, California resident

California is a place to freak out—to redefine boundaries, identities, and attitudes. It is a land that effaces the past to experiment with the novel and unexplored, anticipating the constant changes in mass culture and channeling them into the trends of the future. Gold miners frenzied here in the 1850s, flower-children went wild in the 1960s, ambitious dot-com techno-geeks reached for the good life during the 1990s, and starving would-be actors continue to flock here by the busload. Whether it's gold, free love, IPOs, or stardom, folks still dig deep for riches, imprinting California hype, commerce, industry, art, and insanity on the collective brain of the world. Is California a beach-bumming surf safari or a battleground for well-armed gangs of urban youths? Is it a sprawling therapeutic nature preserve or a smog-filled, concrete nightmare? Is it the ultra-chic home of lunch-doing glamorites or a land of leather bars and pleather sandals? Is it a dream-fulfillment zone or simply a rock climbing, ten-hanging, adrenaline-pumping citrus-soda commercial? It's all of these, baby, and more—it is an image-making machine and a place where maintaining that image means botox, liposuction, and silicone. California is the Golden State, the drawing board for the American Dream. Leave it to the rest of the world to uphold tradition, says California—we're too busy freaking out.

FACTS AND FIGURES

Capital: Sacramento.
State Population: 30,866,851.
Length of Coastline per Resident: 2¾ in.

Length of Los Angeles Roadway per L.A. resident: 114½ in.
Length of the San Andreas Fault: 754 mi.

WHEN TO GO

The myth of California as a haven of warmth and sunshine prevails in Southern California, but fails to account for the immense climatic diversity of the state's chilly mountains, cool northern regions, and searing interior desert. Morning and afternoon fog keeps the North and Central Coast at a temperate 50-70°F for most of the year, while coastal Southern California heats up year-round, but rarely reaches an intolerable swelter. Along the coast, the summer tourist season runs from Memorial Day to Labor Day (May 26-Sept. 1 in 2003). Warm in summer (when campers flood the national parks) and mild in fall, the Sierra Nevada mountains produce heaps of snow from November through March. The Mojave Desert of the state's southern interior scorches in the summer; as in the mountain ski resorts of Tahoe, its main tourist season is the cooler period from September through March. For both the summer-oriented coast and the winter-loving interior, hostels may be cheaper and less crowded in the off-season, but some sights might be closed.

THINGS TO DO

You need something to do? You could climb a half-mile-high sheer granite cliff face overlooking a glaciated valley, or perhaps engage in smoky, hypnotic séances for faux-eastern religious cults in a celebrity-funded shrine. It's still possible to revive the "Summer of Love" in the City by the Bay. Spend a month in a 300 ft.-high redwood tree house with someone named Luna who has held Logging, Inc. at bay for three years, or, if corporate board rooms are more your style, pitch next summer's blockbuster event movie to a room of awed execs. Crawl past the mirages that rise from endless expanses of shimmering sand dunes and frolic in the cool waters with otters, dolphins, and blonde, bronzed beach bums. We'll show you where to start, but you have to seize the opportunities that California presents you and see them to their end. For more specific regional attractions, see the **Highlights** box at the beginning of each chapter.

CITIES

San Francisco (p. 71) and Los Angeles (p. 366), California's primary urban centers, are separated by 419 mi. and a great environmental and cultural divide. They are at opposite poles of California's vast spectrum of climate, landscape, social and political orientation, and lifestyle. The state pits the sprawling L.A. Basin against the great San Francisco Bay, the land of sunshine against the city of fog, the home of freeway lovers against the haunt of ecofreaks, and the workplace of painfully hip media moguls against that of painfully otherwise dot-com execs. L.A. showcases Hollywood, the manufacturer of screen idols, while the Bay nurtures Berkeley, the breeding ground for iconoclasm. Most people tend to gravitate toward one city or the other, but love them or hate them, both are too flavorful not to be tried.

SAN FRANCISCO. San Francisco evokes images of antique cable cars trundling over rolling hills, of pastel houses and earthy hippies, of the sweeping Golden Gate Bridge and ominous Alcatraz Island. As iconic and beautiful as it is, San Francisco is also wacky and unusual. It has inspired its residents to tread off the beaten path, from beatniks and hippies in the **Haight-Ashbury** (p. 110) to Ansel Adams and Imogen Cunningham, whose works show at museums in **SoMa** (p. 100). The city's artistic innovation continues to this day with experimental dance, music, and exhibitions at **Fort Mason** (p. 108) and the **Yerba Buena Center for the Arts** (p. 100). Even the graceful Victorians are given a zany (and very pretty) new life when painted all the colors of the rainbow in the **Castro** district (p. 99), a gay mecca. Vibrant Chicano and Asian-American communities assure an excellent array of delectable dining (p. 88) in the **Mission, Chinatown,** and **Japantown** districts. Parkland, from the **Presidio** (p. 94) to **Golden Gate Park** (p. 97), swaths the city in green, providing dramatic vistas and mellow lounge space.

LOS ANGELES. As the purveyor of much of the world's mass media, L.A.—where every waitress has a headshot and every valet parker a screenplay—holds a special place in the aspirations of many. Thousands head to Hollywood each year to "make it." Most never do, but vacationers can revel in the glitz and glamour that is Hollywood without sacrificing job security. Host to many a movie premiere, **Grauman's Chinese Theater** in Hollywood (p. 393) often sports celebrities, who walk up and down the proverbial red carpet outside the theater. The stars still shine in the **Hollywood Walk of Fame** (p. 395), a sidewalk art display of industry greats, past and present. Unveiling ceremonies for recently added stars are a special treat. If you insist on knowing where to meet the stars and how to propel yourself into their world, check out our insider's scoop in tidbits such as: **So You Wanna Be In Pictures?** (p. 419) and **The Celebrity Tour** (p. 401). It ain't much, but it's a start, kiddo.

Once you're through with Hollywood, you can catch advanced screenings and get tickets for tapings of television shows in **Santa Monica** (p. 396) or work on that tan in the thriving beach communities at Santa Monica and **Venice** (see **Beach Culture,** p. 3). With its wealth of aspiring rock bands and comedy club kings, L.A. has some of the most happening, big time **nightlife** (p. 423) on the planet. And if the unceasing traffic jams wipe the smile off your face, take a daytrip to **Disneyland** (p. 447) to get it surgically reattached. Don't miss the churros!

SAN DIEGO. The southernmost of California's major cities, San Diego is a quieter, more conservative alternative to the tumult of Los Angeles. It hosts a wide selection of museums in **Balboa Park** (p. 480) and two of the world's best zoological habitats in the **San Diego Zoo** (p. 480) and the **San Diego Wild Animal Park** (p. 493). San Diego's beaches are great for surfing (see **Surf,** p. 4) and nurture a laidback waterfront culture (see **Beach Culture,** p. 3). It is a good base for a daytrip to the border town of **Tijuana,** Mexico, the poor man's Sodom and Gomorrah of tequila (p. 497).

LAS VEGAS. A 5hr. shot up I-15 from L.A., Las Vegas (p. 530) is a gloriously overdone sin city, filled with grandiosely outfitted gambling casinos and schmaltzy entertainment spectaculars. Catch the surreal, acrobatic **Cirque du Soleil** in action and gorge yourself at the **buffets** (p. 535) before hitting the Strip for an impassioned surge of **casino hopping** (p. 536). Near Las Vegas (p. 540), rugged **hiking terrain** complements the massive **Hoover Dam** and jet-ski-happy **Lake Mead.**

COASTLINES & TANLINES

The home of the Beach Boys and *Baywatch* offers a far wider range of coastal styles than those pop culture icons might suggest. If you want to careen along the coastal cliffs of the Pacific Coast Highway, bum with the beach bunnies on the sparkling sand, search for the endless summer atop towering waves, or trudge across stunning and secluded shorelines, California is the place to do it.

HIGHWAY 1. Stretching the length of California, the legendary Pacific Coast Highway (Hwy. 1 or PCH) lays the foundation for a magnificent coastal tour (see **Suggested Itineraries,** p. 6). On the North Coast, Hwy. 1 winds along precarious cliffs between crashing surf and towering redwood trees (p. 179). Highlights of the northern route include a meditative stroll to the black sands of **Jones Beach** (p. 186) in the Sinkyone Wilderness or a picnic on the ▓**Mendocino Headlands** (p. 181). In the San Francisco Bay Area, Hwy. 1 passes **Point Reyes National Seashore** (p. 155), where you can stop and stand high on the bluffs over a dramatic drop to the wild, whale-filled ocean. Passing the San Andreas Fault, the highway cuts across the **Golden Gate Bridge** (p. 94) and through the city of San Francisco. Along the Central Coast, the highway skirts laid-back college towns and quirky beach communities (p. 317). The precarious cliff-line crawl past forested **Big Sur** (p. 340), with a stop at **Pfeiffer Beach** (p. 343), offers unbeatable views. In Southern California, the PCH leads to hot surf spots and legendary beach bum haunts, but the most stunning stretch of shoreline is a ferry ride away at **Catalina Island** (p. 437).

BEACH CULTURE. Beach culture is the fleeting sense of laziness that rests at the confluence of boardwalks, wharves, candy parlors, and beach hostels. The beach communities begin in earnest south of San Francisco, lining the coast past Mexico.

On the Central Coast, beach communities crop up in the college towns that party between the redwood forests and the kelp forests. The waterfront in crunchy, liberal **Santa Cruz** (p. 319) has a crowded beach, a wharf under which sea lions bask, and the Boardwalk—a tacky whirligig of aging spin rides and colorful game booths straight out of the 50s. Farther south, **San Luis Obispo** (p. 347) lies near Pismo Beach, which is a more sedate sand-and-pier locale that can become a raging spring break party spot. Beneath the Spanish Revival architecture that dots its hills, ritzy ⬛Santa Barbara (p. 354) has stunning sunsets and raging nightlife.

The Southern California beach scene sacrifices the wacky students and New Age gurus of northern communities to the gods of sun and surf. In the L.A. area, carnivalesque ⬛Venice Beach (p. 398) features an eye-popping kaleidoscope of street vendors, sand sculptors, and chainsaw jugglers. Meanwhile, less frazzled **Santa Monica Beach** (p. 396) crowds with joggers and in-line skaters. Volleyball players spike balls and drinks on **Hermosa Beach** (p. 432), south of L.A. Youthful crowds flock to surf shops at **Huntington Beach** (p. 452) in Orange County and to the noisy bars and grills of San Diego's **Mission Beach** and **Pacific Beach** (p. 483).

SURF. It seems that every other town along the California coast claims the title "Surf City". Most of them are in Southern California, but the Central Coast has a few great surf spots as well. Santa Cruz sensation **Steamer's Lane** (p. 323) and the break next to the pier at **Pismo Beach** (p. 353) near San Luis Obispo rage with waveriders. North of L.A., sleepy **Ventura** (p. 442) rests by some of the dreamiest waves on the coast. Southern California is a surf safari. **Surfrider Beach** in Malibu (p. 399) is the best option near L.A. In Orange County, vets head for the mythical swells of ⬛Huntington Beach (p. 452), while beginners can test the waters at **San Clemente** (p. 454). The San Diego surf scene is equally fantastic, particularly at **Oceanside** (p. 492), Tourmaline and Winandsea Beaches in **La Jolla** (p. 478), and beginner-friendly **Ocean Beach** on Point Loma (p. 478).

WILDERNESS

California is an astoundingly diverse landscape of towering mountains, rugged coastlines, and barren deserts. The vast granite peaks of the **Sierra Nevada mountains** dominate a visually stunning landscape, while austere expanses created by dried lava flows and the natural wonder of **Mount Shasta** (p. 205) characterize the **Cascade Range** of the Northern Interior. The North Coast and the Central Coast feature jagged coastlines and giant redwood trees, while the **Mojave Desert** of Southern California is a desolate landscape of rocks and sand dunes.

HIKING. On the hike to Tall Trees Grove in the North Coast's **Redwood National Park** (p. 192), the towering forest canopy blocks off the misty sunlight and the elements, leaving hikers in quiet, cathedral-like spaces. A trek through **Lassen Volcanic National Park** (p. 199) passes the steaming hydrothermal cauldron of Bumpass Hell and the bubbling waters of Cold Boiling Lake. In **Yosemite** (p. 253), the famed jewel of the Sierra, the narrow staircases of the Mist Trail climb through the dispersed sprays and alluvial rainbows of Vernal and Nevada Falls, while the heady bliss of gazing down from Half Dome vindicates the harrowing scramble to the top. Not to be outdone by their celebrated neighbor, **Sequoia** and **Kings Canyon National Parks** (p. 274) have stunning and less crowded hikes along the Eagle Lake Trail and the easy path through Zumwalt Meadows. Even farther into the Eastern Sierra, the **Whitney Portal Trail** (p. 299) ascends the highest mountain in the contiguous US, and a trek through the **Ancient Bristlecone Pine Forest** (p. 292) in the White Mountains passes among the world's oldest living organisms. In the desert, a scramble along the Skull Rock Interpretive Walk in **Joshua Tree** (p. 520) is a great way to try out bouldering and learn about local flora and fauna.

BIKING. A bike tour of the flat fields of **Wine Country** (p. 151), the region north of San Francisco that produces some of the most celebrated wines in the world, is easy and pleasurable. In **Lake Tahoe,** bikers can take undemanding tours of the lake or get pumped on its nearby winding roads (p. 240). For those who scorn the road, **Mammoth Lakes** (p. 299) becomes a mountain bike park when the snow melts. The most daring ride starts at 11,053 ft. and heads straight down the rocky ski trails.

SKIING. While the attractions of coastal California get all the attention, the heights of the Sierras harvest some of the best powder in North America. **Lake Tahoe** (p. 235) is one of the best places to ski in California. **Squaw Valley,** host of the 1962 Winter Olympics, and the aptly named **Heavenly** are the top resorts. From Southern California, the long journey to Tahoe is daunting, and **Mammoth Lakes** (p. 299), in the eastern Sierra, is a popular alternative. Near Mammoth Lakes, **June Mountain** (p. 287) is lesser known, but well loved by those who venture to it. **Big Bear** (p. 458) provides an easy daytrip from L.A., but the skiing conditions are far inferior to those found in the Sierra Nevada. Cross-country skiers find bliss amid the winter scenery of **Yosemite** (p. 253) and **Sequoia and Kings Canyon National Parks** (p. 274).

WATERSPORTS. The waters of **Lake Tahoe** (p. 235) are the ultimate playground for waterskiers, wakeboarders, and sailors. **Kayakers** can tour tranquil, mineral-rich **Mono Lake** (p. 284) or paddle out to the Pacific Ocean's otter-filled kelp forests near Santa Cruz (p. 319), Monterey (p. 330), or San Luis Obispo (p. 353). **Lake Mead** (p. 541) and **Lake Havasu** (p. 546), just across the border in Nevada and Arizona, respectively, roar with motor boats and jet skis, while the summer sailing at **Big Bear Lake** (p. 458) near L.A. proves a more sedate alternative. **June Lake** (p. 287) is a mountain fishing hot spot, while ocean fisherman harvest the teeming waters off San Diego (p. 488) and all along the coast.

ROCK CLIMBING. Joshua Tree (p. 515) offers footholds for all levels of climbers; its most famed spots are Hidden Valley and Wonderland of Rocks. Experienced climbers tackle the famed granite faces of **Yosemite** (p. 253). Between L.A. and Palm Springs, climbers crank on Tahquitz and Suicide Rocks in rugged **Idyllwild** (p. 463). **Lake Tahoe** (p. 235) has very popular climbing sites of varying difficulty. The spectacular climb of Lover's Leap and the 90 ft. wall at Emerald Bay are two of the most popular spots. The River Gorge in **Owens Valley** (p. 290) and the Buttermilks in **Bishop** (p. 290) are lesser-known but thrilling climbs in the Eastern Sierra.

▨ LET'S GO PICKS

BEST HIPPIE-RUN HOSTEL: Point Reyes Hostel, Marin County (p. 155). Three generations of iconoclasts run this hostel on the gorgeous Point Reyes National Seashore.

BEST PLACE TO STRIKE IT RICH: Gold Country (p. 225). We'll show you how. Then head to **Las Vegas,** NV (p. 530) to lose it all.

BEST SUNSETS: Joshua Tree (p. 515) and **Santa Barbara** (p. 354) provide more than some sand and a pretty ocean view.

BEST SCENIC DRIVE: Marin Headlands, Marin County (p. 151). Ghostly, misty drive west of the Golden Gate Bridge.

BEST CHURROS: Disneyland, Anaheim (p. 447). Mickey and friends dispense these strangely addictive fried treats.

BEST CELEBRATION OF CHRISTOPHER MARLOWE'S WORK: The Oregon Shakespeare Festival, Ashland, OR (p. 219). One guy could never have written all those plays.

SUGGESTED ITINERARIES

THE BEST OF CALIFORNIA: A 3-WEEK EXPLORATION. Start in **San Francisco** (p. 71) and spend 3 days getting a feel for Haight-Ashbury, Chinatown, and Alcatraz. Then head to **Tahoe** (p. 235) for 2 days on the lake—the hiking, biking, watersports, and skiing there are all sensational. Just across the border, test your luck in Nevada's casinos at **Reno** (p. 249). For relief, the breathtaking **Yosemite** (p. 253) is 4hr. away. Spend 3 days traversing its web of trails and bike paths, or admire the scenery from the valley floor. Head back to the coast for 3 days on the Monterey Bay in **Santa Cruz** (p. 319) and **Monterey** (p. 330), taking in both the Beach Boardwalk and the renowned Monterey Bay Aquarium, leaving time for **Carmel**'s Point Lobos (p. 338) or a romp across the gorgeous UC-Santa Cruz campus. A day of camping in scenic **Big Sur** (p. 340) is a great way to experience the redwood forests. Move on to **Santa Barbara** (p. 354) for breathtaking beaches and an afternoon on State St. Next, wander **Los Angeles** (p. 366) for 3 days: see a movie at Grauman's Chinese Theater, get pierced at Venice Beach, and gawk at the Getty Museum. Don't miss the Happiest Place on Earth, **Disneyland** (p. 447), home to roller coasters, Mickey Mouse, and churros. Spend a day in **San Diego** (p. 468) to see the famous Zoo and the Wild Animal Park or hang in Pacific Beach. Head to **Tijuana** (p. 497) in Mexico for a sketchy border town experience. Return to the States for a day in **Joshua Tree National Park** (p. 515) to climb boulders or see some of California's most beautiful sunrises and sunsets. Complete your journey with a day or two in **Las Vegas** (p. 530), where excess is an art form.

GO COASTAL: A 2-WEEK TREK. This scenic drive takes you along Hwy. 1. Start off in **San Francisco** (p. 71) for 3 days in the foggy City by the Bay, spending time at Golden Gate Park, Chinatown and Haight-Ashbury, and doin' time at Alcatraz. Head inland to **Wine Country** (p. 151) for 2 days of wine-tasting and bicycle rides. Travel south to **Santa Cruz** (p. 319) for 2 days of amusement at the beach Boardwalk, visiting UC-Santa Cruz, and strolling the Pacific Garden Mall. Jaunt to **Monterey** (p. 330) for a day at the Monterey Bay Aquarium and another in nearby **Carmel** (p. 338). A day's drive through **Big Sur** (p. 340) promises big views and bigger redwoods. Don't miss Hearst Castle (p. 346) on your day in **Cambria** and **San Simeon** (p. 344). A day in **San Luis Obispo** (p. 347) allows a stop at Pismo Beach (p. 353) or the Seven Sisters rock formations in **Morro Bay** (p. 354). **Santa Bar-**

bara (p. 354) and its splendid mission are good for 2 days of beaches and shopping. From Santa Barbara, take a daytrip to **Channel Islands National Park** (p. 443) or **Ojai** (p. 364), before driving off into the sun.

CAMP, CAMP, CAMP: 2 WEEKS OF THE OUTDOORS. Hiking and camping are the best ways to see California. Even those who don't like to rough it with tent-camping can find nearby hostels or motels and experience the parks on foot during the day. Start with 1 day on **Catalina Island** (p. 437), followed by 2 days in **Joshua Tree National Park** (p. 515) for great hikes and views, including some of the best desert sunsets in the West. In winter, 2 days are well-spent in **Death Valley National Park** (p. 521), when temperatures are bearable, desert wildflowers bloom in March and April. **Sequoia and Kings Canyon National Parks** (p. 274) are a good 2-day stop for hikes through the famous California sequoia trees. The most beautiful park in California is **Yosemite National Park** (p. 253), and a 3-

day stopover allows enough time to hike up Yosemite Falls, ice skate at Curry Village, stargaze from Glacier Point, and (for the truly bold) brave Half Dome's 12hr. ascent. **Lassen Volcanic National Park** (p. 199) has excellent hikes and fewer tourists. Finish up at **Mt. Shasta** (p. 205), where you can hike around the quiet peak and simply contemplate its mystical magnificence.

MISSION IT UP: A 1-WEEK TRIP. This drive through history follows **Father Junípero Serra**'s 18th century foot trail, **El Camino Real**, which connects California's old missions. Start at **Mission San Diego** (p. 486) in the historic Old Town district, and then follow I-5 up the coast to the next stop, **Mission San Juan Capistrano** (p. 454), perhaps the most beautiful of the missions, set amongst the rolling hills of Orange County. A 2hr. drive north through L.A. brings you to the **San Fernando Mission** (p. 411), an amazing re-creation of the original 1797 structure, which has since burnt down. Drive up U.S. 101 to Ventura, where the **Mission San Buenaventura** (p. 443) is still used as a parish church. From there, take U.S. 101 north to discover the coastal serenity at **Mission Santa Barbara** (p. 360), precious Chumash footprints at **Mission Santa Ines** (p. 363), the colorful Native American frescoes at **Mission San Miguel Archangel** (p. 354), and end at the gloriously restored mission in posh **Carmel** (p. 338).

CAMP, CAMP, CAMP

- Mount Shasta
- Lassen Volcanic National Park
- Yosemite National Park
- Kings Canyon National Park
- Sequoia National Park
- Death Valley National Park
- Catalina Island
- Joshua Tree National Park

MISSION IT UP

- Carmel
- San Miguel Archangel
- Santa Ines
- Santa Barbara
- San Buenaventura
- San Fernando
- San Juan Capistrano
- San Diego

LIFE & TIMES

California has the largest population of any US state, and is the third-largest state in the nation by area, bigger than all of Italy. Its border stretches over 800 miles—from Oregon in the north to Mexico in the south. It is about 250 mi. between the Pacific Ocean on its western edge and Nevada and Arizona on its eastern border. This expanse holds both urban and rural riches—California produces more agricultural products than any other US state, although its population is over 91% urban, and only 15% of its land is cultivated. The state's massive population has a broad ethnic mix. Los Angeles has a sizable Japanese-American community, San Francisco's Chinatown is the world's largest Chinese community outside of Asia, and one-third of Mexican-Americans in the US live in California. In California, the "minorities" are the majority.

For centuries, settlers have come to California in search of the elusive and the unattainable. Spanish conquistadors saw in it the utopian paradise depicted in a romance novel, '49ers plumbed its depths for the gloriously imagined Mother Lode, and the naïve and beautiful still quest for stardom on its silver screen. Adventurers flock to the mountains and deserts, and stampedes of 2.2-child families overrun the national parks in their minivans, seeking peace among forests, granite cliffs, and lava beds. Dreamy-eyed, disenfranchised flower children converge on San Francisco's Haight Street, while laid-back tan-seekers chill out by the Santa Monica Pier. Whether it's for the sun, their dreams, or their favorite "herbal remedy," Californians are always reaching for something.

LAND

Snow-capped peaks, fertile valleys, sizzling deserts, endless beaches—California has it all. The jagged granite peaks of the **Sierra Nevada** (p. 225) mountain range dominates much of the eastern third of the state and features one of the country's most popular national parks (**Yosemite,** p. 253) and the continental US's tallest mountain (**Mt. Whitney,** p. 298). Just to the west and running parallel to the Sierras is the enormous San Joaquin or **Central Valley,** one of the most productive agricultural regions in the world. Southeast of the Valley and the mountains lies the harsh climate of the **Mojave Desert** (p. 515). While uninviting, those who can take the heat are rewarded with diamonds in the rough, including **Death Valley** (p. 521), **Las Vegas** (p. 530), and **Joshua Tree National Park** (p. 515). Finally, to the west of everything and running from border to border lies the famed California coast, immortalized by the Pacific Coast Highway, countless movies and books, and several million of the most beautiful sunsets in history.

FLORA & FAUNA

California's ecosystems vary with the state's geography. The plant life is incredibly diverse, from lush forests on the coast to flowering cacti in the Mojave Desert. California's soil also supports many forms of animal life, though the creatures swimming in the Pacific Ocean are perhaps more fascinating for travelers.

PLANTS

SIERRA NEVADA. The trademark **giant sequoias** still tower in small groves within national parks like Yosemite and Kings Canyon; they are the world's largest single organisms and are identifiable by their reddish-brown bark and enormous trunks. The trees can live for up to 3500 years—the small cones alone cling to the branches for almost 30 years. There are not many giant sequoias left, and battles are constantly being fought between developers and environmentalists over the future of the trees. Also common to the area are **ponderosa** and **lodgepole pines,** which have medium sized pine cones and golden, crackled bark. Broad-leafed trees such as **pacific dogwood** and **aspen,** with its milky-white bark, make for beautiful fall foliage. Wildflowers, like the punch-red **Indian paintbrush** and the yellow **monkeyflower,** flourish in the mountains during the warmer months.

MOJAVE DESERT. Cacti abound in this arid region, among them the brightly-flowering cholla, whose "teddy bear" variety looks deceivingly soft and inviting. **Joshua trees** are widely recognizable by their twisted, intertwined branches and upward reaching fronds. They can be found throughout the desert, and are especially abundant in Joshua Tree National Park.

PACIFIC COAST. Relatives of the giant sequoias (and just as rare), **redwoods** are the tallest trees in the world. They too have reddish brown bark, which protects them and allows them to live for over 2000 years. Grape-sized pine cones and flat needles also distinguish the trees. Moving further south along the coast, the rush-like **Monterey cypress** and **pine** are found in coastal bluffs alongside the bright orange state flower, the **California poppy.**

DANGEROUS PLANTS. Poison oak is common at elevations below 5,000 feet. The plant grows as a shrub or vine, with green, shiny, three-pronged leaves that turn red and drop in the fall. Berries are white or greenish-white. Contact with poison oak will cause an irritating red rash; wash skin or clothing immediately with cold water if contact is suspected. Itch-relieving ointments are also a good idea.

ANIMALS

Nice marmot.
  —The Big Lebowski

SIERRA NEVADA. Marmots are found high in the mountains; they are yellow-bellied 20 lb. ground squirrels who very easily become a nuisance when they chew through radiator hoses and camping gear in order to find a warm place to sleep. **Trout** swim in high mountain streams. **Deer** and other ground animals are common, and **grizzly** and **black bears** also roam the forest.

DESERT. Most desert animals are nocturnal, although during the day it isn't hard to spot **kangaroo rats** hopping across the sand or **roadrunners** (gray birds with fluffy heads and straight tails) racing away from wily coyotes and their ACME dynamite.

PACIFIC COAST. Sea lions, otters, and whales swim along California's shore. The former tend to congregate, along with **seals,** near Monterey Bay and the Channel Islands, which are National Marine Sanctuaries. **Gray whales** (or at least their tails and spray) can be seen off the coast from December to March, as they move between the Arctic Sea and their breeding grounds in Mexico. The **California condor,** with a wingspan of nine feet and a life expectancy of up to 40 years, is one of the largest flying birds anywhere. Its future existence was in question until the success of captive breeding attempts in the 1980s, and now almost fifty condors roam about California again, with the total condor population hovering around 200. Condor conservation efforts are spearheaded by environmental groups and zoos such as the ones in San Diego and Los Angeles.

DANGEROUS ANIMALS. The western **diamondback rattlesnake's** painful and dangerous bite is typically harmless. Nonetheless, it makes sense to carry a snake-bite kit, and to watch where hands and legs are going whenever trekking through snake country. Rattlesnakes are typically found in dry areas below 6,000 feet, but have been known to range as high as 8,000 feet. They generally attack only when provoked; do not try to touch or play with them. Cougars, panthers, and coyotes have lost their homes to recent development, and some roam suburban areas at night and in the early morning. Attacks on people are few, but if walking at night, carry a stick and make noise. Bears and sharks are also a concern; for info on how to protect yourself, see **Bears Will Eat You** (p. 45) and **Sharks Will Chew On You** (p. 46).

HISTORY

History? This is California—it just doesn't *do* history. Here, movie stars get face lifts and hippies rebel against tradition, plowing over the wrinkles and monuments of the past. Nevertheless, you can see the relics of Spanish colonialism in the missions and that telltale mark of Westernism—overreaching—in the failed ventures of ghost towns and gold rush monuments.

EARLY YEARS AND EXPLORATION

Before California was California, it was Mexico. And before it was Mexico, or even New Spain, it was home to 100 Native American cultures, descendants of the original Paleo-Siberian immigrants, each with their own political system and language. Most tribes were peaceful and unaggressive and survived by hunting, fishing, and gathering. The tribes lived without all but the most basic agricultural techniques before the arrival of the Europeans.

When the white men in big boats first came upon the region, they conceived of it as a fantasy world they had mapped in their dreams. Landing in Baja California in 1535, colonists under the leadership of infamous conquistador **Hernán Cortés** named the region after the mythical land full of gold and jewels in the Spanish romance *Las Sergas de Esplandian* (1510). In 1542, Spain made its first contact with the tribes of Upper California when Antonio de Mendoza asked explorer **Estévan Juan Rodríguez Cabrillo,** a Portuguese conquistador enlisted in the Spanish navy, to sail up the west coast of North America in a poorly provisioned ship manned by conscripts. His mission to find the mythical Strait of Anian failed, but the exploration party reached latitude 43° on what is now the Oregon coast.

Many more Spanish ships would follow, establishing a cultural presence that remains strong to this day, in everything from architecture to language. The Spanish began to settle the area en masse after 1769. Coastal cities like San Francisco (founded 1776) and Los Angeles (founded 1787) cropped up alongside Catholic **missions,** introduced by Father Junípero Serra.

EARLY 19TH CENTURY

At the beginning of the 19th century, Spain's New World colonies rose in revolt, and California accompanied them. In Mexico, radical priest **Miguel Hidalgo y Costilla** led the indigenous and mestizo populations in a race and class war. The revolutionaries continued even after the capture and execution of Hidalgo, gaining independence for a Mexican state that included California by 1822. With the mission system dissolved by 1833 and regulation from Mexico City ineffective, privileged Mexicans called **rancheros** dominated vast parcels of land, exerting de facto control over California. Staged "revolutionary" battles between ranchero-sponsored factions substituted for governmental checks on power.

BEAR FLAG REPUBLIC

In the following years, a steady trickle of American settlers headed west to the mythical land fancifully described as "edenic" in national newspapers, eager to build their own little houses on the prairie. Responding to the imminent threat of war between the U. S. and Mexico, those settlers along the West coast joined US Captain John C. Fremont in the **Bear Flag Revolt** of 1846, proclaiming California's independence from Mexico. The Bear Flag Republic proved fleeting, as the US soon went to war with Mexico, acquiring California in the process. In the ensuing conflict, the US forced Mexico to surrender. In the 1848 Treaty of **Guadalupe Hidalgo,** Mexico ceded half of its territory, including California and most of what is now the Southwestern US for a paltry sum.

GOLD RUSH

For the US, the timing was golden. Just as the cession became official, James Marshall discovered **gold** at Sutter's Mill near Sacramento (see **Coloma,** p. 233), and the Rush was on. The '49ers, a motley torrent of fortune seekers feverishly searching for the precious metal, flooded the region in 1849; by 1859 they had mined over 28 million ounces of gold, worth $10 billion at today's prices. This massive influx of prospectors caused the non-native population to multiply six-fold within four years. Thousands of settlers had to sail around South America, and those in wagon trains encountered savage winters and Native American attacks while crossing the Rockies and the Sierra Nevada. The most famous of the doomed would-be settlers was the **Donner Party,** forced by the fierce winter of 1846-47 into buffet-madness and all-you-can-eat cannibalism at a snowbound outpost near what is now Donner Lake in the Sierra Nevada (see **This Party Bites!,** p. 248). Following glitter-gilt fantasies, men from around the world flocked to Gold Country. Graveyards and ghost towns have long marked their passing.

Newly independent and economically booming, Gold Rush-era Californians quickly wrote their own constitution and inaugurated John C. Fremont as their first governor a full year before receiving the US Congress's 1850 grant of **statehood.** The completion of a transcontinental telegraph system in 1861 linked California with the East and put the ponies out to pasture. Industrialists founded the Central Pacific Railroad and began to lay tracks eastward, importing and grossly exploiting cheap Chinese labor. The meeting of the Central Pacific and Union Pacific Railroads in 1869 formed the **Transcontinental Railroad,** which made traveling cross-country to California a five-day venture, a far more viable option for fortune-seekers than the month-long coach ride. In the 1870s and 80s, naturalist **John Muir** eloquently advocated conservation of wilderness in the Sierra Nevada Mountains, securing the preservation of Yosemite and Sequoia as national parks in 1890.

EARLY 20TH CENTURY

The **great earthquake** of 1906 set San Francisco ablaze, destroying gas pipes and overturning stoves; the fires destroyed the greater part of the city and killed 452 people. At the same time, an oasis of glitz and gasoline began to flower in the Southern reaches of the state. In 1904, L.A. water bureau superintendent William Mulholland devised a plan to irrigate arid Los Angeles by constructing an aqueduct from the Owens Valley, 250 mi. northeast of the city. The area around the city grew exponentially with the influx of movie studios and nubile hungry young things dreaming of stardom. An extensive **streetcar system,** consisting of over 1150 mi. of track and connecting Los Angeles with four surrounding counties, reached its peak usage in the 1920s. To capitalize on the oil boom of the 1920s, Standard Oil, Firestone, and General Motors bought out and dismantled the streetcars and subways, ensuring the regency of the automobile on newly constructed freeways.

GREAT DEPRESSION & WORLD WAR II

The Great Depression of the 1930s did not deal as harshly with California as with the rest of the country; its farm income sank to half of pre-Depression levels while most other states did worse. Thousands flocked here to escape the impoverished, cropless Dust Bowl of the Southern Plains. These **"Okies"** were perceived as a threat to native Californian workers, and at times local authorities aided farmers in blocking roads against them (as depicted in John Steinbeck's novel *The Grapes of Wrath,* see p. 21). Still, agriculture pressed forward; by 1939, oranges and other produce made California the leading agricultural state in the nation. The grape industry grew following the repeal of Prohibition, and by 1940, California supplied 90% of the nation's wine, table grapes, and raisins. Just across the border, Las Vegas boomed with casinos, hotels, glamour, and sin in the 40s, following its legalization of gambling and loosening of divorce laws a decade earlier.

Three months after the December 1941 Japanese raid on Pearl Harbor, President Roosevelt gave the US military the go-ahead to remove all persons of Japanese ancestry, both American and alien, from the West Coast and relocate them to **internment camps** in the continent's interior. Some historians believe that government and public support for Japanese-American internment was based on greed for their land and resources since many of them owned sizable tracts of farmland in California. Now the internment camps are nothing but a few crumbled building foundations amid the interior wastelands, and a formative memory among California's Japanese-Americans (see **Tule Lake,** p. 215, and **Manzanar,** p. 297).

RADICAL 60S & PSYCHEDELIC 70S

After the war production boom of the 1940s, projects such as the irrigation canals and freeways of Southern California promoted even swifter expansion. In 1964, California redefined the power center of America by overtaking New York as the nation's most populous state. During the early 1960s, the surf culture of Frankie and Annette, Gidget, and the Beach Boys created a carefree, sun-loving image of California that persists to this day. Later in the 1960s, the beach party ended and waves of political upheaval began to shake the college campuses of California. In Berkeley, clashes between students and police over civil rights spawned the **Free Speech Movement,** a precursor to future student activism. Starting in 1965, Cesar Chavez led California grape pickers on a five-year-long strike of California grapes that spread into a campaign for a nationwide grape boycott. In 1967, San Francisco's Haight-Ashbury district declared a **"Summer of Love,"** and young people voiced their disgust with the Establishment by, in Timothy Leary's words, "turning on, tuning in, and dropping out."

However, violence continually marred the flourishing liberal utopianism of the radical 1960s. The summer 1965 riots in **Watts,** Los Angeles, sparked by the arrest of a black man by a white policeman for drunk driving, left four dead and almost 1000 injured. Echo riots also burst through the nation, forcing the country to recognize the severity of urban conditions and the racial tensions within. In the midst of mounting antiwar protests based at the University of California at Berkeley, the black empowerment coalition known as the **Black Panthers** terrorized white California, **Charles Manson** and the Family cult co-opted the hysteria into a series of ritual murders, and leftist golden child **Bobby Kennedy** was murdered in Los Angeles after winning the California primary of the 1968 presidential election. For the benefit of the Establishment, in the very same period, conservative Southern California thrust right-wing powerhouse (and former actor) **Ronald Reagan** into the national political limelight, electing him governor.

In the 1970s, water and fuel shortages as well as the unbearable L.A. smog forced Californians to alter their ways of life, and attitudes all around lost their earlier sunniness. Governor Jerry "Moonbeam" Brown romanced singer Linda Ronstadt while **Proposition 13**, a popular initiative limiting state taxes, captured nationwide attention. The enthusiasm died out, however, when state services were stripped to the bone, and the once-premier public education system plummeted in national rankings for lack of adequate property tax revenue. The Symbionese Liberation Army, the most prominent of a few new revolutionary groups, kidnapped newspaper heiress **Patty Hearst** and temporarily converted her to their cause. In the late 1970s, the People's Temple of San Francisco gained international focus when its leader, **Jim Jones,** poisoned and killed over 1000 members in a mass-suicide service at his religious retreat in Guyana. Meanwhile, **Silicon Valley** in the south San Francisco Bay Area (first pioneered by Hewlett-Packard two decades earlier) began its reign as the capital of the computer world and the mecca for micro-chip enthusiasts across the country.

THE 80S & 90S

In the 1980s, cellular phones jammed airways and BMWs jammed freeways. Illegal immigrants streamed across the border in greater numbers than before. A huge earthquake in 1989 leveled highways in the Bay Area, and two years later a massive fire in Oakland burned over 2000 homes. An enduring statewide drought tested sectional tensions as Southern Californians continued to tap into drying Northern California reservoirs.

The 1990s brought a new wave of racial turmoil and violence to California. In 1992, the **Los Angeles riots,** sparked by the acquittal of the four white police officers accused of beating of Rodney King, revealed a new sphere of racial violence in which Latinos and Asians were added to the tensions between white and black America. The passage of **Proposition 187,** which denied all social services to illegal immigrants, renewed questions of ethnicity and tolerance. Most of the law was eventually struck down by the courts. Meanwhile, the **O.J. Simpson** trial and the media circus that broadcast it into homes across the country revealed the gaping racial divide between black and white perspectives of the effectiveness of the American criminal justice system.

After the University of California system called a halt to all **affirmative action** programs, the general voting public passed **Proposition 209,** which outlawed affirmative action and quotas in state programs like public education and public employment. While the proposition (strongly supported by then-governor Pete Wilson) had been implemented to some degree, court injunction brought things to a screeching halt after a coalition of civil rights groups filed a complaint.

In the aftermath of all of this racial turmoil, Californians found a new way to cope: marijuana. Well, perhaps it is an old way, but the 90s brought about the most comprehensive fight for **marijuana legalization** the state had ever seen. **Proposition 215,** passed by voters in 1996, had allowed individual patients to grow and use marijuana for medical purposes only. However, the law came under a number of legal challenges, and has been stripped down considerably.

The **dot-com boom** consisted of pimply 23-year-old techno-geeks converging on Silicon Valley, forming companies containing some combination of "e," "net," and "tech" in their names, and having millions of dollars thrown at them by crazed venture capitalists still high from the fumes of their brand-new Lexus sport-utility vehicles. During the peak of the dot-com craze in the mid- and late 90s, everyone was riding high on the improvements in productivity and information dissemination that could result from the Internet and new smaller, faster, cheaper computer processors. The NASDAQ stock index kept rising and the money kept appearing magically, and it seemed for a while as though the dot-coms had ushered in a new era of steadily increasing prosperity. And, as usual, the new way of doing things was centered in the state that is all about redefining boundaries—California.

TODAY

The dot-com bubble, which seemed impenetrable for so many years, finally burst as the stock market declined and venture capital dried up in 2000. Layoffs occurred en masse, and many companies went under altogether. The crazed optimism—in Alan Greenspan's words, the "irrational exuberance"—that defined the 90s is gone. That said, the strongest, most innovative high-tech corporations in the world remain in California, and the Silicon Valley is still a hotbed of innovation.

While the dot-com boom has come and gone, political turmoil remains omnipresent in California. The most recent controversial ballot initiative to be approved by the fickle California electorate is **Proposition 22** (passed in March, 2000)—dubbed the "gay marriage ban." Prop. 22 proclaims that only marriages between a man and a woman will be honored in the state. Gay rights activists bemoan the initiative's passage as the latest attempt by religious conservatives to deny homosexuals their fundamental civil liberties, while the authors of the proposition assert that it has allowed Californians to define marriage for themselves.

In Los Angeles one thing you can always count on is a public uproar over the latest **LAPD scandal.** Details first became known in 1999, when it was revealed that officers of the Rampart Police Station—who patrolled an impoverished, mostly minority beat near downtown—were alleged to have been framing, beating, and even shooting innocent people since the mid-80s. The FBI and the US Justice Department have joined local investigators to uncover the details and explore the ramifications of the corruption. So far, dozens of officers have been implicated and relieved of duty, more than 75 tainted convictions have been overturned, and the collective psyche of the City of Angels has been marred by the embarrassing actions of its police officers.

Such foibles didn't keep the state as a whole from prospering during the last economic boom. Crime is down, unemployment is low, cities are thriving, and Governor Gray Davis (elected in 1998) continues to carefully craft his tough-on-crime, tough-on-illiteracy, liberal-yet-not-too-liberal image. Still, there are things that can annoy residents and travelers alike. In 2000 and 2001, the state went through a crippling energy crisis. Governor Davis struggled to keep his state lit and moving as Californians learned to conserve and prepare for frequent blackouts and brownouts. While the power is back on in California, state politicians and energy companies are still reeling from the fallout.

PEOPLE

California is one of the most ethnically diverse states in the US. There is now a non-white majority in the state. The state's Latino population now accounts for a whopping 32 percent of the general population, and this figure will rise to 50 percent by 2040. The population is 12 percent Asian, 7.5 percent African-American, and 1 percent Native American. Minority populations are often denser in urban areas, while outskirts and suburbs are proportionally more Caucasian. Many cities in California, particularly San Francisco and Los Angeles, house ethnic neighborhoods that provide a window into the customs and cultures of faraway lands.

CULTURE

FOOD & DRINK

The 1980s saw the rise of **California Cuisine,** a new gourmet style revolutionized by Alice Waters at Chez Panisse in Berkeley. California Cuisine emphasizes fresh and natural ingredients with strong European, Asian, and Latin American influences. The more pretentious restaurants, such as Chez Panisse and Wolfgang Puck's Spago in Los Angeles, can be quite expensive. However, as always, deals can be found.

Apart from California Cuisine, the state's palate is (in)famous for its reverence of bizarre organic "edibles" like wheatgrass and alfalfa, especially in crunchy Northern California. Organic food junkies have been known to put such ingredients in sandwiches, burritos, and juices. While sprouts should only be handled by professionals, those seeking to live on the edge and do it themselves can find such goods at any organic food store (and there are many), or at **◨Trader Joe's** (☎800-SHOP-TJS/746-7857; www.traderjoes.com).

Also common are bean sprouts, tofu, and something called "pan-Asian fusion," which combines the style and ingredients of Chinese, Japanese, Thai, Cambodian, Vietnamese, Californian, and whatever else is in the kitchen cabinet. Food in the state retains a very strong Mexican influence. Particularly in Southern California, burritos and enchiladas rule the day at regional fast food places (just don't go to Taco Bell), inexpensive *taquerías*, and pricier, fancier restaurants.

CUSTOMS & ETIQUETTE

CIGS & BOOZE

California has the strictest smoking laws in the country. Smoking is banned in all public places, including transportation, bars, and restaurants. At those accommodations, residences, and offices where smoking is allowed, it is a serious *faux pas* to blow smoke anywhere near somebody else's face. It's not unusual for militant bands of nonsmokers to accost (verbally or otherwise) smokers who disrespect their "space." Before reaching for those matches, be sure to ask those near you whether they mind if you light up.

While there is no questioning that California knows how to party, extreme public drunkenness is still not tolerated. Virtually all municipalities have laws on the books for drunk and disorderly conduct. Drunk driving is also a major no-no, and merely being in a car with an open container is illegal.

IT'S ALL GOOD

Laid-back is the word in California. A strange phenomenon known as "California time" means that dinner at 6 only implies that food will be consumed sometime between 7 and midnight. It's not so important when something happens, but rather just that it does, eventually. In addition, the weekend for many begins at noon on Friday and ends at noon on Monday. Dress is generally very relaxed—during the day, shorts and sandals are acceptable for all but the most elite establishments. While you should still mind your pleases and thank-yous, manners and speech are also very laid-back.

THE ARTS

Hollywood is usually considered California's greatest gift to the arts world. Long before the silver screen, however, Monet-trained artists painted the sands of Death Valley and red-tiled missions were constructed overlooking the sea. Even as the curtain opened on the movie age, literary giants penned classic Depression-Era texts and singers crooned about the California girls. From Dorothea Lang to Blink 182, California exudes and accepts artistic expression, in every possible form.

HISTORY

ARCHITECTURE

Californian architecture has historically been connected to the conquistadors and their missionaries. In 1769 **Father Junipero Serra** built Mission San Diego de Alcala, the original Spanish outpost at the edge of the new world. The rancho adobe style with its Spanish tile and interior courtyard fell out of vogue during the Gold Rush years, but was revived with the construction of Stanford University and two-storied, open-balconied Spanish homes. Red-shingled bungalow homes with their bay windows were popularized in San Francisco. In the early 1900s, Californian eclectic architecture embraced a wide variety of styles, opening the double-doors for palatial fantasies like Hearst Castle, the **Julia Morgan** masterpiece. **Nathaniel West** best expressed the jumbled Californian technique when he noted that L.A.'s canyons were lined with "Mexican ranch houses, Samoan huts, Mediterranean villas, Egyptian and Japanese temples, Swiss chalets, Tudor cottages, and every possible combination of these styles." After World War II, Californian architecture became, for better or for worse, synonymous with tract housing, as the cities decentralized and the people fled to the suburbs. **Frank Lloyd Wright**, one of the most experimental architects of the 20th century, did his best to counteract the monotony, building geometric tributes to the human existence.

FINE ARTS

Fine art in California began as a pastime, with tourists pulling out brushes and pencils as they sat along the sea. **Guy Rose** was one of the first Californians to gain international fame as an artist—his impressionist stylings of eucalyptus trees and canyons furthered the popularity of painting out of doors. **Dorothea Lange's** 1930s photos of the working and living conditions of migrant workers helped convince the federal government to build public housing projects. Her 1936 photo *Migrant Mother* became a national symbol of the suffering caused by the Great Depression. In the mid-nineteenth century, **Clyfford Still, Richard Diebenkorn,** and **David Park's** abstract expressionist treatment of representational images stood in coastal contrast to New York's more thoroughly abstract school. Diebenkorn's 1960s *Ocean Park* series of the Santa Monica seashore can be found in many California museums. **Robert Crumb's** dementedly insightful comics about the sex, drugs, and rock 'n' roll scene in San Francisco helped fuel the euphoric introspection of the late 60s counterculture; his cartoon histories of the blues redefined the comic genre. In the 1980s, **David Hockney** gained recognition for his brilliantly hued geometrical perspectives of Californian people and places.

LITERATURE

California has been rooted in literary imagination since its beginnings—the name California was inspired by the fictional Queen Calafia, a character in *Las Sergas de Esplandian* (1510), who reigned over a land of gems and biddies in a mythical 16th-century tropic. In later days, explorers and settlers praised this heralded paradise in verse and in legend, and the literary flow began in earnest with the gold rush. Vestiges of the early California that appeared in the writing of **Bret Harte** and **Mark Twain** can still be seen in the relatively unspoiled hills and ghost towns of Gold Country. Even **Jack London,** Oakland's literary native son, spent time panning for gold and writing pastoral stories on the side. London's 1913 book *The Valley of the Moon* provides an evocative portrait of the Sonoma and San Joaquin Valleys before they were consumed by wineries and agribusiness. Poet **Robinson Jeffers** composed his paeans on the Big Sur coast of Monterey County, where novelist **Henry Miller** set up camp upon returning from Europe.

California's 20th-century urbanization gave its writers a new kind of fertile ground. **Raymond Chandler** and **Dashiell Hammett** depicted the wanderings of hard-boiled, world-weary detectives amid the seamy underbellies of Los Angeles and San Francisco, respectively. With *The Day of the Locust* (1939), **Nathanael West** probed the unglamorous underside of Hollywood, portraying lives warped into empty savagery by a culture of sham and illusion. **John Steinbeck** won the Nobel Prize in 1962 for his insightful representations of the Depression Era. In *The Grapes of Wrath* (1939), he depicted the hard life of Midwesterners displaced to California by drought with a paint-by-numbers symbolism. His descriptions of the Salinas Valley in novels like *East of Eden* (1952) recreated the land as a paradise gone astray. During the 1950s, **Jack Kerouac** and **Allen Ginsberg** combined candid autobiography with visionary rapture to become the gurus of the Beat Generation. They appropriated San Francisco's North Beach (along with New York's Greenwich Village) as a spiritual home to return to after the cross-country wanderings fictionalized in Kerouac's *On The Road* (1957). In the 70s, **Hunter S. Thompson** took the beatniks' road trip motif in a new direction with his narcotic-laden tour through Southern California's barren Mojave Desert and into the City of Sin. **Armistead Maupin's** *Tales of the City* (1978) captured a wacky assortment of characters living on San Francisco's Barbary Lane. Thomas Pynchon's *The Crying of Lot 49* (1966) "went postal" with a different sort of paranoia—potheads, technozoids, and a new slant on stamp collecting. His *Vineland* (1990), an epic mess of pop culture and political conspiracy, romps through California, self-consciously name-dropping every town from Vacaville to Van Nuys. A kinder, gentler author by the name of **Beverly Cleary** invented the *Ramona* series to delight the children of the aforementioned potheads and technozoids.

MUSIC

California's musicians have often been socially engaged: **Jello Biafra** of the Dead Kennedys finished fourth in the 1979 San Francisco mayor's race, the late **Sonny Bono** was a Republican Congressman from Orange County, and **Frank Zappa** served in the Maryland State Legislature. Zappa was also Vaclav Havel's Minister of Culture in the Czech Republic until US Secretary of State **James Baker III** (or Baker's wife, a proponent of censorship in music) forced his resignation.

In Los Angeles, the squeaky-clean **Beach Boys** and **Jan and Dean** warbled harmonized odes to sun and fun in the 1960s, matching their British contemporaries in flair, but with less appreciation for the sublime American blues tradition. The singer-songwriter movement of the 1970s **(Joni Mitchell, Jackson Browne, James Taylor)** eradicated the last traces of political advocacy from the lone-guitarist idiom it had inherited from American folk music. Audiences strained to hear as performers sang and gazed softly into their navels. Bands looking for renewed vigor found it in punk **(X)**, Mexican roots **(Los Lobos)**, or a combination of the two **(The Blasters)**.

From the 1970s to the 1990s, the dissolute tried out several iterations of life in the fast lane. Hollywood produced **The Doors** and their lizard king **Jim Morrison,** the slickly countrified **Eagles,** and the triumphant sleaze of **Guns n' Roses.** The guitar gymnastics of Dutch import **Eddie Van Halen** were epoch-making for pop music technique in the early 1980s, while hair-metal **(Mötley Crüe, Quiet Riot)** and glam-metal **(Poison)** kept the fancy costumes, but toned down rock's bluesiness to a limited number of loud, formulaic gestures.

Hippies established a nationally recognized San Francisco sound in the 1960s, as pot and LSD increased audience tolerance for long, indulgent jams grounded in Afro-Caribbean rhythm **(Santana)**, blues **(Big Brother and the Holding Company,** who launched doomed vocalist **Janis Joplin** to stardom), or folk **(The Grateful Dead).** Baby boomers mustered great enthusiasm for the **Summer of Love** in 1967, as the groovy new sound enhanced the experience of copious sex and drugs. However, the notorious killing of an audience member by Hell's Angels at a 1969 Rolling Stones concert signaled that the "trip" was going bad.

The Bay Area also pulled to prominence several bands that were less dependent on psychedelic motifs. **Sly and the Family Stone's** breathtaking utopian vision of racial integration thumped with the help of slap-bass inventor Larry Graham, and **Creedence Clearwater Revival** of El Cerrito credibly impersonated bayou swamp rats. Meanwhile in suburbia, a sinister breed of short-haired, skateboarding boys pounded punk into shape in the 1980s until it became hardcore **(Dead Kennedys, Black Flag, The Minutemen, Suicidal Tendencies).**

BOOB TUBE & THE SILVER SCREEN

Hollywood has no counterpart. Strictly a West Coast phenomenon, it evokes a bizarre mixture of disdain and jealousy from the New York entertainment world (from whose loins it sprang so long ago) as a glitzy and obnoxious, yet somehow glamorous and trendsetting proxy for legitimate art. "Tinseltown," as it is often called, exerts an increasingly influential hold over global pop culture.

The movie capital of the US had modest beginnings. Before 1910, independent New York filmmakers were continually harassed by a movie trust seeking to drive out competition. The independents moved west and set up shop in sunny Hollywood, then a sleepy sheep-raising town. From there, a quick dash across the Mexican border could foil attempts to confiscate cameras and film. Moreover, they could take advantage of California's almost year-round sun to light shots (artificial lighting had not yet been perfected).

As the balance of movie power began to shift west, the Hollywood studios instituted the **"star system."** For the first time, actors themselves were advertised and used to attract adoring fans to movie after movie. One of the first film divas was Mary Pickford, also known as "America's Sweetheart." Charlie Chaplin, Buster Keaton, Douglas Fairbanks, and that lover of lovers, Rudolph Valentino, soon attained legendary status by virtue of their appearances on the silver screen.

The 1920s witnessed two major developments: sound and scandal. "Talkies," films with sound, were introduced with Al Jolson's *The Jazz Singer* in 1927. Scandals were ushered in when Fatty Arbuckle went on trial for the death of starlet Virginia Rappe. A suspicion that Hollywood was becoming a moral cesspool led to the appointment of Postmaster General Will Hays as "movie czar." His puritanical edicts established a model that "would have suited the strictest of nuns."

Gone With the Wind was the first large-scale Hollywood extravaganza, blazing the way for other studios to utilize exorbitant budgets, flamboyant costumes, and casts of thousands. A less extravagant but equally important film event occurred in 1941, when Orson Welles unveiled his masterpiece, **Citizen Kane,** a work whose innovations expanded contemporary ideas about film's potential. In the 1950s, Cold War era Hollywood bought into the pervasive **Red Scare.** Studios **blacklisted** actors, directors, and screenwriters with the vaguest connection to communist causes for fear of their potentially seditious influence in the national media. Many blacklisted actors and actresses weren't able to find work in Hollywood for years.

The increasing accessibility of **television** magnified the scope and impact of Hollywood's image industry. In the 1960s and 70s, shows like *The Brady Bunch* gave

Americans a shared experience and collective memory of plotlines and theme songs. *Saved by the Bell* gave younger Americans a distorted vision of high school to aspire to, while *Full House* proved to the world that Bob Saget and San Francisco truly could raise a trio of girls. Competition from television studios shifted the focus of the film industry toward big-budget movies that couldn't be produced on the small-screen. *Star Wars* and *E.T.* ushered in the blockbuster age.

CURRENT SCENE

California continues to attract artistic talent; its studios and stages are full, and suburbia's garages spawn new bands daily. Digital television and worldwide movie openings allow California to imprint its consciousness on the rest of the planet.

ARCHITECTURE

The current postmodern focus is minimalist; the current king is **Frank Gehry**. Unique, unorthodox creations fight mass production with their twisting steel frames and angular plywood siding. The **Getty Center,** perched high above its surroundings, is a prime example. The architecture of vending establishments, sadly, has gone in a slightly different direction. "California roadside vernacular" is about architecture imitating life, or at least, architecture imitating produce. Hot-dog shaped hot dog stands and circular doughnut shops will remain, for a while, a roadside staple, welcoming weary (and possibly illiterate) itinerants.

FINE ARTS

California's modern creations are a mixture of styles, textures, and mediums, with artists often dabbling in set design, photography, and the more traditional studio arts. Their labors can be found in studios and galleries in San Francisco and in museums, some, like **The Oakland Museum,** exclusively exhibit Californian residents' work. **Ansel Adams** is the best-known photographer from the state—his representations of Yosemite National Park and the Sierra have graced calendar pages everywhere and are among the most recognized photos in the US.

LITERATURE

Contemporary Americana owes one of its most pervasive catch-phrases to the lonely ennui of Palm Springs's resort culture, which spawned **Douglas Coupland's** *Generation X*. Suburban ennui has been the topic of many recent literary endeavors, as has cyberculture, explored by **Douglas Rushkoff** in works like *Ecstasy Club*. **Bruce Wagner's** *I'm Losing You* shows that Hollywood corruption never goes out of style.

MUSIC

In the early nineties, to the south of L.A. blared the sounds of combative gangsta rap, whose spokesmen **(NWA, Dr. Dre, Eazy E, Ice Cube, Snoop Dogg)** spewed invective straight outta Compton at cops and East Coast rappers. **Eminem** got his start in the underground L.A. hip-hop scene. Rap and hard rock were fused into the diverse Californian late 1980s milieu by leering **(Red Hot Chili Peppers),** grooving **(Fishbone),** and leftist ranting **(Rage Against the Machine).** In the mid 1990s, Los Angeles witnessed the emergence of New Swing, a white, middle-class revival of ethnic rhythms first tapped out during the zoot suit-clad Depression era.

To the north, Oakland's rappers **(Digital Underground, Too $hort, 2Pac)** built the loping Oaktown sound on Graham's hefty bass foundation. These days, newer artists like **Meat Beat Manifesto** bring electronic music into dance clubs all over the US. Ska music, from Jamaica via the UK, found its way to the Californian suburbs in a ska-revival revival, or **third wave;** in 1997, its unvarying upbeats chased radio listeners everywhere with Orange County's **No Doubt,** featuring pop princess Gwen

Stefani, and the pseudo-punk "All-Stars" **Smash Mouth.** Despite the death of lead singer Bradley Nowell in 1996, wildly popular **Sublime** continues putting out their ska-punk-reggae in remix compilations and tours in the form of the **Long Beach Dub All-Stars.** Meanwhile, the pop punk genre finds its hero in the irreverent **Blink 182,** which crafts references to sodomy, masturbation, and bestiality into an art form.

FILM & TV

Throughout the 90s, titanic special effects pictures became vessels in which movie mavens would sink more and more cash; only massive worldwide grosses could rescue them from financial disaster. In this vein, *Men In Black*, *Spiderman*, and George Lucas' later works have blown away summer movie audiences. During this time, the mass-production of television has gone global; patriarchal adolescent fantasy *Baywatch* reigned as the world's most popular television show. Shows like *Beverly Hills, 90210* and *Melrose Place* reinforced the popular idea of California as a superficial blond place of aerobicized bodies, though *Party of Five* gave darker, less tan Northern Californians a celluloid vision of themselves. More recent shows like *Buffy the Vampire Slayer* and its spin-off *Angel* have furthered this trend, fashioning the ironic valley-girl anti-hero as they redefine the moral wasteland of L.A.

SPORTS & RECREATION

BASEBALL

It's still called America's national pastime, and with five teams in the state, baseball excites passions and intrastate rivalries in California. The **San Francisco Giants** with single-season home run king Barry Bonds thrive in their brand-new PacBell Park, which features the occasional dinger hit into the Bay. Across the way, the **Oakland Athletics (A's)** try to pull miracles—and sometimes succeed—with a miniscule payroll. In Los Angeles, the **Dodgers** and media mogul owner Rupert Murdoch compete with the Giants for second place in the National League West, as the lowly **San Diego Padres** look on from the cellar. Oh yeah—rumor has it that Anaheim (in Orange County) has a major league team too, the **Angels.**

FOOTBALL

Major League Baseball's violent and more raucous (and thus more popular) competitor, the National Football League, has three teams in California. Watch the **San Francisco 49ers** reminisce about the glory days of battling with the Dallas Cowboys for supremacy in the National Football Conference. Or go gangsta with the badboy, blue-collar, mother-beating **Oakland Raiders,** who were based in L.A. from 1982-1995 before fickle owner Al Davis moved them back. Los Angeles is devoid of professional football, since the **L.A. Rams** left for St. Louis around the same time that the Raid-uhs packed their bags and headed for the Bay. Few Los Angelinos see any incentive to make the drive to San Diego to see the lowly **Chargers,** whose odds of having a winning season have improved somewhat under new head coach Marty Schottenheimer, although this hardly says much.

There are also two big rivalries in college football. The **Stanford Cardinal** (the color, not the bird) gives the UC Berkeley (known commonly as **Cal**) **Golden Bears** their annual thrashing to great fanfare and poor pranks the weekend before Thanksgiving in mid-November. Down south, the **UCLA Bruins** and the **University of**

Southern California Trojans (and their thoroughly inebriated fans) duke it out for supremacy in the City of Angels each year in early November.

BASKETBALL

The **Golden State Warriors,** who play in Oakland, tend to park their backsides on the doormat of the National Basketball Association. Meanwhile, the **Sacramento Kings,** with standouts Chris Webber and Mike Bibby, are gearing up for another battle for the Western Conference Title. The Kings lost in dramatic fashion last season to the back-to-back-to-back NBA champion **L.A. Lakers,** who, powered by superstars Shaquille O'Neal and Kobe Bryant, tend to make their crosstown bizarro twins, the **L.A. Clippers,** look even worse than they normally do.

SPORTS WITH GOALPOSTS

"Ice" and "indoors" are two words rather unfamiliar to most Californians, but hockey, if it does not thrive, at least survives in the state. In the Bay Area, the **San Jose Sharks,** the Pacific Division champions in the National Hockey League, devour their opponents nightly during the winter. In Southern California, the **Anaheim Mighty Ducks** are the Disney Corporation's original foray into the sporting world (they also own the Angels). The Ducks compete with their crosstown rivals, the **L.A. Kings.** Efforts to popularize soccer (non-American football) are still ongoing. The **San Jose Earthquakes** and **L.A. Galaxy,** both of Major League Soccer, kick it to not-sold-out crowds all summer long.

ADDITIONAL RESOURCES

GENERAL HISTORY

Americans and the California Dream, Kevin Starr. A six-volume series of social, cultural, and political history by the State Librarian of California (Oxford University Press; 1996).

Cadillac Desert: The American West and Its Disappearing Water, Marc Reisner. A look back at how the West was won, one water project at a time (Penguin; 1993).

Bottled Poetry: Napa Winemaking from Prohibition to the Modern Era, James T. Lapsley. A detailed history of the region's growth as a grape-stomping paradise (University of California Press; 1996).

Poet Be Like God: Jack Spicer and the San Francisco Renaissance, Lewis Ellingham and Kevin Killian. An exploration of the literary world in the City by the Bay (Wesleyan University Press; 1998).

FICTION & NON-FICTION

▨ **The Grapes of Wrath** (1939), John Steinbeck.

▨ **On the Road** (1957), Jack Kerouac.

The Maltese Falcon (1930), Dashiell Hammet.

The Loved One (1948), Evelyn Waugh.

The Crying of Lot 49 (1966), Thomas Pynchon.

I'm Losing You (1996), Bruce Wagner.

FILM

For a sliver of real and unreal life in California, watch:

SAN FRANCISCO/BAY AREA

Maltese Falcon (1941). Hard-boiled San Francisco detective Sam Spade (Humphrey Bogart) mixes with a cast of shady characters in pursuit of a golden, jewel-encrusted falcon statue—"the stuff that dreams are made of."

Vertigo (1958). Alfred Hitchcock's complex tale about an altitude-averse San Francisco detective (Jimmy Stewart) and his encounter with a woman eerily troubled by the past. Features Mission Dolores and Mission San Juan Bautista in fantastic supporting roles.

Dirty Harry (1971). Housewife heartthrob Clint Eastwood plays a dangerous San Francisco cop. In 1983 sequel *Sudden Impact*, Harry impales his victim on the merry-go-round unicorn at the **Santa Cruz Beach Boardwalk** (see p. 323).

The Rock (1996). Alcatraz (see p. 105): only one man has ever broken out. Now five million lives depend on two men breaking in. Sean Connery and Nicolas Cage battle California's most famous island prison (except for Disneyland's "It's a Small World" ride).

THE CENTRAL VALLEY

American Graffiti (1973). Director George Lucas put himself on the Hollywood map with this humorous and lyrical rendering of four Modesto high school graduates' misadventures one summer night in 1962.

Psycho (1960). The Hitchcock classic, in which embezzler Janet Leigh has the misfortune to stay in a motel (on a highway between Fresno and Bakersfield) where the caretaker has dangerous, pathological cross-dressing tendencies.

THE COAST

■ **Citizen Kane** (1941). The ultimate classic, loosely based on the life of newspaper giant William Randolph Hearst. Although the film sets the mogul's Xanadu mansion in Florida, its real-world counterpart is **Hearst Castle** (see p. 346).

The Birds (1963). Birds begin attacking residents of **Bodega Bay** (p. 180) in this Alfred Hitchcock thriller.

THE DESERT

Bagdad Cafe (1990). In this offbeat comedy, a German housewife heeds the haunting siren of empty expanses. She dumps her husband in the Mojave and finds an unexpected new life at a small desert motel.

Leaving Las Vegas (1995). A tender romance starring Elisabeth Shue and Nicolas Cage set against a rich backdrop of alcoholism, depression, and prostitution.

Zabriskie Point (1970). Michelangelo Antonioni's counterculture protagonists get down and dirty at Death Valley Monument Zabriskie Point in this bizarre and revolutionary piece. Hang on for the trippy and mind-blowing climax.

LOS ANGELES

■ **L.A. Story** (1991). Steve Martin's love song to the City of Angels. He even gets to roller-blade in the Museum of Art! (See **Los Angeles County Museum of Art,** p. 404.)

Clueless (1995). Alicia Silverstone stars in this meta-fluffy movie about the lives, fashions, and social reverberations of three high school L.A. girls. The plot's similarities to Jane Austen's *Emma* flick this flick into legitimacy.

Chinatown (1974). Jack Nicholson sleuths through a creepy pastel Los Angeles. Robert Towne's script for this Roman Polanski thriller is one of the most studied screenplays in film schools. Hold your breath for the famous last line.

Boyz 'N the Hood (1991). A hard-hitting portrayal of life in the poverty-stricken neighborhoods of South Central Los Angeles. Director John Singleton's debut film.

Speed (1994). Police officer Keanu Reeves displays his sophisticated problem-solving skills by rescuing charming, girl-next-door turned bus driver Sandra Bullock and a vehicle full of passengers from a fiery death on the highways of L.A.

L.A. Confidential (1997). *Chinatown* for the kids: a 1990s retro meta-*film noir* with a sprawling plotline, super-saturated colors, and rotary-sanded editing. Not the real thing, but neither is frozen yogurt.

HOLLYWOOD

■ **Sunset Boulevard** (1950). Dark, satirical drama about a faded silent movie star in love with a cynical young screenwriter played by William Holden. Gloria Swanson, a former silent film queen herself, embodies a culture of self-absorbed decadence in her portrayal of the aging and vainglorious film star.

The Player (1991). Robert Altman's postmodern mirror trick of a motion picture. A menagerie of stars (playing themselves) and visual nods to every film ever made catalyze a cool dissection of morality in show biz.

Rebel Without a Cause (1955). Teen icon James Dean in the quintessential story of disaffected youth. Shot at Hollywood High. Catch the "remake" of this classic in the video for Paula Abdul's song *Rush, Rush,* with Keanu Reeves in the James Dean role.

TRAVEL BOOKS

Best Places to Kiss In Southern California (Beginning Press; 1996), Caroline O'Connell, Megan Davenport, and Deborah Brada.

A Climber's Guide to the High Sierra (Random House; 1993), Steve Roper.

Nature Writings (Library of America; 1997), John Muir, ed. William Cronon.

Wine Country Bike Rides (Chronicle; 1997), Lena Emmery.

SUGGESTED LISTENING

Al Jolson, "California, Here I Come" (1924).

Beach Boys, "California Girls", *Summer Days (and Summer Nights!)* (1965).

Mamas and the Papas, "California Dreamin'", *California Dreamin'* (1966).

Frank Zappa and the Mothers of Invention, *Freak Out* (1966).

Grateful Dead, *American Beauty* (1970).

The Doors, *L.A. Woman* (1971).

Joni Mitchell, "California", *Blue* (1971).

Eagles, "Hotel California", *Hotel California* (1976).

Dead Kennedys, "California Über Alles", *Fresh Fruit for Rotting Vegetables* (1980).

Guns 'n' Roses, "Paradise City", *Appetite for Destruction* (1987).

Ice Cube, "Once Upon a Time in the Projects", *AmeriKKKa's Most Wanted* (1990).

Weezer, "Surf Wax America", *Weezer* (1994).

Lithium Joint, "Encore", *Lithium Joint* (1994).

Green Day, "Welcome to Paradise", *Dookie* (1994).

No Doubt, *Tragic Kingdom* (1995).

Counting Crows, "Long December", *Recovering the Satellites* (1996).

Sublime, "Doin' Time", *Sublime* (1996).

2Pac, "California Love", *All Eyez on Me* (1996).

Red Hot Chili Peppers, *Californication* (1999).

Rage Against the Machine, *The Battle for Los Angeles* (1999).

Aimee Mann, "Red Vines", *Bachelor No. 2* (2000).

Phantom Planet, "California", *The Guest* (2002).

HOLIDAYS & FESTIVALS

National holidays are always a reason to celebrate, and even if Californians don't work as hard as the rest of the country, they feel just as entitled to a day off. Holidays are accompanied by parades and the closing of businesses and mail service. Festivals are focused events celebrating an art form or a piece of cultural history.

DATE IN 2003	HOLIDAY	DATE IN 2003	HOLIDAY
January 1	New Year's Day	September 1	Labor Day
January 20	Martin Luther King, Jr. Day	October 13	Columbus Day
February 17	Presidents' Day	November 11	Veterans' Day
May 26	Memorial Day	November 27	Thanksgiving Day
July 4	Independence Day	December 25	Christmas Day

CALIFORNIA'S FESTIVALS (2003)

DATE	NAME & LOCATION	DESCRIPTION
Jan. 1	▨ Tournament of Roses Parade and Rose Bowl (Pasadena)	Floats made entirely of roses parade down Colorado Ave. from 8-10am. The football champs of the Pac 10 and Big 10 conferences meet in the afternoon for the Rose Bowl.
late Feb.	Chinese New Year Celebrations (SF, L.A.)	Pageants, street fairs, fireworks and dragons usher in the Chinese New Year in these Chinese American communities.
May 5	Cinco de Mayo (everywhere)	Color, costumes, and mariachi bands celebrate Mexican independence throughout the state.
mid-June	Playboy Jazz Festival (L.A.)	Two days of entertainment by top-name jazz musicians of all varieties, from traditional to fusion.
June 24, June 23-24	Pride Day (SF); Gay Pride Weekend (L.A.)	Art, politics, dances, and parades celebrate diversity.
July 4	▨ World Pillow Fighting Championships (Kenwood)	Eager contenders straddle a metal pipe over a mud pit and beat each other to a pulp with wet pillows.
mid-July	National Nude Weekend (Santa Cruz)	Enjoy bands (playing in the buff) or come paint the posing models (on canvas), at the Lupin Naturalist Club.
late July	North Beach Jazz Festival	An assortment of musicians play at this free jazz festival.
3rd week in Sept	Monterey Jazz Festival	Big name blues musicians come to the Bay.
Oct.	Folsom Street Fair (SF)	Pride Day's ruder, raunchier, rowdier brother.
Oct.	▨ World Championship Grape-Stomp (Santa Rosa)	Wine-making on a massive scale in the Sonoma Valley.
Nov. 1	▨ Dia de los Muertos (SF)	Follow the drummers and dancing skeletons to the festive Mexican celebration of the dead.
Nov.	Napa Valley Wine Festival	Wine, music, and theatre for the wine critic in everyone.

ESSENTIALS

FACTS FOR THE TRAVELER

ENTRANCE REQUIREMENTS

Passport (p. 27). Required for citizens of all foreign countries except Canada.
Visa (p. 28). Visitors from the United Kingdom, Ireland, Australia, and New Zealand can travel in the US for up to 90 days without a visa, although you may need to show a return plane ticket. Visitors from Canada do not need a visa, while citizens of South Africa do.
Inoculations: (p. 36).
Work Permit (p. 28). Required for all foreigners planning to work in the US.
Driving Permit (p. 59). Required for all those planning to drive.

EMBASSIES & CONSULATES

US EMBASSIES AND CONSULATES ABROAD

Contact the nearest embassy or consulate for info on visas and permits to the United States. Offices are only open limited hours, so call well before you depart. The US State Department provides contact information for US diplomatic missions on the Internet at http://foia.state.gov/keyofficers.asp. Foreign embassies in the US are located in Washington, D.C., but there are consulates in California that can be helpful in an emergency. For a more extensive list of embassies and consulates in the US, consult the web site www.embassy.org.

AUSTRALIA. Embassy and Consulate: Moonah Pl., **Yarralumla, Canberra,** ACT 2600 (☎02 6214 5600; fax 6273 3191, www.usembassy-australia.state.gov). **Other Consulates:** MLC Centre, Level 59, 19-29 Martin Pl., **Sydney,** NSW 2000 (☎02 9373 9200; fax 9373 9184); 553 St. Kilda Rd., P.O. Box 6722, **Melbourne,** VIC 3004 (☎03 9526 5900; fax 9525 0769); 16 St. George's Terr., 13th fl., **Perth,** WA 6000 (☎08 9202 1224; fax 9231 9444).

CANADA. Embassy and Consulate: 490 Sussex Dr., **Ottawa,** ON K1N 1G8 (☎613-238-5335; fax 688-3101; www.usembassycanada.gov). **Other Consulates:** 615 Macleod Trail SE, Room 1000, **Calgary,** AB T2G 4T8 (☎403-266-8962; fax 264-6630); 1969 Upper Water St., Purdy's Wharf Tower II, suite 904, **Halifax,** NS B3J 3R7 (☎902-429-2480; fax 423-6861); 1155 St. Alexandre St. (mailing address: P.O. Box 65, Postal Station Desjardins, Montréal, QC H5B 1G1), **Montréal,** QC H3B 3Z1; (☎514-398-9695; fax 398-0702); 2 Place Terrasse Dufferin, B.P. 939, **Québec City,** QC G1R 4T9 (☎418-692-2095; fax 692-4640); 360 University Ave., **Toronto,** ON M5G 1S4 (☎416-595-1700; fax 595-0051); 1095 West Pender St., 21st fl., **Vancouver,** BC V6E 2M6 (☎604-685-4311; fax 685-7175).

IRELAND. Embassy and Consulate: 42 Elgin Rd., Ballsbridge, **Dublin** 4 (☎01 668 8777 or 668 7122; fax 668 9946; www.usembassy.ie).

NEW ZEALAND. Embassy and Consulate: 29 Fitzherbert Terr. (or P.O. Box 1190), Thorndon, **Wellington** (☎04 462 6000; fax 478 1701; http://usembassy.org.nz). **Other Consulate:** 23 Customs St., Citibank Building, 3rd fl., **Auckland** (☎04 462 6000; fax 478 1701.

SOUTH AFRICA. Embassy and Consulate: 877 Pretorius St. (mailing address: P.O. Box 9536, Pretoria 0001), **Pretoria** (☎27 12 342 1048; fax 342 2244; http://usembassy.state.gov/pretoria). **Other Consulates:** Broadway Industries Ctr., Heerengracht, Foreshore (mailing address: P.O. Box 6773, Roggebaai, 8012), **Cape Town** (☎021 421 4280; fax 425 3014); 303 West St., Old Mutual Building, 31st fl., **Durban** (☎031 305 7600; fax 305 7691); No. 1 River St., Killarney (mailing address: P.O. Box 1762, Houghton 2041), **Johannesburg** (☎011 644 8000; fax 646 6916).

UK. Embassy and Consulate: 24 Grosvenor Sq., **London** W1A 1AE (☎0207 499 9000; fax 495 5012; www.usembassy.org.uk). **Other Consulates:** Queen's House, 14 Queen St., **Belfast,** N. Ireland BT1 6EQ (☎01232 328 239; fax 248 482); 3 Regent Terr., **Edinburgh,** Scotland EH7 5BW (☎0131 556 8315; fax 557 6023).

CONSULAR SERVICES IN CALIFORNIA

Australia, 2049 Century Park East, 19th floor of the Century Plaza Towers between Olympic Blvd. and Santa Monica Blvd., **Los Angeles,** CA 90067 (☎310-229-4800); and 1 Bush St., #700, at Market St., **San Francisco,** CA 94104 (☎415-536-1970).

Canada, 550 S. Hope St., 9th fl., **L.A.,** CA 90071 (☎213-346-2700).

Ireland, 44 Montgomery St., #3830, **San Francisco,** CA 94104 (☎415-392-4214).

New Zealand, 12400 Wilshire Blvd., #1150, **L.A.,** CA 90025 (☎310-207-1605).

South Africa, 6300 Wilshire Blvd., #600, **L.A.,** CA 90048 (☎323-651-0902).

UK, 11766 Wilshire Blvd., #400, **L.A.,** CA 90025 (☎310-481-0031); 1 Sansome St., #850, at Market St., **San Francisco,** CA 94104 (☎415-617-1300).

TOURIST OFFICES

California Division of Tourism, P.O. Box 1499 Sacramento, CA 95812-1499 (☎916-322-2881, or toll free 800-862-2543; www.gocalif.ca.gov).

DOCUMENTS & FORMALITIES

PASSPORTS

REQUIREMENTS. All foreign visitors except Canadians need valid passports to enter the United States and to re-enter their own country. The US does not allow entrance if the holder's passport expires in under six months; returning home with an expired passport is often illegal, and may result in a fine. Canadians need to demonstrate proof of Canadian citizenship, such as a citizenship card with photo ID.

NEW PASSPORTS. Citizens of Australia, Canada, Ireland, New Zealand, and the United Kingdom can apply for a passport at any post office, passport office, or court of law. Citizens of South Africa can apply for a passport at any office of Foreign Affairs. Any new passport or renewal applications must be filed well in advance of the departure date, although most passport offices offer rush services for a very steep fee.

PASSPORT MAINTENANCE. Be sure to photocopy the page of your passport with your photo, as well as your visas, traveler's check serial numbers and any other important documents. Carry one set of copies in a safe place, apart from the originals, and leave another set at home. Consulates also recommend that you carry an expired passport or an official copy of your birth certificate in a part of your baggage separate from other documents.

If you lose your passport, immediately notify the local police and the consulate of your home government. To expedite its replacement, it helps to have a photocopy of the passport to show as ID and to provide proof of citizenship. In some cases, a replacement may take weeks to process, and it may be valid only for a limited time. Any **visas** stamped in your old passport will be irretrievably lost. In an emergency, ask for **temporary traveling papers** that will permit you to re-enter your home country.

VISAS, INVITATIONS, & WORK PERMITS

VISAS. Citizens of South Africa and some other countries need a visa—a stamp, sticker, or insert in your passport specifying the purpose of your travel and the permitted duration of your stay—in addition to a valid passport for entrance to the US. See http://travel.state.gov/visa_services.html for more information. To obtain a visa, contact a US embassy or consulate.

Canadian citizens do not need to obtain a visa for admission to the US Citizens of Australia, New Zealand, and most European countries (including the UK and Ireland) can waive US visas through the **Visa Waiver Program.** Visitors qualify if they are traveling only for business or pleasure (*not* work or study), are staying for fewer than **90 days,** have proof of intent to leave (e.g. a return plane ticket), possess an I-94W form (arrival/departure certificate attached to their visa upon arrival), and are traveling on particular air or sea carriers. See http://travel.state.gov/vwp.html for more information.

If you lose your I-94 form, you can replace it by filling out form I-102, although it's very unlikely that the form will be replaced within the time of your stay. The form is available at the nearest **Immigration and Naturalization Service (INS)** office (☎800-375-5283; www.ins.usdoj.gov), through the forms request line (☎800-870-3676), or online (www.ins.usdoj.gov/graphics/formsfee/forms/i-102.htm). Mail completed forms to an INS office. See www.ins.usdoj.gov/graphics/howdoi/arrdepart.htm for more information. **Visa extensions** are sometimes granted with a completed I-539 form; call the forms request line (☎800-870-3676) or get it online at www.ins.usdoj.gov/graphics/formsfee/forms/i-539.htm.

All travelers, except Canadians, planning a stay of more than 90 days also need to obtain a visa. For more information, see **Alternatives to Tourism.**

WORK PERMITS. Admission as a visitor does not include the right to work, which is authorized only by a work permit. Entering the US to study requires a special visa. For more information, see **Alternatives to Tourism** (p. 66).

IDENTIFICATION

When you travel, always carry two or more forms of identification on your person, including at least one photo ID; a passport combined with a driver's license or birth certificate is usually adequate. Never carry all your forms of ID together, split them up in case of theft or loss, and keep photocopies in your luggage and at home.

TEACHER, STUDENT, & YOUTH IDENTIFICATION. The **International Student Identity Card (ISIC),** the most widely accepted form of student ID, provides discounts on sights, accommodations, food, and transport; access to a special 24hr. emergency helpline (in North America call ☎877-370-ISIC/4742; elsewhere call US collect ☎715-345-0505); and insurance benefits for US cardholders (see **Insurance,** p. 38). The ISIC is preferable to an institution-specific card (such as a university ID) because it is more likely to be honored abroad. Applicants must be degree-seeking students of a secondary or post-secondary school and must be at least 12 years old. Because of the proliferation of fake ISICs, some services require additional proof of student identity, such as a school ID or a letter signed by your registrar and stamped with your school seal.

The **International Teacher Identity Card (ITIC)** offers teachers the same insurance coverage and similar but limited discounts. For travelers who are 25 years old or under but are not students, the **International Youth Travel Card (IYTC;** formerly the **GO 25** Card) offers many of the same benefits as the ISIC.

Each of the cards costs $22 or equivalent. ISIC and ITIC cards are valid for roughly one and a half academic years; IYTC cards are valid for one year from the date of issue. Many student travel agencies issue the cards (see p. 52), including STA Travel in Australia and New Zealand; Travel CUTS in Canada; SASTS in South Africa; Campus Travel and STA Travel in the UK; and Council Travel and STA Travel in the US. For a listing of issuing agencies, or for more information, contact the **International Student Travel Confederation (ISTC),** Herengracht 479, 1017 BS Amsterdam, Netherlands (☎ +31 20 421 28 00; fax 421 28 10; www.isic.org; istcinfo@istc.org).

CUSTOMS

Upon entering the US, you must declare certain items from abroad and pay a duty on the value of those articles that exceeds the allowance established by US customs. Goods and gifts purchased at duty-free shops abroad are not exempt from duty or sales tax at your point of return and thus must be declared as well; "duty-free" merely means that you need not pay a tax in the country of purchase. Upon returning home, you must similarly declare all articles acquired abroad and pay a duty on the value of articles in excess of your home country's allowance.

MONEY

CURRENCY & EXCHANGE

DOLLAR ($)		
AUS$1= US$0.53		US$1 = AUS$1.87
CDN$1 = US$0.64		US$1 = CDN$1.57
NZ$1 = US$0.46		US$1 = NZ$2.19
SAR$1 = US$0.10		US$1 = SAR$10.44
UK£1 = US$1.52		US$1 = UK£0.66
€1= US$0.97		US$1 = €1.03

The currency chart above is based on August 2002 exchange rates between local currency and Australian dollars (AUS$), Canadian dollars (CDN$), Irish pounds (IR£), New Zealand dollars (NZ$), South African Rand (SAR), British pounds (UK£), US dollars ($), and European Union euros (€). Check the currency converter on financial websites such as www.bloomberg.com and www.xe.com, or a large newspaper for the latest exchange rates.

As a general rule, it's cheaper to convert money in California than at home. While currency exchange will probably be available in your arrival airport, it's wise to bring enough foreign currency to last for the first 24 to 72 hours of a trip.

When changing money abroad, try to go only to banks or other establishments that have at most a 5% margin between their buy and sell prices. Since you lose money with every transaction, **convert large sums** (unless the currency is depreciating rapidly), **but no more than you'll need.**

If you use traveler's checks or bills, carry some in small denominations (the equivalent of $50 or less) for times when you are forced to exchange money at poor rates, but bring a range of denominations since charges may be levied per check cashed. Store your money in a variety of forms; ideally, at any given time you will be carrying some cash, some traveler's checks, and an ATM and/or credit card.

TRAVELER'S CHECKS

Traveler's checks are one of the safest and least troublesome means of carrying funds. American Express and Visa are the most widely recognized brands. Many banks and agencies sell them for a small commission. Check issuers provide refunds if the checks are lost or stolen, and many provide additional services, such as toll-free refund hotlines abroad, emergency message services, and stolen credit card assistance. They are readily accepted throughout the state. Ask about toll-free refund hotlines and the location of refund centers when purchasing checks, and always carry emergency cash.

American Express: Checks available with commission at select banks and all AmEx offices. US residents can also purchase checks by phone (☎888-887-8986) or online (www.aexp.com). AAA (see p. 59) offers commission-free checks to its members. Checks available in US, Australian, British, Canadian, Japanese, and Euro currencies. *Cheques for Two* can be signed by either of two people traveling together. For purchase locations or more information contact AmEx's service centers (☎800-221-7282; in the UK 0800 521 313; in Australia 800 25 19 02; in New Zealand 0800 441 068; elsewhere US collect 801-964-6665).

Visa: Checks available (generally with commission) at banks worldwide. For the location of the nearest office, call Visa's service centers: In the US ☎800-227-6811; in the UK ☎0800 89 50 78; elsewhere UK collect ☎020 7937 8091. Checks available in US, British, Canadian, Japanese, and Euro currencies.

Travelex/Thomas Cook: In the US and Canada call ☎800-287-7362; in the UK ☎0800 62 21 01; elsewhere call UK collect ☎1733 31 89 50.

CREDIT, DEBIT, & ATM CARDS

Where they are accepted, credit cards often offer superior exchange rates—up to 5% better than the retail rate used by banks and other currency exchange establishments. Credit cards may also offer services such as insurance or emergency help, and are sometimes required to reserve hotel rooms or rental cars. **MasterCard** and **Visa** are the most welcomed; **American Express** cards work at some ATMs and at AmEx offices and major airports.

ATM cards are found throughout California. Depending on the system that your home bank uses, you can most likely access your personal bank account from abroad. ATMs get the same wholesale exchange rate as credit cards, but there is often a limit on the amount of money you can withdraw per day (around $500), and unfortunately computer networks sometimes fail. There is typically also a surcharge of $1-5 per withdrawal.

Debit cards are as convenient as credit cards but have a more immediate impact on your funds. A debit card can be used wherever its associated credit card company (usually Mastercard or Visa) is accepted, yet the money is withdrawn directly from the holder's checking account. Debit cards often also function as ATM cards and can be used to withdraw cash from associated banks and ATMs throughout California. Ask your local bank about obtaining one.

The two major international money networks are **Cirrus** (to locate ATMs call ☎800-424-7787 or go to www.mastercard.com) and **Visa/PLUS** (to locate ATMs call ☎800-843-7587 or go to www.visa.com). Most ATMs charge a transaction fee that is paid to the bank that owns the ATM.

GETTING MONEY FROM HOME

If you run out of money while traveling, the easiest and cheapest solution is to have someone back home make a deposit to your credit card or cash (ATM) card. Failing that, consider one of the following options.

WIRING MONEY. It is possible to arrange a **bank money transfer**, which means asking a bank back home to wire money to a bank in California. This is the cheapest way to transfer cash, but it's also the slowest, usually taking several days or more. Note that some banks may only release your funds in local currency, potentially sticking you with a poor exchange rate; inquire about this in advance. Money transfer services like **Western Union** are faster and more convenient than bank transfers—but also much pricier. Western Union has many locations worldwide. To find one, visit www.westernunion.com, or call ☎ 800-325-6000 in the US, in Canada 800-235-0000, in the UK 0800 833 833, in Australia 800 50 15 00, in New Zealand 800 27 0000, and in South Africa 0860 100031. To wire money within the US using a credit card (Visa, MasterCard, Discover), call ☎ 800-225-5227. Money transfer services are also available at **American Express** and **Thomas Cook** offices.

COSTS

The cost of your trip will vary considerably, depending on where you go, how you travel, and where you stay. The most significant expenses will probably be your round-trip (return) **airfare** to California (see **Getting to California: By Plane**, p. 51) and a **railpass** or **bus pass**. Before you go, spend some time calculating a reasonable per-day **budget** that will meet your needs.

STAYING ON A BUDGET. To give you a general idea, a bare-bones day in California (camping or sleeping in hostels/guest houses, buying food at supermarkets) would cost about $30-35; a slightly more comfortable day (sleeping in hostels/guest houses and the occasional budget hotel, eating one meal a day at a restaurant, going out at night) would run $50-70; and for a luxurious day, the sky's the limit. Hostels usually cost $15-20 per day. Cheap motels will run you about $40, but prices rocket to $60 in season at coastal beach towns and ski resorts; the prices of campgrounds range from $5-20. Eating out will cost you $10-20 daily, but you can raid the supermarket for $5-10 per day. A rental car will set you back $35-55 per day, but you can rely on public transportation for considerably cheaper. Also, don't forget to factor in emergency reserve funds (at least $300) when planning how much money you'll need.

TIPS FOR SAVING MONEY. Some simpler ways include searching out opportunities for free entertainment, splitting accommodation and food costs with other trustworthy fellow travelers, and buying food in supermarkets rather than eating out. Do your **laundry** in the sink (unless you're explicitly prohibited from doing so). With that said, don't go overboard with your budget obsession. Though staying within your budget is important, don't do so at the expense of your health or a great travel experience.

PRICE RANGES AND RANKINGS. Our researchers list establishments in order of value from best to worst. Our absolute favorites are denoted by the Let's Go thumbs-up (🖑). Since the best value does not always mean the cheapest price, we have incorporated a system of price ranges into the guide. The table below lists how prices fall within each bracket.

SYMBOL	❶	❷	❸	❹	❺
ACCOMM.	$1-10	$10-20	$20-40	$40-80	$80-120
FOOD	$1-10	$10-20	$20-40	$40-80	$80-120

TIPPING & BARGAINING

In the US, it is customary to tip waitstaff and cab drivers 15-20%, but do so at your discretion. Tips are usually not included in restaurant bills. At the airport and in hotels, porters expect a tip of at least $1 per bag to carry baggage. Unless you are at a flea market, bargaining is generally frowned upon and fruitless in California.

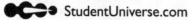

TAXES

Sales tax in California is the equivalent of the European Value-Added Tax. The sales tax rate on normal consumer goods varies by county from 7.25% to 8.5%; there are additional federal taxes on tobacco products and alcoholic beverages. Most grocery items in California are not taxed; clothing items, however, are taxed. *Let's Go* does not usually include taxes in listed prices.

SAFETY & SECURITY

PERSONAL SAFETY

EXPLORING. In California, crime is mostly concentrated in cities, but practice safety measures no matter where you are. L.A., Sacramento, East Palo Alto, and Fresno are the most dangerous cities in California, but that does not mean you cannot or should not visit them. Exercise common sense and be prepared to avoid dangerous situations; wherever possible, *Let's Go* warns of neighborhoods that should be avoided when traveling alone or at night. Tourists are especially vulnerable to crime because they tend to carry large amounts of cash and tend not to be as street-savvy as locals. Avoid unwanted attention by blending in as much as possible; the gawking camera-toter is a more obvious target for thieves than the low-profile traveler. Familiarize yourself with the area before setting out; if you must check a map on the street, duck into a cafe or shop. Always carry yourself with confidence. Be sure that someone at home knows your itinerary and never admit that you are traveling alone.

When walking at night, stick to busy, well-lit streets and avoid dark alleyways. If you feel uncomfortable leave as quickly and directly as you can, but don't allow fear of the unknown to turn you into a hermit.

SELF DEFENSE. There is no sure-fire way to avoid all the threatening situations you might encounter when you travel, but a good self-defense course will give you concrete ways to react to unwanted advances. **Impact, Prepare, and Model Mugging** can refer you to local self-defense courses in the US (☎800-345-5425). Visit the website at www.impactsafety.org for a list of nearby chapters. Workshops (2-3hr.) start at $50; full courses run $350-500. Also, carry a whistle to scare off a would-be attacker or attract attention.

DRIVING. If you are using a **car,** learn local driving signals and wear a seatbelt. Seatbelts in cars and motorcycle helmets on motorcycles and mopeds are required by law in California. Children under 40 lbs. must ride in a specially-designed carseat, available for a small fee from most car rental agencies. Study route maps before you hit the road, and if you plan on spending a lot of time on the road, you may want to bring spare parts. If your car breaks down, wait for the police to assist you. For long drives in desolate areas, invest in a cellular phone and a roadside assistance program (see p. 59). If you are testing car and soul in the heat of the California desert, take special precautions for your drive. See the detailed explanation of **Driving in the Desert,** p. 424. Be sure to park your vehicle in a garage or well traveled area, and use a steering wheel locking device in larger cities. **Sleeping in your car** is one of the most dangerous (and often illegal) ways to get your rest.

For info on the perils of **hitchhiking,** see p. 53.

TERRORISM. In light of the September 11, 2001 terrorist attacks in the Eastern US, there is an elevated threat of further terrorist activities in the United States. Terrorists often target landmarks popular with tourists; however, the threat of an attack is generally not specific or great enough to warrant avoiding certain places

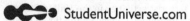

or modes of transportation. Stay aware of developments in the news and watch for alerts from federal, state, and local law enforcement. Allow extra time for airport security and remember that sharp objects in carry-on luggage will be confiscated.

FINANCIAL SECURITY

PROTECTING YOUR VALUABLES. There are a few steps you can take to minimize the financial risk associated with traveling. First, **bring as little with you as possible.** Second, buy a few combination **padlocks** to secure your belongings either in your pack or in a hostel or train station locker. Third, **carry as little cash as possible.** Keep your traveler's checks and ATM/credit cards in a **money belt**—not a "fanny pack"— along with your passport and ID cards. Fourth, **keep a small cash reserve separate from your primary stash.** This should be about $50 sewn into or stored in the depths of your pack, along with your traveler's check numbers and important photocopies.

CON ARTISTS & PICKPOCKETS. In large cities **con artists** often work in groups, and children are among the most effective. Beware of certain classics: sob stories that require money, rolls of bills "found" on the street, mustard spilled (or saliva spit) onto your shoulder to distract you while they snatch your bag. **Don't ever let your passport out of your sight,** especially near the Mexican border. Don't let your bags out of sight; never trust a new "friend" who offers to guard your bag while you are gone. Beware of **pickpockets** in city crowds, especially on public transportation. Also, be alert in public telephone booths: If you must say your calling card number, do so very quietly; if you punch it in, make sure no one can look over your shoulder.

ACCOMMODATIONS & TRANSPORTATION. Never leave your belongings unattended; crime occurs in even the most demure-looking hostel or hotel. Bring your own **padlock** for hostel lockers, and don't ever store valuables in any locker.

Be particularly careful on **buses** and **trains;** horror stories abound about determined thieves who wait for travelers to fall asleep. Carry your backpack in front of you where you can see it. When traveling with others, sleep in alternate shifts. When alone, use good judgment in selecting a train compartment: never stay in an empty one, and use a lock to secure your pack to the luggage rack. Try to sleep on top bunks with your luggage stored above you, if not in bed with you, and keep important documents and other valuables on you. If traveling by **car,** don't leave valuables (such as jewelry or luggage) in it while you are away.

DRUGS & ALCOHOL

In California, as in the rest of the US, the drinking age is a strictly enforced 21. **Never drink and drive**—you risk your own life and those of others, and getting caught results in imprisonment and fines. It is illegal to have an open bottle of alcohol inside a car even if you are not the driver and even if you are not drinking it. Non-prescription drugs of any sort are always illegal. If you carry prescription drugs, it is vital to have a copy of the prescriptions. Cigarette purchasers must be at least 18 years old with photo ID.

HEALTH

Common sense is the simplest prescription for good health while you travel. Luckily, the US has an excellent health-care system and travelers can usually be treated easily for injuries and health problems. Travelers complain most often about their gut and their feet, so take precautionary measures: drink lots of fluids to prevent dehydration and constipation, and wear sturdy, broken-in shoes and clean socks.

BEFORE YOU GO

In your **passport,** write the names of any people you wish to be contacted in case of a medical emergency, and list any allergies or medical conditions. Carry up-to-date, legible prescriptions or a statement from your doctor stating the medication's trade name, manufacturer, chemical name, and dosage. While traveling, be sure to keep all medication with you in your carry-on luggage. For tips on packing a basic **first-aid kit** and other health essentials, see p. 41.

IMMUNIZATIONS & PRECAUTIONS

Travelers over two years old should make sure that the following vaccines are up to date: MMR (for measles, mumps, and rubella); DTaP or Td (for diptheria, tetanus, and pertussis); OPV (for polio); HbCV (for haemophilus influenza B); and HBV (for hepatitis B).

USEFUL ORGANIZATIONS & PUBLICATIONS

The US **Centers for Disease Control and Prevention (CDC)** (☎877-FYI-TRIP/394-8747; fax 888-232-3299; www.cdc.gov/travel) maintains an international travelers' hotline and an informative website. The CDC's comprehensive booklet *Health Information for International Travel*, an annual rundown of disease, immunization, and general health advice, is free online or $25 via the Public Health Foundation (☎877-252-1200). Consult the appropriate government agency of your home country for consular information sheets on health, entry requirements, and other issues for various countries. For detailed information on travel health, including a country-by-country overview of diseases (and a list of travel clinics in the US), try the **International Travel Health Guide,** by Stuart Rose, MD ($19.95; www.travmed.com). For general health information, contact the **American Red Cross** (☎800-564-1234; www.redcross.org).

ONCE IN CALIFORNIA

MEDICAL ASSISTANCE ON THE ROAD

In case of medical emergency, dial ☎**911** from any phone and an operator will send out paramedics, a fire brigade, or the police as needed. Emergency medical care is also readily available in California at any emergency room on a walk-in basis. If you do not have insurance, you will have to pay for emergency and other medical care. (see **Insurance,** p. 38) **Non-emergency care** is available at any hospital or doctor for a fee. Appointments are required for non-emergency medical services.

Those with medical conditions such as diabetes, allergies to antibiotics, epilepsy, and heart conditions may want to obtain a Medic Alert membership (first year $35, annually thereafter $20), which includes a stainless steel ID tag, among other benefits, like a 24hr. collect-call number. Contact the Medic Alert Foundation, 2323 Colorado Ave, Turlock, CA 95382 (☎888-633-4298, outside US ☎209-668-3333; www.medicalert.org).

ENVIRONMENTAL HAZARDS

Heat exhaustion and dehydration: Heat exhaustion can lead to fatigue, headaches, and wooziness. Avoid it by drinking plenty of fluids, eating salty foods (e.g. crackers), and avoiding dehydrating beverages (e.g. alcohol and caffeinated beverages). Continuous heat stress can eventually lead to heatstroke, characterized by a rising temperature, severe headache, and cessation of sweating. Victims should be cooled off with wet towels and taken to a doctor.

Sunburn: It's all about having fun in the warm California sun. But with the pleasure comes the potential for pain—spending just 15min. in the bright sun can result in burns, and the sunburn-prone often burn even on cloudy days. Apply sunscreen liberally. If you get sunburned, drink more fluids than usual and apply an aloe-based lotion.

Hypothermia and frostbite: A rapid drop in body temperature is the clearest sign of overexposure to cold. Victims may also shiver, feel exhausted, have poor coordination or slurred speech, hallucinate, or suffer amnesia. *Do not let hypothermia victims fall asleep.* To avoid hypothermia, keep dry, wear layers, and stay out of the wind. When the temperature is below freezing, watch out for frostbite. If skin turns white, waxy, and cold, do not rub the area. Drink warm beverages, get dry, and slowly warm the area with dry fabric or steady body contact until a doctor can be found.

Earthquakes: Running the length of California, the San Andreas and other faults occasionally shake, rattle, and roll everything in sight. While most earthquakes are mild and harmless, stronger ones do occur in the state every few years. When you feel shaking, simply move away from any objects that could possibly fall on you; when you are indoors, duck underneath a desk or step underneath a doorway. In a car, pull over and wait for the quake to subside.

High altitude: Allow your body a couple of days to adjust to less oxygen before exerting yourself. Note that alcohol is more potent and UV rays are stronger at high elevations.

INSECT-BORNE DISEASES

Many diseases are transmitted by insects—mainly mosquitoes, fleas, ticks, and lice. Be aware of insects in wet or forested areas, especially while hiking and camping; wear long pants and long sleeves, tuck your pants into your socks, and buy a mosquito net. Use repellents containing DEET and soak or spray your gear with permethrin (licensed in the US for use on clothing). To stop the itch after being bitten, try Calamine lotion or topical cortisones. Lyme Disease is a bacterial infection carried by ticks and marked by a circular bull's-eye rash of 2 in. or more. Later symptoms include fever, headache, fatigue, and aches and pains. Antibiotics are effective if administered early. Left untreated, Lyme can cause problems in joints, the heart, and the nervous system. Ticks, responsible for Lyme and other diseases, are a particular danger in the mountains—watch out for them while camping and hiking. If you find a tick attached to your skin, grasp the head with tweezers as close to your skin as possible and apply slow, steady traction. Removing a tick within 24hr. greatly reduces the risk of infection. Do not try to remove ticks by burning them or coating them with nail polish remover or petroleum jelly.

FOOD- & WATER-BORNE DISEASES

Prevention is the best cure: be sure that your food is properly cooked and the water you drink is clean. Virtually all tap water in California is chemically treated and safe for drinking.

Traveler's diarrhea: Results from drinking untreated water or eating uncooked foods. Symptoms include nausea, bloating, and urgency. Try quick-energy, non-sugary foods with protein and carbohydrates to keep your strength up. Over-the-counter anti-diarrheals such as Imodium may counteract the problems. The most dangerous side effect is dehydration; drink 8 oz. of water with ½ tsp. of sugar or honey and a pinch of salt, try uncaffeinated soft drinks, or eat salted crackers. If you develop a fever or your symptoms don't go away after 4-5 days, consult a doctor. Consult a doctor immediately for treatment of diarrhea in children.

Dysentery: Results from a serious intestinal infection caused by certain bacteria. The most common type is bacillary dysentery, also called shigellosis. Symptoms include bloody diarrhea (sometimes mixed with mucus), fever, and abdominal pain and tenderness. Bacillary dysentery generally only lasts a week, but it is highly contagious. Amoebic dysentery, which develops more slowly, is a more serious disease and may cause long-term damage if left untreated. A stool test can determine which kind you have; seek medical help immediately. Dysentery can be treated with the drugs norfloxacin or ciprofloxacin (commonly known as Cipro).

Parasites: Microbes, tapeworms, etc. that hide in unsafe water and food. **Giardiasis,** for example, is acquired by drinking untreated water from streams or lakes. Symptoms include swollen glands or lymph nodes, fever, rashes or itchiness, and digestive problems. Boil water, wear shoes, and eat only cooked food.

OTHER INFECTIOUS DISEASES

Rabies: Transmitted through the saliva of infected animals; fatal if untreated. By the time symptoms (thirst and muscle spasms) appear, the disease is in its terminal stage. If you are bitten, wash the wound thoroughly, seek immediate medical care, and try to have the animal located. A rabies vaccine, which consists of 3 shots given over a 21-day period, is available but is only semi-effective.

Hepatitis B: A viral infection of the liver transmitted via bodily fluids or needle-sharing. Symptoms may not surface until years after infection. A 3-shot vaccination sequence is recommended for health-care workers, sexually-active travelers, and anyone planning to seek medical treatment abroad; it must begin 6mo. before traveling.

Hepatitis C: Like Hepatitis B, but the mode of transmission differs. IV drug users, those with occupational exposure to blood, hemodialysis patients, and recipients of blood transfusions are at highest risk, but it can also be spread through sexual contact or sharing items like razors and toothbrushes that may have traces of blood on them.

AIDS, HIV, & STDS

For detailed information on **Acquired Immune Deficiency Syndrome (AIDS)** in the United States, call the **US Centers for Disease Control's** 24hr. hotline at ☎ 800-342-2437, or contact the **Joint United Nations Programme on HIV/AIDS (UNAIDS),** 20 Ave. Appia, CH-1211 Geneva 27, Switzerland (☎ +41 22 791 3666; fax 22 791 4187).

Sexually transmitted diseases (STDs) such as gonorrhea, chlamydia, genital warts, syphilis, and herpes are easier to catch than HIV and can be just as deadly. **Hepatitis B** and **C** can also be transmitted sexually (see p. 38). Though condoms may protect you from some STDs, oral or even tactile contact can lead to transmission. If you think you may have contracted an STD, see a doctor immediately.

INSURANCE

Travel insurance generally covers four basic areas: medical/health problems, property loss, trip cancellation/interruption, and emergency evacuation. Although your regular insurance policies may well extend to travel-related accidents, you might consider purchasing travel insurance if the cost of potential trip cancellation/interruption is greater than you can absorb. Prices for travel insurance purchased separately generally run about $50 per week for full coverage, while trip cancellation/interruption may be purchased separately at a rate of about $5.50 per $100 of coverage.

Medical insurance (especially university policies) often covers costs incurred abroad; check with your provider. **Canadians** are protected by their home province's health insurance plan for up to 90 days after leaving the country; check with the provincial Ministry of Health or Health Plan Headquarters for details. **Homeowners' insurance** (or your family's coverage) often covers theft during travel and loss of travel documents (passport, plane ticket, railpass, etc.) up to $500.

ISIC and ITIC (see p. 28) provide basic insurance benefits, including $100 per day of in-hospital sickness for up to 60 days, $3000 of accident-related medical reimbursement, and $25,000 for emergency medical transport. Cardholders have access to a toll-free 24hr. helpline (run by the insurance provider **TravelGuard**) for medical, legal, and financial emergencies (☎877-370-4742). **American Express** (☎800-528-4800) grants most cardholders automatic car rental insurance (collision and theft, but not liability) and ground travel accident coverage of $100,000 on flight purchases made with the card.

INSURANCE PROVIDERS. Council and **STA** (see p. 52) offer a range of plans that can supplement your basic coverage. Other private insurance providers in the US and Canada include: **Access America** (☎800-284-8300); **Berkely Group/Carefree Travel Insurance** (☎800-323-3149; www.berkely.com); **Globalcare Travel Insurance** (☎800-821-2488; www.globalcare-cocco.com); and **Travel Assistance International** (☎800-821-2828; www.europ-assistance.com). Providers in the **UK** include **Columbus Direct** (☎020 7375 0011). In **Australia,** try **AFTA** (☎02 9375 4955).

PACKING

Pack lightly: lay out only what you absolutely need, then take half the clothes and twice the money. If you plan to do a lot of hiking, also see the section on **Camping & the Outdoors,** p. 44.

LUGGAGE

If you plan to cover most of your itinerary by foot, a sturdy **frame backpack** is unbeatable. (For the basics on buying a pack, see p. 46.) Toting a **suitcase** or **trunk** is fine if you plan to live in one or two cities or can store things in your car, but otherwise can be burdensome. In addition to your main piece of luggage, a **daypack** (a small backpack or courier bag) is a must.

CLOTHING

For travel in Northern California, pack layers of clothing—mornings and evenings tend to be cold year-round while days can vary drastically. A sweater and light jacket or windbreaker may be necessary even in mid-summer. From late fall to early spring, be sure to bring a rain jacket (Gore-Tex® is both waterproof and breathable) or umbrella and a mid-weight jacket or heavy sweater. Because Southern California is consistently warm and dry, you might be able to get away without much of the rain and cold gear, but be prepared for the occasional fluke cold front. Although heavy jackets are unnecessary on the coast or in the desert, pack heavy-duty gear for a trek into the snow-capped Sierra Nevadas or Cascades. Wherever you go, **sturdy shoes** and **thick socks** can save your feet. **Flip-flops** or waterproof sandals are crucial for grubby hostel showers. You may also want to add one outfit beyond the jeans and t-shirt uniform, and maybe a nicer pair of shoes if you have the room.

CONVERTERS & ADAPTERS

In the United States, electricity is 110V. 220/240V electrical appliances are not compatible with 110V current. Appliances from anywhere outside the US and Canada will need to be used with an **adapter** (which changes the shape of the plug, $10) and a **converter** (which changes the voltage, $20). For more information on converters and adapters worldwide, check out http://kropla.com/electric.htm.

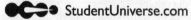

TOILETRIES

Toothbrushes, towels, cold-water soap, talcum powder (to keep feet dry), deodorant, razors, tampons, and condoms are all readily available. If you wear **contact lenses,** bring an extra pair as well as back-up glasses. Also bring a copy of your prescription in case you need emergency replacements.

FIRST-AID KIT

A basic first-aid kit includes: bandages, pain reliever, antibiotic cream, a thermometer, a Swiss Army knife, tweezers, moleskin, decongestant, motion-sickness remedy, diarrhea or upset-stomach medication (Imodium or Pepto Bismol), an antihistamine, sunscreen, insect repellent, burn ointment, and a syringe for emergencies (get an explanatory letter from your doctor).

FILM

Camera stores abound in California, offering many film and developing options. Less serious photographers may want to bring a **disposable camera** or two rather than an expensive permanent one. Despite disclaimers, airport security X-rays *can* fog film, so buy a lead-lined pouch at a camera store or ask security to hand-inspect it. Always pack film in your carry-on luggage, since higher-intensity X-rays are used on checked luggage.

OTHER USEFUL ITEMS

bring a **money belt** and small **padlock.** Basic **outdoors equipment** (plastic water bottle, compass, waterproof matches, pocketknife, sunglasses, sunscreen, hat) may also prove useful. **Quick repairs** of torn garments can be done on the road with a needle and thread; also consider bringing electrical tape for patching tears. If you want to do laundry by hand, bring detergent, a small rubber ball to stop up the sink, and string for a makeshift clothes line. **Other things** you're liable to forget to remember to bring: an umbrella; sealable **plastic bags** (for damp clothes, soap, food, shampoo, and other spillables); an **alarm clock;** safety pins; rubber bands; a flashlight; earplugs; garbage bags; and a small **calculator.**

IMPORTANT DOCUMENTS

Don't forget your passport, traveler's checks, ATM and/or credit cards, and adequate ID (see p. 28). Also check for any of the following, as applicable: a hostelling membership card (see p. 42), driver's license (see p. 28), travel insurance forms, and rail or bus pass (see p. 53).

ACCOMMODATIONS

HOSTELS

Hostels are generally laid out dorm-style, often with large single-sex rooms and bunk beds, although some offer private rooms for families and couples. They sometimes have kitchens and utensils for your use, bike or moped rentals, storage areas, and laundry facilities. There can be drawbacks: some hostels close during certain daytime "lockout" hours, have a curfew, don't accept reservations, impose a maximum stay, or, less frequently, require that you do chores. In California, a bed in a hostel will average around $15-20 per night. Many hostels require proof of foreign citizenship or international travel.

HOSTELLING INTERNATIONAL

It may be worth it to join a hostelling association for its services and the lower rates offered at member hostels. **Hostelling International-American Youth Hostels (HI-AYH)** is the largest of these associations. HI hostels are scattered throughout California, and may accept reservations for a nominal fee via the **International Booking Network** (☎800-909-4776; www.hostelbooking.com). Two comprehensive hostelling websites are www.iyhf.org, which lists contact info for national associations, and www.hostels.com/us.ca.html, which has hostels in California and other resources.

Most HI-AYH hostels also honor **guest memberships**—you'll get a blank card with space for six validation stamps. Each night you'll pay a nonmember supplement (one-sixth the membership fee) and earn one guest stamp; get six stamps, and you're a member. Most student travel agencies (see p. 52) sell HI-AYH cards, as do all of the national hostelling organizations listed below. All prices listed below are valid for **one-year memberships** unless otherwise noted.

Australian Youth Hostels Association (AYHA), Level 3, 10 Mallett St., Camperdown NSW 2050 (☎02 9565 1699; fax 9565 1325; www.yha.org.au). AUS$52, under 18 AUS$16.

Hostelling International-Canada (HI-C), 400-205 Catherine St., Ottawa, ON K2P 1C3 (☎800-663-5777 or 613-237-7884; fax 237-7868; info@hostellingintl.ca; www.hostellingintl.ca). CDN$35, under 18 free.

An Óige (Irish Youth Hostel Association), 61 Mountjoy St., Dublin 7 (☎830 4555; fax 830 5808; anoige@iol.ie; www.irelandyha.org). IR£10, under 18 IR£4.

Youth Hostels Association of New Zealand (YHANZ), P.O. Box 436, 193 Cashel St., 3rd Floor Union House, Christchurch 1 (☎03 379 9970; fax 365 4476; info@yha.org.nz; www.yha.org.nz). NZ$40, under 17 free.

Hostels Association of South Africa, 3rd fl. 73 St. George's St. Mall, P.O. Box 4402, Cape Town 8000 (☎021 424 2511; fax 424 4119; info@hisa.org.za; www.hisa.org.za). SAR45.

Scottish Youth Hostels Association (SYHA), 7 Glebe Crescent, Stirling FK8 2JA (☎01786 89 14 00; fax 89 13 33; www.syha.org.uk). UK£6.

Youth Hostels Association (England and Wales) Ltd., Trevelyan House, 8 St. Stephen's Hill, St. Albans, Hertfordshire AL1 2DY, UK (☎0870 870 8808; fax 01727 84 41 26; www.yha.org.uk). UK£12.50, under 18 UK£6.25, families UK£25.

Hostelling International Northern Ireland (HINI), 22-32 Donegall Rd., Belfast BT12 5JN, Northern Ireland (☎02890 31 54 35; fax 43 96 99; info@hini.org.uk; www.hini.org.uk). UK£10, under 18 UK£6.

Hostelling International-American Youth Hostels (HI-AYH), 733 15th St. NW, #840, Washington, D.C. 20005 (☎202-783-6161; fax 783-6171; hiayhserv@hiayh.org; www.hiayh.org). $25, under 18 free.

HI-AYH COUNCIL OFFICES IN CALIFORNIA

Golden Gate Council, 425 Divisadero St. #307, San Francisco 94117 (☎415-863-1444, travel center ☎415-701-1320; hiayh@norcalhostels.org).

Central California Council, P.O. Box 2538, Monterey 93942 (☎209-383-0686; hiayhccc@aol.com).

Los Angeles Council, 1434 2nd St., Santa Monica 90401 (☎310-393-6263, travel center ☎310-393-3413; hiayhla@aol.com).

San Diego Council, 437 J St., #315 San Diego 92101 (☎619-338-9981; hiayhsd1@aol.com).

OTHER TYPES OF ACCOMMODATIONS

HOTELS

Hotel singles in California generally cost about $35-75 per night, and doubles are $50-100. You'll typically have a private bathroom and shower with hot water, although some cheaper places may offer shared restrooms. Not all hotels take reservations, and few accept traveler's checks in a foreign currency.

BED & BREAKFASTS (B&BS)

For a cozy alternative to impersonal hotel rooms, B&Bs (private homes with rooms available to travelers) range from the acceptable to the sublime. Rooms in B&Bs generally cost $50-70 for a single and $70-90 for a double in California, but on holidays or in expensive locations (such as Napa Valley), prices can soar to over $300. For more info on B&Bs, see **Bed & Breakfast Inns Online,** P.O. Box 829, Madison, TN 37116 (☎615-868-1946; info@bbonline.com; www.bbonline.com), **Inn-Finder,** 6200 Gisholt Dr., #100, Madison, WI 53713 (☎608-285-6600; fax 285-6601; www.inncrawler.com), or **InnSite** (www.innsite.com).

UNIVERSITY DORMS

Many **colleges and universities** open their residence halls to travelers when school is not in session; some do so even during term-time. Getting a room may take a couple of phone calls and require advanced planning, but rates tend to be low.

CAMPING & THE OUTDOORS

With proper equipment, camping is an inexpensive and relatively safe way to experience California's national parks and other scenic areas. California presents a variety of camping alternatives; few areas in the world are as accessible to the traveler. An excellent resource for travelers planning on camping or spending time in the outdoors is the **Great Outdoor Recreation Pages** (www.gorp.com).

USEFUL PUBLICATIONS & RESOURCES

A variety of publishing companies offer hiking guidebooks to meet the educational needs of novice or expert. For information about camping, hiking, and biking, write or call the publishers listed below to receive a free catalog.

Family Campers and RVers/National Campers and Hikers Association, Inc., 4804 Transit Rd., Bldg. #2, Depew, NY 14043 (☎/fax 716-668-6242). Membership fee ($25) includes their publication *Camping Today.*

Sierra Club Books, 85 Second St., 2nd fl., San Francisco, CA 94105 (☎415-977-5500; www.sierraclub.org/books). Publishes resource books on hiking, camping, and women traveling in the outdoors, as well as an array of California-specific hiking books.

The Mountaineers Books, 1001 SW Klickitat Way, #201, Seattle, WA 98134 (☎800-553-4453 or 206-223-6303; fax 223-6306; www.mountaineersbooks.org). Over 400 titles on hiking, biking, mountaineering, natural history, and conservation.

The US Geological Survey, Branch of Information Services, P.O. Box 25286, Denver Federal Center, Denver, CO 80225 (☎888-275-8747; fax 303-202-4693; http://mapping.usgs.gov/mac/findmaps.html). The USGS provides topographical maps of the US that are ideal for hiking and other wilderness activity. All maps are between $4 and 14.

Wilderness Press, 1200 Fifth St., Berkeley, CA 94710 (☎800-443-7227 or 510-558-1666; fax 558-1696; www.wildernesspress.com). Over 100 hiking guides and maps, including dozens for California.

Woodall Publications Corporation, 2575 Vista Del Mar Dr., Ventura, CA 93001 (☎800-323-9076 or 805-667-4100; www.woodalls.com). Woodall publishes the annually updated *Woodall's Campground Directory* ($22).

NATIONAL PARKS

California's 17 national parks contain some of the most spectacular scenery found in the country. The state's most popular park is **Yosemite** (see p. 253), with its extensive trails, jagged peaks, and awe-inspiring waterfalls. However, the wonders of California's national parks do not end there. From the enormous drive-through trees of **Sequoia** and **Kings Canyon** (see p. 274) to the rock-climbing Mecca of **Joshua Tree** (see p. 515), a tour of the wilderness areas of California makes a terrific itinerary for the camping nut (see p. 7) or a fascinating diversion for the city-dweller.

The **National Park Service,** Fort Mason, Bldg. 201, San Francisco, CA 94111 (☎888-GO-PARKS/467-2757; www.nps.gov) provides info on the parks. The NPS sells an annual pass that grants admission to all national parks in the United States for $50 per year. Without a pass, most parks charge admission fees upon entering.

WILDERNESS SAFETY

THE GREAT OUTDOORS

Stay warm, stay dry, and stay hydrated. The vast majority of life-threatening wilderness situations can be avoided by following this simple advice. Prepare yourself for an emergency, however, by always packing raingear, a hat and mittens, a first-aid kit, a reflector, a whistle, high energy food, and extra water for any hike. Dress

in wool or warm layers of synthetic materials designed for the outdoors; never rely on cotton for warmth, as it is useless when wet.

Check **weather forecasts** and pay attention to the skies when hiking. Whenever possible, let someone know when and where you are going hiking, either a friend, your hostel, a park ranger, or a local hiking organization. Do not attempt a hike beyond your ability—you may be endangering your life. See **Health,** p. 35, for information about outdoor ailments and basic medical concerns.

BEARS WILL EAT YOU

If you are hiking in an area that might be frequented by bears, ask local rangers for information on bear behavior before entering any park or wilderness area, and obey posted warnings. No matter how irresistibly cute a bear appears, don't be fooled—they're powerful and unpredictable animals that are not intimidated by humans. If you're close enough for a bear to be observing you, you're too close. If you surprise the bear, speak in low, soothing tones (think Barry White) and back away slowly. Do not run, as tempting as it may be—the bear may identify you as prey and give chase. If you will be traveling extensively in bear-infested areas, consider taking **pepper spray.** If the bear attacks, spray at its face and eyes. Without pepper spray, different strategies should be used with different bear species. Black bears (black coloration, tall ears, no shoulder hump) are carrion eaters—if you play dead, you are giving them a free meal. The best course of action is to fight back—resistance will deter a black bear. If you're standing toe to toe with a grizzly bear, a predator, fighting back will get you killed. Play dead—drop to the ground and shield your face and chest with your arms.

Don't leave food or other scented items (trash, toiletries, the clothes that you cooked in) near your tent. Putting these objects into canisters is now mandatory in some national parks in California, including Yosemite. **Bear-bagging,** hanging edibles and other scented objects from a tree out of paws' reach, is the best way to keep your toothpaste from becoming a condiment. Bears are also attracted to **perfume,** so cologne, scented soap, deodorant, and hairspray should stay at home.

For more information, consult *How to Stay Alive in the Woods*, by Bradford Angier (Macmillan Press, $8).

SHARKS WILL CHEW ON YOU

You are far, far more likely to suffer an injury from a bee sting or a toilet bowl than from a shark attack. Nevertheless, there are generally one or two unprovoked shark attacks per year along the California coast. Sharks hang out near steep drop-offs around sandbars and in prime feeding grounds, often marked by birds diving for fish. Sharks are most active at twilight or in darkness; they are attracted to erratic movements and bright colors. To avoid sharks, do not be mistaken for a seal or a fish. Don't wear shiny jewelry, which simulates the sheen of fish scales, and don't enter the water if you're bleeding.

CAMPING & HIKING EQUIPMENT

WHAT TO BUY...

Good camping equipment is both sturdy and light. Camping equipment is generally more expensive in Australia, New Zealand, and the UK than in North America. Also see **Going Hiking? Outdoor Equipment Tips From a Hiking Expert,** p. 244.

Sleeping Bag: Most sleeping bags are rated by season ("summer" means 30-40°F at night; "four-season" or "winter" often means below 0°F). They are made either of **down** (warmer and lighter, but miserable when wet) or of **synthetic** material (heavier, more durable, and warmer when wet). Prices range $80-210 for a summer synthetic to $250-300 for a good down winter bag. **Sleeping bag pads** include foam pads ($10-20), air mattresses ($15-50), and Therm-A-Rest self-inflating pads ($45-80).

Tent: The best tents are free-standing (with their own frames and suspension systems), set up quickly, and only require staking in high winds. Low-profile dome tents are the best all-around. Good 2-person tents start at $90, 4-person at $300. Seal the seams of your tent with waterproofer, and make sure it has a rain fly. Other tent accessories include a **battery-operated lantern,** a **plastic groundcloth,** and a **nylon tarp.**

Backpack: Internal-frame packs mold better to your back, keep a lower center of gravity, and flex adequately to allow you to hike difficult trails. **External-frame packs** are more comfortable for long hikes over even terrain, as they keep weight higher and distribute it more evenly. Make sure your pack has a strong, padded hip-belt to transfer weight to your legs. Any serious backpacking requires a pack of at least 4000 in^3 (16,000cc), plus 500 in^3 for sleeping bags in internal-frame packs. Sturdy backpacks cost anywhere from $125-420—this is one area in which it doesn't pay to economize. Fill up any pack with something heavy and walk around the store with it to get a sense of how it distributes weight before buying it. Either buy a **waterproof backpack cover,** or store all of your belongings in plastic bags inside your pack.

Boots: Be sure to wear hiking boots with good **ankle support.** They should fit snugly and comfortably over 1-2 pairs of wool socks and thin liner socks. Break in boots over several weeks first in order to spare yourself painful and debilitating blisters.

Other Necessities: Synthetic layers, like those made of polypropylene, and a **pile jacket** will keep you warm even when wet. A **"space blanket"** helps to retain body heat and doubles as a groundcloth ($5-15). Bring a **plastic water bottle. Water-purifica-**

GET CARD. TRAVEL HARD.

SCENIC DRIVE
FOOD + GAS
LOOKOUT

There's only one way to max out your travel experience and make the most of your time on the road: The International Student Identity Card.

 Packed with travel discounts, benefits and services, this card will keep your travel days and your wallet full. Get it before you hit it!

Visit **ISICUS.com** to get the full story on the benefits of carrying the ISIC.

90 minutes, wash & dry (one sock missing).
5 minutes to book online (Detroit to Mom's)

Save money & time on student and faculty
travel at **StudentUniverse.com**

 StudentUniverse.com   **Real Travel Deals**

tion tablets are useful for when you can't boil water. Although most campgrounds have campfire sites, it pays to bring a small **metal grate** or **grill.** For those places that forbid fires or the gathering of firewood, you'll need a **camp stove** (the classic Coleman starts at $40) and a propane-filled **fuel bottle** to operate it. Also don't forget a **first-aid kit, pocketknife, insect repellent, calamine lotion,** and **waterproof matches** or a **lighter.**

...AND WHERE TO BUY IT

The mail-order/online companies listed below offer lower prices than many retail stores, but a visit to a local camping or outdoors store will give you a good sense of the look and weight of certain items.

Campmor, 28 Parkway, P.O. Box 700, Upper Saddle River, NJ 07458 (☎888-226-7667, elsewhere US ☎201-825-8300; www.campmor.com).

Discount Camping, 880 Main North Rd., Pooraka, South Australia 5095, Australia (☎08 8262 3399; fax 8260 6240; www.discountcamping.com.au).

Eastern Mountain Sports (EMS), 1 Vose Farm Rd., Peterborough, NH 03458 (☎888-463-6367 or 603-924-7231; www.shopems.com).

L.L. Bean, Freeport, ME 04033 (US and Canada ☎800-441-5713; in the UK 0800 891 297, elsewhere 207-552-3028; www.llbean.com).

Recreational Equipment, Inc. (REI), Sumner, WA 98352 (☎800-426-4840 or 253-891-2500; www.rei.com).

YHA Adventure Shop, 152-160 Wardour St., London, W1F 8YA (☎020 7025 1900; www.yhaadventure.com). Britain's largest outdoor equipment suppliers.

CAMPERS & RVS

Renting an RV will always be more expensive than tenting or hostelling, but it's cheaper than staying in hotels and renting a car (see **Rental Cars,** p. 56), and the convenience of bringing along your own bedroom, bathroom, and kitchen makes it an attractive option. Rates vary widely by region, season, and type of RV. It always pays to contact several companies to compare vehicles and prices. **El Monte RVs** (☎800-337-2214; www.elmonterv.com) has nine locations in California.

ORGANIZED ADVENTURE TRIPS

Organized adventure tours offer another way of exploring the wild. Tourism bureaus can often suggest parks, trails, and outfitters; other good sources for info are stores and organizations that specialize in camping and outdoor equipment like **REI** and **EMS** (see above).

Specialty Travel Index, 305 San Anselmo Ave., #313, San Anselmo, CA 94960 (☎800-442-4922 or 415-459-4900; fax 415-459-9474; www.specialtytravel.com). Worldwide tours.

AmeriCan Adventures & Roadrunner, P.O. Box 1155, Gardena, CA 90249 (☎800-TREK-USA/873-5872 or 310-324-3447; in the UK 01295 756 2000; fax 310-324-3562; www.americanadventures.com). Organizes group adventure camping and hostelling trips (with transportation and camping costs included).

KEEPING IN TOUCH

BY MAIL

DOMESTIC RATES

First-class letters sent and received within the US take 1-3 days and cost $0.37; **Priority Mail** packages up to 1 lb. generally take 2 days and cost $3.85, up to 5 lb. $7.70. **All days specified denote business days.** For more details, see www.usps.com.

SENDING MAIL HOME FROM CALIFORNIA

Airmail is the best way to send mail home from the United States. **Aerogrammes,** one form of airmail, are printed sheets that fold into envelopes and are available at post offices. Write *"par avion"* or "air mail" on the front. Most post offices will charge exorbitant fees or simply refuse to send aerogrammes with enclosures. **Surface mail** is by far the cheapest and slowest way to send mail. It takes one to three months to cross the Atlantic and two to four months to cross the Pacific—good for items you won't need to see for a while, such as souvenirs or other articles you've acquired along the way that are weighing down your pack. These are standard rates for mail from the United States to:

Australia: Allow 5-7 days for regular airmail home. Postcards/aerogrammes cost $0.70. Letters up to 1 oz. cost $0.80; packages up to 1 lb. $14.50, up to 5 lb. $32.75.

Canada: Allow 5-7 days for regular airmail home. Postcards cost $0.50, aerogrammes $0.50. Letters up to 1 oz. cost $0.60; packages up to 1 lb. $13.25, up to 5 lb. $16.75.

Ireland: Allow 5-7days for regular airmail home. Postcards/aerogrammes cost $0.70. Letters up to 1 oz. cost $0.80; packages up to 1 lb. $14.00, up to 5 lb. $22.75.

New Zealand: Allow 5-7days for regular airmail home. Postcards/aerogrammes cost $0.70. Letters up to 1 oz. cost $0.80; packages up to 1 lb. $12.50, up to 5 lb. $28.75.

The UK: Allow 5-7days for regular airmail home. Postcards/aerogrammes cost $0.70. Letters up to 1 oz. cost $0.80 packages up to 1 lb. $16, up to 5 lb. $32.

SENDING MAIL TO CALIFORNIA

Mark envelopes "air mail" or *"par avion,"* or your letter or postcard will never arrive. In addition to the standard postage system whose rates are listed below, **Federal Express** (☎ 800-247-4747; in Australia 13 26 10; in New Zealand 0800 73 33 39; in the UK 0800 12 38 00; www.fedex.com) handles express mail services from most home countries to the US; for example, they can get a letter from New York to Los Angeles in 2 days for $9.95, and from London to New York in 2 days for UK£25.80.

Australia: Allow 4-6 days for regular **airmail** to the US. Postcards and letters up to 20g cost AUS$1; packages up to 0.5kg AUS$11.50, up to 2kg AUS$38.50. **EMS** can get a letter to the US in 2-5 days for AUS$30. www.auspost.com.au/pac.

Canada: Allow 4-7days for regular **airmail** to the US. Postcards and letters up to 30g cost CDN$0.65; packages up to 0.5kg CDN$5.60, up to 2kg CDN$15.95. www.canadapost.ca/personal/rates/us/default-e.asp.

Ireland: Allow 5-6 days for regular airmail to the US. Postcards and letters up to 25g cost IR£0.57. Add IR£3.40 for Swiftpost International. www.letterpost.ie.

ESSENTIALS

New Zealand: Allow 7 days for regular airmail to the US. Postcards NZ$1.50. Letters up to 200g cost NZ$2; small parcels up to 0.5kg NZ$15.82, up to 2kg NZ$49.56. www.nzpost.co.nz/nzpost/control/ratefinder.

UK: Allow 4 days for airmail to the US. Letters up to 20g cost UK£0.65; packages up to 0.5kg UK£4.55, up to 2kg UK£17.30. UK Swiftair delivers letters a day faster for UK£2.85 more. www.consignia-online.com.

RECEIVING MAIL IN CALIFORNIA

There are several ways to arrange pick-up of letters sent to you while you are abroad. Mail can be sent via General Delivery to almost any city or town in California with a post office. Address General Delivery letters like so:

Kato KAELIN
General Delivery
Beverly Hills, CA 90210 USA

The mail will go to a special desk in the central post office, unless you specify a post office by street address or postal code. Bring your passport or other photo ID for pick-up. If the clerks insist that there is nothing for you, have them check under your first name as well. *Let's Go* lists post offices in the Practical Information section for each city and most towns.

American Express's travel offices throughout the world offer a free Client Letter Service (mail held up to 30 days and forwarded upon request) for cardholders who contact them in advance. Address the letter in the same way shown above. Some offices will offer these services to non-cardholders (especially AmEx Travelers Cheque holders), but call ahead to make sure. *Let's Go* lists AmEx office locations for most large cities in Practical Information sections; for a complete, free list, call ☎800-528-4800.

BY TELEPHONE

CALLING HOME FROM CALIFORNIA

A **calling card** is probably your cheapest bet. Calls are billed collect or to your account. You can frequently call collect without even possessing a company's calling card just by calling their access number and following the instructions. **To obtain a calling card** from your national telecommunications service before leaving home, contact the appropriate company listed below (using the numbers in the first column). To **call home with a calling card,** contact the operator for your service provider in the United States by dialing the given toll-free access number.

You can often also make **direct international calls** from pay phones, but if you aren't using a calling card, you may need to drop coins as quickly as your words. Where available, prepaid phone cards (see below) and occasionally major credit cards can be used for direct international calls, but they are still less cost-effective.

CALLING WITHIN CALIFORNIA

The simplest way to call within the country is to use a coin-operated phone; local calls in California cost $0.35. **Prepaid phone cards,** which carry a certain amount of phone time depending on the card's denomination, usually save time and money in the long run, although they often require a $0.25 surcharge from pay phones. These cards can be used to make international and domestic calls.

Let's Go has recently partnered with ekit.com to provide a calling card that offers a number of services, including email and voice messaging. Before purchasing any calling card, always be sure to compare rates with other cards, and to make sure it serves your needs (a local phone card is generally better for local calls, for instance). For more information, visit www.letsgo.ekit.com.

TIME DIFFERENCES

California is 8 hours behind **Greenwich Mean Time (GMT)**. The entire state observes daylight savings time, so clocks are set forward one hour in the spring and backward one hour in the fall.

BY EMAIL & INTERNET

Though in some places it's possible to forge a remote link with your home server, in most cases this is a much slower (and thus more expensive) option than taking advantage of free **web-based email accounts** (e.g., www.hotmail.com and www.yahoo.com). Travelers with laptops can call an Internet service provider via a **modem.** Long-distance phone cards specifically intended for such calls can defray normally high phone charges; check with your long-distance phone provider to see if it offers this option. Most California cities have public libraries with free Internet terminals. Establishments offering Internet access are listed in the Practical Information sections of major cities. **Cybercafe Guide** locates cybercafes throughout the Golden State (www.cyberiacafe.net/cyberia/guide/ccafe.htm).

GETTING TO CALIFORNIA

BY PLANE

When it comes to airfare, a little effort can save you a bundle. If your plans are flexible enough to deal with the restrictions, courier fares are the cheapest. Tickets bought from consolidators and standby seating are also good deals, but last-minute specials, airfare wars, and charter flights often beat these fares. The keys are to hunt around, to be flexible, and to ask persistently about discounts. Students, seniors, and those under 26 should never pay full price for a ticket.

COMMERCIAL AIRFARES

Airfares to California remain steady throughout the year, except on national holidays, when it's both expensive and difficult to travel. Midweek (M-Th morning) round-trip flights run $40-50 cheaper than weekend flights, but they are generally more crowded and less likely to permit frequent-flier upgrades. Traveling with an "open return" ticket can be pricier than fixing a return date when buying the ticket. If California is only one stop on a more extensive globe-hop, consider a **Round-the-World (RTW)** ticket. Tickets usually include at least five stops and are valid for about a year; prices range $1200-5000. Try **Northwest Airlines/KLM** (☎ 800-447-4747; www.nwa.com) or **Star Alliance,** a consortium of 13 airlines including **United Airlines** (☎ 800-241-6522; www.united.com).

The commercial airlines' lowest regular offer is the **Advance Purchase Excursion (APEX) fare,** which provides confirmed reservations and allows "open-jaw" tickets. Generally, reservations must be made seven to 21 days ahead of departure, with seven- to 14-day minimum stay and up to 90-day maximum stay restrictions. These fares carry hefty cancellation and change penalties (fees rise in summer). Book peak-season APEX fares early; by May you will have a hard time getting your desired departure date. Use **Microsoft Expedia** (msn.expedia.com) or **Travelocity** (www.travelocity.com) to get an idea of the lowest published fares, then use the resources outlined here to try and beat those fares.

The chart below shows sample roundtrip fares between various destinations and either of the two major airport hubs in California—San Francisco (SFO) or Los Angeles (LAX), with LAX typically being the cheaper of the two. Be forewarned that airline prices change frequently; these are just guidelines.

ROUNDTRIP BETWEEN CALIFORNIA AND:	PRICE (IN US$)
Any North American destination	$200-650
UK and Ireland	$350-1100
Sydney, Australia	$900-1200
Auckland, New Zealand	$850-1200
Cape Town or Johannesburg	$950-1400

ESSENTIALS

BUDGET & STUDENT TRAVEL AGENCIES

While knowledgeable agents specializing in flights to California can make your life easy and help you save, they may not spend the time to find you the lowest possible fare—they get paid on commission. Travelers holding **ISIC and IYTC cards** (see p. 28) qualify for big discounts from student travel agencies. Most flights from budget agencies are on major airlines, but in peak season some may sell seats on less reliable chartered aircraft.

Council Travel (www.counciltravel.com). Countless US offices, including branches in Atlanta, Boston, Chicago, L.A., New York, San Francisco, Seattle, and Washington, D.C. Check the website or call 800-2-COUNCIL/226-8624 for the office nearest you. Also an office at 28A Poland St. (Oxford Circus), **London,** W1V 3DB (☎0207 437 7767). Council has been subsumed under STA. However, their offices are still in existence and transacting business.

CTS Travel, 44 Goodge St., **London** W1T 2AD, UK(☎0207 636 0031; fax 637 5328; ctsinfo@ctstravel.co.uk).

STA Travel, 7890 S. Hardy Dr., Suite 110, Tempe AZ 85284 (24hr. reservations and info ☎800-781-4040; www.sta-travel.com). A student and youth travel organization with over 150 offices worldwide, including US offices in Boston, Chicago, L.A., New York, San Francisco, Seattle, and Washington, D.C. Ticket booking, travel insurance, railpasses, and more. In the UK, walk-in office 11 Goodge St., **London** W1T 2PF or call ☎0207 436 7779. In New Zealand, Shop 2B, 182 Queen St., **Auckland** (☎09 309 0458). In Australia, 366 Lygon St., **Carlton** Vic 3053 (☎03 9349 4344).

Travel CUTS (Canadian Universities Travel Services Limited), 187 College St., **Toronto,** ON M5T 1P7 (☎416-979-2406; fax 979-8167; www.travelcuts.com). 60 offices across Canada. Also in the UK, 295-A Regent St., **London** W1R 7YA (☎0207-255-1944).

STANDBY FLIGHTS

Traveling standby requires considerable flexibility in arrival and departure dates and cities. Standby companies sell vouchers rather than tickets, along with the promise to get you to your destination within a certain window of time (typically one to five days). Call in before your specific window of time to hear your flight options and the probability that you will be able to board each flight. You can then decide which flights you want to try to make, show up at the appropriate airport, present your voucher, and board if space is available. Vouchers can usually be bought for both one-way and round-trip travel. You may receive a monetary refund only if every available flight within your date range is full; if you opt not to take an available (but perhaps less convenient) flight, you can only get credit toward future travel. Carefully read agreements with any company offering standby flights. To check on a company's service record in the US, call the Better Business Bureau (☎212-533-6200). It is difficult to receive refunds, and clients' vouchers will not be honored when an airline fails to receive payment in time.

TICKET CONSOLIDATORS

Ticket consolidators, or **"bucket shops,"** buy unsold tickets in bulk from commercial airlines and sell them at discounted rates. The best place to look is in the Sunday travel section of any major newspaper (such as the *New York Times*), where many bucket shops place tiny ads. Call quickly, as availability is typically extremely limited. Not all bucket shops are reliable, so insist on a receipt that gives full details of restrictions, refunds, and tickets, and pay by credit card (in spite of the 2-5% fee) so you can stop payment if you never receive your tickets. For more info, see www.travel-library.com/air-travel/consolidators.html.

TRAVELING FROM THE US & CANADA

Travel Avenue (☎ 800-333-3335; www.travelavenue.com) searches for best available published fares and then uses several consolidators to attempt to beat that fare. Other consolidators worth trying are **Interworld** (☎ 305-443-4929; fax 443-0351); **Pennsylvania Travel** (☎ 800-331-0947); **Rebel** (☎ 800-227-3235; travel@rebeltours.com; www.rebeltours.com); and **Travac** (☎ 800-872-8800; fax 212-714-9063; www.travac.com). Yet more consolidators on the web include the **Internet Travel Network** (www.itn.com); **Travel Information Services** (www.tiss.com); **TravelHUB** (www.travelhub.com); and **The Travel Site** (www.thetravelsite.com). Keep in mind that these are just suggestions to get you started in your research; *Let's Go* does not endorse any of these agencies. As always, be cautious, and research companies before you hand over your credit card number.

TRAVELING FROM THE UK, AUSTRALIA, & NEW ZEALAND

In London, the **Air Travel Advisory Bureau** (☎ 0207 636 5000; www.atab.co.uk) can provide names of reliable consolidators and discount flight specialists. From Australia and New Zealand, look for consolidator ads in the travel section of the *Sydney Morning Herald* and other papers.

CHARTER FLIGHTS

Charters are flights a tour operator contracts with an airline to fly extra loads of passengers during peak season. Charter flights fly less frequently than major airlines, make refunds particularly difficult, and are almost always fully booked. Schedules and itineraries may also change or be cancelled at the last moment (as late as 48 hours before the trip, and without a full refund), and check-in, boarding, and baggage claim are often much slower. However, they can also be cheaper.

Discount clubs and **fare brokers** offer members savings on last-minute charter and tour deals. Study contracts closely; you don't want to end up with an unwanted overnight layover. **Travelers Advantage,** Trumbull, CT (☎ 203-365-2000; www.travelersadvantage.com) specializes in European travel and tour packages. The $60 annual fee includes discounts and cheap flight directories.

GETTING AROUND CALIFORNIA

BY PLANE

It is possible to fly between the Bay Area and Southern California for surprisingly little—in fact, flying is often cheaper than train or bus. **Southwest Airlines** (☎ 800-I-FLY-SWA/435-9792; www.southwest.com) frequently offers $39 or $49 one-way deals between Oakland or San Jose and Los Angeles or San Diego. **United Airlines** (☎ 800-241-6522; www.united.com) also frequently offers deals between the Bay Area and the Southland. Intrastate flights can also be caught from Orange County and Sacramento.

BY TRAIN

Amtrak (☎ 800-USA-RAIL/872-7245; www.amtrak.com) is the only provider of intercity passenger train service in California. The informative website lists up-to-date schedules, fares, arrival and departure info, and makes reservations. **Discounts** on full rail fares are given to seniors 62 years and older (15% off), students with a Student Advantage card (15% off; call 800-962-6872 to purchase the $20 card), travelers with disabilities (15% off), children ages 2 to 15 with a paying adult (50% off), children under 2 (free), and current members of the US Armed Forces, active-duty veterans, and their dependents (25% off). "Rail SALE" offers online discounts of up to 90%; visit the website for details and reservations and for info about **special packages.** Sample fares are listed in the **Practical Information** sections of most California cities.

BY BUS

Buses offer frequent and complete service between cities and towns in California. Often a bus is the only way to reach smaller locales without a car. Sample fares are listed in each city's **Practical Information** section.

Greyhound (☎ 800-229-9424; www.greyhound.com) is the only bus service that operates throughout the entire state. Reserve with a credit card over the phone at least 10 days in advance, and the ticket can be mailed anywhere in the US. Reservations are available only up to 24hr. in advance or at the bus terminal.

Advance purchase fares: Reserving space far ahead of time ensures a lower fare, although expect a smaller discount June 5-Sept. 15. Fares are often reduced for 14-day, 7-day, or 3-day advance purchases on many popular routes. For 3-day advance purchase M-Th, 2 people can ride for the price of 1 ticket.

Discounts on full fares: Seniors with Greyhound Senior Club Card (10% off); ages 2-11 (50% off); Student Advantage card holders (15% off); disabled travelers and an attendant ride together for the price of 1; active and retired US military personnel and National Guard Reserves (10% off with valid ID).

Ameripass: Call ☎ 800-454-7277. Unlimited travel for 7 days ($220), 10 days ($269), 15 days ($340), 30 days ($450), 45 days ($499), or 60 days ($625). There is a student discount. Children's passes are half-price.

International Ameripass: For travelers from outside North America. Call ☎ 800-454-7277 for info. 7 days ($204), 10 days ($254), 15 days ($314), 30 days ($424), 45 days ($464), or 60 days ($499). International Ameripasses are not available at the terminal; they can be purchased in foreign countries at Greyhound-affiliated agencies; telephone numbers vary by country and are listed on the website. Passes can also be ordered at the website, or purchased by calling ☎ 800-229-9424, in **Australia** 049 342 088); in **New Zealand** 064 9 479 65555; in **South Africa** 027 11 331 2911; in the **UK** 044 01342 317 317; or e-mail intlameripass@greyhound.com.

GREEN TORTOISE

Green Tortoise, 494 Broadway, San Francisco, CA 94133 (☎ 800-867-8647; www.greentortoise.com), offers a slow-paced, whimsical alternative to straightforward transportation. Green Tortoise's communal "hostels on wheels"—remodeled diesel buses done up for living and eating on the road—offers aptly named **Adventure Tours.** All tours depart from and return to San Francisco; travelers are responsible for getting to San Francisco themselves. Prices include transportation from San Francisco to the destination, sleeping space on the bus, and tours of the regions through which you pass. Meals are prepared communally; prices listed include the cost of food. Green Tortoise offers trips around Northern California (6

ESSENTIALS

days in July or August, $350, 2 per year), Yosemite National Park (3 days May-Sept., $160; 2 days May-Sept., $130; sporadic trips from Sept.-May), Death Valley National Park (3 days, $160), and the Grand Canyon (9 days May-Sept., $420, 5 per year). Prepare for an earthy trip; buses have no toilets and little privacy. Reserve one to two months in advance, deposits ($100) are generally required; however, many trips have space available at departure. Reservations can be made over the phone or on the web.

ADVENTUREBUS
Adventurebus, 870 Market St., #416, San Francisco, CA 94102 (☎888-737-5263, outside the US 909-797-7366; www.adventurebus.com), runs fun loving tours through cities, towns, and national parks in California and the Southwest US. Transportation in "extremely unconventional" buses driven by knowledgeable guides provides fun and like-minded company. Nine- to 16-day trips run from $300-700.

CONTIKI
For those who want someone else to do the itinerary planning for them, Contiki Travel (☎1-888-CONTIKI/266-8454; www.contiki.com) runs comprehensive 4-6 day bus tours starting at $419. Tours include accommodations, transportation, and some meals.

BY CAR

▨ AMERICAN AUTOMOBILE ASSOCIATION (AAA)

The high priest of California's vehicular demigod. Provides emergency road service (☎800-AAA-HELP/222-4357); to sign up, call 800-JOIN-AAA564-6222 or go to www.aaa.com. Free trip-planning services, maps, and guidebooks, and 24hr. emergency road service anywhere in the US. Offers free towing and commission-free American Express Traveler's Cheques from over 1000 offices across the country, as well as discounts on Hertz car rental (5-20%), Amtrak tickets (10%), and various motel chains and theme parks. AAA has reciprocal agreements with the auto associations of many other countries, which often provide you with full benefits while in the US. Check with your auto association for details. Membership in the California branch costs $46 to join and $17 per year, plus $24 for each additional family member. Costs at other AAA branches are similar in range, but vary in price.

RENTING

Car rental agencies fall into two categories: national companies with hundreds of branches, and local agencies that serve only one city or region. National chains usually allow you to pick up a car in one city and drop it off in another (for a hefty charge, sometimes in excess of $1000). The drawbacks of car rentals include steep prices (a compact car rents for $25-45 per day) and high minimum ages for rentals (usually 25). Most branches rent to ages 21 to 24 with an additional fee, but policies and prices vary from agency to agency. **Alamo** (☎800-327-9633; www.alamo.com) rents to ages 21 to 24 with a major credit card for an additional $20 per day. **Enterprise** (☎800-RENT-A-CAR/736-8222) rents to customers ages 21 to 24 with a variable surcharge. **Dollar** (☎800-800-4000; www.dollar.com) and **Thrifty** (☎800-367-2277; www.thrifty.com) locations do likewise for varying surcharges. **Rent-A-Wreck** (☎800-944-7501; www.rent-a-wreck.com) specializes in supplying vehicles that are past their prime for lower-than-average prices; a bare-bones compact less than eight years old rents for around $20 to $25. There may be an additional charge for a **collision and damage waiver (CDW)**, which usually comes to about $12 to 15 per day. Major credit cards (including MasterCard and American Express) will sometimes cover the CDW if you use their card to rent a car; call your credit card company for specifics.

Because it is mandatory for all drivers in California, make sure with your rental agency that you are covered by **insurance**. Be sure to ask whether the price includes **insurance** against theft and collision. Remember that if you are driving a conventional vehicle on an **unpaved road** in a rental car, you are almost never covered by insurance; ask about this before leaving the rental agency. Insurance plans almost always come with a **deductible** of around $500 for conventional vehicles. This means you pay for all damages up to that sum, unless they are the fault of another vehicle. The excess you will be quoted applies to collisions with other vehicles; collisions with non-vehicles, such as trees, ("single-vehicle collisions") will cost you even more. National chains often allow one-way rentals, picking up in one city and dropping off in another, although there is often a steep additional charge. There is usually a minimum hire period and sometimes an extra drop-off charge of several hundred dollars.

AUTO TRANSPORT COMPANIES

These services match drivers with car owners who need cars moved from one city to another. Would-be travelers give the company their desired destination and the company finds a car that needs to go there. The only expenses are gas, tolls, and your own living expenses. Some companies insure their cars; with others, your security deposit covers any breakdowns or damage. You must be at least 21, have a valid license, and agree to drive about 400 mi. per day on a fairly direct route. Popular transport companies include: **Auto Driveaway Co.,** 310 S. Michigan Ave., Chicago, IL 60604-4298 (☎800-346-2277 or 312-341-1900; www.autodrive-away.com), and **Across America Driveaway,** 9839 Industrial Dr., Highland, IN 46322 (☎800-619-7707; www.schultz-international.com). Offices in L.A. (☎800-964-7874).

 DRIVING PRECAUTIONS. When traveling in the summer or in the desert, bring substantial amounts of **water** (a suggested 5 liters of water per person per day) for drinking and for the radiator. For long drives to unpopulated areas, register with police before beginning the trek, and again upon arrival at the destination. Check with the local automobile club for details. When traveling for long distances, make sure tires are in good repair and have enough air, and get good maps. A **compass** and a **car manual** can also be very useful. You should always carry a **spare tire and jack, jumper cables, extra oil, flares, a torch (flashlight), and heavy blankets** (in case your car breaks down at night or in the winter). If you don't know how to **change a tire,** learn before heading out, especially if you are planning on traveling in deserted areas. Blowouts on dirt roads are exceedingly common. If you do have a breakdown, stay with your car; if you wander off, there's less likelihood trackers will find you.

ON THE ROAD. Tune up the car before you leave, make sure the tires are in good repair and have enough air, and get good maps. **Rand McNally's Road Atlas,** covering all of the US and Canada, is one of the best (available at bookstores and gas stations, $11; California state map $5). If staying in southern California for an extended period of time, it may be worth it to invest in a Thomas Guide ($30) for the county or counties in which you are staying. A **compass** and a **car manual** can also be very useful. Always carry a **spare tire** and **jack, jumper cables, extra oil, flares,** a **flashlight,** and **blankets** (in case you break down at night or in winter). Those traveling long undeveloped stretches of road may want to consider renting a **cell phone** in case of a breakdown. If traveling in the desert, refer to **Desert Survival** (see p. 505) for essential desert driving tips. Also, the California Department of Transportation has a road conditions hotline at ☎800-427-7623.

While driving, be sure to buckle up—seat belts are required by law in California. The speed limit in California varies depending on the road (some freeways have speed limits as high as 70mph, while residential areas are generally 25mph). Heed speed limit signs at all times; not only does it save gas, but most local police forces and highway patrolmen make frequent use of radar to catch speed demons, and fines range from $100-$150. Gas in California costs around $1.40 per gallon, but prices vary widely depending on geographical area and the whims of OPEC. Drivers should take necessary precautions against carjacking, which is a frequently committed crime in the state. Carjackers, who are usually armed, approach victims in their vehicles and force them to turn over their cars. **Sleeping in a car or van** parked in the city is both illegal and extremely dangerous. Don't do it.

NEW CENTRAL HOSTEL

250-bed hostel open all year
bunks and large doubles with regular mattresses • 4 beds per room, private
rooms smoking and nonsmoking rooms

$20*

*per night (depending on bed and season)
travelers' check, VISA, MasterCard accepted
passport and travel documents requested • no membership required

pillows with cases, sheets and blankets provided
laundry • full kitchen
fax service • locker and safety deposit boxes

Check in: 24 hours a day • Check out: by 11 a.m.
No curfew • Parties / social activities

NEW CENTRAL HOSTEL

1412 Market Street
San Francisco, CA 94102
(415) 703-9988
Fax: (415) 703-9986
E-mail: Newcentralhotel@aol.com

☐ **Shared Accommodations**
☐ **Double Rooms**
☐ **Private Rooms**
☐ **Free linen, kitchen**
☐ **Weekly Rates**

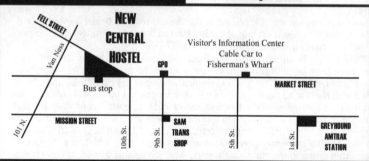

Transportation: city bus stops at front door
Attractions: Fisherman's Wharf, Haight-Ashbury, Union Square, Civic Center,
Golden Gate Bridge and Park, Alcatraz, Cable Cars, restaurants, shopping,
major museums and art galleries, bars, pubs and clubs

Visitor's Information Center, Post Office, hospital and downtown areas are all
within walking distance

HOW TO NAVIGATE THE INTERSTATES. A number of major interstates and highways criss-cross California. Travelers moving north-south have the choice of three major routes. If you're looking for speed, hop on **Interstate 5,** which runs north-south from Oregon through Sacramento, the San Joaquin Valley, Los Angeles, and San Diego on its way to the Mexican border. I-5 is the most direct and fastest route from L.A. to San Francisco (6-8hr.), but it's also deadly boring, affording at best a view of agricultural flatlands and stinky cow pastures. **U.S. 101** winds north-south, much closer to the coast than I-5, through Eureka, Santa Rosa, San Francisco, San Luis Obispo, and Santa Barbara, ending in L.A. With a travel time of eight to 10 hours from San Francisco to L.A., it's slower than I-5, but a considerably more scenic and pleasant drive. The third option is 🎇**Highway 1,** the Pacific Coast Highway, which follows the California coast. Highway 1 is very slow and often traffic-congested, but the scenery is some of the most spectacular in the world, particularly on the breathtaking, cliff-hanging turns of Big Sur (see p. 340). The east-west options are more simple. I-80 heads east from San Francisco to Sacramento and climbs onward to North Lake Tahoe and Reno. To the south, I-10 moves east from L.A. to Palm Springs and Joshua Tree, intersecting on its way with I-15, which cruises northeast to Las Vegas.

DRIVING PERMITS & CAR INSURANCE

INTERNATIONAL DRIVING PERMIT (IDP). If you plan to drive a car while in California, you must be over 16 and have either an American or Canadian drivers license or an IDP.

CAR INSURANCE. Collision insurance is required by state law in California. If you are from outside the United States and want to rent, lease, or borrow a car, you will need a **green card,** or **International Insurance Certificate,** to certify that you have liability insurance. Green cards can be obtained at car rental agencies, car dealers (for those leasing cars), some travel agencies, and some border crossings.

BY TWO WHEELS

BY BICYCLE

Safe and secure cycling requires a quality helmet and lock. A good helmet costs about $40—much cheaper than critical head surgery. U-shaped **Kryptonite** or **Citadel** locks ($30-60) carry insurance against theft for one or two years if your bike is registered with the police. **Bike Nashbar,** P.O. Box 1455, Crab Orchard, WV 25827 (☎800-627-4227), will beat any nationally advertised in-stock price by $0.05, and ships anywhere in the US or Canada. Their techline (☎800-888-2710; open M-F 8am-6pm ET) fields questions about repairs and maintenance. Check out books like: *Best Bike Rides in Northern California,* by Kim Grob (Globe Pequot; $13); and *Mountain Bike! Southern California: A Guide to Classic Trails,* by David Story (Menasha Ridge; $16). For more info on bike trips, contact **Adventure Cycling Association,** P.O. Box 8308, Missoula, MT 59807 (☎800-755-2453; www.advcycling.org). It's a national, nonprofit organization that researches and maps long distance routes and organizes bike tours (75-day Great Divide Expedition $2800, 6-9 day trip $650-800). Annual membership is $30 and includes access to maps and routes and a subscription to *Adventure Cyclist* magazine.

BY MOTORCYCLE

The wind-in-your-face thrill, burly leather, and revving crackle of a motorcycle engine unobscured by windows or upholstery has built up quite a cult following, but motorcycling is the most dangerous of roadtop activities. Of course, safety should be your primary concern. Helmets are required by law in California; wear the best one you can find. Those considering a long journey should contact the **American Motorcyclist Association,** 13515 Yarmouth Dr., Pickering, OH 43147 (☎800-262-5646; www.ama-cycle.org), the linchpin of US biker culture. A full membership ($39 per year) includes a subscription to the extremely informative *American Motorcyclist* magazine, discounts on insurance, rentals, and hotels, and a bad-ass patch for your riding jacket.

BY THUMB

Let's Go strongly urges you to consider the risks before you choose to hitchhike. Hitching means entrusting your life to a randomly selected person who happens to stop beside you on the road. While this may be relatively safe in some areas of Europe and Australia, it is *not* in California. We do not recommend it. Find other means of transportation.

SPECIFIC CONCERNS

WOMEN TRAVELERS

Women exploring on their own inevitably face some additional safety concerns, but it's easy to be adventurous without taking undue risks. If you are concerned, consider staying in hostels which offer single rooms that lock from the inside or in religious organizations with rooms for women only. Stick to centrally located accommodations and avoid solitary late-night treks or metro rides.

Always carry extra money for a phone call, bus, or taxi. **Hitchhiking** is never safe for lone women, or even for two women traveling together. When on overnight or long train rides, if there is no women-only compartment, choose one occupied by women or couples. Look as if you know where you're going and approach older women or couples for directions if you're lost or uncomfortable.

Generally, the less you look like a tourist, the better off you'll be. Dress conservatively, especially in rural areas. Trying to fit in can be effective, but dressing to the style of an obviously different culture may cause you to be ill at ease and a conspicuous target. Wearing a **wedding band** may help prevent unwanted overtures.

Your best answer to verbal harassment is no answer at all; feigning deafness, sitting motionless, and staring straight ahead at nothing in particular will do a world of good that reactions usually don't achieve. The extremely persistent can sometimes be dissuaded by a firm, loud, and very public "Go away!" in the appropriate language. Don't hesitate to seek out a police officer or a passerby if you are being harassed. Memorize the emergency numbers in places you visit, and consider carrying a keychain whistle. A self-defense course will prepare you for a potential attack and raise your level of awareness of your surroundings (see **Self Defense,** p. 33).

For general information, contact the **National Organization for Women (NOW),** 733 15th St. NW, Fl. 2, Washington, DC 20005 (☎202-628-8669; www.now.org), which has branches across the US that can refer women travelers to rape crisis centers and counseling services.

TRAVELING ALONE

There are many benefits to traveling alone, including independence and greater interaction with locals. On the other hand, any solo traveler is a more vulnerable target of harassment and street theft. As a lone traveler, try not to stand out as a tourist, look confident, and be especially careful in deserted or very crowded areas. If questioned, never admit that you are traveling alone. Maintain regular contact with someone at home who knows your itinerary. For more tips, pick up *Traveling Solo* by Eleanor Berman (Globe Pequot Press, $17) or subscribe to **Connecting: Solo Travel Network,** 689 Park Road, Unit 6, Gibsons, BC V0N 1V7, Canada (☎604-886-9099; www.cstn.org; membership $35). **Travel Companion Exchange,** P.O. Box 833, Amityville, NY 11701 (☎800-392-1256 or 631-454-0880; www.whytravelalone.com; $48), will link solo travelers with companions with similar travel interests.

OLDER TRAVELERS

Senior citizens are eligible for a wide range of discounts on transportation, museums, movies, theaters, concerts, restaurants, and accommodations. If you don't see a senior citizen price listed, ask, and you may be delightfully surprised. The books *No Problem! Worldwise Tips for Mature Adventurers,* by Janice Kenyon (Orca Book Publishers; $16) and *Unbelievably Good Deals and Great Adventures That You Absolutely Can't Get Unless You're Over 50,* by Joan Rattner Heilman (NTC/Contemporary Publishing; $13) are both excellent resources. For more information, contact one of the following organizations:

Elderhostel, 11 Ave. de Lafayette, Boston, MA 02111 (☎877-426-8056; www.elderhostel.org). Organizes 1- to 4-week educational adventures for those 55+.

The Mature Traveler, P.O. Box 15791, Sacramento, CA 95852 (☎800-460-6676). Deals, discounts, and travel packages for the 50+ traveler. Subscription $30.

Walking the World, P.O. Box 1186, Fort Collins, CO 80522 (☎800-340-9255; www.walkingtheworld.com), runs trips for 50+ travelers, especially in the Western US.

BISEXUAL, GAY, & LESBIAN TRAVELERS

Although it is generally regarded as a progressive state, prejudice against gays and lesbians is still present in parts of California. Homophobia may be a problem for the openly gay or lesbian traveler, particularly in rural areas. However, many cities in California have large and active queer communities. San Francisco is known for its large homosexual community, Los Angeles has a thriving gay population, and San Diego's Hillcrest district is a significant BGLT center. Smaller outposts of gay culture exist outside the major cities. Palm Springs, known as a resort community for the elderly, increasingly caters to a younger, homosexual clientele. Guerneville, in the Russian River Valley north of San Francisco, is a small town known for its predominately homosexual population. *Let's Go* lists local gay and lesbian info lines and community centers. Listed below are organizations that offer materials addressing some specific concerns. **Out and About** (www.planetout.com) offers a biweekly newsletter addressing travel concerns.

Gay's the Word, 66 Marchmont St., London WC1N 1AB, UK (☎+44 20 7278 7654; www.gaystheword.co.uk). The largest gay and lesbian bookshop in the UK, with both fiction and non-fiction titles. Mail-order service available.

Giovanni's Room, 1145 Pine St., Philadelphia, PA 19107 (☎215-923-2960; www.queerbooks.com). An international lesbian/feminist and gay bookstore with mailorder service (carries many of the publications listed below).

International Lesbian and Gay Association (ILGA), 81 rue Marché-au-Charbon, B-1000 Brussels, Belgium (☎+32 2 502 2471; www.ilga.org). Provides political information, such as homosexuality laws of individual countries.

FURTHER READING: BISEXUAL, GAY, & LESBIAN

Spartacus International Gay Guide 2001-2002. Bruno Gmunder Verlag ($33).

Damron Men's Guide, Damron Road Atlas, Damron's Accommodations, and *The Women's Traveller.* Damron Travel Guides ($14-19). For more info, call ☎800-462-6654 or visit www.damron.com

Ferrari Guides' Gay Travel A to Z, Ferrari Guides' Men's Travel in Your Pocket, and *Ferrari Guides' Inn Places.* Ferrari Publications ($16-20). Purchase the guides online at www.ferrariguides.com.

Gayellow Pages USA/Canada, Frances Green. Gayellow pages ($16). Visit Gayellow pages online at www.gayellowpages.com.

TRAVELERS WITH DISABILITIES

Federal law dictates that all public buildings should be handicapped accessible, and recent laws governing building codes make disabled access more the norm than the exception. However, traveling with a disability still requires planning and flexibility. One should inform airlines and hotels of their disabilities when making arrangements for travel; some time may be needed to prepare special accommodations. Call ahead to restaurants, hotels, parks, and other facilities to find out about wheelchair accessibility. US Customs requires a certificate of immunization against rabies for **guide dogs** entering the country.

In the US, \ Amtrak and major airlines will accommodate disabled passengers if notified at least 72 hours in advance. Hearing-impaired travelers may contact Amtrak using teletype printers (☎800-523-6590 or 800-654-5988). Greyhound buses will provide free travel for a companion; if you are alone, call Greyhound (☎800-752-4841) at least 48 hours, but no more than one week, before you plan to leave and they will assist you. For information on transportation availability in individual US cities, contact the local chapter of the Easter Seals Society.

If you are planning to visit a national park or attraction in the US run by the National Park Service, obtain a free **Golden Access Passport,** which is available at all park entrances and from federal offices whose functions relate to land, forests, or wildlife. The Passport entitles disabled travelers and their families to free park admission and provides a 50% discount on all campsite and parking fees. For further reading, check out *Resource Directory for the Disabled,* by Richard Neil Shrout (Facts on File; $45).

USEFUL ORGANIZATIONS

Mobility International USA (MIUSA), P.O. Box 10767, Eugene, OR 97440 (voice and TDD ☎541–343-1284; www.miusa.org). Sells *A World of Options: A Guide to International Educational Exchange, Community Service, and Travel for Persons with Disabilities* ($35).

Society for Accessible Travel & Hospitality (SATH), 347 Fifth Ave., #610, New York, NY 10016 (☎212-447-7284; www.sath.org). An advocacy group that publishes free online travel information and the travel magazine *OPEN WORLD* ($18, free for members). Annual membership $45, students and seniors $30.

TOUR AGENCIES

Directions Unlimited, 123 Green Ln., Bedford Hills, NY 10507 (☎800-533-5343). Books individual and group vacations for the physically disabled; not an info service.

The Guided Tour Inc., 7900 Old York Rd., #114B, Elkins Park, PA 19027 (☎800-783-5841; www.guidedtour.com). Organizes travel programs for persons with developmental and physical challenges in California and elsewhere in the United States.

MINORITY TRAVELERS

California is a multicultural state, but not always a harmonious one. Although "minority" groups are now the majority in California, there is some anti-immigrant feeling, especially aimed against Mexican immigrants. Tensions between blacks and whites have also been known to flare up in the inner cities, especially in Los Angeles. Be aware that some racial tensions exist, and try to avoid confrontations.

In towns along the US-Mexican border, the Border Patrol for the US Immigration and Naturalization Service (INS) remains on a constant lookout for Mexican nationals who have crossed the border illegally. In border towns, they may pull over anyone who looks suspicious, search their vehicles for smuggled goods and smuggled people, and ask for identification. The INS also runs checkpoints along the interstates south of Los Angeles to catch illegal immigrants. All cars must stop at these points, and the INS workers may search vehicles that arouse suspicion.

TRAVELERS WITH CHILDREN

Family vacations often require that you slow your pace, and always require that you plan ahead. If you rent a car, make sure the rental company provides a car seat for younger children. **Be sure that your child carries some sort of ID.** Tourist attractions, hotels, and restaurants often offer discounts for children. Children under two usually fly for 10% of the adult fare on overseas flights. International fares are usually 25% off for children two to 11. Also consult one of the following books:

Backpacking with Babies and Small Children, Goldie Silverman. Wilderness Press ($10).

Have Kid, Will Travel: 101 Survival Strategies for Vacationing With Babies and Young Children, Claire and Lucille Tristram. Andrews McMeel Publishing ($9).

Kidding Around San Francisco. John Muir ($8).

Trouble Free Travel with Children, Vicki Lansky. Book Peddlers ($9).

DIETARY CONCERNS

Vegetarians should have a food fest in veggie-noshing California. *Let's Go* tries to indicate vegetarian options in restaurant listings; other places to look for vegetarian and vegan cuisine are local health food stores, as well as large natural food chains such as ◼**Trader Joe's** and **Wild Oats**. Vegan options are more difficult to find in smaller towns and inland; be prepared to make your own meals. The **North American Vegetarian Society**, P.O. Box 72, Dolgeville, NY 13329 (☎518-568-7970; www.navs-online.org), publishes info about vegetarian travel, including *Vegetarian Journal's Guide to Natural Food Restaurants in the US and Canada* ($12). Also see Jed Civic's *The Vegetarian Traveler: Where to Stay If You're Vegetarian, Vegan, Environmentally Sensitive.* (Larson Publishing; $16).

Travelers who keep kosher should contact synagogues in larger cities for information on kosher restaurants. Your own synagogue or college Hillel should have access to lists of Jewish institutions across the nation. If you are strict in your observance, you may have to prepare your own food on the road. A good resource is the *Jewish Travel Guide*, by Michael Zaidner (Vallentine Mitchell; $17).

OTHER RESOURCES

USEFUL PUBLICATIONS

Most of California's big coastal cities offer a number of periodicals that provide news and entertainment. In San Francisco, try the *Chronicle*, *SF Weekly*, and the *Bay Guardian*. In L.A., pick up copies of the *Times* and *LA Weekly*. In San Diego, the *Union-Tribune* provides news and the *Reader* has the nightlife scoop.

TRAVEL PUBLISHERS & BOOKSTORES

Hunter Publishing, 470 W. Broadway, fl. 2, South Boston, MA 02127 (☎617-269-0700; www.hunterpublishing.com). Has an extensive catalog of travel guides and diving and adventure travel books.

Rand McNally, P.O. Box 7600, Chicago, IL 60680, (☎847-329-8100; www.randmc-nally.com), publishes road atlases.

Adventurous Traveler Bookstore, P.O. Box 2221, Williston, VT 05495 (☎800-282-3963; www.adventuroustraveler.com).

Bon Voyage!, 2069 W. Bullard Ave., Fresno, CA 93711 (☎800-995-9716, from abroad 559-447-8441; www.bon-voyage-travel.com). They specialize in Europe but have titles pertaining to other regions as well. Free newsletter.

WORLD WIDE WEB

Almost every aspect of budget travel is accessible via the web. At the keyboard, you can make a hostel reservation, get advice on travel hotspots from fellow travelers, or find out how much your flight will cost. Listed here are budget travel sites to start off your surfing; other relevant web sites are listed throughout the book.

WWW.LETSGO.COM Our newly designed website now features the full online content of all of our guides. In addition, trial versions of all nine City Guides are available for download on Palm OS™ PDAs. Our website also contains our newsletter, links for photos and streaming video, online ordering of our titles, info about our books, and a travel forum buzzing with stories and tips.

THE ART OF BUDGET TRAVEL

How to See the World: www.artoftravel.com. A compendium of great travel tips, from cheap flights to self defense to interacting with local culture.

Rec. Travel Library: www.travel-library.com. A fantastic set of links for general information and personal travelogues.

INFORMATION ON CALIFORNIA

GENERAL

California Division of Tourism: www.gocalif.ca.gov. The glossy tourist brochures in e-form, as well as useful maps and regional guides.

Official California Government Page: www.ca.gov. Lists state government services and contact information.

Maps and Driving Directions: www.mapquest.com. Offers thorough street-level maps of the entire country.

THE OUTDOORS

National Park Service: www.nps.gov. A wealth of information on the US National Park system, including maps and reservation information.

California State Parks Official Site: www.cal-parks.ca.gov. Maps and reservation info.

California Surf Reports: www.surfrider.org/cal5.htm. A fairly thorough and frequently updated description of surf conditions up and down the California coast.

The Ski Report: www.skicentral.com/rpt-california.html. Describes ski conditions at major slopes in California.

LOS ANGELES

L.A. Times: www.latimes.com. Full content of the daily newspaper, with free registration.

L.A. Transit Info: www.ladottransit.com. Subway and bus maps, as well as fare info.

SAN FRANCISCO

San Francisco Chronicle: www.sfgate.com/chronicle. The city's largest daily.

San Francisco Transit: www.ci.sf.ca.us/muni/index.htm. Map, schedule, and fare info.

ALTERNATIVES TO TOURISM

Traveling from place to place around the world may be a memorable experience. But if you are looking for a more rewarding and complete way to see the world, you may want to consider Alternatives to Tourism. Working, volunteering, or studying for an extended period of time can be a better way to understand laid-back life in California. From the sun-kissed sands to the towering Redwoods, with their requisite beach bums and adventure-thirsty explorers, California nurtures a number of lifestyles, not all of them out of doors. It takes a certain amount of acclimatization before you can be apathetic about a movie star sighting, or are able to predict exactly how many hours the drive up the Pacific Coast Highway will take. This chapter outlines some of the different ways to get to know California and its varied landscapes and residents. In most cases, you'll feel that you partook in a more meaningful and educational experience—something that the average budget traveler often misses out on.

VISAS & PERMITS

All travelers planning a stay of more than 90 days (180 days for Canadians) need to obtain a visa. **The Center for International Business and Travel (CIBT)**, 23201 New Mexico Ave., NW, #210, Washington, D.C. 20016 (customer service ☎800-925-2428; www.cibt.com) or 6300 Wilshire Blvd., suite 1520, Los Angeles, CA 90048 (☎323-658-5100), secures travel "pleasure tourist," or B-2 visas, to and from all possible countries for a variable service charge (6-mo. visa around $45). If you lose your I-94 form, you can replace it at the nearest **Immigration and Naturalization Service (INS)** office (☎800-375-5283; www.ins.usdoj.gov), although it's very unlikely that the form will be replaced within the time of your stay. Visa extensions are sometimes attainable with an I-539 form; call the forms request line (☎800-870-3676).

Foreign students who wish to study in the US must apply for either a M-1 visa (vocational studies) or an F-1 visa (for full-time students enrolled in an academic or language program). If English is not your native language, you will probably be required to take the **Test of English as a Foreign Language (TOEFL)**, which is administered in many countries. The international students office at the institution you will be attending can give you more specifics. Contact **TOEFL/TSE Publications**, P.O. Box 6151, Princeton, NJ 08541 (☎609-771-7100; www.toefl.org).

If you are a foreigner, you need a **work permit** or "green card" to work in California. Your employer must obtain this document, usually by demonstrating that you have skills that locals lack. Friends in the US can sometimes help expedite work permits or arrange work-for-stay exchanges. Obtaining a worker's visa may seem complex, but it's critical that you go through the proper channels, particularly in parts of California where sentiment against undocumented workers can be strong.

VISA INFORMATION

Visa (p. 28). Visitors from most of Europe, Australia, and New Zealand can travel in the US for up to 90 days without a visa, although you may need to show a return plane ticket. Citizens of South Africa need a visa.

Work Permit (p. 28). Required for all foreigners planning to work in the US.

STUDYING ABROAD

Study abroad programs range from basic language and culture courses to college-level classes, often for credit. In order to choose a program that best fits your needs, you will want to find out what students participate in it and what type of accommodations are provided. In programs that have large groups of students (from your home country) who speak the same language, there is a trade-off. You may feel more comfortable in the community, but you will not have the same opportunity to practice English with native Californians. Dorm life, similarly, provides a better opportunity to mingle with fellow students, but there is less of a chance to experience the local scene. If you live with a family, there is a potential to build lifelong friendships with Californians, but every family is different. Some good resources for finding programs that cater to your particular interests are www.studyabroad.com and www.studyabroaddirectory.com, which have links to various semester abroad programs based on a variety of criteria, including desired location and focus of study.

PROGRAMS IN CALIFORNIA

In order to live the life of a real American college student, you'll have to drink Milwaukee Beast until you puke. Otherwise, consider a visiting student program lasting either a semester or a full year. The best method by far is to contact colleges and universities in your home country to see what kind of exchanges they have with those in California; college students can often receive credit for study abroad. A more complicated option for advanced English speakers is to enroll directly, full-time in an American institution. California is home to a number of outstanding private institutions, such as Stanford and CalTech. The three-tiered state system is among the finest educational programs in the country: the University of California (www.ucop.edu/pathways) has nine campuses, California State University (www.calstate.edu) has 23, and there is a multitude of community colleges. Unfortunately for non-Californians, these state schools have high out-of-state tuition and are extremely popular with residents, who receive priority consideration.

LANGUAGE SCHOOLS

Unlike American universities, language schools are frequently independently-run international or local organizations or divisions of foreign universities that rarely offer college credit. Language schools are a good alternative to university study if you desire a deeper focus on the language or a slightly less-rigorous courseload. These programs are also good for younger high school students who might not feel comfortable with older students in a university program. There are lots of language schools located in California's major cities. Some good programs include:

Eurocentres, 101 N. Union St. suite 300, Alexandria, VA 22314 (☎703-684-1494; www.eurocentres.com) or in Europe, Head Office, Seestr. 247, CH-8038 Zurich, Switzerland (☎+41 1 485 50 40; fax 481 61 24). Language programs for beginning to advanced students with homestays in California. **Language Immersion Institute,** 75 South Manheim Blvd., SUNY-New Paltz, New Paltz, NY 12561-2499 (☎845-257-3500; www.newpaltz.edu/lii). 2-week summer language courses. Program fees are around $1000 for a 2-week course.

Language Studies International, 2015 Center St., Berkeley, CA 94704 (☎510-841-4695; www.lsi.edu) or 1706 5th Ave., San Diego, CA 92101 (☎619-234-2881). Intensive language programs in Berkeley and San Diego for students of all levels. Living options include dorms, homestays, and hotels.

Osako Sangyo University Los Angeles (OSULA) Education Center, 3921 Laurel Canyon Blvd., Los Angeles, CA 91604 (☎818-509-1484; www.osula.com). Offers intensive and general English classes in the suburbs of Los Angeles, in a residential college setting.

FILM SCHOOLS

Hollywood is the cinematic capital of the universe—there is no better place to gain behind-the-scenes experience than in the backlots of Studio City. To this end, there are numerous film schools and colleges with high-caliber film programs in the Los Angeles area, many of which run shorter summer and semester programs. Some good options to check out:

New York Film Academy, 100 E. 17th St., New York, NY 10003 (☎818-733-2600; www.nyfa.com). The Los Angeles location allows would-be actors, filmmakers, and screenwriters the chance to hone their skills on studio sets. Program lengths vary from four weeks to one year, with classes in acting, screenwriting, digital imaging, filmmaking, and 3D animation. Program costs range from $3,000 to $22,500.

University of Southern California School of Cinema-Television, Summer Production Workshop, 850 W. 34th St., Los Angeles, CA 90089-2211 (☎213-740-1742;www.usc.edu/schools/cntv/programs/spw). The world-renowned school's summer workshops offer classes in writing, digital imaging, directing and producing. University housing is available, as are classes for students who have already logged some hours (or years) in the industry.

The American Film Institute, 2021 N. Western Avenue, Los Angeles, CA 90027 (☎323-856-7600; www.afi.com). Committed to "advancing and preserving the art of the moving image," the L.A. branch of the Institute offers seminars and workshops on topics varying from directing to digital TV editing, notably the "Directing Workshop for Women" which was established in 1974. Some programs are free, but housing and meals are not provided. The annual AFI Fest, in the fall, lasts for over a week and has numerous screenings and receptions, featuring established and up-and-coming directors.

WORKING

There are two main schools of thought about working travelers. Some travelers want long-term jobs that allow them to get to know another part of the world in depth (e.g. teaching their native language, working in the tourist industry). Other travelers seek out short-term jobs to finance their travel. They usually seek employment in the service sector or in agriculture, working for a few weeks at a time to finance the next leg of their journey. This section discusses both short-term and long-term opportunities for working in California. Make sure to understand the United States' **visa requirements** for foreign workers. See the box on p. 66 for more information.

Job seekers should look in the classified sections of major daily newspapers such as the *Los Angeles Times* or the *San Francisco Chronicle*. Another option is to seek out temp agencies. It may be possible to volunteer in exchange for room and board in parts of California, such instances are noted in the guide.

LONG-TERM WORK

If you're planning on spending a substantial amount of time (more than three months) working in California, search for a job well in advance. International placement agencies are often the easiest way to find employment abroad. **Internships,** usually for college students, are a good way to segue into working abroad, although they are often unpaid or poorly paid (many say the experience, however, is well worth it). Be wary of advertisements or companies that claim the ability to get you a job abroad for a fee—often times the same listings are available online or in newspapers, or even out of date. It's best, if going through an organization, to use one that's somewhat reputable. Some good ones include:

Council Exchanges, 52 Poland St., London W1V 4JQ UK (☎020 748 2000; www.coun-cilexchanges.org.uk) has a jobs and internships database for US positions.

Alliances Abroad, 702 W. Ave., Austin, TX 78701 (☎888-6ABROAD/227623; www.alli-ancesabroad.com) sponsors internships in San Francisco.

Camp Counselors USA, Green Dragon House, 64-70 High Street, Croydon CR0 9XN UK (☎020 8668 9051; www.workexperienceusa.com) places people aged 18-30 as counselors in summer camps in the US.

AU PAIR WORK

Au pairs are typically women, aged 18-27, who work as live-in nannies, caring for children and doing light housework in foreign countries in exchange for room, board, and a small spending allowance or stipend. Most former au pairs speak favorably of their experience—how it allowed them to really get to know the country without the high expenses of traveling. However, drawbacks include long hours of constantly being on-duty, and the somewhat mediocre pay. In the United States, weekly salaries typically fall well below $200, with at least 45 hours of work expected. In California, as in the rest of the country, au pairs are expected to speak English and have at least 200 hours of childcare experience. Much of the au pair experience really does depend on the family you're placed with. The agencies below are a good starting point for looking for employment as an au pair.

Accord Cultural Exchange, 750 La Playa, San Francisco, CA 94121 (☎415-386-6203; www.cognitext.com/accord).

Childcare International, Ltd., Trafalgar House, Grenville Pl., London NW7 3SA UK (☎020 8906 3116; fax 8906-3461; www.childint.co.uk).

InterExchange, 161 Sixth Ave., New York, NY 10013 (☎212-924-0446; fax 924-0575; www.interexchange.org).

SHORT-TERM WORK

Traveling for long periods of time can get expensive; therefore, many travelers try their hand at odd jobs for a few weeks at a time to make some extra cash to carry them through another month or two of touring around. A common way to make some extra cash in California is picking fruit. Those who try agricultural labor should be prepared for a difficult and character building experience. Go to the local Farm Labor Office for more information. Most agriculture in California is concentrated in the San Joaquin Valley, although regional farms abound up and down the coast, as well. The high season for harvest is May-October. Another popular option is to work several hours a day at a hostel in exchange for free or discounted room and/or board. Most often, these short-term jobs are found by word of mouth, or simply by talking to the owner of a hostel or restaurant. Many places, especially due to the high turnover in the tourism industry, are always eager for help, even if only temporary. Random jobs (moving, working in cafés) can usually be found in bigger cities, like Los Angeles and San Francisco. For something a bit more glamorous, head to Hollywood, where day-jobs as movie extras abound. The organizations listed below offer short-term jobs in popular destinations.

Willing Workers on Organic Farms (WWOOF), P.O. Box 2675, Lewes, UK BN7 1RB (www.phdcc.com/sites/wwoof; $20) allows you to receive room and board at organic farms in California (and other parts of the world) in exchange for help on the farm.

Concession Services Corporation at Yosemite National Park, P.O. Box 578, Yosemite National Park, CA 95389 (☎209-372-1236) hires part time and permanent staff to work in the park.

Travelers Earth Repair Network (TERN), P.O. Box 4469, Bellingham, WA 98227 (www.geocities.com/rainforest/4663/tern.html; $50, $35 students) offers a network of room-and-board options for international travelers.

Bill's Home Hostel, 1040 Cielo Lane, Nipomo, CA 93444-9039 (bdennen@slonet.org) allows travelers free room and board in exchange for two hours of work.

Cenex Central Casting, 220 Flower St., Burbank, CA 91506 (☎818-562-2755) is a reputable casting service which will place extras on movie sets. $20 cash for "photo fee."

VOLUNTEERING

Carefully research a program before committing—talk to people who have previously participated and find out exactly what you're getting into. The more informed you are and the more realistic expectations you have, the more enjoyable the program will be. Most people choose to go through a parent organization that takes care of logistical details, and frequently provides a group environment and support system. There are two main types of organizations—religious (often Catholic), and non-sectarian—although there are rarely restrictions on participation for either. In major cities, small organizations often seek eager volunteers.

Earthwatch, 3 Clocktower Pl. suite 100, Box 75, Maynard, MA 01754 (☎800-776-0188 or 978-461-0081; www.earthwatch.org). Arranges 1- to 3-week programs in the United States and around the world to promote conservation of natural resources. Fees vary based on program location and duration, costs average $1700 plus airfare.

Habitat for Humanity International, 121 Habitat St., Americus, GA 31709 (☎229-924-6935 ext.2551; www.habitat.org). Volunteers build houses in over 83 countries for anywhere from 2 weeks to 3 years. Short-term program costs range from $1200-4000.

The New Conservatory Theatre Center (NCTC), 25 Van Ness Ave., San Francisco, CA 94102 (☎415-861-4914; www.nctcsf.org). The Theatre Centre and School were established in 1981 with the goals of providing entertaining and educational programs for youths and a wide array of performances for the entire community. Always looking for volunteers, from costume designers to ushers to administrative workers.

The Institute for Unpopular Culture (IFUC), P.O. Box 1523, 1850 Union St., suite 4, San Francisco, CA 94123 (☎212-925-6951; www.ifuc.org). Founded as a non-profit in 1989, IFUC seeks to aid artists whose work may not have mass appeal. The Institute sponsors gallery shows, short films, and increased interaction between dot-commers (the money) and artists (the talent), reviving the patron system of old. Volunteers are needed throughout the year to assist with research and administrative work.

Heritage Resource Management Department of US Forest Service, P.O. Box 31315, Tucson, AZ 85751-1315 (☎800-281-9176 or 520-722-2716); www.passportin-time.com) Passport in Time program needs volunteers for archaeological surveys and recording oral histories within the parks.

The Volunteer Center of San Francisco, 425 Jackson Street, San Francisco, CA 94111 (☎415-982-8999). A blanket organization places volunteers with needy non-profits in the Bay Area. For an updated list of weekly volunteer opportunities, call the main line.

FOR FURTHER READING ON ALTERNATIVES TO TOURISM

Alternatives to the Peace Corps: A directory of third world and U.S. Volunteer Opportunities, Joan Powell. Food First Books, 2000 ($10).

Living and Working in America: A Survival Guide, David Hampshire. Survival Books, 1999 ($16).

International Directory of Voluntary Work, Whetter and Pybus. Peterson's Guides and Vacation Work, 2000 ($16).

Work Your Way Around the World, Susan Griffith. Worldview, 2001 ($18).

SAN FRANCISCO

If California is a state of mind, then San Francisco is euphoria. Welcome to the city that will take you to new highs, leaving your mind spinning, your taste buds tingling, your calves aching, and your optic nerves reeling. Though it's smaller than most "big" cities, the City by the Bay more than compensates for its size with a personality that simply won't quit. The dazzling views, the daunting hills, the one-of-a-kind neighborhoods, and the laid-back, friendly people of San Fran add up to create a kind of charisma not to be found anywhere else. The city manages to pack an incredible amount of vitality into its 47 square miles, running from its thriving art community and bustling shops, to the pulsing beats in some of the country's hippest nightclubs and bars. Everyone finds something to love here.

By California standards, San Francisco is steeped in history—but it's a history of oddballs and eccentrics that resonates more today in street culture than in museums and galleries. The lineage of free spirits and troublemakers started back in the 19th century, with the smugglers of the Barbary Coast and the '49ers who flocked here during the mad boom of the Gold Rush. As the last stop in America's great westward expansion, San Francisco has always attracted artists, dreamers, and outsiders. In the 1950s came the Beats—brilliant, angry young writers who captured the rhythms of be-bop jazz in their poetry and their lives. The late 60s ushered in the most famous of San Fran rabble rousers—hippies and flower children, who turned on one generation and freaked out another by making love, not war.

The free spirited tradition continues. Anti-establishment politics have almost become establishment here, as rallies and movements repeatedly fill the city's streets and newspapers. The gay community emerged in the 70s as one of the city's most visible and powerful groups. At the same time, Mexican, Central American, and Asian immigrants have made San Francisco one of the most racially diverse cities in the US. And then in a wave of mid-90s computer-crazed prosperity, young computer workers ditched the bland suburbs of Silicon Valley for the breezes of San Francisco, with upstart Internet companies infiltrating the forgotten spaces of lower-rent neighborhoods. For a while, the Frisco fight was old-timers and hippies vs. dot-commers, but when the Clinton era and the budget surplus went the way of

HIGHLIGHTS OF SAN FRANCISCO

GOLDEN GATE BRIDGE. Yeah, yeah, we know. It's totally cliché, so cliché that it's on two out of three SF postcards. Well, don't hate it because it's beautiful—grab a windbreaker and see for yourself just what all the (justified) fuss is about (p. 94).

A GIANTS GAME AT PACIFIC BELL PARK. Not only do you get to cheer on the Giants (and maybe see a right-field homer make a splash), but the bleacher seats come with fabulous views of the game, the city, and the Bay (p. 117).

MISSION MURALS. This urban street art brilliantly combines artistic excellence, technical perfection, and community politics. Standouts include Balmy Alley and a three-building tribute to guitar god Carlos Santana (p. 99).

ALCATRAZ. Cheesy Bruckheimer flicks aside, "The Rock" is the coolest attraction in the Bay. First a military detention hall and then the original high security civilian prison, this prison has enough ghost stories to keep you up for days (p. 105).

CASTRO STREET ON FRIDAY & SATURDAY NIGHTS. Before they duck into bars or head to SoMa for the clubs, San Francisco's pretty gay boys and girls stroll Castro St. Don't come expecting a freak show—this is high-class and happy (p. 119).

the dodo, high-end yuppification calmed down a bit. Like so many chameleons, San Francisco is changing with the times, but fortunately, some things never do: the Bay is foggy, the hills are steep, and tourists are the only ones wearing shorts. For more coverage of the City by the Bay, see ▨*Let's Go: San Francisco 2003.*

◪ INTERCITY TRANSPORTATION

BY PLANE. Busy **San Francisco International Airport** (**SFO;** general info ☎650-821-8211) is 15 mi. south of downtown by U.S. 101. Plan your transportation from the airport by calling the SFO Travelers Aid (☎650-821-2735; open daily 9am-9pm) or TravInfo (☎817-1717), or by accessing the ground transport section of www.fly-sfo.com, which includes links to the web pages of all public transportation services as well as a driving route planner. **Information booths,** located on the arrivals levels of all terminals and in the international departures terminal, offer detailed fare and schedule info. **Travelers' Aid Society** booths can be found on the departure levels of all terminals. (Both open daily 10am-9pm.)

San Mateo County Transit (**SamTrans;** from the Bay Area ☎800-660-4287, from outside the Bay Area 650-817-1717; www.samtrans.com) runs two buses between SFO (from the lower level, in front of Swissair) and downtown San Francisco. Express bus KX reaches the Transbay Terminal downtown with a few stops along Mission St. and allows only one small carry-on bag per passenger (35min.; 5:30am-12:50am; Adults $3, seniors at off-peak times $1.25, under 17 $1.25). Bus #292 makes frequent stops on Mission St. and allows any amount of luggage (1hr.; 4:30am-12:45am; Adults $2.20, seniors at off-peak times $0.50, under 17 $1.50).

Another option is to take a SamTrans bus to the **Bay Area Rapid Transit (BART)** system, which runs through the city and to other Bay Area destinations. Three BART stops in San Francisco connect to the **San Francisco Municipal Railway (MUNI),** San Francisco's public transportation system. SamTrans bus BX runs from the airport to the Colma BART station just south of the city (20min.; every 20-30min. M-F 5:45am-11:30pm, Sa-Su 6:30am-11:30pm; Adults $1.10, under 17 $0.75, seniors $0.50).

There are many van services which leave from the airport for about $10-15 per person and will take you directly to your lodging. Door-to-door commercial shuttles are the most convenient way of getting downtown from SFO ($10-14). Most shuttles circulate at the airport around the lower level central island—right outside baggage claim—and do not require reservations. You will need to call to arrange for pickup going to the airport. For a complete list of companies, ask at the SFO Info Booth.

Taxis to downtown from SFO depart from the lower level, center island in all terminals—right outside the baggage claim area (about $30). Check free area guides for coupons. Any San Francisco taxi will take you to the airport, but it is better to call for pickup than to try to hail a cab on the street.

BY FREEWAY. If you are driving into San Francisco **from the south,** approach the city directly on **U.S. 101, I-280,** or **Route 1.** I-280 crosses U.S. 101 in South San Francisco and then continues through eastern Potrero Hill to end just southeast of SoMa. U.S. 101 runs along the border of Potrero Hill and the Mission, then bears left through SoMa and becomes **Van Ness Avenue.** Hwy. 1 turns into **19th Avenue** around San Francisco State University and runs through the Sunset, Golden Gate Park, the Richmond, and the Presidio.

From the north, U.S. 101 and Rte. 1 lead over the **Golden Gate Bridge** (southbound-only toll $3). Rte. 1 turns into **19th Avenue,** while U.S. 101 turns into **Lombard Street** in the Marina. From there you have two options. Taking a right on **Divisadero Street** will bring you to the Haight and then the Castro. Alternatively, continuing on Lombard St., turning right on Van Ness Ave., and following it between Pacific Heights and Russian and Nob Hills will bring you to **Market Street** near the Civic Center.

From the east, take **I-5** to **I-580** to **I-80,** which runs across the **Bay Bridge** (westbound-only toll $2) into SoMa and then connects with U.S. 101 just before it runs into Van Ness Ave.

 AREA CODE. The area code in San Francisco is 415.

✴ ORIENTATION

San Francisco is 403 mi. north of Los Angeles and 390 mi. south of the Oregon border. The city proper lies at the northern tip of the peninsula separating the San Francisco Bay from the Pacific Ocean. (For info on other cities surrounding the bay, see **Bay Area and Wine Country,** p. 121).

San Francisco's diverse neighborhoods are loosely organized along a few central arteries. Most neighborhoods are compact enough to explore comfortably on foot. Make a mental note of the steep hills in each district—a two-block detour can sometimes prevent a strenuous climb.

SAN FRANCISCO NEIGHBORHOODS

The following descriptions will move roughly from the tourist-laden western section of downtown San Francisco, to the neighborhoods in the south, and then over to the residential sections in the east. If you find that neighborhood boundaries are getting a bit confusing, don't stress—San Fran, like any living, breathing city, doesn't follow the imaginary lines that books like this one have to rely on. That said, a good map is a must.

FISHERMAN'S WHARF & THE PIERS. The eastern portion of San Francisco's waterfront is one of its most visited—and most reviled—tourist destinations. Aside from the while-you-wait caricature artists, "olde-fashioned fudge shoppes," penny-flattening machines, and novelty t-shirts, the only natives you're likely to find here are the sea lions. **Piers 39** through **45** provide access to some of San Francisco's most famous attractions.

MARINA, FORT MASON, & COW HOLLOW. The residential Marina, between Fort Mason to the east and the whopping Presidio to the west, is home to more young, wealthy professionals than any other part of San Francisco. Neighboring Fort Mason provides the cultural component to the area with theaters and museums. Directly across the lengthy Marina Green near the Presidio stands the awesome **Palace of Fine Arts** and the very fun **Exploratorium** (see p. 108). On the southern border of the Marina, bustling Chestnut and Lombard St. are packed with motels, eateries, and trendy bars. A few blocks farther south, the neighborhood of Cow Hollow houses herds of San Francisco's elite.

NORTH BEACH. On Columbus Ave. at Broadway, shops shift from selling ginseng and roast duck to proffering provolone and biscotti. North of Chinatown lies the legendary Italian community of North Beach, also the birthplace of the **Beat movement.** In the early 1950s, a group of poets and writers including Jack Kerouac, Allen Ginsberg, Maynard Krebs, and Lawrence Ferlinghetti came here to write, drink, and raise some hell. They lashed out at the conformity of postwar America, embraced Eastern religions and be-bop jazz, and lit a fuse that would eventually set off the counterculture explosion of the late 1960s. Today, the Beats have been safely co-opted and commodified in hundreds of English classes and Norton Anthologies, and in 1998, Ferlinghetti was named San Francisco's first poet laureate. Recently, North Beach has experienced a major nightlife surge.

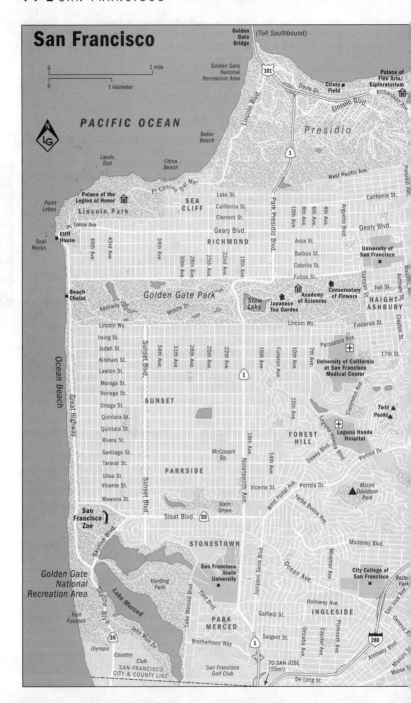

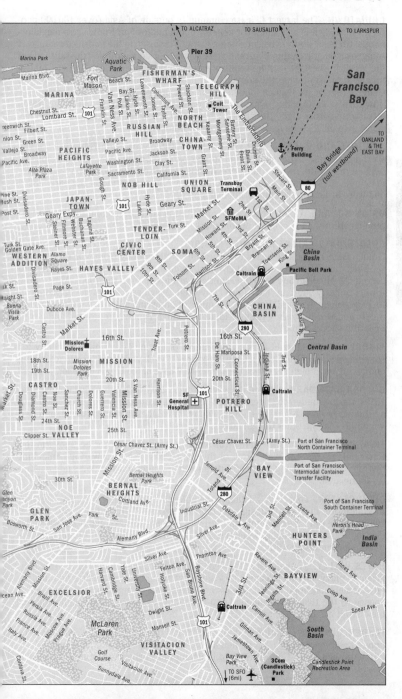

CHINATOWN. The largest **Chinese** community outside of Asia (over 100,000 people), Chinatown is also the most densely populated of San Francisco's neighborhoods. Chinese laborers began coming to San Francisco in the mid-19th century as refugees from the Opium Wars and were put to work constructing the railroads of the West. In the 1880s, white Californians secured a law against further Chinese immigration to prevent the so-called "Yellow Peril." Stranded in San Francisco, Chinese-Americans banded together to protect themselves in this small section of downtown. To this day, Chinatown remains mostly Chinese, although it has attracted visitors since the 1850s, when sailors staggered down from Barbary Coast saloons looking for women, alcohol, and opium.

NOB HILL AND RUSSIAN HILL. In the late 19th century, Nob Hill attracted the West's great railroad magnates and robber barons. Today, their showy mansions make it one of the nation's most prestigious addresses. Russian Hill, to the north, is named after Russian sailors who died during an expedition in the early 1800s and were buried on the southeast crest.

UNION SQUARE. Union's big scene is retail. It is home to mammoth hotels, overpriced eateries, and bevies of panhandlers.

GOLDEN GATE BRIDGE AND THE PRESIDIO. The great swaying span of the Golden Gate Bridge reaches across the San Francisco Bay from Marin County to the Presidio. Originally the northernmost Spanish military garrison, the Presidio served the Mexican and then the American armies up until the 1990s. Most of the former military buildings have been converted to civilian use, but the Presidio can feel hauntingly deserted. However, its miles of paths and hills are wide open to the public and worth a visit. Crissy Field, in particular, is newly renovated and now a beautiful shoreline park.

LINCOLN PARK. Lincoln Park's great chunk of green is positioned perfectly for snapping a shot of the Golden Gate Bridge and the Bay. Rugged terrain for hiking and biking meet high culture at the **California Palace of the Legion of Honor.**

GOLDEN GATE PARK. Golden Gate Park covers 1017 lush acres. Beginning in the 1870s, the city undertook decades of work to transform the desert-like region into a vibrant, green patch of loveliness. Today, nine lakes, a herd of bison, and two windmills (among other things) attract visitors.

FINANCIAL DISTRICT AND EMBARCADERO. Corporate worker bees swarm the Financial District, the Wall Street of the West Coast, where towering banks blot out the sun. A surprising number of parks and architectural standouts add character to the area.

CIVIC CENTER. There's no mistaking the colossal Civic Center with its collection of mammoth, classically-designed buildings arranged around two vast plazas. Home to the opera, symphony, and most of San Francisco's major theaters, the district is grandest at night, when beautifully lit flags and fountains flank bumper-to-bumper limousine traffic.

HAYES VALLEY. To the west of the Civic Center, the hipster haven of Hayes Valley is small, glitzy, and increasingly upscale. Now home to young artists and designers, the neighborhood has not always boasted such a swinging scene. Destruction caused by the 1989 earthquake led to a drastic makeover, and the rough-and-tumble district has become San Francisco's latest beauty queen.

TENDERLOIN. The indistinctly defined region known as the Tenderloin is economic light years away from its neighbors, the upscale Union Square and culturally-endowed Civic Center. Sporadic attempts at urban renewal have done a (small) bit to improve the poverty of the quarter and its residents. Nevertheless, **avoid walking here alone,** especially in the rectangle bordered by Ellis St., Van Ness Ave., Leavenworth St., and Golden Gate Ave.

SOUTH OF MARKET AREA (SOMA). The most well-visited, culturally rich part of SoMa lies north of Folsom St., between 2nd and 4th St. These blocks are filled with the concrete and glass expanses of **Yerba Buena Gardens,** Sony Metreon, and the Moscone Convention Center. The **San Francisco Museum of Modern Art (SFMoMA)** presides over the cultural milieu. Several blocks south, between **Pacific Bell Park** (home of the San Francisco Giants, see p. 117) and the freeway, tiny but vibrant South Park is surrounded by old and new eateries as well as the "cyberspace gulch" of upstart Internet and design companies. The stretch from 7th to 12th streets. along Folsom St., as you head toward the Mission, is known for being hip and clubby with trendy cafes, inexpensive restaurants, myriad clubs, and several establishments dedicated to the wearing and selling of leather.

PACIFIC HEIGHTS. Climbing up Fillmore St. from Japantown brings you straight into Pacific Heights, just southwest of the Marina and Cow Hollow. The abundance of palatial **Victorian homes** in this neighborhood sets a tone of wealth, reflected in the boutiques and eateries.

JAPANTOWN (NIHONMACHI). After it was destroyed by the 1906 earthquake, **Japanese** immigrants moved into the area now called Japantown, a mile west of downtown. For a time, its closely packed homes and shops constituted one of the largest Japanese enclaves outside Japan. Few returned after the community was broken apart by internment during WWII, although the name stuck.

HAIGHT-ASHBURY. East of Golden Gate Park and smack dab in the center of the city, the Haight-Ashbury has aged with uneven grace since its hippie heyday. At one time a haven for conscientious objectors to the Vietnam War, "Hashbury" subsequently embraced drug use and Eastern philosophies during anti-war protests and marches. The hippie voyage reached its apogee in 1967's "Summer of Love," when Janis Joplin, the Grateful Dead, and Jefferson Airplane all made music and love here within a few blocks of one another. Today the counterculture hangs out side-by-side with the over-the-counter culture, especially in the Upper Haight. The Lower Haight still clings to the good ol' days despite the latest additions of Internet cafes and smoothie joints.

CASTRO. Scout's honor, *this* is where the boys are. Much of San Francisco's **gay** male community, along with a much smaller number of hip young lesbians, makes the Castro home. Cruisey bars and cafes are everywhere, same-sex public displays of affection raise nary an eyebrow, and tank tops and chiseled abs are *de rigeur.* Besides being fabulous, the Castro is also pretty.

MISSION. Founded by Spanish settlers in 1776, the Mission district is home to some of the city's oldest structures, as well as some of the hottest young people and places around. Colorful **murals** celebrate the prominent **Latino** presence that has long defined the Mission. The area grows increasingly diverse and gentrified along Valencia St. The area is also home to a cohesive **lesbian** community, and there is a gay male presence.

RICHMOND. Residential Richmond has a rich history of immigration that is slowly turning into a history of yuppification as San Francisco real estate continues its frightening boom. The Richmond has been the traditional home to Irish-, Russian-, and now Chinese-American communities. "Inner Richmond" has been dubbed "New Chinatown," and the abundance of excellent Chinese restaurants justifies the name.

SAN FRANCISCO

ALCATRAZ AND ANGEL ISLAND. Although both Alcatraz and Angel Island once housed prisons, the one on Alcatraz is by far the better known. Because of its location in the middle of the bay, it was thought to be inescapable and was used to house the nation's hardest criminals. Angel Island's history is much calmer, and its shores and trails are perfect for picnicking and hiking.

⊑ LOCAL TRANSPORTATION

BY PUBLIC TRANSPORTATION. San Francisco's main public transportation systems are the **MUNI Metro subway** and **bus system,** which operate throughout the city, and **BART,** which provides wider coverage of the Bay Area and speedy but limited service in San Francisco. Each system is described below and has its own infrastructure, but they are all overseen by the **Metropolitan Transportation Commission** (☎510-464-7700; www.transitinfo.org), which provides transit information for the nine-county San Francisco Bay Area.

A decent public transit system makes San Francisco something of an anomaly in a state full of auto-philes; the Bay Area is the easiest place on the West Coast to explore without a car. The system (particularly the Metro system) may be slower and less developed than its counterparts on the East Coast and in Europe, but the city is so walkable that most find a combination of foot and public transport perfect for getting around.

Most transportation within the city falls under the authority of the **San Francisco Municipal Railway** (**MUNI;** pronounced MEW-nee; ☎673-6864; www.sfmuni.com)—something of a misnomer since the system includes **buses** (electric trolley and diesel), **cable cars** (the only ones in the world still operating), a **subway,** and **streetcars.** The MUNI Metro system, whose cars alternate between subway (below ground) and surface-rail (above ground) transportation at various points in the city, offers more limited but speedier service than the MUNI bus system. Downtown, all six Metro lines (F, J, N, L, M, and K) travel underground along a central artery: **Market Street.** With the exception of the F line, they all travel underground from the **Embarcadero Station,** to at least the **Church Street Station.** The **F** line runs antique streetcars above ground along Market St., from the **Embarcadero** to the **Castro Street Station** and as of just a few months ago also connects to Fisherman's Wharf via the Northern Waterfront/Embarcadero. As they travel "outbound" (i.e. away from the Ferry Terminal and the Embarcadero), they all stop at the **Embarcadero, Powell, Civic Center, Van Ness,** and **Church Street stations;** if you're just traveling along this short downtown stretch, it doesn't matter which car you catch. If you're heading any farther, however, you should take care to snag the appropriate car before the different lines split off from one another. The **J** and **N** emerge from the tunnel at **Church Street,** while the **K, L,** and **M** routes continue underground past **Castro Street** and emerge above ground at the **West Portal Station.**

Single-ride fares on MUNI buses, streetcars, and the subway cost $1 (seniors and ages 5-17 $0.35, under 4 free); if you need one, ask for a **free transfer,** which is valid for 2 additional rides within a 90min. period. Single-ride fares on the cable cars are pricier, at $2 a pop (seniors and disabled $2, $1 9pm-7am with photo ID; children under 6 free; before 7am and after 9pm $1 for adults), with no transfers. **MUNI passports,** sold at the Powell St. Visitors Center and at some accommodations, are valid on all MUNI vehicles, including cable cars (1-day $6, 3-day $10, 7-day $15). The **Weekly Pass** is cheaper ($9), but must be purchased for a single work week and requires an additional $1 to ride the cable cars. The **Monthly FastPass** (adults $35; seniors, disabled, and ages 5-17 $8) includes in-town BART trips (from Embarcadero to Balboa Park) and cable cars.

MUNI's cable cars are a classic emblem of San Francisco. Declared a national historic landmark in 1964, the colorful cable cars are much more about image than practicality. The cars are noisy, slow (9½ mph), expensive (**Fares**, see above), and usually crammed full, making them an unreliable method of getting around. You won't be the first person to think of taking one to Fisherman's Wharf. Still, there is something charming about these relics, and you'll probably want to try them, especially if you have a MUNI passport. To avoid the mobs, the best strategy is to get up early and climb the hills with the sunrise. All lines run daily from 6am to 12:20am. There are three lines from which you can choose.

Golden Gate Ferry (☎923-2000; www.goldengate.org) sails across the Bay to Marin County from the **Ferry Building** at the foot of Market St., east of Pier 1. Ferries serve **Larkspur** (M-F 20 trips per day, first ferry leaves SF 6:35am, last ferry leaves Larkspur 8:15pm. Adults $3.25, seniors $1.60, ages 6-12 $2.45; Sa-Su and holidays 5 trips per day, first ferry leaves SF 10:40am, last ferry leaves Larkspur 5:40pm, $5.30) and **Sausalito** (M-F 9 trips per day, first ferry leaves SF 7:30am, last ferry leaves Sausalito 7:20pm. Adults $5.60, seniors $2.80, ages 6-12 $4.20, under 5 free; Sa-Su 6 trips per day, first ferry leaves SF 11:30am, last ferry leaves Sausalito 6:10pm; $5.30; increased service May-Sept.). Both lines are wheelchair accessible. Kids under five are free with an adult; ages 6-12 get a 25% discount; seniors and disabled get 50% off. Transfers are free between bus routes and ferries.

The **Blue and Gold Fleet** (☎705-8200, tickets ☎705-5555; www.blueandgold-fleet.com) runs to Alcatraz (14 per day; $9.25 round-trip, seniors $7.50, ages 5-11 $6; audio tour $4 extra) and Angel Island (M-F 2 per day, Sa-Su 3 per day; $10.50 round-trip, ages 6-12 $5.50, under 6 free) and between SF and Tiburon, Vallejo, Alameda, and Oakland. The Blue and Gold Fleet also offers an Island Hop to Alcatraz and Angel Island. (Sept.-June daily, May-June M and Th-Su. $35.25, seniors $32.50, ages 5-11 $21, under 5 free; includes audio tour on Alcatraz and TramTour on Angel Island). The **Harbor Bay Ferry** goes between SF and Alameda. (☎510-769-5500; www.harborbayferry.com.) The **Red and White Ferry** has service between SF and Point Richmond (☎673-2900; www.redandwhite.com); the **Baylink Ferry** services SF to Vallejo with a connecting bus to Sacramento. (☎877-643-3779; www.baylinkferry.com.) All ferries leave from the **Ferry Building** near the Embarcadero.

BY REGIONAL PUBLIC TRANSPORTATION. All regional buses operate from the **Transbay Terminal,** 425 Mission St., at 1st St. downtown. An information center on the second floor has maps, displays, and free phone lines for bus information. (☎495-1569. Open daily 4:30am-12:30am.) **Golden Gate Transit** provides regional fixed-route bus service in San Francisco, Marin, and Sonoma Counties. Limited service is also available between Central Marin and Western Contra Costa Counties. (☎923-2000; www.goldengatetransit.org. M-F 6am-10pm, Sa-Su reduced service; $1.50-6.30 depending on distance; discounts for seniors, disabled, and youth.) **Alameda County (AC) Transit** operates bus service to and in Oakland and Berkeley. (☎800-448-9790; www.actransit.org $1.35-2.75 (transbay fares); discounts for seniors, disabled, and youth). **San Mateo Transit (SamTrans)** serves the peninsula with hundreds of daily trips along the Bayshore corridor between Palo Alto and downtown San Francisco. Additional frequent San Francisco service is provided along El Camino Real and Mission St. Hundreds of other daily trips serve San Francisco International Airport, Daly City, Hayward, and 20 other cities throughout the county. (☎800-660-4287 or 650-817-1717; www.samtrans.com. Most routes run daily 6am-6pm; $1-3; discounts for seniors and youth.)

Connections to neighboring cities are well-coordinated and speedy via **BART,** with five lines connecting San Francisco with the **East Bay** (see p. 121), including

Oakland, Berkeley, Concord, and Fremont. All stations provide free maps and schedules and all stops are wheelchair accessible. (☎989-2278; www.bart.org. Service M-F 4am-midnight, Sa 6am-midnight, Su 8am-midnight; times at individual stops may vary. Fare within San Francisco $1.10, to the East Bay up to $4.70.)

Caltrain (in Bay area ☎800-660-4287, from elsewhere 650-817-1717; www.caltrain.com), which leaves San Francisco from the **Caltrain Depot** at 4th & King St. in SoMa (open M-F 5am-midnight, Sa 7am-midnight, Su 8am-10pm), is a regional commuter train that runs south to Palo Alto ($4, seniors and under 12 $2) and San Jose ($5.25, seniors and under 12 $2.50), making many stops along the way. Fares are calculated on the basis of zones and monthly passes are available.

BY BIKE. Despite the hills, San Francisco is a great city to visit on bike or in-line skate. The major hills are predictably punishing. Even the hardiest bike couriers have been spotted walking their bikes up the especially steep grades. Check out our color topographical map of downtown (in the very front and back of this book) to plan a flatter route. The San Francisco Bike and Walking Map also shows street elevations, official (and unofficial) bike routes, vista points, and bike shops. Most modes of public transportation in the Bay Area accommodate bicycles. Beware, when riding on roads also used by cable cars and trains, of getting your tires stuck in their grooves.

The Department of Parking and Traffic runs the **SF Bicycle Program** (☎585-2453), which organizes official, numbered **bike routes** around the city. Rectangular **signs** showing a silhouetted bike and the Golden Gate Bridge mark the routes. Even numbers on the signs refer to north/south routes, with the numbers increasing from east to west; odd numbers refer to east/west routes, with the numbers increasing from north to south; three-digit numbers refer to connector routes; and green signs are for local routes, while signs with a red Golden Gate Bridge icon indicate crosstown routes. These bike paths may run separate from motor vehicle traffic, alongside traffic in the street in a marked bike lane, or with traffic on a street with a wide-curb lane. The SFBP hotline has info on bike lockers, MUNI racks, and safety resources. The non-profit **SF Bicycle Coalition** (☎431-2453; www.sfbike.org) promotes bike use, advocates for transit improvement, and gets members bike shop discounts and other goodies.

Safe and secure cycling requires a quality **helmet** (required by state law) and **lock.** A good helmet costs about $40—much cheaper than critical head surgery. Most rental shops have helmets for very reasonable daily and weekly rates. U-shaped **Kryptonite** or **Citadel** locks ($30-60) carry **insurance** against theft for one or two years if your bike is registered with the police.

BY TAXI. Taxis are not as easy to hail on the street in San Francisco as they are in many American cities, so it's a good idea to call a cab. **San Francisco Yellow Cab** (☎626-2345), **National Cab Company** (☎648-4444), and **Town Taxi** (☎546-1616) are a few of the local taxi companies.

BY CAR. A car is not necessary for getting around the city or area and may be more trouble than it's worth. As evidenced by the terrain, driving in San Francisco demands a certain conscientiousness. Contending with the treacherous **hills** is the first task; if you've arrived in a standard (manual) transmission vehicle, you'll need to develop a fast clutch foot, since all hills have stop signs at the crests. If you're renting, get an automatic transmission. Make sure to stop for cable cars, because they won't stop for you.

Parking in San Francisco is rare and expensive even where legal, and a network of zealous traffic cops doles out copious tickets, despite local protests against the city's outrageous regulations. The many broken parking meters indicate an irate citizenry, but the time limit still applies to such spaces, and you may be ticketed up to three times for one offense. Whatever you do, don't block a sidewalk disabled-access ramp—the ticket is a whopping $250. If you have a car that you'd like to stow while exploring the city, you can leave it parked all day in the residential Richmond or Sunset districts. Also, many suburban BART stations offer free parking. If you want to park near a popular area, your best bet may well be a **parking garage.** Here is a list of car rental agencies.

 City, 1748 Folsom St. (☎877-861-1312), between Duboce and 14th St. Compacts from $29-35 per day, $160-170 per week. Small fee for unlimited mileage. Must be 21; $8 per day surcharge for drivers under 25. Open M-F 7:30am-6pm, Sa 9am-4pm. Additional location: 1433 Bush St. (☎866-359-1331), between Van Ness Ave. and Polk St.

Budget, 321 Mason St. (☎415-928-7864), in Union Sq. Compacts from $30 per day. Must be 21; $20 surcharge per day for drivers under 25. Open M-F 6am-9pm, Sa 6:30am-7pm, Su 6:30am-9pm.

Thrifty, 520 Mason St. (☎415-788-8111), at Post St. Compacts from $27 per day. Unlimited mileage. Must be 21; $25 per day surcharge for drivers under 25. Open daily 7am-7pm.

> **PREVENT RUNAWAYS.** The street signs admonishing you to "Prevent Runaways" refer not to wayward youth but to cars poorly parked on hills. When parking facing uphill, turn front wheels away from the curb, and leave the car in first gear if driving a standard transmission. If your car starts to roll, it will stop (you hope) when the tires hit the curb. When facing downhill, turn the wheels toward the curb and leave the car in reverse. *Always* set the emergency brake.

⚄ PRACTICAL INFORMATION

TOURIST & FINANCIAL SERVICES

Visitor Information: Visitor Information Center (☎415-283-0177 or ☎415-391-2000; 24hr. info recordings 391-2001; www.sfvisitor.org), in Hallidie Plaza, at Powell St. Open M-F 8:30am-5pm, Sa-Su 9am-3pm; phones open M-F 8:30am-5pm.

Consulates: Australia, 1 Bush St. #700, at Market St. (☎415-536-1970). **Ireland,** 44 Montgomery St. (☎415-392-4214), at Sutter St. **UK,** 1 Sansome St. #850, at Market St. (☎415-617-1300).

Currency Exchange: Available at the airport and most banks. **American Express,** 455 Market St. (☎415-536-2600; www.americanexpress.com). Open M-F 8:30am-5pm, Sa 9am-3:30pm. **Bank of America Foreign Currency Services,** 1 Powell St. (☎415-953-5102), at Eddy St., near Market St. Open M-F 9am-6pm, Sa 9am-2pm. **Foreign Exchange Ltd.,** 429 Stockton St. (☎415-677-5100), near Sutter St. Open M-F 9am-5:30pm; Apr.-Sept. Sa 9:15-4:45pm. **Thomas Cook,** 75 Geary St. (☎415-362-3452; www.us.thomascook.com). Open M-F 9am-5pm, Sa 10am-4pm.

LOCAL SERVICES

San Francisco Public Library (www.sfpl.lib.ca.us). **Main Branch,** 100 Larkin St. (☎415-557-4400), between Grove and Fulton St. Open M 10am-6pm, Tu-Th 9am-8pm, F 11am-5pm, Sa 9am-5pm, Su noon-5pm. Other branches in the **Mission,** 300 Bartlett St. (☎695-5090), at 24th St.; in **Chinatown,** 1135 Powell St. (☎274-0275), near Jackson St.; and in **North Beach,** 2000 Mason St. (☎274-0270), at Columbus St.

Ticket Agencies: Tickets.com (☎415-478-2277 or ☎800-225-2277). Open daily 8am-6pm. **TIX Bay Area** (☎433-7827; www.theatrebayarea.org), on Stockton St. between Post and Geary St. Currently in the garage beneath Union Sq. on Geary St. due to construction. Tickets to concerts, clubs, plays, and sports. Half-price tickets often available on day of show (cash only; inquire in person) and on Sa. Carries travel passes and tourist info. Open Tu-Th 11am-6pm, F-Sa 11am-7pm.

Road Conditions: CalTrans, ☎800-427-7623 within California; ☎916-445-7623 elsewhere. **TravInfo,** ☎817-1717.

National Weather Service, ☎650-364-7974.

Laundromats: Brainwash, 1122 Folsom St. (☎415-861-9274), between 7th and 8th St. in **SoMa.** Coffeehouse, restaurant, live music venue, and laundromat. Wash $1.75, dry $0.25 per 8min. Open M-F 7:30am-11pm, Sa-Su 8am-11pm. **Doo Wash,** 817 Columbus Ave. (☎415-885-1222), near Lombard St. in **North Beach.** Video games, pinball machines, pool table, and TV. Wash $1.50, dry $1. Open daily 7am-11pm; last load 9:30pm.

Downtown San Francisco

▲ ACCOMMODATIONS

Adelaide Hostel & Hotel, **33**
Ansonia Abby Hotel, **31**
AYH Hostel at Union Square, **37**
Central YMCA of San Francisco, **41**
The Embassy Hotel, **40**
Fort Mason Hostel, **4**
Golden Gate Hotel, **26**
Green Tortoise Hostel, **14**
Interclub Globe Hostel, **61**
New Central Hotel & Hostel, **53**
Pacific Tradewinds Hostel, **25**
San Remo Hotel, **5**
SoMa Inn, **56**

🍎 FOOD

Ananda Fuara, **52**
Basil, **59**
Bob's Sushi, **3**
Café Bastille, **27**
Café Bean, **28 & 30**
Cafe Venue, **38**
Dottie's True Blue Café, **32**
Golden Gate Bakery, **18**
Grand Palace, **22**
House of Nanking, **19**
Lalitai Thai Restaurant and Bar, **44**
L'Osteria del Forno, **11**
LuLu, **55**
Mario's Bohemian Cigar Store Café, **10**
Millennium, **43**
Patisserie Café, **60**
Pat's Café, **2**
Sotano Grill, **29**
Sushigroove, **9**
Zarzuela, **8**

🎵 NIGHTLIFE/MUSIC

Backflip, **39**
Caffé Trieste, **12**
The EndUp, **57**
Hollywood Billiards, **45**
Hotel Utah Saloon, **58**
The Stud, **62**
Velvet Lounge, **15**
Vesuvio Café, **17**

⭐ ENTERTAINMENT

Biscuits & Blues, **34**
Curran Theatre, **35**
Geary Theater, **36**
Golden Gate Theater, **42**
Herbst Theatre, **46**
Louise M. Davies Symphony Hall, **51**
Lou's Pier, **1**
The Orpheum, **50**
Saloon, **13**
War Memorial Opera House, **48**
Yerba Buena Center for the Performing Arts, **54**

● SIGHTS

Asian Art Museum, **47**
Cable Car Powerhouse and Museum, **20**
City Lights Bookstore, **16**
"Crookedest Street in the World", **6**
Ross Alley, **21**
San Francisco Art Institute, **7**
San Francisco Public Library, **49**
Transamerica Pyramid, **23**
Waverly Place, **24**

Television: ABC (Channel 7, KGO); **CBS** (Channel 5, KPIX); **Fox** (Channel 2, KTVU); **NBC** (4, KRON); **PBS** (9, KQED); **WB** (20, KBWB).

National Public Radio: KQED 88.5 FM; KAWL 91.7 FM.

EMERGENCY & COMMUNICATIONS

Police: ☎553-0123. **Fire:** ☎558-3200. **Poison:** ☎800-876-4766.

24hr. Crisis Lines: AIDS Hotline, ☎800-342-2437. **Crisis Line for the Handicapped,** ☎800-426-4263. **Drug Crisis Line,** ☎415-362-3400. **Rape Crisis Center,** ☎415-647-7273. **Suicide Prevention,** ☎415-781-0500.

Hospitals: Central Public Health Center, 470 27th St. (☎415-271-4263), at Telegraph Ave. in Oakland. Make appointments far in advance. Open M-F 8-11:30am and 1-4pm. **Haight-Ashbury Free Medical Clinic,** 558 Clayton St. (☎415-487-5632), at Haight St. Appointments only. Open M-Th 9am-9pm, F 9am-5pm. **Lyon-Martin Women's Clinic,** 1748 Market St. #201 (☎415-565-7667), at Valencia St. Open for drop-ins Th 1-3pm. Clinic hours: M-Tu and Th-F 8:30am-5pm, W 8:30am-7:30pm.

Internet Access: Most **public library** locations. **The Blue Danube,** 306 Clement St. (☎415-221-9041), at 4th Ave. Internet access $3 per 20min., $5 per 40min., $7 per hr. Open daily 7am-9:30pm. **Chat Cafe,** 498 Sanchez St. (☎415-626-4700), at 18th St. Free with purchase ($2.50 per hr.). Open M-F 6:30am-7:30pm, Sa 8am-7:30pm, Su 8am-6:30pm. **The Crêpe House,** 1755 Polk St. (☎415-441-2421), at Washington St. DSL Internet access $10 per hr. Open Su-Th 7:30am-9:30pm, F-Sa 7:30am-10:30pm.

SAN FRANCISCO

Downtown San Francisco

Post Offices: Bernal Heights Station, 45 29th St., at Mission St. Open M-F 8:30am-5pm. **Postal Code:** 94110. **Chinatown Station,** 867 Stockton St., at Clay St. Open M-F 9am-5:30pm, Sa 9am-4:30pm. **Postal Code:** 94108. **Civic Center: Federal Building Station,** 450 Golden Gate Ave., at Larkin St. Open M-F 8:30am-5pm. **Postal Code:** 94102. **Geary Station,** 5654 Geary Blvd., at 21st Ave. Open M-F 9am-5:30pm, Sa 9am-4:30pm. **Postal Code:** 94121. **Haight-Ashbury: Clayton St. Station,** 554 Clayton St., at Haight St. Open M-F 9am-5:30pm, Sa 9am-4pm. Postal Code: 94117.

PUBLICATIONS

The largest Bay Area **daily** is the *San Francisco Chronicle* ($0.50), run by executive editor Phil Bronstein, Sharon Stone's husband, and owned by the Hearst Corporation. the *San Francisco Examiner*, the paper actually founded by the yellow journalist himself, William Randolph Hearst, has lunchtime and evening editions. The two papers share a Sunday edition ($1.50). The pink *Datebook* section of the Sunday edition is also a worthwhile entertainment resource. Free publications flood San Francisco cafes, visitors centers, and sidewalk boxes, including the progressive *S.F. Bay Guardian* (www.sfbg.com; Wednesdays) and it's major competitor *S.F. Weekly* (www.sfweekly.com). Harder to find, but worth the effort, are two special-interest rags: *Poetry Flash*, available at discerning bookstores, has info on literary happenings in the Bay Area and beyond, while *Bay Area Music (BAM)* magazine is available at the livelier eateries in town.

Various tourist-targeting, coupon-filled free glossies are in sidewalk boxes in the heavily trafficked Fisherman's Wharf and Union Square areas, as well as at Visitors Centers. Among them are the *Bay City Guide, San Francisco Guide,* and *San Francisco Quick Guide.*

⛑ ACCOMMODATIONS

For those who don't mind sharing a room with strangers, San Francisco's better **hostels** (below) are homier, cheaper, and safer than most budget **hotels** (p. 86). Book in advance if at all possible, but since many don't take reservations for summer, you might have to just show up or call early (well before noon) on your day of arrival. Travelers with cars should also consider the **Marin Headlands Hostel,** a beautiful spot just minutes from the city across the Golden Gate Bridge (see p. 94). Some hostels ask for a foreign passport as identification; US citizens are usually welcome but sometimes must prove they are not local residents.

HOSTELS

▧ **Pacific Tradewinds Hostel,** 680 Sacramento St. (☎433-7970; fax 291-8801; www.hostels.com/pt), at Kearny St., in **Chinatown.** While other hostels drift in the doldrums, Pacific Tradewinds plows ahead. Friendly staff and sardine-can intimacy. Linens, laundry, free DSL, no lockout. 2-week max. stay. Reception 8am-midnight. Reservations recommended. Dorms $16-24; double beds $16-22 per person. ❷

▧ **Central YMCA of San Francisco,** 220 Golden Gate Ave. (☎345-6700; fax 885-5439; www.centralymcasf.org), at Leavenworth St. east of Hyde St., in the **Tenderloin.** Opened in 1910, the Tenderloin Y houses 3 floors of hotel space—106 simple rooms, all with TVs, and some with private baths. Energize in the elegant and affordable cafe with complimentary continental breakfast for the free fitness facility's yoga workshops and cardio-kickboxing. Pool, towels, lockers, laundry, mail facilities, and cheap parking. Key and remote deposit $20. Dorms $25; singles $40-50; doubles $50-60; triples $65-78. ❷

▧ **Adelaide Hostel & Hotel,** 5 Isadora Duncan (☎359-1915 or ☎800-359-1915; fax 359-1940; www.adelaidehostel.com; info@adelaidehostel.com), at the end of a little alley off Taylor St. between Geary and Post St., in **Union Square.** Warm hosts, sizable common areas, and reasonable prices make this quiet 18-room oasis the perfect hotel in which to meet a bloke from Australia or a lass from Ireland. Steep stairs let you flex your Frisco calves. All rooms have large windows, TV (some with free 300-channel satellite), and wash basin. Small shared hallway bathrooms. Hostel offers shuttle to SFO each morning ($8). 24 hr. reception. Check-out noon. Reserve online or by phone at least 10 days in advance. Dorms $20; singles and doubles from $55. ❷

AYH Hostel at Union Square, 312 Mason St. (☎788-5604; fax 788-3023), between Geary and O'Farrell St., in **Union Square.** TV, Internet access ($1 per 10min.), and weekly events list with free walking tours, ballgame outings, and a nightly movie. $5 deposit for locker, iron, board game, or key. 21 night max. stay. Reception 24hr. Quiet hours midnight-7am. IBN reservations available. Reserve by phone with credit card or show up around 8am. Tidy and unadorned dorm-style triples and quads $22; nonmembers $25. Private rooms $60; nonmembers $66. Under 13 half-price with parent. ❷

Fort Mason Hostel (HI-AYH), Bldg. #240 (☎771-7277; sfhostel@norcalhostels.org), at the corner of Bay and Franklin St. past the administrative buildings, in **Fort Mason.** Beautiful surroundings give this 160-bed hostel a campground feel. Not a place for partiers—strictly enforced quiet hours and other rules, such as no smoking or alcohol. Movies, walking tours, kitchen, dining room, bike storage. Huge, clean kitchen, and cute cafe with vegetarian dinner ($3). Usually booked weeks in advance, but a few beds are reserved for walk-ins. Minor chores expected. Lockers, laundry (wash $1, dry $1), and parking. Reception 24hr. Check-in 2:30pm. Check-out 11am. No curfew, but lights-out at midnight. IBN reservations available. Dorms $22.50. ❷

Easy Goin' Travel and California Dreamin' Guesthouse, 3145-47 Mission St. (☎552-8452; fax 552-8459; www.easygo.com), at Precita Ave., in **Mission.** The super-friendly staff and excellent amenities more than make up for the slightly removed new location of this independent hostel. Old Haight St. location is no longer associated. 20 dorm-style beds in 4 rooms, and 10 private rooms with 2 double beds each. Additional location at Harrison and 7th. In-room TVs, kitchen, TV lounge, laundry, Internet, bike rental, and travel services. Check-in through the Mission St. location; free shuttle to Harrison and 7th St. $20 security and key deposit. 2-night min. stay. Check-in noon. Check-out 11am. Dorm beds $18-19; private rooms $40-43. Credit cards with $1 surcharge. ❷

Green Tortoise Hostel, 494 Broadway (☎834-1000; www.greentortoise.com), off Columbus Ave. at Kearny St., in **North Beach.** A former brothel, ballroom, and apartment flat sprouted this super mellow and friendly pad. Get to know fellow travelers and crash a keg party or special event in the Fior D'Italia ballroom. Free sauna. Free Internet access. Breakfast and kitchen access included. Storage lockers $1 per day; smaller free lockers under every bed. Laundry (wash $1.25, dry $0.75). Key deposit $20. 10-day max. stay. Reception 24hr. Check-in noon. Check-out 11am. Reservations recommended; call at noon on arrival day for walk-in availability. 4-, 6-, and 8-bed dorms $19-22; private rooms $48-56. No credit cards. ❷

Interclub Globe Hostel, 10 Hallam Pl. (☎431-0540), off Folsom St. between 7th and 8th St., in **SoMa.** From Transbay Terminal, take MUNI bus #12 to 7th and Howard St. Formerly a flophouse, bathhouse, leather bar, drug-den, and hospice, Interclub is now a vibrant hostel. A nice aquarium allows to you sleep with the fishes. 24hr. Internet access. Happening common room has pool table, TV, microwave, and fridge. All rooms have private bath. Refundable key deposit $10. Refundable safety deposit $10. Spare 5 to 8-bed dorms $19, 3 nights $45; private single or double $50; off-season rates reduced. No credit cards or personal checks. Passport required. ❷

SoMa Inn, 1080 Folsom St. (☎863-7522, fax 558-8562), between 6th and 7th St., in **SoMa.** Clean, no-frills rooms on a barren block of Folsom St. Shared hall bath. Kitchen and Internet access. Reception 24hr. Refundable key deposit $5. 8-bed dorms $17; singles $28; doubles $36; triples $66; quads $88. Weekly rates: dorms $99.50; singles $160; doubles $180; triples $330; quads $440. ❷

SAN FRANCISCO

San Francisco Zen Center, 300 Page St. (☎ 863-3136; www.sfzc.org), near Laguna St. in the **Lower Haight**. If rigorous soul searching is not for you but meditative peace of mind sounds appealing, you can stay at the Zen Center as a guest. Breakfast included. Single and double rooms $55-78. Weekly and monthly rates. ❹

New Central Hotel and Hostel, 1412 Market St. (☎ 703-9988), between Van Ness Ave. and Polk St., in **Civic Center**. This conventional, no-frills hostel is dim and austere, but clean. Lockers, TV room, kitchens, laundry, and free linens. Check-in anytime. Check-out 11am. Dorms $15 per night, $95 per week; private room with shared bath $25, with private bath $45. Proof of travel required. ❶

HOTELS

▨ **Ansonia Abby Hotel,** 711 Post St. (☎ 673-2670 or ☎ 800-221-6470; fax 673-9217), between Jones and Leavenworth St., in **Union Square**. Keep this gloriously affordable secret to yourself. Overnight storage and safety deposit, TV and fridge in every room, and access to DSL-equipped computer lab. Free breakfast daily 7-8:30am, dinner M-Sa. Laundry facilities. Check-out 11am. Singles $56-66; doubles $66, with bath $79. Cheap weekly rates (from $211) available Sept.-Apr. for Bay Area summer students. ❹

▨ **The San Remo Hotel,** 2237 Mason St. (☎ 776-8688; www.sanremohotel.com), between Chestnut and Francisco St., in **Russian Hill.** Built in 1906, this hotel has rooms that are small but elegantly furnished with antique armoires, bedposts, lamps, and complimentary (if random) backscratchers. The sparkling shared bathrooms with brass pull-chain toilets harken back to the end of the 19th century. The hotel's penthouse offers a private garden, bathroom, and windowed rooftop room with an amazing view of the city. Friendly staff. Free modem connections. Laundry room (wash $1.50, dry $1). Check-in 2pm. Check-out 11am. Reservations required. Singles $50-75; doubles $60-85; triples $75-90. Penthouse $155 per night; reserve 6-9 months in advance. ❹

▨ **The Red Victorian Bed, Breakfast, and Art,** 1665 Haight St. (☎ 864-1978; www.redvic.com) west of Belvedere St. in the **Upper Haight**. The "Summer of Love" lives on in this B&B and gallery of meditative art. Striving to create peace through tourism, guests come together at breakfast to meditate and chat. All 18 rooms are individually decorated in such themes as sunshine, redwoods, playground, and butterflies. Even the hall bathrooms have their own motifs. Breakfast included. Reception 9am-9pm. Check-in 3-9pm or by appointment. Check-out 11am. Reservations required. Rooms from $72-200, discounts for stays longer than 3 days. ❹

▨ **The Parker House,** 520 Church St. (☎ 621-3222 or ☎ 888-520-7275; www.parkerguesthouse.com), near 17th St., in **Castro.** Serene and stylish. Regularly voted best LGB B&B in the city. A beautiful parlor, with dark wood paneling, grand piano, and flowers galore. Every room has cable and modem ports, but best of all, there are heavenly down comforters and a spa and steam room downstairs. Breakfast included in a sunny porch-room overlooking rose gardens. Parking $15 per day. 2-night min. stay on weekends, 4-night min. stay some holiday weekends. Check-in 3pm. Check-out noon. Reservations recommended. Rooms with shared bath from $119, with private bath from $139. ❺

▨ **The Phoenix,** 601 Eddy St. (☎ 776-1380 or 800-248-9466; fax 673-2696; phoenixhotel@worldnet.att.net; www.thephoenixhotel.com), at Larkin St., in the **Tenderloin.** Self-consciously hip rooms with funky beach resort decor and a gorgeous blue-and-white-tiled swimming pool. "Soothing Sounds" radio, complimentary Pop Tart breakfast by the pool, and access to Crunch Fitness Health Club make this much more than your average dive. Free access to popular Backflip Lounge next door. Parking included. Doubles start at a pricey $145, but may go as low as $99-109 on a slow night. ❸

Inn On Castro, 321 Castro St. (☎ 861-0321; www.innoncastro2.com), near Market St., in **Castro.** Brightly refurbished Victorian exterior complements the cozy living room—the perfect place to enjoy a good book, the Inn's popular full breakfast, or a swig of complimentary brandy. Common kitchen opens onto deck with beautiful, sweeping view of the

East Bay, while the immaculately clean dining area and comfy common lounge are reminiscent of a compulsive friend's apartment. Gay-owned and -operated, but straight-friendly. Parking $15 per day. Reception 7:30am-10:30pm. Singles $100-135; doubles $115-185; patio suite $185; neighborhood apartments $135-250 per night. ❺

The Bed and Breakfast Inn, 4 Charlton Ct. (☎921-9784; info@1stb-bsf.com; www.the-bandb.com), off Union St. between Laguna and Buchanan St., in **Cow Hollow.** One of the more charming accommodations in the city. Everything that you envision a B&B would be, with a garden patio, sherry, and a terrific French breakfast. Innkeeper on duty 6:30am-12:30am. Flexible check-in. Check-out noon. Reservations recommended. Beautiful rooms with twin beds and shared baths $90-125; large rooms with private baths, many with jacuzzis $175; apartment-like suites for 5-8 people $280-380. ❺

Hayes Valley Inn, 417 Gough St. (☎431-9131 or 800-930-7999; www.hayesvalley-inn.com), just north of Hayes St., in **Hayes Valley.** European charm means small, clean rooms and shared baths. Although you will get to know your neighbor, the rooms are well maintained and all have cable TV, phone, and private sink. Some smoking and pet-friendly rooms. Continental breakfast. Check-in 3pm. Check-out 11am. Reservations recommended for summer and holidays. In summer singles $58; doubles $68-$79; queens $78-89; queen turret $88-99. In winter $42/$48-56/$54-61/ $58-66. ❹

Noe's Nest, 3973 23rd St. (☎821-0751; www.noesnest.com), between Noe and Sanchez St., in **Noe Valley.** Feels like a home with all the family memorabilia around. The 7 rooms—all with private bath, phone, cable TV, VCR, and modem ports—are individually themed. Huge breakfast served in the proprietor's kitchen or on the front patio or back garden. Hot tub. Laundry service available. 2-night min. stay on weekends. Flexible check-in and check-out. Reservations required. Singles and doubles $99-195. ❺

The Seal Rock Inn, 545 Point Lobos Ave. (☎752-8000; www.sealrockinn.com), at 48th Ave. opposite the Sutro Baths, in the **Richmond.** Though the area is remote, it's a quiet, attractive place to escape city chaos. Pastel houses with well-kept gardens run right to the beach. Seal Rock's big, clean rooms are a great deal, especially for families. Pool and patio area. Free parking. Check-in 1pm. Check-out 11am. Singles $100-115; doubles $119-134; $10 for each additional person, $5 for each child. One night's advance deposit required by check for weekends and late arrivals. Reduced rates Sept.-May. ❺

The Embassy Hotel, 610 Polk St. (☎673-1404 or ☎888-814-6835; fax 474-4188; embhotelsf@aol.com; www.embassyhotelsf.com), at Turk St. A rare find in **Civic Center**—respectable, affordable and not too far into unpleasant territory. Rooms are neat, if spartan. Free parking, adjoining bar, TV, Internet access, and telephones. Continental breakfast. Singles $85; doubles $119-129. Lower off-season rates. ❺

Metro Hotel, 319 Divisadero St. (☎861-5364), between Oak and Page St., in the **Lower Haight.** Slightly removed from the hubbub, a charming retreat with a sunny backyard garden. Private baths in all rooms. 28-day max. stay. Reception 7:30am-midnight. Check-out noon. Reserve well in advance. Singles $66; doubles $77; triples $120. ❹

El Capitan Hotel, 2361 Mission St. (☎695-1597), between 19th and 20th St., in **Mission.** If you can't get into the guest houses, this is a solid alternative. The owners rent out half of this hotel to discouraged travelers trying to find a place to crash in San Francisco's brutal accommodations market. 24 clean rooms, each with 1 or 2 full beds and color TV. Mostly shared bathrooms (usually 4 rooms to 1 bath). Check-out 11am. Reception 24hr. Singles, doubles, and quads available, $28 per person. No credit cards. ❷

Golden Gate Hotel, 775 Bush St. (☎392-3702 or ☎800-835-1118; fax 392-6202; www.goldengatehotel.com), between Mason and Powell streets., in **Union Square.** John, Renate, and Captain Nemo (the cat) bring brightness and warmth to this gem of a hotel. Wicker chairs, floral bedspreads, antiques, and big bay windows. German, French, and Spanish spoken. Continental breakfast and afternoon tea (4-7pm) included. Garage parking $15 per day. Doubles with sink $85, with bath $130. ❺

◘ FOOD

Strolling and sampling the food in each neighborhood is an excellent way to get a taste for the city's diversity. For the most up-to-date listings of restaurants, try the *Examiner* and the *S.F. Bay Guardian*. The glossy *Bay Area Vegetarian* can also suggest places to graze.

RICHMOND

Some locals claim that Chinese restaurants in the Richmond are better than those in Chinatown. Clement St., between 2nd and 12th Ave., has the widest variety.

Taiwan Restaurant, 445 Clement St. (☎387-1789), at 6th Ave. Watch the cooks fold your dumplings in the window of this yummy, cheap, veggie-friendly spot which serves Northern Chinese cuisine and some mean dim sum. Lines out the door on weekends. Lunch $3.50; dinner $5-8. Open M-F 11:30am-midnight, Sa-Su 10:30am-midnight. ❶

Lee Hou Restaurant, 332 Clement St. (☎668-8070), at 5th Ave. Some of the best dim sum New Chinatown has to offer. Service is basic, but come for the food. 13 pieces of dim sum $8. Lunch $4-10. Open Su-Th 8am-1am, F-Sa 8am-2am. ❷

CASTRO

Slightly posh diners and cafes dominate the Castro's culinary offerings, where little is as cheap as in the nearby Mission. But quality munchies cheaper than Streisand tickets do exist. To find such food, head away from Castro St. along Market St., toward Noe and Sanchez St. Try **Harvest,** 2285 Market St., a "ranch market" with organic food, and outdoor benches. (☎626-0805. Open daily 8:30am-11pm.)

▨ **Welcome Home,** 464 Castro St. (☎626-3600), near the Castro Theatre. If grandma were a drag queen, this would be her kitchen. Dinners $7-10. W all-you-can-eat spaghetti and salad $9. Open M-Sa 8am-10:30pm, Su 8am-4pm. No credit cards. ❷

▨ **La Mediterranee,** 288 Noe St. (☎431-7210), at 16th and Market St. The copper-top tables, lush greenery, and dominant blue hues in this cool spot are like a warm Middle Eastern breeze. A filling phyllo dough combination plate ($9) is as refreshing as the varied colors. Open Su-Th 11am-10pm, F-Sa 11am-11pm. ❸

Marcello's, 420 Castro St. (☎863-3900), across from the Castro Theatre. No-frills joint serves locally adored pizza with a long list of toppings. Slices $2-3; whole pizzas $10-23. Beer $2. Open Su-Th 11am-1am, F-Sa 11am-2am. No credit cards. ❸

MISSION

The Mission is famous for its delicious, authentic Mexican specialties, but the area is home to many other excellent cuisines as well.

▨ **Taquería El Farolito,** 2279 Mission St. (☎824-7877), at 24th St. The spot for cheap and authentic Mexican food—chow down as Latin beats blast through this fast-food joint. Taco Bell this ain't. After any kind of evening activity in Mission, El Farolito is a late-night fix. Tacos $1.75. Open Su-Th 9am-2am, F-Sa 9am-4am. No credit cards. ❶

▨ **Café Abo,** 3369 Mission St. (☎821-6275), near 30th St., directly across from the Safeway. A bizarre conglomeration of art gallery, island getaway, cajun beats, political activism and Yoda paraphernalia, Café Abo has some of the best sandwiches ($8-9) and mouth-watering miniature pizzas ($5-6) in the city. Loosely Italian-inspired and organic whenever possible. Open M-F 7:30am-10pm, Sa 8am-4pm. No credit cards. ❷

Bombay Ice Creamery, 548 Valencia St. (☎431-1103), at 16th St. It's not just the ice cream, but also the food that merits a visit to Bombay. The mango *kulfi* ($2.50) is to die for (get it with rose water and sweet rice noodles). The *bhel* (a puffed rice dish; $3.50) and the *dhai puris* ($3.50) are both delicious. Open Tu-Su 11am-8pm. ❶

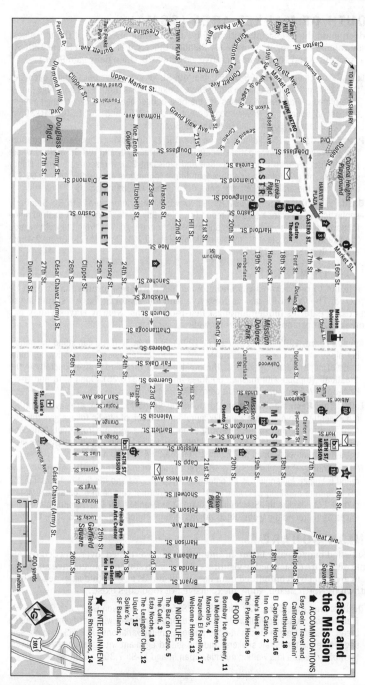

SAN FRANCISCO

Castro and the Mission

▲ ACCOMMODATIONS
Easy Goin' Travel and California Dreamin' Guesthouse, 18
El Capitan Hotel, 16
Inn on Castro, 2
Noe's Nest, 8
The Parker House, 9

◆ FOOD
Bombay Ice Creamery, 11
La Mediterranee, 1
Marcello's, 4
Taqueria El Farolito, 17
Welcome Home, 13

■ NIGHTLIFE
The Bar on Castro, 5
The Café, 3
Esta Noche, 10
The Lexington Club, 12
Liquid, 15
Spike's, 7
SF Badlands, 6

★ ENTERTAINMENT
Theatre Rhinoceros, 14

SOUTH OF MARKET AREA (SOMA)

Hidden amid the industrial hustle and bustle of SoMa are some of the city's best restaurants. For doing it yourself, try **Rainbow Grocery,** 1745 Folsom St., at 13th St., is a worker-owned grocery cooperative. (☎863-0620. Open daily 9am-9pm.)

🖼 **LuLu,** 816 Folsom St. (☎495-5775), near 4th St. An impressive oak-burning oven fires this inventive California Cuisine atmosphere. Unique pizzas (from $14) and huge family-style plates of fire-roasted veggies are the best budget bets on an ever-changing menu of seasonal specialties. Reservations essential. Open M-Th and Su 11:30am-10:30pm, F-Sa 11:30am-11:30pm. Limited menu 3-5:30pm. ❸

Patisserie Café, 1155 Folsom St. (☎703-0557; for cooking classes write chefmohamed@yahoo.com; www.patisseriecafe.com), between 7th and 8th St. A place where you can get a cheap breakfast (coffee and croissant $3), a reasonable lunch (fancy sandwich and dessert $9), or a decadent dinner (appetizers around $6, entrees $9-12) and ponder the artistically experimental decor. Open M-F 8am-5pm. ❷

Basil, 1175 Folsom St. (☎552-8999; www.basilthai.com), near 8th St. Somberly sophisticated ambiance sets the mood for delectably classy Thai–with a dash of spice for upwardly mobile youth. Curries and entrees "from the grill" or "from the wok" include "drunken tofu" and piquant "mussels inferno" (all $9-12). Open M-F 11:30am-2:45pm and 5-10pm, Sa-Su 5-10:30pm. ❸

CIVIC CENTER

This home to opera, musicals and movies has fewer restaurants than would be expected. The Opera Plaza, Van Ness Ave. and McAllister St. have a sprinkling of appetizing eateries hidden amongst fast-food chains. Nearby Hayes Valley has some popular pre-opera offerings as well.

🖼 **Ananda Fuara,** 1298 Market St. (☎621-1994), at Larkin St. If you can stand the annoying piped music, this vegetarian cafe with vegan tendencies offers creative combinations of super-fresh ingredients. The most popular dish and house specialty is the "neatloaf" (topped with mashed potatoes and gravy; $10.25). Open M-Tu and Th-Sa 8am-8pm, W 8am-3pm. No credit cards. ❷

🖼 **Lalitai Thai Restaurant and Bar,** 96 McAllister St. (☎552-5744), at Leavenworth St. Mood-lighting, an elaborate water-lily mural and a touch of plastic foliage give this elegant Thai restaurant an Alice-In-Wonderland, feasting-with-the-frogs feel. Daily and weekly lunch specials ($7.25). Most dinner entrees $11, with veggie options. Reservations recommended. Open M-F 11am-10pm, Sa-Su 4:30-10pm. ❷

Millennium, 246 McAllister St. (☎487-9800), at Larkin St. Though the award-winning menu is vegan, Millennium is an entirely tie-dye-free area and the first restaurant in the US to feature an all-organic wine list. Feast on gourmet cuisine in a romantic, soft-jazz setting. Entrees, like the Szechuan Eggplant Crêpe, range from $13-19 and gather influences from around the globe. Reservations recommended. Open daily 5-9pm. ❹

UNION SQUARE

A satisfied budget eater is rare in Union Square. Overpriced, overcrowded restaurants often lure unsuspecting visitors with the siren song of convenience and leave them groaning with unfulfilled tummies. While not as easy to find as in nearby Chinatown or North Beach, good, inexpensive hot food does exist.

🖼 **Dottie's True Blue Café,** 522 Jones St. (☎885-2767), between Geary and O'Farrell St. French toast tastes so delicately rich since Dottie makes it with her fluffy homemade bread. Despite Calista Flockhart-sized portions, quirky variations like chicken-apple sausage, ceramic turtle salt shakers, and the grilled eggplant with goat-cheese sandwich ($6) often keep a line waiting outside. Open M and Th-Su 7:30am-3pm. ❶

▧ **Café Bean,** 754 Post St. (☎776-6620), and 800 Sutter St. (☎923-9539). The gem planted on Post has sprouted an enormous second location. Steaming eggs and toast ($4), brie and olive sandwich ($6.50), and Dutch pancakes ($4) ready for tourists, business people, and wayward hipsters. Free Internet plug-in with coffee at Sutter St. location. Sutter St. location open M-Sa 6am-7pm, Su 6am-5pm; photo- and postcard-papered Post St. location open daily 6am-2pm. ❶

Sotano Grill, 550 Powell St. (☎989-7131) near Bush St. Green monster enchiladas just like *mamá* used to make, with guitar music and vegetarian tortilla bowls. Black Soup (black bean bowl, $4) or sangria ($6) make this convivial fiesta worth every peso. Live music W-Sa evenings. Open daily 11am-11pm. ❶

FINANCIAL DISTRICT & EMBARCADERO

In the Financial District, eateries are everywhere and cater to the full range of budgets. Corner cafes vend authentic Mediterranean grub at rock-bottom prices. Pedestrian side streets, nestled between banks, are packed with pavement bistros. Sit-down restaurants serve *haute cuisine* with liberal portions of ambience, though you may need an MBA (or at least a well-to-do sugar daddy) to afford more than an appetizer.

▧ **Cafe Venue,** 721 Market St. (☎546-1144), between 3rd and 4th St. Oh, to be a decadent San Franciscan, washing down roasted eggplant on sourdough ($4.50) with a wheatgrass "shot" ($1) to energize an afternoon of Union Square shopping. The people-watching patio juxtaposes Market St.'s bustle, and a similarly diverse menu offers pasta ($6), smoothies ($3), and even spirits in a conspicuously affordable venue. Open M-F 7am-7pm, Sa 8am-5:30pm, Su 11am-5:30pm. No credit cards. ❶

Café Bastille, 22 Belden Pl. (☎986-5673), between Pine and Bush St., and Kearny and Montgomery St. In this strip of pricey pavement cafes, Bastille stands out for its quality food and carefree atmosphere. The menu is filled with light French offerings like crepes ($12.50), steak with wild mushroom pudding ($18.50), mussels and *frites* ($13), and a heavenly chocolate almond dessert crepe ($5). Open daily 11:30am-10pm. ❹

GIMME SUM DIM SUM

Dim sum ("little bits of the heart") are the foods traditionally eaten at a Cantonese or Southern Chinese *yum cha* ("tea lunch"). This heavenly dining experience involves various small dishes eaten in the morning or early afternoon, typically on Sundays, in mass quantities. Waiters and waitresses push carts laden with all sorts of Chinese "finger foods" (from dumplings to chicken feet). Dumplings and buns are steamed, rolls and squares are deep-fried. When they stop at your table, point to whatever looks good (or use the handy mini-menu below). The waiter will stamp a card to charge you by dish.

▧ **Cha Siu Bao.** Steamed BBQ pork buns. Mmm...

▧ **Haar Gao.** Steamed shrimp dumplings.

▧ **Dan Taat.** Tiny tart shells filled with sweet egg custard.

Siu Mai. Shrimp and pork in a fancy dumpling "basket."

Walteep: The classic steamed pork dumplings.

Jiaozi. The classic: steamed pork dumplings.

Dou Sha Bao. Steamed buns filled with sweet red bean paste.

Loh Bak Goh. Mashed turnip patty. Don't knock it until you've tried it.

Fun Gwor. Chicken and mushroom dumplings.

Yuebing: Flaky frosted pastry with bean paste filling.

THE BIG SPLURGE

A TASTE OF THE CLASSICS

In a town where the trends tend toward sophisticated "Cal-Italian" fusion food and new (pricey) twists on old classics, **Pane e Vino** holds down the fort with old-fashioned Italian cuisine. Simplicity is the guardian of great taste at this small Cow Hollow trattoria, where the chefs understand that classics are classic for a reason.

Hailing from Northern Italy, chef and owner Bruno Quercini, guarantees simple, great-tasting dishes in a small, cozy atmosphere. Watch the chef prepare your food in the open kitchen and prepare to be dazzled.

The Ravioli di Magro (spinach and ricotta with fresh tomato) and the Stuffes Branzino (stuffed fish) both come highly recommended, but anything on the menu is bound to be beautiful and delectable. Dine like a native by complementing your meal with a glass or bottle of wine from the restaurant's extensive list, and if there is room, try a great tasting dessert. Appetizers and salads range from $6-12. Pasta from $10-16. Meat and fish from $18-24.

(3011 Steiner St., off Union St. ☎346-2111. Open M-Th 11:30am-2:30pm and 5-10pm, F-Sa 11:30am-10:30pm, Su 5-9:30pm)

CHINATOWN

San Fran's Chinese cuisine is widely held to be unsurpassed outside of Asia. Chinatown is filled with cheap restaurants; in fact, their multitude and superficial similarity may make a choice nearly impossible. Finding vegetarian or vegan food is harder than it might seem; many vegetable dishes use oyster sauce or broth, and rice dishes sometimes include egg. Chinatown's dim sum is not to be missed, and don't forget to venture beyond the bounds of main course dishes; the area is home to many spectacular bakeries, teahouses, and specialty restaurants.

🔲 **House of Nanking,** 919 Kearny St. (☎421-1429), near Columbus Ave. Big, high-quality portions offset a low-key setting and a low-key check in this famous Chinatown institution. Many entrees under $8. Open M-F 11am-10pm, Sa noon-10pm, Su 4-10pm. ❷

🔲 **Golden Gate Bakery,** 1029 Grant Ave. (☎781-2627). Moon cakes, noodle puffs, and vanilla cream buns (all $0.75-$1.50) to make you forget donuts ever existed. Open daily 8am-8pm. No credit cards. ❶

Grand Palace, 950 Grant Ave. (☎982-3705), between Jackson and Washington streets. Chandeliers, plush red cushions, and a meticulously doting waitstaff that serves amazing entrees ($7-10) just right for a pauper's budget. Open daily 7:30am-10pm. ❷

NORTH BEACH

In North Beach, tourism and California cuisine capitalized on the taste of Little Italy, and tourist-geared restaurants sprouted up, offering a unique, *delicioso* taste that blends old and new.

🔲 **L'Osteria del Forno,** 519 Columbus Ave. (☎982-1124), between Green and Union St. Acclaimed Italian roasted and cold foods, plus homemade breads. The tiny dining room is crowded but romantic. Terrific thin-crust pizzas (slices $2.50-3.75, pies $10-17) and focaccia sandwiches ($5-6.50). Open Su-M and W-Th 11:30am-10pm, F-Sa 11:30am-10:30pm. No credit cards. ❷

🔲 **Mario's Bohemian Cigar Store Café,** 566 Columbus Ave. (☎362-0536), at Union St. on the corner of Washington Sq. The Beats frequented this laid-back cafe; these days, locals drop by to have coffee ($1-4) and drinks (wine $4, beer $3). A great place to hang out and grab some first-rate grub (hot focaccia sandwiches $4.25-8; pizza $8.50-11.25; pasta $8.25). Open Su-Th 10am-11pm, F-Sa 10am-midnight. ❷

FISHERMAN'S WHARF

A common, if somewhat overpriced, Wharf meal is a loaf of bread and some clam chowder from a seafood stand.

■ **Pat's Café,** 2701 Leavenworth St. (☎776-8735), at N Point St. One of a string of breakfast joints, Pat's stands out from the crowd—not just because of its bright yellow building—but also for its huge, delicious portions. Burgers, sandwiches, and big breakfast plates (most $4-7) taste just like mom's. Open daily 7:30am-2pm. No credit cards. ❶

Bob's Sushi, 393 Bay St. (☎693-9218), at Mason St. Just 3 blocks inland from the wharf, Bob's offers pristine serenity and some smashing sushi. Sushi from $3. Dinner combos: 2 entrees for $11, or 3 for $13. Open daily 11am-2:30pm and 5-10pm. ❸

NOB HILL & RUSSIAN HILL

■ **Zarzuela,** 2000 Hyde St. (☎346-0800), at Union St. in Russian Hill. Authentic Spanish homestyle cooking and a festively upscale setting make *chorizo al vino* ($4-7) the highlight of the evening. Entrees $10-15. Open Tu-Th 5:30-10pm, F-Sa 5:30-10:30pm. ❸

Sushigroove, 1916 Hyde St. (☎440-1905), between Union and Green St. in Russian Hill. Fiery hues and trance-y disco beats bring self-explanatory Russian Hill chic to this amazingly inexpensive sushi-*sake* joint (most sushi and *maki* $3-7). Valet parking ($10) available on Polk St. Open Su-Th 5:30-10pm, F-Sa 5:30-10:30pm. ❷

MARINA, FORT MASON, & COW HOLLOW

The **Marina Safeway,** 15 Marina Blvd., between Laguna and Buchanan St., is legendary as a spot to pick up more than just groceries. (☎563-4946. Open 24hr.) For purists and puritans, there is a **Real Food Company,** 3060 Fillmore St., on the corner of Filbert St. (☎567-6900. Open daily 8am-9pm.)

■ **Pizza Orgasmica,** 3157 Fillmore St. (☎931-5300), at Greenwich St. in Cow Hollow. With pizzas named "menage a trois" and "doggi style," it's hard not to get excited. Prices can get steep (pies $10-23) so don't miss the all-you-can-eat special (11am-4pm; $6.50). Open Su-W 11am-midnight, Th 11am-2am, F-Sa 11am-2:30am. ❸

■ **Marina Submarine,** 2299 Union St. (☎921-3990), at Steiner St. in Cow Hollow. Often a long (but worthwhile) wait for superlative subs that satisfy in several sizes ($3.70-7). Open M-F 10am-6:30pm, Sa 11am-4:30pm, Su 11am-3:30pm. No credit cards. ❷

Home Plate, 2774 Lombard St., (☎922-4663), off Pierce St. in the Marina. Hard-to-beat, hearty breakfast, brunch, and lunch (most items under $8). Friendly service and scones with homemade strawberry-apple jam with every meal. Open M-Su 7am-4pm. ❷

PACIFIC HEIGHTS

■ **Pizza Inferno,** 1800 Fillmore St. (☎775-1800), at Sutter St. The wild multi-color paint job aside, this is a seriously sophisticated pizza parlor. Lunch specials include a slice of pizza, large salad and soda ($6). Happy hour M-F 4-6:30pm and 10-11pm with 2-for-1 pizzas and pitchers of beer for $11. Open daily 11:30am-11pm. ❷

La Méditerranée, 2210 Fillmore St. (☎921-2956), between Sacramento and Clay St. Narrow, colorful and bustling, La Mediterranee feels like a street in southern Europe. Lunch specials (served until 5pm, about $6.50) and entrees ($7-9) are light, Mediterranean-inspired with a home-cooked taste. Filled phyllo dough ($7.50-9) and quiche of the day ($7) are both must-tries. Open Su-Th 11am-10pm, F-Sa 11am-11pm. ❷

SAN FRANCISCO

JAPANTOWN

Isobune, 1737 Post St. (☎563-1030), in the Kintetsu Bldg., upper level. Eat sushi as it sails by your moat-side seat in America's first sushi boat restaurant. Color-coded plates correspond to item prices ($1.50-3.75). Sake $3. Open daily 11:30am-10pm. ❶

Mifune, 1737 Post St. (☎922-0337), in the Kintetsu Bldg., upper level. Excellent and much-loved noodle restaurant. Choices include *udon* (heavy flour noodles) or *soba* (slender buckwheat noodles). Hot noodles from $4.50; cold noodles from $5.25. *Sake* from $2.80. Open Su-F 11am-9:30pm, Sa 11am-10pm. ❶

HAIGHT-ASHBURY

Squat and Gobble, 1428 Haight St. (☎864-8484; www.squatandgobble.com), between Ashbury St. and Masonic Ave. This popular cafe offers enormous omelettes ($5-7) and equally colossal crepes ($4-7). Lots of salads, sandwiches, and vegetarian options, too. Open 8am-10pm daily. Additional locations: 237 Fillmore St. in the **Lower Haight** and 3600 16th St. in the **Castro**. ❷

Blue Front Café, 1430 Haight St. (☎252-5917), between Ashbury St. and Masonic Ave. This Genie-marked joint is a great place to fill your tummy with starchy goodness. Large portions, flowing conversation, and general wackiness. Down a beer or ginseng chai (both around $2.50), to go with your sizeable wrap ($6) or Middle Eastern meal ($5-8.50). 10% student discount. Open Su-Th 7:30am-10pm, F-Sa 8am-11pm. ❷

Kate's Kitchen, 471 Haight St. (☎626-3984), near Fillmore St. Start your day off right with one of the best breakfasts in the neighborhood (served all day). It's often packed, so sign up on a waiting list outside. Try the "Fruit Orgy," with fruit, yogurt, granola, and honey ($5.25) or anything else on the extraordinarily economical menu ($4-8). Open M 9am-2:45pm, Tu-F 8am-2:45pm, Sa-Su 8:30am-3:45pm. No credit cards. ❷

☉ SIGHTS

GOLDEN GATE BRIDGE & THE PRESIDIO

GOLDEN GATE BRIDGE

When Captain John Fremont coined the term "Golden Gate" in 1846, he meant to name the harbor entrance to the San Francisco Bay after the mythical Golden Horn port of Constantinople. In 1937, however, the colorful name became permanently associated with Joseph Strauss' copper-hued engineering masterpiece—the Golden Gate Bridge. Built for only $35 million, the bridge stretches across 1.2 mi. of ocean, its towers looming 65 stories above the Bay. It can sway up to 27 ft. in each direction during high winds. On sunny days, hundreds of people take the half-hour walk across the bridge; on gloomier days, the crisis counseling phones that dot the sidewalks remind walkers of the bridge's popularity among the depressed. The views from the bridge are amazing, especially those of the city from Vista Point in Marin County. To see the bridge itself, it's best to get a bit farther away: Fort Point and Fort Baker in the Presidio, Land's End in Lincoln Park, Mt. Livermore on Angel Island, and Hawk Hill off Conzelman Rd. in the Marin Headlands all offer spectacular views.

PRESIDIO

When Spanish settlers forged their way up the San Francisco peninsula from Baja California in 1769, they established *presidios*, or military outposts, along the way. San Francisco's Presidio, the northernmost point of Spanish territory in North America, was dedicated in 1776. The settlement stayed in Spanish hands for only 45 years. The deed was then given to Mexico when it won independence from Spain; it was later passed to the US as part of the 1848 Treaty of Guadalupe Hidalgo. Gold fever brought expansion to the outpost; the Presidio gained particular importance during WWII after the attack on Pearl Harbor. Crissy Field's Intelligence School and the Letterman Army Hospital were two of the largest of their kind in the country.

Today, the Presidio is part of the **Golden Gate National Recreation Area (GGNRA),** run by the National Park Service in conjunction with the Presidio Trust. The Presidio Trust is raising funds to make the park self-sufficient by 2013, and coordinating the ongoing renovation and modernization of roads, buildings, and trails in the park.

MAIN POST. The once-grand barracks that make up Main Post are now a semi-historic playground for the San Francisco Film Society and any other non-profit agency willing to fork over funds for a lease. Remnants of the original Spanish settlement are on view in the Officer's Club, one of the many historic buildings that surround the 1776 Parade Ground. The William Penn Mott, Jr. Visitors Center offers free maps, glossy viewbooks, and pocket travel guides about the park's present and past. *(102 Montgomery St. ☎ 561-4323; www.nps.gov/psrf. Open daily 9am-5pm.)*

SAN FRANCISCO NATIONAL CEMETERY. A visit to this 28-acre cemetery will provide history buffs an up close and personal look at the graves of General Frederick Funston, who led the military relief effort after the 1906 earthquake, and the 450 members of the US Army's all-black "Buffalo Soldiers regiment." Maps and registers are available inside the entrance gate. *(Just off of Lincoln Blvd. in the center of the Presidio. P.O. Box 29012, Presidio of San Francisco. ☎ 650-589-7737.)*

FORT POINT. Fort Point, under the Golden Gate Bridge in the northernmost corner of the park, used to be called "the Gibraltar of the West." Once the nation's main coastal defense, it housed a garrison of men and nearly 200 guns and cannons. Today, the cavernous fort is open to the public and boasts half-hearted historical recreations and exhibits. The top tier of the four-story building is windy but the view is worth the climb. Volunteers in Civil War garb give tours and show how to load a cannon, competing with the hardcore surfers for the audience's attention. *(☎ 673-5642; www.nps.gov/fopo. MUNI buses #28 and 29 stop at the Golden Gate Bridge, where dirt paths and paved roads lead down to the fort. Cars take Lincoln Ave. to Long Ave. to Marine Dr.; limited parking. Open F-Su 10am-5pm, schedule may vary due to ongoing "seismic upgrading." Free.)*

LINCOLN PARK

At the northwest end of San Francisco, Lincoln Park has spectacular views of the Pacific and the Golden Gate Bridge. The bulky patch of meandering paths and historical sights is a fabulous place for an afternoon hike or summertime picnic.

CLIFF HOUSE. At the northern tip of Ocean Beach, Lincoln Park begins not with greenery and mountainous paths but with a monument of San Francisco's earlier days. The precarious Cliff House, built in 1909, is the third of that name to occupy this spot—the previous two burned down. It is has slowly deteriorated due to decades of neglect, and plans are in the works to restore the complex to its original glory. The Golden Gate National Recreation Area Visitors Center, housed within the Cliff House, distributes information on Lincoln Park, Ocean Beach, and the entire GGNRA. The helpful staff will give you info on the wildlife of the cliffs and the wild life of the house. Don't feed the coin-operated binoculars that look out over Seal Rocks—instead, head inside and have a free look through the GGNRA telescope. *(☎ 556-8642. Open daily 10am-5pm.)* Along with overpriced restaurants, the Cliff House hosts the **Musée Mécanique,** an arcade devoted to games of yesteryear—not Donkey Kong and Space Invaders, but wooden and cast-iron creations dating back to the 1890s. *(☎ 386-1170. Open daily 10am-8pm; in winter M-F 11am-7pm, Sa-Su 10am-8pm. Entrance free, but most games are $0.25.)* Next to the Musée Mécanique, overlooking the cliffs and the Pacific, rests the **Camera Obscura.** The building has a periscope-like mirrored lens on its roof; as the lens turns in circles, light from outside is bounced down into the "dark room" and onto a concave viewing plate, showing the ocean vistas and nearby Seal Rocks, all at 700% magnification. (☎ 750-0415. *Open daily 11am-sunset, weather permitting—you can't see anything in fog. $2.*)

SUTRO BATHS AND SUTRO HEIGHTS PARK. Adolph Sutro's 1896 bathhouse, known as the Sutro Baths, lies in ruins just north of Cliff House. Up the hill from the intersection of Point Lobos and 48th Ave., and to the east of the Cliff House and the Baths, is spectacular Sutro Heights Park. Sadly underused, the park offers unparalleled views of the city and surrounding watery expanses. A lion-guarded gate recalls the day when the hill was the sight of Adolph's grand private estate.

CALIFORNIA PALACE OF THE LEGION OF HONOR. In the middle of Lincoln Park, between the golf course (which was once a cemetery) and the Land's End wilderness, sits a magnificent enclave of European proportions. The California Palace of the Legion of Honor was built in 1924 after San Francisco's lady-of-the-day, Mrs. Spreckels, fell in love with the temporary "French Pavilion" built on Golden Gate Park for the Panama International Exhibition. The pavilion was a replica of the *Palais de la Legion d'Honneur* on Paris's Left Bank, and Spreckels was determined to build one of equal stature. A copy of Rodin's Thinker beckons visitors into the grand courtyard, where a little glass pyramid recalls another Paris treasure, the Louvre. A thorough catalog of great masters, from the medieval to the modern, hangs inside. Other draws include a pneumatically operated 4500-pipe organ, played in free weekly recitals, and a gilded ceiling from a 15th-century *palacio* in Toledo, Spain. Just outside the Palace, a **Holocaust memorial** offers a sobering reminder of one of Europe's darker historical moments. The memorial depicts the Holocaust as a mass of emaciated victims with a single, hopeful survivor looking out through a barbed-wire fence to the beauty of the Pacific. (☎ 863-3330; *www.legionofhonor.org. Open Tu-Su 9:30am-5pm. Organ recitals Sa-Su 4pm. Adults $8, seniors $6, under 17 $5, under 12 free. $2 discount with MUNI transfer; Tu is free. Free weekly tours Sa in a different language (either French, Spanish, or Italian). Holocaust Memorial: Free to the public.*)

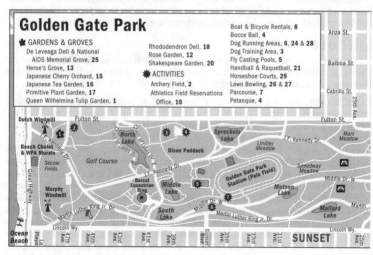

Golden Gate Park

❀ GARDENS & GROVES
De Leveaga Dell & National
AIDS Memorial Grove, **25**
Heroe's Grove, **13**
Japanese Cherry Orchard, **15**
Japanese Tea Garden, **16**
Primitive Plant Garden, **17**
Queen Wilhelmina Tulip Garden, **1**

Rhododendron Dell, **18**
Rose Garden, **12**
Shakespeare Garden, **20**

❀ ACTIVITIES
Archery Field, **2**
Athletics Field Reservations
Office, **10**

Boat & Bicycle Rentals, **8**
Bocce Ball, **4**
Dog Running Areas, **6, 24 & 28**
Dog Training Area, **3**
Fly Casting Pools, **5**
Handball & Raquetball, **21**
Horseshoe Courts, **29**
Lawn Bowling, **26 & 27**
Parcourse, **7**
Petanque, **4**

GOLDEN GATE PARK

In-line skaters, neo-flower children, and sunbathers meet in this lush garden-within-the-city, which spreads 3½ mi. from the Haight to the Ocean, and separates residential Richmond and Sunset districts with 1½ mi. of greenery, north to south. It is bounded by Fulton St. to the north, Stanyan St. to the east, Lincoln Way to the south, and Ocean Beach to the west, except for a strip called the Panhandle, which juts east between Fell and Oak St. into the Haight. Originally the "carriage entrance," it contains the oldest trees in the park. The heavily trafficked section of Hwy. 1 running through the park is called Park Presidio By-Pass Dr. going north and Cross-Over Dr. going south.

Inside, the park is laid out in a sprawling, natural design. Open green meadows, groves of shrubs, and myriad little gardens patch together the larger developed areas, namely, the museum complex in the eastern third of the park, Stow Lake, the Stadium, the golf course, and soccer fields near the western edge. Don't rush through the park—San Franciscans bask in it all weekend long. Intriguing museums and cultural events pick up where the lush flora and fauna finally leave off, and athletic opportunities abound. On Sundays, traffic is banned from park roads, and bicycles and in-line skates come out in full force.

GARDENS & SIGHTS. Despite its sandy past, the soil of Golden Gate Park is rich enough today to support a wealth of flowers, particularly in spring and summer. The **Conservatory of Flowers** is closed for renovations, but the nearby Conservatory Valley, much like the Kew Gardens in London, seems afflicted with obsessive-compulsive disorder—not a bloom is out of place in this unbelievable display of botanic symmetry. Across JFK Dr. from the Conservatory, just south of **Lily Pond,** among the fragile, flowering dogwoods and giant redwoods of **De Laveaga Dell,** rests the **National AIDS Memorial Grove.** The grove is a site for remembrance and renewal, at once somber and rejuvenating. (☎ 750-8340. *Tours Th 9:30am-12:30pm and by special arrangement starting at the Main Portal of the Grove, near the corner of Middle Dr. East and Bowling Green Dr. Free.)*

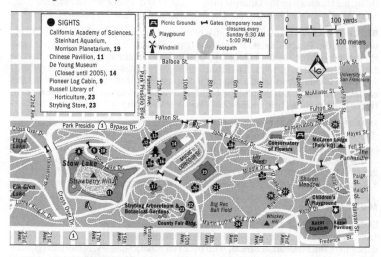

● SIGHTS
California Academy of Sciences,
  Steinhart Aquarium,
  Morrison Planetarium, **19**
Chinese Pavillion, **11**
De Young Museum
  (Closed until 2005), **14**
Pioneer Log Cabin, **9**
Russell Library of
  Horticulture, **23**
Strybing Store, **23**

⬛ Picnic Grounds ⊨ Gates (temporary road
🏛 Playground   closures every
                     Sunday 6:30 AM
🌀 Windmill   - 5:00 PM)
                  ⟋ Footpath

0   100 yards
0   100 meters

The **Strybing Arboretum and Botanical Gardens** is home to 7500 varieties of plants, including collections from Chile, New Zealand, and the tropical, high-altitude New World Cloud Forests. Pretend to munch on faux-prehistoric dinosaur-salad at the **Primitive Plant Garden** near the Friends Gate in the northern part of the Arboretum. On the eastern side, near the **Strybing Store** and **Russel Library of Horticulture,** is the **Garden of Fragrance,** designed especially for the visually impaired—all labels are in Braille, and the plants are chosen specifically for their textures and scents. On the western side is the grand and spacious **Moon Viewing Garden,** perfect for celestial happenings and werewolf sightings. *(On Lincoln Way at 9th Ave. ☎661-1316; www.strybing.org. Open M-F 8am-4:30pm, Sa-Su 10am-5pm. Free guided Tours: From Strybing Store M-F 1:30pm, Sa-Su 10:30am and 1:30pm, from North Entrance W, F, Su 2pm.)*

Near the **Music Concourse** off of South Dr., the **Shakespeare Garden,** filled with crab-apples and red brick, contains almost every flower and plant ever mentioned by the Bard. Plaques with the relevant quotations are hung on the back wall, and there's a map to help you find your favorite hyacinths and rue. *(Open daily dawn-dusk; in winter Tu-Su dawn-dusk. Free.)* The **Rhododendron Dell,** between the Academy of Sciences and John F. Kennedy Dr., honors park designer John McLaren with a splendid profusion of his favorite flower. The 850 varieties bloom the first weeks of spring. Ring-like **Stow Lake** sits in the middle of the park. Cross one of two stone bridges and wreak fruit-filled havoc on the big, green island of **Strawberry Hill.**

SPRECKELS LAKE AND AROUND. Brimming Spreckels Lake, on JFK Dr., is populated by crowds of turtles that pile onto a big rock (also turtle-shaped) to sun themselves. The multi-national collection of gardens and museums in Golden Gate Park would not be complete without something distinctly American...like a herd of bison. A dozen of the shaggy beasts loll about a spacious paddock just west of Spreckels. In the extreme northwest of the park, the **Dutch Windmill** has done its last good turn in the cheery **Queen Wilhelmina Tulip Garden,** which bursts forth color from 10,000 bulbs in March. Rounding out the days of yore is the **carousel** (circa 1912), accompanied by a $50,000 Gebruder band organ. *Let's Go* recommends riding the ◪ostrich or the ◪purple dragon. *Let's Go* does not recommend the frog. *(Open June-Sept. daily 10am-5pm; Oct.-May Tu-W and F-Su 9am-4pm. $1, ages 6-12 $0.25.)*

BEACH CHALET. On the Western edge of the park on the Great Hwy., south of Fulton St., is the Beach Chalet. During the Great Depression, the WPA enlisted the French-born artist Lucien Labaudt to design frescoes for the chalet's walls—the elaborate paintings of 1930s San Francisco were completed just in time for WWII, when the building was used as an army outpost. The walls were restored for the chalet's reopening in 1996, and the building now serves as the official **Visitors Center** for Golden Gate Park. *(☎751-2766. Open daily 9am-7pm.)*

JAPANESE TEA GARDEN. The **Japanese Cherry Orchard** blooms intoxicatingly the first week in April at Lincoln Way and South Dr., near the elegant Japanese Tea Garden, created for the 1894 Mid-Winter Exposition. The oldest Japanese garden in the US, the Tea Garden is a serene collection of wooden buildings, small pools, graceful footbridges, carefully pruned trees, and lush plants. *(☎752-4227. Open daily 8:30am-6pm. $3.50, seniors and ages 6-12 $1.25; free for all daily 8:30-9:30am and 5-6pm.)*

MUSEUMS

▨ **CALIFORNIA ACADEMY OF SCIENCES.** The Academy of Sciences, east of Stow Lake, near 9th Ave., houses several smaller museums specializing in different fields of science. **The Steinhart Aquarium,** with over 600 aquatic species, is more lively than the natural history exhibits. *(Shark feedings M-W and F-Su 10:30am, 12:30, 2:30, 4:30pm. Open ocean fish feedings 1:30pm. Penguin feeding daily 11:30am and 4pm.)* The **Morrison Planetarium** recreates the heavens above with impressive sky shows. *(Sky shows M-F*

2pm, with additional summer showings. $2.50; students, seniors, and ages 6-17 $1.25.) The rest of the Academy is considered the **Natural History Museum**. In the Space and Earth Hall, you can learn how the earth rotates and see a piece of moonrock. The Earthquake room explains all about those shakers famous around the Bay Area, and the Earthquake Theater lets visitors experience a little rock 'n' roll in person. More zaniness lurks down the corridor, where the Far Side of Science gallery pays tribute to Gary Larsen. Moo. *(☎ 750-7145; www.calacademy.org. Open Memorial Day-Labor Day daily 9am-6pm; Labor Day-Memorial Day 10am-5pm. $8.50; students, seniors, and ages 12-17 $5.50; ages 4-11 $2. Extended hours (until 8:45pm) and free entrance 1st W each month.)*

CASTRO

Rainbow flags raised high, out and proud lesbians, gays, bisexuals, and transgendered folk find comfort and fun on the streets of the Castro. The concept, as well as the reality, of an all-queer neighborhood draws queer tourists and their friends from around the world, carrying the already absolutely fabulous Castro scene over-the-top. The people out and about are the main attraction on the picture-perfect streets, and the shops are an added novelty. **Cruisin' the Castro** is a guided tour of the area. Trevor Hailey, a resident since 1972, is consistently recognized as one of San Francisco's top tour leaders. Her 4hr. walking tours cover Castro life and history from the Gold Rush to the present. *(☎ 550-8110; trvrhailey@aol.com; www.webcasro.com/castrotour. Tours Tu-Sa 10am. $40; lunch included. Email or phone reservations required.)* Shoppers, like queens (both the royal and the drag variety), do not climb hills; thus, the steeply sloped areas to the south and west of Castro Village tend to be residential. The vibrantly painted old **Victorians** here are worth wandering for—Collingwood and Noe St. have their share. For architecture without the walk, look for the faux-baroque **Castro Theatre**, 429 Castro St.—not that you could miss it.

MISSION

The Mission is slowly outgrowing its reputation as one of the most underappreciated neighborhoods in the city. Beyond the fabulous food and kickin' nightlife, the Mission is home to a vibrant community of painters and writers struggling to keep themselves and their messages heard in the face of dot-commers and rising rents. The sights in the area require some effort to find, but the rewards are plenty.

MISIÓN DE LOS DOLORES (MISSION DOLORES). Established over two centuries ago and located in the old heart of San Francisco, the Mission Dolores is thought to be the city's oldest building. Founded in 1776 by Father Junípero Serra, it was originally named in honor of St. Francis of Assisi. Later, due to its proximity to the Laguna de Nuestra Señora de los Dolores (Lagoon of Our Lady of Sorrows), the mission became universally known as Misión de los Dolores. Bougainvillea, poppies, and birds-of-paradise bloom in its cemetery, which was featured in Alfred Hitchcock's 1958 film *Vertigo*. *(3321 16th St., at 16th and Dolores St. ☎ 621-8203. Open May-Oct. daily 9am-4:30pm; Nov.-Apr. 9am-4pm. $2, ages 5-12 $1. Mass in English M-F 7:30 and 9am; Sa 7:30, 9am, 5pm; Su 8 and 10am. In Spanish Su noon.)*

MISSION MURALS. A walk east or west along 24th St., weaving in and out of the side streets, reveals the Mission's magnificent murals. (Simply walking up and down Mission St. will yield a taste as well, but the concentration is definitely on 24th.) Continuing the long Mexican mural tradition brought to fame by Diego Rivera and Jose Orozco, the Mission murals have been a source of pride for Chicano artists, schoolchildren, and community members since the 1980s. Standouts include the more political murals of Balmy Alley, off 24th St. between Harrison and Folsom St., a three-building tribute to guitar god Carlos Santana at 22nd St. and Van Ness Ave.

(*Inspire to Aspire*, M. Rios, C. Gonzales, J. Mayorca, 1987), the face of St. Peter's Church at 24th and Florida St. (*500 Years of Resistance*, Isaias Mata, 1993), and the urban living center on 19th St. between Valencia and Guerrero St.

OTHER SIGHTS. La Galeria la Raza celebrates local Chicano and Latino artists with exhibitions and parties. Attached to the gallery is **Studio 24**, a space where Chicano and Latino artists sell artwork, crafts, and jewelry. *(2857 24th St., between Bryant and Florida St. ☎826–8009. Open Tu-Sa noon-6pm. Free.)* **Osento** is a Japanese-style bathhouse for ladies only, with wet and dry saunas, jacuzzi, outdoor dipping pool, sundecks, and meditation room. *(955 Valencia St., between 20th and 21st St. ☎282-6333.Open daily 1pm-1am. Last admission at midnight. 14+. $10-20. No credit cards.)*

SOUTH OF MARKET AREA (SOMA)

To the unititated, South of Market appears to stretch on like an industrial wasteland, but the area is actually home to a good bit of liveliness. This is where the leather and Levi's community began to congregate in the 1940s and 50s. From there, a wild and wonderful nightlife scene emerged. The leather and whips still crack in some bars and clubs, and come out full force at the Folsom Street Fair (see p. 120), but now the area is also home to a wide variety of hip nightlife and vibrant daytime art venues.

YERBA BUENA CENTER FOR THE ARTS. The center runs an excellent theater and gallery space, with many lively programs—emphasizing performance, film, viewer involvement, and local multicultural work. It is surrounded by the **Yerba Buena Rooftop Gardens**, a vast expanse of concrete, fountains, and very intentional-looking foliage next to the redoubtable Sony Metreon. *(701 Mission St., at 3rd St. ☎978-2787; www.yerbabuenaarts.org. Open Tu-Sa 11am-6pm. $6, free 1st Tu of each month; seniors and students $3, free every Th. Free gallery tours with admission Th 5pm and Sa 4pm.)*

ZEUM. Within the gardens but a sight unto itself, this new "art and technology center" is aimed at children and teenagers. Besides studios for claymation and webcasts, ZEUM also has a music performance space and an ice skating and bowling center. The best draw, however, is the **carousel**, created in 1906 and reopened after a 25 year hiatus. *(221 4th St., at Howard St. ☎777-2800; www.zeum.org. Open in summer Tu-Su 11am-5pm, Sa-Su 11am-5pm; off-season Sa-Su 11am-5pm. $7, students and seniors $6, ages 5-18 $5, under 5 free. Carousel open M-Th and Su 10am-6pm, F-Sa 10am-8pm. $2 for 2 rides.)*

█ SAN FRANCISCO MUSEUM OF MODERN ART (SFMOMA). Fascinating from an architectural perspective, as well as for the art it contains, this black and gray marble-trimmed museum houses five spacious floors of art, with emphasis on design, photography, and audiovisuals. Its contemporary European and American collections are impressive—SFMOMA has the most of 20th-century art this side of New York. *(151 3rd St., between Mission and Howard St. ☎357-4000, TTD 357-4154; fax 357-4037; www.sfmoma.org. Open Sept. 3-May 24 M-Tu and F-Su 11am-5:45pm, Th 11am-8:45pm; May 25-Sept. 2 M-Tu and F-Su 10am-6pm, Th 10am-9pm. $10, over 62 $7, students $6, under 13 free. Th 6-8:45pm half-price. Free 1st Tu of each month. 4 free gallery tours per day.)*

HAYES VALLEY

Hayes Valley is the latest San Francisco neighborhood to come into its own. Artists of all types, from architects to fashion and interior designers, have begun to open studios on and around Hayes St. As if a natural extension of the artist community, cafes have sprung up, providing the essential social and caffeine reprieve. Then enter the young trendsetters, and *voilà:* you have yourself a thriving new chic neighborhood. For the most part, the popularity and success of the area has been due to the community's talented artists, both of the culinary and visual sort.

Success has also brought higher prices—starving artists are few and far between. An established contemporary art stronghold, the Bucheon Gallery dazzles the art world with new exhibits every few weeks. The gallery also helps young artists—locals and foreigners alike—find exposure in the who-do-you-know art world. Receptions are open to the public. (540 Hayes St., near Octavia St. ☎863-2891; www.bucheon.com. Open Tu-Sa 11am-6pm, Su noon-5pm. Free.)

CIVIC CENTER

Most of San Francisco's theater scene dominates the beautiful, majestic Civic Center. The palatial **San Francisco City Hall,** modeled after Rome's St. Peter's Basilica, is the centerpiece of the largest US gathering of Beaux Arts architecture. (1 Dr. Carlton B. Goodlett Pl., at Van Ness Ave. ☎554-4000. Open M-F 8am-8pm, Sa-Su noon-4pm.) Overlooking the Civic Center, the **State Building's** grandeur is comparable to City Hall's in both structure and function. Home to the state Supreme Court, it also features a small but interesting art collection in the lobby at the Golden Gate Ave. entrance and an exhibition room near the McAllister St. entrance. (350 McAllister St., between Polk and Larkin St.) The **United Nations Plaza** is sometimes host to the city's **farmer's market** and, most other days, to a general assembly of pigeons. (In summer, the farmer's market pops up on Polk St. W and Su. 5:30am-5:30pm.)

The seating in the glass-and-brass **Louise M. Davies Symphony Hall** was designed to give most audience members a close-up view of performers. Visually, the building is a smashing success, as is the **San Francisco Symphony.** See p. 114 for more info. (201 Van Ness Ave. ☎552-8000; tickets ☎431-5400. Open M-F 10am-6pm, Sa noon-6pm.) The well-regarded **San Francisco Opera Company** (see p. 114) and the **San Francisco Ballet** (see p. 115) perform at the recently renovated **War Memorial Opera House.** (301 Van Ness Ave., between Grove and McAllister St.)

TENDERLOIN

Aptly named, this area host not only to more traditional ladies (and men) of the night, but also to San Francisco specials: transvestite, transsexual, and transgendered streetwalkers. **Do not walk alone here, as the area can be dangerous, especially at night.** Witness the scene more safely by day, and also check out the surprisingly vibrant cultural offerings. The **509 Cultural Center/Luggage Store** (☎255-5971) presents performing arts events, exhibitions, and arts education initiatives at the 509 Cultural Center, 509 Ellis St., and the Luggage Store, 1007 Market St., near 6th St. Started by a group of artists and residents in the late 80s, the group strives to draw on the neighborhood's rich diversity to gain a sense of community. Annual festivals include the "In The Street" theater festival in June. The **Art Institute of California** hosts occasional student shows in its lobby. The place is great for a brief viewing, but don't expect to find a multitude of works—it cannot hold more than fifteen paintings. (1170 Market St. ☎865-0198.)

UNION SQUARE

The three-block radius around Union Square houses prestigious art galleries, the heart of San Francisco's theater district, upscale hotels, several multi-floor shopping centers, and just about every boutique known to man. On the fringes of this radius, however, the homeless and the insane languish unnoticed on the sidewalks of the Tenderloin. Nevertheless, there's plenty of European retail therapy around, most spectacularly at the nine-story **San Francisco Shopping Centre** (notice the spelling) on Market St. at 5th St., where six curving escalators propel you past hundreds of ways to spend money.

GALLERIES. The **Martin Lawrence Gallery** is a modest corner space that displays works by pop artists like Andy Warhol and Keith Haring as well as studies by Pablo Picasso and Marc Chagall. Although Haring once distributed his work for free to New York commuters in the form of graffiti, his art now commands upwards of $13,000—even in print form. *(366 Geary St., between Powell and Mason St.* ☎ *956-0345. Open M-Th 9am-8pm, F-Sa 9am-9pm, Su 10am-6pm.)* **Hang** is a young gallery with attitude housed in a chrome warehouse. It specializes in the rental of paintings and sculpture by emerging Bay Area artists. *(556 Sutter St., between Powell and Mason St.* ☎ *434-4264; www.hangart.com. Open M-Sa 10am-6pm, Su noon-5pm.)* If you're still a couple cents short of owning a Picasso, the newly opened **S.F. Black and White Gallery** transforms a spare urban space into a daily cocktail reception for Bay Area artists. Urban San Francisco chic pervades the gallery, from the breathtaking photographs of the city to The Darkroom's light bar in the back. An photograph can be as low as $30. *(619 Post St., at Taylor St.* ☎ *929-9424. Open daily 9am-9pm.)* **The Academy of Art College** has galleries that showcase student work on a bi-weekly basis. *(688 Sutter St., near Mason St.* ☎ *274-2200. Also at 410 Bush St., between Kearney St. and Grant Ave.* ☎ *274-8680. Open daily 8am-midnight; abbreviated hours during school vacations.)*

FINANCIAL DISTRICT & EMBARCADERO

Although much of modern-day Bay Area business may be conducted online, the city still has its share of pressed suits and corner offices right here. Hidden parks and a handful of sights provide subtle distraction from the overwhelming banking biz. The leading lady of the city's skyline, the **Transamerica Pyramid,** is, according to New Age sources, directly centered on the telluric currents of the Golden Dragon Ley line between Easter Island and Stonehenge. Planned as an architect's joke and co-opted by one of the leading architectural firms in the country, the building earned disdain from purists and reverence from city planners after the fact. Unless you're an employee, tight security means there is no chance of a top-floor view. (600 Montgomery St., between Clay and Washington St.) At the foot of Market St., **Justin Herman Plaza** and its formidable 1971 Vaillancourt Fountain, made of precast aggregate concrete, invite total visitor immersion. Bands and rallyists often rent out the area during lunch. Dubbed "a famous city's most famous landmark" by Herb Caen, the 660 ft. waterfront **Ferry Building,** at the foot of Market St., has lost a bit of grandeur over the years, as bigger and better buildings developed along the Embarcadero and stole the spotlight. A. Page Brown designed the elegant port with repeated archways and Corinthian columns to recall Roman aqueducts.

CHINATOWN

Locals of all backgrounds bargain in Chinatown's markets and feast in its affordable eateries. A distinct mix of Chinese and American that has emerged over time. American politics have blended with Chinese perspectives, while food and desserts have adapted to American cooking styles and tourist tastes.

GRANT AVENUE. The oldest street in San Francisco is Grant Ave., a sea of Chinese banners, signs, and architecture. During the day, Grant Ave. and nearby streets are brimming with tourists, who stop every block to buy health balls and chirping boxes and pretend not to notice the Chinese porn magazines lining some shop windows. At Bush and Grant Ave. stands the ornate, dragon-crested **Gateway to Chinatown,** given as a gift by Taiwan in 1970. "Everything in the world is in just proportion," say the Chinese characters above the gate. Most of the picturesque pagodas punctuating the blocks were designed around 1900 or more recently—not as authentic replicas of Chinese architecture, but to attract Western tourists. While Grant Ave. is the entrance and center of many Chinatown activities, to get a true taste of the neighborhood you must venture off into alleys and side-streets.

ROSS ALLEY. Running from Jackson to Washington St. between Grant and Stockton St., Ross Alley was once lined with brothels and opium dens, and today still has the cramped look of old Chinatown. The narrow street has stood in for the Orient in such films as *Big Trouble in Little China, Karate Kid II,* and *Indiana Jones and the Temple of Doom.* Squeeze into a tiny doorway to watch fortune cookies being shaped by hand in the Golden Gate Cookie Company. *(56 Ross Alley.* ☎ *781-3956. Bag of cookies $3; with "funny," "sexy" fortunes $5.)*

▨**WAVERLY PLACE.** Find this little alley (between Sacramento and Washington St. and between Stockton St. and Grant Ave.) and you'll want to spend all day gazing at the incredible architecture. The fire escapes are painted in pinks and greens and held together by railings made of intricate Chinese patterns. Tourists can also visit **Tien Hou Temple,** 125 Waverly Place, the oldest Chinese temple in the US.

CHINESE CULTURAL CENTER. A stone bridge leads from Portsmouth Square to the other side of Kearny St., where the Chinese Cultural Center operates out of the third floor of the Holiday Inn. The Center houses a gallery of Chinese-American art, displays community exhibits, and sponsors **walking tours** of Chinatown. *(750 Kearny St., on the 3rd fl. of the Holiday Inn; also accessible directly from Portsmouth Sq.* ☎ *986-1822; www.c-c-c.org. Open Tu-Sa 10am-4pm. Heritage Walk Sa and Su 2pm. $15, under 18 $8.)*

NORTH BEACH

North Beach is worth visiting both during the daytime and during its neon-lit evenings. The old Italian community has made way over the years for beatniks, hippies, and you, without compromising its old-world feel.

WASHINGTON SQUARE. Washington Sq., bordered by Union, Filbert, Stockton, and Powell St., is North Beach's *piazza*, a pretty, not-quite-square, tree-lined lawn. The statue in Washington Sq. is of Benjamin Franklin. The wedding site of Marilyn Monroe and Joe DiMaggio, the park fills every morning with men and women from Chinatown practicing *tai chi.* By noon, sunbathers, picnickers, and bocce-ball players take over. At 666 Filbert St., the **Church of St. Peter and St. Paul** beckons tired sightseers to take refuge in its dark, wooden nave. Turn-of-the-century SF philanthropist and party-girl Lillie Hitchcock Coit donated the **Volunteer Firemen Memorial** in the middle of the square after being rescued from a fire as a young girl.

TELEGRAPH HILL. Overlooking Washington Park and North Beach, Telegraph Hill is its own neighborhood. Originally, the steep mount was the site of a semaphore that signaled the arrival of ships in Gold Rush days. Today, tourists hike up the hill to visit **Coit Tower,** which stands 210 ft. high and commands a spectacular view of the city and the Bay. During the Depression, the government's Works Progress Administration employed artists to paint the colorful and surprisingly subversive murals on the dome's inside. *(MUNI bus #39 goes all the way to Coit tower. If driving, follow Lombard St. to the top, where there is free 30min. parking M and F 9am-5pm, Tu-Th and Sa-Su 8am-5pm. Tower:* ☎ *362-0808. Open daily 10am-7pm. Elevator fare: $3.75, over 64 $2.50, ages 6-12 $1.50, under 6 free. Free guided tours of murals Th 10:15am, Sa 11am.)*

SAN FRANCISCO ART INSTITUTE. The oldest art school west of the Mississippi, the San Francisco Art Institute is lodged in a converted mission and has produced a number of American greats including Mark Rothko, Ansel Adams, Imogen Cunningham, Dorothea Lange, and James Weeks, to name a few. Student projects hang throughout the school, and given the place's history, you never know whom you might discover. As you enter, to the left is the **Diego Rivera Gallery,** one wall of which is covered by a huge 1931 Rivera mural. The gallery hosts weekly student exhibits with receptions. Farther down the left hand hallway are the **Walter and McBean Galleries,** which show professional exhibits. Outside these galleries and across the

FROM THE ROAD

FOUND IN THE FOG

A tourist trap is like a gory scene in a horror movie—part of you wants to look at it, but another part is repulsed. When I got to Fisherman's Wharf one sunny weekend afternoon, I immediately gave in to curiosity. I donned shorts, flip-flops, camera and visor, and blended in with the throngs of tourists heading to Pier 39. Thirsty but unwilling to pay $4 for a soda, made impatient by the endless lines, and irritated by the penny-flattening machines and while-you-wait caricature artists blocking the sidewalk, I felt that repulsion had taken over.

I didn't truly appreciate the wharf until the bad weather rolled in. Raised near Newcastle-upon-Tyne, England, (eternalized by soccer-player Paul Gascoigne's one-hit-wonder "The Fog on the Tyne") I was one of the few wharf-goers unfazed by the fog. Wrapped in warm clothing, I wandered along the piers unhindered. The speciality stores and museums became more entertaining without the wait and swirling fog made the Alcatraz tour eerie. The hordes outside the Ghirardelli soda fountain were reduced to a trickle of tourists, and I was able to enjoy my ice-cream in peace while listening to jazz performers, all the while feeling very San Francisco.

–Laura Spence

sunny modern "quadrangle," **Pete's Cafe** serves up cheap burgers and sandwiches ($4.50), making for a nice picnic spot with fantastic views of the bay. *(800 Chestnut St., between Leavenworth and Jones St. ☎ 771-7020 or 800-345-7324; www.sfai.edu. Receptions Tu 5-7pm.)*

CITY LIGHTS BOOKSTORE. Drawn by low rents and cheap bars, the Beat writers came to national attention when Lawrence Ferlinghetti's City Lights Bookstore, opened in 1953, published Allen Ginsberg's *Howl*. Banned in 1956, and then subjected to an extended trial at the end of which a judge found the poem "not obscene," the book and its publisher vaulted the Beats into literary infamy. City Lights has expanded since its Beat days and widely now stocks fiction and poetry, but it remains committed to publishing young poets and writers under its own imprint. Black and white signs beckon visitors to sit down, turn off their "sell-phones," and flip through the books. Index card boxes in the back stairwell hold postings for jobs, housing, and rides, and writers without permanent addresses can have their mail held in the store. See also **Shopping: Books,** p. 111. *(261 Columbus Ave. ☎ 362-8193. Open daily 10am-midnight.)*

FISHERMAN'S WHARF & THE PIERS

Fisherman's Wharf is home to eight blocks of touristy carnivalesque aquatic splendor. Sifting through the while-you-wait caricature artists, "olde-fashioned fudge shoppes," penny-flattening machines, and novelty t-shirts, patrons can catch amazing glimpses of sea lions, Alcatraz, and a rich naval tradition. Piers 39 through 45 provide access to San Fran's most famous attractions. Perhaps the best way to appreciate the wharf is to wake up at 4am, put on a warm sweater, and go down to experience the loading and outfitting of small ships, the animated conversation, the blanket of morning mist, and the incredible view. The western edge, near Municipal Pier, is quieter than the main Wharf piers. For an unusual but still lovely view of the bay, try vigorously bouncing up and down on a giant trampoline while suspended by two bungee cords. ($6, next to Pier 39 on the dock.)

PIER 39. Self-titled "San Francisco's Number One Attraction," Pier 39 is a shamelessly commercial collection of 110 speciality shops, restaurants, fast-food vendors, and entertainment. Even the world-famous sea lions—found by the Eastern tip of the pier—seem to put on a spectacle of splashing and snorting for the benefit of tourists. The **California Welcome Center,** recently relocated to the top of the Marina Plaza stairs, is not to be missed; now part of an Internet cafe, the center offers snacks, info, and occasional discount coupons for attractions in the city and beyond. For a whirlwind city-tour, experience **The Great San Francisco Adventure** at **Pier 39 Cinemax.** In huge-screen format, you can fly over the Golden Gate Bridge, feel a 3.0 scale earthquake, race down Lombard St., watch a 49ers game, and dive to the ocean depths—in only 30 minutes! If that leaves you feeling giddy, head to the end of the pier to unwind with live street performances at **Center Stage,** or a jaunt on the **Venetian Carousel.** *(☎ 981-7437. Shops, attractions, and fast food open Su-Th 10am-9pm, F-Sa 10am-10pm; restaurants open Su-Th 11:30am-10pm, F-Sa 11:30am-11pm. Cinemax: ☎ 956-3456. Shows every 45min. First show 10am. $7.50, seniors $6, children $4.50. California Welcome Center and Internet Cafe: ☎ 956-3493. Open Su-Th 9am-9pm, F-Sa 9am-10pm.)*

PIER 45. Still used by fishermen in the early morning hours, Pier 45 is also home to the **USS Pampanito** (SS-383). In retirement after sinking six enemy ships during its Pacific patrols, this World War II *Balao*-class fleet submarine serves as a National Historic Park museum. *(☎ 775-1943. Open June-Sept. M-Th 9am-6pm, F-Su 9am-8pm; Oct.-May M-Tu and Th-Su 9am-8pm, W 9am-6pm. $7, seniors $5, ages 6-12 $4, under 6 free.)*

GHIRARDELLI SQUARE. Chocolate-lovers' heaven, Ghirardelli Square houses a mall in what used to be a chocolate factory. Don't worry, you don't need a Willy Wonka golden ticket to sample the savory sweets; visit the **Ghiradelli Chocolate Manufactory,** with its vast selection of chocolatey goodies, or the **Ghiradelli Chocolate Shop and Caffe,** with drinks, frozen yogurt, and a smaller selection of chocolates. Both hand out **free samples** of chocolate at the door, but on tourist-heavy days, the Caffe is often less crowded. The **soda fountain,** an old-fashioned ice-cream parlor, serves up huge sundaes ($6.25) smothered with its world-famous hot fudge sauce. *(Mall: 900 North Point St. ☎ 775-5500. Stores open M-Sa 10am-9pm, Su 10am-6pm. Ghirardelli Chocolate Manufactory: ☎ 771-4903. Open Su-Th 10am-11pm, F-Sa 10am-midnight. Soda fountain: Open Su-Th 10am-11pm, F-Sa 10am-midnight. Chocolate Shop and Caffe: ☎ 474-1414. Open M-Th 8:30am-9pm, F 8:30am-10pm, Sa 9pm-10pm, Su 9am-9pm.)*

HYDE STREET PIER. Along with the curving Municipal Pier, Hyde Street Pier encloses an area of the Bay known as the **Aquatic Park.** Sittin' on the dock of the Bay, you can watch the daring locals swim laps in frigid 50 degree water. If you feel like joining them, the **South End Club** and the **Dolphin Club** are open to the public on alternate days for $6.50 when you can thaw out in their sauna. Rich with maritime tradition, Hyde Street Pier is also part of the National Historic Park. The park service offers guided tours of the vessels, schooners and ferryboats are offered along with a boat-building class. *(On Hyde St. ☎ 561-7100. Open 9:30am-5:30pm. $6, seniors $4, ages 12-17 $2, under 12 free, families $13. Guided Pier Walks offered 4 times daily; call for times. Dolphin Club: 502 Jefferson St. ☎ 441-9329. Open W and F 11am-6pm. South End Club: 500 Jefferson St. ☎ 929-9656. Open Tu, Th, and Sa 11am-6pm. Boating Class: ☎ 929-0202.)*

THE CANNERY. Originally the del Monte canning factory, **The Cannery** has been converted into a marketplace-style plaza. Its maze of shady terraces and garden courtyards offers respite from wharfside hubbub and ballyhoo. Among its few restaurants, bars and cafes, the **Belle Roux Voodoo Lounge,** a classy Cajun eatery, and **Cobb's Comedy Club** are well-known favorites. *(Belle Roux Voodoo Lounge: ☎ 771-5225. Cobb's Comedy Club: ☎ 938-4320.)*

ALCATRAZ

The Blue and Gold Fleet (☎ 705-8200, tickets 705-5555; www.blueandgoldfleet.com) runs to Alcatraz (14 per day; $9.25 round-trip, seniors $7.50, ages 5-11 $6; audio tour $4 extra). Ticket lines can be painfully long. Reserve at least a day and preferably a week in advance, especially in summer.

SAN FRANCISCO

BONAPARTE OF THE BAY By nature, California is a populist constituency, putting more questions to voter referendum than any other state—but San Franciscans have made at least one notable exception. From 1853 to 1880, locals recognized the self-proclaimed rule of **Joshua Norton the First, Emperor of the United States and Defender of Mexico.** Norton assumed the grandiose title after tough luck in rice speculation wiped out all his money—and perhaps his sanity as well. He donned an ostrich feather hat and faux-military attire and roamed San Francisco's streets with his dogs, Bummer and Lazarus. When he wasn't busy sending suggestions to Abraham Lincoln, Queen Victoria, and the Czar of Russia, Norton made decrees for San Francisco that included the tradition of having a Christmas tree in Union Square and building a bridge across the Bay. Locals didn't mind his eccentricities; good-natured merchants accepted the money he printed, and the Central Pacific Railroad allowed him to travel for free. The city even footed the bill for his new clothes. When he died, 20,000 people came to wave him on to the next world.

Mention Alcatraz, and most people think of hardened criminals and daring escapes. In its 29 years as a maximum-security federal penitentiary, Alcatraz did encounter a menacing cast of characters—Al "Scarface" Capone, George "Machine Gun" Kelly, and Robert "The Birdman" Stroud among others. There were 14 separate escape attempts—some desperate, defiant bolts for freedom, others carefully calculated and innovative. Only one man is known to have survived crossing the Bay; he was recaptured, while five escapees remain unaccounted for. On the rock, the award-winning cell-house audio tour takes you back to the infamous days of Alcatraz. Listen to the screaming gulls, the booming foghorn, and watch the palm trees blowing in the wind outside. From the dining room window see the glittering hubbub of San Francisco life, and experience some of the isolation that plagued the prison's inmates. But there is more to the history of Alcatraz than gangsters and their antics. A **Park Ranger guided tour** can take you around the island, and through its 200 years of occupation: from a hunting and fishing ground for Native Americans, to a civil war defensive outpost, to a military prison, a federal prison and finally a birthplace of the movement for Native American civil rights. Now part of the **Golden Gate National Recreation Area,** Alcatraz is home to diverse plants and bird lime. The Agave Trail footpath lets you explore these habitats (Sept.-Jan.). For general orientation, the dockside theater gives a 13min. video of the Rock's history and resources. Next door is the bookstore, offering videos, audiotapes, books and gifts to round off the Alcatraz experience. Check the web for occasional book signings by former prisoners (real prisoners, not Sean "hot and leathery" Connery), guards, and residents.

ANGEL ISLAND

The Blue and Gold Fleet (☎ 705-8200, tickets 705-5555; www.blueandgoldfleet.com) runs to Angel Island (M-F 2 per day, Sa-Su 3 per day; $10.50 round-trip, ages 6-12 $5.50, under 6 free).

Picturesque **Angel Island State Park** sits in the middle of San Francisco Bay. A 20min. ferry ride from San Francisco or Marin brings you to rolling hills, biking and hiking trails, and sprawling picnic grounds. The island is a heavenly escape from the bustle of the city, except for those sunny weekends when all of San Francisco heads out there. While many come to enjoy the great views, others visit for the island's rich history. For over 2000 years, Coastal Miwok tribes, native to Marin County, paddled out to Angel Island to hunt and fish. Spaniard Juan Manuel de Ayala "discovered" the island and gave his name to the cove he established as a harbor. The Mexicans used Angel Island to rear cattle until 1859, when it was taken over by the US Army. The forts left by the Army have housed a Civil War encampment, a Spanish-American War quarantine station, a missile site, and an immigration station. From 1910 to

1940, Angel Island served as a holding site for immigrants, mostly Chinese, seeking entry into the US. During WWII, the station was used as a prisoner-of-war camp.

Bring charcoal and some raw food to take advantage of the many public grills that dot the lawn in front of the **Visitor Center** at Ayala Cove. On weekends and summer weekdays, this area fills up with families; but if the screeching of small children is precisely what you're trying to escape, serenity is only a hike away. Just behind the picnic grounds, the Visitor Center has historical exhibits and a free 20min. orientation video. Adjacent to the center, the **Park Ranger Station** offers tours of historic sites, including the Immigration Station, Camp Reynolds, and Fort McDowell. For a leisurely island circuit, the 1hr. **Tram Tour** hits all major historic sites and provides some decent views. With a bit of leg-work, the bike and hike trails allow some escape from the masses and reward with stunning panoramas. **Bikes** can be brought on the ferry, or rented near the docks at Ayala Cove. Bikers are allowed only on the perimeter road and the steeper fire road. The perimeter road balances exhausting uphills with exhilarating downhills. Hikers can troop up several trails to the 781 ft. summit of Mt. Livermore for a bird's eye view of the Bay.

If a day trip isn't enough, you can **camp** at one of the nine eco-friendly hike-in sites. All sites have running water, pit toilets, BBQ, table and food-lockers. Although picnic tables are perched around every corner, food is scarce. You're best off packing meals before coming to the island, but keep in mind that all equipment has to be carried at least 2 mi. to a site.

NOB HILL & RUSSIAN HILL

Lovers of hills and views, welcome to paradise! In a fairly expensive, mostly residential area, the main attractions here are the views and a few noteworthy sights. You'll find more activity as the area merges into Union Sq. and the Tenderloin.

THE CROOKEDEST STREET IN THE WORLD. The famous curves of **Lombard Street** seem to grace nearly half of San Francisco's postcards, and rightfully so. The flowerbeds along the curves are well maintained, and the curves themselves—installed in the 1920s so that horse-drawn carriages could negotiate the extremely steep hill— are one-of-a-kind. From the top of Lombard St., pedestrians and passengers alike enjoy the fantastic view of the city and harbor. The view north along Hyde St.—a steep drop to Fisherman's Wharf and lonely Alcatraz—isn't too shabby, either.

GRACE CATHEDRAL AND HUNTINGTON PARK. The largest Gothic edifice west of the Mississippi, **Grace Cathedral** is Nob Hill's stained-glass studded crown. The castings of its portals are such exact imitations of Lorenzo Ghiberti's on the Baptistery in Florence that they were used to restore the originals. Inside, modern murals mix San Franciscan and national historical events with saintly scenes. The altar of the AIDS Interfaith Memorial Chapel celebrates the church's "inclusive community of love" with a lustrously intricate Keith Haring triptych. Outside, this all-accepting behemoth of Christian modernity looks onto the neatly manicured turf and trees of accepting **Huntington Park,** equipped with a park and playground. *(1100 California St., between Jones and Taylor St. ☎ 749-6300; www.gracecathedral.org. Open Su-F 7am-6pm, Sa 8am-6pm. Services Su 7:30, 8:15, 11am, 3:30pm; M-F 7:30, 8:30am, 12:10, 5:15pm; Sa 9am, 3:30, 5pm. Tour guides available M-F 1-3pm, Sa 11:30am-1:30 pm, Su 1:30-2pm. Suggested donation $3.)* The neat, manicured spot of turf in front of this behemoth of Christian modernity is **Huntington Park,** equipped with a literal playground for the rich.

CABLE CAR POWERHOUSE AND MUSEUM. After the steep journey up Nob Hill, you'll understand what inspired the development of the vehicles celebrated at this museum. More worthwhile as an educational breather than as its own destination, the modest building is the working center of San Francisco's cable car system. Look down on 57,300 ft. of cable whizzing by or view displays to learn more about the cars, some of which date back to 1873. *(1201 Mason St., at Washington St.* ☎ *474-1887. Open Apr.-Oct. daily 10am-6pm; Nov.-Mar. 10am-5pm. Free.)*

MARINA

Pastel stucco houses with lavish gardens, stunning views of Marin, and a high quotient of young beautiful socialites characterize the residential Marina. You would never know that the area was one of the worst struck by the 1989 earthquake, which measured 7.1 on the Richter scale. Massive fires destroyed several buildings in the Marina, but the neighborhood was able to restore its former grandeur. The main attractions stretch along the waterfront across the northern edge of the city.

■ **EXPLORATORIUM.** *Scientific American* called this "the best science museum in the world," and *Let's Go* calls it a mad scientist's dream. Displays include interactive tornados, computer planet-managing, and giant bubble-makers poised to take over the universe. Don't miss demonstrations like the cow's eye dissection or the changing special exhibitions. Within the Exploratorium dwells the **Tactile Dome,** a pitch-dark maze of tunnels, slides, nooks, and crannies designed to help refine your sense of touch. Claustrophobes beware. *(3601 Lyon St.* ☎ *563-7337 or 561-0360; www.exploratorium.edu. Open Memorial Day-Labor Day M-Tu and Th-Su 10am-6pm, W 10am-9pm; Labor Day-Memorial Day Tu and Th-Su 10am-5pm, W 10am-9pm. $10, students and seniors $7.50, disabled and ages 6-17 $6, under 4 free. Free 1st W of each month. Admission included in San Francisco CityPass. Tactile Dome reservations* ☎ *561-0362; reservations@exploratorium.edu. $14. Open during museum hours. Credit card required for reservations; make them at least 1 day in advance. Admission fee includes Exploratorium.)*

■ **WAVE ORGAN.** Past the Golden Gate Yacht Club at the end of a long jetty rests one of San Francisco's best hidden treasures: the Wave Organ, an acoustic environmental sculpture made up of 25 pipes jutting out of the ocean that create musical sounds as waves crash against the pipes. Conceived by Peter Richards, the project was completed in 1986. George Gonzalez, a sculptor and stone mason, designed the seating area around the pipes using granite and marble pieces from an old decimated cemetery. All sorts of carvings can be found if you look closely enough. The music itself is quite subtle, like listening to a sea shell, and is best heard at high tide. If you take the time to sit for a while, tones from the organ will begin to harmonize with the clinking boat masts, fog horns, and seagulls, synthesizing into a sublime oceanic symphony.

■ **PALACE OF FINE ARTS.** With its open-air domed structure and curving colonnades, The Palace of Fine Arts is one of the best picnic spots in the city. It was reconstructed from remnants of the 1915 Panama Pacific Exposition, which had been built to commemorate the opening of the Panama Canal and exemplify San Francisco's recovery from the 1906 earthquake. Shakespearean plays are often performed here during the summer, and the nighttime illumination is glorious. Additionally, the **Palace of Fine Arts Theater,** located directly behind the rotunda, hosts various dance and theater performances, and film festivals. *(On Baker St., between Jefferson and Bay St. next to the Exploratorium. Open daily 6am-9pm. Free. Theater:* ☎ *563-6504; www.palaceoffinearts.com. Call for shows, times, and ticket prices.)*

FORT MASON

Despite its severe facade, the Fort Mason Center is home to some of the most innovative and impressive cultural museums and resources in San Francisco. The Fort's array of outstanding attractions seem to remain unknown to most travelers and locals alike, making it a quiet waterfront counterpart to the tourist blitz of nearby Fisherman's Wharf. The grounds are also home to a popular hostel and the headquarters of the **Golden Gate National Recreation Area (GGNRA).** While not nearly so spectacular as the other lands under the GGNRA's aegis, the manicured lawns make a swell spot for strolling and picnicking. (The eastern portion of Fort Mason, near Gashouse Cove. ☎ 441-3400, ext. 3; www.fortmason.org.)

MUSEUM OF CRAFT AND FOLK ART. The MOCFA brings together a fascinating collection of crafts and functional art (vessels, clothing, furniture, and jewelry) from cultures past and present, near and far, showcasing everything from 19th century Chinese children's hats to unwearable underwear made from Lifesaver wrappers. (Bldg. A., 1st fl. ☎ 775-0990; www.mocfa.org. Open Tu-F and Su 11am-5pm, Sa 10am-5pm. $3, students and seniors $1, under 12 free, families $5. Free Sa 10am-noon and 1st W of each month 11am-7pm.)

AFRICAN-AMERICAN HISTORICAL AND CULTURAL SOCIETY MUSEUM. The African-American Historical and Cultural Society Museum displays historic artifacts and artwork as well as modern works by African and African-American artists. The museum also has a permanent collection by local artists. (Bldg. C, #165. ☎ 441-0640; www.caaac.org/society. Open W-Su noon-5pm. $2, seniors and children $1.)

MUSEO ITALO AMERICANO. The only museum in the country dedicated solely to Italian and Italian-American art, Museo Italo Americano is home to a small collection by artists from several centuries and offers several cultural programs such as language classes and lectures. (Bldg. C, #100. ☎ 673-2200; www.museoitaloamericano.org. Open W-Su noon-5pm. $3, students and seniors $2.)

PACIFIC HEIGHTS

Along Union and Sacramento St., Pacific Heights has the greatest number of Victorian buildings in the city. The Heights sustained serious damage in the 1989 earthquake—Victorian restoration has become a full-fledged enterprise here. Pierce and Clay St., in particular, have an abundance of grand homes. The Public Library offers free tours of Pacific Heights mansions during the summer.

The **Octagon House Museum** was built in 1861 with the belief that the odd architecture would bring good luck to its inhabitants. Its survival of San Francisco's many earthquakes and fires is proof of fortune's favor so far. (2645 Gough St., at Union St. ☎ 441-7512. Open Feb.-Dec. 2nd Su and 2nd and 4th Th of each month noon-3pm. $3 recommended donation.) For church gazers and architecture buffs, St. Dominic's Roman Catholic Church is a looker, with huge statues, ceilings, and breathtaking stained glass windows. (2390 Bush St., at Steiner St. Open M-Sa 6:30am-5:30pm, Su 7:30am-9pm. Mass M-F 6:30, 8am, 5:30pm; Sa 8am, 5:30pm, Su 7:30, 9:30, 11:30am, 1:30, 5:30, 9pm candlelight service.) Once you've hiked up the hills of Pacific Heights, reward yourself with a breather in Alta Plaza, whose colorful flowers and little grassy knolls just beg for a picnic. Alta Plaza, bounded by Jackson, Scott, Steiner, and Clay St., is indeed high and has great views of the surrounding neighborhoods.

JAPANTOWN

Walking all the way through Japantown takes just minutes and is the only way to go. Stores hawk the latest Pokémon paraphernalia, and karaoke bars warble J-pop along Post St. around the Japan Center. The five-tiered **Peace Pagoda,** a gift to the community from the Japanese government, once sat amid cherry trees and a reflecting pool. It is currently in the midst of a slow restoration process to convert its ugly paved lot into an inviting centerpiece of the Japan Center. A brighter example of Japanese architecture is the **Soto Zen Mission Sokoji Buddhist Temple,** where some meditation services are open to the public. (1691 Laguna St., at Sutter St. ☎ 346-7540. Public Zen services Su 8-10:30am. Arrive 15min. early.)

LSD: FROM THE MAN TO THE PEOPLE In 1943, in Basel, Switzerland, Albert Hoffman synthesized a compound called lysergic acid diethylamide (LSD). The new wonder drug was said to cure psychosis and alcoholism. In the early 50s, the CIA adopted LSD for **Operation MK-ULTRA,** a series of Cold War mind control experiments. By the end of the 60s, the drug had been tested on 1500 military personnel in a series of ethically shady operations. Writers Ken Kesey, Allen Ginsberg, and the Grateful Dead's Robert Hunter were first exposed to acid as subjects in government experiments. The CIA soon abandoned the unpredictable hallucinogen, but its effects had been discovered by bohemian proto-hippies in the Haight-Ashbury. Amateur chemists began producing the compound, and prominent intellectuals like Timothy Leary and Aldous Huxley advocated its use as a means of expanding consciousness. In October 1966, the drug was made illegal in California, and Kesey's Merry Pranksters hosted their first public **Acid Test,** immortalized in Tom Wolfe's journalistic novel *The Electric Kool-Aid Acid Test.* Once a secret weapon of the military-industrial complex, acid became an ingredient of the counterculture, juicing up anti-war rallies and love-ins across the Bay Area and the nation.

HAIGHT-ASHBURY

All around Haight and Ashbury St., vestiges of the 60s exist in harmony with chain stores and boutiques. Music and clothing top the list of legal merchandise. Inexpensive bars and ethnic restaurants, action-packed street life, anarchist literature, and shops selling pipes for, um, tobacco, also contribute to groovy browsing possibilities. While the **Upper Haight** tends to attract a younger tourist crowd, the **Lower Haight** is the stomping ground for longtime locals, though visitors are always welcome. Can't you just feel the love?

The former homes of several counterculture legends survive beautifully. Starting at the corner of Haight and Ashbury St., walk up Ashbury St. to #710, just south of Waller St., to check out the house occupied by the **Grateful Dead** when they were still the Warlocks. Look across the street for the **Hell's Angels'** house. Walk back to Haight St., go right three blocks, and make a left on Lyon St., and you can check out **Janis Joplin**'s old abode, 122 Lyon St., between Page and Oak St. Cross the Panhandle, and continue three blocks to Fulton St., turn right, and wander seven blocks toward the park to see where the Manson "family" planned murder and mayhem at the **Charles Manson** mansion, 2400 Fulton St., at Willard St. The **San Francisco Public Library** sponsors a free walking tour focused on the area's pre-hippie incarnation as a Victorian-era resort. (☎557-4266. Tours leave Su 11am from the Park Branch Library at 1833 Page St., near Cole St.)

PARKS. Several parks dot the Haight. You may see police lurking in the bushes—the parks are rumored to be great places to buy pot. **Buena Vista Park,** which runs along Haight St. between Central and Baker St. and continues south, resembles a dense jungle. The lush and exotic fauna provides a private haven for those who want to do their own thing. An unofficial crash pad and community center for San Francisco skaters, Buena Vista is supposedly safer than **Alamo Square,** which lies northeast of the Haight at Hayes and Steiner St. Across Alamo Square's gentle grassy slope, a string of beautiful and brightly colored Victorian homes known as the **Painted Ladies**—subject of a thousand postcards—glow against the backdrop of the metropolitan skyline.

▣ SHOPPING

BOOKS

San Francisco has bookstores to fit every niche market and bibliophilic bent. The highest concentration of small, local stores can be found on **Haight Street** and in the **Mission**. Used bookstores are also abundant along Irving St. in the **Sunset** district and around Columbus Ave. and Broadway in **North Beach**. (For the book trade across the Bay, see **Berkeley: Shopping, p. 129**.)

▣ **City Lights Bookstore**, 261 Columbus Ave. (☎362-8193), near Broadway, in **North Beach**. This Beat generation landmark, famous for promoting banned books in the 1950s and 60s, has a wide selection of fiction, poetry, art, and, of course, Beat literature. Founder and owner Lawrence Ferlinghetti is still committed to publishing and publicizing the work of new authors. Open daily 10am-midnight. See **Sights**, p. 104.

▣ **Green Apple Music and Books**, 506 Clement St. (☎382-2272), at 6th Ave., in **Richmond**. In a city teeming with impressive independent book stores, Green Apple's enormous collection of used books stands out as one of the best. Green Apple's popularity gives it a chaotic marketplace feel—no quiet, comfy-armchair perusing here. The main store covers everything from cooking to transportation; find fiction and a small but significant used CDs section in the **Annex**, 2 doors down at 520 Clement St. Open Su-Th 10am-10:30pm, F-Sa 10am-11:30pm. Annex closes 15min. earlier.

A Different Light Bookstore, 489 Castro St. (☎431-0891), near 18th St., in **Castro**. All queer, all the time, with more-than-plentiful special interest subdivisions, including poetry, travel, and of course, transsexual Asian firefighters. Also the ultimate resource for free Bay Area mags, a popular community bulletin board, and free monthly readings by notable queer authors. Open daily 10am-10pm.

Book Bay Bookstore, Bldg. C., 1st fl. (☎771-1076), in **Fort Mason Center**. Sells donated books at stupendously low prices. Lots of art, film, and performing arts books. Vintage pulp novels. All proceeds benefit the public library. Open daily 11am-5pm.

Phoenix Books and Music, 3850 24th St. (☎821-3477), at Vicksburg St., between Church and Sanchez St., in **Noe Valley**. New, remainder, and used books and CDs. Good artbook selection, great bargains on hardcovers (most $4-15), and yes, a friendly and knowledgeable staff. Open M-Sa 10am-10pm, Su 10am 8pm.

MUSIC

▣ **Amoeba Music**, 1855 Haight St. (☎831-1200), in the **Upper Haight**. *Rolling Stone* dubbed this the best record store in the world. Twice as big as its parent organism in Berkeley, the Haight St. Amoeba stocks an amazing selection of used CDs, plus new music and a parade of vintage concert posters. The store doubles as a venue for free concerts by some big names and a weekly in-house DJ series. Check website for details. Open M-Sa 10:30am-10pm, Su 11am-9pm.

Aquarius Records, 1055 Valencia St. (☎647-2272), at 21st St. in the **Mission**. Tiny store known worldwide for obscure selection of all genres of music and a staff to guide you when you don't know where to start: Japanese Rock or 60s psychedelic folk? Its real specialties are drum & bass, indie, and imports from all over the globe. New and used. Great vinyl section, too. Open M-W 10am-9pm, Th-Su 10am-10pm.

Open Mind Music, 342 Divisadero St. (☎621-2244), at Page St., in the **Lower Haight.** Insane quantities of used vinyl and a fair number of collectibles, but they sell it new, too: dance, down temp, new hip-hop, experimental, lounge music, and even Zeppelin. Listening stations to sample before you buy. Open M-Sa 11am-9pm, Su noon-8pm.

CLOTHES

▨ **Departures From the Past,** 2028 Fillmore St. (☎885-3377), at Pine St., in **Pacific Heights.** Extraordinary collection of genuine vintage clothing for men and women. Particularly impressive range of lingerie (if secondhand lingerie doesn't make you itch). Tons of wacky accessories including but not limited to: costume jewelry, sunglasses, hats, gloves, and bow ties. Open M-Sa 11am-7pm, Su noon-6pm.

Manifesto, 514 Octavia St. (☎431-4778), just north of Hayes St., in **Hayes Valley.** Local designer makes 1950s-inspired clothes for men and women. The retro-looking dresses and shirts are well cut, reasonably priced ($65-150), and more flattering than many of their authentic cousins. Open Tu-F 11am-7pm, Sa 11am-6pm, Su noon-5pm.

American Rag, 1305 Van Ness Ave. (☎474-5214), at Fern St., in **Pacific Heights.** A California vintage clothing institution. Shopaholics will adore big-name retro styles up front while bargain-hunters will be tempted by plentiful racks of true vintage in the back. Even thrift prices aren't great (most pants, skirts, jeans $30-45) but the selection is staggering. Open M-Sa 10am-9pm, Su 10am-7pm.

Getups, 600 Castro St. (☎934-9800), at 19th St., in **Castro.** "Soul Train meets Andy Warhol with a touch of Green Acres," describes the fabulous Miles, who hand-picks every fuzzy hat, feather boa, and vintage jacket that makes up his surprisingly affordable threads. Great selection of trendy new getups for men and women, plus handbags, sunglasses, and "accessories to die for." Open M-Sa 11am-7pm, Su 11am-6:30pm.

TATTOOS & PIERCINGS

California law states that **you must be 18 years old** to get a tattoo. Generally, minors need an adult present for piercing.

Lyle Tuttle's Tattoo Art Studio, 841 Columbus Ave. (☎775-4991), in **North Beach.** Lyle Tuttle opened his modern, clean tattoo studio in the 1960s, permanently decorating the skins of Janis Joplin, Joan Baez, and Cher. While the eminently professional Tuttle, age 71, himself covered in tattoos from head to foot, no longer tattoos behind the bar, his proteges continue the tradition, amidst a small, but impressive collection of tattoo memorabilia—consider it an added bonus if you drop by when someone's under the needle behind the bar. Tattoos from $60. Open daily noon-9pm. No credit cards.

Mom's Body Shop, 1408 Haight St. (☎864-6667), in the **Upper Haight.** This family-run establishment takes great pride in its excellent craftsmanship, proclaiming, "Tattoos like Mom's apple pie." Piercings begin at $20. Tattoos $120 per hr., minimum $60. Open daily in summer noon-9pm; in winter noon-8pm.

EROTICA

▨ **Mr. S. Leather,** 310 7th St. (☎863-7764 or ☎800-746-7677; www.mr-s-leather.com), in **SoMa.** Selections range from 500 types of dildos to a $2900 flying sleep sack/bondage suit. A huge variety of men's leather clothes and a helpful staff make world-wide mail order just as lucrative. Sister store **Madame S,** 321 7th St. (☎863-9447; www.madame-s.com), across the street, specializes in leather and latex "haute fetish couture." Mr. S. open daily 11am-7pm. Madame S open W-Su noon-7pm.

Good Vibrations, 1210 Valencia St. (☎974-8980; www.goodvibes.com), at 23rd St., in the **Mission.** The well-known erotica cooperative for enthusiastic do-it-yourselfers (see their "Make Your Own Dildo" kit). A sex store so tasteful (and we're not just talkin' about the flavored condoms) you could almost take your parents there. Try out "Tester" bottles of lube or observe the progression from wooden cranks to C-cell batteries in a small, but informative display of vibrator evolution dating back to 1910! Must be 18+ to enter. Open Su-W noon-7pm, Th-Sa 11am-8pm.

MISCELLANEOUS

▨ **Imperial Tea Court,** 1411 Powell St. (☎788-6080 or 800-567-5898; www.imperial-teas.com), at Broadway, in **Chinatown.** This oasis of serenity is a must for tea lovers. Exotic scents waft about this little shop's soothing earthen tones and singing rainbow finches. Open Su-M and W-Sa 11am-6:30pm.

Under One Roof, 549 Castro St. (☎503-2300; www.underoneroof.org), between 18th and 19th St. in **Castro.** More sophisticated than your average kitsch shop, Under One Roof donates 100% of the profit from every sale–be it an AbFab magnet, scented bath oil or a Pride holiday ornament–to organizations working to fight AIDS. Sign-up and orientation are simple for the all-volunteer staff that has helped raise over $7 million to date. Open M-Sa 10am-8pm, Su 10am-7pm.

Does Your Father Know?, 548 Castro St. (☎241-9865), between 18th and 19th St. in **Castro.** Your dad told you not to waste your money on touristy trinkets. Now you can show him you didn't listen *and* you're queer! DYFK is stocked with Castro's finest kitschy and trivial junk, from Judy Garland figurines to glow-in-the-dark vibrators. Open M-Th 9:30am-10pm, F-Sa 9:30am-11pm, Su 10am-9pm.

MALLS

San Francisco Shopping Centre (☎495-5656), on Market St. at 5th St., near **Union Square.** Lobbying for an uptown feel, the high-end retailers lacking Union representation have formed a coalition around 6 curving escalators (the only ones in the world) giving shoppers 9 stories' of collective bargaining. Open M-Sa 9:30am-8pm, Su 11am-7pm.

Stonestown Galleria, 19th Ave. and Winston Drive (☎759-2623), between Stern Grove and the SF State University campus. This 2-story shopping mall caters more to spendthrift sophisticates than to students. 250 mall favorites and a grease-laden food court will satisfy mainstream shopping spree needs. Open M-Sa 10am-9pm, Su 11am-6pm.

🎵 ENTERTAINMENT

LIVE MUSIC

The live music scene in San Fran is a vibrant mix of class and brass, funk and punk, hippies and hip-hop, and everything in between. Wailing guitars and scratchy voices still fill the halls of San Francisco's most famous rock clubs, where several stars in the classic rock pantheon got their start. Or if you're in a mellow mood, low-profile, funked-up soul seems to draw today's pimped-out booty shakers and the San Francisco Symphony, with Michael Tilson Thomas as music director, is world class.

The distinction between bars, clubs, and live music venues is hazy. Most bars occasionally have bands, and small venues have rock and hip-hop shows. Start looking for the latest live music listings in *S.F. Weekly* and *The Guardian.* Hardcore audiophiles might also snag a copy of *BAM. The List* is an online calendar of rock gigs all over Northern California (http://jon.luini.com/thelist.txt).

CLASSICAL

Louise M. Davies Symphony Hall, 201 Van Ness Ave. (☎431-5400), near the **Civic Center,** houses the **San Francisco Symphony** in an impressive if controversial structure. The cheapest seats are on the center terrace, directly above the orchestra—the acoustics are slightly off, but you get an excellent (and rare) head-on view of the conductor (and the rest of the audience). Prices vary with performance.

War Memorial Opera House, 301 Van Ness Ave. **San Francisco Opera** (☎864-3330; www.sfopera.com). Tickets from $23. Standing-room-only tickets $10 (cash only) available from 10am on day of performance. Box Office, 199 Grove St. Open M-Sa 10am-6pm and in the Opera House 2hr. before each show.

San Francisco Ballet, (☎703-9400, www.sfballet.com), performances Nov.-May. Standing-room-only tickets $10 (cash only) available from 10am on day of performance. Box office located in the Opera House. Open M-Sa noon-6pm.

Herbst Theatre, 401 Van Ness Ave. (☎392-4400), near the **Civic Center,** provides a plush setting for a year-round schedule of classical soloists, quartets, and smaller symphonies, plus occasional lectures by renowned authors, artists, and other intellectuals.

ROCK & HIP-HOP

■ **Café du Nord,** 2170 Market St. (☎861-5016), between Church and Sanchez St. in **Castro.** Takes you back in time to a red velvet club with speakeasy ambiance. Excellent live music nightly—from pop and groove to garage rock. Local favorites include vintage jazz, blues, and R&B. Special weekly events include the popular M Night Hoot, a showcase of local singing and songwriting talent. Happy hour 6-7:30pm with swank $2.50 martinis, Manhattans, and cosmos. 21+. Cover $5-10 after 8:30pm. Open daily 6pm-2am.

■ **Justice League,** 628 Divisadero St. (☎440-0409, info 289-2038), at Hayes St. in the **Lower Haight.** Live hip-hop is hard to find in San Francisco, but the Justice League fights ever onward for a good beat. M 10pm Club Dred, reggae and dub. W 10pm Bang Bang, soul night. 21+. Tickets at www.ticketweb.com, at **Red Top Clothing,** 1472 Haight (☎552-6494), and at **Open Mind Music** (☎621-2244), at Divisadero and Page St. Cover $5-25, usually $10-14. Usually open daily 9pm-2am.

■ **Bottom of the Hill,** 1233 17th St. (☎626-4455; 621-4455 24hr. club info; www.bottomofthehill.com), between Missouri and Texas St., in **Potrero Hill.** Intimate rock club with tiny stage is the best place to see up-and-comers before they move to bigger venues. Most Su afternoons feature local bands and all-you-can-eat barbecue for $5-10. 21+. Cover $5-10. Open M-Th 3pm-2am, Sa 8pm-2am, Su 4-10pm.

■ **Amoeba Music,** 1855 Haight St. (☎831-1200; www.amoebamusic.com), just east of Stanyan St., in **Upper Haight.** Free concerts in the store—you stand in the aisles. Some fairly well-known acts. Weekly DJ series. Open M-Sa 10:30am-10pm, Su 11am-9pm.

JAZZ & BLUES

Biscuits & Blues, 401 Mason St. (☎292-2583), at Geary St., in **Union Square.** "Dedicated to the preservation of hot biscuits and cool blues," this basement joint will make you feel downright Southern, with fried chicken, sweet potato pie, okra like mama used to make, and live, kickin' blues every night. Entrees $10-12 (smoked turkey and chicken jambalaya with rice and sauce piquante is a must have!). Drinks $3-7. All ages. Tickets $15. Open M-F 5:30pm-midnight, Sa-Su 6pm-midnight.

Lou's Pier 47, 300 Jefferson St. (☎771-5687), at Jones St., in **Fisherman's Wharf.** Live music 7 nights a week makes Lou's the liveliest place on the wharf after dusk. Features over 65 blues bands per month in a jostling upstairs lounge. Happy hour M-F 4-7pm offers beers $2.50-3. 2-drink min. 21+. Cover (up to $10) varies depending on day and time. Open M-Th 4-11pm, F 4pm-1am, Sa noon-1am, Su 4pm-midnight.

Saloon, 1232 Grant Ave. (☎989-7666), between Columbus Ave. and Vallejo St., in **North Beach.** The oldest bar in San Francisco (est. in 1861) still looks like, well, a saloon. Live bands nightly M-F 9:30pm-1:30am, Sa-Su 4-8pm and 9:30pm-1:30am. Cover F-Sa $3-5; 1-drink min. other nights. Open daily noon-2am. No credit cards.

Boom Boom Room, 1601 Fillmore St. (☎673-8000; www.boomboomblues.com), at Geary St., near **Japantown.** Once owned by John Lee Hooker, Boom Boom is known as the city's home to "blues and boogie, funk and bumpin' jazz" and features live music 7 nights a week, often with big-name acts. This place is leading the revival of the 50s Fillmore Jazz scene with style. Cover varies by act. Open daily 4pm-2am.

DANCE

🏛 **Alonzo King's Lines Contemporary Ballet** (☎863-3360; www.linesballet.org), in **Hayes Valley.** Combines elegant classical moves with wild athletic flair to the music of great living jazz, blues, and world music composers. Springtime shows are performed at the Yerba Buena Center for the Arts. Tickets $15-25.

San Francisco Ballet (☎865-2000; www.sfballet.org) shares the War Memorial Opera House with the San Francisco Opera (p. 114). Tickets start at $30; available online or by phone M-Sa noon-6pm. Discounted standing-room-only tickets at the Opera House 2hr. before performances.

Dancer's Group, 3252A 19th St. (☎920-9181; www.dancersgroup.org), at Shotwell St., in the **Mission.** Dedicated to promoting cultural dance and original works. Open M-F 10am-4pm. Call for schedules and prices.

LIVE THEATER

Downtown, **Mason Street** and **Geary Street** constitute **"Theater Row,"** the city's prime place for theatrical entertainment. Fort Mason, near **Fisherman's Wharf,** is also a popular area. For the latest on shows, check local listings in free mags and the newspaper. **TIX Bay Area,** in the garage beneath **Union Square** on Geary St., is a Ticketmaster outlet with tickets and MUNI passes. Assure yourself a seat in advance, or try for cash-only, half-price tickets on the day of the show. (☎433-7827; www.theaterbayarea.org. Open Tu-Th 11am-6pm, F-Sa 11am-7pm.)

Magic Theatre, Bldg. D (☎441-8822; www.magictheatre.org), 3rd fl., in **Fort Mason** (use Fort Mason Center entrance). Sam Shepard served as playwright-in-residence at the Magic Theatre from 1975 to 1985. Today, the theater stages both international and American premieres. W-Th $22-32, F-Su $27-37. Senior and student rush tickets, available 30min. before the show $10. Shows at 8 or 8:30pm. Previews and Su matinees 2 or 2:30pm $15. Call for exact times. Box office open Tu-Sa noon-5pm.

Geary Theater, 415 Geary St. (☎749-2228; www.act-sfbay.org), at Mason St., in **Union Square.** Home to the renowned American Conservatory Theater, the jewel in San Fran's theatrical crown. The elegant theater is a show-stealer in its own right. Tickets $11-61 (cheaper for previews and on weekdays). Half-price student, teacher, and senior tickets available 2hr. before showtime. Box office open Su-M noon-6pm, Tu-Sa noon-8pm.

Theatre Rhinoceros, 2926 16th St. (box office ☎861-5079; open for reservations Tu-Su 1-6pm; www.therhino.org), at South Van Ness Ave., in the **Mission.** The oldest queer theater in the world, the Rhino has been an innovator in the arts community since 1977. The theater emphasizes playwriting by and for the gay, lesbian, bisexual, transgender community. Box office open 1hr. before shows.

The Orpheum, 1192 Market St. at Hyde St., near the **Civic Center.** This famous San Fran landmark hosts the big Broadway shows. 2 sister theaters in the area host smaller shows: **Golden Gate Theatre,** 1 Taylor St., and **Curran Theatre,** 445 Geary St. Box Office at 6th and Market (☎512-7770). Individual show times and ticket prices vary.

FROM THE ROAD

ANYTHING GOES

To truly live and breathe San Francisco, I felt I had to take a yoga class. A friend recommended Yoga Tree but warned that, despite my varsity crew training, this Power Flow class was going to "kick my ass." I had only ever done yoga with the crew team and the hardest part of those sessions was struggling to keep a straight face while we toppled over each other like dominoes.

Waiting for the class to start, I feared impending public humiliation due to my two left feet. Trim, toned, 20-something women in trendy sportswear convulsed in ways my body just doesn't bend. The instructor, Rusty Wells, is so popular that his class has developed a near cult-following. The heat was cranked up to 90°F and we started the sun-salutation to a 6 ft. orange mural of the Hindu God Ganesh. Not only did I survive the 90min. of ujai snorting, sweating and stretching, but found it one of the experiences that defined my San Fran adventure. Growing up in conservative Northern England, the idea of yoga or candlelit Hindi chanting would have been ridiculed. But in this city anything and everything goes—be it Beat culture, strip clubs, or ujai-snorting, Ganesh-worshipping, body- and mind-bending exercise.

–Laura Spence

Yoga Tree: 1234 Valencia at 23rd (☎647-9707), 780 Stanyan at Waller (☎387-4707), and 519 Hayes at Octavia (☎626-9707).

848 Community Space, 848 Divisadero St. (☎922-2385; www.848.com), between Fulton and McAllister St., near the **Upper Haight.** Basically a glorified living room, the 848 serves a steady diet of sexually charged programming. All-night tribal love-ins, sweaty experimental dance troupes, and porn-art stylings. Contact improv classes ($8) and jams ($3) Tu nights. Shows free-$15. No credit cards.

Exit Theater, 156 Eddy St. (☎931-1094, box office 673-5944; www.theexit.org), between Mason and Taylor streets in the **Tenderloin.** Also at 277 Taylor St. between Eddy and Ellis St. 2 locations and 3 venues produce independent and experimental theater for a youthful, urban audience. Special events like Classic Absurdity Theater Festival in February; sassy DIVAfest, 2 weeks in May devoted to "theater of a female persuasion"; and the big daddy of national indie theater, the San Fran Fringe Festival, showcasing 250 performances over 12 days in Sept. Tickets $12-20, $8 and under for San Fran Fringe. No credit cards.

MOVIES

For a complete listing of features and locations, check the weekly papers or call **MovieFone** (☎777-FILM/3456). Keep in mind that San Francisco movie theaters, even the massive AMC-1000, have nowhere near enough parking.

▨ **Castro Theatre,** 429 Castro St. (☎621-6350, automated ☎621-6120; www.thecastrotheatre.com), near Market St., in **Castro.** This landmark 1922 movie palace has live organ music before evening showings. Eclectic films, festivals, and double features. Far from silent—a bawdy, catty, hilarious crowd turns many a movie into *The Rocky Horror Picture Show.* Highlights include the Sing-along Sound of Music, for those who believe Julie Andrews would be much better with chest hair. $8, seniors and under 12 $5. Matinees W and Sa-Su $5. Box office opens 1hr. before 1st show. No credit cards.

▨ **Roxie,** 3117 16th St. (☎863-1087; www.roxie.com), off Valencia St. in the **Mission.** This trendy movie house shows sharp indie films and fashionably foolish retro classics, plus a late-night series of truly disturbing European gore flicks. $7, seniors and under 12 $3. Bargain matinees 1st show W and Sa-Su $4, seniors and kids free. Discount pass (good for 5 shows) $22.

The Lumière, 1572 California St. (☎352-0810 or 885-3201), between Larkin and Polk St., in **Nob Hill.** Indie and art films on 3 screens. $8.75; seniors, children, and 1st show each day $5.75 (before 6pm).

SPECTATOR SPORTS

The **San Francisco Giants** (☎467-8000 or 800-734-4268) play baseball at the newly opened **Pacific Bell Park** in SoMa, near the water off Townsend St. The Giants' season is April through October. Most games sell out before the season even starts, except for 500 seats reserved for day-of-game sale. (Tickets $10-42. Tours of the park $10.) The five-time Super Bowl champion **49ers** (☎468-2249) still play at San Francisco's old-time field—the notoriously windy **Candlestick Park** (☎467-1994). Now officially called **3COM Park**, the stadium is 8 mi. south of the city with its own exit off U.S. 101. MUNI bus #29 will also take you right there. Football pre-season starts in early August. The main season runs from September through the last Sunday in January.

▣ NIGHTLIFE

Nightlife in San Francisco is as varied as the city's personal ads. Everyone from "shy first-timer" to "bearded strap daddy" to "pre-op transsexual top" can find a place to go on a Saturday (or Tuesday) night. The spots listed below are divided into coffeehouses, bars, and clubs, but these lines get pretty blurred in San Francisco after dark. Every other bar calls itself a cafe, every second cafe is a club, and half the clubs in town declare themselves to be lounges. Don't fret—there are 10,000 night spots in the naked city, and you're sure to find something that fits you like a warm leather glove. Ahem. Check out the nightlife listings in *S.F. Weekly*, the *Guardian*, and *Metropolitan*. **Unless otherwise noted, all clubs are 21+ only.**

COFFEEHOUSES

▨ **Vesuvio Café,** 255 Columbus Ave. (☎362-3370), next to Jack Kerouac Alley, in **North Beach.** Jack and his friends started their day by howling like Dharma Bums over pints at Vesuvio and then café-crawled their way up Columbus Ave. The wooden, tiled, and stained-glass bar with an upstairs balcony remains a great place to drink. Draught beers $4.25, bottled beers $3.50, pitchers $9-12. Happy hour M-Th 3-7pm: drinks $1 off, pitchers and bottles of wine $3 off. Open daily 6am-2am. No credit cards.

▨ **Spike's,** 4117 19th St. (☎626-5573; www.spikescoffee.com), between Castro and Collingwood St., in **Castro.** Candy, sweets, and dog-friendly treats at this juice and coffee joint merit walking with Fido away from the center of Castro Village. Neighborly Spike's place is also one of the few cafes with seating. Open daily 6:30am-8pm.

▨ **Caffè Trieste,** 601 Vallejo St. (☎392-6739), at Grant Ave., in **North Beach.** Though every bar in North Beach claims to be a Beat haunt, this is the genuine article. While Vesuvio's is where the gang got trashed, Trieste remained their more mellow living room. The leftovers still hang out in front. It is also where Francis Ford Coppola sat and wrote his *Godfather* screenplay. It hasn't changed much since then—a few new photos of famous patrons on the walls, but the jukebox still plays opera, and it's still the cornerstone of North Beach's remaining Italian community. Live Italian pop and opera concerts every Sa 1:45-6pm (since 1973) alone are worth a stop. Espresso drinks $1.50-3.25. Beer $2-3. Open M-Th and Su 6:30am-11pm, F-Sa 6:30am-midnight. No credit cards.

The Horseshoe Café, 566 Haight St. (☎626-8852), between Steiner and Fillmore St., in the **Lower Haight.** Big-screen TV, movie, and music video projections in the back, DSL Internet access, and plenty of space to read, write, or ruminate over chai iced tea ($2.25), coffee ($1.25), or cookies ($1.25). Open daily 6am-midnight. No credit cards.

BARS & PUBS

▨ **Hotel Utah Saloon,** 500 4th St. (☎546-6300; www.thehotelutahsaloon.com), at Bryant St., in **SoMa.** Excellent and unpretentious saloon—with an original Belgian Bar from 1908—and one of the friendliest crowds around. More than your average bar food, including build your own burgers (from $7). Downstairs stage hosts live rock or country music nightly and one of the best open mics in the city on M (shows begin 8:30-9pm). Beer $3.75. 21+. Show cover $5-7. Open M-F 11am-2am, Sa-Su 6pm-2am.

▨ **Place Pigalle,** 520 Hayes St. (☎552-2671), between Octavia and Laguna St., in **Hayes Valley.** After a long day at work, the designers, boutique owners, and artists of Hayes St. close shop and relax on the vintage velvet sofas at this big, dark, airy bar. Weekend nights the wine flows freely, the music blares, and crowds of 20- and 30-somethings with bohemian sensibilities pack the place beyond capacity. Occasional DJs and a rotating art exhibit liven up the back room. Happy hour daily 4-7pm ($2.75 beer and house red and white wines). Open daily 4pm-2am.

▨ **Hollywood Billiards,** 61 Golden Gate Ave. (☎252-9643), between Taylor and Jones St., in the **Tenderloin.** A buzzing sign and more "provocative" neighbors conceal this upstairs "oasis of serenity," where college students, internationals, and financial district bigwigs have a rackin' good time in San Francisco's oldest pool hall (Su-Th tables $8 per hr., F-Sa $12 per hr.). Guards keep the friendly crowd coming back for cocktails ($4-7) and half-off nights (W ladies, Th students). Happy hour M-F 3-7pm. 21+. Open Su 1pm-2am, M-Th 3pm-2am, F 1pm-3am, Sa 1pm until "God knows when."

▨ **Hush Hush,** 496 14th St. (☎241-9944), at Guerrero St., in the **Mission.** You'll feel oh so hip when you find Hush Hush, since this hotspot is too cool to need a sign. Large leather booths, pool, and local DJs spinning almost every night have everyone whispering about this place. MC Battle 1st Tu of every month. Smile Su with Rock DJs. Look for the blue awning with 496 in white letters. Open daily 6pm-2am. No credit cards.

CLUBS

▨ **SF Badlands,** 4121 18th St. (☎626-9320), near Castro St., in **Castro.** Strutting past the sea of boys at the bar, the Castro's prettiest faces and bodies cruise a futuristic blue-and-chrome dance floor, where Madonna, George Michael, and Destiny's Child—all in enthralling teleprojection—make San Fran Badlands just as amazing as its heart-stealing Dupont Circle twin. Cover F-Sa $2. Open daily 2pm-2am. No credit cards.

Backflip, 601 Eddy St. (☎771-3547), between Larkin and Polk St., in the **Tenderloin.** Hipsters dive into this blue and aqua urban oasis for infamously kitschy and famously cool pool-side parties. Plunge into open mic talent shows Tu 10pm-2am. Beer $4. Cocktails $7. Open Tu-Sa 9pm-2am.

Velvet Lounge, 443 Broadway (☎788-0228), between Kearny and Montgomery St., in **North Beach.** Decked-out 20- and 30-somethings pack this club and thump along to top 40, hip-hop, and house. F occasional live cover bands. No sneakers or athletic wear. Cover usually $10. Open W-Sa 9pm-2am.

Club Deluxe, 1509-11 Haight St. (☎552-6949), west of Ashbury St. in the **Upper Haight.** At this small but swinging retro club, femmes fatales banter with mysterious strangers—and that's just the bar staff. Shiny metal and bluish lights make everyone the star of his own 1940s film noir. Smoky jazz and other live music Th-M. Bossa Nova Su. DJs Tu-W. 21+. Cover varies. Open M-Sa 3pm-2am, Su 1pm-2am. No credit cards.

The Top, 424 Haight St. (☎864-7386), at Fillmore St., in the **Lower Haight.** Host to some of the finest house DJs in SF and beyond. A definite must for turntable loyalists. Su House and M Hip Hop are huge. House on W and F, too. Drum and Bass Tu and Sa. Happy hour 7-10pm. 21+. Cover $5 after 10pm. Open daily 7pm-2am. No credit cards.

Liquid, 2925 16th St. (☎431-8889), at South Van Ness Ave, in the **Mission.** Nightly mix usually includes trip-hop and hip-hop, but mainly house. Young but mellow crowd fills the small space. Meet a cutie and practice those long-forgotten back seat skills; all of Liquid's couches are car seats. 21+. Cover $4-5. Open daily 9pm-3am. No credit cards.

GAY & LESBIAN NIGHTLIFE

▓ **The Bar on Castro,** 456 Castro St. (☎626-7220), between Market and 18th St., in **Castro.** A refreshingly urbane Castro staple with dark plush couches perfect for eyeing the stylish young crowd, scoping the techno-raging dance floor, or watching Queer as Folk on Su. Happy hour M-F 3-8pm (beer $2.25). Su beer $1.75. Open M-F 3pm-2am, Sa-Su noon-2am. No credit cards.

The Café, 2367 Market St. (☎861-3846), between 17th and 18th St., in **Castro.** The Café is chill in the afternoon with pool and pinball, but come evening, it morphs into speaker-pumping, house- and pop-remix bliss, when the dance floor, balcony, and patio crowds rotate in a constant game of see-and-be-seen. Repeat *Guardian* awards for best gay bar. No cover. Open M-F 2pm-2am, Sa-Su 12:30pm-2am. No credit cards.

The Lexington Club, 3464 19th St. (☎863-2052), at Lexington St., in **Mission.** The only bar in San Francisco that is all lesbian, all the time. Jukebox plays all the grrly favorites. Tarot Tu with Jessica. Happy hour M-F 3-7pm. Open daily 3pm-2am. No credit cards.

The Stud, 399 9th St. (☎252-7883), at Harrison St., in **SoMa.** This legendary bar and club (a 35-year-old stallion) recreates itself every night of the week—go Tu for the wild and wacky midnight drag and transgender shows known as "Trannyshack," Th for Reform School boy-cruising party, F for ladies' night, Sa for Sugar's free delicious eye-candy. Crowd is mostly gay. Cover $5-9. Open M, W, F, Su 5pm-2am, Tu 5pm-3am, Th and Sa 5pm-4am. No credit cards.

The EndUp, 401 6th St. (☎357-0827; www.theendup.com), at Harrison St., in **SoMa.** San Francisco institution--complete with outdoor garden and patio--where everyone eventually ends up. DJs spin progressive house for the mostly straight KitKat Th, the pretty-boy Fag F, and the blissful hetero-homo mix during popular all-day Sa-Su parties. Sa morning "Otherwhirled" party 4am. Infamous Su 'T' Dance (27 years strong) 6pm-4am. Cover $5-15. Open Th-F and Su 10pm-4am.

Esta Noche, 3079 16th St. (☎861-5757), at Valencia St., in the **Mission.** The city's premier gay Latino bar hosts regular drag shows. Gringos are asked to refrain from dancing salsa without instruction. Domestic bottles and drafts $2.25. Happy hour daily 4-9pm. Cover F-Su $5-10. Open Su-Th 1pm-2am, F-Sa 1pm-3am. No credit cards.

SEASONAL EVENTS

An astounding array of seasonal events go up in San Francisco no matter what time of year you visit. The summer is especially full, and events like Pride, which can draw crowds of more than 700,000 (as big as the population of the city!) make finding a hotel room or parking space difficult. Events below are listed chronologically. The Visitors Center (☎391-2001) has a recording of current events.

SPRING

San Francisco International Film Festival (☎561-5022), Apr.-May, at Kabuki and Castro theaters. The oldest film festival in North America, showing more than 100 international films of all genres over 2 weeks. Most showings $9.

Cinco de Mayo (☎826-1401), during the weekend nearest May 5. The Mission explodes with colorful costumes and mariachi bands to celebrate Mexican Independence.

Examiner Bay to Breakers (☎359-2800; www.baytobreakers.com), on the 3rd Su in May, starting at the Embarcadero at 8am. The largest foot race in the US, with up to 100,000 participants, covers 7½ mi. in inimitable San Francisco style. Runners win not only on their times but on their costumes as well. Special centipede category.

Carnaval (☎920-0125; www.carnavalSF.com), Memorial Day weekend. San Francisco's take on Mardi Gras, featuring Latino, jazz, and samba Caribbean music and more.

SUMMER

San Francisco International Gay and Lesbian Film Festival (☎703-8650; www.frameline.org), during the 11 days leading up to Pride Day (June 19-29 in 2003), at the Roxie (at 16th and Valencia St.) and Castro Theatre (at Castro and Market St.). California's 2nd-largest film festival and the world's largest lesbian and gay media event. Tickets go very quickly. $6-15.

🏖 **Pride Day** (☎864-3733; www.sfpride.org), on the last Su in June. The High Holy Day of the queer calendar. Officially it's called Lesbian, Gay, Bisexual, Transgender Pride Day, with a parade and events downtown starting at 10:30am. Pink Sa, the night before, brings a sea of bodies to the Castro, where the party actually lasts 12 months.

North Beach Jazz Festival (☎771-2061; www.nbjazzfest.org), the last week of July at venues from Washington Sq. Park to Telegraph Hill. An assortment of musicians play. Every Sa afternoon June-Sept. at the Cannery features free jazz performances. Free-$15.

Nihonmachi Street Fair (☎771-9861), in early Aug., on Post St. between Laguna and Fillmore St. in Japantown. Lion dancers, *taiko* drummers, and karaoke wars.

FALL

🏖 **Ghirardelli Square Chocolate Festival** (☎775-5500; www.ghirardellisq.com), in early Sept., in Ghirardelli Sq. Welcome to chocolate heaven. All kinds of chocolate goodies to be sampled, with proceeds going to Project Open Hand.

Vivas Las Americas! (☎705-5500; www.pier39.com), in mid-Sept. at Pier 39. Music and dance performances celebrating Hispanic heritage.

Folsom Street Fair (☎861-3247; www.folsomstreetfair.com), on the last Su in Sept., on Folsom St. between 7th and 11th St. Pride Day's ruder, raunchier, rowdier brother.

🏖 **Día de los Muertos** (Day of the Dead; ☎821-1155), Nov. 2, Mission. Follow the drummers and dancing skeletons to the festive Mexican celebration of the dead. The party starts in the evening at the Mission Cultural Center, on Mission at 25th St.

WINTER

Festival of Lights (☎362-6355), in Dec., at Union Sq. Festivities lead up to the lighting of a huge menorah.

Messiah (☎864-4000), in Dec., Symphony Hall. At the Symphony, some say San Franciscans can't keep their mouths shut. At the **Sing-It-Yourself-Messiah** (☎564-8086) they don't have to. $30-70.

San Francisco Independent Film Festival (☎931-3456), in Jan. The best of Bay Area indie films at various locations.

Dr. Martin Luther King Jr.'s Birthday Celebration (☎510-268-3777; contact Jackie Keys-Guidry), Jan. 19-21, in Yerba Buena Gardens. Includes a candlelight vigil and "Making the Dream Real" march and rally on Jan. 21 to honor the great civil rights leader.

Chinese New Year Celebration (☎982-3000) and **Parade** (☎391-9680; www.chineseparade.com), during the month of Feb., in Chinatown. North America's largest Chinese community celebrates the Year of the Sheep in San Francisco's largest festival. Flower Fair, Miss Chinatown USA Pageant, a Coronation Ball, and a Community Street Fair. Watch the Parade from Market and 2nd St. to Columbus Ave. Free.

BAY AREA & WINE COUNTRY

Beyond the docks of San Francisco are a number of dynamic complements to the City by the Bay: Berkeley's cafes, Oakland's blues, Wine Country's vineyards, and Silicon Valley's nerds. The bay and the surrounding mountains and rivers shape a sprawl that would otherwise be as disorienting as that of Los Angeles.

HIGHLIGHTS OF THE BAY AREA

TAKE DOWN THE MAN. In the East Bay, **Berkeley** still pulses with vigorous political ferment, visible on the campus of UC Berkeley (p. 127), on Telegraph Avenue (p. 127), and on the shelves of its bookstores (p. 129).

COASTLINE DRIVES. North of San Francisco, the **Marin Coast** (p. 151) has breathtaking drives and seaside views. South of San Francisco, the Pacific Coast Highway glides by the lush farm lands and deserted beaches of **San Mateo County** (p. 146).

WINES AND BIKES. North of San Francisco and inland, tourists rush to the famous wineries of the **Napa Valley** (p. 160); the vineyards in the **Russian River Valley** (p. 174) are more peaceful. Napa is an ideal place for a road bike tour, while **Mount Tamalpais** (p. 158) in Marin is great for mountain biking.

EAST BAY

Longer and older than its Golden Gate neighbor, the Bay Bridge carries the weight of San Francisco traffic east to **Oakland,** where freeways fan out in all directions. The urbanized port city of Oakland sprawls north into the assertively hippie college town of **Berkeley.** The two towns have long shared an interest in political activism, reflected in wonderfully progressive and effective city government and policies. Berkeley, bookish and bizarre as ever, offers boutiques and cafes, while its sister city Oakland echoes with the sounds of a progressive blues and jazz scene.

BERKELEY ☎510

Famous as an intellectual center and a haven for iconoclasts, Berkeley lives up to its well-founded reputation. Although the peak of its political activism occurred in the 1960s and 70s—when students attended more protests than classes—UC Berkeley continues to cultivate consciousness and brainy brawn, even if it is no longer as "Berserkeley" as it once was. The vitality of the population infuses the streets—which are strewn with hip cafes and top-notch bookstores—with a slightly psychotic vigor. While Telegraph Ave., with its street-corner soothsayers, hirsute hippies, and itinerant musicians, remains one of this town's main draws, travelers looking to soak up all that Berkeley has to offer should venture off the main drag.

▐ TRANSPORTATION

Freeway congestion can make driving in the Bay Area frustrating, especially during rush hour. Drivers fortunate enough to reach Berkeley despite the traffic will face

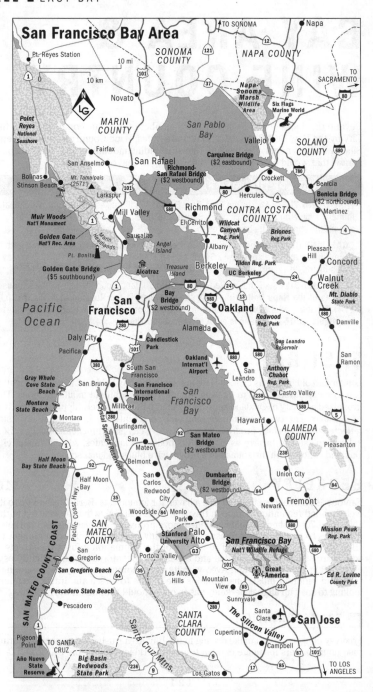

heavy traffic, numerous one-way streets, vexing concrete planters, and an earnest quest for a parking spot—the city's precious holy grail. If you're driving from San Francisco, cross the Bay Bridge on I-80 and take one of the four Berkeley exits. The University Avenue Exit leads most directly to UC Berkeley and downtown. Reasonably priced public lots (most are $12 per day) let you ditch your car and explore on foot.

Public Transportation: Berkeley TRiP, 2033 Center St. (☎644-7665), provides commuter-oriented information on public transportation, biking, and carpooling. They also sell extended-use transit passes and maps. Open Tu-F noon-5:30pm. Satellite office at 2543 Channing Way, open M-F 9am-2pm. Bay Area Rapid Transit (BART; ☎465-2278; www.bart.gov) has 2 Berkeley stops on the Richmond line. The Downtown Berkeley station, 2160 Shattuck Ave., at Center St., is close to the western edge of campus, while the North Berkeley station, at Delaware and Sacramento streets, lies 4 blocks north of University Ave. To get to Southern Berkeley, take the BART to the Ashby stop at the corner of Ashby and Adeline St. (20-30min. to San Francisco, $2.65). Alameda County (AC) Transit city buses #15, 43, and 51 run from the Berkeley BART station to downtown Oakland on Martin Luther King, Jr. Way, Telegraph Ave., and Broadway, respectively (adults $1.35; seniors, disabled, ages 5-12 $0.65; under 5 free; 1hr. transfers $0.25).

Ride Share: Berkeley Ride Board, 1st level of the student store in the Student Union. KALX Radio, 90.7 FM (☎642-5259), broadcasts a ride list daily at 10am and 10pm. Call to put your request on the air for free.

Taxis: A1 Yellow Cab (☎548-0309) and Berkeley Yellow Cab (☎548-2561). Both 24hr.

Car Rental: Budget, 600 Gilman St. (☎486-0806), at 2nd St. Compact car $49 per day with unlimited mileage. Must be 21; under-25 surcharge $20 per day. Open M-F 7:15am-4:45pm, Sa-Su 8:15am-3:45pm.

◧ ⁊ ORIENTATION & PRACTICAL INFORMATION

Just across the Bay Bridge, northeast of San Francisco and north of Oakland, lies Berkeley, a community famous for acting up and acting out. The Marina rests on the western side of Berkeley while Tilden Regional Park climbs the sharp grades to the east. Undergraduates from UC Berkeley tend to do their thing on the campus's south side while older, wiser graduate students stick to the north. Downtown Berkeley, around the BART station at Shattuck Ave. and Center St., is where you'll find banks, public libraries, restaurants, and shops, while Addison St. is fast becoming the area's theater district. The magnetic heart of town, Telegraph Avenue runs south from the Student Union and is lined with bookstores, cafes, palm readers, and panhandlers. North of campus, the Gourmet Ghetto has some of California's finest dining in the area around Shattuck Ave. between Virginia and Rose St. Farther afield, 4th Street, near the waterfront (take MUNI bus #51 bus west) and Solano Avenue to the northwest (take MUNI bus #15 north), are home to yummy eats and yuppie shops. The intersection at College and Ashby avenues (take MUNI bus #51 south) also offers some delectable dining. Quality cafes, music stores, and specialty shops grace the Rockridge district on the border between Berkeley and Oakland (see Oakland, p. 131).

Visitor Information: Berkeley Convention and Visitor Bureau, 2015 Center St. (☎800-847-4823 or 549-7040), at Milvia St. Helpful info and friendly service. Open M-F 9am-5pm. UC Berkeley Visitors Center, 101 University Hall (☎642-5215; www.berkeley.edu), at the corner of University Ave. and Oxford St. Clear, detailed maps and campus info. Guided campus tours depart from the center M-Sa 10am, Su 1pm. Open M-F 8:30am-4:30pm. UC Berkeley Switchboard (☎642-6000) can direct you to info on everything from community events to drug counseling. Open M-F 8am-5pm.

Gay and Lesbian Organizations: UC Berkeley Multicultural BLGA/Queer Resource Center, 305 Eshleman Hall (☎642-6942; http://queer.berkeley.edu), at Bancroft Way and Telegraph Ave. Open Sept.-May M-F 10am-5pm; June-Aug. by appointment. Pacific Center, 2712 Telegraph Ave. (☎548-8283), at Derby St. Counseling and info on community events and housing. Open M-F 10am-10pm, Sa noon-3pm and 7-10pm, Su 6-9pm.

BAY AREA

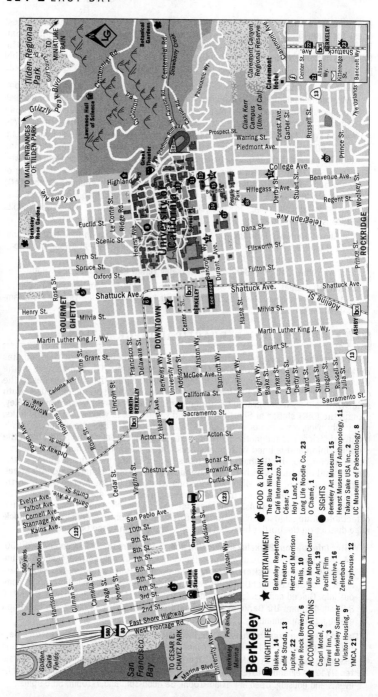

Berkeley

NIGHTLIFE
Blakes, **14**
Caffé Strada, **13**
Jupiter, **22**
Triple Rock Brewery, **6**

ACCOMMODATIONS
Capri Motel, **4**
Travel Inn, **3**
UC Berkeley Summer
Visitor Housing, **9**
YMCA, **21**

ENTERTAINMENT
Berkeley Repertory
Theater, **7**
Hertz and Morrison
Halls, **10**
Julia Morgan Center
for Arts, **19**
Pacific Film
Archive, **16**
Zellerbach
Playhouse, **12**

FOOD & DRINK
The Blue Nile, **18**
Café Intermezzo, **17**
César, **5**
Holy Land, **20**
Long Life Noodle Co., **23**
O Chamé, **1**

SIGHTS
Berkeley Art Museum, **15**
Hearst Museum of Anthropology, **11**
Takara Sake USA Inc., **2**
UC Museum of Paleontology, **8**

Emergency: **Campus Emergency** from campus phones ☎9-911, otherwise 642-3333.

Police: Berkeley Police ☎644-6161 (non-emergency). **Campus Police,** Sproul Hall basement (☎642-6760). Open 24hr.

Crisis Lines: Rape Hotline ☎845-RAPE/7273. Open 24hr. **Suicide Prevention and Crisis Intervention** ☎849-2212. Open 24hr.

Medical Services: Berkeley Free Clinic, 2339 Durant Ave. (☎800-625-4642 or 548-2570; www.berkeleyfreeclinic.org/home.html), at Dana St. 2 blocks west of Telegraph Ave. Served by AC Transit buses #7, 40, 51, 52, and 54. Call for hours of service; the best times to talk to a real person are M-F 3:30-8:30pm, Sa 6-9pm, Su 5-8pm. **STD Clinic and HIV/AIDS Testing:** ☎644-0425. **Dental:** ☎548-2745. **Counseling:** ☎548-2744. **Berkeley Dept. of Health & Human Services,** 830 University Ave. (☎ 644-6500), at 6th St. Medical help on a sliding payment scale. Specialty clinics vary from day to day, so call ahead. Open M-F 8am-5pm. **Berkeley Women's Health Center,** 2908 Ellsworth St. (☎843-6194), 1 block west of Telegraph Ave. Open M and F 8am-noon and 1-5pm, Tu-Th 9am-1pm and 2-6pm.

Internet Access: UC Computer, 2569 Telegraph Ave. (☎649-6089; www.transbay.net). $3 per 15min., $5 per 30min., $7 per hr. Open M-Sa 10am-6pm.

Post Office: 2000 Allston Way (☎649-3155), at Milvia St. Open M-F 9am-5pm, Sa 10am-2pm. **Postal Code:** 94704.

⌂ ACCOMMODATIONS

There are surprisingly few cheap accommodations in Berkeley. The **Berkeley-Oakland Bed and Breakfast Network** (☎547-6380; www.bbonline.com/ca/berkeley-oakland) coordinates some great East Bay B&Bs with a range of rates (singles $50-150; doubles $60-150; twins $85-150). Many travelers stay in San Francisco and make daytrips to Berkeley (**see San Francisco,** p. 84). No-frills motels line University Ave. between Shattuck and Sacramento streets, while the ritzier joints are downtown.

▨ **UC Berkeley Summer Visitor Housing,** in Stern Hall, 2700 Hearst Ave., (☎642-4108; www.housing.berkeley.edu), in Stern Hall, at Highland St. College dorm rooms in a great location. Shared baths. Free Internet access, local phone calls, games, and TV room. Meals and photocopying available. Laundry (wash $1.35). Open June to mid-Aug. Reservations online. Singles $53; doubles $68; 7th night free. ❹

YMCA, 2001 Allston Way (☎848-6800), at Milvia St. Adequate rooms in the co-ed hotel portion of this YMCA make it worthwhile. Shared bath. Use of pool and fitness facilities. Communal kitchen, computer room, and TV lounge. All rooms wired for DSL connection ($5-7 a week). 10-night max. stay; applications available for longer stays. Reception daily 8am-9:30pm. No curfew. Must be 18+. Singles $46; doubles $60; triples $75. ❸

Travel Inn, 1461 University Ave. (☎848-3840), at Sacramento St. Perky pink motel. Clean, comfortable, though sparsely furnished rooms have TVs and phones. Parking and coffee. Laundry available. Reception 24hr. Check-out 11am. Singles $60-70; doubles $65-75; twins $85-95. Discounts on stays over 5 days. ❹

Capri Motel, 1512 University Ave. (☎845-7090), at Sacramento St. Tasteful rooms with cable TV, A/C, and fridge. Must be 18+ with ID. Singles and doubles from $85. ❺

♨ FOOD

Berkeley's **Gourmet Ghetto**, at Shattuck Ave. and Cedar St., is the famous birthplace of California Cuisine. When chef Alice Waters opened *Chez Panisse* in 1971, she introduced the nation to the joys of goat cheese and polenta. Since Berkeley has to

BAY AREA

FROM THE ROAD

THE SOUL OF BERKELEY

A bohemian at heart, I was hell bent on finding the soul of Berkeley. I refused to cut my hair and began to grow a beard. With my guitar, I took to Telegraph, the city's most powerfully pulsing street. "Mind if I set up shop, here?" I asked a street vendor. "Oh, sure," he answered, "street performers: we don't get too many of those anymore." My unamplified chords were swallowed by passing cars but I kept on going.

I was singing for myself, but it seemed hopeless that I'd find what I was looking for. As I tossed out a cover and an original song, no fish were biting. Even the trendy GAP-hippie with the Phish t-shirt paid me no mind. At last, a man interrupted my song to ask the whereabouts of the nearest cell phone store. I was growing disappointed. Four songs later, an old-timer approached me. "Maaan," he sighed, "people ain't got no time; they're all in a rush to get somewhere. I've got all the time in the world." "That's gre—" I tried to interject. "And you know what I'd love to do?" he plowed on. "I'd love to smoke me some bud." I had finally found it: the hidden, hold-over, hung-over, residual heart of the once-hippie town.

—Shawn Snyder

feed thousands of starving students, the area is also home to pizza joints and hamburger stands, although the ghetto mentality makes menu items a bit more interesting. The north end of **Telegraph Avenue** caters to student appetites and wallets with late night offerings along **Durant Avenue.** If you'd rather talk to a cow than eat one, you're in luck because Berkeley does greens like nowhere else. **Solano Avenue,** to the north, is great for Asian cuisine, while **4th Street** is home to more upscale (but cheaper than Gourmet Ghetto) eats. If you've got access to a kitchen or don't like to cook your vegetables anyway, **farmer's markets,** run by the Ecology Center (☎548-3333), sprout up Saturdays at Center St. and Martin Luther King, Jr. Way (open 10am-2pm) and Tuesdays at Derby St. and Martin Luther King, Jr. Way. (Open in summer 2-7pm; off-season 1pm-dusk.)

Café Intermezzo, 2442 Telegraph Ave. (☎849-4592), at Haste St. This veggie-lover's paradise serves heaping salads with homemade dressing, huge sandwiches on freshly baked bread, and tasty soups, all at delicious prices. Salad and sandwich combo $5.50. Sandwiches $5. Salads $3.50-7. Open daily 10am-10pm. No credit cards. ❶

César, 1515 Shattuck Ave. (☎883-0222), just south of Vine St. A great place for wining and dining, with savory tapas ($3-12), *bocadillos* (a small sandwich on french bread; $5-7), desserts ($4-5), and an impressive spirits list. Open daily 11:30am-midnight; kitchen closes Su-Th 11pm, F-Sa 11:30pm. ❷

Long Life Noodle Co. and Jook Joint, 2261 Shattuck St. (☎548-8083), at Kittredge St. You name the noodle, they've got it: Japanese, Chinese, Korean, Thai, Vietnamese noodles, *udon,* ramen, egg, and *soba.* Wok-tossed dishes, soups, and noodles $6-9. Mango Martini $5. Open M-Th 11:30am-9:30pm, F-Su 11:30am-10:30pm. ❸

Holy Land, 2965 College Ave. (☎665-1672), just south of Ashby Ave. War is not the answer; try good food instead. Fantastic Falafel $5. Schuperlative Schwarma $5.75. Pitas $5-6. Lunches $8. Dinner $15-20. Open M-F and Su 11am-9:30pm. ❸

O Chamé, 1830 4th St. (☎841-8783), between Virginia and Hearst streets. Innovative Japanese fusion in a tranquil setting. Become one with a bowl of *soba* or *udon* noodles. Appetizers $5-12 (try the white corn and green onion pancake). Entrees and soups $9.50-20. Open M-Th 11:30am-3pm and 5:30-9pm, F-Sa 11:30am-3pm. ❹

The Blue Nile, 2525 Telegraph Ave. (☎540-6777), between Blake and Dwight streets. Waitresses in traditional gowns slip through beaded curtains serving huge portions of Ethiopian food. Eat *injera* with your fingers while sipping *mes* (honey wine; $2). Entrees $11-13. Open Tu-Su 5-10pm. Reservations strongly recommended on weekends. ❸

⭕ SIGHTS & SEASONAL EVENTS

TELEGRAPH AVENUE

You haven't really visited Berkeley until you've strolled the first five or so blocks of **Telegraph Avenue,** which runs south from Sproul Plaza to Oakland. The action is close to the university, where the street is lined with an assortment of cafes, bookstores, and used clothing and record stores. Businesses come and go at the whims of the marketplace, but the scene—a rowdy jumble of 60s and 90s counterculture—abides. Vendors push tie-dyes, Tarot readings, and handmade jewelry, the homeless and disenfranchised hustle for change, and grizzled characters looking like Old Testament prophets carry on conversations with nobody in particular.

Berkeley's active presses, which can be found in corner boxes and at area cafes, are invaluable for an up-to-date list of around the town happenings. Look in bookstores and bins for the free weekly *East Bay Express* (www.eastbayexpress.com), filled with theater, film, and concert listings. If you can find a recent edition of *Resource*, the guide given to new Berkeley students, grab it (try the Visitors Center at 101 University Hall). The *Daily Californian* (☎548-8300; www.dailycal.org), which publishes on Tuesdays and Fridays in the summer and daily during the academic year, carries university news.

▨**TAKARA SAKE USA INC.** Learn the history and science of *sake* making (through a museum and video) and sample 15 different types of *sake*. The knowledgeable hosts will not laugh in your face when you wobble out the door, another victim of Japan's merciless firewater. *(708 Addison St., just west of 4th St. Take the #51 bus to 4th St. and walk down to Addison St. ☎540-8250; www.takarasake.com. Open daily noon-6pm. Free.)*

FIRST CHURCH OF CHRIST SCIENTIST. Built in 1910, architect Bernard Maybeck's masterpiece is an amalgamation of Gothic, Renaissance, Classical, Japanese, Mediterranean, and industrial architectural styles. *(2526 Dwight St., at Bowditch St. ☎845-7199. Open during services W 8pm, Su 11am; tours at noon on the 1st Su of every month.)*

UC BERKELEY

In 1868, the private College of California and the public Agricultural, Mining, and Mechanical Arts College united as the **University of California.** The 178-acre university was the first of the nine University of California campuses, so by seniority it has sole right to the nickname "Cal." With over 30,000 students and 1350 full professors, the University is especially active when classes are in session, from late August to mid-May. If you'd like to sit in on some classes, track down a **course catalog** and schedule of classes at the campus bookstore or online (www.berkeley.edu). Campus is bounded on the south by Bancroft Way, on the west by Oxford St., on the north by Hearst Ave., and on the east by **Tilden Park.** Remodeling often occurs during academic downtime, so watch for closings. Maps of campus are posted everywhere; the **Visitors Center** (p. 125) hands out campus maps ($0.10) and offers tours.

▨**BERKELEY ART MUSEUM.** BAM is most respected for its collection of 20th-century American and Asian art. Rotating exhibitions showcase more experimental work. *(2626 Bancroft Way, at College Ave. ☎642-0808; www.bampfa.berkeley.edu. Open W and F-Su 11am-5pm, Th 11am-9pm. Adults $6; students, seniors, and ages 12-17 $4. Free Th 11am-noon and 5-9pm.)*

SPROUL PLAZA. In October 1964, students protested the arrest of one of their own who had been distributing civil rights pamphlets in the plaza, and began a series of confrontations that lasted several years. Mario Savio, a student and member of the widely influential Free Speech Movement, famously addressed a crowd from the steps of the plaza, arguing for students' rights to free expression and assembly. He was eventually jailed and expelled from school, but in 1997 the plaza steps were named in his honor. For students, the Plaza is a popular hangout.

SATHER TOWER. Besides the hippies and homeless doing their thing in Sproul Plaza, the most dramatic campus attraction is **Sather Tower,** better known as the **Campanile** (roughly Italian for "bell tower"). A 1914 monument to Berkeley benefactor Jane Krom Sather, at 307 ft. the tower is the tallest building on campus, and the 3rd tallest free-standing clocktower in the world. For a great view, you can ride to its observation level. The tower's 61-bell **carillon** plays during the school year. *(Bell plays M-F 7:10am, noon, 6pm. 45min. concert Su 2pm. Trip up tower $2.)*

LAWRENCE HALL OF SCIENCE. High atop the eucalyptus-covered hills east of the main campus is one of the finest science museums in the Bay Area. Ever-changing exhibits stress hands-on science activities catering to children but fun for all ages. The courtyard offers a life-size model whale, a stunning view of the bay, and stargazing workshops on clear Saturday evenings. Visit the Planetarium for its "Constellations Tonight" show and be sure to check out the outdoor "Forces That Shape The Bay" exhibit. *(On Centennial Dr. Take bus #8 or 65 from the Berkeley BART station and keep your transfer for $2 off admission. Once there, use the University shuttle (☎642-5149; $0.50), or brace yourself for the long, steep walk. ☎643-5708; www.larwrencehallofscience.org. Open daily 10am-5pm. $8; students, seniors, and ages 5-18 $6; ages 3-4 $4.)*

OTHER UC BERKELEY SIGHTS. In the northeastern part of Main campus, the impressive marble **Hearst Greek Theatre,** built in 1903, is modeled after a classical amphitheater in Epidavros, Greece. It is used for university ceremonies and concerts. The Grateful Dead used to play here annually. *(☎642-4864.)* Though the bulk of the impressive collection is rarely, if ever, on display, the **Phoebe Hearst Museum of Anthropology** is a pleasant quick-stop for displays and exhibits from California, ancient Egypt, and pre-Colombian Peru. *(103 Kroeber Hall, at the corner of Bancroft Way and College Ave. ☎643-7648; http://hearstmuseum.berkeley.edu. Open Tu-F 10am-4:30pm, Sa-Su noon-4:30pm. $2, seniors $1, ages 16 and under $0.50.)* The **UC Museum of Paleontology** has a complete Tyrannosaurus rex skeleton. *(Wallace Atrium, 1011 Valley of Life Sciences Building. ☎642-1821; www.ucmp.berkeley.edu. Open M 8am-5pm, Sa-Su 1-5pm. Free.)* The **Botanical Gardens** contain over 13,000 varieties of plant life from around the world, including a huge number of rare and endangered plants. Agatha Christie supposedly came here to examine a rare poisonous plant whose deadly powers she later put to use in a mystery novel. If you took the time to come up to the Gardens, also visit the **Stephen Mather Redwood Grove** across the street. *(200 Centennial Dr., in Strawberry Canyon, midway between the UC Stadium and Lawrence Hall of Science. ☎643-2755; www.mip.berkeley.edu/garden. Labor Day-Memorial Day open daily 9am-5pm except Christmas and the 1st Tu of each month; Memorial Day-Labor Day open daily 9am-7pm. $3, seniors $2, ages 3-18 $1; Th free.)*

PARKS & RECREATION

Berkeley's parks provide respite from the craziness of campus life. North of campus, The ⬛**Berkeley Rose Garden**—built by the Works Projects Administration in the Depression era—spills from one terrace to another in a vast semicircular amphitheater. The roses are pruned in January in preparation for Mother's Day (May 11 in 2003), when the garden is at its glorious peak. (Open May-Sept. dawn-dusk.) Berkeley's biggest confrontation between the People and the Man was not fought over Freedom of Speech or the war in Vietnam, but over a muddy vacant lot between Dwight and Haste St. In April 1969, students, hippies, and radicals christened the

WITH WHAT ARMY? On the night of February 4, 1974, **Patty Hearst,** heiress to the William Randolph Hearst newspaper empire, was abducted from her Berkeley flat by three members of the radical leftist **Symbionese Liberation Army.** She was allegedly coerced and brainwashed under humiliating conditions of confinement. She then began making public statements through tape recordings, condemning the capitalist "crimes" of her parents. The Symbionese Liberation Army extorted $2,000,000 from the Hearst family in the form of a food giveaway to the poor. They also got Patty Hearst to join in at least two robberies, of a San Francisco bank and an L.A. store. The Symbionese Liberation Army never had more than eleven or twelve members, six of whom—including the leader, Donald DeFreeze—were killed in a police shootout and house fire in Los Angeles on May 17, 1974. Hearst remained at large with her captors/confederates, criss-crossing the country. On Sept. 18, 1975, she was captured in San Francisco by the FBI. Hearst was tried and convicted in March 1976 for bank robbery and felonious use of firearms. Sentenced to seven years, she spent three in prison, and was released in February 1979.

patch of university-owned land **People's Park,** tearing up pavement and laying down sod to establish, in the words of the *Berkeley Barb,* "a cultural, political freak out and rap center for the Western world." When the university moved to evict squatters and build a parking garage on the site, resistance stiffened. Governor Ronald Reagan sent in 2000 troops, and the conflict ended with helicopters dropping tear gas on students in Sproul Plaza, one bystander shot dead by police, and a 17-day National Guard occupation. The park's grassy existence represents a small victory over the establishment. At the north end of Shattuck Ave., the basalt face of **Indian Rock** challenges thrill-junkies with short but demanding climbs. For the vertically challenged, side steps lead to an impressive view of the Headlands. (Open daily dawn-dusk.)

In the pine and eucalyptus forests east of the city lies the beautiful anchor of the East Bay park system, **Tilden Regional Park,** east of the city. Hiking, biking, running, and riding trails criss-cross the park and provide impressive views of the Bay Area. The **ridgeline trail** makes for an especially spectacular bike ride. For those looking to frolic without getting sweaty, a 19th-century **carousel** inside the park is a fun option. By car or bicycle, take Spruce St. to Grizzly Peak Blvd. to Canon Ave. AC Transit buses #7 and 8 run from the Berkeley BART station to the entrance at Grizzly Peak Blvd. and Golf Course Dr. (☎ 635-0135. Open daily dawn-dusk.) Also inside the park, Lake Anza's small, sandy beach is a popular swimming spot during the hottest summer days, though not the place to go for a quiet, romantic dip, as **Lake Anza** tends to be brat central. (☎ 843-2137. Open in summer 11am-6pm. $3, seniors and children $2.) At the north end of the park, the **Environmental Education Center** offers exhibits and naturalist-led programs. (☎ 525-2233. Open Tu-Su 10am-5pm. Free.) **Grizzly Peak** and **Inspiration Point** provide breathtaking panoramas of the entire Bay Area. **Wildcat Canyon** is a less developed park than Tilden, with gorgeous hiking through grassy meadows and densely wooded canyons. (Adjacent to Tilden Park. Open daily dawn-dusk.)

▟ SHOPPING

Telegraph Ave. is an excellent source of books, music, and secondhand clothes, along with homemade tie-dye, jewelry, and pipes. Larger-than-life chains seem evil and ominous in this happy land of independent and locally supported stores. The blocks between Blake St. and campus are full of trendy new and vintage clothes. The undisputed champion of the buy-sell-trade music scene is ▨**Amoeba Music,** 2455 Telegraph Ave., near Haste St. Go crazy in the warehouse-sized store with its tons of new and used CDs, including a popular collection of music and mutterings by Telegraph Avenue's least coherent residents. (☎549-1125; www.amoebamusic.com. Open M-Sa 10:30am-10pm, Su 11am-9pm.)

From a bibliophilic standpoint, Berkeley's book trade is the 8th wonder of the world. Leave yourself more time to browse than you think you'll need. Telegraph Ave. is home to some good book nooks, including **Moe's,** 2746 Telegraph Ave., between Dwight and Haste streets., which was featured in *The Graduate* and has four well-arranged floors worth of secondhand knowledge as well as new books at a 10% discount. "More Moe's" has art and antiquarian books on 4th floor. (☎849-2087; www.moesbooks.com. Open daily 10am-11pm.) Just down the street is **Shambhala,** 2482 Telegraph Ave., at Dwight St., which is the incense-foggy place to go for tarot cards, a hazy conversation with someone who will probably know how to read them for you, and a few books on the Kaballah, Tibetan Buddhism, and the Zohar. (☎848-8443. Open daily 11am-8pm.) An inspiring prose paradise beckons on University and Shattuck Ave. The dusty collection at **Serendipity Books,** 1201 University Ave., has earned Bay-wide respect. (☎841-7455. Open M-Sa 9am-5pm.)

🎵 ENTERTAINMENT

ON CAMPUS

🏛 **Zellerbach Playhouse,** near the corner of Bancroft Way and Dana St. Shared by professional dance and theater companies and student ensembles alike, Zellerbach is a community favorite. Summertime shows usually musicals and romantic comedies. Tickets during the academic year $6-12; summer shows $5-10, students and seniors $3-6.

CAL Performances, in Zellerbach Hall (☎642-9988; www.calperformances.berkeley.edu). Info and tickets for concerts, plays, and movies. Open M-F 10am-5:30pm, Sa 10am-2pm.

Hertz and Morrison Halls, on campus (☎642-0527), between Bowditch St. and College Ave. The Berkeley music department hosts noon concerts, including (but certainly not limited to) the African Music Ensemble, the Berkeley Contemporary Chamber Players, the Javanese Gamelan, and the 1991 Grammy-nominated University Chamber Chorus.

OFF CAMPUS

Berkeley Repertory Theater, 2025 Addison St. (☎845-4700). The best-known and arguably the finest theater in the area, with an eclectic repertoire of classics and unknowns. Half-price tickets may be available Tu-Th on the day of the show—line up at the box office at noon. Box office open daily noon-7pm.

Julia Morgan Center for Arts, 2640 College Ave. (☎845-8542), at Derby St., shares space with a preschool and yoga center in a beautiful building that was once a church. Noted for its graceful mix of materials, this building was Morgan's first commission. The theater hosts diverse performances including the **Berkeley Opera** (☎925-798-1300).

Pacific Film Archive, 2575 Bancroft Way (☎642-1124; www.bampfa.berkeley.edu/pfa), near Bowditch St. With a new facility and a huge collection of foreign and indie films, the PFA is a great place to catch a non-Schwarzenegger flick. Adults $7; students $5; seniors, disabled, children under 12 $4.50. Ticket office open M-F 11am-5pm.

🔊 NIGHTLIFE

Because Berkeley is so close to San Francisco proper, when hard-core clubbers need to bump-bump-and-grind they just take the bridge. What Berkeley does offer is an unrivaled array of casual brewpubs and brainy cafes. Crowded at almost any hour of the night or day, they serve as surrogate libraries, living rooms, and lecture theaters; espresso drinks and microbrews loosen the tongues of an already talkative city. Many of the bars have some great live music offerings, as well.

▓ **Caffè Strada,** 2300 College Ave. (☎843-5282), at Bancroft Way. The glittering jewel of the caffeine-fueled intellectual scene. Go to discuss philosophy, or just enjoy the beautiful outdoor terrace. Small latte $2. Most drinks under $2.50. Try the *Strada Bianca*, white hot chocolate ($2). Open daily 6:30am-midnight. No credit cards.

▓ **Jupiter,** 2181 Shattuck Ave. (☎843-8277), near the BART station. Stained glass, church pews, and elaborate Gothic-patterned paneling that you'll only see if the place is empty—but it won't be. Terrific pizza (9 inch pie $8). Live music in the spacious beer garden (Tu-Sa; in winter W-Su). Th Night "Beat Down" offers trance and hip-hop, accompanied by psychedelic projections on a massive brick wall. No cover. Open M-Th 11:30am-1am, F 11:30am-2am, Sa noon-2am, Su noon-midnight.

Blakes, 2367 Telegraph Ave. (☎848-0886), at Durant Ave. A jam-packed and unabashed meat market, but at least the cuts are premium. The pint-sized upstairs has a loud sports bar feel, while the middle floor is mellow. Kick it to the loud beats of local bands downstairs. Appetizers $2-5. Meals $4-8. Beverages from $2.50. Some shows 18+. Cover $2-8. Happy hour daily 4-6pm and 8-10pm. Open daily 11:30am-2am.

Triple Rock Brewery, 1920 Shattuck Ave. (☎843-2739; www.triplerock.com), north of Berkeley Way. Boisterous and friendly, the Rock was the first of Berkeley's many brewpubs. Long and ever-changing menu of ales, stouts, and porters (made 2-3 times a week, through their hands-on 7-barrel process). Award-winning Red Rock Ale $3.25. Open Su-W 11:30am-midnight, Th-Sa 11:30am-1am (later if busy). Rooftop garden closes at 9pm; kitchen closes Su-W 10:30pm, Th-Sa midnight.

OAKLAND ☎510

Led by mayor and one-time US presidential hopeful Jerry Brown, the city of Oakland has launched a public relations campaign to promote the lower prices and sunnier weather across the bay. Indeed, newcomers to the Bay Area too easily forget that Oakland, with 400,000 people, 81 languages, and considerable land mass, is a thriving city in its own right. Although historically less economically blessed than its neighbors, Oakland has a busy commercial center and some beautiful residential neighborhoods. Travelers often fail to incorporate Oakland into their perspective of the Bay Area, even though a nice afternoon downtown, a gourmet dinner in Rockridge, and an incredible live music scene are just a short car or BART ride away.

BAY AREA

▣ TRANSPORTATION

Drivers can take I-80 from San Francisco across the Bay Bridge to I-580 and connect with Oakland **I-980 South,** which has downtown exits at 12th and 19th streets. **TravInfo** (☎817-1717) has traffic updates.

Buses: Greyhound, 2103 San Pablo Ave. (station info ☎834-3213, schedules and reservations 800-231-2222). Buses depart daily to: **L.A.** ($45 one-way); **Sacramento** ($13); **Santa Cruz** ($12). Seniors 10% off, children 50% off. **As always, be careful at night.**

Public Transportation: Bay Area Rapid Transit (**BART:** ☎465-2278; www.bart.gov) is the most convenient way to travel from San Francisco to and within Oakland. BART runs from downtown San Francisco to Oakland's stations at **Lake Merritt** (Dublin/Pleasanton or Fremont trains), **12th Street** (Richmond or Pittsburg/Bay Point trains), **19th Street** (Richmond or Pittsburg/Bay Point trains), **Rockridge** (Pittsburg/Bay Point trains), and **Coliseum** (Dublin/Pleasanton or Fremont trains). **Alameda County (AC) Transit** (☎817-1717, ext. 1111; www.actransit.org). $1.35; seniors, disabled, and ages 5-12 $0.65; under 5 free. 1hr. transfers $0.25. **Transbay** routes to San Francisco ($2.75; seniors, disabled, and ages 5-12 $1.35). All AC buses are wheelchair-accessible and equipped with bike racks. Info about any public transit from **TravInfo** (☎817-1717; TDD 817-1718).

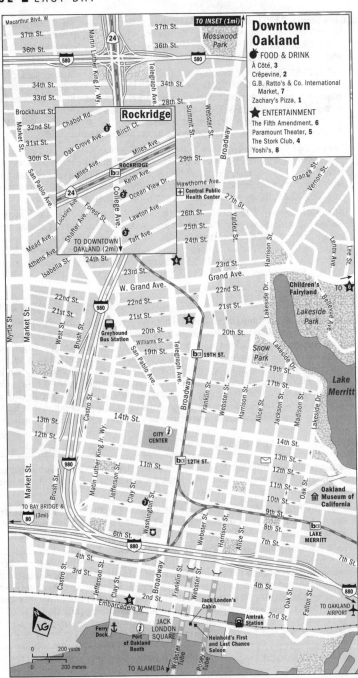

BAY AREA

Macarthur Blvd. W

TO INSET (1mi)

37th St.
37th St.
36th St.
36th St.

Mosswood Park

580
580
24

34th St.
34th St.
33rd St.
28th St.

Brockhurst St.

Market St.
32nd St.
31st St.
30th St.

San Pablo Ave.

Martin Luther King Jr. Wy.

Telegraph Ave.

Summit St.

Webster St.

Broadway

Rockridge

Chabot Rd.
Oak Grove Ave.
Birch Ct.
Miles Ave.
Miles Ave.
ROCKRIDGE
Keith Ave.
Ocean View Dr.
Lawton Ave.
Taft Ave.

29th St.

Hawthorne Ave.
✛ Central Public Health Center

Orange St.
Vernon St.

24
College Ave.
Locksley Ave.
Forest St.
Shafter Ave.

26th St.
25th St.
24th St.

27th St.

Valdez St.

Harrison St.

Lenox Ave.
Lee St.

Mead Ave.
Athens Ave.
Isabella St.
24th St.

TO DOWNTOWN OAKLAND (2mi) ▼

23rd St.
23rd St.

Grand Ave.
22nd St.
21st St.
20th St.

Children's Fairyland
TO ❺

W. Grand Ave.

Lakeside Dr.

Lakeside Park

Bellevue Ave.

980

22nd St.
21st St.
21st St.

20th St.
19th St.

Snow Park

Lake Merritt

Myrtle St.
Market St.
21st St.
22nd St.

West St.
Brush St.

🚌 Greyhound Bus Station
Williams St.

Telegraph Ave.

🚍 **19TH ST.**

17th St.

Lakeside Dr.

13th St.
12th St.

Castro St.
14th St.

Martin Luther King Jr. Wy.

Broadway
Franklin St.
Webster St.
Harrison St.
Alice St.
Jackson St.
Madison St.

Lakeside Dr.

🛈 **CITY CENTER**

14th St.

✉ 13th St.
12th St.

980
Market St.
Brush St.

11th St.
Jefferson St.
Clay St.

11th St.

🚍 **12TH ST.**
11th St.
10th St.
9th St.

Oak St.

Oakland Museum of California

TO BAY BRIDGE & (3mi)
80

🛈
✛
6th St.
880

Washington St.

8th St.
7th St.

🚍 **LAKE MERRITT**

880
7th St.

4th St.
3rd St.

Castro St.
Jefferson St.
Clay St.
Broadway
2nd St.

Franklin St.
Webster St.

4th St.
2nd St.

Fallon St.

TO OAKLAND AIRPORT

Embarcadero W.

★
2nd St.

JACK LONDON SQUARE

Jack London's Cabin

🏢 Amtrak Station

VG

0 ___ 200 yards
0 ___ 200 meters

Ferry Dock
⚓

🛈 Port of Oakland Booth

Webster Tube
Posey Tube

Heinhold's First and Last Chance Saloon

TO ALAMEDA

Downtown Oakland

🍎 **FOOD & DRINK**

À Côté, **3**
Crêpevine, **2**
G.B. Ratto's & Co. International Market, **7**
Zachary's Pizza, **1**

★ **ENTERTAINMENT**

The Fifth Amendment, **6**
Paramount Theater, **5**
The Stork Club, **4**
Yoshi's, **8**

Ferries: Alameda/Oakland Ferry (☎522-3300; www.eastbayferry.com). Purchase tickets on board. Ferries run between Oakland, Alameda, the San Francisco Ferry Building, and Pier 41/Fisherman's Wharf. $5, round-trip $10; seniors and disabled $3/$6; children 5-12 $2.25/$4.50; under 5 free. Free AC and MUNI transfers; MUNI transfers must be validated on ferry.

Taxis: A1 Yellow Cab (☎843-1111). Operates 24hr.

✈ 🚉 ORIENTATION & PRACTICAL INFORMATION

The scarcity of noteworthy sights and cheap and safe accommodations makes Oakland a better daytrip than vacation destination. Oakland's main artery is **Broadway.** Broadway runs northeast, under the I-880 (Nimitz Fwy.) at 5th St., and separates **Old Oakland** (to the west) from **Chinatown** (to the east). The **city center** is at 13th St. and Broadway, but the greater downtown area occupies all of **Lake Merritt,** including Lakeside Park on the north side, and the Lake Merritt Channel on the south side. North-south addresses are numbered to match the east-west cross streets, so 1355 Broadway is between 13th and 14th St. To get to **Jack London Square** and the waterfront from the 12th St. BART stop, just head down Broadway away from the hills. North of downtown, past some of Oakland's poorest slums, are a few Berkeley-esque neighborhoods with boutiques, grocers, and restaurants. **Rockridge,** with its yuppies and manicured lawns, lies toward Berkeley and is accessible from downtown Oakland by BART or AC Transit bus #51.

Visitor Information: Oakland Visitors Information Bureau, 475 14th St. Suite #120 (☎839-9000), between Broadway and Clay. Free maps of the city and brochures. Open M-F 8:30am-5pm. **Port of Oakland Information Booth** (24hr. info ☎814-6000; www.jacklondonsquare.com), on Broadway in Jack London Sq. under the Barnes and Noble bookstore. Info focuses on waterfront sights. Open M-Su 9am-4pm.

Police: 455 7th St. (☎238-3481).

Medical Services: Highland Hospital, 1411 E. 31st St. (☎437-4800, emergency 437-4261), at Beaumont Ave. Emergency care 24hr.

Pharmacy: Leo's Day and Night Pharmacy, 1776 19th St. (☎839-7900), at Broadway. Open M-F 9am-6:30pm.

Post Office: Main Office, 1675 7th St. at Peralta St. Open M 6:30am-midnight, Tu-Th 8:30am-midnight, F 8:30am-11pm. **Postal Code:** 94615.

🏠 ACCOMMODATIONS

Although Oakland is full of motels, few downtown are safe, clean, or economical compared to those in San Francisco and Berkeley. Motels clustered along W. Mac-Arthur Blvd., near the MacArthur BART station, are around $45 per night for a room with private bath. Ask to see the room before checking in. Commercial inns and hotels, are also clustered around Broadway at Jack London Square. For more desirable housing options in Oakland, try one of the beautiful (affordable) B&Bs in the northern part of the city. For information, contact the **Berkeley-Oakland Bed and Breakfast Network** (☎510-547-7726; www.bbonline.com/ca/berkeley-oakland).

B&B on Fairmount, 640 Fairmount Ave. (☎653-7726; www.bbonline.com/ca/fairmount), in Piedmont. Beautiful Victorian home with 3 airy rooms, all with private bath. Tea served in living room with views of the sunset over the hills; huge, homestyle breakfast, made with ingredients from vegetable garden in back, served in the sunny conservatory. 2-night min. stay. 2-week max. stay. Check-in after 3pm. Check-out 11am. Singles from $85; doubles from $95. Every consecutive 7th night is free. No credit cards. ❺

Redwood House B&B, 4244 39th Ave. (☎530-6840; tyler_don@yahoo.com), east of Piedmont. Ornate Victorian house brimming with antiques. Lush house plants, tufted silks, marble surfaces, and stained glass detail around every corner. Master suite with jacuzzi is a steal at $121; smaller but equally luxurious room $100. No credit cards. ❺

🏠 FOOD

All-American staples like burger joints, breakfast diners, and barbecue shacks dominate in Oakland. More gourmet cafes, mostly open for breakfast and lunch, have sprung up on Washington and Clay St. between 7th and 12th St. Oakland's **Chinatown,** west of Broadway around 9th St., features a host of dim sum restaurants, Vietnamese and Cambodian cuisine, and Asian markets. Every Friday from 8am to 2pm, the **Old Oakland farmer's market** (☎745-7100) takes over 9th St. between Broadway and Clay St., offering fresh fruits, vegetables, and some of the best baked goods in the Golden State. A similar **market** takes over a corner of Jack London Sq. on Broadway, near the waterfront. (☎800-949-3276. Su 10am-2pm.)

🥇 **Zachary's Pizza,** 5801 College Ave. (☎655-6385), at Oak Grove Ave. Loyal fans claim Zach's makes the best pizza in the Bay, zealots say west of Chicago, extremists insist it's the best in the world. *Let's Go* won't go that far, but Zach's makes a pretty good pie. Slices under $3. Open Su-Th 11am-10pm, F-Sa 11am-10:30pm. No credit cards. ❶

G.B. Ratto's & Co. International Market, 821 Washington St. (☎832-6503), is a 104-year-old Oakland institution. Speedy, superlative sandwich counter ($3.50-7). Open M-F 9am-6pm, Sa 9:30am-5pm. ❶

Crêpevine, 5600 College Ave. (☎658-2026). Big selection of sweet and savory eggs ($4-8), sandwiches ($6-7), and, of course, crepes ($3-8). Bright, casual space. Open Su-Th 7:30am-11pm, F-Sa 7:30am-midnight. ❷

À Côté, 5478 College Ave. (☎655-6469). Critics rave about the French-inspired menu and velvet decor. Entrees $7-14. Open Tu-Sa 11:30am-2pm and 5:30pm-midnight. ❸

👁 SIGHTS

Haunted by Gertrude Stein's withering observation that "there is no there there," Oakland's tourist literature wages a war of attrition against its former resident, assuring visitors that City Square is "always there for you" and "there is shopping there." Free walking tours of the city (reservations recommended; ☎238-3234; www.oaklandnet.com) highlight the *thereness* of downtown's best sights, including Roslyn Mazzilli's sculpture in City Square's upper plaza, defiantly entitled "There!" For a slightly militant view of the city, take the **Black Panther Legacy Tour.** Former party chief-of-staff David Hillard guides visitors through a first-hand account of the events, locations, and personalities that defined the Party. (☎986-0660; www.blackpanthertours.com. Reservations required for Sa tours. Tickets $20.)

OAKLAND MUSEUM OF CALIFORNIA. The three garden-topped levels of Bauhaus-inspired poured concrete at the Oakland Museum of California showcase the collections of three established area museums, brought together in 1969 to reflect the collective artistic, historical, and environmental legacy of Oakland and California. The **Cowell Hall of History** documents the cultural and political forces that shaped centuries of California dreaming. **The Hall of California Ecology** on the first floor recreates the state's eight biotic zones, and the **Gallery of California Art** includes photography by Ansel Adams, paintings by Richard Diebenkorn, and myriad modern masterpieces. (*1000 Oak St., on the southwestern side of the lake. From the Lake Merritt*

BART station, walk 1 block north on Oak St. toward the hills. ☎ 238-2200 or 888-625-6873, TTY 451-3322; www.museumca.org. Open W-Sa 10am-5pm, Su noon-5pm; 1st F of each month until 9pm. $6; seniors, students, and ages 6-18 $4; under 6 free. 2nd Su of each month free.)

LAKE MERRITT. Lake Merritt was dammed off from the San Francisco Bay in 1869, and now provides a place for sailing, biking, and jogging—not to mention political protest. Activity revolves around **Lakeside Park,** which has the nation's oldest urban bird sanctuary. The **Lake Merritt Boating Center** rents boats, and leads lake tours. *(Park: ☎ 238-7275. Parking $2. Lake: ☎ 238-2196. $10 deposit for boat rentals. Rentals 50% off for seniors and disabled. Open June-Sept. M-F 9am-6pm, Sa-Su 10am-6pm; Oct. M-Su 10:30am-5pm; Nov.-Feb. M-F 10:30am-3:30pm, Sa-Su 10:30am-4pm; Mar.-May M-F 10:30am-4pm, Sa-Su 10:30am-5pm. Boating Center: 568 Bellevue Ave. ☎ 238-2196; www.oaklandnet.com/parks/programs/boating.asp. Lake tours Sa-Su. $1.50, children and seniors $0.75. Canoes and rowboats $6 per hr., kayaks and pedal boats $8 per hr., sailboats $6-8 per hr.)*

JACK LONDON SQUARE. An eight-block commercial district named for Oakland's native son, author of *White Fang* and *The Call of the Wild*, is a nice first stop on the way to other Oakland outings. **Jack London's Cabin,** near Webster St., was the author's home during his 1890s prospecting days. Next to the cabin, the small, wooden **Heinold's First and Last Chance Saloon** has barely changed since London's days, except, presumably, for the addition of the London-themed mural. The same gaslight still burns, the sunken floor and bar from 1906 have never been fixed, and 120-odd years of knickknacks continue to pile up on the walls. *(Cabin: Along the waterfront. Take Broadway south. Event info ☎ 814-6000. Saloon: 56 Jack London Sq., at the foot of Webster St. ☎ 839-6761; www.firstandlastchance.com. $4 pints, $4 well drinks, $7 top shelf. Open M noon-10pm, Tu-Th noon-midnight, F-Sa noon-2am, Su 11am-10pm. No credit cards.)*

CHABOT SPACE AND SCIENCE CENTER. This incredible 2-year-old complex offers stargazing both indoors at the **Planetarium** and outdoors with high-powered telescopes, daily screenings in the **Tien MegaDome Theater,** and interactive exhibits. *(Space and Science Center: 10000 Skyline Blvd, at Skyline Blvd., in Joaquin Miller Park in the Oakland HIlls. ☎ 336-7300; www.chabotspace.org. Open early Sept.-June 30 T-Su 10am-3pm; June 29-Labor Day T-Th 10am-5pm, F-Sa 10am-9pm, Su noon-5pm. $8, students $7, seniors and ages 4-12 $5.50, under 3 free Planetarium and Tien MegaDome Theater: Open same hours as Science Center plus F-Sa 7-9pm. $8.75 for each, students $7.75, ages 4-12 and seniors $6.50, under 3 free. Double and triple venue prices also available.)*

🎵 🎭 **ENTERTAINMENT & NIGHTLIFE**

LIVE MUSIC

The **live music scene** is one of the best reasons to make the Oakland daytrip in the first place. Whether it's West Coast blues, Oaktown hip-hop, or progressive jazz, Oakland's music venues are unsurpassed. Because many artists lack institutional representation, check posters and local papers for shows. *Urban View*, the free Wednesday weekly, and the daily *Oakland Tribune* ($0.50, Su $1.25) are good resources and are available in boxes throughout the city. **Koncepts Cultural Gallery** is an organization that hosts groundbreaking progressive jazz sessions. (☎ 451-5231. Cover $5-25.) The **Paramount Theater,** 2025 Broadway, at 21st St., hosts national music acts like Nina Simone and George Benson. (☎ 465-6400; www.paramounttheater.com. Box office open Tu-F noon-6pm, Sa noon-5pm, and 2hr. before shows.) Safety in Oakland is a constant concern; exercise caution after dark.

■ **The Fifth Amendment,** 3255 Lakeshore Ave. (☎832-3242), at Lake Park Ave. Not the most famous, just the best. Jazz and blues musicians take the stage in this downtown club, where there's never a cover or drink minimum and the crowd is serious about its music. 21+. Shows W-Su usually 9pm. Open daily 3pm-2am.

Yoshi's, 510 Embarcadero W. (☎238-9200; www.yoshis.com), in Jack London Sq. Yoshi's is an upscale institution, bringing together world-class sushi and world-class jazz. Big names command big cover prices; tickets sometimes sell out but are often available at the door. 1-drink minimum. Cover usually $20-25. Local musician nights (usually M) $8-10. Family discount Su matinee: adult (with child) $10, child $5. Seniors and students with valid ID can get half-price tickets for selected shows. Shows M-Sa 8 and 10pm, Su 2 and 8pm. Box office open daily 10:30am-11pm.

The Stork Club, 2330 Telegraph Ave. (☎444-6174). Laid-back country western bar by day, rock party by night. What's more, there's kitschy Christmas decor year-round. 21+. Indie rock, punk, and underground M-Th around 9pm, F-Sa around 10pm. Cover from $5. Open mic Su 9pm with "Girl George." No cover but 2-drink min. Open daily 4pm-2am.

CINEMA & FINE ARTS

The **Paramount Theater,** 2025 Broadway (☎465-6400), at 21st St., is an exquisite Art Deco movie palace. The Paramount shares its stage with the **Oakland East Bay Symphony** and the **Oakland Ballet.** The Symphony performs five Friday concerts yearly, with open rehearsals the preceding Thursday afternoon. The Symphony also sponsors free noon concerts. The ballet performs several programs, including an unconventional *Nutcracker Sweetie.* (Symphony ☎444-0801; www.oebs.org. Ballet ☎893-2300; www.oaklandballet.org. Symphony tickets $15-55. Ballet tickets $8-45. Box office open Tu-F noon-6pm, Sa noon-5pm, and 2hr. before shows.)

Another groovy place to see a movie is the **Parkway Speakeasy Theater,** 1834 Park Blvd., a theater with lounge seating where you can order pizza ($3 per slice), pasta, sandwiches, and wine or beer by the pitcher ($8) or pint ($4) right at your seat. Keep an eye open for special Thrillville features. (☎834-1506; www.picturepubpizza.com. 21+. Tickets $5. *Rocky Horror Picture Show* F midnight 17+. $5. Weekend matinees all ages. $3.) The classic **Grand Lake Theater,** features Wurlitzer organ music before F and Sa evening shows and all the latest, hottest movies. (☎452-3446; www.rrfilms.com. Adults $8.50; children, seniors and matinee $5.) Also, there's the more mainstream **Jack London Cinema,** on Washington St. at Embarcadero. ($8.75, seniors and matinees $5.75.)

SPORTS & SEASONAL EVENTS

Baseball's **Oakland Athletics (A's)** and football's **Oakland Raiders** both play in the **Oakland Coliseum** (☎569-2121), at the intersection of the I-880 (Nimitz Fwy.) and Hegenberger Rd. The Coliseum has its own BART station. The NBA's **Golden State Warriors** play basketball in the **Coliseum Arena,** adjacent to the Oakland Coliseum. (Box office open M-F 10am-6pm, Sa 10am-4pm.)

California Canoe & Kayak, 409 Water St. in Jack London Sq., rents paddling equipment, offers classes, and plans adventure trips. (☎893-7833 or 800-366-9804; www.calkayak.com. Open M-Th 10am-6pm, F-Sa 10am-7pm, Su 10am-5pm. Boat rentals daily 10am-5pm; last boat leaves 4pm. $10-20 per hr., $50-60 per day.)

Lake Merritt's Lakeside Park hosts several festivals over the summer. In June, the **Festival at the Lake** takes over Oakland with a long weekend of international foods, crafts, and music. On Father's Day (June 15 in 2003), **Juneteenth** (☎238-7765) commemorates the anniversary of the Emancipation Proclamation with parades, soul food, blues, and R&B. The park also has **free Shakespeare performances** in summer. (☎415-422-2222 or 800-978-7529; www.sfshakes.org.)

SOUTH BAY

The San Francisco peninsula extends southward into what was once a valley of fruit orchards and is now the center of America's electronics industry. From Palo Alto to San Jose and beyond, the area known as the Silicon Valley seems to make more chips than Frito-Lay.

PALO ALTO   ☎ 650

Dominated by the beautiful 8000-acre Stanford University campus, well-manicured Palo Alto looks like "Collegeland" at a Disney theme park. Stanford's perfectly groomed grounds, sparkling lake, and Spanish mission-style buildings have a manufactured quality that suits the university's speedy rise to international acclaim. The city that Stanford calls home is equally sanitized, with a yuppified downtown strip of restaurants, bookstores, and boutiques. Its nightlife caters to students and suburbanites, while weekday happy hours help singles wind down.

▐ TRANSPORTATION

Palo Alto is 35 mi. southeast of San Francisco, near the southern shore of the bay. Take **U.S. 101** to the University Ave. Exit, or take the Embarcadero Rd. Exit directly to the Stanford campus. Alternatively, motorists from San Francisco can split off onto **I-280 (Junípero Serra Highway)** for a longer but more scenic route. From I-280, exit at Sand Hill Rd. and follow it to the northwest corner of Stanford University.
    The **Palo Alto Transit Center,** on University Ave., serves local and regional buses and trains. (☎323-6105. Open daily 5am-12:30am.) A train-only depot lies on California Ave., 1¼ mi. south of the transit center. (☎326-3392. Open daily 5:30am-12:30am.) The transit center connects to points north via **San Mateo County buses** and to Stanford via the free **Marguerite Shuttle.**

Trains: CalTrain, 95 University Ave. (☎800-660-4287), at Alma St. Street-side stop at Stanford Stadium on Embarcadero Rd. To **San Francisco** ($4.50) and **San Jose** ($3.50). 25% discount M-F 9am-2:30pm. Half-price for seniors and disabled. Operates M-F 5am-midnight, Sa 7am-midnight, Su 8am-10pm.

Buses: SamTrans (☎800-660-4287). To downtown **San Francisco** ($3, under 17 $1.25) and **San Francisco International Airport** ($1.10). To reach Palo Alto from San Francisco, take **SamTrans** express bus KX from the Transbay Terminal in San Francisco to the Stanford Shopping Center. Operates M-F 6am-10pm, Sa-Su 8am-8pm.

Public Transportation: Santa Clara Valley Transportation Authority (☎408-321-2300 or 800-894-9908). Local and county-wide transit. $1.25, seniors and disabled $0.40, ages 5-17 $0.70. Day pass $3, seniors and disabled $1, ages 5-17 $1.75. Express buses $2. The **Marguerite** Shuttle (☎723-9362) provides free service around Stanford University, stopping at red-and-white shuttle stop signs, including the Palo Alto Caltrain. Operates M-F 6am-8pm. The city of Palo Alto provides a free **crosstown shuttle,** operating M-F 7am-6pm, and an **Embarcadero shuttle** operating M-F 6-9am, Sa-Su 11:45am-1:45pm and 3-6pm. (☎329-2520; www.city.palo-alto.ca.us/shuttle).

Taxis: Yellow Cab (☎321-1234 or 800-595-1222). Runs 24hr. $2 per mi.

Car Rental: Budget, 4230 El Camino Real (☎493-6000, reservations 800-527-0700). From $40 per day. Unlimited mileage. Must be at least 21 with credit card. Under 25 surcharge $20 per day. Open M-F 8am-5:30pm, Sa-Su 8am-4:30pm.

Bike Rental: Campus Bike Shop, 551 Salvatierra Ln. (☎325-2945), across from Stanford Law School, allows you to take advantage of Palo Alto's flat boulevards and rolling hills. $15 per day, $20 overnight, helmets $3 (under 18 free). Major credit card or $150-300 cash deposit. Open M-F 9am-5pm, Sa 9am-3pm.

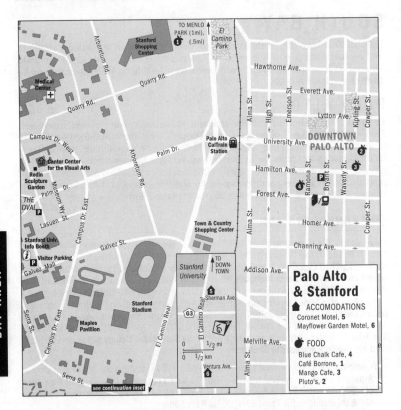

TO MENLO PARK (1mi), (.5mi)
El Camino Park

Stanford Shopping Center

Arboretum Rd.

Medical Center

Quarry Rd.

Quarry Rd.

Campus Dr. West

Cantor Center for the Visual Arts

Rodin Sculpture Garden

THE OVAL

Palm Dr.

Museum Way St.

Lasuen St.

Stanford Univ. Info Booth

Visitor Parking

Galvez Mall

Campus Dr. East

Galvez St.

Serra St.

Maples Pavilion

Campus Dr. East

Stanford Stadium

Serra St.

El Camino Real

Arboretum Rd.

Palm Dr.

Palo Alto CalTrain Station

Hawthorne Ave.

Everett Ave.

Alma St.

High St.

Emerson St.

Lytton Ave.

University Ave.

Hamilton Ave.

Forest Ave.

Alma St.

Ramona St.

Bryant St.

Waverly St.

Kipling St.

Cowper St.

DOWNTOWN PALO ALTO

Homer Ave.

Channing Ave.

Cowper St.

Town & Country Shopping Center

Stanford University

TO DOWN-TOWN

Sherman Ave.

G3

El Camino Real

Addison Ave.

Melville Ave.

Ventura Ave.

0   1/2 mi
0   1/2 km

Alma St.

Palo Alto & Stanford	
▲ ACCOMODATIONS	
Coronet Motel, **5**	
Mayflower Garden Motel, **6**	
● FOOD	
Blue Chalk Cafe, **4**	
Café Borrone, **1**	
Mango Cafe, **3**	
Pluto's, **2**	

see continuation inset

✦ ⁊ ORIENTATION & PRACTICAL INFORMATION

The pristine lawns of residential Palo Alto are not easily distinguished from the manicured campus of Stanford University. Despite its name, **University Avenue,** the main thoroughfare off U.S. 101, belongs much more to the town than to the college. Cars coming off U.S. 101 onto University Ave. pass very briefly through **East Palo Alto,** a community incorporated in 1983 after Palo Alto and Menlo Park had already annexed most of their revenue-producing districts. East Palo Alto once had one of the highest violent crime rates in the nation. The town has cleaned up its act and grown safer in recent years, but you'll find that the contrast with the immaculate tree-lined lawns of Palo Alto is still striking.

Stanford University spreads out from the west end of University Ave. Abutting University Ave. and running northwest-southeast through town is **El Camino Real** (part of Rte. 82). From there, University Ave. turns into Palm Dr., which accesses the heart of Stanford's campus, the **Main Quad.**

Visitor Information: Palo Alto Chamber of Commerce, 325A Forest Ave. (☎324-3121). Open M-F 9am-5pm. **Stanford University Information Booth** (☎723-2053 or 723-2560), across from Hoover Tower in Memorial Auditorium. Free student-led tours daily 11am and 3:15pm; times vary holidays and exam periods. Open daily 8am-5pm.

Police: 275 Forest Ave. (☎329-2406, after hours 329-2413).

Library and Internet Access: Palo Alto Main Library, 1213 Newell Rd. (☎329-2436). Open M-F 10am-9pm, Sa 10am-6pm, Su 1-5pm. **Downtown Branch,** 270 Forest Ave. (☎329-2641). Open M-Sa 11am-6pm. Free.

Post Offices: Main Office, 2085 E. Bayshore Rd. (☎800-275-8777). Open M-F 8am-5pm. **Postal Code:** 94303. **Hamilton Station,** 380 Hamilton Ave. (☎323-2650). **Postal Code:** 94301.

ACCOMMODATIONS

Motels are plentiful along **El Camino Real,** but rates can be steep. Generally, rooms are cheaper farther away from Stanford. More reasonably priced accommodations may be found farther north toward Redwood City. Many Palo Alto motels cater to business travelers and are actually busier on weekdays than on weekends.

Coronet Motel, 2455 El Camino Real (☎326-1081), at California St. Clean, spacious rooms with big windows, cable TV, pool, and kitchens. Cheap considering its proximity to Stanford. Check-out 11am. Singles $75; doubles $85. Weekly rates available. ❹

Mayflower Garden Motel, 3981 El Camino Real (☎493-4433). Spacious, spotless rooms with jaded decor. TV with HBO, fridge, and microwave. Bus stop right outside with regular service to Palo Alto CalTrain depot. Reservations at least a week in advance recommended. Singles $65; doubles $75; $5 per additional person. ❹

Hidden Villa Ranch Hostel (HI-AYH), 26870 Moody Rd. (☎949-8648), about 10 mi. southwest of Palo Alto in Los Altos Hills. Functions as a working ranch and farm in a wilderness preserve. Recent renovations include completely rebuilt dorms and extended living, kitchen, and dining rooms. Heated cabins and 35 beds. Reception 8am-noon and 4-9:30pm. Reservations required for weekends and groups. Open Sept.-May. Dorms $14, nonmembers $17, children $7; private cabins $30-42. ❶

FOOD

Dining in Palo Alto is centered around posh restaurants downtown around University and California avenues. Those watching wallets should stay on University Ave.

Café Borrone, 1010 El Camino Real (☎327-0830), adjacent to Kepler's Books in Menlo Park. Bustling, brasserie-style cafe spills out onto a large patio. Borrone serves freshly baked bread, sinful gateaux ($2-4), coffee drinks, Italian sodas, wine ($5-6 per glass), and beers ($3.75 per pint). Check the chalkboard for daily specials, or choose from a wide range of delicious salads ($4-9), sandwiches ($5-10), and quiches ($6). Open M-Th 7am-11pm, F 7am-midnight, Sa 8am-midnight, Su 8am-5pm. ❷

Blue Chalk Cafe, 630 Ramona St. (☎326-1020). Started by a Stanford Business School student for a project, this elegant restaurant became an instant hit with both students and silicon-professionals. California Cuisine includes shrimp and crab cakes ($9.25), grilled salmon and steaks ($19), and penne pasta with veggie Thai green curry ($15). Open for M-F 11am-2:30pm and Sa 5-10pm. ❸

Pluto's, 482 University Ave. (☎853-1556). Out-of-this-world cafeteria-style restaurant. Design your own salad from heaps of fresh fixings ($5), or choose from grilled meats and veggies to fill a sandwich ($5-6). Open M-Th 11am-10pm, F 11am-11pm, Sa 11:30am-11pm, Su 11:30am-10pm. ❶

Mango Café, 435 Hamilton Ave. (☎325-3229), 1 block east of University Ave. Reggae music and Caribbean cuisine. Seriously spicy Jamaican "jerked joints" ($6) and tropical smoothies ($3.25) served in giant glass bowls. Veggie options. Delicious bread pudding $3. Open M-Sa 11:30am-2:30pm and 6-10pm. ❶

SIGHTS

STANFORD UNIVERSITY

Undoubtedly Palo Alto's main tourist attraction, the secular, co-educational **Stanford University** was founded in 1885 by Jane and Leland Stanford to honor their son, who died of typhoid. The Stanfords loved Spanish colonial mission architecture and collaborated with **Frederick Law Olmsted,** designer of New York City's Central Park, to create a red-tiled campus of uncompromising beauty. (UC Berkeley students sometimes refer to Stanford as "The World's Largest Taco Bell.") The school has produced such eminent conservatives as **Chief Justice William Rehnquist,** and the campus has been called "a hotbed of social rest."

MAIN QUADRANGLE. The oldest part of campus is the site of most undergraduate classes. The walkways are dotted with diamond-shaped, gold-numbered stone tiles that mark the locations of time capsules put together by each year's graduating class. *(Serra St., between Lasuen and Lomita Mall. Free tours at 11:15am, 3:15pm. Depart from Information Booth in Memorial Auditorium.)*

MEMORIAL CHURCH. Memorial Church is a non-denominational gold shrine with stained glass windows and glittering mosaic walls like those of an Eastern Orthodox church. *(Just south of the Main Quad, at Escondido Mall and Duena. ☎ 723-1762; http://religiouslife.stanford.edu/memorial church.)*

HOOVER TOWER. The tower's observation deck has views of campus, the East Bay, and San Francisco. *(East of the Main Quad, near Serra St., between Lasuen and Galvez Mall. ☎ 723-2053. Open daily 10am-5pm. $2, seniors and under 13 $1.)*

IRIS & B. GERALD CANTOR CENTER FOR VISUAL ARTS. The Visual Arts Center displays its eclectic collection of painting and sculpture for free. *(328 Lomita Dr., at Museum Way off Palm Dr. ☎ 723-4177. Open W and F-Su 11am-5pm, Th 11am-8pm. Free.)*

RODIN SCULPTURE GARDEN. The extensive garden contains a stunning bronze cast of Gates of Hell, among other larger figures. It's an ideal spot to enjoy a picnic lunch. *(At Museum Way and Lomita Dr. Free tours Sa-Su 2pm.)*

📷 SHOPPING

Bell's Bookstore, 536 Emerson St. (☎323-7822). Bell's Bookstore, family-run since 1935, is a favorite among locals and Stanfordites. It's packed floor-to-ceiling with old, new, and rare books arranged by subject. Selection includes a large range of hardback and out-of-print texts. Open M-Th 9:30am-5:30pm, F 9:30am-9pm, Sa 9:30am-5pm.

Stanford Shopping Center (☎617-8585 or ☎800-772-9332; www.stanfordshop.com), between campus and El Camino Real. High-street designer clothes, department stores, speciality food shops, and restaurants line tree-shaded avenues. Its patio cafes are perfect for people-watching. Open M-F 10am-9pm, Sa 10am-7pm, Su 11am-6pm.

🎭 ENTERTAINMENT

The Stanford-run *Palo Alto Daily* and the local *Palo Alto Weekly* both contain listings of what's going on all over town. The free *Metro* and the *Palo Alto Daily News,* available in downtown sidewalk boxes, also give the local lowdown.

Dinkelspiel Auditorium (☎ 723-2448), at El Camino Real and Embarcadero. Called "the Dink" by locals, the auditorium holds classical concerts and other events through the Tressider Union ticket office (☎ 725-2787). Open M-F 10am-5pm, Sa noon-4pm.

Stanford Theater, 221 University Ave. (☎324-3700). Dedicated to Hollywood's "Golden Age." Devotes exhibition seasons to directors and stars, such as Billy Wilder and Cary Grant. The Wurlitzer organ plays before and after the 7:30pm show and accompanies silent films every W. Double features $6, seniors $4, under 18 $3.

The Lively Arts at Stanford (☎723-2551; http://livelyarts.stanford.edu) brings semi-big name concerts to Frost Amphitheater and Memorial Auditorium every year, usually at discount prices. The Memorial has Su movies in term-time. $3, students $2.

🅢 NIGHTLIFE

So you're going out on the town in Palo Alto. Do you want to party with Teva-wearing Stanford students or with Silicon Valley professionals still in their work clothes? Truly a dilemma of boundless proportions.

🅜 **Nola,** 535 Ramona St. (☎328-2722). There is a fiesta everyday in this vibrant, super-popular bar. Colorful strings of lights and patio windows open onto a cool, courtyard dining area. Late-night menu offers quesadillas ($7-9), crab cakes ($7), and gumbo ($7) to accompany your cocktails ($6-7). Open daily 5:30pm-2am.

Left at Albuquerque, 445 Emerson St. (☎326-1011). A dot-commer's delight, this Southwestern bar and restaurant is packed with silicon singles the minute the PC factories let out. Margaritas ($6) and over 150 brands of tequila. If you can show proof of the existence of a brand they don't stock (good luck), you drink for free. Happy hour daily 4-7pm. Open Su-Th 11:30am-10pm, F-Sa 11:30am-11pm, bar closes at last call or 2am.

Rose and Crown, 547 Emerson St. (☎327-7673). This low-key pub with an Ace jukebox is good for throwing darts or quietly nursing a Guinness. Authentic British bar menu includes fish and chips ($7-9), bangers and mash ($9), and ploughman's lunch ($7). Open M-F 11:30am-1:30am, Sa noon-1:30am, Su 1pm-1:30am.

BAY AREA

SAN JOSE ☎408

Founded in 1777 in a bucolic valley of fruit and walnut orchards, San Jose was California's first civilian settlement. The area's primary business was agriculture until the middle of the 20th century, when the technology sector began to develop. In 1939, the first computer company, Hewlett-Packard, had modest beginnings—in Dave Packard's garage. Within twenty years, many of San Jose's orchards had been replaced by offices, the moniker "Silicon Valley" already taking hold.

San Jose is the country's foremost center of technological innovation and boasts a growing and wealthy population—its 920,000 residents have the second-highest average disposable income of any US city. However, San Jose's cultural activity has not experienced the same boom as the high-tech gold rush—apart from the musical stylings of the Doobie Brothers, and the Dionne Warwick signature song that *will* get stuck in your head, San Jose offers little on the arts front. And though everyone is wearing a name tag, no one really wants to know your name.

🄵 TRANSPORTATION

Airport: San Jose International, 1661 Airport Blvd. (☎277-5366). Turn right onto Airport Blvd. from Coleman Ave. off I-880 or Guadalupe Pkwy. off U.S. 101. Also accessible by Valley Transit Authority (VTA) light-rail. Free shuttles connect the terminals.

Trains: Amtrak, 65 Cahill St. (☎287-7462 or 800-USA-RAIL/872-7245), to **L.A.** (11hr., $51-78, depending on day/time) and **San Francisco** (1hr., $10-14). **CalTrain,** 65 Cahill St. (☎291-5651 or 800-660-4287), at W. San Fernando Blvd., to **San Francisco** with stops at peninsula cities (1½hr.; every hr. M-F 5am-10pm, Sa 6:30am-10pm, Su 7:30am-10pm; $5.25).

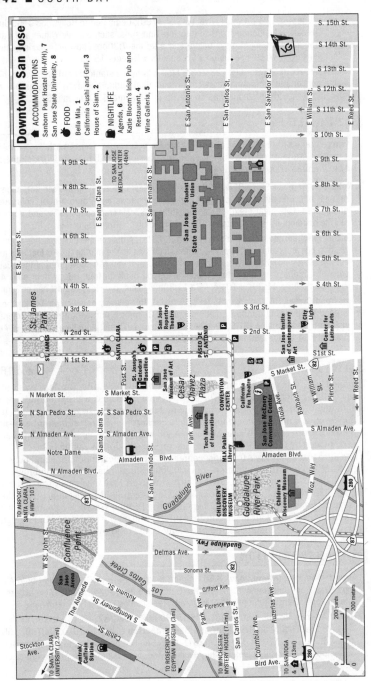

Downtown San Jose

▲ **ACCOMMODATIONS**
Sanborn Park Hostel (HI-AYH), **7**
San Jose State University, **8**

● **FOOD**
Bella Mia, **1**
California Sushi and Grill, **3**
House of Siam, **2**

■ **NIGHTLIFE**
Agenda, **6**
Katie Bloom's Irish Pub and
Restaurant, **4**
Wine Galleria, **5**

TO SAN JOSE
MEDICAL CENTER
(4blk)

San Jose
State University

Student
Union

S. 15th St.
S 14th St.
S 13th St.
S 12th St.
E San Antonio St.
E San Carlos St.
E San Salvador St.
S 11th St.
E Reed St.
E William St.
S 10th St.
E Santa Clara St.
E San Fernando St.
S 9th St.
N 9th St.
N 8th St.
S 8th St.
N 7th St.
S 7th St.
N 6th St.
S 6th St.
N 5th St.
S 5th St.
N 4th St.
S 4th St.
E St. James St.
N 3rd St.
S 3rd St.
St. James
Park
N 2nd St.
San Jose
Repertory
Theatre
S 2nd St.
San Jose Instite
of Contemporary
Art
City
Lights
Center for
Latino Arts
ST JAMES
SANTA CLARA
N 1st St.
S1st St.
Post St.
St. Joseph's
Catedral
Basilica
PASEO DE
ST ANTONIO
S Market St.
N Market St.
San Jose
Museum of Art
S Market St.
Cesar
Chavez
Plaza
CONVENTION
CENTER
California
Fox Theatre
San Jose McEnery
Convention Center
W William
St.
Pierce St.
W Reed St.
N San Pedro St.
S San Pedro St.
Park Ave.
Tech Museum
of Innovation
Viola Ave.
Balbach St.
W St. James St.
N Almaden Ave.
S Almaden Ave.
MLK Public
Library
Almaden Blvd.
S Almaden Ave.
Notre Dame
W Santa Clara St.
Almaden
Blvd.
W San Fernando St.
N Almaden Blvd.
CHILDREN'S
DISCOVERY
MUSEUM
Children's
Discovery Museum
Woz Way
TO AIRPORT,
SANTA CLARA,
& HWY. 101
Guadalupe
River
Guadalupe
River Park
W St. John St.
Confluence
Point
Guadalupe Fwy.
Delmas Ave.
San
Jose
Arena
The Alameda
S Montgomery St.
Autumn St.
Los Gatos Creek
Sonoma St.
Gifford Ave.
Auzerais Ave.
Cahill St.
Amtrak/
CalTrain
Station
TO ROSECRUCIAN
EGIPTIAN MUSEUM (3mi)
TO WINCHESTER
MYSTERY HOUSE (7.5mi)
Park Ave.
Florence Way
San Carlos Ave.
Columbia Ave.
Bird Ave.
Stockton
Ave.
TO SANTA CLARA UNIVERSITY (2.5mi)
TO SARATOGA
& (13mi)
280
87
82
82
280
87
0   200 yards
0   200 meters
BAY AREA

Buses: Greyhound, 70 S. Almaden Ave. (☎295-4151 or 800-231-2222), at Santa Clara St. To **L.A.** (7 hrs., $40) and **San Francisco** (1¼hr., $5). Luggage lockers for ticketed passengers ($2 per 6hr.). Open daily 5am-midnight. The station has security guards.

Public Transportation: Santa Clara Valley Transportation Agency (VTA), 2 N. First St. (☎321-2300), offers ultra-modern buses and a light-rail system. ($1.40, day pass $4; ages 5-17 fare $0.85, day pass $2.50; exact change only.) **Bay Area Rapid Transit** or **BART** (☎510-441-2278) bus #180 serves the Fremont station from 1st and San Carlos St. in downtown San Jose ($2). To **San Francisco** (45-55min., $4.05-4.45).

❊ ORIENTATION

San Jose lies at the southern end of the San Francisco Bay, about 50 mi. from San Francisco (via U.S. 101 or I-280) and 40 mi. from Oakland (via I-880). I-280 is renowned for its roadside scenery along the stretch called Junípero Serra Fwy. and is often less congested than Hwy. 101. (For info on reaching San Jose from San Francisco using public transit, see **CalTrain,** p. 141.)

San Jose is centered around the convention-hosting malls and plazas near the intersection of east-west **San Carlos Street** and north-south **Market Street.** Bars, restaurants, and clubs crowd around 1st St. in the so-called **SoFA District.** The **Transit Mall,** the center of San Jose's bus and trolley system, runs from north to south along 1st and 2nd St. in the downtown area. The grassy grounds of **San Jose State University (SJSU)** (☎924-1000) run several blocks between S. 4th and S. 10th St. Founded in 1857, SJSU is the oldest public college in California.

ⓘ PRACTICAL INFORMATION

Visitor Information: Visitor Information and Business Center: 150 W. San Carlos (☎726-5673 or 888-SAN-JOSE/726-5673, events line 295-2265; fax 977-0901; www.sanjose.org), at Market and San Carlos St. in the San Jose McEnerny Convention Ctr. Free maps. Open M-F 8am-5:30pm, Sa-Su 11am-5pm.

Police: 201 W. Mission St. (☎277-8900 for non-emergency dispatch or 277-2211 for information).

24-Hour Crisis Lines: Rape Crisis (☎287-3000). **Suicide Prevention/Crisis Intervention** (☎279-3312).

Medical Services: San Jose Medical Center, 675 E. Santa Clara St. (☎998-3212), at 14th St. Emergency room (☎977-4444) open 24hr.

Library and Internet Access: Martin Luther King, Jr. Public Library, 180 W. San Carlos St. (☎277-4846), in front of the Convention Center. Internet is free; obtain a login from librarian for access. Get there early to avoid waiting or make a reservation (15, 30 and 60min. time slots available). Open M-W 9am-9pm, Th-Sa 9am-6pm, Su 1-5pm.

Post Office: 105 N. 1st St. (☎292-0487). Open M-F 8:30am-5pm, Sa 7am-12pm. **Postal Code:** 95113.

🏠 ACCOMMODATIONS & CAMPING

County parks with campgrounds surround the city, as do many chain motels. **Mount Madonna County Park ❶,** on Pole Line Rd. off Hecker Pass Hwy., has 117 sites in a beautiful setting, available by reservation or on a first-come, first-camp basis. (☎842-2341 or 842-6761, reservations 355-2201. Sites $15; RVs $25.) The area around **Saratoga ❶,** on Rte. 85, 14 mi. southwest of San Jose, has a number of campsites, as well as miles of horse and hiking trails in **Sanborn-Skyline County Park.** From Rte. 17 South, take Rte. 9 to Big Basin Way and turn left onto Sanborn Rd. (☎867-9959, reservations 355-2201. Open Apr. to mid-Oct. for walk-in camping. Open for day use year-round from 8am to sunset. Sites $8; RVs $25.)

Sanborn Park Hostel (HI-AYH), 15808 Sanborn Rd. (☎ 741-0166), in Sanborn-Skyline County Park, 13 mi. west of San Jose. Those looking for peace and quiet are in luck; this beautiful facility lies among redwoods, golden fields and freshwater ponds. Clean rooms and 39 beds. Linen $0.50. Reception 5am-10:30pm. Check-out 9am. 11pm-7am curfew strictly enforced. Limited wheelchair access; call ahead. Dorms $10, US non-HI-AYH members $12, foreign non-members $13, under 18 $5. ❶

San Jose State University, 375 S. 9th St. (☎ 924-6192), at San Salvador St. Residence halls open to visitors June to early Aug. Shared kitchenette, lounge with billiards, and big-screen TV. Parking $2 per night. Reception 7:30am-10:30pm. Call ahead to reserve. Singles $35, shared doubles $25 per person, shared triples $21 per person. ❸

◖ FOOD

Familiar fast-food franchises and pizzerias surround the campus of SJSU. More international cheap eats lie along **South 1st Street** or near **San Pedro Square**, at St. John and San Pedro St. A **farmer's market** takes place at San Pedro Sq. (late May to mid-Nov. F 10am-2pm.)

House of Siam, 55 S. Market St. (☎ 279-5668). Well-decorated restaurant features excellent Thai entrees (some meatless) $8-15. Beware the spice level! Open M-F 11am-3pm and 5-10pm, Sa-Su 11:30am-10pm. ❸

California Sushi and Grill, 1 E. San Fernando St. (☎ 297-1847). Pacific Rim joint serves up super sushi ($4-5) and rolls ($4-8). Filling tempura, rice, and miso soup lunch ($8.50) and dinner ($13) plates. Open M-F 11:30am-2pm and 5-9pm, Sa 5-9pm. ❷

Bella Mia, 58 S. 1st St. (☎ 280-1993). This self-proclaimed "San Jose Original" has dishes to please all palates (entrees $13-26). Delicious Su brunches (11am-3pm) and special dinner nights (like Murder Mystery and Comedy Cocktail for example; ask the host for tickets). Open M-F 11am-9:30pm, Sa 5-9:30pm, Su 11am-9pm. ❹

◉ SIGHTS

Geographically contained within the Santa Clara Valley and politically bounded by Santa Clara County, the San Jose area lacks organization or a recognizable center. In fact, despite San Jose's efforts to bill itself as the "Capital of Silicon Valley" based on its large population, many of the corporate headquarters of high-tech giants like Intel and Hewlett-Packard are actually in Mountain View and Sunnyvale, just up the peninsula toward San Francisco. These companies are wary of visitors, and tourists will only see anonymous, low-profile buildings of mirrored glass. In San Jose proper, a few well-funded museums are the only real diversions.

WINCHESTER MYSTERY HOUSE. This odd Victorian house is little more than that, but for those with a penchant for the unusual, the (space) ship has landed. Sarah Winchester, the eccentric, if not simply crazy, heir to the Winchester rifle fortune, was convinced by an occultist after the death of her daughter and husband that she was being punished by the spirits of all the men ever killed by her family's guns, and would continue to face vengeance if construction on her home ever ceased. Work on the mansion continued 24hr. a day for over 38 years. A 160 room maze of doors, windows and stairs elaborately designed to "confuse the spirits" is the end result. *(1525 S. Winchester Blvd. Near the intersection of I-880 and I-280, west of town. ☎ 247-2101. Open Oct.-Apr. and June-Aug. daily 9am-7pm; May and Sept. Su-Th 9am-5pm, F-Sa 9am-7pm. Three different tours, each lasting 1-2½hr., depart every 15-30min. $14-24.)*

ROSICRUCIAN EGYPTIAN MUSEUM. Rising out of the suburbs like the work of a mad pharaoh, this grand structure houses an extensive collection of Egyptian and ancient civilization artifacts, including a walk-in tomb and spooky animal mummies. The collection belongs to the ancient and mystical order of the Rosae Crucis, whose past members include Amenhotep IV, Pythagoras, Sir Francis Bacon, Rene Descartes, Benjamin Franklin, and Isaac Newton. The Rosicrucian Order claims to "provide a systematic approach to the study of higher wisdom that empowers you to find the answers to your questions about the workings of the universe and the interconnectedness of all life." Join a free tour by the friendly staff. *(1342 Naglee Ave. at Park Ave. ☎ 947-3635; www.rosicrucian.org. Open Tu-Fr 10am-5pm, Sa-Su 11am-6pm. $9, students and seniors $7, under 10 $5. Under 15 must be accompanied by an adult.)*

TECH MUSEUM OF INNOVATION. This is the most tourist savvy attraction in San Jose, and perfect for little and big kids alike. Underwritten by high-tech firms, the Tech features hands-on cutting-edge science exhibits and an IMAX theater, all in a sleek geometric environment. The most recent addition, "Imagination Playground," is geared toward younger children and includes the latest high-tech toys. *(201 S. Market St. ☎ 294-8324. Exhibits open daily 10am-5pm. $9, seniors $8, ages 3-12 $7; combination tickets for exhibits and one IMAX film: $16, 15, and 13.)*

THE SAN JOSE MUSEUM OF ART. Neighbor to the Tech, this modern museum not only features contemporary art but is itself progressive in design and mission—it recently made admission free to help open the fine arts to the masses. *(110 S. Market St. ☎ 294-2787. Open Tu-Su 11am-5pm, F 11am-10pm. Admission free.)*

OTHER MUSEUMS. The **Children's Discovery Museum,** across from the light-rail station, is filled with hands-on and science-based toys. *(180 Woz Way. ☎ 298-5437; www.cdm.org. Open Tu-Sa 10am-5pm, Su noon-5pm. $6, seniors $5.)* Nearby stands the **San Jose Institute of Contemporary Art (SJICA),** 451 S. 1st St. *(☎ 283-8155; open Tu-Sa noon-5pm)* and the **Center for Latino Arts,** 510 S. 1st St. *(☎ 998-2783; open W-Sa noon-5pm).*

NIGHTLIFE

The brightest spot is the strip of downtown known as the SoFA District on 1st St., which runs north-south. **Bars are 21+ unless otherwise noted.**

Katie Bloom's Irish Pub and Restaurant, 150 S. 1st St. (☎ 294-4408). It's clear why "pub" precedes "restaurant" in the name. Drink imported beers ($4, happy hour 4-7pm $2.75) as Oscar Wilde and James Joyce stare down from their posts at the walls. Extensive space includes many private leather booths as well as rowdier counter spots. Open M-F 11am-2am, Sa-Su 2pm-2am.

Wine Galleria, 377 S. 1st St. (☎ 298-1386). Stands between Cafe Matisse and d.p. Fong Galleries to form a triumvirate of "Art for the Senses." Sample wines by the glass ($5-12) or bottle ($12-600 available; $12-40 is average) as you browse through blown glass sculptures or cuddle on comfy leather sofas. Galleria open Tu-Sa 5pm-12am; Cafe Matisse open M-Th 7:30am-12am, F 7:30am-2am, Sa 8am-2am, Su 9am-12am; d.p. Fong Tu-Sa 1-6pm or by appointment.

Agenda, 399 S. 1st St. (☎ 287-3991). Eat a tasty dish of New American cuisine ($15-27) and then head to the outdoor patio to hear the hottest acid jazz in town for free (non-diners must pay cover). It gets crowded, so plan on eating earlier to get great tables (show starts at 8pm). Upstairs lounge serves 25 microbrews. Open Tu-Sa 5:30pm-2am (kitchen closes at 10pm).

🎵 🎯 ENTERTAINMENT, SEASONAL EVENTS, & SPORTS

For information on entertainment events, look for the weekly *Metro*, available free on downtown street corners. **City Lights,** 529 S. 2nd St. (☎295-4200; www.cltc.org) at William St., offers unique, cutting-edge theater in an intimate and flexible seating space. Local actors put on a variety of performances—classics, adaptations, and some original work. **Camera Cinemas** (☎998-3300) shows art-house, classic, and foreign flicks, as well as film festivals at three locations: **Camera 1,** 366 S. 1st St., **Camera 3,** at S. 2nd and San Carlos St., and **Towne 3,** 1433 The Alameda (☎287-1433). The **cafe** at Camera 3 offers sandwiches like "Tokyo Decadence" (teriyaki-marinated chicken, mozzarella, and veggies on toast, $6) and "Deja vu" (vegan, $5.25). Sandwiches come with blue tortilla chips and salsa. (Open daily 11am-11pm.) The **Student Union and Concert Hall,** 1 Washington Sq. (☎924-1120), at SJSU, hosts concerts and other performances. Concert hall performances are free on Thursdays during the school year.

Topping the list of annual highlights is the May **Blues Festival** (☎924-6262), the biggest, baddest concert in Northern California. On the last weekend in September, the **San Pedro Square Brew-Ha-Ha** fills the downtown area with microbrew sampling, stand-up comedy, and fun for all. (☎279-1775.)

The **San Jose Sharks** (☎287-7070), the city's NHL team, play at the San Jose Arena. Soccer fans can kick it with the **San Jose Earthquakes** (☎260-6300) at Spartan Stadium, on 7th St. off I-280.

NEAR SAN JOSE

SANTA CLARA

Take U.S. 101 to the De La Cruz Exit and follow signs to Santa Clara University. A suburb of a suburb, the small town of Santa Clara lies between San Jose to the southeast and the gargantuan Great America, a Paramount-owned theme park, to the north.

Paramount's Great America theme park is a forest of roller coasters, log rides, and other fiendish contraptions designed to spin you, flip you, soak you, drop you, and generally separate you from your stomach. If you come on a weekday, you'll beat some of the crowds. *(Off U.S. 101 at Great America Pkwy. ☎988-1776. Open June-Aug. Su-F 10am-9pm, Sa 10am-10pm; Mar.-May and Sept.-Oct. Sa 10am-10pm, Su 10am-9pm. $37, seniors and wheelchair-bound $27, ages 3-6 $20. Parking $6.)* Get all wet at Paramount's **Raging Waters,** the area's best collection of waterslides. It's great on a hot day, but don't expect to be the only one seeking a soaking. *(Off U.S. 101 at Tully Rd. Exit. ☎654-5450. Open June-Aug. daily 10am-6pm; May and Sept. Sa-Su 10am-6pm. $23, seniors $16, under 42 in. $19; after 3pm $20, under 42 in. $16.)*

Mission Santa Clara was the first California mission to honor a woman—Clare of Assisi—as its patron saint. The mission was established on the Guadalupe River in 1777, moving to its present site in 1825. The mission church, where summer masses are held, houses a functioning organ. Santa Clara University, which is built around the mission, was established in 1851, making it California's oldest institution of higher learning. Subsequent restorations have refitted the structures to match the beauty and bliss of the surrounding rose gardens and 200-year-old olive trees. *(500 El Camino Real. Mass M-F noon, Su 10am.)*

SAN MATEO COUNTY   ☎650

The bluffs of the San Mateo County Coast obscure the hectic urban pace of the city to the north. Most of the energy here is generated by the coastal winds and waves. The Pacific Coast Highway (PCH) maneuvers its way along a rocky shoreline past colorful beach vistas, generations-old ranches, and the small communities of Pacifica, Half Moon Bay, and Pescadero. The forests of La Honda and the suburban sprawl of Burlingame rest inland. Although it's possible to drive quickly down the coast from San Francisco to Santa Cruz, haste is waste—especially if you drive off a cliff.

◢◣ ⚡ ORIENTATION & PRACTICAL INFORMATION

On this stretch of the Pacific coast, it's good to have a car. Stunning ocean views off **Highway 1** compete with the road for drivers' attentions. Hwy. 1 winds along the San Mateo County Coast from San Francisco to Big Basin Redwoods State Park. This expanse of shore is scattered with isolated, sandy beaches, most of which are too cold for swimming. Keep your eyes peeled for the unmarked, stunning, crowdless beaches along the coast. If traveling by sneaker, you'll have a tougher time. SamTrans services the area only somewhat successfully (see below). Bus route maps are available at CalTrain and BART stations. The shore from Pacifica to Half Moon Bay is serviced by buses #1C, 1L, and 90H.

Public transportation: San Mateo County Transit (SamTrans), 945 California Dr. (within county ☎ 508-6455, elsewhere 800-660-4287; www.samtrans.com). Bus #17 and #294 service Half Moon Bay, on a limited basis. **#17** runs along the coast from El Granada to Half Moon Bay (6am-5:30pm). **#294** runs from Hillsdale to Linda Mar Park-and-Ride and from San Mateo to Pacifica (M-F 5:30am-7:30pm, Sa-Su only from Linda Mar to Half Moon Bay). Bus route maps are available at CalTrain and BART stations; call for specific schedule times. $1.25, seniors and disabled $0.60, ages 5-17 $0.75, under 5 free. Monthly pass $40; seniors and disabled $18, youth 5-17 $22.

Bike Rental: The Bike Works, 20 Stone Pine Ctr. (☎ 726-6708), off Main St. Friendly staff will set you up with a mountain bike. ($7 per hr., $35 per day; helmet included.) Open M-F 10am-6pm, Sa 10am-5pm, Su 11am-4pm.

Visitor Information:

Half Moon Bay Coastside Chamber of Commerce and Visitors Bureau, 520 Kelly Ave. (☎ 726-8380; www.halfmoonbaychamber.org). An amiable staff, lots of brochures, and local bus service maps sit in a Victorian house just east of Rte. 1. Open M-F 9am-4pm.

San Mateo County Convention and Visitors Bureau, Seabreeze Plaza, 111 Anza Blvd. #410 (☎ 800-288-4748). Get off 101 at the Broadway Exit, follow signs to Airport Blvd., take a left, and follow road around to Anza Blvd. Turn left; it's the mirrored building on your right, across the street from the Embassy Hotel. Near SFO, this sleek office offers info on the Central Coast and San Francisco area, including brochures and helpful maps. Open M-F 8:30am-5pm.

San Mateo County Parks and Recreation Department, James V. Fitzgerald Marine Life Reserve, P.O. Box 451, Moss Beach (☎ 728-3584), off Rte. 1, 7 mi. north of Half Moon Bay. Open daily dawn-dusk.

Police: Half Moon Bay: 537 Kelly Ave. (☎ 726-8288). **San Mateo General Information:** ☎ 522-7710.

Library and Internet Access: Half Moon Bay Library, 620 Correas St. (☎ 726-2316), off Main St. Free Internet. Open M-W 10am-8pm, Th 1-8pm, F 10am-6pm, Sa 10am-5pm, Su 1-5pm.

Post Offices: Half Moon Bay: 500 Stone Pine Rd., at Main St. Open M-F 8:30am-5pm, Sa 8:30am-noon. **Postal Code:** 94019. **San Mateo:** 1630 S. Delaware St. Open M-F 8:30am-5pm, Sa 8:30am-12:30pm. **Postal Code:** 94402.

⌂ ACCOMMODATIONS & CAMPING

▧ **HI-AYH Point Montara Lighthouse Hostel,** on Lighthouse Point (☎ 728-7177), at Rte. 1 and 16th St., 25 mi. south of San Francisco and 4 mi. north of Half Moon Bay. SamTrans #294 stops 1 block north of the hostel. Weary travelers will revel in this isolated 45-bed facility with 2 kitchens and serene surroundings. Curfew 11pm; gate locks.

FROM THE ROAD

STRANGE DAY

I decided to venture (fully clothed) to the clothing "optional" Gray Whale Cove Beach, during a much-anticipated solar eclipse. Once there, I found myself surrounded by middle-aged, slightly overweight, naked men. I took notes (ugh...) and one of them mistook me for some sort of expert. "Are you the volunteer they sent?" he asked. "This sea lion is sick but we're not sure what's wrong with it. There's supposed to be some bacterial infection in the water and we're waiting on somebody from Animal Control."

To complicate the already complicated drama, the man was quickly informed by one of his friends that the police were here. I thought they would help the sea lion, but they were here for the guy instead. "I don't know how long this is going to take," he said, "or if I'm going to come back. Can you please stay here as long as possible, watch [the sea lion], make sure nobody gets close or touches him, until help comes. It would mean a lot."

I waited until help arrived and was informed that standard procedure is to see if the sea lion is dead by morning. If it isn't it gets help, if it is, that's the circle of life.

–Shawn Snyder

Make reservations by phone well in advance for weekends, groups, and private rooms. $15, nonmembers $18, children $10; $12 extra for private rooms. ❶

HI-AYH Pigeon Point Lighthouse Hostel, on Rte. 1 (☎879-0633), 6 mi. south of Pescadero. 4 houses, each with a homey common room and equipped kitchen. 53 beds. Chores required. Check-in 4:30pm. Check-out 10am. Lockout 10am-4:30pm. Curfew 11pm. Reservations recommended. Phone reservations 5:30-10pm. Dorms $15, nonmembers $18; extra $15 for 2-person rooms. ❶

Costanoa, 2001 Rossi Rd. (☎879-1100, reservations ☎262-7848; www.costanoa.com), on the east side of Rte 1, 25 mi. south of Half Moon Bay, between Pigeon Pt. and Ano Nueva. The Ritz Carlton of roughing it. All accommodations include access to dry sauna and showers with heated floors. Campsites $30-40; canvas cabins (includes heated mattress) $95-130; lodges $205-240. ❺

Francis Beach Campground, 95 Kelly Ave. (☎726-8820), on Francis Beach. 57 campsites with firepits and picnic tables. Clean bathrooms. June 1-Sept. 30 7-night max. stay; off-season 15-night max. stay. Check-out noon. No reservations. Tent and RV sites $12; seniors $10. Hiker and biker sites $1 per person; 1-night max. stay. Day use of beach $2; seniors $1. Hot showers $0.25 per 2min. ❶

Butano State Park Campground, 5 mi. south of Pescadero (☎879-2040). From the north, take Pescadero Rd. east from Rte. 1 to Cloverdale. From the south, take Gazos Creek from Rte. 1. No showers. Check-out noon. Reservations recommended Memorial Day-Labor Day; call ReserveAmerica (☎800-444-7275). 21 drive-in and 18 walk-in sites $12, seniors $10; trail camp sites $7; day use of park $2. ❶

🍴 FOOD

Despite the area's remote feel, a surprising number of restaurants cater to hungry travelers. Those looking for late-night snacks or planning to picnic along the coast can find a 24hr. **Safeway** at the junction of Hwy. 1 and 92.

3-Zero, 8850 Hwy. 1 (☎728-1411, www.3-zero.com), at the Half Moon Bay Airport. Watch planes take off, while you stay grounded with your huge and hearty down-home style breakfast ($4-8). Menu and owner come equipped with wit and charm. Also serves "launch" (lunch, $5.50-8). Open daily 7am-3pm. ❷

The Flying Fish Grill, (☎712-1125), at Main St. and Rte. 92 in Half Moon Bay. This small roadside cafe serves inexpensive, fresh local seafood. Famous fish tacos $3-5. Other oceanic offerings $7-14. Open Tu-Su 11:30am-8:30pm. ❷

It's Italia Pizzeria, 40 K Stone Pine Ctr. (☎726-4444), off Main St in Half Moon Bay. Turn right off 92, head south on Main St., and Stone Pine Ctr. is on your left. Locals love this upscale pizza joint. It's bright and busy, but a little pricey (small cheese pizza $8.25, pasta and entrees $9-16). Open daily 11:30am-9:30pm. ❸

Jeffrey's, 42 South B St. (☎348-8698), in San Mateo. This hearty independent hamburger joint is somewhere between a dive and a nice family restaurant. Try an avocado burger ($5.50). Open daily 11am-9pm. ❷

Taqueria La Cumre, 28 North B St. (☎344-8989), in San Mateo. This restaurant, which also has a San Francisco branch, has won the "best burrito" award in every major Bay Area magazine. Filling, tasty Mexican meals for under $8.50. Be prepared for long lines at lunchtime. Open Su-Th 11am-9pm, F-Sa 11am-10pm. ❷

🜨 ⚠ SIGHTS & OUTDOOR ACTIVITIES

Wide, sandy, and fairly deserted **state beaches** dot the coast along Rte. 1 (Cabrillo Hwy.) in San Mateo County. Each state beach charges $2 (though this fee is only loosely enforced), a fare which covers admission to *all* state parks for the entire day. All beaches have parking lots and restrooms and are open daily 8am-sunset. Keep your eyes peeled for unmarked beaches along the coast; they're often breathtaking, crowdless spots with free parking. The water is too chilly for most swimmers, and surfers never venture out without full-body wetsuits. Rip currents and undertows are frequent, so be careful if you choose to brave the cold. The creeks near these beaches are often contaminated—signs will be posted at entrances to warn you, but simply staying out of them is generally a good idea.

GRAY WHALE COVE BEACH. This stunning (and startling) beach, shielded by high bluffs from the highway above, used to be one of the more popular *private* nude beaches in the Bay Area. Now legendary as the first "clothing-optional" (as they say in progressive Northern California) *state* beach, Gray Whale Cove offers some of the most gorgeous and not so gorgeous views on the coast. *(12 mi. south of San Francisco, in Devil's Slide. You'll know it by the large parking lot on your left; it's the only one in the Slide. Take SamTrans bus #1L. Open daily 8am-sunset. $2.)*

HALF MOON BAY STATE BEACH. Lining the coast next to town, **Half Moon Bay State Beach** is actually composed of four smaller beaches strung together. The **Coastal Trail,** a paved path perfect for joggers, bikers, and dogwalkers, runs 3 mi. along all four beaches and then continues north. At the end of Kelly Ave., **Francis Beach** lies closest to town and is the southernmost of the four beaches. Although it's the least scenic of the bunch, it is the only one with a campsite (**Francis Beach Campground,** p. 148), a guard station that operates year-round, and wheelchair accessibility. To the north of Francis, the wider and prettier **Venice Beach** is down a flight of stairs at the end of a dirt road leading from Venice Blvd. off Rte. 1. **Dunes Beach** and **Roosevelt Beach** are down a short but steep trail at the end of Young Ave. off Rte. 1. Strong tides and undertows make swimming dangerous at the beaches, but they also create great waves and winds for board- and windsurfing—if you don't want to participate, just watching these sports can be an activity in itself. Windsurfers have to go a ways out to sea to catch the strong gusts because the half-moon shape of the bay protects the shores, making for wonderful picnicking and sunbathing options. *(The beach lines the coast right next to the town of Half Moon Bay. Francis Beach ☎726-8820.)*

DOWNTOWN HALF MOON BAY. The **Community United Methodist Church,** built in 1872, stands as a well-kept example of the city's registered landmarks. The **Half Moon Bay Jail,** just two houses north of the church, was built in 1911 and used as an incarceration facility for the entire county. Today, the austere building houses artifacts from Half Moon Bay's Spanishtown. **Johnston House,** at the south end of Main St., built in 1853 by 49er James Johnston, is the earliest American home still standing along the San Mateo County coastline, as well as one of the few examples of "New

England" salt box architecture on the West Coast. *(Church: at the corner of Johnston and Miramontes St. ☎ 726-4621. Jail: 505 Johnston St. ☎ 726-7084; www.spanishtownhs.org. Open Sa-Su 1-4pm. Johnston House: Drive to south end of Main St., make a left on Higgins Canyon Rd. ☎ 726-0329; www.johnstonhousehmb.org.)*

SAN GREGORIO & POMPONIO STATE BEACHES. These two beaches are dramatically set below the most scenic stretch of Hwy. 1. Of all of the beaches in the area, they are arguably the most picturesque—and often the most deserted. Walk to the southern end of San Gregorio to find little caves in the shore rocks. Between San Gregorio and Pomponio State Beaches, there allegedly rests a gorgeous, less frequented beach at the unmarked turnout at Marker 27.35 along Rte. 1. It's difficult to find without aid; keep an eye out for mysteriously vacant cars parked along the highway. *(San Gregorio: 8 mi. south of Half Moon Bay. Pomponio: 10 mi. south of Half Moon Bay. Both open daily 8am-sunset. $2.)*

PEBBLE BEACH & PIGEON POINT. Though threatening signs attempt to discourage them from doing so, kids tend to pocket handfuls of tiny, smooth pebbles from **Pebble Beach.** Law-abiding parents have been known, however, to mail the stolen stones back to the Half Moon Bay Visitors Center. A paved and level trail heads south from the parking lot along the bluffs; reaching the tidal pools below for exploration requires a bit of a climb down. **Pigeon Point,** 4 mi. south of Pebble Beach, takes its name from a hapless schooner that crashed into the rocky shore on its inaugural voyage in 1853. The point turns heads with its tidepools, 30 ft. plumes of surf, and 115 ft. operating lighthouse (the tallest on the West Coast) which houses 1008 glass prisms. *(Pebble Beach: 19 mi. south of Half Moon Bay, 2 mi. south of Pescadero Rd. Open 8am-sunset. $2. Pigeon Point: 23 mi. south of Half Moon Bay, 6 mi. south of Pescadero Rd. Lighthouse and Point info ☎ 879-2120; hostel info 879-0633. Tours F-Su 10:30am-4pm.)*

AÑO NUEVO STATE RESERVE. This wildlife reserve has several hiking trails that offer views of Año Nuevo Island, the site of an abandoned lighthouse now taken over by birds, seals, and sea lions. Free hiking permits are available at the ranger station by the entrance and at the **Visitors Center** (though seal-viewing permits are only issued up until 3:30pm). The Visitors Center also features real-time videos displaying the animal adventures on the island. From mid-December to late March, the reserve is the mating place of the 15 ft., 4500 lb. **elephant seal.** Like frat boys looking to score, thousands of fat seals crowd the shore, and the males fight each other for dominance over a herd of females. Before mid-August, you can still see the last of the "molters" and the young who have yet to find their sea legs. Don't get too close—if they don't get you, the cops might; law requires staying 25 ft. away at all times. *(50 mi. south of San Francisco, 25 mi. south of Half Moon Bay, and 20 mi. north of Santa Cruz. Park information ☎ 879-0227. Open daily 8am-sunset. Visitors Center: open daily 8:30am-3:30pm. Parking $2; seniors $1. Make reservations by calling ReserveAmerica ☎ 800-444-4445. Tickets go on sale November 15 and are generally sold out within a week or two. 2½hr. guided tours $4.)*

HILLER AVIATION MUSEUM. For the airplane enthusiast, this impressively packed museum features flying machines from past and present, as well as imaginative renditions of future models. *(601 Skyway Rd. From San Francisco take U.S. 101. south to Holly St./Redwood Shores Pkwy. Exit. Go east onto Redwood Shores Pkwy., right onto Airport Rd. and right onto Skyway Rd. ☎ 654-0200. Open daily 10am-5pm. $8, seniors and 8-17 $5, under 8 free.)*

COYOTE POINT RECREATION AREA & MUSEUM. For the animal enthusiast, the recreation area features a small but impressive array of live animals in natural habitats, including an aviary and an aquarium. The park also offers great waterside views of the planes flying into SFO. *(1651 Coyote Point Dr. From San Francisco, take U.S. 101 to*

Poplar Ave. Exit just south of the airport. Follow signs into Coyote Point Recreation Area and Museum. Recreation Area: ☎573-2592. Open in summer 8am-8pm; in winter 8am-5:30pm. Park admission $4 per car. Museum: ☎ 342-7755. Open Tu-Sa 10am-5pm, Su noon-5pm. $3, seniors and ages 13-17 $2, ages 4-12 $1, under 12 free.)

PARKS AND TRAILS. Memorial County Park offers 65 mi. of redwood trails, open to hiking, horseback riding, and some to bicycling, stretching through their three parks. The **Heritage Grove** spans 12 sq. mi. and has the oldest and largest redwood trees in the Santa Cruz mountains. Among the many redwood parks, **Butano State Park** also stands out for its sweeping views of the Pacific Ocean. Its 3200 acres offers 20 mi. of hiking and mountain biking trails off Pescadero Rd., 9 mi east of Rte. 1. For those who prefer concrete, but still want scenic settings, the **Sawyer Camp Trail** is popular among the local bicyclist, rollerblader, jogger, and hiker set. It stretches 10 mi. along the Crystal Springs reservoir. *(Memorial: Pescadero Rd. Go east from Rte. 1 to Cloverdale. ☎879-0212. Visitor Center open May-Sept. daily 10am-4pm. Heritage: Pescadero Rd. to Alpine, make a right. Butano: 5 mi. south of Pescadero. From the north, take Pescadero Rd. east from Rte. 1 to Cloverdale. From the south, take Gazos Creek from Rte. 1 to Cloverdale. ☎879-2040. Sawyer: 1801 Crystal Springs Rd. ☎589-4294. Open M-F. Prior to arrival, visitors with disabilities who need assistance should contact ☎800-777-0369; www.parks.ca.gov.)*

FILOLI ESTATE. If "old money" is your bag, check out this rare, historically important example of an early 1900s country estate, including a pristine Gregorian Revival House and a magnificent 16-acre garden. *(On Canada Road. From San Francisco, take I-280 South to Edgewood Rd. west, turn right on Canada Rd. ☎ 364-8300; www.filoli.org. House and Garden tours Tu-Sa 10am-2:30pm. Closed Oct.-Feb. $10, ages 7-12 $1, under 7 free, students $5.)*

BURLINGAME MUSEUM OF PEZ MEMORABILIA. Admission to the largest public display of Pez Candy Dispensers in the world is (thankfully) free. Enjoy the smaller (bit-sized, really) things in life at this once-in-a-lifetime stop. *(214 California Dr., between Burlingame and Howard Ave. Get off U.S. 101 at Broadway Ave., head west, and turn left on California Dr. Also accessible by CalTrain; get off at the Burlingame Station. ☎347-2301; www.burlingamepezmuseum.com. Open Tu-Sa 10am-6pm.)*

LA HONDA. A winding cross-peninsular trip down Rte. 84 will bring you to the little logging town in the redwoods where author Ken Kesey lived with his merry pranksters in the 1960s, before it got too small and they took off across the US in a psychedelic bus. The shady, scenic drive makes this detour worthwhile, even if you aren't familiar with Kesey's gang, but *Let's Go* recommends reading a copy of Tom Wolfe's ▨*The Electric Kool-Aid Acid Test* before making the journey.

NORTH BAY & WINE COUNTRY

MARIN COUNTY ☎415

Just across the Golden Gate Bridge, the jacuzzi of the bay—Marin (muh-RIN) County—bubbles over with money-making and mantra-spouting residents who help the area strike the perfect balance between upscale chic and counter-culture nostalgia. Despite (or is it because of?) the yuppie reincarnation of the quintessential-San Francisco hippie, Marin is strikingly beautiful, politically liberal, and stinking rich. If the locals seem a little smug, well, why shouldn't they be? The cathedral stillness of ancient redwoods, the sweet-smelling eucalyptus, the brilliant wildflowers, and the high bluffs and crashing surf along Rte. 1 are ample justification for civic pride.

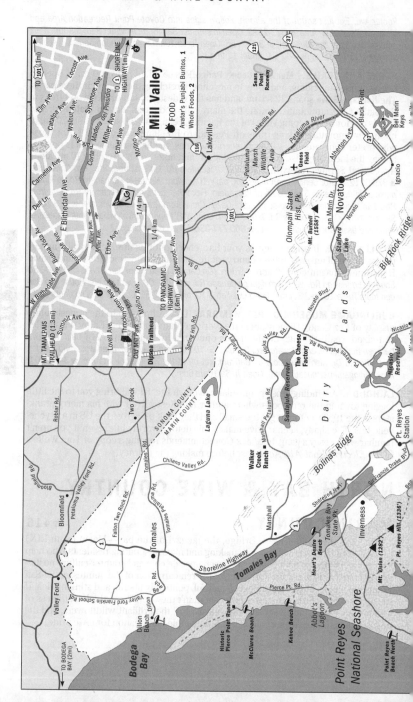

Mill Valley

● FOOD

Avatar's Punjabi Buritos, **1**
Whole Foods, **2**

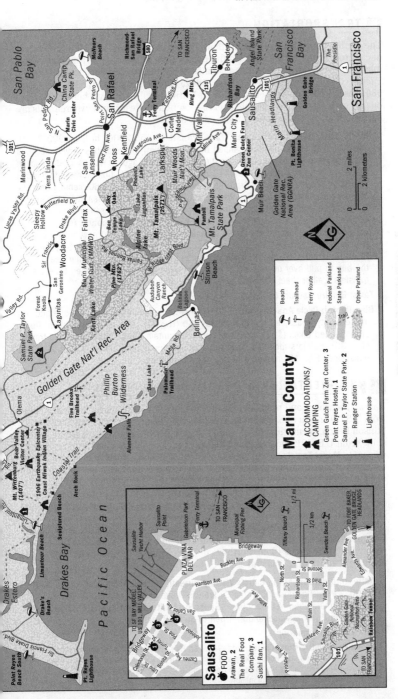

Marin County

ACCOMMODATIONS/ CAMPING
Green Gulch Farm Zen Center, **3**
Point Reyes Hostel, **1**
Samuel P. Taylor State Park, **2**

▲ Ranger Station
ℹ Lighthouse

Beach
Trailhead
Ferry Route
Federal Parkland
State Parkland
Other Parkland

Sausalito

🍴 FOOD
Arawan, **2**
The Real Food Company, **3**
Sushi Ran, **1**

San Pablo Bay

McNears Beach

Richmond-San Rafael Bridge

580

TO SAN FRANCISCO

China Camp State Pk.

Marin Civic Center

Ferry Terminal

San Rafael

Tiburon

Belvedere

Angel Island State Park

San Francisco Bay

Ring Mtn.

131

Paradise Dr.

Richardson Bay

Sausalito

The Presidio

Point San Pedro

N San Pedro Rd.

Lucas Valley Rd.

Marinwood

Terra Linda

Sleepy Hollow

Butterfield Dr.

Drake Blvd.

Fairfax

Woodacre

San Geronimo

Lagunitas

Forest Knolls

Valley Rd.

Samuel P. Taylor State Park

Olema

101

Sir Francis Drake Blvd.

Red Hill Ave.

San Anselmo

Ross

Kentfield

Magnolia Ave.

Corte Madera

Larkspur

Mill Valley

Marin City

Green Gulch Farm

Zen Center

Golden Gate Bridge

San Francisco

1

Muir Woods Nat'l Mon.

Miller Ave.

Muir Beach

Marin Headlands

Pt. Bonita Lighthouse

Golden Gate National Rec. Area (GGNRA)

Sky Oaks

Bon Tempe Lake

Phoenix Lake

Lagunitas Lake

Alpine Lake

Mt. Tamalpais (2571')

Pantoll

Mt. Tamalpais State Park

Marin Municipal Water Dist. (MMWD)

Fairfax-Bolinas Rd.

Pine Mtn. (1762')

Kent Lake

W. Ridge Crest Blvd.

Stinson Beach

Audubon Canyon Ranch

Bolinas

Bolinas Lagoon

Mesa Rd.

Bass Lake

Phillip Burton Wilderness

Golden Gate Nat'l Rec. Area

Five Brooks Trailhead

Palomarin Trailhead

Alamere Falls

Coastal Trail

Arch Rock

Sculptured Beach

Limantour Beach

Drakes Bay

Drake's Estero

Pt. Reyes Lighthouse

Point Reyes Beach South

Sir Francis Drake Blvd.

Drake's Beach

Pacific Ocean

Mt. Wittenburg (1407')

Bear Valley Visitor Center

1906 Earthquake Epicenter

Coast Miwok Indian Village

TO SF BAY MODEL

Bridgeway

Johnson St.

Caledonia St.

Pine St.

Bonita St.

San Carlos Ave.

Gabrielson Park

Sausalito Point

Sausalito Yacht Harbor

Ferry Terminal

TO SAN FRANCISCO

Municipal Fishing Pier

Tiffany Beach

Swedes Beach

Bridgeway

PLAZA VINA DEL MAR

Second St.

Third St.

North St.

Valley St.

Main St.

Richardson St.

Buckley Ave.

Harrison Ave.

Miller Ave.

Alexander Ave.

Edwards Ave.

Crescent Ave.

Sausalito Blvd.

Golden Gate National Recreation Area

TO FORT BAKER, GOLDEN GATE BRIDGE, HEADLANDS

Rainbow Tunnel

TO SAN FRANCISCO

101

0   1/2 mi
0   1/2 km

N

⌐ TRANSPORTATION

The Marin peninsula lies at the northern end of the San Francisco Bay and is connected to the city by **U.S. 101** via the **Golden Gate Bridge.** U.S. 101 extends north inland to Santa Rosa and Sonoma County, while **Highway 1** winds north along the Pacific coast. The **Richmond-San Rafael Bridge** connects Marin to the East Bay via I-**580. Gas** is scarce and expensive in West Marin, so fill up in town before you head out for the coast. Drivers should exercise caution in West Marin, where roads are narrow, sinuous, and perched on the edges of cliffs.

Public Transportation: Golden Gate Transit (☎455-2000, in SF ☎923-2000; www.goldengate.org; phones manned daily 7am-7pm), provides bus service between **San Francisco** and Marin County via the Golden Gate Bridge, as well as local service in Marin. Within Marin County, bus #63 runs on the weekends from Marin City through Sausalito, Mount Tamalpais State Park, and Stinson Beach ($4.60, seniors and disabled $2.30, under 18 $3.45, under 6 free). Bus #65 goes from San Rafael to Samuel P. Taylor Park and Point Reyes Station on weekends ($4.75, seniors and disabled $2.35, under 18 $3.55, under 6 free). **West Marin Stagecoach** (☎454-0964; www.marin-stagecoach.org; phones manned between 8am-5pm) now provides weekday service connecting West Marin communities to the rest of the county. Stops include Pt. Reyes Station, Samuel P. Taylor State Park, Stinson Beach, and Muir Beach. Flag the bus to pull over or drop off between scheduled stops. Free Golden Gate Transit transfers. Call or check the website for specific schedules. $1.50.

Taxis: Belaire Cab Co. (☎388-1234). Open 24hr.

Bike Rental: Cycle Analysis (☎663-9164; www.cyclepointreyes.com), out of a hitch-up in the empty, grassy lot at 4th and Main St. (Hwy. 1) in Point Reyes Station. Rents unsuspended bikes ($30), front-suspension mountain bikes ($35), and child trailers ($25-30). Helmets included. Also does emergency repairs and sets up self-guided tours. Open F-Su 10am-5pm, weekdays by appointment.

✴ ⚡ ORIENTATION & PRACTICAL INFORMATION

National seashore and park land constitutes most of West Marin. **Highway 1** splits from U.S. 101 north of Sausalito and runs up the Pacific coast through Muir Beach, Stinson Beach, Olema, Inverness, and Pt. Reyes. About 4 mi. north of where Hwy. 1 splits from U.S. 101, the **Panoramic Highway** branches off of Hwy. 1 and winds its way up to **Mount Tamalpais** and the Muir Woods. The **Marin Headlands** sit 10 mi. from downtown San Francisco, just across the Golden Gate Bridge. Beaches and coastal wonders line Hwy. 1, which runs along the Marin coast from Marin City and continues north. Slightly inland, Mt. Tamalpais is about 15 mi. northwest of San Francisco; the state park encompasses a large area just inside the coast from Muir Beach to around Stinson Beach. Muir Woods stands about 5 mi. west of U.S. 101 on Hwy. 1. And the **Point Reyes National Seashore,** a near-island surrounded by 100 mi. of isolated coastline, is a wilderness of pine forests, chaparral ridges, and grassy flatlands, about 15 mi. northwest of San Francisco. **Point Reyes Station** sits about 2 mi. north of Olema and about 20 mi. northwest of San Francisco.

Visitor Information: Marin County Visitors Bureau, 1013 Larkspur Landing Cir. (☎499-5000; www.visitmarin.org), off the Sir Francis Drake Blvd. Exit from U.S. 101, near the ferry terminal. Open M-F 9am-5pm. **Sausalito Visitors Center,** 780 Bridgeway Ave. (☎332-0505; www.sausalito.org). Open Tu-Su 11:30am-4pm.

Park Visitor Information:

Marin Headlands Visitors Center, Bldg. 948, Fort Barry (☎331-1540), at Bunker and Field Rd. Talk to the helpful staff about hiking and biking in the park, and pick up permits for free campsites, maps, and trail advice. Also a museum and a store with artifacts, exhibits on the history of the Headlands, and models of military buildings and equipment. Open daily 9:30am-4:30pm.

Point Reyes National Seashore Headquarters (also referred to as **Bear Valley Visitor Center;** ☎464-5100; www.nps.gov/pore), on Bear Valley Rd., ½ mi. west of Olema. Rangers give out camping permits, maps, and sage advice on trails, tides, and weather conditions, and lead guided hikes. The headquarters house excellent exhibits on the cultural and natural history of Pt. Reyes. Open M-F 9am-5pm, Sa-Su and holidays 8am-5pm.

Pan Toll Ranger's Station, 801 Panoramic Hwy. (☎388-2070), in Mt. Tamalpais State Park, about 2½ mi. inland from Stinson Beach. Operates Mt. Tam's campgrounds and trails. Rangers offer suggestions and explain restrictions on the trails. Bus #63 stops at the Ranger's Station.

Muir Woods National Monument Visitors Center (☎388-2596; www.nps.gov/muwo), near the entrance to Muir Woods. Muir Woods trail map $1. Great selection of hiking, biking, and driving maps of Marin and Mt. Tam. Open daily 9am-6pm.

Library and Internet Access: Stinson Beach Library, 3521 Shoreline Hwy. (☎868-0252). Free Internet access. Open M 10am-1pm, Tu 1-5pm and 6-9pm, F 10am-1pm and 2-6pm, Sa 10am-1pm.

Police: ☎258-4610 in San Anselmo. **Marin County Sheriff:** ☎479-2311.

Medical Services: Marin General Hospital and Community Clinic, 250 Bon Air Rd. (☎925-7000, clinic ☎461-7400), in **Greenbrae,** off the U.S. 101 San Anselmo Exit. 24hr. emergency care. Clinic open for appointment only M and Th 8am-7pm, W 9am-7pm, Tu and F 8am-5pm.

Post Office: 15 Calle Del Mar, at Shoreline Hwy. in **Stinson Beach.** Open M-F 8:30am-5pm. **Postal Code:** 94970.

ACCOMMODATIONS

Point Reyes Hostel (HI-AYH) (☎663-8811 or ☎800-909-4776; www.norcalhostels.org), at the Point Reyes National Seashore. Exit west from Hwy. 1 at Olema onto Bear Valley Rd. Take the 2nd left at Limantour Rd. (no sign indicates the turn) and drive 6 mi. into the park. Turn left at the first crossroad at the bottom of a very steep hill. 2 cabins occupy a site near Limantour Beach. Full kitchen, barbecue, and cozy common room. Chores expected. Linen $1; towels $1. Reception open 7:30-10am and 4:30-9:30pm. Quiet hours 10pm-7am. Check-in 4:30-9:30pm. Check-out and chores finished by 10am. Reservations recommended. Dorms $14, under 17 (with parent) $7. Private room available for families with children under 5. ❶

Green Gulch Farm Zen Center, 1601 Shoreline Hwy. (☎383-3134; www.sfzc.org). If your hostel just isn't enlightened enough, Green Gulch's guest student program allows serious students of Zen to stay at the center for $15 per night for a minimum of 5 days and up to 6 weeks. Singles $75-90; doubles $125-140. ❹

CAMPING

The Headlands (☎331-1540; www.nps.gov/goga/camping/index.htm), offers 3 small walk-in (up to 3 mi.) campgrounds with a total of 11 primitive campsites for individual backpackers and small groups. Picnic tables and chemical toilets are available in the backpack camps. Bring your own water and camp stove. No fires allowed. Showers and kitchen ($2 each) at Headlands Hostel. Free outdoor cold showers at Rodeo Beach. 3-day max. stay per site; 9-day max. stay per yr. Reserve up to 90 days in advance. Individual sites free with permit obtained at Headlands Visitors Center (see p. 154). ❶

Kirby Cove (reservations ☎ 800-365-2267), off Conzelman Rd. west of the Golden Gate Bridge, is in the Marin Headlands, but is not administered by the Visitors Center. Accessible by car, it consists of 4 campsites in a grove of cypress and eucalyptus trees on the shore, with fire rings and pit toilets. Kirby Cove is designed for larger groups. No water. 3-day max. stay; 1 weekend reservation per group per yr. Open Apr.-Nov. Sites $25. ❷

Point Reyes National Seashore (☎663-8054; www.nps.gov/pore; open M-F 9am-2pm for phone reservations, walk-in 9am-5pm) has walk-in and boat-in camping only. 2 camps are coastal and 2 are inland—some have exquisite ocean views. Charcoal grills, non-potable running water, and pit toilets. 4-night max. stay. Reservations strongly recommended. Pick up permits at Point Reyes National Seashore Headquarters. Boat-in camping at Tomales Bay; call or check web page for info. Sites $10. ●

Samuel P. Taylor State Park, P.O. Box 251 (☎488-9897; www.parks.ca.gov; Reserve America ☎800-444-7275; www.park-net.com), on Sir Francis Drake Blvd., 15 mi. west of San Rafael in Lagunitas. Family campground in a lush setting beneath stately, second-growth redwoods. Often crowded on weekends. Sites are cool and shady, though not always quiet. Running water, flush toilets, and free hot showers. 7-night max. stay. Check-out noon. Reservations recommended weekends. Sites $12, seniors $10; Walk-in sites 2-night max. stay. $1 per person. Day use parking $2.●

◖ FOOD

Marinites take their fruit juices, tofu, and non-fat double-shot cappuccinos very seriously. Restaurateurs know this and raise both alfalfa sprouts and prices. You can always stock up for the ferry ride home in Sausalito with the organic produce from **Real Food Company,** 200 Caledonia St. (☎332-9640. Open daily 9am-9pm.) In Mill Valley, on the outskirts of town, **Whole Foods,** 414 Miller Ave., specializes in organic groceries. (☎381-1200. Open daily 8am-8pm.)

SAUSALITO

Arawan, 47 Caledonia St. (☎332-0882), is a Thai place which specializes in seafood but also has great curry dishes. Curry under $8. Seafood dishes $12-16. Open daily 11:30am-2:30pm and 5-10pm. ❷

Sushi Ran, 107 Caledonia St. (☎332-3620; www.sushiran.com), is a local favorite. It offers upscale Asian fare, including *sake* bar and vegetarian *maki*. California roll $6.50. Open for M-F 11:30am-2:30pm and 5:30-11pm, Sa 5:30-11pm, Su 5:30-10:30pm. ❺

ELSEWHERE IN MARIN COUNTY

▨ **Avatar's Punjabi Burrito,** 15 Madrona St. (☎381-8293), in Mill Valley. Take chickpeas, rice, chutney, yogurt, and spice. Add tofu and veggies or other things nice. Wrap in yummy Indian bread, and you have a delicious meal for $5.50-8.50. Rice plates and mango lassi also available. Open M-Sa 11am-8pm. ❷

▨ **Bubba's Diner,** 566 San Anselmo Ave. (☎459-6862), in San Anselmo. A local favorite that serves all the essentials with daily specials. "Bubbas famous oyster sandwich" $13. Open M and W-F 9am-2pm and 5:30-9pm, Sa-Su 8am-2:30pm and 5:30-9:30pm. ❸

Theresa and Johnny's Comfort Foods, 817 Fourth St. (☎259-0182), in San Rafael. Serves up huge burgers, salads, grilled sandwiches, omelettes, and pancakes for $3.75-9. Open M-F 7am-2:30pm, Sa-Su 8am-2:30pm. No credit cards. ❷

◖▣ SIGHTS AND OUTDOOR ACTIVITIES

Marin's proximity to San Francisco makes it a popular daytrip destination. Virtually everything worth seeing or doing in Marin is outdoors. An efficient visitor can hop from park to park and enjoy several short hikes along the coast and through the redwood forests in the same day, topping it off with a pleasant dinner in one of the small cities. Those without cars, however, may find it easier to use one of the two well-situated hostels as a base for hiking or biking explorations. Sights are listed in order going northwest from **Muir Beach** to **Bolinas Bay.**

SAUSALITO

Originally a fishing center full of bars and bordellos, the city at Marin's extreme southeastern tip has long since traded its sea-dog days for retail boutiques and overpriced seafood restaurants. **Bridgeway** is the city's main thoroughfare, and practically the only one shown on Sausalito Visitors Center maps. A block away from the harbor and Bridgeway's smug shops, **Caledonia Street** offers more charming restaurants and a few more affordable stores. Perhaps the best thing to see in Sausalito is the view of San Francisco. For the best views of the city, take the ferry or bike across the Golden Gate Bridge.

Half a mile north of the town center is the **Bay Model and Marinship Museum,** 2100 Bridgeway, a massive working model of San Francisco Bay. Built in the 1950s to test proposals to dam the bay, the water-filled model re-creates tides and currents in great detail. (☎ 332-3871. Open Memorial Day-Labor Day Tu-F 9am-4pm, Sa-Su 10am-6pm; Labor Day-Memorial Day Tu-Sa 9am-4pm. Free.)

MARIN HEADLANDS

Fog-shrouded hills just west of the Golden Gate Bridge constitute the Marin Headlands. These windswept ridges, precipitous cliffs, and hidden sandy beaches offer superb hiking and biking within minutes of downtown San Francisco. For instant gratification, drive up to any of the several look-out spots and pose for your own postcard-perfect shot of the Golden Gate Bridge and the city skyline, or take a short walk out to Point Bonita. If you intend to do some more serious hiking or biking, choose one of the coastal trails, which provide easy access to dark sand beaches and dramatic cliffs of basalt greenstone. Either way, bring a jacket in case of sudden wind, rain, or fog.

POINT BONITA. One of the best short hikes is to the lighthouse at Point Bonita, a prime spot for seeing sunbathing California sea lions in summer and migrating gray whales in the cooler months. The cute little lighthouse at the end of the point really doesn't seem up to the job of guarding the whole San Francisco Bay, but has done so valiantly since 1855; in fact, its original glass lens is still in operation. At the end of a narrow, knife-like ridge lined with purple wildflowers, the lighthouse is reached by a short tunnel through the rock and a miniature suspension bridge. Even when the lighthouse is closed, the short walk (1 mi. from the Visitors Center, ½ mi. from the nearest parking) provides gorgeous views on sunny days. *(Lighthouse: 1 mi. from Visitors Center, ½ mi. from nearest parking. Open Sa-M 12:30-3:30pm. Guided walks Sa-M 12:30pm. Free. No dogs or bikes through tunnel.)*

BIG GUNS. Formerly a military installation charged with defending the San Francisco harbor, the Headlands are dotted with machine gun nests, missile sites, and soldiers' quarters dating from the Spanish-American War to the 1950s. **Battery Spencer,** on Conzelman Rd. immediately west of U.S. 101, offers one of the best views of the city skyline and the Golden Gate Bridge, especially around sunset on the (rare) clear day. Farther into the park is the **NIKE Missile Site,** on Field Rd. *(Battery Spencer: On Conzelman Rd. just west of U.S. 101. NIKE Missile Site: On Field Rd., at Fort Berry and Fort Cronkite. ☎ 331-1453. Open W-F and 1st Su of the month 12:30-3:30pm.)*

WILDLIFE. The **Marine Mammal Center,** at Rodeo Beach, is a nonprofit organization dedicated to saving injured, sick, or orphaned marine mammals. *(At Rodeo Beach. ☎ 289-7330; www.tmmc.org. Open daily 10am-4pm. No dogs.)*

OTHER ACTIVITIES. The 1 mi. walk from the Visitors Center down to sheltered **Rodeo Beach,** a favorite of cormorants and pelicans, is easy and pleasant. For more ambitious hiking or biking, a good map is a must. Pick one up at the **Visitors Center** at Bunker and Field Rd. (free-$1.50). The **Wolf Ridge** and **Tennessee Valley** trails are perennial favorites; ask rangers for other suggestions and camping info. Bring a jacket for the sudden descent of rain, wind, or fog.

MOUNT TAMALPAIS & MUIR WOODS

Between the upscale towns of East Marin and the rocky bluffs of West Marin rests beautiful **Mount Tamalpais State Park** (tam-ull-PIE-us). The park has miles of hilly, challenging trails on and around 2571 ft. Mount Tamalpais, the original "mountain" in "mountain bike." The bubbling waterfall on **Cataract Trail** and the **Gardner Lookout** on Mount Tam's east peak are worthy destinations. Visit the **Pan Toll Ranger's Station,** on Panoramic Hwy., for trail suggestions and biking restrictions. Although this is the home of the mountain bike, cyclists that go off designated trails and fire roads risk incurring the wrath of eco-happy Marin hikers. On weekends and holidays, bus #63 stops at the ranger station between the Golden Gate Bridge and Stinson Beach. (☎388-2070. Free. Parking free-$2.)

At the center of the state park is **Muir Woods National Monument,** a 560-acre stand of old coastal redwoods 5 mi. west of U.S. 101 on Hwy. 1. (Open 8am-dusk.) Spared from logging by the steep sides of Redwood Canyon, these massive, centuries-old redwoods are shrouded in silence. The level, paved trails along the canyon floor are lined with wooden fences, but a hike up the canyon's sides will soon take you away from the tourists and face-to-face with the wildlife that is scarce on the forest floor. (☎388-2595. Open 9am-6pm. $2.) Avoid this charge by hiking in 2 mi. from the Pan Toll Ranger Station.

MARIN COAST

Hwy. 1 reaches the Pacific at Muir Beach and then twists its way up the rugged coast. It's all beautiful, but the stretch between Muir and Stinson Beaches is the most breathtaking, especially when driving south on the sheer-drop-to-the-ocean side of the highway. There ought to be a law about allowing such jaw-dropping scenery along such treacherous roads. If you're riding a bike, don't expect the white-knuckled drivers of passing cars to allow you much elbow room.

BEACHES. Sheltered **Muir Beach** is scenic and popular with families. The crowds thin out significantly after a 5min. climb on the shore rocks to the left. Six miles to the north, **Stinson Beach** attracts a younger, rowdier, good-looking surfer crowd, although cold and windy conditions often leave them languishing on dry land. The Bard joins the Stinson Beach crowds from July to October during **Shakespeare at Stinson.** Between Muir Beach and Stinson Beach lies the nudist **Red Rocks Beach,** a secluded spot reached by a steep hike down from a parking area 1 mi. south of Stinson Beach. Tan lines be gone! *(Muir Beach open dawn-9pm. Stinson Beach open dawn-dusk. Shakespeare at Stinson ☎868-1115; www.shakespeareatstinson.org. Bus #63 runs from Sausalito to Stinson Beach on weekends and holidays.)*

ZEN CENTER. Just inland from Muir Beach is the **Green Gulch Farm Zen Center,** an organic farm and Buddhist retreat. Visitors are free to explore the tranquil grounds and gardens, and on Sunday mornings the public is welcome at a meditation lesson (8:15am) and informal lecture on Zen Buddhism (10:15am). Would-be Zen masters are asked to wear dark, loose-fitting clothing for *zazen* meditation. If your hostel just isn't enlightened enough, Green Gulch's guest student program allows serious students of Zen to stay at the center. Students are expected to work in the vegetable gardens and to take part in *zazen* and *sutra* chanting throughout the day. *(1601 Shoreline Hwy. ☎ 383-3134; www.sfzc.org.)*

BOLINAS. Continuing a few mi. northwest from Stinson Beach along Hwy. 1, you'll find the **Audubon Canyon Ranch.** Dedicated to preserving the surrounding lands as well as other areas in Marin and Sonoma counties, the ranch provides educational programs and conducts several research projects. Come watch great blue herons and great egrets nest, or go for a hike on the 8 mi. of trails. Immediately past the lagoon is the unmarked turn-off for the village of Bolinas—a tiny colony of hippies, artists, and writers. Many of the tiny art galleries and eateries that dot the town have no set hours, and watching three generations of hippies walk side by side down the street emphasizes its strong atemporal vibe. Eccentric Bolinas residents have included authors Richard Brautigan *(Trout Fishing in America)* and Jim Carroll *(The Basketball Diaries)*. To graze while you gaze, try Northern California cuisine at **Coast Cafe,** open for breakfast, lunch, and dinner, but don't tell them we sent you. For years, locals hoping to discourage tourist traffic have torn down any and all signs marking the Bolinas-Olema road. Press coverage of the "sign war" won the people of Bolinas exactly the publicity they wanted to avoid, but for now, at least, the town remains authentic in every way that Sausalito is not—and they intend to keep it that way, so don't expect to feel welcomed. But who needs signs anyway? *(Driving north from Stinson Beach, the Bolinas-Olema road is the first left after coming around the lagoon; turn and follow the road to the end. From Olema, take Hwy. 1, and hang a right after (or on) Horseshoe Hill Rd. before the lagoon.)*

POINT REYES

A near-island surrounded by nearly 100 mi. of isolated coastline, the **Point Reyes National Seashore** is a wilderness of pine forests, chaparral ridges, and grassy flatlands. Five million years ago, this outcropping was a suburb of Los Angeles, but it hitched a ride on the submerged Pacific Plate and has been creeping northward along the San Andreas Fault ever since. In summer, colorful wildflowers attract crowds of gawking tourists, but with hundreds of miles of amazing trails, it's quite possible to gawk alone. Hwy. 1 provides direct access to the park from the north or south; Sir Francis Drake Blvd. comes west from U.S. 101 at San Rafael.

The park headquarters are at the **Point Reyes National Seashore Headquarters,** just west of Olema. There, rangers distribute camping permits and can suggest trails, drives, beaches, and picnic areas. (☎ 663-1092; www.nps.gov/pore. Open M-F 9am-5pm, Sa-Su 8am-5pm.) The **Earthquake Trail** is a three-quarters of a mile walk along the infamous San Andreas Fault Line that starts right at Bear Valley. Lovely **Limantour Beach** sits at the end of Limantour Rd., 8 mi. west of the Visitors Center, which runs a free shuttle bus to the beach in summer. The **Point Reyes Hostel** is at the bottom of a steep valley, 2 mi. from the end of Limantour Rd. The dramatic landscape around the hostel is still scarred by a major forest fire that torched the region in 1995. Both Limantour and Point Reyes Beaches have high, grassy dunes and long stretches of sand, but strong ocean currents along the point make swimming very dangerous. Swimming is safest at **Hearts Desire Beach,** north of the Visitors Center on sheltered **Tomales Bay.** To reach the dramatic **Point Reyes Lighthouse** at the very tip of the point, follow Sir Francis Drake Blvd. to its end (20 mi. from the Visitors Center) and head right along the stairway to Sea Lion Overlook. From December until February, migrating gray whales can be spotted from the overlook. (Lighthouse Visitors Center ☎669-1534. Open Th-M 10am-4:30pm.)

SAN RAFAEL

San Rafael is the largest city in Marin County, but it holds little to interest the budget traveler. If you do stop here on your way to or from Northern California, the main strip for eating and shopping lies along **4th Street.**

If you have a car, you might picnic at **China Camp State Park,** an expanse of grassy meadows east of the city. It's named for the ramshackle remains of a Chinese fishing village that once housed thousands of laborers who were forced from the city. (Open daily 8am-8pm; Visitors Center open daily 10am-5pm. Parking $3.) Six miles north of San Rafael is an exit for Lucas Valley Rd., where jedi master George Lucas toils away at **Skywalker Ranch,** crafting the next installment of the Star Wars saga. There's no point in stopping for a sneak preview—Lucas's home and studios are fiercely guarded by Imperial troopers.

■ NIGHTLIFE

If you really wanted to party, you'd head back to the city, but Marin County does offer a number of low-key live music venues and easygoing watering holes. San Rafael probably has the most action, with many more bars than are listed here.

New George's, 842 4th St. (☎457-1515; www.newgeorges.com), in San Rafael, under a movie-style marquee at Cijos St., is the frequent winner of the "best live music and nightlife in Marin" award. The daytime cafe becomes a jumping club by night. Live music Tu-Sa at 9pm. Latin music Su nights. Cover charge varies. Open daily 2pm-2am.

Smitty's Bar, 214 Caledonia St. (☎332-2637), in Sausalito. Has resisted upward mobility to remain a rough around the edges favorite of Sausalito's "boat people." Shuffleboard, pool, 3 TVs, and a wall of bowling trophies to admire. Domestic pints $2.75, schooners $3.75, pitchers $7. Open daily 10am-2am.

No Name Bar, 757 Bridgeway (☎332-1392), in Sausalito. Once a haunt of the Beats, the bar with no name now serves a mixed crowd of tourists and locals. Heated patio out back. Live blues or jazz music most nights—the biggest draw is Dixieland Jazz every Su afternoon (no cover). Rudimentary sandwich menu 11am-4pm. Open 10am-2am.

NAPA VALLEY ☎707

Napa catapulted American wine into the big leagues in 1976, when a bottle of red from Napa's **Stag's Leap Vineyard** beat a bottle of critically acclaimed (and unfailingly French) Château Lafitte-Rothschild in a blind taste test in Paris. While not the oldest, and not necessarily the best, the Napa Valley is certainly the best-known of America's wine-growing regions, in part because the natural hot springs in Calistoga and St. Helena led Gold Rush millionaires to build luxury spas for wealthy vacationers in the 1850s. Around the same time, vintners first planted European vines in the area, but those early producers were crippled in the 1920s by Prohibition, when grapes were supplanted by figs. The region did not begin to reestablish itself until the 1960s, when the now big-name wineries, like Mondavi, first opened. Now firmly established as successful businesses, the big Napa wineries draw a mostly older, well-to-do crowd, but in the midst of the everyday tasting carnival, there are also a lot of young and budget-minded folks looking forward to their fill of chardonnay and a mud bath at the end of the day.

■ ORIENTATION & PRACTICAL INFORMATION

Route 29 (Saint Helena Highway) runs through the Napa Valley north from **Napa** through **Yountville** and **Saint Helena** (where it's called Main St.) to **Calistoga.** Choked with visitors stopping at each winery, the relatively short distance makes for a sur-

X Villa Corona (Mexican)

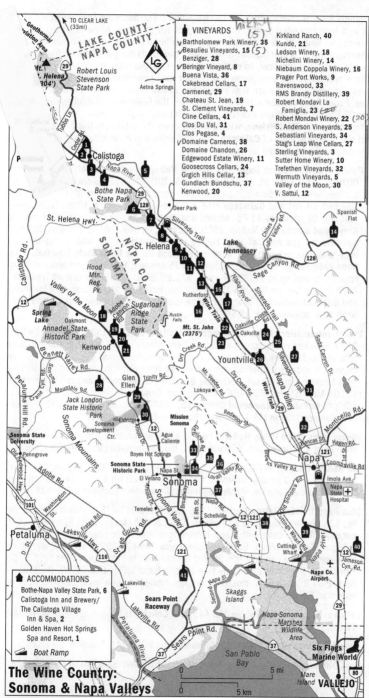

BAY AREA

VINEYARDS

Bartholomew Park Winery, **35**
Beaulieu Vineyards, **15** (5)
Benziger, **28**
Beringer Vineyard, **8**
Buena Vista, **36**
Cakebread Cellars, **17**
Carmenet, **29**
Chateau St. Jean, **19**
St. Clement Vineyards, **7**
Cline Cellars, **41**
Clos Du Val, **31**
Clos Pegase, **4**
Domaine Carneros, **38**
Domaine Chandon, **26**
Edgewood Estate Winery, **11**
Goosecross Cellars, **24**
Grgich Hills Cellar, **13**
Gundlach Bundschu, **37**
Kenwood, **20**

Kirkland Ranch, **40**
Kunde, **21**
Ledson Winery, **18**
Nichelini Winery, **14**
Niebaum Coppola Winery, **16**
Prager Port Works, **9**
Ravenswood, **33**
RMS Brandy Distillery, **39**
Robert Mondavi La Famiglia, **23**
Robert Mondavi Winery, **22** (20)
S. Anderson Vineyards, **25**
Sebastiani Vineyards, **34**
Stag's Leap Wine Cellars, **27**
Sterling Vineyards, **3**
Sutter Home Winery, **10**
Trefethen Vineyards, **32**
Wermuth Vineyards, **5**
Valley of the Moon, **30**
V. Sattui, **12**

ACCOMMODATIONS
Bothe-Napa Valley State Park, **6**
Calistoga Inn and Brewery/
The Calistoga Village
Inn & Spa, **2**
Golden Haven Hot Springs
Spa and Resort, **1**

Boat Ramp

The Wine Country:
Sonoma & Napa Valleys

0   5 mi

0   5 km

prisingly long, if scenic, drive on the weekends. The **Silverado Trail,** parallel to Rte. 29, is a less crowded route, but watch out for cyclists. Napa is 14 mi. east of Sonoma on **Route 12.** If you're planning a weekend trip from San Francisco, avoid Saturday mornings and Sunday afternoons; the roads are packed with like-minded people. Although harvest, in early September, is the most exciting time to visit, winter weekdays are less packed and offer more personal attention. In addition, most accommodations are less expensive in the winter or offer weekend packages. From San Francisco, take U.S. 101 over the Golden Gate Bridge, then follow Rte. 37 East, which intersects Rte. 29, which runs north to Napa.

Yountville and **Saint Helena,** which lie between the relatively busy town of Napa and the soothing spas of **Calistoga,** are well-groomed little villages that each host several small restaurants and trendy shops.

Public Transportation: Napa City Bus, or **Valley Intercity Neighborhood Express (VINE),** 1151 Pearl St. (☎800-696-6443, TDD 226-9722), covers **Vallejo** (M-F 5:20am-8pm, Sa 6:15am-5:30pm, Su 11am-6pm; $1.50, students $1.10, seniors and disabled $0.75) and **Calistoga** (M-F 5:20am-8pm, Sa 6am-6:40pm, Su 9:30am-4:30pm; $2, students $1.45, seniors and disabled $1; free transfers). The nearest **Greyhound** station is in Vallejo, 1500 Lemon St. (☎643-7661 or 800-231-2222). A bus runs to Napa and Calistoga, but it's very slow—almost 3hr. from Vallejo to Calistoga—and does not stop near wineries. To: **Napa** (at the **Napa State Hospital,** 2100 Napa-Vallejo Hwy.; 12:30 and 5:25pm; $8.25 one-way, $15.25 round-trip) and **Calistoga** (5:25 and 8pm; $11.25 one-way, $21.25 round-trip). **Evans Airport Transport,** 4075 Solano Ave. (☎707-255-1559), in Napa, runs daily shuttles from **San Francisco** and **Oakland** airports to downtown Napa. Call for schedules and reservations. SFO-Napa $20, children under 12 $6.

Visitor Information: Napa Conference & Visitors Bureau, 1310 Town Ctr. (☎226-7459; www.napavalley.com/nvcvb.html). Very friendly staff. Free maps and info. Also sells the *Napa Valley Guidebook* ($6) with more comprehensive listings and fold-out maps. Ask about any specials during your visit (they come in daily) and pick up coupons from local businesses. Open daily 9am-5pm. **St. Helena Chamber of Commerce,** 1010A Main St. (☎963-4456), across from Taylor's Refresher. Open M-F 10am-4:30pm. **Calistoga Chamber of Commerce,** 1458 Lincoln Ave. (☎942-6333; www.calistogafun.com). Open M-F 10am-5pm, Sa 10am-4pm, Su 11am-3pm.

Winery Tours: Napa Valley Holidays (☎255-1050; www.napavalleyholidays.com). Afternoon tours $75 per person, $85 with round-trip transportation from San Francisco.

Car Rental: Budget, 407 Soscol Ave. (☎224-7846), in Napa. Cars $40 per day; under 25 surcharge $20 per day. Unlimited mileage. Must be at least 21 with credit card. Promotional specials often available; call Budget Reservation Center at ☎800-537-0700.

Bike Rental: ▧St. Helena Cyclery, 1156 Main St. (☎963-7736). Hybrid bikes $7 per hr., $25 per day; road bikes $15 per hr., $45 per day; tandem bikes $25 per hr., $70 per day. All bikes come with maps, helmet, lock, and picnic bag. Open M-Sa 9:30am-5:30pm, Su 10am-5pm. **Getaway Adventures** (☎942-0332; www.getawayadventures.com), at the corner of Rte. 29 and Lincoln Ave., in Calistoga. $9 per hr., $20 per half-day, $28 per day. Also leads bike tours in Napa Valley. Open M, W, Th, 9:30am-5pm, F-Su 9:30am-6pm, closed rainy days; Nov.-Mar. open fewer hours, usually no later than 5pm.

Police in **Napa:** 1539 1st St. (☎253-4451). In **Calistoga:** 1235 Washington St. (☎942-2810).

Hospital: Queen of the Valley, 1000 Trancas St. (☎252-4411), in Napa.

Post Office: 1627 Trancas St., in Napa. Open M-F 8:30am-5pm. **Postal Code:** 94558.

ACCOMMODATIONS & CAMPING

Rooms in Napa Valley can go fast despite high prices; reserving ahead is best. Try Calistoga first. The quaint town is not a far drive from many wineries and is close to Old Faithful Geyser, the Petrified Forest and Bothe-Napa State Park. It is also the home of many natural, hot-spring spas and was declared one of America's most "distinctive destinations" by the National Trust for Historic Preservation. However, Napa is a bigger city and is closer to the Bay Area. Camping is the least expensive alternative, although the heat can be intense in summer.

Golden Haven Hot Springs Spa and Resort, 1713 Lake St. (☎942-6793; www.golden-haven.com), a few blocks from the main drag, Lincoln St. in Calistoga. More of a nice motel than a resort. Large standard-issue rooms, decorated nicely, with TVs and phones. Rooms with king beds, kitchenettes, jacuzzis, and saunas also available. Mineral swimming pool and hot tub access for all guests. No children under 16. Weekends 2-night min. stay, holiday weekends 3-night min stay. Apr.-Oct. one queen $79; one king with kichenette $125; queen with private sauna $135; king with private jacuzzi $175. Nov.-Mar. M-Th $65/$99/$109/$135. ❺

Calistoga Inn and Brewery, 1250 Lincoln Ave. (☎942-4101; www.calistogainn.com), at the corner of Rte. 29 in Calistoga. 18 clean, simple, country inn double- and queen-sized rooms in the upstairs of an old Victorian house whose downstairs has turned into a microbrewery and restaurant. The walk home from the pub is just a short stumble upstairs. Shared bathrooms. Big breakfast included. No wheelchair access to rooms. Restaurant and bar open 11:30am-11pm. Rooms $75, Sa-Su and holidays $100. ❹

The Calistoga Village Inn & Spa, 1880 Lincoln Ave. (☎942-0991), has clean, basic rooms with cable TV, phones, and private bath. Rooms with jacuzzi also available. Semi-secluded heated mineral pools and hot tub, and on-site spa and restaurant. Doubles $79, doubles with sitting area, kitchenette and Whirlpool tub $159; Nov.-Mar. M-Th rates are $10 and $20 less. 10% discount on all spa treatments to lodging guests. Ask about special room, spa and meal packages. ❹

Bothe-Napa Valley State Park, 3801 Rte. 29 (☎942-4575, reservations 800-444-7275), north of St. Helena. 50 sites near Ritchey Creek Canyon often fill up. Fairly rustic. Toilets. Pool $1, under 17 free. Check-in 2pm. $12, seniors $10. Picnic area day use $2. Hot showers $0.25. Park open daily 8am-dusk. ❶

FOOD

Eating in Wine Country ain't cheap, but the food is usually worth it. Picnics are an inexpensive and romantic option—supplies can be bought at the numerous delis or Safeway stores in the area. Most wineries have shaded picnic grounds, often with excellent views, but most require patronage to use. The **Napa farmer's market,** besides at Pearl and West St., offers a sampling of the valley's other produce. (☎252-7142. Napa Town Center. Open daily 7:30am-noon.)

First Squeeze Cafe & Juice Bar, 1126 First St. (☎224-6762), offers sandwiches, soups, salads, and smoothies. Try their most popular plate, huevos rancheros ($8), or supe-up a fresh fruit smoothie with a shot of gingko biloba or ginseng ($4). Also serves beer and wine. Breakfast every day until 2pm. Free downtown delivery. Open M-F 7am-3pm, Sa-Su 8am-3pm. ❷

Calistoga Natural Foods and Juice Bar, 1426 Lincoln St. (☎942-5822), in Calistoga. One of a few natural foods stores in the area. Organic juices ($3-5), smoothies ($3.50-4.50), sandwiches ($4-7.25), and bargain vegetarian specialties like the Asian veggie stir-fry or steam ($6.50) and the Yummus Hummus wrap ($6.50). Organic groceries also sold. Open M-Sa 9am-6pm, Su 10am-5pm. ❷

BAY AREA

Armadellos, 1304 Main St. (☎963-8082), in St. Helena. Tasty vegetarian-friendly Cali-Mexican dishes (mostly $6-13). Beer and wine available. Open Su-Th 11am-9pm, F-Sa 11am-10pm. ❷

Taylor's Refresher, 933 Main St. (☎963-3486), on Rte. 29 across from the Merryvale Winery, in St. Helena. A roadside stand dishing up big burgers ($4.50-7; vegetarian $6.50) and stellar milkshakes ($3.75) since 1949. Outdoor seating only. Beer and wine served. To avoid the line if ordering to go, make your request at the beer and wine station. Open daily 11am-9pm. ❷

🇿 WINERIES

There are more than 250 wineries in Napa County, nearly two-thirds of which line Rte. 29 and the Silverado Trail in the Napa Valley. Wine Country's heavyweights call this valley home; vineyards include national names such as Inglenook, Fetzer, and Mondavi. Some wineries have free tastings, some have free tours, and all have large selections of bottled wine available for purchase at prices cheaper than in stores—many wineries offer further reduced rates to visitors who purchase a tasting or become a club member. Style and atmosphere, from architecture down to visitor hospitality, vary from estate to estate; experiencing the larger, touristy operations coupled with the smaller name vineyards adds to the fun. No matter their marketing approach, the wineries listed below (from south to north) do card for underage drinkers; **visitors must be 21+ to taste or purchase alcohol.**

A good way to begin your Napa Valley experience is with a tour, such as the ones at **Domaine Carneros** or **Beringer,** or a free tastings class, like the one offered on Saturday mornings at **Goosecross Cellars.**

Kirkland Ranch, 1 Kirkland Ranch Rd. (☎254-9100), south of Napa off Rte. 29. Reminiscent of a ski lodge, this family owned and operated Country Western styled winery has windows overlooking production facilities and family pictures of cattle herding cowboys adorning the walls. Tours are made by appointment. Tastings $5. Any US military personnel or veterans receive 30% off wine purchases.

RMS Brandy Distillery, 1250 Cuttings Wharf Rd. (☎253-9055), ¼ mi. from the Rte. 121 and Rte. 12 intersection. State and federal laws prohibit tastings because of the high alcohol content, but a free informative 1hr. tour and "aroma evaluating" session is offered. The staff is incredibly knowledgeable. Tours every hr. 10:30am-3:30pm. Open daily 10am-4:30pm.

Domaine Carneros, 1240 Duhig Rd. (☎257-0101), off Rte. 121 between Napa and Sonoma. Picturesque estate with an elegant terrace modeled after a French *château.* Owned by Champagne Taittinger and known for its sparkling wines. Free tour and film (daily every hr. 10:15am-4pm) is a great 1st stop info session for a day of wine tasting. No tastings, but wines by the glass $5-10 with complimentary *hors d'oeuvres.* Open daily 10am-6pm.

YOUNTVILLE & NEARBY

Clos Du Val Wine Company, Ltd., 5330 Silverado Trail (☎259-2225; www.closdu-val.com), north of Oak Knoll Rd., in Yountville. Small, stylish grounds attract lots of tourists. Tastings $5; price is applicable towards wine purchase. Free tours by appointment only. Open daily 10am-5pm.

Domaine Chandon, 1 California Dr. (☎944-2280 or 800-934-3975; www.chandon.com), in Yountville. Owned by Moët Chandon of France (the makers of Dom Perignon), this winery produces 4-5 million bottles of sparkling wine annually. The sleek, modern Visitors Center and manicured gardens evoke the spirit of a Zen meditation retreat. There is also a French restaurant on site. Tastings 3 wines for $9, or by the glass $4.50-12. Open daily 10am-6pm.

Stag's Leap Wine Cellars, 5766 Silverado Trail (☎944-2020). "The tiny vineyard that beat Europe's best," says the souvenir glass that comes with the portfolio or flights ($30) tasting. Call in advance to arrange a free 1hr. tour that includes a complimentary tasting. Open daily 10am-4:30pm.

OAKVILLE

Robert Mondavi Winery, 7801 Rte. 29 (☎963-9611 or 800-766-3284; www.robert-mondaviwinery.com), 8 mi. north of Napa. If you are looking to hit one massive, tourist-happy winery, this is it. Beautiful mission-style visitors complex, with 2 tasting rooms selling by the glass ($4-15) and the atmosphere of a luxury summer resort. Offers a variety of tours, differing in length and focus and with various foods. The Vineyard and Winery tour is offered daily every hr. 10am-4pm. Reserve 1hr. in advance. Tour $10, including 3 tastes and *hors d'oeuvres*. The other 6 tours are each given one day per week at 10am or 11am, some only seasonally, and cost $30-95 per person. Open daily 9am-5pm.

Niebaum-Coppola Estate Winery, 1991 St. Helena Hwy. (☎968-1100). The movie giant Francis Ford Coppola and his wife bought the historic 1880 Inglenook Chateau and Niebaum vineyards in 1975. Restoring the estate to production capacity, Coppola also added a Niebaum and Coppola family history museum. Most likely, it will be crowded. $7.50 fee includes 4 tastes and commemorative glass. Free tours given at 10:30am and 2:30pm; summer weekends also 12:30pm. Open daily 10am-5pm.

ST. HELENA & CALISTOGA

Edgewood Estate Winery, 401 St. Helena Hwy. (☎963-7293), in St. Helena. Don't let the lack of cars and crowds outside deter you—a warm, attentive staff and 5 tastes for $4 await within this small, pretty lodge. Garden patio seating for drinkers of wines by the glass. Open daily 11am-5:30pm.

V. Sattui, 1111 White Ln. (☎963-7774 or 800-799-2337; www.vsattui.com), at Rte. 29, in St. Helena. One of the few wineries in the valley that only sells at its winery. The family-owned operation has a gourmet cheese and meat shop. Picnic area for customers. Free tastings. Open daily Mar.-Oct. 9am-6pm; Nov.-Feb. 9am-5pm.

Beringer Vineyards, 2000 Main St. (☎963-7115; www.beringer.com), off Rte. 29, in St. Helena. Huge Gothic Revival estate mobbed with tourists. Historic tours of Rhine House mansion and grounds every 30min., include tasting (10am-5pm; $5, under 21 free). To taste Beringer's better wines, try the reserve room on the 2nd fl. of the Rhine House mansion (samples cost 10% of the wine's price, about $2-10, and will be credited towards wine purchase). Open daily 9:30am-5pm.

👁 ⚠ SIGHTS & OUTDOOR ACTIVITIES

Napa's gentle terrain makes for an excellent bike tour. The area is fairly flat, although small bike lanes, speeding cars, and blistering heat can make routes more challenging, especially after several samples of wine. The 26 mi. **Silverado Trail** has a wider bike path than Rte. 29. ■**St. Helena Cyclery,** 1156 Main St., rents bikes (see **Practical Information,** p. 162).

The annual **Napa Valley Wine Festival** takes place in November. Every weekend in February and March the **Mustard Festival** (☎259-9029; www.mustardfestival.org) lines up different musical or theatrical presentations. **Napa Valley Fairgrounds** (☎942-5111) hosts a weekend fair in August, with wine tasting, music, juggling, rides, and a rodeo. In summer, there are free afternoon concerts at **Music-in-the-Park,** downtown at the riverfront. Contact **Napa Parks and Recreation Office** (☎257-9529) for more info.

CALISTOGA. Calistoga is known as the "Hot Springs of the West." Sam Brannan, who first developed the area, meant to make the hot springs the "Saratoga of California," but he misspoke and promised instead to make them "The Calistoga of Saratina." Luckily, history has a soft spot for millionaires; Brannan's dream has come true, and Calistoga is now a center for luxurious, yet small-scale spas and resorts. His former cottage houses the **Sharpsteen Museum**, 1311 Washington St., which traces the town's development in exhibits designed by a Disney animator. *(☎942-5911. Open daily 11am-4pm; in winter noon-4pm. Free.)*

After a hard day of wine-tasting, the rich and relaxed converge on Calistoga to luxuriate in mud baths, massages, and mineral showers. Be sure to hydrate beforehand; thinned-blood and intense heat do not mix. A basic package consisting of a mud bath, mineral bath, eucalyptus steam, blanket wrap and 25min. massage costs around $80. Salt scrubs and facials are each about $50. Try the **Calistoga Village Inn & Spa** for quality, friendly service. *(☎942-0991. Mud bath treatment $45; 25min. massage $45; 30min. facial $49; ultimate 3hr. package of mud bath treatment, salt scrub, 55min. massage, and mini facial $185.)* **Golden Haven** is one of the less pretentious spas. *(☎942-6793. Mud bath treatment $65, 30min. massage $45, 30min. facial $45.)* Cooler water is at **Lake Berryessa** (☎966-2111), 20 mi. north of Napa off Hwy. 128, where swimming, sailing, and sunbathing are popular along its 169 mi. shoreline.

OLD FAITHFUL GEYSER OF CALIFORNIA. This steamy wonder should not be confused with its more famous namesake in Wyoming, although it performs similarly—it's one of only three faithful geysers in the world. The geyser regularly jets boiling water 60 ft. into the air; although it "erupts" about every 40min., weather conditions affect its cycle. The ticket vendor will tell you the estimated time of the next spurt. *(On Tubbs Ln. off Hwy. 128., 2 mi. outside Calistoga. ☎942-6463. Open daily 9am-6pm; in winter 9am-5pm. $6, seniors $5, ages 6-12 $2, disabled free.)*

MARINE WORLD. This 160-acre Vallejo attraction is an enormous zoo-oceanarium-theme park. It has animal shows and special attractions like the Lorikeet Aviary, the Butterfly Walk, and the Shark Experience. The park was recently purchased by Six Flags. *(Off Rte. 37, 10 mi. south of Napa. ☎643-6722. Vallejo is accessible from San Francisco by BART (☎510-465-2278) and the Blue and Gold fleet (☎415-705-5444). Open Mar.-Aug. daily 10am-10pm; Sept.-Oct. F-Su 10am-6pm. $34, seniors $25, ages 4-12 or under 48 in. $17. Parking $6.)*

OTHER SIGHTS. The Petrified Forest, 4100 Petrified Forest Rd., west of Calistoga. Over three million years ago a volcano erupted 7 mi. northeast of Mt. St. Helens. Molten lava covered the valley in which this forest now lies. The 0.25 mi. trail is wheelchair accessible. *(☎942-6667. Open daily 10am-6pm; winter 10am-5pm. Free.)* Experience an authentic Venetian gondola ride on Napa River with **Gondola Servizio Napa**, 540 Main St., inside Hatt Market. *(☎257-8495. 30min. private ride $55 per couple; $10 each additional person.)* **Napa Valley Wine Train**, 1275 McKinstry St., offers gourmet food, c. 1865, and travels from Napa to St. Helena and back. *(☎253-2111 or 800-427-4124. Train ride 3hr. M-F 11am and 6pm; Sa-Su 8:30am, 12:10, 5:30pm. Ticket and meal plans $35-90. Advance reservations and payments required.)*

SONOMA VALLEY ☎707

Sprawling Sonoma Valley is a quieter alternative to Napa, but home to bigger wineries than the Russian River Valley. Many wineries are on winding side roads rather than a freeway strip, creating a more intimate wine-tasting experience. Sonoma Plaza is surrounded by art galleries, novelty shops, clothing stores, and Italian restaurants. Petaluma, west of the Sonoma Valley, has more budget-friendly lodgings than the expensive wine country.

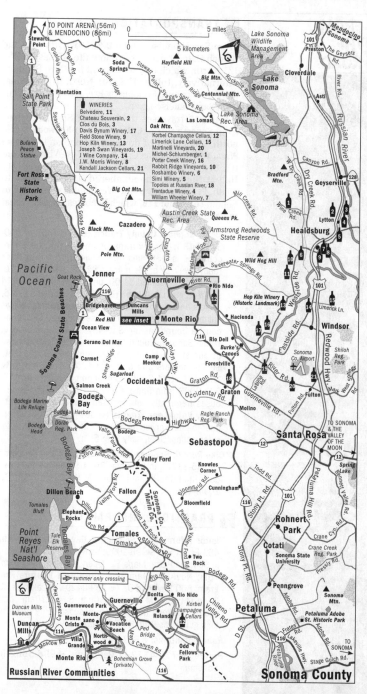

TO POINT ARENA (56mi) & MENDOCINO (86mi)

0   5 miles

0   5 kilometers

Stewarts Point

Soda Springs

Hayfield Hill

Big Mtn.

Rockpile Rd.

Lake Sonoma Wildlife Management Area

Preston

The Geysers Rd.

Cloverdale

Salt Point State Park

Plantation

Skyline Ridge

Stewart Point-Skaggs Springs Rd.

Walters Ridge

Centennial Mtn.

Lake Sonoma

Lake Sonoma Rec. Area

Asti

Bufano Peace Statue

WINERIES
Belvedere, **11**
Chateau Souverain, **2**
Clos du Bois, **3**
Davis Bynum Winery, **17**
Field Stone Winery, **9**
Hop Kiln Winery, **13**
Joseph Swan Vineyards, **19**
J Wine Company, **14**
J.W. Morris Winery, **8**
Kendall Jackson Cellars, **21**

Korbel Champagne Cellars, **12**
Limerick Lane Cellars, **15**
Martinelli Vineyards, **20**
Michel-Schlumberger, **1**
Porter Creek Winery, **16**
Rabbit Ridge Vineyards, **10**
Roshambo Winery, **6**
Simi Winery, **5**
Topolos at Russian River, **18**
Trentadue Winery, **4**
William Wheeler Winery, **7**

Oak Mtn.

Las Lomas

Fort Ross State Historic Park

Fort Ross Rd.

Meyers Grade Rd.

Big Oat Mtn.

Cazadero

Black Mtn.

Cazadero Rd.

Old Cazadero Rd.

Pole Mtn.

Austin Creek State Rec. Area

Queens Pk.

Armstrong Redwoods State Reserve

Sweetwater Springs Rd.

Wild Hog Hill

Bradford Mtn.

W. Dry Creek Rd.

Canyon Rd.

Geyserville

Russian River

128

Lytton

Healdsburg

101

Hop Kiln Winery (Historic Landmark)

Westside Rd.

Limerick Ln.

Windsor

Pacific Ocean

Goat Rock

Jenner

116

Bridgehaven

Red Hill

Ocean View

Serano Del Mar

Carmet

Sugarloaf

Salmon Creek

Guerneville

Duncans Mills

see inset

Monte Rio

River Rd.

Rio Nido

116

Rio Dell

Burke's Canoes

Forestville

Graton Rd.

Graton

Molino

Occidental Rd.

Sonoma Coast State Beaches

Sheep Ridge

Camp Meeker

Bohemian Hwy.

Occidental

Hacienda

Eastside Rd.

Sonoma Co. Airport

Shiloh Reg. Park

Redwood Hwy.

Laguna Rd.

River Rd.

Fulton Rd.

Fulton

Mark West Springs Rd.

Santa Rosa

TO SONOMA & THE VALLEY OF THE MOON

Bodega Marine Life Refuge

Bodega Bay

Bodega Harbor

Doran Reg. Park

Bodega Head

Bodega

Freestone

Bodega Highway

Ragle Ranch Reg. Park

Valley Ford Cutoff

Sebastopol

12

Estero Americano

Valley Ford

Knowles Corner

Todd Rd.

Cunningham

Bloomfield Rd.

12

Spring Lake

Bennett Valley Rd.

Dillon Beach

Tomales Bluff

Elephant Rocks

Fallon

Bloomfield

Sonoma Co. Marin Co.

Fallon Two Rock Rd.

1

Dillon Beach Rd.

Valley Ford Rd.

Petaluma Valley Ford Rd.

Stony Pt. Rd.

116

101

Rohnert Park

Crane Cyn Rd.

Point Reyes Nat'l Seashore

Tule Elk Reserve

Tomales

Petaluma Rd.

Tomales-Petaluma Rd.

Two Rock

Bodega Ave.

Cotati

Sonoma State University

Crane Creek Reg. Park

Pressly Rd.

Tomales Bay

Stony Pt. Rd.

D St.

Penngrove

Sonoma Mtn.

Petaluma

Adobe Rd.

Petaluma Adobe St. Historic Park

TO SONOMA

summer only crossing

Duncan Mills Museum

Duncan Mills

116

Cazadero Hwy.

Moscow Rd.

Guernewood Park

Monte Cristo

Villa Grande

Monte-sano

Guerneville

Vacation Beach

North-wood

Ped Bridge

Mays Canyon Rd.

El Bonita

Rio Nido

Rolands

Korbel Champagne Cellars

12

Rio Nido Rd.

Odd Fellows Park

Chileno Valley Rd.

Petaluma

116

Lakeville Hwy.

Frates Rd.

TO SONOMA

Stage Gulch Rd.

Russian River Communities

Bohemian Grove (private)

116

Sonoma County

BAY AREA

FROM THE ROAD

DRINK TO YOUR MIND

n my life, I had been to one wine tasting party (with a reputed expert no ess), and had definitely consumed ny fair share of the fermented grape beverage—surely, then, I was prepared for wine country. However, as I wandered into the wineries around Sonoma Valley, I slowly realized how ittle I knew.

It wasn't at all that I was being ridiculed or ignored. Quite the contrary, in fact. The staff was warm and receptive to all of my questions, no matter how elementary they were. Nonetheless, my ignorance of the language of winemaking made me feel a bit uncomfortable.

In the beginning, I would look over the tasting menu and choose the wine with the most awards or the highest price. Sometimes I would simply ask the server to choose. They were happy to oblige (especially when I mentioned cost as a criterion), but I wanted to feel more instrumental in the process. The approach wasn't wrong, just weak. As I asked more questions, tasted more wines, and read more information, I began to feel like I knew a bit more about wine and what I was doing. The whole process became much less intimidating.

I discovered that a few hundred wine types exist in the world, but that most Californian wines are made from about a dozen major ones, known as varietals. Though soil, climate, and the hand of the winemaker all play important roles in creating a wine's flavor, certain characteristics of each varietal come through in a wine no matter what. By law, at least 75% of a

⌨ TRANSPORTATION

From San Francisco, take **U.S. 101 North** over the Golden Gate Bridge, then follow Rte. 37 East to Rte. 121 North, which crosses Rte. 12 North to Sonoma. Alternatively, follow U.S. 101 North to Petaluma, then cross over to Sonoma by Rte. 116. Allow 1-1½hr. from San Francisco.

Route 12 traverses the length of Sonoma Valley, from **Sonoma** through **Glen Ellen** to **Kenwood** in the north. The center of downtown Sonoma is **Sonoma Plaza**, which contains City Hall and the Visitors Center. **Broadway** comes to a dead end in front of City Hall at Napa St. The numbered streets run north-south. **Petaluma** lies to the west and is connected to Sonoma by **Route 116,** which becomes **Lakeville Street** in Petaluma.

Buses: Sonoma County Transit (☎576-7433 or 800-345-7433; www.sctransit.com) serves the entire county. Bus #30 runs from **Sonoma** to **Santa Rosa** (daily every 1½hr. 6am-4pm; $2.05, students $1.70, seniors and disabled $1.00, under 6 free); buses #44 and #48 go to **Petaluma** (M-F; $1.75, students $1.45, seniors and disabled $0.85). A **"SummerPass"** allows unlimited summer rides for those under 18 ($20) and can be bought at the Safeway on Mendocino Ave. Within Sonoma, county buses stop when flagged down at bus stops (M-Su 8am-4:25pm; $0.95, students $0.75, seniors and disabled $0.45). **Golden Gate Transit** (☎541-2000 from Sonoma County or 415-923-2000 from San Francisco, TDD 257-4554) runs buses frequently between **San Francisco** and Santa Rosa. **Volunteer Wheels** (☎800-992-1006) offers door-to-door service for people with disabilities. Call for reservations. Open daily 8am-5pm.

Bike Rental: Sonoma Valley Cyclery, 20093 Broadway (☎935-3377), in Sonoma. Bikes $6 per hr., $25 per day; includes helmet. Open M-Sa 10am-6pm, Su 10am-4pm.

🛈 PRACTICAL INFORMATION

Visitor Information: Sonoma Valley Visitors Bureau, 453 E. 1st St. (☎996-1090; www.sonomavalley.com), in Sonoma Plaza. Maps $2. Open June-Oct. daily 9am-7pm; Nov.-May 9am-5pm. **Petaluma Visitors Program,** 800 Baywood Dr. (☎769-0429), at Lakeville St. Open May-Oct. M-F 9am-5:30pm, Sa-Su 10am-6pm; shorter weekend hours in the off-season. The free visitor's guide has listings of restaurants and activities.

Road Conditions: ☎817-1717.

Police: ☎778-4372 in Petaluma, ☎996-3602 in Sonoma.

Hospital: Petaluma Valley, 400 N. McDowell Blvd. (☎ 781-1111).

Post Office: 617 Broadway (☎ 800-275-8777), at Patten St., in Sonoma. Open M-F 8:30am-5pm. **Postal Code:** 95476. Also at 120 4th St., in Petaluma. Open M-F 8:30am-5pm, Sa 10am-2pm. **Postal Code:** 94952.

ACCOMMODATIONS & CAMPING

Pickings are pretty slim for lodging; rooms are scarce even on weekdays and generally start at $85. Less expensive motels cluster along **U.S. 101** in Santa Rosa and Petaluma. Campers with cars should try the **Russian River Valley** (see p. 174).

Redwood Inn, 1670 Santa Rosa Ave. (☎ 545-0474), in Santa Rosa. Clean, comfortable rooms and suites with kitchenettes, cable TV, phones, and bath. Singles $55; doubles $65. Prices $5 less in winter. Ask about AARP and AAA discounts. ❹

Sonoma Creek Inn, 239 Boyes Blvd. (☎ 939-9463 or 888-712-1289), traveling west off of Hwy. 12, in Sonoma. 10min. from the Sonoma Plaza, restaurants, and wineries. Colorful rooms with kitchenette, cable TV, phone, and full bath. Rooms $89-159. ❺

Sugarloaf Ridge State Park, 2605 Adobe Canyon Rd. (☎ 833-5712; www.parks.ca.gov), off Rte. 12, north of Kenwood in the Mayacamas Mountains. 49 sites, with tables and fire rings, around a central meadow with flush toilets and running water, but no showers. In summer and fall, take advantage of the day/night sky observing at Ferguson Observatory inside the park; see www.rfo.org for details. Reserve through ReserveAmerica (☎ 800-444-7275; www.reserveamerica.com). Sites $12, seniors $10; day use $2. No credit cards at the park, but ReserveAmerica accepts MC/V. ❶

San Francisco North/Petaluma KOA, 20 Rainsville Rd. (☎ 763-1492 or 800-992-2267; www.koa.com), in Petaluma off the Penngrove Exit. Suburban camp with 300 sites plus a recreation hall with activities, a petting zoo, a pool, a store, laundry facilities, and a jacuzzi. Hot showers. Lots of folks, many families. Check-in 1pm. Check-out 11am. 1 week max. tent stay. Reservations recommended. 2-person tent sites $31-35; each additional adult $5, child $3. RVs $38-41. Cabins (sleep 4; no linens) $55-60. ❸

FOOD

Fresh produce is seasonally available directly from area farms or at roadside stands and farmer's markets. *Farm Trails* maps are free at the Sonoma Valley Visitors Bureau. Those in the area toward the end of the summer should ask about the ambrosial **crane melon,** a tasty cross hybrid of fruits, grown only on the

wine must be made from a specific varietal in order to list that varietal on the label. Each varietal (and its wines) has specific, distinguishing attributes. For example, the white grape Chardonnay produces rich, crisp, complex wines. Most are dry and full-bodied with medium acidity and smell faintly like apples, melons, or figs. Cabernet Sauvignon, a red grape, can make a velvety wine. Sometimes hints of cedar, black currants, or stewed fruit are discernible. Once I knew what to expect, it became fun to compare the variations of scents and flavors within varietals and between different varietals.

After grasping the concept of varietals and memorizing their typical characteristics, I learned how soil and climate subtly affect flavor. Vineyards fall into distinct geographical regions called appellations. Topography, climate, and soil define each area and impart characteristics to the grapes grown under these conditions. For a winemaker to include an appellation on the label, 85% of the wine must come from that area. Trying to detect differences in similar wines from various appellations became a game.

The most important bit of information I learned, however, was the differences in bottle sizes. Buying anything larger than a Jeroboam (3 liters or 4 glasses) left me far too drunk to taste what I was drinking anyway. The 15 liter Nebuchadnezzar would have to wait for larger crowds. To really compare wines and develop a critical palate, I had to restrict my tasting. It's worth it though, for at my next wine tasting party I'll be the "reputed" expert." *Salud!*

—Eliza Dick

Crane Farm north of Petaluma. The **Sonoma Market,** 520 W. Napa St., in the Sonoma Valley Center, is an old-fashioned grocery store with deli sandwiches ($5-7) and *very* fresh produce. (☎996-0563. Open daily 6am-9pm.) For inexpensive fruit, head to the **Fruit Basket,** 18474 Sonoma Hwy. (☎996-7433. Open daily 7am-7pm. No credit cards.) All things generic can be found at **Safeway,** 477 W. Napa St. (☎996-0633. Open 24hr.)

▓ **Sonoma Cheese Factory,** 2 Spain St. (☎996-1931 or 800-535-2855; www.sonoma-jack.com), in Sonoma. Forget the wine for now—take a toothpick and enjoy the free cheese samples. You can even watch the cheese-making process in the back room. Sandwiches ($4.50-5.50). Open daily 9am-6pm. ❷

√ ▓ **The Vasquez House,** 414 First St. E. (☎938-0510), in El Paseo de Sonoma. Inconspicuously tucked behind touristy shops, this historic house hides a library and a miniscule tea room serving coffee, tea, and lemonade ($0.75) and freshly baked "indulgences" ($1). Open W-Su 1:30-4:30pm. No credit cards. ❶

Maya, 101 E. Napa St. (☎935-3500), in Sonoma. Brings Yucatan spirit to Sonoma. The festive decor, mouth watering food, and extensive wine and tequila menu are impressive. No wonder Maya won 2002 Best New Restaurant in Sonoma County. Entrees $6-19. Live music Th 9:30pm-12:30am in summer (no cover). Open M 4-9pm, Tu-Th and Su 11:45am-9pm, F-Sa 11:45am-10pm; in winter Su and M 4-9pm. ❸

Murphy's Irish Pub, 464 First St. E. (☎935-0660; www.sonomapub.com), in El Paseo de Sonoma. A sign here reads, "God created whiskey to keep the Irish from ruling the world," but Murphy's reigns supreme in the land of food and drink. Burgers, stews, salads, sandwiches ($7-9), and beer ($4). No Bud, so don't ask. Live music Th-Sa 8pm, Su 6pm. Open Su-Th 11am-11pm, F-Sa 11am-midnight. ❷

Sonoma Meritage, 522 Broadway (☎938-9430), in Sonoma. This bistro serves up the best breakfast in town ($6-10) and a mouth-watering weekend brunch (around $10). Try homemade gelatos and sorbet flavors like Rosepedal. Lunch specials $8-9. The Oyster Bar is a favorite. Pastas and entrees $13-$24. Brunch Sa-Su 11:30am-3pm. Open M and Sa-Su 11:30am-3pm and 5:30-9pm, W-F 8am-11am and 5:30-9am. ❹

◢ WINERIES

Sonoma Valley's wineries, near Sonoma and Kenwood, are less touristy but just as elegant as Napa's. As an added bonus, many of the tastings of current vintages in the Sonoma Valley are complimentary. Near Sonoma, white signs will help guide you through backroads. They are difficult to read but indicate the wineries' general directions. Take a close look at the *Let's Go* map or bring an extra one along on the ride (they're all over the place and free), as the signs will often desert you when they're most needed.

IN & AROUND SONOMA

▓ **Gundlach-Bundschu,** 2000 Denmark St. (☎938-5277; www.gunbun.com). Established in 1858, Gundlach-Bundschu is the 2nd oldest winery in Sonoma and the oldest family-owned and run winery in the country. Its unpronounceable name is offset by fragrant wines and a setting of pronounced loveliness. In summer hosts many outdoor events, such as the Mozart series. Tours of the wine storage caves Sa-Su every hr. 11am-3pm or by appointment. Free tastings daily 11am-4:30pm and during evening events.

Buena Vista, 18000 Old Winery Rd. (☎252-7117; www.buenavistawinery.com), off E. Napa St. The oldest premium winery in the valley. Famous stone buildings are preserved just as Mr. Haraszthy built them in 1857 when he founded the California wine industry. Theatre shows July-Sept. Historical presentations July 1st-Labor Day 11am and 2pm. Self-guided tours. Tastings ($5, including glass) daily 10am-5pm.

Ravenswood, 18701 Gehricke Rd. (☎938-1960; www.ravenswood-wine.com), in Sonoma. Edgar Allan Poe himself would have approved of the red Zinfandels here, which are often described as "gothic." "Unwimpy" wines produced by a surprisingly light-hearted group who believe "wine should also be fun." Price of tastings ($4) is applicable to wine purchase (and well worth it). Tours by appointment at 10:30am. Open daily 10am-4:30pm.

GLEN ELLEN

☒ **Benziger,** 1833 London Ranch Rd. (☎935-4046 or 888-490-2379; www.benziger.com). This winery is known for its big, buttery, rich and accessible wines. Tourists flock here for the acclaimed 40min. tram ride ($5) through the vineyards, which runs in the summer at 11:30am, noon, 12:30, 1:30, 2, 3, 3:30pm. Self-guided tours lead from the parking lot through the vineyards and peacock aviary. Tastings of current vintage free, limited $5, reserves $10. Open daily 10am-5pm.

KENWOOD

Kunde, 10155 Sonoma Hwy. (☎833-5501; www.kunde.com), near Kenwood. On hot afternoons, the cave tours at Kunde offer a cool break from the California sun. Known for its Chardonnays. Free tastings. Open daily 10:30am-4pm.

Ledson Winery and Vineyards, 7335 Sonoma Hwy. (☎833-2330; www.ledson.com). A relatively new vineyard, known as a Merlot estate, that does not market its wines. Every summer weekend, noon-4pm, they host free music concerts and offer a BBQ meal ($12). Home to many benefits and shows throughout the year. Free tastings daily 10am-5pm.

Kenwood, 9592 Sonoma Hwy. (☎833-5891; www.kenwoodvineyards.com). One of few wineries using organic grapes. Known for its Jack London Wolfe wine (they buy the grapes from his estate). Free tastings of current vintage, $5 for private reserves. Free 15min. tours daily 11:30am and 2:30pm. Open M-F 10am-4:30pm.

BAY AREA

◎ SIGHTS & SEASONAL EVENTS

SONOMA STATE HISTORIC PARK. Within the park, an adobe church stands on the site of the **Mission San Francisco-Solano,** the northernmost and last of the 21 Franciscan missions. It marks the end of the El Camino Real, or the "Royal Road." Built in 1826 by Padre Jose Altimira, the mission has a fragment of the original California Republic flag, the rest of which was burned in the 1906 post-earthquake fires. *(E. Spain and 1st St., in the northeast corner of town. ☎938-9560. Open daily 10am-5pm. $1, children under 16 free. Includes Vallejo's Home, the barracks, and Petaluma Adobe.)*

GENERAL VALLEJO'S HOME. The site is often referred to by its Latin name, *Lachryma Montis,* meaning "Tears of the Mountain." This "Yankee" home of the famed Mexican leader, who also was mayor of Sonoma and a California senator, is open for tours of the museum, pond, pavilions, and gardens. The grounds are garnished by a serene picnic area designed in part by Vallejo and his wife. *(¾ mi. northwest of Sonoma Plaza on Spain St. ☎938-9559. Open daily 10am-5pm. $1, children under 16 free.)*

JACK LONDON STATE PARK. Around the turn of the 20th century, hard-drinking and hard-living Jack London, author of *The Call of the Wild* and *White Fang,* bought 1400 acres here, determined to create his dream home. London's hopes were frustrated when the estate's main building, the Wolf House, was destroyed by arsonists in 1913. London died three years after the fire and is buried in the park, his grave marked by a volcanic boulder intended for the construction of his house. The nearby **House of Happy Walls,** built by his widow in fond remembrance of Mr. London, is now a two-story museum devoted to the writer. The park's scenic 0.5 mi.

Beauty Ranch Trail passes the lake, winery ruins, and quaint cottages. There are many longer trails that provide a greater challenge. Take **Lake Trail** (1 mi.) from the parking lot to the lake. There, follow **Mountain Trail** (0.35 mi.) to a lovely vista point. Continue on Mountain Trail all the way to the Park Summit (2.6 mi.) or circle around Woodcutter's Meadow on the **Fallen Bridge Trail** (1.3 mi.) to return. *(Take Hwy. 12 4 mi. north from Sonoma to Arnold Ln. and follow signs. ☎ 938-5216. Park open daily 9:30am-7pm; in winter 9:30am-5pm. Museum open daily 10am-5pm.)* **Sonoma Cattle and Napa Valley Trail Rides** also amble through the fragrant forests. *(☎ 996-8566. 2hr. ride $55.)*

SEASONAL EVENTS. Sonoma Plaza hosts festivals and fairs nearly every summer weekend. **Kenwood** heats up **July 4,** when runners gather for the Kenwood Footrace, a tough 7½ mi. course through hills and vineyards. A chili cook-off and the **World Pillow Fighting Championships** pass the rest of the day. Eager contenders straddle a metal pipe over a mud pit and beat the hell out of each other with wet pillows.

SANTA ROSA   ☎ 707

Famed horticulturist Luther Burbank once said of Santa Rosa (pop. 140,000), "I firmly believe, from what I have seen, that this is the chosen spot of all the earth, as far as nature is concerned." Of course, whatever Luther envisioned gave way long ago to the concerns of developers, who cast tract housing here and shopping malls there, effectively hiding Santa Rosa's commercial dominance over Sonoma County under a veil of suburban torpor.

■ ◪ ORIENTATION & PRACTICAL INFORMATION. Santa Rosa is at the intersection of **U.S. 101** and **Route 12,** 57 mi. north of downtown San Francisco. **Cleveland Avenue** marks the city's western edge. The town center is occupied by a mall, which interrupts A St. and 2nd through 5th St. **Mendocino Avenue** and **4th Street** define the bustling yet spotless downtown area. The **Railroad Square** area, bounded by **4th, 5th,** and **Wilson Streets,** houses Santa Rosa's trendiest shops and most charming cafes. The neighborhoods surrounding the city's heart are not some of the safest. **Exercise caution after dark.**

Greyhound buses, 435 Santa Rosa Ave., 4 blocks from 2nd St., run to San Francisco. (☎ 545-6495 or 800-231-2222. 4 per day; $12 one-way, $24 round-trip.) **City Bus** (☎ 543-3333) covers the main streets of Santa Rosa for $1; carry exact change and get a schedule at the Visitors Bureau. To rent **bikes,** call **Rincon Cyclery,** 4927 Sonoma Hwy., at Rte. 12. They rent mountain and road bikes, hybrids, and tandems—the shop is near off-road trails. (☎ 800-965-2453. Open M-F 10am-6pm, Sa-Su 10am-5pm. $7 per hr., $25 1st day, $20 per additional day, $100 per week. 2hr. minimum. Tandems $10/$14/$150. Free maps.) The **Greater Santa Rosa Convention and Visitor Bureau,** 9 4th St., at Wilson St. in the old North-West train depot, sells maps and brochures for $1. (☎ 577-8674 or 800-404-7673; www.visitsantarosa.com. Open M-F 8:30am-5pm, Sa-Su 10am-3pm.) The **Sonoma County Wine and Visitors Center,** 5000 Roberts Lake Rd., east of U.S. 101, in Rohnert Park, sells maps of most area wineries and a tasting directory. (☎ 586-3795. Open daily 9am-5pm.) Other local services include: **police** (☎ 543-3600); **Santa Rosa Memorial Hospital,** 1165 Montgomery Dr. (☎ 546-3210); and **Post Office,** 730 2nd St., between D and E St. (☎ 528-2209. Open M-F 8am-6pm, Sa 8am-2pm.) **Postal Code:** 95402.

▐ ACCOMMODATIONS. Santa Rosa offers basic road-side motels in addition to a few swanky downtown lodgings. **The Redwood Inn ❹,** 1670 Santa Rosa Ave., offers limited local calls and cable TV in impeccably clean rooms. Breakfast snacks, coffee and kitchenette are also provided in each room. (☎ 545-0474. Singles $45; doubles $65. 10% discounts for AAA members.) **The Country Inn ❹,** 2363 Santa Rosa

Ave., has tidy rooms with cable TV, phones, refrigerators and coffee. There is also an outdoor pool. (☎546-4711. Singles M-F $55, weekends $65; doubles M-F $65, Sa-Su $75; prices drop $5 in winter. 10% discount for seniors.) The historic **Hotel La Rose ❺**, 308 Wilson St., is located in Railroad Square, which adds to its charm and price. Rooms come with cable TV, phones, a continental breakfast, and access to a roof-top jacuzzi. Check-in after 3pm; check-out by noon. (☎579-3200. Rooms from $179 in summer; $144 in winter. AAA and AARP members receive 10% off, and Saver's Club and Quest Card holders receive 50% off.)

🖸 FOOD. Fresh produce can be found at the Wednesday night **farmer's market** at 4th and B. St. (Open W 5-8:30pm.) **Organic Groceries**, 2481 Guerneville Rd., near Fulton St., has every organic food you've ever heard of in bulk quantities. (☎528-3663. Open M-F 9am-8pm, Sa-Su 10am-7pm.) **The Rose Pub & Restaurant ❸**, 2074 Armory Dr., serves classic, old-world Irish dishes like Kerry Pie ($9), as well as seafood options such as black tiger shrimp ($14). Puffed pastry filled with potatoes, carrots, mushrooms, and peas in a curry sauce ($9) will delight vegetarians. (☎546-7673. Open Tu-Sa 3-10pm; kitchen open 4pm.) **Mixx ❹**, 135 Fourth St., has modern American dishes infused with Mediterranean, Asian, and Southwestern spices. (☎573-1344. Lunch $9-16. Dinner $18-26. Open M-Sa 11:30am-2pm and 5:30-9pm. Reservations are welcome and suggested for weekend evenings.)

🖸 🎵 SIGHTS & ENTERTAINMENT. The **Luther Burbank Home & Gardens,** at Santa Rosa and Sonoma Ave., is a great place to stop and smell the chamomile or pet the lamb's ears (herbal, not animal). At the age of 26, the horticulturist Burbank fled to California from Massachusetts to carry out his maniacal plant-breeding experiments, with the aim of improving the quality of plants and thereby increasing the world's food supply. He created over 800 new varieties of plants, some of which are exhibited in his gardens and greenhouse. (☎524-5445. Gardens open Apr.-Oct. daily 8am-7pm; Nov.-Mar. 8am-5pm. House open Apr.-Oct. T-Su 10am-4pm. Tour every 30min. until 3pm. Tour $3, under 12 free.)

Luther Burbank Center for the Arts, 50 Mark West Springs Rd., is the new state-of-the-art home for big name music concerts, as well as other lesser-known talent. The 2002 summer season hosted artists like Jewel, Diana Ross, Art Garfunkel and Roseanne. (☎546-3600; www.lbc.net. Box office open M-Sa noon-6pm.) The **Redwood Empire Ice Arena,** 1667 W. Steele Ln., is decorated with original Snoopy stained glass artwork. (☎546-7147. $5.50, under 11 $4.50; skate rental $2.) If you're tired of working for peanuts, get some sympathy next door at **Snoopy's Gallery,** which continues the ice rink's artistic theme. Every souvenir imaginable is sold here. Good grief! (Open daily 10am-6pm.) Haven't had enough? You're in luck. Visit the new **Charles M. Schulz Museum,** One Snoopy Pl. (☎579-4452; www.charlesmschulzmuseum.org), that opened in August 2002. Here the work and legacy of Mr. Schulz and the Peanuts gang are celebrated and officially preserved.

If you are biking or driving, Sonoma County's backroads offer scenery that surpasses even that on Rte. 12. **Bennett Valley Road,** between Kenwood and Santa Rosa, **Petaluma Hill Road,** between Petaluma and Santa Rosa Ave., and **Grange/ Crane Canyon Road,** connecting the two, offer particularly good views of the countryside. If you are on a bike, remain aware of drivers; the surroundings can distract you from the blind turns and hills. Drivers along these routes should be especially alert for bicyclists.

Annual events include the **Dixieland Jazz Festival** (☎539-3494; www.sonomacountydixiejazz.org), with non-stop music and dancing on the last weekend in August. **The Green Music Festival** at Sonoma State University, 1801 East Cotati Ave. in Rohnert Park, is a celebration of music, art and ideas. Events scheduled throughout July-August. (☎546-8742. M-F between 9am-6pm. Tickets $8-48.) The **Sonoma**

BAY AREA

County Fair is a two-week extravaganza from late July through early August. In the in the first weekend of October, Santa Rosa celebrates local food, wine and artists at the **October Harvest Fair.** There are over 500 wines represented. ($5 admission. An additional $6 buys a wine glass and two tastes.) Also in the fall, the ⬛**World Championship Grape Stomp Contest** offers much more than fragrant, dirty feet. Live jazz and bluegrass music, horse rides and a petting-zoo draw locals and tourists alike. (Sonoma County Fairgrounds ☎545-4203; www.sonomacountyfair.org.)

RUSSIAN RIVER VALLEY ☎707

The Russian River Valley is a well-kept secret. Though many of its wineries have been operating nearly as long as their counterparts to the southeast, they are neither as well known nor as frequently visited. Along with small, intimate vineyards, the area is home to beautiful coastline, second-growth redwoods, and a scenic river, making it ideal for hiking and biking. In quiet Sebastopol, hippies and farmers coexist peacefully, biding their time until the next great social reckoning or marijuana raid. Unpretentious Guerneville is a small, gay-friendly community that plays host to those who want the Great Outdoors without having to sacrifice nightlife. Farther north and east, Healdsburg is a town of beauty and bucks, as well as a good base for winery exploration.

◪ ORIENTATION & PRACTICAL INFORMATION

The **Russian River** winds through western Sonoma County before reaching the Pacific Ocean at Jenner. The river flows south, roughly following **U.S. 101** until **Healdsburg,** where it veers west. A number of small towns line this western stretch of river, including **Guerneville, Monte Rio,** and **Forestville.** This area is quite compact by California standards; none of the towns are more than a 40min. drive apart. **Sebastopol,** not a river town itself, claims kinship to those towns because of its location on **Route 116,** "the road to the Russian River." To reach Sebastopol, travel west on **Route 12** from Santa Rosa.

Buses: Golden Gate Transit (in Sonoma ☎541-2000, in San Francisco 415-923-2000) connects the Russian River area and the Bay Area. Free explanatory maps at visitors centers. Bus #78 heads north from Freemont between Mission and Howard to **Sebastopol** (2hr.; 4:17, 4:55, 5:19pm; $6.30). Morning buses to Santa Rosa available. **Sonoma County Transit** (☎576-7433 or 800-345-7433) has a county-wide route (#20) from Santa Rosa Ave. to the Russian River area. Leaves from 2nd St. and B St. (M-F 10 per day 5am-8pm, Sa-Su 3 per day 10:30am-6:45pm; to Sebastopol $1.50, to Guerneville $2.)

Bike Rental: Bicycle Factory, 195 N. Main St. (☎829-1880), Sebastopol. Mountain bikes $8 per hr., $24 per day (with helmet, lock, and water bottle). Open M-F 10am-6:30pm, Sa 10am-5pm, Su 10am-4pm.

Visitor Information: Sebastopol Area Chamber of Commerce, 265 S. Main St. (☎823-3032). Open M-F 9am-5pm. **Healdsburg Chamber of Commerce,** 217 Healdsburg Ave. (☎433-6935). Open M-F 9am-5pm, Sa-Su 10am-2pm. **Guerneville Chamber of Commerce and Visitors Bureau,** 16209 1st St. (24hr. info line ☎869-9000). Open Su-W 9:30am-7pm, Th-Sa 9:30am-8pm.

Post Office: Sebastopol, 290 S. Main St. Open M-F 8:30am-5pm. **Postal Code:** 95472. **Healdsburg,** 409 Fosscreek Circle (☎433-9276). Open M-F 8:30am-5pm. **Postal Code:** 95448.

ACCOMMODATIONS & CAMPING

The Russian River Valley's least expensive option is camping, for the tourist industry on the Russian River caters to a well-heeled, elegant, B&B-staying crowd. Nonetheless, there are a couple of indoor options that won't break the bank.

Johnson's Beach Resort, on 1st St. (☎869-2022), in the center of Guerneville. The family-run resort emphasizes that they are and always have been a place for families. The Resort is a throw-back in time: burgers, hot dogs, and beers are all the same price ($1.50) and crooners, like Sinatra, play on the speakers. Canoes ($7 per hr., $20 per day), paddle boats ($7 per hr.), and inner-tubes ($3 per day) are the cheapest on the river. The campground looks like a parking lot, but the friendly atmosphere more than makes up for it. The **Russian River Jazz Festival** is held here. Free river access. Recreation and laundry room available. Reservations only for cabin rentals of 1 week or more. Open May 15th-Oct. 15th. Sites $12, each additional person $2; RVs $20-25; well-worn cabins with fridge and TV $50-60. No credit cards. ❶

River Village Resort & Spa, 14880 River Rd. (☎869-8130 or 800-529-3376; www.rivervillageresort.com), Guerneville. A delightful venue with pool and spa treatment across the street from the Russian River. Rooms are uniquely decorated with hand-crafted furniture and art. Pets allowed in designated cottages. Offers many concierge services. Ask about winter packages and senior rates. Reservations advised for weekends and holidays; minimum stay may be required. 20 units $90-195. ❺

The Willows, 15905 River Rd. (☎869-2824 or 200-953-2828), Guerneville. Directly on the Russian River, staying here is more like camping in someone's backyard than in the woods, but many amenities, like free canoes and kayaks, outdoor jacuzzi and sauna, and use of a semi-outdoor kitchen, are all included. The atmosphere caters to a youthful adult, party-going crowd and welcomes all kinds—"hate stops here"—except pets. The scene gets a little wild; leave the kids at home. Sites May-Sept. $25 per person, $20 per person for 3 or more nights. Rooms $79-139; in winter $10-20 less. ❷

Faerie Ring, 16747 Armstrong Woods Rd. (☎869-2746), just south of Armstrong Woods State Reserve, 1½ mi. north of Guerneville. Privately operated, gay-friendly campground has quiet sites with tables and fire rings. Hot showers. Reservations recommended, especially on weekends. Children welcome, ask where appropriate sites are located. Recreation room, some exercise equipment. Rooms in the mobile home lodge and cabins $45-65. Sites Oct.-Apr. $15; RVs $20. May-Sept. $5 more. Upper-level tent sites $5 extra, but may be worth the extra distance from the road. ❷

FOOD

The health-conscious Russian River Valley sprouts good and good-for-you restaurants. The entire area is overflowing with food fit for the gods.

Willow Wood Cafe, 9020 Graton Rd. (☎823-0233) in Graton, off Rte. 116. This out-of-the-way cafe and country market is more than worth the detour. Food so fresh, you'd think they harvest for each individual order. Try the polenta with goat cheese ($6.75) for dinner or the delectable roast pork tenderloin sandwich ($7) for lunch. Chai ($2.75) comes in big ceramic bowls. Open M-Th 8am-9pm, F-Sa 8am-9:30pm. ❷

Screamin' Mimi's, 6902 Sebastopol Ave. (☎823-5902), Sebastopol. Unless your mouth is too full, you'll be screamin' praises for the best ice cream and sorbet around ($2-3.75). This colorful shop makes rich delights such as its signature Mimi's Mud (espresso, fudge, and Oreo). They also have a full line of coffees and teas. Open June-Sept. daily 11am-11pm; Oct.-May Su-Th 11am-9:30pm, F-Sa 11am-11pm. ❶

BAY AREA

East-West Cafe, 128 N. Main St. (☎829-2822), Sebastopol. Mediterranean platters make this the best local vegetarian-friendly restaurant. Weekday breakfast specials $6. Free-range chicken or tofu fajitas $8. Thai iced tea and ginger honey lemonade. Wine and beer available. Open M-F 7:30am-9pm, Sa 8am-9pm, Su 8am-8pm. ❷

Sparks, 16248 Main St. (☎869-8206), Guerneville. Serves organic vegetarian and vegan fare. The menu is always changing but look forward to unique plates like oyster, mushroom, and summer vegetable kebobs drizzled in savory Brazilian sauce ($12) and seasonal beverages like hibiscus and mint cooler sweetened with chicory syrup ($1.50) or sangria ($4.50). Cooking classes M-W. Open Th-Su 5:30-9pm, Sa-Su 10am-3pm. ❸

🜛 SIGHTS

The **wineries** in the Russian River Valley are typically smaller, more remote, and less crowded than those in Napa and Sonoma. The *Wine Country Map of the Russian River Wine Road,* free at every visitors center and Chamber of Commerce in Wine Country, has an excellent map and lists every winery in the area, complete with hours, services, and products. Here are some favorites highlighted. Traveling a few miles northwest along Rte. 116 from Sebastopol brings visitors to **Forestville.** This is the site of **Topolos at Russian River Vineyards,** 5700 Rte. 116 (Gravenstein Hwy.), known most for their Zinfandels and efforts toward an all organic vineyard. Complimentary tasting and restaurant dining is offered. (☎887-1575 or 800-867-6567. Restaurant open W-Su 11:30am-2:30pm and 5:30-9:30pm; tasting room open daily 11am-5:30pm.) Just outside Guerneville, the **Korbel Champagne Cellars,** 13250 River Rd., bubble with popular free tours, which cover the cellars, brewery, rose gardens, and tasting room. A deli offers gourmet sandwiches for $6. (☎824-7000. Tours daily 10am-3:45pm. Tastings daily 9am-4:30pm; in winter 9am-4pm.) The unpretentious **Hop Kiln Winery,** 6050 Westside Rd., in Healdsburg, is a historic landmark. Visitors are welcome to complimentary wine, olive oil, and chutney tastings. (☎433-6491. Open daily 10am-5pm for tasting, grounds close at 5:15pm.) Those with an interest in art will feel right at home at **Roshambowinery,** 3000 Westside Rd., 3 mi. south of Healdsburg. It overlooks miles of vines, framed by rolling golden and green mountains. (☎888-535-WINE/9463. Open Su-M and W-Sa 10:30am-4:30pm. Gallery openings 4-8pm as announced.) Fountains abound at the more intimate **Trentadue Winery,** 19170 Geyserville Ave., 1 mi. south of Geyserville. Tourists can either watch winemaking in action (although tours are dependent on available personnel) or picnic under a canopy of grape leaves, clematis, and potato lion. (☎433-3104. Tasting room open daily 11am-4:30pm.) Also in Geyserville, the award-winning **Château Souverain,** 400 Souverain Rd., at the Independence Ln. Exit, offers wine tasting to the country club elite. The chic cafe looks out on the palatial winery and its magnificent expanse of vineyards. (Tasting room ☎888-809-4637; cafe 433-3141. Tastings daily 10am-5pm. Cafe open daily 11:30am-2:30pm and F-Su 5:30-8pm.)

Burke's Canoe Trips rents canoes to make the 10 mi. trip to Guerneville. This fee includes a ride back; Burke's runs two buses every 30min. to shuttle people. (☎887-1222. Canoes $42 per day. No credit cards; call ahead for return service to your car. Open May-Oct. M-F 9:30am-6pm, Sa-Su 9am-6pm.) **Russian River Kayaks,** 2030 Rte. 116, has a private landing right on the river. (☎865-2141. Kayaks or bikes $5 per hr., $15 for 4hr., $25 per day. Open M-Sa 8am-5:30pm, Su 10am-4pm; later returns can be arranged.) Just 10min. north of Guerneville, the **Armstrong Woods State Park** (☎869-2015) and its manifold redwoods rise from Sonoma's golden hills. Hiking, biking, and horseback riding opportunities abound. The 1 mi. **Pioneer Trail,** starts at the Visitors Center parking lot and skirts Fife Creek. For a challenging trek take the **East Ridge Trail** (6.8 mi.), which climbs 1600 ft.

◙ NIGHTLIFE

Guerneville is *the* night spot in the Russian River Valley. It is predominantly a gay scene, although no one is made to feel unwelcome. ◙**Stumptown Brewery,** 15145 River Rd., 1 mi. east of Guerneville, is a funky venue with unique in-house brews ($4-7). Live music and an outdoor patio looking out over the Russian River. One piece of advice: don't ring the bell. (☎ 869-0705. Open daily noon-2am. Cash only.) The **Rainbow Cattle Co.,** 16220 Main St., has a few posters of men in thongs on the wall, stickers stating "Hate Stops Here" and proudly welcomes everyone. (☎ 869-0206. Open daily 6am-2am.)

Sebastopol's **Apple Blossom Festival,** in late April, has entertainment, crafts, and food. The **Sebastopol Music Festival** (☎ 800-648-9922) also occurs at this time. There are free concerts each Sunday from 2-4pm, June-August, on the plaza in Healdsburg. The **18th Festival of Art and Wine** (☎ 824-8717), in Duncan Mills, occurs in late June. The **Russian River Valley Winegrowers Grape to Glass Weekend** (☎ 522-8726), in mid-August, is the big event of the season, when over 30 wineries offer free tours and tastings. The **Russian River Jazz Festival** is a major event at Johnson's Beach Resort, blasting trombone, trumpet, and piano melodies down the river the weekend after Labor Day. (☎ 869-3940. Tickets from $26.)

BAY AREA

THE FAR NORTH

California's vast, oft-forgotten Far North offers a peaceful escape from the crowding and congestion that typifies California life. Small and friendly towns dot the countryside, and the coastal and mountain wilderness is some of the most remote in the state. The Far North stretches from Mendocino County north along the coast to the Oregon border and east into the rich, densely forested Cascades. Along the way, the region offers plenty of activities for the small-town enthusiast, the nature-lover, and the outdoor adventurer.

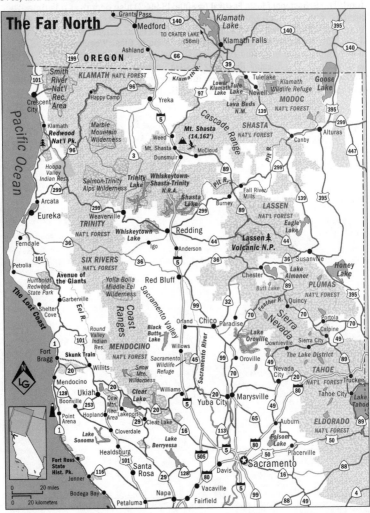

The Far North

THE NORTH COAST

Wind-swept and larger than life, the North Coast may well be the crown jewel of California's natural wonders. Redwoods stretching beyond skyscrapers, prairies as gold as sun-kissed honey, and black sand beaches still undiscovered by tourists defy human comprehension. The traveler will marvel at the unchanging, isolated feel of this stunning region, whose pre-historic forests and dread-locked hippies inhabit a land that time forgot.

The North Coast begins in the San Francisco Bay Area and continues to the Oregon border. Roadtrip voyagers on the North Coast can take one of two scenic highway routes. Hwy. 1 (see below) offers coastal views of the shores of Marin, Sonoma, and Mendocino Counties. One hour north of Fort Bragg, Hwy. 1 turns sharply inland and travels miles away from the coast, merging with U.S. 101 for the journey north. Prior to this juncture, U.S. 101 meanders through the heart of California's wine country on its way to sleepy farmlands and the stopover town Ukiah.

The shore the highways leave behind, which is known as the Lost Coast (see p. 185), offers some of the most rugged scenery in the state. Lost Coast marijuana farmers are (in)famous for cultivating what smokers consider to be some of the kindest bud in the world, but there are heavy penalties for growing on federal land. The inland leg of U.S. 101 brings travelers to the Avenue of the Giants, home of the redwoods that make the region famous. Past Eureka and Arcata, U.S. 101 winds along the coast again, as redwoods tower alongside, protected by the long strips of Redwood National and State Parks (see p. 192).

HIGHWAY 1:
THE PACIFIC COAST HIGHWAY

Easy driving it is not, but Highway 1 (the Pacific Coast Highway, or PCH) is one of the world's most breathtaking stretches of road. North of San Francisco, the famous highway snakes along rugged cliffs between pounding surf and monolithic redwoods. Drivers will appreciate opportunities to recover from the heart-stopping journey in quaint coastal hamlets. Be prepared, however, for slow trailers on the road and sky-high prices for food and accommodations. The least expensive options are outdoors: camping, hiking, and picnicking. However, the coast is home to some of the loveliest inns and B&Bs around, which may persuade travelers to splurge after a week in the wilderness. For more on Hwy. 1, see **Central Coast**, p. 317, and **Bay Area**, p. 121.

BODEGA. The highway winds its way out of the Bay Area via San Rafael, nearing the breathtaking Point Reyes National Seashore (see **Marin,** p. 151). Continuing north, Hwy. 1 takes a brief inland turn before meeting the ocean again at surf haven Bodega Bay. On the Sonoma coast west of Bodega Bay, the **Bodega Head Loop** is a short coastal hike with pristine beach and ocean views. To reach the 1.5 mi. trail from the town **Bodega Bay,** turn left on E. Shore Rd. Turn west on Bay Flat Rd. and continue around the Bay. Continue past Spud Point Marina to Bedge Head parking, where the trailhead is located. The small town of Bodega Bay keeps its seafaring roots alive in the form of incredibly fresh salmon and crab at oceanside restaurants. The **Visitors Center,** 850 Coast Hwy. 1, has info on the North Coast. (☎707-875-3866. Open M-Th 10am-6pm, F-Sa noon-8pm, Su 11am-7pm.) Both the towns of Bodega Bay and Bodega, 1½ mi. away, were featured in Alfred Hitchcock's 1963 film *The Birds*. See pictures at the Visitors Center.

Sonoma Coast State Beach begins just north of Bodega Bay off Hwy. 1. The 5000 acres of land offer 16 mi. of beach, spectacular views, and a variety of spots in which to picnic, hike, and camp. Nonetheless, don't venture too far into the ocean—unpredictable currents make these beaches dangerous for swimming and surfing (see **Sleeper Waves,** p. 187). The two most popular coastal campgrounds are **Bodega Dunes ❶** (hot showers, 98 sheltered sites $12) and **Wright's Beach ❷** (sites $16). Call ReserveAmerica for reservations at ☎800-444-7275 or 875-3483.

FARTHER NORTH. Heading up, Hwy. 1 hits Jenner, where the Russian River enters the ocean. Jenner's **Goat Rock Beach,** is the site of the famous harbor seal rookery. Twelve miles up the coast from Jenner is **Fort Ross State Historic Park.** (☎707-847-3286. Entrance fee $2.) A lonely walled fort clinging to the ocean bluffs, **Fort Ross** marked the eastern limit of former imperial Russia. Russians migrated here from outposts in Alaska to hunt otters and find farmland, but had to leave in 1841 after they had hunted the otters to near extinction and lost vast sums of money. **John Sutter,** of mill and creek fame, bought the fort for a song, primarily to get the redwood threshing table inside. The fort now houses a small museum and a comprehensive bookstore. (Museum open daily 10am-4:30pm. Free with $2 entrance fee to park.) The park features the only reconstructed Russian buildings in the continental US and has 6 mi. of sandy beaches. Hwy. 1 is usually closed in this area at least once per year due to spring rains, but Fort Ross is accessible via detour. Fort Ross may be accessed by bus as well as car. The **MTA Coast Bus** runs one weekday loop daily from Point Arena to Santa Rosa. (☎800-696-4682. $6.75-$11, students $5.50-8.75, seniors 50% discount.) Take the MTA's daily coast run from Point Arena on the way to Santa Rosa and get off at Fort Ross (see **Sonoma Valley: Practical Information,** p. 166). Camping is also available in the Fort Ross Historic State Park. **Reef Campground and Day Use Area ❶,** 2 mi. south of the Fort, offers 21 primitive campsites with fire rings and picnic tables. (First-come, first-served only. Water spigots. Flush toilets. Dogs allowed. Open Apr.-Nov. Sites $12; day use $2.) **Salt Point State Park ❶,** north of Fort Ross, 20 mi. from Jenner, offers 6000 acres, including 6 mi. of rugged North Coast. There are 109 sites with firepits and picnic tables. (☎707-847-3221, reserve through ReserveAmerica 800-444-7275. No showers. Dogs allowed. Drinking water and toilets. Open for day use sunrise-sunset. Sites $12.)

Farther north on Hwy. 1 in Mendocino County, the fog-shrouded **lighthouse** and museum of **Point Arena** deserve a stop. The original building dates from 1869, but the 115 ft. lighthouse is vintage 1906, built after the San Francisco earthquake demolished the original. (☎707-882-2777. Open daily 11am-3:30pm. Free, guided tour $5.) Point Arena has 46 tent sites and hike/bike sites at **Manchester State Beach ❶.** (☎707-937-5804. Flush toilets. Sites $9, seniors $7; day use $5.)

BOONVILLE. Twenty-seven miles to the east over Mountain View Rd. is **Boonville**, where the main attraction is the rapidly fading local language **Boontling.** This language, which is basically a complex slang, is only known by a few old timers who are "white-oakin" (working hard) to keep it alive. Get some "bahl gorms" (good food) at **Boont Berry Farm ❷**, 13981 Rte. 128. They serve avocado, cheese, and chicken sandwiches ($4.75-5.75) and are known for their BBQ tofu on brown rice ($6.50 per lb.) A cup of "horn of zeese" (coffee) can be had for under $1. (☎707-895-3576. Open M-Sa 10am-6pm, Su noon-6pm.)

MENDOCINO ☎707

Teetering on bluffs overlooking the ocean, isolated Mendocino (pop. 1107) is a charming coastal community of art galleries, craft shops, bakeries, and B&Bs. The town's weathered wood shingles, white picket fences, and clustered homes seem out of place on the West Coast; perhaps that's why Mendocino was able to masquerade for years as the fictional Maine village of Cabot Cove in the TV series *Murder, She Wrote.*

◢◤ ORIENTATION AND PRACTICAL INFORMATION. Mendocino sits on **Highway 1,** right on the Pacific Coast, 30 mi. west of U.S. 101 and 12 mi. south of Fort Bragg. Although driving is the easiest way to reach Mendocino, once there, the tiny town is best explored on foot (plentiful street parking available). Mendocino, like all northern coast areas, can be very chilly. Travelers should prepare for 40-70°F temperatures.

The nearest **bus station** is two hours away in Ukiah. Greyhound runs two buses per day to Ft. Bragg. Mendocino Stage provides a shuttle service along the north Mendocino coast. It also runs buses between Ft. Bragg and Ukiah. (☎964-0167. 2 per day, $10.) **Mendocino Transit Authority,** 241 Plant Rd. makes one round-trip daily between Santa Rosa, Ukiah, Willits, Fort Bragg, and Mendocino. (☎800-696-4682. One-way $16, round-trip $26.50.) **Fort Bragg Door-to-Door Taxis** has an on-call passenger van service. (☎964-8294. Runs daily 10am-2am.)

For **visitor information,** contact the **Ford House,** 735 Main St., in Mendocino Village. (☎937-5397. Open in summer daily 11am-4pm; winter schedule depends on volunteers.) For **park-related general information,** call ☎937-5804, or go to the **MacKerricher State Park Visitor Center,** 3 mi. north of Fort Bragg. (☎964-8898. Open M-Th 11am-6pm, F-Su 10am-6pm; in winter Sa-Su 11am-3pm.) **Catcha Canoe and Bicycles, Too!** at Hwy. 1 and Comptche Rd., specializes in hand-crafted, redwood canoe rentals but also rents top quality bikes and kayaks. Call ahead for tide info. (☎937-0273. Canoes $18 per hr., $54 per day; bikes $10 per hr., $30 per day; kayaks $12 per hr., $36 per day. Open daily 9am-5:30pm.) **Lost Coast Kayaking** gives fantastic guided tours of Van Damme State Park. (☎937-2434. 2hr.; $45 per person. Tours available daily 9, 11:30am, 2pm. Reservations are necessary but walk-ins can get lucky sometimes. Open May-Oct.) For clean clothes, head to **Colombi Laundromat,** 647 Oak St., in Fort Bragg. (☎964-5773. Wash $1.75, 8min. dry $0.25. Open daily 7am-11pm.) **Internet access** is available at the **Regional Branch Library of Mendocino,** 499 Laurel St., on the corner of N. Whipple St. and Laurel St., three blocks east of Main St. in Fort Bragg. (Open Tu-W 11am-7:45pm, Th-F 11am-5:45pm, Sa 10am-4:45pm.) Emergency services include the **police** (☎961-0200) with a station in Fort Bragg, the **sheriff** (☎963-4086), and a **rape crisis line** (☎964-4357). **Mendocino Coast District Hospital** is located at 700 River Dr. (☎961-1234), Ft. Bragg. Find the **Post Office** at 10500 Ford St., two blocks west of Main St. (☎937-5282. Open M-F 7:30am-4:30pm.) **Postal Code:** 95460.

⌐ ACCOMMODATIONS. ◪**Jug Handle Creek Farm ❶,** 5 mi. north of Mendocino off Hwy. 1, across the street from the Jughandle State Reserve, is a beautiful 133-year-old house sitting on 40 acres of gardens, campsites, and small rustic cabins. Guests have access to the beach and trails in Jug Handle State Reserve (see **Sights,** p. 183). One hour of chores (or $5) is required per night. (☎964-4630. 30 beds. No linen. Reservations recommended in summer, walk-ins welcome. Dorms $20, students $14, children $9; sites $9; cabins $28 per person.) **Nicholson House Inn ❺,** 951 Ukiah St., is in the heart of town, right next to great restaurants and just a block from the ocean. Phones, TV, and breakfast are available in the Hospitality Living Room. (☎937-0934 or 800-962-0934. 2 night min. stay on weekends, 3 night min. stay on holidays. All reservations are to be paid in full in advance. Rooms $90-174; $5 less in winter.) Less expensive and less eye-pleasing options can be found in Fort Bragg. The most budget-friendly option is **Colombi Motel ❸,** 647 Oak St., five blocks east of Main St. It has clean single and double units with cable TV, a phone, and private bath; some units also have a full kitchen. (☎964-5773. Motel office inside market. Check-out 11am. Singles $45; doubles $55.) There are also hundreds of campsites nearby; interested travelers should call ReserveAmerica (☎800-444-7275) to make reservations, which are strongly advised in summer. **MacKerricher State Park campground ❶,** 3 mi. north of Fort Bragg, has excellent views of tidepool life, passing seals, sea lions, and migratory whales, as well as 9 mi. of beaches and a murky lake for trout fishing. Around this lake is **Lake Cleone trail**—a short (1 mi.), easy hike that features thick cypress trees and a pretty marsh. Access the trail from Cleone Camp or Surfwood Camp. (☎937-5804. Showers, bathrooms, and drinkable water. Sites $12; day use free.) Woods and, usually, fog shelter 30 sites at **Russian Gulch State Park campground ❶,** 2 mi. north of town on Hwy. 1. Campers have access to a beach, redwoods, hiking trails, and a 35 ft. waterfall. The **Falls Loop trail** (7 mi.) will take you to the rushing water. This trail is no secret but it will take you through a scattering of old-growth redwoods and reward you with the rock pounding falls. (☎937-5804. Showers and flush toilets. No hookups. Open Apr.-Oct. Sites $12, seniors $10; hike/bike $1; day use $2.)

☐ FOOD. All of Mendocino's breads are freshly baked, all vegetables locally grown, all wheat unmilled, all coffee cappuccino, and almost everything expensive. Most restaurants close at 9pm. Picnicking on the Mendocino Headlands is the cheapest option and should be preceded by a trip to **Mendosa's Market,** 10501 Lansing St., the closest thing in Mendocino to a real supermarket. It's pricey of course, but most items are fresh and delicious. (☎937-5879. Open daily 8am-9pm.) **Tote Fête ❶,** 10450 Lansing St., has delicious tote-out food, and the crowds know it. An asiago, pesto, and artichoke heart sandwich ($4.75) hits the spot. The Tote Fête Bakery in the back has a flowery garden and a small, serene fountain. (☎937-3383. Open M-Sa 10:30am-7pm, Su 10:30am-4pm; bakery open daily 7:30am-4pm.) **Lu's Kitchen ❷,** 45013 Ukiah St. west of Lansing St., is a local favorite. It serves cross cultural vegetarian cuisine in an informal, outdoor atmosphere. (☎937-4939. Prices range $5-10. Open daily 11:30am-5:30pm. Closed Jan.-Mar. and on very rainy days.) **Mendocino Cookie Co. ❶,** 10450 Lansing St., offers a caffeine fix and sugar high at once with a doubly potent super large latte ($3) and tasty white chocolate chip and macadamia cookie ($1.25). The Cookie Co. sells muffins, scones, and croissants as well. Everything is freshly baked. (☎937-4843. Open daily 6:30am-5:30pm.) **Cafe Beaujolais ❺,** 961 Ukiah St., bakes fresh brick-oven bread daily and has a remarkable garden that welcomes wandering. (☎937-5614. Dinner $19-25. Bakery open daily 11am-4pm and 5:45-9pm. Garden open daily 11am-4pm. Closed in Dec.) **Albion Inn ❻,** 3790 N. Hwy. 1, south of Mendocino, has a spectacular ocean view and award winning food. The menu changes periodically, but always count on roasted garlic caesar salad ($8), lime & ginger prawns ($24), and grilled pacific king salmon ($23) to satisfy taste buds. (☎937-1919 or 800-479-7944. Reservations suggested. Open M-F 5:30-9pm, Sa-Su 5-9pm.)

◐ ▣ SIGHTS AND ENTERTAINMENT. Mendocino's greatest attribute lies 900 ft. to its west, where the earth comes to a halt and falls off into the Pacific, forming the impressive coastline of the ▣**Mendocino Headlands.** The windy ¼ mi. stretch of land that separates the town from the rocky shore remains an undeveloped meadow of tall grass and wildflowers, despite its obvious value as a site for more multi-million dollar vacation homes.

In **Fort Bragg,** the **Skunk Train,** at Hwy. 1 and Laurel St., offers a jolly, child-friendly diversion through deserted logging towns and a recuperating forest. (☎964-6371 or 800-777-5865. 9:30am, 2pm; off-season 10am.) A steam engine, diesel locomotive, and vintage motorcar take turns running between Fort Bragg and Willits via Northspur. Round-trip rides include a short break in Northspur and an hour in Willits. Schedule changes necessitate calling ahead for reservations. (Half day $29-39, children $16-18; full day $45/25.)

Poor drainage, thin soil, and ocean winds have created an unusual bonsai garden 3 mi. south of town at the **Pygmy Forest** in **Van Damme State Park ❶** (camping $12; day-use $2). The Pygmy Forest, off Hwy. 1 past the park (after turning left, drive 3½ mi. to a parking lot and look for a sign) is open for free to hikers. The **ecological staircase** at **Jug Handle State Park** is a terrace of five different ecosystems, each roughly 100,000 years older than the one below it and formed by a combination of erosion and tectonic uplift.

An abundance of hot springs in the Mendocino area proves once and for all that the region is a natural paradise. **Orr Hot Springs,** 13201 Orr Springs Rd., is just east of Mendocino, off Comptche Ukiah Rd. Those wishing to simmer their stress away should take the North State St. Exit off U.S. 101. Sauna, steam room, and gardens make the world disappear at this clothing-optional resort. (☎462-6277. 18+. Day-use $20. Open daily 10am-10pm.) In July, enjoy the **Mendocino Music Festival,** a two-week mêlée of classical music, opera, and cultural dance. Tickets for some events go quick. (☎937-2044; www.mendocinomusic.com. Tickets $15-40.)

AVENUE OF THE GIANTS ☎707

About 10 mi. north of Garberville off U.S. 101 in the **Humboldt Redwoods State Park,** the Avenue of the Giants winds its way through 32 mi. inhabited by the largest living organisms above ground level. Hiking, swimming, fishing, biking, and rafting opportunities abound in this rugged area. A generous portion of lurid, 1950s-style tourist traps also share the region, lining the roadway with their tacky billboards.

◪ PRACTICAL INFORMATION. Greyhound (☎923-3388 or 800-231-2222) runs **buses**—two north and two south daily—out of Garberville to Eureka ($14), Portland ($59), and San Francisco ($34). Meet the bus behind the Six Rivers National Bank, 432 Church St., one block east of Redwood Dr.

The **Humboldt Redwoods State Park Visitors Center,** just south of Weott on the Avenue, has a very knowledgeable staff and free brochures highlighting the Avenue's groves, facilities, trails, bike routes and providing camping safety tips. The center also has hands-on displays for kids about area wildlife. (☎946-2263. Open Apr.-Oct. daily 9am-5pm; Oct.-Apr. Th-Su 10am-3pm.) The **Garberville-Redway Chamber of Commerce,** 773 Redway, Garberville, offers information on local events and attractions. (☎800-923-2613. Open M-F 10am-5pm.) The **Post Office** is at 368 Sprowl Creek Rd. (☎923-2652. Open M-F 8:30am-5pm.) **Postal Code:** 95542.

FAR NORTH

ACCOMMODATIONS & CAMPING. The **Brass Rail Inn ❹**, 3188 Redwood Dr., Redway, housed a brothel in 1939, but is now a perfectly respectable motel. (☎923-3931. Singles $50; doubles $60.) **The Redway Inn Motel ❹**, 3223 Redwood Dr., has bright, clean rooms with cable TV and coffee. (☎923-2660. Singles $50; doubles $60.) Farther north on the Avenue, the **Madrona Inn ❹**, 2907 Ave. of the Giants, in Phillipsville, has pink cottages, some with kitchens and two bedrooms. (☎943-1708. Cottages $55-100. Pets $5.) In Myers Flat, the bed and breakfast **Myers Inn ❺**, has homey bedrooms and offers boating and fishing tours. Hot breakfast included. (☎943-3259 or 800-500-6464; www.myersinn.com. Rooms $125-150.)

To sleep directly among the giants, camping is the best bet. In **Humboldt Redwood State Park ❶**, camping options are plentiful. Each developed campsite offers coin showers, flushable toilets, and fire rings. (☎946-2409. Sites $12.) The most remote site, wildlife-filled **Albee Creek ❶**, on Mattole Rd. 5 mi. west of U.S. 101, near Rockefeller Forest, has access to biking and hiking trails and is open year-round. **Hidden Springs ❶**, near Myers Flat, is situated on a hillside in a mixed forest and has 154 semi-secluded sites. Few hiking trails start directly at the campsite, but the South Fork of Eel River is a short hike away. (Open mid-May through mid-Oct.) **Burlington ❶** is next to the Visitors Center, but is haunted by the drone of the nearby freeway. (Open mid-May through Sept.) **Richardson Grove State Park ❶** (☎247-3318), off U.S. 101 8 mi. south of Garberville, has sites with toilets and showers. Call ReserveAmerica (☎800-444-7275) for reservations at any of the above.

FOOD Nearby Garberville offers a number of civilized eating options. **Sentry Market**, on Redwood Dr., is the largest supermarket for miles. (☎923-2279. Open daily 7am-10pm.) Locals highly recommend **Calico's Cafe ❷**, on Redwood Dr. next to Sherwood Forest Motel, for its homemade pastas, though it offers salads and grill items as well. Try the garlicky fettucine gorgonzola ($9) made from scratch. (☎923-2253. Open M-Th 8am-9pm, F-Sa 8am-10pm, Su 11am-9pm.) **Nacho Mama's ❷**, at Redwood Dr. and Sprowl Creek Rd., is an organic Mexican fast-food stand that people love for its healthy burritos, dolphin-free albacore tacos, and refreshing soy wildberry or peach frosties that taste as good as yo mama's. (☎923-4060. Entrees $3-9. Open M-Sa 11am-7pm.) For a 100% all-ranch burger ($5-8) stop by the **Chimney Tree Coffee Shop ❷**, 1111 Avenue of the Giants, just south of Phillipsville. There is also a hokey "hobbit" trail and burnt-out,"Chimney," redwood for the kids. (☎923-2265. Open M-Su 10:30am-7pm.) In Myers Flat, **Knight's ❸** is a promising choice. They are best known for their steaks and pasta dishes. (☎943-3411. Breakfast $4-9. Lunch $5-13. Dinner $17-20. Open daily 8am-9pm.)

SIGHTS & SEASONAL ACTIVITIES Scattered throughout the area are several tourist traps, such as **Eternal Tree House, Confusion Hill** (a vortex of mystery where the laws of gravity no longer apply; free), the **Drive-Thru Tree** ($1.50), and plenty of Bigfoot merchandise. Young children will be entertained by a train ride through the redwoods ($3). Hiking can be a more satisfying way to enjoy the redwoods' magnificence. To do longer trails, maps should always be in hand; they are available at the Visitors Center ($1) or at any of the campsites (see p. 183).

There are a number of short day-hikes. Half a mile north of Miranda, the **Stephens Grove Trail** is an easy 0.7 mi. walk. Stephens Grove was a campsite until a flood in 1964 destroyed it, and signs of the old campground can still be seen. Farther north, south of the Visitors Center, the 0.5 mi. **Kent-Mather** loop trail begins at the **Garden Club of America Grove** and wanders through redwood sorrel and sword and lady ferns. Look for ospreys near the river. At **Founder's Grove,** the 0.5 mi. nature trail loop features the 1300-1500 year old **Founder's Tree,** and the former tallest tree in Humboldt Redwoods State Park, the fallen **Dyerville Giant,** whose massive trunk stretches the length of 60 human bodies and whose three-story rootball looks like a mythical ensnarlment of evil.

Uncrowded trails wind through **Rockefeller Forest** in the park's northern section, which contains the largest grove of continuous old-growth redwoods in the world. The **Grasshopper Peak Trail,** a strenuous 14 mi. round-trip hike, starts at the Big Tree parking lot 4 mi. west of the Avenue on Mattole Rd. This is a hilly, all-day backcountry hike. This journey will take you 3379 ft. high to enjoy a gorgeous 360 degree panoramic view. **Grasshopper Trail Camp** is near the summit for overnight campouts. (Primitive sites. Pit toilets. $1 per person. Register in advance at headquarters.)

With its sizable population of artists, Garberville's **art festivals** are a big draw. **Jazz on the Lake** and the **Summer Arts Fair** begin in late June, followed by **Shakespeare at Benbow Lake** in late July. Early August brings a marathon of jammin' on the banks of the Eel River with **Reggae on the River,** a wild three-day festival. For more info on events, call ☎ 800-923-2613 or the Chamber of Commerce (see **Practical Information,** p. 183).

LOST COAST   ☎707

The Lost Coast can elude even the most observant visitor. When Hwy. 1 was built, the rugged coastline between Usal and Ferndale had to be bypassed and the highway moved inland; hence, this part of the coast was "lost" to modernization, leaving the jagged mountains, rocky shores, and black sand beaches comparatively untouched. Bring a map and 4WD because many roads are unpaved, steep, and poorly marked; it can be easy to get, well, lost. Be careful when exploring—you don't want to wander into someone's **marijuana farm.** Leave Humboldt County's marijuana farmers' cabins and crops alone. Be especially careful around harvest time, usually October and November.

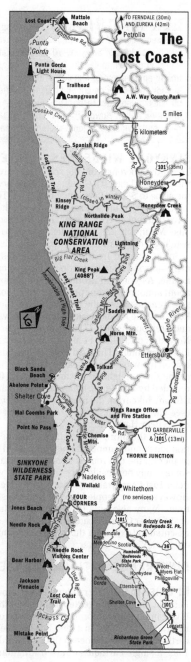

The Lost Coast

ELK MACHISMO Easy to spot thanks to their massive size and signature cream-colored rumps, Roosevelt elk have rebounded from near extinction to populate the prairies of Sinkyone Wilderness State Park and Redwood National and State Parks. In the fall, male elks (bulls) put their sheikh skills to the test in rivalries to control an entire group of females, known as a "harem." A challenger bull approaches an already spoken-for harem and bugles, urinates, and kicks up turf in a show of desire. If the sheikh-in-residence answers the challenge, some poor cream-rump could end up losing an antler. However, one of the bulls usually backs down before things escalate to an antler clash, as should visitors who make the mistake of getting too close.

SINKYONE WILDERNESS STATE PARK

To get to Sinkyone from the south, take Hwy. 1 to Usal Rd. (where Hwy. 1 starts to turn toward Leggett). Coming from the north, take U.S. 101 to Redway and follow the signs to **Shelter Cove** along Briceland-Thorn Rd. Ten miles farther is a four-way intersection: to the left is Usal Rd., which eventually leads to Usal Beach, along a drive that makes Hwy. 1 seem like child's play (4WD required). To the right is Chemise Mountain Rd., which leads back to Shelter Cove. Allow 2hr. to travel the winding wooded route with occasional vistas of the rugged Lost Coast.

Straight ahead from the intersection is Bear Harbor Rd., another treacherous drive—a road so narrow it only fits one car at a time—crafted for the fearless or insane. As you pull around the numerous blind hairpin turns, don't be bashful about announcing your presence with a sound honk of the horn. Dodging the man-size trenches down the mountain road, you will come across **Jones Beach, Needle Rock,** and the **Needle Rock Visitors Center,** which offers maps ($1), camping permits, and firewood. (☎986-7711. Visitors Center open hours vary; always closes at 5pm. No water; pit toilets. 14-night max. stay. Sites $12. First-come, first-camp. Usually fills in summer.) The road eventually leads to **Bear Harbor,** getting even more difficult on the way. The dedicated, however, will find their reward in the rustic beauty of the three neighboring campgrounds (**Orchard, Railroad,** and **Bear Harbor**). Surrounded by lush ferns, black sand, and transplanted eucalyptus trees, the sites are a 0.5 mi. hike from the road. Be prepared to share your space with the **Roosevelt elk** (see **Elk Machismo,** above). The blocked-off road to **Jones Beach** is just two mi. down Bear Harbor Rd.

One of the more popular Lost Coast beaches, **Usal Beach ❶** has a self-registration kiosk and camping areas (unmarked sites $12, trail camps $2). About 300 ft. farther up the dirt road is a short bridge and turn-off leading to a parking area and some windy beachside sites (no drinking water). The southern trailhead of the difficult **Lost Coast Trail** begins at Usal and leads 52 mi. up the coast to **Mattole River.** However, most people hike the Lost Coast north to south so that the wind is with them. Many also only travel from the **Mattole Campgound** to **Black Sands Beach,** near Shelter Cove, because that 24 mi. stretch hugs the coast. Again, trail maps are essential for exploring this wilderness and are available at state parks or the Needle Rock Visitors Center.

KING RANGE NATIONAL CONSERVATION AREA

▪ **ORIENTATION.** Stretching 24 mi. along the coast between Shelter Cove and Petrolia, the **King Range National Conservation Area** provides some of the best primitive camping in California. It is also one of North America's most unstable mountain ranges, as it sits on a fault line between three different tectonic plates. Intense earthquakes push the ocean floor skyward an average of 10 ft. every 1000 years. In 1992, a single earthquake raised King Range almost 4 ft. in a matter of minutes.

Home to many clean creeks, beaches, and an abandoned lighthouse, the area also provides varied possibilities for exploration on trips that can take anywhere from one to several days. 4WD vehicles are necessary to traverse many of the roads. **King Peak Road** travels through dense forest in the central part of the conservation area and leads to **Lightning, Saddle Mountain,** and **Horse Mountain Creek** trailheads, and the **Horse Mountain** and **Tolkan** campsites. It can only be traveled by 4WD vehicles, and no motor homes or trailers are permitted north of Hurse Mountain Campground. **Chemise Mountain Road** meanders through Douglas fir and leads to Roosevelt elk at the **Hidden Valley** trailhead (where the southern **Lost Coast Trail** begins), **Nadelos and Wailaki campsites,** and the **Sinkyone Wilderness State Park.** Use low gears on downgrades, watch for oncoming traffic on one-lane stretches, and pull over to allow cars behind you to pass.

⚑ CAMPING. Camping permits are required at all campgrounds for commercial outfitters but not for individuals or families. Fire permits are required for everyone and can be purchased at the **King Range Bureau of Land Management (BLM)** office, on Shelter Cove Rd., 7 mi. from Shelter Cove. (☎986-5400; www.ca.blm.gov/arcata. Open M-Sa 10am-5pm.) Permits may also be obtained at many local general stores, such as the nearby one in Petrolia. **A.W. Campground ❶,** between Honeydew and Mattole on Mattole Rd., is managed by Humboldt County and sits on the Mattole River. It has flush toilets and showers (sites $12). **Horse Mountain Camp ❶,** which is not located by the trailhead, is the most remote developed campground. Its 9 sites are windy, cool, and lacking water. **Tolkan ❶** is windy, secluded, and on a steep ridge. (13 sites, picnic tables, pit toilets, fire rings, no water. No RVs. Sites $7.) **Mattole Beach Campground ❶,** at the northern part of King Range, is at the end of Lighthouse Rd., 45min. north of Honeydew off Mattole Rd. There are pit toilets but no drinking water. (Sites $5, free day use.)

◎ 🄼 SIGHTS & HIKES. The windy, flat beach is framed by steep grass-covered mountains and rolling dunes. Here campers can enjoy the **Mattole River Estuary,** a nursery for young salmon and home to egrets and brown pelicans, or take off on the rather challenging **Lost Coast Trail** (25 mi. one-way to Shelter Cove, allow three days). Although it is possible to hike the trail one way and then backtrack to your vehicle, most campers use the **shuttle service** (see **Shelter Cove,** p. 188). The trek is long, but you will be rewarded with ever-changing vistas of mountains and coastline, as well as views of sea lions, shore birds, and black-tailed deer. All drinking and bathing water is supplied by the fresh water streams that run through the area. The ridge trails have no water, so if you plan a side hike, come prepared. You may also see a black bear, especially if your camp is not clean. Bear canisters are required on all King Range land and can be rented at the BLM office ($15). Always be on the lookout for poison oak, ticks, and rattlesnakes. Some of the trail is impassable during high tide; it is necessary to check **tide tables.** Do this at the King Range BLM, or buy them in Garberville or Petrolia. It's a good idea to stop by the BLM office and calling ahead to let them know your plans.

SLEEPER WAVES. Sleeper waves are overpowering waves that crash ashore and then forcefully pull back whatever or whomever they happen upon. Many beaches have posted warnings about such dangerous currents, and it is safest to simply stay out of treacherous waters. However, if yanked in by a sleeper wave, **do not swim toward shore.** Doing so will only tire you out in a futile battle against the current. Instead, swim parallel to the beach until you're out of the wave's clutches.

GESTURE OF INDULGENCE

The **Gingerbread Mansion Inn** is home to the most opulent room not only in Ferndale, but perhaps in Northern California. The Empire Suite takes up the entire third floor and is one grandiose gesture of indulgence. At $385 per night, it had better be.

This delightful Bed and Breakfast will be the stuff of wistful memories in years to come. In addition to a richly decorated boudoir (and bathrooms with claw-footed tubs), the breakfast experience is the work of a gourmet chef. Deliciously prepared morning meals are often decorated with edible wildflowers. To see some live flowers, head to the gorgeous rose garden, whose sights and scents provide the setting for an invigorating stroll. Afternoon tea, held from 4-6pm, welcomes visitors upon their return. The lowest rate is $150 for Zipporah's room; which is a cozy vision of Victorian style. (400 Berding St. ☎786-4000 or 800-952-4136l; http://gingerbread-mansion.com. Check-in 3-6pm, check-out 11am. Singles deduct $20 from room rates; triples add $40.)

The northern 24 mi. of Lost Coast trail ends in Shelter Cove at **Black Sands Beach,** which is open to beachcombing only at low tide. Do not attempt a swim here; the riptides will pull you out into the deep blue sea. From Black Sands Beach, those not wanting to make the entire Lost Coast trek but still wanting to see some of the action can hike north to Big Flat (8.5 mi.). It is all beach hiking and impassable during high tide, but is still a favorite of hardcore surfers seeking "killer" waves and camping enthusiasts enjoying the large coastal terrace. From Big Flat, a great inland day hike is **Rattlesnake Ridge Trail,** which leads to the fern shrouded canyon of Big Flat Creek (4 mi. one-way to Bear Hollow Camp).

Hikes abound in King Range. Three miles into the Lost Coast Trail, from Mattole, lies the **Punta Gorda Lighthouse.** It was first lit in 1917 and was known as the Alcatraz of lighthouses because of its remote location and reputation for being the station with which to punish deviant keepers. Allow half a day for the journey there and back, as most of the trail is slow-going sand hiking. **King Peak Trail** climbs 4,087 ft. to reach a panoramic view of endless forested peaks and more than 100 mi. of Pacific coastline. The hike is a moderate, steady climb from Lightning trailhead (2 mi. one-way) or a very gradual ascent from Saddle Mountain trailhead (5 mi. one-way). There is a spring near the top at Maple Camp for water.

SHELTER COVE

The tamest part of the wild Lost Coast, Shelter Cove was once a trading post. Native Americans bartered with each other here and settlers built a shipping port for fishing and wood products. Shelter Cove, on Point Delgada, is still home to a tiny community of fishermen and now welcomes vacationers as well. Tourists can view sea lions perched on coastal rocks at **Sea Lion Rock,** along lower Pacific Dr., or inspect tidepools and a historic lighthouse at **Mal Coombs Park,** next to Mario's Marina. Pick up news and advice at the **Shelter Cove Deli ❷,** 492 Machi Rd., the only place in town where you can get fish 'n' chips ($6.75), Shelter Cove souvenirs, a tide table, and aspirin all at once. The closest thing in town to an information booth, the deli also provides details on over 100 campsites next to the marina and runs shuttle services that take hikers from Black Sands Beach parking lot to the trailhead at Mattole Beach. (☎986-7474. Shuttles to be arranged, $125 per vehicle. Tent sites $16, RVs with full hookups $27. Open M-F 7am-8pm, Sa-Su 6am-8pm.) With bath and TV, the rooms at the **Shelter Cove Beachcomber Inn ❹,** 412 Machi Rd., are the best deals on this stretch of coast. Some have kitchens and fireplaces. (☎986-7551 or 800-718-4789. Singles from $55.) For an unobstructed ocean view and pet friendliness, stay at **Shelter Cove Motor Inn ❺**, 205 Wave Dr. All rooms have a small kitchenette and an ocean view. (☎986-7521 or 888-570-9676; www.sheltercovemotorinn.com. One queen bed $88; family units $120 in the summer, $75-105 in the winter. 10% discount for AOPA, AARP and AAA members.) The pricier **Oceanfront Inn and Lighthouse ❺**, 10 Seal Ct., also has seaside rooms and is closer to **Mario's Marina**, 533 Machi Rd. (☎986-1401), where the only open-daily restaurant and the site for chartering and launching boats are located. (☎986-7002. Rooms with kitchen available. All have private beach access and a private deck overlooking the ocean. One queen bed $125; the private lighthouse suite $175.) The **Cove Restaurant ❸** is on the Inn's first floor. (☎986-1197. Lunch $7-13, dinner $12-19. Open 11:30am-9pm.)

FERNDALE

The northernmost Lost Coast town of **Ferndale** (pop. 1320) exemplifies small-town perfection. The amphitheater-like **cemeteries** near **Russ Park** on Ocean Ave. give a sense of the town's history and provide a breathtaking view of the Victorian town and its grazing dairy cattle. The accommodations here are mainly exorbitantly priced B&Bs, but if you have been saving for a splurge, this is the place. One option is California's oldest B&B, the **Shaw House ❺**, 703 Main St. Founded in 1860, the Carpenter Gothic Revival-style home offers 7 rooms, a sit-down hot breakfast, and afternoon tea. (☎786-9958; www.shawhouse.com. Check-in between 4-6pm, check-out at 11am. Rooms in summer $85-165; in winter $75-165.)

🗹**Village Baking and Catering ❶**, 472 Main St., is worth a stop off the highway. Try the incredible Special Turkey Sandwich with homemade artichoke relish ($4.25), sip coffee drinks ($1-2.25), or delight in gooey sticky buns for under $2. (☎786-9440. Open M-Sa 7am-3pm, Su 7am-1:30pm.)

One of Ferndale's most curious features, the annual Arcata Kinetic Sculpture Race (see **Arcata: Sights,** p. 192), is revered at the studio of the event's founder, **Hobart Galleries**, 393 Main St., at Brown St. Down the street, the **Kinetic Sculpture Museum** is undergoing construction and renovation as the future Ferndale Community Center, though it will still display treasured artifacts from races past. Pieces constructed entirely from license plates will make you wonder how they ever managed to move at all, let alone travel 38 mi.

EUREKA ☎707

Eureka (pop. 27,218) was born out of the demands of mid-1800s gold prospectors, who wanted a more convenient alternative to the tedious overland route from Sacramento. The Humboldt Bay provided such a route, and Eureka was thus founded. As there is no more gold to be found and the lumber business has been stifled in order to protect the area's natural treasures, Eureka's survival is now based on fishing and tourism. The town may not be as appealing as some of its more attractive neighbors, but Old Town Eureka is regaining some of its historic attraction. Sitting next to the harbor are quaint shops, restaurants, and art galleries in old Victorian-style buildings. Don't judge Eureka only by driving through on Hwy. 101. The city's perimeter may reek of stinky pulp, but out of the center of Eureka wafts the powerful, alluring smell of old-town charm.

🔳🗹 **ORIENTATION & PRACTICAL INFORMATION.** Eureka straddles **U.S. 101**, 12 mi. south of Arcata and 280 mi. north of San Francisco. To the south, U.S. 101 is referred to as Broadway. In town, U.S. 101 is called 4th St. (heading south) and 5th St. (heading north).

FAR NORTH

Greyhound buses depart twice per day for San Francisco ($33-35) from 1603 4th St. at Q St. (☎442-0370 or 800-231-2222. Open M-F 9am-2pm, 3:30-5:45pm and 8-10pm.) The **Humboldt Transit Authority,** 133 V St., runs regional buses between Scotia and Trinidad ($1.40-2) via Arcata. Most buses pick up passengers along 5th St. or Broadway. (☎443-0826. 133 V St. Open M-F 8am-noon and 1-4:30pm.) The **Eureka/Humboldt Visitors Bureau,** 1034 2nd St., will answer specific questions. (☎443-5097 or 800-809-5908, out-of-state 800-346-3482. Open M-F 9am-5pm.)

Eureka's **Chamber of Commerce,** 2112 Broadway, has information and brochures. Ask about any discounts they may be offering. (☎442-3738 or 800-356-6381. Open M-F 8:30am-5pm, Sa-Su 10am-4pm.) An **ATM** is at the **Bank of America,** near the corner of E and 4th St. and at the **Eureka Co-op** on 5th St., at L. St. **Summer Street Laundromat** is at 111 Summer St. (☎443-7463. Wash $2-4.75, dry $0.25 per 7min. Open daily 7am-9pm.) Eureka has **police** (☎441-4044) and **fire departments** (☎441-4054). The **Eureka General Hospital** is at 2200 Harrison Ave. (☎445-5111 ext. 4699). The **Post Offices** are located at 337 W. Clark St., near Broadway St. (☎442-1768; open M-F 8:30am-5pm and Sa noon-3pm) and 514 H St. at 5th St. (☎442-1828. Open M-F 8:30am-5pm.) **Postal Code:** 95501.

⌂ ACCOMMODATIONS & CAMPING. Travelers will find many budget motels off U.S. 101, but most are unappealing; be selective. It is not recommended to walk around alone at night, especially along Broadway. Old Town Eureka is more suitable for evening dinners and strolls. For an indulgent night, a hidden haven can be found above ◪**Cafe Waterfront ❺,** in Old Town at First and F St. The restaurant owns two plush Victorian rooms with a kitchen and breakfast nook to share. It feels like a private harbor-view apartment. (☎444-1301. Breakfast included. Rooms in summer $125-175; winter $100-150.) **Motel 6 ❸,** 1934 Broadway, lies south of town off U.S. 101 and offers satellite TV. (☎445-9631. Singles $46-50; doubles $52-56; additional person $3. Rates may vary in July and Aug.) Pricey but dependable, the **Red Lion Hotel ❺,** on U.S. 101 at the northern edge of town, has immaculate rooms. (☎445-0844. Singles $89; doubles $94. $10-15 discounts for AAA members.) Most of the area's camping is closer to Arcata than Eureka. **Big Lagoon County Park ❶,** 20 mi. north of Eureka on U.S. 101, is a favorite. The park has 32 sites with flush toilets, drinking water, and a big lagoon for swimming, canoeing, and kayaking. (☎445-7652. No hookups. Sites $12, day-use $2; arrive early to beat the rush.)

◖ FOOD. Eureka Co-op, 1036 5th St. at L St., sells bulk grains, organic produce, and deli foods. (☎443-6027. Open M-Sa 7am-9pm, Su 8am-9pm.) There are also two **farmer's markets** that run in summer and fall. (Old Town Gazebo June-Oct. Tu 10am-1pm; Henderson Center July-Oct. Th 10am-1pm.) **Ramone's Bakery and Cafe ❶,** 209 E St., between 2nd and 3rd St., specializes in homemade truffles, fresh-baked pies, and the ever-popular "Chocolate Sin," a chocolate and liqueur torte. Sandwiches ($4), soups ($3), and salads ($4) are also available. (☎445-2923. Open M-Sa 7am-6pm, Su 8am-4pm.) Across the street, experience a taste of Italian tradition at **Gabriel's ❹,** 216 E St. Stuff yourself with pastas ($11-15) and pizzas and calzones ($11-13), but save room for homemade desserts like cannolis and spumoni ($5-7). (☎445-0100. Entrees $14-40. Open M-Th 11:30am-2:30pm and 5-9pm, F-Sa 11:30am-2:30pm and 5-10pm, Su omelette buffet 10am-1pm.) **Saffire Rose Cafe ❷,** 520 2nd St., is located in the Historic Vance Hotel. Dine inside an old-fashioned brass elevator and listen to live Jazz every Fri. and Sat. night. Grilled panini sandwiches ($6-9) and salads ($6-10) are offered for both lunch and dinner, and there is a dinner buffet special on weekend nights. (☎441-0805, Open daily 9am for coffee, breads, and pastries, Su-Th 11am-9pm, F-Sa 11am-midnight.) **Cafe Marina ❸,** 601 Startare Dr., is off U.S. 101 at the Samoa Bridge Exit (Rte. 255). From there, take the Woodley Island Exit north of town. Outdoor dining on the marina is the perfect way to enjoy their fresh seafood, like the spicy blackened snapper. The polished bar is a night spot for local fishermen. (☎443-2233. Lunch $10-15. Dinner $13-18. Open in summer daily 7am-10pm; off-season daily 7am-9pm.)

◙ VICTORIANS, DUNES, & ART. Eureka is very proud of its bevy of restored **Victorian homes,** a few of which are worth driving past (self-guided tour maps are available at the Chamber of Commerce). Some of the more handsome houses are now expensive B&Bs. If you drive by, don't miss the oft-photographed, dramatically stark **Carson Mansion,** which belonged to a prominent logger in the 1850s. **Art galleries,** Eureka's main claim to fame, cluster downtown. Checkout **First Street Gallery,** 422 1st St. (☎443-6363), **The Ink People Gallery,** 411 12th St. (☎442-8413), or the **Morris Graves Museum of Art,** 636 F St. (☎442-0278) for their interesting collections. Ask the Chamber of Commerce about current exhibits. The **dunes recreation area,** in Samoa off Rte. 255 (past the cookhouse and left at Samoa Bridge, on the north end by the jetty), was once a thriving dune ecosystem. Now, this peninsula offers beach access and dune hiking.

ARCATA ☎707

Arcata is like Berkeley without San Francisco. At the intersection of U.S. 101 and Rte. 299, Arcata (ar-KAY-ta; pop. 16,300) typifies the laid-back, stress-free existence that characterizes the North Coast. Check out the town's many murals, Victorian homes, and characters living "alternative" lifestyles. Arcata's neighbor, Humboldt State University, focuses on forestry and marine biology (Earth First! was founded here). All over Humboldt County, students and would-be students get baked in the sun—and on the county's number-one cash crop.

⚠ PRACTICAL INFORMATION. Arcata Chamber of Commerce, 1635 Heindon Rd., has visitor information. (☎822-3619. Open daily 9am-5pm.) An **ATM** is at **U.S. Bank,** 953 G St. Just like the bank, the most convenient **laundromat** is M.O.M.'s, 5000 Valley West Blvd. (☎822-1181. Open daily 7:30am-9:30pm.) **Adventure's Edge,** 650 10th St., rents outdoor equipment. (☎822-4673. Tents $20 for the first 3 days, $3 per additional day. Sleeping bags $14 for the first 3 days, $2 each additional day. Sea kayaks $30 same day return, $35 per 24hr. Cross-country ski packages $18 per 3 days. Open M-Sa 9am-6pm, Su 11am-5pm.) Other services include **Mad River Hospital,** 3800 Janes Rd. (☎822-3621), and the **Post Office,** 799 H St. (☎822-3570. Open M-F 8:30am-5pm.) **Postal Code:** 95521.

⌂ ACCOMMODATIONS & CAMPING. Arcata has many budget motels off U.S. 101 N at the Giuntoli Exit. One of these is **Motel 6 ❸,** 4755 Valley West Blvd. It is clean and quiet, and offers cable TV, pool, and A/C. (☎822-7061. Singles Su-Th $40, F-Sa $45, off-season singles $42; 2nd adult $6 extra, 3rd and 4th $3 each.) A classier, pricier dig is the historic **Hotel Arcata ❹,** 708 9th St., in the town's center. (☎826-0217 or 800-344-1221. Su-Th singles $70; doubles $120, F-Sa $75-140.)

For those with cars, camping is easy near Arcata. The popular **Clam Beach County Park ❶,** on U.S. 101, 7½ mi. north of Arcata, has dunes and a huge sand beach with seasonal clam digging; call ahead. (☎445-7651. Campsites with water and pit toilets $8, entrance fee for hikers and cyclists $3.) **Patrick's Point State Park ❶,** 15 mi. north of Arcata, is an excellent spot for watching whales and seals. It has 124 sites with terrific ocean views, lush vegetation, and treasure-hunting in the beach's tidepools and agates. (☎677-3570. Showers and flush toilets. No dumpsite. $12 per vehicle; no hookups. Day use $2 per car. Reservations are strongly recommended; make them through ReserveAmerica at ☎800-444-7275.)

◘▣ FOOD & ENTERTAINMENT. Golden Harvest Cafe ❷, 1062 G St., a popular breakfast venue, caters especially to vegetarians and vegans. All dishes $4-8. (☎822-8962. Open M-F 6:30am-3pm, Sa-Su 7:30am-3pm.) **Crosswinds ❷,** 860 10th St., in a restored Victorian home, offers a number of breakfast and lunch variations in large portions. Vegan substitutes are available for all meat used in the Mexican, Italian, and Californian specialties, which cost $5-9.25. (☎826-2133. Open Tu-Su 7:30am-2pm.) The **Arcata Co-op ❷,** a crunchy supermarket on 8th St. at I St., sells tofu, tempeh, ginseng cola, and soy milk. (☎822-5947. Open daily 7am-9pm.) **Folie Douce ❹,** 1551 G St., is a chic venue for dinner and drinks with a seasonal menu. (☎822-1042. Appetizers $8-9. Wood-fire oven pizza $9-12. Entrees $16-27. Kitchen open Tu-Th 5:30-9pm, F-Sa 5:30-10pm; bar stays open late. A **farmer's market,** offering tie-dyed dresses, candles, and the usual fresh produce, livens up the Arcata Plaza on Saturdays (Apr.-Nov. 9am-1pm). Several local bands playing at full volume make the affair a weekly party.

As a college town, Arcata maintains its share of bars, most of which are on 9th St. in the town square. **Humboldt Brewery,** 856 10th St. at I St., is a popular local microbrewery with an extensive collection of sports memorabilia lining the walls. Unusual beers like the Red Nectar Ale go well with a game of pool. (☎826-2739. Open Tu 4pm-midnight, W-Sa noon-midnight.) **Jambalaya Restaurant and Saloon ❹,** 915 H St., at 9th and H St., is a great place to hang with locals, eat a fine meal ($13-21, seasonal menu), and listen to occasional live jazz and blues. (☎822-4766. Open Tu-Su from 5pm until late.)

◙ SIGHTS & SEASONAL EVENTS. Experience Arcata by taking a **walking tour** around the **Arcata Plaza,** in the center of town near the intersection of 8th and H St. The plaza offers folk music on the weekends and an annual **Summer Solstice Festival** (on the weekend nearest the summer solstice). The Natural History Museum (13th and G St.) is a short walk from the plaza and home to an impressive collection of whale skulls. Nearby **Redwood Park,** at 14th and Union St., contains lots of nooks for picnicking among the giants. Behind the park lies the **Arcata Community Forest,** which has picnic spaces, lush meadows, redwoods, and hiking trails (free). Camping is illegal here, although the rule is often broken. A former "sanitary" landfill, the 75-acre **Arcata Marsh and Wildlife Sanctuary** lies at the foot of I St., across from Samoa Blvd. Visitors can wander the trails around the lake or take a tour to see how this saltwater marsh/converted sewer system works with treated waste. Take **Sanctuary Trail** (2 mi.; 1hr.) on the northern edge of Humboldt Bay for great bird watching opportunities. (☎826-2359. Tours Sa 8:30am and 2pm; meet at info center. Open daily 9am-5pm.)

The 32-year-old **Kinetic Sculpture Race,** held annually over Memorial Day weekend, is Humboldt County's oddest festival. A few dozen insane and/or intoxicated adventurers attempt to pilot unwieldy homemade vehicles on a grueling three-day, 38 mi. trek from Arcata to Ferndale on road, sand, and water. Past vehicles are on display at a museum in Ferndale (see p. 189).

REDWOOD NATIONAL & STATE PARKS ☎707

With ferns that grow to the height of humans and redwood trees the size of skyscrapers, Redwood National and State Parks, as John Steinbeck said, "will leave a mark or create a vision that stays with you always." The redwoods in the parks are the last remaining stretch of the old growth forest that used to blanket two million acres of Northern California and Oregon. Wildlife runs rampant here, with black bears and mountain lions in the backwoods and Roosevelt elk grazing in the meadows. While a short tour of the big sights and the drive-through trees will certainly give visitors ample photo opportunities, a more memorable way to experience the redwoods is to head down a trail into the quiet of the forest, where you can see the trees as they have been for thousands of years.

AT A GLANCE

AREA: 112,613 acres . **CLIMATE:** Cool and foggy.	**GATEWAYS:** Orick (p. 197), Klamath (p. 198).
FEATURES: Redwoods, Fern Canyon, Battery Point Lighthouse.	**CAMPING:** Developed and undeveloped sites. (See p. 195.)
HIGHLIGHTS: Whale-watching off the Coastal Trail, hiking to the Tall Trees Grove.	**FEES & RESERVATIONS:** Free. $2 per day for Jedediah Smith, Del Norte Coast, and Prairie Creek Redwoods. $2 per day per car for daytime parking.

■ ORIENTATION

Redwood National and State Parks is an umbrella term for four contiguous redwood parks. **Redwood National Park** (between Klamath and Orick) is the southernmost of four; the others, from south to north, are **Prairie Creek Redwoods State Park, Del Norte Coast Redwoods State Park,** and **Jedediah Smith Redwoods State Park.** The tiny town of **Orick** marks the southern limit of the parks. Just south of town is an extremely helpful ranger station. **Crescent City,** with park headquarters and a few basic services, is at the northern end of the park region.

■ TRANSPORTATION

Orick and **Klamath** border the national forest to the south and north. **U.S. 101** traverses most of the parks. The slower but more scenic **Newton Drury Parkway** runs parallel to U.S. 101 for 31 mi. from Klamath to Prairie Creek (watch for bikers).

■ PRACTICAL INFORMATION

FAR NORTH

Entrance Fees: No charge to enter, but $2 per car for day-use of parking and picnic areas. South of Orick are free off-highway areas; ask at visitors centers for locations.

Buses: Greyhound, 500 E. Harding St., Crescent City (☎464-2807). To **San Francisco** (2 per day, $58.50-62.50) and **Portland** (2 per day, $60.50–64.50). Open M-F 7-10am and 5-7:30pm, Sa 7-8:15am and 7-7:30pm. No credit cards.

Auto Repairs: AAA Emergency Road Service (☎800-222-4357). 24hr.

Visitor Information:

Redwood Information Center (☎464-6101, ext. 5265), on U.S. 101, 1 mi. south of Orick. Shows an informative video on redwoods. Free park maps useful; more detailed maps for sale as well. Info on trails and campsites doled out by enthusiastic and helpful rangers. Open daily 9am-5pm.

Redwood National Park Headquarters and Information Center, 1111 2nd St., Crescent City (☎464-6101, ext. 5064). Headquarters of the entire national park, although ranger stations are just as well informed. Open daily 9am-5pm. Closed Su in winter.

Prairie Creek Information Center (☎464-6101, ext. 5301), on the Newton Drury Scenic Pkwy. in Prairie Creek Redwood State Park Campground. Open in summer M-Th 9am-5pm, F-Su 9am-6pm, when volunteers are available; in winter daily 10am-5pm.

Crescent City-Del Norte County Chamber of Commerce, 1001 Front St., Crescent City (☎464-3174). Free coffee, brochures, and coupons. Very knowledgeable staff to assist you with your travel plans. Open M-Sa 9am-7pm.

Hiouchi Ranger Station (☎464-6101, ext. 5067), on U.S. 199 across from Jedediah Smith Redwoods Park. Open June-Sept. daily 9am-5pm; Oct. Sa-Su depending on staff availability.

Six Rivers National Forest Station (☎457-3131), on U.S. 199 in Gasquet, has info about recreation opportunities in the Smith River National Recreation area and nearby campgrounds Panther Flat, Grassy Flat, and Big Flat. Open in summer M-Sa 8am-4:30pm, in winter M-F 8am-4:30pm.

Jedediah Smith State Park Information Center (☎464-6101, ext. 5113), on U.S. 199 across from the Hiouchi Ranger Station in the campground. Open in summer daily 9am-5pm.

REDWOOD CHAINSAW MASSACRE Rising up hundreds of feet above the ground, the trees in Redwood National Park have towered in lush profusion for 150 million years. Native Americans called these lofty giants "the eternal spirit" because of their 2000-year lifespan, ability to adapt to climatic changes, and resistance to insects, fire, and even lightning. The redwoods were indeed almost invincible—until the era of logging. With money on their minds (1 tree builds 22 houses) and saws in their hands, loggers chopped 96% of the virgin coast redwoods in one century. Despite the economic boom that the logging industry brought to the area's small towns, conservationists fought back to maintain the forest ecology. Concerned citizens began buying redwood plots from loggers in the 1920s, and in 1968 the Redwood National Park was formed by the federal government, preserving these quiet giants for the next few hundred generations. Present-day activists insist that the Pacific Lumber Co., which still harvests the trees outside of national park areas, must stop their programs entirely. In order to get their point across, Earth First! volunteers stage "tree sits," sometimes spending months 180 ft. high in the trees.

ATM: Bank of America, 240 H St. at 2nd St. in Crescent City.

Laundromat: 101 Laundromat and Dry Cleaners, 503 L. St. (☎464-9230). Wash $1.75, dry $0.25 per 8min.

Road Conditions: ☎800-427-7623.

24-Hour Rape Crisis Line: ☎445-2881.

Medical Assistance: Sutter Coast Hospital, 800 E. Washington Blvd., Crescent City (☎464-8511).

Internet: Advanced Cyberworks, 415 Hwy. 101, Crescent City (toll free ☎877-418-7999). $5 per 30min., coffee included. Open M-F 10am-6pm, Sa by appointment.

Post Office: Crescent City: 751 2nd St. (☎464-2151). Open M-F 8:30am-5pm, Sa noon-2pm. **Postal Code:** 95531. **Orick:** 121147 U.S. 101 (☎488-3611). Open M-F 8:30am-noon and 1-5pm. **Postal Code:** 95555. **Klamath:** 141 Klamath Blvd. (☎482-2381). Open M-F 8am-4:30pm. **Postal Code:** 95548.

▀ ACCOMMODATIONS

Ravenwood, 151 Klamath Blvd., off U.S. 101 (☎482-5911 or toll free 866-520-9875). Clean rooms with a more modern decor. Conveniently located next to a market, cafe and laundromat. Doubles $48; family unit $95. ❸

Camp Marigold, 16101 U.S. 101 (☎482-3585 or 800-621-8513), 3 mi. north of Klamath Bridge. Stay in a log cabin with full kitchen and cable TV. RV hookups available. One-bed studios $48; doubles $78; six-person lodge $195. ❸

The Historic Requa Inn, 451 Requa Rd., west off U.S. 101 (☎482-1425 or toll free 866-800-8777). This bed and breakfast has a glorious view overlooking the Klamath River. Take in the picturesque scenery in front of the fire in the Victorian-styled parlor or through your lace-curtained bedroom window. Each bathroom has a claw-footed tub and the Inn offers evening dining to guests. Rooms $69-95. ❺

Redwood Youth Hostel (HI-AYH), 14480 U.S. 101 (☎482-8265), at Wilson Creek Rd. 7 mi. north of Klamath. This 30-bed hostel is run by a friendly, young family. Chores and rules (no shoes inside) keep the house immaculate. Kitchen and 2 ocean-view sundecks. No sleeping bags allowed, so bring your own sleepsack or rent linen ($1). Check-in 4:30-9:30pm. Check-out 10am. Lockout 9:30am-4:30pm. Day storage available. Curfew 11pm. Reservations recommended in summer. Dorms $14, under 17 $7. Advance payment required. ❶

Patrick Creek Lodge & Historic Inn, 13950 Hwy. 199, Gasquest (northeast of Hiouchi). Established in 1926, this lodge is a home-away-from-home for travelers. Fish along the famous, undammed Smith River, hike or kayak by day, and enjoy a toasty fire and self-titled "creative cuisine" at the lodge by night. Singles $43; doubles $80; suites $90; cabin for two $120, for four $160, extra persons $10 ea. ❸

📷 CAMPING

Redwood National Park offers several backcountry campsites; all are free and accessible only by hiking from roads or parking lots. **Nickel Creek campground,** at the end of Enderts Beach Rd. outside Crescent City, has ocean access and toilets, but no showers or water. **Flint Ridge ❶** is off the end of Redwood National and State Parks Coastal Dr., and has neither water nor showers, but toilets are available. Exit U.S. 101 and head toward the ocean. There are also State Park campsites, which are easily accessible and have all the amenities except electricity. Call ReserveAmerica (☎800-444-7275) for reservations, which are necessary in summer (sites usually $12). North of Crescent City on U.S. 199 is **Jedediah Smith Redwoods State Park ❶.** Amenities include picnic tables, grills, water, restrooms, showers, and RV hookups. Campfire programs and nature walks also offered during the summer. (Campsites are $12, $2 for day use, and $1 for hikers/bikers without vehicles at designated campsites.)

The **Del Norte Coast Redwoods State Park** offers magnificent ocean views and inland camping at Mill Creek Campground, where space is usually available. Camping in **Prairie Creek Redwoods State Park** is possible at Elk Prairie, where elk munch away and generally ignore photo-flashing tourists as long as the cameras stay at a distance (see **Elk Machismo,** p. 186). Camping is also possible at Gold Bluffs Beach, where the sound of the rolling Pacific will gently pacify you. Smith River National Recreation Area at **Six Rivers National Forest** (☎457-3131) has several campgrounds. **Big Flat Campground ❶** is 14 mi. up South Fork Rd. off U.S. 199 ($8; no hookups.). Before Big Flat there are river access trails along South Fork Rd. Two great finds at one stop, called Second Bridge/Forks, are at the ¼ mi. marker. From the restroom/parking area take the left trail to reach a great beach with swimming, fishing, and rafting opportunities. Take the right trail to enjoy the view of the Middle and South Forks of the Smith River converging. Situated directly on the Smith River, **Panther Flat ❶,** on U.S. 199, 25 minutes north of Crescent City, has water and showers. (Day-use picnic area, sites $15 in summer, $10 in winter.)

🍴 FOOD

There are more picnic tables than restaurants in the area, so the best option for food is probably the supermarket. **Orick Market** has reasonably priced groceries. (☎488-3225. Open M-Sa 8am-7pm, Su 9am-6pm.) In Crescent City, head to the 24-hour **Safeway,** 475 M St. (☎465-3353), on U.S. 101 between 2nd and 5th St.

If cooking is not included in your travel plans, there are some restaurants in the area. Hungry visitors can grab breakfast or lunch at the ▨**Wild Rocket Juice Bar & Cafe ❶,** 309 U.S. 101, in Crescent City. The fresh vegetables in the Rocket's scrumptious wraps ($5) and salads ($4-6) are all from locally based Reese Hydro Farms. (☎464-2543. Drive-thru available. Open M-F 6am-6pm, Sa 9am-3pm.) The **Palm Cafe ❷,** on U.S. 101, is the only place to eat in Orick, and welcomes locals and visiting hikers and bikers to a mom-and-pop environs. Their homemade fruit, coconut, and chocolate pies are delicious. (☎488-3381. Open daily 5am-8pm.) **Glen's Bakery and Restaurant ❶,** at 3rd and G St., was opened in 1947 and has always been a family affair. As the multitude of dedicated regulars demonstrate, locals just love the basic diner fare, including huge pancakes ($3) and sandwiches ($4-6.50). Breakfast served anytime. (☎464-2914. Open Tu-Sa 5am-6:30pm.)

FAR NORTH

FAR NORTH

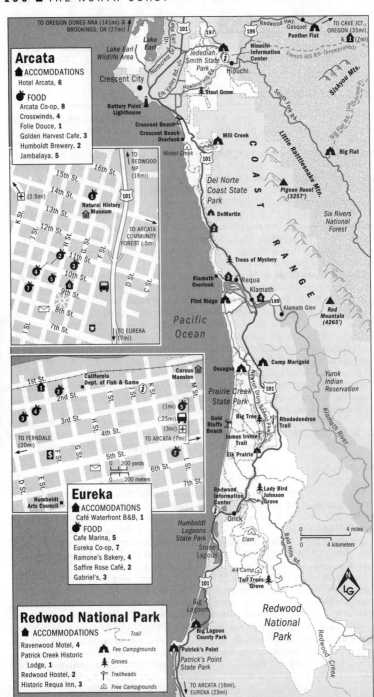

TO OREGON DUNES NRA (141mi) &
BROOKINGS, OR (27mi)

Redwood Hwy.
Gasquet

TO CAVE JCT.,
OREGON (35mi)
& ___ (7mi)

Panther Flat

101

197

199

French Hill Rd. (unimproved)

Lake Earl
Wildlife Area

Lake Earl

Jedediah
Smith State
Park

Hiouchi
Information
Center

Hiouchi

Siskyou Mts.

Crescent City

Howland Hill Rd.

Stout Grove

South Fork Rd.

Big Flat Rd. (unimproved)

Arcata

🏠 **ACCOMODATIONS**

Hotel Arcata, **6**

🍎 **FOOD**

Arcata Co-op, **8**
Crosswinds, **4**
Folie Douce, **1**
Golden Harvest Cafe, **3**
Humboldt Brewery, **2**
Jambalaya, **5**

Battery Point
Lighthouse

Crescent Beach
Crescent Beach
Overlook

Nickel Creek

101

Mill Creek

Del Norte
Coast State
Park

DeMartin

2

Big Flat

Little Rattlesnake Mtn.

Pigeon Roost
(3257')

C O A S T   R A N G E

Six Rivers
National
Forest

16th St.

15th St.

14th St.

13th St.

12th St.

11th St.

10th St.

9th St.

8th St.

7th St.

K St.

J St.

H St.

G St.

F St.

D St.

C St.

(2.5mi)

TO
REDWOOD
NP
(16mi)

101

Natural History
Museum

TO ARCATA
COMMUNITY
FOREST (.5mi)

1

2

3

4

5

7

6

TO EUREKA
(7mi)

Trees of Mystery

Klamath
Overlook

3

Requa

Klamath

4

169

Klamath Glen

Red
Mountain
(4265')

Flint Ridge

Pacific
Ocean

Camp Marigold

Ossagon

Prairie Creek
State Park

101

Yurok
Indian
Reservation

Klamath River

1st St.

2nd St.

3rd St.

4th St.

5th St.

6th St.

7th St.

California
Dept. of Fish & Game

Carson
Mansion

K St.

M St.

J St.

H St.

G St.

F St.

E St.

D St.

1

2

3

4

5

7

(1mi)

(.25mi)

(3mi)

TO FERNDALE
(20mi)

TO ARCATA (7mi)

0   200 yards

0   200 meters

Humboldt
Arts Council

Eureka

🏠 **ACCOMODATIONS**

Café Waterfront B&B, **1**

🍎 **FOOD**

Cafe Marina, **5**
Eureka Co-op, **7**
Ramone's Bakery, **4**
Saffire Rose Café, **2**
Gabriel's, **3**

Gold
Bluffs
Beach

Big Tree

James Irvine
Trail

Rhododendron
Trail

Elk Prairie

Redwood
Information
Center

Orick

Lady Bird
Johnson Grove

Humboldt
Lagoons
State Park

Stone
Lagoon

Elam

4 miles

4 kilometers

44 Camp

Tall Trees
Grove

Redwood National Park

🏠 **ACCOMODATIONS**

Ravenwood Motel, **4**
Patrick Creek Historic
  Lodge, **1**
Redwood Hostel, **2**
Historic Requa Inn, **3**

〜 Trail
🏠 Fee Campgrounds
🌲 Groves
⊤ Trailheads
⌂ Free Campgrounds

101

Big
Lagoon

Big Lagoon
County Park

Patrick's Point

Patrick's Point
State Park

TO ARCATA (16mi),
EUREKA (23mi)

Redwood
National
Park

Bald Hills Rd.

Redwood Creek

N
LG

HIKING

In the parks, you may gather berries for personal consumption, but all other plants and animals are protected—even feathers dropped by birds of prey are off-limits. **California fishing licenses** (one-day licenses $23) are required for fresh and saltwater fishing off any natural formation, but fishing is free from any manmade structure (check out Battery Point in Crescent City). There are minimum-weight and maximum-catch requirements specific to both. Call the Fish and Game Department (☎ 445-6493) to obtain a permit.

The redwoods are best experienced on foot. The parks span 40 mi. of coast and two counties, with information centers and unique attractions throughout. The National Park Service and the California Department of Parks and Recreation conducts many ranger-led activities for all ages in the summer (see **Visitor Information,** p. 193 or call the Redwood Information Center at ☎ 464-6101). Hikers should take particular care to wear protective clothing—**ticks** (see **Insect-Borne Diseases,** p. 37) and **poison oak** (see **Dangerous Plants,** p. 9) thrive in these dark places. **Roosevelt elk** roam the woods and are interesting to watch but dangerous to approach, as invaders of their territory are promptly circled and trampled (see **Elk Machismo,** p. 186). Also be on the lookout for the **black bears** and **mountain lions** that inhabit the park. Before setting out, get advice and trail maps at the Visitors Center.

ORICK AREA

The Orick Area covers the southernmost section of Redwood National and State Parks. The **Visitors Center** lies on U.S. 101, 1 mi. south of Orick and ½ mi. south of the Shoreline Deli (the Greyhound bus stop). A popular sight is the **Tall Trees Grove,** accessible by car to those with permits (free from the Visitors Center) when the road is open. Allow at least three to four hours for the trip. From the trailhead at the end of Tall Trees Access Rd., off Bald Hills Rd. from U.S. 101 north of Orick, it's a 1¼ mi. hike down (about 30min.) to some of the tallest trees in the world. The return hike up is steep—allow an hour. If the road is closed, hardy souls can see these giants by hiking the 16 mi. round-trip from **Dolason Prairie Trail** to **Emerald Ridge Trail,** which connects with **Tall Trees Trail.**

Orick (pop. 650) is a somewhat desolate town overrun with souvenir stores selling burl sculptures (over-crafted and expensive wood carvings) and cows (which outnumber the people). However, it also has a post office and a market for campfire groceries. **Patrick's Point State Park ❶,** 15 mi. south of Orick along U.S. 101, offers one of the most spectacular views along the coast, and merits a day or two for campers and nature enthusiasts heading north to the redwoods (sites $12; day-use $2). During **whale-watching** season (Nov.-Dec. and Mar.-May), the towering cliffs of the point provide great seats for observing the migration of gray whales.

PRAIRIE CREEK AREA

The Prairie Creek Area, equipped with a **ranger station, visitors center,** and **state park campgrounds,** is perfect for hikers, who can explore 75 mi. of trails in the park's 14,000 acres. Be sure to pick up a trail map ($1) at the ranger station before heading out; the loops of criss-crossing trails may be confusing without one. Starting at the Prairie Creek Visitors Center, the **James Irvine Trail** (4.5 mi. one-way) winds through a prehistoric garden of towering old-growth redwoods of humbling height. Snaking past small waterfalls that trickle down 50 ft. fern-covered walls, the trail ends at **Fern Canyon** on **Gold Bluffs Beach. Rhododendron** (7.8 mi. one-way) is another choice pick because of its beautiful blossoms and its many possibilities—if you get tired you can take the convenient switchback, **South Fork Trail.** The less ambitious can cruise part of the **Foothill Trail** (0.8 mi. one-way) to the 1500-year-old **Big Tree** or elk-watch on the meadow in front of the ranger station. The 306 ft. high behemoth, **Big Tree,** is a satisfying substitute for those who don't want to make the long trek to **Tall Trees Grove** (see **Orick Area,** above).

FAR NORTH

The **Elk Prairie Trail** (1.4 mi. one-way) skirts the prairie and loops around to join the nature trail. The **Revelation Trail** is accessible to people with disabilities and frequented, every now and then, by the stray elk.

KLAMATH AREA

The Klamath Area to the north consists of a thin stretch of parkland connecting Prairie Creek with Del Norte State Park. The town itself consists of a few stores stretched over 4 mi., so the main attraction here is the spectacular coastline. The **Klamath Overlook,** where Requa Rd. meets the steep **Coastal Trail** (8 mi.), is an excellent **whale-watching** site with a fantastic view (provided it's fog-free) but also can be crowded by North Coast standards.

The mouth of the **Klamath River** is a popular commercial fishing spot (permit required; contact the Redwood Visitors Info Center, ☎464-6101, ext. 5064) in fall and spring, when salmon spawn, and in winter, when steelhead trout do the same. In spring and summer, sea lions and harbor seals congregate along Coastal Dr., which passes by the remains of the **Douglas Memorial Bridge,** and then continues along the ocean for 8 mi. of incredible views. Kitsch meets high-tech at **Trees of Mystery**, 15500 U.S. 101 N., just north of Klamath. It is a 0.8-mile walk through a maze of curiously shaped trees and elaborate chainsaw sculptures that talk and play music. There is also a small, free Native American museum that displays ornate costumes, baskets, and tapestries, and (of course) a souvenir shop. The tourist trap's latest addition, the **Sky Trail,** is a multi-million dollar gondola snaking up the hill to offer an exclusive bird's eye view of the towering trees. A 200 ft. tall Paul Bunyan and his blue ox Babe, mark the entrance to the sight. Be sure to pick up a 20% discount card at the Crescent City Chamber of Commerce. (☎482-2251 or 800-638-3389. Trail open daily 8am-6:30pm; gift shop and museum 8am-7:30pm. $15, seniors $12, children $8, parties of 5 or more get a 20% discount.)

CRESCENT CITY AREA

An outstanding location from which to explore the parks, Crescent City calls itself the city "where the redwoods meet the sea." The **Battery Point Lighthouse** is on a causeway jutting out from Front St. Turn left onto A St. at the top of Front St. It houses a museum open only during low tide. The curious should consult guides about the resident **ghosts,** in which they claim not to believe. (☎464-3089. Open Apr.-Sept. W-Su 10am-4pm, tide permitting. $2, children $0.50.) From June through Aug., the national park offers **tidepool walks,** which leave from the Enderts Beach parking lot. (Turn-off 4 mi. south of Crescent City; call ☎464-6101, ext. 5064 for schedules.) The trailhead is at the **Crescent Beach Overlook** on Enderts Beach Rd., just off U.S. 101. A scenic drive from Crescent City along **Pebble Beach Drive** to **Point Saint George** snakes past coastline that looks transplanted from New England; craggy cliffs, lush prairies, and an old lighthouse add to the atmosphere.

Annual highlights include the **World Championship Crab Races,** featuring races and crab feasts on the 3rd Sunday in February. The Sea Cruise, a parade of over 500 classic cars, happens over three days on the 1st or 2nd weekend in October. Call the Crescent City/Del Norte County Chamber of Commerce (☎800-343-8300) for information regarding any of these events.

HIOUCHI AREA

This inland region, known for its rugged beauty, sits in the northern part of the park region along U.S. 199 and contains some excellent hiking trails, most of which are in **Jedediah Smith Redwoods State Park.** Several trails lie off Howland Hill Rd., a dirt road easily accessible from both U.S. 101 and U.S. 199. From U.S. 199, turn onto South Fork Rd. in Hiouchi and right onto Douglas Park Rd., which then turns into Howland Hill Rd. From Crescent City, go south on U.S. 101, turn left onto Elk Valley Rd., and right onto Howland Hill. Drive through **Stout Grove** which, some say, makes the **Avenue of the Giants** pale in comparison. From here one can also take the wheelchair-accessible **Stout Grove Trail** (0.5 mi.) and admire the ancient redwoods up close. The trailhead is near the eastern end of Howland Hill Rd., and the paved section is just past the trail. The **Mill Creek Trail** is a moderate 4 mi. hike with excellent swimming, accessible from the Mill Creek Bridge on Howland Hill Rd. and from the footbridge in the Jedediah Smith campground during summer. The more strenuous **Boy Scout Trail** off Howland Hill Rd. splits after 3 mi.; the right path goes to the monstrous Boy Scout Tree, and the left ends at Fern Falls. Two miles west of Jedediah State Park on U.S. 199 lies the Simpson-Reed Grove, a circular trail through an old stand of redwoods.

The untapped beauty of **Six Rivers National Forest** (☎457-3131) is directly east of Hiouchi. The Smith River, the state's last major undammed river, rushes through rocky gorges as it winds its way from the mountains to the coast. The area offers the best salmon, trout, and steelhead fishing around; excellent camping awaits on the riverbanks. There are also numerous hiking trails throughout the forest.

NORTHERN INTERIOR

The voyage through the relatively unpopulated and infrequently visited Northern Interior sweeps across vast plains, over rocky hills, and along swift rivers. Gold Country, a sprinkling of towns unpretentiously devoted to remembering the mass migration of the Gold Rush, lies east of Sacramento amid this beautiful landscape. The Cascade Mountains interrupt the expanse of farmland to the southeast with quiet peaks, lush wilderness, and two enormous glaciated mountains (Shasta and Lassen). Ancient and recent volcanic activity has left behind a surreal landscape of lava beds, mountains, lakes, waterfalls, caves, and recovering forest areas.

LASSEN VOLCANIC NATIONAL PARK ☎530

One link in a chain of active and dormant volcanic regions that make up the "Ring of Fire" along the Pacific Rim, Lassen Volcanic National Park owes its status as the Cascade Range's most geothermally active area to a massive pocket of molten magma about 10 mi. beneath its surface. As tectonic plates collided and fed the magma pool, tremors, streams of lava, black dust, and a series of enormous eruptions ravaged this area in 1914, climaxing a year later when Mt. Lassen spewed a seven mile high cloud of smoke and ash into the sky. The attention this eruption received facilitated the establishment of the area as a national park in 1916. Even now, volcanic effects are evident in Lassen's unearthly pools of boiling water, its barren stretches of moonscape, and its occasional sulfur stench. But the eruptions also brought about a flurry of new growth, both of natural flower beds and fauna.

FAR NORTH

AT A GLANCE

AREA: 106,372 acres.

CLIMATE: Fairly cold in the summer (sometimes with near-freezing temperatures at night), Lassen gets snowed-in during the winter, and most of the roads are blocked off.

FEATURES: Cold Boiling Lake, Mt. Lassen, the Devastated Area.

HIGHLIGHTS: Witness Bumpass Hell, smell Sulphur Woods, take in the view from Panorama Point.

GATEWAYS: Redding (p. 204).

CAMPING: Camping 7- to 14-day max. stay, Backcountry 14-day max. stay.

FEES & RESERVATIONS: $10 entrance fee for vehicles, $5 for walk-ins and cyclists, is valid for 7 days. $20 annual fee. Free wilderness permit is required for backcountry camping.

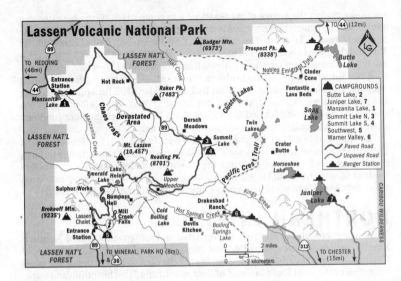

Lassen Volcanic National Park

CAMPGROUNDS
Butte Lake, 2
Juniper Lake, 7
Manzanita Lake, 1
Summit Lake N, 3
Summit Lake S, 4
Southwest, 5
Warner Valley, 6
⁓ Paved Road
⁓ Unpaved Road
▲ Ranger Station

TRANSPORTATION

The park can be easily reached from **Redding**, via Rte. 44 (see p. 204), and Red Bluff, via Rte. 36. Primary access to the park is on **Route 89**, which connects to both Rte. 44 and Rte. 36 north and south of the park, respectively. Only two dirt roads enter the park from the south, at **Chester** (71 mi. from Red Bluff on Rte. 36), one leading north to Juniper Lake and the other northwest to Warren Valley.

ORIENTATION

Lassen National Park is located squarely in the middle of Lassen National Forest, about 50 mi. east of Redding (via Rte. 44) and Red Bluff (via Rte. 36). Rte. 89 winds through the major attractions on the west side of the park. The park's east side is less developed. The **Pacific Crest Trail** passes right through the center of the park, intersecting with Warren Valley in the south.

PRACTICAL INFORMATION

Information Stations: There are three information stations in Lassen, all offering wilderness permits, publications, and information about the entire park: **Southwest Info Station**, right at the south entrance on Rte. 89 (☎595-3308; open June-Sept. daily 9:30am-5:30pm); the **Loomis Museum**, at Manzanita Lake near the north entrance (☎595-4444, ext. 5180; open June-Oct. daily 9am-5pm); and **Park Headquarters**, in Mineral. (☎595-4444. Open daily 8am-4:30pm.)

Fees & Reservations: Entrance fee to the park is $10 per vehicle, valid for 7 days, and $5 per walk-in or biker. Backcountry camping requires a free wilderness permit.

WHEN TO GO. Lassen is one of the least visited national parks and is fairly quiet until July, when the summer tourists show up. The park is open year-round; rangers ski to work when the roads close. Those visiting Lassen in the winter should have previous outdoors experience.

ACCOMMODATIONS & CAMPING

INSIDE THE PARK

Because of the danger of rock slides and lava flows, there are few permanent structures in the park. The only option for indoor lodging in Lassen is the upscale **Drakesbad Guest Ranch ❺**, in Chester. This 110-year-old guest ranch isn't cheap, but you do get three meals a day and scenic and secluded surroundings. Take Rte. 36 to Chester, turn right at the firehouse, and follow the signs. (☎529-1512, ext. 120. Open June-Oct. Singles and doubles from $120 per person; bungalows from $140 per person.) Fortunately, **camping** in the park is beautiful and abundant. Unfortunately, you may experience near-freezing night temperatures, even in August. Check the snow situation before leaving; campgrounds often remain closed well into the summer. All sites are doled out on a first-come, first-camp basis; register on site. **Backcountry camping ❶** is limited to 14 days per year, and you'll need a free wilderness permit. Fires are prohibited, as is the use of all soaps (including biodegradable ones) in the lakes. Using portable propane or gas stoves is allowed. Avoid camping near Bumpass Hell, Devil's Kitchen, and other intimidatingly named areas that suddenly spew boiling lava or hot steam. A list of restricted areas, as well as explicit rules concerning safety and ecology, is available at ranger stations.

▨ **Summit Lake North,** 6700 ft., 17½ mi. south of the Manzanita Lake entrance. Summit Lake's deep blue glitters through the pine trees surrounding 46 popular sites. Summit Lake North and its cousin on the other side are usually the first to fill up. Drinking water and flush toilets. 7-day max. stay. Open July-Sept. Sites $14. ❶

▨ **Summit Lake South,** 6700 ft., just around the lake from the Summit North campground. All 48 sites have the same views as North Summit. Lots of trails begin here. Drinking water, no showers, no flush toilets. 7-day max. stay. Open July-Sept. Sites $12. ❶

Manzanita Lake, 5900 ft., just inside the park border, near the northwest entrance. Most sites have some privacy, but choose wisely. Pay phone, concession services, boating without motor, drinking water, flush toilets, laundry, showers, dump station, and gas. 14-day max. stay. Open early June-late Oct. 179 sites $14; late Sept.-close $8. ❶

Butte Lake, 6100 ft., 6 mi. south on a dirt road from Rte. 44, 17 mi. east of Old Station. New water treatment plant now provides piped drinking water. 46 spots most of the year, 101 during late summer once all the snow melts. On the lake, with flush toilets and swimming, boating, and fishing access. Open late May-late Sept. Sites $12. ❶

OUTSIDE THE PARK

The nearest indoor accommodations are 12 mi. north in **Old Station.** Less costly motels are in **Redding,** 50 mi. west on Rte. 44, (see p. 204); **Red Bluff,** 50 mi. west on Rte. 36, (see p. 199); and **Chester,** southeast on Rte. 36. **Lassen National Forest,** which surrounds the park, has several developed campgrounds. Six line Rte. 89 for the first 10 mi. north of the park. Campgrounds are generally open late April or late May through October. **Big Pine ❶**, 4500 ft., is the closest. (Piped water, vault toilets. 19 sites $10.) **Bridge ❶**, 4000 ft. and **Cave ❶**, 4300 ft., both have drinking water and trailer-only sites for $11, although tents may be used if you don't mind bumpy ground. Two campgrounds sit on Rte. 36 near the southwest park entrance in the Almanor Ranger District (☎258-2141). A number of campgrounds dot the southwestern shore of **Eagle Lake,** in the eastern part of Lassen National Forest. **Christie, Merrill,** and **Aspen Grove** have piped water and are in the Eagle Lake Ranger District. (☎257-4188. Sites $13-15.) **McCarthy Point ❹**, once an active fire lookout, has since been converted into a guest cabin. Accommodations include a kitchen and a bedroom accommodating up to six. (☎258-2141. Lookout Su-Th $40, F-Sa $60. Security deposit $200. Reserve ahead.)

FAR NORTH

▐ FOOD

The budget Lassen meal consists of groceries bought in one of the outlying towns. For prepared meals, try the **Lassen Chalet,** an inexpensive cafeteria-style restaurant and gift shop just inside the Mineral entrance. Their large burgers ($4-6) are filling fuel, but are only available until 5pm. (☎595-3376. Open daily 9am-6pm; late May-late June and Sept. to mid-Oct. 9am-4pm.) At the park's other end, the **Manzanita Camper Service Store,** at the Manzanita Lake Campground, sells pricey groceries, a small selection of grill foods, postcards, fishing licenses, informative guides, gasoline, and helpful maps, and also launches seaworthy boats. (☎335-7557. Open daily 8am-8pm; late May-late June and Sept. to mid-Oct. 9am-5pm.)

◉ ▐ SIGHTS & HIKES

Lassen is very drivable: roadside sights are clearly numbered for tourists, and most are accessible from Rte. 89. Drivers can pick up the *Lassen Road Guide,* a booklet keyed to roadside markers ($5), at any park entrance ranger station. A comfortable drive through the park (including a few stops) should take about 2hr., but allow a full day to accommodate short hikes.

FROM THE LOOMIS MUSEUM VISITORS CENTER. There are a few easy, relaxing walks in the area surrounding the Loomis Museum Visitors Center, at Rte. 89's north entry into the park. The hike to **Crags Lake** starts 500 yd. from the Visitors Center and runs 1.75 mi. one-way, climbing 700 ft. (2-4hr. round-trip). The intermediate walk opens into magical vistas frequently enough to keep hikers motivated for the trek. At the end of the hike, an emerald lake sits at the bottom of a huge gray bowl that looks like it was formed by the crash of a massive spaceship. Similarly short, easy hikes look up and around to Lily Pond (1 mi. interpretive hike) and around Reflection Lake (0.7 mi.), both across the street from the Visitors Center. The 1.6 mi. loop trail around Manzanita Lake makes for a relaxing stroll.

ALONG ROUTE 89. Coming from the south on Rte. 89, the first sight (or smell) is **Sulphur Works,** where the earth hisses its grievances. The guard rails may prevent you from getting burned, but if the wind changes direction, you're likely to get a face full of rotten-egg mist. The boardwalk is wheelchair accessible. About 4½ mi. north, **Emerald Lake,** when partially thawed by the sun, shimmers with bright green, icy cold 300 ft. deep waters around a snowy center. Swimming is fine for fish, but too cold (40°F) for the warm-blooded. No fishing is allowed.

Things heat up again about a half-mile past Emerald Lake. The 1.5 mi. hike to **Bumpass Hell,** the largest group of hot springs west of Yellowstone, wanders through the park's largest hydrothermal area. Pick up a guide ($0.50) at the trailhead. Bumpass Hell is a massive cauldron of muddy, boiling, steaming water where the man who discovered it lost his leg; to avoid any danger to your own life and limb, stay on the trail. In spite of year-round snow, the water always appears to boil at **Cold Boiling Lake** due to its placement above a flatulent fissure. (4 mi. farther north; easier access from King's Creek.)

Mount Lassen is the world's largest plug-dome volcano. From the parking area, a little over 1 mi. from Bumpass Hell, it's a steep 2.5 mi., 4-5hr. trek to the 10,457 ft. summit. Even if it's sunny and 90°F, take along extra clothes (especially a windbreaker) for the gusty crest, as well as sunblock and lots of water. Solid shoes are important, too; 18 in. of snow can clog the upper 2 mi. of trail even in summer. Guidebook available at trailhead ($0.50). Those opting out of the hike can still get excellent views at **Panorama Point,** a pull-off 1 mi. from Mt. Lassen trailhead with a sweeping view of Reading Peak, Mt. Harkness, and Lake Almanor.

About 5 mi. from Mt. Lassen is the **King's Creek Picnic Area,** near the wildflower-filled King's Creek meadow. From here, trails loop back toward more southerly destinations on Rte. 89, heading to Cold Boiling Lake (0.8 mi.) and Bumpass Hell (4 mi.), or to Crumbaugh Lake (1.3 mi.), all the way to Southwest Campground (5.3 mi.). A little farther north on Rte. 89, at mile marker 32, is the trailhead to King's Creek Falls, Summit Lakes, and Drakesbad. The trail to King's Creek Falls follows the idyllic, cascading King's Creek 1.5 mi. to the rushing falls. **Summit Lake** can be reached on foot from here or on Rte. 89, 5 mi. farther on. A little farther north, **Dersch Meadow** is a good place to spot grazing deer and circling birds of prey.

A little over 3 mi. from Summit Lake, a short trail leads to what is left of **Devastated Area,** the forested area that was completely annihilated by debris spewed out of Mt. Lassen in 1915. Conifers have reclaimed the land here, and as the forest nears maturity, it is becoming difficult to see that damage was done. In a decade or so, the forest will be virtually as it was before the eruption. **Hot Rock** sits 2 mi. down the road. The 300-ton boulder once was a part of Mt. Lassen, but was swept down with a massive lava flow to its current location. Though it never melted from the lava, the rock got so hot that it boiled the mud around it for months.

Heading up to the north end of the park, check out **Chaos Crags and Jumbles,** 6 mi. from Hot Rock, a broken, messy field of rock that avalanched off of several volcanic domes. The final stop, at the northernmost end of Rte. 89, is the **Loomis Museum,** which showcases an extensive collection of photographs of the blast.

OVERNIGHT HIKES. A network of trails explores much of the wilder eastern portion of the park, rising and dipping through coniferous forests, hidden lakes, and the occasional lava bed. Of the 150 mi. of trails (including a stretch of the **Pacific Crest Trail;** see **From Crest to Crest: the Trail of the West,** p. 242), the **Manzanita Creek Trail,** near Manzanita Lake campground, and the **Horseshoe Lake** area, east of Summit Lake, are customarily dry throughout the summer. Both make enjoyable overnight trips. **Manzanita Creek Trail** parallels a lovely creek that runs through rolling woodlands, bearing scant resemblance to the boiling cauldrons to the south. To the east, the Horseshoe Lake area is rich in ice-cold lakes and deer-filled pine forests. Trails leading east also begin at Hat Lake (Old Emigrant Trail), Summit Lake, and at the Kings Creek Falls trailhead. Alternately, the same trails can be taken west by starting out at Juniper Lake or Drakesbad, accessed by dirt roads from Chester. Wilderness permits are required for backcountry camping.

By mid-summer, the shallow waters of Lake Manzanita and Lake Summit can warm to swimming temperatures. Several lakes in the park have native **rainbow trout;** Hat Creek is a renowned trout stream. A state license is required to go **fishing,** and some areas may have additional rules—Manzanita, for example, has "catch and release" and barbless hook policies.

NEAR LASSEN

Three wilderness areas are less-traveled than neighboring Lassen. Pick up a free **wilderness permit** from the US Forest Service. Buy a topographic map of the area ($4) at one of the ranger stations—it is invaluable for finding trails and figuring out what the heck you're staring at. All wilderness areas are no-trace, so everything packed in must be packed out.

CARIBOU WILDERNESS

Caribou Wilderness, a gently-graded plateau, borders the park to the east. For the easiest border access, take Rte. 44 or 36 to Hwy. A-21 for 14 mi., then take Silver Lake Rd. to the **Caribou Lake Trailhead.** Its many quiet, clean lakes support water lilies and wildflowers in early summer and treat hikers to solitude. The more deso-

FAR NORTH

late **Cone Lake Trailhead** can be reached by taking Forest Service Road (F.S.) 10, off Rte. 44 north of County Hwy. A-21. For the ultimate in isolated beauty, make the trek to the **Hay Meadows Trailhead.** Head north on F.S. 10 from Rte. 36 (near Chester), then turn left after 14 mi. F.S. 10 can be rough—a 4WD vehicle is necessary.

THOUSAND LAKES WILDERNESS

Thousand Lakes Wilderness (and all the trout in those lakes) can be accessed from F.S. 16 off Rte. 89. Seven miles from Rte. 89, the road forks; F.S. 16 continues to the left to **Magee Trailhead,** a strenuous trail that leads to Magee Peak, 8594 ft., and deserted Magee Lake. Insect repellent is a must. **Tamarack Trailhead** is easier and travels to Lake Eiler via Eiler Butte. Going north, take F.S. 33 N25 and hook left just after Wilcox Rd. When the road forks, turn left onto F.S. 33 N23Y. This 7 mi. stretch of road requires 4WD. **Subway Cave,** off Rte. 89, 3¼ mi. north of Rte. 44, invites exploration of its 1300 ft.-long lava tubes. The cave is pitch-black and cool with uneven footing, so bring a friend, sturdy shoes, a sweater, and a lantern or strong flashlight with extra batteries.

ISHI WILDERNESS

The spectacular Ishi Wilderness, named for the last survivor of a Yahi Yana tribe, comprises rugged terrain at a lower altitude, making it friendly to off-season exploration. Take Rte. 36 from Red Bluff 15 mi. to Plum Creek Rd., and turn right on Ponderosa Way. This rough road skirts the eastern edge of the wilderness, where most trailheads lie. Ishi is a series of river canyons with dense islands of Ponderosa pine and sunburnt grasslands in the south; it's very hot in the summer. **Mill Creek Trailhead** runs along the 1000 ft. canyon, where gentle waters await swimmers. Keep an eye out for red-tailed hawks and golden eagles. The Tehana Deer Herd, the largest migratory herd in California, spends its winters in Ishi (not so fast, Elmer—hunting isn't allowed). The **Deer Creek Trail** is another scenic hike, with a trailhead at the southern end of the Ishi Wilderness on Ponderosa Way.

REDDING   ☎530

Touting itself as "Another California," Redding (pop. 72,906) is "yet another town" near supreme camping and recreational opportunities. Redding's position at the crossroads of I-5 and Rte. 44 and 299, as well as its quantity of hotels and restaurants, make it a convenient, if not essential, supply stop for Shasta Lake, Lassen Volcanic National Park, and Trinity Wilderness to the west.

🛈 PRACTICAL INFORMATION. Redding is on I-5, 160 mi. north of Sacramento and 100 mi. south of Yreka. Shasta Lake is 16 mi. north of Redding on I-5, and Mt. Shasta is 60 mi. north. There is an unstaffed **Amtrak train** station at 1620 Yuba St. (☎800-USA-RAIL/872-7245). Buy a ticket on the train or directly through Amtrak. Trains depart to: Sacramento (4hr., 4 per day, $26); San Francisco (6hr., 3 per day, $40); Portland (12-13hr., 1 per day, $77). **Greyhound buses,** 1321 Butte St. (☎241-2531 or 800-231-2222), at Pine St., depart from the 24hr. station to: Sacramento (3-4hr., 9 per day, $23); San Francisco (5-7hr., 8 per day, $35); Portland (9-10hr., 4 per day, $54). **Enterprise,** 361 Cypress St., rents compact **cars** for $32 per day with 100 mi. included, $0.20 per additional mile. Renters must be 21+ with major credit card. (☎223-0700. Under-25 surcharge $10 per day. Open M-F 7:30am-6pm, Sa 9am-noon.) Get informed at the **Visitors Center,** 777 Auditorium Dr., off Rte. 299 at the Convention Center Exit. (☎225-4100 or 800-874-7562; www.visitredding.com. Open M-F 8am-5pm.) Call the **Shasta Lake Ranger District,** 14225 Holiday Rd., for local conditions or camping info. (☎275-1589. Open M-F 8am-5pm.) Other services include: **police,** 1313 California St. (☎225-4200); **Redding Medical Center,** 1100 Butte

St. (☎ 244-5400), at East St.; and the **Post Office,** 2323 Churn Creek Rd. (☎ 223-7523. Open M-F 8:30am-5:30pm, Sa 9am-3pm.) **Postal Code:** 96049.

🖪🖸 ACCOMMODATIONS & FOOD. Before heading to a motel, pick up a free vacation planner at the Visitors Center for a variety of coupons for area and state accommodations. Standard, inexpensive, reliable rooms can be found at **Motel 6 Central Redding ❸,** 1640 Hilltop Dr. Take the Rte. 44 east Exit in downtown Redding for Hilltop Dr. south. Rooms have phone, cable TV, coffee, and access to an outdoor pool. (☎ 221-1800. Singles and doubles $44-54.) **Oak Bottom campground ❷,** 1200 ft., on Rte. 299, 13 mi. west of Redding on beautiful Whiskeytown Lake, has beaches and swimming areas. The camp has 100 sites with solar-powered showers but no hookups. (Reservations ☎ 800-365-2267, dispatch 241-6584, campground headquarters 359-2344. May-Sept. waterfront tents $18, interior $16; Oct.-Apr. $8/ $7. RVs $14.) There are numerous campgrounds on **Shasta Lake ❶,** 1100 ft. (Take the Gilman Rd. Exit on I-5. Sites $10-16.) **Buz's Crab ❷,** 2159 East St., next to Safeway, has the best seafood in the area. Fish (and oysters, and calamari) and chips ($3-8); hot crab sandwich ($6.25). (☎ 243-2120. Open daily 11am-9pm.)

MOUNT SHASTA ☎ 530

It's easy to contemplate Mount Shasta from a distance—you can see its peak from 100 mi. away. Shasta attracts nature buffs and thrill-seekers, mineral-bath pilgrims, and extreme sports enthusiasts, all entranced by silent night visions of its 14,161 ft. of bare, snow-covered rock. Something about Shasta's solitary rise from the earth gives it a particular resonance among all those who encounter it. One Shasta worshipper in 1873 spoke of the mountain as "lonely as God, white as a winter moon," a description that stuck, and is now engraved on the Mt. Shasta plaque in the base city of Mt. Shasta (pop. 3806).

Shasta Indians believed that a great spirit dwelled within the volcano, and modern-day spiritualists are drawn to the mountain by its mystical energy. In 1987, thousands of New Age believers converged here to witness the great clerical event of Harmonic Convergence, which climaxed when a resident turned on her TV set and saw an angel displayed on the screen. Perhaps unaware of the theological implications, climbers come to challenge the ice-covered slopes, while over-stressed yuppies come for the region's fragrant air and peaceful atmosphere. The town of Mount Shasta is moderately touristy in a New Age sort of way: vegetarian restaurants, spiritual bookstores, and Shasta pilgrims crowd the streets.

F A R N O R T H

⬛🔟 ORIENTATION & PRACTICAL INFORMATION

The town of Mt. Shasta is 60 mi. north of Redding on **Interstate 5,** 50 mi. west of Lassen Volcanic National Park and 275 mi. north of San Francisco. If traveling by car, the town can be used as a base for exploring Lava Beds, Lassen, Burney Falls, and the Shasta Recreation Area.

Trains: Amtrak's closest station is the unattended one in Dunsmuir (9 mi. south on I-5), 5750 Sacramento Ave. (☎ 800-872-7245). Trains depart to: **Portland,** OR (10½hr., 1 per day, $82); **Redding** (2hr., 1 per day, $15); **San Francisco** (8½hr., 1 per day, $51).

Buses: Greyhound (☎ 800-231-2222), flag stop in the parking lot at 4th St. and Mt. Shasta Blvd. To **San Francisco** ($47-50) and **Redding** ($12-13).

Public Transportation: Siskiyou Stage (☎ 800-247-8243) offers minibus transit between Weed, Mt. Shasta (next to the Black Bear Diner in the Mt. Shasta Shopping Center), and Dunsmuir. Operates M-F; call for times. $1.25.

Visitor Information: Mount Shasta Visitors Center, 300 Pine St. (☎800-397-1519). Open daily 9am-5pm. **Shasta-Trinity National Forest Service,** 204 W. Alma St. (☎926-4511), is across the railroad tracks from the intersection of Alma St. and Mt. Shasta Blvd. Find out which campgrounds and trails are open, and grab maps, info, and fire and wilderness permits. Outside is a trail register that mountain climbers and day hikers must sign. Open M-Sa 8am-4:30pm, Su 10am-3pm. **Shasta Lake Information Center** (☎275-1589), 10 mi. north of Redding at the Montaingate Wonderland Blvd. Exit off I-5. **Whiskeytown Unit Visitor Information** (☎246-1225; www.nps.gov/whis), 8 mi. north of Redding, at the intersection of Rte. 299 and Kennedy Memorial Dr. Open daily 9am-5pm; in winter 10am-4pm.

ATM: Bank of America, 100 Chestnut St. (☎926-8950 or 800-521-2632). Open M-Th 10am-4pm, F 10am-5pm.

Equipment Rental: House of Ski and Board, 316 Chestnut St. (☎926-2359), 1 block behind Mt. Shasta Blvd. Rents, sells, and services ski, climbing, and snowboarding equipment at reasonable rates. Boots, bindings, and skis $15-18 per day. Snowboard and boots $20-25 per day. Snowshoes $10-15 per day. Open M-F 9am-6pm, Sa 8am-6pm, Su 10am-5pm. A **cycle shop** is in the same building and rents mountain bikes; $18 half-day, $22 full-day; 3rd day free. **5th Season,** 300 N. Mt. Shasta Blvd. (☎926-3606), rents camping gear, outdoor equipment, skis, and bikes. Sleeping bag with pad $18 for 3 days; $6 each additional day. 2-person tent $40 for 3 days. Ski rental (boots, bindings, and poles) $40 for 3 days. Bike rentals $36-48 per day. Also offers mountain-climbing and alpine touring equipment. Open M-F 9am-6pm, Sa 8am-6pm, Su 10am-5pm; in winter daily 8am-6pm.

Weather, Climbing, and Skiing Conditions: 24hr. Weather ☎842-4438. **Climbing Conditions** ☎926-9613. **Ski Report** ☎926-8686.

Library and Internet Access: Mount Shasta Library, 515 E. Alma St. (☎926-2031). Internet access free for 1hr. Open M and W 1-6pm, Tu noon-6pm, Th and Sa 1-5pm.

Laundromat: Mount Shasta Laundromat, 302 S. Mt. Shasta Blvd., opposite Berryvale Natural Foods. Wash $1.25 ($2.50 for largest machines); 10min. dry $0.25.

Police: 303 N. Mt. Shasta Blvd. (☎926-7540), at Lake St.

Crisis Lines: Notify the sheriff (☎841-2900 or 800-404-2911) of missing climbers.

Hospital: Mercy Medical Center, 914 Pine St. (☎926-6111).

Post Office: 301 S. Mt. Shasta Blvd. (☎926-1343). Open M-F 8:30am-5pm. **Postal Code:** 96067.

▌ ACCOMMODATIONS

▨ **Alpenrose Cottage Guest House,** 204 E. Hinckley St. (☎926-6724; www.hostels.com/alpenrose), near the KOA driveway. Roses, wind chimes, a sundeck with view of Mt. Shasta, and bulletin boards full of Shasta info (both spiritual and practical) give this cottage a homey appeal. Joyful owner Betty Brown is friendly and helpful. Wood-burning stove, open kitchen, TV room, and library. Hummingbird viewing in summer. Free laundry. With 4 beds available, reservations are highly recommended, especially in summer. $35 per person, $30 for multiple nights; $60 per couple. No credit cards. ❸

▨ **Shastao,** 3609 N Old Stage Rd. (☎926-4154). A "philosophical hermitage" owned and operated by 2 philosophy Ph.Ds with interests in Eastern and Western Religion and Philosophy, yoga, music, and conversation. 2 guest rooms (Bodhidharma and Radha-Krishna Rooms) have personalized libraries and amenities geared toward introspection and tantric romance, respectively. Breakfast and vegetarian dinner, conversation, and yoga instruction complementary. Individuals $75, couples $125. ❹

Finlandia Motel, 1612 S. Mt. Shasta (☎926-5596). A clean, 2-level motel presumably of Finnish origin. Deluxe rooms have vaulted ceilings and bathtubs and access to a spa and sauna, economy rooms are more like standard motel rooms. Some rooms have mountain views. Kitchens available for both deluxe and economy rooms. Economy singles from $41; doubles from $47; with kitchen from $53. Deluxe singles and doubles from $67. In summer and winter $3 extra. ❸

CAMPING

The US Forest Service (☎926-4511) runs a few area campgrounds. The campgrounds closest to town, however, are primarily commercial. Pick up a campground map from the Visitors Center. No-fee campgrounds require a campfire permit, available at the Forest Service station.

Lake Siskiyou Campground (☎926-2618 or 888-926-2618; www.lakesis.com), 3 mi. southwest of town. Flee I-5 via Lake St. Exit, follow Hatchery Lane ¼ mi., then go south on Old Stage Rd. and W.A. Barr Rd. This family-oriented campground has beach access, encourages swimming, and rents paddleboats, motorboats, and canoes. Coin-operated laundry, flush toilets, hot showers. Reservations recommended. Tent sites $18; RV sites with full hookup and TV $25. ❷

McBride Springs Campground, 5000 ft., 5 mi. east of Mt. Shasta off Everett Memorial Hwy. 9 drive-up sites with views, water, and hiking access. Well-maintained outhouses. 7-night max. stay. Sites $10. ❶

Panther Meadow, 7500 ft., sits on Mt. Shasta 8 mi. down the road from McBride Springs, and offers astounding views. High elevation means it is cold at night, even during the summer. 10 walk-in sites with pit toilets; no water. 3-night max. stay. Free. ❶

Castle Crags State Park, 2000 ft., (☎235-2684 or 800-444-7275), 15 mi. south of Mt. Shasta on I-5 (take the Castella Exit). A large, clean, low elevation campground. 67 tent and RV sites are spacious, though some are a bit too close to the interstate for comfort. Rock climbing on the crags, swimming, fishing, and hiking opportunities. Facilities include water, flush toilets, hot showers, and an interpretive center. Sites $12. ❶

FOOD

Shasta has many grocery stores, the largest of which is **Ray's Food Place,** 160 Morgan Way, in the Mt. Shasta Shopping Center off Lake St. near I-5. (☎926-3390. Open daily 7am-11pm.) In the summer, **produce stands** across the street provide cheaper, fresher fruits and veggies. The **Mount Shasta Supermarket,** at the corner of Chestnut and E. Alma St., is a pricier specialty store. (☎926-2212. Open M-Sa 8am-7pm, Su 8am-6pm.) **Berryvale Natural Foods,** 305 S. Mt. Shasta Blvd., caters to the health-conscious with organic produce, soy products, and enough tie-dye to make you dizzy. (☎926-1576. Open M-Sa 8:30am-8pm, Su 10am-6pm.)

Laurie's Mountain View Cafe, 401 N. Shasta Blvd. (☎926-4998). Tiny cafe with sunny patio, huge baked goods, fantastic sandwiches (salmon, pesto, and cheese $7), and incredible smoothies. Microbrews and imported beers. Live music from 7pm on weekends. Fish and chips (F) and BBQ (Sa) with live music in summer F 5-8pm. Open Su-Th 7am-4pm, F-Sa 7am-8pm; Nov.-May daily 7am-4pm. No credit cards. ❷

Black Bear Diner, 401 W. Lake St. (☎926-4669). Busy diner with crowds of folksy locals, visiting hikers, and hippies. Friendly waitstaff and huge portions that are "unbear-ably filling." Hungry Bear's Breakfast is 3 eggs, sausage, hash browns, 2 biscuits, and a slab of ham ($8). Dinners are heaping plates of comfort food ($8-11). Vegetarian options. Locations in Redding and Yreka, too. Open daily 5:30am-11:30pm. ❷

FAR NORTH

Lily's, 1013 S. Mt. Shasta Blvd. (☎926-3372). Hiding in a little white house with a picket fence is perhaps the most extensive and creative menu in town. Meals are a small splurge, but fairly priced considering the quality and preparation. For breakfast, both vegetarian eggs benedict ($8) and non-veggie eggs Benedict Arnold ($9) are enticing. Try the "Chicken Rosie," with raspberries, hazelnut liqueur, and cream ($16), or the ribeye steak ($17). Open in summer daily 7am-10pm; in winter 8am-9pm. ❹

👁 🏔 SIGHTS & OUTDOOR ACTIVITIES

The mountain attracts people climbing to new heights by car, foot, chair lift, pick-axe, or spiritual force. Everyone can enjoy Mt. Shasta without breaking a sweat, if they let their cars do the work. The **Everitt Memorial Highway** provides excellent views of the mountain as it winds 14 mi. from the town of Mt. Shasta to the Ski Bowl trailhead. Parking is available at Bunny Flats and at the end of the road. A number of **day hikes** begin along the Everitt Highway, including the 2 mi. steep hike to Grey Butte from Panther Meadow Campground, and another 2 mi. hike through Red Butte to Squaw Meadows from the Old Ski Bowl (0.7 mi. from Panther Meadow). The **Horse Camp Trail**, at Horse Camp, is another short but interesting hike. It begins at Bunny Flat and goes 2 mi., affording great views of Avalanche Gulch and the Red Banks.

FISH, ROCKS, AND BOOKS. The **Mount Shasta State Fish Hatchery,** ½ mi. west of I-5, monitors the production of nearly 10 million baby trout every year. Throw food in the ponds and spark a feeding frenzy. Don't jump in, no matter what the fish say. Guided tours are provided. *(3 Old State Rd. ☎926-5508. Closed Jan. and Feb. Open daily 7am-dusk. Free.)* Next door, the **Sisson Museum** has exhibits on the area's geology and history. *(☎926-5508. Open Apr.-Oct. M-Sa 10am-4pm, Su 1-4pm. Free.)* For a more literary experience, start at the **Village Books Bookstore.** Info about the latest New Age activities in the area is posted on the bulletin board out front. Step inside to peruse the spiritual book collection or enjoy the small coffeehouse. *(320 N. Mt. Shasta Blvd. ☎926-1678 or 800-344-0436. Open M-Sa 9:30am-9pm, Su 11am-5pm.)*

MOUNT SHASTA SKI PARK. Downhill skiers tackle the intermediate-level ski trails of **Mount Shasta Ski Park.** Cross-country skiers can try the **Ski Parks Nordic Center** or go solo for challenging backcountry skiing (maps and info from ranger service; see **Visitor Information,** p. 206). In summer, experienced **mountain bikers** wishing to challenge the mountain can take a chair lift from Mt. Shasta Ski Park and co-o-o-ast down. Logging roads in the national forests make excellent backcountry biking trails. Climbers of all skill levels love the park's outdoor wall. Those left unsatisfied can go **paragliding** or **mountain boarding.** *(Ski Park: 10 mi. east of I-5. ☎926-8600 or 800-754-7427; www.skipark.com. Lift tickets $33, ages 8-12 and over 64 $17, under 8 $7. Super Tu adult tickets $26. Night skiing W-Sa 4-10pm $20/$13/$3. Ski rental packages from $21. Nordic Center: Trail pass and rental $22/$18/$9. Biking: $12/$4/$8, rentals $20 for 6hr. Climbing: 2 climbs $5, 3hr. $12. Paragliding: $75 for tandem flight. Hours vary by season.)*

CLIMBING MOUNT SHASTA

All climbers must stop at the US Forest Service (see p. 206) for weather updates, climbing conditions, safety registration, a wilderness permit (free), a summit pass for climbs over 10,000 ft. ($15), and the mandatory human waste pack-out system. All adventurers should stop by for the most up-to-date maps and information before venturing into the wilderness. Mt. Shasta rangers are particularly knowledgeable, friendly, and helpful, whether you're going for a jump in a lake, an afternoon hike, or a trip to the summit. Parking is free at Bunny Flat, home of the most popular trailhead, but costs $5 at Clear Creek, Brewer Creek, and North Gate.

Mt. Shasta, at 14,162 ft., is not an easy climb, and unlike Mt. Whitney, requires mountaineering skills even on its easiest route. Weather conditions are notoriously unpredictable. There are 17 trails leading to the Shasta summit, each with its own rewards and challenges. The most popular and accessible route is **Avalanche Gulch,** which starts at Bunny Flat, on the mountain's southwest side, off Everitt Memorial Hwy. A short, steep trail leads to Horse Camp, where hikers will find the historic **Sierra Club Cabin.** In the summer, the cabin is occupied by a caretaker. This is a good place to set up **base camp ❶** for the necessary early morning ascent. ($5 fee to tent near the cabin, $3 for a bivy sack; no accommodations in the cabin itself.) Alternately, first-night **camping ❶** is permitted on the Bunny Flat parking lot or anywhere in the surrounding area, as long as you have a wilderness permit (see p. 206). While the climb can be done in one day, most first-time climbers choose to spend the night at Helen Lake (10,443 ft.). Though Avalanche Gulch is not a technical climb, it does require crampons and an ice pick, even in summer. Some significantly more difficult technical climbs also start at Bunny Flat, as well as at North Gate, Brewer Creek, and Clear Creek. Since Mt. Shasta City is at a mere 3,500 ft., acclimating to Shasta's extreme elevations probably necessitates some miniclimbs on the mountains before attempting to summit.

BEYOND MOUNT SHASTA

Castle Crags State Park (☎ 235-2684), off I-5, 15 mi. south of Shasta, is an awesome wilderness with beautiful trails, rivers, and lakes. When viewed from I-5, this massive mountain of rock looks like the fortification for an epic castle. It's not just a model, however; you can step in and feel the magic for yourself. Spanning the area are 28 mi. of well-maintained hiking trails. For great views of Mt. Shasta, try the strenuous 2.7 mi. **Castle Crags Trail,** accessible from the Vista Point parking area, which tops out on Castle Dome, 2250 ft. higher than the trailhead. Buy a topographical map of the area from the ranger station ($1). Stop at Indian Spring on the way up to fill up on ice-cold mountain water. The **Pacific Crest Trail** (see **From Crest to Crest: the Trail of the West,** p. 242) runs for 19 mi. through the wilderness, offering access to several serene alpine lakes. Access the trail at the south fork of Sacramento Rd.; maps and permits are available at the Forest Service. Be cautious: much of the stone here is dangerous and unstable. Nearby **Cantara Loop** has good beginner's rock faces, and **Pluto Caves** have fun lava tubes. There is also an outdoor climbing wall at the Mt. Shasta Ski Park (see p. 208). For more climbing info, call **5th Season** (☎ 926-3606) or the **US Forest Service** (☎ 926-4511). Camping is free in the area of the Shasta-Trinity National Forest surrounding the Castle Crags Wilderness, and the state park runs a full service campground. Abutting the wilderness area is **Castle Lake,** which offers beautiful hiking trails as well as fishing, swimming, and camping (although there is a restriction within 200 ft. of the lake).

Stewart Mineral Springs ❶, 4617 Stewart Springs Rd., in Weed, is a popular spiritual destination. Mr. Stewart was brought here on the brink of death and attributed his subsequent recovery to the healing energy of the water. Whether or not there's any truth to this, an afternoon spent relaxing in the saunas and hot tubs is, at the very least, a luxury. (☎ 938-2222; www.stewartmineralsprings.com. Open Su-W 10am-6pm, Th-Sa 10am-10pm; in winter daily 10am-6pm. Tent sites and RVs $15; motel rooms $45, with kitchen $49-79; cabins $59.)

The **McCloud River Area,** 10 mi. east of the town of Mt. Shasta on I-5, is perfect for swimming, boating, hiking, and camping. Thirteen miles of fairy-tale rivers, complete with three storybook waterfalls and meadows, make this a fantasy-filled area for afternoon sun worship and wildlife viewing. Acquired by the US Forest Service in 1989, the area is growing in popularity, but many trails and facilities are still unmarked. Forest Service rangers have helpful maps with detailed directions.

FAR NORTH

The **Squaw Valley Creek Trail** is an enjoyable, gentle 5 mi. trail south of McCloud. An abundance of unique vegetation and a thick carpet of moss lines the creek, itself a wonder of waterfalls and pools suitable for fishing and swimming. The trailhead is located 9 mi. south of McCloud; follow the signs to Squaw Valley Creek Rd. For a simple hike gushing with views, go to the **Falls of the McCloud River,** on Rte. 89, 6 mi. east of McCloud; follow signs to Fowlers Campground. At the fork, take a right. One mile down is a parking area with a large pine tree in the center. From here, head directly across the street toward the roar of falling water. In this short walk up the river there are three waterfalls worthy of snapshots. The trail is not strenuous, but there are sheer cliffs and no guard rails; exercise extreme caution. A 30min. hike from the falls (or the left fork in the road) leads to **Fowlers Camp ❶**, 3600 ft., the only overnight campsite in the area. This spot has toilets, picnic units, drinking water, and handicap facilities. (First-come, first-camp. Sites $12.)

AREA LAKES

The area's numerous lakes are almost as popular as its mountains. Around Mt. Shasta are alpine lakes great for secluded swimming and fishing, including **Deadfall Lake, Castle Lake, Toad Lake,** and **Heart Lake. Lake Siskiyou,** which is controlled according to water needs in the area, is less remote and more crowded (beach use $1). The ranger station has info on dozens of lakes and rivers in the area.

LAKE SHASTA. Thirty minutes south of Mt. Shasta on I-5 (15min. north of Redding), Lake Shasta is not only the largest reservoir in California, but also the chillest place to kick back. All sorts of watercraft explore the 450 mi. of sapphire blue shoreline. Campgrounds and picnic areas pepper the coast. However, this lake remains a beach-less haven, best enjoyed by exiting the car and hopping into some form of flotation device. Visitors can enjoy a stop at the **Shasta Dam,** at the southern end of the lake. Three times taller than Niagara Falls, the Shasta is the second-largest dam in the US after the Grand Coulee in Washington State. In it is enough concrete to build a sidewalk around the Earth. It was built from 1938-1945 as the "Keystone of the Central Valley Project." Tourists gasp at the panoramic mountain views. Visit the **Dam Visitor Center,** in the Dam Park. (☎275-4463. Open daily 9am-4pm. For security reasons, dam tours have been cancelled.)

WHISKEYTOWN UNIT. Eight miles west of Redding is this home to the popular **Whiskeytown Lake and Recreation Center.** The lake's beaches, marinas, campsites, and hiking trails are easily accessible from Rte. 299. It's not quite Coney Island, but in peak summer season the lakeside snack bars are packed, and the surf bustles with boats. The recreation area boasts many well-maintained primitive and developed **campgrounds ❶.** However, RV campers are often dismayed to find that their sites are basically in a crowded parking lot with minimal shade. Entry into the area is $5 per vehicle for a day, $10 for a week.

The **Whiskeytown Unit Visitors Center,** at Rte. 299 and Kennedy Memorial Dr., south of the lake, has day use permits. Reserve campsites through Biospherics (☎800-365-2267; http://reservations.nps.gov). Pick up backcountry camping permits and hiking permits at Park Headquarters. (☎246-1225. 14-day max. stay. Camping permits $10. Open daily 9am-6pm; in winter 10am-4pm.) The **Oak Bottom Campground,** off Rte. 299, has 22 RV sites and 100 developed tent sites near a beach, picnic area, snack bar, and marina, as well as drinking water and flush toilets. RV sites have similar facilities (no hookup) and lake access, but they aren't too scenic. (Sites May 15-Sept. 15 $16, lakeside $18; Sept. 16-May 14 $8.) The park headquarters directs visitors to a number of first-come, first-served primitive **campsites ❶,** all $10 per night ($5 in winter). Nearby **Oak Bottom Marina** rents ski boats, sailboats, patio boats, and canoes for reasonable rates. (☎359-2269. Canoes $21 for 3hr.; sailboats $42 for 3hr. Open M-Th 7am-8pm, F-Su 7am-9pm.)

YREKA
☎ 530

Yrekan rebels taught us this lesson in December 1941: to get political attention from chichi southern California and the space cadets of northern Oregon, take to the streets with shotguns, barricade roads, write a declaration of independence, set up a provisional government, and declare yourself a state. Three days after this little "rebellion," the situation was shelved in the wake of a certain bombing at Pearl Harbor. Alas! Yreka's 15 minutes came and went as the temporary capital of The Great State of Jefferson: a "state that never was and never will be, but that has lived in men's minds for a hundred years." Even today, some continue to assert Jefferson's independence; just south of Yreka on I-50, a farmer painted "State of Jefferson" proudly across his barn, hoping passing motorists would take note.

Now, Yreka (why-REE-ka; pop. 7500) chugs along a more modern track with standard shopping malls, one-night motels, and cheap lube jobs. Home to a high-quality county museum and many other dependable establishments, Yreka is a good place to stop on your way to somewhere else.

■■**7 ORIENTATION & PRACTICAL INFORMATION.** Yreka is conveniently stationed on I-5, 20 mi. south of the Oregon border, and 40 mi. north of the town of Mt. Shasta, and 260 mi. north of Sacramento. Greyhound (☎842-3145; open daily 8am-5pm) buses roll to **Redding** (2hr., 3 per day, $21-23), **Mt. Shasta** (50min., 1 per day, $10-11), **Portland** (8-9hr., 2 per day, $65), and **San Francisco** (9-10hr., 3 per day, $57). **Enterprise**, 1275 S. Main St., rents compact cars for $32 a day will 100 free mi., $0.20 each additional mi. (841-0525. Must be 21 with a major credit card. Under 25 surcharge $10 per day. Open M-F 8am-5pm, Sa 9am-noon.) The **Chamber of Commerce**, 117 W. Miner St., gives the lowdown on its hometown. (☎842-1649; www.yrekachamber.com. Open M-F 9am-5:30pm, Sa 11am-4pm, Su noon-5pm; in winter M-F 9am-5pm.) Other services are available at: **Klamath National Forest Headquarters** and **Clouds National Forest Ranger**, 1312 Fairlane Rd. (☎842-6131; open M-F 8am-4:30pm); **24hr. General Counseling and Rape Crisis** (☎842-4068); **Domestic Violence** (☎842-4068; call collect from anywhere); the **hospital**, 444 Bruce St. (☎842-4121); and the **Post Office**, 401 S. Broadway (☎842-9372; open M-F 8:30am-5pm), at Center St. **Postal Code:** 96097.

7 ACCOMMODATIONS. Gas stations, motels, and inns flank Main St. The south end of Main St. is most promising for high-value accommodations. The **Klamath Motor Lodge ❸**, 1111 S. Main St., is a friendly spot with large clean rooms, phones, microwaves, popcorn, cable TV, A/C, fridge, coffee, and a pool with a grassy picnic area with a barbecue. (☎842-2751 or 800-551-7255. Singles from $44, in winter $21; doubles $47/$42.) The **Miner's Inn ❹**, 122 E. Miner St., right off I-5, is a Best Western a step above the standard Interstate motor lodge. Spacious, spotless rooms have cable TV, phone, and coffee, while several suites are two bedroom apartments with kitchens. The well-managed, if corporate, grounds feature two heated pools and a large conference center. (842-4355. Singles and doubles $62-72, suites with kitchen $92, in winter $3 less.)

☐ FOOD. The fare ranges from truck-stop convenience to New Age soul-enriching nutrients and famously "quaint" rail-town tourist taverns. At Main and W. Minor St. are two 24hr. family restaurants with standard Denny's-style fare. Without 24hr. convenience, but with New Age flute music, **Nature's Kitchen ❷**, 412 S. Main St., has a fresh flower on every table, a smile on every employee, and a fresh lemon slice in every glass of ice water. The room and waitstaff are bright and sunny, and prices are heavenly. A Monterey jack and avocado sandwich with a sesame-and-garlic seasoned salad or bowl of soup is only $5.50. An organic bakery and espresso bar are also one with this establishment. (☎842-1136. Open M-Sa

8am-3pm.) Another local favorite, **Poor George's Family Restaurant ❶,** 108 Oberlin St., just west of Main St., is sweet and friendly. Inside are homemade pie, a jukebox, paintings of bald eagles, and other slices of Americana. Seniors and skaters alike munch on burgers ($3.50-6), sandwiches ($4-6), salads ($3-6), and steak and eggs ($8). Breakfast is served all day. (Open M-F 6am-7:45pm, Sa-Su 7am-1:45pm.)

LAVA BEDS NATIONAL MONUMENT ☎530

At first glance, Lava Beds National Monument appears to be a stark sea of sagebrush, arid grasses, and craggy rocks. But beneath this 72 sq. mi. expanse lies a complex web of more than 400 lava-formed caves and otherworldly tunnels. Cool, quiet, and often eerie tubes are the product of lava flows from the Mammoth crater around 30,000 years ago, and range from 18 in. crawl spaces to 80 ft. cathedrals. As the outer layer of a flow contacts the colder ground or air around it, it hardens and creates a sheet that insulates the molten lava inside. The hot, fluid lava continues to flow away, leaving hollow conduits under the earth after the lava flow ceases.

In spring and fall, nearby Tule Lake Refuge provides a stopover for migratory birds, some of which come from as far away as Siberia. The fall migration is particularly spectacular, when a million ducks and half a million geese literally darken the sky. In winter, this is the best place in the contiguous US to see a bald eagle.

For people, however, Lava Beds and the Tule Lake Refuge appear to be a challenging destination, due mostly to their remoteness and harsh climate: expect blistering heat and little water in the monument. Local accommodations are sparse, and those seeking less desolate motels should plan on making the drive to Mt. Shasta (see p. 205) or Klamath Falls, OR (see p. 215).

▟ ◪ ORIENTATION & PRACTICAL INFORMATION

Although cold weather can pervade the high desert climate at any time of the year, summer weather tends to be arid, with hot days and cool nights. It takes a day to really appreciate the park, and you'll need a car not only to access the park but also to explore its northern areas. The nearest spot to catch a bus, rent a car, or find a hospital is across the Oregon border in **Klamath Falls** (p. 215), 50 mi. north of Lava Beds. **Redding** (p. 204) and **Medford,** OR also offer these services but are a few hours away. There is no public transportation to the area. Tulelake **police** is located at 24th St. and C St. (☎800-404-2911 or 667-5284).

Lava Beds is southwest of the blink-and-you'll-miss-it town of Tulelake (pop. 1000) and northeast of Mt. Shasta. The **Visitors Center** is in the southeast corner of the park. There are two northern entrances near Tulelake. The **southeast entrance** (25 mi. south of town) is closest to the Visitors Center. The two **east entrances** are closer to Klamath Basin Wildlife Refuge and the Oregon border. Access roads to the national monument and Visitors Center are clearly marked. The **north entrance** is on Rte. 139. The road to the **northeast entrance** leaves Rte. 139 about 8 mi. southeast of Tulelake, and winds through the wilder northern areas of the monument for 25 mi. to the Visitors Center. Visitors coming from the south on I-5 must take a circuitous route, following U.S. 97 North, then Rte. 161 East to S. Hill Rd. For cheap gas, hop over the Oregon border on Rte. 139 North to Merrill.

Lava Beds Visitors Center, in the park's southeastern corner, near a cluster of accessible caves, has exhibits on Modoc culture and gives daily tours. Summer presentations on the lava tubes, wildflowers, and the Modoc tribe are given at the nearby outdoor theater. The well-informed staff lends flashlights to explorers (free; return them by 5:30pm, in winter by 4:30pm) and sells hardhats for $3.25. **Bring plenty of water and food**—there are no concessions at the monument. (☎667-

2282; www.nps.gov/labe. Open May 26-Sept. 1 daily 8am-6pm; Sept. 2-May 25 8am-5pm. Center tours daily 10am and 2pm. Outside tours daily 9pm. $5 per vehicle.)

🏠 🍴 ACCOMMODATIONS, CAMPING, & FOOD

The only developed campground in Lava Beds is **Indian Well ❶**, opposite the Visitors Center. Though it must have been a hellish walk across the jagged volcanic rocks to reach this long-used Indian camp in the old days, you can now drive up to sites, featuring flat ground, picnic tables, firepits, and a fantastic view of the stars. Even drinking water and flush toilets are available May-October. (☎ 667-2282. 43 sites. No reservations accepted. $10.) The monument has two **wilderness areas,** one on each side of the main north-south road, for backcountry **camping ❶**. A wilderness permit is not required within the park. Cooking is limited to stoves, and camps must be at least 1 mi. from trailheads, roads, and parking areas and 150 ft. from cave entrances. **Modoc National Forest** borders the monument on three sides, and offers free off-road **camping ❶**. Nearby are **Medicine Camp** and **Hemlock campgrounds ❶;** both have water, flush toilets, and opportunities to fish, swim and boat (sites $7). More info is available at the **Modoc National Forest Doublehead Ranger Station,** 1 mi. south of Tulelake on Rte. 139. and across from a set of metal silos. (☎ 667-2246. Open M-F 8:30am-4:30pm.)

There are a few roadside motels in Tulelake. Each is fairly isolated, set between agricultural fields and Rte. 139. The best of the bunch is the **Ellis Motel ❸,** 2238 Rte. 139, 1 mi. north of Tulelake, which sits alone behind a manicured lawn with only a row of large shady trees between it and the highway. There are 11 small, simple rooms, some with kitchens. (☎ 667-5242. Singles from $35; doubles from $45.)

Jock's, at Modoc and Main St., is a decently sized but slightly overpriced grocery store. (☎ 667-2612. Open M-Sa 7am-8pm, Su 9am-6pm.) **Captain Jack's Stronghold Restaurant ❷,** 5 mi. south of Tulelake, 1 mi. south of the turn-off to Lava Beds, serves homemade soups and breads, and has a sizable salad bar. The diverse menu, prime location, and welcoming floral decorations attract locals and tourists. (☎ 664-5566. Breakfast and lunch $6-8. Dinner $8-13. Open Feb.-Nov. Tu-W 7am-8pm, Th-Sa 7am-9pm, Su 9am-8pm.)

👁 ⛰ SIGHTS & OUTDOOR ACTIVITIES

SPELUNKING. The lava beds, (mostly) linear lava tubes, offer novice cavers relatively easy expeditions into the underground. That is not to say, however, that the caves aren't pitch black, perfectly silent, and generally spooky; though never more than a few hundred feet below the surface, the caves give a sense of isolation and, at times, fear, that few other experiences provide. Hardhats, on sale at the Visitors Center (see p. 212) for $3.25, or other helmets, are essential unless you're under 12 inches tall: the unusually sharp ceilings have an uncanny affinity for human heads. Another necessary cave-going accessory is a sweatshirt or jacket; the sun-swept desert can be scorching, but the caves below are cool and damp. Cave tours, leaving from the Visitors Center (mid-June to Sept. 1 daily 2pm), explain the fascinating phenomena associated with the caves. Solo exploring is not recommended but is allowed; bring steely nerves and *at least* two flashlights. Inquire at the Visitors Center for guidelines and information.

There are over 400 caves in the park, with nearly three dozen available for public exploration. (All caves are public, but under the Cave Protection Act, only a few can have their location disclosed. Feel free to look for the other 400 or so if you know what you're doing.) The **Mushpot Cave,** in the middle of the Visitors Center's parking lot, has a short, well-lit, self-guided trail that will acquaint visitors with cave formations. South of the Visitors Center is perhaps the best and most surreal

FROM
THE
ROAD

AFRAID OF THE DARK?

My echoed laugh returned to me, warming the damp 42°F chill for a second. "What the hell am I doing here?" I asked myself, about a thousand feet inside Valentine Cave. Man has sent himself into space and has gone to the depths of the ocean—but at this moment, in this cave, there seemed nothing more absurd and contradictory to self-preservation than putting myself into exactly the situation I was in: subterranean burial, deep within a lava tube. This thought alternated with overpowering flashlight paranoia. I'd take four steps forward then stare at the lantern's beam. Is it getting weaker? Yes, it's getting weaker. No, it isn't. Am I talking to myself? Take four steps forward. Repeat.

My heart had barely settled when I nervously started into Golden Dome. Just past the twilight zone, I squinted, shook my head, and put my flashlight's beam back onto what had caught my eye: a man was seated sideways to me, at the edge of my sight, 400 ft. into the cave. What was he doing here, alone, in the dark? I didn't care to ask, and started back, quietly so as not to disturb his silent meditation. But then I wondered: maybe he's hurt, or even dead? I walked back, and called out, "Hello?" No answer. "HELLO?" I advanced, an impending sense of heroism only faintly overcoming an impending sense of doom. But wait, the head...is separate from the torso. Disbelief passed into humiliation as it quickly became obvious the "man" was a pile of rocks. Strange things you see down here, alone...

—Carleton Goold

of the area's "public" caves, **Valentine Cave,** with unnaturally smooth walls and a frozen waterfall. Townsend Bats return to the **Skull Ice Cave,** 3½ mi. north, every February. On an equally eerie note, this cave is where a rancher found two human skeletons chilling alongside wagonloads of bighorn sheep skulls. The floor of the cave is covered with ice, which undoubtedly attracted the animals. The ice has since been gated off, but the 80 ft. tall ceilings are still worth it. On the 2¼ mi. **Cave Loop Road,** which starts and finishes at the Visitors Center, there are 20 caves with little more to guide you than an entrance stairway. Parking is available at each entrance. **Sentinel Cave** has crisscrossing tunnels, skylights, and two entrances for added fun and confusion. Though **Golden Dome** is structurally unremarkable, be sure to inspect the lavacicles on the yellow hydrophobic bacteria-encrusted ceiling. The most complex of the Cave Loop and the other public tunnels is the **Catacombs Cave,** with over 1 mi. of interconnected passageways, some of which require a good deal of crawling. Bring a technical map, available at the Visitors Center ($4.50), and allow 4-6hr. for this one.

HIKING. Trails of varying difficulty wander through the park. Hikers should keep in mind that the area is essentially a desert, with little shade and extreme heat. The **Whitney-Butte Trail** goes through rocky brush to the black Callahan Lava Flow, a 3.5 mi. (one-way) route from the trailhead at Merrill Cave. The **Mammoth Crater** is more a sight than hike, but offers all the benefits of a huge volcanic crater with none of the annoying molten rock and exploding cinder. For an overnight hike, the Lyons Trails traverses 10 mi. from Skull Cave to Hospital Rock over the rocky, hot plain in the park's eastern reaches. Consult a ranger before you go.

Four miles north of the Visitors Center is **Schonkin Butte.** The steep 0.75 mi. ascent takes about 30min. and leads to a working fire lookout that gives a broad view of the landscape's greens and golds and the massive white face of Mt. Shasta. Close to Lava Bed's northern entrance is **Captain Jack's Stronghold,** the natural lava fortress where Modoc warriors held back Colonel Wheaton's troops during the Modoc War. Go only if your interest in history and imagination is strong: few traces of the struggle remain. A beautiful example of the lengths to which man will go to leave his mark, **Petroglyph Point,** just outside the northern entrance, is a cliff wall of a former island covered with a large collection of native rock carvings. Native Americans had to paddle across a lake to the cliff, where they engraved mountain- and human-like images. A few carvings from before 1950, such as Japanese characters engraved by prisoners of the internment camps, are also historic. Sadly, the ugly barbed wire fence guarding the walls prevents further efforts to leave inscrutable messages for posterity.

BEYOND LAVA BEDS

The **Klamath Basin National Wildlife Refuge** teems with waterfowl. The **Tule Lake** and **Lower Klamath National Wildlife Refuges** are the two areas of the basin that are most accessible from Lava Beds. The drive from Tulelake to Lava Beds runs through the Tule Lake refuge, which is visible from Rte. 161 just north of Tulelake. The area is a bird-watcher's paradise. Over a million birds come through the refuge each year, including bald eagles and pelicans; the best time to see the eagles is fall and especially winter. The **Lower Klamath and Tule Lake Wildlife Refuge Visitors Center and Headquarters,** on Hill Rd., 4 mi. south of Rte. 161 and 18 mi. north of Lava Beds Visitors Center, has a small **museum** with a high-quality slide show and many a stuffed bird or beast. A canoe route starting from the museum is open July-September, and has two marked miles of "trails" for quiet and up-close observation. (☎667-2231. Open M-F 8am-4:30pm, Sa-Su 10am-4pm.) Car tours are available in the Tule Lake and Lower Klamath Refuges. The "Tule Lake tour" is best. A 10 mi. trail open to hiking, biking, and cross-country skiing meanders through the Klamath Marsh Refuge. The still waters and low mountains make perfect photographic backdrops for images of the active wildlife. Thanks to the National Audobon Society and other activists, former President Theodore Roosevelt declared this fragile wetlands the first-ever wildlife refuge.

For a taste of the dark side of American history, you can visit the remains of a Japanese internment camp, where more than 18,000 Japanese-Americans were held by the US government during WWII. The camp is in Newell, 4 mi. north of Petroglyph Point, but is referred to as the **Tule Lake site.** There is not much left to see of the camp except a plaque, a couple of ruined buildings, and old fence-lines.

CRATER LAKE & KLAMATH FALLS ☎541

The deepest lake in the US, the 7th deepest in the world, and one of the most beautiful anywhere, Crater Lake is one of Oregon's signature attractions. Formed about 7700 years ago in an eruption of the huge Mt. Mazama, it began as a deep caldera and gradually filled itself with centuries worth of melted snow. The circular lake plunges from its shores to a depth of 1936 ft.; though it remains iceless in the winter, its banks, which loom as high as 2000 feet above the 6176 ft. lake surface, are snow-covered until July. Visitors from all over the world circle the 33 mi. Rim Drive, carefully gripping the wheel, enchanted by the impossibly blue water. Klamath Falls, one of the nearest cities, makes a convenient stop on the way to the park and houses most of the services, motels, and restaurants listed below.

▐ TRANSPORTATION

Route 62 skirts the park's southwestern edge as it arcs 130 mi. between Medford in the southwest and Klamath Falls, 56 mi. southeast of the park. West of the park, Rte. 62 follows the Upper Rogue River. To reach Crater Lake from Portland, take I-5 to Eugene, then **Route 58** east to **U.S. 97** south. From U.S. 97, **Route 138** leads west to the park's north entrance, but Crater Lake averages over 44 ft. of snow per year, and snowbound roads usually keep the northern entrance closed as late as July. The roads to **Rim Village** stay open year-round. Before July, enter the park from the south. **Route 62** runs west from U.S. 97 about 40 mi. south of the park, through the small town of **Fort Klamath** and on to the south access road that leads to the caldera's rim. Another 20 mi. of travel from the intersection of Rte. 62 and U.S. 97 brings you right to Klamath Falls.

FAR NORTH

IN RECENT NEWS

WHO'S THE SUCKER?

Farmers in the dusty Klamath basin have counted on dependable irrigation from the Klamath River since 1905. But for several years before the summer of 2001, the Klamath Basin worked up a deep debt in precipitation, receiving only about half of its 11 in. average. Environmentalists took notice, and alerted the federal government. Citing possible extinction of suckerfish and coho salmon populations if water levels declined any further, the US Bureau of Reclamation shut down irrigation water to 1400 farmers downstream in Southern Oregon and Northern California.

Over the course of the chaotic summer, farmers forcibly opened headgates four times, and armed federal agents had to be called in. Snowpack and slightly improved rainfall ensured water releases in 2002. To some extent, though, the damage was already done; younger farmers in Tule Lake have already left for wetter pastures. Fueling the flames was a pronouncement by the National Academy of Sciences finding that the science behind the conclusion that lowered water would kill the fish was "baseless." Complicating matters further, saving water for the fish deprived waterfowl of it and bald eagles in the Lower Klamath Basin. No solution seems readily available—some turn to the Bible, while others feel the government should buy out farmers. In any case, tension is building, as the drought, though lessened, is by no means over, and signs attesting to the frustration of the farmers remain: "Remember your oath: people before fish."

Trains: Amtrak (☎884-2822 or 800-USA-RAIL/872-7245; www.amtrak.com). Follow Klamath Ave. until you see signs for the station. Open daily 7:30-11am and 8:30-10pm. To **Portland** (7hr., 1 per day, $36-60); trains continue north.

Buses: Greyhound, 3817 U.S. 97 N, in Mollie's Truck Stop (☎882-4616). To **Eugene** (10hr., 1 per day, $40) and **Redding** (4hr., 1 per day, $30). Open M-F 8am-1am, Sa 6-9am and midnight-12:45am.

Public Transportation: Basin Transit Service (☎883-2877), runs 6 routes. Runs M-F 6am-7:30pm, Sa 10am-5pm. $0.90, seniors and disabled $0.45.

Taxis: Classic Taxi (☎850-8303). $2 base, $2 per mi. 24hr.

Car Rental: Budget (☎885-5421), at Klamath Falls airport. From S 6th St., go south on Washburn Dr. and follow the signs. M-F $30 per day, $0.25 per mi. after 100 mi. Sa-Su $26 per day, 100 free mi. per day. Open M-F 7am-10pm, Sa-Su 8:30am-6pm.

⚡ PRACTICAL INFORMATION

Tourist Information: Chamber of Commerce, 507 Main St. (☎884-0666 or 800-445-6728; www.klamath.org). Open M-F 8am-5pm.

Outdoor Information: William G. Steel Center (☎594-2211, ext. 402), 1 mi. from the south entrance. Open daily 9am-5pm. **Crater Lake National Park Visitors Center** (☎594-3100 or 594-3000; www.nps.gov/crla), on the lake shore at Rim Village. Open daily June-Sept. 8:30am-6pm.

Park Entrance Fee: Cars $10, hikers and bikers $5. Free with Golden Eagle Passport.

Laundromat: Main Street Laundromat, 1711 Main St. (☎883-1784). Wash $1.25, dry $0.25 per 12min. Open M-Sa 8am-8pm; last wash 7pm.

Police: 425 Walnut St. (☎883-5336).

Crisis and Rape Crisis Line: ☎800-452-3669. 24hr.

Hospital: Merle West Medical Center, 2865 Daggett Ave. (☎882-6311). From U.S. 97 North, turn right on Campus Dr., then right again onto Daggett. 24hr. emergency room.

Library and Internet Access: Klamath County Library, 126 S 3rd St. (☎882-8894). Has 6 slow computers with 1hr. free Internet access. Open M-Tu and Th 10am-5pm, W 1-8pm, F-Sa 10am-5pm, Su 1-5pm.

Post Office: Klamath Falls, 317 S 7th St. (☎800-275-8777), at Walnut St. Open M-F 7:30am-5:30pm, Sa 9am-noon. **Crater Lake,** in the Steel Center. Open M-Sa 9am-noon and 1-3pm. **Postal Code:** 97604.

ACCOMMODATIONS & CAMPING

Klamath Falls has plenty of affordable hotels that make easy bases for Crater Lake. If you'd rather live in the trees, **Forest Service campgrounds ❶** (usually about $5) line **Route 62** through Rogue River National Forest to the west of the park. The park itself contains two campgrounds, both of which are closed until roads are passable. **Backcountry camping ❶** is allowed in the park; a backcountry permit, free from the Steel Center, is required.

Mazama Campground (☎594-2255), near the park's south entrance off Rte. 62. Tenters and RVs swarm this monster facility when it opens in mid-June, and some don't leave until it closes in Oct. Mostly tent sites. Few electrical hookups. Loop G is more secluded and spacious, but opens later in the year. Toilets, laundry, telephone. A general store and gas, open daily 7am-10pm. No reservations. 213 sites. Tents $15; RVs $17; electric hookups $19. Showers $0.75 for 4min. ❶

Townhouse Motel, 5323 S 6th St. (☎882-0924), 3 mi. south of Main St. on the edge of strip-mall land. Offers clean, comfy rooms at good prices. Cable, A/C, no phones. Rooms from $30. ❷

Lost Creek Campground (☎594-2255), in the southeast corner of the park, 3 mi. on a paved road off Rim Dr. 16 mid-sized sites set amid pines. Water, toilets. No reservations. Usually open mid-July to mid-Sept.; check with Steel Center. Tent sites $10. ❶

Collier Memorial State Park and Campground (☎783-2471), 30 mi. north of Klamath Falls on U.S. 97, offers small tent and RV sites with little privacy near the Williamson River. The brilliant green lichen hanging off the timber is a highlight—ironically, as a logging museum is just south of the campground. Toilets, showers, laundry. Sites $15; full hookups $18. ❶

Williamson River Campground, farther down the road from Collier Memorial State Park and Campground, offers tent sites with pit toilets and no water for $6 per night. ❶

Union Creek Resort (☎560-3565), just south of the Rogue River Gorge on Rte. 62, in Union Creek. Has cozy, woody rooms. Microwave and fridge but no phones. Office open 8am-9pm. Rooms without private bath $40-50; cabins $55-95. ❸

FOOD

Eating cheap ain't easy in Crater Lake, with dining limited to a cafeteria, restaurant, and cafe in Rim Village. **Klamath Falls** has some affordable dining and a **Safeway** at Pine and 8th St., one block north of Main St. (☎882-2660. Open daily 6am-11pm.) A lot of eats in Klamath Falls go hand in hand with billiards; if you're a pool shark, Main St. between 5th and 7th St. is the place to go. The **Fort Klamath General Store,** 52608 Rte. 62, offers canned goods, sells gas, and houses a cafe. (☎381-2263. Open daily 7am-10pm; in winter 7am-8pm.)

Waldo's Mongolian Grill and Tavern, 610 Main St. (☎884-6863). This large restaurant and lounge might play techno or reggae even if most patrons are wearing Stetson hats. The food is standard Mongolian BBQ; the lounge has just about every equipment-intensive bar game (pool, shuffleboard, etc.) known to man. Youthful bar scene weekends. Medium bowl $8.50, all-you-can-eat $10. Grill open M-Sa 11am-9pm; tavern M-Th 11am-11:30pm, F-Sa 11am-1am. ❷

Plentiful Bakery, 2918 Altima Dr. off S 6th St. (☎273-6622). Basic homemade goodness hits the spot in this small cafe. Be like the locals and have soup and a sandwich for $5.50, or stick with salad ($3-6). Open daily 6am-9pm. ❶

Cattle Crossing Cafe (☎381-2344), on Rte. 62, in Fort Klamath. Waffle breakfasts ($3-7), burgers ($5-7), and dinners ($7-14) are capped off by mouth-watering homemade pie ($2.75 a slice). Open Apr.-Oct. daily 9am-6pm. ❷

FAR NORTH

⚠ OUTDOOR ACTIVITIES

The area around Crater Lake is filled with all sorts of outdoor adventures. With ample options for hiking and biking, as well as easy access to the backcountry regions outside the park, you may feel overwhelmed with options. A good jumping-off point is the Steel Center (see **Outdoor Information,** p. 216), or up at the Rim Village, where the Information Center and the Crater Lake Lodge are located. **Crater Lake Lodge** (☎594-2255; reservations 830-8700) is a few hundred yards east of **Sinnott Memorial Overlook** in the rim village. Rooms are very expensive, but fun in the lodge can be had for free: make a quick visit to the rustic "great hall," rebuilt from its original materials, and warm yourself by the fire or relax in a rocking chair on the observation deck. The friendly staff will be happy to help you find any info that you need about the lake.

DRIVING. Rim Drive, usually not open until mid-July, loops 33 mi. around the rim of the caldera, high above the lake. Pull-outs are strategically placed along the road wherever a view of the lake might cause an awe-struck tourist to drive off the cliff. Don't despair when the caldera walls block sight of the lake: the views of Cascade volcanoes as distant as Mt. Shasta, 100 mi. south, will console your eyes.

HIKING. Most visitors never stray far from their vehicles as they tour the lake, so hiking provides a great way to get away from the crowds. Trailheads are scattered along the rim, so just park and hike away from the road. The Steel Center has a trail map and info about which trails are closed due to weather. **Watchman Peak Trail** (0.75 mi. one-way) begins on the west side of the lake. It is short, but yields a great view of Wizard Island, one of two active cinder cones in the lake. **Mount Scott Trail** (5 mi. round-trip) is 17 mi. clockwise from Rim Village. Although steep, the ascent to the top of 9000 ft. Mt. Scott and the historic fire tower on top affords a beautiful panoramic view of the lake. **Cleetwood Cove Trail** (2.25 mi. round-trip) is the only route to go to the water and is the park's most traveled trail. It drops 700 ft. in 1 mi. to get to the shore.

ON THE LAKE. In the summer, park rangers lead hour-long boat tours from the Cleetwood Cove trailhead. Aside from giving a comprehensive history of the lake and its formation, the tours provide breathtaking views of both **Wizard Island,** a cinder cone rising 760 ft. above the lake, and **Phantom Ship Rock,** a spooky rock formation. (Tours run late June to mid-Sept. 7 times daily 10am-4:30pm. $19.25, under 11 $11.50.) The boat tours provide foot access to the island, which can be hiked for a view into its crater. Landlubbers may prefer picnics and fishing (artificial lures only) at the bottom of the trail. Though the lake (supposedly without outlet, though many contend the Rogue River drains out the bottom) was virtually sterile when modern man found it, it has since been stocked with rainbow trout and kokanee. If you walk down to the lake at Cleetwood Cove you can take a dip, but the lake's melted snow reaches a maximum temperature of only 50°F.

BACKCOUNTRY EXPLORATION. A hiking trip into the park's vast **backcountry** leaves all the exhaust and tourists behind. Hiking or climbing inside the caldera is prohibited. Other than near water sources, dispersed **camping ❶** is allowed anywhere in the area, but is complicated by the absence of water and the presence of bears. Get info and required backcountry permits for free at either visitors center. Part of the **Pacific Crest Trail** begins from the trailhead ¾ mi. west of the south entrance. The ultimate backcountry trail passes through the park and three backcountry campsites, giving great views of mountain meadows, old-growth timber, and, of course, the lake. Another excellent loop begins at the **Red Cone trailhead** on the north access road, passing the less-traveled **Crater Springs, Oasis Butte,** and **Boundary Springs trails.** However, it is impaired by the snow until July and opens only at the discretion of the ranger. Contact the Steel Center for more information.

UPPER ROGUE RIVER

If you prefer your water more vertical than anything the lake can offer, try the Upper Rogue, easily accessible from Rte. 62 southwest of Crater Lake. Emerging from a spring on the northern slope of Mt. Mazama, the river contends with the area's many lava flows by raging through scenic gorges, passing through huge waterfalls and cataracts, and even going underground for a stretch. Despite all this, the fish are doing all right, especially in places like **Casey State Park,** 46 mi. southwest of the park, where the angling is good but crowded.

One hundred seventy-three foot **Mill Creek Falls** drops into a deep canyon downstream of the **Avenue of Giant Boulders,** where a huge jumble of rocks offers navigational puzzles for the feet and sublime **sunning** for your back. The pools formed between cascades also make for equally great **splashing around.** From Rte. 62, easy, short trails to both sites are accessible from a trailhead; follow signs to "Mill Creek Falls/Prospect Access Road," about 32 mi. southwest of Crater Lake on Rte. 62.

Things get steamier for the Rogue the closer it approaches Mt. Mazama: lava flows are clearly at work in both the **Natural Bridge** and the **Rogue River Gorge.** The bridge performs a natural, but still frightening, disappearing act over part of the river when it descends into a lava tube and reappears 200 ft. downstream. In the Gorge, the river is forced through a lava flow and gets very angry about it, smashing through in a series of short but raging waterfalls. The Gorge and Natural Bridge are about 20 and 23 mi. southwest of Crater Lake on Rte. 62, respectively.

ASHLAND, OREGON ☎ 541

Set near the California border, Ashland mixes hip youth and British literary history to create an unlikely but intriguing stage for the world-famous Oregon Shakespeare Festival. From mid-February to October, drama devotees can choose from 11 plays—several of them written by dramatists other than Shakespeare—which are performed in Ashland's three elegant theaters. But to locals and the outdoorsy, Ashland is far more than a town crazy for an old, dead bard: unexpected in every way, it's a small (pop. 20,000) town crammed between mountains to the west and east and culturally smeared somewhere between liberal Portland and new-age Northern California; the dining and partying befits a town ten times its size. To add to the fun, the surrounding area is packed with all the biking, boating, and hiking one could ever hope for. Ashland is the perfect place to linger a few more days or weeks than you'd originally planned.

▐▀ JOURNEY'S END

I pray you, stay not, but in haste to horse.
  —*All's Well That Ends Well,* II.v

Ashland is located in the foothills of the Siskiyou and Cascade Ranges, 285 mi. south of Portland and 15 mi. north of the California border, near the junction of **I-5** and **Route 66.** Cutting through the middle of town on a northwest-southeast axis is **Route 99.** It becomes **North Main Street** as it enters town from the west, then splits briefly into **East Main Street** and **Lithia Way** as it runs through the walkable downtown. Farther south, Main St. changes name again to **Siskiyou Boulevard,** where Southern Oregon University (SOU) is flanked by affordable motels.

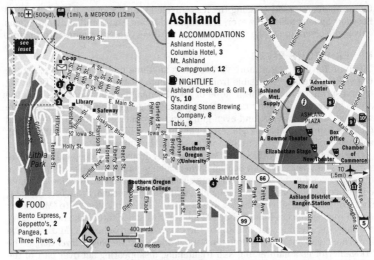

Ashland

■ ACCOMMODATIONS
Ashland Hostel, **5**
Columbia Hotel, **3**
Mt. Ashland
    Campground, **12**

■ NIGHTLIFE
Ashland Creek Bar & Grill, **6**
Q's, **10**
Standing Stone Brewing
    Company, **8**
Tabú, **9**

● FOOD
Bento Express, **7**
Geppetto's, **2**
Pangea, **1**
Three Rivers, **4**

Buses: Greyhound, 2073 N. Rte. 99, (☎482-8803). Pickup and drop-off at Mr. C's Market, at the intersection of Rte. 99 N and Valley View Rd., which extends from I-90 Exit 280. To: **Portland** (8hr., 3 per day, $43); **Sacramento** (7hr., 3 per day, $45); **San Francisco** (11hr., 3 per day, $49).

Public Transportation: Rogue Valley Transportation (RVTD; ☎779-2877), in Medford. Bus schedules available at the Ashland Chamber of Commerce. The #10 bus runs between the transfer station at 200 S Front St. in **Medford** and the plaza in Ashland (35min.), then makes several stops on a loop through downtown Ashland. In-town fare $0.25. #10 runs through Ashland every 30min. daily 5am-7pm.

Taxis: Yellow Cab (☎482-3065, 800-527-0700). $2.50 base, $2 per mi. 24hr.

Car Rental: Budget, 3038 Biddle Rd. (☎779-0488), at the airport in Medford. $30 per day, $0.20 per mi. after 200 mi. Must be 21 with credit card. Under-25 surcharge $10.

➡ 🔒 HERE CEASE MORE QUESTIONS

'Tis time I should inform thee farther.
    —*The Tempest*, I.ii

Visitor Info: Chamber of Commerce, 110 E Main St. (☎482-3486; www.ashlandchamber.com). Also, there is an **info booth** in the center of the plaza. Open summer M-Sa 10am-6pm, Su 11am-5pm.

Outdoor Information: Ashland District Ranger Station, 645 Washington St. (☎482-3333), off Rte. 66 by I-5 Exit 14. Offers Pacific Crest Trail maps ($2) and tips (free), as well as up-to-date sno-park info. Ranger station open M-F 8am-4:30pm. For the inside scoop on the outdoors, it's better to talk to the people at Ashland Mountain Supply.

Equipment Rental: 🎒 Ashland Mountain Supply, 31 N Main St. (☎488-2749; www.ashlandmountainsupply.com). Rents internal frame backpacks and many other "accessories" (ice axes, helmets, etc.) for $5 per day. Mountain bikes $13 for 2hr., $30 per day. Cash deposit or credit card required. Copious and multidisciplinary (climbing, fishing, skiing, biking) outdoors knowledge, free; can refer fishing guides for almost every local river. Open daily 10am-6pm.

Laundromat: Main Street Laundromat, 370 E Main St. (☎ 482-8042). Wash $1.25, dry $0.25 per 8min. Open daily 7am-11pm, last wash at 10pm.

Pharmacy: Rite Aid, 2341 Ashland St. (☎ 482-7406). Open M-F 8am-9pm, Sa 9am-7pm, Su 10am-6pm.

Police: 1155 E Main St. (☎ 482-5211).

Crisis Line: ☎ 779-4357 or 888-609-4357. 24hr.

Hospital: Ashland Community Hospital, 280 Maple St. (☎ 482-2441). 24hr. emergency service.

Library and Internet Access: the newly expanded **Ashland Library,** 410 Siskiyou Blvd. (☎ 482-1151), at Gresham St. 30min. Internet access free. Open M-Tu 10am-8pm, W-Th 10am-6pm, F-Sa 10am-5pm. **Evo's Java House,** 376 E Main St. (☎ 482-2261), also offers free access, and once or twice a week you can check your mail while listening to live folk, punk, metal, or maybe a duet.

Post Office: 120 N 1st St. (☎ 800-275-8777), at Lithia Way. Open M-F 9am-5pm. **Postal Code:** 97520.

⚑ TO SLEEP, PERCHANCE TO DREAM

Now spurs the lated traveler apace to gain the timely inn.
   —*Macbeth,* III.iii

In winter, Ashland is a budget traveler's paradise of motel vacancy and low rates; in summer, every room in town fills in the blink of an eye and rates rise sky high. The nearest state park offering a decent-sized campground is the **Valley of the Rogue State Park ❶,** about 30 mi. north on I-5.

▓ **Ashland Hostel,** 150 N Main St. (☎ 482-9217). A Victorian parlor and sturdy bunks play host to PCT hikers, theater-goers and other Ashland visitors in search of entertainment, whether it be outdoors or in. Laundry and kitchen. Check-in 5-10pm. Lockout 10am-5pm. Reservations recommended. Dorms $20; private rooms $50. In winter dorms $18; private rooms $45. ❷

Columbia Hotel, 262½ E Main St. (☎ 482-3726 or 800-718-2530). Oozes with charm; don't expect a full-service chain hotel. A reading alcove and morning tea round out this historic home turned Euro-style hotel. Only 1½ blocks from theaters. June-Oct. rooms $65; private baths begin at $95. Mar.-June $49-89. 10% HI discount in off-season. ❹

Relax Inn, 535 Clover Lane (☎ 482-4423 or 888-672-5290), just off I-5 at Exit 14 behind a 76 gas station. The small building conceals recently remodeled rooms with cable TV and A/C. Singles $43; doubles $52. ❸

▓ **Mt. Ashland Campground,** about 25min. south of Ashland off I-5 Exit 6. Follow signs to Mt. Ashland Ski Area, and take the high road from the west end of the lot at the sign for Grouse Gap. 7 sites in the forest overlook the valley and Mt. Shasta. Can be snowy as late as June. Fire pits and pit toilets, no drinking water. Suggested donation $3. ❶

♥ FOOD OF LOVE

Give them great meals of beef and iron and steel, they will eat like wolves and fight like devils.
   —*Henry V,* III.vii

The incredible selection of foods available on North and East Main St. has earned Ashland a great culinary reputation. Even the ticketless come from miles around to dine in Ashland's excellent (although expensive) restaurants. Beware of the pre-show rush—a downtown dinner planned for 6:30pm can easily become a late-night affair, as pushy theater-goers fight to finish by 8:15pm. In lieu of prepared food, **Ashland Community Food Store Co-op,** 237 N 1st St. at A St., has a lively spirit, great organic produce, and natural foods. (☎482-2237. Open M-Sa 8am-9pm, Su 9am-9pm. 5% senior discount.) Cheaper groceries are available at **Safeway,** 585 Siskiyou Blvd. (☎482-4495. Open daily 6am-midnight.)

■ **Morning Glory,** 1149 Siskiyou Blvd. (☎488-8636), offers ambience galore, with a fire-place and bookcases inside and outside rose-entwined wooden porticos. Everyone from tourists to regulars to professors to students loves it; there will probably be a wait on weekends. Grab a book, wait, and you'll be well rewarded for your patience. Breakfast and lunch $8.50-11.50. Open daily 7am-2pm. ❷

Three Rivers, 1640 Ashland St. (☎482-0776). Great, cheap Indian food. The tandoori chicken and the rest of the buffet are very tasty. All-you-can-eat lunch buffet $7, dinner buffet $8. Open M-Su 11:30am-2:30pm and 5-9pm. ❷

Pangea, 272 E Main St. (☎552-1630), offers a menu of creative, filling wraps and grilled panini sandwiches. The Wrap of Khan is an enormous meal ($7). Almost any-thing on the menu can be made without meat. Open daily 11am-9pm. ❷

Bento Express, at the corner of Granite St. and N Main St., is a tiny restaurant offering large portions of rice and cheap *bento* lunches to go. *Bao* and potstickers $1.75. *Bento* meals $4.25. Open M-Sa 11am-5pm, Su noon-4pm. ❶

Geppetto's, 345 E Main St. (☎482-1138). An intimate dining room, also a wicker bas-ket-lover's paradise. Have a pesto or smoked salmon omelette ($8), "World Famous Eggplant Burger" ($5), or dinner from $10.50. Open daily 8am-midnight. ❸

▨ DRINK DEEP ERE YOU DEPART

Ashland remains a cultural center even after the festival ends. Local and touring artists alike play throughout the year to the town's enthused audiences. The **Oregon Cabaret Theater,** at 1st and Hagardine St., stages light musicals in a cozy former church with drinks, dinners, and Sunday brunch. (☎488-2902; www.oregoncaba-ret.com. Box office open M and F-Sa 11am-2pm and 3-6pm, W 3-6pm, Th 11am-2pm and 4-6pm, on performance nights Su 4-8pm. Tickets $15-23, food not included; dinner and brunch reservations required 48hr. in advance.) Small groups, such as the **Actor's Theater of Ashland** (☎535-5250), **Ashland Community Theatre** (☎482-7532), and **Southern Oregon University's (SOU)** theater department (☎552-6346) also raise the curtains sporadically year-round. Ashland also finds space for great music. When in town, the traveling **Rogue Valley Symphony** performs in the Music Recital Hall at SOU and at Lithia Park. (☎552-6398. Tickets from $31, stu-dents $10.) In July and August, the **State Ballet of Oregon** graces the stage in a vari-ety of venues Monday nights. Monday nights in late June find the **Palo Alto Chamber Orchestra** giving hit performances at the Elizabethan Stage, weather permitting. (☎482-4331. Tickets $10.)

Tabú, 76 Will Dodge Way (☎482-3900). Choice acoustics and a great bar sheltered from the dance floor give this place a trendy and classy feel. Dance salsa Th and Sa, or shake it to house/techno on Fr. Cover $2-3. Open for dinner M-Tu 5-10pm, W-Su 11:30am-3pm and 5-10pm. Club open Th-Sa 10pm-2am, and *tapas* served until 2am.

Q's, 140 Lithia Way (☎488-4880). One of the best billiard halls in Oregon, with cool decor and many a brew to even out mismatched games. M pool tournaments, Th col-lege night. Open Su-M about 11am-1am, Th-Sa 11am-2:30am.

Ashland Creek Bar & Grill, 92 N Main St. (☎482-4131). Mellow out on the huge out-door deck and groove to blues, ska, or reggae every F-Sa. But on W nights, $2 pints and a resident DJ are the perfect recipe for a huge and crazy party. 21+ after 9pm. Cover $1-3. Open M-Th and Su 11am-1am, F 11am-2am, Sa 11am-8pm.

Standing Stone Brewing Co., 101 Oak St. (☎482-2448), has family dining by day, Latin jazz Su afternoon. M night brings the blues. The friendly steel brewing vats surround and hint at the excellent organic beer inside. Glass $2.50, pint $3.50. Open daily 11:30am, closes sometime between 10pm and 2am.

MIDSUMMER MADNESS

The Oregon Shakespeare Festival (☎482-4331; www.osfashland.org.) was begun in 1935 by local college teacher Angus Bowmer as a nighttime complement to the daytime boxing matches at the **Chautauqua Dome.** Today, the site of the dome is the festival's featured theater; instead of local college students, professional actors perform 11 plays in repertory, five or six of which are contemporary and classical works. Performances run on the three Ashland stages from mid-February through October, and any boxing now is over scarce tickets. The 1200-seat **Elizabethan Stage,** an outdoor theater modeled after an 18th-century London design, is open from mid-June to mid-October, and hosts three Shakespeare plays per season. The **Angus Bowmer Theater** is a 600-seat indoor stage that shows one Shakespearean play and a variety of dramas. The **New Theater,** awaiting a $7 million donor for a name, seats 250-350 and serves as a modern replacement for the aging **Black Swan** theater. 2003 brings 11 plays to the Ashland stages, including *Romeo and Juliet* and *The Piano Lesson* in the Angus Bowmer, *Antony and Cleopatra* and *Lorca in a Green Dress* in the New Theater, and *Richard II* and *A Midsummer Night's Dream* in the Elizabethan.

In mid-June, the **Feast of Will** celebrates the annual opening of the Elizabethan Stage with dinner and merry madness in Lithia Park. ($12. Call the box office for details.) **Festival Noons,** a mix of lectures, concerts, and talks held in the courtyard just outside the Elizabethan Stage, occur almost every day at noon beginning in mid-June. Mostly free, but some require tickets ($2-10) available at the box office.

TICKETS. Ticket purchases are recommended six months in advance. The **Oregon Shakespearean Festival Box Office,** 15 S Pioneer St., is next to the Elizabethan and Bowmer Theaters, and across the street from the New Theater. (☎482-4331; www.osfashland.org. Open M 9:30am-5pm, Tu-Su 9:30am-8:30pm.) General mail-order and phone ticket sales begin in January; many weekend shows sell out within the first week. Tickets cost $22-39 for spring previews and fall shows, summer shows $29-52, plus a $5 handling fee per order for phone, fax, or mail orders. Children under 6 are not admitted to any shows. Those under 18 receive discounts of 25% in the summer and 50% in the spring and fall. For complete ticket info write **Oregon Shakespeare Festival,** P.O. Box 158, Ashland, OR 97520, or visit the web site.

Last-minute theater-goers should not abandon hope. At 9:30am, the box office releases any unsold tickets for the day's performances. Prudence demands arriving early; local patrons have been known to leave their shoes in line to hold their places. When no tickets are available, limited priority numbers are given out. These entitle their holders to a designated place in line when the precious few returned tickets are released (1:30pm for matinees, 6pm for evening shows). For those truly desperate for their Shakespeare fix, the box office also sells 20 clear-view **standing room tickets** for sold-out shows on the Elizabethan Stage ($11, available on the day of the show). Half-price **rush tickets** are occasionally available 1hr. before performances not already sold out. Some half-price matinees are offered in the spring and in October, and all three theaters hold full-performance **previews** in the spring and summer at considerable discounts. If you're willing to go through a scalper, unofficial ticket transactions take place all the time just outside the box office. Ticket officials advise those "buying on the bricks" to check the date and time on the ticket carefully and pay no more than the face value.

BACKSTAGE TOURS. Backstage tours provide a wonderful glimpse of the festival from behind the curtain. Tour guides (usually actors or technicians) divulge all kinds of anecdotes—from the story of the bird songs during an outdoor staging of *Hamlet* to the time when a door on the set used for most every stage entrance and exit locked itself midway through the show, provoking over 30min. of hilarious improvising before it was fixed during intermission. (2hr. tours leave from the Black Swan Tu-Sa 10am. Call box office in case of changes. $12, ages 6-17 $7.50; no children under 6.)

◪ THE GILDED MONUMENTS

LITHIA PARK. Before it imported Shakespeare, Ashland was naturally blessed with **lithia water,** which has dissolved lithium salts once reputed to have miraculous healing powers. It is said that only one other spring in the world has a higher lithium concentration. To try the water, hold your nose (to avoid sulfur salts) and head for the circle of fountains in plaza center. Besides aquatic phenomena, Lithia Park has free concerts, readings, nature walks around hiking trails, a Japanese garden, and swan ponds. On summer weekends, there is an artisans' market.

EMIGRANT LAKE PARK. Scads of kids and kids-at-heart flock to the 280 ft. **waterslide** at **Emigrant Lake Park,** 6 mi. east of town on Rte. 66. Popular for boating, hiking, swimming, and fishing, the park offers fantastic views of the valley. (Slide info ☎ 774-1200, ext. 2145. Park open daily 8am-sunset. Waterslide open May-Sept. daily noon-6:30pm. $3 entry fee. Ten slides for $5 or unlimited slides for 3hr. $10-12.)

MT. ASHLAND. If your muscles demand a little abuse after all this theater-seat lolly-gagging, head out to Mt. Ashland for some serious **hiking** and **biking.** One of the best options for those looking for a long days' worth of downhill is a shuttle to the Mt. Ashland Ski Lodge, 6200 ft., that allows a 15-25 mi. ride down to Ashland, 1800 ft. **Bear Creek Bicycles,** 1988 Hwy. 99 N, across from a car dealership offers the service and Jackson County bicycle maps ($3); you'll have to rent your mountain bike elsewhere, though. (☎ 488-4270. Sa-Su 9:30am. $10.) Both hiking and biking on and around Mt. Ashland require a Northwest forest pass, available at the ranger station for $5 per day. The Ranger Station can also provide an excellent and comprehensive guide to hiking and biking in the area for free. The folks at the **Adventure Center** (see **Equipment Rental,** p. 220) can give tips on biking trails. There is access to the **Pacific Crest Trail.** Take Exit 6 off I-5 and follow the signs along the Mt. Ashland Access Rd. for 7¼ mi. to the sign denoting the Rogue River National Forest Boundary. This section of the Pacific Crest Trail begins to climb Mt. Ashland, passing through forests and meadows covered with wildflowers, and ends at the Grouse Gap shelter.

For a more strenuous hike, try the **Wagner Butte Trail** (5.25 mi. one-way). From Ashland, take Rte. 99 north of town to Rapp Rd. in Talent. Turn left and drive 1 mi. to the junction with Wagner Creek Rd. and then 8 mi. to Forest Rd. #22. Turn left and drive 2 mi. to the trailhead across from a parking area. This trail climbs 3000 ft. through a landslide area and stands of old-growth fir to the top of Warner Butte, offering breathtaking views on sunny days. **Horn Gap Mountain Bike Trail** (3 mi. one-way or 9 mi. loop) provides fun for those on wheels. To reach the trailhead from Lithia Park, take Granite St. along Ashland creek 1 mi. to Glenview, and park alongside the road. This is the upper trailhead; the lower trailhead is 4 mi. down the road. This ride offers both incredible views of Mt. Ashland, and technical fun in steep slopes and several slalom courses.

THE SIERRA NEVADA

The Sierra Nevada nurtures some of the most breathtaking scenery anywhere. It marks the 450 mi. line along which two gigantic plates, the Pacific and North American, collided four hundred million years ago. Stretching from the stifling Death Valley to just below the Oregon border, the range is a living record of the tireless work of the elements—a product of Lassen volcanic activity hundreds of millions of years ago and granite-smoothing glaciation a mere few thousand years ago. The region's highlights include the crystalline waters of Lake Tahoe, the giant tufa formations of Mono Lake, and the enduring enormity of Sequoia National Park's redwoods, but the entire range is worthy of homage and scrutiny, and millions of visitors eagerly undertake the pilgrimage every year.

Temperatures in the Sierra Nevada are as diverse as the terrain. Even during the generally warm summer, overnight lows can dip into the 20s (check local weather reports). Normally, only U.S. 50 and I-80 are open during the snow season. Exact dates vary from year to year; check with a ranger station for road conditions, especially from October through June. In summer, protection from exposure to ultraviolet rays at high elevations is necessary; always bring sunscreen and a hat. For additional outdoors advice, see **Essentials: Camping and the Outdoors,** p. 46.

HIGHLIGHTS OF THE SIERRA NEVADA

LAKE TAHOE. Tahoe hosts world-class **skiing** (p. 243) and some of the state's best **water sports** (p. 240), **biking** (p. 241), **hiking** (p. 241), and **rock climbing** (p. 242).

YOSEMITE. Join the herd of tourists at Yosemite National Park, where you can hike **Half Dome** (p. 265), watch climbers squeezing up **El Capitan** (p. 264), or retreat to the beautiful **backcountry** (p. 268) to enjoy the park in peace.

SEQUOIA & KINGS CANYON. Sequoia and Kings Canyon National Parks feature incredible views from **Moro Rock** (p. 281), great backcountry hiking and camping in **Zumwalt Meadow** (p. 281), and the **deepest canyon in the United States** (p. 282).

OWENS VALLEY. Stand among the **oldest living things on Earth** (p. 292) and slide down the **largest land-locked sand dunes in the world** (p. 293).

CLIMB EVERY MOUNTAIN. Inyo National Forest offers the **tallest mountain in the contiguous US** (p. 297), as well as the remnants of one of the country's most romantic periods (p. 297) and one of its most shameful (p. 297).

GOLD COUNTRY

In 1848, California was a rural backwater of only 15,000 people. The same year, sawmill operator James Marshall wrote in his diary: "This day some kind of mettle...found in the tailrace...looks like goald." Word started to get around about the untold riches buried in the hills, but skepticism by the press muted the swelling excitement until President James K. Polk, in December 1848, declared the rumors to be true. By the end of the next year, some 90,000 miners from around the world had jumped at Marshall's discovery and headed for California and its Mother Lode, a 120 mi. expanse of gold-rich seams. "Gold fever" brought on a stampede of over half a million prospecting men and families over the next decade. Many of the first prospectors found the rumors to be quite accurate, and made fortunes mining easily-accessed surface gold, further fueling the rush. These stores were rapidly depleted, however, and few of the subsequent prospectors struck it rich. Miners, sustained by dreams of instant wealth, worked long and hard, but most could

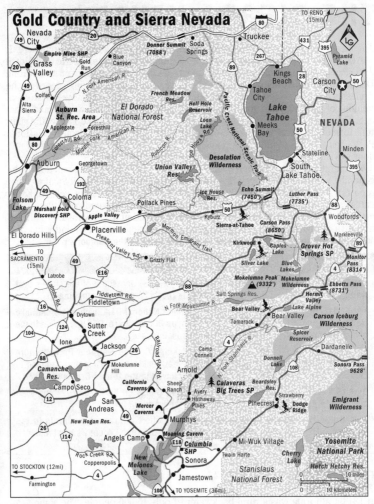

Gold Country and Sierra Nevada

barely squeeze sustenance out of their fiercely guarded claims. Many miners died of malnutrition. Mark Twain described the diet as "Beans and dishwater for breakfast, dishwater and beans for dinner. And both articles warmed over for supper." In Coloma, during one miner's funeral, a mourner spotted "color" (gold) in the open grave. In the ensuing gold frenzy, the coffin was quickly removed, and everyone in attendance, including the preacher, took to the ground with shovels.

Five years after the big discovery, the panning gold was gone, and miners could survive only by digging deeper and deeper into the rock. All but a few mines were abandoned by the 1870s, along with most of the towns around them. Nonetheless, the frenzy brought a vast entrepreneurial population to California, whose gold lust, when directed toward other pursuits, helped create what is now one of the most economically prosperous states in the Union.

While gold remains buried deep in them thar hills, today the towns of Gold Country make their money mining tourist traffic. Gussied up as "Gold Rush Towns," they solicit tourists traveling along the appropriately numbered Rte. 49, which connects dozens of small Gold Country settlements. Prepare for stomach-dropping roads and jaw-dropping views when traveling Rte. 49; travelers without an off-road vehicle should be wary of straying too far from the highway. Traffic from the coast connects with Rte. 49 via I-80 through Sacramento, which serves as an apt starting point for a Gold Country tour. If you tire of Gold Country lore, vine-yard touring, river rafting, and spelunking are popular in the area. Most of Gold Country is about 2hr. from Sacramento and 3hr. from San Francisco.

SONORA
☎209

A band of roaming prospectors from Sonora, Mexico were the first to stumble upon gold in the canyons around present-day Sonora. The settlers named their small mining encampment after their homeland and created a famously wild Mexican frontier town. The thousands of white Gold Rush 49ers who later flooded the area wouldn't stand for Mexicans mining their diggings, and they began enforcing a steep foreigner mining tax, driving out the original miners in a few short years. Things settled down as gold became scarce and tourists became plentiful, and today gold panning is for weekends—the hordes of straw-hatted, gap-toothed prospectors are probably antiquing.

■ 🛈 ORIENTATION & PRACTICAL INFORMATION. The drive to Sonora takes about 2½hr. from **Sacramento** (100 mi.), and 3½hr. from **San Francisco** (130 mi.). Sonora's layout is complicated by the fact that two highways enter the town from three directions. **Washington Street** runs north-south through town, and at the north end becomes Rte. 49 North. At the south end, it branches, and the east fork becomes Rte. 108. In the middle of town, Washington St. intersects with **Stockton Street,** which becomes Rte. 49 South.

The **Visitors Bureau,** 542 W. Stockton Rd., gives out several local publications with lots of information. (☎533-4420 or 800-446-1333; www.thegreatun-fenced.com. Open M-F 9am-7pm, Sa 10am-6pm, Su 10am-5pm.) Other services include: **police** (☎532-8143); **Tuolumne General Hospital,** 101 Hospital Rd. (☎533-7100; 24hr. emergency care); and the **Post Office,** 781 S. Washington St. (☎536-2728. Open M-F 8:30am-5pm, Sa 10am-2pm.) **Postal Code:** 95370.

🝙 🕻 ACCOMMODATIONS & FOOD. Many roadside motels and hotels are east of Sonora on Rte. 108. Built in 1896, the Spanish-style **Sonora Days Inn ❶,** 160 S. Washington St., stands apart from most standard chain motels in its age and authenticity. Spacious rooms all have A/C and cable TV, and some have fridges and microwaves. Rooms in the inn are large, with floral wallpaper and colonial furniture. The hotel also houses a rooftop pool, steakhouse, and saloon. (☎532-2400 or 800-329-9466. Doubles $60-70; lower in winter.) **Camping** is abundant in the Stanislaus National Forest (seep. 269), 15 mi. east of Sonora on Rte. 108. The Mi-Wuk Ranger District is closest to town, but has few developed campgrounds. **Fraser Flat ❶,** 4800 ft., 25 mi. east on Rte. 108 to the Spring Gap turnoff, then 3 mi. north on Rd. 4N01, has 38 sites near the South Fork Stanislaus. (Piped water, vault toilets. Open May-Sept. Sites $13.) **Dispersed camping ❶** is free and does not require a permit in most of the forest, though campfire permits are often required.

Wilma's Cafe ❷, 275 S. Washington St., named for the wooden pig perched atop the pie case, has pink pig paraphernalia galore. Pig out on Wilma's delicious pies ($3), hickory-smoked barbecue burgers ($6-7), homemade soups ($2-4), or vege-tarian options. Saloon makes a good watering hole. (☎532-9957. Open Su-Th

IN RECENT NEWS

THE MODERN GOLD RUSH

Of all the job opportunities open to freshly minted college grads, dredging for gold in the Mother Lode or creassing bedrock for hard rock mines is a notably less popular choice than it was 150 years ago, when California was populated overnight by zealous prospectors stricken with gold fever. Today, a sizable but little-known group of latter-day prospectors has emerged, many possessing the same wild determination as their predecessors. The US Geological Survey estimates that around 12% of the world's gold is located in the U.S., much of it in California; at current prices of about $310 per ounce, that adds up to about $100 billion in ore, good enough to get many people excited.

What makes modern gold prospecting an endeavor worth pursuing, however, is that—as in the days of the 49ers—if you find gold on public land, it's yours (usually). The Bureau of Land Management distributes claims on 20-acre parcels on unprotected public lands for an annual fee of $100. Just stake your claim, literally, with four poles, and seek out the nearest BLM office in a hurry. Joining an organization like the Gold Prospectors Association of American (GPAA) ☎909-699-4749; www.goldprospectors.org), can give you access to private lands, though these have often been heavily scoured already. Before getting flush with gold fever, however, heed the sage advice of the BLM: "[The gold prospector] must be prepared to undergo physical hardships...and not be discouraged by repeated disappointments."

6:30am-10pm, F-Sa 6:30am-midnight.) **Banny's Cafe ❸**, 83 S. Stewart St., a block east of Washington St., has eclectic, moderately priced lunches ($6-11) and dinners ($11-15) that fuse Mediterranean, Southwestern, and Asian flavors. Entrees like the wasabi ginger salmon filet ($10) and the mango chipotle pork loin ($9) are welcomed variants to the standard Gold Country cuisine. (☎533-4709. Open M-Sa 11am-3pm and 4:30-9pm, Su 4-8pm.)

◙ ▨ SIGHTS & ACTIVITIES. Columbia State Historic Park is an entirely preserved 1850s mining town. Take Rte. 49 North from Sonora to Parrot's Ferry Rd. and look for signs to the park. Once the "Gem of the Southern Mines" and rich in placer gold (loose gold found in rivers), Columbia supported 5000 people and 150 saloons, shops, and other businesses, putting over $1 billion into the local economy. Now Columbia supports the tourist industry. The only transportation option in the park is horse and buggy. (☎532-4301. Open daily 9am-4:30pm. Free.) Just 10min. south of Sonora in Jamestown, **Railtown 1897 State Historic Park** is remarkable as a restored and operating 19th-century railroad roundhouse. Heading south on Rte. 49 to Jamestown, the park is 1 mi. south on 5th St. The park's trains have been featured in dozens of films and television shows. Tours and weekend train rides are offered. (☎984-3953. Open daily 9:30am-4:30pm. Free.) Visit the Stanislaus National Forest (seep. 269) for outdoor recreation, with fine hiking, fishing, mountain biking, and rafting opportunities. Gear up at the **Sierra Nevada Adventure Co.,** 173 S. Washington St. (☎532-5621. Kayaks and canoes from $45 per day.)

CALAVERAS COUNTY ☎209

Unsuspecting Calaveras turned out to be literally sitting on a gold mine—the richest, southernmost part of the "Mother Lode"—when the big rush hit. Over 550,000 lb. of gold were extracted from the county's earth during its heyday. A journalist from Missouri named Samuel Clemens, a hapless miner but a gifted spinner of yarns later known as **Mark Twain,** allegedly based "The Celebrated Jumping Frog of Calaveras County" on a tale he heard in Angels Camp Tavern. Life in this area has since imitated (or capitalized on) art; Calaveras has held annual **frog-jumping contests** in the third week of May every year since 1928. (www.frogtown.com. 4-day fair $11-13 per day.)

A drive along scenic **Route 49** is a great way to glimpse Calaveras County. **San Andreas,** at the juncture of Rte. 26 and 49, is the county hub and most densely populated area, but isn't very big. The **Cala-**

veras County Information Center, in downtown Angels Camp, is a great historical resource. (☎ 736-0049 or 800-225-3764; www.visitcalaveras.org. Open M-F 9am-6pm, Sa 11am-6pm, Su 11am-4pm.) Just south of Angels Camp on Rte. 49 is **Tuttletown,** Mark Twain's one-time home, now little more than a historic marker, a grocery store, and a well of stories.

OUTDOORS. Calaveras County encompasses dramatically varied landscape, from the rolling foothills of the Sierra in the west to 8000 ft. peaks in Stanislaus National Forest (see p. 269) in the east. Excellent outdoor recreation is available in the Forest, and also in **Calaveras Big Trees State Park,** just inside Stanislaus National Forest on Rte. 4, about 35min. from Angels Camp. (☎ 795-3840, reservations 795-2334. Day use $2, seniors $2.) Featuring two timeless groves of Giant Sequoia, the world's oldest and biggest living organisms, and over 6000 acres of forest, stream, and lake along the Sierra's western slope, the park is a destination for those seeking natural spectacles. There are three primary trails. **North Grove** (1 mi.), from the Visitors Center parking lot, is a gentle, heavily traveled stroll to the first big trees ever discovered by European settlers. About 10 times as many trees (over 1000) can be found at the end of the more challenging, and hence quieter 3.5 mi. **South Grove Trail.** Just after Beaver Creek Bridge along South Grove Trail is the trailhead to **Bradley Grove** (2.5 mi.), which provides a chance to see young sequoias, about 30 years old, planted by the former caretaker of the South Grove. **Fishing** is permitted in the Stanislaus River and Beaver Creek with a license, though there are some catching restrictions. **Camp** at **North Grove ❶** or **Oak Hollow ❶** with piped water, flush toilets, and showers (sites $12). In winter, family-friendly skiing at **Bear Mountain** is the major draw. The mountain features 67 runs and 1900 vertical feet, made nice with 30 ft. of snow coming down each winter. (☎ 753-2301. Day passes $43, ages 13-23 $36, ages 8-12 $15, ages 65-74 $10, under 7 and over 74 free.)

CAVERNS. Most who flocked to Calaveras County throughout its history of settlement were interested in what was in the ground. Today, many are more interested in what isn't: solid earth. A labyrinthine limestone cave network snakes through the Calaveras underworld, offering visitors an exciting chance to see what lies beneath. Three caverns have been developed for visitors. To get to the most popular cavern from Angel's Camp, travel 10min. east on Rte. 4 to Parrott's Ferry Rd., then turn right and continue 1 mi. to Moaning Cavern Rd. **Moaning Cavern,** 5350 Moaning Cave Rd., is a vast vertical cave. There are three ways to explore the giant chamber. The most popular 45min. walking tour descends 234 steps to about 160 ft. below the earth's surface, to the point where the remains of prehistoric people who had fallen into the chamber a long time ago were found. Those over 18 (or over 12 with parental consent) on the fast track can rappel down the cavern to the same point. Reservation-only 3hr. adventure tours start where the rapelling trip ends, venturing into the cavern's dark passages. (☎ 736-2708. Open daily 9am-6pm; in winter M-F 10am-5pm, Sa-Su 9am-5pm. Stairs $10, children $5; rappel $45; adventure trip $60-100.) **Mercer Cavern,** off Rte. 4 on Sheep Rd. in Murphys, is filled with elaborate crystalline formations. All tours are 45min. and descend by walkway into ten-million year old chambers. (☎ 728-2101. Open Su-Th 9am-5pm, F-Sa 9am-6pm; in winter Su-Th 10am-4:30pm. Tours $10, ages 5-12 $6.) During the Gold Rush, **California Caverns,** at Cave City, 9 mi. from San Andreas off Mountain Ranch Rd., served as a naturally air-conditioned bar and dance floor, and a shot of whiskey could be purchased for a pinch of gold dust. The caverns sobered up on Sundays for church services, and one stalagmite served as an altar. Walking tours and "wild cavern expedition trips" explore cramped tunnels, waist-high mud, and underground lakes. (☎ 736-2708. 1hr. walking tour $10, ages 3-13 $5; 2hr. expeditions $99, ages 8-16 $65.)

SIERRA NEVADA

THE BIG SPLURGE

A HUT OF ONE'S OWN

Renting one of the Forest Service's three huts is an exceptional deal for groups. These structures range from small shacks to large mountain chalets, and are found in the heart of Eldorado National Forest.

Robbs Hut was built in 1938, and served as a forest service fire lookout until 1976. It provides a great base for cross-country skiing in the winter and mountain biking in the summer, and sleeps up to six people comfortably. There is no access to water or utilities, but the hut does have an outdoor barbecue and outdoor toilet.

The **Van Vleck Bunkhouse** sits on the edge of a glorious 40-acre meadow. The last remnant of a cattle ranch, the bunkhouse provides a great view of the Crystal Range and easy access to hiking, bird watching, fishing, mountain biking, and horseback riding. Water, propane lights, and a wood stove sweeten the deal for six lucky campers.

The **Loon Lake Chalet,** overlooking the Loon Lake Reservoir, can accommodate up to 20 people in its second-story warming room and third-story loft. The chalet is heated and has a small kitchen, gas fireplace and vault toilets.

All three huts provide a change of pace for those sick of pitching tents and waking up to the roar of nearby RV engines. (Info ☎ 644-2349, reservations 877-444-6777. Robbs Hut $45. Van Vleck Bunkhouse $55. Loon Lake Chalet $65.)

WINERIES. Winemaking is as old a pursuit as gold prospecting in the county, as the nine flourishing vineyards attest. Most are located on Rte. 49, just north of San Andreas, and on Rte. 4, near Murphys. Almost all of the vineyards have tasting rooms, offering free samples and a chance to purchase a bottle, and often some gourmet food. The largest vineyard in the county, **Stevenot Winery,** on Sheep Ranch Rd., off Main St. in Murphys, has won hundreds of awards for its bold creations. (☎ 728-3436. Main tasting room open daily 10am-5pm. 2nd tasting room at 451 Main St., in Murphys, open daily 10:30am-5:30pm.) **Ironstone Vineyards,** on Six Mile Rd., 1½ mi. south of Main St., is another large vineyard, producing 250,000 cases a year. Outstanding visitor facilities include a museum, tasting room, demonstration kitchen, gallery, and caverns. (☎ 728-1251. Free 45min. tours daily 11:30am, 1:30, 3:30pm. Sa additional tour 2:30pm. Tasting room open daily 11am-5pm.)

SUTTER CREEK ☎ 209

Sitting in the heart of Gold Country, Sutter Creek markets itself more as an alternative to the Wine Country of Napa and Sonoma than as a Gold Rush throwback, resulting in a more affluent tourist set than those found in many other Rte. 49 towns. History buffs and gold fanatics can still get their fill, however; this former mining encampment, named after the river named after the pioneering prospector John Sutter, was one of the Gold Rush's few success stories. Buried in the quartz rock around town were some of the richest gold stores in the Mother Lode, yielding fortunes for mine owners like Leland Stanford, who used his earnings to start a railroad business, become governor, and found a university.

Sutter Creek is in the heart of Gold Country, 30 mi. south of Placerville on Rte. 49, 67 mi. from Sacramento via Rte. 50 to Rte. 49, and 90 mi. west of South Lake Tahoe. In town, Rte. 49 becomes Main St., where the majority of historical sights and commercial activity can be found. **Amador Rapid Transit System** (☎ 223-2877) sends two **buses** per day to and from Sacramento to Rancho Murieta, where another bus can take you to Sutter Creek for $1. Visitor information, including a downtown walking tour map, can be found at the **Sutter Creek Visitors Center,** at the end of Eureka St., in Knight's Foundry. (☎ 267-1344. Open M-Sa 8am-4:30pm.) Other services in Sutter Creek include the **police** (☎ 267-5646), and the **Post Office,** 3 Gopher Flat Rd., near Main St. (☎ 267-0128. Open M-F 8:30am-5pm.) **Postal Code:** 95685.

There are well over a dozen B&Bs within walking distance of town, including **Grey Gables ❺**, 161 Hanford St. (☎267-1039) and **Foxes ❺**, 77 Main St. (☎267-5882). The typical bed and breakfast decor and amenities apply, here for about $130-250 per night. Somewhat lower priced rooms can be found at the **Sutter Creek Inn ❺**, 75 Main St., a cute, well-decorated Greek Revival house on a relaxing yard, claiming to be California's first B&B. (☎267-5606. Doubles with bath from $82.)

Food in town tends toward the pricey side, with a number of restaurants specializing in fine dining and expensive wines. **The Back Roads Coffeehouse ❶**, 74 Main St., is open for lunch and dinner, serving light lunch fare, fresh baked pastries and bagels, and espresso-based drinks. (☎267-0440. Open M-F 5:30am-4pm, Sa-Su 7am-4pm). The **Sutter Diner ❷**, 291 Hanford St., smokes its beef brisket for over 10hr. and uses a homemade BBQ sauce on its ribs. Most dishes cost $7-10. (☎267-1551. Open M 7am-2pm, W-Su 7am-8pm.)

The majority of sights in town are on Main St. The **Monteverde General Store,** on Randolph St., one block from Main St., was once something akin to the modern-day Wal-Mart, but is now a museum. (☎267-5647. Open Th-F 11am-4pm, Sa-Su noon-5pm. Donation requested.) Still in operation, **Knight's Foundry,** at the end of Eureka St., built and serviced hard rock mining equipment. Operating with water power, just as in 1873, the shop is unique. (☎267-0201. Call for a tour.) **Sutter Gold Mine,** 1 mi. north of town on Rte. 49, takes you into an abandoned hard rock gold mine, exploring abandoned mining equipment and explaining how to tell real gold from the fool's variety. (☎736-2708. Open daily 9am-5pm. 1hr. family tours $10, 3½hr. deep mine exploration $99 by reservation only.) Before Napa and Sonoma became California's wine country, the Sierra foothills were the state's biggest producer. Prohibition hit the region hard, however, and it is only recently that the area's 40 **vineyards** have begun to prosper again. **Sutter Ridge,** 14110 Ridge Rd., 1 mi. south on Rte. 49 and 2½ mi. east on Ridge Rd., is run by a 4th-generation wine making family that grows their own grapes on 170 acres. (☎267-1316. Open F-Su 11am-4:30pm.) **Argonaut Winery,** 13825 Willow Creek Rd., 11 mi. from town, northwest via Rte. 49 and south via Willow Creek Rd., is a small vineyard with weekend tastings. (☎245-5567. Open Sa-Su 10am-5:30pm.)

PLACERVILLE

☎530

In its Gold Rush prime, Placerville (pop. 9301) was the third-largest town in California. Now it's a friendly, well-stocked stop en route to somewhere else. The town preserves its past in a restored historic district of eateries and antique shops.

▆▐ ORIENTATION & PRACTICAL INFORMATION. About one-third of the way from Sacramento to Lake Tahoe on U.S. 50, Placerville is strategically positioned to snare campers, boaters, and skiers. Most streets, like **Main Street,** run parallel to U.S. 50. **Route 49** also bisects the town, running north to Auburn (10 mi.), and south toward Calaveras County.

Greyhound (☎800-231-2222) **bus** service to Placerville makes drop-offs and pickups at 222 Main St. at Pacific St., going to Reno (6hr., 1 per day, $20) and Sacramento (1½hr., 2 per day, $12). At **Enterprise,** 583 Placerville St., cars are $32 per day, 100 mi. included, or $42 per day with unlimited mileage. (☎621-0866. Under-25 surcharge $10 per day.) The **Chamber of Commerce,** 542 Main St., has maps and info. (☎621-5885. Open M-F 9am-5pm.) Other services are **police,** 730 Main St. (☎642-5210; www.hangtowncops.org), and **Post Office,** 3045 Sacramento St., south of U.S. 50. (☎642-5280. Open M-F 8:30am-5pm, Sa 8:30am-noon.) **Postal Code:** 95667.

ACCOMMODATIONS & FOOD. One of the best deals in this consistently overpriced town is the **National 9 Inn ❹**, 1500 Broadway, which has spotless new rooms and comfortable queen beds. (☎622-3884. Singles Su-Th $45, F-Sa $55-75; doubles $50-65/65-75.) **Camping** is plentiful in the Eldorado National Forest, east of town. **Sand Flat ❶**, 3800 ft., is on Rte. 50, 28 mi. east of town. (Vault toilets, water. Sites $12.) Dispersed **camping ❶** is free and does not require a permit, although campfire permits are required for wood fires and stoves.

The historic ⬛**Placerville Coffee House ❶**, 594 Main St., dates from 1859. High stone walls, numerous nooks and crannies (including a 150 ft. walk-in mine shaft), and offbeat displays of local artwork call to mind a dusty mansion. (☎642-8481. Sandwiches $4-5. Fresh fruit smoothies $1.50-3.50. Espresso $1.50-2.50. Th-Sa live jazz, folk, blues, Celtic, comedy, and acoustic bands; W open mic. Open Su-Tu 7am-6pm, W-Sa 7am-11pm.) For a *Dukes of Hazzard* experience, saunter into ⬛**Poor Red's ❸**, on El Dorado's Main St., 5 mi. south of Placerville on Rte. 49. Quite the Boss Hogg scene, this authentic BBQ place is always packed. Their famous two-glass "Golden Cadillac" (responsible for three percent of the total American consumption of galliano) is only $3.25. (☎622-2901. $12 per rack of ribs. Open M-F 11am-2pm and 5-11pm, Sa 5-11pm, Su 2-11pm.) **Sweetie Pies ❷**, 577 Main St., is known for its huge cinnamon buns, full espresso bar, light lunches (sandwiches $6), and extensive breakfast menu ($4-7). Homemade pie by the slice ($3.25) is sweet and delicious. (☎642-0128. Open M-F 6:30am-4pm, Sa 7am-3pm, Su 7am-noon.) Placerville was once known as "Hangtown, USA" because of its reputation for handing out speedy justice at the end of a rope. Now the **Historic Hangman's Tree**, 305 Main St., is a friendly neighborhood bar with a life-size replica of a hanging dead man (George) outside, and a life-size ghost (Willy) inside. (☎622-3878. Open daily 6am-whenever.) Alternatively, forage for fresh food at the **farmer's market** in the Ivy House parking lot. (Open Th 5-8pm, Sa 8am-noon.)

SIGHTS & OUTDOOR ACTIVITIES The hills around Placerville are filled with fruit and good cheer. By bike and car, travelers tour the apple orchards and wineries off U.S. 50 in the area known as **Apple Hill**. The fall is particularly busy with apple-picking celebrations. **Gold Hill** (☎626-6522) features peaches, plums, and citrus fruits for the plucking. A complete listing and map of orchards is available from the Chamber of Commerce (see p. 231). Locals claim that **Denver Dan's**, 4454 Bumblebee Ln. (☎644-6881), has the best prices, while **Kid's**, 3245 N. Canyon Rd. (☎622-0084), makes the best apple pie in the area. Most orchards are open only September-December, but **Boa Vista Orchards**, 2952 Carson Rd. (☎622-5522), is open year-round, selling fresh pears, cherries, and other fruits. For free wine tasting, try **Lava Cap Winery**, 2221 Fruitridge Rd. (☎621-0175. Open daily 11am-5pm.) You can also visit **Sierra Vista Winery**, 4560 Cabernet Way (☎622-7221; open daily 10am-5pm) or **Boeger Winery**, 1709 Carson Rd. (☎622-8094. Open daily 10am-5pm.) There are nearly 20 maintained trails in the Placerville Ranger District of the **Eldorado National Forest**. About 50 mi. east of town, the **Bryan Meadows Trail** passes 3 mi. through lodgepole pine to meet the Pacific Crest Trail. From the same trailhead access the **Sayles Canyon Trail** (4.5 mi.), which leads to a mountain meadow. To get to the trailhead, take Rte. 50 east 48 mi. to Sierra-at-Tahoe Rd., continue 2 mi. to Bryan Rd., turn right, and go another 2½ mi. The **Information Center**, 3070 Camino Heights Dr., in Camino, 9 mi. east of Placerville on Rte. 50, dispenses info and permits. (☎644-6048. Open daily 8am-5pm; in winter M and Th-Su 8am-5pm.)

SIERRA NEVADA

COLOMA
☎530

The 1848 Gold Rush began in Coloma at John Sutter's water-powered lumber mill, operated by James Marshall. Today, the town (pop. 175) tries its darndest to hype up this claim to fame, but the effort just makes tiny Coloma feel like a deserted amusement park. The town revolves around the **James Marshall Gold Discovery State Historic Park.** Near the site where Marshall struck gold is a replica of the original mill. (☎622-1116. Open daily 8am-dusk. Day use $2 per car, seniors $1; walk-ins $1, under 16 free. Display your pass in your car or be ticketed.) Picnic grounds across the street surround the **Gold Discovery Museum,** 310 Back St., which presents the events of the Gold Rush through dioramas and film. (☎622-3470. Open daily 8am-5pm; in winter 10am-4pm.) **Camping** can be found 2 mi. downstream at **Camp Lotus ❷,** 700 ft., on Basie Rd. off Lotus Rd. The sites are large and shady. (Water, flush toilets, free hot showers, nearby store. Sites Su-Th $18, F-Sa $24.)

The real reason to come to Coloma may be the natural attractions. The **American River's** class III currents, among the most accessible rapids in the West, attract thousands of rafters and kayakers every weekend. Farther north along Rte. 49, the river flows into **Folsom Lake** and a deep gorge perfect for hiking and swimming. Many of the **rafting** outfitters in the county offer tours in the waters surrounding Coloma. Contact **Ahwahnee** (☎800-359-9790), **Motherlode River Trips** (☎800-427-2387), **Oars Inc.** (☎800-346-6277), or **Whitewater Connection** (☎800-336-7238)—whichever floats your boat. (Half-day from $69-79, full-day from $89-109.)

NEVADA CITY
☎530

New Age meets ages past in Nevada City, a town in the Sierra foothills full of rustic hippies and gaping tourists. Although the tourist board seems hellbent on creating the illusion of yesteryear, the eccentricity of current residents belies the mining town image. Draped across hills, the city's winding streets modulate its luster.

Many buildings in the town are of historical interest, including the dozens of **Victorian homes,** the **National Hotel** (claiming to be the nation's oldest in continual operation), and the historic **Firehouse.** There is a museum in the firehouse with exhibits on mining, pioneer life, the Nisenan and Maidu Indians, and the once-large Chinese population. (Open daily 11am-4pm; in winter M-Tu and Th-Su 10am-3pm.) A walking tour map is available from the **Chamber of Commerce** at the end of Commercial St., near the Shell station and bank. (☎265-2692 or 800-655-6569. Open M-F 9am-5pm, Sa 11am-4pm.) Most historical buildings in Nevada City have been transformed into cappuccino bars, New Age bookstores, and vegetarian eateries.

Nevada City's health-conscious congregate to refuel at **Earth Song,** 135 Argall St., a natural foods market and cafe where vegetarians stock up on soy burgers, Welsh and Cornish cuisine, and organic produce. (☎265-9392. Market open daily 8am-9pm. Cafe open daily 11am-3pm and 5-8pm.) Another popular hangout is **Cafe Mekka ❷,** 237 Commercial St. Admire its metallic decoration, browse among the children's books, modernist art, and chaises, munch on a mighty fine artichoke heart, pesto, and brie sandwich ($7), or sip coffee with the evening crowd. (☎478-1517. Open M-Th 7am-11pm, F 7am-12:30am, Sa 8am-12:30am, Su 8am-11pm.) The **Outside Inn ❹,** 575 E. Broad St, is a redesigned 40s-era motel catering to outdoor enthusiasts. (☎265-2233. A/C, library with maps and recreational info, patio, grill and swimming pool, and Internet in every room. Rooms from $65, with kitchenette from $90.) US Forest Service and California Parks Department operate **campgrounds** east of town on Rte. 20. **Scotts Flat ❷** has wooded RV and tent camping near a popular lake. (☎265-5302. Water, flush toilets, hot showers. Sites $14-23.) Unimproved, free sites are available at **Bowman Lake ❶,** 16 mi. north on Rte. 20.

History awaits you at the **Empire Mine State Historic Park,** on the Empire St. Exit off Rte. 20 west of town. Peering down the cool, dark mine shaft, you may wonder if you'd go 12,400 ft. down for a chance at the big money—5.8 million ounces of gold were extracted from the mine during its 106 years of production. The estate and woods make peaceful hikes, but beware of poison oak, rattlesnakes, and mountain lions. Tours are offered on summer weekends. (☎273-8522. Open May daily 9am-5pm; June-Aug. 9am-6pm; Sept.-Apr. 10am-5pm. $1, under 17 free.)

The Nevada City area has trails for hikers of every ability. The **Nevada City Ranger Station,** 631 Coyote St., of the Tahoe National Forest, provides information on recreation and camping. (☎265-4531. Open M-Sa 8am-4:30pm.) Take the **Loch Leven Trail** (3.6 mi.) to the Loch Leven chain of granite-bed glacial lakes. The trailhead is just east of the Big Bend Visitors Center, at the Big Bend Exit off I-80 east from Nevada City. **Bridgeport State Park,** in Penn Valley off Rte. 20, features an easy 1.25 mi. hike over the largest covered bridge in the West and around the river canyon. Search for a free souvenir during the park's gold-panning demonstration. Swimming holes line the **Yuba River,** which has been immortalized in song by countless folk. Enjoy them by hiking the Independence Trail and discovering personal freedom in skinny dipping. Whitewater rafting and kayaking are great ways to experience the rugged beauty of the area. **Wolf Creek Wilderness,** 595 E. Main St. (☎477-2722), in Grass Valley, rents kayaks year-round and runs multiple kayaking trips and clinics. They also rent snowshoes and cross-country skis. In the winter, snowshoe tours and avalanche clinics are held here.

SIERRA BUTTES AREA ☎530

A craggy ridge of volcanic peaks north of Donner Pass, the Sierra Buttes are the highlight of the **Lakes Basin Recreation Area,** a stretch of wilderness spanning Plumas and Tahoe National Forests. The mountains and over 40 glacial lakes in the area are among the least traveled outdoors destinations in the state. Hiking trails lead through the small but beautiful range, while the fishing and boating in the lakes are good and quiet. The area is 6 mi. north of Sierra City. Five miles east of Sierra City, on the corner of Rte. 49 and Gold Lake Hwy., lies **Bassetts Station,** an all-purpose establishment that has offered **lodging ❹,** dining, gas, and supplies for over 125 years. Stop in for info. (☎862-1297. 3 rooms $70-75. Open daily 7am-9pm.)

The Gold Lake Hwy. leads to **Gold Lake,** 6 mi. from Rte. 49 past Bassetts Station. The adjacent **Gold Lake Pack Station** offers guided horseback rides around the area. (☎283-2014. $23 per hr.) The turn-off for **Frasier Falls** is 6 mi. from the Bassetts Station, across from the first lake turn-off. Follow signs for 4 mi. to the Frasier Falls parking lot; the falls are a 30min. walk. There are six **campgrounds** along the route from the Bassetts turn-off to Frasier Falls, all marked by signs. Most have toilets but no water or showers, and all are first-come, first-camp. Some sites charge $13, but many are free. **Gold Lake ❶** and **Snag Lake ❶** are especially beautiful campgrounds. For those in the mood for more cushy digs, the **Gold Lake Lodge ❺** has rustic cabins, and also includes a great breakfast and dinner, and easy access to many hiking trails. (2-night min. stay. Cabins from $95.)

The **Sierra Buttes** themselves rise farther up Gold Lake Rd., amid a series of small alpine lakes. For trail access, take the Sardine Lake turn-off 1 mi. north of Rte. 49, bear right past Sardine Lake, and continue 1½ mi. past Packer Lake.

LAKE TAHOE ☎530/775

Tahoe's natural beauty attracts outdoor fanatics from across the globe, who are eagerly supported by a burgeoning entertainment and hotel industry. After roads were cut into the forested mountain terrain, new money arrived with casinos, summer homes, and motels. Now, everyone can enjoy Tahoe's pure blue waters, tall pines, and high-rises silhouetted by the deep auburn glow of the setting sun. In a town without an off-season, visitors can revel in an array of activities from keno to kayaking. An outdoor adventurist's dream in any weather, Tahoe has miles of biking, hiking, and skiing trails, long stretches of golden beaches, lakes stocked with fish, and many hair-raising whitewater activities.

▐ TRANSPORTATION

Buses: Greyhound, 3794 Montreal Rd. (☎530-543-1050 or 800-231-2222), in the Tahoe Colony Inn at Raley's Shopping Center. To **San Francisco** (3 per day, $27-29) and **Sacramento** (3 per day, $21-23). Station open daily 8am-7pm.

Trains: Amtrak (☎800-USA-RAIL/872-7245) runs a bus from its San Joaquin and Capitol train routes to Pre-Madonna Casino off I-15 and Whiskey Pete's Casino in **Stateline, NV.** These trips are long and costly. Call for rates, which fluctuate greatly.

Public Transit: Tahoe Casino Express (☎800-446-6128) provides shuttle service between the Reno airport and South Shore Tahoe casinos (daily 6:15am-12:30am; $19, round-trip $34, up to 2 children under 12 free). **Tahoe Area Regional Transport** or **TART** (☎550-1212 or 800-736-6365; www.laketahoetransit.com) connects the western and northern shores from Incline Village to Tahoe City to Tahoma (Meeks Bay in summer). Stops daily every hr. or ½hr. 6:30am-6pm, depending on the route. Buses also run out to Truckee and Squaw Valley several times per day. Exact fare required. $1.25, day pass $3. **South Tahoe Area Ground Express** or **STAGE** (☎541-6328) operates around South Tahoe and hourly to the beach. It connects Stateline and Emerald Bay Rd. $1.25, day pass $2, 10-ride pass $10. Most casinos operate free shuttle services along U.S. 50 to California ski resorts and motels. A summer bus program connects STAGE and TART at Meeks Bay daily 6am-midnight.

Car Rental: Enterprise (☎775-586-1077), in the Horizon lobby in Stateline, NV. Must be 21+ with credit card. From $41 per day, $199 per week with unlimited mileage.

▞ ORIENTATION

In the northern Sierra on the California-Nevada border, Lake Tahoe is a 4hr. drive from San Francisco. Lake Tahoe rests 118 mi. northeast of Sacramento and 35 mi. southwest of Reno on I-80. From the Carson City and Owens Valley area, **U.S. 395** runs north-south 20 mi. from Tahoe's eastern shore.

The lake is divided into two main regions, known as **North Shore** and **South Shore.** The **North Shore** includes Kings Beach, Tahoe City, Tahoe Vista, and Incline Village, while the **South Shore** has Emerald Bay, South Lake Tahoe City, and Stateline. Proclaimed "The Most Beautiful Drive in America," **U.S. 50** combines with **Routes 28 and 89** to form a 75 mi. asphalt ring around the lake; the complete winding, sloping loop takes nearly 3hr. Rte. 89 is also known as **West Lake Boulevard** and **Emerald Bay Road,** while Rte. 29 becomes **North Lake Boulevard** and **Lakeshore Drive** in Tahoe City and on the western shore, and **South Lake Tahoe Boulevard** turns into **Highway 50.**

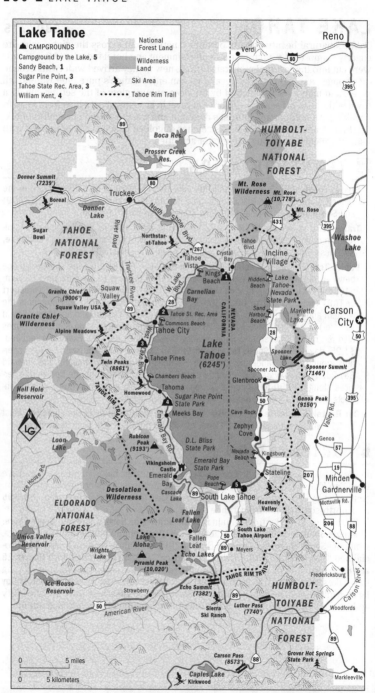

Lake Tahoe

▲ CAMPGROUNDS
Campground by the Lake, **5**
Sandy Beach, **1**
Sugar Pine Point, **3**
Tahoe State Rec. Area, **3**
William Kent, **4**

National
Forest Land

Wilderness
Land

Ski Area

•••••• Tahoe Rim Trail

SIERRA NEVADA

Road conditions in Tahoe can be treacherous from September to May, when tire chains may be required and a 4WD vehicle is highly recommended. As Tahoe is a popular weekend destination, traffic is fierce on Friday afternoons and Sunday evenings. During winter, cars on the way to or from Tahoe City ski resorts pack the roads around 9am and 5pm. If there is road work near the small town of Tahoe City, forget trying to get there on either Rte. 28 or 89 from the South Shore.

⁊ PRACTICAL INFORMATION

Tahoe is littered with tourist information and visitors centers, often with more than one in each town. Brochures offer valuable lodging and dining coupons, as well as information about Tahoe's thriving wilderness activities.

TOURIST & INFORMATION SERVICES

US Forest Service Visitors Center, 870 Emerald Bay Rd. (☎573-2600), 2 blocks north of S. Lake Tahoe on Rte. 89. Supervises campgrounds and recreation trails. Mandatory wilderness permits for backcountry hiking available. Open M-F 8am-4:30pm.

Lake Tahoe Visitors Center (☎573-2674), 3 mi. north of S. Lake Tahoe on Rte. 89. Hiking trailheads and detailed maps of the area. Sells permits for entering Desolation Wilderness. Camping fee $5 per person per night, $10 per person for 2 or more nights, $20 for 1-year pass. Under 12 free. Reservations ($5) are available for overnight permits June-Sept. Open daily 8am-5pm; with extended summer hours.

Visitor information: ☎573-2674. **Lake Tahoe/Douglas Chamber of Commerce,** 195 U.S. 50 (☎775-588-4591; www.tahoechamber.org), in Stateline, NV. Open daily 9am-5pm. **Tahoe North Visitor Resort Association,** 950 N. Lake Blvd. (☎583-3494). Staff helps with reservations. Open M-F 7am-9pm, Sa-Su 9am-3pm. **Incline Village and Crystal Bay Visitors Bureau,** 969 Tahoe Blvd. (☎800-GO-TAHOE/468-2463; www.gotahoe.com). Open M-F 8am-5pm, Sa-Su 10am-4pm.

LOCAL SERVICES

Banks: US Bank, 705 N. Lake Blvd. (☎583-2346), in Tahoe City. Open M-Th 9am-5pm, F 9am-6pm. **Bank of the West,** 2161 Lake Tahoe Blvd. (☎531-3390), in S. Lake Tahoe. Open M-Th 9am-5pm, F 9am-6pm, Sa 9am-1pm. **Both have 24hr. ATMs.**

Library and Internet Access: South Lake Tahoe Library, 1000 Rufus Allen Blvd. (☎573-3185). Open Tu-W 10am-8pm, Th-Sa 10am-5pm. **Tahoe City Library,** 740 N. Lake Blvd. (☎583-3382). Open Tu and Th-F 10am-5pm, W noon-7pm, Sa noon-4pm. Free.

Laundromat: The Big Tree Cleaners, 531 N. Lake Blvd. (☎583-2802), in Tahoe City. Wash $1.50, dry $0.25 for 10min. Open M-F 9am-6pm. **Uncle Bob's Laundromat,** 2180 Lake Tahoe Blvd. (☎542-1910), in S. Lake Tahoe. Wash $1.25-1.50, dry $0.25 for 8min. Open daily 7am-10pm.

EMERGENCY & COMMUNICATIONS

Road Conditions: California ☎800-427-7623; Nevada ☎702-793-1313.

Police: Sheriff's offices are located at 1352 Johnson Blvd. (☎542-6100), in S. Lake Tahoe; 2501 N. Lake Tahoe Blvd. (☎581-6310), in Tahoe City.

Crisis Hotlines: General ☎800-992-5757. **Gamblers Anonymous** ☎583-8941. **Tahoe Women's Services** ☎546-3241.

Medical Services: Barton Memorial Hospital at 3rd St. and South Ave. (☎541-3420), in S. Lake Tahoe. **Incline Village Community Hospital,** 880 Alder Ave. (☎775-833-4100, in Incline Village. **Tahoe Forest Hospital,** at Donner Pass Rd. and Pine Ave. (☎587-6011), in Truckee.

SIERRA NEVADA

Post Office: Tahoe City, 950 N. Lake Blvd. #12 (☎800-275-8777), in the Lighthouse Shopping Center. Open M-F 8:30am-5pm, Sa noon-2pm. **Postal Code:** 96145. **South Lake Tahoe,** 212 Elk Point Rd. (☎588-5419). Open M-F 8:30am-5pm, Sa 10am-2pm. **Postal Code:** 96151.

AREA CODE. The area code for Lake Tahoe is 530 unless otherwise specified. The Nevada side is 775.

┃ ACCOMMODATIONS

The strip off U.S. 50 on the California side of the border supports the bulk of the South Shore's motels. Particularly glitzy and cheap in South Lake Tahoe, motels also line the quieter area along **Park Avenue** and **Pioneer Trail.** The North Shore offers more woodsy accommodations along **Route 28,** but rates are especially high in Tahoe City, where lodgings are booked solid and well in advance for weekends and holidays at sky-high prices. Fall and spring are the most economical times of the year to visit Tahoe because of the off-season bargains. Look for discount coupons in newspapers. Nearby campgrounds are a good option in warmer months.

▧ **Tahoe City Inn,** 790 N. Lake Blvd. (☎581-3333 or 800-800-8246; www.tahoecity-inn.com), next to Safeway in Tahoe City. Deluxe rooms sporting glass block walls, jacuzzis, and mini-fridges. Comfy queen beds, coffeemakers, and cable TV complete the package. Rooms with VCRs are more costly, but visitors get free access to extensive video library. Late Apr. to mid-June and late Sept.-late Nov. Su-Th $49, F-Sa $66; extra bed $10. Prices rise during peak season. ❹

▧ **Doug's Mellow Mountain Retreat,** 3787 Forest Ave. (☎544-8065), in S. Lake Tahoe. From the north turn left onto Wildwood Rd., and after 3 blocks take a left on Forest Ave.; it's the 6th house on the left. Easygoing Doug supplies a modern kitchen, BBQ, and fireplace. Internet access $5 per hr. Bedding included. No curfew. Flexible checkout times. Dorms $15 per person; private rooms available. Discounts for stays over a week. ❶

Tamarack Lodge, 2311 N. Lake Tahoe Blvd. (☎583-3350 or 888-824-6323), 3 mi. north of Tahoe City, across from Star Harbor. Clean lodge in the woods. Outdoor BBQ and fireplace, phones, cable TV, and friendly management. Rooms from $44. ❸

Cedar Glen Lodge, 6589 N. Lake Blvd. (☎546-4281 or 800-500-8246; www.cedarglen-lodge.com), in Tahoe Vista. Modest rooms with numerous amenities. Private beach access, pool, and indoor and outdoor hot tub and sauna. Grounds include BBQ pits, playground, flowers, and a rabbit hutch. Newspaper and continental breakfast. Cottages with kitchens also available. Open daily 8am-8:30pm. Singles from $65. ❹

Royal Inn, 3520 Lake Tahoe Blvd. (☎800-556-2500), in S. Lake Tahoe. Queen beds and desk space, along with a cable TV. Continental breakfast, laundry facilities. Singles Su-Th $35; doubles $59. Weekends and holidays see greatly inflated rates, but mention that *Let's Go* brought you here—you may be handsomely rewarded. ❺

Firelite Lodge, 7035 N. Lake Tahoe Blvd. (☎800-934-7222), in Tahoe Vista. Modern quarters with kitchenette, pool, and spa. Call ahead for reservations. Open daily 8am-10pm. Singles in summer and winter from $59; off-season singles begin at $49. ❹

┃ CAMPING

At its Visitors Center, the **US Forest Service** provides up-to-date information on camping (see **Tourist and Information Services,** p. 237). *North Tahoe Truckee This Week,* a free publication, prints info about grounds. **Route 89** is scattered with state campgrounds from Tahoe City to South Lake Tahoe. In July and August campgrounds are often booked, so reserve well in advance; call the **National Recreation Reservation System** or **NRRS** (☎877-444-6777; www.reserveusa.com) for US Forest Service campgrounds; the **California Campground Reservation System** or **CCRS** (☎800-444-7275 or 619-452-1950) for California State Parks; or the **National Park Reservation System** (☎800-365-2267). The NRRS and CCRS charge a non-refundable reservation fee and require a credit card. Backcountry camping is allowed in designated areas with a permit from the Forest Service (see **Tourist and Information Services**, p. 237). The only year-round backcountry campground is **General Creek ❶** in Sugar Pines State Park; others are generally open Memorial Day to Labor Day.

The 63,960 acres of **Desolation Wilderness** on the western side of Lake Tahoe are free of substantial human presence. Camping here is only for the experienced. The heavily protected area boasts glacial lakes and valleys, granite peaks, and subalpine forests that comprise some of the region's most breathtaking vistas. To maintain the grounds, Congress has introduced new permit costs and zoning regulations as part of the Recreation Fee Demonstration Program. The **Granite Chief Wilderness** is a less traveled area. Next to the Alpine Meadows and Squaw Valley ski resorts, the wilderness overlooks the Lake Tahoe Basin. Visitors are free to day hike without a wilderness permit. Free campfire permits are required and issued by the US Forest Service (see **Tourist and Information Services,** p. 237). The **Mount Rose Wilderness,** one of the nation's newest, is located in the northeast area of the Lake Tahoe Basin (accessible via Rte. 431) and can be traversed without a permit.

▧ **Tahoe State Recreation Area** (☎583-3074), at the northeast end of Tahoe City on Rte. 28. 1 acre of land along the lake and road, with a long pier. Water, flush toilets, showers ($5). Open May-Nov. 38 sites $15-16; $1 per dog per day. ❶

▧ **Sugar Pine Point State Park** (☎525-7982), on the west shore, 1 mi. south of Tahoma, and across Rte. 89, just a few mi. north of Meeks Bay. Popular grounds include tennis courts, cross-country ski trails, bike trails, nature center, the historic Ehrman mansion, and lakeside dock. Water, BBQ pits, and flush toilets. Hot showers $0.50. 175 sites $16; day use $2, seniors $1. ❷

William Kent (☎583-3642), on Rte. 89, 2 mi. south of Tahoe City, is one of the most popular campgrounds on the west shore. Beach access across Rte. 89. Clean flush toilets and water. Open June-Labor Day. 92 sites $16. ❷

Campground by the Lake (☎542-6096), 1150 Rufus Allen Blvd., in S. Lake Tahoe. City-run campground operates over 160 sites on 35 acres, just across from beach and picnic areas. Free casino shuttle, showers and flush toilets included. Open Apr. 1-Oct. 31. Sites $18; RV hookups $25; pets an additional $1. ❷

Sandy Beach (☎546-7682), off Rte. 28 in Tahoe Vista. Rocky soil beneath pine trees and adjacent to a sandy beach. Hookups, water, flush toilets, and showers. 44 very visible sites $15-20; pets $1.50 per day. ❷

◻ FOOD

In the south, the casinos offer perpetually low-priced buffets, but bar and grilles and burger joints dot the lakeshore, promising reasonable prices, similarly large portions, and much better food. Groceries are cheaper on the California side. Try **Safeway,** in S. Lake Tahoe, at Lake Tahoe Blvd. and Johnson St. (open 24hr.), or in Tahoe City at 850 N. Lake Blvd. (open daily 7am-10pm). Alternatively, you could go *au naturel* at **New Moon Natural Foods,** 505 W. Lake Blvd., just south of Tahoe City. (☎583-7426. Open M-F 10am-7pm, Sa-Su 10am-6pm.)

Red Hut Waffles, 2749 Lake Tahoe Blvd. (☎541-9024), and 227 Kingsbury Rd. (☎588-7488). Homestyle cooking. Waffle piled with fruit and whipped cream $5.75. Bottomless coffee $1.25. Open daily 6am-2pm. No credit cards. ❷

Lakehouse Pizza, 120 Grove St. (☎583-2222), in Tahoe City. The kitchen turns out small but tasty pizzas from $9. Standard breakfast specials $3-7. California salad and sandwiches $7. Open M-Th 8am-10pm, F-Sa 8am-11pm. ❷

The Fire Sign Cafe, 1785 W. Lake Blvd. (☎583-0871), 2 mi. south of Tahoe City, 100 yd. south of TART stop. Big breakfasts served in a woodsy location. Large omelettes, with home fries and a muffin, for only $6. Daily lunch deals. Open daily 7am-3pm. ❷

Fast Eddie's Texas-Style BBQ, 690 N. Lake Blvd. (☎583-0950), in Tahoe City. The beef brisket ($15) takes 10hr. to cook—you get it in 10min. Everything is slow-cooked with oak firewood, and you can taste the difference. Open daily 11am-10pm. ❸

Sprouts Natural Foods Cafe, 3123 Harrison Ave. (☎541-6969), at the intersection of Hwy. 50 and Alameda Ave. All-natural food in unnaturally large portions; this place keeps everyone satisfied. Try the breakfast burrito with avocados ($5), or the tasty smoothies ($3-3.75). Open daily 8am-10pm. ❶

◪ OUTDOOR ACTIVITIES

SUMMER ACTIVITIES

BEACHES

Many beaches ring Lake Tahoe, providing the perfect setting for a day of sunning and people-watching. Parking generally costs $5; bargain hunters should leave cars in turnouts on the main road and walk to the beaches.

NORTH SHORE. Sand Harbor Beach, south of Incline Village, has gorgeous granite boulders and clear waters that attract swimmers, sunners, and scuba divers in droves. The parking lot ($5) is usually full by 11:30am. **Commons Beach Park,** in the heart of Tahoe City just off N. Lake Tahoe Blvd., contains a playground for kids, an acre of beach for sunbathing, and access to lake waters for swimming. City planners intend to add a bike trail, more beach, and picnic areas. **Kings Beach** has volleyball nets, picnic tables with grills, a basketball court, and a playground. Jet-skis, sailboards, and kayaks can be rented at both beaches. Parasailing and waterskiing are also available.

SOUTH SHORE. Pope Beach, at the southernmost point of the lake off Rte. 89, is a pine-shaded expanse of shoreline that becomes less trafficked on its east side. **Nevada Beach,** 3 mi. north of South Lake Tahoe, is close to the casinos off U.S. 50, offering a sagebrush sanctuary with a picturesque view of sun-kissed mountains. **Zephyr Cove Beach,** about 15 mi. north of South Lake Tahoe, has completely renovated its impressive facility, hosting a youthful crowd keen on beer, beaches, and bikinis. It is also the launch site for the M.S. Dixie II, which cruises the lake.

WEST SHORE. Meeks Bay, 10 mi. south of Tahoe City, is family-oriented, social, and equipped with picnic tables, volleyball, motorboat and kayak rental, camping areas, and a store. In summer, the Tahoe City and South Tahoe buses connect here. Five miles south of Meeks Bay, the **D.L. Bliss State Park,** 17 mi. south of Tahoe City on Rte. 89, has a large beach on the small Rubicon Bay. Stand atop Rubicon Point and peer into the crystalline lake. The trailhead of the Rubicon Trail leads to the peaceful Vikingsholm mansion. Parking here ($5) is very limited, so check at the Visitors Center at the entrance or look to park on the road and walk in. **Chambers Beach,** between Homewood and Tahoma, draws an energetic crowd of families and young hipsters who occupy the public volleyball nets. Visitors of **Emerald Bay** often marvel at the pristine beauty of the scene. Circled by neat rows of green pines, the bay boasts the distinction of being named a National Natural Landmark, and affords access to Vikingsholm and the "Tea House" on Fannette Island.

HIKING

Hiking is a great way to explore the Tahoe Basin. The Visitors Center and ranger stations provide detailed info and maps for all types of hikes. Backcountry users must obtain a wilderness permit from the US Forest Service (see **Tourist and Information Services,** p. 237) for any hike into the Desolation Wilderness; only 700 hikers are allowed in this area on any given day. Due to erratic weather conditions in the Sierra, hikers should always bring a jacket and drinking water. Buy a topographical map before you go and ask where the snow has (or has not) melted—it's not usually gone until July, and finding a trail under a foot of hard snow is next to impossible. **Alpenglow Sport Shop,** 415 N. Lake Blvd., in Tahoe City, carries an array of equipment and sells great trail maps, but any found at the numerous outdoorsy stores are adequate. (☎ 583-6917. Open M-F 10am-6pm, Sa-Su 9am-6pm.)

After decades of work, the 165 mi. **Tahoe Rim Trail** has been completed, but upkeep and maintenance continues daily. The hiking trail encircles the lake, following the ridge tops of the Lake Tahoe Basin. Hiking is moderate to difficult, with an average grade of 10%. On the western shore, it is part of the Pacific Crest Trail. Trailheads abound throughout the region, so consult visitors centers for those nearest you. Frequently trafficked trailheads include Spooner Summit at the U.S. 50/Rte. 28 junction and Tahoe City off Rte. 89 on Fairway Dr.

NORTH SHORE. The **Granite Chief Wilderness,** behind Squaw Valley, is a great option; its rugged hiking trails and mountain streams wind through secluded forests and fields of wildflowers. The **Stateline Lookout,** running 0.5 mi., provides a knowledgeable staff and telescope views of the lake. From Rte. 28, go north on Reservoir Dr., make a right on Lakeshore, and a left on Forest Service Rd. 1601. Watch trout breed at Martis Creek Lake on the 3 mi. **Wildlife Creek Wildlife Area Loop,** just south of Truckee. Take Rte. 267 9 mi. north from Kings Beach. The **Marlette Lake Trail** begins at Spooner State Park, NV, at the junction of U.S. 50 and Rte. 28. It leads 5 mi. through the moderately difficult terrain of the Tahoe Rim Trail from Spooner Lake to Marlette Lake. At 10,778 ft., **Mount Rose,** in the Toiyabe National Forest, is one of the tallest mountains in the region as well as one of the best climbs. (Info ☎ 775-882-2766. Open M-F 8am-4:30pm.) The 6 mi. trek starts out as an easy dirt road hike but becomes a rocky scramble after mile three. Take Rte. 431 from Incline Village to the trailhead, which is 1 mi. south of the summit.

SOUTH SHORE. The southern region of the basin offers many moderate to strenuous hiking trails. Many visitors find the picturesque **Emerald Bay** to be an essential stop and photo opportunity. This crystal-clear pocket of the lake embraces Tahoe's only island and most photographed sight—tiny, rocky Fannette. The alpine lakes and dramatic waterfalls make this a mini-paradise. **Emerald Bay State Park,** which connects to the Desolation Wilderness, offers hiking and biking trails of varying difficulty, camping, and terrain for rock climbing. The parking lot collects a $3 day use fee. One of the best hikes in Tahoe is the **Rubicon Point Trail,** which wraps 5 mi. around the beach and granite cliffs of Emerald Bay. The trailheads are at D.L. Bliss Park and Vikingsholm. The **Eagle Falls Trail** is accessible from the Vikingsholm's parking lot by hiking to Eagle Lake (1 mi.) and into the Desolation Wilderness. (Permits required for this hike, and there is a fee for overnight camping; for details on these regulations, see p. 238.)

Those looking for a more leisurely excursion will enjoy the nature trails around the Taylor Creek Visitors Center, north of South Lake Tahoe on Rte. 89. The **Lake of the Sky Trail** (0.5 mi. round-trip) is dotted with informative signs about the origins of the lake, its early inhabitants, and its current animal inhabitants.

SIERRA NEVADA

FROM CREST TO CREST: THE TRAIL OF

THE WEST As the longest hiking path in America, the **Pacific Crest Trail (PCT)** snakes, swerves, and scales up 2638 mountainous miles from Mexico to Canada, passing through all sorts of climates from deserts to sub-Arctic regions along the way. True to its name, the PCT always keeps to the crests—the trail maintains an average elevation of over 5000 ft. The trail dishes out quality as well as quantity; there's an amazing view from the summit of **Mount Whitney** (14,494 ft.), the highest peak in the contiguous United States. Although the PCT was begun in 1968, the trailblazing task was so immense that it was not officially completed until 1993.

No matter how much of the trail you choose to take on, proper supplies, conditioning, and acclimatization are vital. The **Pacific Crest Trail Association** (☎916-349-2109 or 888-728-7245; www.pcta.org) gives tips on how to prepare for the journey. Contact them at 5325 Elkhorn Blvd., Box 256, Sacramento 95842.

Lower and **Upper Echo Lakes,** off U.S. 50 south of Tahoe, are a smaller, wilder version of Tahoe; granite tablets and pine trees tower around the lakes, producing an unmatched feeling of seclusion. **Echo Chalet,** 2 mi. west of U.S. 50 near the top of Echo Summit, operates **boat** service across the lake. (☎659-7207. Runs daily 8am-6pm. No reservations. One-way $7 with at least 2 people; pets $3.) This is the most affordable way to satiate motorboat-borne desires. From the drop-off point, a well-maintained trail (part of the Pacific Crest Trail) skirts the north side of the lakes to the Upper Lake boat landing and into the Desolation Wilderness. Day hiking wilderness permits are available at the chalet; mandatory overnight permits are issued at the forest service (see **Wilderness Permits,** p. 237). Another 2 mi. along U.S. 50, just before Twin Bridges, is the **Horsetail Falls** trailhead. The waterfalls here make those at Eagle Lake look like leaky faucets. To access them, you'll have to make the short (1.3 mi.) but tough hike through the slippery canyon. Inexperienced hikers should beware—each year, several people have to be rescued by US Forest Service helicopters.

ROCK CLIMBING

The **Alpenglow Sport Shop,** 415 N. Lake Blvd., in Tahoe City, provides free rock and ice climbing literature, and rents climbing shoes for $8 a day. (☎583-6917. Open M-F 10am-6pm, Sa-Su 9am-6pm.) **Headwall Climbing Wall,** at Squaw Valley, offers several challenging routes in the Cable Car Building. (☎583-7673. Open daily 10am-5pm. $12 per day, indoor shoe rental $4 per day.)

There are many popular climbs in Lake Tahoe, but climbing should never be undertaken without knowing the ropes—proper safety precautions and equipment are a must. Those unprepared for dangerous climbs can try bouldering at **D.L. Bliss State Park** and at **Split Rock** in Donner Memorial State Park. The climbing at **Donner Summit** is world-renowned. Along Old Hwy. 40 by Donner Pass, climbers ascend **School Rock** (beginner) or the precarious **Snow Shed** (advanced). A host of popular climbing spots are scattered through South Shore and the Donner Summit area. The super-popular **Ninety-Foot Wall** at Emerald Bay, **Twin Crags** at Tahoe City, and **Big Chief** near Squaw Valley are some of the more famous area climbs. **Lover's Leap,** in South Lake Tahoe, is an incredible (and an incredibly crowded) climb of two giant cliffs. East of South Lake Tahoe off U.S. 50, **Phantom Spires** has amazing ridge views, while **Pie Shop** has great exposure.

SEEING THE SIGHTS

Heavenly Mountain (see **Winter Activities,**p. 243) whisks visitors at 13 ft. per sec. to Heavenly's summit. (☎775-586-7000. Runs daily 10am-sunset. $20, ages 6-12 $12.)

Squaw Valley (see below) also offers a scenic tram ride that climbs to the mountaintop High Camp, with a year-round ice-skating rink, tennis club, pool, spa, mountain bike and hiking trails, and the world's highest bungee jumping tower. Restaurants and shops at the top are pricey. (Runs daily June-Aug. 10am-9pm, Sept. 10am-4pm. $17, under 12 $5; after 5pm $8.)

For a closer view of the waters, the **M.S. Dixie II Paddlewheeler** cruises Lake Tahoe in style from its Zephyr Cove dock, at 760 Hwy. 50. With up to five tours per day, the ride includes a video of the ecosystem that thrives under the lake's calm surface. (☎775-589-4906. Tours $24. Dinner/dancing $49. Breakfast $27. Champagne brunch $29.) On the North Shore, the **Tahoe Gal,** 850 N. Lake Tahoe Blvd., in the Lighthouse Shopping Center, makes a floating foray into Lake Tahoe with five daily cruises. The Happy Hour Cruise offers discounted drinks and two adults for the price of one. (☎800-218-2464. Happy hour cruise 4:30pm. Tickets $20.)

WINTER ACTIVITIES

DOWNHILL SKIING

With its world-class alpine slopes, knee-deep powder, and notorious California sun, Tahoe is a skier's mecca. There are approximately 20 ski resorts in the Tahoe area. The Visitors Center provides info, maps, publications like *Ski Tahoe* (free) and *Sunny Day* (free, with excellent area maps), and coupons (see **Tourist and Information Services,** p. 237). For daily ski info updates, use www.tahoesbest.com/skitahoe. All the major resorts offer lessons and rent equipment. Lifts at most resorts operate daily 9am-4pm; arrive early for the best skiing and shortest lines. Prices do not include ski rental, which generally costs $15-20 for a full day. Skiers on a tight budget should consider night skiing or half-day passes. Numerous smaller ski resorts offer cheaper tickets and shorter lines. **Diamond Peak Ski Resort** (☎775-832-1177), off Country Club Dr. in Incline Village, has a snowboard park and is on the beach, while **Sugar Bowl** (☎426-9000), 3 mi. east on Old Hwy. 40 off I-80 at Soda Springs Exit, recently doubled in size. Skiing conditions range from bikini days to frost-bitten finger days, and snow (artificial or otherwise) might cover the slopes into early summer. Off-season skiing may not compete with winter skiing for snow quality, but it's generally much cheaper. **Rates listed below are for winter.**

▧ **Squaw Valley** (☎583-5585 or 888-SNOW-321/766-9321; www.squaw.com), off Rte. 89, north of Alpine Meadows. Site of the 1960 Olympic Winter Games, and with good reason—the groomed bowls make for some of the West's best skiing. 4200 acres of terrain across 6 Sierra peaks. The 32 ski lifts—including the 110-passenger cable car and gondola—access high-elevation runs for all levels. Open late Nov.-June 1. Full-day lift ticket $56, half-day $39, seniors and 13-15 $28, over 76 and under 12 free. Night skiing (until mid-Apr. daily 4-9pm) $20. Non-skiing cable car ride $16, after 4pm $65.

▧ **Alpine Meadows** (☎583-4232 or 800-441-4423), on Rte. 89, 6 mi. northwest of Tahoe City. An excellent, accessible family vacation spot and local hangout with more than 2000 skiable acres. Not as commercial as Squaw, it has long expert bowls with good powder skiing, but few beginner runs. Full-day lift ticket $54, ages 7-12 $10, ages 65-69 $30, over 70 $8, under 6 $6. Basic ski rental $27, under 13 $18.

GOING HIKING?
Outdoor Equipment Tips from a Wilderness Expert

THE BASICS. A map of the area and a simple compass are critical for not getting lost. A knife and sunscreen should always be brought along. Carry at least one liter of water (two liters is preferable) and drink regularly to avoid cramps and dehydration.

FOOTWEAR. Appropriate hiking footwear provides stability and support for your feet and ankles while protecting them from the abuses of the environment. Mid-weight hiking boots are a good all-around choice, but appropriate footwear may range from running shoes to heavyweight boots depending on the environment and support desired.

PACK. The best packs will have a padded waist belt that allows you to carry pack weight on your hips and lower body rather than shoulders. When trying on packs, loosen the shoulder straps, position the waist belt so that the top of your hips (the bony iliac crest) is in the middle of the belt, and then tighten the shoulder straps. Ideally, the straps will attach to the pack slightly above (and off) the shoulders, preventing the pack weight from being borne by the easily fatigued muscles of your shoulders and back. For day-hikes, a pack with a capacity of 1000-2000 cubic inches (16-32L) is recommended.

CLOTHING. Go synthetic. Cotton clothing absorbs a lot of moisture and dries slowly, leaving a wet layer next to your skin which conducts heat away from your body roughly 20 times faster than dry clothing. Blue jeans are the worst. Nylon and polyester are the most common synthetic materials, absorb little moisture, and dry extremely fast.

RAIN GEAR. Waterproof/non-breathable rain gear is generally the best way to go. While it does not breathe and traps your sweat next to your body while you hike, it is cheap—jackets run $25-50. This raingear is impervious to liquid water, but allows water vapor (sweat) generated by the body to pass through to the outside and thus keeps you more comfortable. Gore-Tex is still considered the best waterproof/breathable barrier, but there are a variety of similar products which perform admirably.

SURVIVAL. Always be prepared for the unexpected night out. Carrying waterproof matches, a head lamp/flashlight, extra clothes, and extra food will keep you warm and comfortable during the night. A whistle is a powerful distress signal and can save your life if you become immobilized. Bring a basic first aid kit—at a minimum this should include an over-the-counter painkiller (aspirin, ibuprofen); a long, 2-4 in. wide elastic bandage for wrapping sprained ankles, knees, and other joints; and the basics for treating a wound: antibiotic ointment, gauze, small bandages, medical tape, and band-aids.

OTHER TIPS. Always purify water taken from backcountry sources. Iodine is cheap, easy, and compact. Hiking time can be estimated using the following guidelines: A reasonably fit individual can expect to travel 2-3 mi. (3-5km) per hour over level ground and descents, 1-2 mi. (2-3km) per hour on gradual climbs, and only about 1 mile (1.6km)—or 750-1000 feet (200-300m) of elevation—per hour on the steepest ascents.

Matt Heid was a Researcher-Writer for *Let's Go: Alaska and Western Canada 1993, Europe 1995,* and *New Zealand 1998.* He is the author of *101 Hikes in Northern California* and *Camping and Backpacking the San Francisco Bay Area,* both available from Wilderness Press.

Heavenly (☎ 775-586-7000), on Ski Run Blvd. off U.S. 50 (South Lake Tahoe Blvd.), is the largest and most popular resort in the area, with over 4800 skiable acres, 29 lifts, and 84 trails. Over 10,000 ft. high, it is Tahoe's highest ski resort. Few shoots or ridges. Its lifts and slopes straddle the California-Nevada boundary and offer dizzying views of both. Full-day lift ticket $57, ages 13-18 $47, seniors and ages 6-12 $29.

Rose (☎ 800-SKI-ROSE/754-7673), 11 mi. from Incline Village on Rte. 431, is a local favorite because of its long season, short lines, and intermediate focus. Full-day lift ticket $45, seniors $25, ages 13-17 $35, ages 6-12 $12, over 70 (midweek) and under 6 free; half-day $35, ages 13-17 $30. Tu 2 for 1 tickets, W student discounts.

Boreal (☎ 426-3663), on I-80, 10 mi. west of Truckee, opens earlier than most resorts and saves skiers the drive to Tahoe. Voted "Best Place to Snowboard" by locals. Mostly beginner and intermediate slopes are good for snowboarding. 9 lifts and 41 trails. Open Nov.-Apr. Ski 9am-9pm. Full-day lift ticket $34, ages 5-12 $10, over 60 $18, over 70 and under 5 free. Call about midweek discounts and night skiing.

Northstar (☎ 562-1010; www.skinorthstar.com), on Rte. 267, 13 mi. north of Tahoe City, is a family-oriented ski area with lots of beginning and intermediate trails. 200 new acres on Lookout Mountain cater to advanced skiers. Dining available at 6 restaurants on or near the mountain. Full-day lift ticket $5, ages 13-22 $44, under 13 $17.

CROSS-COUNTRY SKIING & SNOWSHOEING

One of the best ways to enjoy the solitude of Tahoe's pristine snow-covered forests is to cross-country ski at a resort. For more detachment, rent skis at an independent outlet and venture onto the thick braid of trails around the lake. **Porters** (☎ 587-1500), at the Lucky-Longs Center, in Truckee, and 501 N. Lake Blvd., in Tahoe City (☎ 583-2314; open daily 8am-6pm), rents skis for $9-12.

Royal Gorge (☎ 426-3871), on Old Hwy. 40 below Donner Summit, is the nation's largest cross-country ski resort, with 90 trails covering 170 mi. of beginner and expert terrain. Warming huts provide a respite during your trek. **Spooner Lake,** at the junction of U.S. 50 and Rte. 28, offers 57 mi. of machine-groomed trails and incredible views. (☎ 775-749-5349. $15, children $3; mid-week special $11.)

Snowshoeing is easier than cross-country skiing, and allows you to traverse more varied terrain. Follow hiking or cross-country trails, or trudge off into the woods (bring a map). Equipment rentals are available at sporting goods stores for about $15 per day. Check local ranger stations for ranger-guided winter hikes.

▶ NIGHTLIFE

There are varying degrees of nightlife in Lake Tahoe. In Tahoe City, most of the nightlife is centered around the pub scene. On the South Shore, however, it's a little more glitzy—that's where you find the late-night gambling and dancing. To get in, you'll need a state ID or license; international residents need passports.

Caesar's Palace, 55 U.S. 50 (☎ 888-829-7630). Roman themed casino, sportsbook, restaurants, and clubs. Within Caesar's, popular **Club Nero** (☎ 775-586-2000) is hot for dancing, with M $2 drinks. Cover $5-25. Open daily 9pm-early morning.

The Brewery, 3542 S. Lake Tahoe Blvd. (☎ 544-2739). Stop in and try one of the 6 microbrews on tap. Sassy Bad Ass Ale packs a fruity punch, and pizzas (starting at $9) come crammed with as many toppings as you want. Laid-back atmosphere makes this spot a favorite for locals. Open daily 11am-10pm; later hours during peak seasons.

SIERRA NEVADA

NEAR LAKE TAHOE

The area surrounding Lake Tahoe is a rare find in the High Sierra: a pristine mountain setting with nearby outposts of urbanization, offering the best of both worlds. Lake Tahoe and Donner Lake glitter in both sun and snow. Innumerable outdoor recreation opportunities reel in visitors by the score; after the sun goes down, they all head to beachside barbecues, the dimly lit yuppie bars of Tahoe City, or the glitzy gambling of South Lake Tahoe and Reno, just across the Nevada border.

TRUCKEE & DONNER LAKE ☎ 530

Truckee (pop. 10,950), throughout the history of Western settlement, has served as a gateway through the High Sierra for those traveling from the east. In the early 1800s, settler parties heading to California were forced to abandon their wagons—a dangerous and costly sacrifice—before crossing the treacherous Sierra Nevada range. In 1844, one such party encountered an encampment of Paiute Indians and their leader, a man they named Chief Truckee. The party forged a strong friendship with Truckee, who helped them find what would later become Donner Pass, the first wagon route across the Sierras. From then on, Truckee served as a rugged camp before the crossing. The discovery of gold nearby in 1844, and the arrival of the transcontinental railroad in 1863, brought further expansion to the town. Nonetheless, today as in the late 1800s, it is tourism to Lake Tahoe that truly keeps Truckee (and its reputation as a mountain gateway) alive.

Lying two miles west of Truckee and encircled by gray granite cliffs is Donner Lake, the site where the ill-fated Donner Party got snowed in by an early winter. Travelers will notice numerous memorials to the gruesome event, when members of the party resorted to cannibalism for survival (see **This Party Bites!**, p. 248), but will likely find Donner Lake much more fun than the pioneers did. Warmer than Tahoe, the lake has become a popular place for swimming, boating, and hiking. The **Tahoe National Forest** also offers a host of recreational opportunities.

✳ 🛈 ORIENTATION & PRACTICAL INFORMATION

Truckee lies just off I-80 in the Sierra Nevada, 100 mi. northeast of Sacramento, 33 mi. west of Reno, and 15 mi. north of Lake Tahoe on Rte. 89. The town is about a 3hr. drive from San Francisco. **Donner Pass Road** (part of Rte. 89), the main drag, leads east into downtown, where it becomes Commercial Row, and west to Donner Summit and Donner Lake, where it is known as **Old Highway 40.** Be extremely cautious along Donner Pass—there are not always barriers along the cliffside edge of the road. In summer, potholes make for a harrowing drive. In winter it is usually closed due to snow and ice; stick to I-80.

> **Trains: Amtrak** at Railroad St. and Commercial Row (☎ 800-USA-RAIL/872-7245), in Truckee. Trains depart to: **Reno** (1hr., 1 per day, $18); **Sacramento** (4½hr., 1 per day, $70); **Salt Lake City** (12hr., 1 per day, $110). Service to and from **San Francisco** via Emeryville (5hr., 3 per day, $33). Station is unstaffed; order tickets in advance.
>
> **Buses: Greyhound,** 10065 Donner Pass Rd. (☎ 800-231-2222), in the Visitors Center. To: **Reno** (4 per day, $10); **Sacramento** (6 per day, $21-23); **San Francisco** (6 per day, $35). **Tahoe Area Regional Transit (TART)** (☎ 800-736-6365) buses to and from Tahoe City from the train station 4 times a day (departs Tahoe YMCA every 2hr. 7:30am-1:30pm and at 3:45pm; departs Truckee 8:30, 10:30am, 12:45, 1:45, 3pm).

Public Transportation: In town, the **Truckee Trolley** (☎587-7451) runs M-Sa 9:15am-5:15pm between Truckee-Tahoe airport, major stops in town, Donner Lake and Donner Park, and West End Beach. In winter the trolley runs daily 7am-6pm and hits ski destinations. **Dial-a-Ride** (☎587-7541) will take you anywhere in town M-F 8am-5pm for $3.

Auto Repairs: AAA Emergency Road Service (☎800-222-4357).

Visitor Information: Truckee-Donner Chamber of Commerce, 10065 Donner Pass Rd. (☎587-2757; reservations 800-548-8388), across from Commercial Row, at the train station. Brochures, maps, and a sign-up list for the commemorative Donner Party Hike in early Oct. Open daily 8:30am-5:30pm. **US Forest Service Truckee Ranger District,** 10342 Hwy. 89 North (☎587-3558; www.r5.fs.fed.us/tahoe/tkrd), off I-80. Info on camping and recreation in Tahoe National Forest as well as ranger-led activities. Open June-Aug. M-Sa 8am-5pm; Sept.-May M-F 8am-4:30pm.

24hr. ATM: Bank of the West, 10069 Bridge St. (☎582-3070), 1 block north of downtown. Open M-Th 9am-4pm, F 9am-6pm.

Equipment Rental: The Sports Exchange, 10095 W. River St (☎582-4510), across the tracks from Old Town. In summer, rents kayaks (single $30 per day, double $40) and mountain bikes and helmets ($25 per day). In winter offers ski packages ($20 per day), snowboard packages ($20 per day), and snowshoes with poles ($10 per day). Discounts on multi-day rentals. Climbing gym on site (day pass with shoes $10). Open daily 10am-6pm.

Weather Conditions: ☎546-5253. **Road Conditions:** ☎800-427-7623.

Police: ☎582-7838.

Medical Services: Tahoe Forest, 10121 Pine Ave. (☎587-6011), at Donner Pass Rd.

Post Office: Truckee, 10050 Bridge St. (☎800-275-8777), on Rte. 267, 1 block north of Commercial Row. Open M-F 8:30am-5pm, Sa 11am-2pm. **Postal Code:** 96161. **Donner Station,** 11415 Deerfield. Open M-F 9am-4:30pm. **Postal Code:** 96162.

ACCOMMODATIONS & CAMPING

As a ski town in winter and host to Donner Lake and Lake Tahoe tourists in the summer, it's almost always the high season in Truckee, meaning lodging is hard to get and expensive (doubles start at $100-150 per night). In business for 125 years, the historic **Truckee Hotel ❸,** 10007 Bridge St., was designed in the European fashion—wash basins in the rooms, baths in the hall—back when Victorian sensibilities reigned. Rooms are spotless, restored to their original look, and thanks to the shared baths, the best lodging deal in town. (☎800-659-6921. Rooms with shared bath from $50, with private bath from $80.)

Seventeen **campgrounds** lie within 12 mi. of Truckee. The US Forest Service (☎587-3558) operates northern and southern sites along Rte. 89, and also along Stampede Meadows Rd., off I-80 at the Hirshdale Exit. **Campsites ❶,** 5600-6000 ft., clustered around Boca and Prosser Reservoirs, offer boating and fishing. (All have free water except Boca and Davies Creek. Sites $12.) The campsites along Rte. 89 south are the most popular, offering easy access to Lake Tahoe. **Granite Flat ❶,** 5920 ft., is 3 mi. south. (Water and vault toilets. 75 sites $14.) **Goose Meadow ❶,** 6068 ft., is 5 mi. south. (Water and vault toilets. 25 sites $12.) Stop at the ranger station on Rte. 89 just off I-80 for maps and info. (Open M-Sa 8am-5pm; in winter 8am-4:30pm.) **Donner Memorial Park ❷,** 12593 Donner Pass Rd., is an expansive campground. Scenic views of Donner Lake and Donner Summit and flush toilets and hot showers make this site especially popular. (153 sites $16.) All campgrounds recommend reservations, especially on weekends. (MISTIX ☎800-444-7275.)

SIERRA NEVADA

THIS PARTY BITES! It's hard to pass through Donner Lake without seeing numerous memorials to the Donner Party. The fuss began when 87 midwesterners (led by the Donner family) headed for the comfort of California in April 1846. The ill-fated group took a "short-cut" advocated by the daring but reckless adventurer Lansford Hastings. The party hacked through the wilderness, losing cattle and abandoning wagons as they went. Although the area was brushed with barely a foot of snow the year before, the onset of an early winter at Truckee (later Donner) Lake in December devastated the group. Trapped by 22 ft. of snow and without powder skis, many turned to cannibalism before they were rescued. Only 40 survived. The Donner Party is remembered in the **Donner Memorial State Park** (☎582-7892), 3 mi. west of Truckee, and on countless t-shirts. To get to the park, take I-80 to the Donner Lake Exit, then go west on Old U.S. 40 until you reach the park entrance. The park includes the **Emigrant Trail Museum,** which documents the infamous incident with multimedia flair c. 1975. There's also the **Annual Donner Party Hike** (☎587-2757), which ritually reenacts the fateful journey every October (dinner not included).

◙ FOOD

Though human flesh is no longer being served in the region, you can take your pick of touristy restaurants and coffee shops in Truckee, or forage at the 24hr. **Safeway** supermarket on Rte. 89, 1 mi. west of downtown. The **Treat Box Bakery ❶,** 11400 Donner Pass Rd., is an ideal spot for picnic packing. Eat in the cafe or order from their selection of fresh sandwiches ($4-5). Pies ($11), breads ($3), and cakes (from $17) are homemade. (☎587-6554. Open daily 5am-9pm.) **Squeeze-In ❷,** 10060 Commercial Row, across from the fire station, offers 57 varieties of omelettes ($7-9) and 23 different sandwiches ($6-7) named after colorful locals like Luscious Lucy and Captain Avalanche. (☎587-9814. Open daily 7am-2pm. Cash only.)

◉ 🔼 SIGHTS & ACTIVITIES

The local **historical society** (☎582-0893) oversees a short town trail, as well as a small museum in the **Old Truckee Jail** on Jibbom St. Although many Old West criminals were tarred and feathered, the lucky ones were locked up in this wood-and-stone prison until its closure in 1964, when it held the distinction of the oldest continuously run jail in the US. (Open June-Oct. daily 11am-4pm. Free.) One of 25 known specimens, Truckee's **Rocking Stone,** at the corner of High St. and Spring St., no longer rocks since it was cemented in place, but you can imagine how fun it must have been to tip a 17 ton boulder with your pinky finger.

The city of Truckee lies outside the Truckee Ranger District of the **Tahoe National Forest** and just east of **Donner Memorial State Park.** In total, the Tahoe Forest has 630 mi. of hiking trails, over 20,000 surface acres of fishable lakes and reservoirs, nearly 100 mi. of the Pacific Crest Trail, 1500 mi. of lakes and streams, and mountain peaks along the Pacific Crest rising up to 9000 ft. **Fishing** is popular along the Truckee River, Donner Lake, and at the Boca and Stampede Resevoirs, east on I-80 at the Hischdale Exit. Several day and extended **hikes** depart from the Donner Summit Trailhead, 8 mi. west of town on I-80 at the Boreal Ridge Rd. Exit. The easy 0.5 mi. **Glacier Meadow Loop Trail** details the effects of glacial action on the landscape. The **Summit Lake Trail** follows the PCT north for 2 mi. through beautiful forest to an I-80 underpass, where it branches off to tranquil, trout-filled Summit Lake. Continuing on the PCT 1 mi. past this intersection will take you to the difficult **Warren Lake Trail** (7 mi. one-way), which crosses a saddle (8570 ft.) and descends to a lake, where you can fish or camp. The **Commemorative Overland Emi-**

grant Trail traces the emigration path of many 19th century settlers. The 15 mi. moderate trail through pines and over creeks, from Alder Creek Rd. to Stampede Reservoir, is good for hiking and great for **mountain biking.** Take I-80 to Rte. 89 north, proceed 2¼ mi. to Alder Creek Rd., turn left and go 3 mi. to the trailhead. No wilderness permits are required in Tahoe National Forest for day use or camping, but campfire permits are required in undeveloped sites for both fires and stoves.

Despite its morbid namesake, the popular **Donner Memorial State Park** is the local playground, with hiking trails, picnic areas, and scenic Donner Lake. On the lake's west end is a crowded public beach. A roped-off swimming area, volleyball court, tennis courts, sandy beach, and grassy picnic lawn (day use $2) make this place feel like a little Lake Tahoe. The Donner Memorial is a chilling reminder of the extreme winter that gave rise to the Donner tragedy. Beseiged by families from all over the world photographing themselves in front of it, the 20 ft. high monument is as tall as the height of snowfall that stormy winter. Next door, the **Emigrant Trail Museum** is at the entrance to the park. (Open daily 9am-5pm. $2, ages 6-12 $1.)

In the winter, local ski, snowboard, snowplay, and extreme-sports resorts open to thousands of outdoors enthusiasts. **Boreal,** 8 mi. west of town on I-80 at the Boreal Exit, has perhaps the lowest prices in the area and is open until 9pm. (☎426-3666. Day pass $34, ages 60-69 $15, ages 5-12 $10, under 5 and over 70 free.) **Soda Springs,** at the Soda Springs Exit of I-80 west of Truckee, specializes in tubing, snowboarding, sledding, and snowshoeing, but has ski runs. (☎426-1010. Day pass for all runs $22, ages 8-17 $16, under 7 and over 70 free.) There are five designated **Sno-Play** areas, including one at Donner Lake and Donner Summit. **Cold Stream Adventures** (☎582-9090) offers snowmobile rentals and dogsled tours.

RENO
☎ 775

Reno, with its decadent casinos cradled by snow-capped mountains, captures both the natural splendor and capitalist frenzy of the West. Acting as the hub of northern Nevada's tourist cluster, that includes nearby Lake Tahoe and Pyramid Lake, this self-proclaimed "biggest little city in the world" does a decent job of compressing the gambling, entertainment, and dining experience of Las Vegas into a few city blocks. Built as much around the allure of a quick buck as a quick break-up, the city rose to prominence as a celebrity destination, where getting a divorce was easier than making a hard eight on the craps table. Whatever your reason for visiting, Reno continues to be the Sierra's alternative to Vegas, attracting gamblers who crave the rush of hitting it big without the theme-park distractions.

◾ TRANSPORTATION

Flights: Reno-Tahoe International Airport, 2001 E. Plumb Ln. (☎328-6400), on U.S. 395 at Terminal Way, 3 mi. southeast of downtown. Most major hotels have free shuttles for guests; otherwise take bus #13. Taxis from downtown to the airport $9-11.

Trains: Amtrak, 135 E. Commercial Row (☎800-872-7245 or 329-8638). Ticket office open daily 8:30am-4:45pm. Arrive 30min. in advance to purchase tickets. 1 train per day travels to **Sacramento,** continuing on to **San Francisco** via bus.

Buses: Greyhound, 155 Stevenson St. (☎322-2970 or 800-231-2222), half a block from W. 2nd St. Open 24hr. Higher prices F-Su. To **Las Vegas** (1 express per day, $72) and **San Francisco** (17 per day, $30-33).

Public Transportation: Reno Citifare (☎348-7433) serves the Reno-Sparks area. Main terminal at 4th and Center St. Runs daily 5am-7pm, although city center buses operate 24hr. Buses stop every 2 blocks, and service runs to the airport. $1.25, seniors and disabled $0.60, ages 6-18 $0.90. Carson City $3 one way.

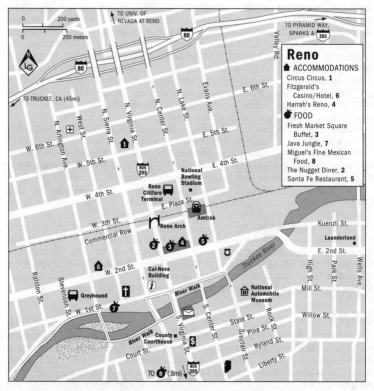

Reno

♠ ACCOMMODATIONS
Circus Circus, **1**
Fitzgerald's
 Casino/Hotel, **6**
Harrah's Reno, **4**

🍴 FOOD
Fresh Market Square
 Buffet, **3**
Java Jungle, **7**
Miguel's Fine Mexican
 Food, **8**
The Nugget Diner, **2**
Santa Fe Restaurant, **5**

Taxis: Yellow Cab, ☎ 355-5555. **Reno-Sparks Taxi Cab,** ☎ 333-3333.

Car Rental: Savers Rent-a-Car, 1201 Kietzke (☎ 786-6444 or 888-432-3455). 23+ with liability insurance. $23 per day, 150 mi. included. Credit card or $300 cash deposit required. Open daily 8am-7pm.

✳🛈 ORIENTATION & PRACTICAL INFORMATION

Only 14 mi. from the California border and a 443 mi. desert sprint north of Las Vegas, Reno sits at the intersection of **I-80** and **U.S. 395,** which runs along the eastern slope of the Sierra Mountains and the scenic Truckee River. Scan West Coast papers or internet travel sites for "gamblers' specials" on bus and plane fare.

Most major casinos are "downtown" on Sierra and Virginia St., between 2nd and 4th St. The wide and neon-lit streets in downtown Reno are heavily patrolled in summer, but **avoid walking alone** near the northeastern corner at night. Virginia St. south of the Truckee River has cheaper accommodations and good food, and is serviced by the #1 bus running from downtown Reno to the Meadowood Mall. In the adjacent city of Sparks, to the northeast, several casinos line I-80. *Reno/Tahoe Travel Planner,* available at the Visitors Center, has a local map and is an excellent city guide. **The official drinking and gambling age is 21,** but enforcement varies.

Visitor Information: Reno-Sparks Convention and Visitors Center Cal-Neva Building, 100 N. Virginia St. (☎800-367-7366; www.playreno.com or www.renolaketahoe.com), on the 2nd floor of the Cal-Neva Building. Pamphlets, a Reno Historical Society exhibit, and the Reno-Sparks Chamber of Commerce on the 16th floor. Open daily 9am-5pm.

Quick Cash: ATMs in most casinos. Most charge $1.50 for out-of-state withdrawals.

Library and Internet Access: Downtown Reno Library, 301 S. Center St. (☎327-8300). Free public Internet access against the soothing backdrop of an indoor fountain. Open M-W 10am-8pm, Th-F 10am-6pm, Sa 10am-5pm; Su noon-5pm.

Marriage: Men and women over 18 (and those 16-17 with a parental OK) can pick up a marriage license at the **Courthouse,** 75 Court St. (☎328-3274), for $50 (cash)—all you need is a partner and an ID. Open daily 8am-midnight, including holidays. Numerous chapels in Reno are eager to help you tie the knot.

Divorce: To obtain a divorce permit, you must be a resident of NV for at least 6 weeks and pay a $150 fee. Permits are available at the courthouse divorce office M-F 8am-5pm; an uncontested divorce may take up to 4 months. Call ☎328-3535 for info.

Laundromat: Launderland & Coin-op Laundry, 680 E. 2nd St. (☎329-3733). Wash $1.75-4.50, drying is free. Open daily 7am-10pm; last load 9pm.

Road Conditions: ☎877-687-6237.

24-Hour Crisis Lines: General Counseling and Rape Crisis, ☎800-992-5757. **Compulsive Gamblers Hotline,** ☎800-522-4700.

Medical Services: St. Mary's Hospital, 235 W. 6th St. (☎770-3000; in emergency 770-3188), near Arlington Ave. Open 24hr.

Post Office: 50 S. Virginia St. (☎800-275-8777), Open M-F 8:30am-5pm; Sa 10am-2pm to pick up packages only. **Postal Code:** 89501.

▚ ACCOMMODATIONS

While weekend prices at casinos are usually on the high side, gambler's specials, weekday rates, and off-season discounts provide some great, cheap rooms. The prices below don't include Reno's **12% hotel tax.**

Harrah's Reno, 219 N. Center St. (☎800-427-7247). A Reno staple, Harrah's provides big, clean rooms in a central location. 2 towers of rooms, 6 restaurants, an arcade, and a health club leave little to be desired. The casino attracts large crowds, and houses Planet Hollywood's Reno branch: a great place to grab a mixed drink. Call ahead for rates and availability. Rooms M-Th from $49, F-Su $89. ❹

Fitzgerald's Casino/Hotel, 255 N. Virginia St. (☎800-535-LUCK/5825). Resting at the base of the Reno arch, this 351-room hotel and casino offers cheap, clean rooms right at the heart of the city. Airport shuttle service ($2.65) and free valet parking for guests. Rooms S-Th $30, F-Sa $50. ❸

Circus Circus, 500 N. Sierra St. (☎329-0711 or 800-648-5010). As the family casino of Little Sin City, entertainment for all can be found in this 1,500-room hotel. Acres of casinos, restaurants, a workout room, carnival activities, and a real live big top. Rooms are posh and quiet. Rooms Su-Th from $34-129, F-Sa from $60. Call for discounts. ❹

CAMPING

To escape the constant jingle of slot machines in Reno, campers can drive to the woodland campsites of **Davis Creek Park ❶**, 17 mi. south on U.S. 395, then follow the signs ½ mi. west. (☎849-0684. Showers and toilets. Open daily 8am-9pm, but campers can self-pay at the gates at any time of day. Free picnic area open daily 8am-9pm, with volleyball courts and trout-packed Ophir Creek Lake. Sites $13; each additional car $5; pets $1.) After camping at the base of Slide Mountain, hike its Ophir trail, which ascends over 4,000 ft. to meet the Tahoe Rim Trail. The difficult climb is 6.1 mi. You can also camp along the shore at **Pyramid Lake ❶**. To stay closer to Reno, park and plug in your RV at **KOA ❶**, 2500 E. 2nd St., near the Reno Hilton. (☎888-562-5698. Campers can swim in the Hilton's pool. Hookups $29.)

FOOD

Eating in Reno is cheap, but the quality doesn't have to be. To ensure that gamblers don't stray from their tables and slots, casinos offer a wide range of all-you-can-eat buffets and 99-cent breakfasts. Buffet fare can be greasy and overcooked, but you can find a good combination of quality and cost. Escaping the ubiquitous buffets is worthwhile, as inexpensive eateries provide Mexican and Basque food.

Miguel's Fine Mexican Food, 1415 S. Virginia St. (☎322-2722). Miguel's Mexican fare is praised by locals and critics alike. A substantial lunch menu ($6-9) offers delicious food in handsome servings. The taquitos ($3) and sopapillas (3 for $1) are scrumptious. Entrees $5-10. Open Su noon-8pm; Tu-Th 11am-9pm; F-Sa 11am-10pm. ❷

Fresh Market Square Buffet (☎786-3232), second floor in **Harrah's.** Prime rib, crab legs, and shrimp run along the numerous buffet tables. In addition to the cooked-to-order prime cut of beef, diners can sample Asian cuisine, pizza, traditional American fare, and desserts. Breakfast buffet $7. Lunch $7. Dinner $11. Champagne brunch Sa-Su 8am-2pm $11. Open M-F 7am-2pm and 4-9pm, Sa-Su 8am-2pm and 4-9pm. ❸

Santa Fe Restaurant, 235 Lake St. (☎323-1891), in the Santa Fe Hotel, in the heart of downtown. When the Basques migrated from the Pyrenees, they brought their cuisine with them. Hearty, Americanized portions are served up family style. Oxtail, beef tongue, and pigs feet alternate as side dishes, while top sirloin steak, chicken, and pork chops are mainstays. Lunch $11. 7-course dinner $15. Open daily 11am-2pm and 6-9pm. ❸

Java Jungle, 246 West 1st St. (☎329-4484), just past West St., along the river. The fun jungle theme finds an outlet with numerous plants and giraffe prints. Enjoy your coffee ($1.25), espresso or sandwich ($5) on the outdoor patio in view of Wingfield Park. For $1.75, the Italian sodas are a great way to cool off in the summer: choose from over 30 flavors. Open Su-Th 6am-11pm, F-Sa 7am-midnight; extended summer hours. ❶

The Nugget Diner, 233 N. Virginia St. (☎323-0716), Treat yourself at this crowded greasy spoon in the back of the tiny Nugget Casino. The "Awful Awful" burger comes with all the trimmings and heaps of fries for only $3.50. Breakfast, served all day, is cheap and fast. Open M-Tu 7am-11pm, W-Su 7am-4am. ❶

ENTERTAINMENT & SEASONAL EVENTS

Reno is a big adult amusement park. Many casinos offer free gaming lessons; minimum bets vary between establishments. Drinks are usually free if you're gambling, but alcohol's inhibition-dropping effects can make betting a bad experience.

Almost all casinos offer live nighttime entertainment, but most shows are not worth the steep admission prices. **Harrah's,** represents an exception, by carrying on with its **dinner shows** in Sammy's Showroom. For $32.50, Harrah's offers dinner at one of its restaurants and a performance by headlining impersonator Gordie Browne, named "Entertainer of the Year" by the *Sacramento Bee.* At **Circus Circus,** 500 N. Sierra (☎329-0711), a small circus above the casino performs "big top" shows every half-hour. Shows are listed in the weekly *Showtime. Best Bets* and *Fun & Gaming* provide listings of discounted local events. The *Nevada Events & Shows* section of the Nevada Visitors Guide lists sights, museums, and events. More info is in the *Reno Gazette-Journal* and *News & Review.*

There's far more to Reno than its casinos. In late November, Reno's **River Holiday and Festival of Trees** (☎334-2262 or 334-2414) uses the Truckee River Walk and the island setting of Wingfield Park to celebrate the holiday spirit. The park is decorated with lights and trees, as artists sell their wares, performers entertain crowds, and children are treated to a visit from Santa.

Cultural events heat up in the summer, such as the popular five-year-old **Artown** festival (☎322-1538; www.artown.org), held every July for the entire month. The event features dance, jazz, painting, and basketry, and everything is free. In August, local Basque traditions, dancing, food, and music break through the seams of the blanketing casino culture at Reno's annual **Basque Festival** (☎787-3039).

The first week in August roars into chrome-covered, hot-rod splendor with **Hot August Nights** (☎356-1956), a celebration of classic cars and rock 'n' roll. The annual **Reno Rodeo** (☎329-3877), one of the biggest in the West, gallops over eight days in late June. In September, the **Great Reno Balloon Race** (☎826-1181), in Rancho San Rafael, and the **National Championship Air Races** (☎972-6663; www.air-race.org), at the Stead Airport, draw an international group of contestants who take to the sky. Also in September, Virginia City hosts **Camel Races** (☎847-0311) on the weekend after Labor Day, where camels and ostriches race through town.

NATIONAL PARKS & FORESTS

Far from the urban centers and industry of coastal California, the central Sierra nurtures the wilderness in its unbridled majesty. Clear streams flow through seemingly endless forests, while high Sierra peaks remain untrammeled by human feet. This rugged wilderness is the legacy of a long standing conservation movement pioneered by John Muir in the late 19th century (see **The Naturalist,** p. 268). The two main park areas in the Sierra Nevadas are Yosemite National Park (near Stanislaus National Forest and Mono Lake) and Sequoia and Kings Canyon National Parks (framed by the Sierra National Forest to the north and Sequoia National Forest to the south). National parks may conserve the natural surroundings, but they also attract adventure-hungry tourists from around the world. Those seeking solitude may need to explore the less-heralded treasures of the more remote areas.

YOSEMITE NATIONAL PARK ☎209

In 1868, a young Scotsman named John Muir arrived by boat in San Francisco and asked for directions to "any place that is wild." Anxious to run this crazy youngster out of town, Bay Area folk directed him to the heralded lands of Yosemite. The wonders that Muir beheld there sated his wanderlust and spawned a lifetime of conservationism. His efforts won Yosemite its national park status in 1890. Sequoia and Kings Canyon earned the same reward that year.

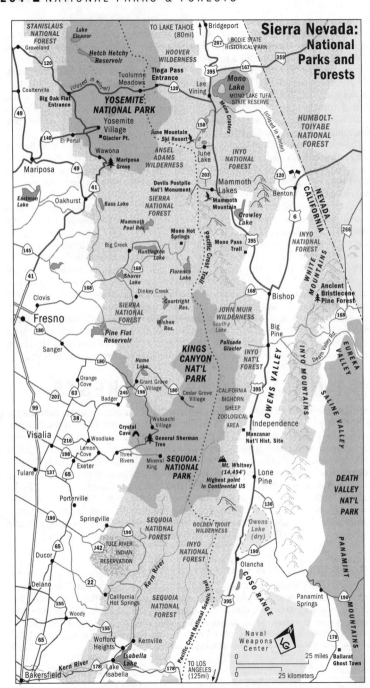

Host to its own full-service hospital, kennel, daycare center, Lions and Rotary Clubs, seven religious congregations, a golf shop, one of the grandest hotels in California, and more informative programs than PBS, Yosemite and its more than four million yearly visitors have given rise to a small city, in the middle of one of the most awesomely wild regions in America. With a park roughly the size of Rhode Island, however, and a "civilized" spread of about 6%, most of Yosemite remains tranquil. And despite the endless rows of tents, RVs, and SUVs, the bustling heart of it all, Yosemite Valley, still lives up to its old name: "The Incomparable Valley."

AT A GLANCE

AREA: 1189 sq. mi.

CLIMATE: Temperate forest.

FEATURES: Tuolumne Meadows, Mariposa Grove, Yosemite Valley.

HIGHLIGHTS: Hike to Glacier Point, photograph Bridalveil Falls, raft on the Merced River.

GATEWAYS: Mariposa, Sonora (p. 227), Mammoth Lakes (p. 299), Oakhurst, and Merced (p. 313).

CAMPING: Reservations necessary to get a spot. 7-night max. stay in the Valley and Wawona, 14-night max. stay elsewhere. Permits needed for camping in the high country within the Park.

FEES & RESERVATIONS: Necessary 7-day pass $10 per hiker, biker, or bus rider; $20 per car. Annual pass $40. National park passes also accepted here.

ORIENTATION

In all, Yosemite covers 1189 sq. mi. of mountainous terrain, most of which is completely rugged and wild, and some of which is quite developed. The center of activity in the park, **Yosemite Valley,** hosts the park's most enduring monuments, including **El Capitan, Half Dome,** and **Yosemite Falls.** The immense valley and all its granite monoliths were carved out by glaciers over thousands of years. Facing the sheer southern wall of the valley and incomparable 360-degree views, **Glacier Point** brims all summer with tourists and their cars. **Tuolumne** (ta-WALL-um-ee) **Meadows,** in the park's northeastern corner, is an alpine meadow surrounded by snow-capped peaks and swift streams. **Mariposa Grove** is a forest of giant sequoia trees at the park's southern end. Wawona, just north of Mariposa Grove, is a historic, upscale development that features museums, the Wawona hotel, and a golf course. The rest, for the most part, is wild. (7-day pass $10 per hiker, biker, or bus rider; $20 per car. Annual pass $40. National park passes accepted.)

Yosemite Concession Services provides some discounts to holders of Golden Age and Golden Eagle national park passes (2-for-1 bike rental; 2-for-1 greens fee at Wawona Golf). Inquire at the visitors centers of gateway towns like Mariposa, Sonora, Mammoth Lakes, Oakhurst, or Merced for additional discounts.

TRANSPORTATION

Yosemite lies 200 mi. east of San Francisco (a 3½hr. drive) and 320 mi. northeast of L.A. (a 6-9hr. drive, depending on the season). It can be reached via Rte. 140 from Merced, Rte. 41 from Fresno, or Rte. 120 from Manteca or from Lee Vining.

BY BUS OR TRAIN. Yosemite runs public **buses** that connect the park with Fresno, Merced, and Mariposa. **Yosemite VIA** runs buses from the Merced bus station at 16th and N streets to Yosemite. (☎384-1315 or 800-VIA-LINE/842-5463. 7:10, 9, 10:50am, 5:15pm; weekends and holidays 7, 8:45, 10:30am, 5:15pm; $20.) Buses also make stops in Cathy's Valley, Mariposa, Midpines, and El Portal. VIA also meets Amtrak trains from San Francisco arriving at the Merced train station. Tick-

SIERRA NEVADA

ets can be purchased from the driver. (☎384-1315. Buses throughout the day M-F 8am-5pm. Fares include Yosemite entry.) **Yosemite Gray Line (YGL)** also runs buses to and from Fresno/Yosemite International Airport, Fresno hotels, and Yosemite Valley ($20). A service called **YARTS** (☎877-989-2787 or 372-4487) provides four daily trips to Yosemite from Merced, making similar stops as VIA along the way, and sends one bus a day along Rtes. 120 and 395, hitting Mammoth and June Lakes, Lee Vining, and Tuolumne Meadows. ($20 round-trip from Merced, Mammoth and June Lakes, Lee Vining, Tuolumne Meadows; other fares less. Fares include Yosemite entry. Buses depart Merced bus station 7, 8:45, 10:30am, 5:25pm.) **Amtrak** runs a **bus** from Merced to Yosemite (4 per day, $10). Amtrak **trains** (☎800-USA-RAIL/872-7245) run to Merced from SF (3½hr., 5 per day, $22-29) and L.A. (5½hr, 4 per day, $28-51). The trains connect with the waiting YGL bus.

An excellent way to see both the essential sights and more remote spots is to take a trip with **Incredible Adventures,** 35 Brosnan St. #2, San Francisco 94110. Catering to young, spirited backpackers, the energetic, informative guides lead incredible hiking and sightseeing trips. (☎415-642-7378 or 800-777-8464; www.incadventures.com. 3-day/3-night trips depart from San Francisco June-Oct. W and Su; $200 including meals, entrance fee, equipment, transportation, and tax. 2-day trips $150. Daytrips run throughout the year; $93 with free hotel or hostel pick-up.) **Green Tortoise** sends its "hostels on wheels" from San Francisco on two- (Apr.-Sept.) and three-day (June-Oct.) tours of Yosemite (for details, see p. 54).

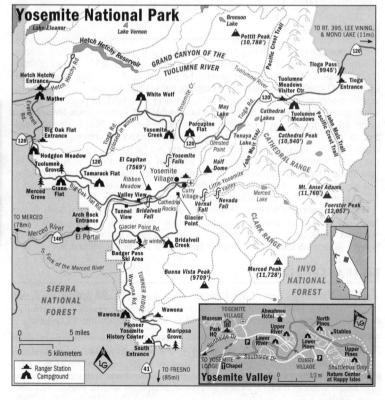

Yosemite National Park

The best bargain in Yosemite is the **free shuttle bus system,** which runs in Yosemite Valley, and, in summer, in between Wawona and Mariposa Grove, and Tioga Pass and Tenaya Lake. Comfortable but often crowded, the buses have knowledgeable drivers and wide viewing windows. (Daily every 10min. 7am-6pm, every 20min. 6-10pm.) **Hikers' buses** run daily to Glacier Point and to Tuolumne Meadows/Lee Vining. (☎372-1240. Late June-Labor Day, $20.50 round-trip.) To get to the shuttle, drive into the Valley and park near Curry and Yosemite Villages.

The closest airport to Yosemite is **Fresno International (FYI),** 4995 E. Clinton Way (☎559-621-4500), which is international only in that it has some flights coming in from Mexico. Most flights are from western cities, like L.A., San Francisco, and Las Vegas. Five national rental car agencies serve the airport and VIA runs buses from the terminal to the park.

BY CAR. As is usually true in the US, driving is the most convenient way to enter the park, though it's likely others know this as well, so expect traffic. Be sure to fill the tank before heading out, as there is no gas in Yosemite Valley (except for emergency gas at the Village Garage). There are overpriced 24hr. gas stations at Crane Flat, Tuolumne Meadows, and Wawona. Within the Valley, there is really no reason to drive, since the shuttle system is free and very convenient, and the bus drivers are quite knowledgeable about the area. Drivers intending to visit the high country in spring and fall should have snow tires (sometimes required even in summer). Of the five major approaches to the park, **Route 120** to the Big Oak Flat entrance is the curviest. A less nauseating alternative is Rte. 41 from Fresno into the valley, featuring the famous **Inspiration Point.** The eastern entrance, **Tioga Pass,** is closed during snow season but makes an awe-inspiring summer drive, with snow often lasting until July. (For info on winter driving, see **Wintertime in Yosemite,** p. 267.)

BY BICYCLE. Cycling into the park is permitted from any of the entry points, and will land you half-off the regular admission price. Cycling is also an excellent way to see Yosemite Valley. Many sights are within 2 mi. of the valley center, and the 12 mi. of valley trails are paved, smooth, and flat, allowing for excellent cycling tours. One popular bike trail is the wide, paved road from the valley campgrounds to Mirror Lake (3 mi. round-trip), which is closed to motorized vehicles. Yosemite's bike paths are ideal for leisurely rides and circumventing automobile traffic; serious cyclists should not expect a workout. Off-road mountain biking is not permitted in the park, though all paved roads are open to cyclists.

■ PRACTICAL INFORMATION

General Park Information (24hr. ☎372-0200; general info www.nps.gov/yose, visitor info www.yosemite.org). Info on weather, accommodations, and activities. All visitors centers have free maps and copies of *Yosemite Guide*. **All hours listed are valid late May-Sept. unless otherwise noted.**

Camp Reservations: ☎800-436-7225; www.reservations.nps.gov.

Yosemite Valley Visitors Center (☎372-0200), in Yosemite Village. Sign language interpreter in summer. Books, maps, exhibits, and the new *Spirit of Yosemite* orientation film. Open daily 8am-6pm.

WHEN TO GO. Yosemite's moderate climate makes it a comfortable destination year-round. Less snow means more tourists, however, and the park is generally overrun from June to Sept. Those seeking a quiet visit to this national wonder should consider going during the colder winter months.

BRAVING THE WILDERNESS
Camping & Hiking in California's Public Lands

A vast amount of land in California is public, available and accessible to everybody. For the budget traveler, this means cheap camping accommodations and hiking excursions in the glorious California backcountry. Here is an overview of California's public lands:

NATIONAL PARKS. Run by the federal government, national parks are designated to preserve and protect the land in its natural state. Regulations are strict—car camping is permitted only in designated sites, trail quotas are often in effect for overnight trips into the backcountry, and dogs are never permitted on the trail. National parks are the most expensive public lands to visit—entrance fees run $5-20 and campgrounds $15-20 per night. (www.nps.gov.) In California, **Yosemite National Park** is unlike anywhere else on Earth—don't miss it. The hike to do is the 17-mile round-trip to the summit of Half Dome. In **Sequoia/Kings Canyon,** avoid the masses in Giant Forest and discover the magnificent trees instead in lightly-traveled Redwood Canyon.

STATE PARKS. State parks are generally small, protect a wide variety of natural features, and are common along the coast. As with national parks, roads are good and regulations are strict—car camping is permitted only in designated campgrounds ($12-15), backcountry camping (when possible) is allowed only at designated trail camps (fees charged), and dogs are prohibited on park trails. Entrance fees ($3-5) are usually charged. All state park campgrounds operate on the same reservation system—call 1-800-444-PARK/7275 or online at www.reserveamerica.com. (www.parks.ca.gov.)

NATIONAL FORESTS. Run by the federal government (Department of Agriculture), national forests are managed by the U.S. Forest Service (USFS) for a variety of purposes—logging, ranching, hunting, and hiking are all permitted—and regulations are generally few. Primitive camping (free) is permitted virtually anywhere on national forest land away from main roads. Roads are generally poor, commonly unpaved, and often challenging and confusing to navigate. National forest maps ($6-10) are essential for navigation, and available primarily at USFS ranger stations (typical hours Mon.-Fri. 9am-430pm). The USFS also maintains numerous designated campgrounds. (www.fed.fs.us.)

NATIONAL FOREST WILDERNESS AREAS. Managed to protect the land's wild aspect, designated wilderness areas are much like national forests but with a few more restrictions. No roads exist, and all motorized vehicles are prohibited. Wilderness permits are required in all but the most remote areas and can be obtained free at any nearby ranger station. Due to heavy use, the wilderness areas in the Sierra Nevada are more heavily managed and trail quotas are often in effect. The USFS publishes wilderness-specific maps indicating trails and topography, available at local ranger stations.

OTHER AGENCIES. City and county parks are common in the San Francisco and Los Angeles areas, are almost all day-use only, and charge entrance fees ($3-6). The Bureau of Land Management (www.blm.gov) manages unforested public lands and have regulations similar to national forests. They are common throughout the desert region of Southern California.

Matt Heid was a Researcher-Writer for *Let's Go: Alaska and Western Canada 1993, Europe 1995,* and *New Zealand 1998.* He is the author of *101 Hikes in Northern California* and *Camping and Backpacking the San Francisco Bay Area,* both available from Wilderness Press.

Wilderness Center, P.O. Box 545, Yosemite National Park 95389 (☎372-0308; www.nps.gov/yose/wilderness), in Yosemite Village. Wilderness permit reservations up to 24 weeks in advance (☎372-0740, $5 per person per reservation, M-F 9am-4pm), or first-come, first-served (free). 40% of backcountry quota is held for first-come, first-camp on the day of. Staff cannot plan your trips, but have tons of info for those who are prepared. Bear canisters, maps, and guidebooks for sale. Open daily 8am-5pm.

Tuolumne Meadows Visitors Center (☎372-0263), on Tioga Pass Rd. 55 mi. from Yosemite Village. The high-country headquarters, with visitor services. Open in summer daily 9am-7pm; in spring and fall 9am-5pm; closed in winter. **Wilderness Center,** off Tioga Rd. on the road to Tuolumne Lodge, issues permits. Open daily 8am-5pm.

Big Oak Flat Info Station (☎379-1899), on Rte. 120 W. in Crane Flat. Open daily 9am-5pm. Wilderness permits available daily 8am-noon and 1-5pm.

Wawona Info Station (☎375-9501), on Rte. 41, 6 mi. from the southern entrance near the Mariposa Grove, on the Wawona Hotel grounds. Large selection of books. Open daily 8:30am-4:30pm. Wilderness permits issued.

LOCAL SERVICES

Auto Repairs: Village Garage, (☎372-8320) in the center of the village. Open daily 8am-5pm. Cars towed 24hr. Emergency gasoline available. AAA accepted.

Bike Rental: Yosemite Lodge (☎372-1208) and **Curry Village** (☎372-8319) for $5.25 per hr., $20 per day. Wheelchairs also available at both shops for $5 per hr., $20 per day. Driver's license or credit card required as security deposit. Both open daily 9am-6pm, weather permitting; open on a limited basis after Labor Day.

Equipment Rental: Yosemite Mountaineering School (☎372-8344 or 372-8436), on Rte. 120 at Tuolumne Meadows. Sleeping bags $10 per day, backpacks $8 per day; 3rd day half-price. Climbing shoes rented to YMS students only. Driver's license or credit card required for deposit. Rock climbing classes daily. Open daily 9am-5pm. For info on ski and snowshoe rental, see **Wintertime in Yosemite,** p. 267.

24-Hour ATM: Bank of America, in Yosemite Village. Bank also has a check-cashing service. Open daily 8am-4pm. Also ATMs in Village Store, Curry Village market, Wawona store, and in El Portal.

Gas Stations: There is no gas in Yosemite Valley. Tank up in **Crane Flat** (open daily 8am-8pm), El Portal, **Wawona** (9am-6pm), or **Tuolumne Meadows** (8:30am-5pm) before driving into the High Sierra—prices rise with the elevation. All 24hr. with credit card.

Laundromat: Laundry facilities open at **Housekeeping Camp.** Wash $1.25, 10min. dry $0.25. Open daily 8am-8pm. In winter, laundry facilities available at **Camp 6,** across the street from the Village Store. Open daily 7am-10pm.

Swimming Pools: At Yosemite Lodge and Curry Village. $2 per day; free for guests at the Ahwahnee Hotel, Yosemite Lodge, and Curry Village. Open daily 10am-6pm.

Showers: Housekeeping Camp $2, children $1.50, includes towel and soap. Open daily 24hr. **Curry Village** (free for guests). Open 24hr. Also at **Tuolumne Meadows** and **White Wolf Lodges** ($2). Open daily noon-3:30pm.

Weather and Road Conditions: ☎372-0200. Open 24hr.

EMERGENCY & COMMUNICATIONS

Medical Services: Yosemite Medical Clinic (☎372-4637), two blocks from the eastern end of Yosemite Village. 24hr. emergency room. Walk-in urgent care M-Sa 8am-7pm. Scheduled appointments M-F 8am-5pm, Sa 9am-noon. **Dental services** (☎372-4200 or 372-4637) available next to the Medical Clinic.

Internet Access: Yosemite Bug Hostel (☎966-6666), on Rte. 140, 30 mi. west of Yosemite in Midpines (see p. 262). Internet access $1 for 8min.

IN RECENT NEWS

A NEW FRAMEWORK

On December 28, 2001, environmentalists rejoiced as the object of eight years and $22 million in scientific research, political lobbying, and special interest wrangling—the Sierra Nevada Framework, a sweeping plan to severely restrict logging in 11.5 million acres of Sierra National Forest and—was given the go-ahead by the Bush administration's Under Secretary of Agriculture, Mark Rey. Parties involved in crafting the Clinton-era plan were concerned that Rey, a political conservative and former logging lobbyist, would mitigate or overturn the Sierra Framework in the interest of the region's logging industry. Just four days after having breathed a collective sigh of relief, however, many of the environmentalists' original suspicions were validated when the newly-appointed director of the Forest Service's Pacific Southwest region, Jack Blackwell, purportedly under Rey's direction, announced a "broad review" of the Sierra Framework, with special attention on the effects of the new restrictions on the logging industry, recreation, and cattle grazing.

The original Sierra Framework was a sweeping set of restrictions on commercial and recreational use of the region's 11 national forests, with the aim of restoring the health and diversity of the forest ecosystems. Over 50 years of logging had significantly diminished the health of the Sierra forests, with the most alarming impact on the "old-growth" forests made up of thick lodgepole pines and aspens. This has had a negative impact on species that make their home in the old-growth ecosystem,

Post Office: Yosemite Village, next to the Visitors Center. Open M-F 8:30am-5pm, Sa 10am-noon. Lobby open 24hr. **Curry Village,** near the registration office. Open Memorial Day-Labor Day M-F 11:30am-2:30pm. **Yosemite Lodge,** open M-Th 11:30am-2:45pm, F 11:30am-4:30pm. **Wawona,** open M-F 9am-5pm, Sa 9am-1pm. **Tuolumne Meadows,** open M-F 9am-5pm, Sa 9am-1pm. **Postal Code:** 95389.

📷 CAMPING

One of the first impressions of Yosemite during the summer will probably be of the endless "tent cities" in the Valley. Don't expect to get a spot without reservations, which have to be made well in advance for summer visits. (☎800-436-7275, TDD 888-530-9796, outside the US 301-722-1257; http://reservations.nps.gov. Reservations available by phone or website daily 7am-7pm or mail NPRS, P.O. Box 1600, Cumberland, MD 21502. Reservations available up to 5 months in advance.) Cancellation lotteries are held at the campground reservations office in Curry Village (daily 8am and 3pm), but the odds are against you. Camping is plentiful and usually easily available in the surrounding national forests; these are good alternatives if you can't get a spot in Yosemite. During the summer, there is a seven-night maximum stay for those in the Valley or at Wawona, and a 14-night maximum stay for campers outside the Valley (except Wawona). All drive-in campsites provide picnic tables, firepits or grills, a cleared tent space, parking, and a food storage area. Natural stream water (serving Tamarack Flat, Yosemite Creek, and Porcupine Flat) must be boiled, filtered, or treated to prevent giardia (an intestinal disease; see **Food- and Water-borne diseases,** p. 37). Iodine water treatments can be bought at any supply store. Backcountry camping is prohibited in the Valley but encouraged outside of it (see **Backcountry,** p. 268). Toilet facilities are everywhere, but only vault toilets are available at Tamarack Flat, Yosemite Creek, and Porcupine Flat. No RVs allowed in walk-in sites, and they're not advised in Tamarack Flat, Yosemite Creek, or Porcupine Flat. Dump stations are available in the Valley (all year) and Wawona and Tuolumne Meadows (summer only). Only Upper Pines and Sunnyside, in the Valley, and Wawona and Hodgon Meadow campgrounds are open year-round; the rest are open in the summer, usually June-September.

IN YOSEMITE VALLEY

All drive-in campsites require reservations, which should be made as far in advance as possible, up to five months prior to camping. **All Valley campgrounds completely fill every summer night.**

Sunnyside (also Camp 4), 4000 ft., at the western end of the Valley, past Yosemite Lodge. 35 sites fill up before 9am most mornings. Pervaded by a climbing culture with seasoned adventurers swapping stories of exploits on vertical rock faces. Be prepared to meet new friends, since every site is filled with 6 randomly assembled people. Water, flush toilets, and tables. First come, first camp. Limited parking. $5 per person. ❶

Lower Pines, 4000 ft., in the busy eastern end of Yosemite Valley. Commercial, crowded, and plagued by the noises of cars. Next to **North Pines** campsite (4000 ft., open Apr.-Sept., 81 sites) and the **Upper Pines** campsite (4000 ft., 238 sites). Water, toilets, tables, and showers. Open Mar.-Oct. Sites $18. All require reservations. ❷

BEYOND YOSEMITE VALLEY

Outside the Valley, campsite quality vastly improves.

▩ **Hodgdon Meadow,** 4900 ft., on Rte. 120 near Big Oak Flat Entrance, 25 mi. from Valley. Warm enough for winter camping. 105 thickly wooded sites provide some seclusion even when the campground is full. Water, toilets, and tables. Sites May-Sept. $18; Oct.-Apr. first-come, first-camp $12. ❷

Tuolumne Meadows, 8600 ft., on Rte. 120, 55 mi. east of the Valley. Drive into the sprawling campground or escape the RVs in the 25 sites saved for walk-in hikers. Ranger programs every night. Pets allowed in western section only. 152 sites require advance reservations, 152 saved for same-day reservations. Open July-Sept., depending on snowpack. Drive-in sites $18; backpacker sites $3 per person. ❶

Wawona, 4000 ft., off Rte. 41, 1 mi. outside Wawona. 93 open, unshaded sites near the South Fork of the Merced River. Water, flush toilets, and tables. Pets allowed. May-Sept. reservations required; Oct.-Apr. first-come, first-camp. Sites $18. ❷

Tamarack Flat, 6300 ft., 23 mi. northeast of the Valley. Take Rte. 120 east on Tioga Rd. and follow the rough road for 3 mi. (If your car can take it; not recommended for RVs and trailers.) 52 rustic drive-in sites. Fewer amenities, but campers can enjoy peace and quiet far from the crowds. First-come, first-camp. Open June-Sept. Sites $8. ❶

Bridalveil Creek, 7200 ft., 25 mi. south of the Valley on Glacier Point Rd. Peaceful grounds convenient to Glacier and Taft Points; 2 mi. walk to beautiful McGurk Meadow. 110 sites. First-come, first-camp. Open July-early Sept. Sites $12. ❶

Porcupine Flat, 8100 ft., 15 mi. from Tuolumne Meadows off Tioga Rd. The front section of the camp is accessible to RVs. First-come, first-camp. Open late July-Sept. 52 sites $8. ❶

like the endangered California spotted owl and Yosemite toad. Environmentalists also argue that the selective cutting of these large-diameter trees increases the risk of devastating forest fires, like those seen in Colorado and Arizona in 2002. Naturally fire-resistant because of their size, old growth forests provide a light-blocking canopy that keeps the forest floor from getting too dry, and also keeps highly-flammable smaller trees and shrubbery from proliferating. The framework was to set aside 40% of the forest land for old-growth development, banning all logging of trees over 12 in. in diameter. In most of the rest of the forest land, logging was to be banned on trees over 20 in. in diameter.

Opponents argue that without the ability to log large-diameter trees, California's logging industry will be crippled. Without economic incentive to thin out forests, the fire hazard would increase, adding injury to insult for already economically-devastated logging towns in the Sierra. In reality, proponents of the plan assert, logging only makes up 4% of the Sierra's employment, and the thinning of valuable thick-trunk trees does more harm than good in preventing massive forest fires. As the debate continues, the future of vast forests of the Sierra Nevada remains uncertain. It is certain, however, that the devastating, unprecedented fires that have raged through the country in the last several years are but the most immediately pressing evidence that the US's forestry policy is in need of a change.

White Wolf, 8000 ft., off Rte. 120 east, 31 mi. from the Valley. 8000 ft. up with lots of boulders to lounge on. Open late July-early Sept., depending on snow. 74 sites $12. ❶

Crane Flat, 6200 ft., centrally located on Big Oak Flat Road near the Tioga Pass turnoff. Surrounded by meadows and boulders, these 166 well-spaced sites tend to fill up later than other sites in the area. Open June-Sept. Reservations required. Sites $18. ❷

🛏 ACCOMMODATIONS

INSIDE THE PARK

When American Transcendentalist Ralph Waldo Emerson visited Yosemite in 1884, the park's accommodations were so simple that he was awakened in the morning by the clucking of a hen climbing over his bed. These days, Yosemite's accommodations have become much more comfortable, but at times you may feel as if you need to be a dignitary of Emerson's stature to get a room in the valley. Spring and summer rates are high (suites at the luxurious Ahwahnee Hotel start at $360 in season), and space is tight. Advance reservations are necessary and can be made up to one year in advance by calling ☎ 559-252-4848. Rates fluctuate, but tend to be higher on weekends and during the summer (those given below are for summer weekends). Check-in hovers around 11am. **All park lodgings provide access to dining and laundry facilities, showers, and supplies.**

🏅 Curry Village (☎ 252-4848), 2 mi. southeast of Yosemite Village. 627 accommodations, featuring pool (open 10am-6pm), nightly shows at the amphitheater, snack stands, cafeteria, and an ice rink from Nov.-Feb. Ranger programs nearly every night feature stories about the history of Yosemite. Standard motel room $112; cabin with bath $92, without bath $77; canvas tent cabin $54. ❹

Housekeeping Camp (☎ 372-8338), ¼ mi. west of Curry Village. Canvas-capped concrete "camping shelters" hold up to 4 people (6 with cots) and include 2 bunk beds, a double bed, a picnic table, a firepit with grill, lights, and outlets for $56. ❹

Tuolumne Meadows Lodge (☎ 372-8413), on Tioga Pass Rd., in the northeastern corner of park. In the high country, these rustic cabins are more tranquil than in the village, and offer easy access to the backcountry. Canvas-sided cabins, wood stoves, no electricity. Maid service $4. Cabins $59; additional adult $8.25, child $4. ❹

White Wolf Lodge (☎ 372-8416), on Tioga Pass Rd. in the western area of the park. Scenic and remote. Open late June to early Sept. Cabins with bath $88; tent cabin doubles $55; each additional person $8.25. ❹

Yosemite Lodge (☎ 372-1274), west of Yosemite Village and directly across from Yosemite Falls. Lodge rooms are spacious, with private patios and A/C. Lodge rooms $120-140; standard rooms $112; each additional person $11.50. ❺

OUTSIDE THE PARK

Lodging in the park may be convenient, but it's also expensive and hard to get, especially during the summer months. For the same price as a canvas cabin in the valley, you can find high-quality hotel accommodations in quiet and scenic areas. For more info on gateway towns and accommodations, access the **Yosemite Area Traveler Information (YATI)** web site (www.yosemite.com). YATI has computer terminals at the Yosemite Valley Visitors Center (see p. 257), the Greater Merced Chamber of Commerce (see p. 313), the Yosemite Sierra Visitors Bureau (see p. 257), and the Tuolumne County Visitors Bureau (see p. 259).

🏅 Yosemite Bug Hostel on Rte. 140 in Midpines (☎ 966-6666; www.yosemitebug.com), 25 mi. west of Yosemite. Look carefully for sign. A woodsy, spirited resort spot. International backpacking crowd lounges in hammocks. Beer on tap, kitchen, library, cafe with great food, glorious swimmin' hole with a waterfall. Offers outdoor expeditions in winter, mountain bike rental, and rafting trips. Discounts on public transportation (45min., $10 round-trip) to park. Internet access $1 for 8min. Dorm beds $16; tent sites $17; family and private rooms with shared bath $40-70; private rooms with bath $55-115. ❷

Evergreen Lodge, 33160 Evergreen Rd. (☎379-2606), 7 mi. off Rte. 120, 1 mi. before park entrance. Over 80 years old and near the quieter Hetch Hetchy region, these spacious cabins have porches, an outdoor patio and grill, and an on-site restaurant, bar, deli, and market. Standard cabins $79; family cabins $89; large family cabins $104. $10 extra during the busy season. ❹

Yosemite View Lodge on Rte. 140 (☎379-2681 or 888-742-4371; www.yosemite-motels.com), 2 mi. east of El Portal just outside the park. Descend from the mountains and loiter in luxury. Huge hotel squats on the banks of the Merced River. 3 pools, 6 jacuzzis, high-vaulted wood ceilings, kitchenettes in every room. Rooms $125-155. ❺

FOOD

The Yosemite Lodge and the Village Store (both open June-Sept. daily 8am-10pm; Oct.-May 8am-9pm), at Wawona (open daily 8am-8pm), Crane Flat (open daily 8am-8pm), El Portal (open daily 8am-8pm), and Tuolumne Meadows (open 9am-6pm) have slim supplies of pricey groceries. Consider buying all of your cooking supplies, marshmallows, and batteries in Merced or Fresno en route to the park.

IN YOSEMITE VALLEY

Yosemite's center of commerce is crammed with people at lunchtime. It may be more pleasant to carry your meal somewhere more peaceful.

Mountain Room Restaurant (☎372-9033), in Yosemite Lodge. Outstanding views of Yosemite Falls from nearly every seat in the restaurant. Great, filling portions of hearty American fare $20-30. Open daily 5:30-9pm, in winter weekends only. ❺

Ahwahnee Dining Room (☎372-1489). Linen tablecloths, 34 ft. high ceilings, chandeliers, and strictly enforced dress codes make this an option if the market is rising. Elegant and expensive American fare $30-50. Open M-F 7-10:30am,11:30am-3pm, 5:30-9pm; Su brunch 7am-3pm. Bar open 11am-11pm. Reservations recommended. ❻

Degnan's Delicatessen (☎372-8437), in Yosemite Village. Inside a convenience store and adjacent to an ice cream parlor/pizza place. Huge sandwiches and small veggie sandwiches $5.75. Now offering coffee-shop fare as well. Open daily 7am-5pm. ❷

Taqueria, in Curry Village next to the gift store and grocery store. Reheated, relabeled, and repriced Taco Bell fare. Tostada $4. Tacos $2.50. Open daily 11am-5pm. ❶

BEYOND YOSEMITE VALLEY

Other restaurants in the park are generally in the hotels. Check Yosemite's publications for smorgasbords and lunchtime bargains. Tuolumne Meadows and White Wolf Lodges both have moderately upscale dining facilities offering hearty, American-style food. Tuolumne Meadows also has a grill with lower priced but still filling food. Wawona has an expensive restaurant in its hotel and also a snack shop in the golf shop. Glacier Point has a snack shop. Call ☎372-1000 for current dining information. Cheaper, often better dining opportunities can be found just outside of the park. The **Yosemite View Restaurant ❸,** on Rte. 140 at the Yosemite View Lodge in El Portal, fancies itself fine dining. A gleaming wood building, it has a high wooden ceiling, a stone fireplace, and lots of tourists. Fuel up at its breakfast buffet for $10. (☎379-9307. Open daily 7-11am and 6-10pm.) Seven miles down the road at the **Cedar Lodge Restaurant ❸,** on Rte. 140 in El Portal, food is also available. (☎379-2316. Entrees $9-19. Open daily 7am-10pm; lounge serves until 1am.)

⚡ OUTDOOR ACTIVITIES

BY CAR OR BICYCLE. Although the view is better if you get out of the car, you can see a large portion of Yosemite from the bucket seat. The **Yosemite Road Guide** ($4 at every visitors center) is keyed to roadside markers and outlines a superb tour of the park—it's almost like having a ranger tied to the hood. Spectacular panoramas are omnipresent during the drive east along **Route 120 (Tioga Pass Road).** This stretch of road is the highest highway strip in the country; as it winds down from Tioga Pass through the park's eastern exit, it plunges nearly 1 mi. to reach the lunar landscape of Mono Lake. The drive west from the pass brings you past **Tuolumne Meadows** with its open spaces and rippling creeks, to shimmering Tenaya Lake. No less incredible are the views afforded by the southern approach to Yosemite, **Route 41.** Most recognizable is the Wawona Tunnel turnout (also known as **Inspiration Point**), which most visitors will immediately recognize as the subject of many Ansel Adams photographs. **El Capitan,** a gigantic granite monolith (7569 ft.), looms over awestruck crowds. If you stop and look closely (with binoculars if possible), you will see what appear to be specks of dust moving on the mountain face—they are actually world-class climbers inching toward fame. At night their flashlights shine from impromptu hammocks hung from the granite. Nearby, **Three Brothers** (three adjacent granite peaks) and misty **Bridalveil Falls** pose for hundreds of snapshots every day. A drive into the heart of the Valley leads to **Yosemite Falls** (the highest in North America at 2425 ft.), **Sentinel Rock,** and mighty **Half Dome.**

Glacier Point, off Glacier Point Rd., opens up a different perspective on the Valley. This gripping overlook, 3214 ft. above the valley floor, can stun even the most wilderness-weary traveler. Half Dome rests majestically across the Valley, while Nevada Falls looks deceptively peaceful from such a distance. When the moon is full, this is an extraordinary (and very popular) place to visit. Arrive at sunset and watch the fiery fade of day over the valley: the sky dims, the stars appear, the bottom sides of clouds in the east begin to glow bright silver, and from behind some nearby mountains the blinding full moon crosses the horizon.

To investigate Yosemite's most famous flora, take the short hiking trail through the giant sequoias of **Mariposa Grove.** This interpretive walk begins off Mariposa Grove Rd., at the Fallen Monarch, a massive trunk lying on its side, and continues to both the 209 ft. tall, 2700 year old Grizzly Giant and the fallen Wawona Tunnel Tree. Ancient Athens was at its height when many of these trees were saplings.

SUMMERTIME IN YOSEMITE

DAY HIKING IN THE VALLEY. To have the full Yosemite experience, visitors must travel the outer trails on foot. A wealth of opportunities rewards anyone willing to lace up a **pair of boots,** even if only for a daytrip. But these trails are well populated—at nearly any point in the day you may find yourself stuck behind groups of other tourists on trails. Hiking just after sunrise is the best—and sometimes the only—way to beat the crowds. But even then, trails like Half Dome are already busy. A colorful trail map with difficulty ratings and average hiking times is available at the Visitors Center ($0.50; see **Yosemite Valley Visitors Center,** p. 257). The **Mirror Lake Loop** is a level 3 mi. walk to Mirror Lake (0.5 mi.) and up Tenaya Creek and back. **Bridalveil Falls,** another Ansel Adams favorite, is an easy 0.25 mi. stroll from the nearby shuttle bus stop, and its cool spray is as close to a shower as many Yosemite campers ever get. This trail, as well as **Lower Yosemite Falls Trail,** is wheelchair accessible. The **Lower Yosemite Falls Trail** is a favorite of all ages and starts just opposite the Yosemite Lodge. On moonlit nights, mysterious moon-bows can sometimes be spotted here. **Upper Yosemite Falls Trail,** a back-breaking 3.5 mi. trek to the windy summit, rewards the intrepid hiker with an overview of the 2425 ft. drop. Those with energy to spare can trudge on to **Yosemite Point** or **Eagle Peak,** where views of the valley below rival those from more-heralded Glacier Point. The trail begins with an extremely steep, unshaded ascent. Leaving the marked trail is not a wise idea—a sign warns, "If you go over the waterfall, you will die."

From the Happy Isles trailhead, the **John Muir Trail** leads 211 mi. to Mt. Whitney, but most visitors prefer to take the slightly less strenuous 1.5 mi. **Mist Trail** past the base of **Vernal Falls** to the top of **Nevada Falls.** This is perhaps the most popular day-use trail in the park, and with good reason—views of the falls from the trails are outstanding, and the drizzle that issues from the nearby water-assaulted rocks is more than welcome during the hot summer months. Grab a shuttle from the Visitors Center. From Nevada Falls, the trail continues to the base of **Half Dome,** Yosemite's most recognizable monument and a powerful testament to the power of glaciation. Dedicated hikers trek to the top and enjoy the breathtaking vista of the Valley. The hike is 17 mi. round-trip, rises a total of 4800 vertical ft., and takes a full day (6-12hr.). Don't attempt this hike unless you are in top shape and have done strenuous hikes before. If you want to make it a two-day excursion, **camping** ❶ is available at Little Yosemite Valley, with a wilderness permit. The final 800 ft. of the walk is a steep climb up the east side of the famous rock face. Equipped with cables, this precarious final challenge is well worth the thrill of sitting on top of the world. Enthusiasts of all ages and global origins share high-fives with adrenaline-silly strangers and help each other out with cheers like "You're almost there!"

Although you'll have to share your achievement with the multitudes who drive to **Glacier Point,** the steep 5 mi. hike will earn you the right to truly savor the unbelievable views. The 3200 ft. ascent is grueling, making the snack bar at the top nearly irresistible. You can find the trailhead on Southside Dr., 1 mi. southwest of the village. The wildflower-laden **Pohono Trail** starts from Glacier Point, crossing Sentinel Creek (spectacular **Sentinel Falls,** the park's second-largest cascade, lies to the north) on its way to **Taft Point, Dewey Point,** and other secluded lookouts. A concession bus leaves from the valley in the morning for the **Four Mile Trail** (4.75 mi.) and the **Panorama Trail** (8 mi.), both of which also start at Glacier Point.

DAY HIKING OUTSIDE THE VALLEY. Tioga Rd. slices through the park, making its way into high country usually inaccessible to day hikers. From the west, the lush **White Wolf** trails, near the campground, are generally flat, and head to fishing and swimming at **Harden** (3 mi. northwest) and **Lukens Lakes** (1 mi. southeast, uphill). The 4 mi. hike down to **North Dome,** providing great views of Yosemite Valley and Half Dome, isn't too difficult, but the hike back up is more strenuous. The trailhead is 5 mi. past where Tioga Rd. crosses Yosemite Creek. At a turn off on your left about 8 mi. from the creek crossing, the hike to **Mt. Hoffmann** (10,850 ft.) is a moderate 3 mi. to the top of the geographic center of the park. Along the way, you'll pass gorgeous **May Lake.** Halfway between the turn-off for Mt. Hoffmann and Tenaya Lake is the pullout for **Olmstead Point,** a must-see vista of Tenaya Canyon, stretching out to Yosemite Valley, with views of the backside of Half Dome. Two miles farther east is **Tenaya Lake,** a large, clear alpine lake perfect for swimming.

The destination for most hikers on Tioga Rd. is **Tuolumne Meadows** (8600 ft.), a park village in the real high country. A huge number of greatly rewarding day hikes weave through the region. The 4 mi., 1000 ft. ascent hike to **Cathedral Lakes** will take you to a nice swimming spot with an incredible view of the unmistakable Cathedral Peak. **Elizabeth Lake** is a short, steep 2 mi. haul to another outstanding mountain lake, situated at the base of Unicorn Peak. The Visitors Center has info on the many hiking opportunities in the region. Visitors should try unfamiliar trails—scarcely a hike exists in Yosemite that doesn't give hikers jaw-dropping views and quiet moments of harmony. For a taste of "real" rock climbing without

SIERRA NEVADA

the requisite equipment and training, Yosemite day hikers and climbers clamber up **Lembert Dome** above Tuolumne Meadows. This gentle (by rock climbing standards) incline riddled with foot- and hand-holds is nonetheless a solid granite face.

For views rivaling those of the Valley—without the hordes of tourists—head to the much less visited **Hetch Hetchy Reservoir**. This sparkling valley provides up to 300 million gallons of water each year to San Francisco and other areas. Take Rte. 120 west to the Big Oak Flat Entrance, then turn right (1 mi.) on Evergreen Road. Continue for 16 mi. and park by the O'Shaughnessy Dam. The area boasts several idyllic day hikes, but backcountry access can be even more stunning. Permits are available one day before or the day of the hike at the Hetch Hetchy entrance, or make reservations for $5 per person (☎209-372-0740). The **Wapama Falls** trail (2.5 mi.) is a fairly easy hike with spectacular views at every turn. The trail continues to **Rancheria** (an additional 4 mi.), a popular place to camp. **Bring bear canisters—the bears here are more aggressive than in other backcountry locations.**

OTHER ACTIVITIES. The world's best **climbers** come to Yosemite to test themselves at angles past vertical. If you've got the courage, you can join the stellar rock climbers by taking a lesson with the **Yosemite Mountaineering School** (see p. 259). Basic rock climbing classes (mid-Apr. to Oct.) teach simple skills like bouldering, rappelling, and ascending an 80 ft. high cliff. Reservations are useful and require advance payment, although drop-ins are accepted. (☎372-8344. Open in Curry Village daily 8:30am-noon and 1-5pm; in Tuolumne Meadows daily 9am-5pm. Classes in Curry Village 8:30am; 3-6 people $70, individual courses $170. Intermediate lessons on weekends and alternating weekdays $80-90.) Guided **horseback rides** start at $46 per half-day. There are stables at: Yosemite Valley (☎372-8348; open Easter-Oct. daily 7:30am-5pm); Wawona (☎375-6502; open daily 7:30am-5pm); and Tuolumne Meadows. (☎372-8427. Open daily June-Sept. 7:30am-5pm.)

Fishing is allowed from April through November in any of Yosemite's lakes, streams, or rivers, but don't expect to catch anything. Anglers may obtain a fishing license from grocery or sporting goods stores in Yosemite Valley, Wawona, Tuolumne, or White Wolf. (Non-resident 10-day license $30, under 16 fish free. There are also 2 free fishing days per season. Consult the *Fishing in Yosemite National Park* handout for specific guidelines.) Tackle is available at the **Village Sport Shop**. (☎372-1286. Open daily 8:30am-6pm.) Those frustrated with Yosemite's fishing can **bird-watch** instead; the Visitors Center gives out field checklists.

Rafting is permitted on the Merced River (10am-4pm) when deemed safe, but no motorized crafts are allowed. Rafts can be rented at the Curry Village Recreation Center. For organized rafting trips, **All Outdoors**, 1250 Pine St. #103, Walnut Creek 94596 (☎925-932-8993 or 800-247-2387) leads trips on the north fork of Stanislaus River (leave from Calaveras Big Trees State Park), the Merced River (Mt. View Store, Midpines), the Kaweah River (Kaweah General Store), and Goodwin Canyon (Stanislaus River Park, Sonora). Most full-day trips cost $119 during the week and $144 on weekends. **Swimming** is allowed throughout the park except where posted. Those who prefer their water chlorinated can swim in the public pools at Curry Village and Yosemite Lodge. (Open daily 10am-6pm. $2 for non-guests.)

ORGANIZED ACTIVITIES. Open-air tram tours (☎372-1240) leave from Curry Village, the Ahwahnee Hotel, Yosemite Lodge, and the Village Store. Tickets are available at lodging facilities and the Village Store tour desk. The basic 2hr. **Valley Floor Tour** points out Half Dome, El Capitan, Bridalveil Falls, and Happy Isles. (Departs daily 10, 11am, 1, 2, 3pm. $17.50, seniors $15.75, ages 5-12 $9.50.) The 4hr. **Glacier Point Tour** climbs 3200 ft. to the point for a view of the valley 7300 ft. below. (Runs June-Oct. daily. Departs 8:30, 10am, 1:30pm from Yosemite Lodge. $20.50, ages 5-12 $11). The **Moonlight Tour,** on nights with a full (or nearly full) moon, offers unique nighttime views of the valley (2hr., $17.50).

Park rangers lead a variety of informative hikes and other activities for visitors of all ages. Daily **junior ranger** (ages 8-10) and **senior ranger** (ages 11-12) activities allow children to hike, raft, and explore aquatic and terrestrial life. (Free. Reservations required in advance through the Yosemite Valley Visitors Center, see p. 257.)

Rangers also guide a number of free walks. **Discover Yosemite Family Programs** address a variety of historical and geological topics. (3hr., daily 9am, most wheelchair accessible.) Rangers also lead strenuous, 4-8hr. **Destination Hikes** into the high country from Tuolumne Meadows. Other free, park-sponsored adventures include 1½hr. **photographic walks,** which are lesson-adventures led by professional photographers. (Sign up and meet at the Ansel Adams Gallery; seep. 268). **Sunrise photo walks** leave most mornings from the Yosemite Lodge tour desk (free). The **Glacier Point Sunset Photo Shoot** is offered Thursday nights from June to September. Bring lots of film; this is an incredible spot, especially at sunset. Late in the day the Valley rests in blues and purples. The workshop with a professional photographer is free, but the scenic tram ride up to the point is not. (Departs 1hr. before the meeting time and returns 4hr. later; $20.50.) However, you can drive yourself and meet the group at the Glacier Point Amphitheater.

WINTERTIME IN YOSEMITE

The cold dramatically transforms Yosemite's landscape in its quietest season, as the waterfalls turn to ice and snow masks the meadows. The Sierra are known for heavy winter snowfall; Yosemite is no exception. But, unlike much of the range, Yosemite Valley remains accessible year-round. **Route 140** from Merced, a designated all-weather entrance, is usually open and clear. Although Tioga Pass and Glacier Point Rd. invariably close at the first sign of snowfall, **Route 41** from the south and **Route 120** from the west typically remain traversable. Verify road conditions before traveling (☎372-0200), and carry chains. Many valley facilities remain open even during the harshest winters. Camping is generally permitted in Lower Pines, Sunnyside (Camp 4), Hodgdon Meadow, and Wawona; most indoor accommodations offer big reductions. Park tours move "indoors" to heated buses; even the Merced and Fresno buses (see **Transportation,**p. 255) operate road conditions permitting. Many say this is the best time to find peace amid Yosemite's treasures.

Cross-country skiing is free, and several well-marked trails cut into the backcountry of the valley's South Rim at Badger Pass and Crane Flat. Both areas have markers on the trees so trails can be followed even under several feet of snow; this same snow transforms many summer hiking trails into increasingly popular **snowshoe trails.** Rangers host several snowshoe walks, but the serene winter forests are perhaps best explored without guidance. Snowshoes and cross-country skis can be rented from the **Yosemite Mountaineering School** (seep. 259). **Badger Pass Rental Shop** (see below) also rents winter equipment and downhill skis. Backcountry skiers can stay at one of the two **ski huts,** Ostrander Ski Hut, 9 mi. south of Badger Pass, and Glacier Point Hut, at the end of Glacier Point Rd. Both provide heated accommodations and meals, and require reservations (☎327-8444).

The state's oldest ski resort, **Badger Pass Ski Area,** on Glacier Point Rd. south of Yosemite Valley, is the only downhill ski area in the park. The resort's powder may not rival Tahoe's, but its family-fun atmosphere fosters learning. Free shuttles connect Badger Pass with Yosemite Valley. (☎372-8430. Lifts open 9am-4:30pm. Group ski lessons $22 for 2hr., private lessons from $44. Rental packages $18 per day, under 12 $13. One-day lift tickets M-F $22, Sa-Su $28, under 12 daily $13.)

Ice skating at Curry Village is a beautiful (if cold) experience, with Half Dome towering above an outdoor rink encircled by snow-covered pines. (Open in winter M-F noon-9:30pm, Sa-Su 8:30am-9:30pm. $5; skate rental $2.) **Sledding** and **tobogganing** are permitted at Crane Flat, off Rte. 120.

SIERRA NEVADA

THE NATURALIST When **John Muir** was 29, a piece of metal struck his eye in the industrial shop where he worked as an inventor. The accident left Muir blind, and the month that he struggled with his condition became a time of profound personal epiphany. Muir's blindness left him with an expanded sense of vision; he vowed that if he ever recovered his sight, he would use it to observe nature's beauty. And recover he did. In subsequent years, Muir later claimed, "I wandered afoot and alone" with no concern as "to which one of the world's wildernesses I first should" come upon. In 1868, Muir's travels led to Yosemite, and he formed a life-long devotion to the Valley. Partly because of his advocacy, Congress created Yosemite National Park in 1890. Years later, Muir's writing caught the eye of President Theodore Roosevelt, who visited the naturalist in Yosemite. Often called the "Father of our National Park System," Muir was one of the nation's first and most influential conservationists.

BEYOND YOSEMITE VALLEY: THE BACKCOUNTRY

Most folks never leave the Valley, but a wilder, more isolated Yosemite awaits those who do. The Wilderness Center in Yosemite Valley offers maps and person-alized assistance for those who choose to leave the Valley. (For advice on keeping yourself and the wilderness intact, see **Essentials: Wilderness Safety,**p. 46.) Topo-graphical maps and hiking guides are especially helpful in navigating Yosemite's nether regions. Equipment can be rented or purchased at the Mountaineering School at Tuolumne Meadows (see p. 259) or at the Mountain Shop at Curry Vil-lage, but backpacking stores in major cities are less expensive.

Backcountry camping is prohibited in the Valley (those caught face a $60 fine and park eviction), but is generally permitted along the high country trails with a free wilderness permit (see p. 259); each trailhead limits the number of permits available. For an alternative to backcountry camping, the wildly popular **High Sierra Camps** allow multi-day hikers to sleep on mattresses, eat real food, and take showers (see Camping, above). There is a 40% quota held on 24hr. notice at the Yosemite Valley Visitors Center, the Wawona Ranger Station, and Big Oak Flat Sta-tion (see **Visitor Information,**p. 257). Popular trails like Little Yosemite Valley, Clouds Rest, and Half Dome fill quickly. (Permits free; reservations $3. Call ☎372-0740 or write Wilderness Permits, P.O. Box 545, Yosemite National Park 95389.)

In the high country, many hikers stay at undeveloped mountain campgrounds, which offer a few bear lockers and company. Hikers can also store food in hanging bear bags (see **Bears Will Eat You,**p. 45) or in rented plastic canisters from the Yosemite Valley Sports Shop ($5 per day). Canisters are highly recommended and mandatory in some areas—bear-bagging is considered mainly a delay tactic.

With over 800 mi. of trails, backcountry hiking opportunities are virtually limit-less. Many of the most popular trails start from Happy Isles Nature Center, in the Valley, and Tuolumne Meadows. Heading off from the Nature Center is the extraordinary 211 mi. **John Muir Trail,** which connects with the Pacific Crest Trail at Tuolumne Meadows, then heads south to the summit of Mt. Whitney in Kings Can-yon and Sequoia National Park, the highest peak in the lower 48 states. Making a go at any portion of this trail, including the 27 mi. journey to Tuolumne Meadows from the Valley, makes for an unforgettable experience. The entire trail takes any-where from three weeks to a few months.

👁 🎵 SIGHTS & ENTERTAINMENT

There are ranger-led activities, ranging from nature walks to historical presenta-tions to star-gazing, every day of the week at nearly every park village. Almost all of the activities are free. Pick up a copy of *Yosemite Today* or check local bulletin boards and ranger stations for schedules and information.

The **Ansel Adams Gallery,** next to the Visitors Center, is an artsy gift shop/activity center featuring work by the famous wilderness photographer. Sign up for a fine-print viewing to see the precious stuff—most likely you'll be shown around with a group of people, but occasionally the staff will give private showings. The gallery offers free camera walks three times a week leaving at 9am from the village. (☎372-4413; www.anseladams.com. Open daily 9am-6pm.) The **Art Activity Center,** in Yosemite Village, takes pride in its artist-in-residence program and offers an art instruction class. Classes offer different types of art, from watercolor to sketching to acrylic. (☎372-1442. Open daily 10am-5pm. Class offered daily 10am-2pm. Advance signup recommended. Supplies are not included, but are for sale.)

Just behind the gallery, Native American cultural events take place in the **Miwok-Paiute Village.** The village is a melange of Native American sweatlodges, round-houses, *umachas* (homes), placards describing indigenous fauna, and a diorama that recycles hokey narration when you press the red button. The large *Hangie* (roundhouse) is a humbling piece of construction that still serves as a cultural center for local Miwok and Paiute Indians (village open dusk to dawn). Further interpretive information can be garnered at the **Yosemite Village Museum,** next to the Visitors Center. Inside is a reconstruction of one moment in Ahwahnee village life, Indian craft demonstrations, and a display of the park's enormous art collection, including some restaurant-bathroom-style pieces of Yosemite-related subject matter. (Open daily 10am-noon, 1-4pm.) Pick up the guide at the Visitors Center and tour the resting places of Native Americans and Anglos who played important roles in forming the park at the **Yosemite Cemetery,** across from the museum.

In 1903, John Muir gave President Theodore Roosevelt a now-famous tour of Yosemite. The renowned thespian Lee Stetson has assumed Muir's role, leading 1hr. hikes along the same route (free). Stetson also presents **The Spirit of John Muir,** a one-man show (90min.; W and F 8pm; $7, seniors $6, under 12 $3) and **Conversation with a Tramp** (Tu, Th, and Sa 8pm; $7, seniors $6, under 12 $2). Stetson has recently begun a new show reenacting the encounter between Muir and Roosevelt entitled **The Tramp and the Roughrider.** There are six different theatrical presentations, which change from year to year. (M-F 8pm; $6, seniors $5, under 12 $3.)

STANISLAUS NATIONAL FOREST ☎209

Once overrun with gold prospectors, Stanislaus has since quieted down, to the point where it is one of the more untroubled regions in the Sierra, especially compared to its southeastern neighbor, Yosemite. Preserving nearly 900,000 acres of central Sierra forest, including nearly 200,000 acres of untrammeled wilderness, over 7000 campsites, 811 miles of rivers and streams, 480 mi. of trails, innumerable crystalline lakes, and vast stretches of pine, Stanislaus is brimming with undisturbed recreational opportunities. The park is organized into four ranger districts, Calaveras, Groveland, Mi-Wok, and Summit, and also encompasses parts of the Carson-Iceberg, Emigrant, and Mokelumne federal wilderness areas.

Maps, brochures, permits, and advice can be found at **Park Headquarters,** 19777 Greenly Rd., across from the county library, in Sonora. (☎532-3671; www.r5.fs.fed.us/stanislaus. Open M-F 8am-5pm; in winter M-F 8am-4:30pm.) Permits are required for overnight trips into the wilderness areas and for building campfires outside of developed campsites in the rest of the forest. Distributed camping is permitted throughout most of the national forest, and requires no permit or fee. The exception is in many recreation areas, like Pinecrest and Alpine Lake, and in wilderness areas, where a permit is required. Of the developed campsites, only Pinecrest and Pioneer Trails (a group site) accept reservations; other sites are available on a first-come, first-camp basis.

SUMMIT DISTRICT. Encompassing a large section of the Emigrant Wilderness, the family-friendly Pinecrest Recreation Area, a number of glacial lakes, and subalpine meadows, the Summit Ranger District serves as both an entry point into the backcountry and a venue for less-remote fishing, camping, biking, and nordic skiing. The **ranger station,** 1 Pinecrest Lake Rd., off Rte. 108 at Pinecrest Lake, has info on all the camping and recreational activities in the area. (☎965-3434. Open daily 8am-5pm; in winter M-Sa 8am-4:30pm.) The district hosts 21 campgrounds, most at 6000-7000 ft. elevations. Campsites abound to the east along Rte. 108. **Cascade Creek ❶,** 6000 ft., 11 mi. from Pinecrest, and **Niagara Creek ❶,** 6600 ft., 16 mi. from Pinecrest on Eagle Meadow Rd., both have beautiful, forested sites (12 and 10 sites respectively, $5) with fire rings and vault toilets, but neither have running water. **Pinecrest ❷,** the largest campsite in the district, is right next to the Pinecrest Recreation Area, offering swimming, fishing, boating, and hiking opportunities. The 200 campsites have drinking water and flush toilets. (Reservations ☎800-280-2267, TDD 800-879-4496. Open May-Oct. Sites $19.) The only free campground is **Beardsley Dam ❶,** 3400 ft., which is right on the Beardsley Reservoir, just off Beardsley Rd., and has 26 sites. **Herring Creek ❶,** 7350 ft., with seven sites, and **Herring Reservoir ❷,** 7350 ft., with 42 sites, both on Herring Creek Rd. off Rte. 108, are on the donation system, however, so pick your price. All sites are open May- Oct.

Pinecrest Lake, about 30 mi. east of Sonora on Rte. 108, is popular with families. The alpine lake, set amidst granite mountains and pine trees, serves as a small resort area, offering a swimming area, fishing pier (and rainbow trout stocking), picnic sites, and a 4 mi. hiking trail around the lake. **Boat rentals** are available at the marina. (Kayaks $6 per hr., sailboats $22 for 2hr., paddleboats $9 per hr. Motorboats $25 for 2hr. Party boats $175 per day.) Every June, the lake hosts a **fishing celebration** (☎532-3671) that includes a fishing and casting contest and a free lunch (yes, there is such a thing, but it's hot dogs, not fish).

Route 108 is a 60 mi. drive northeast through the forest, starting in Sonora and ending at the Sonora Pass on the border of the Toiyabe National Forest. The drive itself is quite scenic and rich in history. Pick up an audio cassette tour at the ranger station to play in your car as you make the trip. There are several easy, enjoyable **self-guided trails** available at the Sonora ranger station (but beware: the numbered stakes that dot the trails are confusing). The trail names are generally more fantastic than the events they describe. The **Trail of the Gargoyles,** a 3 mi. round-trip hike east of the station off Rte. 108 on Herring Creek Rd., is lined with shapely geological formations, documenting nature's labor in lava flows, lahar (hardened mud), and ash. The **Trail of the Ancient Dwarfs,** a 2½ mi. loop on Herring Creek Rd, off Rte. 108, 15 mi. east of Pinecrest, provides great views of the mountain range as it follows a line of natural bonsai trees. Most of the more challenging hikes require some prolonged time in the wilderness. Many backcountry hikes into the Emigrant and Carson-Iceberg Wildernesses start along Rte. 108; obtain a wilderness permit, topographical maps, and more information at the ranger station. For stunning views of the **Stanislaus River** and its dammed reservoir, take Rte. 108 18 mi. east of Pinecrest to **Donnell Vista.** The popular and excellent **Gooseberry-Crabtree Trail** is a 15 mi. gravel and dirt road **mountain biking** loop that makes a difficult 2000 ft. ascent but rewards the tenacious biker with awesome vistas.

CARSON-ICEBERG WILDERNESS. Bordered to the north by Rte. 108, to the south by Rte. 4, and to the east by Rte. 395, Carson-Iceberg is 160,000 acres of volcanic peaks, granite canyons, sinuous creeks, and solitude. While the high elevations, steep terrain, and scarcity of lakes eliminate this region from most itineraries, adventurous travelers are rewarded with unspoiled wilderness terrain—all to themselves. Most visitor activity is concentrated near the region's lakes, including **Highland Lakes,** on Highland Lakes Rd. off Rte. 4, the **Lake Alpine,** on Rte. 4, and the nearby **Silver Valley trailhead,** which leads into several small adjoining lakes, and

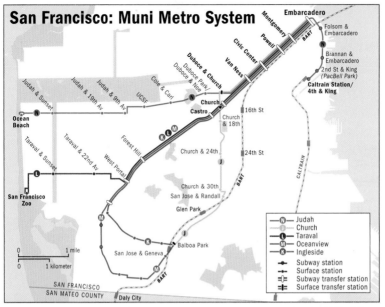

San Francisco: Muni Metro System

Judah & Sunset
Judah & 9th Av
Judah & 19th Av
UCSF
Cole & Carl
Duboce & Church
Duboce Park
Duboce & Noe
Van Ness
Civic Center
Powell
Montgomery
Embarcadero
Folsom & Embarcadero
Brannan & Embarcadero
2nd St & King (PacBell Park)
Caltrain Station/ 4th & King

Ocean Beach
Church
Castro
16th St
Church & 18th

Taraval & Sunset
Taraval & 22nd Av
West Portal
Forest Hill
Church & 24th
24th St

San Francisco Zoo
Church & 30th
San Jose & Randall
Glen Park

San Jose & Geneva
Balboa Park

SAN FRANCISCO
SAN MATEO COUNTY
Daly City

0   1 mile
0   1 kilometer

N — Judah
Church
L — Taraval
M — Oceanview
K — Ingleside
Subway station
Surface station
Subway transfer station
Surface transfer station

CALTRAIN
BART

San Francisco: BART System

Pittsburg/ Bay Point
Concord

CONTRA COSTA COUNTY

Richmond
El Cerrito del Norte
El Cerrito Plaza
North Berkeley
Berkeley
Ashby
MacArthur
19th St/Oakland
Oakland City
West Oakland
Lake Merritt

Pleasant Hill
Walnut Creek
Lafayette
Orinda

MARIN COUNTY

San Francisco Bay

Embarcadero
Montgomery St
Powell St
Civic Center
16th St/Mission
24th St/Mission
Glen Park
Balboa Park
Daly City
Colma
S San Francisco
San Bruno

SAN FRANCISCO

Caltrain

Fruitvale
Coliseum/ Oakland Airport
Oakland International Airport
San Leandro
Bay Fair
Castro Valley
Hayward
South Hayward
Union City
Fremont

Dublin/ Pleasanton

ALAMEDA COUNTY

San Francisco Bay

San Francisco International Airport

Millbrae

SAN MATEO COUNTY

Richmond-Daly City/Colma
Pittsburg/Bay Point-Daly City/Colma
Fremont-Daly City
Fremont-Richmond
Dublin/Pleasanton-Daly City
New Airport Extension   CalTrain

0   4 miles
0   4 kilometers

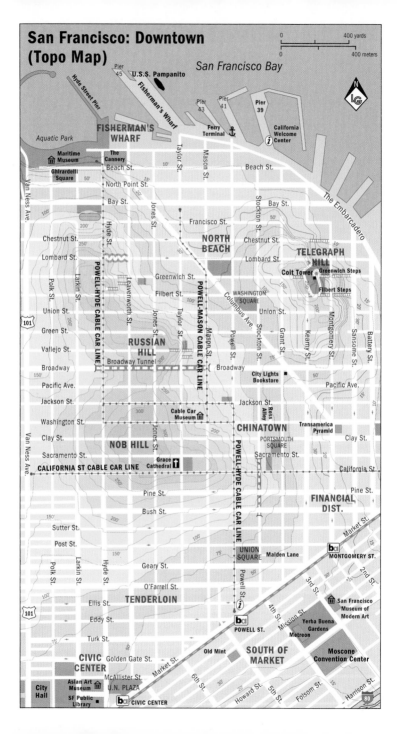

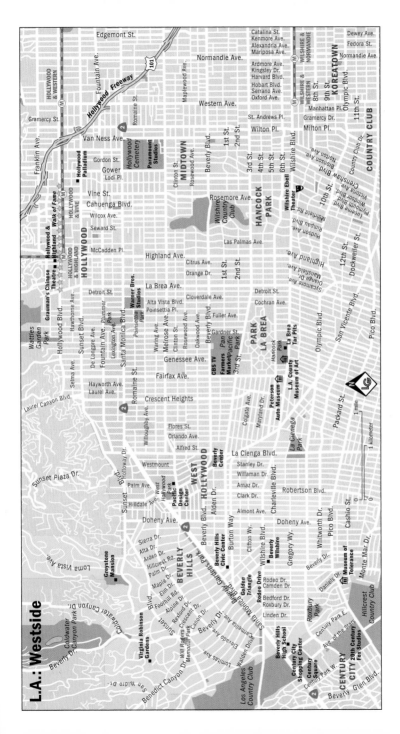

L.A.: Westside

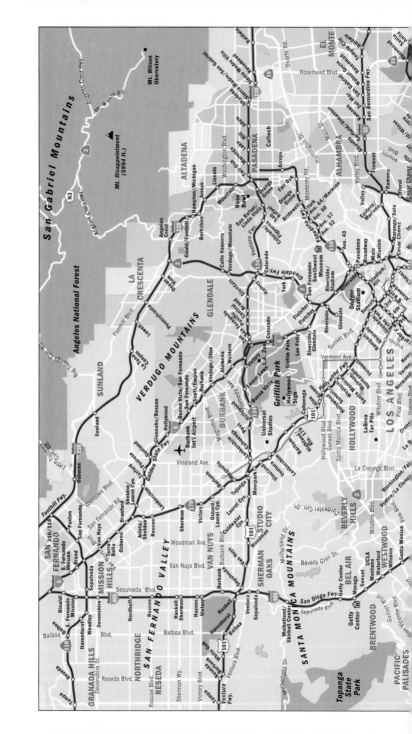

Metropolitan
Los Angeles

- Metro Green Line
- Metro Blue Line
- Metro Red Line

0 — 2 miles
0 — 2 kilometers

Pacific Ocean

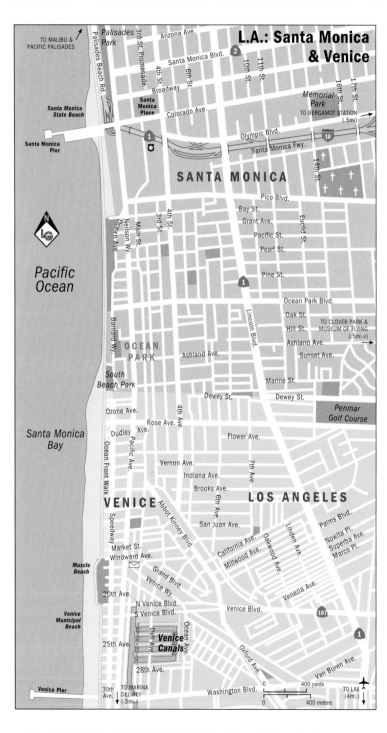

Mosquito Lakes, 8 mi. east of Lake Alpine. One hundred ninety-five miles of back-country hiking extends from trailheads along Rte. 108 and Rte. 4. Stanislaus Peak and Sonora Peak are accessible from the Pacific Crest Trail (for more info, see **From Crest to Crest: the Trail of the West,** p. 242), and give persevering climbers a humbling panorama of the Sierra. The Pacific Coast Trail includes a 5 mi. round-trip cross-country scramble from **Saint Mary's Pass,** 1 mi. before **Sonora Pass** on Rte. 108. It has a great view of the Central Valley, but the 3000 ft. climb is tiring. All mechanized vehicles, including bicycles, are prohibited in the wilderness.

CALAVERAS DISTRICT. In the northwest corner of the forest, the Calaveras Ranger District is blessed with some quieter lakes, easy to intense high elevation hikes, the best rock climbing around, and the raging North Fork Stanislaus River. The **ranger station,** 5341 Rte. 4, at Hathaway Pines, contains the Dardanelles, a series of volcanic by-products. (☎795-1381. Open M-F 8am-5pm, Sa 8:30am-2pm; in winter M-F 8am-4:30pm, Sa 9am-1pm.) **Wa Ku Luu Hep Yoo Campground ❶,** on Boardscrossing-Sourgrass Rd. off Rte. 4 in Dorrington, is shady and cool and has water, flush toilets, and hot showers. The camp is on the site of an ancient Miwok village and features a number of preserved artifacts. (Open June-Oct. 49 sites $13.) **Rock climbing** can be found at Box Canyon, on Rte. 4; over 250 mi. of day and extended hikes branch off from Rte. 4 and the popular district lakes.

GROVELAND DISTRICT. Covering the area south of Sonora and west of Yosemite, Groveland District is best known for its run of the Tuolumne Wild and Scenic River and its lakeside recreation. The **Ranger Station,** 24545 Rte. 120, is 9 mi. west of Groveland. (☎962-7825. Open M-Sa 8am-5:30pm, Su 8am-4:30pm; in winter 8am-4:30pm; Apr.-May closed Sa.) **The Pines ❶,** 3200 ft., 9 mi. west of Groveland on Rte. 120, is the closest campground to the entrance. The 12 sites have piped water and vault toilets. (Open year-round. Sites $10.) **Cherry Lake Campground ❶,** 4700 ft., 20 mi. down Cherry Lake Rd. off Rte. 4, has 46 sites, water, and access to boating and fishing on Cherry Lake. (Open Apr.-Oct. Sites $12.) **Cherry Creek Canyon,** a bit scarred from a fire, is north of Cherry Lake just west of Yosemite. The glacier-carved canyon has space for hikers. A bridge crossing the South Fork Tuolumne on Rte. 120 marks the site of the popular swimming **Rainbow Pool,** once a resort until it burned down in the 1950s. Short hikes criss-cross the area, but the only extended hikes are in the Emigrant Wilderness. A trailhead at **Eagle Meadow** leads down to Coopers Meadow and **Three Chimneys,** a brick-red volcanic formation.

SIERRA NATIONAL FOREST ☎209

Breathtaking landscape, spanning from the foothills of the San Joaquin Valley to the cold peaks of the High Sierras, and a favorable backpacker-to-fannypacker ratio characterize the 1.3 million acres of the Sierra National Forest. Nearly half of the forest is federally-designated wilderness, offering near complete solitude, while the region's rivers and lakes serve as recreational centers, primarily for fishing enthusiasts. Information on these centers, popular spots, and the 60 campgrounds in the forest can be obtained at the **Sierra National Forest Supervisor's Office,** 1600 Tollhouse Rd., off Rte. 168 just outside the gateway town of Clovis. (☎297-0706. Open M-F 8am-4:30pm.)

A **backcountry permit** is required for all of the designated wilderness areas (Ansel Adams, Dinkey Lakes, John Muir, Kaiser, and Monarch), which constitute 46% of the forest. Obtain permits for the Ansel Wilderness by writing the Mariposa/Minarets District and permits for the John Muir and Kaiser Wilderness areas by writing the Pineridge/Kings River Ranger District (for addresses, see below). Trailhead quotas are in effect from July to Labor Day. Forty percent of the permits are offered daily first-come, first-served, but quotas fill quickly. It is also possible to write away for an advance reservation ($5 per person).

NORTHWESTERN MARIPOSA DISTRICT. Information on the northwestern Mariposa District can be obtained by calling or writing the **Mariposa/Minarets Ranger District Office,** 57003 Rd. 225, North Fork, P.O. Box 10 93643. (☎ 877-2218. Open M-F 8am-4:30pm.) In summer, parched San Joaquin Valley residents throng **Bass Lake,** taking advantage of fishing, boating, and waterskiing opportunities. Fishing is definitely the main draw, however: the lake is stocked with salmon, catfish, trout, crappie, bluegill, and, surprisingly enough, bass. **Lupine** and **Cedar Campgrounds ❷** are open year-round for strong-willed ice fishers or wintertime Yosemite patrons. (Sites $16.) Some of the best **hikes** in the Sierra are also nearby. **Nelder Grove,** off Sky Ranch Rd. from Rte. 41, contains a campground (once used for thousands of years by the Southern Sierra Miwuk Indians) and a 1 mi. trail through 106 seldom-visited sequoia. Another trail affords the rare opportunity to see the Bull Buck Tree, a 246 ft. giant, without the gaping tourists who crowd to such natural monuments in other parts. The lonely **Willow Creek Trail,** which passes both Angel Falls and the aptly named **Devil's Slide Waterfall** en route to McLeod Flat Rd., and the meandering Mono Trail are other options. (Take Rte. 41 to the Bass Lake turn-off and follow Rd. 222 about 4 mi. to the parking lot at the trailhead.) **Forks ❷** is a pleasant campground, right by the lake, with flush toilets. (Sites $16.)

KINGS RIVER DISTRICT. The far reaches of the Kings River District rise to 13,000 ft. at the Sierra Crest. Most of the region's activity centers around the Dinkey Creek area and the Pine Flat Reservoir. The **Kings River Trail,** beginning at the end of Garnet Dike Rd. on the north side of Kings River, is the most popular in the area, passing tranquil wilderness. The 269 ft. **Boole Tree,** at the end of Converse Basin Rd., 5 mi. past Grant Grove off Rte. 180, is the largest giant sequoia outside of the national parks system. Four free **camping** sites, located along Kings River, are open during the summer. **Whitewater rafting** on the Kings River is popular, especially in spring. **Kings River Expeditions** offers a variety of guided trips; get a group together to reduce costs. (☎ 233-4881. Open M-F 8am-5pm.) Trail bikes and 4WD vehicles raise dust on five off-highway routes that provide access to camping and fishing.

PINERIDGE DISTRICT. Easily accessible from Rte. 168, the Pineridge District is the forest's most popular region due to its wealth of opportunities for swimming, boating, biking, rafting, fishing, hiking, and camping. **Camp Edison ❷** is one centrally located, private campground that has its own marina, tree and trout farm, and lake access. There are 252 sites with electric hookup, flush toilets, showers, tables, and fire pits. (☎ 841-3134. Sites from $20.) The **Pineridge/Kings River Ranger District Office,** 29688 Auberry Rd., P.O. Box 559, Prather 93651, is one of the forest's busiest centers. The office gives weekly ranger talks and guided hikes followed by marshmallow roasts—call for details. (☎ 855-5355. Open daily 8am-4:30pm.)

HUNTINGTON LAKE. Just one reservoir in the Big Creek Hydroelectric system developed by Southern California Edison, Huntington Lake, 21 mi. farther east along Rte. 168, is known for its excellent boating and summertime regattas, windsurfing, waterskiing, and fishing (yes, the water is the main attraction). The best hiking from the lake ventures into the Kaiser and Dinkey Lakes Wilderness Areas, for day and overnight trips. Seven campgrounds cluster around the lake; register at the **Eastwood Visitor Center,** at the junction of Rte. 168 and Kaiser Pass Rd. Past Kaiser Pass, the road becomes narrow and slightly treacherous—honk your horn on the sharp, blind turns. The terrain at the end of this road is definitively High Sierra—alpine lakes, flowers, and craggy summits. Mountain bikers enjoy dozens of trails, from the leisurely Tamarack Trail to the 66 mi. Dusy/Ershin Rd.

SIERRA NEVADA

SEQUOIA NATIONAL FOREST ☎ 559

The Sequoia National Forest is on the southern end of the majestic Sierra Nevada range, which continues its southward march 60 mi. below the park boundary before petering out in the Mojave Desert. It is bounded on the north by the Kings River, on the west by the San Joaquin Valley, on the east by the Owens Valley, and on the south by Telephone Ridge. The Kern River slices through its southeast region. The forest is best known for its 38 groves of towering giant sequoia trees, and for the Hume Lake Dam, the first multiple arch concrete dam built in the US.

The **forest headquarters,** 900 W. Grand Ave., Porterville, on Rte. 65 in Porterville, has detailed maps of the forest ($4.30) featuring the national forest's six designated wilderness areas. There is a park fee to enter the northern forest. (☎784-1500. Open M-F 8am-4:30pm.) Backcountry excursions to the **Golden Trout Wilderness** require wilderness permits, available at the Tule River district ranger's office. The **Hume Lake Ranger District Office,** 35860 E. Kings Canyon Rd., on Rte. 180 in Dunlap, 32 mi. east of Fresno near the forest entrance, provides camping info. (☎338-2251. Open Memorial Day-Labor Day M-Sa 8am-4:30pm; Labor Day-Memorial Day M-F 8am-4:30pm.)

Camping in the forest is abundant, quiet, and occasionally free. In the Hume Lake District, **Big Meadow ❶** (7600 ft.), 13 mi. southeast of Grant Grove on Big Meadow Rd. from Generals Highway, has 25 sites suitable for tents and trailers for no charge, though there's no water available. More popular sites in the area include **Stony Creek ❷** and **Upper Stony Creek ❶** (6400 ft.), both 14 mi. southeast of Grant Grove on Generals Highway. Both can be reserved in advance, though many sites are first-come first-served. (☎877-444-6777. Stony Creek sites $16, Upper Stony Creek $12.) Like the name implies, **Quaking Aspen ❶** (7000 ft.) campground, in the Tule River/Hot Springs District, is surrounded by beautiful quaking aspen. (Water, toilets, hiking, and fishing. Sites $14.)

Kern River Outfitters runs two-day **whitewater rafting trips** on the Lower Kern for about $300 per person, day and half-day trips on the Upper Kern for $100-150, and serious three-day trips on the North Fork Kern, Class V rapids and all, for $750-800. (☎800-323-4234; www.kernrafting.com.) Whitewater Voyages gives kayaking instruction and also has Kern and Kings River rafting trips. (☎800-488-7238; www.whitewatervoyages.com. 2-4 day kayaking courses $250-500; rafting $100-200 per day.) The northern section of Sequoia National Forest surrounds **Kings Canyon Highway,** the road connecting to Kings Canyon National Park's Grant Grove area. The **Hume Lake District** contains the awesome remnants of what used to be the largest grove in the world before the logging industry destroyed it.

Hiking in the district is beautifully quiet. There is a strenuous 40 mi. stretch of the Pacific Crest National Scenic Trail that passes through the forest on its 2600 mi. journey between Canada and Mexico (see **From Crest to Crest: The Trail of the West,** p. 242). More relaxing, the Trail of 100 Giants is a 35min. walk in the southern section of the forest, bespeckled with interpretive placards. The trail is evenly paved, and you can still see many giant sequoias, making it perfect for wheelchairs and strollers. The **Sherman Pass Trail** and the **Boone Meadow Trail** are attractive alternatives to the main trails for more experienced hikers, and the 2¼ mi. **Packsaddle Cave Trail** (trailhead is 16 mi. north of Kernville on State Mtn. 99) takes you to its namesake, the Packsaddle Cave. These trails are "OHV," meaning that hikers occasionally share the road with off-road vehicles and horses. One hundred and fifty miles of **backcountry hiking** is to be found in the Golden Trout Wilderness, accessible on Rte. 190 and Rte. 395, and Monarch Wilderness, accessible on Rte. 180. These areas are remote and unforgiving; expeditions require serious preparation.

EASTERN SIERRA

While the western side of the Sierra descends slowly over a foothill region before flattening into the Central Valley, the eastern side drops off precipitously, its jagged rock faces forming a startling silhouette against the skies. Although barely visible through the smog from the San Joaquin Valley to the west, the peaks of the High Sierra tower over Owens Valley to the east and contrast ominously with the desert to the south. The sharp drop-off is a result of the lifting and faulting processes that shaped the Sierra ridge 10 million years ago. The Sierra's eastern slope traces the fault line along which the Owens Valley once collapsed, exposing 14,000 ft. tall slabs of rock to glaciation. Watered by cool ocean air, the western slope is carpeted by dense forests at middle elevations. The clouds dissipate before they can cross the range, however, leaving the eastern side remarkably arid.

SEQUOIA & KINGS CANYON
NATIONAL PARKS   ☎ 559

Protected from deforestation nearly as soon as it was discovered by European Americans, Sequoia National Park, which was expanded in the 1940s to include Kings Canyon to the north, is the nation's 2nd oldest national park. The park's most popular attractions are its groves of giant sequoia, which stand as the earth's largest organisms. The largest specimen of giant sequoia, the General Sherman tree, in Giant Forest, weighs over 2.7 million lb. and has a base circumference of over 100 ft. In that same small grove stand four of the world's five largest trees, each about as old as Western civilization. The behemoths cover only a small portion of the parks, which stretch north-south along the lower part of the Sierra range, from the foothills to the sequoia groves on the middle elevations along the parks' western slope to the soaring peaks of the high Sierras on the eastern border. Also within the parks' boundaries are Kings Canyon, the deepest in North America, the 6000 ft. Kern Canyon, and an abundance of meadows, creeks, and peaks.

Most of these sights can be reached by car or by short walking expeditions, but two-thirds of the parks are completely undeveloped, providing hardy hikers with 800 mi. of beautiful backcountry trails. The park entrance fee is $5 for bicycles, pedestrians, and individuals on buses; $10 for cars. Both of these passes are valid in both parks for seven days. You can also purchase an annual pass for $20.

AT A GLANCE	
AREA: 864,411 acres.	**GATEWAYS:** Fresno (p. 314), Visalia, Three Rivers.
CLIMATE: Temperate redwood forests.	
FEATURES: General Sherman Tree, Moro Rock, Grizzly Falls.	**CAMPING:** Some campgrounds take reservations.
HIGHLIGHTS: Drive through Tunnel Log, spelunk in the Crystal Cave, hike through Redwood Mountain Grove.	**FEES & RESERVATIONS:** Entrance fee for 7 days for those on foot, bike, or motorcycle $5. $10 7 day entrance fee per vehicle. Annual pass $20.

◣ ORIENTATION

The parks' most popular sights are concentrated in four areas: **Giant Forest** and **Mineral King** in Sequoia, and **Grant Grove** and **Cedar Grove** in Kings Canyon. Beautiful backcountry comprises the northern two-thirds of Kings Canyon and the eastern two-thirds of Sequoia. Seasonal changes are dramatic in this part of the Sierra. Anything beyond the frontcountry of Generals Highway is only accessible during the summer, as snow can last throughout the year on some peaks. Dogwood, aspen, and oak display brilliant colors in the fall. Snow season is from November-March, although trails may have snow as late as mid-June. Spring here is unpredictable, bringing late storms, low fog, and runoff flooding as well as falling rock.

✈ INTERCITY TRANSPORTATION

By car, the two parks can only be accessed from the west. From **Fresno,** Rte. 180 runs east 60 mi. to Kings Canyon's Grant Grove entrance and terminates 30 mi. later in Cedar Grove at the mouth of the Canyon itself. The road to Cedar Grove is typically closed from late October to May due to the threat of winter storms and falling rocks. From **Visalia,** Rte. 198 winds its way past Lake Kaweah to Sequioa's Ash Mountain entrance, where it becomes the Generals Highway, named for its route between the General Grant and General Sherman Trees. An especially serpentine and sometimes unpredictable speedway, Rte. 198 snakes through 130 spine-tingling turns and 12 major switchbacks as it ascends 2000 ft. Drivers using the southern entrance should expect intermittent delays between Hospital Rock and Giant Forest due to road repairs. Barring long delays, however, the drive from Ash Mountain through Sequoia's Giant Forest to Grant Grove takes about 2hr. In winter, **Generals Highway** is usually covered by over 15 ft. of snow, defying plows and monster trucks. The road is usually open from mid-May to Oct., permitting entrance deeper into the forest. Rte. 198 branches into the **Mineral King** turn-off just before the main entrance into the park. This drive is punctuated by high-country panoramas, but drivers should beware—the poor road maintenance and endless switchbacks make it difficult to steer straight. No gas is officially sold in the park, so be sure to fill up before entering. In a pinch, Hume Lake and Kings Canyon Lodge, in Sequoia National Forest to the northwest of the park, sell gas for a premium. During the winter, entries points to Grant Grove and Giant Forest, and Generals Highway connecting the two, are usually kept open, except when the weather makes for hazardous conditions. Tire chains may be required. The only park access from the east is by trail; enter either park from the **John Muir Wilderness** and the **Inyo National Forest,** both accessible from spur roads off U.S. 395. Hikers venturing in from the east should secure their backcountry permits in advance.

◧ LOCAL TRANSPORTATION

There is no public transportation to the parks, but the **free shuttle system** goes from Wuksachi Village in Sequoia National Park to Lodgepole, the General Sherman Tree, and back. (every hr., daily 9am-5pm.) Check schedules at Visitors Centers and bulletin boards. Visitors interested in renting horses can contact the stables at Wolverton Pack Station (☎565-3039), Grant Grove (☎335-9292), Cedar Grove (☎565-3464), Mineral King (☎561-3039), or at Horse Corral (☎565-3404). All are open daily mid-May to mid-June (Mineral King) from 8am-6pm and offer guided rides ($20 per hr., $75-80 per day). Rates vary; call for info. Bicycles, off-road vehicles, and snowmobiles are not permitted on hiking trails or in the backcountry.

⁇ PRACTICAL INFORMATION

Camping supplies, amenities, gas, and groceries in the parks are no-frills and expensive. The **San Joaquin Valley** (see p. 305), **Three Rivers** (8 mi. southwest on Rte. 198), and **Visalia** (25 mi. southwest on Rte. 198) offer a better selection.

WHEN TO GO. The moderate climate of the region means the parks are overrun with tourists in the summer. Nonetheless, this is the best time for hikes and water activites.

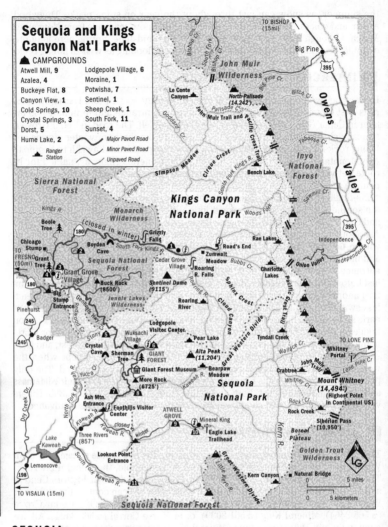

Sequoia and Kings Canyon Nat'l Parks

▲ CAMPGROUNDS

Atwell Mill, **9**	Lodgepole Village, **6**
Azalea, **4**	Moraine, **1**
Buckeye Flat, **8**	Potwisha, **7**
Canyon View, **1**	Sentinel, **1**
Cold Springs, **10**	Sheep Creek, **1**
Crystal Springs, **3**	South Fork, **11**
Dorst, **5**	Sunset, **4**
Hume Lake, **2**	

▲ Ranger Station

〰 Major Pavod Road
〰 Minor Paved Road
〰 Unpaved Road

SIERRA NEVADA

SEQUOIA

Visitor Information: Foothills Visitors Center (☎565-4212), at the park headquarters. Open daily 8am-5pm. **Lodgepole Visitors Center** (☎565-3782), on Generals Hwy. 4 mi. east of Giant Forest. Open May-Sept. daily 8am-6pm; Oct.-Apr. 9am-4:30pm; wilderness permits available 7am-4pm in summer, self-registration in winter. **Mineral King Ranger Station** (☎565-3764), 1 mi. before the end of Mineral King Rd., is the headquarters for the remote Mineral King region of the southern park, replete with maps, hiking info, books, first aid, and wilderness permits. Open May-Sept. daily 7am-4:30pm.

Gas: Gasoline is not available in the park. The nearest option is in Three Rivers, Hume Lake, or Kings Canyon Lodge, a 15min. drive from Grant Grove in Kings Canyon.

Auto Repair: AAA Emergency Road Service (☎800-400-4222).

Markets: Lodgepole's market is well stocked with food and outdoors supplies. (Open Oct.-April daily 9am-4:30pm; May 9am-6pm; June-Sept. 8am-8pm.) Two stores in Three Rivers, **Village Market** (open M-Sa 8am-8pm, Su 9am-6pm) and **Three Rivers Market** (open daily 7:30am-8pm), offer better selections on food, camping gear, and prices. Fresno and Visalia are larger cities, well endowed with stores and supplies. **Silver City Resort** (☎561-3223) in Mineral King has some supplies.

Showers: Opposite Lodgepole Visitors Center. $3. Open May-Sept. daily 8am-7:45pm; Oct.-Apr. 9am-5:45pm. Closed daily 1-3pm.

Laundromat: Wash $1.25; dry $0.25 per 10min. Open Oct.-Apr. daily 9am-4:30pm; May daily 9am-6pm; June-Sept. 8am-8pm.

Medical Services: Kaweah Delta Hospital (☎624-2000), off Rte. 198, in Visalia.

Post Office: At Lodgepole. Open M-F 8:30am-1pm and 1:30-4pm. A stamp machine is in the lobby (open 24hr.). General delivery mail to: Sequoia National Park, CA. **Postal Code:** 93262.

KINGS CANYON

Visitor Information: In addition to providing info, the following Visitors Centers sell self-guided tours (1-2 mi., 1-2hr.). Different crowd-pleasing tours include Congress Trail, Mineral King, General Grant Tree and Trail, and the Zumwalt Meadow Trail. Daily walks, talks, and slide shows at Grant and Cedar Groves begin in June.

Grant Grove Visitors Center (☎565-4307), Grant Grove Village, 2 mi. east of the Big Stump entrance by Rte. 180. Books, maps, local wilderness permits and exhibits. Nightly campfire programs and daily hikes. Open daily 8am-5pm; in winter 8am-5pm.

Cedar Grove Ranger Station (☎565-3793), 30 mi. farther down Rte. 180 by Kings River. Near trailheads into Kings Canyon high country; a ½ mi. south of Cedar Grove Village. Books, maps, and first aid. Open mid-June to Labor Day daily 9am-5pm; in fall Sa-Su 9am-5pm.

Road's End Kiosk (info ☎565-3791), 6 mi. east of Cedar Grove Village, issues wilderness permits, and sells maps and bear canisters. Open daily 7am-4pm; in winter self-register.

Gas: The nearest options are at **Hume Lake Christian Camp** (☎335-2000), 10 mi. from Grant Grove, and **Kings Canyon Lodge** (☎335-2405), 13 mi. from Grant Grove. Emergency only gas is available at Grant Grove Market.

Auto Repair: Attendants at Grant Grove (☎335-5500) can handle minor repairs and lockouts. For major repairs or service outside the Grant Grove area, call **Michael's** (☎638-4101), in Reedley. **AAA Emergency Road Service** (☎800-400-4222).

ATM: At Grant Grove Market and Cedar Grove Market. $2 surcharge.

Markets: Grant Grove Market, Cedar Grove Market, and the **Hume Lake General Store** carry a limited selection of camping basics and groceries. Grant Grove Market is open daily 8am-8pm, in winter 9am-6pm. Cedar Grove Market daily 9am-5pm, and the Hume Lake General Store is open Su-F 8am-7pm, Sa 8am-10pm.

Showers: Cedar Grove Village: $3 per person, towel $1. Open daily 9am-5pm. **Grant Grove Village:** $3 per person, towel $1. Open daily 11am-4pm.

Laundromat: Cedar Grove Village. Wash $1; dry $0.25 per 15min. Open daily 9am-5pm.

Medical Services: Fresno Community Hospital (☎459-6000), at Fresno and R St.

Post Office: Grant Grove Village (☎335-2499), near the Visitors Center. Hours vary widely, but generally M-Sa 8:30am-noon or early afternoon. A stamp machine and mailbox are next to the Visitors Center year-round. General delivery to: Kings Canyon National Park, CA. **Postal Code:** 93633. **Hume Lake,** at the Hume Lake Christian Camp. Open June-Oct. M-F 9:30am-4:30pm, Sa 9am-2pm. **Postal Code:** 93628.

S
I
E
R
R
A

N
E
V
A
D
A

IN RECENT NEWS

BLAZING FIRES

While threats from fellow humans took the top headlines in the summer of 2002, a natural threat, the forest fire, often came in a close second. By mid-July, over 4 million acres, had burned, about three times average. Over 600,000 acres in Arizona, 500,000 acres in Colorado, and nearly 150,000 acres in California had been ravaged by fires. Thousands were evacuated, hundreds of homes were lost, and the Forest Service expected to pay $1 billion dollars. Several arrests were made in connection with some fires, including a high school freshmen, a Forest Service employee, and an unemployed firefighter seeking work. Some are pointing fingers at a less likely suspect: Smokey the Bear.

Well, few are criticizing Smokey's earnest pleas to be careful with your campfires and cigarette butts, but a growing number, including officials at the Forest Service, are taking issue with the "stamp out forest fires" mantra that has, since the 1930s, been the standard line and common practice, a mantra that was iconized in the anthropomorphized grizzly. Forest fires, as terrible as Disney made them out to be, are an integral part of the forest ecosystem, and the program of complete suppression that Forest Service has until recently held is now being seen as the primary cause behind the unnaturally large and hot fires that burned much of the West.

In an undisturbed state, forest fires are a natural clearing mechanism for the forest floor. Lightening starts off a fire, which burns off the vegetation on

⚠ CAMPING

Although campgrounds fill quickly, you should be able to drive up late and snatch a spot on most non-holiday weekends. Only Lodgepole, in Sequoia, fills regularly, partly because of its proximity to Giant Forest Village and partly because it's one of only two campgrounds in either park that accepts summer reservations (the other is Dorst). Both Lodgepole and Dorst prefer campers to reserve ahead, even if unreserved sites are available. Most campgrounds are open from mid-May to October, with a 14-night maximum stay during the summer and one month total per year. There are no RV hookups in the parks, but dump stations are available at Potwisha, Lodgepole, Dorst, and Princess. Contact a ranger station for more info, or call ☎565-3351 for a 24hr. recording. Dorst and Lodgepole can be reserved by calling ☎800-365-2267. **Backcountry camping** is free with the requisite permit (see **Practical Information**, p. 276). Black bears, though usually not aggressive toward humans, are common in both parks. In developed campsites, all odorous items should be locked away in bear boxes. Backcountry campers can rent a bear canister at visitors centers. For more information, see **Bears Will Eat You**, p. 45.

SEQUOIA

Buckeye Flat, 2800 ft., past park headquarters, a few mi. from the Ash Mountain entrance on Rte. 198. Access road is a narrow dirt strip with views of mountains above and white water below. Closed to RVs. All 28 sites are spacious and lie in a grove of low-lying trees and stark outcroppings of rock. Flush toilets and drinking water. Sites $14. Open year-round. ❶

Potishwa, 2100 ft., is a full-service campground nearby with 42 well-spaced sites where RVs are welcome. No hookups but dump stations available. Flush toilets and drinking water, a good choice when the temperature drops due to its lower elevation (like Buckeye Flat). Sites $14. ❶

Atwell Mill, 6650 ft., **and Cold Springs,** 7500 ft., 20 mi. along Mineral King Rd. in the Mineral King area. Secluded, with pit toilets, but offer piped water and picnic tables for the 61 tent sites that overlook a stream. Steep, winding roads and a ban on trailers keep the RVs away. Store, restaurant, showers, and phones are 3 mi. away in Silver City. There has been a recent problem with marmots; check ranger postings to see if the area is secure. Closed in winter. Sites $8. ❶

South Fork, 3600 ft., on South Fork Rd. 13 mi. from Rte. 198. 10 sites near ranger station, a river, and some backcountry roads. Pit toilets, no drinking water. Not recommended for trailers or RVs. Sites $8. ❶

Dorst, 6800 ft., 12 mi. north of Giant Forest and 8 mi. north of Lodgepole. Huge campground (200+ sites) convenient to Sequoia attractions. The wide paved road and woodchip paths give rise to gentle hills, a small stream, and huge pines. Because of its choice location, it is on the reservation system—be sure to call for one (☎800-365-2267) during the summer weekends. Pay phone. Closed in winter. Sites $16. ❷

KINGS CANYON

▨ **Sunset, Azalea,** and **Crystal Springs,** 6500 ft., are within a stone's throw of Grant Grove Village (and all the services therein) but remain quiet. Sunset (200 sites) features gentle wooded hills and brilliant western views of the San Joaquin Valley, but it is often closed unless other sites start to overflow. Azalea (113 sites), open year-round (free in winter), has a calm feel and a trailer dump station. Crystal Springs (62 sites) is the smallest and most remote. Like Sunset, it is also frequently closed. All offer flush toilets, water, and plenty of privacy. Sites $14. ❶

Sheep Creek, Sentinel, Canyon View, and **Moraine,** 4600 ft., on Rte. 180 at the Kings River near Cedar Grove, 32 mi. east of Grant Grove. Store, food, laundry, and showers nearby. Within a few mi. of Road's End and Kings Canyon trailheads. Sheep Creek (111 sites) has more secluded tent sites in the back of the campground. Sentinel's 82 sites are flatter and near the Cedar Grove Amphitheater. Sheep Creek's most secluded and rustic sites are in the back areas as well. Moraine, with its canyon vistas, serves primarily as overflow and opens only on the busiest weekends. Close to Cedar Grove, all have flush toilets, water, and dump stations. Access roads and campgrounds usually closed Oct.-May. Canyon View accepts reservations from groups only. Sites $14. ❶

▐ OTHER ACCOMMODATIONS

Although indoor lodging can't compare with camping in price, some deals are to be had, especially in the outlying towns. When traveling in a group, look for hotels with suites or cabins, which usually work out to be significantly less per person than doubles. The **Kings Canyon Park Service** (☎335-5500; P.O. Box 909, Kings Canyon National Park 93633) is in charge of accommodations and reservations in the park. **Grant Grove Lodge and John Muir Lodge ❸** (☎335-5500; www.sequoia-kingscanyon.com), in Grant Grove Village, has wooden structures with canvas tops, no

the forest floor, leaving most of the large, old growth trees intact. This process clears out dead wood scraps a serious fire threat when accumu lated. By erecting fire lookouts through the nation and suppressing any fire almost immediately, the For est Service halted an important natu ral process, resulting in the buildup o large stores of "fuel" on the fores floor. Now, when a blaze starts, the size and heat of the fires is enough to burn even the biggest fire-resistan trees, and an abundance of fue allows the fires to spread quickly.

The answer to this problem may be the increasingly-popular practice o "prescribed" and "controlled" burns Started by trained forest firefighters under controlled conditions, thes fires aim to reduce ground fuel with out leveling the ecosystem or endan gering communities. Though successful, these fires have critics Controlled burns are often hard to control. In 2000, over 20 homes in Northern California were destroyed in a Bureau of Land Management fire run amok, and about 260 homes were lost in a Los Alamos burn. Also these burns are expensive, especiall when considering the enormity of fo est land that needs regular treatmen Yet controlled burns are the onl method we have for preventing vastl more destructive fires like those see in 2002. This realization ha prompted Congress to budget $3 bi lion for fuel reduction programs. Pe haps forest stewardship has proved to be a Pandora's box; in attempting to control the land, we've disturbed system not so easily brought bac into balance.

electricity, and communal baths (from $40), rustic wooden cabins with or without electricity ($47 or $57), and cabins with private bath and electricity (from $90). The cheapest motel accommodations still hover at higher rates at the **Cedar Grove Lodge** ❺ in Cedar Grove Village. (☎565-0100; reservations 335-5500. Rooms $90.)

Outside of the park, small spots can be a better value but are still pricey. Motels and lodges abound in **Three Rivers,** 6 mi. west of the park on Rte. 198. Larger **Visalia,** 30 mi. southwest of the park on Rte. 198, is home to standard accommodations and a few finds. Built in 1876, **Ben Maddox House** ❺, 610 N. Encinia St., is a four-room ground-level bed & breakfast built out of sequoia trees. Appreciated and uncommon amenities include 14-foot ceilings, a pool, patio, and spa, full breakfast, complementary beverages, and in-room Internet connections. (☎800-401-9800. Singles $85-95; doubles $90-110.)

▨**The Sierra Lodge,** 43175 Sierra Dr./Rte. 198 (☎561-3681), in Three Rivers. Just outside the parks with spacious rooms with high ceilings, valley and river view, large pool, BBQ, refrigerators, coffeemakers, library/lounge, kitchenettes, fireplaces, and balconies. The suite/apartments can quarter a small army. 17 rooms and 5 suites feel more like a condo resort than a motel. Continental breakfast included. Rooms from $49, $39 in the winter; suite/apartments (with full kitchen and large fireplaces) $100-160. ❸

The Sequoia Motel, 43000 Sierra Dr./Rte.198 (☎561-4453; www.sequoiamotel.com), in Three Rivers. This newly remodeled motel has 11 distinctive rooms and 4 cabins, with more in the making. Owned by a family with a green thumb and an interior decorator. Pool, picnic area, extensive garden. "The Library" (named for its previous book wallpaper), the smallest of the rooms, has several windows, a patio, and private bath. Rooms from $60; 6-person "house" $135-170. ❹

◪ FOOD

Believe it or not, the majority of visitors to the parks are not camping, and they usually rely on the plain and expensive fare provided courtesy of the US Department of the Interior. If you have a small camp stove, some BBQ briquettes (available at park markets), or don't mind a cold meal, however, you can stock up on provisions at a park market (see Practical Information) or in Three Rivers. **Village Market** in Three Rivers may produce an affordable meal if you're cooking for a group. (☎561-4441. Open M-Sa 8am-8pm, Su 9am-6pm.) Campers, of course, can cook up from the comfort of their nesting grounds.

Grant Grove Restaurant (☎335-5500), in Grant Grove Village. Coffee shop atmosphere. Good portions of standard fare: pancakes with eggs, club sandwiches, steaks. Meadow view dining. Breakfast $4-7. Lunch $5-8. Dinner $8-16. Open daily 7am-7pm. ❸

The Pizza Factory, 40915 Sierra Dr. (☎561-1018), in Three Rivers. It's a chain, but these people know how to make a good pizza, slightly sweet and always fresh. Play in their arcade as you eat. Large sandwiches $4-5. Pizzas $12-15. Tu night special (large pizza, breadsticks, pitcher of soda) $15. Open M-Sa 11am-10pm, Su noon-10pm. ❷

Anne Lang's Emporium, 41651 Sierra Dr. (☎561-4937), in Three Rivers. The lingering scents of potpourri and coffee permeate the air in this country store, florist, notary public, and deli. Terraces overlook the Kaweah River. Large sandwiches ($5) come with potato salad and fruit. Soups $2-3. Open M-F 9:30am-5:30pm, Sa-Su 10am-5pm. ❶

◉ ⋔ SIGHTS & HIKES

SEQUOIA

Giant Forest is the center of activity in Sequoia and hosts the largest specimens of giant sequoia trees, including the biggest, General Sherman. The grove was named by John Muir, who explored the area at length, recounting his epiphanous experiences to the American public in his plea for conservation, *My First Summer in the Sierra*. Branching off eastward from the Giant Forest Museum on Generals Highway, the 3 mi. dead-end road to Moro Rock and Crescent Meadow also offers access to many other wonders, including a testament to the long and storied relationship between trees and automobiles: the **Tunnel Log** (2¾ mi. from village), a fallen sequoia with a trunk big enough for cars to drive through.

GENERAL SHERMAN TREE. The tallest of the park's marvels, this towering pine was discovered in 1879 and named by a Civil War veteran after William Tecumseh Sherman, the stone-faced Union general who led a fierce campaign to split the south. Standing 275 ft. tall, measuring 102 ft. around at its base, and weighing in at over 1385 tons, it looms as the world's largest living thing. Many sequoias are over 3000 years old; their extensive root systems, fire-resistant bark, and insect-repelling juices make them the ultimate survivors. The 2 mi. **Congress Trail,** the park's most popular trail, boomerangs around General Sherman and other trees named for US political stars, and passes through the heart of the grove. The 0.7 mi. **Big Trees Trail** is a short, wheelchair accessible loop that starts at the Giant Forest Museum and explores some of the most impressive trees and a parade of informative panels. Trail guides to Giant Forest are available at all visitors centers in the park. (see **Practical Information,** p. 276.)

MORO ROCK. Recently toured and admired by President Bush, the granite monoliths and meadows of the Giant Forest area are perhaps more impressive than the trees that made it famous. The region's most spectacular view awaits atop Moro Rock, 2 mi. from the village, where a 400-step granite staircase leads to a stunning 360-degree view of the southern Sierra. If the arduous climb up the stairs doesn't leave you breathless, the view most certainly will—the Great Western Divide lies to the east, and foothills recline into the San Joaquin Valley to the south and west.

CRESCENT MEADOW. At the end of Crescent Meadow Rd. rests this fabulous bed of flora, which Muir called "the gem of the Sierra." Its emerald grasses are dotted with ruby and amethyst wildflowers gleaming against the cedars and sequoia that line the drive. The Park Service requests that you stay on marked trails, so frolicking and the like are out. Although human voices often shatter the serenity, a quick hike to **Tharp's Log,** a hollowed-out sequoia that served as a home to the first Anglo settler in the area, guarantees a peaceful view of the meadow. For ultimate serenity, venture out from the High Sierra trailhead to Mt. Whitney, 71 mi. to the east.

CRYSTAL CAVE TOURS. Nine miles from Giant Forest Village on Rte. 198 is Crystal Cave, discovered by two trail construction workers fishing on their day off in 1918 and one of the few caves on Sequoia's western side open to the public. Reached by a half-mile hike from the road, the cave is lined with smooth limestone stalagmites and stalactites, moistened by a dark underground stream, and inhabited by hordes of Mexican free-tailed bats. Tours last 45min., and proceed from room to room along lighted walkways, stopping often to describe the cave's internal structure. Marble Hall, the cave's largest chamber, is 141 ft. long and over 40 ft. high. The temperature inside is a constant 50°F, so wear warm clothing. (☎565-3135. Tickets must be purchased 1½hr. in advance at the Lodgepole or Foothills Visitors Centers. Tours given Memorial Day-Labor Day daily every 30min. 11am-4pm; Labor Day-Memorial Day Su-M and F-Sa every hr. 11am-4pm. Tours $8, seniors $6, children $4, under 6 free.)

OTHER ACTIVITIES. For those seeking the underground scene, **Boyden Cavern** lies on Rte. 180, 10 mi. west of Cedar Groves, in Kings Canyon itself. (☎209-736-2708. 45min. tours run Apr.-Nov. every hr. 10am-5pm. $9, ages 3-13 $4.50, under 3 free. National park entrance fee required. No reservations necessary.) Whitewater rafters should contact **Kaweah White Water Adventures,** on Rte. 198 in Three Rivers. (☎561-1000 or 800-229-8658. Class 3 rapids, half-day $50 per person; classes 4 and 5, full-day $110 per person.)

HOW DO I GET A TREE NAMED AFTER ME?

Up until the 1920s it was as simple as waving a paintbrush, a hammer, a nail, and declaring "MY TREE!" Pioneers, visitors, and tough guys would post makeshift plaques on random trees and proclaim ownership or at least namesakehood. This may account for the abundance of trees named after Civil War generals, all of which were Union generals until The Daughters of the Confederacy feistily plastered up the names of two enduring Southern heroes.

In 1933, Dr. Morton W. Fraser, a long-time fan of the forest, was buried beneath a tree in Giant Forest, now named Burial Tree and etched with a small tombstone. Another two-tree combo grew in such a way that a swampy cesspool of scum/water collected between them. Rumor has it that a ranger once found a couple of black bears kicking back in this pool on a hot summer day; he called the tree Bear's Bathtub.

KINGS CANYON

GRANT GROVE. The most developed portion of Kings Canyon is Grant Grove, named for its commanding attraction, the General Grant Tree. The 3500-year-old general, the third-largest sequoia in the world (267½ ft.), is famed for its prototypical shape. It has been designated the "Nation's Christmas Tree" and serves as the only living shrine to the American war dead. Just north of the park entrance on Rte. 180 lies the **Big Stump Basin Trail,** a 1 mi. self-guided walk through an old logging camp. Scars left by early loggers are still visible.

The **Grant Tree Trail,** just past the Sunset campground, consists of a half-mile loop and a glance at the mammoth sequoia. The trail is the best way to see the huge Fallen Monarch (another felled sequoia), which once housed a saloon and a stable and has been laying on the forest ground undecayed for an unimaginably long time, and the 24 ft. wide Centennial Stump, which stubbornly resisted nine days of hacking. When the tree arrived at the 1876 Centennial Exposition in Philadelphia, Easterners refused to display it, dismissing it as "another California hoax."

Hidden behind the Visitors Center parking lot is the steep, narrow road to **Panoramic Point** (RVs prohibited). If the road is closed, use the 2 mi. North Boundary Trail (1 mi. west of Grant Grove Village) to access Pan Point. In addition to affording awesome mountain and lake views, the point serves as the trailhead for the 2 mi. hike. Tremendous views can also be had from **Buena Vista Peak,** a 1 mi. hike from Generals Highway, 7 mi. south of Grant Grove, and **Big Baldy,** a 2 mi. hike from the trailhead, which is 8 mi. south of the grove. **Park Ridge Trail** is one of the most scenic and well-marked treks in the park. The 1.5 mi. round-trip hike along the **Dead Giant Loop** borders national park and national forest lands, and provides interpretive information on the differences in land management between the two.

CEDAR GROVE. The most incredible sights in Kings Canyon lie east of Grant Grove. The combined efforts of ancient glaciers and the South Fork Kings River has carved the park's topography and made it deeper even than the Grand Canyon. One can approach the canyon's towering granite walls from Cedar Grove. Although accessible via U.S. 180, Cedar Grove is nevertheless one of the park's most secluded areas. Sheer rock walls dominate the views, and at the bottom of the canyon, the Kings River glistens like a champagne supernova.

Once within the grove, you can explore the Kings River's banks and marvel at the depth of the canyon (8200 ft. in spots). **Zumwalt Meadows,** accessible via a 1½ mi. trail loop, has a rocky site from which bears and mule deer can be seen foraging in the flora below. It's perfect for the hiker who wants a moderate trail. A guide is available at the trailhead. **Roaring River Falls** and **Mist Falls** are at their best in late spring and early summer, when the streams that feed them are swift and swollen. Roaring River Falls is easily reached by road; Mist Falls requires a relaxed 4hr.

hike. The breathtaking **Grizzly Falls,** located 7 mi. west of Cedar Grove, is a leisurely 50-yard walk from the highway.

Road's End is exactly that, a naturally U-shaped glacial valley at the end of Rte. 180 with parking for those entering the backcountry. The most popular backcountry foray from Road's End is the **Rae Lakes Loop,** which traverses a sampling of the Sierra's best: glaciated canyons, gentle meadows, violent rapids, and inspiring lakes. Travel clockwise to avoid a daunting uphill grade. Trails into the High Sierra also depart from here. Campgrounds pace the four- or five-day trek at 7 mi. intervals. Obtain permits at the **Road's End Kiosk** (see **Practical Information,** p. 277).

🔖 HIKES

In the backcountry, visitors should be wary of bears, which are adorable, fuzzy, and very dangerous (see **Bears Will Eat You,** p. 45). **Group tours** led by the park's pack stations (☎563-3445) provide safety in numbers. The fashionable guide to backcountry safety, *Backcountry Basics*, is available at the Visitors Center.

After being dwarfed by an army of redwoods named after dead American politicos and military men in Sequoia, conquering a trail or two is a good way to reinflate the ego. Near Giant Forest, **Little Baldy Trail** starts at Little Baldy Saddle, 9 mi. north of General Sherman on the Generals Highway, and climbs 1.7 mi. with a 700 ft. vertical ascent to a rocky summit. The more challenging **Garfield Trail** climbs 4.5 mi. to the Garfield sequoia grove from South Fork Campground. **Middle Fork Trail** starts on a dirt road turnoff on Buckeye Flat campground road, and heads from the foothills to deep into higher elevations, passing Moro Rock.

Redwood Mountain Grove, the world's largest grove of redwood trees, lies near Quail Flat, 6 mi. south of Grant Grove and 4 mi. north of Giant Forest Village. A 7 mi. trail forms two loops through the grove along Redwood Creek, a tributary of the Kaweah River's North Fork, which is surrounded by blooming azaleas in May and June. The **Muir Grove,** west of the Dorst campground, is less pristine but more accessible. **Mist Falls** heads out from Road's End on 5 mi. of relatively flat hiking to a grand waterfall. The long and strenuous **Don Cecil** and **Hotel Creek Trails,** which begin within walking distance of the village, head toward Cedar Grove and the awesome canyon, making full-day hikes.

The extensive system of backwoods trails presents even more spectacular views. The 7 mi. **Marble Falls Trail** begins by the Potwisha campground and twists through hills to a 2000 ft. peak at **Marble Falls.** The moderately strenuous hike from the Lodgepole Visitors Center to the glistening **Twin Lakes** (13.6 mi. round-trip) reminds visitors that some of the beauty of the park can be found in the little things as well: flowers, brooks, and chipmunks. A few trails lead deep into the park, connecting with the Pacific Crest Trail along the parks' eastern border and crossing into Inyo National Forest. Inquire with a ranger about the High Sierra Trail and the Woods Creek Trail.

The Mineral King area was acquired by the park system in 1978 after lawsuits prevented the Walt Disney Corporation from building a ski resort on the site. Some of the best scenery in the park has been preserved for those willing to brave the winding drive, complete with blind corners and steep drop-offs. The valley is 7500 ft. deep, with steep trails leading up to mountain lakes and meadows. A booming mining area in the 1800s, the region now offers magnificent day and backcountry hiking and climbing. The walk to **Aspen Flat** from Mineral King Pack Station is an easy, rewarding day hike, flanked by soda springs and wildflowers. Perhaps the most astounding view of the region is the sink hole of Eagle Creek, where it completely disappears underground—no one knows where the water ends up. The **Eagle Lake Trail** (6.8 mi. round-trip), which starts 1 mi. down the road from the Ranger Station, brings you to this impressive work of nature.

LEE VINING & MONO LAKE ☎760

As the snow thaws in June, Rte. 120 in the stunning Tioga Pass opens to motorists, making the town of Lee Vining (pop. 315) a great—if a bit expensive—Yosemite gateway, or a getaway of its own. The town's focus is the preservation of its sacred Mono Lake. Sitting at the western flank of the Great Basin desert, home to similarly saline lakes like Pyramid and The Great Salt Lake, Mono Lake is sustained by freshwater inflows from surrounding mountains. Without any outlet, evaporation is the sole equilibrating force in the lake, but since salts and minerals are left behind as the lake dries, salinity has built up to two to three times ocean levels. This process of drainage and evaporation has been going on for nearly a million years, making Mono Lake one of the oldest in the Western Hemisphere. The lake has a lunar appearance as the result of towers (similar to giant drip sandcastles) of calcium carbonate called tufa, which form when calcium-rich springs well up in the carbonate-filled salt water.

Today, Mono supports not only its own delicate and unique ecosystem but also the water needs of greater metropolitan L.A. Although Mono Lake's water has always been too salty to use, its freshwater inflows are extremely pure. L.A.'s rapid growth, scarcity of freshwater supplies, and political might resulted in these inflows being completely diverted in 1941. By 1982, the lake's levels had dropped 50 ft., its volume had halved, and its salinity had doubled. Delicate tufa were exposed, withering the riparian forests, and endangering the California shore gulls. Increased salinity impaired brine shrimp reproduction and devastated the trout stock of adjacent streams, some of which were close to drying out. As if these ecological problems were not enough, massive quantities of newly exposed alkaline dust polluted local air in frequent dust storms. In the past 20 years, however, locals and lake-lovers alike have rejoiced to see the combined efforts of Congress, the US Forest Service, the Audubon Society, and the Mono Lake Committee succeed in reducing the flow south to one-half its previous output. Consequently, the lake level has risen more than 15 ft., and the residents of Lee Vining can breathe easy again without having to think about what might be in the air.

⊞⁊ ORIENTATION & PRACTICAL INFORMATION

Lee Vining provides stunning access to Yosemite via Inyo National Forest, and the best access to Mono Lake and Bodie. Lee Vining is 70 mi. north of Bishop on U.S. 395 and 10 mi. west of the Tioga Pass entrance to Yosemite. Bodie is 28 mi. northwest of Lee Vining off U.S. 395. Addresses in Lee Vining consist only of P.O. Box numbers, so general directions or cross-streets are provided instead.

▓ **Mono Lake Committee and Lee Vining Chamber of Commerce** (☎647-6595; www.monolake.org; lodging, dining, and local services www.leevining.com), at Main and 3rd St., Lee Vining, in the orange and blue clay building. Like a friendly eco-gift shop with exhibits, posters, articles, books, as well as extensive lake and preservation info. Walking and canoe tours (see **Sights and Activities,** p. 286). Open daily late June-Labor Day 9am-10pm; Labor Day-late June 9am-5pm.

Mono Basin National Forest Scenic Area Visitors Center (☎873-2408; www.r5.fs.fed.us/inyo/vvc/mono/), Inyo National Forest, off U.S. 395 ½mi. north of Lee Vining. Housed in a new structure (with large, angled skylights) that resembles a modern-day cathedral or *Architectural Digest* centerfold, a testament to the community's care for the basin. Interpretive tours, an informative film, free patio talks, and info on Mono County's wilderness areas. Topographical maps ($6-20) and free wilderness permits available. Open M-F 9am-5:30pm; in winter M-F 9am-4pm. Summer tours of the center's exhibits and the lake's South Tufa Grove (3 times daily, $3, under 18 free).

Kayak Rental: Caldera Kayaks (☎935-4942; www.calderakayak.com), at Crowly Lake Marina, Mammoth Lakes. Kayaks $20 per half-day, $30 per day. Natural history kayak tour of Mono Lake (full day $60).

ATMs: There are 3 machines in Lee Vining: in the Mobile station on the southern end of town, in the Chevron station on the northern end of town, and in the Lee Vining Market, near Main and 4th St.

Laundromat: Mono Vista RV Park (☎647-6401), at the north end of the town. Wash $1.25; dry $0.50. Showers $1.75 for 5min. Open 9am-6pm.

Weather: ☎935-7663.

Internet Access: At the Chamber of Commerce. $2 for 15min.

Post Office (☎647-6371), on 4th St., Lee Vining, in the big brown building. Open M-F 9am-2pm and 3-5pm. **Postal Code:** 93541.

ACCOMMODATIONS

When Tioga Pass is open (early June-Sept.), Lee Vining is an ideal stop on the way from Reno or Death Valley to Yosemite, making hotel vacancies scarce on Friday afternoons and holidays. Even if you do get a room, lodging and meals are always expensive; camping and picnics are cheaper alternatives. Many hotels and campgrounds are closed in winter; call ahead. Most cheap options are on **Main Street,** or 10 mi. south of town on the 14 mi. **June Lake Loop** (see p. 287).

El Mono Motel (☎647-6310), at Main and 3rd St., offers a slice of modern California: fake Spanish name, white stucco exterior, espresso bar, and art nouveau posters in the lobby. Clean, bright rooms have cable TV but no phone. Pets allowed. Open Apr.-Oct. Singles with shared bath $49. ❸

Inn at Lee Vining (☎647-6300), at Main and 2nd St. Follow signs to The Kings Inn. Sheltered from street noise, cabin-like motel rooms have painted walls, colorful quilts, wicker chairs, and brand-new beds and carpets. Continental breakfast $5. $35 deposit required for pets. Rooms from $45. Kitchen $10 extra. ❸

Tioga Lodge (☎647-6423 or 888-647-6423), 2 mi. north of Lee Vining on the western shore of Mono Lake. Each cabin-like room in this complex is decorated with some turn-of-the-century Sierra theme. All rooms have excellent views of the lake. Idyllic small meadow has a swing, gazebo, and creek. Singles $95; doubles $105. ❺

Gateway Motel (☎647-6467 or 800-282-3929; www.yosemitegatewaymotel.com), in the center of town. Each standard room has a great view of Mono Lake; several have balconies. Phone, cable TV, coffee, and spa. 18 rooms from $89; in winter $49. ❺

CAMPING

None of the area's campgrounds take reservations, but sites are ubiquitous, so a pre-noon arrival time will almost always guarantee a spot, and an afternoon arrival probably will too. Most sites are clustered west of Lee Vining along Rte. 120.

Inyo National Forest Campgrounds ❶, close to town. Many campgrounds are on Rte. 120 heading into town. **Lundy** and **Lee Vining Canyons** are the best locations for travelers headed for Mono Lake. No water. Open May-Oct. Sites $7. The **June Lake Loop** area south on U.S. 395 has 6 sites (see **Camping,** p. 288). Most sites $13; **Bloody Canyon Trailhead** free. First-come, first-camp.

Ellery Lake, on Tioga Pass Rd. at Rte. 120 across from Tioga Pass Resort. 12 first-come, first-camp sites near a brook. Running water, chemical toilets. Sites $13.

SIERRA NEVADA

🍴 FOOD

The food offerings in town are limited, as most restaurants are in hotels. **Lee Vining Market,** on U.S. 395 at the southern end of town, is the closest thing to a grocery store. (☎647-1010. Open Su-Th 7am-9:30pm, F-Sa 7am-10pm.) **Tioga Gas Mart,** at the intersection of Rte. 120 and Rte. 395, is not your average gas station. It offers fancy coffees, chai, mixed drinks, pizza, deli, grilled food, groceries, a gourmet food selection, and 93-octane gas. The picnic area overlooks Mono Lake. (☎647-1088. Open daily 7am-10pm. Gas 24hr.)

Nicely's (☎647-6477), on Rte. 395 3 stores north of the Visitors Center, has hot sandwiches ($6-7), burgers ($5-7), and monster salads ($7-9). A local favorite with the ambience of a diner. Open daily 6am-10pm; in winter closed W. ❷

Mono Cone (☎647-6606), on Rte. 395 at the northern end of town, is a local institution whose opening signals the beginning of summer. Their corn dogs ($2), floats ($3), and frosty cones ($1.50) are the best in town. Open daily 11am-7pm. ❶

👁 🏔 SIGHTS & ACTIVITIES

BODIE. One of the best-preserved ghost towns in the country, Bodie was "the most lawless, wildest, and toughest mining camp the West has ever known," though it doesn't look that way now. Named after Waterman S. Body, who discovered gold here in 1859, the town's heyday was from 1877 to 1881, when it was home to 10,000 people, 65 saloons, 750 million modern-day dollars in gold and silver, numerous opium dens, and, in its most treacherous times, up to one homicide per day. "Good-bye God, I'm going to Bodie!" was the rallying cry of the day. Bodie survived until 1932, when the toughest town in the West was destroyed by the infamous Bodie Bill, a 2½ year-old child who leveled 90% of the town with one match. The remaining ten percent, however, is now a ghost town: absolutely genuine and brimming with romantic appeal. *(Off U.S. 395 32 mi. north of Lee Vining, then 13 mi. east on Hwy. 270. Open Memorial Day-Labor Day daily 9am-7pm; Labor Day-Memorial Day daily 9am-4pm. $1. Self-guide booklet $1.)* The **Bodie Museum** is the small home to some Wild West stories and artifacts. *(Open daily 10am-5pm. For more info, call Bodie State Historic Park at ☎647-6445, or write P.O. Box 515, Bridgeport 93517.)*

MONO LAKE. In 1984, Congress set aside 57,000 acres of land surrounding Mono Lake and named it the **Mono Basin National Forest Scenic Area** (☎873-2408). To get there, take U.S. 395 South to Rte. 120, then go 4 mi. east and take the Mono Lake South Tufa turn-off 1 mi. south to Tufa Grove. For a $3 fee (Golden Eagle, Golden Age, and Golden Access passes accepted), travelers may investigate the **South Tufa Grove,** which harbors an awe-inspiring hoard of calcium carbonate formations. Free summer tours led by knowledgeable naturalists depart from the South Tufa parking lot daily at 10am, 1, and 6pm. The tufa towers pierce the smooth surface of this solemn sea. Five miles north of Lee Vining on U.S. 395, and 1 mi. east on Cemetery Rd. is **Mono Lake County Park,** a public playground with a boardwalk trail to the tufa towers (wheelchair accessible) and a smaller tufa grove, as well as bathrooms, picnic tables, and swings. Rangers lead a number of free hikes throughout the summer, including bird watching excursions, a hike to Panum Volcano, and stargazing trips. Inquire at the Visitors Center (☎647-3044) about schedules.

The Mono Lake Committee offers **canoe tours** of the lake that include a crash course in conservation and Mono's natural history. (☎647-6595. 1hr. tours depart from South Tufa at Mono Lake mid-June to early Sept. Sa-Su at 8, 9:30, 11am; birdwatching is better on earlier tours. Arrive 30min. early for lifejacket fitting and photos of placid reflections. Tours $17, ages 4-12 $7. Reservations required.) Caldera Kayaks offers full-day **kayak tours and rentals** (see p. 285).

In this arid basin, summertime high noon inspires tourists to seek shade. The 20min. slide show presentation at the Mono Lake Committee is beautifully done, informative, rabble-rousing, and free. The US Forest Service Scenic Area Visitors Center shows a film that requires less thought from viewers. ($3; includes 20min. film, exhibits, and access to South Tufa area.) The **Mono Basin Historical Society Museum** (☎ 647-6461), in Guss Hess Park, Lee Vining, is a great way to get informed about the Basin's rich past. In the old Mono Lake schoolhouse, this museum has the standard balance of Gold Rush trinkets and Native American artifacts.

HIKING. The unique terrain of this geological playground makes it a great place for hikers of all levels. Easier trails include the ¼ mi. boardwalk to tufa and lake, **Old Marina Area Trail,** 1 mi. north of Lee Vining on Rte. 395, the **Lee Vining Creek Trail,** which begins behind the Mono Basin Visitors Center, and the **Panum Crater Trail,** 5 mi. south on U.S. 395 near the South Tufa turnoff. Those undaunted by the prospect of a punishing trek should head 10 mi. east of U.S. 395 on Rte. 120, where an exceptionally steep trail leads 1 mi. to the glistening **Gardisky Lake.** Another peaceful but tough hike starts at **Lundy Lake,** off U.S. 395, 7 mi. north of Lee Vining, and leads to **Crystal Lake** and the remains of an old mining town. The hike gains 2000 ft. in its 3 mi. ascent, and the well-maintained trail offers little shade. Bring plenty of sunscreen and bug spray. Other moderate-to-difficult trails depart from Lundy Lake, including the 5.4 mi. trail though **Lundy Canyon** to 20 Lakes Basin and the 3.2 mi. trail up out of Lundy Canyon to **Lakes Canyon.**

JUNE LAKE LOOP ☎ 760

While there certainly is dramatic and expansive wilderness around June Lake, the townsfolk in this glacier-carved valley off Rte. 395 have their focus squarely set on the smaller lakes and mountains forming the June Lake Loop enclave. This means that hiking, rock climbing, mountain biking, and the like tend to take a backseat to the activities that this nook does best: fishing in the summer and skiing in the winter. From the last Saturday in April to the end of October, the four beautiful lakes that the loop traces become altars to the cult of fishing. Locals and thousands of visitors flock to the town's marinas in a vigilant quest for the elusive monster trout, a trophy, or simply dinner. In the winter, the family-friendly June Mountain and the slopes around the loop make for excellent skiing and snowsports, with smaller crowds and lower fees than at Mammoth.

■₄ ▐ **ORIENTATION & PRACTICAL INFORMATION**

Just off U.S. 395, 7 mi. south of Lee Vining, the 14 mi. June Lake Loop winds by Grant, Silver, Gull, and June lakes before rejoining U.S. 395. In June Lake Tow, Boulder Dr. is also referred to as Main St. Addresses in the June Lake Loop consist only of P.O. Box numbers; general directions or cross streets are provided instead.

Buses: CREST (☎ 800-922-1930) buses from **Carson City, Nevada** to June Lake firehouse Tu, Th, F $13. Greyhound makes stops in Carson City from around the country. Reserve CREST tickets in advance.

Boat Rental: June Lake Marina (☎ 648-7726) has 6-horsepower (half-day $37, full-day $42) and15-horsepower (half-day $47, full-day $52) motorboats. Open daily 6am-7pm. **Gull Lake Marina** (☎ 648-7539) has motorboats (half-day $34, full-day $40), large pontoon boats (half-day $90, full-day $150), and paddleboats. ($10 per hr.)

Visitor Information: June Lake Chamber of Commerce (☎ 648-7584; www.junelakecalifornia.com) offers tourist info. Open M-F 8am-5pm. Another info kiosk at the south entrance. **June Lake Properties** makes reservations (☎ 648-7705).

Auto Repair and Service: June Lake Automotive (☎ 648-7542), **Fred Sebald's Body Shop** (☎ 648-7343), and **Silver Lake Automotive** (☎ 648-7252).

Laundromat: Carson Peak Laundromat, across from the Fern Creek Lodge. Wash $1.50; 10min. dry $0.25. Open 8am-9pm.

Frontier Pack Train (☎648-7701). Guided horseback trips including overnight packing trips. $25 per hr., half-day $50, all-day $80.

Weather: 24hr. snow report (☎619-934-6166 or 213-935-8866).

Emergency: 24hr. Sheriff (☎932-7451) or **Forest Service** (☎647-6525).

Post Office: on Boulder Dr. (☎648-7483), across from Trout Town Joe Cafe. Open M-F 9am-2pm and 3-5pm. **Postal Code:** 93529.

ACCOMMODATIONS

As befits a resort town, there are plenty of places to stay, many of them very nice, only a few of them affordable. Still, prices are significantly lower than in Mammoth Lakes, and the many cabins, condos, and suites available mean cheap and comfortable lodging is within reach for larger groups and families. A 12% bed tax applies to all indoor accommodations.

Fern Creek Lodge, on Rte. 158 (☎648-7722 or 800-621-9146; www.ferncreek-lodge.com), 13 mi. from Lee Vining, 2 mi. past June Lake Town. Apartment units and cabins, some small and rustic, some like full-sized houses. All come with fully-equipped kitchens and cable TV. 2-person cabin $50-55; 14- to 16-person cabin $210-220. ❸

Boulder Lodge, on Boulder Dr. (☎648-7533; www.boulderlodge.com), near the beginning of June Lake. Spacious, clean rooms. Sitting area, cable TV, private bath, pool table, small arcade, sauna, recreation facilities, and indoor pool. Most lake-view rooms have patios with great views of June Lake. Doubles from $60; suites from $90. ❹

Reverse Creek Lodge, on Loop Rd. (☎648-7535 or 800-762-6440; www.reversecreek-lodge.com), has chalets, big log cabins, and small cabins, all with private bath, kitchens, cable TV, and a patio with a barbecue grill. A-frame chalets (for up to 6 people) are larger, include 2 full baths, gas fireplaces and grills, and look out on nearby Carson Peak. Small cabins $65; 2-bedroom cabins $100; chalets $125-140. ❹

June Lake Motel, on Boulder Dr. (☎648-7547, reservations only 800-648-6835; www.junelakemotel.com), is a fisherman's dream. Large facility has multi-unit cabins, condos, motel rooms with and without kitchens, and full houses for rent. Besides a jacuzzi, sauna, BBQs, and cable TV, it also offers a fish-cleaning station, fish freezing, fish rags, and free ice. Motel rooms double from $62; triples with kitchen from $72; cabins $90-135; well-equipped lake-view condominiums from $145. ❹

June Lake Villager Motel, (☎648-7712 or 800-655-6545; www.junelakevillager.com), on Boulder Dr. Standard motel rooms, kitchenette rooms, suites, and cabins, with exceptionally low mid-week rates in winter. Fish cleaning station, ice, VCRs, coffeemakers, relaxing patio with grill. For the winters there is firewood for rooms with fireplaces and an indoor jacuzzi. Singles from $50, with kitchen from $70; cabins from $120. In winter singles from $35, with kitchen from $50; cabins from $100. ❺

CAMPING

Camping is a more affordable option in the June Lake Loop. There are six Inyo National Forest campgrounds, as well as a few privately operated sites. Most campsites are open only during fishing season (last Saturday in Apr.-Oct. 31).

Grant Lake Resort (☎648-7964), 7600 ft., off Rte. 158 toward Lee Vining, in the most remote part of the June Lake Loop. Atypical resort has a tackle shop, marina, and boat rental (half-day $30, full-day $35). Each site has water, hookup, and firepit. Most sites have decent shade, and many overlook Grant Lake. Lake is big and somewhat less crowded, making for good fishing. For reservations, send a check for camping fee to P.O. Box 627, June Lake 93529. Open late Apr.-Oct. Tent sites $13, seniors $10. ❶

Oh! Ridge Pine Cliff Resort (☎648-7558), 7600 ft., by the June Lake shore. Private RV and campground not affiliated with the NFS campground. The resort has a general store, gas, propane, laundry (8am-8pm), basketball court, and showers. Mainly RVers with some tent sites. No cooking grills supplied, so bring one or a camp stove if tenting. Open mid.-Apr.-Oct. On-site trailer rentals $160-400 weekly, full RV hookup $20, water and electric hookup $16, tent sites $12. ❶

Oh! Ridge Campground, 7600 ft., is right next door to the Resort and has access to a swimming beach and flush toilets. Campers may find these sites a bit quieter; the campground rarely fills and there are few RVs. Open Apr.-Nov. Sites $13. ❶

June Lake Campground, 7600 ft., next to the marina. On a busy lake, near shops and a restaurant, this tree-lined campground makes up for in lakeside access what it loses in tranquility. 28 sites, 6 for walk-in tent campers only. Water, flush toilets. Sites $13. ❶

Silver Lake Campground, 7200 ft., a National Forest site. Right on the lake and near a number of trailheads, the grassy campsites don't have much shade, but do have room. 63 sites with flush toilets, water. Good fishing access. Open late Apr.-Oct. Sites $13. ❶

⬛ FOOD

The **June Lake General Store** is a supermarket, hardware store, liquor store, and deli, all in one yellow building. (Open daily 9am-7pm.) Options outside of June Lake are the small supermarket at **Fern Creek Lodge** (☎648-7722; open daily 6am-9pm; in winter 7am-8pm) or the **Silver Lake Resort Store.** (Open daily 7am-9pm.)

Tiger Bar, Knoll Ave. and Rte. 158 (☎648-7551; www.junelakeloop.com/menu/thetigerbarcafe). Good Mexican fare, as well as standard American food, all reasonably priced. The quirky decor features black-and-white photos of the area. Small gaming area with a pool table, TV, and pinball machine. Huge Tostada Grande $7.25. Burgers with fresh-made fries or chips $6.25-7.75. Full breakfasts $4-7. American-style dinners $9-15. Open daily 8am-midnight; kitchen open until 10pm. ❷

Trout Town Joe, 2750 Boulder Dr. (☎648-1155), across from the post office. June Lake's finest (and only) coffeehouse. Panini sandwiches ($7), a wide variety of great coffees ($1.50-3), assorted pastries, and a friendly atmosphere will convince you it warrants the title. Open M-F 6am-3pm, Sa-Su 6am-6pm. ❷

Eagle's Landing Restaurant, at the Double Eagle Resort (☎648-7897), 2 mi. outside of June Lake, is *the* place to go to treat yourself. Surpisingly inexpensive fine dining with mountain views from every table. You can grab a drink at the **Eagle's Nest Saloon,** and watch a game on their 42 in. plasma screen TV. The house specialty is rotisserie chicken basted in lemon-herb garlic and barbecue sauce ($14). Logger-type breakfasts $6-11. Burgers $6-7. Sandwiches $7-9. Open daily 7am-9pm. ❸

◎ ⚑ SIGHTS & ACTIVITIES

In the summer months, all minds in June Lake are on one thing—**fishing.** The June Lake Loop (State Rte. 158) traces the outer edge of four bountiful lakes: **June Lake** (☎648-7726), closest to the South June Lake Junction with Rte. 395; **Gull Lake** (☎648-7539); **Silver Lake** (☎648-7525); and the expansive **Grant Lake** (☎648-7964) to the north. There are also a number of fishable streams in the loop, like Rush Creek and Alger Creek, and lakes only accessible on foot or by horse. Each of the four main lakes has its own marina that rents motorboats ($40-50 per day), has a tackle shop, and sells California fishing licenses (required for anyone over 16). The lakes are stocked twice a month with rainbow, brook, and German brown trout. Although all the lakes yield big fish every day, many people prefer Gull and Grant Lakes. June Lake is a popular spot for sunbathing, swimming, and recreational boating. Quieter **Walker Lake** and **Parker Lake** are accessible by short hikes from trailheads just north of Grant Lake. **Rush Creek, Agnew Lake,** and **Gem Lake** can all be accessed on the **Rush Creek Trail,** which starts across from the Silver Lake campground, and is 2.2 mi. to Agnew Lake and 3 mi. to Gem Lake.

There are a few moderate day **hikes,** most leading to trout-filled lakes, and some excellent backcountry trails into the Ansel Adams Wilderness, where you connect to the John Muir Trail. Across from the June Lake firehouse, the trail to **Yost Lake** is a moderate 5 mi. hike through the aspen and fir forest of the June Mountain Ski Area. The separate **Yost Creek Trail,** departing about 1 mi. south of Silver Lake, will take you to Yost Lake or Fern Lake, which are both beautiful and quiet. About a mile into the hike, the trail forks near a waterfall; the right branch leads a steep 1.5 mi. to Fern Lake, while the left trail is a moderate 2.5 mi. hike to Yost Lake. Much of the backcountry can be explored on **horseback.** Contact the **Frontier Pack Train** (see **Orientation and Practical Information,** p. 287) for more information.

Increasingly popular but still much less crowded than Mammoth Mountain, **June Mountain Ski Resort** has traditionally catered to families, though the recently opened JM2UNBOUND "enhanced terrain" parks, catering to the extreme-sports snowboarding crowd, promises to change the atmosphere a bit. Excellent powder, tremendous views, and short if any lines make this an attractive alternative to the larger resort to the south. It's also less expensive to ski here. (☎ 648-7733. Day pass $45, ages 19-23 $40, ages 13-18 $35, children and seniors $25.)

BISHOP & OWENS VALLEY ☎ 760

Bishop's great location and numerous accommodations and food make it a popular stop for visitors to recharge en route to the surrounding lakes, mountains, and desert. The largest city in the Eastern Sierra, this resort town has many of the things missing in the rest of the region, like international cuisine, bookstores, and coffeehouses; and some of the things that aren't, like casinos, stripmalls, and fast food. As for in-town attractions, fishing in the clear blue lakes of Bishop Creek Canyon, bouldering in the Buttermilks, and joining in on one of the many seasonal events and festivals are all popular. The Owens Valley, in which Bishop resides, is wedged between the Sierras and the dry and exceptionally high 10,000-14,000 ft. White Mountains. In the early 20th century, the Owens Valley's freshwater streams began providing the water for the budding semi-desert city of L.A., leading to the water scandal that the movie *Chinatown* grossly fictionalized (see **Film,** p. 23).

🛈 PRACTICAL INFORMATION

Bishop is located on Rte. 395 in between Lee Vining, 62 mi. north, and Lone Pine, 57 mi. south. Via the Tioga Pass, the town is 140 mi. from Yosemite. L.A. is 270 mi. south via Rte. 395.

Bus: Greyhound has canceled service to the Eastern Sierra, but you can take it to Carson City, where **CREST** (☎ 800-922-1930) runs Tu and Th-F at 2pm, arriving in Bishop at 6:30pm. One-way fare $20.

Public Transportation: Dial-A-Ride (☎ 872-1901 or 800-922-1930). Round-trip within Bishop city limits $0.75, to areas just outside the city $1.30. Shuttles to **Mammoth Lakes** ($3.50) and **Crowley Lake** ($3). By special arrangement, they will drop you at a trailhead (prices vary). Call the day before for schedules and reservations; there is limited seating. Open M-Th 8am-5pm, F-Sa 8am-midnight (last call 11:30pm).

AAA Emergency Road Service: ☎ 800-400-4222.

Visitor Information:

    Bishop Area Chamber of Commerce and Visitor's Bureau, 690 N. Main St. (☎ 873-8405; fax 873-6999; www.bishopvisitor.com), at the City Park. Area maps and info. Get a free copy of the *Vacation Planner* for up-to-date listings of special events. Open M-F 9am-5pm, Sa-Su 10am-4pm.

SIERRA NEVADA

White Mountain Ranger Station, 798 N. Main St. (☎873-2500; www.r5.fs.fed.us/inyo/vvc/whitemtn). Excellent lists of campgrounds and trails throughout Inyo. Weather report and message board. Permits reservable up to 6 months in advance and must be picked up by 10am on the day of departure. Walk-in permits are held open for all trails. Open late June-Sept. 15 daily 8am-5pm; Sept. 16-late June M-F 8am-4:30pm.

Fishing Licenses: Available at **K-Mart,** 910 N. Main St. (☎873-3800). Open daily 8am-10pm. Also available at sporting goods stores.

Bank: Bank of America, 536 N. Main St. (☎800-338-6430). Open M-Th 9am-5pm, F 9am-6pm, Sa 9am-1pm. **24hr. ATM.**

Laundromat: The Wash-Tub, 236 N. Warren St. (☎873-6627). Wash $1.25, 10min. dry $0.25. Open daily 7am-10pm; last load 8pm. Showers $4.

Road Conditions: Caltrans, ☎800-427-7623.

Police: 207 W. Line St. (☎873-5866).

Hospital: Northern Inyo Hospital, 150 Pioneer Ln. (☎873-5811), at W. Line St. 24hr. emergency care.

Library and Internet Access: Inyo County Public Library, 210 Academy Ave (☎873-5115). Free 30min. terminals. Open M-Th 10am-8pm, F 10am-6pm, Sa 10am-1pm.

Post Office: 595 W. Line St. (☎873-3526 or 800-275-8777). Open M-F 8:15am-4:45pm, Sa 10am-2pm. **Postal Code:** 93514.

ACCOMMODATIONS

Those traveling in groups, especially those looking to fish, may find a cabin is the best option. **Bishop Creek's Cardinal Village Resort** (☎873-4789), 16 mi. west of Bishop on Rte. 168, the **Bishop Creek Lodge** (☎873-4484), on South Lake Rd., and **Paradise Resort** (☎387-2370), on Rte. 2, provide such accommodations. Hotels are plentiful in Bishop, but cheap hotels are not. If you want to save money, you may be better off camping in or near Bishop.

El Rancho Motel, 274 Lagoon St. (☎872-9251 or 888-872-9251), 2 blocks west of Main St. A quintessential motel; drive up to your door. 16 rooms with TV, A/C, coffeemakers, and refrigerators. Kitchen $8 extra. Singles $40-50; doubles $50-60. Prices lowest Nov. to mid-Apr. ❸

Elms Motel, 233 E. Elm St. (☎873-8118 or 800-848-9226). These 2 room cottages are dirt-free, quiet, and come with A/C, coffeemakers, and cable TV. City Park is right next door. Fish cleaning facilities. Singles $37; doubles $42. Nov.-Mar. prices $5 less. ❸

Chalfont House, 213 Academy St. (☎872-1790). This pleasant bed and breakfast is worth the few extra bucks. Built in 1898, it has hardwood floors, patchwork quilts, and a potbelly stove in the parlor. Antique store on site. Excellent breakfast plus evening refreshments. Singles and doubles from $65. ❹

CAMPING

Most campgrounds around Bishop are well kept and near major roads. Sites have a consistent flow of campers throughout the summer but are especially crowded during the **Mule Days** celebration over Memorial Day weekend (book a year in advance; see **Entertainment,** p. 294).

There are over 30 **Inyo National Forest** campgrounds in the Bishop Ranger District (most open May-Oct.). The closest campgrounds to town can be found on or near Rte. 395 just north and south of Bishop. Closest is **Town Campground ❷** (formerly Schober Lane), 4100 ft., 1 mi. south, where 150 grassy tent and RV spots sit next to a golf course and come with water, showers, laundry, recreation facilities, and even a TV room and arcade. The private **Millpond ❶**, 4500 ft., 6 mi. north of Bishop on Saw Mill Rd., has 60 cool and shady spots near Millpond County Park, a creek, and recreational facilities. Both Town Campground and Millpond are run by the same company. (☎873-8522. Open Mar.-Oct. Sites $16.) About 12 mi. southwest of town on Rte. 168, near Bishop Creek, are a number of public campgrounds. The large **Four Jeffrey ❶**, 8100 ft., campground is southeast of Forks and has similar amenities as its neighbors for the same price; it's also wheelchair accessible (sites $12). For lakeside camping, **North Lake ❶**, 9500 ft., and **Sabrina Lake ❶**, 9000 ft., both have great scenery, trail access to the John Muir Wilderness, swimming, and fishing, of course. These chilly sites have water and vault toilets. (North Lake open June-Sept. Sabrina Lake open May-Sept. Sites $11.) Free camping can be found 8½ mi. north on Rte. 395 and 5 mi. west on Round Valley Rd. at **Horton Creek's ❶**, 5000 ft. Fifty-three unshaded sites have no potable water and vault toilets.

Some of the best camping in the area is found north of town, between Bishop and Mammoth Lakes, on Rte. 395, at **Rock Creek Lake ❶**, 7,000-10,000 ft. Thirteen campgrounds with over 300 sites adjoin the lake and creek, nearly all of which are secluded and shady. There is excellent fishing, mountain biking, and hiking in the area. Most sites have piped water and flush toilets. (Open May-Oct. Sites $12.)

🌄 FOOD

Stock up on groceries at **Vons Supermarket,** 900 N. Main St. (☎873-4396. Open 6am-1am.) As usual, fast food chains abound.

Western Kitchen, 930 N. Main St. (☎872-3246). Surprisingly, along with all the usual American fare, this Western Kitchen also serves some delicious dishes from the East. Go for a ham steak ($7) or choose from an extensive list of Thai specialties (curries $7.50), depending on your mood. Open daily 6am-9pm. ❷

Erik Schat's Bakery, 763 N. Main St. (☎873-7156). A popular and tasty bakery that's been in town for a long time. Breads and pastries ($3-4) are baked fresh daily and served with good coffee. Salads, sandwiches, and soups also on the menu. Try the sheepherder's bread. Open daily 6am-10pm; in winter 7am-6pm. ❶

Kava Coffeehouse, 206 N. Main St. (☎872-1010). A hip spot to scarf healthy meals and slurp fresh smoothies. Outstanding coffee. The wares of local artisans grace cabinets along the walls. A favorite spot for local climbers and other outdoor athletes. Every Tu night is chess night (5-8pm). Open daily 6am-4pm, though hours can vary. ❶

🏔 OUTDOOR ACTIVITIES

EAST OF BISHOP

The mountains forming the Owens Valley, some of the highest on the continent, are a backpacker's Eden. In the other half of Inyo National Forest, which is split by U.S. 395, the yellow sands of the **White Mountains** rise to heights rivaling the Sierra. Because of the great variation in elevation, the abundance of pristine alpine lakes and streams, and the odd geological forces that have shaped some of the country's best rocks to climb, nearly any outdoor experience is possible. If you want to tackle the tough 1 mi. climb to the top of White Mountain itself (14,246 ft.), park your car (preferably 4WD) on White Mountain Rd., 22 mi. from Rte. 168. Unlike Mt. Whitney, a day-use permit is unnecessary, yet one can get nearly as high.

Scattered across the face of the White Mountains are California's **bristlecone pines,** the oldest living organisms on the planet. Gnarled, twisted, and warped into fantastic shapes, the trees may grow only one inch every 100 years. The slow growth at extreme altitudes (up to 12,000 ft.) has allowed the "Methuselah" specimen in the Schulman Group to survive for 4700 years (to prevent vandalism, they don't tell you which one it is). To get to the **Ancient Bristlecone Pine Forest,** follow Rte. 168 off U.S. 395 at Big Pine for 12 mi. Turn left at the sign to the Bristlecone Pine Forest and the White Mountains Research Station. The 11 mi. paved road takes you to **Schulman Grove,** at nearly 10,000 ft. Before the grove, 8 mi. down the road, you'll come to **Sierra View Overlook,** from where you can see the expansive Sierra Range, including parts of Yosemite and Mt. Whitney. Two short hikes head out from Schulman. The moderately strenuous 4.5 mi. Methuselah Walk and easy 1 mi. Discovery Trail lead through the hills. The drive to Patriarch Grove, home of some of the most astonishing trees, is a beautiful but unpaved 12 mi. from Schulman. The end of the road will take you to a trailhead for a 5 mi. hike to the summit of White Mountain Peak, doable in an intense day of hiking for the acclimated.

Moving past the Inyos from Deep Springs Valley (home of the lake and the college), the uninhabited **Eureka Valley** lies southeast of Inyo and northwest of Death Valley, in the Death Valley National Park. Its magnificent and haunting sand dunes are the tallest landlocked dunes in the country. If the sand is cool, flip off your shoes, climb to the top of the dunes, and roll down. The friction between the sand you disturb and the nearly 700 ft. of grains beneath makes a bizarre, deep sound. Local Native Americans called it "the singing of the sands." Roads lead into the valley from the Owens Valley near Big Pine and various points on the Nevada side, but none are reliable and not even the proverbial wild horses could drag you through when the road is washed out or snowed in. Check with the Death Valley Visitors Center (see p. 523) for specifics, and see **Desert Survival,** p. 505 for desert travel tips. Since it is a part of the national park, a $10 entry fee applies.

WEST OF BISHOP

A lot of fun can be had in the nearby Big Pine Canyon and Bishop Creek Canyon, to the south and west, and in Buttermilk Country and Rock Creek, to the west and northwest. To access Big Pine Canyon, head south on Rte. 395 to Big Pine, then head west on Crocker St. for 10 mi. to get to **Big Pine Canyon,** which guide Big Pine Creek through the thick groves of Jeffery Pines. This area is home to the southernmost glaciers in the US, remnants from the last ice age that once shaped much of the landscape. The largest of these glaciers is **Palisade Glacier,** which is about 2 mi. in length and many hundred feet thick. The **North Fork Trail** is a popular destination for hikers as well as rock and ice climbers. The trail passes Lakes #1, 2, and 3 as well as the stone cabin of Hollywood legend Lon Cheney before getting to the Palisade Glacier. The hike to the glacier and back is a long and challenging 18 mi. with a 2500 ft. ascent to 12,400 ft. **Fishing** enthusiasts favor Big Pine's seldom-traveled **South Fork Trail,** which leads to lakes laden with trout. The path is rather obscure, especially from Willow Lake (4 mi. from trailhead) to Brainard Lake (5 mi.).

Follow Line St. to Rte. 168, 14 mi. west of Bishop, to the lakes and campgrounds of **Bishop Creek Canyon.** At the north end of the canyon, 16 mi. down the highway, the road forks at **Intake 2,** an old electric power station where you can fish and stroll. Turning left at the fork will take you to **South Lake,** while going straight will take you to **Sabrina Lake,** both beautiful mountain reservoirs teeming with fish and near a number of hiking trails. At the end of the road heading to South Lake, hikers can fork onto the **Bishop Pass Trail,** which connects to leisurely trails that lead to Green, Treasure, and Chocolate Lakes and mountain meadows filled with wildflowers. More adventurous hikers can forge deeper into the wilderness along the trail and tackle some of the nearby 13,000 ft. peaks, including **Mount Agassiz.** The trail eventually connects to the John Muir Trail to Mt. Whitney.

From the Intake 2 fork, continue west 4 mi. to **Sabrina Basin** for secluded hiking and fishing opportunities. Steeper switchbacks off the main trail lead to the less populated **George Lake,** from where you can continue on to a number of 13,000 ft.

SIERRA NEVADA

lakes. Easier access to a secluded lake can be found down a narrow, one-way dirt road heading north to North Lake just before Lake Sabrina. From the campground here, **Lamark Lakes Trail** heads through wildflowers and rough rock to the lakes, while **Piute Pass** follows the north fork of Bishop Creek. Sabrina, North, and South Lakes provide spectacular **trout fishing.** The official angling season spans May-October. Contact the Chamber of Commerce (☎ 873-8405) for tournament and general fishing info. Tackle and taxidermy are available at Parcher's Resort, Bishop Creek Lodge, and Cardinal Village on North Fork Trailhead. (**Camping ❶** sites near Sabrina and South Lakes with piped water $12.) Serious hikers may want to connect here with the Inyo Segment (11,000 ft.) of the **John Muir Trail,** which connects Yosemite Valley with Mt. Whitney. The trail is 8 mi. west of the **White Mountain Visitors Center,** 798 N. Main St. (☎ 873-2500), in Bishop, which offers permits.

Seven miles down Rte. 168, a turnoff for Buttermilk Rd. will take you to some world-famous boulders in **Buttermilk Country.** Named for the dairy farms that once refreshed stagecoach parties heading through the region, the area is characterized by giant granite boulders, good for playing around, and great for rock climbing and mountain biking. About 4 mi. down the road, you'll come to the **Peabody Boulders,** the most celebrated of the outcroppings. Across from the boulders, **Grouse Mountain** (8100 ft.) is open for leisurely exploration and moderate-intensity climbing.

The recreation areas along **Rock Creek Canyon** are frequented year-round. Hair-raising precipices, plunging canyons, and velvet wildflowers mesmerize photographers and casual onlookers alike. Take U.S. 395 24 mi. north of Bishop, turn west on Rock Creek Rd., and continue up Rock Creek Canyon to the end of the road (park at Mosquito Flat). **Little Lakes Valley** is surrounded by 13,000 ft. peaks and lakes full of trout. A relaxed trail from Mosquito Flat explores the Valley's lakes and meadows. **Mono Pass Trail,** which branches off from the Little Lakes trail about ¼ mi. from the trailhead, leads to beautiful **Ruby Lake** and its staggering sheer granite walls, continues to Mono Pass, and connects with the John Muir Trail. There are numerous campgrounds on the way to **Mosquito Flat ❶,** and plenty of day-parking at each of the five trailheads (sites with toilets $12).

In winter, the evergreen forests and lake basins of this "range of light" (as Muir described the Eastern Sierra) make for spectacular **cross-country skiing.** Bishop Creek and Rock Creek drainages are the best areas. **Rock Creek Lodge** (☎ 935-4170) has groomed trails and a ski school. The ranger station has info (see p. 291).

🎵 ENTERTAINMENT

Although raging activity and unbridled excitement permeate everyday life in Bishop, several annual events add even more spice to this swinging metropolis. Haul your ass to town during Memorial Day weekend for the largest mule event in the world, **Mule Days** (☎ 872-4263). View 110 mule sporting events, 40,000 mule-obsessed fans, 700 mules, and the famous Mule Days Parade, which is long enough to be listed in the Guinness Book of World Records. The **Hotrods, Hippies & Polyester 50s-70s Dance** (☎ 873-3588) grooves every February, and the **Air Show** usually flies by on Fourth of July weekend. The City Park (behind the Visitors Center) has hosted **evening concerts** in the gazebo for 40 consecutive summers. (June-Aug. M 8-9pm. Free.) Food, games, and fun characterize the massive **Tri-County Fair** (☎ 873-3588) in late August or early September. Nearly every weekend in the summer has something going on, so contact the Visitors Center for details.

LONE PINE ☎ 760

Flanked to the west by the boundless High Sierra and the other-worldly Alabama Hills, the south by the unrivaled Mt. Whitney, and the east by Death Valley, it's no wonder that Hollywood has opened a franchise in Lone Pine (pop. 2016). For those who didn't grow up admiring Western heroes like Roy Rodgers and The Lone Ranger, *Gladiator* and, regrettably, *Gone in 60 Seconds,* are a few recent examples of the over 300 films and TV shows shot in this striking landscape. More than anything else, the natural wonders surrounding Lone Pine stir up the awe, reverence, excitement, and twinge of fear that the great Western frontier has so powerfully evoked throughout American history, and which has been so frequently glamorized on screen. Hikers, mountaineers, anglers, mountain bikers, rock climbers, and artists are drawn to this mythical American wilderness. Once in town, however, myth and legend take a back seat to a serious outdoor experience.

■■ ■ ORIENTATION & PRACTICAL INFORMATION

Straddling U.S. 395, Lone Pine is the first Sierra town northeast on Rte. 136 from Death Valley. Independence, the county seat, is 15 mi. north, while Bishop is 60 mi. north. L.A. is 4hr. away, 212 mi. south along U.S. 395, and southwest along Rte. 14. Yosemite is a 5-6hr., 210 mi. drive north on U.S. 395. Upon reaching Lone Pine, U.S. 395 becomes Main St.; Washington St. is one block west.

Buses: Since Greyhound has canceled service to the Eastern Sierra, getting to Lone Pine by bus is rather difficult. You can take Greyhound or Amtrak to Carson City, where **CREST** (☎800-922-1930) departs on Rte. 395 Tu and Th-F at 2pm, and arrives in Bishop, 60 mi. north of Lone Pine, at 6:30pm. A separate, non-connecting bus passes through Bishop on its way to Lone Pine on M, W, F. Contact CREST to figure out the best way to match up buses.

Airport: Inyokern Airport (IYK), in Inyokern (☎377-5844), 70 mi. south on Rte. 395. Daily service to and from Los Angeles International Aiport by United Airlines (www.ual.com). $200-300 round-trip.

Car Rental: Lindsey Automotive, 361 S. Washington St. (☎876-4789). Rates from $60 per day. 150 mi. included. Must be at least 21 with credit card. Open daily 8am-5pm. After-hours service available for a charge.

Auto Repairs: Don's Garage, 840 S. Main St. (☎876-4415). Open daily 8am-7pm.

AAA Emergency Road Service: ☎872-8241.

Visitor Information:

Interagency Visitors Center (☎876-6222), at U.S. 395 and Rte. 136, about 1 mi. south of town. Joint venture between a number of agencies, including the Forest Service and University of California. Excellent maps and guidebooks, plus small exhibits. Informative handouts on hiking in the area. Open July-Sept. daily 8am-5:50pm; Oct.-June 8am-4:50pm.

Chamber of Commerce, 126 S. Main St. (☎876-4444 or toll-free 877-253-8981; www.lone-pine.com), in Lone Pine. Same services as the Visitors Center. Cheerful, knowledgeable employees. Open M-Sa 9am-5pm.

Mount Whitney/Inyo National Forest Ranger Station, 640 S. Main St. (☎876-6200; www.r5.fs.fed.us/inyo/vvc/index.htm), in Lone Pine. Programs on regional wildlife and history. Topographical and trail maps for backcountry camping. Gives out **wilderness permits,** which are free and required in the backcountry. All trails within the Ansel Adams, John Muir, Dinkey Lakes, and Golden Trout have overnight usage quotas (usually 10-30 people). Reserve permits up to 6

SIERRA NEVADA

months in advance for the quota season, May 1-Nov. 1 ($5); self-register in the winter. 40% of trail quotas saved for walk-ins during the quota season. **Mt. Whitney** has 60 overnight and 130 day-use permits, all of which must be reserved in advance (no walk-ins). A lottery is held every Feb. where day and overnight permits are issued. Contact the ranger station or visit the website for an application, which must be mailed or faxed in. Some spots are usually left over, and can be reserved beginning in May. Station open daily 7am-noon and 1-4:30pm. **Wilderness Reservations,** P.O. Box 430, Big Pine 93545 (☎888-374-3773; fax 938-1137).

Laundromat: Coin-Op Laundromat, 105 W. Post St., just off Main St. Wash $1.25, 12min. dry $0.25. Open daily 6:30am-9pm. Change machines.

Showers: Kirk's Barber Shop, 114 N. Main St. (☎876-5700; $4), or on the mountain at **Whitney Portal** store ($3).

Police: Inyo County Sheriff, Lone Pine Substation, S. Washington St. (☎876-5606); County Headquarters (☎878-0383).

Hospital: Southern Inyo, 501 E. Locust St. (☎876-5501).

Library and Internet Access: Lone Pine Public Library (☎876-5031), on S. Washington St. Open M-Tu and Th-F 9am-noon and 1-5pm, W 6-9pm, Sa 10am-1pm. 1hr. per day.

Post Office: 121 Bush St. (☎876-5681), between Jackson and Main St. Open M-F 9am-5pm. **Postal Code:** 93545.

ACCOMMODATIONS

Many clean but high-priced motels are available here. Weekdays are cheapest, but rates fluctuate widely depending on demand; make reservations or arrive early.

■ **Historical Dow Hotel,** 310 S. Main St. (☎876-5521, reservations 800-824-9317; www.dowvillamotel.com). Built during Lone Pine's Hollywood heyday to house pouty movie stars, the welcoming lobby of this old hotel boasts several couches, a TV, tea and coffee bar, and a fireplace. Pool and jacuzzi open 24hr. Next to the more upscale **Dow Villa Motel ❺,** with newer rooms and more amenities. Great mountain views. Hotel double rooms with shared bath start at $38, private baths $52. Motel rooms, some sleeping up to 6 people $80-115. ❸

Alabama Hills Inn, 1920 S. Main St. (☎876-8700; www.alabamahillsinn.com/), 1 mi. south of Lone Pine. Named for the frequently filmed hills nearby, this new motel is close to Peter's Pumpkin and Wounded Knight. Clean, standard hotel rooms all have mountain views. Cable, fridge, and microwave. Heated pool open 24hr. Continental breakfast included. Singles Apr.-Oct. from $59; Nov.-Mar. $49. $10 extra for double, patio, or balcony. AAA discount 10%. ❹

De La Cour Ranch, 2½ mi. past Lubken Canyon Rd. on Horseshow Meadow Rd. (☎876-0022), off Whitney Portal Rd. in Lone Pine. Secluded, spacious cabin with bedroom/living room, full kitchen, and bathroom. Futon and loft sleep 4 inside, 2 tent bungalows sleep another 4. Feels like home. Cabin $150, weekly $750. Reserve in advance. ❺

CAMPING

Camping is cheap, scenic, and conveniently located. As with motels in the area, make reservations or arrive early.

■ **Whitney Portal Campground** (Mt. Whitney ranger ☎876-6200, reservations 800-280-2267), 8000 ft., on Whitney Portal Rd., 13 mi. west of town. Surrounding evergreens, a rushing stream, and phenomenal views make this an exceptional campground. Campground hosts Nicki and Jim are happy to chat. Served by the **Whitney Portal Store,** which carries light food, guidebooks, and outerwear. (Open June-Sept. daily 7am-9pm.) Pay phone and a small restaurant (burgers $6). 7-night max. stay. Some sites reserved for first-come, first-camp. Open May-Oct. Sites $14; group sites $30. ❶

Diaz Lake Campground, 3700 ft., on U.S. 395 (☎876-5656), 2 mi. south of Lone Pine. 200 quiet, tree-lined sites overlooking Diaz Lake. Watersports fanatics will love the sites on the lake's far shore—the shoreline facilitates smooth watercraft launches. Grills, flush toilets, and showers. 15-day max. stay. Sites $14. ●

Portagee Joe, 3800 ft., ½ mi. from Lone Pine, on Whitney Portal Rd. Tree-lined camping by a small stream. 15 sites. Water and vault toilets. Sites $10. ●

Lone Pine Campground (reservations ☎877-444-6777), 6000 ft. Take Whitney Portal Rd. from Lone Pine for about 7 mi. 38 immaculate sites in close proximity to numerous trailheads and stellar views of the soaring granite faces. Water and vault toilets. 14-day max. stay. Open Mar.-Nov. Sites $12, seniors $6. ●

☕ FOOD

Lone Pine has its share of coffee shops and 24hr. mini-marts, but not much else. Grab groceries in town at **Joseph's Bi-Rite Market,** 119 S. Main St., which also has a hearty, if heavy, hot deli. (☎876-4378. Open daily 8am-8pm.) Most restaurants are nondescript, but cheap, decent fare is available.

P.J.'s Bake and Broil, 446 Main St. (☎876-5796). Down-to-earth food and prices. BBQ beef sandwich ($5.50) is a great post-climb treat. A favorite of the locals, it's the only restaurant open and serving breakfast all day. Open F-Sa 24hr., Su-Th 7am-10pm. ❷

Pizza Factory, 301 S. Main St. (☎876-4707). The friendly people at the Factory churn out fresh, hot pizzas in minutes. The slightly sweet dough tastes delicious, whether you eat your own mini (4 slices; $4) or share a large (10 slices; $10.50). Pasta, calzones, deli sandwiches, beer and wine. Open Su-Th 11am-10pm, F-Sa 11am-10pm. ●

Seasons Restaurant, on the corner of Rte. 395 and Whitney Portal Rd. (☎876-8927). The most upscale restaurant in town, serving "continental" type cuisine ($10-25) including some excellent seafood entrees. Good selection of California and imported wines. Open daily 5-10pm; in winter closed Su. ●

◉ SIGHTS

With the craggy edges of **Mount Whitney** as the star of the show, the parts of the bordering **Inyo National Forest** form a suitable supporting cast. All of the Sierra's tallest peaks are here, with many of them towering over 14,000 ft.

Well before Whitney Portal, along Whitney Portal Rd., is **Movie Road,** which leads to the scenic **Alabama Hills.** A bouldered dreamscape of golden-brown granite formations, the hills were the stage set for fictionalized Hollywood cowboy 'n' Indian tales like the 1920s *How the West Was Won.* In all, over 250 Westerns were filmed here, including such television shoot-'em-ups as *Bonanza* and *Rawhide,* and, more recently, countless SUV commercials. Recent flicks include *Maverick, Star Trek: Generations,* and *Gladiator.* The Chamber of Commerce dispense a **movie location map** that will help you find where any film was shot. Lone Piners celebrate the Hills' glamorous career with the annual **Lone Pine Film Festival** (☎876-4314), every Columbus Day weekend, where only films shot in the region are screened.

The **Eastern California Museum,** 155 N. Grant St., off Market St. in Independence, has a collection featuring local Paiute and Shoshone handicrafts, preserved equipment used by locals to construct the Los Angeles aqueduct, and a display on the Manzanar internment camp. Next door is a recreation of a small 1880s pioneer village, Little Pine. (☎878-0258. Open Su-M and W-Sa 10am-4pm. Donation $1.)

On U.S. 395, between Lone Pine to the south and Independence to the north, lies the **Manzanar National Historic Site,** symbolic of one of the most shameful chapters in American history. Previously known as a "relocation" camp, it was the first of 10 internment centers that the US established after Japan's 1941 attack on Pearl Harbor to contain Japanese Americans, whom the government saw as enemy sympathizers. From March 1942-1945, 10,000 people were held here. Aggressively and conspicuously ignored by the government, the camp is reduced to a few building foundations and some barbed wire. On the last Saturday of every April, an annual pilgrimage of former internees is held at the camp's cemetery. The day of remembrance and education is open to the public.

Once a big lake used to transport bullion from the nearby gold mines, **Owens Dry Lake,** 5 mi. south of town on Rte. 395, is now a big, mineral-rich, multi-colored dry lakebed. In the 1920s, freshwater streams that fed the river were diverted to the L.A. aqueduct, leaving the 75 sq. mi. lake to dry up under the sun. The pinkish hue at lake bottom is from bacteria. The dry salts exposed when the water disappeared have caused a serious dust problem in the area; in fact, the Environmental Protection Agency has deemed the area around Owens Lake the dustiest in the US.

One of the best-preserved ghost towns in the state, **Cerro Gordo** (☎876-1860), or "Fat Hill," was once producing nearly 10,000 lb. of silver a day, all bound for L.A., where it accounted for one-third of all business transactions in the Port of L.A. in the late 1800s. Today, the town's remains are private property. Nonetheless, they are open to the public, featuring old time hotels, offices, a brothel, mining structures and a museum. Cerro Gordo is 8 mi. down a dirt road from Keeler, off Rte. 270 south of Lone Pine. Call ahead if you want to visit.

⚠ HIKING

Climbing Mt. Whitney requires significant preparation, both in terms of physical endurance and logistics. Unlike most other Inyo trails, the main Mt. Whitney trail is on a reservation-only system, meaning no first-come, first-served permits are issued during the quota season, May 1-November 1. The trail is so popular that it has been put on lottery system. Throughout the month of February, lottery applications (available at www.r5.fs.fed.us/inyo/vvc/wild_permits/permits.htm or by calling ☎873-2483) are accepted for both day and overnight use permits. Overnight hikers have about a 60% chance of getting a spot, while day hikers have about a 90% chance, though these odds are highly dependent on dates and group size. A few permits go unissued every year, and can be reserved beginning in May.

One of the most popular trails in the nation, the **Mount Whitney Trail** to the highest point in the lower 48 states, is full of adventurers, both experienced and amateur, looking for bragging rights. The trailhead for **Mount Whitney** is at 8365 ft. and ascends over 6000 ft., and hikers should be wary of the effects of altitude. Hike slowly and allow extra time in your itinerary, but most importantly, spend some time hiking at higher altitudes; altitude sickness is a miserable affliction. Many campers spend a few days in the area before attempting higher climbs. Also remember that this is bear country. Ingenious bears are adept at breaking into cars and ripping apart backpacks (see **Bears Will Eat You,** p. 45). Rent a bear-proof food container at one of the ranger stations ($10 plus deposit). The **Whitney Trailhead Ranger Station** (☎876-6200) is on Whitney Portal Rd., 13 mi. west of Lone Pine. The 11 mi. trek to the top of Mt. Whitney usually takes two to three days, though the very fit and acclimated can summit and return in one long day. While more of a strenuous hike than a mountain climb, this non-technical route is feasible only in late spring and summer when there is no ice. The mountain can become quite cold, especially at night, so only attempt the journey with proper outerwear. Hiking permits for both day and overnight use are required. Write to the **Mount Whitney Ranger Station** at 640 S. Main St, Lone Pine, CA 93545. Include your desired dates and the number of your party. For rock climbers, Mt. Whitney's **East Face** is a year-round challenge. A backcountry route to the Mt. Whitney summit, the **Cottonwood Lakes Trail** (10,000 ft. at the trailhead) squeezes over 40 mi. between the forests that abut the John Muir Wilderness and Sequoia National Park, passing some of the most incredible nature in the country along the way. Follow Whitney Portal Rd. for 4 mi. from Lone Pine and take Horseshoe Meadow Rd. 20 mi. to the trailhead. The trail is on the quota system from June-September 15.

Many moderate **day hikes** explore the Eastern Sierra out of the Whitney Portal. The hour-long hike along **Horseshoe Meadow Trail** to **Golden Trout Wilderness** passes several dozen high mountain lakes that mirror the Inyo Mountains. **Horseshoe Meadow** has camping ❶ (sites $6) and equestrian facilities ($12 per horse). The **Meysan Lake Trail** is a tough 4.7 mi. haul from Whitney Portal to an exquisite high-altitude lake. Consider buying a topographical map, as the trail can be difficult to follow at times. The **Whitney Portal Trail** offers a more challenging, 6hr. hike from the Lone Pine campground to Whitney Portal campground. The trail follows Lone Pine Creek to the densely forested higher altitudes and offers incredible views of Mt. Whitney and the Owens Valley.

If you've got bulletproof muscles and high-octane willpower, you may want to dig into one of the toughest races in the world. Each spring, Lone Pine hosts the **Death Valley to Mt. Whitney Race** for both runners and cyclists. The arduous trek departs from Stovepipe Wells (elevation 5 ft.) in Death Valley and struggles over an undulating 100 mi. course to the 8300 ft. Whitney Portal. Day one is 78 mi.; day two climbs the last 22 mi. This brutal exercise makes a marathon look like a giddy April stroll. Speaking of marathons, Lone Pine stages a standard marathon, the high elevation **Wild Wild West Marathon,** considered the 7th most difficult in the nation, the previous weekend. Interested athletes can enter by contacting the **Chamber of Commerce** (see p. 295). For those of you yawning, there is also a 135 mi. Badwater (Death Valley) to Whitney **ultra marathon** (☎ 510-528-3263) in sweltering late July. This invitation-only odyssey usually takes two to three days for the world's top endurance athletes to complete, while the unimaginably tough winners tend to finish in just over a full day of pain. You're unlikely to find a more intense athletic event anywhere, ever.

MAMMOTH LAKES ☎ 760

Home to one of the most popular ski resorts in the United States, the town of Mammoth Lakes (pop. 5305) has transformed itself into a giant year-round playground. Snowfall averages over 350 in. a year, creating about 3500 acres of skiable terrain. High altitudes mean that snow lasts as late as July some years, cutting the off-season down to four months. As soon as the snow is gone, mountain bikers invade the town by the thousands to take on Mammoth Mountain; skateboarders come to test their skills in some of the stiffest competitions in the country; and fisherfolk come to the magma-warmed creeks to catch some hot fish. There is fun nearly every hour of the day and every day of the week The nightlife is lively and entirely full of athletes who come to this alpine paradise to have mammoth fun.

SIERRA NEVADA

⬅ TRANSPORTATION

Bus: CREST (☎ 800-922-1930) runs buses Tu and Th-F at 2pm from **Carson City,** arriving in **Mammoth Lakes** around 5:20pm. Fare $17.

Airport: Reno/Tahoe International (☎ 775-328-6400). Served daily by major carriers. Mammoth Shuttle provides bus connections to town (see below).

Public Transit:

Inyo-Mono Dial-A-Ride (☎ 872-1901) provides service to **Bishop, Bridgeport, Lee Vining, June Lake,** and **Crowley Lake** from Mammoth Lakes McDonald's and Bishop K-Mart M, W, Sa; fare depends on location.

Mammoth Shuttle Service (☎934-3030) provides on-call service M-Th 8am-midnight, F-Sa 8am-2am. Within town $5, each additional person $2; to lodge $10, each additional person $3.

Mammoth Area Shuttle or **MAS** (☎934-3030) offers a red line shuttle to town and the main lodge. During ski season, shuttles connect to chairlifts every 15min. 7am-midnight. Free. In summer, a shuttle every 20min. 7:30pm-5:30pm goes from main lodge to **Reds Meadow, Devils Post Pile,** and 8 other stops in the forest. The shuttle is mandatory to enter these areas from 7am-7pm. Last run out of Reds Meadow 8pm. Day pass $5, good for duration of trip if camping.

YARTS (☎800-636-6684; www.yarts.com) runs daily between **Yosemite Valley** and **Mammoth Lakes,** stopping at Lee Vining along the way. Departs from Mammoth Inn at 7am. Round-trip to Yosemite $20.

Sierra Express (☎924-8294) is a door-to-door shuttle service that runs anywhere from 7am-2am. Rates fluctuate.

Car Rental: U-SAVE, 452 Old Mammoth Rd. #1J (☎934-4999 or 800-207-2681). 4WD vehicles from $62 per day with 150 mi. included, or $372 per week with 1050 mi. included; $0.25 each additional mi. Compacts from $42/252. Rentals available at the **Chevron** (☎934-8111), next to the Post Office. Cars $40-90 per day, 150 mi. included; $0.25 each additional mi.

Auto Repairs: AAA Emergency Road Service: ☎800-400-4222.

■ ⛶ ORIENTATION & PRACTICAL INFORMATION

Mammoth Lakes is on U.S. 395, 160 mi. south of Reno, 325 mi. north of L.A., and 40 mi. southeast of the eastern entrance to Yosemite. Rte. 203 runs through the town as **Main Street** and then veers off to the right as **Minaret Road.** After Minaret Rd., Main St. becomes Lake Mary Rd. In the winter, the roads from L.A. are jammed with weekend skiers making the 6hr. journey up to the slopes.

Equipment Rental: Footloose Sports Shop, 3043 Main St. (☎934-2400), rents ski packages from $35 per day; snowboard packages from $25 per day; mountain bikes from $30 per day. Ski tuning, boot fitting, and trail info. Open M-F 8am-7pm, Sa 7am-8pm, Su 7am-6pm. **Rick's Sport Center,** 3241 Main St. (☎934-3416). Daily rod rental $10. 10-day non-resident license $30, yearly pass $80. Package fishing deal (waders, booties, fins, and float tube) $30 per day. Fly-fishing lessons available. Open daily 6am-8pm; off-season 7am-7pm.

Visitor Information: Inyo National Forest Visitors Center and Chamber of Commerce (☎924-5500; www.visitmammoth.com), on Rte. 203 west of U.S. 395, north of town. Area info and discounts on accommodations and food; offers *Mammoth Times* ($0.50), free video, exhibits, and walks. Accommodations reservations. Open daily 8am-5pm.

Bank: Bank of America, 3069 Main St. (☎934-6830). Open M-Th 9am-4pm, F 9am-6pm. **24hr. ATM.**

Laundromat: Mammoth Lakes Laundromat (☎934-8207), on Laurel Mountain Rd., 1 block off Main St. Wash $1.25, snappy 7½min. dry $0.25. Friendly staff. Open M-Sa 8:30am-6:30pm, Su 8:30am-5pm. Last wash 1½hr. before closing.

Weather: ☎934-7669.

Ski Conditions: Mammoth Mountain Snow Conditions (☎934-6166). **Mammoth Mountain Ski Area** (☎934-2571). **June Mountain Ski Area** (☎648-7733).

Medical Services: Mammoth Hospital, 185 Sierra Park Rd. (☎934-3311). Offers 24hr. emergency care.

Post Office: 3330 Main St. Open M-F 8:30am-5pm. **Postal Code:** 93546.

ACCOMMODATIONS

As with most ski resorts, lodging is much more expensive in the winter. Condo rentals are a comfortable choice for groups of three or more, starting at $100 per night. **Mammoth Reservation Bureau** (☎800-462-5571; www.mammothvacations.com) can make rental arrangements. For lone travelers, dorm-style motels are the cheapest option. Make reservations far in advance.

Davison St. Guest House, 19 Davison Rd. (☎924-2188), off Main St. Perched on the hill, Davison houses one of the best views in town. Friendly management, kitchen, fireplace, and huge common room with couches, TV/VCR, and stereo. Clean and homey. Dorms $18; private rooms $35-50. In winter dorms $22-27; private rooms $53-87. ❷

Swiss Chalet, 3776 Viewpoint Rd. (☎934-2403 or 800-937-9477), just off Main St. 21 hilltop motel rooms with vaulted wood ceilings and stunning mountain views. Immaculate rooms with cable TV, refrigerator, ski rack, and coffee. Old-fashioned appearance with hand-painted wooden signs outside each door. Sundeck, indoor jacuzzi, and sauna are amazing. Rooms $60-75; in winter $80-95. ❺

Holiday Haus, 3905 Main St. (☎934-2414). Spacious and clean standard rooms and cabins, some with fireplaces and kitchens. Centrally located with spa on site. One of the best deals in town. Summer M-Th doubles from $45; in winter from $50. Suite for up to 6 with kitchen from $60 in winter. ❹

CAMPING

There are nearly 20 Inyo Forest public **campgrounds** ❶ (sites $13-15) in the area, at Mammoth Lakes, Mammoth Village, Convict Lake, Red's Meadow, Agnew Meadow, and June Lake. All sites have piped water, and most are near fishing and hiking. Interested parties should contact the **Mammoth Ranger District** (☎924-5500) for info. Reservations can be made for New and Old Shady Rest, and at nearby Sherwin Creek (☎877-444-6777; www.reserveusa.com).

Twin Lakes, 8600 ft., ½ mi. off Lake Mary Rd., about 2 mi. outside town. In a pine forest, the 95 magnificent sites are near fishing and swimming at Twin Lakes. General store nearby with the essentials and showers. Perfect view of Twin Falls rushing into the southern end of Upper Twin Lake. Piped water and flush toilets. 7-night max. stay. Open June-Nov. Sites $14. Showers $2. ❶

New Shady Rest, 7800 ft., on Rte. 203 across from McDonald's. A 5min. walk into the heart of town. Camping isn't the same when you can see the Golden Arches through the trees, but the sites are densely wooded and manage to feel remote. 14-night max. stay. 94 sites $13. ❶

Lake Mary, 8900 ft., on Lake Mary Loop Rd. Camping can't get much better than this: clear water, trout jumping into your boat, beaches to relax on, and a general store for when you get tired of roughin' it. 14-night max. stay. Open June to mid-Sept. 48 sites $14. ❶

FOOD & NIGHTLIFE

Fast food franchises exert monopolistic control over cheap meals, but adventurous palates need not despair. Some places have prices as high as the neighboring peaks, but others are more down to earth.

▨ **Schat's Bakery and Cafe,** 3305 Main St. (☎934-6055). Arguably the best bakery in town, with cappuccino ($2.25) or 1 lb. loaf of succulent sourdough ($3). Inside the bakery, the **Vermeer Deli ❷** is perfect for picnic assembly, with famously fresh sandwiches ($7). Deli open daily 10am-2pm. Bakery open M-F 5:30am-6pm, Sa-Su 5:30am-6pm. ❶

Whiskey Creek (☎934-2555), at Lake Mary and Minaret St. Large bar area with live entertainment (Th-Sa) and an aura of dimly-lit sophistication. Meaty American fare with some international influences (Chinese five spice duck $18; rare tuna with wasabi mashed potatoes $21; prime rib dinner $23). Microbrews $3. Happy Hour M-F 5-7pm with drafts $1. Bar open daily 5pm-1:30am; kitchen open daily 5:30-10pm. Open in winter 5-10pm. ❺

Nick-n-Willies Pizza & Subs, 76 Old Mammoth Rd. (☎934-2012). The best pizza in town, and the subs aren't bad either. Wide variety of toppings, including chipotle, sun dried tomatoes, feta cheese, and pesto. Cheese slice $2.50, small pizza $9. Subs, like the Hot Pizzawich (sauce, pepperoni, mushrooms, olives, red onions, and mozzarella) $6-7. Open daily 11:30am-9pm. ❶

Base Camp Cafe, on Main St. (☎934-3900), across from the Post Office. Excellent and inexpensive breakfast, lunch, and dinner. Breakfast and "Breakfast Lite" can be had for as little as $2. Sandwiches ($4-6) include a delicious California chicken roll (grilled chicken, avocado, bacon, swiss cheese, and garlic mayo on a French loaf). Brown bag lunches $7 (call ahead). Open daily 6am-10pm. ❷

⊙ SIGHTS

There's plenty to see in Mammoth Lakes, much of which is accessible by the **MAS shuttle service** (see p. 299). Rte. 203 and the nearby **campground ❶** (sites $12-14) are operational only in summer and may open as late as July in years with heavy snows. In an effort to keep the area from being completely trampled, rangers have introduced a shuttle service between the parking area at the Mammoth Mountain Inn and the monument center, which all visitors—drivers and hikers alike—must use from 7am-7pm (day pass $5).

DEVIL'S POSTPILE NATIONAL MONUMENT AND RAINBOW FALLS. An intriguing geological formation of basalt columns 40-60 ft. high, the Devil's Postpile was formed when lava oozed through Mammoth Pass thousands of years ago and then cooled, cracking into hexagonal formations when the pressure of solidifaction was more powerful than the flow of lava. After the magma cooled, ancient glaciers exposed and polished the posts. A pleasant 3 mi. walk from the Devil's Postpile Monument, the middle fork of the San Joaquin River drops 101 ft. into a glistening green pool at Rainbow Falls. There is also much to do beyond Postpile-gazing; take a stroll around Sotcher Lake, steep in Fisher Creek Hot Springs, or hike a part of the John Muir Trail to fully appreciate the marvels of the park. To really get to know the Postpile, camp at one of the six area campgrounds (7600-8400 ft.), all of which have piped water. *(From U.S. 395, the Devil's Postpile/Rainbow Falls trailhead can be reached by a 15 mi. drive past Minaret Summit on Rte. 203. Driving in is prohibited, however; take the shuttle bus. Guided ranger walks daily 11am. Camp sites ❷ $16. Shuttle passes valid for the duration of the trip for campers, mention this when purchasing.)*

FUN WITH VOLCANOES. From the shuttle stop, it's an easy 0.25 mi. jaunt to the **Inyo Craters,** spectacular water-filled volcanic blast holes that are a favorite spot for area waterfowl. The craters are only about 500 years old, active reminders of the area's shaky underground history. The trailhead can be reached from Mammoth Scenic Loop Rd., a gently winding thoroughfare that leads to sights between Rte. 203 and U.S. 395. A 10 mi. **mountain biking** loop explores the craters up close.

Obsidian Dome lies 14 mi. north of Mammoth Junction and 1 mi. west of U.S. 395 on Glass Flow Rd. (follow the sign to Lava Flow). This vast blob of solid volcanic glass was formed by the quick chilling of volcanic lava around 1000 years ago.

🏔 OUTDOOR ACTIVITIES

HIKING

Day hikes in the area are clustered around the Mammoth Lakes Basin and Reds Meadow. A quick 0.5 mi. hike from the Twin Lakes turn-off on Lake Mary Rd. culminates in spectacular views of Owens Valley and Crowley Lake from the **Panorama Dome.** Lake Mamie has a picturesque picnic area and many short hikes leading out to Lake George, where exposed granite sheets attract climbers. For short but stunning hikes through wildflowers and amazing scenery, trek the **Crystal Lake Trail** (2.5 mi.) or the **Barrett Lake Trail,** both of which leave from the Lake George entrance parking lot. **Horseshoe Lake** is a popular swimming spot and also the trailhead for the impressive Mammoth Pass Trail. The fork in the trail leads to **McLeod Lake** on the left or **Red's Meadow** on the right. In Agnew Meadows (take the shuttle), moderate trails lead to the tranquil **Shadow** (3.5 mi.) and **Ediza** (6.5 mi.) lakes from the campground. Also departing from Agnew Meadows is a very challenging day hike or a great overnighter, the trail to **Thousand Island Lake.** (10 mi.) **Mammoth Sporting Goods** (☎934-3239) and **Sandy's Ski & Sport** (☎934-7518) can equip more experienced hikers with gear and info on more challenging climbs.

FISHING

Not one of the over 100 lakes near town (60 are within a 5 mi. radius) actually goes by the name of Mammoth Lake. The area's largest, most beautiful lake, the 1 mi. long **Lake Mary,** is popular for boating, sailing, and fishing. Anglers converge on the Mammoth area each summer to test their skills on some of the best **trout lakes** in the country. Permits are required for anyone over 16 (the Visitors Center has info on other regulations) and can be expensive for non-residents. Fanatics will find the frequent fishing derbies well worth the price of entry, but less competitive types might prefer to try their luck at the area's serene and well-stocked backcountry waters. Manmade reservoir **Crowley Lake** in Owens Valley, 12 mi. south of town, is a fishing mecca, yielding over 80 tons of rainbow trout each summer and attracting a city's worth of people on opening day. (☎935-4301. Motorboat rental $55 per day; parking included. Parking without rental $6 per day. **Campsites ❷** with full hookup $25.) Just south of town on Rte. 395, **Convict Lake** is deep and home to some monster trout, but its clear water and windy surroundings can make catching one a challenge. (☎934-3800. Fishing boats $15 per hour, $65 per day. Camping sites $13.) **Owens River,** south on Rte. 395 to Benton Crossing Rd. and then 3 mi. to a bridge and a dirt road that follows the river, is a great spot for fly fishing.

The trout-filled **Hot Creek Geothermal Area,** 5 mi. south of town off U.S. 395 at Hot Creek Rd., also allows catch-and-release fishing. The waters here are warmed by the liquid magma sending up steam from miles below the creek bed following a toasty volcanic blast. Hungry trout bathe in these warm waters year-round. Several trails lead to the springs, but be careful—a close look may result in a severe burn. Tours of the hot springs and trout hatchery are given (open daily 8am-4pm).

🎵 ENTERTAINMENT

Mammoth is like a Mountain Dew commercial come to life—extreme activities abound, from wall-climbing to dogsledding. **Mammoth Mountain High Adventure** gets people up high. The stately climbing wall stands like a modern-day shrine to extreme sports, beckoning both the inexperienced and the professional. (☎924-5683. Open daily 10am-6pm. $6 per climb, $13 per hr., $22 per day; discount for groups of 3 or more.) The **Map and Compass Course** has more of an outdoor sleuth/guerrilla warfare approach to freedom. Explore and hike through a freelance course. ($15 round trip for 2hr. course; includes compass rental and map and introductory lesson.) Swing, tightrope walk, and rappel to freedom in the **High Ropes Course.** (4hr.; Th-Sa 1pm, Su 10am. $43, group rate $40 per person.)

Visitors can ride the **Mammoth Mountain Gondola** for a view miles above the rest. (☎934-2571. Open daily 8am-4pm. Round-trip $16, children $8; day pass for gondola and trail use $25. Round-trip chair ride only $10, children $5.) Exit the gondola at the top for a mountain biking extravaganza of more than 80 mi. of twisted trails in **Mammoth Mountain Bike Park,** where the ride starts at 11,053 ft. and heads straight down on rocky ski trails. (☎934-0706. Helmets required. Open 9am-6pm. 1 day pass $29, children $15. Unlimited day pass and bike rental $62/31.) In case you somehow exhaust your recreation opportunities, a bus also runs daily to **Yosemite National Park** (see **Transportation,**p. 299) from the mountain lodge.

Basically every weekend in every season Mammoth is host to some wild festival, from triathlons to skateboarding contests, dogsledding to canoe races—it's like a year-round summer camp. The **Mammoth Festival of Beers and Bluesapalooza** chugs truckloads of over 40 microbrews and piles of BBQ dishes to the sounds of some of the country's best blues in early August. (☎934-0606. Unlimited beer and 4 food coupons $36; music only $28.) The **Mammoth Lakes Jazz Jubilee,** in mid-July, is a local favorite. (☎934-2478. Day entry $30, 3 day pass $60.) The **Mammoth Motorcross Race** (☎934-0642), in late June, is one of the area's most popular athletic competitions, and the **National Mountain Biking Championships** (☎934-0651), in early September, attracts nearly 50,000 people. Winter festivities include some cross-country ski races, a **Snowshow Play Day** (☎934-7566) in February, a **Winterfestival** (☎934-6643) in March, and a **marathon** (☎934-2442) in late March.

SKIING & WINTER RECREATION. With 150 downhill runs, 28 lifts, and miles of nordic trails, Mammoth is one of the country's premier winter resorts. The season extends from November to June; in a good year, downhill skiing can last through July. Visiting during a slow time (avoiding weekends and major holidays) keeps costs lower. Rent skis in town (see **Equipment Rental,** p. 300); resort-run shops usually charge 10-20% more. Mammoth Mountain lift tickets can be purchased at the **Main Lodge,** at the base of the mountain on Minaret Rd. (☎934-2571. Open daily 7:30am-3pm.) Day passes are available for everyone. (Experienced day pass $45, teens $35, children $22, seniors $22. Beginners $25 for all ages.) Group ski lessons are available for all levels ($54) and beginners ($35) every day. A special first-timers package includes rentals, day pass, and a lesson for $78. A free **shuttle bus (MAS)** transports skiers between lifts, town, and the Main Lodge (see p. 299). The US Forest Service provides info and tips on the area's cross-country trails.

Mammoth has miles of trails and open areas for **snowmobiles.** The **Mammoth Lake Snowmobile Association** maps out open and restricted areas. Visitors over 16 years old with a driver's license can rent snowmobiles at **Center Street Polaris DJ Snowmobile.** (☎934-4020. Open M-Sa 8am-4:30pm. One-rider 2hr. $85, 4hr. $167; two-rider $115/245.) Mammoth has lately pioneered **bobsledding;** although runs are slow enough for non-Olympians, they can be exhilarating, especially at night. **Bobsledz,** on Minaret Rd. halfway to the lodge, can hook you up. (☎934-7533. Open daily 10am-4pm; in summer 4:30-7:30pm.)

June Mountain Ski Area, at U.S. 395 North and Rte. 158 West, 20 mi. north of Mammoth Lakes, has less stellar skiing and correspondingly shorter lines than Mammoth. (☎648-7733. Lift tickets $45, ages 19-23 $40, ages 13-18 $35, children and seniors $25. Lift tickets are available in the Tram Haus next to the parking lot.

THE CENTRAL VALLEY

California's Central Valley minds its own agribusiness. Lifestyles here are conservative, unadorned, and far removed from the spotlight that scrutinizes the Valley's kooky western neighbors. Known as one of the most fertile and productive regions in the world, the San Joaquin Valley stretches from the Tehachapi Range south of Bakersfield to just north of Stockton, where it becomes known as the Sacramento Valley. From there, the Valley continues on northward past Chico, before it is engulfed by the Cascades. The land is flat, the air is oven-hot, and the endless fields and rows of fruit trees are broken only by hordes of cars racing up and down the razor-straight slashes of I-5 and Rte. 99. No other place in the state seems so irreconcilable with the idea of California that dominates popular imagination.

SACRAMENTO   ☎916

Sacramento (area pop. 1.9 million) is the distinctive capital of a highly distinctive state. In 1848, Swiss emigré John Sutter, fleeing debtor's prison back home, purchased 48,000 dusty acres from the Miwok tribe for a few trinkets. His trading fort became the central pavilion for the influx of gold miners to the Valley in the 1850s. Over the next century, mansions and suburban bungalows gradually changed the landscape, paving the way for future residents Ronald Reagan and the Brady Bunch. Sacramento balances the nonstop bustle of San Francisco to the west with the tranquility of the mountains to the east, remaining as slow-paced as any small town (especially in summer, when temperatures can soar to 115 degrees). But don't let the city's slowness fool you; **exercise caution at night.**

⎅ TRANSPORTATION

Airport: Sacramento International (☎929-5411; http://airports.co.sacramento.ca.us), 12 mi. north on I-5. 2 terminals host 12 airlines serving hundreds of destinations worldwide. Cabs are expensive ($22-25 to downtown); vans are cheaper ($9-10); call **Super-Shuttle** for pick-up (☎800-258-3826). **Yolo Bus** (☎530-666-2877) runs public buses downtown. (Every hr. 5am-10pm, $1.25.)

Trains: Amtrak, 401 I St. (☎800-USA-RAIL/872-7245), at 5th St. To: **San Francisco** (2hr., 5 per day, $18); **Reno** (3hr., 5 per day, $23); **L.A.** (8-9hr., 4 per day, $42); and **Seattle** (8½hr., 1 per day, $110). Station open daily 4:45am-11:30pm. **Be careful around the station at night.**

Buses: Greyhound, 715 L St. (☎800-231-2222), between 7th and 8th St. To: **San Francisco** (2-3hr., 20 per day, $13-14); **Reno** (3hr., 12 per day, $21-23); **Seattle** (16-20hr., 5 per day, $59-62); **L.A.** (7-9hr., 15 per day, $42-45). Lockers available. Open 24hr. **Be careful around the station at night.**

Public Transit: Sacramento Regional Transit Bus and Light Rail, 1400 29th St. (☎321-2877; www.sacrt.com). Provides transportation in town 5am-10pm, light rail 4am-midnight. Fare in city center $0.50. Outer destinations $1.50 (free transfer); seniors, disabled, and ages 5-12 $0.50. Day passes $3.50.

Taxis: Yellow Cab (☎444-2222 or 800-464-0777). Open 24hr.

Car Rental: Enterprise, 2700 Arden Way (☎486-9900). Cars from $30 per day. Must be 21 with major credit card. Open M-F 7:30am-6pm, Sa 9am-4pm.

Bike Rental: American River Bike Shop, 9203 Folsom Blvd., also 256 Florin Rd., and 2645 Macaroni Ave. (☎427-6199). Bikes $4 per hr., $20 per day. Grab a friend for a tandem ride ($6 per hr., $30 per day). Open M-F 10am-6pm, Sa-Su 10am-5pm.

✦⚡ ORIENTATION & PRACTICAL INFORMATION

Sacramento is at the center of the **Sacramento Valley.** Five major highways converge on the capital of California: **I-5** and **Route 99** run north-south, **I-80** runs east-west between San Francisco and Reno, and **U.S. 50** and **Route 16** bring traffic westward from Gold Country. Numbered streets run north-south and lettered streets run east-west in a grid. The street number on a lettered street corresponds to the number of the cross street (2000 K St. is near the corner of 20th St.). The capitol building, parks, and endless cafes and restaurants occupy the **downtown area** around 10th St. and Capitol Ave.

Visitor Information: Sacramento Convention and Visitor Bureau, 1303 J St., #600 (☎264-7777; www.sacramentocvb.org/visitors). Congenial. Open M-F 8am-5pm.

Police: 900 8th St. (☎264-5471; www.sacpd.org), at I St.

Medical Services: UC Davis Medical Center, 2315 Stockton Blvd. (☎734-2011), at Broadway.

Crisis Hotline: Suicide Prevention and Crisis Response (☎368-3111). Open 24hr.

Library and Internet Access: Sacramento Library, 828 I St. (☎264-2700), between 8th and 9th St. Free Internet access 30min. per person per day. Open M 10am-6pm, Tu-Th 10am-9pm, Sa 10am-5pm, Su noon-5pm.

Post Office: 801 I St. (☎556-3415). Open M-F 8am-5pm. **Postal Code:** 95814.

⌂ ACCOMMODATIONS

Sacramento has many hotels, motels, and B&Bs, but waves of lawyers, businesspeople, and politicians can flood accommodations, making it hard to find a room. Advance reservations are always a good idea. The cheap hotels that line **West Capitol Avenue** in nearby West Sacramento may be a bit seedy, so be choosy. Within Sacramento proper, **16th Street** is home to many hotels and motels. Rates fluctuate seasonally, but standard chain hotel and motel rooms usually go for $50-150 per night. **Camping** is most popular with RVers, but tent sites are usually available, even in the metropolitan area. **KOA Sacramento ❷** is centrally located. Take I-80 west of downtown and Exit at West Capitol Ave. (☎371-6771, reservations 800-562-2747. Campsites $25-28; RV sites with full hookup $33-36; Cabins $43-55.)

◪ **Sacramento Hostel (HI-AYH),** 900 H St. (☎443-1691, reservations 800-909-4776 ext. 40), at 9th St. Looks more like an upscale, elegant B&B than a hostel, with high sloping ceilings, a grand mahogany staircase, and a stained-glass atrium. Huge modern kitchen, 3 large living rooms, library, TV/VCR, and an extensive selection of video rentals ($1). Dorm-style rooms are spacious, immaculate, and beautifully decorated. Guests are given 1 brief chore in the morning. Laundry. Check-in 7:30-10am and 5-10pm. Check-out 9:30am. Hostel closed 10am-5pm. Doors lock at 11pm, so speak to the receptionist before going out. Dorms $16-18 for HI-AYH member, $19-21 for nonmembers. Family, couple, and single rooms available. Group rates. ❷

Vagabond Inn Midtown, 1319 30th St. (☎454-4400; www.vagabondinn.com), between M and N St. A clean, well-maintained chain motel with comfortable rooms and below-market rates. Rooms have cable TV, phone, and free newspapers. Doubles from $50; online rates as low as $42. ❸

Courtyard by Marriott, 4422 Y St. (☎455-6800), at the UC Davis Medical Center. A full-fledged luxury hotel at a relatively low price. Grounds have exercise room, pool, whirlpool, laundry, restaurant, cocktail lounge, and coffee shop. Rooms include cable TV, irons, hairdryers, and high-speed Internet connections. Doubles from $80. ❺

🔲 FOOD

Food in Sacramento is plentiful and good, thanks to a hip midtown, new immigrant populations, and a dose of Californian culinary inventiveness. Most eateries are on **J Street** or **Capitol Avenue** between 19th and 29th St. Old Sacramento is filled with gimmicky restaurants that tend to be on the more expensive side.

🔳 **The Fox and Goose,** 1001 R St. (☎443-8825), at 10th St. Situated in a glass factory built in 1913 and renovated in the 1970s, the Fox and Goose has fostered a unique atmosphere blending authentic English public house atmosphere with some elements of American alternative culture. Great brunch and night spot; filling meals served three times a day. Serves everything from a proper pot of tea to European beer ($3), bangers ($5), pasties ($5), and fish and chips ($6). Open mic nights, live bands, and live magic every night. Open M-F 7am-2pm and 5:30pm-midnight, Sa-Su 8am-2am. ❶

Cafe Bernardo, 2726 Capitol Ave. (☎443-1189), at 28th St. This pleasant and hip cafe serves up light, fresh fare cafeteria-style for breakfast, brunch, lunch, and dinner. Outdoor seating allows full appreciation of summer evenings. Delectable sandwiches ($6-8), salads ($2-7), and soups ($2-4). Open Su-Th 7am-10pm, F-Sa 7am-11pm. ❷

33rd St. Bistro, 3301 Folsom Blvd. (☎455-2233), at 33rd. St. Opened by two classically-trained chef brothers who weren't afraid to experiment. Mixes flavors of the Pacific Northwest, American South, Mediterranean, and Caribbean seamlessly and successfully. Popular and busy, this bistro has gained a wide local following for its carefully designed dishes as well as its reasonable prices. Entrees $9-17. Desserts $4-5. Open Su-Th 8am-10pm, F-Sa 8am-11pm. ❸

The Central Valley

CENTRAL VALLEY

Maalouf's Taste of Lebanon, 1433 Fulton Ave. (☎972-8768), east of downtown. Mixing Middle Eastern and Mediterranean influences, Lebanese food is bold, fresh, and flavorful, and this is definitely the place to go for kebab and schwarma sandwiches ($3-5), and appetizer favorites like kibbe and falafel ($2-4). Open M-Sa 11am-9:30pm. ❶

Rubicon Brewing Company, 2004 Capitol Ave. (☎448-7032), at 20th St. Cool, laid-back microbrewery with decent, standard pub food. Patrons can watch the brewing process from the dining area, and the results are worth trying (pint $3). Sandwiches $4-6; Rubicon wings $6.25 for a dozen. Su brunch. Open M-Th 11am-11:30pm, F 11am-12:30am, Sa 9am-12:30am, Su 9am-10pm; kitchen closes earlier. ❶

◉ ◭ SIGHTS & OUTDOOR ACTIVITIES

Sacramento has traditionally been more of a pit stop on the way to the lakes and mountains in the east, but people are realizing there are plenty of reasons to stay. Debates about immigration, welfare, water shortages, and secession rage daily in the elegant **State Capitol,** at 10th St. and Capitol Ave. For a brief treatment of recent debates in California politics, see p. 14. Watch for the modernist portrait of iconoclastic former Gov. Jerry Brown, which contrasts amusingly with the formal portraits of California's other governors. (☎324-0333. 1hr. tours depart daily every hr. 9am-4pm. Free tickets distributed in Room B27 on a first-come, first-serve basis.) Colonnades of towering palm trees and grassy lawns make **Capitol Park** an oasis in the middle of downtown's busy bureaucracy. The **State Historic Park Governor's Mansion,** at 16th and H St., was built in 1877, serving as the residence of California's governor and his family until then-governor Ronald Reagan opted to rent his own pad. (☎324-0539. Open daily 10am-4pm. Hourly tours $1, under 16 free.)

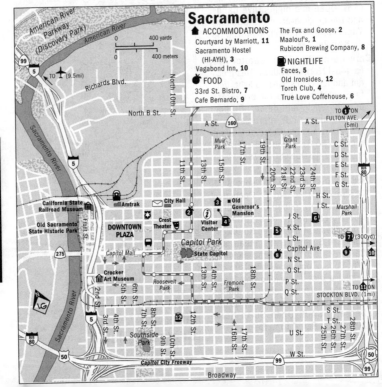

Sacramento

♠ ACCOMMODATIONS
Courtyard by Marriott, **11**
Sacramento Hostel (HI-AYH), **3**
Vagabond Inn, **10**

♦ FOOD
33rd St. Bistro, **7**
Cafe Bernardo, **9**

The Fox and Goose, **2**
Maalouf's, **1**
Rubicon Brewing Company, **8**

◗ NIGHTLIFE
Faces, **5**
Old Ironsides, **12**
Torch Club, **4**
True Love Coffeehouse, **6**

Old Sacramento, which attracts nearly five million visitors annually, has been refurbished to resemble its late 19th-century appearance, but wooden sidewalks and horse-drawn carriages are not enough to mask the roaring freeway or the sky-scrapers. Attractions include a Discovery Museum, restored riverboat, California's first theater, Old Eagle, and a military museum. The world-renowned 100,000 sq. ft. **California State Railroad Museum,** at 2nd and I St., exhibits 23 historic locomotives and offers train rides. (☎445-6645. Open daily 10am-5pm. $3, under 16 free. 1hr. train rides from the Train Depot in Old Sacramento Apr.-Sept. weekends; $6, ages 6-12 $3, under 6 free).

The **Crocker Art Museum,** 216 O St., between 2nd and 3rd St., exhibits 19th-cen-tury European and American oil paintings, Asian art, and contemporary California art, including works by Brueghel, Rembrandt, and Jacques-Louis David. (☎264-5423. Open Tu-W and F-Su 10am-5pm, Th 10am-9pm. $5.50, seniors $4.50, ages 7-17 $3, under 7 free. Tours available; book a week in advance.) Chimps, hippos, giraffes, lions, and white tigers are among the nearly 400 critters chilling out at the **Sacramento Zoo,** at the William Land Park at Parkland Drive and Sutterville Rd. The zoo's emphasis is on the protection of endangered species and the careful recre-ation of natural habitats. (☎264-5888; www.saczoo.com. Open daily 10am-4pm. $5.50, weekends and holidays $6; ages 3-12 $3.75/$4.25; under 3 free.)

The rushing waters of the American River flow quite close to Sacramento, and their gurgle calls adventuresome **river rafters.** Rent rafts at **American River Raft Rent-als,** 11257 S. Bridge St., in Rancho Cordova, 14 mi. east of downtown on U.S. 50. Exit on Sunrise Blvd. and take it north 1½ mi. to the American River. (☎635-6400. Open daily 9am-6pm; rentals available until 2pm. 4-person raft $38; kayak $27. $2 launch fee, $3 per person for return shuttle.)

The **American River Recreation Trail and Parkway,** spanning over 30 mi. from Dis-covery Park to Folsom Lake, is a nature preserve where you can still glimpse the downtown skyline. Five million people a year visit to cycle, jog, swim, fish, hike, and ride horses. You can enter the trail in Old Sacramento or at designated entrance points along the river. **Folsom Lake State Recreation Area,** 25 mi. east of town on I-80 (take Douglas Blvd.), hosts a giant, 11,000 acre reservoir offering swimming, boating, fishing, and water-skiing, and surrounding hills with over 100 mi. of trails. (☎988-0205. Open daily 6am-10pm. $6 per vehicle.)

🎵 ENTERTAINMENT

Sacramento bustles with free afternoon concerts and cheap food in summer. The Friday edition of the *Sacramento Bee* contains a supplement called *Ticket,* which gives a rundown of events, restaurants, and night spots. For weekend music and activities, check the free weeklies, such as *Sacramento News and Review* and *Inside the City.* The free *Alive and Kicking* has schedules and information about music and arts throughout the city. **Bass tickets,** 1409 28th St. Suite 206 (☎453-2730; www.tickets.com) is the largest ticket vendor in the area; call them for event times, locations, and prices.

Aside from the ubiquitous multiplexes, Sacramento has a good number of art and **film** theaters. The **Crest Theater,** at 10th and K St., was built in 1913 as a vaude-villian stage and is now a theater reminiscent of the golden age of Sacramento's theater district. Inside are three cinemas with palatial stairways, gilded ceilings, crystal chandeliers, and decadent paisley carpet. It is the premiere local venue for big name musical performances (contact Bass for tickets). Three cinema screens show recent independent films. (☎442-7378. $7.50, children, seniors, and matinee shows $5.) Since 1942, the **Sacramento Theatre Company,** 1419 H St. (☎443-6722), has been staging classic and contemporary plays. Seven productions, often lesser-known critical hits, go up each year from September to May.

If you're visiting Sacramento in the spring, catch a **Sacramento Kings** basketball game. The Kings play at the Arco Arena, 1 Sports Pkwy. (☎928-6900. To order sin-gle-game tickets by phone, call ☎649-8497, 530-528-8497, or 209-485-8497.)

Friday Night Concert Series (☎442-2500), at Cesar Chávez Park, 10th St. and I St.. Live bands, food stands, and beer gardens. In summer every F 5-9pm.

Sacramento Heritage Festival (☎481-2583). The biggest outdoor musical event to come to town each year. Two days of all kinds of music, food, and drink. Early June. $7.

Dixieland Jazz Jubilee (☎372-5277). Over 100 bands play every Memorial Day weekend in late May, attracting over 100,000 listeners.

International Street Fair, on 11th St. between J and L St. A celebration of Sacramento's multi-ethnicity. Food, vendors, kids' activities, and performances. Mid-July 5-9pm.

Shakespeare Lite (☎442-8575), St. Rose of Lima Park, 7th St. and K St. Comedic abridged versions of the Bard's work. Pack a picnic. June to mid-July Th noon-1pm.

California State Fair (☎263-3000; www.bigfun.org). This agriculturally inclined fair doesn't skimp on spinning rides, fairway food, and pig races. Mid-Aug. to early Sept. Tickets $7, seniors $5, children $4.50.

■ NIGHTLIFE

Capital-dwellers slither among brass and mahogany of the Gold Rush era while enjoying the highly refined moving images and coffee beverages of more recent eras. Sacramento's midtown entertainment parlors afford a view of city residents who are odder-looking and more frequently body-pierced than their fellow citizens in the government. The **Fox and Goose** (see p. 307) is a splendid nightlife option.

True Love Coffeehouse, 2406 J St. (☎492-9002), at 24th St. A warm, cozy hangout thriving on the pulse of Sacramento alternative culture, especially the music scene. A small stage is given over to all sorts of entertainment, from MST2k movie screenings to waffle night to performances by one of a dozen or so regular bands and visitors. Usually no cover, but some performances $6-7. Open Su-Th 5pm-midnight, F-Sa 5pm-3am.

Torch Club, 904 15th St. (☎443-2797), at I St. The ultimate blues and bluegrass venue in town. Blues legends rambling through town and local upstarts attract hardcore soul music enthusiasts. Deep wailing and foot-stomping exuberance gives these tunes a redemptive, releasing vitality. Live bands play every night. 21+. Cover varies, but often free. Open daily 10am-2am.

Old Ironsides (☎443-9751), at 10th and S St. A local favorite. Grease up and groove on the dance floor, or throw back a few in the bar area. Meaty meals $5-11. Drafts $1.50. Live bands of all types Tu and Th-Sa, disco parties Su. 21+. Cover F-Sa $5-7, usually no cover Tu. Open M-Sa 9am-2am, Su 6pm-2am.

Faces, 2000 K St. (☎448-7798), at 20th St. *The* gay club in Sacramento. High-stylin' with 5 huge areas (dance, video, social bar, microbrew bar, and patio). Sand volleyball court. Su afternoon BBQ 5:30pm. Occasional amateur stripteases Su and Th nights (and every night, if you pound enough Heineken). 21+. Open daily 3pm-1:45am.

CHICO ☎530

Essentially, Chico (pop. 55,437) is a small town that wakes up and rocks out with wild college kids. As the home of the Sierra Nevada Brewing Company, this place knows how to please visitors, not only with its numerous bike trails and swimming holes in the incomparable Bidwell Park, and its hip and lively downtown, but also with its wickedly cheap beer. Say it with us, people: *cheap beer!* The residents of Chico apparently put all that beer to good use: it was recently named one of the "Top 10 places to retire in the US," and Cal State Chico is perennially one of Playboy's "Top 10 Party Schools." While the point is to enjoy either the cheap beer or the outdoors (but not both at the same time), visitors to Chico can find that there are all sorts of delights in this town of earthly pleasures.

Chico

⌂ ACCOMMODATIONS
Thunderbird Lodge, 7
Town House Motel, 2

◗ NIGHTLIFE
Blue Room, 5
Brick Works, 6

◗ FOOD
Burger Hut, 1
Madison Bear
Garden, 4
Naked Lounge, 3
Sierra Nevada
Brewing Co., 8

⚡ 🏨 PRACTICAL INFORMATION & CHEAP BEER. The **Amtrak train** station (☎342-0221) is just a platform on Orange St., at W. 5th St. Trains go to Sacramento (2hr., 4 per day, $19) and San Francisco (5½hr., 3 per day, $30). **Greyhound,** 450 Orange St. (☎343-8266), at the Amtrak station, sends **buses** to: Red Bluff (1hr., 4 per day, $9-10); Sacramento (2½hr., 3 per day, $14-15); and San Francisco (5-6hr., 3 per day, $30-32). The **Chamber of Commerce,** 300 Salem St., at 3rd St., has wall-to-wall tourist brochures and a friendly staff. (☎891-5556 or 800-852-8570; www.chicochamber.com. Open M-F 9am-5pm, Sa 10am-3pm.) Other services include **police,** 1460 Humboldt Rd. (☎895-4912) and **Enloe Hospital,** 1531 W. 5th St. (☎895-9111), at Esplanade St. **Bar X Liquors,** 915 Main St., supplies lots of beer and liquor (but no kegs). If you want anything they don't have, they will order it the last week of each month. (☎342-6741. Open M-F 7:30am-2am, Sa 8am-2am, Su 8am-midnight.) The **Post Office** is at 550 Vallombrosa Ave. (☎343-2068. Open M-F 8am-5:30pm, Sa 9:30am-12:30pm.) **Postal Code:** 95926.

⌂ 🏕 🏨 ACCOMMODATIONS, CAMPING, & CHEAP BEER. As a big college town, Chico has plenty of inexpensive hotels and motel rooms to offer, many for as low as $40 a night. **Town House Motel ❸,** 2231 Esplanade St., is a clean and quiet remodeled motel close to downtown. Standardish rooms have cable TV and A/C. (☎343-1621. Singles from $40; doubles from $45.) **Thunderbird Lodge ❸,** 715 Main St., in downtown, has large clean rooms with brown shag carpet and white walls. (☎343-7911. Singles $40-50; doubles $55-65.) The closest place to get beer is at **Chevron,** 110 W. 9th St., at Main St. (☎891-8055. Open 24hr.)

For camping, pick up a useful camping brochure at the Chamber of Commerce. It will likely direct you to **Lake Oroville,** 30 mi. from Chico on Rte. 99 South (9 mi. from Oroville Dam Exit), and its fishing, swimming, boating, and 35 mi. bike trail. **Bidwell Canyon ❷** is very close to the water and used mostly by RVs. (☎534-2409. Full hookup $20, with no tent discount.) **Loafer Creek ❷** is more forested than Bidwell, with a beach and swimming area. (Reservations ☎538-2219. Sites $16.) Camping is abundant in the Lassen and Plumas National Forests, both a short distance east of Chico. Lassen has numerous campgrounds on Rte. 32, about 35 mi. north of Chico, near Lake Almanor.

⌂⊠ FOOD & CHEAP BEER. It is hard not to find great tasting, ridiculously inexpensive food and drink in Chico, given the unrelenting demand for it placed by the college population. Declared a "legend" by Chico *News and Review*, **Burger Hut ❶**, with locations at 933 Nord Ave. and 2451 Forest Ave., makes the best burger in town for about as cheap as it gets. The "Student Special," a flame-kissed burger, fries, and soda, is the best bet at $3.60. (☎891-1418. Open M-Th 10am-9pm, F-Sa 10am-10pm, Su 11am-9pm.) **Madison Bear Garden ❷**, 316 2nd St., at Salem St., is marked by its spicy atmosphere and huge party potential. An enormous outdoor patio and cheap beer garden, dance floors, pool tables, and a horse and buggy hung from the ceiling make this a hot spot for hundreds of rowdy cheap beer guzzlers. (☎891-1639. Burgers, salads, and sandwiches $5-7. Pint of beer $1 Sa 9pm-1am. Occasional live bands Th-Sa 9pm-1:30am. Open Su-W 11am-midnight, Th-Sa 11am-2am. Kitchen closes at 10pm.) Cheap beer also flows at the sedate and classy **Sierra Nevada Brewing Co. ❸**, 1075 E. 20th St., home of the brand's brewery, a tap room, and grill. Tours of the brass-and-mahogany brewery are a great way to get acquainted with the spirit of the brew gods. Some may come to try the chili-lime chicken, the blackened shark, or the vegetarian options, but they can't deny themselves the 11 different Sierra Nevada brews on tap for $2.50 a pint. Lunch ($5-10) and top-notch dinner ($6-20) are served at the brewpub. (☎345-2739. Tours M-F and Su 2:30pm, Sa noon-3pm. Live music M, Su and some other nights $10-20. Pub open Tu-Th and Su 11am-9pm, F-Sa 11am-10pm.) For a more subdued atmosphere, head to the artsy, relaxed **Naked Lounge ❶**, 118 W. 2nd St., where the coffee is made from the highest grade beans on the planet, stimulating conversation and the central nervous system. (☎895-0676. Espresso $1.75. Open daily 7am-11pm.)

◙⌂⊠ SIGHTS, ACTIVITIES, & PLACES TO DRINK CHEAP BEER. Most of the residents of Chico would agree that the two best things to do in Chico are indulge in the youthful revelry of this party school town after dark, and frolic in its awesome playground, Bidwell Park, during the day. There are a good number of sights in the historic, walkable downtown; pick up a copy of the downtown walking tour guide at the Visitors Center. The highlights of the tour include: a stroll around **Cal State Chico**'s campus, at W. 2nd and Normal; a swing over to the **National YoYo Museum**, at Broadway and W. 3rd (☎893-1414; open M-Sa 10am-5:30pm, Su 11am-4pm; don't miss the National YoYo Contest in early Oct.; free); and a tour through man-of-influence John Bidwell's historic **mansion**, 525 Esplanade. (☎895-5144. Tours on the hour from noon-4pm, Sa-Su 10am-4pm. $1, under 16 free.) Entertainment options in town include two excellent independent movie theatres: **Pageant Theater**, 351 E. 6th St. (☎343-0663), with sofas in the front row; and **El Rey Theater** (☎342-2727), 230 W. 2nd St., a restored single-screen Vaudevillian theater nearly 100 years old. The **Blue Room**, 139 W. 1st St., shows bold, often unconventional plays to an appreciative audience. (☎895-3749. Tickets $5-10.) For live music of the rock, rap, and indie pop sort, and also Top 40-type dancing, try **Brick Works**, 191 E. 2nd St. (☎895-7700. Tickets $5-20.) The **Senator Theater**, 517 Main St. (☎894-8621), is the big venue in town, with a stated mission "to increase human happiness." Community plays and small, medium, and big name acts are up all year. The **Concert in the Park Series** shows free musical and theatrical performances at Downtown Park Plaza, at 5th and Main St. (☎345-6500. Aug. F 7-8pm.)

Bidwell Park (☎895-4972) is the nation's 3rd largest municipal park, with over 3600 acres. Without a doubt, the park is the most enjoyed and cherished of Chico's attractions, and this is clearly visible in the throngs who flock to its trails, parks, golf course, and swimming holes on balmy summer days. Take East Ave. north from Rte. 99 as it curves east; follow signs into Upper Bidwell Park. The gurgling sound of joyful swimmers will lead you to nearby **Bear Hole.** The park is divided into an upper and lower section, the upper part being largely undisturbed canyon-land, while the lower part is a more developed area, where people enjoy jogging, biking, playing baseball, and sunning. In the upper part, **North Rim Trail,** on Wild-wood Ave. upon entering the park, explores the hardy, rugged terrain. In the lower part, **One-Mile Recreation,** near downtown by 4th St., is a great spot for picnicking, playing frisbee, or loafing around while drinking cheap beer. The **Chico Creek Nature Center,** 1968 E. 8th St., is a museum and interpretive center for the park, exploring and preserving its natural life. (☎891-4671. Open Tu-Su 11am-4pm. Free talks, exhibits, and nature walks.)

MERCED

☎209

The wide streets of downtown Merced (pop. 63,893) project an order and openness shared by the entire town. The friendly atmosphere makes Merced one of the best places to stop off in before heading for Yosemite's northern entrance.

■■ **ORIENTATION & PRACTICAL INFORMATION.** Situated on Rte. 99, Merced maintains a small-town image along its quaint Main St., while the area north of Bear Creek hosts standard mall and restaurant chains. As the "Gateway to Yosemite," Merced's public transportation into the park is excellent. Greyhound **buses,** 710 W. 16th St. (☎722-2121 or 800-231-2222), run to Yosemite frequently, especially during the summer ($20). Buses to San Francisco (every 3hr., $26) and to L.A. (every 2hr., $29) are also available. The regional **YARTS** provides bus trips directly to Yosemite ($20). Call ahead to ask about schedules, which vary widely (☎877-989-2787; www.yosemite.com/yarts). Amtrak **trains,** 355 W. 24th St., run to L.A. and Reno, among other destinations. (☎800-USA-RAIL/872-7245. Open daily 7:15am-8:45pm.) Public transportation within Merced, called **The Bus** (☎384-3111 or 800-345-3111), may be flagged down at any street corner along designated routes. (Runs M-F 7am-6pm, Sa 9am-5pm. Single fare $1, all-day pass $3.) The **Merced Chamber of Commerce** and the **California Welcome Center,** 690 W. 16th St., have Yosemite road conditions, travel and activities information, and well as maps and brochures detailing local restaurants, accommodations, and transportation options. (Chamber of Commerce ☎384-7092. Open M-F 8:30am-5pm; Welcome Center ☎284-2791. Open M-Sa 8am-5pm.) Other services include: **police,** 611 W. 22nd St. (☎385-6912); **Mercy Hospital and Health Services,** 2740 M St. (☎384-6444; open 24hr.); and the **post office,** 2334 M St. (☎800-275-8777; open M-F 7:30am-5:30pm.) **Postal Code:** 95340.

■■ **ACCOMMODATIONS & FOOD.** The friendly hosts of the eight-bed ■**Merced Home Hostel** ❶ pick up guests from the bus and train stations between 5 and 9pm. Visitors must call in advance; without reservations, the address is not disclosed. (☎725-0407. Members $14; non-members $17.) Advertising the lowest prices in town, the **Happy Inn** ❸, 740 Motel Dr., has a pool and average rooms and is conveniently yet noisily located just off Rte. 99. (☎722-6291. Breakfast, satellite TV, and local calls included. Small rooms $32; regular rooms $40-55.)

While fast-food joints are abundant, especially along Olive Ave., cheap home-grown eats can also be found. Pleasant **Mandarin Shogun** ❷, 1204 W. Olive Ave., offers an all-you-can-eat buffet (lunch $5.95, dinner $7.95; seniors 10% discount) with a variety of entree and dessert choices. (☎722-6313, delivery 722-1881. Open Su-Th 11am-2:30pm and 5-9:30pm, F-Sa 11am-2:30pm and 5-10pm.) **La Nita's** ❷, 1327 W. 18th St., serves tasty Mexican dishes and good margaritas. (☎723-2291. Entrees $6-10. Open Tu-Sa 9am-9:30pm, Su 8am-9:30pm.)

IN RECENT NEWS

BUILDING A FUTURE

A couple of years ago, downtown Fresno was not a place you felt safe in during the night, nor a place you'd want to shop at or visit during the day. When the suits went home after work, the area cleared out. Weekend entertainment was found in the surrounding wilderness and in nearby cities; Fresno locals wouldn't dream of returning to their city for play. As a city built-up by leapfrog development and the creation of shopping centers, complimented by tract housing spreading outward from the city center, Fresno's downtown became neglected and outdated.

Slowly, things are changing. With the recent completion of a 12,500 seat, $46 million Triple A ballpark, Fresno is attempting to revitalize a downtown that had, of late, fallen into disrepair. Also, the city government has mandated that governmental agencies seeking relocation move downtown. Moreover, they have begun work on a $120 million courthouse, a $200 million medical center, and a $50 million office tower. Eventually, they hope that these buildings will draw business back into the downtown area, making it a safe, vibrant cultural and culinary center for locals and tourists alike. Until then, come for a Grizzlies game at the stadium, and enjoy the intimate and economical attraction of minor league baseball. Soon there will be stores for pre-gaming, and bars and clubs for seeking solace after the ninth inning.

🔲 **SIGHTS.** As the "Gateway to Yosemite," Merced functions primarily as a rest stop and portal to the great wilderness. Tucked away in the Merced area, however, are two interesting attractions. The old **Courthouse,** 21st and N St., houses a museum with free tours. Volunteer residents recall personal and public anecdotes that transform a typical small-town museum into a discovery of American quirks and inventions. (☎722-6291. Open W-Su 1-4pm.) To the northwest of Merced is the **Castle Airport** and **Air Museum,** 5050 Santa Fe Dr., in Atwater. Aviation buffs and history enthusiasts can wander among the 40 restored aircraft on museum grounds or visit the small collection of Air Force paraphernalia. (☎723-2178. Open May-Sept. 9am-5pm; Oct.-Apr. 10am-4pm. Adults $7, seniors and teens $5.)

FRESNO ☎559

Fresno (pop. 430,000) struggles to balance its agricultural past with its ever-growing urban population. Truly an asphalt jungle, Fresno is dusty, hot, and in many places crime-ridden. However, some interesting attractions, decent digs, and cheap eats are available for travelers on their way to the mountains.

🚩 **PRACTICAL INFORMATION.** Greyhound **buses,** 1033 Broadway Ave. (☎268-1829), run to San Francisco five times a day ($24) and L.A. six or more times daily ($22). Amtrak **trains,** 2650 E. Tulare St. Bldg. B, also run to San Francisco and L.A., and are slightly more expensive than Greyhound. (800-872-7245/USA-RAIL. Open daily 7:15am-8:45pm.) Local transportation is provided by **Fresno Area Express,** commonly known as **FAX.** Visit the transportation offices at the Manchester Shopping Center at Sheilds and Blackstone Ave. for schedules and routes. The **Fresno County and City Chamber of Commerce,** 2331 Fresno St. (☎495-4800; www.fresnochamber.com; open M 9am-5pm, Tu-Th 8am-5pm, F 8am-4:30pm) and the **Convention and Visitor Bureau** (☎233-0836; open M-F 8am-5pm) both have information on accommodations, food, and attractions. The main **Post Office** is located at 2601 E. Olive Ave. (Open M-F 8:30am-4pm.) **Postal Code:** 93721.

🛏🍴 **ACCOMMODATIONS & FOOD.** Chain motels line the highways that run through Fresno; the most inexpensive accommodations can be found off Rte. 99. The **Red Roof Inn ❸,** 5021 N. Barcus Ave. (☎276-1910 or 800-RED-ROOF/733-7663) has large, clean rooms, but lots of noise from Rte. 99. (Pool, cable TV, A/C, laundry, pets allowed. Singles with queen bed from $45.) **Piccadilly Inn ❺**, 2305 W. Shaw, is a great high-end place. Well-removed from the main arteries, rooms at the Piccadilly Inn are not only quiet, but spacious and well-maintained. Pool, spa, cable TV, A/C, laundry, banquet rooms, and restaurant all add to the luxury. (☎ 226-3850. Singles start at $85.)

The trendy Tower District, on E. Olive Ave. between N. Palm Ave. and N. Blackstone Ave., is Fresno's best bet for good eats. The **Daily Planet ❸**, 1121 N. Wishon, masters contemporary American flavor in a dining room with an art deco flare. (☎ 266-4259. Dinner entrees $10-17.) **Cafe Revue ❶**, 620 E. Olive Ave., is the place to see and be seen. A friendly staff serves up coffeehouse favorites in a chic cafe and patio area. (☎ 449-1844. Drinks and pastries $1-4. Open M-Th 7am-11pm, F 7am-midnight, Sa 7:30am-midnight, Sun 7:30am-11pm.)

◙ SIGHTS. If you have time for only one thing in Fresno, stop by the **Baldasare Forestiere Underground Gardens,** on Shaw St., one block east of Rte. 99. Forestiere migrated to Fresno from Sicily around the turn of the century with the intention of making profits from farming, but found hardpan instead of fertile topsoil. So he moved underground, gardens and all, to escape the heat. His hilarious descendants now lead tours through his 40-room house. (☎ 271-0734. Tours W-Sun at 10am, noon, and 2pm during the summer; Sa-Su at noon and 2pm fall-spring. Adults $8, seniors $7, teens $6.) Fresno also offers the fantastic **Fresno Art Museum**, 2233 N. First St. at Clinton Ave. Exhibits include rotating local talent and permanent collections. (☎ 441-4220. Open Tu-F 10am-5pm and Sa-Su 12pm-5pm. Adults $4, seniors and students $2. Free every Tu.) **Roeding Park** and **Chaffee Zoological Gardens,** on Olive Ave. one block east of Rte. 99, are great for picnics or entertaining children. (☎ 498-2671. Park entrance $1, zoo entrance: adults $6, seniors $4. Open Mar.-Oct. 9am-5pm; Nov.-Feb. 10am-4pm.)

BAKERSFIELD ☎ 661

Virtually every West Coast commercial outlet that has opened in the past twenty years still has a home in Bakersfield (pop. 230,771). Although convenient for the scores of long-haul truckers looking for a place to rest on the road to Fresno, Bakersfield is more of a pit stop than a tourist locale. While Bakersfield is one of the fastest growing cities in California, there's not much for tourists besides cheap motels and chain stores.

⚑ PRACTICAL INFORMATION. The **Greater Bakersfield Chamber of Commerce** helps out at 1725 Eye St., on the corner of 18th and I St. (☎ 327-4421. Open M 9am-5pm, Tu-F 8am-5pm.) Bakersfield is serviced by **Golden Empire Transit (GET)**, a reliable public transportation system. (☎ 869-2GET; www.getbus.org. Single fare $0.75; one day pass is $1.75.) Other services include: **police**, 1601 Truxtun Ave. (☎ 327-7111); **Bakersfield Memorial Hospital**, 420 34th St., at Union Ave. (☎ 327-1792; open 24hr.); and the **Post Office**, 1730 18th St. (☎ 861-4346). **Postal Code:** 93302.

⌂ⓒ ACCOMMODATIONS & FOOD. Bakersfield's reputation as a great overnight stop is well earned, as it teems with inexpensive hotels. Cheap, clean, and safe chain motels cluster at the Olive St. Exit off Hwy. 99 North. Non-chain options include the **California Inn ❸**, 3400 Chester Ln., behind Carl's Jr. at Real Rd., which offers a pool, spa, and sauna, as well as mini-fridges, TV, and laundry. (☎328-1100. Singles $45.) Or try **E-Z 8 Motels ❸**, 5200 Olive Tree Ct., with TV, pool, and a friendly staff. (☎392-1511. Singles $34; doubles $47.)

🔲Maitia's Basque Cafe ❹, 4420 Coffee Rd., has offered a delicious sampling of local basque flavor since 1946. Lunch is less expensive, but less traditional. (☎587-9055. Dinner $13-22. Open daily 11am-9pm.) For a sweeter taste of Bakersfield tradition, head over to **Dewar's ❶**, 1120 Eye St. The candy shop and soda fountain have been open since 1909, and all their treats are an art perfected. Ice cream and floats $1-5. (☎322-0933. Open Su-Th 10am-9pm, F-Sa 10am-10pm.)

◪ SIGHTS. Country music fans should do-se-do over to **Buck Owens' Crystal Palace**, 2800 Buck Owens Blvd., a restaurant, theater, and museum. Live music and dancing on W-Sa nights is popular with locals and tourists alike. (☎328-7560. Open M-Sa 5pm-midnight, Su 9:30am-2pm. $6-10 cover. Entrees $7-27.) The 16-acre **Kern County Museum** complex has over 50 structures dedicated to Kern County's history and culture. Buildings focus on local themes, including agriculture, community development, and native cultures. New for 2003 is the interactive petroleum exhibit. (www.kcmuseum.org. Open M-F 8am-5pm, Sa 10am-5pm, Su noon-5pm. Ticket office closes daily at 3pm. Adults $6, seniors and students $5, children $4.)

THE CENTRAL COAST

Although the popular image of the California dream is manufactured by the media machine in L.A., the image itself comes from the Central Coast. The 400 mi. stretch of coastline between L.A. and San Francisco embodies all that is purely Californian: rolling surf, dramatic cliffs, self-actualizing New Age adherents, and always a hint of the off-beat. This is the solitary magnificence that inspired John Steinbeck's novels and Jack Kerouac's musings. Among the smog-free skies, sweeping shorelines, dense forests, and plunging cliffs, there is a point where inland farmland communities and old seafaring towns intersect, beckoning citified residents to journey out to the quiet drama of the coast. The landmarks along the way—Hearst Castle, the Monterey Bay Aquarium, Carmel, the historic missions—are well worth visiting, but the real point of the Central Coast is the journey itself.

HIGHLIGHTS OF THE CENTRAL COAST

BIG SUR. The quiet forests and roaring coastline of Big Sur (p. 340) continue to inspire mystics and weirdos.

MONTEREY BAY AQUARIUM. The elaborate displays at the immense aquarium (p. 335) create habitats for delicate sunfish, luxuriant kelp forests, and critters of the deep.

HEARST CASTLE. At San Simeon, media mogul William Randolph Hearst's hilltop mansion (p. 346) fabulously commemorates its builder's wealth.

SANTA BARBARA. Built in a graceful Spanish style, the hilly city of Santa Barbara (p. 358) is full of carefree living, crazy nightlife, and stunning coastal environs.

SANTA CRUZ. Mixing college town ease with coastal breeze, Santa Cruz (p. 319) unites New Age crazies, surfers, and trippy students with fog-drenched forests, a bustling downtown, and a tacky beachside milieu.

PACIFIC COAST HIGHWAY

The quintessential Californian road, the **Pacific Coast Highway** (known to Angelenos as **PCH,** to other Californians as **Highway 1,** and on maps as **Route 1**), stretches along the majority of the state's coastline. Begun in 1920, the PCH required 10 million dollars and 17 years to complete. From San Francisco, Hwy. 1 slips along the craggy shorelines of San Mateo County to loopy Santa Cruz and sedate Monterey. South of Monterey, the highway follows the 90 mi. strip of sparsely inhabited coastline known as **Big Sur** (p. 340). Climbing in and out of Big Sur's mountains, Hwy. 1 inches motorists to the edge of jutting cliffs that hang precipitously over the surf. William Randolph Hearst's **San Simeon** (p. 344), anchors the southern end of Big Sur. From **San Luis Obispo** (p. 347), the route winds past vineyards, fields of wildflowers, and miles of beaches on the journey southward to genteel **Santa Barbara** (p. 354). The highway curves from Santa Barbara to lazy, surf-crazed Ventura and finally skirts the coastal communities of L.A. From Santa Cruz to Ventura, state parks and national forests offer peaceful campgrounds and daring recreation. The **Bay Area** (see p. 121), **North Coast** (see p. 179), and **Los Angeles** (see p. 366) sections have more on the route of Hwy. 1.

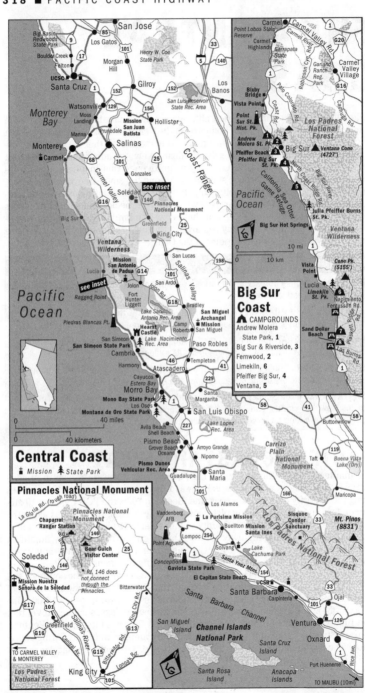

Big Sur Coast

▲ CAMPGROUNDS

Andrew Molera
State Park, **1**
Big Sur & Riverside, **3**
Fernwood, **2**
Limekiln, **6**
Pfeiffer Big Sur, **4**
Ventana, **5**

0   10 mi

0   10 km

Central Coast

♦ Mission   ♣ State Park

0   40 miles

0   40 kilometers

Pinnacles National Monument

* Rt. 146 does
not connect
through the
Pinnacles.

CENTRAL COAST

SANTA CRUZ

☎ 831

One of the few places where the 1960s catchphrase "do your own thing" still applies, Santa Cruz (pop. 56,000) simultaneously embraces macho surfers, aging hippies, free-thinking students, and same-sex couples. The atmosphere here is fun-loving but far from hedonistic, intellectual but not even close to stuffy. This small city has enough Northern California cool and Southern California fun for all, whether you find it in gobbling cotton candy on the Ferris wheel or sipping wheatgrass at poetry readings.

Along the beach and boardwalk, tourism and surf culture reign supreme. Nearby Pacific Ave. teems with independent bookstores, cool bars, trendy cafes, and pricey boutiques which provide a relatively safe, and pleasant hangout for local teens and travelers alike. On the inland side of Mission St., the University of California at Santa Cruz (UCSC) sprawls luxuriously across miles of rolling forests and grasslands filled with prime biking routes and wild students. Restaurants offer avocado sandwiches and industrial coffee, while merchants hawk UCSC paraphernalia alongside fliers for courses that ask "Should you kill your superego?" Be careful about visiting on Saturday or Sunday, since the town's population virtually doubles on summer weekends, clogging highways as daytrippers make their way to and from the Bay Area.

☞ TRANSPORTATION

Buses: Greyhound, 425 Front St. (☎423-1800 or 800-231-2222). To: **L.A.** (6 per day, $40); **San Francisco** (5 per day, $11); **San Jose** (M-Th 5 per day, $6). Open daily 8:30-11:30am and 1-6:45pm, as well as during late bus arrivals and departures.

Trains: Amtrak (☎800-872-7245). The closest train station is in **San Jose,** which is reachable by bus.

Public Transportation: Santa Cruz Metropolitan Transit District (SCMTD), 920 Pacific Ave. (consumer service line open M-F 8am-4pm ☎425-8600, TDD 425-8993; www.scmtd.com), in the Pacific Garden Mall. The free *Headways* has route info. $1, seniors and disabled $0.40, under 46 in. free; day pass $3, $1.10, free. Buses run daily 6am-11pm.

Taxis: Yellow Cab (☎423-1234). Initial fee $2.25, each additional mi. $2. Open 24hr.

Bike Rental: The Bike Shop of Santa Cruz, 1325 Mission St. (☎454-0909). Mountain or round-the-town bikes $10 per hr., $40 per day. 2hr. minimum rental. $5 off rentals and 10% off parts or accessories to Hostel International members. Open daily 9am-6pm. **Family Cycling Center,** 912 41st Ave. (☎475-3883). Trailers and beach cruisers $15 per day M-F, mountain bikes $25 per day, super-lites $40 per day. Open M-Sa 10am-6pm, Su 10am-5pm.

◪ ◪ ORIENTATION & PRACTICAL INFORMATION

Santa Cruz is on the northern tip of Monterey Bay, 65 mi. south of San Francisco on Hwy. 1. Passing through westside Santa Cruz, Hwy. 1 becomes **Mission Street.** The **University of California at Santa Cruz (UCSC)** blankets the hills inland from Mission St. Southeast of Mission St. lies the waterfront and the downtown. Down by the ocean, **Beach Street** runs roughly east-west. The narrow **San Lorenzo River** runs mainly north-south, dividing the Boardwalk scene from quiet, affluent residences. **Pacific Avenue** is the main street downtown. Along with **Cedar Street,** Pacific Ave. carves out a nightlife niche accessible from the beach motels. Resident-traffic-only zones, one-way streets, and dead-ends can make Santa Cruz highly frustrating to navigate by car. Park at a motel or in free 2hr. public lots off Pacific Ave. to avoid the cash-guzzling beach-vicinity lots and meters.

CENTRAL COAST

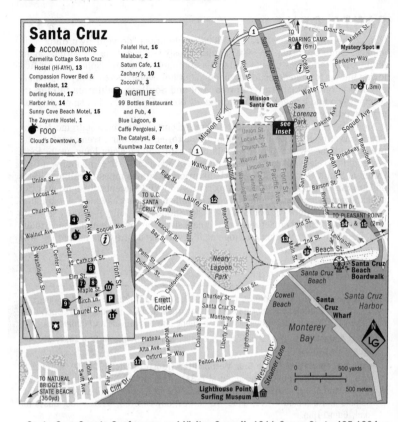

Santa Cruz

🏠 ACCOMMODATIONS
Carmelita Cottage Santa Cruz
Hostel (HI-AYH), **13**
Compassion Flower Bed &
Breakfast, **12**
Darling House, **17**
Harbor Inn, **14**
Sunny Cove Beach Motel, **15**
The Zayante Hostel, **1**
🍴 FOOD
Cloud's Downtown, **5**

Falafel Hut, **16**
Malabar, **2**
Saturn Cafe, **11**
Zachary's, **10**
Zoccoli's, **3**

🍴 NIGHTLIFE
99 Bottles Restaurant
and Pub, **4**
Blue Lagoon, **8**
Caffe Pergolesi, **7**
The Catalyst, **6**
Kuumbwa Jazz Center, **9**

Santa Cruz County Conference and Visitor Council, 1211 Ocean St. (☎425-1234 or 800-833-3494; www.santacruzca.org). Extremely helpful staff. Publishes the free *Santa Cruz County Traveler's Guide* with helpful information and discounts. Cyclists should pick up the extensive "bike adventure kit." Open M-Sa 9am-5pm, Su 10am-4pm.

Downtown Info Center, 1126 Pacific Ave. (☎459-9486). Open daily noon-6pm. An information **kiosk** sits in front of the Cowell's Beach boardwalk. (☎421-9552). Open July 1-Labor Day daily 10am-5pm.

California Parks and Recreation Department, 600 Ocean St. (☎429-2850), across from the Holiday Inn. Info on camping and beach facilities in Santa Cruz; for reservations, call ReserveAmerica (☎800-444-7275). Open M-F 8am-5pm.

Library: 224 Church St. (☎420-5730). **Internet access** available in 1hr. sessions at no cost–get there early. Open M-Th 10am-9pm, F 10am-6pm, Sa 10am-5pm, Su 1-5pm.

Bi-Gay-Lesbian Organizations: Lesbian, Gay, Bisexual, and Transgender Community Center, 1328 Commerce Ln. (☎425-5422; www.diversitycenter.org), north of Pacific Garden Mall. Publishes *Manifesto* and distributes the *Lavender Reader,* a quarterly journal. Extremely helpful staffers supply info about events, outings, and general concerns. Open daily; call for hours.

Laundry: Ultramat, 501 Laurel St. (☎426-9274). Santa Cruz's 1st laundromat cafe. Wash $1.75, dry $0.25 per 7min. Morning wash special $1 9:30-11:30am. Open daily 7am-midnight.

Weather Conditions: ☎656-1725. Operated by the Bay Area National Weather Service out of Monterey. Automated weather report 24hr.

Police: 155 Center St. (☎471-1131). Open 24hr.

Crisis Lines: Women's Crisis Line (☎685-3737). Open 24hr. **Suicide Prevention Service** (☎458-5300). Open 24hr.

Medical Services: Santa Cruz Dominican Hospital, 1555 Soquel Dr. (☎462-7700). Take bus #71 on Soquel Dr. from the Metro Center. Open 24hr.

Post Office: 850 Front St. (☎426-8184). Open M-F 8:30am-5pm, Sa 9am-4pm. **Postal Code:** 95060.

🏠 ACCOMMODATIONS

Like many beach towns, Santa Cruz gets packed solid during the summer, especially on weekends. Room rates skyrocket and availability plummets. Surprisingly, the nicer motels tend to have the more reasonable summer weekend rates, but more expensive rates at other times. Reservations are always recommended. Shop around—price fluctuation can be outrageous. Camping may be the best option for the budget traveler.

Carmelita Cottage Santa Cruz Hostel (HI-AYH), 321 Main St. (☎423-8304), 4 blocks from the Greyhound stop and 2 blocks from the beach. Centrally located, but in a quiet neighborhood, this 40-bed Victorian hostel is run by a young staff. Kitchen, common room, and storage lockers available. Chores required. Linen provided. July-Aug. 3-night max. stay. Reception 8-10am and 5-10pm. Lockout 10am-5pm. Strict curfew 11pm. Call for reservations, but no refunds after 48hr. prior to booking. Dorms $20, members $17, ages 12-17 $15, ages 4-11 $10, ages 3 and under free. ❷

Harbor Inn, 645 7th Ave. (☎479-9731), near the harbor and a few blocks north of Eaton St. A beautiful 19-room hotel well off the main drag. Summer weekend rates are likely to be below the absurd prices extorted by other motels. Rooms have queen-sized beds, cable TV, microwaves, and fridges. In late June, you can pick Santa Rosa plums from the trees out back. Check-in 2-7pm; call to arrange late check-in. Check-out 11am. Reservations recommended. Rooms Su-Th from $75-115, F-Sa from $75-175; off-season Su-Th from $65-105, F-Sa from $75-115. ❺

Compassion Flower Bed & Breakfast, 216 Laurel St. (☎466-0420). Beautifully restored Victorian home in lively downtown. Gourmet breakfast, fand jacuzzi. Garden patio. Run by a female couple and their children who take extra care to run an environmentally friendly house. Vegan, vegetarian and special diets catered to. 2 night min. stay may be required. Rooms in summer $125-175; in winter $110-$155. ❺

Darling House, 314 West Cliff Dr. (☎458-1958). A 1910 ocean-front mansion on lovely gardens. Hardwood interiors and ocean views. Continental breakfast. Sa stays usually require 2 night min. Rooms from $95. Check with Visitors Center for discounts. ❺

Sunny Cove Beach Motel, 1610 E. Cliff Dr. (☎475-1741), near Schwan Lagoon. Far from downtown, but pleasant, well-kept suites have kitchens and cable TV. Outdoor pool. Market and beach 1 block away. Pets allowed. Rooms Su-Th $60-100, F-Sa $80-130. Weekly rates available. ❺

The Zayante Hostel, on East Zayante Rd. (☎335-4265), across the street from the market, near Felton. The former nightclub hosted folk-rock legends in the late 50s, 60s and 70s and was famous for hippie pool parties. Now the funky hand-built, wooden structure caters to those looking for a place to rest their heads and warm their bellies with a country breakfast ($1) cooked on a wood burning stove. Outdoor rustic cabins have beds underneath makeshift skylights, with leafy vines creeping through the walls. Plan on meeting a variety of characters, some traveling and some just hanging out indefinitely. Linens provided, but not a bad idea to bring your own. Dorms $16. Cash only. ❷

CAMPING

Reservations for state campgrounds can be made through ReserveAmerica (☎800-444-7275) and should be made early. Sites below are listed geographically, moving north toward Santa Cruz and then past Santa Cruz into the mountains. New Brighton State Beach and Big Basin Redwoods State Park, two of the more scenic spots, are both accessible by public transportation. As with any other kind of lodging in Santa Cruz, campgrounds fill up quick and early.

■ **Big Basin Redwoods State Park**, 21600 Big Basin Way (☎338-8860), in Boulder Creek, 23 mi. northwest of Santa Cruz. Go north on Rte. 9 to Rte. 236 through Boulder Creek. Although it is removed from the delights of Santa Cruz, Big Basin offers the best camping from Point Reyes to Big Sur. The mountain air helps cool off its 80 mi. of trails, including the 2-day (30 mi.) Skyline-to-the-Sea Trail (trailhead parking $5). To reserve one of the 145 campsites with showers or one of the 35 tent cabins, call ReserveAmerica ☎800-444-7275; for tent cabins call 800-874-8368. $5 non-refundable reservation fee. Reservations for all options required well in advance during the summer. Sites $12; day use sunrise to sunset $5 per car. Backcountry sites $5 including parking. ❶

Sunset State Beach, 201 Sunset Beach Rd. (☎763-7063), in Watsonville, on Hwy. 1, 16 mi. south of Santa Cruz. Take the San Andreas Rd. Exit and turn right onto Sunset Beach Rd. Wind through eucalyptus-lined roads and end up by a stunning beach. Reservations highly recommended in summer. 90 sites $12; day use 6am-sunset $3. ❶

Manresa Uplands State Beach Park, 205 Manresa Rd. (☎761-1795), in La Selva Beach, 13 mi. south of Santa Cruz. Take Hwy. 1 and Exit at San Andreas Rd. Veer right and follow San Andreas Rd. for 4 mi., then turn right on Sand Dollar Rd. 64 walk-in "tents only" Sites $12; day use 6am-10pm $3 per car. ❶

New Brighton State Beach, 1500 Park Ave. (☎464-6329), in Capitola, 4 mi. south of Santa Cruz off Hwy. 1. On a coastal bluff, wave breakers murmur to 112 sites (4 bike sites). Showers available. June-Sept. 7-night max. consecutive stay; Oct.-May 15-night max. consecutive stay. Check-out noon. Reservations required. Sites $12; day use from sunrise to 10pm is $3 per car. RV sites available; no hookups. ❶

FOOD

Santa Cruz offers an astounding number of budget eateries. The healthful restaurant community goes out of its way to embrace vegans—tofu can be substituted for just about anything. Fresh local produce sells at the **farmer's market** at Lincoln and Cedar St. downtown. (Open W 2:30-6:30pm.)

■ **Zoccoli's**, 1534 Pacific Ave. (☎423-1711). This phenomenal deli makes sandwiches for $4-5. Daily pasta specials ($6.75) come with salad, garlic bread, cheese, and salami. Only the freshest ingredients. Open M-Sa 10am-6pm, Su 11am-5pm. ❷

■ **Malabar**, 1116 Soquel Ave. (☎423-7906), at Seabright Ave. Healthy, vegetarian Sri Lankan cuisine. Incredible flatbread served by candlelight with ghee and garlic ($2.50). Hefty entrees are reasonably priced ($5-9). Open M-Th 11am-2:30pm and 5:30-9pm, F 11am-2:30pm and 5:30-10pm, Sa 5:30-10pm. No credit cards. ❷

Zachary's, 819 Pacific Ave. (☎427-0646). With excellent potatoes, freshly baked bread, and enormous omelettes, laid-back and earthy Zachary's will fill you with reasons to laze about at the beach for the rest of the day. Basic breakfast (2 eggs, oatmeal-molasses toast, and hash browns) for under $5. Beware of the crowds here on weekends. Open Tu-Su 7am-2:30pm. ❶

Saturn Cafe, 145 Laurel St. (☎429-8505, for downtown lunch delivery 429-9069), at Pacific Ave. At this planetary-punk themed restaurant, hard-working waitstaff do their best to keep your table clean and your coffee fresh. Excellent vegetarian meals. Veggie breakfast plates like tofu scramble with fakin' bacon or veggie sausage and pancakes (can be made vegan) $6. Open M-F 11:30am-2:30pm, Sa-Su 11:30am-3:30pm. ❷

Falafel Hut, 309 Beach St. (☎423-0567), across the street from the start of the Boardwalk. A good place for a quick late-night snack, it serves a variety of Middle Eastern and American dishes. The Lebanese owners pride themselves on their falafel sandwiches ($4.25), but the chicken ($5) is hard to beat. Open daily 11am-11pm. ❶

Cloud's Downtown, 110 Church St. (☎429-2000). Modern and friendly atmosphere. Fresh California Cuisine with a Pacific Rim influence. Usually a more mature, affluent crowd or those looking to impress their dates. Salads $5-12. Main dishes $9-20. Open M-Th 11:30am-10pm, F-Sa noon-11pm, Su noon-10pm. F-Sa bar open until 2pm. ❸

👁 SIGHTS

SANTA CRUZ BEACH BOARDWALK. Santa Cruz has a great beach, but the water is frigid. Without wetsuits for warmth, many casual beachgoers catch their thrills on the Boardwalk, a three-block long strip of over 25 amusement park rides, guess-your-weight booths, shooting galleries, and corn-dog vendors. The boardwalk is a gloriously tacky throwback to 50s era beach culture, providing a loud and lively diversion—one that seems to attract every sun-drenched family, couple, and roving pack of teenagers in California. Highly recommended is the Giant Dipper, a 1924 wooden roller coaster, where Dirty Harry met his enemy in 1983's *Sudden Impact*. If stomach-turning rides don't sound very appealing, there's always Buccaneer Bay Miniature Golf or video games inside Neptune's Kingdom. While the Boardwalk is relatively safe, be cautious of the surrounding community at night— a handful of people live or loiter on the streets. *(Boardwalk open daily Memorial Day-Labor Day, plus many off-season weekends and holidays. Rides $30 per 60 tickets, most rides 4 or 5 tickets; all-day pass $25 per person. Some height restrictions. Miniature golf $4.)*

UNIVERSITY OF CALIFORNIA AT SANTA CRUZ (UCSC). Five miles northwest of downtown sprawls this 2000-acre campus, accessible by many buses (#10, 12, 16, 19, 91) car, or bicycle (for those who brave the uphill climb). When it was built in the late 1960s, then-governor Ronald Reagan's plan to make UCSC a "riot-proof campus" (free of a central point where radicals could inflame a crowd) had a beneficial side effect in promoting the university's decentralized and forested layout. Although the campus appears tranquil, with university buildings sitting uncrowded amid spectacular rolling hills and redwood groves, Santa Cruz is famous (or infamous) for its fervent leftist politics and conspicuous drug culture. Once the "safety school" of the UC system, UCSC now regularly turns away scores of aspiring Banana Slugs (the school's mascot). Student-led tours of the campus are available by reservation only. If you drive onto the campus on weekdays, make sure you have a parking permit. Trails behind the campus are perfect for day hikes. The UCSC **Arboretum** grows some of the world's rarest flowers and is considered one of the finest in the state. Many are also impressed by the UCSC **Farm & Garden,** where students of the Center for Agroecology and Sustainable Food Systems are hard at work growing acres of vegetables, plants and flowers. The UCSC **Seymour Marine Discovery Center,** at Long Marine Laboratory, is also a fascinating spot for nature lovers. Located on the bluffs overlooking Monterey Bay, current scientific research is made into exhibits for the public to observe and touch. *(For UCSC campus tours call ☎429-2231; M-F 8am-5pm. Parking permits ($4) and maps available at police station.*

CENTRAL COAST

Arboretum open daily 9am-5pm; free. Seymour Marine Discovery Center: 100 Shaffer Rd. ☎ 459-3799. Adults $5, students, seniors and children ages 6-16 $3, 1st Tu of every month free.)

SURFER STATUE & SANTA CRUZ SURFING MUSEUM. The bronze Surfer Statue, just southwest of the lighthouse on W. Cliff Dr. near Steamer's Lane, is a monument "dedicated to all surfers, past, present, and future." This inspirational figure, erected in 1992, is often graced with a *lei*. Inside the lighthouse itself is a small surfing museum, which opened in 1986. The main room displays vintage artifacts, photos, and videos, concentrating on the personal stories of local surfers from the 1920s to the present. *(☎ 429-3429. Open Su-M and W-Sa noon-4pm. Free.)*

SANTA CRUZ WHARF. Jutting off Beach St. is the longest car-accessible pier on the West Coast. Seafood restaurants and souvenir shops will try to distract you from the expansive views of the coast. Munch on candy from local favorite Marini's (☎ 423-7258) while watching the sea lions who hang out on rafters beneath the end of the pier. *(Parking $1 per hr., under 30min. free. Disabled patrons free.)*

MISIÓN DE EXALTACIÓN DE LA SANTA CRUZ. This peaceful, fragrant adobe church and garden offer contemplative quiet. *(126 High St. Turn north on Emmet St. off Mission St. Open Tu-Sa 10am-4pm, Su 10am-2pm. Donation requested.)*

☞ ♨ BEACHES & ACTIVITIES

The **Santa Cruz Beach** (officially named Cowell Beach) is broad, reasonably clean, and generally packed with volleyball players. If you're seeking solitude, you'll have to venture farther afield. Away from the main drag, beach access points line Hwy. 1. Railroad tracks, farmlands, and dune vegetation make several of these access points somewhat difficult, but correspondingly less crowded. Maps of these beaches are listed in the *Santa Cruz Traveler's Guide*, available at the Visitors Center (see **Practical Information,** p. 320). Many of the sites listed under **Camping,** p. 322, let out onto pristine and unfrequented beaches. Folks who want to exercise their right to **bare everything** should head north on Hwy. 1 to the **Red, White, and Blue Beach,** down Scaroni Rd. Sunbathers must be 18 or accompanied by a parent. (Day use $10 per person; after 3pm $15 per person. Beach open Feb.-Oct. daily 10am-6pm.) If you're averse to paying for the privilege of an all-over tan, try the **Bonny Doon Beach,** off Hwy. 1 at Bonny Doon Rd., 11 mi. north of Santa Cruz. Magnificent cliffs and rocks surround this windy and deserted spot.

To try your hand at riding the waves, contact the **Richard Schmidt Surf School,** or ask around for him at the beach. Schmidt is much respected by the locals, who say that he can get anyone surfing. (☎ 423-0928. 1hr. private lesson $80, 2hr. group lesson $80. Lessons include equipment.) The best vantage points for **watching surfers** are along W. Cliff Dr. Although the beach is packed with wetsuited hopefuls, patient observers will soon identify the more experienced surfriders. To learn more about the activity, stop in at **Steamer's Lane,** the popular name for the deep water off the point where surfers have flocked since Hawaiian "Duke" Kahanamoku kick-started California's surf culture here 100 years ago. Or, check out the more remote "Hook" along **Pleasure Point,** slightly north of Santa Cruz in Live Oak.

Around the point at the end of W. Cliff Dr. is **Natural Bridges State Beach.** Only one natural bridge remains standing, but the park offers a pristine beach, awe-inspiring tidepools, and tours during monarch butterfly season (Oct.-Mar.). In November and December, thousands of the stunning *lepidoptera* swarm along the beach and blanket the nearby groves in their orange hues. (☎ 423-4609. Open daily 8am-dusk. Parking $3, seniors $2, disabled $1.)

Outdoor sports enthusiasts will find ample activities in Santa Cruz. Parasailing and other pricey pastimes are popular on the wharf. **Kayak Connection,** 413 Lake

Ave., has ocean-going **kayaks** at reasonable rates. Rentals include paddle, life jacket, and a wetsuit. Brief instruction accompanies all rentals; you must provide ACA certification for a closed-deck kayak unless you go to **Elkhorn Slough**—a beautiful estuary where it is safe for unexperienced kayakers to used a closed-deck kayak. Elkhorn Slough is an incredible spot with an amazing array of wildlife, more experienced kayakers will enjoy it just as much as beginners. Beware of cheap rental agencies without instruction sessions, since closed-deck ocean kayaking can be dangerous. (Kayak Connection ☎479-1121. Open M-F 10am-5pm, Sa-Su 9am-6pm. Open-deck single $33 per day, closed-deck single $37. 4½hr. lessons $45. Tours also available from $25-48.) You can try **rock climbing** on 13,000 sq. ft. of artificial terrain at **Pacific Edge**, 104 Bronson St. #12. The gym includes a weight room, a sauna, and showers. (☎454-9254. Open M 4-10pm, Tu and Th 8am-10pm, W and F 11am-10pm, Sa 10am-9pm, Su 10am-7pm. Offers packages to suit the needs of climbers of all skill levels. Day pass for experienced climbers $14; class for beginners $31.50, kids $14.50.)

🎵 🍷 ENTERTAINMENT & NIGHTLIFE

Underage kids and those asking for spare change flock to downtown, especially along Pacific Ave. Nevertheless, this strip also is home to a host of bustling coffee shops and a few laid-back bars. There are comprehensive weekly events listings in the free local publications *Good Times* and *Metro Santa Cruz*, and also in the *Spotlight* in Friday's *Sentinel* (all available at cafes and bookstores). The Boardwalk bandstand offers free summertime Friday concerts, usually by oldies bands, around 6:30 and 8:30pm. The Santa Cruz Parks and Recreation Department (see **Practical Information,** p. 320) publishes info in the free *Summer Activity Guide.*

🏠 **Caffe Pergolesi,** 418A Cedar St. (☎426-1775). Chill coffeehouse/bar with a series of small rooms and a spacious patio for reading, writing, or socializing. Cheerful color scheme and intimate tables give "Perg's" a supremely friendly atmosphere. 4 varieties of hot chocolate. $3 pints daily 7-9pm. Large coffee for the price of a small M-F 1-3pm. Open M-Th 6:30am-11:30pm, F-Sa 7:30am-midnight, Su 7:30am-11:30pm.

🏠 **99 Bottles Restaurant and Pub,** 110 Walnut Ave. (☎459-9999). This modest but lively bar in the heart of downtown offers standard bar meals (burgers $7) and 99 different types of beer. Happy hour M-F 4-6pm, beers $3, pitchers $8.75; Tu and W also 10pm-close; on "Thirsty Thursday," Happy hour extends until close. Open M-Th 11:30am-1:30am, F-Sa 11:30am-2am, Su 11:30am-midnight. Kitchen closes at 10pm.

Kuumbwa Jazz Center, 320 Cedar St. (☎427-2227; www.kuumbajazz.org). Known throughout the region for great jazz and innovative off-night programs. Those under 21 are welcome in this small and low-key setting. Coffees, sodas, beer and wine. The big names play here on M; locals have their turn on F. Tickets ($10-20) sold through **Logos Books and Music,** 1117 Pacific Ave. (☎427-5100; open daily 10am-10pm), as well as at www.ticketweb.com. M shows 7 and 9pm; F 8pm.

Blue Lagoon, 923 Pacific Ave. (☎423-7117). Mega-popular gay-straight club has won all awards from "best bartender" to "best place you can't take your parents" from the local press. Bar in front, 3 pool tables in back, and people dancing everywhere. Happy Hour with $3 drinks daily 6-9pm. Su Bloody Marys $3. Stronger-than-the-bouncer drinks $3-4. Cover $2-5. Open daily 4pm-1:30am.

The Catalyst, 1011 Pacific Ave. (☎423-1338). The town's primary music/dance venue draws national, college, and local bands. Pool and darts upstairs, deli and bar downstairs. Sandwiches $4-8. Cover and age restrictions vary widely with show ($5-30; as young as 16+); adjacent bar area strictly 21+. Shows W-Sa. Open M-Sa 9am-2am, Su 9am-5pm. Food served daily 9am-3pm and 9am-10pm on show days.

SEASONAL EVENTS

Whale-watching season, Dec.-Mar. Boats depart from the Santa Cruz Municipal Wharf. Trips $5-30; some guarantee sightings. For more info, contact the Santa Cruz Visitor Infocenter (☎425-1234).

Migration Festival (☎423-4609), at the Natural Bridges State Park. In early Feb., celebrate the journeys of migrating elephant seals, salmon, shorebirds, whales, and monarch butterflies that pass through the Central Coast. Music, crafts, and booths.

Santa Cruz Blues Festival (☎479-9814; www.santacruzbluesfestival.com). 2 days in late May. Big-name blues. $30, children under 12 $20.

Lesbian, Gay, Bisexual, Transgender Pride Day (☎761-9652), 1st Su in June. Now in its 25th year. Parade, music, and speakers.

Surf City Classic (☎420-5273; santacruzwharf.com), late June. More than 150 classic surf vehicles roll into the beautiful Santa Cruz Municipal Wharf. These so-called "woodies" generate a fine fuss. 50s and 60s theme music and food adds to the fun.

Musical Saw Festival, at Roaring Camp Railroads, Felton (☎335-4484), late June. Musicians and listeners are invited to workshops for jam and open mic sessions featuring performances of musical saws and folk instruments from around the world.

Shakespeare Santa Cruz, at UCSC (☎459-2159), mid-July to Sept. Nationally acclaimed, innovative outdoor festival. All-show passes available.

Santa Cruz Hot and Cool Jazz Fest (☎888-474-7407), 3 days in mid-July. Jazz artists from the West play in 4 venues along the beach. Boardwalk concerts are free, concerts at Coconut Grove and Seaside Bowl $15-25 each.

Cabrillo Music Festival (☎426-6966), first 2 weeks in Aug. Held downtown in the Civic Auditorium, the festival brings contemporary and classical music to the Central Coast. Purchase tickets ($15-35) in advance for good seats.

NEAR SANTA CRUZ   ☎831

Santa Cruz is surrounded by gently sloping hills that make hiking a delight; the paths are only mildly strenuous and the scenery is magnificent. To the north, **Big Basin Redwoods State Park,** the first (and some say the best) of the California state parks, offers trails that novices can enjoy. South of Big Basin, the gorgeous **Henry Cowell Redwoods State Park** (see p. 322) has trails suitable for daytrips. Bikers get a kick among the second-growth redwoods of **Niscene Marks State Park.** Heading south from Santa Cruz on Hwy. 1, take the Seacliff Beach Exit, cross over the highway, and turn right on Soquel Ave. The park will be on your left. **Ano Nuevo State Reserve,** on New Years Creek Rd., in Pescadero, is home to enormous seals that can be viewed on a 3 mi. (round-trip) trek across uneven sandy terrain. The Visitors Center also offers Naturalist-led tours. (☎879-2025. Open 8am-sunset.)

In Felton, the **Roaring Camp Railroads,** on Graham Hill Rd., runs an old steam-powered passenger train on a spectacular route from Felton through the redwoods to Bear Mountain and holds seasonal historic celebrations. (☎335-4484. Round-trip $15, ages 3-13 $10.) To reach Felton, take Rte. 9, which passes through Henry Cowell Redwoods State Park. In Felton, take Graham Hill Rd. southeast and bear south to Roaring Camp as indicated by road signs.

Santa Cruz county is home to "renegade" **wineries.** Calling the area "The anti-Napa," local wine-makers are highly experimental, and follow their instincts to create concoctions such as "sulphiteless" and "gingseng" wine. However odd these wines may sound, many are winning awards and having financial success. Make sure to take advantage of this unique opportunity and go tasting! Pick up a map at the Visitors Center, or contact the **Santa Cruz Mountains Winegrowers Association** (☎479-9463; www.scmwa.com) for more information.

SALINAS & SALINAS VALLEY ☎831

The heart of John Steinbeck Country beats in Salinas, an agricultural town 90 mi. south of San Francisco and 25 mi. inland from Monterey. Steinbeck, the renowned author (the first of two Americans to win both the Pulitzer and Nobel Prizes) lived here until he was 17. This is where Steinbeck set *East of Eden* and *The Red Pony*, where many of the characters he created are from, and where his ashes are buried. Aside from echoes of Steinbeck's writing and a highly acclaimed rodeo, Salinas offers travelers pieces of Great Depression and World War II era culture. For most, the town is a brief diversion while driving along U.S. 101 or Rte. 68 to Monterey.

South of Salinas, U.S. 101 stretches out toward faraway San Luis Obispo, running through the wide, green Salinas Valley, where the towns of Gonzales, Soledad, Greenfield, and King City (all 10-15 mi. apart) serve mainly as farming communities and truck stops. Framed by the rolling San Lucia mountain range, acre upon acre of lettuce, artichokes, broccoli, cauliflower, carrots, grapes, and chili peppers thrive here in the self-proclaimed "salad bowl of the world." Driving down U.S. 101, beware the speed trap around King City, where wily highway patrolmen are known to flag down drivers who don't obey the speed limit on their own. For a more intimate, scenic, take smaller roads like Rte. 146. Rising above the greenery are the points of the Pinnacles, an old volcanic crater with incredible rock formations and wildlife attractions.

⍰ PRACTICAL INFORMATION

Trains: Amtrak, 11 Station Pl. (☎422-7458 or 800-827-7245), in Salinas. Offers bus/train combo and train-only service. To: **L.A.** (bus/train $46-69; train only $54-94) and **San Francisco** (bus/train $16-24). Waiting room open Tu-Sa 11am-8pm.

Buses: Greyhound, 19 W. Gabilan St. (☎424-4418 or 800-231-2222), in Salinas, 1 block from the MST Center. Several buses per day to: **L.A.** ($38.50-40.50); **San Francisco** ($17.25-18.25); **Santa Cruz** ($10.25-11.25). Open daily 4am-11:30pm.

Public Transportation: Monterey-Salinas Transit or **MST,** 110 Salinas St. (☎424-7695), at Central Ave. in Salinas. Fare per zone $1.75; seniors, ages 5-18, and handicapped $0.85. One-zone day pass $3.50/$1.75. Multiple-zone day pass $7/$3.50. Same-zone transfers free up to 2hr. Bus #20 or 21 will take you to Monterey. (See listing for MST in **Monterey: Practical Information,** p. 331.)

Visitor Information: Salinas Valley Chamber of Commerce, 119 E. Alisal St. (☎424-7611), in Salinas, has city maps ($2) and plenty of info on the Salinas Valley and Monterey Peninsula. Open M 9:30am-5pm, Tu-F 8:30am-5pm. At the **King City Chamber of Commerce and Agriculture,** 203 Broadway (☎385-3814), in King City. Staff members are available to answer questions but are short on brochures, just as the region is short on tourist activities. Open M-F 10am-noon and 1-4pm.

Road Conditions: ☎800-427-7623. Available 24hr.

Police: Salinas (☎758-7321); King City (☎385-8311).

Medical Services: Salinas Valley Memorial Hospital, 450 E. Romie Ln., Salinas (☎757-4333).

Post Office: Salinas, 100 W. Alisal St. (☎770-7142). Open M-F 8:30am-5pm. For General Delivery, use the post office at 1011 Post Dr. **Postal Code:** 93901. **King City,** 123 S. 3rd St., at Bassett St. Open M-F 8:30am-4:30pm. **Postal Code:** 93930.

⍔ ACCOMMODATIONS

Generally, the farther south from Salinas accommodations are, the lower their prices will be. Salinas has several expensive hotels, but standard chain motels cluster at the E. Market St. Exit off U.S. 101.

▨ **Traveler's Hotel,** 16½ East Gabilan St. (☎ 758-1198), is the best moderately-priced option in Salinas. Recently renovated hotel with cable TV, mini-fridge, coffee maker and private bath. Coin-operated laundry. No off-street parking. Singles $55-66; doubles $88-110. 10% AARP and military discounts. ❹

El Dorado Motel, 1351 N. Main St. (☎ 449-2442 or 800-523-6506), near the California Rodeo. Clean rooms with cable TV, private baths. Laundry facilities on site. Apr.-Sept. singles $55-72; doubles $66-83. Oct.-Mar. singles $55; doubles $66. ❹

Greenfield Inn, 22 4th St. (☎ 674-5995), has small rooms with TV, bath, and upper lofts for additional beds. Singles $35; each additional person $5. ❸

Fireside Inn, 640 Broadway (☎ 386-1010), in King City, has a gigantic tree growing through its office, which is open daily 8am-2pm and 4-10pm. Doubles with TV, refrigerator, and bath from $40. ❸

⛺ CAMPING

There is no camping at **Pinnacles National Monument** (☎ 389-4485), but east of the monument is **Pinnacles Campground Inc.** ❶, a privately owned campground with 78 tent sites (6-person max.), 15 group sites, 36 RV sites, a pool, flush toilets, and hot showers. (☎ 389-4462. 4-night max. stay. $7 per person. Electrical hookups $2 extra.) All sites are first-come, first-camp. There are five other campgrounds on the east side of Pinnacles: **Bolado Park** ❶, 27 mi. north of the park (☎ 628-3421; $7.50 per vehicle, $12 per RV); **Hollister Hills State Vehicular Recreation Area** ❶, 35 mi. north (☎ 637-3874; $6 per vehicle); **Mission Farm RV Park** ❷, 40 mi. north (☎ 623-4456; $20 per tentsite, $28 per RV); **KOA Campground** ❷, 50 mi. north (☎ 623-4263; $28.30 per tentsite or RV, $33.60 for full hookup); and **Fremont Peak State Park** ❶, 52 mi. north (☎ 623-4255; $3 per vehicle). Be warned—there is no road access from the east side of the park to the west side (the drive is 70 mi.), although it is possible to hike through. Camps to the west of the park are **Paraiso Hot Springs** ❷, 25 mi. west (☎ 678-2882; $30 per person); **Arroyo Seco** ❷, 45 mi. west (☎ 678-2882; $16 per site); **Salinas Valley Fairgrounds** ❶, in King City (☎ 385-3243; trailers and RVs only; $9.50-15 per night); **San Lorenzo Regional Park** ❷, in King City (☎ 384-5964; $16 per tent site, $19 per RVs, $21 for full hookup); and **Cuidad del Rey Motel and Trailer Park** ❷, 2 mi. south of King City (☎ 385-4828; $15 per tent site, $25 per RV site).

🍴 FOOD

Pass the fast food joints lining the freeway and you'll find fresh greens in Salinas eateries. Those stopping in Old Salinas by the Steinbeck Center will sing the praises of the popular **First Awakenings** ❷, 171 Main St. Priding themselves on fresh food and good service, it is no wonder that weekend mornings often see lines outside the doors. Try their gourmet apple cinnamon pancakes ($6) or one of their egg dishes—crepes, omelettes, frittatas, or the "your way" option for $4.25-7.25. (☎ 784-1125. Open daily 7am-2pm.) The more traditional greasy-spoon diner would be **Sang's Cafe** ❷, 131 Main St. Large homestyle breakfasts $4.25-9. (☎ 424-6012. Open Tu-Sa 6:30am-2:30pm.) For a more upscale lunch or dinner try the **Monterey Coast Restaurant and Brewery** ❸, 165 Main St., which serves tasty American fare—burgers, sandwiches, and pizza—with a few more sophisticated entrees like pork chops with red wine, apples and potatoes ($14). Vegetarians options include artichoke, sun-dried tomato and goat cheese pizza ($8.50). They also craft their owns brews and have live jazz Sundays at lunch. (☎ 758-2337. Open Su-Th 11am-11pm, F-Sa 11am-midnight.) **Hullaballoo** ❹, 228 S. Main St. is more expensive ($9-25) but has more options and very large portions. They also have a cafe in the Steinbeck Center. (☎ 775-4738. Open M-F 11:30am-4pm, F-Sa 4-10pm, Su-Th 4-9pm.)

🔊 STEINBECK & SEASONAL EVENTS

The town of Salinas salivates over internationally recognized hometown author John Steinbeck. The enormous **National Steinbeck Center**, 1 Main St. (☎796-3833; www.steinbeck.org), brings 37,000 sq. ft. of mice to pet, plants to smell, and stories to hear, all evocative of Steinbeck's inspiration: the Salinas Valley. One does not have to be a Steinbeck lover or even have read any of his legendary works to appreciate the interactive and provocative trip into Steinbeck's world of American small-town culture. The Center is usually teeming with schoolchildren who love the Center's hands-on multimedia approach. Those desiring a more relaxing atmosphere will find it in the art gallery, with work depicting the Salinas area. The Center is constructing a 6,500 sq. ft. exhibit called "Valley of the World" to celebrate Salinas's other claim to fame—agriculture—due to open summer 2003. The nearby **gravesite** at 758 Abbot St. and **Steinbeck House**, 132 Central St., are less dazzling but more intimate ways to enter Steinbeck's world. (Center open daily 10am-5pm. $10, seniors and students $8, ages 13-17 $7, ages 6-12 $6, ages 5 and under free.)

Salinas's biggest non-literary tourist pull is the **California Rodeo Salinas**, on North Main St. at Laurel Dr. The rodeo is the fourth-largest in the world, attracting wrestlers, riders, cows, and bulls from across the West in the third week of July. While the rodeo lasts for only four days, related events, including **cowboy poetry readings at the Fox Theatre**, take place May-July. (P.O. Box 1648, Salinas, CA. 93902. ☎800-549-4989; www.carodeo.com. $11-18, season tickets $60-72.)

PINNACLES NATIONAL MONUMENT ☎831

Towering dramatically over the dense, dry brushwood east of Soledad, Pinnacles National Monument comprises the spectacular remnants of an ancient volcano. Set aside as a national monument in 1908, it preserves the erratic and unique spires and crags that millions of years of weathering carved out of prehistoric lava flows. Thirty miles of hiking trails wind through the park's low chaparral, boulder-strewn caves, and pinnacles of rock, many of which make for great but dangerous climbing and caving (flashlights are required on cave trails). **Bench Trail** is an easy, 1.9 mi. path with access to park facilities from Pinnacles Campground, Inc., along Chalone Creek. At the end of that hike, one can link up to **Bear Gulch or Old Pinnacles. Bear Gulch** is a moderate, 1 mi., shaded, bottom valley walk connecting the Bear Gulch Visitors Center and Chalone Creek. **Old Pinnacles** is also a shaded walk along canyon bottom but slightly easier and longer (2.3 mi.). Both trails will lead towards cave exploring options: **Bear Gulch Cave Trail** and **Balconies Cave Trail**, respectively. The **High Peaks Trail** runs a strenuous 5.6 mi. across the park between the east and west entrances, offering amazing views of the surrounding rock formations. A magnificent array of **wildflowers** blooms in the spring, and the park offers excellent **bird-watching** all year long. Pinnacles has a wide range of wildlife, including mountain lions, bobcats, coyotes, rattlesnakes, golden eagles, and peregrine falcons. Since Pinnacles is far from city lights and has very few clouds, the **night sky** over the monument puts on quite a show. The park headquarters is at the eastern entrance, taking Rte. 25 to Rte. 146, but maps, water, and restrooms are also available at a station on the west side off Rte. 146 from U.S. 101. (Headquarters ☎389-4485. Open daily 7:30am-9pm. Park entrance $5.)

The **Mission Nuestra Señora de la Soledad (Our Lady of Solitude)**, 36641 Fort Romie Rd., in Soledad, off Arroyo Seco, was built in 1791. Floods destroyed the building, but it was restored in the 1950s and today has a small museum. An annual fiesta is held the last Sunday in October, and an annual barbecue takes place on the last Sunday in June. (☎678-2586. Open W-M 10am-4pm.)

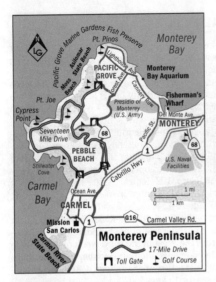

Monterey Peninsula
- ◠ 17-Mile Drive
- ⊓ Toll Gate ⚲ Golf Course

Between Salinas and Monterey, 4 mi. off Hwy. 68 on River Rd., is the home of many movie-star animals, **Wild Things,** 400 River Rd. See how animals are trained for film, television, live productions, or education work and what it takes to house and maintain them. (www.wildthingsinc.com. Tours daily 1pm daily; June-Aug. also 3pm. Adults $10, ages 14 and under $8.)

MONTEREY ☎ 831

Monterey (pop. 33,000) makes good on its public claim to have preserved more of its heritage than any other Californian city. Although luxury hotels and tourist shops abound, and the *Cannery Row* of Steinbeck fame has all but vanished, a number of important sites bear witness to the city's—and the state's—fabled history. The "Path of History," marked by little yellow medallions embedded in the sidewalks, passes by such landmarks as Colton Hall, the site of the California Constitutional Convention in 1849, and the Robert Louis Stevenson House, where the author found shelter for a time in 1879. Most of this heritage owes its preservation to Monterey's other distinguishing feature: abundant wealth. Multi-million dollar homes and golf courses line the rocky shoreline and droves of luxury cars cruise the pristine city streets, cutting a sharp contrast with Monterey's gritty, industrial past.

▬ TRANSPORTATION

Motorists can approach Monterey from **U.S. 101** via Rte. 68 west through Salinas, or directly from coastal **Highway 1.** The relative isolation of Monterey does little to insulate the city from prodigious summer traffic jams, and the abundant one-way signs and complicated traffic signals don't help matters much. Alternatively, park for free in the Del Monte Shopping Center and explore by foot and shuttle. Monterey's primary attractions are within walking distance or a bus ride from **Alvarado Street.** Bicycling is also a great way to see the peninsula, but exercise caution on the narrow, twisting roads and on the often windy coast. Expensive lots or free 1hr. street parking are available for those traveling by car.

Airport: Monterey Airport (☎648-7000; www.montereyairport.com). From Hwy. 1, take Rte. 68 1½ mi. east and Exit onto Olmsted Rd. Small airport with intrastate and national service. Rental car agencies: **Avis** (800-331-1212), **Budget** (800-527-0770), **Hertz** (654-3131), and **National** (227-7368).

Buses: Greyhound (☎373-4735 or 800-231-2222) departs from Monterey Bay Gas, 1042 Del Monte Ave. To: **Santa Cruz** (1hr., 3 per day, $10.25); **San Francisco** (4-8hr., 3 per day, $16.25); and **Santa Barbara** (7hr., 3 per day, $34.25).

Public Transportation: Monterey-Salinas Transit or **MST,** 1 Ryan Ranch Rd. (☎899-2555, TDD 393-8111. MST phone lines open M-F 7:45am-5:15pm, Sa 10am-2:30pm.) The free *Rider's Guide,* available on buses, at motels, and at the Visitors Center, contains route info. MST serves the region from Watsonville in the north (where it connects to SCMTD; see **Santa Cruz**, p. 319) to Carmel in the south, as well as inland to Salinas. Many buses stop at the **Transit Plaza** downtown, where Munras Ave., Tyler, Pearl, Alvarado, and Polk streets converge. MST has 4 zones, each encompassing 1 or 2 towns. Fare per zone $1.75; seniors, ages 5-18 and disabled $0.85. Same-zone transfers free up to 2hr.; exact change required. Between Memorial Day and Labor Day, MST offers 2 extra services: The **Waterfront Area Visitors Express (WAVE)** goes to Monterey sights from the Del Monte Shopping Center for free; **Bus #22** runs twice daily May-Oct. between Monterey and Big Sur ($3.50; seniors, ages 5-18, and disabled $1.75).

Taxi: Yellow Cab (☎646-1234). Initial charge $2; each additional mi. $2.

Bike Rental: Bay Bikes, 640 Wave St. (☎646-9090), on Cannery Row directly on the waterfront bike path, **Recreation Trail.** There is also a smaller, usually less crowded location on the bike path near **Fisherman's Wharf.** Bikes $10 first 2hr., $4 each additional hr.; daily rates $22. Includes lock and helmet. Open daily 9am-7pm. Will deliver and retrieve bikes for day rentals to hotels.

✦ ? ORIENTATION & PRACTICAL INFORMATION

The Monterey Peninsula, 116 mi. south of San Francisco, consists of **Monterey, Pacific Grove** (a largely residential community), and **Pebble Beach** (an exclusive nest of mansions and golf courses). **Alvarado Street** runs north-south through Old Monterey, and is home to most of the area's nightlife scene. Parallel to it is **Pacific Street,** a main traffic thoroughfare. At its northern end stand luxury hotels and the gigantic DoubleTree Conference Center; beyond the brick plaza lies a large parking lot, the marina, and Fisherman's Wharf. Perpendicular to Alvarado St., **Del Monte Avenue** runs roughly northeast to the coast; on the other side, **Lighthouse Avenue** leads northwest out through Pacific Grove, where it turns into **Central Avenue** and then leads back to Lighthouse Ave., and ends at the Point Piños Lighthouse.

Visitor Information: Monterey Peninsula Visitor and Convention Bureau, 150 Olivier St. (☎657-6400, 649-1770, or 888-221-1010; www.montereyinfo.org). Free pamphlets and *Walkabout Map.* The 120-page *Visitor's Guide* ($6) lots of info. Open M-F 8:30am-5pm. There is also a smaller **Visitors Center,** 401 Camino El Estero (☎649-1770). Open May-Sept. M-F 10am-6pm, Sa-Su 10am-5pm; Oct.-Apr. daily 10am-5pm.

Library: 625 Pacific St. (☎646-3930), diagonally across from City Hall. Pleasant courtyard. 2hr. free parking and **Internet access.** Open M-Th 9am-9pm, F 9am-6pm, Sa 9am-5pm, Su 1-5pm.

Laundromat: Wash n' Dry, 619 Lighthouse Ave., Wash $1.50, dry $0.25 per 10min. Self-service. Change machine. Soap $0.50. Open 24hr.

Road Conditions: ☎800-427-7623.

Police: 351 Madison St. (☎646-3830), at Pacific St.

Crisis Lines: Rape Crisis (☎375-4357). 24hr. **Suicide Prevention** (☎649-8008). 24hr.

Post Office: 565 Hartnell St. (☎372-4003). Open M-F 8:30am-5:00pm, Sa 10am-2pm. **Postal Code:** 93940.

▗ ACCOMMODATIONS

Inexpensive hotels line **Lighthouse Avenue** in Pacific Grove (bus #2 or some #1), and on the 2000 block of **Fremont Street** in Monterey (bus #9 or 10). Others cluster along **Munras Avenue** between downtown Monterey and Hwy. 1. The cheapest hotels in the area, are in the less-appealing towns of Seaside and Marina, just north of Monterey. Note that prices fluctuate dramatically depending on the day and concurrent local events.

Monterey Carpenter's Hall Hostel (HI-AYH), 778 Hawthorne St. (☎649-0375), 1 block west of Lighthouse Ave. This 45-bed hostel is fairly new and perfectly located. Although it lacks the quaint, homey feel of many other California hostels, it makes up for any deficiencies of character with clean, modern facilities, and a comfortable living room with a piano, library, and games. Lockout 10am-5pm. Curfew 11pm. Small chore requested. Reservations essential June-Sept. Dorms $20, non-members $23, ages 7-17 $15.50, under 6 $11.50; private rooms for up to 4 from $54. Free parking lot adjacent. ❷

Del Monte Beach Inn, 1110 Del Monte Blvd. (☎649-4410), in Monterey, near downtown and across from the beach. Victorian-style inn with pleasant rooms with TV. Near a fairly loud road. Continental breakfast and tea in sunny main room. Hall phone. Check-in 2-8pm. Reservations recommended. Rooms with shared bath Su-Th $55-66, F-Sa from $77; rooms with private bath and one with kitchenette $88-99. ❹

Butterfly Grove Inn, 1073 Lighthouse (373-4921). 28 rooms with TV, phones and private bath. Continental breakfast and pool. Ocean views, full kitchens, fireplaces, and jacuzzi available. Summer rates $99-179; winter rates from $69. ❺

Sunset Inn, 133 Asilomar Blvd. (☎375-3936), in Pacific Grove. In a quiet neighborhood less than 1 mi. from the ocean. Rooms have cable TV, phones, and private bath. Some have a fireplace and jacuzzi. Continental breakfast included. Prices can skyrocket, so reserve ahead. If rooms are available, walk-ins may receive lower prices. Rooms Apr.-Sept. Su-Th from $119, F-Sa from $149; Oct.-Mar. Su-Th from $59, F-Sa $79. ❺

♥ CAMPING

Camping is an excellent option for the budget traveler in expensive Monterey. Call the Monterey Parks line (☎755-4895 or 888-588-2267) for camping info and ReserveAmerica (☎800-444-7275) for reservations.

Veterans Memorial Park Campground (☎646-3865), in Via Del Rey, 1½ mi. from downtown. Take bus #3. From Rte. 68, take Skyline Forest Dr. and turn left onto Skyline Dr. From downtown, go south on Pacific St., turn right on Jefferson St., and follow the signs. On a hill with a view of the bay. Playground, barbecue pits, and hot showers, but no hookups. 40 sites available on first-come, first-camp basis; arrive before 3pm in summer and on weekends. 3-night max. stay. Walk-in sites $5; with vehicle $18. ❶

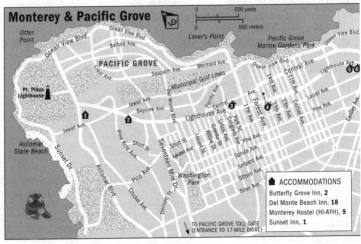

Monterey & Pacific Grove

▲ ACCOMMODATIONS
Butterfly Grove Inn, **2**
Del Monte Beach Inn, **18**
Monterey Hostel (HI-AYH), **9**
Sunset Inn, **1**

Laguna Seca Recreational Area (☎ 758-3604 or 888-588-2267), on Rte. 68 near the racetrack, 10 mi. east of Monterey. This hilly, oak-strewn camp overlooks valleys and the auto racetrack. Of the 174 campsites, 99 have hookups. If nobody is on duty, pitch your tent and rangers will come by and collect. Restrooms, BBQ pits, tables, and hot showers. Reservations accepted 5 or more in advance. Sites $18; hookups $22. ❷

🗔 FOOD

Once a booming spot for the canned sardine industry (hence the name Cannery Row), Monterey Bay now yields squid, crab, red snapper, and salmon. Seafood is bountiful, but it may be expensive—an early-bird special (usually 4-6:30pm) may ease the pain in your wallet. **Fisherman's Wharf** has smoked salmon sandwiches ($7) and free chowder samples. Don't despair if you loathe seafood—this is also the land of artichokes and strawberries. Free samples of fruit, cheese, and seafood are at the **Old Monterey Market Place,** on Alvarado St. (☎ 655-2607. Open Tu 4-8pm.) **Whole Foods,** 800 Del Monte Ctr. off Munras Ave. (☎ 333-1600), is a grocery store offering sandwiches made with fresh, gourmet ingredients ($6). Its location at the Del Monte Shopping Center makes it a convenient stop for picnic supplies before catching the WAVE or a bus to town.

CANNERY ROW & DOWNTOWN

Kalisa's, 851 Cannery Row, across from the Monterey Aquarium. This simple yellow structure may not look like much but, it has a Steinbeck connection (it was La Ida Cafe in *Cannery Row*) and features belly dancing from time to time. Hearty, healthy, and inexpensive sandwiches and salads ($4.50-6.75). The homemade ice cream ($2.50) will also please the palate. Open M-Sa 8:30am-8pm, Su 8:30am-7pm. ❷

Amarin Thai Cuisine, 807 Cannery Row (☎ 373-8811), near the aquarium in a complex of touristy shops. Fresh and unique California-style Thai food. Many vegetarian dishes such as tofu with vegetables and chili pepper sauce ($13). Lunch $6-11, dinner $10-13. Open M and W-Sa 11:30am-3:30pm and 5:30-9:30pm, Su noon-3:30pm. ❸

Old Monterey Cafe, 489 Alvarado St. (646-1021), Serves breakfast anytime ($4-10). Try their Old Monterey banana pancakes $5.50 or cinnamon raisin swirl french toast $6. Burgers and sandwiches are $5-7. Huge salads, like the Athenian greek, $9.50. ❷

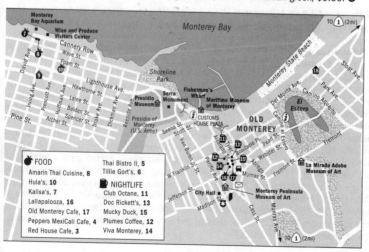

🍎 FOOD	Thai Bistro II, **5**
Amarin Thai Cuisine, **8**	Tillie Gort's, **6**
Hula's, **10**	🎵 NIGHTLIFE
Kalisa's, **7**	Club Octane, **11**
Lallapalooza, **16**	Doc Rickett's, **13**
Old Monterey Cafe, **17**	Mucky Duck, **15**
Peppers MexiCali Cafe, **4**	Plumes Coffee, **12**
Red House Cafe, **3**	Viva Monterey, **14**

Lallapalooza, 474 Alvarado St. (☎645-9036). This American dinner house and martini bar serves up portions that are a bit pricey but immense ($8.25-22). Excellent service and trendy, "olive-themed" (to say the least) decor. Many simply sample the slew of specialty martinis $6-9). Open M-Th 4pm-midnight, F-Sa 4pm-12:45am, Su 4-11pm. ❹

LIGHTHOUSE AVENUE AREA

■ **Thai Bistro II,** 159 Central Ave. (☎372-8700), in Pacific Grove. Graced with good service and a patio ringed with flowers, this bistro offers a comfortable atmosphere and quality thai cuisine. Mixed vegetable curry and tofu $8. Lunch combos ($6) come with soup. Open daily 11:30am-3pm and 5-9:30pm. ❷

■ **Tillie Gort's,** 111 Central Ave. (☎373-0335). This vegetarian mecca has been in the biz for over 30 years, which is some indication just how good the food is. Large portions of fresh dishes like the Mexican fiesta salad ($8.25), eggplant francese ($7.75) or spinach ravioli ($8.25), and sweet treats like berry cheesecake or chocolate vegan cake (each $4.50) will please even non-vegetarians. Beer and wine also served. Open daily 8am-10pm; Nov.-May weekdays open 11am. ❷

Red House Cafe, 662 Lighthouse Ave. (☎643-1060). Simple American favorites with a European gourmet flair. Only the freshest ingredients from local growers are used here. Patience is a virtue and usually a necessity to get a table and your meal; each dish is carefully prepared. Small dinner plates $8-11. Daily entree specials about $17. Open Tu-Su 8am-3pm, Th-Sa 5pm-8pm. No credit cards. ❸

Peppers MexiCali Cafe, 170 Forest Ave. (☎373-6892) between Lighthouse Ave. and Central St. Serves fresh-Mex fare, like snapper Yucatan ($11) and chicken caribe fajitas ($10), for lunch and dinner in a fun and lively setting decorated with "pepper" art. Reservations strongly recommended in evenings. Beer, wine, and margaritas available. Open M-Sa 11:30am-10pm, Su 4-10pm. ❸

Hula's, 622 Lighthouse Ave (☎655-4852). Try Hawaiian inspired dishes like macadamia encrusted ono and fresh island fisti ($13). Or have a wrap or rice bowl ($8). Beer, wine, and sake available. Open T-Sa 11:30am-2:30pm and 5-11pm, Su 5-10pm. ❸

◎ SIGHTS

■ **MONTEREY BAY AQUARIUM.** The biggest of Monterey's attractions, this extraordinarily impressive aquarium feeds on the committed community interest in marine ecology. The facility provides visitors with a window (literally) into the most curious creatures of the Pacific. Gaze through the **world's largest window** at an enormous marine habitat containing green sea turtles, giant ocean sunfish, large sharks, and impressive yellow- and blue-fin tuna to learn about how they live and how we can help them keep living. Don't miss the graceful and mesmerizing jellyfish—a new exhibit connecting the shape, movement, and beauty of jellyfish to various art forms provokes and stretches one's curiosity and imagination. Eager tourists scuttle for a glance at the **sea otters** during feeding time, a living kelp forest housed in a two-story-tall glass case, a petting zoo of damp bay denizens (stingrays included), and a **shorebird aviary.** The matter-of-fact environmental impact awareness theme running throughout will open your eyes. Arrive with a surfeit of patience; the lines for tickets, admission, viewing, and food can be as unbelievable as the exhibits themselves. Pick up tickets the day before and save 20-40min. *(886 Cannery Row. ☎648-4888 or 800-756-3737; www.montereybayaquarium.org. Open June to early Sept. and holidays daily 9:30am-6pm; early Sept. to late May 10am-6pm. $18; students, seniors, and ages 13-17 $15 with ID; disabled and ages 3-12 $8. Audio tour in English, German, French, Japanese and Spanish $3.)*

CANNERY ROW. Lying along the waterfront south of the aquarium, this was once a depressed street filled with languishing sardine-packing plants. The three-quarter mile row has been converted into a different commercial venture of tourist-packed mini-malls, bars, and a pint-sized carnival complex. All that remains of the earthiness and gruff camaraderie celebrated by John Steinbeck in *Cannery Row* and *Sweet Thursday* are a few building facades: 835 Cannery Row was the Wing Chong Market, the bright yellow building next door is where *Sweet Thursday* took place, and Doc Rickett's lab, 800 Cannery Row, is now owned by a private men's club. For a series of interpretive looks at Steinbeck's Cannery Row, take a peek at the **Great Cannery Row Mural.** Local artists have covered 400 ft. of a construction-site barrier on the 700 block with depictions of Monterey in the 1930s. The 2nd floor bayview "Taste of Monterey" **Wine and Visitors Center** offers a taste of the county's burgeoning wine industry with well-priced bottles and winery maps. The wide variety of regional wine to taste and to buy, plus the knowledgeable staff and inspiring view, makes it a good starting place for tasting tours. *(700 Cannery Row. ☎ 888-646-5446. 6 tastings $5; can go towards wine purchases. Open daily 11am-6pm.)*

MARITIME MUSEUM OF MONTEREY. Ship models, photos, navigation tools, logs, and other paraphernalia sketch the history of Monterey, as does the free 14-minute film. The museum's centerpiece is the original Fresnel lens of Point Sur Lighthouse: the entire lens is a two-story structure of gear-works and cut glass that was later replaced by the electric lighthouse. *(5 Custom House Plaza, across from Fisherman's Wharf in downtown Monterey. ☎ 373-2469. Open Tu-Su 11am-5pm. $5; seniors, ages 13-17, military, and disabled $2.50; under 12 free with an adult.)*

OTTER POINT. Catch a glimpse of otters in the wild from several nearby spots, including this one. Touching an otter is illegal, and "harassing" one in Monterey Bay may lead to a $10,000 fine. *(In Pacific Grove, 2½ mi. south from the Coast Guard Pier.)*

MONTEREY STATE HISTORIC PARK (PATH OF HISTORY WALKING TOUR). Monterey's early days spawned a unique architectural trend that incorporates Southern details, like wraparound porches, with Mexican adobe characteristics, such as 3 ft. thick walls and exterior staircases. The Path of History, which snakes through the downtown with its yellow sidewalk medallions, passes by numerous historic buildings, including the *Royal Presidio Chapel*, built in 1794, and the *Larkin House*, home to the US consul to Mexico during the 1840s. Walking the path unguided or with the paper brochure costs nothing, but a tour led by the state park rangers is worth the extra money, since the historical details and anecdotes attached to each building are not printed entirely in any brochure. *(Tours leave daily from Maritime Museum at 10:30am and Cooper Museum Store at 2pm. ☎ 649-7118. Houses open daily 10am-5pm; in winter 10am-4pm. Tours $5.)*

OTHER SIGHTS. The **Monterey Peninsula Museum of Art** has two locations. The Civic Center branch holds changing shows, mostly of California artists. *(559 Pacific St. ☎ 372-5477. Open W-Sa 11am-5pm, Su 1-4pm. $5, students and military $2.50, under 12 free.)* **La Mirada**, off Fremont across from Lake El Estero, has exhibits on California history, and collections of regional Asian and Pacific Rim art. *(720 Via Mirada. ☎ 372-3689. Open W-Sa 11am-5pm, Su 1-4pm. $5, students and military $2.50, under 12 free.)*

SEASONAL EVENTS

Laguna Seca Raceway (☎ 800-327-7322; www.laguna-seca.com), on Rte. 68 east of Monterey. Late May through early Oct. (office open M-F 8am-5pm). The raceway hosts the Monterey Sports Car Grand Prix (late July), Historic Automobile Races (late Aug.), and Monterey Grand Prix Indy Car World Series (early Oct.).

AT&T National Pro-Am Golf Tournament (☎ 800-541-9091; www.attpbgolf.com), at Pebble Beach (☎ 649-1533), Jan. 28-Feb. 3. Celebrity and PGA tour match-ups.

Monterey Bay Blues Festival (☎394-2652; www.montereyblues.com). Brings big-name blues musicians to the Bay in late June.

Monterey Bay's Theatrefest (☎622-0700; www.pacrep.org), Between the Customs House and the Pacific House at the head of Fisherman's Wharf; late June to early Aug. Free afternoon theater Sa-Su 11am-5pm; evening shows $15, students and seniors $8.

Annual Winemaker's Celebration (375-9400; www.montereywines.org). In early Aug. Over 25 Monterey County wineries pour new releases and special wines. Also featuring educational exhibits on topics like grapevine pruning and cork display, as well as live music and silent auction.

Monterey County Fair (☎372-5863; www.montereycountyfair.com), at Monterey County Fairgrounds, mid-Aug. Livestock exhibitions, live music, amusement park, and food.

Monterey Jazz Festival (☎373-3366; www.montereyjazzfestival.org). Top names in jazz show up in mid-Sept. Legends like Miles Davis and Dizzy Gillespie are part of the festival's history and help explain why this is the longest running jazz festival in the world.

▨ OUTDOOR ACTIVITIES

Several companies on Fisherman's Wharf offer critter-spotting boat trips around Monterey Bay. The best time to go is during gray whale migration season (Nov.-Mar.), but the trips are hit-or-miss at any time of year. If lucky, you may spot up to hundreds of dolphins frolicking in the current generated by the bow of the boat. On the other hand, nothing but desolate stretches of ocean may be all one sees. **Chris's Fishing Trips,** 48 Fisherman's Wharf, offers has 2-3hr. daily whale watching tours. (Adults $25, under 13 $20. May-Nov. 11am and 2pm. Gray whale migration 2hr. tours Dec.-Apr. Adults $18, under 13 $12. Fishing boat chartering: tuna (requires full day) $150; salmon (¾ day) $50; rock cod, halibut and sea bass (¾ day) $40. ☎375-5951. Open daily 4am-5pm.)

The local swells may not be the stuff of legends, but they provide a good (and cold) testing ground for enthusiastic water-goers. **On The Beach Surf Shop,** 693 Lighthouse Ave., rents surfboards, boogie boards, and wetsuits just a few steps from the water. (Surfboard rentals $10 per half day, $20 per day. Boogie boards $5 per half day, $10 per day. Wetsuits $6 per half-day, $12 per day. ☎646-9283. Open M-Th 10am-7pm, F-Sa 9am-8pm, Su 10am-6pm.) Sea kayaking on top of kelp forests and among prancing otters can be a heady experience. **Monterey Bay Kayaks,** 693 Del Monte Ave., provides rentals, instruction, and tours. (☎373-5357 or 800-649-5357. Call for lesson information. Rentals $30 per person, includes gear, wetsuit, and instruction. 3 hr. beach tours given by biologist cost $55 per person. Open daily 9am-6pm; in summer extended hours F-Sa 9am-8pm.)

There are several designated **bike paths** in the area. The best is the **Monterey Peninsula Recreation Trail,** which follows the coast for approximately 20 mi. from Castroville to Asilomar St. in Pacific Grove. Bikers can then continue through Pacific Grove to Pebble Beach along famous **17 Mile Drive.** The Recreation Trail shares the road with cars after Lover's Point, 2.5 mi. from Fisherman's Wharf and it can be windy. However, the biking, running, or in-line skating effort is rewarded with spectacular views of pristine coastline dotted with cyprus trees and marine life.

▨ NIGHTLIFE

Monterey knows how to cut loose at night, although some areas of the peninsula quiet down early. The main action is downtown along Alvarado St., but there are a few Lighthouse Ave. bars as well. Pickings are slim for those under 21, but covers are reasonable or nonexistent.

🔲 **Mucky Duck British Pub,** 479 Alvarado St. (☎655-3031). Empty front window booths might fool you, but many patrons are in the back beer garden, listening to music, having a smoke, or staying warm around a coal burning fire. Monterey locals have voted their beer the city's best for 6 years in a row. Come early to avoid waits. Live music and karaoke during the week from 5, 6, or 8pm; DJ weekends 9pm. Quiz night Tu 8pm—win cash prizes. Parking lot in back. Open daily 11:30am-2am.

🔲 **Club Octane,** 321-D Alvarado St. (☎646-9244), on the 2nd floor at Del Monte Ave. Strobe lights and heavy smoke machines throb like teenage hormones in this extensive club. 2 bars and dance floors with different DJs. Pool tables and a smoking deck. Male and female burlesque M 9:45pm. Strict dress code—no hats, no tennis shoes, no beach flip-flops. Parking structure adjacent. Cover F and Sa $5, Su and M $7, W and Th free. Back room opens 11pm. Open M and W-Su 8pm-1:30am.

Viva Monterey, 414 Alvarado St. (☎646-1415). An intense crowd lives it up amid creative wall art. Liquid creations like "Swedish Passion" start at $5. 3 black-lit pool tables. No cover for live, usually alternative rock, music. Th nights bring a drum or listen to the "Circle of Rhythm" jam session where professionals and amateurs alike pound out beats. Open Su-M and W-Sa 7:30pm-2am, Tu 3:30pm-2am. Shows M-Sa 9:30pm.

Doc Rickett's, 180 East Franklin St. (649-4241). Named after Ed Ricketts, the famous marine biologist friend and literary character of Steinbeck. Offers comedy 9-10:30pm and dancing F-Sa, sushi grill ($5-25) every night, and live entertainment M-W. No cover. Open M-Sa 5pm-2am.

Plumes Coffee, 400 Alvarado St. (☎373-4526). Brightly lit cafe hosts a hip crowd posing on tiny chairs. Central location makes for a popular under-21 night spot. Espresso, American coffee, and tea $2; latte $2.50. Gourmet sandwiches ($5) and pastries ($2) also available. Open Su-W 6:30am-11pm, Th-Sa 6:30am-midnight.

NEAR MONTEREY

☎831

Monterey's neighbors to the west and north have more dramatic coastlines and more impressive surf than the beaches of Monterey itself. Around the northern end of the peninsula, the beach runs uninterrupted for nearly 4 mi., first as **Pacific Grove Municipal Beach,** then as **Asilomar State Beach.** Bus #2 stops within four blocks of the ocean in Pacific Grove. The numerous tide pools along the rocky shore are intriguing places to explore.

SUNSET DRIVE. West of Monterey in Pacific Grove, Sunset Drive provides a free, 6 mi. scenic alternative to 17 Mile Drive (see below). Appropriately, Sunset Dr. is the best place in the area to watch the sun go down. People arrive a full two hours before sunset in order to secure front row seats along the road, also known as Ocean Blvd. At the western tip of the peninsula stands **Point Piños Lighthouse,** the oldest continuously running Pacific Coast lighthouse, which now houses exhibits on Coast Guard history. (☎648-3116. Open Th-Su 1-4pm. Free.)

PACIFIC GROVE. Pacific Grove took root as a Methodist enclave over 100 years ago, and many of the Victorian houses are still in excellent condition. This unpretentious town (which falls eerily quiet at night) has a beautiful coastline, numerous lunch counters, and lots of antique and artsy home furnishing stores. Browse in second-hand clothing, book, and music stores along Lighthouse Ave., or outlet-shop-till-you-drop at the **American Tin Cannery,** on Ocean View Blvd., near New Monterey. In addition, Pacific Grove houses thousands of **monarch butterflies** from October to March. Look, but don't touch: bothering the butterflies, the signs warn, is a $1000 offense. The **Pacific Grove Museum of Natural History,** at Forest and Central Ave. one block north of Lighthouse Ave., has year-round exhibits on Monarchs and other local wildlife. The stuffed birds and whale room are top-notch. (☎648-5716. Open Tu-Su 10am-5pm. Free.)

THE LOCAL STORY

HANGING 10 & OTHER SURFER FAUX PAS

Brian, a 19-year-old surfer dude originally from San Jose, was spotted with his longboard and wet-suit at Carmel City Beach.

Q: How long have you been surfing?
A: 'Bout 12 years.

Q: And exactly how long did it take you to actually stand up on the board and "catch a wave"—is that the proper terminology nowadays?
A: No that's fine, some people still say that....And it took me a good year until I could really ride a wave.

Q: But how long did it take you to even stand up on the board? [It took our researcher 2hr.]
A: I think just about anyone could do it in a day with some instruction.

Q: [Feeling validated—he said *day*] What are the big rules of surfing?
A: The biggest one is that up-wave surfers have the right of way. So, like, if someone is on a wave before you then it's his and you can't get in his way.

Q: Now getting back to the issue of jargon or slang, you said that some people will say "catch a wave." What are some other examples of contemporary surfing parlance?
A: Um, like what do you mean?

Q: I mean, what words would you use to describe a fantastic surfing expedition? "Gnarly," "rad," "wicked?" And does anyone say "hang ten"?
A: [Pensive] I guess I say "killer" a lot and call going out to surf a "sesh" [short for session]. "Hang ten" is not something I hear.

17 MILE DRIVE. The famous 17 Mile Drive meanders along the coast from Pacific Grove through **Pebble Beach** and the forests around Carmel. Once owned by Del Monte Foods, Pebble Beach has become the playground of the fabulously well-to-do. Its enormous, manicured golf courses creep up almost to the shore's edge, in bizarre contrast to the dramatically jagged cliffs and turbulent surf. The drive is rolling, looping, and often spectacular, although plagued by slow-driving tourists and a $7.50 entrance fee. To drive in and out as you please in one day, present your receipt to the guard and have him or her record your license plate number. Save money by biking it (bicyclists and pedestrians allowed in for free) or drive along Sunset Dr. instead (see above). Along the drive, make sure to stop at **Fanshell Overlook** to see massive harbor seals and their pups rest up on the pure white shore, and at the **Lone Cypress,** an old, gnarled tree growing on a rock promontory, valiantly resisting the onslaught of determined, jostling photographers. The image of this tree, prevalent in Northern California, is now the official logo of the Pebble Beach community.

CARMEL ☎831

Moneyed Californians migrate to Carmel (pop. 4400) to live out their fantasies of small-town life, molding the small community to their aspirations. The town is officially named Carmel-by-the-Sea, but tourists and residents alike generally drop the last three words. Carmel has pristine beaches, a main street lined with boutiques and art galleries, and a carefully manufactured and maintained aura of quaintness. Local ordinances forbid address numbers, parking meters (though police chalk tires to keep careful track of how long cars have been parked), franchise stores, live music in bars, billboards, and, at one time, eating ice cream cones outside—all considered undesirable symbols of urbanization. All this effort to make Carmel absolutely *precious* ends up imparting a saccharine feeling. The white sand beaches of Carmel and the extraordinary mission are beautiful, and your heart may race with the prospect of seeing resident and former mayor Clint Eastwood, but the town proper may simply be too snooty for some.

◪ PRACTICAL INFORMATION

Carmel lies at the southern end of the Monterey Peninsula off **Highway 1,** 126 mi. south of San Francisco. The town's main street, **Ocean Avenue,** cuts west from the freeway to (surprise) the ocean. All other east-west avenues are numbered, ascending toward the south. **Junípero Avenue** crosses Ocean Ave. downtown and leads south to the mission at **Rio Road**. Free town maps are available at most hotels and the Visitors Center. A public lot on the corner of Junípero Ave. and 3rd St. has **free all-day parking**.

Public Transportation: Monterey-Salinas Transit or **MST** (☎899-2555, TDD 393-8111). Buses #4, 5, and 24 go through Carmel. Bus #22 runs to Big Sur (2 daily). Schedules available at the Monterey info and transit centers. Fare per zone $1.75, seniors, disabled, and ages 5-18 $0.85, same-zone transfers free up to 2hr.

Bike Rental: Bay Bikes (☎646-9090), based in Monterey, delivers for free to Carmel on 24hr. notice. Bikes $22 per day, includes helmet and bike lock. Open daily 9am-7pm.

Visitor Information: Carmel-by-the-Sea Business Association (☎624-2522), on San Carlos St. between 5th and 6th St., on 2nd fl. of Eastwood Bldg. Free city maps available here and all over town. Open M-F 9am-5pm; plaza kiosk open W-Su 11am-4pm.

Internet Access: Mail Mart (☎624-4900), at Dolores Ave. and 5th St. $6 for 30min., $10 per hr. Open M-F 8:30am-6pm, Sa 9am-4pm.

Post Office: (☎800-275-8777), 5th St. between San Carlos St. and Dolores Ave. Open M-F 9am-4:30pm, Sa 10am-2pm. **Postal Code:** 93921.

ACCOMMODATIONS

The **inns** and **lodges** (there are no motels) in Carmel offer only double-occupancy rooms (below $90 only on mid-week specials or winter), and usually include full breakfasts. A 15min. bus ride to Monterey will yield some lower rates at places with less charm. Camping is illegal within city limits, and no state parks are nearby. There is, however, a private campground 4½ mi. east at **Saddle Mountain Ranch ❷**, 27625 Schulte Rd. The 50 popular sites have showers and swimming pool access. (☎624-1617. Reserve in advance. $25.) Here is a sampling of Carmel's posh and pricey inn selection:

Wayfarer Inn, 4th and Mission St. (624-2711 or 800-533-2711). Nestled in Carmel village, the Wayfarer has immaculate, simple English-country styled rooms with TV, VCR, phone, refrigerator, fireplace and private bath. Buffet breakfast for guests in the morning. Mid-week specials ($89) through the Visitors Center. Rooms June 21-Sept. 30 weekdays $129-189, weekends $159-229; Oct 1-June 20 $89-139/$119-159. Special events weekends are summer rates plus $50. ❺

Coachman's Inn, San Carlos at 7th St. (☎624-6421 or 800-336-6421). Many rooms have fireplaces. Outdoor patio, hot tub, and sauna available for all guests. English Country rooms $135-250. Check Visitors Center for mid-week deals. ❺

The Green Lantern Inn, Seventh and Casanova (☎624-4292 or 888-414-4392). Modeled after an English country cottage, this quaint inn includes TV, phone, refrigerator, and private bath. They also serve an expanded continental breakfast buffet and afternoon wine and cheese. Street parking. Rooms $129-229; in winter $85-229. ❺

FOOD

Em Le's, Dolores Ave. (☎625-6780), between 5th and 6th St. This cafe is known for its fabulous breakfasts. Omelettes with potatoes or cottage cheese and toast $7-9; unique French toast $8.50, $6.50 for a half-order. Many lunch options $5-9. Dinner selection features a variety of meats ($14-20). Breakfast served until 11am. Open daily 6:30am-3pm, F-Sa 5pm-10pm. ❷

A Little Pizza Heaven, Dolores Ave. (☎625-3190), between 7th and 8th St., offers casual dining in a cozy atmosphere. Serves incredibly fresh pasta ($8-12) and gourmet brick-oven pizza ($7-20). Beer and wine available. Open W-M 4-8:30pm. ❸

Jack London's, Dolores Ave. (☎ 624-2336), between 5th and 6th St. Salads $5-9, fish or fowl ($7-9), burgers and sandwiches (from $7). Get a shrimp fajita or teriyaki chicken breast for $11 as an Early Bird special4:30-6:30pm. Sit in the courtyard or near the action-packed bar. Open daily 11:30am-12:30am; only night-owl menu in town served 10pm-midnight. ❷

👁 🌀 SIGHTS & BEACHES

🏞 **POINT LOBOS RESERVE.** This extraordinary 550-acre state-run wildlife sanctuary is popular with skindivers and day hikers. Otters, sea lions, seals, brown pelicans, and gulls are visible from paths along the cliffs (bring binoculars). Point Lobos has tide pools and marvelous vantage points for watching the winter whale migration. Scuba access. No dogs. *(On Hwy. 1, 3 mi. south of Carmel. Park on Hwy. 1 before the tollbooth and walk or bike in for free. Accessible by MST bus #22. ☎ 624-4909. Open Apr.-Oct. daily 9am-7pm; Nov.-Mar. 9am-5pm. $4 per car, seniors $3; map included. Day-use free for campers registered with one of the state parks. Free daily nature tours; call for times. Divers must call ☎ 624-8413 or email ptlobos@mbay.net for reservations. Dive fee $7.)*

MISSION BASILICA SAN CARLOS BORROMEO DEL RÍO CARMELO. It may be a mouthful to say, but it is a marvel to see. Established at its present site in 1771 by Father Junípero Serra, "the great conquistador of the cross," the mission converted 4000 Native Americans before it was abandoned in 1836. Fastidiously restored in 1931, the mission's marvels continue to receive attention with the help of wealthy tourists' donations. Complete with a stone courtyard, Mudéjar bell tower, luscious gardens, and a daily mass, the mission is one of the most extensive in the system today. Buried here are Father Serra and over 2300 Native Americans. The 3 museums display the original silver altar furnishings, handsome vestments, and a library. *(3080 Rio Rd. and Lausen Dr., off Hwy. 1. ☎ 624-1271. Open daily 9:30am-5:30pm. $4, 5-17 $1, under 5 free.)*

CENTER FOR PHOTOGRAPHIC ART. The Center is housed in the Sunset Cultural Center, which was once occupied by Friends Photography run by Weston and Ansel Adams. The photographer set considers the Center's exhibits to be topnotch; they include work by local and international artists, as well as celebrities. Recent exhibitors include David Lynch, Graham Nash, and Dennis Hopper. *(San Carlos St. between 8th and 9th St. ☎ 625-5181; www.photography.org. Open Tu-Su 1-5pm. Free.)*

BEACHES. The northern Big Sur coast truly begins at Carmel City Beach, at the end of Ocean Ave., a pristine crescent of white sand framing a cove of chilly, azure waters. The beach ends abruptly at the base of distant red cliffs, which make a fine grandstand for sunsets. The **Carmel River State Beach,** just south of City Beach, is even windier and colder than Carmel City Beach, but it is blessed with better surf and smaller crowds. Bring a jacket or sweater, even in summer. *(Walk about 1 mi. along Scenic Rd., or drive to the end of Carmelo St. off Santa Lucía. Parking lot closes at dusk.)*

BIG SUR ☎ 831

Host to crowded campsites usually booked seven months in advance and a handful of expensive restaurants, Big Sur's big appeal is its outdoor offerings—an array of terrain including redwood forests with fresh water rivers, and rocky shores with crashing surf on golden sand beaches. As Big Sur is more of a region than a precise destination, there may be no signs to announce that you are in fact in Big Sur, but you'll know you're there because it's the first time you'll see any signs of civilization for miles in either direction.

▲ ORIENTATION

Monterey's Spanish settlers simply called the entire region below their town *El Sur Grande*—the Large South. Today, Big Sur is a more explicitly defined coastal region bordered on the south by San Simeon and on the north by Carmel. The coast is thinly inhabited, dotted with a few gas stations and exorbitant "getaway" hotels. Almost everything—fuel, food, beer, toiletries—costs more in Big Sur than anywhere outside it. Last-chance stops for the thrifty are at the supermarket complex on Rio Rd. in Carmel to the north and the market in Morro Bay to the south.

Despite its isolation, Big Sur can be reached by public transit in the summer (see below for details). The drive from Carmel to Big Sur on Hwy. 1 is simply amazing but curvy and crowded, so go slowly and find a time (early mornings recommended) when traffic won't interfere with your enjoyment of the splendor.

Spring is the optimal time to visit Big Sur, when the wildflowers are in full bloom. No matter what the season, warm and cold weather clothing is necessary—mornings are typically cool and foggy, afternoons sunny, and evenings chilly.

ⓘ PRACTICAL INFORMATION

In general, it's best to plan a trip to Big Sur ahead of time and bring all necessary supplies along. In town, there is a Shell **gas station** and an **ATM** (near the Post Office), but visitors are better off taking care of such matters in Carmel to the north or Cambria to the south before going to Big Sur. As places in Big Sur do not have street addresses, general directions are provided.

Public Transportation: Monterey-Salinas Transit (MST) (☎899-2555). Bus #22 through Big Sur leaves from the Monterey Conference Center and runs as far as Nepenthe, 29 mi. south of Carmel, stopping at various points en route. Limited space for bikes; call ahead. 2 per day May-Oct. Fare per zone $1.75, seniors and under 18 $0.85.

Visitor Information: Big Sur Chamber of Commerce (☎667-2100; www.bigsurcalifornia.org; mailing address P.O. Box 87, Big Sur 93920). Open M, W, F 9am-1pm. Leave a message any time to have a Big Sur travel brochure sent to you. **Big Sur Station** (☎667-2315), ½ mi. south of Pfeiffer Big Sur entrance on Hwy. 1. Multi-agency station includes the State Park Office, the US Forest Service (USFS) Office, and the CalTrans Office. It provides permits and maps, and dispenses info on hikes and campfires. Open June-Sept. daily 8am-6pm; Oct.-May 8am-4:30pm.

Road Conditions: ☎800-427-7623. **Highway Patrol:** ☎805-549-3261.

Ranger Dispatch: ☎649-2810.

Post Office: 47500 Hwy. 1 (☎667-2305), next to the Center Deli in Big Sur Center. Open M-F 8:30am-5pm. **Postal Code:** 93920.

▲ CAMPING

Camping in Big Sur is heavenly, but neglecting to bring equipment is a big mistake. Be warned: site availability reflects the high demand for camping in the area. Reserve in advance by calling ReserveAmerica. (☎800-444-7275. $7.50 non-refundable fee.) If all sites below are booked, check with the **US Forest Service.** Camping is free in the Ventana Wilderness, a backpack-only site at the northern end of Los Padres National Forest (permits at Big Sur Station). Detailed trail maps are necessary for this kind of backcountry camping; ask Big Sur rangers for essential information on current conditions.

■ **Ventana Big Sur** (☎ 667-2712), on Hwy. 1, 30 mi. south of Carmel. 80 shady sites in a gorgeous redwood canyon with picnic tables, fire rings, and water faucets. Hot showers. Reservations should be made at least 2 weeks in advance. Sites for 2 people and 2 vehicles Su-Th $25, F-Sa $35; each additional person $4, 5-person max. ❷

Andrew Molera State Park (☎ 667-2315), on Hwy. 1, 5 mi. north of Pfeiffer Big Sur next to a horse ranch. A level 0.75 mi. trail leads to hike-in, tent-only campgrounds. 18 first-come, first-served sites. Beach, ornithology center, and pit toilets. No showers. 3-night max. stay. Sites $2; day use $2 when entrance booth attended. ❶

Big Sur Campground and Cabins (☎ 667-2322), on Hwy. 1, 26 mi. south of Carmel on the Big Sur River. Hot showers and laundry. Reservations recommended. Sites for 2 people $26, with RV hookup $29; each additional person (5-person max.) and leashed dogs $4; day use $10. 4 tent cabins $50; 13 cabins $90-180. ❷

Riverside Camp (☎ 667-2414), right next door to the Big Sur Campground, has sites with a little more dust for similar prices. Reservations can be made for $4. 2 people and 1 vehicle $28, each additional person (ages 5 and older) and dogs $3; additional untowed vehicle $6. Electricity and water hookup $4. 2 cabins ($105) and 5 rooms ($60-115) are also available (no pets). ❷

Fernwood Resort and Campground (☎ 667-2422), on Hwy. 1, 2 mi. north of the Post Office downhill from the Fernwood Bar and Grill (see p. 342). In a redwood forest on the Big Sur River, the 63 campsites and 2 swimming holes on the river are small and exposed, but beautifully situated. Trails lead from the campground into the state park. Hot showers. Campground office open 8am-6pm. Reservation fee $4. Sites for up to 6 people $24; 2 people and 1 vehicle with hookup $27; walk-in sites $8 per person. Additional people $4 each; vehicles $5; dogs $3. ❷

Pfeiffer Big Sur State Park (☎ 667-2315), on Hwy. 1, 26 mi. south of Carmel, just south of Fernwood Park campgrounds. The diverse wildlife and terrain, the beautiful Big Sur River, and several hiking trails ensure that all 218 campsites fill up in advance. No hookups. Firepits, picnic tables, softball field and hot showers. Trail maps available ($1). Reservations essential in summer. Park open sunrise-sunset. Sites $12, seniors $10, disabled $6; bike-ins $1, day use $5. 2nd vehicle $3, dogs $1. ❶

⬛ FOOD

Grocery stores are at Big Sur Lodge (in Pfeiffer Big Sur State Park), Pacific Valley, and Gorda, and some packaged food is sold in Lucia and at Ragged Point, but it's better to arrive prepared because prices in Big Sur are generally high.

■ **Big Sur Restaurant and Bakery** (restaurant ☎ 667-0520, bakery 667-0524), just south of the Post Office, by the Shell gas station and the Garden Gallery. Simple restaurant has garden seating and serves 12" woodfire pizza ($9-14) and dishes using free range meats and fresh local vegetables ($12-23). The bakery specializes in organic breads and pastries. Beer and wine available. Open daily 8am-8pm, until 9pm if busy. ❸

■ **The Roadhouse** (☎ 667-2264), off Hwy.,1 north of mi. 48 marker. A relatively new dining venue with a lively, intimate atmosphere and flavorful food. Small, selective menu changes frequently. Patio seating available. Soups and salads $6-7. Entrees $11-15. Desserts $5-6. Beer and wine. Open M and W-Su 5:30-9pm. ❸

Fernwood Bar and Grill (☎ 667-2422), on Hwy. 1, 2 mi. north of the Post Office. Great outdoor patio under redwood canopy. Chicken breasts, veggie burritos, and hamburgers from $6.50. Weekend breakfast and BBQ specials, often with live music ($8-10). Also has full bar and small grocery store. Open daily 11am-10pm. Bar open Su-Th 11am-12:30am, F-Sa 11am-2am. Grocery store open daily 8am-10pm. ❷

Center Deli and General Store (☎667-2225), 1 mi. south of Big Sur Station, beside the Post Office. This is where you will find the most reasonably priced goods in the area. $3.25-5 sandwiches include veggie options like avocado and egg salad. Pasta salads $5 per lb. Open daily 7:30am-8pm. ❶

Ceilo (☎667-4240), off Hwy. 1, 30 mi. south of Carmel, just south of Big Sur Station. Situated high on a gentle mountain next to the Ventana Resort, Ceilo, Italian for sky, is aptly named. It is one of the most chic and costly restaurants in the area, but, unlike at many other similar establishments, you are not just paying for the view—the food and atmosphere are first-rate as well. If dinner entrees ($25-34) are above your budget, try a smaller plate ($8-12). Lunches feature salads ($9-15), sandwiches ($11-12), and main courses ($15-17) like oak grilled flat iron steak. Open daily 11:30am-9pm. ❺

◉ ⚠ SIGHTS & OUTDOOR ACTIVITIES

Big Sur's state parks and **Los Padres National Forest** beckon outdoor enthusiasts of all types. Their **hiking** trails penetrate redwood forests and cross low chaparral, offering even grander views of Big Sur than those available from Hwy. 1. The northern end of Los Padres National Forest, accessible from Pfeiffer Big Sur, has been designated the **Ventana Wilderness** and contains the popular **Pine Ridge Trail**, which runs 12 mi. through primitive sites and the Sikes Hot Springs. The Forest Service ranger station supplies maps and permits for the wilderness area (see **Practical Information,** p. 341).

Within **Pfeiffer Big Sur State Park** are eight trails of varying lengths ($1 map available at park entrance). **Pfeiffer Falls** (1.4 mi. round-trip) and **Valley View** (2 mi. round-trip) are both short, easy hikes. Pfeiffer Falls is a scenic hike through redwoods along Pfeiffer Big Sur Creek, which ends at a 60 ft. waterfall. The Valley View Trail, from Pfeiffer Falls, offers views of Pt. Sur and Big Sur Valley. **Oak Grove Trail** is a bit more challenging, at 3 mi. round-trip from the Big Sur Lodge, and intersects with the Pfeiffer Falls trail. It features redwood groves, oak woodlands and dry chaparral. The strenuous **Mt. Manuel Trail** (8 mi. round-trip) begins at the Oak Grove Trail and is a steep, dry climb to the 3379 ft. Manuel Peak. **Buzzard's Roost Trail** is a rugged 2hr. hike up torturous switchbacks, but at its peak, hikers are rewarded with panoramic views of the Santa Lucia Mountains, the Big Sur Valley, and the Pacific Ocean.

Big Sur's most jealously guarded treasure, USFS-operated **Pfeiffer Beach,** was closed indefinitely in 2002. If it is open during your visit, travel 1 mi. south of Pfeiffer Burns State Park and roughly 10½ mi. north of Julia Pfeiffer Burns State Park. Turn off Hwy. 1 at the stop sign just past the bridge by Loma Vista. Follow the road 2 mi. to the parking area, where a path leads to the beach. An offshore rock formation protects sea caves and seagulls from the pounding ocean waves. Other beaches can be found at **Andrew Molera State Park** (5 mi. north of Big Sur station; $2 day use), **Sand Dollar Beach** (33 mi. south of the Big Sur station near Kirk and Plasket Creek campsites; $5 day use), and **Jade Cove** (36 mi. south of Big Sur station; free). Roughly at the midpoint of the Big Sur coast lies **Julia Pfeiffer Burns State Park,** where picnickers find refuge in the redwood forest and sea otters in McWay Cove. (Backcountry camping permits at Big Sur Station. No dogs. Day use free.) At the point where McWay Creek flows into the ocean is a spectacular 80 ft. waterfall, visible from a semi-paved path 0.3 mi. from the park entrance. **Ewoldsen Trail** (4.5 mi. round-trip) starts in redwoods at McWay Creek, follows McWay Canyon and climbs, at times steeply, upwards to reveal coastal views. **Tan Bark Trail** starts east of Hwy. 1 at Partington Cove. The 5.5 mi. round-trip hike traverses oaks and redwoods to the Tin House and has excellent coastal views. To shorten the trip, take the road at the end of the trail. It leads back to Hwy. 1, 1 mi. south of the trailhead.

Many state park trails are usually crowded, but solitude seekers can avoid the crowds by following highway turn-offs that lead to secluded inlets with terrific rock formations and crashing waves. Or escape the parks altogether and spend some time learning about one of the area's most celebrated former residents—Henry Miller. The **Henry Miller Memorial Library,** just south of Nepenthe and Cafe Kevah, displays books and artwork by the famous author. (☎667-2574; www.henrymiller.org. Open W-Su 11am-6pm and by special arrangement.) The library sells books and hosts concerts like the **Big Sur Jazz Festival** and readings such as the **West Coast Championship Poetry Slam.** There is also an interesting sculpture garden, featuring a computer and wire crucifix and a mammoth cocoon, among other things. Miller's casual reminiscences and prophetic ecstasies made hundreds of readers aware of Big Sur. Many readers of his more explicit works came to Big Sur seeking a nonexistent sex cult that he purportedly led. While the sex cult has ceased to be a big boon to the area, the cult of history suffices quite nicely.

CAMBRIA & SAN SIMEON ☎805

The original settlers of the southern end of the Big Sur coast were awestruck by the stunning pastoral views and rugged shoreline, reminiscent of the eastern coast of England. In homage to the natural beauty of their homeland, they named this equally stunning New World site Cambria, the ancient Roman name for Wales. Today art galleries, restaurants, and amicable townies help create a pleasant afternoon away from Hwy. 1.

Neighboring New San Simeon is a somewhat lurid strip-town with few roads and many motels beside spectacular beaches. It is the last stop for travelers heading northward to Big Sur or those making the pilgrimage to majestic Hearst Castle. Old San Simeon is north of New San Simeon and consists only of a 150 yr. old store, **Sebastian Store,** and the private homes of Hearst Corporation ranchers. Driving along this stretch of Hwy. 1, the last thing one would expect to see is a castle that would put Disney to shame. Newspaper tycoon William Randolph Hearst built **Hearst Castle,** his extravagant abode, over 29 years (1919-1948), and invited the rich and famous to visit him (and often his mistress Marion Davies) there.

■ PRACTICAL INFORMATION

Public Transportation: Central Coast Area Transit (CCAT), (☎781-4472 or 541-2228). Bus #8 runs from San Luis Obispo to Morro Bay ($1-1.50). Connect (ask driver for transfer, there is an additional $0.75 fee) to #12 for Cambria ($1-1.50) and San Simeon ($1-1.75); you may have to flag buses to get them to stop. There is no Su service. Carry exact change. **Cambria Village Transit** (☎927-0468) is a free trolley service through Cambria (every 30min.; July-Sept. 15 M and Th-Su 9am-6pm, Sept. 16-June 30 M and F-Su 9am-6pm). Currently, there is no public transportation to Hearst Castle.

Visitor Information: Cambria Chamber of Commerce, 767 Main St. (☎927-3624), provides maps of the area. Open daily 9am-5pm. **San Simeon Chamber of Commerce,** 250 San Simeon Dr. (☎927-3500 or 800-342-5613), on the west side of Hwy. 1; look for tourist info signs. Open Apr.-Oct. M-Sa 9am-5pm; Nov.-Mar. M-F 10am-2pm.

24hr. ATM: Bank of America, 2258 Main St., in Cambria.

Sheriff: ☎800-834-3346.

Library and Internet Access: Cambria Branch Library, 900 Main St. (☎927-4336), in Cambria. Open Tu-Th 10am-7pm, F 10am-5pm, Sa 10am-4pm.

Post Offices: Cambria, 4100 Bridge St. (☎927-8610). Open M-F 9am-5pm. **Postal Code:** 93428. **San Simeon** (☎927-4156), on Hwy. 1, in the back of Sebastian's General Store (which also has gas pumps). To get there, take the road opposite the entrance to Hearst Castle. Open M-F 8:30am-noon and 1-5pm. **Postal Code:** 93452.

⚡ ACCOMMODATIONS & CAMPING

Cambria has lovely but pricey B&Bs. Budget travelers will have better luck in San Simeon. The arrival of Motel 6 set off a pricing war that has led to wildly fluctuating rates, so it is always a good idea to call ahead. Beware of skyrocketing prices in summer, when tourists storm the castle.

▨ **Bridge Street Inn,** 4314 Bridge St. (☎927-7653), in Cambria. Originally built in the 1890s for the preacher of the church next door, this newly renovated house includes sunny and sparklingly clean rooms with sturdy bunks. White picket fence encloses a yard with volleyball and croquet. Pleasant living room with fireplace. Continental breakfast and linen included. Reception 5-9pm. Dorms $19; private rooms $40-$70. ❷

Creekside Inn, 2618 Main St. (☎927-4021 or 800-269-5212), in Cambria. Look for yellow country cottage-like building. Some rooms have balconies overlooking the creek; all have TVs and VCRs. Singles and doubles $59-99; summer weekends $79-139. ❺

Sands Motel, 9355 Hearst Dr. (☎927-3243 or 800-444-0779), in San Simeon, west of Hwy. 1 near the beach. All rooms have cable TV and coffee makers, some have VCRs and fridges. Coffee, muffins, and juice served in the morning. Indoor heated pool. Standard room (one king bed) May-Sept. $65-80; July-Aug. weekends up to $115; Oct.-Apr. $40-65. ❹

Motel 6, 9070 Castillo Dr. (☎927-8691), in San Simeon off Hwy. 1 at the Vista del Mar Exit. Gotta love chain consistency. New, clean, and comfy. Big rooms with 2 queen beds and cable TV. Singles May-Sept. Su-Th $65, F-Sa $80; Oct.-Apr. $45-55. Extra person (up to 4) $6 each. ❹

▨ **San Simeon State Beach Campground** (☎927-2053), just north of Cambria on Hwy. 1. **San Simeon Creek** has showers at its 134 developed sites near the beach. Neighboring **Washburn** sits on a hill overlooking the ocean and has primitive camping. Pit toilets and cold running water. For reservations, call ReserveAmerica (☎800-444-7275). Sites $12; day use $3 8am-sunset. ❶

🍴 FOOD

Food is more plentiful in Cambria than in San Simeon. Though most places have pre-established opening and closing times, they may close early if it is slow, so plan ahead, especially if you want to dine after 8:30pm. Groceries are available at **Soto's Market,** 2244 Main St., Cambria. (☎927-4411. Open M-Th 7am-8pm, F-Sa 7am-9pm, Su 8am-6pm.) Buy fresh local produce at the Cambria **farmer's market,** on Main St. next to the Veteran's Hall every Friday afternoon. (Open 2:30-5:30pm.)

▨ **Robin's,** 4095 Burton Dr. (☎927-5007), in Cambria. Many San Luis Obispo residents consider this the only reason to go to Cambria. Eclectic international cuisine in a craftsman-style bungalow with outdoor gardens. Entrees $10-19. Sandwiches $7-9. Veggie options like thai curry tofu ($12). Extensive wine list. Reservations recommended for evenings. Open June-Sept. daily 11am-10pm; Oct.-May 11am-9pm. ❸

Bistro Solei, 1980 Main St. (☎927-0887). Offers an intimate, welcoming dining atmosphere and specializes in creative dishes, all made from scratch and changing seasonally. Su brunch features live music. Entrees $15-24 but early birds (5-6:30pm), pay less. Open M-Th 5-9pm, F-Sa 5-9:30pm, Su 10am-12:30pm and 5-9pm. ❹

Creekside Gardens Cafe, 2114 Main St. (☎927-8646), in Cambria, at the Redwood Shopping Center. Locals frequent this petite eatery for hearty "California country cookin'." Indoor or patio dining. Pancakes $5-6.50. Desserts ($2-3) made fresh daily. Open M-Sa 7am-2pm, Su 7am-1pm. No credit cards. ❶

Main St. Grill, 603 Main St. (☎927-3194), in Cambria. Extremely popular eatery serves fast, cheap, quality grill food in a spacious, sports-themed restaurant. The patio seating is pleasant on a sunny day, but vegetarians be warned—rows of meat cook on the open-air grill. Burger $3.50, baby-back ribs $9. Beer available. Open M-F 11am-10pm, Sa-Su 11am-11pm. No credit cards. ❷

The Hamlet at Moonstone Gardens, (☎927-3535), off Hwy. 1, approximately 4 mi. north of Cambria at Moonstone Gardens. A spectacular ocean view and lovely outdoor seating for lunch and evening bar. Soft crooners often play to a more mature dinner crowd. Features live music, like its summertime "Sunset Jazz" series Th 8-11pm ($7). Luncheon specials, like quiche lorraine ($7.50) orcalamari and chips ($9.50). Bowls of chowder $5. Main entrees $11-28. Kitchen open 11:30am-9pm, F-Sa until 9:30pm. Bar often open until 11pm. ❹

French Corner Cafe and Bakery, 2214 Main St. (☎927-8227). A cute little, um, corner cafe and bakery modeled after Parisian cafes and boulangeries. Seeded baguette $3. Croissant au chocolate $2. Cafe au lait $2.50. Open daily 7am-6pm. ❶

◉ HEARST CASTLE

*On Hwy. 1, 3 mi. north of San Simeon and 9 mi. north of Cambria. Info ☎ 927-2020, reservations through DESTINET 800-444-4445, international reservations 916-638-5883, wheelchair accessible reservations 927-2020. **Tours:** Call in advance, as tours often sell out. 4 different daytime tours, each leaving approximately every 30min., depending on demand. 1¾hr. Tour 1, the "Experience Tour," $14, ages 6-12 $7; tours 2, 3, 4 $10 each, ages 6-12 $5, under 6 free. Evening tours feature costumed docents acting out the Castle's legendary Hollywood history (2hr.; $20, ages 6-12 $10). Each tour involves 150-370 staircase steps.*

Casually referred to by founder William Randolph Hearst as "the ranch," Hearst Castle (as tourists and locals refer to it today) is an indescribably decadent conglomeration of castle, cottages, pools, gardens, and Mediterranean *esprit* towering high above the Pacific. Officially referred to as the Hearst San Simeon Historic Monument, it does indeed stand as a monument to Hearst's unfathomable wealth and Julia Morgan's architectural genius. Young Hearst caught a bad case of art collecting fever at age 10 traveling in Europe with his mother, and he spent the rest of his life gathering Renaissance sculpture, tapestries, and ceilings. Ms. Morgan, the first woman to receive a certificate in architecture from the Ecole des Beaux-Arts in Paris, orchestrated all of this into a Mediterranean mélange. Scores of Hollywood celebs flocked to the castle (by invitation only) to bask in Hearst's hospitality—as long as they behaved. But while countless memorable cast parties were held on these grounds, the only things ever filmed here and mass-distributed were 30 seconds of *Spartacus* and the end of a Kodak Funsaver commercial.

Before going to see the castle, your experience may be enhanced by stopping by the **Visitors Center** at the base of the hill, which features a surprisingly frank portrait of Hearst's failed days at Harvard University, his central role in yellow journalism, and the scandals of his life. At one point, Hearst's mistress, Marion Davies, had to sell her jewels so that construction of her indebted lover's mansion could continue without interruption. Tours are run by the State Parks Department and are a strictly hands-off experience. The banisters or staircases are the only things you may touch in the castle. **Tour One** covers the photogenic Neptune Pool, the opulent Casa del Sol guest house, fragrant gardens, and the main rooms of the house; this is the best bet for first-time visitors. **Tours Two, Three,** and **Four** cover the living quarters and gardens in greater depth—these tours are recommended for those already familiar with Tour One. Tour One also includes a viewing of the 40min. National Geographic documentary "Hearst Castle—Building the Dream," which details on a five-story screen how the architectural wonder became a reality. Alternatively, you can view scenes from one of the greatest American films of all time: Orson Welles's *Citizen Kane*, which is commonly thought to be based at least in part on Hearst's life. (☎927-6811. *Films show daily every hour on the half-hour 9:30am-5:30pm. Tickets $7, under 12 $5.)*

BEACHES & OUTDOOR ACTIVITIES

Big Sur's dramatic coastline comes to a stunning end in San Simeon. Sea otters, once near extinction, now live in the kelp beds of **Moonstone Beach,** on Moonstone Dr. off Hwy. 1 toward San Simeon. Along this stretch of coast, surfers are occasionally nudged off their boards by playful seals (and far more rarely, by not-so-playful great white sharks, who thrive in these waters; see **Sharks Will Chew on You,** p. 46). Scenic **Leffingwell's Landing** offers the best spot for **whale-watching.** (Open Dec.-Apr. 8am-sunset.) Call **Virg's Landing** for info. (☎927-4676.) In addition to providing the best swimming for miles, **San Simeon** and **Hearst State Beaches,** just across from Hearst Castle, are ideal for cliff climbing and beachcombing.

SAN LUIS OBISPO   ☎805

San Luis Obispo (pop. 42,300) is pronounced "san-LEW-is oh-BIS-bow," and condensed to SLO, pronounced "slow." With its sprawling green hills and its proximity to the rocky coast, SLO is a town that lives up to its name, but by no means stands still. This area grew into a full-fledged town only after the Southern Pacific Railroad laid tracks here in 1894. Ranchers and oil refinery employees make up a significant percentage of today's population, and California Polytechnic State University (Cal Poly) students add a young, energetic component to the mix. Along the main roads in downtown, the hip, laid-back students mingle with locals in outdoor eateries, trendy shops and music-filled bars, topping it all off with a dose of wheatgrass and bee pollen.

TRANSPORTATION

Trains: Amtrak, 1011 Railroad Ave. (☎541-0505 or 800-USA-RAIL/872-7245), at the foot of Santa Rosa Ave., 7 blocks south of Higuera St. To: **L.A.** ($31); **San Francisco** ($36); **Santa Barbara** ($18-20). It is cheapest if you make reservations at least a week in advance. Open daily 5:45am-8:30pm. Ask for special rates for frequent riders.

Buses: Greyhound, 150 South St. (☎543-2121 or 800-231-2222), ½ mi. from downtown. To get to downtown from the station, walk west on South St., then north on Higuera St. To **L.A.** (5-6hr., 6 per day, $32) and **San Francisco** (6-7hr., 6 per day, $37). Luggage storage $2 per day. Open daily 7:30am-9:30pm.

Public Transportation: The **Central Coast Area Transit** or **CCAT** (☎541-2228) links SLO to: **Morro Bay** (#8, #12; $1.50); **Los Osos** (#11, #12; $0.75-$1); **Pismo Beach** (#10, $1); **Paso Robles** (#9, $1.75). Unlimited use day pass $3. Buses depart from City Hall at Osos and Palm St. On Sa, only buses #10 (south to Santa Maria) and #12 (north to San Simeon) are operational. **SLO Transit** (☎541-2877) runs buses throughout the city, and they go faster than the acronym would suggest. Fare $0.75, seniors $0.35; free transfers. Buses run M-F 6am-11pm, Sa-Su 8am-6pm; Sa-Su only buses #3 and 5 are operational. SLO Transit also offers a **free trolley** service around downtown. Runs Su-W and F-Sa noon-5pm, Th noon-9:30pm. Additional service to hotels along Monterey St. **Ride-On** (☎459-3616) offers safe rides for $4 as well as many other shuttle services. Safe rides F and Sa 9pm-3am,

Car Rental: Thrifty, 2750 Broad St. (☎544-3777). Cars start at $39 per day with unlimited mileage within California. Must be 21+; under 25 pay $5 per day surcharge. Open M-F 7am-9pm, Sa 8am-5pm, Su 9am-9pm.

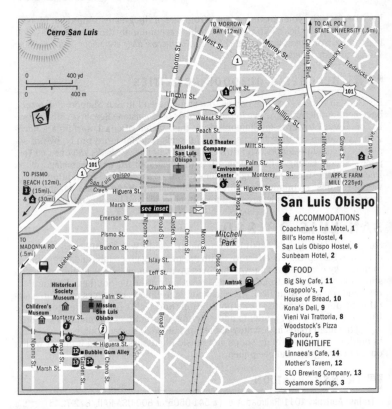

San Luis Obispo

ACCOMMODATIONS
Coachman's Inn Motel, **1**
Bill's Home Hostel, **4**
San Luis Obispo Hostel, **6**
Sunbeam Hotel, **2**

FOOD
Big Sky Cafe, **11**
Grappolo's, **7**
House of Bread, **10**
Kona's Deli, **9**
Vieni Vai Trattoria, **8**
Woodstock's Pizza Parlour, **5**

NIGHTLIFE
Linnaea's Cafe, **14**
Mother's Tavern, **12**
SLO Brewing Company, **13**
Sycamore Springs, **3**

■ 🔀 ORIENTATION & PRACTICAL INFORMATION

San Luis Obispo is the heart of the Central Coast. It sits inland on **U.S. 101,** burrowed among ranch-laden mountains. This small town serves as a hub between Morro Bay, 12 mi. north on Hwy. 1, and Avila Beach, Shell Beach, and Pismo Beach, all about 12 mi. south on Hwy. 1.

Downtown, **Monterey and Higuera Street** (north-south) and **Broad and Garden Street** (east-west), are the main drags. Walking here is easy and there is plenty of cheap parking. One hour **free parking** is available on streets and in parking structures downtown at the Palm St. (at Morro St.) and Marsh St. (at Chorro St.) lots.

Visitor Information: Visitors Center for the Chamber of Commerce, 1039 Chorro St. (☎781-2777). Watch for signs on U.S. 101. Staff and brochures. Open Su-M 10am-5pm, Tu-W 8am-5pm, Th-F 8am-8pm, Sa 10am-8pm. **State Parks Office,** 3220 S. Higuera St., #311 (☎549-3312). Open M-F 8am-5pm.

Laundromat: California Coin Laundry, 552 California Blvd. (☎544-8266). Wash $2, dry $0.25 per 8-10min. Open 24hr.

Weather Conditions: ☎541-6666. **Road Conditions:** ☎800-427-7623.

Police: 1042 Walnut St. (☎781-7317).

CENTRAL COAST

Crisis Line: (☎800-549-8989). Counseling and referrals 24hr.

Hospital: SLO General Hospital, 2180 Johnson Ave. (☎781-4871).

Library and Internet Access: San Luis Obispo Branch Library, 995 Palm St. (☎781-5989), on the 2nd fl. Open M-W 10am-8pm, Th-Sa 10am-5pm. **SLO Perk,** 1028 Chorro St. (☎541-4616). $1.50 per 15min., $5 per hr. Open daily 7am-6pm.

Post Office: 893 Marsh St. (☎543-3062). Open M-F 8:30am-5:30pm, Sa 9am-5pm. **Postal Code:** 93405.

ACCOMMODATIONS

Hotel rates in San Luis Obispo fluctuate daily, depending on the weather, the season, the number of travelers that day, even on the position of the moon. There is less fluctuation in nearby **Pismo Beach** and **Morro Bay,** but the average prices are the same. It is often cheapest to stay in hotels downtown during the week and hostels during the weekends. However, make a reservation well in advance during summer weekends and events. (Cal Poly commencement is in mid-June.)

San Luis Obispo (HI-AYH), 1617 Santa Rosa St. (☎544-4678; www.hostelobispo.com). Convenient location just 1 block from the Amtrak station (exit to your right) and 3 blocks from downtown. Small space and friendly staff create a tight-knit atmosphere. The relaxing common room is great for conversations with fellow travelers. Free homemade sourdough pancakes daily 7:30am. Linen provided, towel $0.50. Laundry $2. Reception 7:30-10am and 4:30-10pm. Lockout 10am-4:30pm. Dorms $18, non-members $20. Private family room for 2-4 adults $50-80 (children are half price); F-Sa in summer add $5 for private room. No credit cards. ❷

Bill's Home Hostel, 1040 Cielo Ln. (☎929-3647), in Nipomo, 30 mi. south of SLO. Exit 101 on Tefft St., take a left on Orchard and a right on Primavera. Cielo Ln. is on the left. Travelers fleeing the city will find a base camp near the Pismo Dunes here at Bill's cluttered retreat. Those without cars can take a long walk into town for public transport. Check-in by 9pm. Donation of $12 can be replaced with work on the farm. ❶

Sunbeam Hotel, 1656 Monterey St. (☎543-8141). Looks like an apartment complex. Rooms have cable TV, A/C, fridges, phones, coffee makers. May-Sept. M-Th rooms $39, F-Sa $79-99; Oct.-Apr. $36-39. ❹

Coachman Inn Motel, 1001 Olive St. (☎544-0400). A few blocks from downtown, near the Hwy. 101 S. Exit. Sizable, immaculate rooms have cable TV and fridges. Singles May-Sept. $35-45; doubles $50. Oct.-Apr. singles $25-30; doubles $32-35. In summer weekend prices can rise to $140. ❸

Peach Tree Inn, 2001 Monterey St. (☎543-3170 or 800-227-6396). Cozy, creekside country-style inn, located on the edge of town. Rooms with TV, telephone and continental breakfast. Singles May-Sept. Su-Th $35-70, F-Sa $70-160. Prices higher Oct.-Apr. Discounts for AAA and AARP members, as well as midweek. ❹

CAMPGROUNDS

All state park sites can be reserved through ReserveAmerica (☎800-444-7275) up to seven months in advance. For a list of more campsites in the area, contact State Parks Information (see **Practical Information,** p. 349). In summer, you need reservations at beach parks; especially crowded parks require reservations year-round.

Montaña de Oro State Park (☎528-0513), on Pecho Rd., 4 mi. south of Los Osos, 12 mi. from SLO via Los Osos Valley Rd. 50 primitive sites in a gorgeous, secluded park. Outhouses and cold running water (but bring your own drinking water). Reserve weeks in advance Memorial Day-Labor Day. Sites $10. ❶

THE BIG SPLURGE

VERGIN' ON TACKY

The **Madonna Inn**, in south SLO, is probably the only hotel in the world that sells postcards of each room. Alex S. Madonna, the contractor behind the construction of much of U.S. 101 and I-5, decided in 1958 to build a Queen Anne-style hotel of 12 rooms fit for the most discerning material girl. He put his wife, Phyllis, in charge of the design. By 1962, the vision had grown into a hot-pink behemoth of 101 rooms on 2200 acres of land. The men's room is truly a work of art, featuring a giant laser-operated waterfall that doubles as a urinal.

Every room has its own theme. Take a holiday in the Caveman Room, or express yourself in the Daisy Mae Room. One room even has a working waterwheel for a headboard. Even non-guests can cherish coffee and a bun from the Madonna's own oven or dine on steak in bubble-gum pink booths surrounding a giant gold caste tree, illuminated with flower shaped electric bulbs. You can also check out the photo album of the rooms in the reception area. At night, there's swing music from 7-11pm in the lounge to keep things hoppin'. (100 Madonna Rd., off U.S. 101, take the Madonna Rd. Exit. ☎543-3000. Rooms from $127-320.)

Morro Bay State Park (☎772-7434), 12 mi. west of SLO on Hwy. 1. Popular park between the ocean and forest with 135 developed sites, 30 with hookups. Hot showers and running water. Sanitary disposal station. Reserve year-round. Sites $12; with hookup $18. ❶

Morro Strand State Beach (☎772-2560), off Hwy. 1, at the northern edge of Morro Bay. 81 contiguous sites along a beautiful stretch of sandy beach. Toilets and water, but no hot showers. Your receipt will allow you to use the showers at Morro Bay State Park without paying another entrance fee. Sites $12. ❶

Pismo Beach State Park (☎489-1869), on Hwy. 1, just south of scenic Pismo Beach. **North Beach** has 103 tent sites with water, showers and restrooms. Sanitary disposal. **Oceano** has 40 tent sites and 42 RV hookups. Water, flush toilets, showers. North Beach sites are larger and closer to the beach. Call for reservations. Sites $13; RV sites $18. ❶

🍴 FOOD

Higuera Street and its cross streets are lined with restaurants and cafes. One can find cheap, greasy spoon fare as well as many healthy, organic choices. The area south of the mission along the creek is popular with lunchtime crowds. A **farmer's market** takes over Higuera St. every Thursday 6:30-9pm.

Big Sky Cafe, 1121 Broad St. (☎545-5401). Voted "Best Restaurant in SLO" in a recent magazine poll, Big Sky delivers with vegetarian-friendly food. Sandwiches $6-9. Choice local wines $4-6 per glass. Margaritas or swanky kir royales $3.50. Call for reservations for 6 or more between 4:30-6pm. Open M-Sa 7am-10pm, Su 8am-9pm. ❷

House of Bread, 858 Higuera St. (☎542-0255). Enticing smells will lure you into this warm bakery, which uses chemical-free Montana wheat in its delicious bread products. Free samples provide ample opportunity for choosing favorites. Raspberry pinwheel or huge cinnamon roll $2. Open M-W and F-Sa 7am-7pm, Th 7am-9pm, Su 9am-5pm. ❶

Grappolo's, 1040 Broad St. (☎788-0260). This new Italian restaurant and bar is Art Deco chic on San Luis Obispo Creek. Dishes range from $8-17 and the wine list is one of the most extensive in town. After dinner head downstairs to the dimly lit, basement bar. Kitchen open Su-Th 11:30am-9pm, F-Sa 11:30am-11pm; bar open until 2am. ❸

Woodstock's Pizza Parlour, 1000 Higuera St. (☎541-4420). This hangout invariably sweeps annual best pizza awards. Young crowd keeps it lively into the night. Lunch specials, like all-you-can-eat pizza and bottomless soda, $6. Single slices $1.75, whole pies $5.25-13.50. Toppings $0.50-$1.50. Happy hour M-W 8-11pm with pitchers of beer $4-8, slices $1.25. Open Su-Th 11am-midnight, F-Sa 11am-1am. ❷

Vieni Vai Trattoria, 690 Higuera St. (☎544-5282). Homemade organic pasta and ravioli with lots of vegetarian sauces ($8-12). Half-order portions are plenty for mid-sized appetites. Also serves dishes with seafood, chicken and veal ($14-17) and pizza ($9-12). Full bar. Open daily 11am-11pm. ❸

Kona's Deli, 726 Higuera St. (☎783-7171). No-nonsense deli offers basic sandwiches for $2.75-5. This deli pays homage to the surfers of Hawaii with funky decor and music. Open daily 10am-10pm (often 9pm in the summer). No credit cards. ❶

🔆 SIGHTS

MISSION SAN LUIS OBISPO DE TOLOSA. San Luis Obispo grew around the Mission San Luis Obispo de Tolosa, and the city continues to engage in celebrations and general lunchtime socializing around its front steps. Founded in 1772, the mission was at one time covered in white clapboards and crowned with a steeple to emulate that of a New England church. In the late 1800s, however, the town made an effort to revive the mission's Spanish origins, and by the 1930s it was fully restored. It still serves as the Catholic parish church for SLO. The mission also houses a small museum, which displays objects from the early days of the mission and a small collection of Chumash pot shards and arrowheads. (☎543-6850. Open daily early Apr.-late Oct. 9am-5pm; late Oct.-early Apr. 9am-4pm. $2 donation requested.) The mission faces Mission Plaza, where Father Serra held the area's first mass. At the edge of the plaza sits the **SLO Art Center,** 1010 Broad St., with lectures, art classes, and multimedia exhibits by regional artists. (☎543-8562. Open Tu-Su 11am-5pm. Free, but donations are appreciated.)

SLO HISTORICAL SOCIETY MUSEUM. One million dollars of city money have transformed the old public library, 696 Monterey St., into a modern, professionally-mounted ethnographic museum. Meticulously crafted dioramas and state-of-the-art interactive displays depict eras of San Luis Obispo's history, catering to younger audiences. The museum gives special emphasis to local Native American civilization, perhaps attempting to compensate for the less prominent coverage next door in the mission museum. (☎543-0638. Open W-Su 10am-4pm.)

OTHER SIGHTS. The nearby **Jack House,** 536 Marsh St., is a restored Victorian residence with the original 19th-century furnishing inside and a gazebo and garden outside. (☎781-7308, tour info 781-7300. Open Feb.-Nov. 1st Su of the month 1-4pm; June-Aug. also open Th 2-5pm. 45min. tours $2.) Kids may like to check out the **SLO Children's Museum,** 1010 Nipomo St., to get some "education through exploration." (☎544-5437. Open Tu-Sa 11am-5pm, Su noon-5pm. $5, under 2 free.) A gurgling 14 ft. waterwheel and shady deck await visitors to the **Apple Farm Mill,** 2015 Monterey St. Alternately churning ice cream and flour, the mill provides free samples of cider from a local farm and complimentary tea on the deck. It is also the home of a restaurant, bakery, gift shop and inn. (☎544-2040, gift shop 541-0369, dining reservations 544-6100. Gift shop and bakery open daily 7am-9pm, F-Sa 7am-10pm.)

🎭 🎪 ENTERTAINMENT & NIGHTLIFE

One half of SLO's population is under the age of 24, so the town can't help but party. It gets particularly wild after the Thursday night **farmer's market,** along Higuera St. between Nipomo and Osos St., which is more of a raging block party than a produce bazaar. **San Luis Little Theater,** 888 Morro St., has performances by

THE LOCAL STORY

POLY CULTURE

Jon studies agriculture and business at Cal Poly while Corey is a student of viti-culture at Cal Poly.

Q: What are the top five reasons to attend Cal Poly?

J: Unique majors, location, weather, affordability, a diverse student body.

C: Great department of my interest, location, fun parties, cool people, and hot girls.

Q: What are some unique majors?

J & C: Viti-culture (grape growing and wine-making); Soil Science; Ornamental Agriculture; Meat or Cheese (under the umbrella of Food Science).

Q: Can you describe a typical student at Cal Poly?

J & C: There are a couple of major groups but it is hard to classify or to depict the average student because there are so many people, with so many different interests.

Q: So give me a few stereotypical groups.

J & C: Definitely surfers. Then you have an intriguingly large number of "campus crusaders," who are hard-core Christians. There are some "Granola" kids, but many students are just really passionate about their studies.

Q: Why is that?

J: You have to pre-decide your major in order to apply. You apply to a specific college.

Q: Intense. What are the top five things students can do in the area?

J & C: Outdoor recreation covers numbers one-four. Number five would be drinking.

local thespians. (☎786-2440. Shows Th-Sa 8pm, Su 2pm. $14, students and seniors $12; Th $10.) The **Palm Theater,** 817 Palm St., screens artsy and revival films at odd times; call for schedule. (☎541-5161. $6.50, seniors and children $4, matinees $4; M night $4.) Standard Hollywood flicks often run at the grand **Art Deco Freemont Theatre,** 1035 Monterey St., designed in 1942 by the preeminent Southern Californian architect Charles Lee. The main theater maintains the original murals, but there's no air conditioning. ($7.50, seniors and children $4.75; matinees before 5:30pm $4.75.) Weekdays slow down a bit, as the students rescue their grades. Consult the free weekly *New Times* regarding other local happenings; nightlife options range from disco dancing to live big bands, and from pool clubs to gallery openings.

Mother's Tavern, 725 Higuera St. (☎541-8733). This Yukon decorated bar and restaurant, with lofty ceilings and mounted animal heads, draws mostly Cal Poly students who pile in for the W night disco party ($3 after 10pm). Also offers 80s nights ($3) and karaoke (free). Happy Hour M-F 3-6pm. Live music Th-Sa usually draws more mature crowds along with the under 30 year olds. 21+ after 9pm. Live music cover $3-7. Open daily 11:30am-1:30am; kitchen closes 9pm.

SLO Brewing Company, 1119 Garden St. (☎542-0380). Winner of the World Beer Cup 2000 for its incredible Amber Ale, the Brewing Co. also features amazingly good porter ("Cole Porter" $3.75 per pint). Happy Hour M-F 4-5:30pm (half-price draft pitchers). Live funk, reggae, and rock Th-Sa (cover varies) in the downstairs. Seven billiard tables upstairs: $6 per hr., but half-price Su-W and before 6pm Th-Sa. Downstairs open M-W 11:30am-midnight, Th-Sa 11:30am-1:30am, Su 11:30am-9pm. Upstairs open M-W 4pm-midnight, Th-F 4pm-1:30am, Sa noon-1:30am, Su noon-midnight.

Linnaea's Cafe, 1112 Garden St. (☎541-5888). Evening hangout for the artsy set. Displays local artists' works on the walls and features music nightly at 8:30pm; jazz F-Su during the school year. No cover, but a hat is passed around after each performance. Open M-Sa 7am-midnight, Su 7am-3pm and 7pm-midnight. No credit cards.

Sycamore Springs, 1215 Avila Beach Dr. (☎595-7365), 1 mi. south of Avila Beach. Cal Poly students and vacationers alike come here to unwind at a SLO pace. Private outdoor redwood hot tubs with sulfurous mineral water operate 24hr. a day for round-the-clock relaxation. Reservations recommended between 8pm-3am, especially on weekends. M-F between 4-6pm (non-holidays) $10 per person per hr., children $6; all other times $12.50 per person per hr., children $7.50.

BEACHES SOUTH OF SAN LUIS OBISPO

Two beaches just southwest of San Luis Obispo exist in relative obscurity to the passer-by; no signs announce their existence to the masses. The well-frequented and swimsuit optional **Pirate's Cove** has unusually warm water, which is fortunate for the nude bathers' pleasure and pride. Take U.S. 101 south from San Luis Obispo and take the Avila Rd. Exit. Follow signs for Avila Beach, but turn left on Cave Landing Rd. Park in the dirt lot and take a path (500 yd.) to the cove. The shore of **Shell Beach,** 1 mi. down U.S. 101 south of Avila Beach and Pirate's Cove, is the launching point for many a kayak. Take the Shell Beach Exit and turn left on Shell Beach Rd. A right on Cliff Ave. will lead to Ocean Blvd. Park at the gazebo and climb down the stairs to the rocky ocean shore.

Avila and **Pismo Beaches** are both more developed and more crowded than Shell Beach. Avila is known for its gaggle of fishermen. The adjoining city streets seem determined to mimic the boardwalk atmosphere of Pismo. Avila Beach is on the left after Cave Landing Rd. Pismo Beach, 1½ mi. south of Shell Beach, is the most developed and congested beach in the area; the lines for the public restrooms are practically social events. This raging spring break party spot is accessible by **Central Coast Area Transit** (☎541-2228) as well as **Greyhound** (☎800-231-2222). Rent all kinds of beach equipment at **Beach Cycle Rentals,** 150 Hinds Ave., next to the pier. (☎773-5518. Open daily 9am-dusk.) At day's end, when the sun sets behind the hills that jut into the sea, Pismo Beach lights up with a gorgeous sand-on-fire effect.

Pismo Dunes (☎473-7223), south of Pismo Beach on Grover Beach, is a State Vehicular Recreation Area, where for a $4 day use (6am-11pm) fee, you can take your car or all-terrain vehicle (ATV) down onto the dunes and burn rubber to your heart's content. You can rent ATV equipment from **BJ's ATV,** 197 Grand Ave. (☎481-5411. Open daily 8am-5pm. M-F $75-125 for 2hr., Sa-Su $40-75 per hr.) But keep your speed down to 15 mph, or pay a stiff $900 fine. At the south end of the park is **Oso Flaco Lake ❶,** accessible by hiking. Camping here is an option for the serious budget traveler. On the weekends, though, the sounds of squealing tires and revving engines drown out the surf. (☎473-7223. Sites $6, seniors $4, walk-ins $1).

SEASONAL EVENTS

Believe it or not, SLO hosts the most rollicking **Mardi Gras** this side of the Mississippi, celebrated the Saturday before Ash Wednesday. Thousands flock in for the fiesta. (Info ☎541-2183.) The **Mozart Festival,** in late July and early August, is also a favorite. Concerts play at the Cal Poly theatre, the Cohan Center, the mission, local wineries, and local churches. (For info, call ☎781-3008 or write 1160 Marsh Street #310, San Luis Obispo, CA 93401. Tickets ☎756-2787 or 888-233-2787. $15-30, student rush tickets 30min. before show $7.50.) The acclaimed **Central Coast Shakespeare Festival** runs two Shakespeare plays for six weeks at the SLO City Playhouse. (☎546-4224. Starting the first or second week in July Th-Su. $14, students and seniors $12. No credit cards.) The four-day **International Film Festival** features independent films, documentaries, and seminars. (☎546-3456; www.slofilmfest.org. 1st week of Nov. $5 per screening.)

NEAR SAN LUIS OBISPO ☎805

Gray whales, seals, otters, dolphins, and the occasional orca frequent **Montana de Oro State Park** (☎528-0513), 30min. west of SLO on Los Osos Valley Rd. The 8000 acres and seven miles of shoreline remain relatively secluded. **Spooner's Cove,** ¾ mi. north of Coralina Cove, has tidepools and offers free whale watching from the bluffs above at the Bluff's Trail trailhead. You can get more info about hikes at the **Ranger Office** in the old ranch house. (☎772-7434. Open in summer daily 8:30am-9:30pm; in winter M-Th 8:30am-3:30pm, F-Su noon-4pm.)

The **wineries** around SLO are well-respected. **Paso Robles,** 25 mi. north of SLO on U.S. 101, is vintner central. The **Paso Robles Chamber of Commerce,** 1225 Park St., has a list of wineries, including visiting hours, tours, and tastings. (☎238-0506. Open M-F 8:30am-5pm, Sa 10am-4pm.) The SLO Chamber of Commerce has similar info on the wineries (see **Practical Information,** p. 349). Wild Horse, Justin Winery, Edna Valley and Steven Ross are some of the most renowned labels. To do tasting in San Luis Obispo proper, try Cental Coast Wineries at 712 Higuera St. (☎544-8761. Local winemakers host tastings Th 6-9pm. Tasting $4. Open Su-W 11am-6pm, Th 11am-9pm, F-Sa 11am-8am.)

Mission San Miguel Archangel is 43 mi. north of San Luis Obispo in San Miguel, just off U.S. 101; take the San Miguel Exit. The 1818 complex has colorful frescoes, painted in 1821 by Monterey's Esteban Munras and a team of Native American artists. (☎467-3256. Open daily 9:30am-4:30pm. $1 donation requested.)

MORRO BAY   ☎805

*CCAT bus #8 and #12 serves Morro Bay from SLO. (Info ☎541-2228. 7 M-F, $1.) Motels here are often cheaper than in SLO. **Morro Bay Chamber of Commerce,** 880 Main St., has maps and listings of accommodations. (☎772-4467 or 800-231-0592. Open M-F 8:30am-5pm, Sa 10am-3pm.) For campground info, see **SLO: Camping,** p. 350.*

The Seven Sisters, a chain of small ex-volcanoes, are remnants of a time when SLO County was a hotbed of volcanic activity. Today the lava that once flowed here forms dramatic shorelines along Hwy. 1 from Morro Rock to SLO. The northernmost sister, Morro Rock, and three large smoke-stacks from an electric company shadow the tiny burg of Morro Bay, just to the north of its namesake park.

Morro Bay State Park, is home to coastal cypresses that are visited by Monarch butterflies from November-early February. The park's **Museum of Natural History** flexes its curatorial might on the aquatic environment and wildlife of the coastal headlands. A bulletin board near the entrance lists a variety of free nature walks led by park docents. *(☎772-2694. Open daily 10am-5pm. $2, under 17 free.)* South Bay Blvd., which links the town and the park, winds through the new **Morro Bay National Estuary,** a sanctuary for great blue herons, egrets, and sea otters. You can park on the deserted end of the Marina lot and either take the trail or rent a kayak or canoe to roam through the estuary. *(☎772-8796. Open 9am-5pm. Kayaks $8 per hr.; canoes $12 per hr.)* For a perfect picnicking opportunity, pack a basket and paddle out in your canoe to the sand dunes for lunch. Check for tides to avoid (or take advantage of) numerous sandbars.

The **Embarcadero,** an area along the beach, is the locus of Morro Bay activity and fish 'n' chips bargains. The **Morro Bay Aquarium,** 595 Embarcadero, has over 100 live ocean critters and a seal-feeding station. *(☎772-7647. Open daily 9:00am-6:30pm; in winter daily 9:30am-5:30pm. $2, ages 5-11 $1.)* Morro Bay's pride and joy is the **Giant Chessboard,** in Centennial Park on Embarcadero across from Southern Port Traders. The board is 256 sq. ft., with 18 to 20 lb. carved redwood pieces. *(Call the Morro Bay Recreation office at ☎772-6278 to set up a game. $17 per game for non-residents.)*

SANTA BARBARA   ☎805

Santa Barbara (pop. 92,500) epitomizes worry-free living. The town is an enclave of wealth and privilege, true to its soap opera image, but in a significantly less aggressive way than its SoCal counterparts. It is also home to many people with native Chumash ancestry, descendants of the Spanish and Mexican settlers. Spanish Revival architecture decorates the hills that rise over a lively pedestrian district. State Street, Santa Barbara's main drag, is a sanitized, palm-lined promenade lined with inexpensive cafes and thrift stores as well as glamorous boutiques and galleries. Santa Barbara's golden beaches, museums, historic missions, and scenic drives make it a frequent weekend escape for the rich or famous and an attractive destination for surfers, artists, and backpackers alike.

◨ TRANSPORTATION

Driving in Santa Barbara can be bewildering, as dead-ends, one-way streets and congested traffic abound. Beware of intersections on State St. that surprise motorists with quick red lights. Many downtown lots and streets offer 1¼hr. of **free parking,** including two underground lots at Pasco Nuevo, accessible by the 700 block of Chapala St. All parking is free on Sundays. **Biking** is a nice alternative; most streets have special lanes. The **Cabrillo Bikeway** runs east-west along the beach from the Bird Refuge to the City College campus. MTD buses run throughout the city.

Flights: Santa Barbara Municipal Airport (☎683-4011; www.flysba.com), in Goleta. Offers intrastate and limited national service.

Trains: Amtrak, 209 State St. (☎963-1015; schedule and fares 800-USA-RAIL/872-7245). **Be careful around the station after dark.** To **L.A.** (5-6hr., 2 per day, $20-25) and **San Francisco** (7hr., 3 per day, $48-68). Reserve in advance. Open daily 6:30am-9pm. Tickets sold until 8pm.

Buses: Greyhound, 34 W. Carrillo St. (☎962-2477), at Chapala St. To **L.A.** (2-3hr., 9 per day, $13) and **San Francisco** (9-10hr., 8 per day, $32). Open M-Sa 5:30am-8pm and 11pm-midnight, Su 7am-8pm and 11pm-midnight.

Santa Barbara Metropolitan Transit District (MTD), 1020 Chapala St. (☎683-3702), at Cabrillo Blvd. behind the Greyhound station. Bus schedules available at this transit center (and visitors center), which serves as the transfer point for most routes. Open M-F 6am-7pm, Sa 8am-6pm, Su 9am-6pm. $1, seniors and disabled $0.50, under 5 free; transfers free. The MTD runs an electric, purple **crosstown shuttle** from the Franklin Center on Montecito St. to Mountain and Valerio, running through the transit center on Chapala St. Runs M-F starting 7am-6:30pm. $1. The **downtown-waterfront shuttle** along State St. and Cabrillo Blvd. runs every 10min. Su-Th 10:15am-6pm, F-Sa 10:15am-8pm. Stops designated by circular blue signs. $0.25.

Taxis: Yellow Cab Company (☎965-5111). Open 24hr.

Car Rental: U-Save, 510 Anacapa St. (☎963-3499). Cars start at $22 per day with 150 free mi., $134 per week with 1050 free mi.; each additional mi. $0.20. Must be 21+ with major credit card. Open M-F 8am-6pm, Sa 8am-2pm.

Bike Rental: Beach Rentals, 22 State St. (☎966-6733). Surreys, choppers, quadsports, slingshots, regular mountain bikes and beach cruisers ($10-28 for 2hr.) as well as boogie-boards, scooters and in-line skates ($5-15) are available. Rentals include safety gear. Open daily 8am-8pm.

✳ ◪ ORIENTATION & PRACTICAL INFORMATION

Santa Barbara is 92 mi. northwest of Los Angeles and 27 mi. from Ventura on **U.S. 101** (Ventura Fwy.). Since the town is built along an east-west traverse of shoreline, its street grid is slightly skewed. The beach lies at the south end of the city, and **State Street,** the main drag, runs northwest from the waterfront. All streets are designated east and west from State St. The major east-west arteries are U.S. 101 and **Cabrillo Boulevard;** U.S. 101, normally north-south, runs east-west between Castillo St. and Hot Springs Rd.

Santa Barbara

ACCOMMODATIONS
Cabrillo Inn, **13**
Hotel State Street, **11**
Traveler's Motel, **1**
Motel 6, **2** & **14**
Santa Barbara International
Tourist Hostel, **12**

FOOD
The Natural Cafe and
Juice Bar, **8**
Pacific Crepes, **5**
Palazzio, **3**
The Taj Cafe, **4**

NIGHTLIFE
Club 634, **7**
The Hourglass, **6**
O'Mally's, **9**
Q's Sushi A-Go-Go, **10**

Visitor Information: Tourist Office, 1 Garden St. (☎965-3021), at Cabrillo Blvd. near the beach. Hordes of folks clambering for maps and brochures. 15min. free parking in summer and on weekends. Open July-Aug. M-Sa 9am-6pm; Su 10am-6pm; Sept.-Nov. and Feb.-June M-Sa 9am-5pm, Su 10am-5pm; Dec.-Jan. M-Sa 9am-4pm, Su 10am-4pm. Outdoor computer kiosk open 24hr. **Hotspots,** 36 State St. (☎564-1637 or 800-793-7666), is an espresso bar with free tourist info, hotel reservation service, and an **ATM.** Cafe open 24hr.; tourist info M-Sa 9am-9pm, Su 9am-4pm.

Bi-Gay-Lesbian Organization: The Pride Foundation: Gay and Lesbian Resource Center, 126 E. Haley St. #A-11 (☎963-3636). Counseling for alcohol and drug abuse. AIDS hotline, testing, and social services. Open M-F 9am-5pm.

Laundromat: Mac's Laundry, 501 Anacapa St. (☎966-6716). Pink-and-purple wonder features ever-entertaining Spanish TV. Wash $1.25, dry $0.25 per 15min. Open daily 6am-midnight; last load 10:30pm.

Police: 215 E. Figueroa St. (☎897-2300).

Hospital: St. Francis Medical Center, 601 E. Micheltorena St. (☎962-7661), 6 blocks east of State St.

Library and Internet Access: Santa Barbara Public Library, 40 E. Anapamu St. (☎962-7653). Open M-Th 10am-9pm, F-Sa 10am-5:30pm, Su 1-5pm.

Post Office: 836 Anacapa St. (☎800-275-8777), 1 block east of State St. Open M-F 8am-6pm, Sa 9am-5pm. **Postal Code:** 93102.

ACCOMMODATIONS

A 10min. drive north or south on U.S. 101 rewards with lodging cheaper than that found in Santa Barbara proper. Trusty **Motel 6 ❹** is always an option. In fact, Santa Barbara is where this glorious chain of budget-friendly motels originated. There are two locations: at the beach at 443 Corona del Mar Dr. (☎564-1392), and north of the main drag at 3505 State St. (☎687-5400). Prices are more expensive by the beach ($76-86, based on 2 person occupancy). The State St. location starts at $68-80 in the summer and $55 in the winter. All Santa Barbara accommodations are more expensive on the weekends (peaking in July and August and on holidays) as a flood of tourism drowns out competitive rates.

Hotel State Street, 121 State St. (☎966-6586), on the main strip 1 block from the beach and next to the train station. Welcoming, comfortable, and meticulously clean European-style inn offers a good, cheap night's sleep. Common bathrooms are pristine. Rooms have sinks and cable TV; a few have skylights. Continental breakfast included. Reservations recommended. Rooms $50-70; $5-10 higher July-Aug. ❹

Santa Barbara International Tourist Hostel, 134 Chapala St. (☎963-0154). This newly-built facility has a great location for action: it is near the train station, the beach, and bustling State St. Bike and surfboard rentals available. Laundry. Internet $1 per 20min. Ask about 2-3 day camping trips to surrounding areas. Reservations recommended; call or e-mail sbres@bananabungalow.com. 12 rooms sleeping 6-8 people, 5 private rooms with 1 double bed. Dorms $18-20; private rooms $45-55. ❷

Traveler's Motel, 3222 State St. (☎687-6009). Take bus #6 or 11 from downtown. Although it's a bit far from the action, this motel is clean and spacious, and has pastel, floral bedspreads to soften the atmosphere and sweeten your stay in the gosh-darn prettiest l'il place on State St. Cable TV, A/C, direct-dial phones, microwaves and fridges. Complimentary fruit and coffee 7am-10am. Singles June-Sept. Su-Th $55-70, F-Sa $129-149; Oct.-May $40/$69-99. Palatial rooms with full kitchenettes $10 more; each additional person (up to 4) $5. ❺

Cabrillo Inn, 931 E. Cabrillo Blvd. (☎966-1641 or 800-648-6708). Directly across from East Beach, 1 mi. south of Sterns Wharf at State St.. This is the best oceanfront value in town. The ocean is visible from 38 out of 39 rooms. 2 swimming pools and ocean-view lounge where continental breakfast is served. 2-night stay is required on all weekends. Rooms May-Sept. Su-Th from $109, F-Sa $139; Oct.-Apr. $89/$109. Rooms will full ocean view, add $30; suites, add $60. Vaction home rentals by the week and month are also available. ❺

CAMPING

State campsites can be reserved through ReserveAmerica (☎800-444-7275), up to seven months in advance, to reach **Carpinteria Beach State Park ❶,** 12 mi. south of Santa Barbara, follow signs from U.S. 101, entrance is at the end of Palm Ave., or take bus #20 or #21 express to Carpinteria. It has 261 developed sites with hot showers. (☎684-2811. Sites $12; with hookup $18; day use $2.) There are two other state beaches within 30 mi. of Santa Barbara, but these are not served by buses. All three are scrunched between the railroad tracks and U.S. 101.

El Capitán ❶, north of Santa Barbara off U.S. 101, has 140 well-kept sites, some with views of the Channel Islands. However, it usually fills up months in advance. (☎968-1033. Sites $12.) **Refugio ❶** has 84 crowded, wheelchair-accessible sites just steps from the beach. (☎968-1033. Sites $12.) **Gaviota ❶,** off Hwy. 101 at 10 Rugio Beach Rd., is first-come, first-served and offers 43 sites in a parking lot environment but it is near the beach and has a marsh. (☎968-1033. Sites $12. Cash only.)

FOOD

Santa Barbara may well have more restaurants per capita than anywhere else in America, so finding a place to eat is not exactly a problem. State and Milpas St. both have many places to eat; State St. is hipper, while Milpas St. is cheaper. Ice cream lovers flock to award-winning **McConnel's ❶,** 201 W. Mission St. (☎569-2323. Scoops $2.50. Open daily 10am-midnight.) There's an open-air **farmer's market** packed with bargains on the 4500 & 600 blocks of State St. (in summer Tu 4-7:30pm; in winter 3pm-6:30pm), and another on Santa Barbara St. at Cota St. (Sa 8:30am-12:30pm). **Tri-County Produce,** 335 S. Milpas St., sells fresh produce and prepared foods. (☎965-4558. Open M-Sa 9am-7:30pm, Su 9am-6pm.)

▨ Palazzio, 1026 State St. (☎564-1985). They say that "people don't usually leave here hungry," and you certainly shouldn't buck the trend. The depiction of the Sistine Chapel on the ceiling is nearly as impressive as the enormous pasta dishes ($11-13 for half portion, $16-18 for full) and the simply amazing garlic rolls. Tally your own intake at the serve-yourself wine bar. Open Su-Th 11:30am-3pm and 5:30-11pm, F-Sa 11:30am-3pm and 5:30pm-midnight. ❸

Pacific Crepes, 705 Anacapa St. (☎882-1123). Parlez-vous francais? If not, you'll have to wing it. This comfortable, classy French cafe is not only filled with the delicious smells of a full menu of crepe creations, but is authentique—owned and run by a French couple qui ne parle que francais (speak French only, mon ami). The heavenly "Brittany" is topped with fresh strawberries and blueberries, fruit sauce, and ice cream—a perfect dessert ($6.25). Lunch and dinner special $15. Beer, wine and champagne available. Open Su-Tu and Th-Sa 9am-9pm. ❷

The Taj Cafe, 905 State St. (☎564-8280). Enjoy traditional village-style Indian cooking with all natural ingredients. Taj has tasty items like tandoori chicken in a sweet, tangy mango sauce ($10). Lunch specials $5.50-7.50. Many vegetarian entrees ($6.50-8). Open M-Th 11:30am-3pm and 5-10pm, F-Sa 11:30am-3pm and 5-11pm. ❷

The Natural Cafe and Juice Bar, 508 State St. (☎962-9494). Casual dining with a sophisticated, health-bent appeal. A variety of salads, sandwiches, and hot entrees ($5-8). Smoothies with supplements like protein powder or bee pollen will keep you charged all day (from $2.75). Open Su-Th 11am-9:30pm, F-Sa 11am-10pm. ❷

◉ SIGHTS

Santa Barbara is best explored in three sections—the beach and coast, swingin' State St., and the Missionary Mountains. Essential to discovering local events and goings-on is the *Independent*, published every Thursday and available at city newsstands. The downtown-waterfront **shuttle** ($0.25) runs from the beach up State St. The **Visitors Center,** 1 Garden St., at Cabrillo Blvd., has a map and peppy, pamphlet-bearing employees. Pick up *Santa Barbara's Red Tile Tour*, a walking tour guide (free at the Visitors Center; $0.25 inside the courthouse).

COASTAL SANTA BARBARA

Recently revamped, Santa Barbara's supreme coastal drive is along Cabrillo Blvd., the first leg of the city's "Scenic Drive." Follow the green signs as they lead you on a loop into the mountains and around the city, winding through the hillside bordering the town along Alameda Padre Serra. This part of town is known as the American Riviera for the wealth that resides here.

SANTA BARBARA ZOO. The delightfully leafy habitat has such an open feel that the animals seem kept in captivity only through sheer lethargy. A mini-train provides a park-tour. There's also a miniaturized African plain where giraffes stroll lazily, silhouetted against the Pacific. (*500 Niños Dr., off Cabrillo Blvd. from U.S. 101. Take bus #14 or the downtown-waterfront shuttle. ☎962-5339. Open daily 10am-5pm. $8, seniors and ages 2-12 $6, under 2 free. Train $1.50, children $1. Parking $2.*)

SEA CENTER. Stearn's Wharf, at the foot of State St., is the oldest working pier on the West Coast, housing the newly renovated Sea Center and some restaurants and shops. The center is now a working lab with hands-on exhibits for visitors. (*At State St. and Cabrillo Blvd. ☎962-0885. Sea Center open daily 10am-5pm. Touch tank open daily noon-5pm. $4, seniors and ages 13-17 $3 ages 3-12 $2. First 1½hr. parking on wharf free.*)

BEACHES & ACTIVITIES. The Santa Barbara beaches are breathtaking, lined on one side by skyrocketing palm trees and on the other by the endless sailboats in the distance at the local harbor. **East and Leadbetter beaches** flank the wharf on each side. **Skater's Point Park**, along the waterfront on Cabrillo Blvd., south of Sterns Wharf, is a free park for skateboarders. Helmets and gear are required. **Beach Rentals** will rent beachgoers a retro surrey: a covered, Flintstone-esque **bicycle.** You and up to eight friends can cruise along the beach paths in this stylish buggy. (*22 State St. ☎966-6733. Open daily 8am-8pm. Surreys $15-28 per 2hr., depending on number of riders. For other rental options, see **Practical Information**, p. 355*) **Beach House,** 10 State St., rents surfboards and body boards plus all the necessary equipment. (*☎963-1281. Surfboards $7-35; body boards $4-16; wet suits $3-16. Credit card required.*) **Paddle Sports,** 100 State St., offers kayak rentals and lessons. (*☎899-4925. Open in summer daily 7am-6pm; in winter Tu-F noon-6pm, Sa-Su 10am-5pm. Rentals $20-40 for 2hr., $40-60 per day.*) Across the street from the Visitors Center is idyllic **Chase Palm Park,** a beautiful public parkland complete with a vintage 1916 Spillman carousel. (*Carousel operates 10am-6pm. $2.*)

BEST SUNSET. For the best sunset view in the area, have a drink (soda $3.75-4.50, beer and wine $5.50-12) at the bar at the Four Seasons Biltmore Hotel. Appetizers also available for $9-100 (Beluga caviar costs $100). This five-star lodging is beautifully decorated and just a l'il bit steep for the most travelers, but the view of the Pacific is priceless. Free live music is also often featured in the evenings. (*Take Hwy. 101 South to Channel Dr. Exit. 1260 Channel Dr., Montecito. ☎969-2261. Park across the street or else valet parking will run $50, including tip.*)

STATE STREET

State St., Santa Barbara's monument to city planning, runs a straight, tree-lined two miles through the center of the city. Among countless shops and restaurants are some cultural and historical landmarks that should not be missed. Everything that doesn't move—malls, mailboxes, telephones, the restrooms at the public library—has been slathered in Spanish tile.

SANTA BARBARA COUNTY COURTHOUSE. To take in the city's architectural homogeneity and a killer view of the ocean, go up the elevator in the courthouse to the observation deck. Compared to the more prosaic Mission Revival buildings found elsewhere in California, the courthouse is a work of genius with its sculpted fountain, sunken gardens, historic murals, wrought-iron chandeliers, and hand-painted vaulted Gothic ceilings. (*1100 Anacapa St. ☎962-6464. Open daily 10am-5pm; tower closes 4:45pm. Tours M-Sa 2pm, M-Tu and F also 10:30am. Free.*)

SANTA BARBARA MUSEUM OF ART. The museum has an impressive collection of classical Greek, Asian, and European works spanning 3000 years. The 20th-century and Hindu collections are particularly impressive. Over 90% of the works in the permanent collection were gifts from Santa Barbara's wealthy residents. *(1130 State St. ☎ 963-4364. Open Tu-Th and Sa 11am-5pm, F 11am-9pm, Su noon-5pm. Tours Tu-Su noon and 2pm. $6, students and ages 6-16 $3, seniors $4. Free Th and 1st Su of each month.)*

ARLINGTON CENTER FOR PERFORMING ARTS. This combination live performance space and movie theater comfortably seats 2018 people. The murals over the entrance of the Spanish-Moorish building depict scenes from California's Hispano-Mexican era. Its tower is one of the few structures in this low stucco town to rival the palm trees in height, and the actual theater space resembles a Mexican village. Call the box office for info on upcoming events. *(1317 State St. ☎ 963-4408. Movie tickets $8, seniors and ages 2-12 $5; 1pm matinee and twilight show before 6pm $5.)*

OTHER SIGHTS. At the corner of Montecito Ave. and Chapala St. stands the famed **Moreton Bay Fig Tree.** Brought from Australia by a sailor in 1877, the tree's gnarled branches now span 160 ft.; it can provide shade for more than 1000 people at once. If you'd rather drink than stand in the shade with 999 other people, sample award-winning wine at the **Santa Barbara Winery.** *(202 Anacapa St. ☎ 963-3646. Open daily 10am-5pm. Tours daily 11:30am and 3:30pm. Tastings $4 for 6 wines.)*

MOUNTAINS AROUND SANTA BARBARA

Up in the northern part of town, things get considerably more pastoral. In addition to awe-inspiring, rugged mountain terrain, multi-million dollar homes populate the land, adding well manicured lawns and shrubbery to the landscape.

MISSION SANTA BARBARA. Praised as the "Queen of Missions" when built in 1786, the mission was later restored after the 1812 earthquake and assumed its present incarnation in 1820. Towers containing splayed Moorish windows stand around a Greco-Roman temple and facade, and a Moorish fountain bubbles outside. The museum contains items from the mission archives. The main chapel is colorful and solemn; visitors are welcome to (respectfully) drop in on mass. Today the Mission is not only a museum and parish, but also an infirmary and Franciscan friary. For more on missions, see p. 7. *(At the end of Las Olivas St. Take bus #22 ($1 one-way or $3 day pass). ☎ 682-4149. Open daily 9am-5pm. Self-guided museum tour starts at the gift shop. $4, under 12 free. Mass M-F 7:30am, Sa 4pm, Su 7:30, 9, 10:30am, noon.)*

SANTA BARBARA MUSEUM OF NATURAL HISTORY. Unlike in a typical museum, the only way to get from one exhibit to the next is by going outside—you can learn while taking in the sun. It was built to be a museum of comparative oology (no, not zoology), but the founder's wishes were overturned by a Board of Trustees who thought that devoting the space to the study of eggs was silly. So, they hatched the current exhibitions, which include the largest collection of Chumash artifacts in the West, a natural history gallery, and a planetarium. *(2559 Puesta del Sol Rd. Follow signs to parking lot or take bus #22. Museum: ☎ 682-4711, astronomy hotline ext. 405. Open daily 10am-5pm. $6, seniors and ages 13-17 $6, under 12 $4, under 2 free. Planetarium shows in summer daily 1, 2, 3pm; in winter W 3pm, Sa-Su 1, 2, 3pm. Admission plus $2.)*

SANTA BARBARA BOTANICAL GARDEN. Far from town, but not far from Mission Santa Barbara or the Museum of Natural History, the botanical garden offers an amazing array of non-native vegetation along easy, meandering paths. Five miles of hiking trails wind through 65 acres of native Californian trees, wildflowers, and cacti. The garden's water system was built by the Chumash and is now one of the last vestiges of the region's native heritage. *(1212 Mission Canyon Rd. ☎ 682-4726. Open Mar.-Oct. M-F 9am-5pm, Sa-Su 9am-6pm; Nov.-Feb. M-F 9am-4pm, Sa-Su 9am-5pm. Tours*

M-Th and Sa at 2pm, Su-Th 10:30am; special demonstrations F and Su at 2pm, Sa at 10:30am. $5; students, seniors, and ages 13-19 $3; ages 5-12 $1 under 5 free.)

HIKING. Very popular **Inspiration Point** is a 3.6 mi. round-trip hike and climbs 800 ft. Half of the hike is an easy walk on a paved road. The other half is a series of mountainside switchbacks. The reward is a extensive view of the city, the ocean and the Channel Islands on a clear day. Following the creek upstream will lead to **Seven Falls.** *(From Santa Barbara Mission drive toward the mountains and turn right onto Foothill Rd. Turn left onto Mission Canyon Rd. and go 1 mi. Bear left onto Tunnel Rd. and drive 1¼ mi. to its end.)* **Rattlesnake Canyon Trail** is a moderate 3.5 mi. round-trip hike to Tunnel Trail junction with a 1000 ft. gain. It passes many waterfalls, pools, and secluded spots, but is a highly popular trail—expect company. *(From Santa Barbara Mission drive toward the mountains and turn right onto Foothill Rd. Turn left onto Mission Canyon Rd. and go ½ mi. Make a sharp right onto Las Conas Rd. and travel 1¼ mi. There is a large sign indicating the trailhead on the left side of the road.)* The trek from the **Cold Springs Trail** to **Montecito Peak** (7.3 mi. round-trip, 2462 ft. elevation gain) or to **Camino Cielo** (9 mi. round-trip, 2675 ft. elevation gain) are considerably more strenuous, with great views. *(From U.S. 101 South, take Hot Springs Rd. Exit, and turn left. Travel 2½ mi. to Mountain Dr. Turn left and stop 1¼ mi. by the creek crossing.)* For a more extensive listing of trails, try the Botanical Garden gift shop or the Visitors Center in town. Another option is to join the local **Sierra Club** on their group hikes. *(For more information call ☎ 564-7892. Social hike, at Santa Barbara Mission, 6:15pm. Strenuous hike, at Hope Ave. by the Bank of America, Sa-Su 9am. Led by expert hikers; free.)*

UNIVERSITY OF CALIFORNIA AT SANTA BARBARA (UCSB). This beautiful outpost of the UC system is stuck in Goleta, a shapeless mass of suburbia, gas stations, and coffee shops. The excellent **art museum** is worth visiting. It houses the Sedgwick Collection of 15th- to 17th-century European paintings (including a Bellini *Madonna and Child*) and hosts innovative contemporary exhibits. *(Museum off U.S. 101. Take bus #11. ☎ 893-2951. Open Tu-Sa 10am-4pm, Su 1-5pm. Free.)*

OTHER NEARBY SIGHTS. The beach at **Summerland** is east of Montecito and accessible by bus #20. Its biggest food attraction is **The Big Yellow House,** a Victorian-estate-turned-restaurant. It is reported to be inhabited by two ghosts: Hector haunts the wine cellars, while his mistress sticks to the women's bathroom upstairs. Ask to eat in the bedroom with the secret door. *(108 Pierpoint Ave. ☎ 969-4140. Open Su-Th 8am-9pm, F-Sa 8am-10pm.)* **Rincon Beach,** 3 mi. southeast of Carpinteria, has some of the county's best surfing. **Gaviota State Beach,** 29 mi. northwest of Santa Barbara, also has good surf. You can **whale-watch** from late November to early April, when the Pacific grays migrate.

◘ SEASONAL EVENTS

One of the most special events in Santa Barbara is not organized by human hand. Starting in October, and assembling most densely from November to February, hoards of **monarch butterflies** cling to the eucalyptus trees in Ellwood Grove, just west of UCSB, and at the end of Coronado St., off Hollister Ave.; take the Glen Annie/Storke Rd. Exit off U.S. 101. Other events include:

Hang Gliding Festival (☎ 965-3733; www.flyaboveall.com), Mesa Flight Park, early Jan.

Santa Barbara International Film Festival (☎ 963-0023; www.sbfilmfestival.com), late Feb.-early Mar. Sponsored by the Arlington Center, among others (see p. 360). Premieres US indies and foreign films and boasts of celebrity patronage. Passes can be purchased online or by phone.

Gay Pride Parade (☎ 884-2974), on a Sa in mid-July. The 1-day festival held on Leadbetter Beach celebrates the local gay community.

I Madonnari Italian Street Painting Festival (☎569-3873), Memorial Day weekend. Professional and amateur chalk paintings decorate the Old Mission Courtyard. An Italian tradition since the 16th century.

Summer Solstice Parade and Fair (☎965-3396), on the Sa nearest June 21. Pre-Bacchanal fun on State St. No words (on posters), no vehicles, no religious faith symbols, and no animals allowed. It's a pagan thing.

Old Spanish Days Fiesta (☎962-8101), early Aug. Spirited fiesta, celebrated for the last 75 years, with rodeos, carnivals, parades, dancing, live flamenco guitar everywhere, and plenty of margaritas and sangria.

Music Academy of the West, 1070 Fairway Rd. (☎897-0300; www.musicacademy.org), holds a series of inexpensive concerts throughout the summer. Stop by for a brochure.

Santa Barbara International Jazz Festival (☎966-3000), early Sept. Big names in jazz.

▮ SHOPPING

State Street is a shopping mecca with two miles of mildly trendy shops and the upscale **Paseo Nuevo Mall,** between Cañon Perdido St. and Ortega St. Local craftspeople line Cabrillo Blvd. for the **Arts and Crafts Show,** where they sell their hand crafted wares every fair-weathered Sunday from 10am to dusk.

▨ **Scavenge,** 418 State St. (☎564-2000). Half clothing store, half garage sale, this bargain shopper's dream store carries everything from framed Monet and Degas prints to screwdriver and ratchet sets. Find that perfect chinese lantern or a new pink tutu. Also sells retail clothing and shoes. Prices range from $1-100. Open Su-Th 11am-10pm, F 11am-midnight, Sa 10am-midnight.

As Seen on TV, 1125 State St. (☎564-4100). Late-night infomercials open new horizons of consumer cravings: love handle removal and the clearest pores a teenager has ever known. The most popular items are the roller-hose ($25) and sewing genie ($40). Watch the products advertised on in-store TVs. Open M-Sa 10am-8pm, Su 10am-7pm.

2000 Degrees, 1206 State St. (☎882-1817). Feeling left out of the California art scene? Then experience the Santa Barbara ceramics circuit at this paint-your-own studio. Pay $7 workshop fee and paint as many pieces of bisqueware as you can buy. Prices range from $2-60; a decent send-home-to-Mom mug is $6.50 (they'll even ship it home for you). Open M-W 11am-6pm, Th-Su 10:30am-7pm, Su noon-6pm.

▮ ▮ ENTERTAINMENT & NIGHTLIFE

Every night of the week, the clubs on **State Street,** mostly between Haley St. and Canon Predido St., are packed. This town is full of those who love to eat, drink, and be mirthful. Consult the *Independent* to see who's playing on any given night. Bars on State St. charge $4 for beer fairly uniformly; search for specials.

The Hourglass, 213 W. Cota Street (☎963-1436), in a residential part of town. With 9 spas total, pick an intimate indoor bath or watch the stars from a private outdoor tub. No alcohol allowed. Towels $1. 2 people $25 per hr.; each additional person $7. $2 student discount; children free with parent. Open Th-Su 5pm-midnight.

Q's Sushi A-Go-Go, 409 State St. (☎966-9177). A tri-level bar, 8 pool tables, and dancing. Stomach some sushi ($3.50-13.50). Accompany with *sake* for $3.50. Happy Hour M-Sa 4-7pm includes 20% off sushi plates and half-priced drinks and appetizers. M Brazilian night. W karaoke. Cover F-Sa after 9pm $5. Open daily 4pm-2am.

Club 634, 634 State St. (☎564-1069). Cocktails, dancing and 2 large patios. Live bands and DJs. Su and W karaoke, Th $3 Red Bull and vodkas, F 5-8pm $1.50 select beers. Occasional cover. Open M-F 2pm-2am, Sa-Su noon-2am.

O'Mally's, 525 State St. (☎564-8904). An Irish pub/sports bar. DJs and dancing. Cover about 5 times per year during major local events. Open daily 1pm-1:30am.

NEAR SANTA BARBARA   ☎805

LOS PADRES NATIONAL FOREST

Once the land of the Chumash Indians and condors, the vast **Los Padres National Forest** (district office ☎968-6640) stretches north of Santa Barbara into San Luis Obispo County and beyond. Los Padres is a leader in wildlife recovery programs, reintroducing many endangered plants and birds, such as the bald eagle and the falcon. The **San Rafael Wilderness** alone contains 125 mi. of trails and a sanctuary for the nearly extinct California condor. **Cachuma Lake,** 15 mi. from U.S. 101 on Rte. 154, is a gorgeous, dark emerald colored water source for the area, as well as a **campsite ❶** and recreational area (day use $5). Ask for trail information at the entrance. The nearby **Chumash painted cave** is 20min. north of Santa Barbara. Take U.S. 101 to Rte. 154 to Painted Cave Rd. Go past the village and down into the oak glen. The cave is up on the right; parking is scarce. The impressive red ochre handiwork of native shamans dates to 1677. There are many outdoors opportunities in the area (see **Santa Barbara: Camping,** p. 357). The **Adventure Pass,** needed in all recreation areas in the forest, is available at the **Santa Barbara Ranger Office,** 3505 Paradise Rd. Take Rte. 154 for 10 mi. to Paradise Rd., and turn right; the office is 5 mi. ahead. (☎967-3481. Open M-Sa 8am-4:30pm. Pass $5 per day, $30 per year.)

SANTA YNEZ VALLEY

To the northwest of Santa Barbara along Rte. 154 lies the lovely **Santa Ynez Valley,** home to thousands of acres of vineyards, hundreds of ostriches, and Michael Jackson's **Wonderland Ranch,** ostensibly named after Lewis Carroll's fantasy world. The free *Santa Barbara County Wineries Touring Map,* available at the Santa Barbara Visitors Center, gives comprehensive listings. One of the prettiest vineyards is **Gainey Vineyard,** 3950 E. Rte. 246, at Rte. 154. (☎688-0558. Open daily 10am-5pm. Tours daily 11am, 1, 2, 3pm. Tastings fee of $5 includes 9 tastes and logo glass.)

Solvang Village rises, somewhat oddly, off Rte. 246, in all its Danish-styled-thatched-roofed glory. Crammed with northern European gift shops, restaurants and *conditoris* (bakeries) this Disney-esque town is a kind of tribute to its ancestors and a peculiar tourist attraction. The **Solvang Bakery,** 460 Alisal Rd. claims to be "Solvang's favorite coffeehouse." (☎688-4939. Open daily 7am-6pm; in summer F-Sa until 8pm.) Next door is the graceful **Mission Santa Ines,** 1760 Mission Dr.. Look for the footprint of a Chumash child in the Chapel of the Madonnas and pay respects to the graves of 1700 Chumash people. (☎688-4815. Open daily 9am-7pm; in winter 9am-5pm. $3, under 16 free.) Four miles west, at the intersection of Rte. 246 and U.S. 101, is the town of **Buellton,** home of **Pea Soup Andersen's ❶** since 1924, where the split pea soup is thick, hot and fresh. (☎688-5581. Soup $3.50. All-you-can-eat servings of soup plus a thick milkshake, $7. Open daily 7am-10pm.)

Farther to the northwest, at the juncture of Hwy. 1 and Rte. 246, is the city of **Lompoc,** home of the nation's largest producer of flower seed. The acres upon acres of blooms, which peak near the end of June, are both a visual and an olfactory explosion. Lompoc holds a **flower festival** at the season's peak, usually the last weekend in June (info ☎735-8511). **La Purisma Mission State Park,** 2295 Purisma Rd., follow Rte. 246, the entrance is off Mission Rd., has the most fully restored of Father Serra's missions, and 12 mi. of maintained trails. (☎733-7781. Open daily 9am-5pm. Parking $5.) For more info on missions, see p. 7.

CENTRAL COAST

THE ANTI-GURU Jiddu Krishnamurti may not have had Deepak Chopra's knack for self-promotion, nor was he ever able to whittle his spiritual teachings down to seven bite-sized laws, but there's no doubting Krishnamurti's influence in spreading Eastern philosophy worldwide. It all started on a beach in Madras (now Chennai), India, where the charismatic Englishwoman and theosophist **Annie Besant** (known for her friendship with Gandhi) picked out the 14-year-old Krishnamurti from the crowd and proclaimed him the coming World Teacher—the vehicle for the reincarnation of Christ in the West and Buddha in the East. Annie Besant adopted the boy and raised him in Britain in the tradition of the **theosophists,** who melded Eastern and Western religious thought into a belief both in the direct and often mystical experience of God and in the underlying unity of the universe. In 1922, when Krishnamurti came to the Ojai Valley, he had an awakening that eventually led him to repudiate his status as World Teacher—much to the dismay of his ardent throng of followers. He felt that man could not arrive at truth through any organized religion, nor through any guru or priest. This conviction became the core of his teaching: "The truth is a pathless land." Until his death in 1986, Krishnamurti traveled the world speaking to large audiences. His home and headquarters was in Ojai, but Krishnamurti established foundations in India, Europe, and elsewhere in the US. The Krishnamurti Foundation of America in Ojai continues to publish all of Krishnamurti's writings and talks.

OJAI
☎ 805

Lying only 80 mi. north of L.A., Ojai (OH-hi) is a pleasant retreat from the city. Wooded valleys and mountain vistas have long been known to make mystics out of passers-through. The town has capitalized on age-old traditions and made them new age: Ojai is now home to chi-chi health spas, organic farms, and non-denominational spiritual centers.

⊞ 🖍 ORIENTATION & PRACTICAL INFORMATION. The Ojai Valley sits 15 mi. north of Ventura, just east of the Santa Ynez Mountains and just south of Los Padres National Forest. To reach Ojai from L.A., take U.S. 101 North, following signs for Santa Barbara; take the Rte. 33 Exit. Fifteen miles of leafy roads lead to Ojai, where Rte. 33 becomes Ojai Ave., the town's east-west spine. If you want to give your car a rest, the city of Ojai runs a **trolley** along Ojai Ave. (Runs M-F 7:15am-5:40pm, Sa-Su 9:05am-4:53pm. $0.25.) The **Ojai Valley Visitor Center,** 150 W. Ojai Ave., has maps and info on Ojai's art galleries, antique shops, campgrounds, and spa services. (☎646-8126. Open M-F 9:30am-4:30pm, Sa-Su 9am-3pm.)

🛏 ACCOMMODATIONS. The **🏠Ojai Farm Hostel ❶**, P.O. Box 723, Ojai 93024, epitomizes the town's earthy aura—any fruit in the organic orchard is yours for the pickin'. They offer free pickup in Ventura, two TV rooms (complete with video library), and free use of bikes. There are two lodge-type accommodations with a total of 12 beds; one is for couples and women, the other for men. Call ahead for required reservations or to be picked up free from the Ventura bus station; the location will not be disclosed to anyone not staying at the hostel. (☎646-0311; www.hostelhandbook.com/farmhostel. $15 per person. Proof of international travel required.) **Capri Motel ❷**, 1180 E. Ojai Ave., is situated in a perfect locale—tall palms frame the pool and jacuzzi. (☎877-589-5860. Rooms with cable TV, A/C, and balconies. Continental breakfast included. Doubles $75-110; suites $85-135. Weekly discounts available.) The **El Camino Motel ❸**, 406 W. Ojai Ave., has 20 rooms with cable, phones and some kitchen units. Call ahead for rates and reservations. (☎646-4341. Singles $55-65; doubles $65-70.) The other option for the budget traveler is roughing it at camp sites, which are plentiful in the surrounding areas (see **Santa Barbara: Camping,** p. 357).

▣ 🄰 **SIGHTS & HIKES.** Ojai was once the playpen of the Hollywood elite, who came to romp in the spas and natural hot springs. But when Eastern luminary Jiddu Krishnamurti had a spiritual awakening under an Ojai tree (see **The Anti-Guru,** p. 364), the town attached a glow of enlightenment to the sheen of glamor. Today, many visitors forego body wraps, masks, and scrubs ($55-200) at Ojai spas, and come to free their minds for free. The international **Krotona Institute of Theosophy,** 2 Krotona Hil operates a quiet library, with classes on theosophy and comparative religion. (☎646-2653. Open Tu-F 10am-4pm, Sa-Su 1-4pm.) Other spiritual centers are the **Krishnamurti Library,** 1130 McAndrew Rd. (☎646-4948; open W-Su 1-5pm) and the **Meditation Mount,** on Reeves Rd., which has a meditation room and garden. (☎646-5508. Open daily 10am-dusk. Free.)

For a scant $2, trace the history of the area, Chumash to New Age, at the **Ojai Valley Museum,** 130 W. Ojai Ave. (☎640-1390. Open W-F 1-4pm, Sa-Su 10am-4pm.) The **Ojai Center for the Arts,** 113 S. Montgomery St., has art, dance, poetry readings, workshops, and theater. (☎646-0117. Open daily noon-4pm.) **Bart's Books,** on the corner of Canada St. and Matilija St., could only exist in Ojai. This open-air shop has bookshelves outside the gates on the street; after-hours browsers pay for their selections by dropping coins in a box. The books are cheap and plentiful, though the selection is better inside. (☎646-3755. Open Tu-Su 10am-5:30pm.)

A 10min. drive south of town on Rte. 33 leads to the **Old Creek Ranch Winery,** 10024 Old Creek Rd. Built in 1981 on the site as an 1880's historic winery—the oldest in Ventura County—this winery offers handmade premium wines. Buy a bottle and enjoy the quiet of the valley. (☎649-4132. Open for tasting Sa-Su 11am-5pm.)

Ojai is also the southernmost gateway to **Los Padres National Forest** (see p. 363). Get maps, camping info, and an Adventure Pass ($5 per day, $30 per year) at the **Los Padres Ojai Ranger Office,** 1190 E. Ojai Ave. (see p. 458). Ask about trails to the **Punchbowls,** small water holes that sit like pools on the mountain, close to local waterfalls and "moon rocks." (☎646-4348. Open M-F 8am-4:30pm.)

LOS ANGELES

The greater L.A. area (pop. 9.9 million; 4753 sq. mi.), stretching from Antelope Valley in the north to Catalina Island in the south with a desert basin center, two mountain ranges, and 76 mi. of dazzling coastline, is the epicenter of the "California Dream." Some see in its sweeping beaches and dazzling sun a demi-paradise, a land of opportunity where the most opulent dreams can be realized. Others point to its congestion, smog, and crime, and declare L.A. a sham—a converted wasteland where media-numbed masses go to wither in the sun.

California's largest city has been plagued with crises: race riots, earthquakes, floods, and homelessness. What could explain the Angeleno's loyalty in the face of such catastrophe? Perhaps it's the persistence of L.A.'s mystique, the veneer of a city whose most celebrated industry is the production and dissemination of images. The glitter of the studios, the mammoth billboards on Sunset Strip, and the glamour of Rodeo Drive all attest to the resilience of L.A.'s fixation.

In a city where nothing seems to be more than 30 years old, the latest trends curry more respect than the venerable. Many come to this historical vacuum to make (or re-make) themselves. And what better place? Without the tiresome duty of bowing to the gods of an established high culture, Angelenos are free to indulge not in what they must, but in what they choose. The resulting atmosphere is delicious with potential. Some savor L.A.'s image-bound culture, while others may be appalled by its excess. Either way, it's one hell of a show.

HIGHLIGHTS OF LOS ANGELES

TINSELTOWN. Hollywood (p. 393) was the cradle of the American film industry. Here, the Hollywood sign presides above historic theaters and bars frequented by stars and as-yet-undiscovered hopefuls.

BEACH LIFE. An extensive beach culture thrives in **Santa Monica** (p. 396) and **Venice** (p. 398), where surfing, in-line skating, and beach volleyball mesh with wild cultural oddities in a non-stop circus sideshow.

STUDIOS. Television studios cluster in the smog-filled **San Fernando Valley** (p. 411), along with the world-famous **Universal Studios** theme park.

MUSEUMS. L.A.'s museums are among the nation's finest, from the **Museum of Tolerance** (p. 401) to the **Getty** (p. 403) to the **Norton Simon Museum of Art** (p. 412) to the **Los Angeles County Museum of Art** (p. 404). In Santa Monica, the **Bergamot Station Art Center** (p. 397) is a conglomeration of galleries that include the Santa Monica Museum of Art and the Gallery of Functional Art.

PAR-TAY. West Hollywood (p. 405) is the heart of L.A.'s thriving gay community and home to the **Sunset Strip,** center of the hippest **nightlife** (p. 423).

THE CITYSCAPE. The greatest view of the Hollywood sign and the city sprawl can be had by driving—or walking, god forbid—to the top of **Griffith Park** (p. 409), which is also home to a planetarium and the L.A. Zoo.

TASTE. Arguably tasteful **shopping** (p. 416) and **dining** (p. 387) culture flourishes along Melrose Avenue in West Hollywood and along the Third Street Promenade in Santa Monica. If you'd rather eat than taste, jump into L.A's rockin' **diner** scene. Among the best are Duke's Coffee Shop (p. 388) and Canter's (p. 423).

DOWNTOWN EXISTS! Downtown (p. 405) is home to L.A.'s **historic center,** the bustling **Grand Central Public Market** (p. 387), the **Museum of Contemporary Art** (p. 407), and many gleaming monoliths.

✈ INTERCITY TRANSPORTATION

BY PLANE. Los Angeles International Airport (LAX) is in **Westchester**, about 15 mi. southwest of Downtown and 10 mi. south of Santa Monica. LAX can be a confusing airport, but there are electronic information kiosks everywhere with Chinese, English, French, German, Japanese, Korean, and Spanish. **LAX information** (☎310-646-5252) will help Spanish and English speakers. **Airport police** (☎310-646-7911) are there 24hr. a day. **Traveler's Aid,** an info and referral service for airport info, transportation and accommodation suggestions, and major transit emergencies, is in all terminals. (☎310-646-2270. Open M-F 8:30am-noon and 1-5pm.) There is also a **First Aid Station.** (☎310-215-6000. Open daily 7am-11pm.) Currency exchange is available at **International Currency Exchange (ICE) Currency Services,** in all terminals. However, local American Express offices generally offer more attractive exchange rates (see **Currency Exchange,** p. 377). Cell phones geared for international business travelers can be rented here. (☎310-417-0366. Open daily 7am-11pm.)

Besides renting a car, there are several other **transit** options from the airport. Before hopping into any of the vehicles below, check with the place at which you plan to stay; many accommodations offer deals on transportation from the airport.

Metro Rail Subway: The **Metropolitan Transit Authority (MTA)** oversees subway and bus transportation, including the local DASH buses. Call ☎800-COMMUTE/266-6883 or see www.mta.net. Take the **Green Line Metro Rail shuttle,** leaving every 10-15min., from any terminal to the Green Line Metro Rail Aviation station. (Open daily 4:30am-11:30pm.) From **Aviation** to: **Long Beach,** take the Green Line rail to the Rosa Parks station at Imperial and Wilmington, and switch to the Blue Line rail heading south to Long Beach; **Redondo Beach,** take the Green Line west to the end of the line; **Downtown,** go east to Rosa Parks, change to the Blue Line and head north until it meets the Red Line's 7th/Metro Center. From there, head northwest toward Hollywood.

MTA Buses: Orange signs highlight the traffic island where shuttle "C" transports bus-bound passengers to the **transfer terminal** at Sepulveda and 96th St. **Westwood/UCLA,** #561 (M-F 6am-midnight, Sa-Su 8am-midnight). **Downtown,** #42 (M-Sa 5am-11pm, Su 7am-11pm). After hours, bus #40 picks up this route and runs all night. Also try the #439 express (every 40min. daily 5am-10pm). **Long Beach,** #232 (M-F 5:15am-11pm, Sa-Su 6am-11pm). **West Hollywood** and **Beverly Hills** #220 (hourly; M-F 6:30am-7:30pm, Sa-Su 7:30am-7:30pm). **Hollywood,** from West Hollywood, #217 along Hollywood Blvd. (every 10 min.; M-Sa 4am-midnight, Su 5am-midnight), or #12 along Sunset Blvd. (every 12 min.; M-F 5am-1am, Sa 6am-1am, Su 6:30am-11pm), or #4 along Santa Monica Blvd. (every 15-20min.; 24hr.).

Taxis: Follow yellow signs. Cabs are costly; fare from airport to Hollywood $40; to Santa Monica $25. (For more info, see p. 375.)

BY TRAIN. Amtrak rolls into **Union Station,** 800 N. Alameda St. (☎213-683-6729 or 800-USA-RAIL/872-7245), at the northwestern edge of Downtown L.A. Opened in May 1939, Union Station brought together the Santa Fe, Union Pacific, and Southern Pacific railroads. The station has been featured in a number of films, including *Bugsy* and *The Way We Were.* From the station, take bus #33 to **Santa Monica** (3 hr., 12 per day, $24-30) and along the coast to **San Francisco** (12hr., 10am, $59-78), but it's faster and cheaper to take the San Joaquin route, which requires a bus coach to Bakersfield (9½ hrs., 3 per day, $46-57).

BY BUS. If coming by **Greyhound Bus** (☎800-231-2222 or 213-629-8401), consider bypassing its Downtown station, 1716 E. 7th St. at Alameda St. (☎213-629-8536), which is in an extremely rough neighborhood. If you must get off in Downtown, be very careful near 7th and Alameda St., one block southwest of the station, where

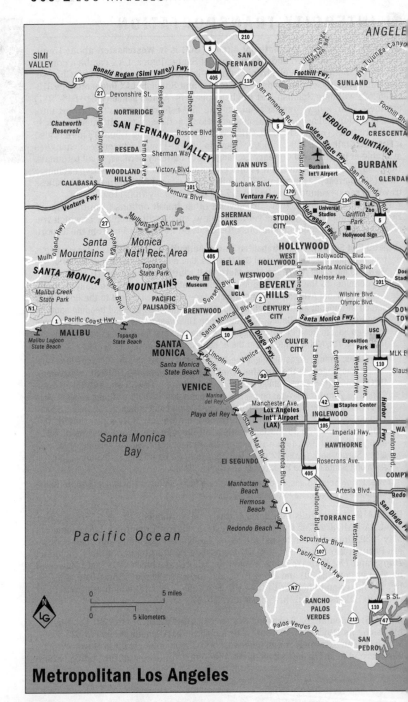

Metropolitan Los Angeles

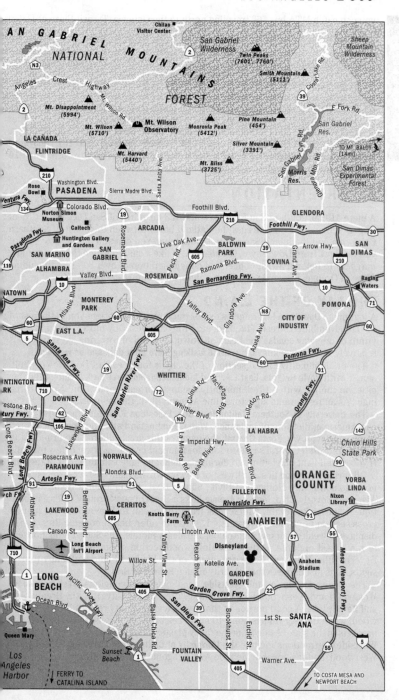

you can catch MTA bus #60 traveling north to the Gateway Transit Plaza at Union Station. The new terminal in Hollywood, 1715 N. Cahuenga Blvd. (☎323-466-1249), is in a great location and is close to many hotels, restaurants, and sights.

> **Greyhound Routes: Santa Barbara** (6 per day; $12, round-trip $22); **San Diego** (11 per day; $13, round-trip $23); **San Francisco** (8 per day; $42, round-trip $78). Open Su-Sa 6:30am-9:30pm. **Tijuana,** Mexico (4hr.; $15, round-trip $25). Route maps $2.

BY CAR. The city is criss-crossed by over a dozen freeways that can seem confusing. However, stick to the main six and it's smooth sailing—other than the bumper to bumper traffic. The **I-5 (Santa Ana Freeway, Golden State Freeway, and San Diego Freeway),** the **I-405 (San Diego Freeway), I-110 (Harbor Freeway), U.S. 101 (Hollywood Freeway),** and the **Highway 1 (Pacific Coast Highway)** all run north-south. The **I-10 (San Bernardino Freeway)** runs east from the city.

✦ ORIENTATION

A mere 419 mi. south of San Francisco and 133 mi. north of San Diego, the City of Angels spreads its wings across the flatland basin between the coast of Southern California and the inland San Gabriel Mountains. You can still be "in" L.A. even if you're 50 mi. from Downtown. Greater L.A. is like a club to which the surrounding burgs try to belong, a vast conceptual conglomeration of over 80 cities, including those in Orange, Riverside, San Bernardino, and Ventura counties.

THE LAY OF THE L.A.ND

A legitimate **Downtown** Los Angeles exists, but it won't help orient you to the rest of the city. Numbered streets (1st, 2nd, etc.) run east-west Downtown, forming a labyrinth of one-way roads. The heart of Downtown, full of towering skyscrapers, is relatively safe on weekdays, but **avoid walking there after dark and on weekends.**

The predominantly Latino section of the city is found east of Downtown's Indiana St. with **Boyle Heights, East L.A.,** and **Montebello. Monterey Park** is one of the few cities in the US with a predominantly Asian-American population. Not surprisingly, Asian restaurants and stores line Atlantic Blvd., the main drag.

The **University of Southern California (USC), Exposition Park,** and the mostly African-American districts of **Inglewood, Watts, Huntington Park,** and **Compton** stretch south of Downtown. **South Central,** the name of this area, suffered the brunt of the 1992 riots. South Central's is notorious for rampant crime—it attracts few tourists. If you're hell-bent on visiting, go during daylight and take valuables out of the car.

Glittering **Hollywood** lies northwest of Downtown. Its main east-west drags (from north to south) are Hollywood Blvd., Sunset Blvd., Santa Monica Blvd., Melrose Ave., and Beverly Blvd. **Melrose Avenue** links a chain of quasi-trendy cafes and boutiques. **Sunset Boulevard,** which runs from the ocean to Downtown, presents a cross-section of virtually everything L.A. has to offer: beach communities, lavish displays of wealth, famous nightclubs, and sleazy motels. The **Sunset Strip,** hot seat of L.A.'s best nightlife, is the West Hollywood section of Sunset Blvd. closest to Beverly Hills. **Hollywood Boulevard,** home of the Walk of Fame and many tourist sights, runs just beneath the celebrity-ridden **Hollywood Hills.**

The region known as the **Westside** encompasses prestigious **West Hollywood,** Westwood and Westwood Village, Century City, Culver City, Bel Air, Brentwood, and **Beverly Hills.** A good portion of the city's gay community resides in West Hollywood, while Beverly Hills is home to many celebrities and some of the highest tax brackets in the state. Aside from the fancy plastic surgeons and residential estates, Westside's attractions include the **University of California at Los Angeles (UCLA),** in Westwood, and fashionable Melrose Ave. hangouts in West Hollywood. The name

West L.A. is a municipal distinction that refers to Westwood and the no-man's land inland of Santa Monica that includes Century City (the corporate and shopping district on what used to be the 20th Century Fox backlot). The area west of Downtown and south of West Hollywood is known as the **Wilshire District,** named after its main boulevard. **Hancock Park,** an affluent residential area, covers the northeast portion of the district and intersects with Fairfax, a large Jewish community.

The **Valley Region** sprawls north of the Hollywood Hills and the Santa Monica Mountains. For most people, the valley is, *like*, the **San Fernando Valley,** where almost two million people wander among malls and TV studios. The valley is also home to **Burbank** and **Studio City,** which include the lion's share of today's movie studios. The basin is bounded to the north and west by the Santa Susanna Mountains and Rte. 118 (Ronald Reagan Fwy.), to the south by Rte. 134 (Ventura Blvd.), and to the east by I-5 (Golden State Fwy.). The **San Bernardino Valley,** home to about two million, stretches eastward from L.A. south of the San Gabriel Mountains. This valley is largely industrialized and heavily plagued by the county's famed smog, although it is home to **Pasadena** and its famed Rose Parade.

Eighty miles of beaches line L.A.'s **coastal region. Zuma,** the inspiration for the 1975 Neil Young album of the same name, is northernmost, followed by **Malibu,** which lies 15 mi. up the coast from **Santa Monica.** Farther south is the distended beach-side freak show known as **Venice.** The beach towns south of Venice include **Manhattan, Hermosa,** and **Redondo Beaches** (see p. 359). South across the Palos Verdes Peninsula is **Long Beach** (see p. 363), a port city of half a million people with a large gay population. Farthest south are the **Orange County** (see p. 445) beach cities: Seal Beach, Sunset Beach, Huntington Beach, Newport Beach, and Laguna Beach.

L.A. COMMUNITIES

HOLLYWOOD. Nowhere is the myth/reality divide more dramatic in Los Angeles than in the sharp contrast between the movieland glamor associated with Hollywood's name and the unromantic squalor of its present existence. In truth, Hollywood has long since ceased to be the home of the American movie industry. All the major studios (except Paramount, see p. 418) moved over the Hollywood Hills in the 1930s to the roomier locale and lower taxes of the San Fernando Valley. What remains are a few fragments of the silver screen industry: the Academy Awards, the star-studded Walk of Fame, a handful of historic theaters that host a few premieres, and an aura of decayed nostalgia that brings in visitors by the busload despite the relatively high proportion of pimps, panhandlers, and porn shops. For a brief history of Hollywood, see **The Boob Tube and the Silver Screen,** p. 18.

SANTA MONICA. The most striking characteristic of Santa Monica (pop. 87,000) is its efficiency. It is safe, clean, and unpretentious—and you can usually find a parking spot. Santa Monica is also easily navigable on foot or by bus. Its residential areas, once heavily populated by screen superstars, are just blocks away from its main districts. The **Third Street Promenade** is the city's most popular spot to shop by day and schmooze by night, and the nearby beaches are packed. Many find that a drive down Ocean Ave. leaves them with the eerie feeling that they are on a set. Santa Monica issues almost 1000 permits yearly to production companies who want to capture the Gold Coast on film. *(From Downtown L.A., it takes about 30min. (with no traffic) to reach Santa Monica on MTA #33 or 333 or on I-10 (Santa Monica Fwy.). Santa Monica's efficient **Big Blue Bus (BBBus)** system connects to other L.A. bus routes.)*

VENICE. Venice is a carnivalesque beach town where guitar-toting, wild-eyed, tie-dyed residents sculpt masterpieces in sand and compose them in graffiti, all before heading to the beach to slam a volleyball. Grab a corn dog and head onto Ocean Front Walk; a stroll through in-line skating, bikini-flaunting, tattooed Venice is truly a memorable experience. *(To get to Venice from Downtown L.A., take MTA #33 or 333 (or 436 during rush hour). From downtown Santa Monica, take Santa Monica BBBus #1 or 2. Avoid hourly meter feedings by parking in the $5-per-day lot at Pacific Ave. and Venice Blvd.)*

MARINA DEL REY. Venice's neighbor to the immediate south is older, more expensive, and considerably more sedate. While Marina del Rey does have a swimming beach, it spurns sunbathing in favor of boating. Once a duck-hunting ground, the area was used as an oil field in the late 1930s and was reincarnated in 1965 as a yacht harbor. Marina del Rey is now the largest manmade marina in the world, with 6000 pleasure boats and 3000 boats in dry storage.

MALIBU. Malibu makes its southern neighbor Santa Monica look like a carnival: Malibu is *the beach*. It has no amusement parks and no boardwalk—just sand, mountains, and surf. Although Tom Cruise, Bob Dylan, Martin Sheen, Diana Ross, Sting, and Cher are just a few of Malibu's better-known residents, it is not a see-and-be-seen type of town. The quiet shores and the 27 mi. of beautiful beaches that run along the 20000 and 30000 blocks of the **Pacific Coast Highway** (**PCH**; Hwy. 1 north from Santa Monica) will soothe the sunburnt soul.

BEVERLY HILLS. The very name Beverly Hills evokes images of palm-lined boulevards, tanned and taut skin, and million-dollar homes with pools shaped like vital organs. Beverly Hills glows in the televised mystique of expensive hotels, ritzy boutiques, and movie stars galore. These perceptions are not far from the truth. Although many silver screen starlets no longer call 90210 their postal code, Beverly Hills is still a spectacle of opulence and class. You can live it up on a budget here simply by being as showy as the town. Throw on your Sunday best, slip on the shades, and make clerks work for the money they think you have.

WESTWOOD & UCLA. Wedged between the exclusive neighborhoods of Brentwood and Beverly Hills, Westwood is a mecca for young and fun-loving travelers, mostly because it is home to the University of California at Los Angeles (UCLA) and its many thousands of students. Westwood Village (on, around, and between Gayley, Westwood, and Kinross Ave.) hosts myriad movie theaters, boutiques, outdoor cafes, and coffeehouses. Most cater to college kids, though some are rather upscale. Overall, Westwood is very clean, safe, and hip.

BEL AIR, BRENTWOOD, & PACIFIC PALISADES. Home to many celebrities, these three residential communities don't offer much to the economizing traveler in terms of accommodations or food, but the **Getty Museum** and a scenic drive along **Sunset Boulevard.** are two free ways to experience the best the area has to offer. Veer off Sunset Blvd. onto any public (non-gated) road to see tree-lined rows of well-spaced six-bedroom homes—living here is as costly as in Beverly Hills.

WILSHIRE DISTRICT. L.A.'s culture vultures drive south from Hollywood to peruse the Wilshire District's museums, which glorify everything from tar to Model Ts. **Museum Row** is on the Miracle Mile (Wilshire Blvd. from Fairfax to La Brea Ave.). Developed in the 1920s, the city's first shopping district was designed for those arriving in those new-fangled gizmos called automobiles.

WEST HOLLYWOOD. Once considered a no-man's land between Beverly Hills and Hollywood, West Hollywood is now a city unto itself, as well as the proud abode of Los Angeles's gay community—the city was one of the country's first to be governed by openly gay officials. Though spanning only 2 sq. mi., the area is packed with more restaurants, galleries, boutiques, theaters, and clubs than most cities. The section of Santa Monica Blvd. around San Vicente Blvd. is its oldest gay district. It is home of the legendary 1½ mi. stretch of Sunset Blvd.

known as the **Sunset Strip** (between Doheny Dr. and Crescent Heights Ave.). From its heyday in the 1940s and 50s, the Strip has been a den of L.A.'s rock 'n' roll scene in the 60s and a haven for burnouts in the 70s. Today it is the epitome of diversity, as the opulent from the Westside mix with the quaint from the east—creating the ultimate L.A. nightlife (see **Nightlife,** p. 423). To experience it all, park along the street or in a pay lot and walk or take the **CityLine,** which runs at night along Santa Monica Blvd. (☎800-447-2189. Su-F $0.25, Sa $0.50.)

DOWNTOWN. Say "downtown" to Angelenos and they'll wince—either because they don't know what you're referring to, they know but don't go there, or they work there and are none too happy about it. It is L.A.'s netherland—the place over there. Mayor James Hahn and City Hall strive valiantly to project Downtown as a paradigm of L.A.'s culture and diversity, but the Westside powers have a solid grip on the culture, and the neighborhoods in L.A. County are sharply defined by homogeneity of race and class. Downtown, an uneasy truce prevails between the bustling financiers and the street population, but visitors should be cautious—the area is especially unsafe after business hours and on weekends.

GRIFFITH PARK & GLENDALE. Five times larger than New York's Central Park, Griffith Park is an expansive 4107 acres and the site of many outdoor diversions ranging from golf and tennis to hiking. The L.A. Zoo, the Griffith Observatory and Planetarium, Travel Town, a bird sanctuary, and 52 mi. of trails decorate the dry hills. The park stretches from above North Hollywood to the intersection of Rte. 134 (Ventura Fwy.) and I-5 (Golden State Fwy.). Several of the mountain roads through the park (especially the Vista Del Valle Dr.) offer panoramic views of Downtown L.A., Hollywood, and the Westside. Sadly, heavy rains have made them unsafe for cars, but foot traffic is allowed on most (open daily 5am-10pm).

SAN FERNANDO VALLEY. All the San Fernando Valley wants is a little respect. Yet it can't seem to shake the infamy it gained for breeding the Valley Girl, who started a worldwide trend in the 1980s with her huge hair, and, like, omigod, totally far-out diction. The Valley has been mocked by actors on *Clueless* and *Beverly Hills 90210*, and is often overlooked in City Hall's affairs. It might not be the Westside, but it is more than just a satellite of L.A. After all, most movies and television shows are produced here, not in Hollywood. With its cookie cutter houses and strip malls, the Valley marks the suburban ritual elevated to its highest form.

PASADENA. Every New Year's Day in the US, masses of hung-over, snowbound TV viewers jealously watch the blessed few who march through sunny Pasadena for the Tournament of Roses Parade and **Rose Bowl** football game. While for the nation Pasadena is the home of the Rose Bowl, for Californians, it is a serene, ritzy suburb. With its classy museums, graceful architecture, lively shopping district, and idyllic weather, Pasadena lacks only a coastline. **Old Town,** the Promenade of Pasadena, combines intriguing historic sights with a lively entertainment scene.

ⴲ LOCAL TRANSPORTATION

Nowhere is the god *Automobile* revered more than in L.A., making the City of Angels a transportation hell. Sometimes it seems like all 3.7 million residents are out crowding the freeways at once, leaving little room for clean air, patience, and sanity. The greatest density of Mercedes-Benzes outside Europe can be seen in L.A., and there's no shortage of vehicles affixed with BMW, Audi, or Lexus emblems either. Hand-in-hand with cell phone use, driving takes up a major chunk of any self-respecting Angeleno's day. Those who can afford to invest heavily, since one's car gives the first impression—too often when stopped in traffic.

The roadways are disgustingly jammed and poorly planned. Though renting a car is expensive, especially if you are under 25, it is the best way to navigate these monstrous counties. If you must forego the rental, use the subway and then the bus to navigate L.A. See the **Practical Information** sections for **Hollywood,** p. 379, and **Santa Monica,** p. 380, for info on getting around in those areas of the city.

PUBLIC TRANSPORTATION

In the 1930s and 40s, General Motors (GM), Firestone, and Standard Oil bought up streetcar companies and ran them into the ground, later destroying the rails. This increased dependence on buses and, later, on cars. In 1949, GM was convicted in federal court of criminal conspiracy—but there are still no trolleys.

Six **Metropolitan Transit Authority (MTA) Metro Customer Centers** are available to point mass transit users in the right direction. They have MTA schedules and route maps, as well as a friendly staff to help plan your trip. **Downtown:** Arco Plaza, 515 S. Flower St., Level "C" (open M-F 7:30am-3:30pm); Gateway Transit Center, Union Station E. Portal (open M-F 6am-6:30pm). **East L.A.:** 4501-B Whittier Blvd. (open Tu-Sa 10am-6pm). **San Fernando Valley:** 14435 Sherman Way, Van Nuys (open M-F 10am-6pm). Centers are also located in Baldwin Hills and Wilshire.

For travelers who know where they want to go, MTA provides informative telephone and online assistance. (☎ 800-COMMUTE/266-6883; www.mta.net. Open M-F 6am-8:30pm, Sa-Su 8:30am-6pm.) MTA's hotline covers the metro rail subway and bus routes, as well as DASH connections. L.A. County's commuter rail, **Metrolink,** is under separate management (see below).

BY DASH. The local **DASH shuttle** ($0.25), designed for short distance neighborhood hops, serves major tourist destinations in many communities, including Downtown, Hollywood (along Sunset Blvd.), Fairfax, Midtown, Crenshaw, and Van Nuys/Studio City, as well as Venice in the summer (☎ 213-808-2273; www.ladottransit.com. Open M-F 9am-5pm, Sa 10am-2pm).

BY MTA BUS. Nary an Angeleno will suggest moving about L.A. in anything but a car, but L.A.'s buses are not altogether useless. The MTA used to be known as the RTD (Rapid Transit District), and some of its older buses may still be labeled as such. The name change was apt—most L.A. buses are not rapid by any modern definition of the word. Given the over 200 routes and several independent municipal transit systems that connect to the MTA, it's no easy task to study the timetables. Ninety percent of MTA routes have wheelchair-accessible buses. Appropriate bus stops are marked with the international symbol for disabled access.

Using the MTA to sightsee in L.A. can be frustrating, because attractions tend to be quite spread out. Those determined to see *everything* in L.A. should get behind the wheel of a car. If this is not possible, base yourself in Hollywood (where there are plenty of sights and bus connections), make daytrips, and have plenty of change for the bus. Bus service is dismal in the outer reaches of the city and 2hr. journeys are not unusual. Transferring often involves waits of an hour or more, and L.A. traffic congestion frustrates everyone.

MTA's basic fare is $1.35 (transfer $0.25), seniors and disabled $0.45 (transfer $0.10); exact change is required. Weekly passes ($11) are available at customer service centers and local grocery stores. Transfers can be made between MTA lines or to other transit authorities. **Unless otherwise noted, all route numbers are MTA;** BBBus stands for Big Blue Bus and indicates Santa Monica buses (p. 380).

BY SUBWAY. L.A.'s system of light-rail connections is spreading its tendrils, although it is still far from complete. Where rails do exist, they can often save commuters time otherwise wasted in traffic snarls, and several stations have park-and-ride lots available. The **Blue Line** runs from Downtown to the southern L.A. communities and Long Beach. The **Green Line** goes along I-105 from Norwalk to

Redondo Beach, with shuttle service to LAX at Aviation/I-105. The **Red Line** runs from Downtown through Hollywood to the San Fernando Valley; other branches go west to Wilshire and east to Union Station. A one-way trip costs $1.35, with transfers to bus and rail $1.60; seniors and disabled $0.45, with transfers $0.55. All lines run daily 5am-11pm (info ☎800-266-6883/COMMUTE; www.mta.net).

BY METROLINK TRAIN. Metrolink trains run out of the city from Union Station to Ventura and Orange Counties (M-F), and to Riverside via San Bernardino, Santa Clarita, and Antelope Valley (M-Sa). One-way fares are $4-10.25, depending on the destination. You can only buy them from machines in the station within 3hr. of your departure time. Discounts are available if traveling Saturday or during off-peak hours (8:30am-3:30pm and after 7pm). Beware—trains come and go up to 5min. ahead of schedule. For more info, call ☎800-371-5465.

BY TAXI. If you need a cab, it's best to call Independent (☎213-385-8294 or 800-521-8294), L.A. Taxi/Yellow Cab Co. (☎800-711-8294 or 800-200-1085), or Bell Cab (☎888-235-5222). Be prepared to wait at least 15min. Fare is about $2 per mi. anywhere in the city and approximately $30-35 from the airport to Downtown.

NON-PUBLIC TRANSPORTATION

■**BY CAR.** L.A. may be the most difficult city in the U.S. to get around in without a car. It may also be the most difficult city in which to **rent** a car for younger travelers. Most places will not rent to people under 21, and the ones that do are likely to impose a surcharge that only movie stars can afford to pay (nearly double the standard rate). Drivers between 21 and 25 will incur a lower surcharge.

Nationally known agencies are reputed to have more dependable cars, but the high demand for rental cars assures that even small local companies can survive, and many have much lower rates than the big guys. They are worth looking into, but be forewarned: although you may be planning a budget trip, car rental is not the thing to be thrifty with. National agencies will replace a broken-down car hassle-free; if you want to use a local place, it might be wise to make sure that they will do the same. Local rental companies might quote a very low daily rate and then add extra fees when you return the car. The prices quoted below are intended to give a rough idea of what to expect; ask about airline-related discounts.

There are many paid lots in L.A. (about $7) and most accommodations offer free parking. Metered parking is on every major street, however authorized hours vary so be sure to read all the signs over and over and over again. A quarter buys you anywhere from 7½-30min. The **Automobile Club of Southern California,** 2601 S. Figueroa St., at Adams St., has additional driving info and maps. Club privileges are free for AAA members and cost $2-3 for nonmembers. Their *Westways* magazine is a good source for daytrip or vacation planning. (☎213-741-3686, emergency assistance 800-400-4222. Open M-F 9am-5pm. Other offices in greater L.A.)

Avon, 7080 Santa Monica Blvd. (☎323-850-0826; www.avonrents.com), at La Brea Blvd. Cars $29 per day with 150 mi. free, $175 per week with 750 mi. free, or $600 per month with 1000 mi. free. Collision Damage Waiver $9 per day. No under-25 surcharge. Open M-F 6am-7pm, Sa-Su 7am-5pm.

Avis, 11901 Santa Monica Blvd. (☎310-914-7700), between Barrington Ave. and Bundy St. Economy cars $34 per day or $169 per week with unlimited mileage. CDW $9 per day. Will not rent if under 25. Pick-up available nearby. Open M-F 8am-5pm, Sa 8am-2pm, Su 9am-2pm.

Thrifty (☎310-645-1880 or 800-367-2277; www.thrifty.com), at L.A. airport. Prices vary daily, but drop as low as $25 per day with unlimited mileage in CA, NV, and AZ. CDW $9 per day. Under-25 surcharge $20 per day. Open 24hr.

Alamo (☎310-649-2242 or 800-327-9633; www.alamo.com), at L.A. airport. Prices vary with availability; generally $27-35 per day or $110-155 per week, both with unlimited mileage. CDW $9 per day. Under-25 surcharge $25 per day. Open 24hr.

Enterprise (☎310-649-5400 or 800-RENT-A-CAR; www.enterprise.com), at L.A. airport. Economy cars $23-40 per day or $169 per week, both with unlimited mileage. CDW $9 per day. Under-25 surcharge $10 per day. Open M-Su 6am-10pm.

Lucky, 8620 Airport Blvd. (☎310-641-2323 or 800-400-4736). Provides free transportation to and from LAX. Economy cars $20-30 per day with 150 mi. or $109-169 per week with 1050 mi. included. CDW $9 per day. Under-25 surcharge $5-15 per day. Open daily 8am-6pm.

Universal Rent A Car, 920 S. La Brea Ave. (☎323-954-1186). Cars from $19.99 per day with 150 mi. free, $129 per week with 1050 mi. free. No under-25 surcharge. Open daily 9am-6pm.

FREEWAYS. The freeway is perhaps the most enduring image of L.A. No matter what may separate Angelenos—race, creed, or class—the one thing that unites everyone is the freeway system, a maze of 10- and 12-lane concrete roadways. "Caught in traffic" is the all-purpose excuse for tardiness, guaranteed to garner knowing nods and smiles of consolation from co-workers and acquaintances. In planning your route, note that heavy traffic moves toward Downtown from 7 to 10am on weekdays and streams outbound from 4 to 7pm. However, since L.A. has a huge population that doesn't work 9-to-5, traffic can be as bad at 1pm as it is at 6pm. But no matter how crowded the freeway is, it's almost always quicker and safer than taking surface streets to your destination, unless traveling under the guidance of a seasoned local (many of whom know tried-and-true shortcuts).

Uncongested freeways offer the ultimate in speed and convenience; the trip from Downtown to Santa Monica can take as little as 20min. A nighttime cruise along I-110 (Harbor Fwy.) past Downtown can be exhilarating, as the road whizzes through the tangle of interchanges and the lights of L.A.'s skyscrapers. For freeway info, call **CalTrans** (☎213-897-3693) and refer to the **L.A. Overview map.**

BICYCLES. Unless you have legs and lungs of steel, a bicycle in L.A. is useful only for recreational purposes. Air quality is poor, distances are long, and drivers aren't used to looking out for cyclists. Always wear a helmet; it's illegal to bike on the road without one. For those who really want to explore by bike, the people of **L.A. Bike Tours,** 6733 Hollywood Blvd., offer the best advice as well as tours of Hollywood, Beverly Hills, and Venice Beach that range from 3hr. to an entire day ($30-75). Advanced rides to the Hollywood Sign, the Getty, and a two-day coastal adventure to Santa Barbara are all available by request. (☎323-466-5890 or 888-775-2453; www.labiketours.com. Prices include bike rental and snack.)

If you are not in a group, it's best to rent a bike from L.A. Bike Tours ($15-20 per day or $50-60 per week) and stick to one of many designated bike paths. The most popular route for the casual rider is the **South Bay Bicycle Path,** which runs from Santa Monica to Torrance (19 mi.), winding over the sandy beaches of the South Bay past sunbathers and spandex-clad in-line skaters. The path continues to San Diego. The new **L.A. River Bike Path** runs from Long Beach to Dodger Stadium. The **Nichols Canyon** to **Mulholland Drive Path** attracts many local riders. It also gives a mini-tour of celebrities' homes. Other bike paths include: **San Gabriel River Trail,** a 37 mi. pedal along the river with views of the San Gabriel Valley; **Upper Rio Hondo** (9 mi.) and **Lario Trails** (22 mi.), which are free of traffic; and **Kenneth Newell Bikeway,** a 10 mi. glide through residential Pasadena. For the more serious rider the **Donut Ride** in **Palos Verdes** in South Bay provides hill after hill after hill.

BY WALKING AND HITCHHIKING. L.A. pedestrians are a hapless breed. Unless you're running in the L.A. Marathon, moving from one part of the city to another on foot is a ludicrous idea—distances are just too great. Nevertheless, some colorful areas such as Melrose, Westwood, the Santa Monica Promenade, Hollywood, and Old Pasadena are best explored by foot. Just remember that Californians will stare (and possibly run) you down, and cops may ticket you for setting foot in a crosswalk without a "Walk" signal. For coastal culture lovers, Venice Beach is one of the most enjoyable (and popular) places to walk, with nearby sights and shopping areas. **LA Now,** the publication of the Convention and Visitor Bureau, has an excellent list of walking tours (see **Practical Information: Publications,** p. 379). Since some of the best tour companies are one-person operations, schedules and prices are not written in stone. Look for theme tours (e.g., Graveyard) of celebrity homes geared toward your obsessions. The **Los Angeles Conservancy** (☎213-623-2489; www.laconservancy.org) offers 2½hr. tours of the Downtown area every Saturday at 10am. Tours cost $8; advance reservations are required. Call **Tree People** (☎818-753-4600) for info about Sunday walking tours in Coldwater Canyon Park. Once the sun sets, those on **foot,** especially outside West L.A. and off well-lit main drags, should exercise caution, particularly when alone. Plan your pedestrian routes very carefully—it is worth a detour to avoid passing through heavily crime-ridden areas. **If you hitchhike, you will probably die.** It is exceptionally dangerous, not to mention illegal. There are many other options. Don't even consider it.

⏏ PRACTICAL INFORMATION

TOURIST & FINANCIAL SERVICES

Visitor Information:

L.A. Convention and Visitor Bureau, 685 S. Figueroa St. (☎213-689-8822; www.visitl-anow.com), between Wilshire Blvd. and 7th St. in the Financial District. Staff speaks English, French, Spanish, and Japanese. Detailed bus map of L.A. available. California road map $3. Distributes *LA Now,* a free booklet with tourist and lodging info. Open M-F 8am-5:30pm.

National Park Service, 401 W. Hillcrest Dr. (☎818-597-9192), in Thousand Oaks, in the Conejo Valley. Info on the Santa Monica Mountains (including outdoor activities and special events) in *Outdoors,* a quarterly events calendar. Open daily 9am-5pm.

Sierra Club, 3435 Wilshire Blvd. #320 (☎213-387-4287), between Normandy and Vermont St. Hiking, biking, skiing, and backpacking info. Stores throughout L.A. Sells 4-month event schedules for $10; call for locations. Open M-F 10am-6pm.

Budget Travel:

STA Travel, 7280 Melrose Ave. (☎323-934-8722; tele-booking 800-777-0112), has services for travelers but no gear. Open M-Sa 10am-6pm.

Los Angeles/Santa Monica HI-AYH, 1434 2nd St. (☎310-393-3413), in Santa Monica next door to the hostel. Info and supplies for travelers. Guidebooks, backpacks, money belts, rail passes, and ISICs. Open M-F 10am-5pm, Sa 9am-5pm.

Consulates: Australia, 2049 Century Park East, 19th fl. (☎310-229-4800). Open M-F 9am-5pm; visa desk open M-F 9am-1pm. **South Africa,** 6300 Wilshire Blvd. #600 (☎323-651-0902). Consulate and visa desk open M-F 9am-noon. **UK,** 11766 Wilshire Blvd. #1200 (☎310-481-0031). Open M-F 8:30-11:30am for visas, 8:30am-noon and 2-4pm for consular services, 8:30am-5pm for all other business.

Currency Exchange: At most airport terminals (see **Intercity Transportation,** p. 367), but rates are exorbitant. **American Express** offices have better rates, but charge $5 to change currency and charge a 1% fee on traveler's checks. AmEx **Beverly Hills,** 327 N. Beverly Hills Dr. (☎310-274-8277). Open M-F 10am-6pm, Sa 10am-3pm. Also in **Pas-**

adena, 269 S. Lake Ave. (☎ 626-449-2881 or 888-533-7283). Open M-F 8:30am-6pm, Sa 10am-2pm. Other locations in **Torrance** and **Costa Mesa. Banknotes Exchange,** 520 S. Grand Ave. L 100 (☎213-627-5404), has no fee for changing currency; charges a 3% fee for traveler's checks. Open M-F 9am-5:30pm, Sa 9am-1pm.

LOCAL SERVICES

Central Public Library, 630 W. 5th St. (☎213-612-3200, events line 213-228-7040), Downtown between Grand Ave. and Flower St. Present ID with current local address to get a library card; reading room open to all card holders. Library houses foreign-language books, weekly exhibits, and activities including readings, films, and workshops. Tours M-F 12:30pm, Sa 11am and 2pm, Su 2pm. Open M-Th 10am-8pm, F-Sa 10am-6pm, Su 1-5pm. Validated parking available at 524 S. Flower St. with L.A. library card.

Ticket Agency: Ticketmaster (☎213-480-3232), charges high per-ticket fees. A better bet is to contact the box office directly.

Surf Conditions: Recorded info on Malibu, Santa Monica, and South Bay (☎310-457-9701). Most FM radio stations have a surf report at noon.

Weather Conditions: Detailed region-by-region report (☎213-554-1212).

Highway Conditions: Recorded info may help you stave off an afternoon parked on the freeway (☎800-427-7623). KFWB 980 AM has reports every 10min. for those driving.

LOCAL MEDIA

Television Stations: ABC (Channel 7); **CBS** (Channel 2); **Fox** (Channel 11); **NBC** (Channel 4); **KTLA/WB** (Channel 5); **UPN** (Channel 13).

National Public Radio: 91.5 FM for all considerable things.

Other Radio Stations: Old School/R&B "Hot" 92.3 FM; **Pop/Rock/Top 40** "Star" 98.7 FM; **Pop/Top 40** KIIS 102.7 FM; **Soft Rock** 103.5 FM; **Rock** KROQ 106.7 FM; **Oldies** 101.1 FM; **Classic Rock** 104.3 FM; **Smooth Jazz** "The Wave" 94.7 FM.

EMERGENCY & COMMUNICATIONS

Rape Crisis: ☎310-392-8381.

24hr. Pharmacy: Sav-On, 3010 S. Sepulveda Blvd. (☎310-478-9821), in West L.A. For other 24hr. locations, call ☎800-627-2866.

Hospitals: Cedars-Sinai Medical Center, 8700 Beverly Blvd. (☎310-855-5000, emergency 423-8644). **Good Samaritan Hospital,** 616 S. Witmer St. (☎213-977-2121, emergency 977-2420). **UCLA Medical Center,** 10833 Le Conte Ave. (☎310-825-9111, emergency 825-2111).

AREA CODES. L.A. is big. Really big. There are many area codes. Here's a handy guide to them:

213 covers Downtown L.A.

323 covers Hollywood, Vernon, Huntington Park, Montebello, and West Hollywood.

310 covers Santa Monica, Malibu, and Westside.

310 and **562** cover southern and eastern L.A. County.

626 covers the San Gabriel Valley and Pasadena.

818 covers Burbank, Glendale, San Fernando Valley, Van Nuys, and La Cañada.

909 covers the eastern border of L.A. County.

Planned Parenthood (☎323-226-0800). Various locations in the city; call for the nearest one. Birth control, prenatal care, STD treatment, abortions, pregnancy testing, HIV testing, and counseling. Call 1 week in advance for appointments. Hours and fees vary.

Free Clinics: Hollywood-Sunset Free Clinic, 3324 W. Sunset Blvd. (☎323-660-7959). Provides general medicine, family planning, and psychiatric care for people without an insurance policy or HMO. No mandatory fees. Appointments only; call M, W, or F 10am-noon to schedule. **Valley Free Clinic,** 6801 Coldwater Canyon (☎818-763-8836), in North Hollywood. Women's health, birth control, medical counseling, drug addiction services, and free HIV testing. Appointments only; call weeks in advance M-F 10am-4pm.

Post Office: Central branch at 7101 S. Central Ave. (☎800-275-8777). Open M-F 7am-7pm, Sa 7am-3pm. **Postal Code: 90001.**

PUBLICATIONS

The free *L.A. Weekly*, which comes out on Thursdays, is the definitive source of entertainment listings, and is available at shops, restaurants, and newsstands. L.A. has a number of "industry" (i.e. movie) papers; the best-known are *Variety* and *The Hollywood Reporter*. The *Los Angeles Times* (newsstand $0.25, Su $1.50) defeats all rivals. The *Times* "Calendar" section has the scoop on the current L.A. scene. *The Los Angeles Sentinel* is L.A.'s largest **African-American** paper. UCLA's **student** paper, *The Daily Bruin*, comes out during the school year. Four of the most popular **gay and lesbian** entertainment magazines are *Fab!*, *Vibe*, *The Frontiers*, and *Edge*. L.A. also has numerous foreign-language publications. The **Spanish** *La Opinión* is the largest, but two **Korean** papers (*The Korean Central Daily* and *The Korea Times*) each have circulations approaching 75,000. The *International Daily News* and the *Chinese Daily News* serve the **Chinese**-speaking community. L.A.'s gargantuan newsstands offer not only muscle, car, sports, fashion, and skin mags, but also many foreign-language publications. **World Wide,** 1101 Westwood Blvd., at Kinross Ave., is a fine example. (Open daily 7am-midnight.)

HOLLYWOOD PRACTICAL INFORMATION

Public Transit: Important buses: **#2** and **#3** run along Sunset Blvd., **#4** along Santa Monica Blvd., **#10** along Melrose Ave. Fare $1.35, transfers $0.25. 1-month pass $42, weekly $11.

Parking: Ample amount of metered parking on the street. 30 min. for $0.25. Lots of public lots charging from $1.50 per hr. to $10 per night. Public lot north of Hollywood Blvd. at Cherokee St. offers 2hr. free with each additional hour $1 for up to 3 more hours.

Currency Exchange: Cash It Here, 6565 Hollywood Blvd. (☎323-464-2718), at Whitley St. 1% commission. Open 24hr. M-F, Su 8am-6pm; Sa hours vary.

Police: 1358 N. Wilcox Ave. (☎213-485-4302).

24hr. Pharmacy: Rite-Aid, 7900 W. Sunset Blvd. (☎323-876-4466), in Hollywood.

Hospital: Queen of Angels Hollywood Presbyterian Medical Center, 1300 N. Vermont Ave. (☎213-413-3000). Emergency room open 24hr.

Internet Access: Many L.A. coffeehouses have **CaféNet** computers, which have Internet access but not text-based email. These Hollywood locations have both: **Cyber Java,** 7080 Hollywood Blvd. (☎323-466-5600). $2.50 per 15 min, $9 per hr. or $45 for a 10hr. card. Open M-F 7am-11:30pm, Sa-Su 8am-11:30pm. **@coffee,** 7200 Melrose Ave. (☎323-938-9985). Happy hour before 11am $5 per hr; after 11am $2 per 10min., $5 per 30min., $7 per hr. includes a coffee. Open M-Sa 8am-8pm, Su 9am-7pm. **Kinkos,** 9334 Wilshire Blvd. (☎310-271-1258). $0.20 per min. Open M-Th 7am-11pm, F 7am-8pm, Sa 8am-6pm, Su 9am-10pm.

Post Office: 1615 Wilcox Ave. (☎800-275-8777). Open M-F 8:30am-5:30pm, Sa 8:30am- 3:30pm. **Postal Code: 90028.**

SANTA MONICA PRACTICAL INFORMATION

Public Transit: Santa Monica Municipal Bus Lines (☎310-451-5444). With over 1000 stops in Santa Monica, L.A., and Culver City, the "Big Blue Bus" (BBBus, as featured in *Speed*, see p. 23) is faster and cheaper than the MTA. Fare for most routes $0.50; transfer tickets for MTA buses $0.25; transfers to other BBBuses free. Important buses: **#1** and **2** connect Santa Monica and Venice via Santa Monica Blvd. and Wilshire Blvd. respectively; **#3** goes to the L.A. airport; **#10** provides express service from downtown Santa Monica (at 7th St. and Grand Ave.) to Downtown L.A. **The Tide Shuttle** runs to downtown ($0.25). Signs with route info litter downtown Santa Monica. Runs every 15min. M-F noon-10pm.

Equipment Rentals: Perry's Beach Rentals, Ocean Front Walk (☎310-458-3975; www.actionsportsrentals.com), in the eye-catching blue buildings north and south of the pier and just before Venice Beach. Main location at 930 Ocean Front Walk. In-line skates and bikes $6 per hr., $18 per day; tandem bikes $10 per hr., $22 per day; boogie boards $3 per hr., $8 per day. Student discounts offered. Free beverage with rental. On-site cafe (burgers $4.25). Open daily 9am-dark. **Skate City,** 111 Broadway (☎310-319-9272), rents in-line skates for $5 per hr., $10 per day. Open Su-W 10:30am-6pm, Th-Sa 10:30am-8pm. **Blazing Saddles Bike Rentals,** 320 Santa Monica Pier (☎310-393-9778), is a bike rental bonanza with mountain and road bikes ($6-11 per hr., $18-30 per day). Tandems and baby seats also available. Helmets, locks, and racks included. Open M-F 9am-7:30pm, Sa-Su 9am-8pm.

Parking: 6 lots flank the 3rd St. Promenade, 3 are accessible from 4th St., and 3 from 2nd St. First 2hr. free, each additional 30min. $0.50. Santa Monica Place Mall has free parking for up to 3hr. ($3 flat fee after 5pm); others are metered ($0.50 per hr.). Downtown streets have meters as well (also $0.50 per hr.). All-day beachside parking $6-10.

Currency Exchange: Western Union, 1454 4th St. (☎310-394-7211), at Broadway. Open M-F 9am-6pm, Sa 9am-3pm.

Library: L.A. Public Library, Santa Monica branch, 1343 6th St. (☎310-458-8600), at Santa Monica Blvd. Open M-Th 10am-9pm, F-Sa 10am-5:30pm, Su 1-5pm.

Medical Services: Santa Monica/UCLA Medical Center, 1250 16th St. (☎310-319-4765). Emergency room open 24hr.

Police: 1685 Main St. (☎310-395-9931).

Post Office: 1248 5th St. (☎800-275-8777), at Arizona Blvd. Open M-F 9am-6pm, Sa 9am-3pm. **Postal Code:** 90401.

■ ACCOMMODATIONS

Cheap accommodations in Los Angeles are often unsafe. It can be difficult to gauge quality from the exterior, so ask to see a room before committing. For those willing to share a room and a bathroom, hostels are a saving grace, although Americans should be aware that many only accept international travelers. These hostels require an international passport, but well-traveled Americans with proof of travel (passports, out-of-state identification, or plane tickets often do the trick) may be permitted to stay. It never hurts to ask for off-season or student discounts, and occasionally managers will lower prices to snare a hesitant customer.

In choosing where to stay, the first consideration should be location. If you don't have wheels, decide which element of L.A. appeals to you the most. Those visiting for beach culture should choose lodgings in Venice or Santa Monica. Avid sightseers will be better off in Hollywood or the more expensive (but cleaner and nicer) Westside. Downtown has public transportation connections, but is unsafe after dark. Even those with cars should choose lodgings proximate to their interests to keep car-bound time to a minimum. **Listed prices do not include L.A.'s 14% hotel tax.**

HOLLYWOOD

Staying in Hollywood puts you smack in the middle of it all, which is a blessing for some and a curse for others. Though the area is crawling with people by day, avoid hanging out on street corners late at night. Always exercise caution while scouting out one the budget hostels on or around Hollywood Blvd., especially east of the main strips. Overall, the accommodations are generally good and a much better value than most others in L.A.

Hollywood Bungalows International Youth Hostel, 2775 W. Cahuenga Blvd. (☎888-259-9990; www.hollywoodbungalows.com), just north of the Hollywood Bowl. Deep in the hills of Hollywood, this newly renovated mini-compound cultivates a wacky summer camp atmosphere, with spacious rooms and nightly jam sessions. Pool, weight room, big screen TV, and mini-diner. Cable and VCR in all rooms. Internet access. Meals offered 3 times per day (breakfast $3.50; dinner $10). Lockers $0.25. Linen and parking included. Laundry ($1.25 wash; $0.75 dry). On-site Universal Rent-a-Car (see p. 376). Check-in 24hr. $14 airport shuttle. Stay 3 nights for free one-way transportation to airport. **Passport and international airline ticket or college ID required.** 6- to 10-bed co-ed dorms with bathroom $15-19; private doubles for up to 4 people $59. ❷

USAHostels Hollywood, 1624 Schrader Blvd. (☎323-462-3777 or 800-524-6783; www.usahostels.com), south of Hollywood Blvd., west of Cahuenga Blvd. Stay for more than a day at the hostel and get free pickup from airport, bus, and train stations. This lime-green and blue-dotted chain hostel is packed with young people looking to have some fun. Special events are offered 7 nights a week, highlighted by free comedy W and Su. Purchase a raffle ticket in exchange for a beer or a shot. Beach shuttles run T, Th, and Su free of charge. To use lockers, bring your own lock or buy one for $3. All-you-can-eat pancakes, linen, and parking included. Dinner $5. **Passport or proof of travel required.** Dorms (6-8 beds) with private bath $17; private rooms for 2-4 people $38-46. Prices discounted $1-2 during winter off-season. ❷

Orange Drive Manor, 1764 N. Orange Dr. (☎323-850-0350). This pleasant, converted mini-mansion in a quiet residential neighborhood is the perfect tranquil retreat. Don't be confused by the lack of a sign—this house is your hostel. Cable TV lounge and limited kitchen with microwave and fridge. Spacious, clean rooms with antique furniture. Internet access. Lockers $0.75. Parking $5 per night. Reservations recommended. **US citizens and non-students permitted.** Dorms (4-6 beds), some with private baths, $19-23; private rooms $37-47. Minimal discount with ISIC card. No credit cards. ❸

Student Inn International Hostel, 7038½ Hollywood Blvd. (☎323-469-6781 or 800-557-7038; www.studentinn.com), on the Walk of Fame. Hands down the most economical choice around. Free pickup from airport, bus, and train stations. Small kitchen, cable TV lounge, free Internet access, scanner and printer, discounted tickets to theme parks. Free lockers (bring a lock). 3 small meals a day and linen included. Work at reception in exchange for a night's stay. Call far in advance for reservations. **International passport required.** Dorm $16 per night. Rooms with 2 double beds and private bath $45 per night. Flash your *Let's Go* book and get $2 off the price of a bed. ❷

Liberty Hotel, 1770 Orchid Ave. (☎323-962-1788), south of Franklin Ave. Small hotel located on a quiet and clean residential street only 1 block north of Hollywood Blvd. Free coffee and parking; coin laundry. Add $5 for microwave and fridge or just use the ones in the lobby. Reception 8am-11pm. Check-out 11am. Some rooms have A/C and either tile floors or carpet. King bed or 2 full-size beds $45-60 for 1-4 persons. ❸

Hollywood International Hostel, 6820 Hollywood Blvd. (☎323-463-0797 or 800-750-6561; www.hollywoodhostels.com). Front-row seats overlooking the Walk of Fame and the new Kodak Theatre. Lounge with TV, billiards, and old arcade games. Loopy starlets and aspiring screenwriters make the hostel a volatile soap opera. Discounted tours and car rentals. Small kitchen. Toast and tea breakfast. Lockers $0.25. Laundry ($1 wash;

$0.50 dry). Reception open 24hr. Reserve ahead with credit card. Free pickup from plane, train, and bus. Linens included. **International passport required.** Single-sex 2- to 4- bed dorms with shared bath $18; private rooms $32. Weekly dorms $112. ❷

Hollywood International Hotel, 1921 N. Highland Ave. (☎323-876-6544). This pink adobe abode was the site of Hollywood's oldest hostel until it began welcoming drugs and prostitution. Under new management, it has cleaned up its act. Distance from Hollywood makes it quiet. 2 kitchens. Lounge with billiards and TV. Internet access. Laundry ($1 wash; $0.75 dry). 4- to 6-bed dorms $18. Private rooms $45-63. ❸

SANTA MONICA & VENICE

Accommodations in Santa Monica and Venice range from cheap oceanfront hostels to expensive oceanfront hotels. Depending on the hostel/hotel, the tax on your room may be 8.5% or 14%. Everything fills quickly in summer; book early. Drivers should look for accommodations that include parking or consider staying farther from the beach where there is more street parking as overnight parking is very limited. For those venturing into L.A. proper, the city center is connected to Santa Monica by the MTA or Santa Monica's Big Blue Bus (**BBBus,** see p. 380).

▣ **Los Angeles/Santa Monica (HI-AYH),** 1436 2nd St. (☎310-393-9913; www.hilosangeles.org), Santa Monica. Take MTA #33 from Union Station to 2nd St. and Broadway, BBBus #3 from LAX to 4th St. and Broadway, or BBBus #10 from Union Station. Next door to the associated **SaMo Travelers Center.** Welcoming travelers of all backgrounds and ages, and only one block from the promenade, this hostel can afford to be choosy. Righteous enough to enforce a no-alcohol policy and 10pm-8am quiet hour. Rooms are small but common spaces well kept and well attended. Newly renovated kitchen, 2 nightly movies, library, central courtyard. Various breakfast foods served 7:30-10:30am ($2-4). Safe deposit boxes and lockers. Laundry wash $1, dry $0.75. Pay garages nearby. 24hr. security and check-in. 10 consecutive day max. stay. In summer, reserve well in advance by phone or at www.hiayh.org. 4-10 bed dorms $25-27, non-members $28-30; private doubles $67-73. Group packages available for 8+ people. ❷

Cadillac Hotel, 8 Dudley Ave., Venice (☎310-399-8876; www.thecadillachotel.com), directly off the Ocean Front Walk, in Venice. $11 airport shuttle. Discounted car rental with free pickup. Free parking. Sauna, rooftop sundeck with spectacular view, and well-equipped gym. Rooms have TVs and private baths. Internet access $1 per 10min. Laundry $0.75 wash, $0.50 dry. Reservations recommended. 4 person dorms $25. Work in exchange for night stay. "Family room" with queen and bunk $99; standard room $89. Requires 2 out of 3 of the following: valid driver's license, credit card, or passport. ❷

Venice Beach Cotel, 25 Windward Ave., (☎310-399-7649; www.venicebeachcotel.com), above St. Mark's Restaurant, in Venice. From the L.A. airport, take BBBus #3, transfer to #2, get off at the Venice Beach post office, and walk 1 block toward shore. International staff and guests make the cramped quarters lively and livable. Outdated BYOB bar area opens nightly 7pm. Free tea and coffee. Use of tennis rackets, table tennis, and boogie boards ($20 deposit). Breakfast $1.25-$3.50. Linen included. No laundry. $5 key deposit. Reception and security 24hr. Reservations always recommended. 3, 4, and 6 bed dorms with ocean view and bath $17; doubles (some with private bath, TV, and view) $35-49; triples with bath and view $60. **Passport** required. ❷

Share-Tel Apartments, 20 Brooks Ave., (☎310-392-0325; www.share-tel.com), half a block from the beach, in Venice. Folks in their mid-20s and up crowd this hostel and smoke on the patio. For the location, amenities, and price Share-Tel beats many. Dorm rooms have baths and kitchenettes. Toast and tea breakfast. Free coffee and tea 24hr. $5 BBQ Sa-Su 7-9pm. Lockers $0.50 per opening. Linen and key deposit $20. 24hr. check-in. 4-8 bed dorms $20, weekly $125. Private rooms use dorm bath. Private twin $46, $300 weekly; doubles $50, $330 weekly. Weekly prices lower in winter. No credit cards. **Valid international passport** with proof of travel or **student ID** required. ❷

Santa Monica and Venice

♠ ACCOMMODATIONS

Cadillac Hotel, 12
Hostel California, 14
Hotel California, 7
Santa Monica HI-AYH, 4
Share-Tel Apartments, 8
Venice Beach Cotel, 11

♦ FOOD

Aunt Kizzy's Back Porch, 16
Big Daddy's, 10
Big Dean's "Muscle-In" Cafe, 6
Bread & Porridge, 2
Britannia Pub, 3
Fritto Misto, 5
Rose Cafe and Market, 13
Sidewalk Cafe, 9
Tony P's Dockside Grill, 15
Toppers Restaurant and
    Cantina, 1

LOS ANGELES

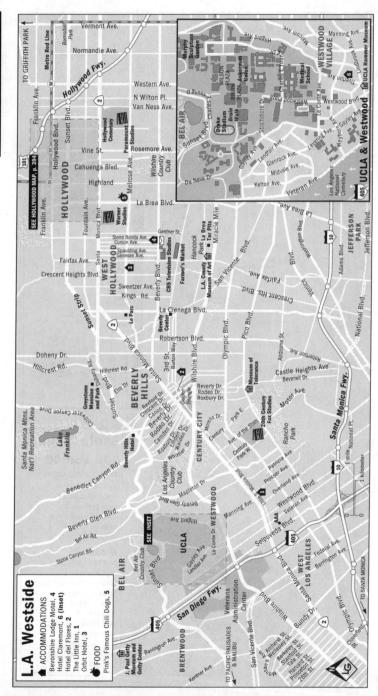

L.A. Westside

▲ ACCOMMODATIONS
Bevonshire Lodge Motel, 4
Hotel Claremont, 6 (Inset)
Hotel del Flores, 2
The Little Inn, 1
Orbit Hotel, 3

● FOOD
Pink's Famous Chili Dogs, 5

■ J. Paul Getty Museum and Getty Center

UCLA & Westwood

SEE HOLLYWOOD MAP, p. 394

TO GRIFFITH PARK

Metro Red Line

Barnsdall Park

Vermont Ave.

Normandie Ave.

Hollywood Fwy.

Franklin Ave.

Western Ave.

N Wilton Pl.

Van Ness Ave.

Hollywood Blvd.

Sunset Blvd.

Vine St.

Cahuenga Blvd.

Highland

HOLLYWOOD

Hollywood Cemetery

Paramount Studios

Rosemore Ave.

Wilshire Country Club

Melrose Ave.

La Brea Blvd.

Fountain Ave.

Warner Studios

Santa Monica Blvd.

Gardner St.

Sierra Bonita Ave.
Curson Ave.

Spaulding Ave.
Genesee Ave.

Fairfax Ave.

Crescent Heights Blvd.

WEST HOLLYWOOD

CBS Television Studios

Beverly Blvd.

Farmer's Market

Hancock Park

Miracle Mile

L.A. County Museum of Art

La Brea Tar Pits

San Vicente Blvd.

Sweetzer Ave.

Kings Rd.

La Cienega Blvd.

Beverly Center

Robertson Blvd.

Olympic Blvd.

Pico Blvd.

Washington Blvd.

JEFFERSON PARK

Adams Blvd.

Jefferson Blvd.

Fairfax Ave.

Sunset Strip

Le Parc

Doheny Dr.

Hillcrest Rd.

Hillcrest Rd.

3rd St.

Burton Way

Wilshire Blvd.

Museum of Tolerance

Castle Heights Ave.

Beverwil Dr.

Santa Monica Fwy.

Santa Monica Mtns.
Nat'l Recreation Area

Greystone Mansion and Park

Elm Dr.

Beverly Dr.

Rodeo Dr.

Rexford Dr.

Crescent Dr.

Canon Dr.

Camden Dr.

Roxbury Dr.

Walden Dr.

BEVERLY HILLS

Golden Triangle

Moreno Dr.

Park E.

20th Century Fox Studios

Motor Ave.

Rancho Park

Lake Franklin

Coldwater Canyon Drive

Benedict Canyon Rd.

Beverly Hills Hotel

Los Angeles Country Club

Maplton Dr.

CENTURY CITY

Ave. of the Stars

Century Park W.

Patricia Ave.

Prosser Ave.

Overland Ave.

Westwood Blvd.

Veteran Ave.

Beverly Glen Blvd.

Mapleton Dr.

Beverly Glen Blvd.

Bel Air Rd.

Stone Canyon Rd.

BEL AIR

Bel Air Country Club

Hilgard Ave.

SEE INSET

UCLA

Gayley Ave.

Landfair Ave.

WESTWOOD

Le Conte Dr.

Manning Ave.

Sepulveda Blvd.

405

Veterans Administration Center

San Diego Fwy.

405

BRENTWOOD

Barrington Ave.

Kenter Ave.

Sunset Blvd.

Gayley Ave.

Stanton Blvd.

WEST LOS ANGELES

Santa Monica Blvd.

Federal Ave.

Barrington Ave.

Wilshire Blvd.

Bundy Dr.

TO SANTA MONICA

TO PACIFIC PALISADES & MALIBU

San Vicente Blvd.

S. Amherst Ave.
Wellesley Ave.
Beverley St.
Stanton St.
Tulia St.
Harvard St.
Princeton St.
26th St.

Cloverdale

Olympic Blvd.

2

1 mile National Pl.

1 kilometer

INSET (UCLA & Westwood):

Manning Ave.

Hilgard Ave.

Malcolm Ave.

Tiverton Ave.

Manning Ave.

Lindbrook Dr.

WESTWOOD VILLAGE

UCLA Hammer Museum

Murphy Sculpture Garden

WILSON PLAZA

BRUIN PLAZA

Ackerman Union

Medical School

Westwood Plaza

Bruin Walk

Charles E. Young Dr.

Strathmore Dr.

Levering Ave.

Le Conte Ave.

Weyburn Ave.

Gayley Ave.

BEL AIR

Drake Stadium

Sunset Blvd.

De Neve Dr.

Charing Cross Rd.

Hilgard Ave.

Glenrock Ave.

Midvale Ave.

Kelton Ave.

Landfair Ave.

Veteran Ave.

Los Angeles National Cemetery

405

Hostel California, 2221 Lincoln Blvd., (☎310-305-0250; kschmahle@aol.com) park free in lot off Lucille Ave., 1 block north of Venice Blvd, in Venice. Take MTA #33 or 333 from Downtown. Free airport pickup. Walk 1 mi. to the beach or rent a bike ($8). Pool table, big-screen TV, kitchen, and laundry. Linen included. Key deposit $5. Co-ed and single-sex dorms. Military style 30-bunk barrack $13.50; tight, dark 6-bed dorms $17; doubles $43. 1 day free for weekly bookings in the dorms only. Prices increase slightly July-Oct. **Passport** with proof of travel or **out-of-state driver's license** required. ❶

Hotel California, 1670 Ocean Ave., (☎310-393-2363 or 866-571-0000; www.hotelca.com) Steps from the ocean, this newly renovated hotel is a great deal for its beachfront location. All rooms include satellite TV, mini-fridge, and surfboard shaped carpets. Suites with kitchenettes, dining tables, pull-out bed, stereo, and balcony available. Private beach access for all guests. Standard room with queen or two doubles $169 in the high season. 20% off if stay 7+ nights. Credit card required. ❺

WESTSIDE: BEVERLY HILLS & WESTWOOD

The snazzy and safe Westside has excellent public transportation to the beaches. The area's affluence, however, means less bang for your buck; there are few hostel-type accommodations. Those planning to stay at least one month in summer or six months during the school year (Sept.-June) can contact the **UCLA Off-Campus Housing Office,** 350 De Neve Dr. (☎310-825-4491; www.cho.ucla.edu), where a roommate bulletin board lists students who have a spare room, as well as sublets and rentals. UCLA's student newspaper, the *Daily Bruin*, lists even more info (available around campus or at www.dailybruin.ucla.edu).

▨ **Orbit Hotel and Hostel,** 7950 Melrose Ave. (☎323-655-1510; www.orbithotel.com), west of Fairfax Ave. in West Hollywood. Opened by 2 young L.A. locals 3 years ago, Orbit deserves top honors for location and livability. Fashion-conscious furniture and large room fans. Spacious retro kitchen and big-screen TV lounge area, small courtyard, and a late-night party room. Free breakfast. Free TV show tickets. Internet access. Car rental $20 per day. Parking available. 6-bed dorms $17; 4-bed dorms $20. Private rooms with TV and bath $45. Dorms accept international students with **passport** proof only. ❷

Hotel Claremont, 1044 Tiverton Ave. (☎310-208-5957 or 800-266-5957), in Westwood Village near UCLA. Pleasant and inexpensive. Owned and operated by the same family that built the hotel over 60 years ago. Clean rooms with antique dressers, ceiling fans, private baths, and phones. Microwave and free coffee in the lobby next to a pleasant, Victorian-style TV lounge. Daily maid service. Reservations recommended, especially in June. Singles $45; doubles $51; 2 full-size beds for up to 4 people $60. ❸

The Little Inn, 10604 Little Santa Monica Blvd. (☎310-475-4422). Classic old school motel off a little dirt road. Clean, color-coordinated rooms. A/C, cable TV, and fridges. Parking included. Check-out 11am. 1 bed (up to 2 people) $50; 2 beds $55. Additional guests $5 per person. During the high season expect prices to rise $10. *Let's Go* readers get special rates Sept. 20-July 1 (excluding major holiday periods). ❸

Bevonshire Lodge Motel, 7575 Beverly Blvd. (☎323-936-6154). Seconds from CBS Studios, the staff welcomes many *The Price is Right* contestant hopefuls to the newly renovated rooms. A/C, mini-fridge, cable TV, daily maid service, and parking included. Pool and courtyard. Singles and doubles $55-65; 5-person suites (2 doubles and a single) $70-80. King bed with kitchen for 2 people $61-71. 10% ISIC discount. ❹

Hotel del Flores, 409 N. Crescent Dr. (☎310-274-5115), in Beverly Hills. 3 blocks from Rodeo Dr., this vintage hotel hosts shoppers and up-and-comers. The only budget place in Beverly Hills; hotels next door charge twice as much. Most rooms with TV, fans, and fridges. Shared baths on 2nd floor are pleasant and well-lit. Very limited street parking. Check-out noon. Singles with shared bath from $55; doubles with shared bath $55-75, with private bath $65-75. 2 beds (sleeps 4) with private bath $125-135. Weekly rates available. ISIC or student ID discount. Mention *Let's Go* for a 5% discount. ❸

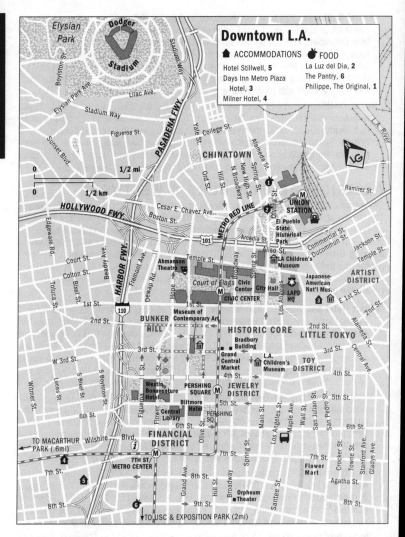

Downtown L.A.

🏠 ACCOMMODATIONS 🍴 FOOD

Hotel Stillwell, **5**
Days Inn Metro Plaza
   Hotel, **3**
Milner Hotel, **4**

La Luz del Dia, **2**
The Pantry, **6**
Philippe, The Original, **1**

DOWNTOWN

Downtown L.A. is probably not the best place to look for accommodations. Although busy and fairly safe by day, the area empties and becomes less safe at night. If you have an overwhelming desire to stay Downtown, some affordable lodgings can be found in the area. If possible, remember to travel in groups.

Milner Hotel, 813 S. Flower St. (☎ 213-627-6981 or 800-827-0411). Take the Prime Shuttle ($13) from the airport, bus, or train station, and get reimbursed when you stay at this centrally located Downtown spot. Small, well-furnished rooms with A/C, cable TV, and continental breakfast. Singles $50-70; doubles $60-80. ❸

Hotel Stillwell, 838 S. Grand Ave. (☎213-627-1151 or 800-553-4774). A sensible option. The historic building has been restored and refurbished with modern conveniences. In-house Indian and Mexican restaurants and Hank's Bar. A/C and cable TV. Parking $3.75 per day. Weekly rooms fill quickly. Singles $56, weekly $285; doubles $67/$371. Prices include tax. Rooms are $35 and $45 plus tax with ISIC card. ❹

Days Inn Metro Plaza Hotel, 711 N. Main St. (☎213-680-0200 or 800-223-2223), at Cesar Chavez Ave., near Union Station. Hidden in a plaza, the glass entry doors open onto a fine hotel. Big rooms with TVs and refrigerators. Parking and continental breakfast. Singles $69; doubles $85. $10 per each additional person. ❹

🏕 CAMPING

L.A. has no campgrounds convenient to public transportation. Even drivers face at least a 45min. commute from Downtown. One nearby L.A. County campground, **Leo Carrillo State Beach ❶** (☎310-457-1324), lies on Hwy. 1 (the PCH), 20 mi. north of Malibu. It has 100 developed sites with flush toilets and showers ($12). Nearby **Point Mugu** has 57 sites at **Sycamore Canyon ❶** with flush toilets and showers ($12) and 75 primitive sites at the **Thornhill Broome ❶** area with chemical toilets and cold showers ($12). **Malibu Creek State Park ❶,** off Las Virgenes Rd., 6 mi. north of Hwy. 1, has 50 sites with flush toilets and showers ($15). Call ☎818-880-0367 for info, and ReserveAmerica (☎800-444-7275) for required reservations.

🍴 FOOD

Eating in Los Angeles, the city of the health-conscious, is more than just *eating*. Thin figures and fat wallets are a powerful combination—L.A. lavishes in the most heavenly and healthy recipes. There are restaurants where the main objective is to be seen and the food is secondary, as well as those where the food itself seems too beautiful to be eaten. And though few are struck by the beauty of a wrapped (veggie) burger, L.A. elevates fast food and chain restaurants to heights unknown in the rest of the country—chains are a way of life, as Angelenos want quality and convenience. For the supreme burger-and-fries experience, try ▧**In 'n' Out Burger,** a beloved chain symbolized by a '57 Chevy. **Mel's Diner** and **Johnny Rocket's** revive the never-really-lost era of the American diner; their milkshakes are a heady experience. All **Fatburgers** come with frank witticisms, free of charge. The current craze is lard- and cholesterol-free "healthy Mexican"—▧**Baja Fresh** leads the pack. Californians crave pizza at the **California Pizza Kitchen. Quizno's** reheats its fresh baked bread for sub lovers. Surfer meets Mexican at Hawaiian-born **Wahoo's Fish Tacos.** If you're looking to cook, ▧**Trader Joe's** specializes in budget gourmet food. They save by doing their own packaging and, as a result, you get amazing deals like $4 bottles of choice Napa wines. There are 84 locations; call ☎800-SHOP-TJS/746-7857 to find the nearest one. (Most open daily 9am-9pm.)

Of course, food in L.A. isn't just about California Cuisine. The range of culinary options is a direct result of the city's ethnic diversity. Jewish and Eastern European food is most prevalent in Fairfax; Mexican in East L.A.; Japanese, Chinese, Vietnamese, and Thai around Little Tokyo, Chinatown, and Monterey Park; and seafood along the coast. Listings of **late-night** restaurants and cafes are on p. 423.

MARKETS. L.A.'s enormous public markets give the visitor a first-hand look at the variety and volume of foodstuffs available here. ▧**Farmer's Market,** 6333 W. 3rd St., Wilshire District, at Fairfax Ave., has over 160 produce stalls, as well as international food booths, handicraft shops, souvenir stores, and a phenomenal juice bar. Take lunch upstairs to the **Beverly Hills Art League Gallery** and munch among the paintings of local amateur artists. There's delectable produce, but bargains are becoming increasingly rare. (☎ 323-932-8616. Open M-Sa 9am-7pm, Su 10am-6pm.) A less touristy and less expensive source of produce is the **Grand Central Public Market,** 317 S. Broadway, a large baby blue building Downtown, between 3rd and 4th St. Grand Central has more than 50 stands selling produce, clothing, housewares, costume jewelry, vitamins, and fast food. This vast space is always riotously busy and entertaining. (☎ 213-624-2378. Open daily 9am-6pm.) **◙Trader Joe's** specializes in budget gourmet food. They save by doing their own packaging and, as a result, you get amazing deals like $4 bottles of choice Napa wines. There are 84 locations (most of them in the trendier neighborhoods); call ☎ 800-SHOP-TJS/746-7857 to find the nearest one. (Most open daily 9am-9pm.)

HOLLYWOOD

Aspiring screenwriters and starlets still constitute much of Hollywood's population. Most are single, hungry, and nearly broke after paying the rent on their bungalows. As a result, Hollywood offers the best budget dining in L.A. As an added bonus, if you're in the right place at the right time, you may see celebrities chowing on the same lunch special as yours. **Hollywood** and **Sunset Boulevards** have excellent international cuisine, while **Fairfax Avenue** hosts Mediterranean-style restaurants and kosher delis. **Melrose Avenue** is full of chic cafes, many with outdoor people-watching patios. As Hollywood is the heart of L.A.'s pounding nightlife, many of its best restaurants are open around the clock (see **Late-Night Restaurants,** p. 423).

◙ **Duke's Coffee Shop,** 8909 Sunset Blvd. (☎ 310-652-3100), in West Hollywood. The legendary Duke's is the best place to see hung-over rockers looking for breakfast. If the seats don't testify to it, the walls will—they are plastered with autographed album covers. Communal, canteen-style tables are a regular meeting place. Try "Sandy's Favorite" (with green peppers, cubed potatoes, and scrambled eggs) for $7.25. Entrees $5-11. Attendant parking in rear $1. Open M-F 7:30am-8:30pm, Sa-Su 8am-3:30pm. ❷

◙ **Roscoe's House of Chicken and Waffles,** 1514 Gower St. (☎ 323-466-7453). The downhome feel and all-day menu makes this dive a popular spot for regular folk and celebs alike. Try "1 succulent chicken breast and 1 delicious waffle" ($6.90). Be prepared to wait on weekends. Open Su-Th 8:30am-12am, F-Sa 8:30am-4am. ❷

Chin Chin, 8618 Sunset Blvd. (☎ 310-652-1818; www.chinchin.com), in West Hollywood. Other locations in Brentwood, Beverly Hills, Studio City, Marina del Rey, and Encino. Sunglassed celebrities lounge on the patio. Extremely popular with lunchtime crowds for its handmade "dim sum and then sum" ($10.75). Chinese chicken salad ($8) is the sort of Chinese-Californian cuisine befitting a restaurant whose name means "to your health." Open Su-Th 11am-11pm, F-Sa 11am-1am. ❷

Pink's Famous Chili Dogs, 709 N. La Brea Ave. (☎ 323-931-4223; www.pinkshollywood.com), at Melrose. More of an institution than a hot dog stand, Pink's has been serving up chili-slathered dogs since 1939. Rumor has it Orson Welles scarfed down 15 dogs in one sitting. Try the special "Ozzy Osbourne Dog" for $4.45. Chili dogs $2.40; chili fries $2.20. Open Su-Th 9:30am-2am, F-Sa 9:30am-3am. No credit cards. ❶

Pshaw's Bistro, 6099 W. Sunset Blvd. (☎ 323-871-2546). On the second floor of a corner mall is some of the very finest French food in all of Los Angeles. The cozy but dimly lit dining room and garden patio are the perfect romantic oasis. Entrees start at $12. Open M-Sa 5-10pm, Su 11am-6pm. ❸

SANTA MONICA

Giant table umbrellas sprouting from sidewalks and patios along the 3rd St. Promenade and Ocean Ave. herald Santa Monica's upscale eating scene. Most side streets have equally good food. Menus give a nod to (high spending) health buffs by offering organic and vegetarian choices.

■ **Fritto Misto,** 601 Colorado Ave. (☎310-458-2829), at 6th St. This "Neighborhood Italian Cafe" lets you create your own pasta ($6+). Made-to-order menu ($10-14), and cheery waitstaff. Vegetarian entrees $8-11. Daily hot pasta specials $8. Weekend lunch special (all-you-can-eat calamari and salad; $10). Omelettes Su 11:30am-4pm ($7-8). Open M-Th 11:30am-10pm, F-Sa 11:30am-10:30pm, Su 11:30am-9:30pm. ❷

Big Dean's "Muscle-In" Cafe, 1615 Ocean Front Walk (☎310-393-2666), a few steps from the Santa Monica Pier. Sun, sand, sauerkraut, and *cervezas!* Home of the management-proclaimed "burger that made Santa Monica famous" ($5.75).Veggie burgers $4.75. Happy hour M-F 4-8pm with $2 domestic beers. Open M-F 10am and Sa-Su 10:30am until dark, or until the everybody-knows-your-name regulars empty out. ❶

Toppers Restaurant and Cantina, 1111 2nd St. (☎310-393-8080), sits atop the landmark Radisson Huntley Hotel. Ride the glass elevator, found just inside and to the right of the 2nd St. entrance, up to "R" (for Restaurant) for some drinks and a long look out the window. You can't top this deal: it's short on cost and long on coast. Happy hour daily 4:30-7:30pm is a great bargain: buy 1 drink (sodas $1.50; half-pitcher of margarita $5.75), and get $2 Mexican appetizers. If you are looking for a full meal after happy hour the mostly Mexican entrees run from $12-17. Open daily 6:30am-1am. ❸

Britannia Pub, 318 Santa Monica Blvd. (☎310-458-5350), 1 block from 3rd St. Promenade. This is a quality pub where the regulars rule. Signs of supremacy of the old British Navy cover the walls. Beer-battered mushrooms $4.25, club sandwich $6.25, and the *British Weekly* absolutely free. Beer $3.75-5. Happy hour (M-F 4-7pm) gets you $0.50 off everything. Karaoke Tu, Th, Sa and Su. Open daily 11am-1:30am. ❶

Bread & Porridge, 2315 Wilshire Blvd. (☎310-453-4941), in Santa Monica. A breakfast (all day) and lunch (after 11am) spot. Buttermilk, banana, strawberry, chocolate chip, blueberry, pecan, and mixed 4-stack pancakes $5-6.25. 12 kinds of omelettes $8-10. Sandwiches and entrees $7-12. Oatmeal $4.55. Open daily 7am-2pm. ❷

VENICE & MARINA DEL REY

Venetian cuisine runs the gamut from greasy to ultra-healthy, as befits its beachy-hippie crowd. The boardwalk has cheap snacks in fast food fashion. Hit boardwalk cafes and restaurants during happy hour for specials on food and drink.

■ **Rose Cafe and Market,** 220 Rose Ave. (☎310-399-0711), at Main St. Gigantic rose painted walls, local art, industrial architecture, and a gift shop might make you think this is a museum, but the colorful cuisine is the main display. Healthy deli specials, including sandwiches ($6-8) and salads ($4-7) available from 11:30am. Limited menu after 3pm. Open M-F 7am-7pm, Sa 8am-7pm, Su 8am-5pm. ❷

■ **Aunt Kizzy's Back Porch,** 4325 Glencoe Ave. (☎310-578-1005), in Marina Del Rey. In a vast strip mall at Glencoe Ave. and Mindanao Way. Done up to look like a back porch, Aunt Kizzy's is a little slice of Southern heaven. Specialties like Cousin Willie Mae's smothered pork chops come with cornbread and fresh veggies. Save room for Aunt Kizzy's $3 sweet potato pie. Dinner $12-13. Brunch $8. All-you-can-eat brunch buffet $13 (Su 11am-3pm). Open M-Th 11am-9pm, F-Sa 11am-11pm, Su 11am-10pm. ❸

TOURING THE BURGER KINGDOM Los Angeles has spurred many tasteless trends, but few realize that it's also the birthplace of perhaps the world's furthest sweeping trend, one guaranteed to leave a curious taste in your mouth: good ol' American fast food. Unlikely as it sounds, this obsessively health-conscious city spawned some of the nation's greasiest, most cholesterol-packed grub. An international synonym for fast food, **McDonald's** was founded by Angeleno brothers Richard and Maurice McDonald in 1937 (serving, incidentally, hot dogs only). The oldest standing golden arches still glare proudly at 10807 Lakewood Blvd. in Downey, which has walk-up rather than drive-thru service. A small museum pays tribute to the oldest operating franchise in the world. (The brothers granted Ray Kroc exclusive US franchising rights.) Home to the original double-decker hamburger, the oldest **Bob's Big Boy**, 4211 Riverside Dr. (☎818-843-9334), in Burbank, still looks as sleek and streamlined as the day it opened in 1949. Check out the car-hop service (Sa-Su 5-10pm). **Carl's Jr.** started off as a Downtown hot dog stand at Florence and Central Ave. in 1941, and the **Denny's** and **Winchell's** chains also got their start in the L.A. Basin.

Big Daddy's, 1425 Ocean Front Walk (☎310-396-4146), cross Market Ave. With surfboard tables and the Beach Boys blaring, this is the ultimate beach food shack. These grillmasters will serve up anything the heart desires but can't quite handle. $1 menu includes hot dogs, pizza, vanilla ice cream, and more. Burgers $4+. Fried everything (zucchini $4; calamari $6). Churros from an authentic Mexican machine with chocolate, strawberry, or caramel sauce center $2. Open M-F 11am-9pm, Sa-Su 8am-10pm. ❶

Sidewalk Cafe, 1401 Ocean Front Walk (☎310-399-5547), just north of Windward St. Right on the boardwalk, location gives this spot deserved attention. Regulars recommend the Timothy Leary (sauteed mushroom and avocado cheeseburger; $8.50). The Junior Review (hot dog and fries; $6) and Olympiad (grilled cheese and fries; $7) are less expensive. Big, social bar (pints $3). Sunset happy hour (name gives the time) with appetizer and drink specials. Open Su-Th 8am-midnight, F-Sa 8am-1am. ❷

Tony P's Dockside Grill, 4445 Admiralty Way. (☎310-823-4534). Palace of steak and seafood. Spectacular marina views. Tavern is decorated with tapes and TVs. Lunch entrees $7-9, dinner entrees $10-22. Martinis handshaken at your table ($7). Open M-Th 11:30am-11pm, F 11:30am-12:30am, Sa 9am-1:30am, Su 9am-11pm. ❹

MALIBU

Cheap eats are hard to come by at Malibu's shoreside restaurants, which charge as much for their view as for their food. **Malibu Chicken** ❷, 22935 PCH, downstairs from Malibu Ocean Sports (see p. 399), has sandwiches named after old beach-movie idols, like "Gidget" (grilled chicken breast; $8) and "Big Kahuna" (chicken breast, eggplant and feta; $8). The "Dora" (2 chickens, 4 large sides, salad, and bread; $22) could feed a family. (☎310-456-0365. Open daily 11:30am-9pm.) **Duke's Malibu** ❸, 21150 PCH, at Las Flores Canyon Rd., serves reasonably priced fare in its "Barefoot Bar," where you can sit with your feet in the sand and watch the Pacific pound the cliffs. Entrees ($8-20) are half-price during happy hour. (☎310-317-0777; www.hulapie.com. Happy hour M-Th 4-7pm, F all night. Barefoot bar open M-F 11:30am-midnight, Sa-Su 11:30am-1am; kitchen closes 10pm.)

BEVERLY HILLS

Yes, there is budget dining in Beverly Hills—it just takes a little looking to find it. An important tip: do not eat on Rodeo Dr. and stay south of Wilshire Blvd.

■ **Al Gelato,** 806 S. Robertson Blvd. (☎310-659-8069), between Wilshire and Olympic St. Popular among the theater crowd, this homemade gelato spot also does large portions of pasta with a delicious basil tomato sauce. Giant meatball ($4.75) and rigatoni ($11). Just stick to the gelato ($3.75-5.75)and made-to-order cannoli ($4.50) for dessert. Open Tu, Th, Su 10am-midnight; F-Sa 10am-1am. No credit cards. ❶

Nate n' Al Delicatessen, 414 N. Beverly Dr. (☎310-274-0101). For 55 years, this delicatessen (no mere deli) has been serving up hand-pressed potato pancakes ($8.75), blintzes ($9), and reuben sandwiches ($11.50). The waitresses wear pink pinstripes and there's a bottle of Hebrew National Deli Mustard on every table. Open daily 7am-9pm. ❸

Ed Debevic's, 134 N. La Cienega Blvd. (☎310-659-1952). Jammed wall to wall with 50s memorabilia, Ed Debevic's was the inspiration for Jack Rabbit Slims of *Pulp Fiction* fame. Entrees $7-10. Full bar. Open Su-Th 11:30am-10pm, F-Sa 11:30am-midnight. ❷

WESTWOOD & UCLA

Westood Village, the triangular area just south of the University of California at Los Angeles (UCLA) and bordered by Weyburn, Glendon, and Broxton, caters to the tens of thousands of students who live in the area. Westwood overflows with good buys and beer. If you're down to your last few bucks, head to **Jose Bernstein's** ❶, 935 Broxton Ave., for $4 burritos. (Open Su-Th 11am-1am, F-Sa 10am-2:30am.)

🏅 **Sandbag's Gourmet Sandwiches,** 11640 San Vicente Blvd. (☎310-207-4888), in Brentwood. Other locations in Westwood (☎310-208-1133) and Beverly Hills (☎310-786-7878). The perfect place for a healthy, cheap lunch that comes with a complimentary chocolate cookie. Try the "Sundowner" (turkey, herb stuffing, lettuce, and cranberries). Most sandwiches $5.75. Open daily 9am-4pm. ❷

🏅 **Diddie Riese Cookies,** 926 Broxton Ave. (☎310-208-0448). Cookies baked from scratch every day. Popular late-night spot. Well worth the wait for a $1 ice cream sandwich. A buck also buys you 3 cookies and milk, juice, or coffee. Open M-Th 7am-midnight, F 7am-1am, Sa noon-1am, Su noon-midnight. ❶

Gypsy Cafe, 940 Broxton Ave. (☎310-824-2119). Modeled after a sister spot in Paris, this cafe's fare is more Italian than French (penne cacciatore $8.25), and its mood is more Turkish than Italian (hookahs for rent, $10 per hr.). Don't expect fast food—the bountiful buffet is terrific, and the elegant atmosphere encourages customers to linger. Mediterranean kabobs $9. The tomato soup ($5) is famous throughout Westwood. Beer $3.50-4.50, wine $4.50. Open Su-Th 7am-2am, F-Sa 7am-3am. ❷

Westwood Bistro, 1077 Broxton Ave. (☎310-824-7788). This modern and chic bistro offers superb French, Italian, and Asian cuisine. The always popular patio lends itself to a casual yet elegant dining experience. Salads $5-12. Entrees $9-15. Beer $2.50-5; wine $18 and up. Open Su-Th noon-10pm, F-Sa noon-11pm. ❸

WILSHIRE DISTRICT

The Wilshire District's eateries are sadly out of step with its world-class museums. Inexpensive (and often kosher) restaurants dot Fairfax Ave. and Pico Blvd., but health nuts should stay away—there's no keeping cholesterol down in these parts.

Nyala Ethiopian Cuisine, 1076 S. Fairfax Ave. (☎323-936-5918), south of Olympic Blvd. The Fairfax area is known for its kosher delis, but it's also the backbone of L.A.'s Ethiopian community. Nyala combines traditional African influences with L.A.'s hip atmosphere, but as far as the food goes, there's no fusion, just large plates of spongy crepe (*injera*) topped with spicy stews (lunch $7.50, dinner $10.50). The vegetarian lunch buffet (M-F 11:30am-3pm) is a steal at $5.35. Open M-Th 11:30am-11pm, F-Su 11:30am-2am. ❸

The Apple Pan, 10801 W. Pico Blvd. (☎310-475-3585), 1 block east of Westwood Blvd. across from the Westside Pavilion. Suburban legend has it that *Beverly Hills 90210*'s Peach Pit was modeled after The Apple Pan. Paper-plated burgers $4-6; pies $4. Open Tu-Th & Su 11am-midnight, F-Sa 11am-1am. No credit cards. ❶

FROM THE ROAD

BATMAN BY DAY, CLOONEY BY NIGHT

Max was spotted in costume as Batman outside of Grauman's Chinese Theatre on Hollywood Blvd.

Q: So Batman, how long have you been working outside Grauman's Chinese Theatre?

A: About a year now. I'm actually George Clooney's stand in, I'll show you a script from the movie we are doing (pulls out script). It's called *Solaris*, you gotta see this, you like psychological thrillers?

Q: I love them. How'd you land that job?
A: Well, 'cause I look exactly like him.

Q: You obviously have the experience as Batman...
A: Obviously [laughs]. Technically speaking, I have actually fought crime. I've caught two purse snatchers and had five fights in this suit.

Q: WOW!
A: I have been on the news and everything else. I'm about as close to Batman as you can get.

Q: How do you feel about the success of Spiderman?
A: I like that.

Q: It must be good for the superhero world?
A: Yes it is.

Q: Do you have aspirations for leaving the Bat wings and getting into acting full time?
A: Well it's kind of hard. I'm having a real hard time due to the fact that I look so much like Clooney, it's hard to get an agent to take me seriously. So, double for him.

DOWNTOWN

Financial District eateries vie for the businessperson's coveted lunchtime dollar. Their secret weapon is the lunch special, but finding a reasonably priced dinner can be a challenge. (It may not be a good idea to stick around that late, anyway.)

🟨 **Philippe, The Original,** 1001 N. Alameda St. (☎213-628-3781; www.philippes.com), 2 blocks north of Union Station. The French dip sandwich was accidentally invented here in 1918 when Philippe unintentionally dropped a sliced French roll into a roasting pan filled with juice still hot from the oven. The sandwich has been the staple of Philippe's menu ever since. Choose from pork, beef, ham, turkey ($4.25) or lamb ($4.50). Top it off with a large slice of pie ($2.75) and a cup of coffee ($0.09), and you've got a colossal meal at this L.A. institution. Free parking. Open daily 6am-10pm. ❶

🟨 **The Pantry,** 877 S. Figueroa St. (☎213-972-9279). Since 1924, it hasn't closed once—not for the earthquakes, not for the riots (when it served as a National Guard outpost), and not even when a taxicab drove through the front wall. There aren't even locks on the doors. Known for its large portions, free cole slaw, and fresh sourdough bread. Giant breakfast specials ($6). Lunch sandwiches $8. Open 24hr. No credit cards. ❷

La Luz Del Dia, 1 W. Olvera St. (☎213-628-7495), on the circular walking path of the El Pueblo Historic Park Plaza kiosk. Be serenaded by a mariachi band while enjoying homemade tortillas. Everything is authentic—from the outpost-style building to the menu. Meal plates, including rice and beans, are $5-6. Open daily noon-10pm. ❷

Zucca Ristorante, 801 S. Figueroa St. (☎213-614-7800), in the financial district. This bright, classy, and perfectly located Italian restaurant is very popular among the local business set. Pizza $10-13. Pasta $14-16. Pesce $14-15. Open M-F 11:30am-2:30pm and 5-11pm, Sa 5-11pm. ❸

SAN FERNANDO VALLEY

Burbank is packed with eateries that are themselves often packed with stars venturing out in search of lunch. The rules of star-watching state that you can stare at the celebrities all you want, but don't bother them or ask for autographs.

🟨 **Miceli's,** 3655 W. Cahuenga Blvd. (☎323-851-3344), in Burbank. Would-be actors serenade dinner guests. Don't worry about losing your appetite during the Broadway and cabaret numbers—waiters must pass strict vocal auditions. Pizza, pizza, or lasagna $10-15. Open M-Th 11:30am-11pm, F-Sa 11:30am-midnight, Su 3-11pm. ❸

Dalt's Grill, 3500 W. Olive Ave. (☎818-953-7750), in Burbank, at Riverside. Classic, classy, and cool American grill. Burgers and sandwiches $7-8. Chicken fajita caesar salad $9. Full bar. Beer $4.50-$5.75. Happy hour Sa-Th 4-8pm, F 4-10pm. Open M-Th 11am-midnight, F-Sa 11am-1am (bar open until 2am), Su 10am-midnight. ❷

PASADENA

Eateries line **Colorado Boulevard** from Los Robles Ave. to Orange Grove Blvd. in Old Town, making it Pasadena's answer to Santa Monica's 3rd St. Promenade.

▨ **Fair Oaks Pharmacy and Soda Fountain,** 1516 Mission St. (☎626-799-1414), at Fair Oaks Ave. in South Pasadena. This old fashioned drug store, with soda fountain and lunch counter, has been serving travelers on Rte. 66 since 1915; now, a bit of Pasadena's upscale boutique flavor has crept into the establishment. Hand-dipped shakes and malts $4.25. Deli sandwiches $5.50. Patty melts $6. Soda fountain open M-Sa 9am-10pm, Su 11am-9pm; lunch counter open Su-F 11am-5pm, Sa 11am-8pm. ❷

Pita! Pita!, 927 E. Colorado Blvd. (☎626-356-0106), at Lake Ave. Never has the pita deserved so many exclamation points! Appetizer of green olives, yellow pepper, and toasted pita tasty and free. Lunch dishes $7-8. Spicy chicken pita $6. Lamb kebab $6. Daily lunch specials $4-7. Open Su-Th 11am-9pm, F-Sa 11am-10pm. ❷

Holly Street Bar & Grill, 175 E. Holly St. (☎626-440-1421), between Marengo and Arroyo Pky. Contemporary eatery with leopard-print seating. The elegant dining experience is often complimented by live jazz. Salads $9. Entrees $8-24. Full bar. Beer $3.50-4, cocktails $6. Open M-Th 11am-2:30pm and 4:30-9pm, F and Sa 11am-2:30pm and 4:30-10:30pm (bar open until 2am), Su 10am-2:30pm and 4:30-9pm. ❹

◉ SIGHTS

HOLLYWOOD

Exploring the Hollywood area takes a pair of sunglasses, a camera, some cash, and a whole lot of attitude. It is best to drive through the famous Hollywood Hills and then park and explore **Hollywood Boulevard** on foot. Running east-west at the foot of the Hollywood Hills, this strip is the center of L.A.'s tourist madness. The boulevard itself, home to the Walk of Fame, famous theaters, souvenir shops, and museums is busy day and night, especially around the intersection of Highland St. and Hollywood Blvd. and then west down Hollywood Blvd.

HOLLYWOOD SIGN. Those 50 ft. high, 30 ft. wide, slightly erratic letters perched on Mt. Lee in Griffith Park stand as a universally recognized symbol of the city. The original 1923 sign, which read HOLLYWOODLAND, was an advertisement for a new subdivision in the Hollywood Hills. The sign was taken over by the Chamber of Commerce in 1949 and three decades later was replaced by a steel replica unveiled for Hollywood's 75th anniversary. The sign has been a target of college pranks—having it read everything from "Hollyweird" to "Ollywood" (after the infamous Lt. Col. Oliver North). A fence keeps you at a distance of 40 ft. (*To get as close to the sign as possible requires a strenuous 2.5 mi. hike. Use the Bronson Canyon entrance to Griffith Park, following Canyon Dr. to its end. Parking is free. The Brush Canyon Trail starts where Canyon Dr. becomes unpaved. At the top of the hill, follow the road to your left; gaze at Hollywood on one side and the Valley on the other; the sign looms just below. For those not interested in hiking, drive north on Vine St., turn right on Franklin Ave., left on Beachwood and drive up until you are forced to drive down.*)

GRAUMAN'S CHINESE THEATRE. Formerly Mann's, this 75-year-old theatre is back to its original name because of local efforts to establish a Hollywood historical culture. Loosely modeled on a Chinese temple, the theater is a hot spot for movie premieres, recently including *Star Wars Episode 2: Attack of the Clones.*

The exterior columns were imported from China, where they once supported a Ming Dynasty temple. Setting foot in the theatre means stepping into the footprints of more than 200 celebrities cemented in the courtyard, plus Whoopi Goldberg's dreadlocks, R2D2's wheels, and George Burns's cigar. *(6925 Hollywood Blvd., between Highland and La Brea Ave.* ☎ *323-461-3331. Free.)*

KODAK THEATRE. The centerpiece of the brand-new Hollywood & Highland complex, this huge $94 million theatre was built specifically as the new and permanent home of the Academy Awards. Designed to achieve the utmost of intimacy between performers and spectators the seating capacity ranges from 2,200 for live theatre to 3500 for concerts and award shows. In 2002 it hosted the finale of the wildly popular American Idol TV show. *(6801 Hollywood Blvd. Box office* ☎ *323-308-6363. Open M-Sa 10am-6pm.)*

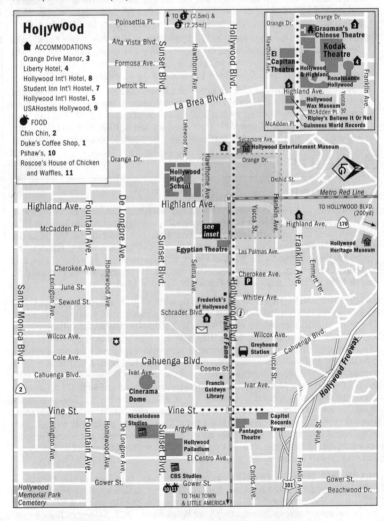

Hollywood

🏠 ACCOMMODATIONS
Orange Drive Manor, **3**
Liberty Hotel, **4**
Hollywood Int'l Hotel, **8**
Student Inn Int'l Hostel, **7**
Hollywood Int'l Hostel, **5**
USAHostels Hollywood, **9**

🍎 FOOD
Chin Chin, **2**
Duke's Coffee Shop, **1**
Pshaw's, **10**
Roscoe's House of Chicken and Waffles, **11**

WALK OF FAME. Pedestrian traffic mimics L.A. freeways along Hollywood Blvd. as tourists stop midstride to gawk at the sidewalk's over 2000 bronze-inlaid stars, which are inscribed with the names of the famous, the infamous, and the downright obscure. Stars are awarded for achievements in one of five categories—movies, radio, TV, recording, and live performance; only Gene Autry has all five stars. The stars have no particular order so don't try to find a method to the madness. Recent inductees include Muhammad Ali (in front of the Kodak Theatre). To catch today's (or yesterday's) stars in person, call the Chamber of Commerce for info on star-unveiling ceremonies. (☎ 323-469-8311; www.hollywoodchamber.net. Free.)

HOLLYWOOD BOWL & MUSEUM. The Hollywood Bowl is synonymous with picnic dining and summer entertainment in a beautiful hillside atmosphere. All are welcome to listen to the L.A. Philharmonic at rehearsals on Mondays, Tuesdays, Thursdays, and Fridays. The Bowl also hosts a summer jazz concert series. The small but cozy museum has several exhibits, as well as listening stations where you can swoon to the Beatles, Dylan, and BB King, all of whom played the Bowl in the 60s. (2301 N. Highland Ave. ☎ 323-850-2058, concert line 850-2000; www.hollywoodbowl.org. Open July-Aug. Tu-Sa 10am-8:30pm; Sept.-June Tu-Sa 10am-4:30pm. Free.)

HOLLYWOOD HERITAGE MUSEUM. The museum provides a glimpse into early Hollywood filmmaking. In 1913, famed director Cecil B. DeMille rented this former barn as studio space for Hollywood's first feature film, *The Squaw Man*. Antique cameras, costumes worn by Douglas Fairbanks and Rudolph Valentino, props, vintage film clips, and other memorabilia fill the museum. The surrounding hills provide an ideal picnic area. (2100 N. Highland Ave, across from the Hollywood Bowl. ☎ 323-874-2276; www.hollywoodheritage.org. Open Sa-Su 11am-3:45pm; call ahead. $3, ages 3-12 $1, under 3 free. Ample free parking, except during Bowl events.)

HOLLYWOOD ENTERTAINMENT MUSEUM. This landmark offers a behind-the-scenes look at the four arts of entertainment—radio, television, film, and recording. A Goddess of Entertainment statue welcomes visitors. It's a treasure chest of authentic set designs, costumes, and props, and a lesson in the how-to's of the business. The original sets from *Star Trek* and *Cheers* deserves ooh- and aah-ing. The *Cheers* bar is functional and open for drinks for Monday Night Football and Super Bowl Sunday. See where the stars carved their initials in the bar during the final episode. (7021 Hollywood Blvd. ☎ 323-465-7900. Museum open June-Aug. daily 10am-6pm; Sept.-May Th-Tu 11am-6pm. Tours every 30min., last tour begins at 5pm. $8.75, students $4.50, seniors $5.50, ages 5-12 $4, under 5 free. Parking $2. Cheers cover $5.)

ALTERNA-MUSEUMS. The sometimes dead-on, sometimes questionable reality of the **Hollywood Wax Museum**'s 200+ life-sized pop icon figures has visitors droning, "That looks nothing/just like...." Choose your own object of distraction, from Legends to Super Heroes and Blockbusters to Chart Toppers. Don't miss the Hall of Presidents and the Horror Chamber. (6767 Hollywood Blvd. ☎ 323-462-5991. Open Su-Th 10am-midnight, F-Sa 10am-1am. $10.95, seniors $8.50, ages 6-12 $6.95, under 6 free.) **Guinness World of Records** has the tallest, shortest, heaviest, most tattooed, and other curious superlatives, all on display. (6764 Hollywood Blvd. ☎ 323-463-6433. Open Su-Th 10am-midnight, F-Sa 10am-1am. $10.95, seniors $8.50, ages 6-12 $6.95, under 6 free; combined admission with wax museum available.) **Ripley's Believe It or Not!** "odditorium" was created to prove that Ripley was not "the world's biggest liar." Displays include an actual section of the Berlin Wall and the world's largest tire. (6780 Hollywood Blvd. ☎ 323-466-6335. Open Su-Th 10am-11pm, F-Sa 10am-12am. Regular admission $10.95, military, seniors, and AAA $9.95, ages 6-12 $7.95, under 6 free.) **Frederick's of Hollywood,** a lingerie store, gives a free peek at celebrity-worn corsets and bosom-boosting bras in its mini-museum including those of the Fembots and Pamela Anderson. Look hard

FROM THE ROAD

BREAKING IT DOWN

Two hundred years ago, Americans were told to head west to the New Frontier. It was a place where one could get rich and start a new life. Little has changed. Countless numbers of people still flock to Los Angeles to chase their dream and try to make it big. Many of these people choose Venice Beach and Santa Monica as the starting point.

A leisurely stroll up Ocean Front Walk and through the Third Street Promenade provides ample opportunity to see artists showcasing their talent. However, unless you want to participate, don't get too close. One Saturday afternoon I found myself drawn to a small crowd surrounding an L.A. Lakers-clad break-dancer on the promenade. This guy was good—so good that within minutes the crowd had grown to hundreds. Soon thereafter he announced that he needed the help of a few male assistants. I tried to make myself as small as possible—at 6'5" this was not an easy task.

Sure enough I was spotted and soon found myself in the middle of a circle that seemed more like a black hole. In a team huddle the performer assured us that all we had to do was follow the instructions and we would be fine. We broke the huddle and took our places. The show began. I was relieved, for all we were doing was standing in one spot, occasionally helping him fly through the air, but more often than not just watching as he moon-walked, break-danced, and spun on his head to the much deserved applause of the crowd.

Then my worst fears were realized.

enough and you will find Forrest Gump's boxers. *(6608 Hollywood Blvd. ☎323-957-5953. Open M-F 10am-9pm, Sa 10am-7pm, Su 11am-6pm.)*

CAPITOL RECORDS TOWER. The tower is the pre-eminent monument of the modern recording industry. The cylindrical building, constructed in 1954, was designed to look like a stack of records, with fins sticking out at each floor (the "records") and a needle on top, which blinks H-O-L-L-Y-W-O-O-D in Morse code. *(1750 Vine St., just north of Hollywood Blvd.)*

EL CAPITÁN THEATRE. "Hollywood's First Home of Spoken Drama" this cinema house hosted the 1941 Hollywood premiere of *Citizen Kane*. Restored by Walt Disney Co. in 1991, it now features exotic Indian 1920s interior decoration and Disney movies. Movies are not shown every day; call in advance for showtimes. *(6838 Hollywood Blvd. ☎323-467-9545 or 800-347-6396; www.elcapitantickets.com. Tickets $9.50, ages 3-11 and seniors $6, matinee $6, live shows or special exhibit tickets $13-22, kids $11-20. Parking $4 with validation.)*

SANTA MONICA

Given the cleaner waters and better waves at beaches to the north and south, Santa Monica is known more for its shoreside scene than its shore. Filled with gawkers and hawkers, the area on and around the carnival pier is the hub of local tourist activity. The fun fair spills over into the pedestrian-only **Third Street Promenade,** where street performers and a farmer's market make for cinematic "crowd" scenes. Farther inland, along Main St. and beyond, a smattering of galleries, design shops, and museums reveal the city's love for art and design.

THIRD STREET PROMENADE. This ultra-popular three-block stretch is *the* major walking, shopping, people-watching, and movie-viewing thoroughfare around. Before taking its present form (fashionable boutiques and yuppie cafes), 3rd St. was known as one of L.A.'s artsier areas, and it is still home to the city's better book and music stores (see **Shopping,** p. 416). On Wednesday and Saturday mornings, the area is transformed into a farmer's market. The strip truly comes alive at night, when street artists arrive and the ivy-lined mesh dinosaur sculptures light up. Young adults with clipboards often sign people up for free movie passes. After all, this is the film screening capital of the world.

SANTA MONICA PIER & PACIFIC PARK. The famed pier is the heart of the Santa Monica Beach and home of the carnivalesque family funspot Pacific Park, where the fun meets the sun and "the rides meet the tides." Roller coaster lovers and ferris wheel fanatics 4 ft. and taller can have some fun for a few bucks among the sticky-fingered kids and sunburned parents who populate the pier. Along the pier, amidst pizza joints and souvenir shops, look for free TV show tickets (the variety and late-night kinds) near the north entrance. Buy temporary hipness at booths along the strip in the form of a painless henna tattoo for $5-20 or pose for a portrait from one of many very talented artists for $20. *(Off PCH on the way to Venice Beach from Santa Monica Beach. ☎310-656-8886; www.santamonicapier.com. Open in summer M-Th 11am-11pm, F-Su 11am-12:30am; in winter F-Sa 11am-12:30am, Su 11am-9pm. Ticket window closes 30min. before the park closes. Tickets $1.50 each, most rides 2-3 tickets; day passes $16, children under 42 in. $9. Twilight Dance Series July-Aug. Th 7:30pm (free); for info, call ☎310-458-8900. Parking off PCH $8 per day.)*

MAIN STREET. Beginning at Colorado Ave., Main St. struts its stuff all the way to Venice. Sporting galleries and designer knick-knack shops, it is much artsier and more urbane than the Promenade but no more pretentious. On Main St., window-shopping need not stop at the window. The historic, Victorian-style Roy Jones House that contains the **California Heritage Museum** contrasts with the design-happy Main St. architecture surrounding it. The museum has several restored rooms and hosts temporary exhibits. *(2612 Main St., ½ mi. south of Pico. ☎310-392-8537. Open W-Su 11am-4pm. $3, students and seniors $2, under 12 free. Parking free.)*

BERGAMOT STATION ARTS CENTER. Once a train depot, these converted warehouses are now helping to move contemporary L.A. area artists—painters, sculptors, mixed-media designers, and photographers—to higher ground. While the art is pricey, the viewing is free and fabulous. The **Gallery of Functional Art** sells inspired art object creations such as toasters-turned-wall lamps and the more affordable fork-chops. The **Santa Monica Museum of Art,** in building G-1, exhibits the work of emerging artists. Featured art rotates regularly. Bergamot Station also houses a reasonably priced Gallery Cafe, as well as a Colleagues Gallery with more affordable works. *(2525 Michigan Ave., near the intersection of Olympic and Cloverfield Blvd. ☎310-586-6467. Santa Monica Museum of Art open Tu-Sa 11am-6pm, Su noon-5pm; call ahead, because it often closes for installation changes. Suggested donation to $3, students and seniors $2; galleries free. Gallery Cafe open M 9am-4pm, Tu-F 9am-5pm, Sa 10am-5pm.)*

MUSEUM OF FLYING. On the airstrip of the Santa Monica Airport, this small hangar museum features WWI single-seat fighters, a "footprints on the moon"

The performer suddenly came over to me and whispered two words in my ear: "Follow me."

"What does that mean?" I asked myself. But it was too late. He had just finished another dance in the center of the circle and was calling me over—it was my turn. I now had to put on my dancing shoes and break-dance for the crowd—alone. I did the first thing that came to mind. I laid down on the ground and did a back somersault.

I stood up to the delayed applause of the crowd—apparently it appeared as though I had smacked my head on the concrete so no one wanted to applaud until it was clear I was okay. My time in the spotlight was over, and not too soon. Though my performance is unlikely to land any roles in showbiz at least I was able to leave with the knowledge that one day I might see an L.A. Lakers-clad artist on TV, and if so I can say that I danced in his show.

–James Kearney

KNOCKING KNEES

Joe Nucci, a retired limo driver, was heard with his guitar on Venice Beach.

Q: What brings you and your guitar to Venice Beach?
A: Well, there's quite a history of performance. The number one performer from Venice is Jim Morrison. The Doors was born on Venice Walkway. It's also a place where you can be homeless and an artist and get a little bit of respect—not much, but a little.

Q: So do you just come out when you feel like playing a little guitar?
A: Right now I just come out to make a few dollars and try to meet some girls [laughs].

Q: An enjoyable time?
A: Oh yeah, I have the sun and the beach, I can lie in the hot sand. I like to swim up in Malibu at Point Dume, the water is much clearer.

Q: How long have you been out here in Venice?
A: Well I actually grew up in Pittsburgh but I have been out here since 1979. I used to drive a limo. I drove Kim Basinger one night with her sister in Georgia. At the end of the run Kim grabs my hand and holds it in both of her hands, she was giving me a tip which turned out to be 100 dollars, (she) looks me right in the eyes and goes, "Oh Joe, you were fantastic tonight". Then I heard this knocking sound, it was my knees.

tribute to the Apollo missions, and an aircraft simulator. The Air Traffic Control station allows you to listen to real time transmissions from local air towers. *(Donald Douglas Coop N. St., at the end of 28th St. ☎ 310-392-8822. Open W-Su 10am-5pm. $7, students with ID and seniors $5, ages 3-16 $3. Virtual reality simulator pass $2.)*

OTHER SIGHTS. The paved **beach path** is a mini-freeway of cyclists, skaters, and runners, stretching 20¼ mi. between Santa Monica and Torrance Beaches. Under the first few planks of the Santa Monica Pier sits the **UCLA Ocean Discovery Center,** where the kiddies can get their fingers fishy in the "touch tank" and watch ocean movies. *(☎310-393-6149. Open July 1-Labor Day Tu-F 3-6pm, Sa 11am-6pm, Su 11am-5pm; Labor Day-June 30 Sa-Su 11am-5pm. $3, children under 2 free.)* At the Santa Monica Senior Recreation Center is the **Camera Obscura,** which uses convex lenses to project a 360-degree bird's-eye view of the beach onto a screen in a dark room—well worth the 10 seconds it takes to see. *(1450 Ocean Ave. Open M 9am-2pm, Tu-F 9am-4pm, Sa-Su 11am-4pm. Free.)*

VENICE

At the turn of the 20th century, Abbot Kinney envisioned a re-creation of Italy's Venice on the California coast—a touch of Old World charm, with mustached gondoliers working the canals and the social elite strolling on an elegant oceanside promenade. Instead, Kinney ended up with a massive dose of New World neuroses. **Ocean Front Walk,** Venice's main beachfront drag, is a seaside three-ring circus of fringe culture. Street people converge on shaded clusters of benches, evangelists drown out off-color comedians, and bodybuilders of both sexes pump iron in skimpy spandex outfits at **Muscle Beach,** 1800 Ocean Front Walk, closest to 18th St. and Pacific Ave. Fire-juggling cyclists, master sand sculptors, bards in Birkenstocks, and the **"skateboard grandma"** define the spirit of this playground population. Vendors of jewelry, henna body art, snacks, and beach paraphernalia overwhelm the boardwalk.

To untangle your wits after the initial barrage of gaudy Venice, you can people-watch from one of the cafes or juice bars and check out life in the fast lane on the bike path stretching from Santa Monica. **Boardwalk Skates,** 201 Ocean Front Walk, rents bikes and skates. *(☎310-450-6634. Bikes or skates $5 per hr., bikes $15 per day, Skates $12 per day for Let's Go readers; tandem bike $7 per hr., $20 per day. Open M-F 10:30am-7pm, Sa-Su 10am-7:30pm.)* Or cross the bike path to **Venice One-Stop Beach Rental** in the bright yellow boxcar and receive a free map and drink voucher. (Bikes or skates $5 per hr., $8 for 2hr., $12 per day.) Those who think they got game can play ball at the popular basketball court at 18th St. and Ocean Front Walk, which is featured in the movie *White Men Can't Jump*.

Toward Culver City is the **Museum of Jurassic Technology,** 9341 Venice Blvd., just west of Robertson Blvd. The museum is not really reachable on foot from the beach. By car, take I-10 to Robertson Blvd. South; from Robertson Blvd., turn left onto Venice Blvd. The museum is about four blocks down Venice Blvd. The museum walks a fine line between an elaborate practical joke and a profound statement on the ultimate inaccessibility of history. It is unlike any museum you have ever visited, with an unapologetic and unexplained juxtaposition of exhibits as incongruous as mole rat skeletons, fake gems, and trailer park art. To describe it as such doesn't really do justice to the creeping feeling that, despite the professional displays, portentous audio narration, and deadpan introductory slide show, *this may all be a load of utter baloney.* Maybe, maybe not. Attempting to decide for oneself is a unique and delightfully maddening experience. (☎310-836-6131. Open Th 2-8pm, F-Su noon-6pm. Requested donation $4, students and seniors $2.50, active military $1.50.)

MARINA DEL REY

For a low-key slice of seaside life in L.A., take a walk along the marina or drive down to **Fisherman's Village** (at the eastern end of Fiji Way off Lincoln Blvd.), a small but pleasant wharf-meets-strip-mall that is home to a handful of restaurants, gift shops, and boating stores. Although the Village does not warrant a full daytrip, it's a wonderful way to spend a relaxing weekend afternoon in a boat or kayak rented from **Marina Boat Rentals,** 13719 Fiji Way (☎310-574-2822), which offers great rates on four-person powerboats and sailboats ($30-100 per hr. depending on size), eight-person electric boats ($60 per hr.), single and double kayaks ($12 and $20 per hr.), and three-person pedal boats ($15 per hr.). No experience is necessary for most rentals, but you should call in advance for reservations. Relax afterward on the central patio, where locals crowd in to hear live music on weekend nights and some weekend afternoons.

MALIBU

North of Santa Monica along the PCH, the traffic lightens and the cityscape gives way to overwhelming stretches of sandy shoreline. Stop along the coast and you may see dolphins swimming in packs close to shore—or at least packs of surfers trying to catch a wave. Malibu's beaches are clean and relatively uncrowded—easily the best in L.A. County for surfers and swimmers alike. You can jet through the wave tubes at **Surfrider Beach,** a section of Malibu Lagoon State Beach north of the pier at 23000 PCH. Walk there via the Zonker Harris Access Way (named after the beach-obsessed Doonesbury character) at 22700 PCH. **Malibu Ocean Sports,** 22935 PCH, across from the pier, rents surfboards ($10 per hr., $25 per day), kayaks (single $15 per day; double $20 per day, $50 per day), boogie boards ($12 per day), and wetsuits ($10 per day), and also offers surfing lessons ($100 for 2hr. lesson and full-day gear) and tours. (☎310-456-6302. Open daily 9am-7pm.)

Corral State Beach, a tiny windsurfing and swimming haven off the side of the road, lies on the 26000 block of PCH. The larger and generally uncrowded **Point Dume State Beach** (main entrance near 29000 PCH, look for signs) is just north of Corral State Beach, offering better currents for scuba-diving. Along the 30000 block of PCH lies **Zuma Beach,** L.A. County's northernmost, largest, and most user-friendly county-owned sandbox. The central location makes sections #5-7 a big draw for swarms of local kids, while distance from the one and only entrance makes sections #9-11 less crowded. Swimmers should stay as close as possible to manned lifeguard stations; because of the strong **riptide**, rescue counts are high. **The Zuma Cafe ❶**, 30066 PCH, rents boogie boards ($5 per hr.), kayaks ($15 per hr.), and bikes ($10 per hr.) among other things. Breakfast ($2.50-6), burgers ($3.50) and hot dogs ($2.50) allow for quick beach re-fueling. (☎310-457-3143. Open daily 7:30am-6pm.) The free street parking is coveted, so expect to use the beach lot ($6, after 6pm $2). Although it's disguised as a deli, **Malibu Ranch Market**, 29575 PCH, in the Zuma Beach Plaza at Busch Rd., rents boogie boards (small $7 per day, large $9) and sells deli sandwiches, snacks, and alcohol. (☎457-0171. Open M-Th 7:30am-10:30pm, F 7:30am-11pm, Sa 8am-11pm, Su 8am-10pm.)

BEVERLY HILLS

Conspicuous displays of wealth can border on the vulgar in this storied center of extravagance and privilege. Residential ritz reaches peaks along the mansions that line the blocks of Beverly Dr. The heart of the city, known for its flashy clothing boutiques and jewelry shops, is in the **Golden Triangle**, a wedge formed by Beverly Dr., Wilshire Blvd., and Santa Monica Blvd., centering on **Rodeo Drive.** Built like an old English manor house, Polo Ralph Lauren (444 N. Rodeo Dr.) stands out from the white marble of the other stores. The divine triple-whammy of Cartier (370 N. Rodeo Dr.), Gucci (347 N. Rodeo Dr.), and Chanel (400 N. Rodeo Dr.) sits on some of the area's prime real estate, where rents are as high as $40,000 per month.

At the south end of Rodeo Dr. (the end closest to Wilshire Blvd.) is the all-pedestrian shopping complex of **2 Rodeo Drive**, a.k.a. **Via Rodeo**, which contains Dior, Tiffany, and numerous salons frequented by the stars. Although it fakes European antiquity, the promenade was constructed in the last decade—cobblestone street, lampposts, and all. Across the way is the venerable **Beverly Wilshire Hotel**, 9500 Wilshire Blvd. (☎310-275-5200), whose old and new wings are connected by **El Camino Real** and its Louis XIV gates. The hotel lobby gives you a good idea of just how extravagant the rooms might be.

North of ritzy Rodeo Dr. is Santa Monica Blvd., which gives the Hills a little bit of nature to complement the shopping. A series of small but pleasant parks line the boulevard. One such park contains the most varieties of **cacti** in one place in the world. Although it's a dusty patch, the cactus plants are an interesting sight, between N. Camden and N. Bedford Dr. on Santa Monica Blvd.

MUSEUM OF TELEVISION & RADIO. Complete with a radio broadcast studio and two theaters, this museum's biggest highlight is its library, which holds 117,000 television, radio, and commercial programs. You can request your favorite tube hits, and five minutes later the library staff will have the full-length episodes ready and waiting for your viewing pleasure at your own private screening station. Caricatures of television stars decorate the walls, and there is always someone watching *I Love Lucy*. *(465 N. Beverly Dr. ☎310-786-1000. Open W and F-Su noon-5pm, Th noon-9pm. Donation $6, students and seniors $4, under 13 $3. 2hr. free parking in the museum's lot off Little Santa Monica Blvd.)*

CIVIC CENTER. Just outside of the main area is the **Beverly Hills City Hall**, 455 N. Rexford Dr., just below Santa Monica Blvd., which would look out of place anywhere but here. This Spanish Renaissance building was erected during the Great Depression, and is now engulfed by Beverly Hills's new white phoenix of a Civic Center, which took nine years to build at a cost of $120 million. The **Beverly Hills Library**, 444 N. Rexford Dr., has an interior adorned with Thai marble but only an average collection of books. *(City Hall ☎310-285-1000. Library ☎213-288-2220.)*

BEVERLY HILLS HIGH. It may only be a local public high school, but it is still a mild marvel. The indoor swimming pool is open in the summer, operated by Parks and Recreation, and has a sliding floor cover that converts the pool into a basketball court. That very floor is where Jimmy Stewart and Donna Reed danced the aquatic Charleston in *It's a Wonderful Life.* The school today is still quite a popular filming location. *(241 Moreno, between Olympic Blvd. and Spalding. ☎310-201-0661. Pool open in summer M-F noon-9pm.)*

BEVERLY HILLS HOTEL. The hotel is a pink, palm-treed array of 182 rooms and suites and 21 poolside bungalows, hidden among 12 acres of tropical gardens, that are as famous as the starlets who romanced here. Marilyn Monroe reportedly had trysts with both JFK and RFK in these bungalows. The hotel is home to the **Polo Lounge,** where countless industry deals have been negotiated. Owned by the Dorchester Group, rooms run from $345-445, Bungalows from $405-4,215, and suites from $745-4,700. *(9641 Sunset Blvd. ☎310-276-2251.)*

MUSEUM OF TOLERANCE. Just south of Beverly Hills is the sobering Museum of Tolerance. This hands-on, high-tech museum has interactive exhibits on the Holocaust, the Croatian genocide, the L.A. riots, and the US civil rights movement. Visit the Point of View Diner, a re-creation of a 50s diner that serves a menu of controversial topics on video jukeboxes. You can pick up a "passport" of a child from Nazi-occupied territory and later in the museum plug it into computer kiosks that will provide the biography (read: awful fate) of your cardholder. Artifacts from concentration camps and original letters from Anne Frank are in the 2nd floor Multimedia Learning Center. Required orientation sessions run every 10-12min. The main floor of the museum, with its sound- and light-guided displays, takes about 2hr. to get through—patience is encouraged. The Museum has hosted speeches by many influential world figures including President George W. Bush and the Dalai Lama and has held discussions concerning Civil Rights vs. Civil Liberties after the terrorist attacks on September 11, 2001. Diagonally across the street is the **Simon Wiesenthal Center** for Holocaust research. Holocaust survivors speak of their experiences Sunday through Thursday at 1, 2, and 3pm. *(9786 W. Pico Blvd., at Roxbury St. Museum ☎310-553-8403 or 800-900-9036; www.wiesenthal.com. Open M-Th 11:30am-4pm, F 11:30am-1pm, Su 11am-5pm. $9, seniors $7, students and ages 3-10 $5.50. Free parking. Wheelchair accessible.)*

CELEBRITY TOUR

The reason why all the maps to stars' homes only seem to show dead stars is that while the privileged may still *shop* here, most no longer *live* here. The area still houses many a multi-millionaire and lives up to the well-manicured ideal that visitors expect, but the real fame and money has since moved away from the hype to areas that afford privacy (see **Bel Air, Brentwood, and Pacific Palisades,** p. 403).

A conspicuous way to tour the city is in the 1914 trolley car replica operated by the Beverly Hills Chamber of Commerce (☎310-248-1000). The 40min. **tour of the city and stars' homes** costs $5 and leaves from the corner of Rodeo Dr. and Dayton (every hr. June-Sept. Tu-Sa 1-5pm). For a cooler approach, go solo with a star map ($8), sold along Sunset Blvd. but not within Beverly Hills, or take the following *Let's Go* abbreviated tour (consult the L.A. Westside map for reference).

Elvis had two homes in L.A. He purchased the first, at 1174 Hillcrest, shortly after his marriage to Priscilla in 1967, but quickly relocated to 144 Monovale because it offered more privacy. Today, Priscilla still lives near those old memories at 1167 Summit Dr. The 55-room **Greystone Mansion** at nearby 905 Loma Vista Dr., just off Doheny, was the most expensive home in Beverly Hills in the 1920s. The mansion was built by oil mogul **Edward Doheny** for his son, who was found dead with his male secretary only a few weeks after moving in, giving rise to unconfirmed rumors that the two were lovers. Now owned and operated by the city, the Tudor and Jacobean revival house with its two gatehouses and glorious gardens is used extensively as a filming location, most notably in *The Witches of Eastwick*, *Ghostbusters*, and *The Bodyguard*. (☎310-550-4654. Open daily 10am-6pm; gardens free.) Head back to Sunset Blvd., make a right, and then make a left on Elm Dr. The estate at 722 N. Elm Dr. has been owned by **Elton John** and **Prince**, and was most recently the site of the **Menendez** murders. **Frank Sinatra** owned the house at nearby 915 Foothill Rd., one street west of Elm Dr. Head back to Sunset Blvd. again, make a left, and another left onto Roxbury Dr. Aw-shucks actor and icon **Jimmy Stewart** resided at 918 Foothill Rd. If you dig serious power, have a glance at the walls of the massive **David Geffen** mansion, 1801 Angelo Dr. Follow Roxbury Dr. north as it turns into Hartford, make a left onto Benedict Canyon, and another left on Angelo Dr. to the media god's mansion. Now, turn back to Benedict Canyon, make a left, then a right onto Tower. **Jay Leno**, at 1151 Tower Rd., lives just around the corner from the home of **Heidi Fleiss**, 1270 Tower Grove Dr. Head back down Benedict Canyon toward Sunset Blvd., make a right, and then another right onto Carolwood. **Barbra Streisand** lived at 301 Carolwood, and the house at 355 Carolwood is where **Walt Disney** lived until his death. Turn back to Sunset Blvd. and head toward Westwood, making a left on the tiny and windy Charing Cross. The estate at 10236 is the **Playboy Mansion.** Charing Cross becomes N. Mapleton, site of the largest and most extravagant residence in Beverly Hills: producer **Aaron Spelling's** mansion, 594 N. Mapleton, is larger than the Taj Mahal. Wife Candy Spelling's closets reportedly take up an entire wing.

WESTWOOD & UCLA

UNIVERSITY OF CALIFORNIA AT LOS ANGELES (UCLA)

Directly north of Westwood Village and west of Beverly Hills. To drive to the campus, take I-405 (San Diego Fwy.) to the Wilshire Blvd./Westwood Exit and head east into Westwood. Take Westwood Blvd. north off Wilshire Blvd., and go through Westwood Village and directly into the campus. By bus, take MTA #2 along Sunset Blvd., #21 along Wilshire Blvd., #320 from Santa Monica, or #561 from the San Fernando Valley, or Santa Monica BBBus #1, 2, 3, 8, or 12. Parking pass ($6) is valid all day at 14 different parking structures. Maps free.

Get a feel for mass academia UC-style at this 400-acre campus sprawling in the foothills of the Santa Monica Mountains. A prototypical California university, UCLA sports an abundance of grassy open spaces, dazzling sunshine, and pristine buildings. Once voted the #1 jock school in the country by *Sports Illustrated*, UCLA also boasts an illustrious film school whose graduates include James Dean, Jim Morrison, Oliver Stone, Francis Ford Coppola, and Tim Robbins.

UCLA and Westwood are navigable on foot, so pay for a parking pass from campus information stands at any entrance, then park and walk. UCLA parking cops live to ticket unsuspecting visitors. **Tours** are offered by the Alumni Center, which is directly north of Westwood Plaza and parking structures #6 and 8. (☎310-825-8764. Tour times vary seasonally.) One great outdoor highlight is the **Murphy Sculpture Garden** (in the northeast corner of campus), which contains over 70 pieces by such major artists as Auguste Rodin, Henri Matisse, and Joan Miró.

UCLA HAMMER MUSEUM OF ART. The UCLA Hammer Museum houses the world's largest collection of works by 19th-century French satirist Honoré Daumier and the collection of late oil tycoon Armand Hammer, with works by Rembrandt, Monet, and Pissarro. The museum's true gem is Vincent Van Gogh's *Hospital at Saint Rémy*. Hammer purportedly wanted to donate his collection to the L.A. County Museum of Art, but demanded that the works be shown together in a separate wing. The museum refused, telling Hammer to build his own place—which he did. The center hosts traveling exhibitions throughout the year, as well as free summer jazz concerts and seasonal cultural programs. *(10899 Wilshire Blvd.* ☎ *310-443-7000 or TDD 310-443-7094. Open Tu-W and F-Sa 11am-7pm, Th 11am-9pm, Su 11am-5pm. Summer jazz concerts F 6:30-8pm. $5, seniors $3, under 17 free, Th free. Free tours of permanent collection Su 2pm, of traveling exhibits Th 6pm, Sa-Su 1pm. 3hr. parking $2.75, $1.20 each additional 20min.)*

FOWLER MUSEUM OF CULTURAL HISTORY. The Fowler displays artifacts from contemporary, historic, and prehistoric cultures. The fact that it preserves Native American remains for their archaeological value (there are laws protecting Native Americans' rights to sacred burial) is controversial. *(In Haines Hall.* ☎ *310-825-4361. Open W and F-Su noon-5pm, Th noon-8pm. $5, students and seniors $3, under 17 free; Th free.)*

ACKERMAN UNION. With all practical needs met by Ackerman Union services (which includes a campus credit union and post office), there's no need for students ever to leave campus. Visitors are free to enjoy the **Food Court** which features a grill, a pizza place, and a smoothie bar. For those who are interested in such risky ventures, a ride-share board on the first floor posts information on drivers and riders going everywhere from Vegas to Miami. The huge **UCLA Store** swallows up most of the ground floor with a bevy of UCLA paraphernalia, a newsstand, a grocery store, and the always-essential Clinique counter. *(308 Westwood Plaza, downhill from the quadrangle on Bruin Walk.* ☎ *310-206-0833. Store open M-Th 7:30am-7pm, F 7:30am-7:30pm, Sa 8am-7pm, Su noon-5pm. Union open mid-June to late Sept. daily 10am-11pm; late Sept. to mid-June 8am-11pm.)*

TICKETS. The **UCLA Central Ticket Office** sells tickets for on-campus arts events (including concerts and dance recitals), UCLA sporting events, and discounted tickets to local movie theaters and water parks (discounts not limited to UCLA affiliates). It also has a Ticketmaster outlet. *(*☎ *310-825-2101; www.cto.ucla.edu.)* The renowned School of Film and Television Archive sponsors various film festivals, often with foreign films and profiles on groundbreaking filmmakers. *(*☎ *310-206-3456; www.cinema.ucla.edu. Double features $6, students $4; select films free.)*

BEL AIR, BRENTWOOD, & PACIFIC PALISADES

These three residential communities don't offer much to the budget traveler in terms of accommodations or food, but a stop at the Getty Museum or a scenic drive along Sunset Blvd. are two free ways to experience the best the area has to offer. Veer off Sunset onto any public (non-gated) road to see tree-lined rows of well-spaced six-bedroom homes that make living here as costly as Beverly Hills.

J. PAUL GETTY MUSEUM & GETTY CENTER

1200 Getty Center Dr. Take I-405 (San Diego Fwy.) to the Getty Center Dr. Exit. Public transportation is strongly recommended: take either Santa Monica BBBus #14 (for info call ☎ *310-451-4444) or MTA #561 (for info call* ☎ *800-266-6883) to Sepulveda Blvd.* ☎ *310-440-7300; www.getty.edu. Free; headset audio guides $3. Open Su, Tu-Th 10am-6pm, F-Sa 10am-9pm. Parking reservations required Tu-F before 4pm. ($5 per car); no reservations necessary for college students, weekends, or after 4pm. A "panorami-tram" takes visitors up the hill to the museum. Off-site parking, also serviced by shuttle (10min.), is free.*

Above Bel Air and Brentwood in the Santa Monica Mountains lies a modern Coliseum, "The Getty." Indeed, the 16,000 tons of travertine marble used to build this museum came from the same quarry as that of the Coliseum. Wedding classical materials to modern designs, renowned architect Richard Meier designed the $1 billion complex, which opened to the public in 1997. The museum consists of five pavilions overlooking the Robert Irwin-designed Central Garden, a living work of art that changes with the seasons. The pavilions contain the permanent Getty collection (including Vincent Van Gogh's *Irises*), Impressionist paintings, Renaissance drawings, and a fantastic Rembrandt collection. The Getty also hosts gallery talks by local artists, lectures, films, and a concert series. The "Friday Nights at the Getty" program features plays, films, and readings.

OTHER SIGHTS

SKIRBALL CULTURAL CENTER. Dedicated to the preservation of Jewish culture, this institution rests minutes north of the Getty. It contains one of the world's largest collections of Judaica, a children's Discovery Center, and interactive exhibits. Call for the schedule of concerts and lectures. *(2701 N. Sepulveda Blvd. ☎310-440-4500. Open Tu-Sa noon-5pm, Su 11am-5pm.)*

BEL-AIR CELEBS

SEEING STARS. Many of today's stars live in Bel Air, Brentwood, and Pacific Palisades. The best way to see their cottages and compounds is to pick up a star map, available at the Santa Monica Pier, local newsstands, or from vendors along Sunset Blvd. However, you'll probably only see the stars themselves on screen. Lurking around their neighborhoods might get you a peek at their landscaping or a picture of their mailbox, but it's doubtful you'll ever see them taking out the trash.

Next to UCLA is **Bel Air,** home of the *Beverly Hillbillies* mansion, at 750 Bel Air Rd. A few blocks up from the former home of **Sonny and Cher,** at 364 St. Cloud. **Elizabeth Taylor** is right around the corner at 700 Nimes Rd. A few blocks away is **Nicolas Cage's** place at 363 Copa De Oro. Back in the golden days, Bel Air was the locus for glamorous celebs, including **Judy Garland** at 924 Bel Air Rd., **Alfred Hitchcock** at 10957 Bel Air Rd., and **Lauren Bacall** and **Humphrey Bogart** at 232 Mapleton Dr.

Further west on Sunset Blvd. is **Brentwood,** home to many a national scandal-starter. **O.J. Simpson's** estate at 360 Rockingham Pl. was repossessed and auctioned off for a meager $2.63 million. Consequently, the famous accusé no longer lives here. However, America's greatest accuser, former White House intern **Monica Lewinsky,** resides in southern Brentwood at 12224 Darlington Ave. A one-time White House favorite herself, **Marilyn Monroe** was found dead at her home at 12305 Fifth Helena Dr. in 1962. Celeb-studded Brentwood also includes the homes of **Michelle Pfeiffer, Harrison Ford, Meryl Streep,** and **Rob Reiner.**

The considerably more secluded **Pacific Palisades** brings the stars closer to the ocean and farther from the *paparazzi.* **Kurt Russell** and live-in love **Goldie Hawn** reside at 1422 Capri Dr. **Whoopi Goldberg** is in town at 1461 Amalfi Dr., just down the road from **Steven Spielberg,** who lives in the house at 1513-1515 Amalfi Dr. that belonged to David O. Selznick while he was producing *Gone with the Wind.* **Arnold Schwarzenegger** and **Maria Shriver,** who loved their lot so much they bought out their neighbors for $5.4 million, practice family fitness at 14205, 14209, and 14215 Sunset Blvd. **John Travolta** and **Kelly Preston** are stayin' alive at 735 Bonhill Rd.

WILSHIRE DISTRICT

HANCOCK PARK. A good place to orient yourself to the myriad sights of the Wilshire District is the well-manicured **Hancock Park,** which sprawls from Ogden Dr. to Curson Ave. between Wilshire Blvd. and 6th St. The park contains two famous museums and is adjacent to many other sights and smells. Picnickers should be wary of the odorous tar pits, which may conflict with your otherwise sweet-smelling lunchmeat. *(Park open daily 6am-10pm. Free.)*

LOS ANGELES COUNTY MUSEUM OF ART (LACMA). At the western end of Hancock Park, LACMA's renowned collection contains "more than 110,000 works from around the world, spanning the history of art from ancient times to the present." Opened in 1965, LACMA is the largest museum on the West Coast, with six main buildings around the **Times-Mirror Central Court.** The **Steve Martin Gallery,** in the Anderson Building, holds the famed benefactor's collection of Dada and Surrealist works, including R. Magritte's *Treachery of Images.* (This explains how Steve was able to roller skate through LACMA's halls in *L.A. Story;* see p. 23.) The latest addition is **LACMA West,** and its **Children's Gallery.** The museum sponsors free jazz, chamber music, film classics and documentaries, and a variety of free daily tours. *(5905 Wilshire Blvd. General info ☎ 323-857-6000, Docent Council 857-6108; www.lacma.org. Open M-Tu and Th noon-8pm, F noon-9pm, Sa-Su 11am-8pm. $7, students and seniors $5, under 18 $1; free 2nd Tu of each month. Free jazz F 5:30-8:30pm, chamber music Su 6-7pm. Film tickets $7, seniors $5. Parking $5, after 7pm free. Wheelchair accessible.)*

PETERSEN AUTOMOTIVE MUSEUM (PAM). This slice of Americana showcases one of L.A.'s most recognizable symbols—the automobile. Something of a time-travel showroom, PAM is the world's largest car museum and the nation's 2nd-largest history museum (after the Smithsonian). 300,000 sq. ft. showcase 130 of history's finest and wildest rides. The museum also features 1920s service station, a 1950s body shop, and a 1960s suburban garage. *(6060 Wilshire Blvd., at Fairfax. ☎ 323-930-2277. Open Tu-Su 10am-6pm; Discovery Center closes at 5pm. $7, students and seniors $5, ages 5-12 $3, under 5 free. Full-day parking $6.)*

GEORGE C. PAGE MUSEUM OF LA BREA DISCOVERIES. The smelly **La Brea Tar Pits,** which fill the area with an acrid petroleum stench, provide the inspiration for this museum. Mistaking the pits for a lake, thirsty mammals of bygone geological ages drank from these pools of water only to find themselves stuck in the tar that oozed below. Most of their one million recovered bones are on display here, along with reconstructed Ice Agers and murals of prehistoric L.A. The only human unearthed in the pits stands out in holographic horror—discovered in 1914, the La Brea woman, standing no more than 4'8", was presumably thrown into the tar 9000 years ago after having holes drilled into her skull. A viewing station exists at Pit 91 where archaeologists continue their digging. *(5801 Wilshire Blvd., at Curson Ave. Wilshire Blvd. buses stop in front of the museum. ☎ 323-857-6309. Open M-F 9:30am-5pm, Sa-Su 10am-5pm. Tours of grounds 1pm, museum tours Tu-Su 2:15pm. $6, students and seniors $3.50, ages 5-12 $2; 1st Tu of each month free. Parking $5 with validation.)*

WEST HOLLYWOOD

Melrose Avenue, running from Santa Monica Blvd. at the edge of West Hollywood into Hollywood, lined with restaurants, art galleries, and shops, is home to the hip. The choicest stretch is between La Brea and Fairfax Ave. While much sold here is used ("vintage"), none of it is really cheap (see Shopping, p. 416). North of the Beverly Center is the **Pacific Design Center,** 8687 Melrose Avenue (☎ 310-657-0800; www.pacificdesigncenter.com), a sea-green glass complex nicknamed the Blue Whale and constructed in the shape of a rippin' wave. In addition to 125 design showrooms, which mostly showcase home and furnishing projects, this rich man's Home Depot has a public plaza and 350-seat amphitheater called the Silver Screen, which stages free summer concerts and art exhibits (call for schedules).

DOWNTOWN

Downtown is spotted with people but lacks any overpowering energy. Pick up two detailed **Angels Walk** brochures (available at the Visitors Center, central library, and museums) which organize "symbolic and whimsical" sites around the financial district (Historic Core Walk) and the Civic Center (Main Walk) into two connecting 15-point walking tours modeled on Boston's Freedom Trail—except that city planners, not revolutionary heroes, dictated its course. Each guide has a map and helpful MTA information. The **Los Angeles Conservancy** (www.laconser-

THE INSIDER'S CITY

LITTLE TOKYO

Angelenos of Japanese ancestry live elsewhere—like suburban Gardena—but Little Tokyo is still an active cultural center, as well as home to fantastic and unique architecture.

1 **Little Tokyo Visitor Center,** 307 E. 1st St. (☎213-613-1911) has maps and info.

2 **Japanese Village Plaza,** 300 block E. 2nd St., is a wild florid fusion of shopping-mall Americana and Japanese design.

3 **Japanese American National Museum,** 369 E. 1st St., is housed in a Buddhist temple and an accompanying building designed by Roy Obata (see p. 407).

4 **Japanese American Cultural & Community Center,** 244 S. San Pedro St., is a showcase of community art (see p. 407).

5 **Japan America Theatre,** opens its handwoven silk *doncho* (curtain) to cultural events like Kabuki theater.

6 **A Thousand Cranes,** 120 S. Los Angeles St. (☎213-629-1200), overlooks Japanese gardens and serves shabu-shabu and tempura.

vancy.org) also offers free, printable self-guided walking tours geared toward architectural landmarks on its website as well as a variety of docentled Saturday tours featuring Downtown's historic buildings. (☎213-623-2489. Tours $8. Make reservations at least 1 week in advance.)

The **DASH Shuttle** runs six lines Downtown that cover most of the major tourist destinations. ($0.25; see p. 373. References in the listings below are for M-F travel.) If driving, park in a secure lot, rather than on the street. Due to expensive short-term parking ($1.50 per 20min.) and reasonable day rates ($5-10), it's best to park in a public lot and hit the pavement on foot. Parking rates decrease in the early morning, late at night, and on weekends. The **L.A. Visitors Center,** 685 S. Figueroa St., is gushing with answers to your travel queries, with pamphlets for every place you could possibly want to visit. (Open M-F 8am-5pm, Sa 8:30am-5pm. See p. 377.)

EL PUEBLO HISTORIC PARK. The historic birthplace of L.A. is now known as **El Pueblo de Los Angeles Historical Monument,** bordered by Cesar Chavez Ave., Alameda St., Hollywood Fwy., and Spring St. (DASH B). In 1781, 44 settlers established a pueblo and farming community here; today, 27 buildings from the eras of Spanish and Mexican rule are preserved.

The **Plaza** (1825-30), with its century-old Moreton Bay fig trees and huge *kiosko*, is the center of El Pueblo. The cheapest churros (2 for $1), as well as pictures on a stuffed pony are offered here. Walk down **Olvera Street,** which resembles a colorful Mexican marketplace, and bargain at *puestos* (vendor stalls) selling everything from Mexican handicrafts and food to personalized t-shirts. The street is the site of the Cinco de Mayo and Día de los Muertos celebrations of L.A.'s Mexican population (see **Seasonal Events,** p. 414). The **Avila Adobe** (c. 1818), 10 E. Olvera St., is the "oldest" house in the city; its adobe was reinforced by concrete to meet earthquake regulations. On the first floor of the **Sepulveda House** (1887) is the **Visitors Center,** where you can join a free walking tour or take a map and steer yourself. Upon request, view *Pueblo of Promise,* an 18min. history of L.A. (☎213-628-1274. Tours W-Sa 10, 11am, noon.)

CHINATOWN. Today's **Chinatown** (DASH B), roughly bordered by Yale, Spring, Ord, and Bernard streets, is home to less than five percent of the city's Chinese population. With its pagoda-like gates, pedestrian lanes, restaurants, and kitsch vendors, it can be quite vibrant during the day, but for a more authentic experience of Chinese-American culture, visit Monterey Park, 6 mi. to the east. Pick up walking tour maps at the **Chinatown Heritage and Visitors Center.** *(977 N. Broadway. ☎213-617-0396. Open M-F 9:30am-5pm.)*

CIVIC CENTER. The **Civic Center,** (DASH B and D) is a solid wall of bureaucratic architecture sitting south of El Pueblo, bounded by the Hollywood Fwy. (U.S. 101), Grand Ave., 1st, and San Pedro St. Unless you have a hearing for that parking violation you got in Hollywood, there isn't much reason to go inside. One of the best-known buildings in the Southland, **City Hall,** 200 N. Spring St., "has starred in more movies than most actors."

Tours of the **Music Center** are offered weekdays and show the three-theatre complex as performance schedules permit. *(135 N. Grand Ave.* ☎ *213-972-7211; www.music-center.org.)* The **Dorothy Chandler Pavilion,** the old site of the Academy Awards, houses the L.A. Opera. *(☎213-972-8001; www.laopera.org.)* The **Mark Taper Forum** and the **Ahmanson Theatre** are also on site. *(☎ 213-628-2772; www.taperahmanson.com.)*

LITTLE TOKYO & THE ARTS DISTRICT. Southeast of the Civic Center, east of 2nd and San Pedro St., lies **Little Tokyo** (DASH A). Founded with the opening of a Japanese restaurant in 1886, Little Tokyo served as the spiritual, cultural, and commercial center for Japanese immigrants and their descendants until deportation during WWII. After returning from interment camps, many Japanese-Americans moved to the suburbs, but successful efforts to rejuvenate the area have lead it to regain its traditional status as a community center (see **The Insider's City,** at left).

The Japanese American Cultural and Community Center is home to a plaza designed by the renowned Isamu Noguchi, the quiet James Irvine Garden and its 170 ft. stream, and the Doikazi Gallery of calligraphy, *ikebana* (flower displays), and other traditional art forms. *(244 S. San Pedro St.* ☎ *213-628-2725. Gallery open Tu-F noon-5pm, Sa-Su 11am-4pm. $3. See left.)* The **Japanese-American National Museum,** 369 E. 1st St., has a Resource Center with interactive computers and access to WWII relocation camp records. *(☎213-625-0414; www.janm.org. Open Tu-W and F-Su 10am-5pm, Th 10am-8pm. Resource Center closes at 5pm. $6, seniors $5, students and ages 6-17 $3, under 5 free; Th after 5pm and first Th of each month free.)*

The Frank Gehry-renovated **MOCA at The Geffen Contemporary,** 152 N. Central Ave., was once the garage for the LAPD fleet. The "Temporary Contemporary" became permanent to the delight of its adoring public, and the city now leases its space for $1 per year. Summer Thursday nights offer free top-notch jazz and cheap munchies. *(☎213-626-6222; www.moca.org. Open Tu-W and F-Su 11am-5pm, Th 11am-9pm. $8, students and seniors $5, under 12 free; Th 5-8pm free. Admission good for both Downtown MOCA locations. Shuttle transportation between the 2 locations offered.)*

OTHER SIGHTS. To see L.A.'s history etched in stone, check out the sides of the **L.A. Times** building between 1st and 2nd St. and on the corner of Spring St. Bargain hounds can haggle to their hearts' delight in the **Fashion District,** which is bordered by 6th and 9th St. along Los Angeles St. On Saturdays, these small, open-front wholesale stores sell their flimsy brandname (e.g. "DNKY") knockoffs individually. Get sequin tube tops, push-up bras, colored contacts (non-prescription), or packs of socks for cheap. The **Cooper Building,** 860 S. Los Angeles St., is a good first stop. The equally well-stocked **Grand Central Public Market** (see **Food,** p. 387) has its own stars in the sidewalk out front, each bearing the name of a Chicano celebrity—a *rambla de fama* to complement Hollywood's. An L.A. fixture, the market is one of the best spots to taste some local flavor.

SOUTHERN DISTRICTS. The **Financial District** (DASH B and C) is a fusion of glass and steel, where gigantic offices crowd the busy Downtown (bounded roughly by 3rd, 6th, Figueroa St., and Olive St.). The **Library Tower,** 633 W. 5th St., is the tallest building in L.A. at 1017 ft., and the **Westin Bonaventure Hotel,** 404 S. Figueroa St., has appeared in *Rain Man, In the Line of Fire,* and *This Is Spinal Tap.* The easily amused can spend hours in the high-speed elevators. Don't scoff at them; the view from the 32nd floor is better than the view from most helicopters. Just a bit southeast of the Bonaventure is the historic **Biltmore Hotel,** 506 S. Grand Ave., a $10 million, 1000-room hotel designed by Schultze and Weaver (best known for New

York's Waldorf-Astoria). It was a filming location for *Dave*, *Independence Day*, *Ghostbusters*, and *The Sting*, which featured scenes in the Crystal Ballroom.

Before **Bunker Hill** sprouted skyscrapers, it was a residential area with expensive Victorian homes. The one remaining relic from this era is **Angel's Flight,** "the shortest railway in the world." *(Runs daily 6:30am-10pm, $0.25.)* On the southwest side of the hill along 5th St. are the Bunker Hill Steps—a fantastic, florid maze of escalators, stairs, and landings modeled after the Spanish Steps in Rome.

MUSEUM OF CONTEMPORARY ART (MOCA). The Museum of Contemporary Art (MOCA), 250 S. Grand Ave., in the California Plaza, is a celebrated piece of modern architecture. Arata Isozaki found inspiration for the facade's curve in L.A.'s favorite daughter, Marilyn Monroe. The most compelling collection of Western modern visual art ever curated is now on permanent display at MOCA's Downtown locales. Thursday nights play host to free musical entertainment. *(☎213-626-6222; www.moca.org. Open Tu-W and F-Su 11am-5pm, Th 11am-8pm. $8, students and seniors $5, under 12 free; Th 5-8pm free. Art talks led by local artists at noon, 1, 2pm; free with admission.)*

NEAR DOWNTOWN

EXPOSITION PARK

Southwest of Downtown, off Rte. 110, bounded by Exposition Blvd., Vermont Ave., Figueroa, and Martin Luther King Jr. Blvd. From Downtown, take DASH shuttle F or MTA #81 or 442. From Hollywood, take MTA #204 or 354 down Vermont Ave. From Santa Monica, take MTA #20, 22, 320, or 322 on Wilshire Blvd.; transfer to #204 at Vermont Ave. Parking: at Figueroa St. and Exposition Blvd. ($5).

Once an upscale suburb, Exposition Park began to decline around 1900, plummeting to its lowest point in the 1920s, as wealthier citizens moved west. This population vacuum was filled by immigrants, who were barred from the Westside by homeowners' associations. The resulting low-cost, high-density housing further depressed the neighborhood. The deterioration was counteracted when the Olympic Games came to town in 1932, and the neighborhood was revitalized again for the 2nd Olympic Games at the park in 1984. Today, the entire area could use another Olympic makeover. Its museums are generally safe and well visited, but **visitors should exercise caution outside the park, especially at night.**

CALIFORNIA SCIENCE CENTER (CSC). Dedicated to the sciences of California, the interactive exhibits in this spiffy new building educate kids and adults alike about West Coast issues: earthquakes, smog, traffic, and studio production. A display on California's fault lines has a jarring rendition of a magnitude 8.3 earthquake. You can even design your own earthquake-proof buildings. Ironically, McDonald's sponsors a nutrition display. *(700 State Dr. ☎323-SCIENCE/724-3623; www.casciencectr.org. Open daily 10am-5pm. Free.)* The five-story, 70 ft. wide **IMAX Theater** shows 45min. films on nature, space, and special effects. *(☎213-744-7400. Shows every hr. M-Th 10am-5pm, F-Su 10am-7pm. $7, students and seniors $5.25, ages 4-12 $4.25. Discounts for more than 1 ticket. Evening shows often sell out; call ☎213-744-2019 to reserve tickets, $2 surcharge.)* The CSC's formal **rose garden** is the last remnant of the blessed days when the park was a horticultural exposition. The garden has over 19,000 specimens of 200 varieties of roses surrounding green lawns, gazebos, fountains, and a lily pond. *(Open Mar. 16-Dec. 31 daily 8:30am-5pm. Free.)*

OTHER MUSEUMS. The **California African-American Museum** showcases the history of African Americans and their experience in California via rotating exhibits. *(600 State Dr. ☎213-744-7432; www.caam.ca.gov. Open Tu-Su 10am-5pm. Free.)* The **Natural History Museum,** which has exhibits about pre-Columbian cultures and American history until 1914, features "habitat halls" with North American and African mammals and dinosaur skeletons. The hands-on **Discovery Center** allows visitors to interact

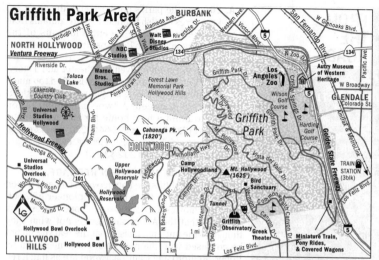

Griffith Park Area

with animals and fossils in various ways. *(900 Exposition Blvd. ☎ 213-743-4861. Open 10am-5pm daily. $8, seniors and ages 13-18 $5.50, ages 5-12 $2, under 5 free; free 1st Tu of each month. Pavilion of Wings $3, students and seniors $2, ages 5-12 $1.)*

GRIFFITH PARK & GLENDALE

Five times larger than New York's Central Park, Griffith Park is an expansive 4107 acres, and the site of many outdoor diversions, ranging from golf and tennis to hiking. The L.A. Zoo, the Griffith Observatory and Planetarium, Travel Town, a bird sanctuary, and 52 mi. of hiking trails decorate the dry hills. The park stretches from the hills above North Hollywood to the intersection of Rte. 134 (Ventura Fwy.) and I-5 (Golden State Fwy.). Several of the mountain roads through the park (especially Vista Del Valle Dr.) offer panoramic views of Downtown L.A., Hollywood, and the Westside.

Griffith Park, the nation's largest municipal park, is surprisingly rugged for its urban location—north of Hollywood and east of Universal City. The 5 mi. hike to the top of Mount Hollywood, the highest peak in the park, is quite popular. For information on this and other trails, stop by the **Visitors Center and Ranger Headquarters**, 4730 Crystal Spring Dr. (☎323-913-4688, emergency 323-913-7390. Park open daily 5am-10pm.) The park has designated equestrian trails and numerous places to saddle up. No experience is necessary, and guides are provided. **Circle K Stables**, 914 Mariposa St., Burbank, is open weekends, takes customers first come, first served, and accepts cash only. (☎818-843-9890. Open daily 7:30am-6pm; in winter closes at 4:30pm. $18 1st hr., $12 each additional hr.)

PLANETARIUM & OBSERVATORY. The white stucco and copper domes of the castle-like mountaintop observatory are visible from around Griffith Park, and the observatory parking lot affords a terrific view of the Hollywood sign. You may remember the planetarium from the James Dean film *Rebel Without A Cause.* Unfortunately, the observatory and planetarium are closed until 2005, when they will re-open with an additional 35,000 sq. ft. The grounds will remain open. *(Drive to the top of Mt. Hollywood on Vermont Ave. or Hillhurst St. from Los Feliz Blvd., or take MTA #180 or 181 from Hollywood Blvd. ☎323-664-1181, recording 323-664-1191; www.griffithobs.org. Free parking, use Vermont St. entrance to Griffith Park. Grounds open in summer daily 12:30-10pm; in winter Tu-F 2-10pm, Sa-Su 12:30-10pm.)*

FROM THE ROAD

ON LOCATION

One thing I've taken for granted as an avid TV and movie watcher is the dedication and expertise of those who we don't see on screen. Sitting at home on my sofa, I would marvel at the beauty of the skyline caught by the camera or the spectacular architecture of that Downtown building. What I didn't truly realize until taking the Universal Studios and Warner Brothers behind the scene tours is that the beautiful skyline was painted on an enormous canvas and the Downtown building was built with painted aluminum siding. The same skyline will be re-painted by a set designer to look like a highway running through the Arizona desert for the next motion picture and the building will appear in hundreds of scenes, each time looking like a setting from a completely different part of the world. All the while, we will not notice. Even on the tours we do not notice until the tour guide points it out and shows us various scenes from different movies on the TV in the golf cart. Eventually the air is filled with sounds of "oh my gosh, it is, look..." and the tour guide drives on with a wide smile on his face. It would cost a studio hundreds of millions of dollars more if they had to fly to every location required for film. Instead, the set designers create the location on the studio lots and the audience never knows the difference. A successful movie definitely requires talented actors, powerful producers, and creative directors, but the work of the designers and the manipulation of the camera is the true beauty of film making. Sometimes it takes a tour to appreciate it.

–James Kearney

L.A. ZOO. At the park's northern end, the zoo's 113 well-kept acres furnish habitats for rare animals from around the world. The recent additions of the Komodo dragon and the Red Ape Rain Forest, featuring the orangutan, are very popular. The Children's Zoo has an interactive adventure theater and a storytime area. During summer, the heat is often too much for the animals—viewing all your favorites is certainly not guaranteed. A two-year construction project to build a new home for the sea lions is underway. *(333 Zoo Dr. ☎ 323-644-4200; www.lazoo.org. Open Sept.-June daily 10am-5pm; July-Aug. daily 10am-6pm. $8.25, seniors $5.25, ages 2-12 $3.25.)*

AUTRY MUSEUM OF WESTERN HERITAGE. The Autry Museum blurs the line between fact and fiction of the Old West in its exhibits on pioneer life, outlaws, and movies. City slickers and lone rangers may discover that the American West is not what they thought—the museum insists that the real should not be confused with the reel. Still, costumes worn by Robert Redford and Clint Eastwood are as much relics as the authentic saddles and spurs of California's first cowboys, the *vaqueros.* Check out the Holdout Arm Cheating Device for concealing cards, and the extensive Colt firearms collection in the Community Gallery. *(4700 Western Heritage Way. ☎ 323-667-2000. Open Tu-W and F-Su 10am-5pm, Th 10am-8pm. $7.50, students and seniors $5, ages 2-12 $3; Th after 4pm and the 2nd Tu of each month free.)*

FOREST LAWN CEMETERY. A rather twisted sense of celebrity sightseeing may lead some travelers to Glendale, where they can gaze upon stars who won't run away when chased for a picture. Among the illustrious dead are Clark Gable, George Burns, and Sammy Davis, Jr. The cemetery also has reproductions of Michelangelo pieces, as well as the "largest religious painting on earth" (the 195 ft. by 45 ft. *Crucifixion*), transported from Europe in sections wrapped around telephone poles. Forest Lawn allegedly inspired the "Whispering Glades Cemetery" (of Evelyn Waugh's novel *The Loved One*), where death and showbiz combine to transform sorrow and spirituality into something more marketable and cliched. *(1712 Glendale Ave. From Downtown, take MTA #90 or 91 and get off just after the bus leaves San Fernando Rd. to turn onto Glendale Ave. By car from I-5 or the Glendale Fwy., take Los Feliz Blvd. south to Rte. 2 (Glendale Ave.). ☎ 800-204-3131. Grounds open Mar.-Oct. daily 8am-6pm; Nov.-Feb. 8am-5pm. Mausoleum open 9am-4:30pm.)*

TRAVEL TOWN MUSEUM. At the very northern tip of the park, this museum is the resting place of several antique train sections, given by the railroad companies to the children of L.A. Locomotives pulling freight cars, passenger cars, and cabooses are shined by kiddie shoes daily as visitors are invited to climb aboard. The museum's collection no longer exhibits airplanes, but automobiles and fire engines (1869-1940) historically connected to L.A. are still on display. Children will demand to take the train ride. Tours of a first-class passenger train are conducted on the 3rd weekend of each month. *(5200 Zoo Dr. ☎ 323-662-5874. Open M-F 10am-5pm, Sa-Su 10am-6pm. Free. Train ride $2, seniors $1.25, children 13 and under $1.50; free on the 1st weekend of the month.)*

SAN FERNANDO VALLEY

Movie studios are the defining feature of the San Fernando Valley. Passing Burbank on Rte. 134 (the Ventura Fwy.), you will see some of the Valley's most lucrative words: **Universal, Warner Bros., NBC,** and **Disney**. To best experience the industry, attend a **free TV show taping** or take one of the tours offered by most studios.

◪UNIVERSAL STUDIOS. A movie and television studio that happens to have the world's first and largest movie-themed amusement park attached, Universal Studios Hollywood is the most popular tourist spot in Tinseltown. Located north of Hollywood in its own municipality, Universal City (complete with police and fire station), the park was born as a public tour of the studios in 1964. It has since become a full-fledged amusement park with riding attractions and live shows featuring Universal brand names. The signature Studio Tour provides riders with an insider's view of America's movie tradition as it wanders through backlots past blockbuster sets including *The Great Outdoors*, *Jurassic Park*, and the infamous Bates Motel from *Psycho*, among many others. However, for some the tour plays second fiddle to the park's interactive adventures. The movie itself may have bombed, but the live stunts at the *Waterworld* spectacular are impressive. Travel through time with Doc Brown in *Back to the Future: The Ride*, fly with *E.T.* on his journey across galaxies, or endure the heat of the blazing inferno in *Backdraft*. *(Take Rte. 101 to Universal Center Dr. or Landershim Blvd. Exits. Or take MTA bus #420 bus west from Downtown or east from the Valley. ☎818-622-3801. Open July-Aug. M-F 9am-9pm, Sa-Su 9am-10pm; Sept.-June M-F 10am-6pm, Sa-Su 9am-7pm. Last tram leaves at 6:15pm; in off-season 4:15pm. Tours in Spanish daily. $45, ages 3-9 $35. Parking $8.)*

UNIVERSAL CITY WALK. If, miraculously, you manage to retain some energy (or cash) after a tour of Universal Studios, or you just want to stroll in the sun, head to the adjacent shopping, food, and entertainment strip. The City Walk offers 65 cool things to do and 22 places to eat. The mammoth green guitar outside the Hard Rock Cafe and the colossal 18-screen Cineplex Odeon movie theater set the precedent for this larger-than-life window-shopping extravaganza. *(City Walk parking $8. Full refund if you buy 2 movie tickets before 6pm, $2 refund after 6pm.)*

MISSION SAN FERNANDO REY DE ESPAÑA. One of the few L.A. sights with any history is the San Fernando Mission, in Mission Hills. It was founded in 1797 by Padre Fermin Lasuen, but no structures remain from the original. The building that stands today is an amazing re-creation. The grounds, with museum and gift shop, are beautifully kept and definitely worth a visit. *(15101 San Fernando Mission Blvd. ☎818-361-0186. Mass M-Sa 7:25am, Su 9 and 10:30am. Open daily 9am-4:15 pm. $4, seniors and ages 7-15 $3.)*

SIX FLAGS THEME PARKS. At the opposite end of the Valley, 40min. north of L.A. in Valencia, is **Magic Mountain.** Not for novices, Magic Mountain has the hairiest roller coasters in Southern California, if not the world. **X,** the park's latest addition forces riders to flip, spin, and rotate 360 degrees, creating a legitimate flying phenomenon. **Goliath** provides a 3min., 85 mph thrill and an underground tunnel. Other highlights of the park include: **Revolution,** a smooth metal coaster with mind-blowing loops; **Colossus,** California's largest wooden roller coaster; the world's largest looping roller coaster, **Viper; Tidal Wave** (stand on the bridge for an impromptu shower); **Deja Vu,** a coaster with a "boomerang" track; the suspended **Batman;** and the 100 mph **Superman** (meaning 6½ seconds of weightlessness). Temperatures here frequently soar above 100°F in the summer, so bring plenty of bottled water. Next door, Six Flags' waterpark **Hurricane Harbor** features the world's tallest enclosed speed slide. (☎661-255-4111. Open daily Apr.-Labor Day, hours vary; open weekends and holidays Sept.-Mar. $43, seniors and under 48 in. tall $27, under 2 free. Parking $7. **Hurricane Harbor:** ☎661-255-4527. Open May-Sept., hours vary. $22, seniors and under 48 in. tall $15, under 2 free. Combo admission to both parks $53.)

PASADENA

The splendidly helpful **Convention and Visitors Bureau,** 171 S. Los Robles Ave., is a useful first stop in Pasadena, with its numerous promotional materials and guides to regional events. (☎626-795-9311; www.pasadenacal.com. Open M-F 8am-5pm, Sa 10am-4pm.) The city provides **free shuttles** approximately every 15min. that loop between Old Town and the Downtown area around Lake Ave. Each of the twelve buses has a theme (i.e., performing arts, Arroyo Seco desert, multiculturalism) reflected in its decor. (☎626-744-4055. Shuttles run Downtown M-Th 11am-7pm, F 11am-10pm, Sa-Su noon-8pm; uptown M-F 7am-6pm, Sa-Su noon-5pm.)

ROSE BOWL. In the gorge that forms the city's western boundary stands Pasadena's most famous landmark. Home to "the granddaddy of them all"—the annual college football confrontation between the champions of the Big Ten and Pac 10 conferences, and the NCAA Football National Championship every four years—the Rose Bowl is the regular-season venue for UCLA Bruins football and Major League Soccer's L.A. Galaxy (see **Seasonal Events,** p. 414). (991 Rosemont Blvd. ☎626-577-3100. **Bruins info:** ☎310-825-2949; www.cto.ucla.edu. **Galaxy info:** ☎626-432-1540.) The bowl also hosts an enormous monthly **swap meet,** with over 2200 vendors, that attracts well over 20,000 people. (☎323-560-7469. Held the 2nd Su of each month 9am-4:30pm. Spectators $6, under 12 free. Bargain hunters $10, admitted at 7:30am; call ahead for $15 VIP admission at 6am.)

■**NORTON SIMON MUSEUM OF ART.** The recently revamped museum features a world-class collection, chronicling Western art from Italian Gothic to 20th-century abstract, with paintings by Raphael, Van Gogh, Monet, Picasso, and others. The Impressionist and Post-Impressionist hall is particularly impressive, as is the collection of Southeast Asian sculptures Simon's eclectic taste gives the collection flair. Don't miss the sculpture garden, by California landscape artist Nancy Goslee Power. (411 W. Colorado Blvd., at Orange Grove Blvd. Take MTA bus #180 or 181 west on Colorado Blvd. between Lake and N. Orange St. or #180 south on Lake St. between Washington and Colorado St. ☎626-449-6840; www.nortonsimon.org. Open W-Th and Sa-Su noon-6pm, F noon-9pm. $6, seniors $3, students with ID and children under 12 free. Wheelchair accessible.)

FENYES ESTATE. Built in 1905, the estate sits on the same grounds as the **Pasadena Museum of History** and the Pasadena city archives. It houses an impressive collection of Renaissance furniture, Egyptian sculpture, and local art amassed by Eva Scott Fenyes. Exhibitions rotate regularly. (470 W. Walnut St., off Orange Grove Blvd. ☎626-577-1660. Museum tours Th-Su every hour 1-3pm. $6, students and seniors $5.)

ARTS... The **Pasadena Playhouse,** founded in 1917, nurtured the careers of William Holden and Gene Hackman, among others. Restored in 1986, it now offers some of L.A.'s finest theater. (39 S. El Molino Ave., between Colorado Blvd. and Green St. ☎626-356-

7529. *For more info, see* **Theater,** *p. 421.*) Housed in the concrete labyrinth of the Pasadena Center, the **Pasadena Civic Auditorium,** at Colorado Blvd., is the centerpiece of the city's Spanish-influenced architecture. The Auditorium hosted television's **Emmy Awards** each year until 1998, when they were moved to Los Angeles. Since it is a rented venue, events are forever changing, but as of late, this 3000-seater has played host to the NAACP Image Awards and the Pasadena Symphony. *(300 E. Green St. ☎ 449-7360. Box office open M-Sa 10am-5pm.)* If you're sick of the arts, you can work off your intermission snacks at the **Pasadena Ice Skating Center,** which holds public skate sessions every evening Wednesday through Saturday. *(310 E. Green St., in the Pasadena Center. ☎ 626-578-0801. Schedule varies; call ahead.)*

...AND SCIENCES. Some of the world's greatest scientific minds do their work at the **California Institute of Technology (CalTech).** Founded in 1891, CalTech has amassed a faculty that includes several Nobel laureates and a student body that prides itself both on its staggering collective intellect and its practical jokes. These jokes range from the simple (unscrewing all the chairs in a lecture hall and bolting them in backwards) to the immensely elaborate (adding a message to the Rose Bowl scoreboard during the game). *(1201 E. California Blvd., about 2½ mi. southeast of Old Town. ☎ 626-395-6327. Tours daily.)* **NASA's Jet Propulsion Laboratory,** about 5 mi. north of Old Town, executed the journey of the Mars Pathfinder. Ask to see pictures of the face of Mars. *(4800 Oak Grove Dr. ☎ 818-354-9314. Free tours by appointment.)*

OTHER SIGHTS. Besides spectator sports, Pasadena's main draw is **Old Town,** bound approximately by Walnut St. and Del Mar Ave., between Pasadena Ave. and Arroyo Pkwy. This vibrant shopping and dining mecca, which proudly calls itself "trendy," also includes **Central Park** and 12 parking garages. The **Plaza Pasadena** is the shopping mall just east on Colorado Blvd.—stop in if only to beat the heat. On the northern side of Plaza Pasadena is the beautiful **City Hall,** 100 N. Garfield Ave., complete with an open courtyard, lush gardens, and a fountain. *(☎ 626-744-4228.)*

NEAR PASADENA

HUNTINGTON LIBRARY, ART GALLERY, AND BOTANICAL GARDENS. This institute was built in 1910 as the home of Henry Huntington, who made his money in railroads and California real estate. Its stunning gardens host 150 acres of plants. (Picnicking and sunbathing among the greens is strictly forbidden.) The library holds one of the world's most important collections of rare books, as well as British and American manuscripts, including a Gutenberg Bible, Benjamin Franklin's handwritten autobiography, a 1410 manuscript of Chaucer's *Canterbury Tales,* and a number of Shakespeare's first folios. The art gallery is known for its 18th- and 19th-century British paintings. The Virginia Steele Scott Gallery has American art, the Arabella Huntington Memorial Collection displays Renaissance paintings and 18th-century French decorative art, and tea is served in the Rose Garden Tea Room. *(1151 Oxford Rd., between Huntington Dr. and California Blvd. in San Marino, south of Pasadena, about 2 mi. south of the Allen Ave. Exit from I-210. From Downtown L.A., take MTA bus #79 out of Union Station to San Marino Ave. and walk ½ mi. (45min. trip). ☎ 626-405-2100. Open Memorial Day to Labor Day Tu-Su 10:30am-4:30pm; in winter Tu-F noon-4:30pm, Sa-Su 10:30am-4:30pm. $10, seniors $8.50, students $7, under 12 free; 1st Th of each month free.)*

SOUTHWEST MUSEUM. Recent remodeling and innovative exhibits give this Highland Park museum the attention it deserves. The palatial Spanish-Moorish building has Native American cultural artifacts, including a Tlingit totem pole. *(234 Museum Dr. Take MTA bus #83 along Broadway to Museum Dr. By car, take the I-110 (Pasadena Fwy.) to Ave. 43 and follow the signs. ☎ 323-221-2164. www.southwestmuseum.org. Open Tu-Su 10am-5pm; library open W-Sa 10am-5pm. $6, students and seniors $4, ages 7-18 $3.)*

RAGING WATERS. Beat the heat with 50 acres of slides, pools, whitewater rafts, inner tubes, fake waves, and even a fake island (this is L.A., after all). Hurl yourself over the seven-story waterslide **Drop Out** or rush down **Speed Slide.** *111 Raging Waters Dr. At I-10, Rte. 210, and 57. ☎909-802-2200. Open May-Sept. Su-Th 10am-8pm, F-Sa 10am-9pm; Mar-Apr. hours vary. $27, under 48 in. tall $15, under 2 free; after 4pm $17, under 48 in. tall $10. Parking $6; lockers $4-6.)*

◘ SEASONAL EVENTS

▓ Tournament of Roses Parade and Rose Bowl (☎626-449-7673), in Pasadena. New Year's Day, Jan. 1, is always a perfect day in Southern California. Some of the wildest New Year's Eve parties happen along Colorado Blvd., the parade route. If you miss the parade, which runs from 8-10am, you can still see the floats on display that afternoon and on Jan. 2 at the intersection of Paloma and Sierra Madre ($1). The champs of the Pac 10 and Big 10 conferences meet on the afternoon of Jan. 1 for the Rose Bowl; and every 4 years, the NCAA Football National Championship is held here. Only a few end-zone tickets are available to the public; call ☎626-449-4100 after Nov. 1.

Chinese New Year Parade (☎213-617-0396), in Chinatown. Fireworks and dragons usher in this Chinese celebration.

UCLA Mardi Gras (☎310-825-6564), at the athletic field. Billed as the world's largest collegiate activity (a terrifying thought). Festivities run from 7pm-2am on Fat Tuesday, which is in mid-May. Proceeds go to charity.

Playboy Jazz Festival (☎310-449-4070), at the Hollywood Bowl. 2 days of entertainment by top-name jazz musicians of all varieties, from traditional to fusion. Sorry, no bunnies. Call Ticketmaster (☎213-381-2000) for prices.

Gay Pride Celebration (☎323-969-8302), funded by the Christopher Street West Association, the last or second-to-last weekend in June, in West Hollywood. L.A.'s lesbian and gay communities celebrate in full effect. Art, politics, dances, and a big parade to top it all off. Tickets $12.

Shakespeare Festival/L.A. (☎213-481-2273), in Hollywood, Downtown, Rancho Palos Verdes, and Pasadena, in June and July. This theater company aims to make Shakespeare accessible to all. Willpower to Youth program performs Shakespeare adaptations (early Aug.). Canned food donation accepted in lieu of admission at performances within the city of L.A. Palos Verdes shows in the last 2 weeks of July are $15-18.

Día des los Muertos, along Olvera St., Downtown, Nov. 1. Rousing Mexican cultural celebration for the spirits of dead ancestors revisiting the world of the living. Food, vendors, costumes, and Halloween accoutrements.

Los Posados (☎213-485-9777), along Olvera St., Downtown, in Dec. This celebration includes a candlelight procession and the breaking of a piñata.

Whale-watching is best Dec.-Mar., as the Pacific grays migrate south. For the past few years, 90% of the world's blue whale population has summered off the Channel Islands (see p. 443). Boats depart from Ventura, Long Beach, and San Pedro.

▓ L.A. BY REGION

So you've dropped your bags off, grabbed a bite to eat, and maybe even seen some of the sights. Now the real fun begins. From basketball to bookstores, cafes to clubs, L.A.'s got something for you. Below are a few handy charts of L.A.'s best options. There's shopping—including music (p. 416), books (p. 416), clothes (p. 417), and novelties (p. 417); entertainment—including cinemas (p. 419) and live theaters (p. 421); and nightlife—including late-night restaurants (p. 423), coffeehouses (p. 424), bars (p. 425), clubs (p. 426), and LGB nightlife (p. 427). They're grouped by region, so if you find yourself looking for a movie in Hollywood, or craving a late-night snack in the Valley, you'll know where to go.

HOLLYWOOD (& AROUND)

SHOPPING	
Counterpoint Records (p. 416)	Music
Hollywood & Highland (p. 418)	Malls
☒ Samuel French (p. 416)	Books
Skeletons in the Closet (p. 417)	Novelties
Studio Wardrobe Dept. (p. 417)	Clothes

ENTERTAINMENT	
El Capitan (p. 420)	Cinema
☒ Grauman's Chinese (p. 420)	Theater
☒ Pacific Cinerama Dome (p. 420)	Cinema
Pantages (p. 421)	Theater

NIGHTLIFE	
Akbar's (p. 427)	LGB
Arena (p. 426)	Club

NIGHTLIFE (CONT.)	
Barney's Beanery (p. 423)	Late-Nite
☒ Beauty Bar (p. 425)	Bar
The Coach and Horses (p. 425)	Bar
Daddy's (p. 425)	Bar
☒ Derby (p. 426)	Club
☒ Fred 62 (p. 423)	Late-Nite
G.A.L.A.X.Y. Gallery (p. 424)	Coffee
Groundling Theater (p. 424)	Comedy
Martini Lounge (p. 426)	Club
☒ The Room (p. 425)	Bar
Standard Lounge (p. 425)	Bar
Stir Crazy (p. 424)	Coffee
☒ The 3 of Clubs (p. 425)	Bar

WEST L.A.

SHOPPING	
Beverly Center (p. 418)	Mall
Century City Complex (p. 418)	Mall
City Rags (p. 417)	Clothes
☒ Moby Disc (p. 416)	Music
Rhino Records (p. 417)	Music
Westside Pavilion (p. 418)	Mall

ENTERTAINMENT (CONT.)	
Geffen Playhouse (p. 421)	Cinema
LACMA's Bing Theater (p. 421)	Theater
Mann's Village Theatre (p. 420)	Theater
Nuart Theatre (p. 420)	Theater

NIGHTLIFE	
Cow's End (p. 424)	Coffee
Maloney's (p. 425)	Bar

WEST HOLLYWOOD, FAIRFAX, & SUNSET STRIP

SHOPPING	
Aardvark's (p. 417)	Clothes
Baby Jane of Hollywood (p. 418)	Novelties
☒ Book Soup (p. 416)	Books
A Different Light (p. 416)	Books
☒ Dudley Doo-Right (p. 417)	Novelties
Out of the Closet (p. 417)	Novelties
Retail Slut (p. 417)	Clothes
Vinyl Fetish (p. 416)	Music

NIGHTLIFE	
☒ Abbey Cafe (p. 427)	LGB
☒ Canter's (p. 423)	Late-Nite
Comedy Store (p. 424)	Comedy
Micky's (p. 427)	LGB

NIGHTLIFE (CONT.)	
☒ Miyagi's (p. 425)	Bar
Key Club (p. 426)	Club
L.A. Improv (p. 424)	Comedy
☒ Largo (p. 426)	Club
Laugh Factory (p. 425)	Comedy
Mel's Drive In (p. 423)	Late-Nite
The Palms (p. 427)	LGB
Rage (p. 427)	LGB
☒ Rainbow Grill (p. 423)	Late-Nite
Roxy (p. 426)	Club
7969 Peanuts (p. 427)	LGB
WEHO Lounge (p. 424)	Coffee
Whisky A Go-Go (p. 426)	Club

THE SAN FERNANDO VALLEY

SHOPPING	
☒ Moby Disc (p. 416)	Music
☒ Samuel French (p. 416)	Books

ENTERTAINMENT	
☒ Loews Cineplex (p. 420)	Cinema

ENTERTAINMENT (CONT.)	
Pasadena Playhouse (p. 421)	Theater

NIGHTLIFE	
Bob's Big Boy (p. 423)	Late-Nite
Jerry's Famous Deli (p. 423)	Late-Nite

▢ SHOPPING

In L.A., shopping isn't just a practical necessity; it's a way of life. Popular shopping areas like Santa Monica's Third Street Promenade, Pasadena's Old Town, the Westside Pavilion, and the Century City Mall are lined with identical chain boutiques with the latest cookie-cutter fashions. Nevertheless, a number of cool specialty shops with more one-of-a-kind items are tucked away from the shuffle. Remember, dahling, when the going gets tough, Angelenos go shopping.

BOOKS

L.A. might not seem like the most literary of cities. After all, while subway commuters in other cities immerse themselves in the newspaper, Angelenos caught in an early-morning traffic jam listen to news radio. The front shelves of most L.A. bookstores are lined with Hollywood bios and practical guides on how to become a star. But fear not, hungry literati, you don't have to resort to the ubiquitous Barnes and Noble megastores just yet.

▨ **Book Soup,** 8818 Sunset Blvd. (☎310-659-3110; www.booksoup.com), in **West Hollywood.** A maze of new books in every category imaginable, with especially strong film, architecture, poetry, and travel sections. The comprehensive newsstand that wraps around the building includes industry mags and international newspapers. The Addendum next door carries sale items and lots of hardcover art, photo, and design books at reduced prices. Main store open daily 9am-midnight; Addendum open daily noon-8pm.

▨ **Samuel French Bookshop,** 7623 Sunset Blvd. (☎213-876-0570), in **Hollywood;** and 11963 Ventura Blvd. (☎818-762-0535), in **Studio City.** Get prepped for your audition at this haven for entertainment industry wisdom: acting directories, TV and film reference books, trade papers, and a vast selection of plays and screenplays. Lists local theaters that are currently casting. Occasional script signings by local playwrights. Hollywood location open M-F 10am-6pm, Sa 10am-5pm; Studio City location open M-F 10am-9pm, Sa 10am-6pm, Su noon-5pm.

A Different Light, 8853 Santa Monica Blvd. (☎310-854-6601; www.adlbooks.com), in **West Hollywood.** The nation's largest gay and lesbian bookseller has an incredibly diverse selection: gay fiction and classics, biography and autobiography, self-help, travel, law, and queer theory. The shop also has videos, magazines, music, gift items, readings, and book signings. Open daily 11am-10pm.

MUSIC

Used music stores are a dime a dozen, especially in **Westwood** and along **Melrose Ave.** Many of the stores buy old CDs and tapes, which makes for good selections of "rejections." Below are some diamonds in the mix.

▨ **Moby Disc,** 2114 Wilshire Blvd. (☎310-828-2887), in **Santa Monica;** 14622 Ventura Blvd. (☎818-990-2970), in **Encino;** and 28 E. Colorado Blvd. (☎626-449-9975), in **Pasadena.** At the great white whale of used CD stores, the odds for good finds are in your favor. Fairly non-discriminating in buying used CDs. Smaller new CD and used cassette sections. Open daily 11am-8pm.

Counterpoint Records and Books, 5911 Franklin Ave. (☎323-957-7965; www.counterpointrecordsandbooks.com), in **Hollywood.** One of L.A.'s best vinyl collections and a smaller collection of used CDs and tapes. They have everything from blues to punk. Counterpoint doubles as a used bookstore, and its walls are crammed with both popular and obscure titles. Open M-Th 11am-11pm, F-Sa 11am-midnight, Su 1-8pm.

Vinyl Fetish, 7305 Melrose Ave. (☎323-935-1300), in **West Hollywood.** The LP collection you wish you owned. Top-rate rock, funk, industrial, ska, punk, new wave, and disco. Records $5-20, depending on condition and rarity. CDs, tapes, books, t-shirts, stickers, pins, and other accessories. Open daily 11am-10pm.

Aron's, 1150 N. Highland Ave. (☎323-469-4700), in **Hollywood,** between Santa Monica and Sunset Blvd. Well loved for its massive new and used CD collection, which ranges from ska to showtunes. Open Su-Th 10am-10pm, F-Sa 10am-midnight.

Mr. Musichead, 709 N. Sierra Bonita (☎323-658-7625), in **West Hollywood,** at Melrose St. Although Mr. Musichead has a collection of 60s and 70s rock and jazz, it's better known for posters and collectibles from the same era. Open daily 11am-7pm.

Rhino Records, 2028 Westwood Blvd. (☎310-474-8685), in **West L.A.** Specializes in the obscure, the alternative, and those never-played promotional albums that couldn't find a home. Strong blues, jazz, exotica, and dance sections. Definitive collection of titles on the excellent Rhino label specializing in re-issues. Open M-Th 10am-11pm, F-Sa 10am-midnight, Su 10am-9pm.

CLOTHING

It's a fashion war out there, and you've got to look your best. Fashion in the City of Angels is one-half glitz, one-half retro, and both halves acutely aware that this is *not* New York—black just doesn't cut it. Your mission is to look like heaven at one hell of a low price. Unfortunately, with so many overpriced boutiques in L.A., that's not always easy. Check out some of the great spots below.

Aaardvark's, 7579 Melrose Ave. (☎323-655-6769), in **West Hollywood;** and 85 Market St. (☎310-392-2996), in **Venice.** Used gear galore from practical used Levi's ($20-25) to fabulously funky wigs ($20). Lots of hats, leather jackets, and dresses from any decade. Open M-Th noon-8pm, F-Sa 11am-9pm, Su noon-7pm.

Retail Slut, 7308 Melrose Ave. (☎323-934-1339; www.retailslut.com), in **West Hollywood,** is a mecca for all manner of punks and goths. It's the place to find fetish gear, or just a cool spot to browse a huge selection of earrings and body-rings. Open M-Th 11am-9pm, F-Sa 11am-10pm, Su noon-8pm.

City Rags, 10967 Weyburn Ave. (☎310-209-0889), in **Westwood Village.** This small but well-stocked 70s retro-wear-house has a friendly staff and great bargains on vintage stuff that's actually wearable. If they don't have what you need, they can hunt it down. Shirts $12-16; pants $18-30. Open Su-Th 11:30am-8pm, F-Sa 11:30am-10pm.

The Studio Wardrobe Department, 1357 N. Highland Ave. (☎323-467-9455), in **Hollywood.** Everything, including the register, is vintage in this brick-walled warehouse of denims, furs, and polyesters. Known for its 25 items for $1 and 25 pairs of jeans for $5 sales. No refunds or exchanges. Open Su-Th 10am-10pm, F-Sa 10am-midnight.

NOVELTIES

L.A. has its share of eccentrics, and they've got to shop somewhere. Some are a little morbid, some may be a little too explicit, but none make apologies for what they sell or how they sell it.

Dudley Doo-Right Emporium, 8200 Sunset Blvd. (☎323-656-6550), in **West Hollywood.** Cartoonist Jay Ward's old production office is now cluttered with memorabilia based on his characters, *Rocky and Bullwinkle, George of the Jungle,* and *Dudley Doo-Right.* T-shirts $16-20, stuffed animals $10+, show scripts $8.50, storyboards $15.95. Open Tu, Th, and Sa 11am-5 pm. No credit cards.

Out of the Closet, 8224 Santa Monica Blvd. (☎323-848-9760), in **West Hollywood.** With 15 stores in the L.A. area, this is the sugar-daddy of resale retail. They've got anything you need in at least one of their stores. Profits from the sale of used clothing, electronics, and furniture are donated to the AIDS Healthcare Foundation. Look for OOC's trademark neon storefronts, or call for other locations. Open M-Sa 10am-7pm, Su 10am-6pm.

Skeletons in the Closet, 1104 Mission Rd. (☎323-343-0760), in **Downtown.** It's actually the L.A. Coroner's gift shop, and yes, it's as terrifically tasteless as it sounds. Sells personalized toe tags and beach towels with body outlines, among other morbid memorabilia. All profits go to drunk driving programs. Open M-F 8am-4:30pm.

Baby Jane of Hollywood, 7985 Santa Monica Blvd. (☎323-848-7080), in **West Hollywood,** at Laurel St. in the French Market Restaurant. Baby Jane carries more than just your typical array of old movie posters, classic records, vintage tabloids, and autographed glossies ($25-75). It also has a huge collection of *Pez,* old film industry collectibles, and shots of celebs in, shall we say, revealing poses. Open daily noon-8pm.

MALLS

Mall-shopping in L.A. is not just for the Valley Girl, and your retail-going experience need not be as unpleasant as, say, a trip to the Valley. Going to the mall can (and should) be a full-day activity, as you will need a few hours to see and be seen. Many shopping complexes are open-air, which can make shopping a stroll down a sunny, tree-lined walkway. The hub of the 'til-you-drop spots is West L.A., with these malls at the head of the pack:

Century City Shopping Complex, 10250 Santa Monica Blvd. (☎310-277-3898), in **West L.A.,** just southwest of Beverly Hills. Offers 140 stores, boutiques, and cafes, but few come just for the shops. Its well-manicured, labyrinthine walkways are a good place to spot celebrities. It also features the incredibly popular 14-screen AMC Century Theater (☎310-289-4262).

Westside Pavilion, 10800 W. Pico Blvd. (☎310-474-5940 or 0408), in **West L.A.,** has 150 shops and restaurants, including mall standards Banana Republic, Barnes & Noble, Nordstrom, and Robinson's May. And what would an L.A. mall be without a movie theater? This one features Westside Pavilion Cinemas.

Beverly Center, 8500 Beverly Blvd. (☎310-854-0070), in **Beverly Hills,** at La Cienega Blvd. Perhaps the prime example of bigger, better, more, more, more. A monstrous neon megalith smack-dab in the middle of the city, complete with voyeuristic escalators snaking up the building's glass siding; the display windows are quite showy. Attached to the Beverly Center is the nation's 1st (and the world's 2nd) **Hard Rock Cafe** (☎310-276-7605; open Su-Th 11:30am-11pm, F-Sa 11:30am-midnight).

Hollywood & Highland, 6801 Hollywood Blvd. (☎323-960-2331), in **Hollywood.** Representing the rejuvenation of Hollywood, and based on the 1916 movie *Intolerance.* The Babylon Court of this 64,000 sq. ft. complex takes center stage, serving as an outdoor gathering place and event venue, with its arch perfectly framing the Hollywood sign.

⚑ ENTERTAINMENT

There are many ways to indulge in the glitz that the entertainment capital of the world holds so dear. **Shopping** (see p. 416), for example, is a major pastime in the L.A. area, one that has been crafted into what some might call an art. For off-hours fun, L.A. features some of the trendiest, celeb-frenzied **Nightlife** (p. 423) imaginable. For amusement parks, see the listings for **Disneyland** (p. 447), **Knott's Berry Farm** (p. 449), **Magic Mountain** (p. 411), and **Universal Studios** (p. 411).

FILM & TELEVISION STUDIOS

A visit to the world's entertainment capital isn't complete without some exposure to the actual business of making a movie or TV show. Fortunately, most production companies oblige. **Paramount** (☎323-956-5000), **NBC** (☎818-840-3537), and **Warner Bros.** (☎818-954-1744) offer 2hr. guided tours that take you onto sets and through backlots. The best way to get a feel for the industry is to land yourself tickets to a TV taping. Tickets are free, but studios tend to overbook, so holding a ticket does not always guarantee that you'll get into the taping. Show up early.

NBC, 3000 W. Alameda Ave., at W. Olive Ave. in Burbank, is your best spur-of-the-moment bet. Show up at the ticket office on a weekday at 8am for passes to Jay Leno's **Tonight Show,** filmed at 5pm the same evening (2 tickets per person, must be 16+). The line starts getting long at 3pm. Studio tours run on the hour. (☎818-840-3537. M-F 9am-3pm; $8, ages 5-12 $4.) Many of NBC's "Must-See TV" shows are taped at **Warner Bros.,** 4000 Warner Blvd. (☎818-954-6000), in Burbank. Sitcoms such as the *Drew Carey Show* and *Everybody Loves Raymond* are taped from August to May—call the studio at least five business days in advance to secure tickets. NBC's *Friends* no longer films in front of a public audience. Call for information on the VIP tour. As it is the only major studio still in Hollywood, **Paramount's** tours are very popular. (Every hr. M-F 9am-2pm. $15.)

A **CBS box office,** 7800 Beverly Blvd., next to the farmer's market in West Hollywood, hands out free tickets to Bob Barker's game-show masterpiece *The Price is Right* (taped M-Th) up to one week in advance. (☎323-575-2458. Open non-taping days M-Th 9am-5pm, taping days M-Th 7:30am-5pm.) Audience members must be over 18. You can request up to 10 tickets on a specific date by sending a self-addressed, stamped envelope to *The Price is Right* Tickets, 7800 Beverly Blvd., L.A. 90036, about four to six weeks in advance.

If all else fails, **Audiences Unlimited, Inc.,** 100 Universal City Plaza, Building 4250, Universal City 91608 (☎818-506-0067; www.tvtickets.com), is a great resource. To find out which shows are available during your visit, send in a self-addressed, stamped envelope or check the website.

MOVIES

Countless theaters show films the way they were meant to be seen: in a big space, on a big screen, and with top-quality sound. It would be a cinematic crime not to take advantage of the incredible experience of movie-going in L.A.

The gargantuan theaters at **Universal City,** as well as those in **Westwood Village** near UCLA, are incredibly popular, especially on weekends. Lines at all the best theaters are very long, especially for new releases. In **Santa Monica,** there are 22 screens within the three blocks between Santa Monica Place and Wilshire Blvd. along the 3rd St. Promenade.

SO, YOU WANNA BE IN PICTURES? Honey! Baby!

Sweetheart! You don't have to be beautiful and proportionally perfect to grace celluloid—just look at Tom Arnold or Lili Tomlin. The quickest way to get noticed is to land yourself a job as an extra—no experience necessary. One day's work will land $40-130 in your pocket and two meals in your tummy. Step One is to stop calling yourself an extra—you're an "atmosphere actor" (it's better for both your ego and your resume). Step Two is to contact a reputable casting service. **Cenex Central Casting,** 220 S. Flower St., Burbank 91506 (☎818-562-2755), is the biggest, and a good place to start. You must be at least 18 and a U.S. citizen or have a Resident Alien/ Employment Authorization card. Step Three is to show up on time; you'll need the clout of DeNiro before you can waltz in after call. Don't forget to bring $20 in cash to cover the "photo fee." Step Four is to dress the part: don't wear red or white, which bleed on film and render you unusable. Finally, after you collect three **SAG** (Screen Actors Guild; 5757 Wilshire Blvd., L.A. 90036; ☎323-937-3441) vouchers, you'll be eligible to pay the $1272 to join showbiz society. See you in the movies!

Devotees of second-run, foreign-language, and experimental films are rewarded by the Santa Monica theaters away from the Promenade. Foreign films play consistently at the eight **Laemmle Theaters** in Beverly Hills (☎310-274-6869), West Hollywood (☎323-848-3500), Santa Monica (☎310-394-9741), Pasadena (☎626-844-6500), and Downtown (☎213-617-0268).

L.A.'s giant movie industry does not, surprisingly, include world-class film festivals like Cannes or Sundance. On the other hand, the city hosts a number of smaller, less expensive, and more accessible film showcases, including the **Annual L.A. International Gay and Lesbian Film Festival, Outfest** (☎323-960-9200; www.outfest.org; each film $8-12) in July, and the **Asian Pacific Film and Video Festival** (☎213-680-4462, ext. 68; each film $8, seniors and students $5), in May. The largest film festival in the area is the pricey late-Oct. **Annual AFI L.A. International Film Festival,** which shows 150 shorts, documentaries, and features from around the world. (In the US ☎323-856-7707, elsewhere 323-856-7709; www.afifest.com. $50 for full-week matinee pass; $250 for the entire festival.)

If you'd like to ogle the stars as they walk the red carpet into the theater for a **premiere,** call the four premiere-hounds: **Grauman's Chinese** (about 2 per month); **El Capitan** (Disney films only); **Mann's Westwood;** and the **Bruin,** 948 Broxton Ave. (☎310-248-6266), in Westwood. For info on what's playing in L.A., call ☎323-777-3456, or read the daily Calendar section of the *Los Angeles Times*.

MOVIE THEATERS

▦ **Loews Cineplex Cinemas** (☎818-508-0588), in **Universal City,** atop the hill at Universal City Walk. Opened in 1987 as the world's largest cinema complex, its 18 wide-screen theaters and Parisienne-style cafe put all competition to absolute shame. Tickets $9, seniors and under 13 $6; before 4pm $6.75. Full refund on parking with purchase of 2 regular admission tickets before 6pm M-F; $2 parking rebate on all other shows.

▦ **Pacific Cinerama Dome,** 6360 Sunset Blvd. (☎323-466-3401), in **Hollywood,** near Vine St. The ultimate movie screen, measuring 3 times the size of normal screens. The spectacular sound system rumbles stomachs and pierces ears nightly. Tickets $8.50, seniors and under 12 $5, 1st 3 shows daily $5.

▦ **Grauman's Chinese Theatre,** 6925 Hollywood Blvd. (☎323-464-8111), in **Hollywood.** Hype to the hilt. A must-see. For details, see **Hollywood Sights,** p. 393. Tickets $10, ages 3-12 and over 65 $6.50, 1st show of the day $7.50. Parking $6.50.

El Capitan, 6838 Hollywood Blvd. (☎323-467-7674 or 800-347-6396), in **Hollywood,** across from Grauman's. Glitz straight out of *Fantasia*. Disney movies, live Disney stage shows and exhibitions. Tickets generally $9.50, seniors and children $6. Parking in lot behind the theater on Hawthorne Ave., $4 with validation.

Mann's Village Theatre, 961 Broxton Ave. (☎310-208-0018), in **Westwood.** One auditorium, one big screen, one great THX sound system, a balcony, and Art Deco design. Watch the back rows and balcony for late-arriving celebrities. Tickets $10, students $7.50, seniors and under 12 $6.50, shows before 6pm $6.

REVIVAL THEATERS

Nuart Theatre, 11272 Santa Monica Blvd. (☎310-478-6379), in **West L.A.,** just west of 1-405 (the San Diego Fwy.), at Sawtelle Ave. Perhaps the best-known revival house. The playbill changes nightly. Classics, documentaries, and modern films. *The Rocky Horror Picture Show* screens Sa night at midnight with a live cast. Tickets $9, seniors and under 12 $6. Discount card (5 movie tickets for $30).

LACMA's Bing Theater, 5905 Wilshire Blvd. (☎323-857-6010), in the **Wilshire District,** at the L.A. County Museum of Art. Classic films on the big screen, at times for less than a video rental. Shows Tu 1pm and F-Sa 7:30pm only. Tickets on Tu $2, seniors $1; weekend tickets $8; students, seniors, and museum members $6.

LIVE THEATER

The wondrously dramatic spectacle that is Broadway never quite made it across the Rockies, so the live theater scene isn't quite the spectacle it is in New York. On the other hand, 115 "equity waiver theaters" (under 100 seats) offer a dizzying choice for theater-goers, who can also take in small productions in museums, art galleries, universities, parks, and even garages. For the digs on what's hot, browse the listings in the *L.A. Weekly.*

Geffen Playhouse, 10886 LeConte Ave. (☎310-208-5454), in **Westwood.** Off-Broadway and Tony award-winning shows in a cozy space. Tickets range $28-46; student rush tickets ($10) 1hr. before show.

Pasadena Playhouse, 39 S. El Molino Ave. (☎626-356-7529 or 800-233-3123), in **Pasadena.** California's premier theater and historical landmark has spawned Broadway careers and productions. Tickets $35-60. Call for rush tickets. Shows Tu-Su.

Pantages, 6231 Hollywood Blvd. (☎323-468-1770, Ticketmaster ☎213-365-3500), in **Hollywood,** across the street from the red Metro line's Hollywood/Vine station. Hosted the premieres of *Cleopatra* and *Spartacus.* Newly remodeled theatre is again a hotspot for big Broadway performances and cabaret acts. Tickets from $12. Parking $5-8.

LIVE MUSIC

L.A.'s music venues range from small clubs to massive amphitheaters. The **Wiltern Theater** (☎213-380-5005) shows alterna-rock/folk acts. The **Hollywood Palladium** (☎323-962-7600) is of comparable size, with 3500 seats. Mid-size acts head for the **Universal Amphitheater** (☎818-777-3931). Huge indoor sports arenas, such as the **Great Western Forum** (☎310-330-7300) and the newer **Staples Center** (☎213-742-7100), double as concert halls for big acts. Few dare to play at the 100,000-seat **Los Angeles Memorial Coliseum and Sports Arena**—only U2, Depeche Mode, Guns 'n' Roses and the Warped Tour have filled the stands in recent years. Call Ticketmaster ☎213-480-3232 to purchase tickets for any of these venues.

🎵 **Hollywood Bowl,** 2301 N. Highland Ave. (☎323-850-2000), in **Hollywood.** The bowl hosts a summer music festival from early July to mid-Sept. Although sitting in the back of this outdoor, 18,000-seat amphitheater makes the L.A. Philharmonic sound like it's on a transistor radio, bargain tickets and a panoramic view of the Hollywood Hills from the bowl's south rim make it worthwhile. Free open house rehearsals by the Philharmonic and visiting performers M-Tu and Th-F. Parking at the bowl is limited and pricey at $11. It is better to park at one of the lots away from the bowl and take a shuttle (parking $5, shuttle $2.50; departs every 10-20min. starting 1½hr. before showtime). There are lots at 10601 and 10801 Ventura Blvd., near Universal City; 1626 N. La Brea Ave., at the corner of Hollywood Blvd.; and 5333 Zoo Dr., at the L.A. Zoo in Griffith Park. MTA bus #163 runs from Burbank and Hollywood and bus #156 goes west from Downtown or east from the valley. Call Ticketmaster (☎213-480-3232) to purchase tickets.

Music Center, 135 N. Grand Ave. (☎213-972-7211), in **Downtown,** at the corner of 1st St. in the heart of the city. Includes the Mark Taper Forum, the Dorothy Chandler Pavilion, and the Ahmanson Theatre, and in the fall of 2003, the Gehry-designed Walt Disney Concert Hall. Performance spaces host the L.A. Opera, Broadway and experimental theater, and dance. Parking $7 after 6pm, but you pay less at the many lots nearby.

THE LOCAL STORY

LENTIL SOUP

Miguel was working behind the scenes in the kitchen, as Head Chef at the Rainbow Grill.

Q: How long have you been working at Rainbow Bar and Grill?

A: Over thirty years

Q: What are some of your favorite memories from the last thirty years?

A: I really liked John Belushi and Led Zeppelin was great. We had a party for Elton John a long time ago. At the Rainbow you never know when they are going to come over.

Q: How much have things changed in this area over the years?

A: The Rainbow is hopping better today than before, but different crowds, the music has changed. We used to have a lot of Rock 'n' Roll now we have different kinds of music and different kinds of people.

Q: What was your favorite time?

A: I think the old days were better, I really believe that. Well, probably because I was younger [laughs].

Q: Tell us about that last fateful night of your friend John Belushi.

A: John Belushi came by the night he died, he walked in here around nine o'clock. He used to sit in the kitchen with us, he had some lentil soup and some spaghetti with meatballs. Then he went upstairs with, I think Rob DeNiro and probably went to the dance floor or whatever. I got up the next day and heard that he died. It was unbelievable because I saw him the night before. It was pretty sad. You know, I've never made lentil soup since. I really liked John Belushi a lot, he was one of my favorite guys, he was a good guy.

SPECTATOR SPORTS

Exposition Park and the often dangerous city of **Inglewood**, southwest of the park, are home to many sports teams. The **USC Trojans** football team plays at the **Los Angeles Memorial Coliseum**, 3939 S. Figueroa St. (tickets ☎213-740-4672), at Martin Luther King Blvd., which seats over 100,000 spectators. It is the only stadium in the world to have the honor of hosting the Olympic Games twice. The torch that held the Olympic flame still towers atop the Coliseum's roof. Basketball's doormat, the **Los Angeles Clippers** (☎213-742-7500), and the dazzling, star-studded 2002 NBA Champion **Los Angeles Lakers** (☎310-426-6031) play at the new **Staples Center**, 1111 S. Figueroa St. (☎213-742-7100; box office 213-742-7300), along with the **Los Angeles Kings** hockey team (☎888-546-4752) and the city's women's basketball team, the impressive **Los Angeles Sparks** (☎310-330-3939). Tickets for these games are in high demand (Lakers season runs Nov.-June; Sparks June-Aug.). Kings tickets start at $20, Lakers at $23, and Sparks at $5. For tickets, call Ticketmaster ☎213-480-3232.

Elysian Park, about 3 mi. northeast of Downtown, curves around the northern portion of Chavez Ravine, home of **Dodger Stadium** and the popular **Los Angeles Dodgers** baseball team. Single-game tickets ($6-21) are a hot commodity during the April-October season, especially if the Dodgers are playing well. Call ☎323-224-1448 for info and advance tickets.

EXTREME! SPORTS

Perris Valley Skydiving, 2091 Goetz Rd. (☎909-657-1664 or 800-832-8818), in **Perris Valley,** near Riverside. Take I-10 East to Rte. 605 South to 91 East to 215 South; exit on D St. and take it to Goetz Rd. (1¾ hr.). Not the most budget-savvy activity, but this is the place to fulfill that urge to leap 12,500 ft. and experience the thrill of a lifetime. Accommodates experienced jumpers and 1st-timers, who jump with a skydiving instructor strapped (tightly!) to their backs. After a 1min. free-fall, enjoy a 4min. descent. Dives $199-299. Group discounts and lessons available.

Hollywood Star Lanes, 5227 Santa Monica Blvd. (☎323-665-4111), in **Hollywood.** The site of several scenes from 1998's *The Big Lebowski,* locals call it "the best thing to do after 2am besides...sleep." Cool shoes, as always (mandatory rental $1.50). Games $2.75 per person; weekdays 10am-5pm $2. Tu 10am-2pm 3 games $5, 9pm-2am 3 games $6. Open 24hr.

■ NIGHTLIFE

LATE-NIGHT RESTAURANTS

Given the unreliability of the L.A. club scene and the short shelf-life of cafes, late-night restaurants have become reliable hangouts. The mainstay of L.A. nightlife, they're the place where underage club kids come trolling among the token celebs.

■ **Canter's,** 419 N. Fairfax Ave. (☎323-651-2030), in **Fairfax.** An L.A. institution, this deli has been the heart and soul of the historically Jewish Fairfax community since 1931. Grapefruit-sized matzoh ball in chicken broth is the best ever ($4.50). Giant sandwiches $8-9. Visit the Kibbitz Room nightly for live rock, blues, jazz, and cabaret-pop (from 9pm). Cheap beer ($1.50). Open 24hr.

■ **Fred 62,** 1850 N. Vermont Ave. (☎323-667-0062), in **Los Feliz.** "Eat now, dine later." Headrests and toasters at every booth. Hip, edgy East L.A. crowd's jukebox selections rock the house. The waffles ($4.62—all prices end in .62) are divine. Open 24hr.

■ **The Rainbow Grill,** 9015 Sunset Blvd. (☎310-278-4232; http://rainbowbarand-grill.com), in **West Hollywood,** next to the Roxy. Dark red vinyl booths, dim lighting, and loud music set the scene. An insane rainbow of guests play their parts. Marilyn Monroe met Joe DiMaggio on a blind date here. Brooklyn-quality pizza $6; calamari $8; grandma's chicken soup $3.50. Open M-F 11am-2am, Sa-Su 5pm-2am. Free parking.

Barney's Beanery, 8447 Santa Monica Blvd. (☎323-654-2287), in **Hollywood.** Barney's has been around since 1920—and it shows. Over 600 items on the menu, 125 bottled beers, and 28 on draft. If they don't have it, you don't need it. Janis Joplin and Jim Morrison were regulars. Pool and ping-pong tables. Experience the loud, riotous karaoke nights Su, M, W 9:30pm-1am. Happy hour M-F 4-7pm (well drinks and house wines $2.50; appetizer $3). Valet parking $1.50. Open daily 11am-2am. See **Hollywood Canteens,** (p. 428).

Mel's Drive In, 8585 Sunset Blvd. (☎310-854-7200), in **West Hollywood;** also at 1660 North Highland Ave. (☎323-456-2111), in **Hollywood** with more limited hours. The 1950s-style diner is a picture-perfect re-creation of the era. The original Mel's (in **Modesto, Northern California**) was in the movie *American Graffiti,* and this is as artfully constructed as a Hollywood set. Play your part by ordering a cheeseburger, fries, and a vanilla milkshake—all for under $10. Free valet parking. Open 24hr.

Bob's Big Boy, 4211 Riverside Dr. (☎818-843-9334), in **Burbank.** Don't miss this classic 1940s spot, where a sculpture of Bob welcomes you. The oldest remaining establishment of the once large chain was declared a State Point of Historical Interest in 1993. Daily specials $7-9. Burgers $6-7. F 6-10pm is Classic Car Night, Sa-Su 5-10pm offers a car hop service. Open 24hr.

Jerry's Famous Deli has multiple locations, including 8701 Beverly Blvd. (☎310-289-1811), in **West Hollywood;** 10925 Weyburn Ave. (☎310-208-3354), in **Westwood;** and 12655 Ventura Blvd. (☎818-980-4245), in **Studio City.** An L.A. deli with a 90s twist—meaning a sleek design and sky-high prices. Note the menu's height—Jerry is rumored to have wanted "the longest menu possible while still maintaining structural integrity." There's always something on it for a 4am snack. Sandwiches $8-13. Open Su-Th 7am-2am, F-Sa 24hr.

COFFEEHOUSES

In a city where no one eats very much for fear of rounding out that bony figure, espresso, coffee, and air are vital dining options. Here you'll find the hip younger crowd that doesn't earn enough to hit the restaurants. Bring a book and hide behind it while scoping out everyone else.

▨ **Un Urban Coffeehouse,** 3301 Pico Blvd. (☎310-315-0056), in **Santa Monica.** 3 separate rooms of campy voodoo candles, Mexican wrestling masks, musty books, and leopard-print couches. Iced mocha blends $3.50, Italian sodas $2. Open mic comedy Th 7:30pm, open mic songwriters F 8pm, music showcase Sa 7pm. Sign-up for open mic ½hr. before. No cover. Open M-Th 7am-midnight, F 7am-1am, Sa 8am-1am, Su 8am-7pm.

Cow's End, 34 Washington Blvd. (☎310-574-1080), in **Venice.** With its asymmetrical whole-pane windows, uneven brick floor, and scantily clad beach patrons, the Cow's End is riotously popular. Sandwiches from $5.50. Smoothies from $3.75. Live music F 8pm. Open daily 6am-midnight.

Stir Crazy, 6917 Melrose Ave. (☎323-934-4656), in **Hollywood.** By day, crazy students read up on their crazy literary heroes. By night, crazier people talk up a crazy social scene. Crazy cappuccinos ($2.50), served to the crazy sounds of Glenn Miller. Crazy "signature" sandwiches $5.50. Open daily 9am-12:30am. No credit cards.

Bourgeois Pig, 5931 Franklin Ave. (☎323-464-6008; www.bourgeoispig.com), in **Hollywood.** Writers tap their screenplays into laptops and conference with their agents as they sip coffee ($1.75-4.25). At night, locals lounge between the rich blue walls and in the intimate Moroccan backroom space. Open daily 9am-2am. No credit cards.

WEHO Lounge, 8861 Santa Monica Blvd. (☎310-659-6180), in Out of the Closet, **West Hollywood.** The 1st coffeehouse/AIDS info center. Plush sofas, art on the walls. Next to main gay strip. Lots of club traffic. Many gay men, but all types chat it up on the outdoor patio. Free oral HIV testing M-F 6-10pm, Sa-Su 3-6pm. Open daily 10am-midnight.

G.A.L.A.X.Y. Gallery, 7224 Melrose Ave. (☎323-938-6500), in **Hollywood,** also at 2804 Main St. (☎310-314-1440), in **Santa Monica.** Much more than just a coffee shop, this spacious tobacco store has art on display, a super-comfy couch, and an enormous bong and hookah display for all your tobacco needs. Acid jazz jams on some weekend nights. Hemp coffee $1.75. 18+. Cover varies. Open M-Sa 11am-10pm, Su noon-9pm.

COMEDY CLUBS

The talent may be imported from New York, but it doesn't change the fact that L.A.'s comedy clubs are the best in the world. Although prices are steep, it's worth the setback to catch the newest and wackiest comedians, guffaw as famous veterans hone new material, or preside over the latest trends in stand-up comedy.

▨ **L.A. Improv,** 8162 Melrose Ave. (☎213-651-2583), in **West Hollywood.** L.A.'s best talent, like Robin Williams and Jerry Seinfeld, have shown their faces here; Drew Carey and Ryan Stiles often join the show. Dinner at the restaurant (entrees $6-14) includes priority seating for the show. 18+. Cover $10-15. 2-drink min. Shows Su-Th 8pm, F-Sa 8:30 and 10:30pm. Bar open daily until 1:30am. Reservations recommended.

Groundling Theater, 7307 Melrose Ave. (☎323-934-9700; www.groundlings.com), in **Hollywood.** The best improv and comedy "forum" in town. The Groundling's alums include Pee Wee Herman and many current and former *Saturday Night Live* regulars like Will Farrell, Julia Sweeney, and Chris Kattan. Don't be surprised to see *SNL* producer Lorne Michaels sitting in the back. Lisa Kudrow of *Friends* got her start here, too. Mostly polished skits. Cover $7-18.50. Shows Tu and Th 8pm, F-Sa 8 and 10pm, Su 7:30pm.

Comedy Store, 8433 Sunset Blvd. (☎323-656-6225), in **West Hollywood.** The shopping mall of comedy clubs: 3 rooms each feature a different type of comedy. Main Room has big names and prices ($15-20). Original Room features mid-range comics ($15). Belly Room has real grab-bag material (no cover). 21+. 2-drink min., drinks from $4.50. Shows at 8 and 9pm. Open daily until 2am. Reserve up to a week in advance.

The Laugh Factory, 8001 Sunset Blvd. (☎323-656-1336), in **West Hollywood.** Young talent—you can say you saw them here first. Daily themed showcases, Tu is open mic night for the 1st 15 people in line at 5pm. 18+. Cover T-Th $10, F-M $12. 2-drink min. Shows M 8pm, Tu 5pm, W 8pm & 10pm, Th-Su 8pm, 10pm, midnight.

The Ice House, 24 N. Mentor Ave. (☎626-577-1894), in **Pasadena.** The 30-year-old granddaddy of clubs, its alums pop in occasionally. The Annex has stand-up F-Sa 8 and 9:45pm ($12). 21+. Cover $8.50-12.50; 2-drink min. Reservations recommended.

BARS

While the 1996 film *Swingers* may not have transformed every bar into The 3 of Clubs, it has had a sadly homogenizing effect on L.A.'s hipsters. Grab your retro-70s polyester shirts, sunglasses, goatees, and throwback Cadillac convertibles, 'cause if you can't beat them, you have to swing with them, daddy-o. **Unless otherwise specified, bars in California are 21+.**

■ **Beauty Bar,** 1638 Cahuenga Blvd. (☎323-464-7676), in **Hollywood.** A combination bar and beauty parlor. It's like getting ready for the prom all over again, except that the drinking starts before rather than after. Drinks like "Shampoo" are $5-7. Smoking room with hair-setting seats. Manicures, "up 'dos," and henna tattoos Th-Sa nights with a specialty drink ($10). DJ nightly at 10pm. Open Su-W 9pm-2am, Th-F 6pm-2am, Sa 8pm-2am.

■ **Miyagi's,** 8225 Sunset Blvd. (☎323-656-0100), on **Sunset Strip.** With 3 levels, 5 sushi bars, and 7 liquor bars, this Japanese-themed restaurant, bar, and lounge is the latest Strip hotspot. "*Sake* bomb, *sake* bomb, *sake* bomb" $4.50. Open daily 5:30pm-2am.

■ **The 3 of Clubs,** 1123 N. Vine St. (☎323-462-6441), in **Hollywood.** In a small strip mall beneath a "Bargain Clown Mart" sign, this simple, classy, spacious, hardwood bar is famous for appearing in 1996's *Swingers.* DJ F-Sa, live bands Th. Open daily 7pm-2am.

■ **The Room,** 1626 Cahuenga St. (☎323-462-7196), in **Hollywood.** A speakeasy that empties into an alley, the very popular Room almost trumps The 3 of Clubs. No advertising, no sign on the door. 2nd location in **Santa Monica** at 14th St. and Santa Monica Blvd. Open daily 8pm-2am.

Standard Lounge, 8300 Sunset Blvd. (☎323-822-3111), in **Hollywood,** in the Standard Hotel. Exclusively for the connected and the gorgeous. Reservations highly recommended. Open daily 10pm-2am.

Daddy's, 1610 N. Vine St. (☎323-463-7777), in **Hollywood,** between Hollywood and Sunset Blvd. Large, New York-style lounge. Low-to-the-ground booths, candle lighting, and the cheapest jukebox in town. Sip $5 drinks and $4 beers to the mellow stylings of Al Green. Open M-F 7pm-2am, Sa 8pm-2am, Su 9pm-2am.

The Coach and Horses, 7617 Sunset Blvd. (☎323-876-6900), in **Hollywood.** Former speakeasy turned pub dive. The bartenders know all the local legends. Aspiring stars retreat here to drown post-audition sorrows. Alfred Hitchcock was a regular. Beer $4-5. Open M-Sa 11am-2pm, Su 5pm-2am. See **Hollywood Canteens,** p. 428.

The Lava Lounge, 1533 N. La Brea Ave. (☎323-876-6612), in **Hollywood.** Fun bar with outdoor motif—surf rock and Pacific Island sounds. Sip a Blue Hawaiian ($7) under a twinkling star ceiling. Entertainment from 10pm. Cover up to $5. Open daily 9pm-2am.

Maloney's, 1000 Gayley Ave. (☎310-208-1942), in **Westwood Village.** This UCLA *Cheers*-style hangout is a favorite among the Bruins. No college town prices (beers $3-6, drinks $4-9), but students still cling to the bar and watch ESPN on the big screen TVs. Full lunch and dinner menu. Su 2-for-1 draft beers. Open daily 11:30am-2am.

CLUBS

L.A. is famous for its club scene. With the highest number of bands per capita in the world, most clubs are able to book top-notch acts night after night. The distinction between music and dance clubs is a bit sketchy in L.A.—most music clubs have DJs a few times a week, and many dance clubs occasionally have live music. Most prevalent and popular, however, are club "events" that promoters design for specific venues. These events give a venue its temporary character—promoters often move their events to different clubs, creating a caravan effect among diehard fans. Thus, club venues may host completely different crowds nightly.

L.A. clubs are often expensive, but many are still feasible for budgeteers. Coupons in *L.A. Weekly* (see **Publications,** p. 379) and those handed out in bushels inside the clubs can save you a bundle. To enter the club scene, it's best to be at least 21—it also helps to be a beautiful woman. Nevertheless, if you're over 18 and your plastic surgery appointment isn't until next week (or you happen to have a Y chromosome), you can find a space to dance, but it may mean a hefty cover charge in a less desirable venue. **All clubs are 21+ unless otherwise noted.**

Largo, 432 N. Fairfax Ave. (☎323-852-1073), in **West Hollywood.** Elegant and intimate sit-down (or, if you get there late, lean-back) club. Original rock, pop, and folk sounds along with comedy acts. Cover $2-12. Open M-Sa 8:30pm-2am.

Derby, 4500 Los Feliz Blvd. (☎323-663-8979), in **Hollywood.** The concept of the Derby was conceived by Cecil B. DeMille in the 1920s. Today this joint is still jumpin' with the kings of swing. Ladies, grab your snoods, because many dress the 40s part. Choice Italian fare from Louise's Trattoria next door. Full bar. Free Lindy Hop and East Coast swing lessons Sa 7:30pm. Cover $5-10. Open daily 7pm-2am.

Key Club, 9039 Sunset Blvd. (☎310-274-5800), on **Sunset Strip.** A colossal, crowded multimedia experience complete with black lights, neon, and a frenetic dance floor. Live acts and DJ productions, depending on the night. 4 full bars. Cover $10-55. Open on club nights 10pm-2am, live music nights 7pm-2am.

Roxy, 9009 Sunset Blvd. (☎310-278-9457, box office 310-276-2222), on **Sunset Strip.** Known as the "Sizzling Showcase," it's one of the best-known Sunset Strip clubs. Bruce Springsteen got his start here. Live rock, blues, alternative, and occasional hip-hop. Many big tour acts. All ages. Cover varies. Opens at 8pm.

Whisky A Go-Go, 8901 Sunset Blvd. (☎310-652-4205), in **West Hollywood.** Historically, this is the great prophet of L.A.'s music scene. It hosted progressive bands in the late 70s and early 80s, and was big in the punk explosion. The Doors, Janis Joplin, and Led Zeppelin all played here. All ages welcome all the time. Cover M-Th $10, F-Su $12-15. 5-6 hard rock/alternative bands play F-Su 8pm-2am. Shows begin after 8pm.

Martini Lounge, 5657 Melrose Ave. (☎323-467-4068), in **Hollywood.** More people sip beer than martinis, and more people mingle than dance. Music from reggae to trance. Live bands and DJ promotions. Cover up to $10. Shows at 8pm. Open daily until 2am.

Arena, 6655 Santa Monica Blvd. (☎323-462-0714), in **Hollywood.** Paired with sister club **Circus,** this club lends itself to frenzied techno and Latin beats. Gay night Sa, drag shows at midnight. Cover $10-15. Open Su-Th 9pm-2am, F-Sa 9pm-4am.

GAY & LESBIAN NIGHTLIFE

While the Sunset Strip features all the nightlife any Jack and Jill could desire, gay men and lesbians may find life more interesting a short tumble down the hill on **Santa Monica Boulevard.** Still, many ostensibly straight clubs have gay nights; check *L.A. Weekly* or contact the Gay and Lesbian Community Services Center. Free weekly magazine *fab!* lists happenings in the gay and lesbian community. **Motherload,** 8499 Santa Monica Blvd. (☎310-659-9700), and **Trunks,** 8809 Santa Monica Blvd. (☎310-652-1015), are two of the friendliest and most popular bars. Neither has a cover and both are open until 2am. **All clubs are 21+ unless otherwise noted.**

▨ Abbey Cafe, 692 N. Robertson Blvd. (☎310-289-8410), in **West Hollywood,** at Santa Monica Blvd. This cafe becomes a lounge, bar, and dance club as the moon rises. Impeccable service, tasteful decor. Open daily noon-2am.

Micky's, 8857 Santa Monica Blvd. (☎310-657-1176), in **West Hollywood.** Large, popular spot filled with delectable men. Music is mostly Top 40 dance. Serves lunch M-Sa 11am-3pm and hot go-go boys Tu-F and Su. "Cocktails with the stars" (many of them porno stars) Th 6-8:30pm. Happy hour M-F 5-9pm. Cover $3-5. Open daily 11am-2am.

Rage, 8911 Santa Monica Blvd. (☎310-652-7055), in **West Hollywood.** Its glory days have passed, but this institution rages on with nightly DJs 'til you drop. Mostly gay men; some lesbians during the day. Full lunch and dinner menu served daily noon-9pm. Happy hour (beer $2) M-F 2-8pm. Th 18+. Open daily noon-2am.

7969 Peanuts, 7969 Santa Monica Blvd. (☎323-654-0280), in **West Hollywood.** Sometimes a strip club, sometimes a drag show, sometimes a go-go dance party—not for the faint of heart. Call for the crazy schedule. Most nights feature a mixed gay and lesbian crowd. Many nights 18+. Cover varies. Open daily 10pm-2am.

The Palms, 8572 Santa Monica Blvd. (☎310-652-6188), in **West Hollywood.** Pool room and full bar with lots of drink specials, like Tu $3 frozen drinks. DJ Th-Sa; music ranges from house to disco to salsa. Men are welcome, but may feel very alone. W 9pm-midnight $1 drinks. Su Beer Bust $0.50 drafts and free buffet. Open daily 2pm-2am.

Akbar, 4365 Sunset Blvd. (☎323-665-6810), in **Silver Lake,** at Fountain St., next to a McDonald's. Out of the way and hard to find, but that's what makes it "a neighborhood oasis" for Arabian nights (and knights). Mostly but not exclusively gay. Great jukebox, friendly, laid-back scene. Happy hour F 6-8pm ($3 beers), vinyl spin Tu with $3 margaritas. Open Su-Th 7pm-2am, F 6pm-2am.

HOLLYWOOD CANTEENS
Where the famous stars boozed, binged, & blacked out

Bogart. Sinatra. Hepburn. Gable. Monroe. The greatest livers of a generation were destroyed here. Those who say L.A. has no sense of history need look no further than the bottom of their cocktail glass at these venerable (and still standing) Old Hollywood bars. Here's looking at you, kid!

Barney's Beanery, 8447 Santa Monica Blvd. (☎323-654-2287), in West Hollywood. Some like it hot—especially Marilyn Monroe. While filming the picture of the same name, she'd drop at this rough-and-tumble Rte. 66 roadhouse for chili. Janis Joplin partied here the night she died. Happy hour M-F 4-7pm. Open daily 11am-2am.

Chez Jay, 1657 Ocean Ave. (☎310-395-1741), in Santa Monica. A tiny, crusty beachside dive festooned with Christmas lights, red check tablecloths, and pictures of Sinatra. Why not? Ol' Blue Eyes dented the red vinyl here regularly in his day. Open M-F 6pm-2am, Sa-Su 5:30pm-2am.

Coach & Horses Pub, 7617 W. Sunset Blvd. (☎323-876-6900), in Hollywood. A dark, tiny ye olde hole in the wall where Richard Burton used to start his benders. If you feel like following suit, start early on a weekday. On F and Sa nights the hipsters invade, armed with apple martinis and leather pants. Open M-Sa 11am-2am, Su 5pm-2am.

The Gallery Bar at the Biltmore Hotel, 506 S. Grand Ave. (☎213-612-1532), in Downtown L.A. Glide into wood-paneled elegance, sip a martini, and wonder what really happened to the Black Dahlia. This was, after all, the last place aspiring starlet Beth Short (nicknamed for her pin-up quality black dresses) was seen alive. Back in 1947, a doorman tipped his cap to her and five days later, her severed body made her the most famous victim of an unsolved murder case in city history. Open daily 4:30pm-1:45am.

Formosa Cafe, 7156 Santa Monica Blvd. (☎323-850-9050), in Hollywood. This Suzy Wong boîte is equal parts black lacquer and 8"x10" glossies. The more than 250 star headshots plastering the walls are rumored to have been dropped off in person. Cozy up in a booth like Lana Turner used to and drink all you want, but avoid the greasy "Chinese" food. Open M-F 4pm-2am, Sa-Su 6pm-2am.

Musso & Frank Grill, 6667 Hollywood Blvd. (☎323-467-7788), in Hollywood. Where Bogie boozed, Sinatra swilled, and Bukowski blew his cash. The drinks ain't cheap, but oh, what ambience! Honeyed light, high-backed booths, and curmudgeonly red-jacketed waiters. The martini is hands-down the city's best. Raymond Chandler immortalized Musso's gin and lime juice drink in "The Long Goodbye." Open Tu-Sa 11am-10:45pm.

The Polo Lounge at the Beverly Hills Hotel, 9641 Sunset Blvd. (☎310-276-2251), in Beverly Hills. Ask to be seated in the patio section, order up a Singapore Sling, and dream about the days when Kate Hepburn and Marlene Dietrich held court here. Come F mornings and see why this place coined the term "power breakfast"—tables on the outer edge of the terrace are a classic place for movie deals to be struck. Open daily 7am-1am.

Trader Vic's at the Beverly Hilton Hotel, 9876 Wilshire Blvd. (☎310-274-7777), in Beverly Hills. A dim, linen tablecloth tiki bar that George Hamilton allegedly singled out as a great place for celebrity affairs owing to its two entrances. The house cocktails' $10 price tags are more than made up for in presentation—the pina colada comes in a whole pineapple; a gardenia graces the scorpion bowl. Open Su-Th 5pm-2am, F-Sa 5pm-1am.

Stephanie L. Smith was a researcher-writer for Let's Go: California 1997 *and* New Zealand 1998. *She worked as a freelancer for CitySearch Los Angeles, reviewing restaurants, bars, and attractions, and is now working in Hollywood as the features editor/writer for the online division of Channel One News.*

AROUND L.A.

Once you leave the city limits of Los Angeles (or, some might argue, even the Westside), the glam-factor drops considerably. The cities and neighborhoods in southern L.A. and Orange counties are a little hotter and a lot less cool. But while they lack the glitz of L.A. proper, they more than compensate for it with their beauty, especially along the coast. In fact, some of the most awe-inspiring spots in all of the L.A. area lie south of the city in the hills of Palos Verdes, 22 mi. west in the waters off Santa Catalina Island, on the trails of the northern Santa Monica National Recreation Area, and all along the beaches of the South Bay. And if the lush rolling hills in yuppified Orange County don't cause you to burst out in song, the legendary merriment of Disneyland just might do the trick.

HIGHLIGHTS OF L.A. & ORANGE COUNTIES

BEACH LIFE. Beach communities, both relaxed and loud, line South Bay (p. 429). Beach volleyball thrives at **Hermosa Beach** and **Manhattan Beach.** The beach communities of Orange County (p. 446) have legendary surfing and a fun sand scene, primarily at **Huntington Beach** and **San Clemente.**

CATALINA ISLAND. 22 mi. offshore rests beautiful, lush Catalina (p. 437). Great hiking, camping, and snorkeling are a brief ferry ride from the mainland.

AMUSEMENT. Anaheim hosts such family fun centers as **Disneyland** (p. 447) and **Knott's Berry Farm** (p. 449).

MISSION SAN JUAN CAPISTRANO. The crumbling religious abode (p. 454) is the most beautiful mission in California, as well as a famous roost for swallows.

WILDERNESS. Big Bear (p. 458), **Idyllwild** (p. 463), and the **San Gorgonio Wilderness** (p. 462) are tracts of mountainous terrain with excellent hiking above the smog of L.A. Ski resorts operate at Big Bear in winter, and the sailing is excellent in summer; Idyllwild attracts rock climbers to Tahquitz and Suicide Rock; and San Gorgonio has miles of untouched backcountry.

SOUTHERN L.A. COUNTY

Head to L.A. County's southern communities for the most precious of Southern Californian souvenirs: a tan. Easily accessible by public transportation or a 30min. hop down I-405 (San Diego Fwy.), these beach towns are more casual and less congested than the metropolis to the north. South Bay provides a haven for surfers, beach volleyball players, and sun worshippers, and the sandy campsites and snorkeling spots off Catalina Island are the closest it gets here to tropical paradise. Although Long Beach's urban sprawl overshadows its stretch of shoreline, the city fosters a growing nightlife and shopping scene underneath the industrial facade.

SOUTH BAY   ☎310

All activity in South Bay revolves around the sand, and a cloudy sky is reason enough not to get up in the morning. **Manhattan Beach** is the best kept of L.A. County beaches, and its town is the most yuppified. Immediately to the south lies **Hermosa Beach,** the site of the Miller-sponsored pro volleyball championships and various other beer-inspired activities. Sweet waves, a popular boardwalk, and

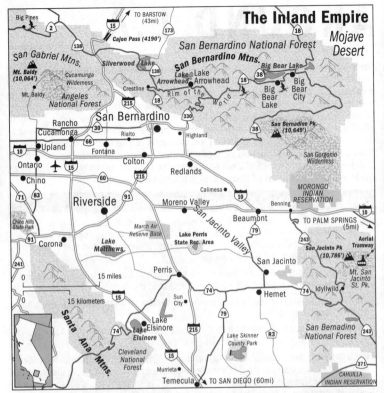

swimsuit competitions add to Hermosa's festive atmosphere. **Redondo Beach** is smaller and more commercial than its northern neighbors. Ritzy **Rancho Palos Verdes** is a different breed of coastal town, but down below the haughty cliffs are sandboxes overrun by gaggles of eager skaters, volleyball players, surfers, and sunbathers. **San Pedro** is home to Worldport L.A., the nation's busiest harbor, and is better known for its history and marine life than for its beaches.

■ ⁊ ORIENTATION & PRACTICAL INFORMATION

To reach this strip of beaches, take I-405 (San Diego Fwy.) and follow signs to your destination, or hop on Hwy. 1 South from Los Angeles. The communities are a few miles apart along the Pacific Coast Highway. Manhattan Beach, Hermosa Beach, and Redondo Beach pop up one after another as you head straight down the coast from L.A. Rancho Palos Verdes and San Pedro are slightly farther apart, around the bend that separates the Santa Monica Bay from the San Pedro Bay.

> **Public Transportation: Bus #439** leaves L.A.'s **Union Station** for Manhattan, Hermosa, and Redondo Beach. #444 leaves Union Station as well, and serves W. Torrance, Rolling Hills Estates, and Rancho Palos Verdes, while #445-447 serve San Pedro. #232 travels from the L.A. Airport to Long Beach, making stops at South Bay beaches.

Car Rental: Robin Hood, 1209 N. Sepulveda Blvd., in Manhattan Beach. Will beat other companies' prices by 15%. $27 per day; out-of-county $40. Ages 18-21 must have proof of liability insurance; under-25 surcharge $10 per day. Credit card and cash deposit required. (☎546-8977 or 800-743-2992. Open M-F 7am-6pm, Sa 8am-5pm.) **Omni Rental,** 2800 Via Cabrillo Marina (☎831-7368). Guests at the HI-AYH hostel get discounted rates. Compact $30 per day, $170 per week. 200 free mi. per day. Credit card required. Open M-F 7:30am-6:30pm, Sa 8am-4pm, Su 8am-3pm.

Visitor Information: Manhattan Beach: Chamber of Commerce, 425 15th St. (☎545-5313). Open M-F 9am-5pm. **Hermosa Beach:** Chamber of Commerce and Visitor Information Center, 1007 Hermosa Ave. (☎376-0951; www.hbchamber.net). Open M-F 9am-5pm. **Redondo Beach:** Chamber of Commerce, 200 N. Pacific Coast Hwy. (☎376-6911 or 800-282-0333). Open M-F 8:30am-5pm. **San Pedro:** Chamber of Commerce, 390 W. 7th St. (☎832-7272 or 888-447-3376). Open M-F 9am-5pm. **South Bay Community Pages** (www.commpages.com) has links to each city's events.

Equipment Rental: Each community has at least a few stores that rent **bikes** ($6-9 per hr.), **in-line skates** ($6 per hr.), and **surfboards** ($7-8 per hr.). Some also rent volleyballs, boogie boards, umbrellas, and beach chairs. These include: **Ocean Gear,** 920 Manhattan Ave., in Manhattan Beach. (☎798-7896; surfboards $25 per day; open daily 10am-7pm); **Jeffers Rentals,** 39 14th St., in Hermosa Beach (☎372-9492; surfboards $25 per day, boogie boards $15 per day, wet suits $10 per hr.; ID and credit card required; open daily 9am-6pm); **Marina Rentals,** 505 N. Harbor Dr., in Redondo Beach. (☎318-2453. Bikes $18 per day. Open M-F 10am-7pm, Sa-Su 9am-8pm.)

Weather and Surf Conditions: ☎379-8471.

Medical Services: South Bay Free Clinic, 2114 Artesian Blvd. (☎318-2521, appointment desk 376-0791), in Redondo Beach. Hours vary slightly, but the clinic is generally open M, W, F 8am-5pm, Tu and Th 10am-7:30pm. **Beach Cities Ambulatory Center,** 514 N. Prospect Ave. (☎376-9474), in Redondo Beach.

Police: Redondo Beach, 401 Diamond St. (☎379-2477); **San Pedro,** 2175 Gibson Blvd. (☎548-7605).

Post Offices: Redondo Beach, 1201 N. Catalina Ave. Open M-F 8:30am-5pm, Sa 8:30am-3:30pm. **Postal Code:** 90277. **San Pedro,** 839 S. Beacon St. Open M-F 8:30am-5pm, Sa 9am-noon. **Postal Code:** 90731.

ACCOMMODATIONS

South Bay's hostels represent two extremes in beach living: the contemplative roost at San Pedro and the party-going pad at Hermosa Beach. Motels in budget range pepper the Pacific Coast Highway.

Los Angeles South Bay (HI-AYH), 3601 S. Gaffey St., Bldg. #613 (☎831-8109), in San Pedro's in Angels Gate Park (entrance across from 36th St.). The 180-degree view from the hilltop location is unbeatable, but the hostel was once an army barrack and the living quarters are simple. Kitchen, TV room. Linen $2 (no sleeping bags allowed). Laundry. Strictly enforced 7-night max. stay. Parking included. Reception 7am-noon and 1pm-midnight; in winter 7am-noon and 4-11pm. Reservations in advance with credit card. 16-bed dorms $20; semi-private rooms with 2-3 beds $23; private rooms $45. Members receive $3 discount. International or out-of-state residents preferred. ❷

Los Angeles Surf City Hostel, 26 Pier Ave. (☎798-2323), in Hermosa Beach's Pier Plaza, in the center of the local scene. Free airport pickup 8am-8pm, $10 drop-off. Take bus #439 to 11th and Hermosa St., walk 2 blocks north, and make a left on Pier Ave. Young, international clientele. Discount car rentals, showers, Internet access, kitchen,

TV lounge, and downstairs bar. Includes boogie boards, breakfast, and linen. Laundry. Key deposit $10. 28-night max. stay. 3-day max. stay for US citizens. No parking. Reservations recommended. Passport required for all guests. 4- to 6-bunk dorms May-Nov. $17; Dec.-Apr. $15.50. Private rooms $45. ❷

Moon Lite Inn, 625 S. Pacific Coast Hwy. (☎540-4058), in Redondo Beach, 2 blocks from the ocean. Lots of amenities: TV, A/C, fridge, microwave, phone, and parking. Show your *Let's Go* book for a 1-bed rate of $50-65. 2 beds $65-85; king-sized bed with beautiful marble jacuzzis $95. ❹

🔆 FOOD

Each South Bay community offers a ridiculous amount of quality places to eat great food. Restaurants by the beach are packed with California kids re-fueling after a day in the sand and surf.

🦈 **Wahoo's Fish Tacos,** 1129 Manhattan Ave. (☎796-1044), in Manhattan Beach. Opened by 2 Hawaiian surfers, this funky little shack has decal stickers all over its formica counters and plywood walls. It's close to the sand, cheap, and a mug of Ono Ale is just $2. Wahoo's offers any 2 tacos or enchiladas for only $5. Get it with fish, chicken, steak or vegetarian. Some will die for the Maui Bowl ($7). 18 other locations in Southern California. Open M-Sa 11am-10pm, Su 11am-9pm. ❶

The Kettle, 1138 N. Highland Ave. (☎545-8511), in Manhattan Beach. The Kettle is steaming with tasty, heaping platefuls of home-style cooking. Come nightfall, surfers invade. The menu is only a guide—creativity is encouraged. Salads and sandwiches $6.50-8. "Hangover" omelette $7. Beer and wine served until midnight. Open 24hr. ❷

The Spot, 110 2nd St. (☎376-2355; www.worldfamousspot.com), in Hermosa Beach. Opened in 1977, this is the L.A. area's oldest vegetarian restaurant, still a favorite of the resident New Age population. Turn a blind eye to the vinyl floral tablecloths and concentrate on the fat-free and non-dairy-based menu. Tempeh, tofu, and tahini definitely hit the spot. "Inflation buster" combos $5-7. Open daily 11am-10pm. ❷

Good Stuff, 1286 The Strand (☎374-2334), in Hermosa Beach, at 13th St. Other locations at 1617 Pacific Coast Hwy. (☎316-0262), in Redondo Beach, and 1300 Highland Ave. (☎545-4775), in Manhattan Beach. As advertised, the food is good stuff (or at the very least fresh), and the view of the ocean is phenomenal. Burgers $6-8. Salads $3-9. Breakfast served until 5pm. Open daily 7am-9pm. ❷

👁 🏖 SIGHTS & SEASONAL EVENTS

MANHATTAN, HERMOSA, & REDONDO BEACHES. About 20 mi. south of downtown L.A., the **Pacific Coast Highway** (Hwy. 1) swings by the sand at **Manhattan Beach,** generally favored for surfing, and continues through **Hermosa Beach,** the most popular urban beach in L.A. County. The Hermosa beach community has the same spirit found in Venice, although in Hermosa it is of a more upscale variety.

Manhattan Beach's main drag, **Manhattan Avenue,** is lined with popular cafes and shops. At the end of the Manhattan Beach Pier, on a fishing plank with a mean view of the shore, the **Roundhouse Marine Studies Lab** has seven aquaria with Santa Monica marine life, including a shark aquarium and tide pool touch tanks. (☎379-8117. Open M-F 3pm-dusk, Sa-Su 10am-dusk. $1.) Manhattan is the place for a serious game of **beach volleyball,** which celebrated its first professional championships on these sands in 1960. Dubbed the Wimbledon of beach volleyball, the **Manhattan Beach Open** draws crowds to the pier in late July. The courts on the corner of **Marine and Highland Avenues** are the elite training grounds for young players.

In Hermosa Beach, **Pier Plaza,** at the end of Pier Ave. between Hermosa Ave. and the beach, is the center of the beach scene. South Bay's best bars, cafes, and surf boutiques sit in a small, car-free promenade. **The Strand** is the bike path that runs along Manhattan Ave. from Hermosa to Marina del Rey until it hits the bike/skate path along Ocean Front Walk, which stretches north to Santa Monica. In August, the **International Surf Festival** (☎305-9546) storms Manhattan Beach with lifeguarding and sand castle competitions. Anyone can enter for a fee. The **Hermosa Beach Open,** in late August awards more prize money than any other beach volleyball tournament. Call the Hermosa Beach Community Center (☎318-0280) for info.

Redondo Beach is a little farther south and a little less upscale than its northern neighbors. The main attractions are the pier, boardwalk, and marina complex. Adjacent **King Harbor** shelters thousands of pleasure boats and hosts some excellent sport fishing. The **Monstad Pier** supports an assortment of restaurants, bars, clubs, and the local fishing community.

RANCHO PALOS VERDES. For a dose of Southern California's floral profusion, head to **South Coast Botanic Gardens,** 26300 Crenshaw Blvd., off Hwy. 1 in Rancho Palos Verdes. This former county landfill has metamorphosed into an 87-acre garden, where over 75% of the plants are drought-resistant. There's a tram on weekends. (☎544-6815. Romp in the roses daily 9am-5pm. $5, students and seniors $3, ages 5-12 $1; free 3rd Tu of each month. Tram $2.) On a cliff sits the all-glass **Wayfarer's Chapel,** 5755 S. Palos Verdes Dr. The chapel was designed by Frank Lloyd Wright's son, **Lloyd Wright.** Like his father, Wright combines architecture with its natural surroundings. (☎377-1650. Open daily 7am-5pm, but closes for weddings and services. Free.)

SAN PEDRO. Farther south and east, at the end of Rte. 213, still water, tidepools, and a nearby harbor draw families to **Cabrillo Beach.** (Beach parking $6.50; free parking in surrounding neighborhood.) The **Cabrillo Marine Museum,** 3720 Stephen White Dr., presents touch tanks, marine history exhibits, and a rather disturbing view of pickled squid and whale skeletons. (☎548-7562. Open Tu-F noon-5pm, Sa-Su 10am-5pm. $2, children and seniors $1.)

Cafes and antique shops line **6th Street.** The **Fort MacArthur Military Museum,** 3601 Gaffey St., is a nearly intact coastal fortification. (☎548-7705. Open Sa-Su noon-5pm. Free.) At the end of Gaffey St. is the **Korean Friendship Bell,** in the 64-acre **Angel's Gate Park,** a popular daytime recreation spot but not the place for twilight strolls. The bell was featured in 1995's *The Usual Suspects.*

☑ NIGHTLIFE

The predominantly young crowd in South Bay keeps the nightlife bumping. There are over 50 bars around the **Hermosa Beach Pier;** many lie along Hermosa Ave.

Lighthouse Cafe, 30 Pier Ave. (☎372-6911), in Hermosa Beach, in Pier Plaza. Frequented by bronzed volleyball players, this cool dance club features nightly music ranging from reggae to 80s. Reasonably priced munchies. No cover. Su jazz brunch 11am-3pm. Open M-F 6pm-2am, Sa-Su 10am-2am.

Cafe Boogaloo, 1238 Hermosa Ave. (☎318-2324), in Hermosa Beach. Blues, and California Cuisine with Louisiana soul. Full bar with 27 microbrews on tap ($3). Nightly shows begin around 8pm, weekends 9pm. Cover Th-Sa $5-10. Dinner from $10 (5-11pm). Happy hour daily 4-7pm. Open M-F 5pm-1am, Sa 3pm-2am, Su 11am-1am.

Catalina Coffee Company, 126 N. Catalina Ave. (☎318-2499; www.catalinacoffee.com), in Redondo Beach. Every beach town has its Bohemian coffeehouse, but this one stands out for its classiness. Couches, Internet access, and mystery library. Coffee beans roasted on site ($1.50-4), teas ($2.25), gourmet sandwiches ($6) and baked goods ($1-4). Open daily 6am-10pm.

LONG BEACH ☎562

Long Beach (pop. 430,000), as its Chamber of Commerce proudly proclaims, is "the #1 container shipping port in the world," and nothing could be more evident to the first-time visitor. The breakwater created by the massive shipping harbor keeps the waves tiny. But the beaches are pristine, and the thriving entertainment district helps make up for the inescapable views of 10-story loading cranes, diesel trucks, and container barges.

⚓🔟 ORIENTATION & PRACTICAL INFORMATION

Long Beach is 24 mi. south of downtown L.A. and down the coast from South Bay. To reach Long Beach from L.A. by **public transit,** take the Metro blue line from the L.A. airport, take the green line and transfer to the blue line at Imperial from downtown, or take bus #232 ($1.35). By **car,** take the I-405 (San Diego Fwy.). Exit at the I-710 (Long Beach Fwy.), which runs to Long Beach.

Long Beach's main tourist attractions lie by the bay. **Pine Avenue,** the backbone of downtown, runs north from the bay, and **Ocean Boulevard** runs west to the boutiques of Belmont Shores. **Exercise caution in inland areas of Long Beach.**

Buses: Greyhound, 1498 Long Beach Blvd. (☎218-3011 or 800-231-2222). Buses run to: **L.A.** ($8.25-9.25); **San Diego** ($14); **San Francisco** ($42). Open daily 5:30am-8:30pm.

Public Transportation: Long Beach Transit (LBT), 1963 E. Anaheim St. (☎591-2301), is the nation's safest transit agency. Most buses stop downtown at the newly renovated **Transit Mall,** on 1st St. between Pacific Ave. and Long Beach Blvd. High-tech bus shelters have route maps and video screens with bus info. $0.90, students $0.75, seniors $0.45, transfers $0.10-0.35. **Long Beach Passport,** 1963 E. Anaheim St. (☎591-2301), a separate division of the LBT, offers free service along Ocean Blvd. and Pine Ave., as well as to the Queen Mary (every 15min.). One route runs from downtown to Belmont Shores ($0.90). Most routes operate daily 6am-midnight.

Car Rental: Budget, 249 E. Ocean Blvd. (☎495-0407), and at Long Beach Airport (☎421-0143). Cars with unlimited mileage $40 per day. Must be 21 with major credit card. Under-25 surcharge $20 per day. Open M-F 7:30am-6pm, Sa-Su 8am-4pm.

Bike Rental: Bikestation (☎436-2453), at 1st St. and the Promenade, downtown. Bikes $5-7 per hr., $20-28 per day. Open M-F 6am-7pm, Sa-Su 9am-6pm.

Equipment Rental: Long Beach Windsurf Center, 3850 E. Ocean Blvd. (☎433-1014). In-line skates ($10 per hr.), as well as kayaks, sailboards, and wetsuits. Open M and W-F 11am-6pm, Sa 10am-6pm, Su 10am-5pm.

Auto Repair: AAA Road Service, 4800 Airport Plaza Dr. (☎496-4130, emergency help 800-400-4222). Open M-F 9am-5pm.

Visitor Information: Long Beach Convention and Visitors Bureau, 1 World Trade Ctr., #300 (☎436-3645 or 800-452-2829), at Ocean Blvd. and I-710 (Long Beach Fwy.). Tons of help and free brochures. Open M-F 8am-5pm.

Laundromat: Super Suds, 250 Alamitos Ave. (☎436-1859). The Disneyland of laundromats. Wash $1.25 per lb., dry $0.50. Open daily 7am-10pm.

Police: 100 Long Beach Blvd. (☎435-6711).

Post Office: 300 N. Long Beach Blvd. (☎800-275-8777). Open M-F 8:30am-5pm, Sa 9am-2pm. **Postal Code:** 90802.

ACCOMMODATIONS

Daytrips to Long Beach from L.A. are cheap and easy, something to keep in mind when considering an overnight trip in a place where good budget accommodations are scarce. Nevertheless, there are a few reasonably priced surf motels along Ocean Blvd. between Belmont Shores and downtown. The **Beach Plaza Hotel ❹**, 2010 E. Ocean Blvd., at Cherry Ave., has a bright turquoise exterior to match the ocean water. Clean rooms have cable TV and fridges, and there is a pool and private access to the beach. (☎437-0771. Reservations recommended. Doubles $80-130, with ocean view and kitchenette $150-180. Prices include parking.)

FOOD & NIGHTLIFE

The horde of eateries lining Pine Ave. between 1st and 3rd St. aren't all as expensive as the valets along the sidewalk might lead you to believe. There are equally budget-smart eateries in Belmont Shores. Buy cheap produce at the **open air market** on Promenade St. (Open F 10am-4pm.) Long Beach supports a vibrant blues and jazz scene; try the **Blue Cafe,** 210 Promenade St. (☎983-7111), on any given night, or **Captains Quarters,** 5205 E. Pacific Coast Hwy. (☎498-2461), on Friday and Saturday nights. Most **gay and lesbian** night spots are around East Broadway and Falcon Ave.

The Omelette Inn, 108 W. 3rd. St. (☎437-5625). "Good food prepared with your health in mind," brags the menu's organic-egg-in-sunglasses logo. For the health-conscious, there are egg white omelettes, brown rice, and veggie bacon strips. (There's real hickory smoked bacon, too.) Omelettes, sandwiches, and burgers $5-7. Early bird specials ($4) served until 9am. Open daily 7am-2:30pm. ❷

The Shorehouse Cafe, 5271 E. 2nd St. (☎433-2266), Belmont Shores. Wicker beach furniture and wooden ceiling fans add to a comfy diner setting where you can order "anything at anytime." The menu is vast and reasonably veggie-friendly. Great for lunch or late-night meals. Omelettes made with your choice of tasty fillings (from $4.25). Huge burgers $7-8. Pasta $12-14. Open 24hr. ❷

The Library, 3418 E. Broadway (☎433-2393). This gay-friendly library is, well, much like a library—with attitude. Books line the walls (Danielle Steel to Bertoldt Brecht $1-10), and studious types settle into plush antique seats. Cup of gourment coffee $1.50. Italian soda $2.75. Live music Su and W 8:30pm, F 9:30pm. Sa-Su breakfast omelette bar 7am-1pm. **The Gift Horse** annex sells local art and other items. Open M-Th 6am-midnight, F 6am-1am, Sa 7am-1am, Su 7am-midnight. ❶

Alegría, 115 Pine Ave. (☎436-3388). *Cocina Latina* with *tapas* bar. Excruciatingly hip Miró-inspired interior. Menu is a bit pricey for the pennywise, but tapas are $2.25-7, and flamenco, salsa, or Latin jazz plays nightly. Entertainment begins at 8pm. Happy hour daily 3:30-6pm (drinks $2, tapas $1). Must be 21+ after 9:30pm. Open M-Th 11:30am-11pm, F-Sa 11:30am-2am, Su noon-10pm.

Shannon's Bayshore, 5335 E. 2nd St. (☎433-5901), Belmont Shores. One of the liveliest of 2nd St.'s many night spots. For decades, drunk Long Beach residents have carved their names and those of their lovers into the wood bar. Dollar bills are pasted above the bar. As you carve, swig Shoot-the-Root, a shot of root beer schnapps in a cup of beer ($3.50). Pool table $0.50. Happy Hour daily 11am-7pm with $2.75 drafts and well drinks. Free food M-F 4-7pm. Open daily 11am-2am.

👁 SIGHTS & SEASONAL EVENTS

Shipping is the central occupation of Long Beach; tourism is clearly an after-thought. Beach life is, well...not a thought at all. Waves here are minimal due to the breakwater created by the busy port. The shipping center does have some attractions. To get a hold on the city's cargo, cross the majestic **Vincent Thomas Bridge** to central San Pedro ($0.50, free from the other direction).

QUEEN MARY. A 1934 Cunard luxury liner has been transformed into a swanky hotel with art exhibits, historical displays, and upscale bars. There are still rem-nants of the days when she was a troop ship during WWII (Hitler offered the high-est honors to anyone who could sink her). A tour of the ship is definitely worth it—otherwise, you won't be able to see much more than the engine room, the deck, and the gift shops. *(At the end of Queensway Dr. Parking for over 1hr. $8; you can also park downtown and take Passport C from Pine Ave. ☎435-3511. Open daily 10am-6pm. $19, seniors $17, children $15.)*

LONG BEACH AQUARIUM OF THE PACIFIC. A $117 million, 156,735 sq. ft. cele-bration of the world's largest and most diverse body of water, the aquarium is sit-uated atop one of the world's busiest and most polluted harbors. Just when you think you're too old to enjoy a place like this, the fish dazzle you. Meet the crea-tures of the deep who struggle every day to coexist with Long Beach's flotsam, jet-sam, and effluvium. Among the 12,000 displaced inhabitants of the Pacific Ocean are seals, sea lions, sea otters, sharks, and jellies. *(100 Aquarium Way. ☎590-3100; www.aquariumofpacific.org. Open daily 9am-6pm. $19, seniors $15, children $10.)*

MUSEUM OF LATIN AMERICAN ART. The MoLAA is making critics say "ooh-la-la" for showing work by artists who are well known in their own countries but not in the US. The drab exterior does not reflect the superb contemporary art inside, but plans are in the making to give the place an architectural rebirth. *(628 Alamitos Ave. ☎437-1689; www.molaa.com. Open Tu-Sa 11:30am-7pm, Su 11am-6pm. $5, seniors and students $3, under 12 free. Family art workshops Su noon-4pm; $7.50, students $5.)*

LONG BEACH MUSEUM OF ART. The original museum, built at the turn of the 20th century by famed Pasadena architects Greene and Greene, is now augmented by a new building built in the style of the original. The museum features rotating exhibits as well as videos by its grant recipients. Evening concerts held outside in the summer. *(2300 Ocean Blvd., on the waterfront. ☎439-2119. Open Tu-Su 10am-5pm. $5, students $4; free 1st F of the month. Summer garden concerts Th 7-10pm; $27.50-75.)*

NAPLES ISLAND. Like Venice Beach, Naples Island was planned around a series of canals. Unlike those in Venice Beach, the canals are still in use—the Rivo Alto canal even has gondoliers. *(Moonlight cruises: ☎433-9595; www.gondolagetawayinc.com. 1hr. bread-and-cheese cruise for 2 $65, most popular 5-11pm.)* It also harbors **Alamitos Bay,** from whence the *S.S. Minnow* set sail on its infamous 3hr. tour (according to the opening sequence of *Gilligan's Island*).

BEACHES. In Long Beach's upscale, uptown neighborhood, the family-oriented beach of **Belmont Shores** is reputed to be the city's best. Park at meters near the intersection of Ocean Blvd. and La Verne St. ($0.25 for 15min., 10hr. max.)

SEASONAL EVENTS. The Parade of a Thousand Lights features a display of deco-rated boats along the harbor in mid-Dec. The **Long Beach Toyota Grand Prix** (☎436-9953) revs along downtown streets in early Apr. Summer sounds jazz up down-town at **Jazz Fest** in mid-Aug. (☎424-0013), and the **Day of Music** jazz and blues extravaganza is held in mid-Sept. (☎435-2525). For more on seasonal events, con-tact the Convention and Visitors Council (see p. 434).

CATALINA ISLAND
☎ 310

Only 22 mi. off the coast of Southern California lies the island paradise of Catalina. In winter, hotel rooms are cheap, but the round-trip crossing still plagues piggy-banks. Home to a casino without gambling, a memorial without a dead body, and a 3rd Street without a 1st or 2nd, Avalon is the island's biggest town (1 sq. mi), a gateway to unbeatable snorkeling, beautiful camping and hiking sites, and protected wildlife. The potential for profit has not been lost upon the hotel owners and merchants. Tourists leaving the boat are deluged by offers of tram tours and boat trips. The rampant commercialism is mitigated by two facts: 88% of the island is owned by a non-profit group dedicated to Catalina's conservation, and the tours *do* take you to some of the most beautiful and unspoiled land in the L.A. area. The conservation group goes to lengths to ensure that the land remains natural—bike permits are required, and tours are limited to the main roads. The island's best sights are outside Avalon, so try to get inland or on the water. Hiking is free (get a mandatory pass from the campground office) and snorkeling is great and cheap.

⬛ TRANSPORTATION

Ferries: Without a yacht, the usual way to get to Catalina is via the **Catalina Express.** Shuttles depart from San Pedro (1hr.); Long Beach (1hr.); Dana Point (1½hr.) to Avalon, or San Pedro (1½hr.) to Two Harbors. Even though there are over 30 departures each day, reservations should be made in advance. (☎800-618-5533; www.catalinaexpress.com. Round-trip $40-45, seniors $37-40, ages 2-11 $31-33, under 2 $3.) **Catalina Explorer,** 34671 Puerto Pl., serves travelers from Dana Point to Avalon and Two Harbors. (☎877-432-6276; www.catalinaexplorerco.com. 1½hr.; departs daily 9am, returns 5pm. $40, seniors $36.50, ages 3-11 $30.) **Catalina Passenger Service,** 400 Main St., in Balboa, ferries vacationers once a day on the *Catalina Flyer* catamaran from Newport Beach to Avalon. (☎800-830-7744; www.catalinainfo.com. 1¼hr.; daily 9am, return 4:30pm; round-trip $39, seniors $36, ages 3-12 $26, under 2 $3.)

Public Transportation: Santa Catalina Island Company runs a bus between **Avalon** and **Two Harbors,** stopping at a few campgrounds en route (2hr.; daily 10:30am, return 4pm; $20). **Catalina Explorer** runs a **water shuttle** between the towns; it takes off from the boat dock where the cross-channel boats arrive. (June-Sept.; daily 11am, return 3:30pm. One-way $13, round-trip $25.) Call the Visitor Bureau (☎510-1520) for more info. **The Island Hopper,** a tram that leaves from Island Plaza on Metropole St., will take you to the Botanical Gardens or the Casino ($1).

Bike Rental: Brown's Bikes, 107 Pebbly Beach Rd. (☎510-0986), 360 ft. from the boat dock. Single-speed bikes $5 per hr., $12 per day; 21-speed mountain bikes $9/$20; 6-speed tandems $12/$30. Open in summer daily 9am-6pm; in winter 9am-5pm. **Island Rentals,** 125 Pebbly Beach Rd. (☎510-1456), rents **golf carts** ($30 per hr. with $30 deposit); must be 21+ to drive. Open in summer daily 8am-6pm; in winter daily 8am-5pm.

✴ ⁊ ORIENTATION & PRACTICAL INFORMATION

Visitor Information: Chamber of Commerce and Visitor Bureau, P.O. Box 217, Avalon 90704 (☎510-1520; www.catalina.com), on the left side of Avalon's Pleasure Pier. Open in summer daily 8am-5pm; off-season M-Sa 8am-5pm, Su 9am-3pm. **Catalina Island Conservancy,** 125 Claressa Ave., P.O. Box 2739, Avalon 90704 (☎510-2595). This non-profit group owns 88% of Catalina. Hiking permits (free), maps ($0.25), and trail advice available here. Open daily 9am-5pm. **Biking permits** ($50, families $75) are required outside of Avalon. They can be obtained at the Conservancy, as well as the Catalina airport and the Two Harbors Visitors Center (☎510-2880).

THE BIG SPLURGE

WRIGLEY'S WONDER

In 1921 William Wrigley, the Chicago Cubs owner and bubble gum magnate, built his home on Catalina Island, on a mountain he named after his wife. In his abode atop Mt. Ada, he entertained the Prince of Wales, as well as Presidents Calvin Coolidge and Warren Harding.

Wrigley's gorgeous, white and green-roofed Georgian colonial home has been converted to the **Inn on Mt. Ada,** so now everyone can drink in the delicious views previously reserved for politicians and members of the upper-crust. On clear days, one can see across the 85-mile San Pedro Channel to Long Beach.

Most rooms have ocean views and fireplaces (one also has a private deck), and run from $300-640. Along with a room and a view, you also get breakfast, lunch, fresh fruit, champagne, and freshly baked cookies. Guests are given golf carts to make the three-minute drive into Avalon, and to zoom around. (398 Wrigley Rd. No children under 14. 2-night min. required on weekends and holidays. ☎510-2030.)

Tours: Santa Catalina Island Company (SCIC) (www.scio.com) is ubiquitous on the island, and runs major sightseeing tours, as well as campgrounds, hotels, and restaurants. On the island, tram tours run $10-80, boat trips $25-100.

ATM: US Bank, 303 Crescent Ave. **SCI Information Center** ATM across from Green Pier on Catalina St.

Laundromat: Catalina Coin Laundry, in the Hotel Metropole shopping arcade across from Vons. Wash $1.50, 15min. dry $0.25.

Showers: Public facilities on Casino Way across from the Tuna Club. Entrance $1, each 5min. $1. Assorted preening implements $0.25-3 each; bring a towel. Open Su-Th 7am-7pm, F-Sa 7am-8pm; off-season daily 7-11am and 3-5pm.

Emergency: Police ☎510-0174; **fire** (☎510-0203); **hospital** (☎510-0700).

Post Office: (☎310-510-0084). Arcade Bldg., between Metropole and Sumner St. **Postal Code:** 90704.

■ ACCOMMODATIONS

Hoteliers on the island know they have a captive audience and tons of demand; in summer, accommodation prices skyrocket way out of budget range, even in mediocre Avalon digs. Summer is peak season, and on most weekends, and some weekdays, there are no accommodations available on the island at all. **Call as far in advance as possible**—a month is recommended—to make sure you won't have to bed down with the bison and wild boar.

Hermosa Hotel (☎510-1000), 131 Metropole St., whose motto is "sleep cheap," is an exception to Avalon prices. Offers clean, inexpensive rooms, some with ocean views, in a relaxed atmosphere maintained by the friendly management. 2-night min. stay on weekends. 18+. Double occupancy $25-65 with shared bath, $35-85 with private bath, $45-100 with kitchen. Rates depend on day and season. ❸

Hotel Atwater, 125 Sumner St. (☎800-851-0217), is the next cheapest lodging option on the island. Rooms in summer $67-88; off-season $49+. ❹

Catalina Beach House, 200 Marilla Ave. (☎310-510-1078), has delightful rooms at reasonable prices. Doubles in summer $65-75; in winter $25-35. ❹

Zane Grey Pueblo Hotel, 199 Chimes Tower Rd. (☎800-3-PUEBLO/378-3256). The Hopi Indian-style Pueblo that Grey built in 1926 is now a delightful B&B. Perched on a hillside, the ocean views are spectacular, as are the grounds. Living room has a fireplace. 16 rooms have private baths. Rooms in Apr.-Oct. $135-150; Nov.-Mar. $80-95. ❺

PHONE CODES. All seven-digit phone numbers on Catalina begin with **510.** Locals may often give phone numbers with only four digits (1234), requiring confused mainlanders to supply the missing ones (☎510-1234).

CAMPING

While no wilderness camping is permitted, the five campgrounds on Catalina each offer distinct camping experiences. You must check in at Two Harbor Visitors Center at the foot of the pier. Required reservations at any of the five campgrounds can be made at www.catalina.com/camping. A two-night minimum stay applies from July-Aug., and on holiday weekends at Hermit Gulch and Little Harbor. Unless otherwise noted, the camping charge is $12 per adult and $6 per child; discounts may be available November to March. Hermit Gulch is closest to Avalon, but you can get closer to nature at the other four campgrounds, all run by Two Harbors Management (☎510-2800). To get to any of these sites from Avalon, take the shuttle bus; you may have to hike 1½ mi. from the nearest stop.

Hermit Gulch (☎510-2000), a 1½ mi. walk from the Avalon boat landing, is populated by carousing campers. Hot showers, flush toilets, a coin microwave, BBQs, a vending machine, and a limited number of stoves and lanterns ($5). No gear? No problem—they also rent teepees ($30), tents ($10-16), and sleeping bags ($11). ❶

Blackjack is comprised of 11 large, secluded pine forest sites. The camp has cold showers, running water, and fire rings, but prepare for large herds of buffalo to amble by. ❶

Two Harbors campground, ¼ mi. from Two Harbors, has the most popular beach camping, with 54 campsites, cold showers, chemical toilets, and rental gear. Tents $10-25; sleeping bags $11. Nov.-May 2- or 4-bunk "Catalina Cabins" $30. ❶

Little Harbor, south of Two Harbors, on the western side of the island. 16 incredible beach sites offer a secluded cove, potable water, picnic tables, and chemical toilets. ❶

FOOD

Avalon, centered on **Crescent Avenue,** is Catalina's largest town and is the island's restaurant and recreation scene. Crescent Ave. curves along Catalina harbor, arcing from the pier where cross-channel boats arrive at the iconic Avalon Casino. Eateries and bars line the street (paved with tile and off-limits to cars and golf-carts), affording patrons spots to eyeball the sand and bottle-blue water. **Green Pleasure Pier** intersects Crescent Ave., and bustles with fish 'n' chip joints and cotton-candy vendors. Many of the larger restaurants host live music and karaoke nightly, and basic, cheap food is easy to find. For make-your-own materials, visit **Vons,** 121 Metropole St. (☎510-0280. Open daily 7am-10pm.)

Antonio's, 230 Crescent St. (☎510-0008), is the seaside home of the island's best pizza. Walls are adorned with colorfully defaced one-dollar bills and floors are strewn with peanut shells. Huge pizzas $12-17. Open M-Th 8am-11pm, F-Su 8am-midnight. ❷

Casino Dock Cafe, 2 Casino Way (☎510-2755), at the end of the Via Casino, lying in the shadow of the Casino and overlooking the placid harbor, has one of the best views in Avalon. Burgers $3.50-5. Swordfish sandwich $7. Beer $3-4. Live music in summer Sa-Su 3-6pm. Open M-F 8am-5pm, Sa-Su 8:30am-6:30pm. ❶

Pancake Cottage, 118 Catalina Ave. (☎510-0726), puts the breakfast grills on Crescent Ave. to shame. Breakfast special (2 pancakes, 2 eggs, 3 strips of bacon) $6. Sandwiches $6-8. Open M-F 6:30am-1pm, Sa-Su 6am-1:30pm. ❷

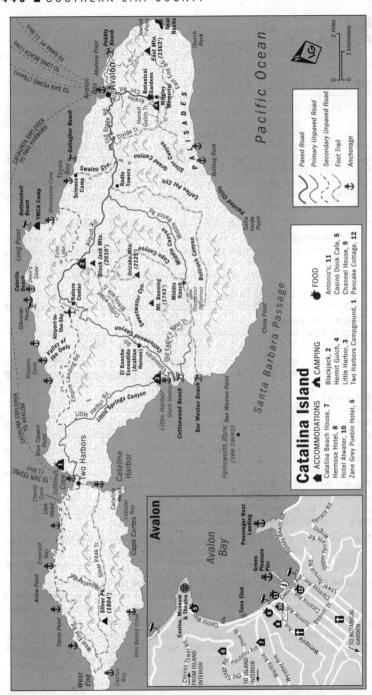

Catalina Island

Pacific Ocean

Santa Barbara Passage

Paved Road
Primary Unpaved Road
Secondary Unpaved Road
Foot Trail
⚓ **Anchorage**

Catalina Island

▲ **ACCOMMODATIONS**
Catalina Beach House, **7**
Hermosa Hotel, **8**
Hotel Atwater, **10**
Zane Grey Pueblo Hotel, **6**

▲ **CAMPING**
Blackjack, **2**
Hermit Gulch, **4**
Little Harbor, **3**
Two Harbors Campground, **1**

🍴 **FOOD**
Antonio's, **11**
Casino Dock Cafe, **5**
Channel House, **9**
Pancake Cottage, **12**

Avalon

Avalon Bay

AROUND L.A.

TO LONG BEACH (1.5hr)
TO DANA PT (3hr)
TO SAN PEDRO (75min)

CATALINA EXPLORER TO TWO HARBORS

Abalone Point
Pebbly Beach
Jewfish Point
Seal Rocks
Church Rock
East Mtn. (1563')
Avalon
Botanical Gardens
Wrigley Memorial Rd.
Hermit Gulch Tr.
Avalon Canyon Rd.
Old Stage Rd.
Divide Tr.
Gallagher Beach
Toyon Bay
Swains Cyn.
Science Camp
Radio Towers
Grand Canyon
Silver Canyon
Coffee Pot Cyn.
Bulldog Rock
Painted Cliffs
Salta Verde Point
P A L I S A D E S
Moonstone Cove
Long Point
Buttonshell Beach
YMCA Camp
Cabrillo Beach
Gibraltar Point
Echo Lake
Airport Rd.
Black Jack Mtn. (2010')
Devil's Slide
Nature Center
Airport-in-the-Sky
Valley of the Owls
Rippers Cove
Empire Landing Rd.
Cottonwood
Black Jack Tr.
Orizaba Mtn. (2125')
Cape Canyon
Middle Ranch Rd.
Mt. Banning (1743')
Sweetwater Cyn.
Middle Ranch
Bullrush Canyon
Thompson Reservoir
China Point
El Rancho Escondido (Arabian Horses)
Escondido Rd.
Old Eagle's Nest Tr.
Cottonwood Canyon
Little Harbor Rd.
Little Springs Canyon
Cottonwood Beach
Bar Weston Beach
Shark Harbor
Little Harbor
Ben Weston Point
Bar Weston Point
Farnsworth Bank (sea caves)
CATALINA EXPLORER TO AVALON
TO SAN PEDRO (1.5hr)
Two Harbors
Isthmus Cove
Cherry Cove
Lion Head
Catalina Head
Catalina Harbor
Cape Cortes Bay
Lobster Bay
Blue Cavern Point
Emerald Bay
Arrow Point
Stony Point
West End Rd.
Boushay Rd.
Silver Peak Tr.
Silver Pk. (1804')
West End
Cactus Bay
Iron Bound Cove
Chimes Tower Rd.
Casino, Museum & Theatre
Tuna Club
Casino Way
Stage Rd.
Old Stage Rd.
TO ISLAND INTERIOR
Old Stage Rd.
Metropole Ave.
Marilla Ave.
Whitley Ave.
Beacon St.
Sumner Ave.
Upper Terrace Rd.
Lower Terrace Rd.
Clarissa Ave.
Catalina Ave.
Crescent Ave.
Pebbly Beach Rd.
Terrace Rd.
Whitley Terrace Rd.
TO BOTANICAL GARDEN
Green Pleasure Pier
Passenger Boat Landing

2 miles
2 kilometers

Channel House, 205 Crescent Ave. (☎510-1617), serves Continental cuisine in its elegant dining hall and secluded patio overlooking the sea. Lunch $8-16. Dinners $15-25. Full bar. Early bird specials M-Th 4:30-6pm. Open M-Th 11am-3pm and 4:30-9pm, F 11am-3pm and 5-9:30pm, Sa-Su 10am-3pm and 5-9:30pm. ❹

👁 🏔 SIGHTS & ACTIVITIES

The **Santa Catalina Island Company** runs a slew of tours. The **Skyline** or **Inland Motor** tours are your best bets; go to the Discovery Tours Center at Catalina St. and Crescent Ave. (Skyline Tour $21, seniors $18.50, children $10.50. Inland Motor Tour $36, seniors $31.75, children $18.) The best way to see underwater life is to snorkel. Before going down below, gather dive gear at **Catalina Diver's Supply** (☎510-0330 or 800-353-0330), on the left-hand side of Pleasure Pier (mask, snorkel, and fin package or wetsuit $7 for 2hr., $11 per day). **Lover's Cove** is the most convenient snorkeling spot, and an excellent place to pick up on the tips shouted out by guided tours. You might get to swim among tiger sharks. Rent near the cove from **Catalina Snorkeling Adventures.** (☎510-8558. Open Apr.-Oct. Mask, snorkel, and fins $2.50 per hr., $5 per day; wetsuits $5/$10; deposit required.) The best place to snorkel is among the red garibaldi in the kelp forests off **Casino Point.** For privacy and no boats, walk past the Casino to private **Descano Beach** (day use $1-2). You can rent equipment just before the beach at **Descano Beach Ocean Sports.** (☎510-1226. Mask, snorkel, and fins $3 per hr., $6 per day; wetsuits $6/$11; single kayak $11/$45.) Those unable to, unwilling to, or uninterested in snorkeling can take **Glass Bottom Boat Trips** (30min.; $8-10, seniors $7-9, ages 2-11 $5-5.25) or the fantastic submarine **Undersea Tour** (45min.; $21-25, seniors $19-22, ages 2-11 $10.75-12.50).

The **Casino Building,** at the end of Crescent Ave., was never a gambling den; William Wrigley, Jr. built it for $2 million as a ballroom dancing hall in 1929 (*casino* means "gathering place" in Italian). The architectural tour of the building is well worth it. (☎510-7400. Tours $9.75, seniors $8.50, children $5.) You can also sneak a peek at the building's elegant art deco murals by catching a film in the 1000-seat **Avalon Theater;** nightly showings include a free concert on the antique page organ. (☎510-2414. Film showings 7 and around 9pm. $8.) The casino hosts occasional **jazz concerts** and a **New Year's Eve bash** that re-creates the Catalina of the 1930s and 40s, when it was a palace for the sultans of swing. Ask about the **Silent Film Festival** (June; for tickets, call ☎510-2414) and the **Halloween Costume Ball** (☎888-330-5252). Beneath the casino is the **Catalina Island Museum,** with exhibitions on island history, Native American inhabitants, and author/filmmaker Zane Grey. (☎510-2414. Open daily 10am-5pm. $2.50, seniors $2, ages 6-11 $1, under 6 free.) **Zane Grey's Avalon pueblo** is now a hotel overlooking the Casino from the high bluffs above.

At the end of Avalon Canyon Rd. (2 mi. outside Avalon), you can pick up the hilly **Hermit Gulch Trail,** a 3.5 mi. loop past canyons, secluded coast, and the **Wrigley Memorial.** The last is a monolithic remembrance of the gum magnate, who once owned the island, minus his dead body, which was removed from the island in the 1940s (the body is now at **Forest Lawn Cemetery,** p. 374). Past the memorial is the 38-acre **Botanical Gardens.** (☎510-2288. Open daily 8am-5pm. $3 donation.) The Gardens grow eight plant species native to Catalina as well as a vast, otherworldly cactus garden; a trek to the top of the cactus garden rewards hikers with sweeping views across the blue Pacific, extending all the way to the mainland on a clear day. The Memorial and Gardens are accessible by walking or taking the **Island Hopper** (p. 437) straight up Arroyo Canyon Rd. from Avalon. Bison and wild boars inhabit the area along the 4 mi. **Black Jack-Cape Reservoir Loop.** The two or three hundred buffalo here are the descendants of the 25 originally ferried over for the filming of Zane Grey's 1924 film *The Vanishing American*. The rigorous 8 mi. **Black Jack Trail** leads to Little Harbor. Pick up either of the last two trails at the Black Jack Junction, accessible by the **airport shuttle** (round-trip $14.50).

VENTURA ☎ 805

The Central Coast's southernmost city, Ventura (pop. 102,000) is blessed with cultural and historical treasure. Visitors to "California's Rising Star" flock to the recently revitalized downtown, now home to numerous restaurants, shops, museums and galleries. An emerging cultural district for performers of all genres is gaining much support, though most of the culture goes inside after dark. A short drive from downtown lies Ventura Harbor, a bustling center of activity with over 30 restaurants and shops, concerts, and festivals. To best locate all that Ventura has to offer, pick up the historic walking tour map from the Visitors Bureau.

⬛🔢 ORIENTATION & PRACTICAL INFORMATION. Ventura lies 30 mi. south of Santa Barbara off U.S. 101. **Main Street** runs east-west in the historic downtown area on the east side of town, intersecting with **California Street,** which runs down to the pier. **Ventura Harbor** lies south along the coast; from downtown, take Harbor Blvd. to **Spinnaker Drive.**

Pick up maps and helpful information at the **Ventura Visitors Bureau,** 89 S. California St. (☎ 648-2075 or 800-333-2989; www.ventura-usa.com. Open M-F 8:30am-5pm, Sa 9am-5pm, Su 10am-4pm.) Those interested in visiting the **Channel Islands National Park** (see p. 443) should seek out the **National Park Visitors Center,** 1901 Spinnaker Dr. (☎ 658-5730. Open M-F 8am-5pm, Sa-Su 8am-5:30pm.) **Cycles 4 Rent,** 239 W. Main St., rents bikes. (☎ 652-1114. $21 per half day, $30 per full day. Open by appointment only.) Other services include the **police,** 1425 Dowell Dr. (☎ 339-4400); the **County Hospital,** 3291 Loma Vista Rd. (☎ 800-746-8885); and the **Post Office,** 675 E. Santa Clara St. **Postal Code:** 93001.

🏠🏕 ACCOMMODATIONS & CAMPING. Prior to its rejuvenation Ventura was treated exclusively as a stopover point along the coastal routes. As a result, the destination has a number of budget motels, particularly along East Thompson Avenue, though many are decades old and in desperate need of renovation. A good bet is the **Rex Motel ❹,** 2406 E. Thompson Blvd. (☎ 643-5681. Singles $46-79; doubles $54-84. Weekly rates available.) For something fancier, try the **Clocktower Inn ❺,** 181 E. Santa Clara St. Once a firehouse, the Clocktower Inn is located minutes away from the heart of the city. Free continental breakfast. (☎ 805-652-0141. Some rooms with balconies and fireplaces. Singles and doubles $80-130.)

Beach camping is in no short supply around Ventura, but conditions lean toward the primitive. Reservations can be made through ReserveAmerica (☎ 800-444-7275) and should be made months in advance. **McGrath State Beach Campground ❷,** just south of town in Oxnard, is a popular spot with 174 campsites ($22).

🍴🎭 FOOD & ENTERTAINMENT. You'll find cheap food in Ventura along **Main Street,** in the heart of historic downtown. **Franky's ❷,** 456 E. Main St., is a Ventura institution, offering healthy, delectable pita pockets ($7.50), turkey burgers ($6.50), and music and art shows. (☎ 648-6282. Open daily 7am-3pm.) **Top Hat ❶,** 299 E. Main St., at Palm St., is a burger shack serving chili cheeseburgers ($2.15), hot dogs ($1) and fries ($1) to a neverending local crowd. (☎ 643-9696. Open Tu-Sa 10am-6pm.) **Jonathan's at Peirano's ❹,** 204 E. Main St., is popular Mediterranean spot. Its beautiful patio, adjacent to a well-manicured park and large fountain make for a pleasant dining experience. (☎ 648-4853; www.jonathansatpeiranos.com. Lunch entrees $9-15. Dinner entrees $12-25. Open Tu-Th 11:30am-2:30pm and 5:30-9:30pm, F-Sa 11:30am-2:30pm and 5:30-10pm, Su 5:30-9pm.) If the desire for pasta strikes, try **Capriccio Restaurant ❷,** 298 Main St, at the corner of Main and

Palm. This quiet, warm, red-bricked Italian restaurant is popular among both the lunch and dinner crowd. Some patio seating is available. (☎ 643-7115. Lunch entrees $7-9. Dinner entrees $9-12. Open M-Th 11:30am-8:45pm, F-Sa 11:30am-10pm, Su 12:00pm-8:45pm.) One of the few late-night establishments, **Nicholby's Upstairs,** 404 Main St., offers a happy hour with $2.50 well and draft drinks. Wednesday's "Hump Night" features live crab races and casino games. (☎ 653-5320. $3 cover F-Sa 8-10pm. Open W-Sa 7pm-1:30am.)

🔊 🎵 **SIGHTS & HIKES.** Billed as California's "Gold Coast," the clean beaches near Ventura roar with fantastic surf. **Emma Wood State Beach,** on Main St. (take State Beaches Exit off U.S. 101), and **Oxnard State Beach Park,** about 5 mi. south of Ventura, are quiet and peaceful. On the other hand, **San Buenaventura State Park,** at the end of San Pedro St., entertains families and casual beach-goers with its volleyball courts and nearby restaurants. **Surfer's Point,** at the end of Figueroa St., has the best waves around, but novices should start at **McGrath State Beach,** about 1 mi. south of Ventura down Harbor Blvd. Pick up insider surfing tips and Patagonia outlet gear at **Real Cheap Sports,** 36 W. Santa Clara St. (☎ 650-1213. Open M-Sa 10am-6pm, Su 10am-5pm. For info on surf sessions call ☎ 648-2662 or check out www.surfclass.com.)

Inland from Ventura Harbor and next to Olivas Park Golf Course, on Olivas Park Dr., is the **Olivas Adobe.** The restored 1847 home of Raymundo Olivas now stands as a tribute to the rancho period of Ventura's history. Olivias was not only one of the richest ranchers in California, but also an early host to the budget traveler. Next to the visitors' beds, Raymundo placed bowls of coins from which guests could draw some pocket change. (☎ 644-4346. Open daily 10am-4pm. Docent tours Sa-Su 10am-4pm, daily self-guided tour with map. Recommended donation $0.50.)

Mission San Buenaventura, 211 E. Main St., still functions as a parish church, although it also houses a tiny museum of treasures from Father Junípero Serra's order. (☎ 643-4318. Open M-Sa 10am-5pm, Su 10am-4pm. $1 donation requested.) Across the street is the **Museum of History and Art,** 100 E. Main St., which has one permanent and two rotating exhibits, including quarter-life-size George Stuart Historical Figures. (☎ 653-0323; www.vcmha.org. Open Tu-Su 10am-5pm. $4, seniors $3, ages 6-17 $1, under 6 free.)

CHANNEL ISLANDS NATIONAL PARK ☎ 805

Ventura serves as a point of departure to the desolate Channel Islands, which are home to ancient Chumash sites, historic ranches, kelp forests, seals, and wildflowers. The **Channel Islands National Park Visitors Center,** 1901 Spinnaker Dr., has info, in addition to an observation tower that looks out on the islands, an indoor tide pool, a native plant garden, and other exhibits. (☎ 658-5730. Open May-Sept. M-F 8am-5pm, Sa-Su 8am-5:30pm; Oct.-Apr. M-F 8am-4pm, Sa-Su 8am-4:30pm.)

The park consists of five islands. **Anacapa** is composed of three islets and is home to 265 species of plants. **Santa Cruz** is renowned for pristine beaches, lonely canyons, and grassy hills. **Santa Rosa** is the second largest island and is inhabited by the island fox and spotted skunk. **San Miguel** nurtures an eerie fossilized caliche forest and thousands of seals. Tiny **Santa Barbara** is only one square mile and cultivates the live-forever, a plant found only on this island.

Unfortunately, unless you happen to own your own boat, you'll have to call one of the park's "official concessionaires" to take you to the islands. **Island Packers,** 1691 Spinnaker Dr., in Ventura Harbor, has a virtual monopoly on island transport, with rates up to $215. The concessionaires go to each of the islands and offer various diversions on each, such as camping, hiking, kayaking, and tours. (Recorded info ☎642-7688. Both daytrips and overnight camping excursions depart around 8am. Anacapa daytrip $37, overnight $48. Santa Cruz daytrip $42, overnight $54. Santa Rosa daytrip $62, overnight $80. Santa Barbara daytrip $49, overnight $75. San Miguel overnight only $90. An Island Cruise with no landing available for $24. Reserve well in advance at ☎642-1393.)

All recreational gear must be rented in advance. Three-hour guided kayaking tours, a safe and enjoyable way to see wildlife and island formations, are run by **Aqua Sports,** 1955 Hogan Dam Rd., in Valley Springs. (☎800-773-2309; www.island-kayaking.com. Tours $85.) For snorkel and dive gear, try **Pacific Scuba Center,** 480 S. Victoria Ave., in Oxnard. (☎805-984-2566; www.pacificscuba.com. Scuba package $40 first day, $20 each additional day. Snorkel package with mask, snorkel, fins, boots, and gloves $29 first day, $10 each additional day.) **Camping ❶** at the islands requires your own gear, food, and water. (Reservations ☎800-365-2267; www.reservation.nps.gov. Sites $10.)

The best part of a Channel Islands trip can be the **boat ride.** Most trips see pods of common dolphins playing in the boat wake. Sea lions, birds, flying fish, and whales can also be spotted en route to the islands. **Island Packers** runs whale-watching tours as well as island tours. (Grey whale: Dec. 26-Mar. 31 daily 9am and 1pm; 4hr.; $24. Humpback and blue whale: July-Aug. Sa 9am and 1pm; 7-8hr.; $58.)

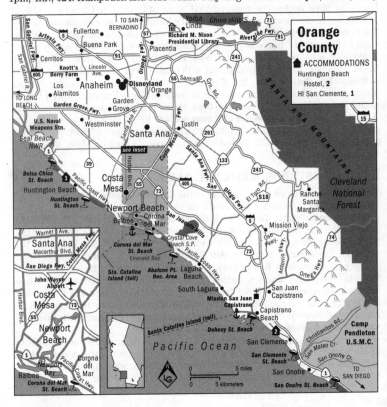

ORANGE COUNTY

Directly south of L.A. County lies Orange County (pop. 2.75 million). Composed of 34 cities, it is a microcosm of Southern California: dazzling stretches of sandy shoreline, bronzed beach bums, endless strip malls, frustrating traffic snarls, and the stronghold of the late Walt Disney's ever-expanding cultural empire. One of California's staunchest Republican enclaves, Orange County supports big business and its economy shows it. It is also one of the safest areas in the country.

Disneyland is the premier inland attraction; home to dancing disney characters in the midst of the suburban sprawl. The self-proclaimed "Happiest Place On Earth" is now even happier as a result of the construction of California Adventure and Downtown Disney. Orange County's aesthetic appeal increases as one moves closer to the shore. A drive down the Pacific Coast Highway (PCH to locals) from Huntington Beach to Laguna Beach is well worth it. The coast runs the gamut from the budget and party-friendly surf burg of Huntington Beach to the opulent excess of Newport Beach and the artistic vibe of Laguna. A little farther south lies the quiet mission of San Juan Capistrano, set amidst rolling hills that spill onto the laid-back beaches of Dana Point and San Clemente.

AROUND L.A.

▟ TRANSPORTATION

Airport: John Wayne Orange County, 18601 Airport Way, Santa Ana (☎949-252-5006), 20min. from Anaheim. Newer, cleaner, and easier to get around than the L.A. Airport; domestic flights only.

Trains: Amtrak (☎800-USA-RAIL/872-7245; www.amtrakcalifornia.com). Stations (from north to south): **Fullerton,** 120 E. Santa Fe Ave. (☎714-992-0530); **Anaheim,** Anaheim Station Parking Lot, 2150 E. Katella Blvd. (☎714-385-1448); **Santa Ana,** 1000 E. Santa Ana Blvd. (☎714-547-8389); **Irvine,** 15215 Barranca Pkwy. (☎949-753-9713); **San Juan Capistrano,** 26701 Verdugo St. (☎949-240-2972).

Buses: Greyhound (☎800-231-2222) has 3 stations in the area: **Anaheim,** 100 W. Winston Rd., 3 blocks south of Disneyland (☎714-999-1256; station open daily 6:30am-9pm); **Santa Ana,** 1000 E. Santa Ana Blvd. (☎714-542-2215; open daily 6am-8:30pm); and **San Clemente,** 2421 S. El Camino Real. (☎949-366-2646. Open daily 7am-8:30pm.)

Public Transit: Orange County Transportation Authority (OCTA), 550 S. Main St., Orange. Thorough service is useful for getting from Santa Ana and Fullerton Amtrak stations to Disneyland and for beach-hopping along the coast. Long Beach, in L.A. County, serves as the terminus for several OCTA lines. Bus #1 travels the coast from Long Beach to San Clemente (every hr. until 8pm). Buses #25, 33, and 35 travel from Fullerton to Huntington Beach; #91 goes from Laguna Hills to Dana Point. (☎714-636-7433; www.octa.net. Fare $1, day pass $2.50.) **Info center** open M-F 6am-8pm, Sa-Su 8am-5pm. **MTA Info** (☎213-626-4455 or 800-266-6883). Phone lines open daily 5am-10:45pm. MTA buses run from L.A. to Disneyland and Knott's Berry Farm.

▟ PRACTICAL INFORMATION

Visitor Information: Anaheim Area Visitors and Convention Bureau, 800 W. Katella Ave. (☎714-765-8888), in Anaheim Convention Ctr. Lodging and dining guides. Open M-F 8am-5pm. **Huntington Beach Conference and Visitors Bureau,** 417 Main St. (☎714-969-3492 or 800-729-6232). If the helpful staff doesn't know something, they'll find someone who does. Good maps and brochures. Open M-F 9am-5pm. **Newport Harbor Area Chamber of Commerce,** 1470 Jamboree Rd. (☎949-729-4400), in Newport Beach. Offers free maps and info. Open M-F 8:30am-5pm; 24hr. automated answering service. **Newport Visitors Bureau,** 3300 West Coast Hwy. (☎949-722-1611 or 800-942-6278), in Newport Beach. Maps and brochures of area attractions and events and an eager-to-help staff. Open M-F 8am-5pm; in summer also Sa-Su 11am-4pm. **San Clemente Visitors Center,** 1100 N. El Camino Real (☎949-492-1131), in San Clemente. Open M-F 8:30am-5pm, Sa 10am-3pm, Su 10am-2pm.

Gay-Lesbian Community Center: 12832 Garden Grove Blvd., suite A (☎714-534-0862), in Garden Grove. Open M-F 9am-10pm.

Surf and Weather Conditions: ☎213-554-1212.

Police: Anaheim, 425 S. Harbor Blvd. (☎714-765-1900). **Huntington Beach,** 2000 Main St. (☎714-960-8811).

Crisis Lines: Sexual Assault Hotline (☎714-957-2737). **Orange County Referral Hotline** (☎714-894-4242).

Medical Services: St. Jude Medical Center, 101 E. Valencia Mesa Dr., Fullerton (☎714-871-3280). **Lestonnac Free Clinic,** 1215 E. Chapman Ave. (☎714-633-4600). Open Tu-F 9am-5pm.

Post Office: 701 N. Loara St., Anaheim (☎800-275-8777), 1 block north of Anaheim Plaza. Open M-F 8:30am-5pm, Sa 9am-3pm. **Postal Code:** 92803.

> **ORANGE COUNTY AREA CODES. 714** in Anaheim, Fullerton, Fountain Valley, Santa Ana, Orange, Garden Grove; **949** in Newport, Laguna, Irvine, Mission Viejo, San Juan Capistrano, and surrounding areas; **310** in Seal Beach.

ANAHEIM ☎714

Anaheim (pop. 300,000) was considered, in the late 1950s, the city of the future. Californians flocked to Orange County's capital city, where booming industry and Uncle Walt's dream machine created jobs and revenue galore. Today, the city is best known as a place to go if you want to have fun. Though most roads in Anaheim do lead to Disneyland, other venues make it a great place for entertainment. The Mighty Ducks play hockey at Arrowhead Pond and the Angels play baseball at Edison Field. The new House of Blues and The Grove attract the best in music. Disney recently built a new theme park called "California Adventure," adjacent to Disneyland. The frontier sights of California Adventure combined with the new "Downtown Disney" provide an enclave of restaurants, shops, and shows.

ACCOMMODATIONS

The Magic Kingdom is the sun around which the Anaheim solar system revolves, so budget motels and garden-variety "clean comfortable rooms" flank it on all sides. Keep watch for family and group rates posted on marquees, and seek out establishments offering the 3-for-2 passport (3 days of Disney for the price of 2). The good news about the California Adventure construction is that it inspired hotel owners to revamp their establishments; the bad news is that hotel prices have gone up as a result.

Fullerton (HI-AYH), 1700 N. Harbor Blvd. (☎738-3721), in Fullerton, 15min. north of Disneyland. Shuttle from L.A. airport $21. OCTA bus #43 runs along Harbor Blvd. to Disneyland. In the woods and away from the thematic craziness of nearby Anaheim. Enthusiastic, resourceful staff invites questions but forbids drinking. Offers services, including ISICs. Kitchen, Internet access, relaxing living room, communal bathrooms. Linen $2. Free laundry. 7-night max. stay. Check-in 8-11am and 4-11pm. No curfew.

Reservations encouraged. Open June 1-September 30. Single-sex and co-ed dorms $16.50, non-members $19.50 (including taxes). ❷

Econolodge, 1126 W. Katella Ave. (☎533-4505; www.econolodge.com), in Anaheim, at the southwest corner of Disneyland. Clean, newly revamped rooms with HBO, phones, and A/C. Balconies offer a good view of Disney's nightly fireworks. Small pool, many kids. Reservations recommended; 10% discount with Internet reservations. Singles $79; doubles $99. In winter singles $69; doubles $89. ❺

◼ FOOD

Anaheim is more mini-mall than city. There are countless fast food places to choose from, but hold out for one of the inexpensive ethnic restaurants in the strip malls that line Anaheim's streets. Many specialize in takeout or will deliver to your motel room.

Rutabegorz, 211 N. Pomona Blvd. (☎738-9339; www.rutabegorz.com), in Fullerton. With a name derived from the unloved rutabaga and a style acquired from the worship thereof, this hippie-cum-hipster joint supplies a 20-page menu (printed on recycled newsprint, of course). Crepes, curries, quesadillas, and club sandwiches are all fresh and veggie-licious. Heaping salads with homemade dressings $4-9. Mexican casserole $7. Smoothies, veggie juices, and coffee drinks $1.50-4. Open M-Th 11am-10pm, F-Sa 11am-11pm, Su 4-9pm. ❷

Angelo & Vinci's Cafe Ristorante, 550 N. Harbor Blvd. (☎879-4022), in Fullerton. Prepare for opera—arias, masks, even "backstage dining." Padded red chairs, iron-rod table lamps, and indoor awnings are all part of the Sicilian motif. The food is unmistakably the stuff of family recipes (Cannelloni Vinci $10.75), with more than enough to feed the family at the lunch buffet ($6). Su champagne brunch ($9) 11am-3pm. Open Su-Th 11am-9:45pm, F-Sa 11am-11:45pm. ❸

El Pollo Inka, 400 S. Euclid Blvd. (☎772-2263), in Anaheim. Locals congregate under a back-lit mural of Machu Picchu and devour Anaheim's best Peruvian food. The *arroz con pollo* (rice and chicken; $8) is delicious, and the *mazzomorra morada* (purple corn pudding; $2.50) makes an excellent dessert. Live Andean music Sa 8-10pm. Open M-Th 11:30am-9pm, F 11:30am-11pm, Sa noon-11pm, Su noon-9pm. ❷

◉ ♫ SIGHTS & ENTERTAINMENT

DISNEYLAND

*Main entrance on Harbor Blvd., and a smaller one on Katella Ave. May be approached by car via I-5 to Katella Ave. From L.A., MTA bus #460 travels from 4th and Flower St. (about 1hr.) to the Disneyland Hotel (service to the hotel begins at 4:53am; service back to L.A. runs until 1:20am). Free shuttles link the hotel to Disneyland's portals, as does the Disneyland monorail. The park is also served by Airport Service, OCTA, Long Beach Transit, and the Gray Line (see **Practical Information,** p. 445). Parking $8. ☎781-4565; www.disneyland.com. Disneyland open Su-Th 8am-11pm. F-Sa 8am-midnight; hours may vary; call ahead. California Adventure open Su-Th 9am-10pm, F-Sa 9am-10:30pm. Disneyland passport $43, ages 3-9 $33, under 3 free; allows repeated single-day entrance into the park. Two- and three-day passes are also available. California Adventure passports $43, ages 3-9 $33, under 3 free. Combination tickets available. Lockers west of the ticket booths outside the main entrance and at the lost and found facility on Main Street, USA.*

Disneyland calls itself the "Happiest Place on Earth," and there is a part of everyone that agrees. Your almighty wallet, of course, may not. Even though the admission is steep, this is probably the best place in Southern California to spend your money. Weekday and off-season visitors will undoubtedly be the happiest, but the enterprising can wait for parades to distract children from the epic lines. Walt's innovative Disney team has finally arrived at the line-busting solution they have been looking for: the **FastPass** program. FastPass lets you pick up a reservation ticket by inserting your park ticket into a vending machine at designated attractions. Then you may return at a specific time to walk right on and ride. If you are willing to ride without your friends **Single-Rider** tickets allow you to skip almost the entire line. Tickets only available at a few rides. *Guide to the Magic* lists parade and show times, as well as important shopping information.

MAIN STREET, USA. This is a children's-book walk through the golden age of small-town America. Disney and his designers skewed the perspective on Main Street so that the street seemed longer upon entering and shorter upon exiting, thereby creating visitor anticipation and making the walk to the car less daunting after a long day. Main Street's shops stay open an hour after the park itself closes, but don't be fooled into thinking you'll get your souvenirs on the way out—everyone else has the same idea.

FANTASYLAND. The geographical and spiritual center of the park, Fantasyland contains the trademark castle as well as the scintillating **Matterhorn Bobsleds,** and numerous kiddie rides like the trippy **It's A Small World,** which will fiendishly engrave its happy, happy song into your brain. This area is best enjoyed when the rides light up at night, the kiddies go home, and you have twenty bucks to blow on the addictive $2.50 *churros* (sugary sticks of fried dough).

ADVENTURELAND. To the left of Main Street is the home of **Tarzan's Treehouse,** a walk-through attraction that replaced the Swiss Family Robinson Treehouse. The **Indiana Jones Adventure** is just next door. Pass the time in line by decoding the inscriptions inside the Temple of Maya (hint: the ride is sponsored by AT&T). Indiana Jones fans' palms will sweat when an animatronic Harrison Ford suggestively says, "You were good in there...very good." The **Jungle Cruise** next door has a new landing with a swing band to entertain the poor souls languishing in the hot sun. For lunch, the **Bengal Barbecue** offers chicken and beef skewers ($3), tasty breadsticks ($2), and cold grilled bananas ($4).

NEW ORLEANS SQUARE. In the left corner of the park are the best shops and dining in Disneyland. Find New Orleans cuisine at the **French Market** (dinner $7) or the much more expensive **Blue Bayou,** where there seems to be a surcharge for atmosphere. The low-key but entertaining rides are evocative of authentically Southern lazy afternoons. Try the creepy, campy **Haunted Mansion,** or the ever-popular, if now politically-corrected, **Pirates of the Caribbean.**

FRONTIERLAND. Wild West fetishists will find amusement galore here, especially on **Big Thunder Mountain Railroad.** Grab a bite at the **River Belle Terrace,** famous for its Mickey Mouse shaped pancakes. The **Mark Twain riverboat** tours around Tom Sawyer's Island, which looks suspiciously like a clever way to isolate harmful children on an island away from smart adults (see **Alcatraz,** p. 93).

CRITTER COUNTRY. Most of the park's cuter things lurk in this section, where the main attraction is **Splash Mountain,** a soaking log ride past singing rodents and down a thrilling vertical drop. Its host, **Brer Rabbit,** originated in the humor-filled "Uncle Remus" stories of the Reconstruction-era South. You might enjoy the snapshot they take of your horror-frozen face on the way down.

MICKEY'S TOONTOWN. At the rear of the park, this cartoon playland provides the key source of fun for the 10-and-under crowd. Mickey and Co. can often be found strolling about, followed by a stampede of kids in hot pursuit. Disney seems to be phasing out Mickey's old-school compadres like Donald, Goofy, and Chip 'n' Dale, in favor of hi-tech new kids Ariel, Simba, Aladdin, and Belle.

TOMORROWLAND. To the right of Main Street is this futuristic portion of the park, recently remodeled after Disney executives recognized that its supposed imagination of the future was gloriously stuck in the 1950s. Though the **Astro-Orbiter**—rockets that circle around moving planets—will thrill young children, the overwhelming favorite of the rush-seeking set is still **Space Mountain,** the darkened roller coaster that travels beneath a mountain of sheer exhilaration. **Star Tours** promises a routine shuttle to Endor, but delivers an exciting simulation ride.

CALIFORNIA ADVENTURE. Just recently, Disneyland introduced its new kid brother, "California Adventure," to the Southern California theme park family. The park features ambitious attractions divided into four districts. **Sunshine Plaza,** the gateway to the park, is anchored by a 50-ft.-tall sun enlivened by a wealth of red, orange, and yellow lights at night. Built as a shrine to the greatest state of them all, **Golden State** offers an 8-acre mini-wilderness, a citrus grove, a winery, and even a replica of San Francisco. **Paradise Pier** is dedicated to the so-called "Golden Age" of amusement park—with rides such as **California Screamin'** and **Mulholland Madness**. Finally, the **Hollywood Pictures Backlot** realizes your aspirations to stardom without those embarrassing before-you-were-famous potato chip commercials hanging over your head. Admission to California Adventure is not included in admission to Disneyland, but combined passes are available (see p. 447).

K(NOT)T DISNEYLAND

Back in 1932, Walter Knott combined a red raspberry, a blackberry, and a loganberry to make a boysenberry, marking the future site of **Knott's Berry Farm.** Naturally, his popular roadside stand quickly grew into a restaurant. When he imported the Old Trails Hotel (from Prescott, AZ) and the last narrow gauge railroad in the country to form "Ghost Town," the precursor to the first theme park in America was born. After the opening of Disneyland in Anaheim in 1955, Knott's Farm added more rides and other theme sections such as Fiesta Village. Knott's is a local favorite and aims at being "the friendliest place in the West." It has long since given up on being the happiest place on Earth. The park's highlights include roller coasters like **Montezuma's Revenge, Boomerang,** and **Ghostrider,** the largest wooden roller coasters in the West. The latest addition is **Xcelerator,** bringing you from 0 to 80 mph in three seconds. If you are brave enough try **Supreme Scream,** the tallest thrill ride of its kind, where you will fall 30 stories in three seconds. The Doolittle-ish **Birdcage Theater** is where Steve Martin got his start, and now showcases special seasonal entertainment. At Halloween, the park is rechristened Knott's Scary Farm, and at Christmas, Knott's Merry Farm. The food inside is what you'd expect; the best deal, **Mrs. Knott's Chicken Dinner Restaurant** (☎714-220-5080), is outside the park. The Mrs. offers soup, salad, corn, biscuits, chicken, and dessert (the specialty is—surprise—boysenberry pie) for only $10. Prepare to line-up. *(8039 Beach Blvd. at La Palma Ave., 5 mi. northeast of Disneyland. From downtown L.A., take MTA bus #460 from 4th and Flower St.; 1¼hr. If driving from L.A., take I-5 south to Beach Blvd., turn right at the end of the Exit ramp and proceed south 2 mi. Recorded info ☎220-5220. Open Su-Th 9am-10pm, F-Sa 9am-midnight; hours may vary; call ahead. $38, seniors and ages 3-11 $28, under 3 free; after 4pm all ages $17. Summer discounts available. Parking $8.)*

SOAK CITY USA. This 13-acre water park marks Knott's latest effort to make a splash in the already drenched local theme park scene. Its 21 water rides and attractions are fashioned after the longboards and surf woodies and waves of the 1950s Southern Californian coast. *(Next to Knott's Berry Farm. ☎220-5220. Open Su-Th 10am-6pm, F-Sa 10am-8pm; hours may vary; call ahead. $20, ages 3-11 $14, under 3 free.)*

RICHARD NIXON LIBRARY & BIRTHPLACE. Farther inland in Yorba Linda is this highly uncritical, privately funded monument to Tricky Dick. The first native California president was born in this house, which has now become an extensive museum. Rotating exhibits cover such fashionable topics as "Barbie as First Lady" with the presidents' wives all dolled up and "Secret Treaties" from Westphalia to Spy Paraphernalia. Skeptics can investigate the Watergate Room. Throughout the museum are letters from "small Republicans" to their big GOP idol, who was laid to rest here alongside his wife. Museum curators consistently portray Nixon as a victim of circumstance, plotting enemies, and his own immutable honor. *(18001 Yorba Linda Blvd. ☎ 993-5075. Open M-Sa 10am-5pm, Su 11am-5pm. $6, seniors $4, ages 8-11 $2, under 8 free.)*

CRYSTAL CATHEDRAL. Seating 3000 faithful in Garden Grove, the cathedral is where Dr. Robert H. Schuller's weekly TV show *Hour of Power* is taped. The Crystal Cathedral's own Ministry of Traffic provides the opportunity for In-Car Worship at a huge outdoor television. *(12141 Lewis St. ☎ 971-4013. 45min.-1hr. tours M-Sa 9am-3:30pm. English services Su 9:30 and 11am; Spanish service 12:45pm. Free. Broadcast on KCAL-TV, channel 9 in Orange County.)*

HSI LAI TEMPLE (INTERNATIONAL BUDDHIST PROGRESS SOCIETY). Notorious for its involvement in a Clinton-Gore fund-raising scandal, Hsi Lai's recent political abstinence has hardly extinguished "Buddha's Light" from its halls. The Bodhisattva Hall up the stairs from the main gate anticipates the main shrine with miniature *bodhisattva* sculptures lining the walls. For a dollar, you can get your fortune-cookie readings or *dharma* (translated as "religion" or "duty"). In the main shrine are three huge enamel Buddhas, each holding a different symbolic object. Toss pennies at a bell in the Statue Garden; hit it one, two, or three times and receive increasing levels of health, intelligence, and prosperity. Informative signboards along the pathways and in front of shrines make the largest Chinese Buddhist temple outside China as much a museum as a place of worship. Don't forget that it is the latter, too—no shorts or tank tops may be worn in the main shrine. *(3456 S. Glenmark Dr., Hacienda Heights. From Anaheim, take Rte. 57 north to Rte. 60 west; Exit Hacienda Blvd. and go south to Glenmark Dr. ☎ 626-961-9697. Vegetarian lunch buffet ($5) M-F 11:30am-1:30pm, Sa-Su 11:30am-2:30pm. Services Sa 1:30pm, Su 10:30am.)*

SOUTH COAST PLAZA. 3333 Bristol St. (☎714-435-2000), in Orange County. True shopaholics head to this mother of all malls. The 300 stores and a 1.6-acre garden path in the mall are impressive, and the novice L.A. shopper will appreciate free maps and inter-plaza shuttles. *(Open M-F 10am-9pm, Sa 10am-7pm, Su 11am-6:30pm.)*

SPORTS. For more evidence of Disney's world domination, catch a game by one of the teams they own: The major league **Anaheim Angels** play baseball from early April to October at **Edison Field.** *(☎ 940-2000 or 800-626-4357. General tickets $6-25.)* To check out some NHL action catch a **Mighty Ducks** hockey game at **Arrowhead Pond.**

ORANGE COUNTY BEACH COMMUNITIES

Taking town planning to the extreme, Orange County's various beach communities have cleaner sand, better surf, and less madness than their L.A. County counterparts. Other than the ocean view, sights are scarce along the 35 mi. stretch of Hwy. 1 between Huntington Beach and San Clemente, with the exception of the graceful Mission San Juan Capistrano. L.A. residents seek refuge among Orange County's natural wonders—its surf, coastal cliffs and wooded canyons.

⌐ ACCOMMODATIONS

Orange County's prime coastline and pricey real estate impose a dearth of bargain rates. Those without multi-million dollar summer homes in the area can try their luck along the Pacific Coast or Newport Blvd. in Newport Beach.

▨ **Huntington Beach Colonial Inn Youth Hostel,** 421 8th St. (☎714-536-9206), in Huntington Beach, 4 blocks inland at Pecan Ave. Take OCTA #29 (which also goes to Knott's) or #50. This large, early 20th-century yellow and blue house was once a brothel. Things have quieted down since the neighbors moved in (quiet hours after 11pm). Common bath, large kitchen, reading/TV room, coin-op laundry, Internet access, deck, and surfboard shed. Linen and breakfast included. Key deposit $20. Americans 1-week max. stay. Check-in 7am-11pm. No lockout. Reserve 2 days in advance for summer weekends. 3-4 person dorms $22; doubles $50. **International passport required; American college IDs accepted on space-available basis.** ❷

HI San Clemente Beach (HI-AYH), 233 Ave. Granada (☎949-492-2848; www.hostelweb.com/sandiego/sanclemente.htm), in San Clemente, 2 blocks west of El Camino. Within walking distance of the shore. This surfer's haven is so laid-back it's almost comatose. Patio, comfy couches, and entertainment center. Lockers, laundry, kitchen, Internet access. 14-day max. stay. Reception 8-10:30am and 5-11pm. Quiet hours 11pm-7am. Open May 1-Oct. 31. 20-bed male dorm, 14-bed female dorm, and private room with 3 beds ($2 surcharge per person). Dorms $14, nonmembers $17. ❶

Balboa Inn, 105 Main St. (☎949-675-3412; www.balboainn.com), on the sand at Newport. This recently renovated historical landmark offers rooms with ocean or bay views and is only a short drive from area attractions. Relax in the pool or jacuzzi. Continental breakfast and room service offered. Room rates start at $119. ❺

⌐ CAMPING

Orange County's state beaches have campgrounds, but they are somewhat cramped and crowded. Reservations are required for all sites (reservation fee $7). Reserve through ReserveAmerica (☎800-444-7275) a maximum of seven months in advance, and as soon as possible in the summer. Beachside camping outside official campgrounds is both illegal and unsafe.

Doheny, 25300 Dana Point Harbor Dr. (☎714-496-6171), in Dana Point, along Hwy. 1. The most popular Orange County campground. Fire rings, grills, volleyball nets, bike and in-line skate rental. Beachfront sites $12. ❶

San Clemente, 3030 Del Presidente (☎949-492-3156), in San Clemente. From I-5 North, Exit at Christianitos, turn right onto Del Presidente, and left onto Calafia after ¾mi.; from I-5 South, Exit at Calafia. Ocean bluffs, nature trail, and coin-operated hot showers draw all kinds of folks. Hookups at 72 sites. Sites $12, with hookup $18. ❶

⌐❘ FOOD & NIGHTLIFE

Orange County's restaurants tend toward California Cuisine of the light and seafood-oriented variety.

Laguna Village Market and Cafe, 577 S. Coast Hwy. (☎949-494-6344), in Laguna Beach. The restaurant is housed in an open-air gazebo, but its oceanfront terrace is the main draw. Lap up the view, along with some seafood or the house specialty Village Huevos ($9.50). Calamari plate $9. After your meal, check out local art in the surrounding gazebo. If you want a toe-ring, this is the place. Open daily 8:30am-dark. ❷

Ruby's (☎714-969-7829), at the end of the Huntington Beach Pier. Go back in time for a great burger ($6) and a fabulous ocean view at this 1950s-style diner. ❷

Cafe Zoolu, 860 Glenneyre (☎949-494-6825), in Laguna Beach. This small evening restaurant offers an opportunity to dine on the freshest fish possible in a bustling yet quaint atmosphere, undoubtedly enhanced by leopard print chairs and red-stone walls. It is best to pick from the seafood specials. Nothing prepares you for Alaskan halibut ($26) like ahi tar-tar ($15). Open Tu-Su 5pm-close. ❺

The Dutch Bakery, 32341 Camino Capistrano (☎949-489-2180), in San Juan Capistrano. Located in the Vons Center plaza, this bakery provides the best sandwiches you will ever have. Choose from a selection of chicken, turkey, ham, salami, and roast beef all made on fresh baked ciabatta bread. The chicken paisano (with havarti cheese, tomato, lettuce, and paisano mayo; $6) is unbeatable. Wash it down with a strawberry banana smoothie ($3). Open M-F 6am-4pm, Sa 7am-3pm. ❷

The Cottage, 308 N. Coast Hwy. (☎949-494-3023), at Cliff Dr., across from the Laguna Art Museum, in Laguna Beach. In a turn-of-the-century "board and batten" beach home, The Cottage is a Laguna landmark. Overflowing portions of home-style cooking (surfer's breakfast $9) and omelettes galore assure that guests are fed like family. Prices go up for dinner. Breakfast served daily until 3pm. Open daily 7am-3pm and 5-9pm. ❸

Streetlight Espresso Café, 201D Main St. (☎714-969-7336), in Huntington Beach. Streetlight is as bohemian as Huntington Beach gets. This non-denominational cafe hosts Christian rock bands F-Sa nights. Its board games get regular play. Super-sweet white chocolate mocha ($3-3.50) is a godsend. Sandwiches $4.50; cup of soup $4.50. Open M-Th 6am-midnight, F 6am-1am, Sa 7am-midnight, Su noon-midnight. ❶

The Boom-Boom Room, 1401 S. Coast Hwy. (☎949-494-7588), at Mountain St., in Laguna Beach. Lively gay hangout has international reputation, pool tables, live DJs, and a "surfing, muscle-bound, cruising, tanned" clientele. Boom-Boom specials include "Beer Busts" (Su and Th 4-8pm) with $1.50 drafts. Open daily noon-2am.

◪ ◎ BEACHES & SIGHTS

Apart from pre-fabricated amusement park joy, fun in the sun Orange County-style revolves around the Pacific—along the Pacific Coast Highway (PCH). On average, the beaches are cleaner, less crowded, and more elegant than those in L.A. County. Nevertheless, visitors should not be lulled off-guard by the swishing coastal waters. As in any city, pedestrians should take extreme care after dusk.

HUNTINGTON BEACH

From L.A., take the I-405 south to Hwy. 39 (Beach Blvd.). Follow Hwy. 39 south to PCH, then turn right (north). The pier is on the left at intersection of the PCH and Main St.

This prototypical Surf City, USA is a beach bum playground. This town has surf lore galore, and the proof is on the **Surfing Walk of Fame** (the sidewalk along PCH at Main St.) and in the **International Surfing Museum,** 411 Olive St. (☎714-960-3483. *Open 5 days weekly, call for details. $2, students $1.)* You can join the wave-riding for about $40 per hour for an instructor, board, and wetsuit. Inquire at any of the local surf shops or make an appointment with the lifeguard-staffed **Huntington Beach Surfing Instruction** (☎714-962-3515). The pier is the best place to watch the continuing cavalcade of official surfing contests. By night, H.B.'s bars become a beach party brouhaha. **Duke's Barefoot Bar** (☎714-374-6446), at the foot of the pier, is the major beach landmark, and **Perq's,** 117 Main St. (☎714-960-9996), is Orange County's oldest blues house. **Main St.,** Huntington Beach's central lane, is a surf shop superstore. Locals lament the loss of familiar establishments. Malls and shiny new bars have replaced the luster of Huntington's grimy, surfing underside.

NEWPORT BEACH & BALBOA PENINSULA

From L.A., take I-405 or the I-5 (San Diego Fwy.) south to Hwy. 55 (Costa Mesa Fwy.) and head west. Hwy. 55 turns into Newport Blvd., the main drag leading to the peninsula.

Multi-million dollar summer homes are packed along Newport Harbor, the world's largest leisure-craft harbor, while the beach is crowded with young scantily clad hedonists. The Newport Pier is an extension of 22nd St. at West Balboa Blvd.

BALBOA PENINSULA. The sands of Newport Beach run south onto the Balboa Peninsula, separated from the mainland by Newport Bay. The peninsula is only two to four blocks wide and can be reached via the PCH. Ocean Front Walk, which extends the length of the peninsula, is the best place to stroll. The Balboa Pier, flanked by beautiful sands, is at Main St. and East Balboa Blvd. At the end of the peninsula, **The Wedge** is a body-surfing mecca, pounded by 20 ft. tall waves.

On the opposite side of the peninsula, at the end of Main St., is the ornate **Balboa Pavilion.** Once a sounding ground for Big Band great Benny Goodman, it is now a hub for harbor tours and whale watching. The double-deck *Pavilion Queen* and smaller *Pavilion Paddy* offer 45min. *($6, children $1)* and 90min. *($8, children $1)* cruises. The *Catalina Flyer* leaves for Catalina Island at 9am and returns at 4:30pm March-November. *(☎949-673-5245. Call for reservations and for Dec.-Feb. schedule. Round-trip $37, ages 3-12 $21, under 3 $3.)* A harborside mêlée, **Funzone** stretches its Ferris wheel and bumper cars west of the pavilion. *(Open daily 10am-10pm.)*

Most of the crowds navigate Newport Beach and the Balboa Peninsula by bicycle, 5-person bicycle surrey, or in-line skates. Stands everywhere rent all necessary gear. *(Bikes $5-7 per hr., $15 per day; skates $3-6 per hr., $15 per day; boogie boards $5-6 per day.)* Bikers should pick up *Bikeways*, a map of trails in Newport Beach, at the Visitors Center (see p. 445).

BALBOA ISLAND. Across the harbor from the pavilion is Balboa Island, a haven for ice cream shops (locally famous for Balboa bars and frozen bananas), artsy gift boutiques, and bikini shops. A vintage **ferryboat** travels there from the peninsula. *(☎673-1070. Ferry runs daily every 5min., but expect a delay at rush hour. Car and driver $1.25, each additional passenger $0.50, children $0.25; bikes $0.40-0.75.)* The island is also accessible from the PCH via the Jamboree Rd. bridge. The island's outermost sidewalk, which traces the shore, is a popular place for morning walks and runs (no biking or skating permitted).

OTHER SIGHTS. Newport's **Harbor Nautical Museum,** aboard the 190 ft. *Pride of Newport*, 151 E. Pacific Coast Hwy., displays Newport maritime history and extraordinary model ships. *(☎949-673-7863. Open Tu-Su 10am-5pm. Free.)* A few miles east, in what was formerly Corona del Mar, is the **Sherman Library and Gardens,** 2647 E. Pacific Coast Hwy., where pristine botanical collections range from desert cacti and succulents to tropical blooms. *(☎949-673-2261. Gardens open daily 10:30am-4pm. Library open M-F 9am-4:30pm. $3, ages 12-16 $1, under 12 free.)*

Just inland, above the PCH and between MacArthur Blvd. and Jamboree Rd., sits **Fashion Island.** Divided into seven courts, this outdoor mall has all the amenities of a regular mall and allows you to get a tan while shopping.

LAGUNA BEACH

From Los Angeles, take I-405 south to Hwy. 133 (Laguna Canyon Rd.). Follow Hwy. 133 to Laguna Beach.

Punctuated by rocky cliffs, coves, and lush hillside vegetation, this town's character is decidedly Mediterranean and artsy. **Ocean Avenue,** at the Pacific Coast Hwy., and **Main Beach** are the prime parading areas. **Westry Beach,** which spreads south of Laguna just below Aliso Beach Park, and **Camel Point,** between Westry and Aliso, form the hub of the local gay community. For beach access, park on residential streets to the east and look for "Public Access" signs between private properties.

From the turn of the century, Laguna has been an artists' colony. The latest incarnation of the original 1914 Laguna Beach art association is the **Laguna Art Museum,** 307 Cliff Dr. The collection showcases local and state art, including some excellent early 20th-century Impressionist works. Pick up the museum's guide to local art, which lists information on over 100 **art galleries** in the immediate Laguna Beach area. (☎ 494-8971; www.lagunaartmuseum.org. Tours daily 2pm. Open Tu-Su 11am-5pm. $5, students and seniors $4, children under 12 free.)

SAN JUAN CAPISTRANO

From L.A. take the I-5 south to the Ortega Hwy., make a right and follow it downtown.

The **Mission San Juan Capistrano,** 30min. south of Anaheim on I-5, is the most touching physical space in Orange County. Established by Father Junípero Serra in 1776, this is considered the "jewel of the missions." Although most of the original structure collapsed in the earthquake of 1812, this is the only standing site where Serra himself is known to have said mass, and the oldest building still in use in the state. The crumbling walls of the beautiful **Serra Chapel** are warmed by a 17th-century Spanish altar and Native American designs. Gregorian chants evoke the spiritualism that Serra once envisioned. The mission is best known as a home to the swallows, who nest in mid-March. (☎ 949-248-2048. Besides English, self-guided tours available in Italian, Spanish, and German; call ahead. Open daily 8:30am-5pm. $6, seniors $5, ages 3-12 $4.) **The Swallows Inn,** 31786 Camino Capistrano (☎ 949-493-3188), has been a local hub in San Juan for over 50 years. It is home to the largest chili cook-off in the country and is the best place to catch the **Swallows Day Parade** in March.

DANA POINT & SAN CLEMENTE

To get to Dana Point from L.A., take the I-5 (San Diego Fwy.) south to PCH. Follow PCH toward Dana Point Harbor. For San Clemente from L.A., take the I-5 south to El Camino. Exit in San Clemente. Don't miss your exit; there are no exits for 30min. through Camp Pendleton.

Dana Point's spectacular bluffs were popularized in namesake Richard Henry Dana's *Two Years Before the Mast.* The Harbor is packed with pleasure craft and serves as a point of departure for Catalina Island. The point's **swimming beach** lies at Salt Creek and the Strands.

The neighboring **San Clemente,** a "small Spanish village by the sea," has the waves of Huntington and Newport minus the beach party raves. As host to Camp Pendleton, the town determines its character as much by the military presence as by the surf. Farther south is **San Onofre State Beach** and its "Trestles" area, a break point, and therefore a prime surfing zone for experienced thrill-seekers.

WILD RIVERS WATERPARK

If you haven't had enough amusement park action, make a splash at **Wild Rivers Waterpark,** 8770 Irvine Center Dr., in Irvine, off I-405. With 40 waterslide rides and two wave pools, this attraction is a welcome alternative to a cold shower. (☎ 949-768-9453. Open daily 10am-8pm. $23, ages 55+ $10, ages 3-9 $18. Parking $5.)

SEASONAL EVENTS

Strawberry Festival (☎ 714-638-0981), in downtown Garden Grove on the village green. Late May. Garden Grove is the US's leading producer of strawberries, and the festival includes some arduous strawberry pie-eating contests.

Festival of Arts and **The Pageant of the Masters,** 650 Laguna Canyon Rd. (info ☎ 949-494-1145, tickets 800-487-3378; www.foapom.com), in Laguna Beach, take place together in the Irvine Bowl July-Aug. Life literally imitates art in the pageant as residents who have rehearsed for months don the makeup and costumes of figures in famous paintings and pose for 90-second tableaux. Festival grounds open daily 10am-11pm; $2, seniors $1. Pageant shows nightly 8:30pm; tickets $10-50. For reservations, contact the Festival of Arts, P.O. Box 1659, Laguna Beach, 92652.

Sawdust Festival, 935 Laguna Canyon Rd. (☎949-494-3030; www.sawdustfestival.org), across the street from The Pageant of the Masters, July-Aug. Lots of local art. Festival grounds open daily 10am-10pm. Tickets $6.50, ages 6-12 $2, under 6 free.

Christmas Boat Parade of Lights (☎949-729-4400), the week before Christmas, in Newport Harbor. Over 200 boats and zillions of lights create a dazzling display.

EAST OF L.A.

L.A.'s huddled masses who yearn to be free—and breathe free—often pack up their kids, cell phones, and cares, and head for the hills. Granite mountains, scenic hiking trails, campgrounds, and scented pine forests repose a mere 45min. drive above and beyond the inversion layer (the altitude at which the smog ends).

In the mountains, outdoor activities abound at all times of the year, but winter is definitely the high season. While the Sierra Nevada resorts around Lake Tahoe (p. 203) and Mammoth Lakes (p. 273) are destinations of choice for serious California skiers, daytrips to the smaller resorts of the San Bernardino mountains have become increasingly popular. Temperatures typically allow ski resorts to operate from November through April (always call ahead to check conditions). Even when the snow melts, the coastal mountains are an ideal getaway. The Angeles and San Bernardino National Forests sprawl across majestic mountains and have many campgrounds, hiking trails, and mountain villages.

ANGELES NATIONAL FOREST

National forests cover about one quarter of L.A. County north of Pasadena and east of Valencia. Cradling the northern edge of the L.A. Basin and the San Gabriel Valley are the San Gabriel Mountains, whose highest peak, Mt. San Antonio ("Mt. Baldy"), tops out at 10,064 ft. This area is popular year-round, attracting mountain bikers, anglers, bird watchers, and hikers. Harsh weather and frequent brush fires often rearrange the place, but rangers give helpful directions. Skiers will probably find Big Bear more worthwhile than the closer resorts at Mt. Baldy (☎909-982-0800) and Mt. High East and West (☎760-249-5808).

🔁 PRACTICAL INFORMATION

The national forest is divided into three ranger districts: Los Angeles River, San Gabriel River, and Santa Clara. Each houses a district office, a visitors center, a work center, and an information station, each with info specific to the district. For general forest information, call ☎626-574-5200 or visit the Forest Headquarters (see below). In an **emergency,** contact the Angeles National Forest Dispatcher (☎818-447-8999 in the Arcadia area, 661-723-7619 in the Lancaster area). All ranger stations listed below are open Monday through Friday 8am to 4:30pm.

Angeles National Forest: Headquarters, Supervisor's Office, 701 N. Santa Anita Ave. (☎626-574-1613), in Arcadia. Comprehensive forest maps ($6-8).

Los Angeles River Ranger District, 5600 Oak Grove Park. (☎818-790-1151), in Flintridge. Visitors center: **Chilao,** on Rte. 2 (Angeles Crest Hwy.), 26 mi. from La Cañada (☎626-796-5541). Open Sa-Su 9am-5pm. This is the south-central area of the forest, north of Pasadena. Gateway to the Angeles National Forest via Rte. 2. 25 campgrounds in this district; many are high country camps. Works with the **Tujunga Work Center,** 12371 N. Little Tujunga Canyon Rd. (☎818-899-1900), in San Fernando. Covers the west end of the San Gabriel Mountains. Hiking, horseback-riding and 5 campgrounds.

San Gabriel River Ranger District, 110 N. Wabash Ave. (☎626-335-1251), in Glendora. Visitors center: **Mount Baldy,** on Mt. Baldy Rd. north of Ontario. Open daily 8am-4:30pm. The southeastern district of the forest has 8000 ft. peaks, hiking trails, the San Antonio Falls, and scenic Glendora Ridge Rd. 4 developed campgrounds.

Santa Clara Ranger District, 30800 Bouquet Canyon Rd. (☎805-296-9710), in Saugus, northwest of the main forest. The district has 2 Visitors Centers: **Big Pines,** on the east end of Rte. 2 (Angeles Crest Hwy.) near the turn-off for Valyermo (☎249-6911; open F-Sa 9am-4pm); **Grassy Hollow,** also on Rte. 2, 6 mi. west of Wrightwood (☎626-821-6737; open Sa-Su 10am-4pm). Pyramid, Elizabeth, and Castaic Lakes have boating and fishing. 22 campgrounds, some have been vandalized. This district also has the **Mojave River Work Center,** P.O. Box 15, 29835 Valyermo Rd. (☎661-944-2187), in Valyermo, in the northeastern part of the San Gabriel Mountains. Open M-F 8:30am-5pm.

CAMPING

The US Forest Service maintains an array of well-groomed hiking trails and camping facilities. Many of the 557 mi. of trails cross each other, so maps are vital. Most campsites run by the Forestry Service are free, though parked vehicles must display an **Adventure Pass** ($5, available at ranger stations, visitor centers, and various local retailers; see p. 458). Campsites run by concessionaires are $10-15 per night. Sites are first-come, first-camp (14-night max. stay), and many are closed in the winter. There are many campgrounds along Big Pines Hwy. which are convenient and free but offer little seclusion. A site beyond the front country affords more privacy and security, though probably no drinking water or bathrooms.

Chilao Recreation Area, 5300 ft., off Rte. 2, 26 mi. northeast of La Cañada, on the left. Visitors center 1 mi. north of the campground offers walks, talks, and children's activities. South of Three Points (Pacific Coast Trail) and Devil's Canyon trailheads. 111 sites have fire rings, tables, water, and toilets, but no hookups. Sites $12. ❶

Buckhorn, 6300 ft., on Rte. 2, 26 mi. southwest of Wrightwood and 36 mi. northeast of La Cañada, has 40 sites surrounded by lush ferns and towering redwoods. Near Burkhart Trailhead. All have fire rings, tables, water, and toilets, but no hookups. Open June-Nov. Sites $12. ❶

Spunky, 3300 ft., on Spunky Canyon Rd. From I-5 in Valenicia, take Magic Mtn. Pkwy. Exit, drive east to Valencia Blvd. and continue 2 mi., turn left to Bouqet Canyon Rd., and continue 14 mi. to Spunky Canyon Rd. Near the Pacific Coast Trail, this campsite allows for easy access to backcountry hiking. ❶

Glen Trail Camp, 2000 ft., off Rte. 39 North. The end of the West Fork National Bike Trail (16 mi. round-trip). Walk or bike in from a gate. Physically challenged can get a driving permit; contact the San Gabriel Ranger Station (☎626-335-1251). 10 free sites. ❶

SIGHTS & OUTDOOR ACTIVITIES

HIKING & CLIMBING. Situated just outside the national forest in a county park, the **Devil's Punchbowl** entices hikers and climbers alike with its spooky sandstone formations. (Take Longview Rd. from Hwy. 138 to Devil's Punchbowl Rd., where a right turn will take you into the park.) For a moderately easy and scenic morning or afternoon hike, try **Charlton Flat to Vetter Mountain** (3 mi.). Heading off from near the Charlton Flat picnic area (off Rte. 2), the uphill trail climbs past pine and oak and a wide variety of birds and flowers, to an old fire lookout point on Vetter Mountain, providing fine views of surrounding landscape. A different trailhead from Charlton Flat leads to **Devil Peak**, another short and enjoyable hike. A popular moderate full day hike leads from **Vincent Gap to Mt. Baden-Powell** (8 mi.), the 9400 ft. peak named after British officer Lord Baden-Powell. The trail climbs 2800 ft. through ancient pines, and summits to spectacular views of the San Gabriel range, including Old Baldy and, on clear days, the looming desert. The trailhead is located in the Vincent Gap parking lot, off Rte. 2, 52 mi. from La Cañada. The **Blue Ridge Trail** to **Mt. Baldy** (12 mi.), the highest peak in the San Gabriel range at 10,064 ft., is a challenging, high elevation hike that should only be attempted by the fit. Those who summit, however, will be rewarded with unsurpassed views of the alpine country. To reach the trailhead, drive 1½ mi. west of Big Pines on Rte. 2 to Blue Ridge Road. It is 3 mi. to the Blue Ridge campground and the trailhead.

The three- to five-day **Gabrielino Trail** (53 mi. round-trip) connects Oak Grove Park and the north end of Windsor Ave., in La Cañada Flintridge. The five-day **Silver Moccasin Trail** (53 mi. one-way), once a rite of passage for adventurous Boy Scouts, is now a popular backcountry route. The trail connects Chantry Flats with Vincent Gap, crossing forest, stream, mountain, and canyon. Long hikes such as these necessitate **trail camping**. Fortunately, it is free and legal, but fire permits are required (available at ranger stations) and camping is not allowed within 200 ft. of any stream. There are also numerous opportunities to hike a portion of the renowned **Pacific Crest Trail** (see **From Crest to Crest: The Trail of the West**, p. 218). Trailheads are scattered along the length of the **Hwy. 2** (Angeles Crest Hwy.).

MEDITATION. Visitors in search of a more contemplative experience may care to stop at the Benedictine **St. Andrews Abbey** in the village of **Valyermo**. Three-day weekend retreats, including room and board, begin at $130, and focus on diverse theological themes like spirituality in modern cinema and the writings of C.S. Lewis. A ceramic craftworks helps to support the abbey. Visitors are welcome at mass. Rooms with air conditioning are also available on a regular basis for $60 per person per night. (Retreat office ☎661-944-2178; www.valyermo.com. Take Valyermo Rd. from Hwy. 138. Open daily 10am-4pm; mass daily noon-1:30pm.)

The **Descanso Gardens**, 1418 Descanso Dr., is in nearby La Cañada, by the intersection of Rte. 2 and 210. The garden includes the world's largest camellia forest, a historic rose collection, and manmade waterfalls. Events ($7-10) include tutorials on home gardening, bug displays, and cool night walks. (☎818-952-4400. Open daily 9am-5pm. $5, students and seniors $3, ages 5-12 $1.)

SAN BERNARDINO NATIONAL FOREST

The San Bernardino National Forest makes up 800,000 acres of pristine mountainous public lands on the outer edge of Southern California's urban expanse. The mountains host five federally-designated wilderness areas—Cucamonga, San Gorgonio, Bighorn Mountain, San Jacinto, and Santa Rosa—with largely undisturbed snow-capped peaks, desert transition zones, deep canyons, green(ish) meadows, and crystal-blue lakes. Outside the wilderness areas are more developed attractions like Big Bear and Arrowhead Lakes. For detailed information on exploring, pick up a Visitor Guide at the Big Bear Discovery Center (see p. 458).

AT A GLANCE

AREA: 737,280 acres.

CLIMATE: Temperate forest.

FEATURES: Big Bear, San Gorgonio Wilderness Area, Arrowhead Lakes.

HIGHLIGHTS: Ski in Big Bear Lake by summer, ski Big Bear Mountain by winter, hike the forest all year long.

GATEWAYS: San Bernardino (p. 462), Big Bear (below), Los Angeles (p. 335).

CAMPING: Camping is permitted at US Forest Service sites throughout the area. Also allowed at more remote sites with free visitors permit available at Ranger Station.

FEES & RESERVATIONS: Recreational use of national forest land requires an Adventure Pass (p. 458).

BIG BEAR   ☎909

Big Bear Lake serves as a gateway to the San Bernardino wilderness and a destination unto itself. In the summer, the central lake provides ample opportunities for fishing and sailing, while the nearby mountains and forest offer some enjoyable hikes and well-preserved campgrounds. The village surrounding the lake is a quiet outcropping of civilization, with accommodations mainly geared toward the skiing set, which arrives en masse from L.A. and elsewhere around December.

■ ⚡ ORIENTATION AND PRACTICAL INFORMATION

To reach Big Bear, take **I-10** to **Route 30** in San Bernardino. Take 30 north to **Route 330** (Mountain Rd.),which turns into **Route 18,** a winding 30-45min. ascent. Rte. 18 hits the west end of Big Bear Lake and forks into a continuing Rte. 18 branch along the south shore, where it is called Big Bear Blvd., and Rte. 38 along the north shore. A less congested route approaches from the east via I-10 to Redlands and then **Route 38** to Big Bear Lake. Driving time from L.A. is about 2½hr., barring serious weekend traffic or road closures. The loneliest route to Big Bear Lake curls across the high desert along Rte. 18 through the Lucerne Valley, from **I-15** in Victorville. Weekend day skiers should wait until after 6pm to head home in order to avoid the 4pm rush. Driving to Big Bear should not be attempted during the winter without checking road conditions with **CalTrans.** (☎427-7623; www.dot.ca.gov.) **Mountain Area Regional Transit Authority or MARTA** runs two **buses** per day from the Greyhound station in San Bernardino to Big Bear. (☎584-1111. $5, seniors and disabled $3.75.) Buses also run the length of Big Bear Blvd. (End-to-end trip 1hr.; $1, students $0.75, seniors and disabled $0.50.) MARTA also operates **Dial-A-Ride.** ($2, students $1.50, seniors and disabled $1.)

The **Big Bear Chamber of Commerce,** 630 Bartlett Rd., in the "village," dispenses glossy brochures and arranges lodging and ski packages. (☎866-4608; fax 866-5412; www.bigbearchamber.com. Open M-F 8am-5pm, Sa-Su 9am-5pm.) The **Big Bear Lake Resort Association** has info on lodging, local events, and ski and road conditions. (☎866-7000 or 800-424-4232; www.bigbearinfo.com. Open M-F 8am-6pm, Sa-Su 9am-5pm.) **Big Bear Discovery Center** or **BBDC,** on Rte. 38 4 mi. east of Fawnskin and 1¼ mi. west of the Stanfield Cutoff, is a ranger station that sells and the **National Forest Adventure Pass** ($5), which is required for vehicles at camping sites that charge no additional fee. (☎866-3437. Open Apr.-Sept. daily 8am-6pm; Oct.-Mar. daily 9am-5pm.) The National Forest Adventure Pass can be purchased at ranger and information stations throughout the state, as well as through a number of private vendors or at www.fsadventurepass.org. In **emergencies,** call ☎383-5651 to reach a ranger station. **Internet Access** is available at Big Bear Public Library,

41930 Garstin Dr. (☎866-0162. Open M-Tu noon-8pm, W-F 10am-6pm, Sa 9am-5pm.) The **Post Office,** 247 Sandlewood, is off Big Bear Blvd. **Postal Code:** 92315.

ACCOMMODATIONS

In the winter, budget accommodations are next to impossible to find, but in the summer bargains abound. For rooms below $50 a night, however, you'll usually have to head into San Bernardino (see p. 462). Big Bear Blvd. is lined with lodging possibilities, and groups can find the best deals by sharing a cabin. **Mountain Lodging Unlimited** arranges lodging and lift packages. (☎800-487-3168. Packages from $100 per couple. Open in ski season 7am-midnight; off-season 9am-midnight.)

Robinhood Inn, 40797 Lakeview Dr. (☎866-4643 or 800-990-9956). Chalet-style motel with a courtyard, complete with spa and barbecue. Fireplaces, kitchenettes, and coffeemakers in many rooms. John Wayne once stayed here. Singles and doubles begin at $54 in summer and $62 in winter; suites sleeping up to 6 under $90. ❹

Hillcrest Lodge, 40241 Big Bear Blvd. (☎866-7330, reservations 800-843-4449; www.hillcrestlodge.com). Pine paneling and skylights give these cozy rooms a ritzy feel at a reasonable price. Jacuzzi, cable TV, and free local calls. In winter, small rooms $48-79; 4-person units and suites $79-139. In summer, small rooms $48-70; 4-person units with kitchen $90-140; 2-bedroom suites with hearth and kitchen $100-150. ❸

The Village Resort, 41060-41082 Big Bear Blvd. (☎866-4978). Reasonable prices, friendly hosts, and an on-site market and surf & turf restaurant are nice extras. Kitchenettes in some units. Singles and doubles $70-80 on weekdays, $90-100 on weekends; 2-room units with kitchenette $90-110; cabins for up to 6 people $100-120. ❹

Embers Lodge, 40229 Big Bear Blvd. (☎866-2371; www.emberslodge.com). Simple studios, some with kitchens, fireplaces, TVs, and phones for 2-8 people. Dec.-Mar. Su-Th $65, F-Sa $95-120; Apr.-Nov. Su-Th $25, F-Sa $40-70. ❸

CAMPING

Camping is permitted at US Forest Service sites throughout the area. Several of the sites listed below accept reservations through the National Recreation Reservation Service (☎877-444-6777; www.reserveusa.com) or the US Forest Service (☎800-280-2267). Most are open from May to Nov. Campers can tent on US Forest Service land, at least 200 ft. from water and roads and ¼ mi. from developed areas. Get info about Remote Camping Areas and Yellow Post Sites, and obtain the free visitors permit at the Big Bear Discovery Center (see **Practical Information,** p. 458).

Pineknot, 7000 ft., on Summit Blvd., south of Big Bear. Amid thick woods, these 52 sites are secluded and cool. At the base of steep Snow Summit, mountain bikers rule the single-track. Flush toilets and water. Wheelchair accessible. Sites $18. ❷

Hanna Flats, 7000 ft., on Forest Rd., 2½ mi. northwest of Fawnskin. Lush vegetation surrounds 88 roomy sites. Hiking, water, pit and flush toilets. Sites $17. ❷

Holcomb Valley, 7400 ft., 4 mi. north on Forest Rd., then east for ¾ mi. These 19 sites have pit toilets and no water. Near the Pacific Crest Trail (see **From Crest to Crest: the Trail of the West,** p. 218). Sites $10. ❶

FOOD

Food can get pricey, so those with kitchens should forage at **Stater Bros.,** 42171 Big Bear Blvd. (☎866-5211. Open daily 7am-11pm.) Many of the cutesy village eateries offer all-you-can-eat specials.

IN RECENT NEWS

ADVENTURES IN TAXING

The National Forest Adventure Pass is a recreation pass for visitors using the Cleveland, Angeles, Los Padres, and San Bernardino National Forests. The pass is available per day $5 or per year $30. A visitor is only required to purchase a pass when parked on the forest for recreational purposes. If a visitor is driving through the forest but not stopping a pass is not required. In 1996 Congress passed legislation authorizing national forests to collect fees from visitors for recreation use. The fees are collected from sales of the Adventure Pass. The forest service argues that such a pass is necessary, as a result of the increase in tourism and the 30% budget cut since 1994. Essentially there are few dollars available to maintain facilities in the forests, including public restrooms and hiking trails. At least 80% of the fees collected are invested in the local forest in maintaining sites and facilities and protecting resources and habitats. Others argue, however, that the forest Service is already supported through taxes and that one should not be required to buy an Adventure Pass. The Forest Service simply replies that there is not enough money from the appropriated dollars to pay for the maintenance of the forests. The issue awaits further congressional debate. For now, failure to display a pass may result in your being fined up to $100.

Mongolian Palace, 40797 Lakeview Dr. (☎866-6678), just off Big Bear Blvd. Design your own dish from the all-you-can-eat buffet of fruits and vegetables and gorge on it for lunch ($8) or dinner ($10). Open Su-Th 11am-9pm, F-Sa 11am-9:30pm. ❷

Virginia Lee's, 41003 Big Bear Blvd. (☎866-3151). A motley collection of hot dogs, tamales, ice cream, fancy hot chocolate, and potato and pasta salads make the menu as this tasty little roadside shack. Most everything $2-4. Open W-Su 10am-4pm. ❶

Grizzly Manor, 41268 Big Bear Blvd. (☎866-6226). A local favorite for breakfast. Get some combination of the breakfast staples of eggs, pork, and potatoes for $4-7 or just say t'hell with it and get "The Mess" ($7). Open W-F 7am-2pm, Sa-Su 6am-2pm. ❷

La Paws, 1128 W. Big Bear Blvd. (☎585-9115), in Big Bear City. A fun little family-run spot serving authentic and inexpensive Mexican specialties and American favorites (burritos $5). Open daily 7am-8pm. ❶

◪ OUTDOOR ACTIVITIES

SUMMER RECREATION

The **National Forest Adventure Pass** (p. 458) is required for parking at a trailhead, though not at picnic areas.

HIKING. Although hiking often takes a back seat to higher velocity recreation in Big Bear, the trails in the surrounding mountains are a superb way of exploring the San Bernardino wilderness. Maps, trail descriptions, and the *Visitor's Guide to the San Bernardino National Forest* are available at the Big Bear Discovery Center. Perfect for an afternoon stroll, the 3.5 mi. **Alpine Pedal Path** runs its gentle, paved course from the Stanfield Cutoff on the lake's north shore to the Big Bear Discovery Center. The moderately difficult 2.4 mi. **Castle Rock Trail,** starting 1.1 mi. east of the dam on Hwy. 18, is a short but steep haul, finishing atop a colossal granite blob (the final rock scramble can be a tad risky). The views of Big Bear Lake and the surrounding area are stupendous. A more challenging day hike, **Cougar Crest Trail** (5 mi.) ascends from ½ mi. west of the Discovery Center on Rte. 38 to meet the Pacific Coast Trail, and continues east to the summit of Bertha Peak (8502 ft.), affording unobstructed views of desert. Serious hikers may want to catch a longer piece of the **Pacific Crest Trail (PCT),** which extends 2638 mi. from Mexico to Canada, and is moderately difficult in this area. (For more info, see **From Crest to Crest: the Trail of the West,** p. 218.) The trail runs east of the lake; the Big Bear Discovery Center can direct hikers to any of the multiple entry points in the area.

BIKING. When the snow melts, **mountain biking** takes over in Big Bear. In the San Bernardino National Forest, mountain biking is allowed on all public trails except the PCT and within the designated wilderness areas. Grab a *Ride and Trail Guide* at the Discovery Center and at **Snow Summit**, 1 mi. west of Big Bear Lake, which runs lifts in summer so adrenaline monsters can grind serious downhill terrain. (☎866-4621. $10 per ride, day pass $20; ages 7-12 $5 per ride, day pass $10. Helmet required. Open M-F 9am-4pm, Sa 8am-5pm, Su 9am-5pm.) **Team Big Bear,** 476 Concklin Rd., operating out of the **Mountain Bike Shop** at the base of Snow Summit, rents bikes and sponsors several organized bike races each summer. (☎866-4565. $9 per hr., $27 for 4hr., $50 per day; helmet included. For more race info, call Apr.-Oct. daily 9am-5pm, or write Team Big Bear, Box 2932, Big Bear Lake, CA 92315.) **Big Bear Bikes,** 41810 Big Bear Blvd. rents at comparable prices. (☎866-2224. Open daily 10am-5pm, extended F-Sa hours if it's busy.)

FISHING. Stocked during fishing season with a mighty supply of rainbow trout, fishing in Big Bear Lake takes over as the main attraction for the summer. State **fishing** licenses are available at area sporting goods stores (day $10, season $28). Any part of the lake will afford good fishing, but only the north shore is accessible to everyone; the south shore is mostly private property. The dam at the west end of the lake is reputed to be very good. For stocking information, updated weekly, call ☎562-590-5020. **Boats** can be rented at any one of Big Bear's marinas, including **Holloway's Marina and RV Park,** 398 Edgemor Rd., on the south shore. (☎800-448-5335; www.bigbearboating.com. Full day $50-175.)

OTHER "ADVENTURES". If you don't have the patience to watch wildlife in the national forest, head over to **Moonridge Animal Park,** south of Big Bear Blvd. at the end of Moonridge Rd. (☎584-1171. Open May-Oct. daily 10am-5pm; Nov.-Apr. 10am-4pm. $4.50, ages 3-10 $3.) This care center for wounded and abandoned animals has the only big bears in Big Bear: **grizzlies.** The featured attraction is named Harley in honor of his sponsors, the Inland Empire chapter of the Harley-Davidson Club. **Magic Mountain Recreation Area,** 800 Wild Rose Ln., west of Big Bear Lake Village, operates an **alpine slide** (☎866-4626. Open M-F 10am-8pm, Sa 10am-9pm. 1 ride $4, 5 rides $15), **waterslide park** (1 ride $1, 10 rides $7, unlimited rides $12), a **snowplay hill** in the winter for all sorts of snow sliding (day pass $18), and **miniature golf** course for summer visitors. (Open daily 10am-9pm. $4, under 13 $3) Local wildlife can be observed in its natural habitat at the **Bowling Barn,** 40625 Lakeview Dr. (☎878-2695); mating rituals proceed next door at **Alley Oops** in the form of karaoke and dancing. (Both open daily Su-Th 10am-11pm, F-Sa 10am-1am. $4.25 per game, children $3.25; shoes $2.75.)

WINTER RECREATION

When conditions are favorable, ski areas run out of lift tickets quickly. **Tickets** for the resorts listed below may be purchased over the phone through Ticketmaster (☎714-740-2000). Driving the crowded mountain roads to popular destinations can challenge both vehicle and driver. Gas stations are scarce on the way up the mountain, and signs notify drivers of tire chain requirements. Call CalTrans (☎800-427-7623) for info on road conditions.

Cross-country skiing along Big Bear's many trails is a popular way to breeze through the mountain's wintertime scenery. Rent skis, boots, and poles at **Big Bear Bikes,** 41810 Big Bear Blvd. (☎866-2224), for $14 per day; trail information is free. The **Rim Nordic Ski Area,** across the highway from Snow Valley, is an undulating network of cross-country ski trails. This is a national forest area, so an Adventure Pass ($5) is required (see p. 458). Open in winter when snow conditions permit.

The following resorts cater to **downhill skiing and snowboarding:**

Big Bear Resort (☎585-2519 or 800-BEAR-MTN/232-7686; www.bearmtn.com), 1½ mi. southeast of downtown Big Bear Lake. 12 lifts, 4 mountain peaks, and 32 trails cover 195 acres of terrain, including huge vertical drops and acres of undeveloped land suitable for adventurous skiers. More expert runs than other area slopes. Lift tickets $39, holidays $49. Skis $23, snowboards $30. New skier/snowboarder packages include group lesson, lift ticket, and equipment rental.

Snow Summit (☎866-5766, reservations 909-866-5841; www.snowsummit.com), 1 mi. east of Big Bear Lake. 12 lifts (including 2 high-speed quads) serve over 31 runs. The Summit has a well-rounded assortment of beginner runs, snowmaking, and night skiing capacities. Lift tickets $41 ($50 on holidays), ages 13-19 $34, ages 7-12 $13. Skis $22, snowboards $30; deposit required.

Snow Valley (☎867-2751, snow report 867-5151), near Running Springs. 12 lifts, 800-5000 ft. runs, snowmaking, night skiing, and a skate park in the summer. The most family-oriented resort in Big Bear, with a children's obstacle course and beginner trails. Lift ticket $37, ages 6-13 $23. Ski rental $17, snowboard $30.

SAN GORGONIO WILDERNESS AREA

The rugged 60,000-acre San Gorgonio Wilderness Area is set aside from the rest of the San Bernardino National Forest and protected from development. Almost 100 mi. of trails converge on remarkable summits, the highest of which, **San Gorgonio** (dubbed "Old Grayback" for its barren summit), is at 11,500 ft. the tallest in California outside the Sierras. On a clear day, the panoramic summit includes the southern Sierras, Mexico, the Pacific Ocean, and the Mojave Desert. There are no campgrounds within the Wilderness Area, but backcountry camping is allowed.

To forge into the backcountry, you must have a **wilderness permit.** Obtain these for free up to three months in advance in person at the **Mill Creek Ranger Station,** near Methone, about 40 mi. west of Big Bear on Rte. 38 (☎909-794-1123. Open for info and cancellations M-F 8am-4:30pm, Sa-Su 6:30am-3pm; in winter M-F 8am-4:30pm, Sa-Su 7am-3:30pm) or at the **Barton Flats Visitor Information Center,** on Rte. 38 about 25 mi. from Big Bear (☎909-794-4861. Open for info and cancellations W-Su 8am-4:30pm). Open fires are not allowed in the wilderness area.

All but the toughest pack animals will need two days to traverse Mt. San Gorgonio (typical routes are 30 mi. long). Consult rangers at Barton Flats or Mill Creek for indispensable local info and excellent topographical maps ($4). The **South Fork Trail,** a challenging 22 mi. haul, is the most popular way to reach the summit, though the **Fish Creek Trail** will start you off higher and get you to the top quicker. The **Vivian Creek Trail** is the shortest and steepest path to the top. While backcountry camping is free, parking isn't. Anyone who uses a trail needs an **Adventure Pass** for each day of parking (see p. 458). The dry, thin air quickly dehydrates hikers, so bring ample water.

If you prefer seeing San Gorgonio from the road, there are a handful of campgrounds along a 5 mi. stretch of Rte. 38 near Barton Flats Visitor Center. **San Gorgonio** and **Barton Flats Campgrounds ❶,** near the Visitors Center, are the most expensive ($15) and have showers; **Heart Bar ❶,** toward Big Bear, is the cheapest ($10). Sites fill up fast on summer weekends, and reservations (☎800-280-2267) are recommended for the more developed campgrounds.

SAN BERNARDINO   ☎909

San Bernardino (pop. 181,718), the seat of America's largest county, is a generic southern California smog-bowl. Inexpensive food and lodging are available for those en route to a more palatable destination.

◪ PRACTICAL INFORMATION. MARTA **buses** (☎584-1111) run to Big Bear via Arrowhead (3hr., 2 per day, $5). For a **taxi**, call YellowCab (☎884-1111). The Metrolink **trains**, 1204 W. 3rd St., connect L.A. and San Bernardino with 15 trains running daily on weekdays and 8 on weekends. (☎800-371-5465. Call M-F 4:30am-10:30pm, Sa-Su 9am-9pm. $6-8, $11.25-15 round-trip.) The **San Bernardino Convention and Visitors Bureau,** 201 North E. St. #103, at the 2nd St. Exit off Rte. 215 North or the 3rd St. Exit off Rte. 215 South, has the *Inland Empire Adventure Guide!* and maps. The dearth of brochures reflects the area's level of tourist activity. (☎889-3980. Open M-Th 7:30am-5:30pm, F 7:30am-4:30pm.) Other services include: **police** (☎384-5742) and **San Bernardino Community Hospital,** 1805 Medical Ctr. Dr. (☎887-6333), with 24hr. emergency care. **Internet Access** is available at San Bernardino Public Library, 555 W. 6th St. (☎381-8201. Open M-W 10am-8pm, Th-Su 10am-6pm.) **Post office** can be found at 390 W. 5th St., downtown. (☎800-275-8777. Open M-F 8am-5pm.) **Postal Code:** 92401.

▐▐ ACCOMMODATIONS, FOOD, & THE FIRST MCDONALD'S. The area along Mt. Vernon Ave. (old Rte. 66) is not so safe, so out-of-towners should stick to either the north end of town or Hospitality Ln., which crosses Waterman Ave. just north of I-10. At the **Budget Inn ❸,** 1280 S. E St., the rooms have fridges, and breakfast is included. (☎888-0271. Singles $33; doubles $38.) **Motel 6 ❸,** 1960 Ostrems Way, at the University Pkwy. Exit off Rte. 215, is near Cal State University. (☎887-8191. Singles $40; doubles $46.) The three-star **Hilton San Bernardino ❺,** 285 E. Hospitality Ln., is reasonably priced (for a Hilton) and offers all of the amenities of an upscale hotel. (☎889-0133. Singles and doubles $100-$130.) In 1936, the **Stater Bros. Markets** chain was founded in nearby Yucaipa, and now there are 46 of the stores in the county. Several local branches can supply provisions for the long drive ahead: 1085 W. Highland Ave. (☎886-1517; open daily 7am-11pm), 648 W. 4th St. (☎888-0048; open daily 7am-10pm), and 277 E. 40th St. (☎866-4517; open daily 7am-10pm). **Hogi Yogi ❶,** 4595 University Pkwy. (☎887-7812), serves tasty sandwiches (regular "hogi" $3-4) and frozen yogurt (small "yogi" $2.15) with your choice of mix-in. The original **McDonald's** once stood at 1398 N. E St., but don't expect 15-cent burgers anymore. The only thing offered at this historic site is a growing display of Golden Arches memorabilia.

IDYLLWILD & SAN JACINTO MOUNTAINS ☎909

Unlike the teeming resort hubs of Palm Springs and Big Bear, Idyllwild refuses to become a tacky tourist town in spite of its many attractions. Set amidst the scrub and stocky pines of the San Jacinto range, Idyllwild offers outdoor enthusiasts many steep and dusty challenges. Hundreds of miles of well-maintained hiking trails, including routes to the nearly 11,000 ft. summit of Mt. San Jacinto, surround the town. Full-service and wild backcountry campgrounds abound, as well as chalet-style accommodations for the less rugged. The monstrous granite of Tahquitz Rock and Suicide Rock tests rock climbers of all abilities. Suspended more than 6000 ft. above the desert, this mountain town not only escapes the incinerating heat that besieges Palm Springs but also enjoys snowy, blustery winters.

◪◪ ORIENTATION & PRACTICAL INFORMATION

From L.A. to the west or Palm Springs to the east, the swiftest approach to Idyllwild is via **I-10** and **Highway 243** south from Banning. This spectacular Palms-to-Pines Hwy. climbs 6000 ft. from the desert to temperate alpine climate. The Palm Springs Aerial Tramway offers the only **public transportation** to Mt. San Jacinto.

There is a network of trails leading from the tram into Idyllwild—buy a map to the San Jacinto National Forest while in Palm Springs. For more info on the tramway, see **Practical Information,** p. 464, or **Palm Springs: Sights and Activities,** p. 471.

Idyllwild Chamber of Commerce, 54295 Village Center Dr. (☎659-3259; www.idyllwild.org), downstairs in the *Town Crier* building across from the Idyllwild Inn. Info and restaurant coupons. Open M-F 10am-4pm.

San Jacinto Ranger Station (US Forest Service), 54720 Pine Crest Ave. (☎659-2117). Maps of hiking trails and campgrounds $1-4. Free mandatory wilderness permits for day hiking and overnight backpacking in the San Jacinto National Forest. Buy an Adventure Pass ($5) if you plan to park your car on U.S. Forest Service property, which includes all picnic sites and trailheads. Open daily 8am-4:30pm.

Mt. San Jacinto State Park and Wilderness Headquarters, 25905 Rte. 243 (☎659-2607). Free mandatory wilderness permits available. Maps $1-8. Open M-Th 8am-5pm, F-Sa 8am-10pm.

Aerial Tram Info (☎619-325-1391), on Tram Rd. off North Palm Canyon Dr. in **Palm Springs.** Tram from Palm Springs to Mt. San Jacinto runs every 30min. Round-trip fare $19, seniors $17, children 5-12 $12.50. Open M-F 10am-8pm, Sa-Su 8am-8pm.

Gear: Nomad Ventures, 54414 N. Circle Dr. (☎659-4853), sells a vast array of hiking, camping, and climbing gear. Rock climbing shoe rentals $7.50 per day. Open M-F 9am-5:30pm, Sa 8am-6pm, Su 9am-5pm. Closed Tu-W in Winter.

Emergency: Riverside Mountain Rescue Unit, Inc. (☎654-6200). Search-and-rescue missions for injured or lost hikers in the San Jacinto mountains.

Police: Banning Sheriff (☎922-7100). Open 24hr.

Library and Internet Access: Idyllwild Public Library, 54185 Lower Pinecrest (☎659-2300). Open M and F 10am-6pm, W 11am-7pm, Sa 10am-4pm.

Post Office: 54391 Village Center Dr. (☎800-275-8777), in the Strawberry Creek shopping center. Open M-F 9am-5pm. **Postal Code:** 92549.

▐ ACCOMMODATIONS & CAMPING

Hiking and camping enthusiasts could stay here for weeks on a pittance. **Idyllwild Lodging Information** (☎659-5520) gives a rundown of options. Campsite reservations can be made for Forest Service sites by calling ☎800-280-CAMP/2267. For State Park campsites at Idyllwild or Stone Creek, call ☎800-444-PARK/7275, or go to www.reserveamerica.com. Sites fill up quickly in summer, make reservations or plan on arriving early. Check with the rangers for other camping options.

Atipahato Lodge, 25525 Scenic Highway 243. (☎888-400-0071; www.atipahato.com). Cozy and romantic, each of the rooms at this alpine chalet has a kitchenette and private balcony. The lodge owns five acres of private land for quiet, moonlit strolls. Rooms with one queen bed $55 during the week, $65 on the weekends. Two beautiful cabins, complete with jacuzzi baths, fireplaces, and full kitchens are available for $150 a night. ❸

Knotty Pine Cabins, 54340 Pine Crest Dr. (☎659-2933), off Rte. 243 north of Idyllwild. Eight different cabins are available, each with kitchens or kitchenettes, dishes and utensils, linens, BBQs, TVs and VCRs. Cabins with one queen bed $56-79. $8 discount with a two-night stay midweek. ❸

Dark Canyon Campground, 5800 ft., located 6 mi. north of Idyllwild on Rte. 243. This Forest Service Campsite is tucked away amid tall pines and large rocks. RVs up to 22 ft. in length are welcome. 22 sites with water, fire pits, vault toilets, and access to hiking trails. Nearby sites at **Fern Basin** (6300 ft., 22 sites) and **Marion Mountain** (6400 ft., 22 sites) are just as lovely. Both are accessible to RVs up to 15 ft. All sites $10. ❶

Idyllwild Campground, 5400 ft., located off Rte. 234 just south of Idyllwild. This State Park Campsite offers a few more amenities, but less seclusion. Nonetheless most of the 30 sites are quiet and pretty. Water, restrooms, coin-operated showers, and fire rings. Sites $12-16. ❶

🔲 FOOD

Restaurant prices rise with the altitude, making the supermarket an attractive option. **Fairway Supermarket,** in the Strawberry Creek shopping center off Village Center Dr., has reasonable prices. (☎659-2737. Open spring-fall M-Sa 9am-9pm, Su 9am-7pm; in winter M-Sa 9am-8pm, Su 9am-7pm.) If cooking doesn't sound appealing, some pricier options serve up wonderful treats.

The Bread Basket, 54710 N. Circle Dr. (☎659-3506; www.thebreadbasket.net). European-styled bakery is one of Idyllwild's most beloved eateries. Breakfast omelettes are a hearty morning option ($6-10), but the Bread Basket's real specialties are its sandwiches ($7-10). Monthly wildflower teas. Open Su-Th 8am-8pm, F-Sa 8am-9pm. ❷

Restaurant Gastrognome, 54381 Ridgeview (☎659-5055; www.thegnome.com). "The Gnome," as locals fondly refer to it, serves up an excellent array of steaks, seafoods, and pasta in a cozy atmosphere. Dinner entrees $12-18. Open Su-Th 11:30am-2:30pm for lunch, daily 5-9:30pm for dinner. ❸

Idyllwild Pizza Company, 54391 Village Center Dr. (☎659-5900), next to the Post Office. Relaxed, family-style atmosphere. Pizzas $8-20. Open spring-fall Su-Th 11:30am-8:30pm, F-Sa 11:30am-9pm. Winter open daily 11:30am-8pm. ❸

Squirrel's Nest, 25980 Rte. 243. (☎659-5274). This small restaurant offers fresh California grill specialties, for eating at the counter or to go. The breakfast burritos are especially filling ($4-5.25). Open Th-Tu 11am-7pm. ❶

👁 📍 SIGHTS & SEASONAL EVENTS

Visitors come to this largely undiscovered town to explore the rough alpine terrain of the San Jacinto range. Hundreds of miles of established trails snake through the boulder-strewn slopes, and the glacier-polished granite of Tahquitz and Suicide Rock are crawling with buff rock climbers. Importantly, the comparatively high altitude keeps the temperature reasonable even when Palm Springs swelters in the hellish torment below. Winters sometimes dump glorious powder on the San Jacinto range, and cross-country skiers occasionally have cause to frolic here.

The **Palms-to-Pines Highway,** the section of Rte. 243 that connects Rte. 74 with I-10, rises from the low Colorado Desert into the sky. The highway not only offers spectacular views, but also a fascinating opportunity to examine the ecological transformation of the desert into a temperate alpine climate. Though Idyllwild is only 26 mi. from I-10, plan to set aside time for the steep and curvy road, as well as to stop at one of the many roadside vista points.

The **Ernie Maxwell Scenic Trail** (2.5 mi.) is a scenic, downhill path through the forest, great for day hikes. This is one of the few trails that does not require a wilderness permit. From downtown Idyllwild, take the free shuttle up to Humber Park to the trailhead. The trail will take you back to the town center. More serious backpackers can travel a section of the 2600 mi. **Pacific Crest Trail** (55 mi. lie in the San Jacinto District; for more info, see **From Crest to Crest: the Trail of the West,** p. 218). The trail picks up at Rte. 74 1 mi. east of Rte. 371 or at Black Mountain's scenic **Fuller Ridge Trail,** which is a strenuous hike (16 mi. round-trip) to the 10,840 ft. summit of Mt. San Jacinto. Or go to the top of Mt. San Jacinto from Devil's Slide (16 mi. round-trip). Views from the lower portion of **Devil's Slide Trail** out to Tahquitz Peak and the Valley below are excellent. On summer weekends the limited number of permits for this area run out very quickly, so get to the ranger station early (see **Practical Information,** p. 464). Those who want peak views with only a moderately strenuous hike should try the **Deer Spring Trail** out to Suicide Rock (3.3 mi. one-way), which continues out to Strawberry Junction Campground.

Idyllwild ARTS, 52500 Temecula Dr. (☎659-2171), at the end of Toll Gate Rd. off Rte. 243, gives free dance, drama, and music performances, as well as exhibitions and workshops. ARTS emphasizes Native American arts and crafts. The **Jazz in the Pines** festival is every August. (☎659-3774. Tickets $20-25.) Sophisticates may imbibe culture and bubbly during the fall's **Art Walk and Wine Tasting,** in which participants tour the art galleries of Idyllwild and enjoy wines along the way. Contact the Idyllwild Gallery of Fine Art for details. (☎659-1948 or 888-882-5264.)

NORTH OF L.A.

Government legislation ensures a prime hiking and camping in the vast expanse of park land north of Los Angeles. Unspoiled coastline, chaparral, and rolling hills stretch from the Santa Monica Mountains to the end of the Central Coast.

SANTA MONICA MOUNTAINS NATIONAL RECREATION AREA   ☎805

"Recreation area" is a suitably vague term for this collection of private and public lands. The best place for info is the **National Park Service Visitors Center,** 401 W. Hill-crest Dr., Thousand Oaks, off U.S. 101 at the Lynn Rd. Exit. (☎370-2301. Open daily 9am-5pm.) Call to request *Outdoors,* the recreation area's quarterly calendar of events and programs. Reserve state-run campsites through ReserveAmerica (☎800-444-7275). **Leo Carrillo ❶, Point Mugu ❶,** and **Malibu Creek ❶** all cost $12. You can backcountry camp at **Topanga State Park** on a first- come, first-served basis.

HIKING TRAILS. These hills sport more than 570 mi. of hiking trails of widely varying difficulty, so ask a ranger for advice before heading out. *Hike Los Angeles, Vol. 1 and Vol. 2* ($10 each, sold at the Visitors Center), feature the most popular walks in the park, with relevant info about the area's ecology and history. If **Malibu Creek** looks vaguely like the set of *M*A*S*H,* that's because it was. Much of the set was dismantled after the television show's shooting ended in 1982, and more of it was destroyed in subsequent fires, but an easy 1.5 mi. hike from the Crags Rd. trailhead leads to the remaining jeep and ambulance. The flat area above the bank was the helipad. Die-hard outdoor enthusiasts might want to taste the pain of the **Backbone Trail,** a 70 mi., three-to-five-day journey from Pt. Mugu to Sunset Blvd. in Pacific Palisades. Consult a ranger before going.

WILD, WILD WEST. The National Park Service administers the **Paramount Ranch Site,** which was used as a location for several Paramount films between 1927 and 1953. Director Cecil B. DeMille and actors Gary Cooper and Mae West all worked here. The ranch served as colonial Massachusetts in *The Maid of Salem* (1937), ancient China in *The Adventures of Marco Polo* (1938), and early San Francisco in *Wells Fargo* (1937). After purchasing the property in 1980, the US Park Service revitalized the old movie set, and it is now open to visitors. Rangers conduct regular tours. In summer, Paramount Ranch screens silent movies from the 1920s with live musical accompaniment; call for dates. *(To reach the ranch, take U.S. 101 to the Kanan Rd. Exit (in Agoura Hills). Continue for half a mile and turn left onto Cornell Way, veer right onto Cornell Rd., and continue 2½ mi. to the entrance on the right.)*

SATWIWA. On the western edge of the recreation area lies Rancho Sierra Vista/Satwiwa. At one time, a nearby Chumash village had the name Satwiwa, which means "the bluffs." Park rangers or special Native American guests host "fire circles" as part of the fascinating twilight program at the **Native American Indian Culture Center.** The 8 mi. hike from this site down through Big Sycamore Canyon to the sea is one of the park's most rewarding. (*Culture Center* ☎ *375-1930. Open Sa-Su 9am-5pm. Fire circles Sept. 1-May 31 Sun 6:30-8pm; June 1-Aug 31 Sa 6:30-8pm.*)

SAN DIEGO

San Diegans are fond of referring to their garden-like town as "America's Finest City." This claim is difficult to dispute—San Diego (pop. 1,130,000) has all the virtues of other California cities without many of their frequently cited drawbacks. No smog fills this city's air, and no sewage spoils its silver seashores. Its zoo is the nation's best, and the temperate year-round climate is unbeatable.

The city was founded when the seafaring Spanish extended an onshore leave in 1769 and began the first permanent European settlement on the West Coast of the United States. San Diego remained a nondescript town until it became the headquarters of the US Pacific Fleet following the attack on Pearl Harbor in 1941. As a result, over a dozen naval and marine installations exist in and around the city, and the military presence shapes both the economy and the somewhat conservative local culture. Indeed, much of the skyline is composed of the superstructures of colossal aircraft carriers. Today, high-tech industries have fueled an impressive renaissance, as well as an explosion in ethnic and economic diversity. It is the country's sixth and California's second-largest city, and one of the fastest-growing.

HIGHLIGHTS OF SAN DIEGO

ZOOS. The **San Diego Zoo** (p. 480) and **San Diego Wild Animal Park** (p. 493) are some of the best places in the world to view animals in captivity.

BEACHES. Coronado Island (p. 482), **Mission** and **Pacific beaches** (p. 483), and **La Jolla Shores** (p. 485) are fabulous ocean-side spots.

CULTURE. History buffs go to **Old Town** for museums, historic buildings (some reputedly haunted), and the **Mission Basilica San Diego de Alcalá** (p. 486), while museum lovers head to **Balboa Park** and the **El Prado Museums** (p. 480).

✈ INTERCITY TRANSPORTATION

San Diego rests in the extreme southwest corner of California, 127 mi. south of Los Angeles and 15 mi. north of the Mexican border. Three freeways link the city to its regional neighbors: **I-5** runs south from L.A. through the North County cities of Oceanside and Carlsbad and skirts the eastern edge of downtown on its way to Mexico; **I-15** runs northeast through the desert to Las Vegas; and **I-8** runs east-west along downtown's northern boundary, connecting the desert with Ocean Beach. The downtown core is laid out in a grid, making it easy to navigate. In **North County,** the **Pacific Coast Highway** runs parallel to I-5, known as Old Hwy. 101, 1st St., or Carlsbad Blvd., depending on location.

Airport: San Diego International (Lindbergh Field), at the northwest edge of downtown. Call the Travelers Aid Society (☎231-7361) for info. Society open daily 8am-11pm. Bus #2 goes downtown ($2), as do cabs ($8).

Trains: Amtrak, 1050 Kettner Blvd. (☎239-9021 or 800-872-7245), just north of Broadway in the historic Santa Fe Depot. To **L.A.** (10 trains daily, 6am-8:30pm, $27). Station has info on bus, trolley, car, and boat transportation. Ticket office open daily 5:15am-10:20pm. Additional $10 for reservations.

Buses: Greyhound, 120 W. Broadway (☎239-8082 or 800-231-2222), at 1st St. To **L.A.** (30 per day 5am-11:35pm; $15, round-trip $25) and **Tijuana** (16 per day 5am-11:35pm; $5, round-trip $8). Ticket office open 24hr.

✦ ORIENTATION

The epicenter of San Diego tourism is historic **Balboa Park.** It is home to the world-famous **San Diego Zoo** and a cluster of diverse museums and cultural attractions. Northeast of the park is the stylish **Hillcrest** neighborhood. In addition to being the city's gay enclave, Hillcrest also has great restaurants and shopping. The reinvigorated **Gaslamp Quarter** sits in the southern section of downtown between 4th and 6th streets. The Gaslamp has many of San Diego's signature theaters and nightclubs, as well as fine restaurants. Just north of downtown in the southeast corner of the I-5 and I-8 junction lies a little slice of old Mexico known as **Old Town.** Discriminating travelers may find Old Town's touristy kitsch a bit contrived, but the fantastic Mexican food and lively scene make this place more than worth the visit. Downtown San Diego is surprisingly safe, but nevertheless, always exercise reasonable caution and avoid the somewhat run-down far-eastern section of downtown that abuts I-5, as well as the district south of the Gaslamp.

San Diego Bay opens up south of downtown and is bounded by glorious **Coronado Island.** While often exasperatingly touristy and too pricey for most budget travelers, Coronado offers sunny outdoor fun like surfing and cycling. Northwest of town sits the collection of shiny beaches and man-made inlets known as **Mission Bay.** The beaches west of the bay, and those north and south, are some of the finest urban beaches in America. And don't forget to get splashed by crashing and spurting marine mammals at the original **Sea World.** A jaunt up the coast leads to the swanky tourist haven of **La Jolla** (p. 485). But don't be fooled by the profusion of upscale shops and Euro-designer brand names: **La Jolla Cove** has excellent snorkeling, **La Jolla Shores** is the cleanest of the San Diego beaches, and the surrounding parkland is a great place to spend a warm afternoon. Up the coast beyond La Jolla are the laid-back and sun-soaked beach communities of the **North County** (p. 488).

▐ LOCAL TRANSPORTATION

PUBLIC TRANSPORTATION. The city of San Diego provides fairly extensive public transportation through the **San Diego Metropolitan Transit System (MTS).** MTS's automated 24hr. information line, **Info Express** (☎685-4900), has info on San Diego's buses, trains, and trolleys. To talk to live people, visit the **Transit Store** at 1st Ave. and Broadway, which has bus, trolley, and ferry tickets and timetables, as well as a free pamphlet with tips for riding. Be sure to pick up a one, two, three or four day **Day Trippers Pass** if you plan to be using public transit of any kind more than once. (Open M-F 8:30am-5:30pm, Sa-Su noon-4pm. One-day pass $5, two-day $8, three-day $10, four-day $12.) The **Regional Transit Information Center** is also a good source, although it can be difficult to get through. (☎233-3004. Open M-F 5:30am-8:30pm, Sa-Su 8am-5pm.) **Bus** fares range from $0.50 to $3.50 depending on the route. Bus transfers are good for 1½hr. after they are issued. They require exact fare, but accept dollar bills. All buses are wheelchair-accessible. If getting to a bus stop is a problem, call the door-to-bus-stop service **DART.** (☎887-841-DART/3278. $2.25. Operates M-F 5:30am-8pm.) The **COASTER** sends trains daily between San Diego (downtown and Old Town) and the coastal communities of Solana Beach, Encinitas, Carlsbad, and Oceanside. (☎800-COASTER/262-7837; www.sdcommute.com. $3.50-4.75 one-way, 10-trip passes $29-43.)

The bright red **San Diego Trolley** consists of two lines leaving from downtown for El Cajon, San Ysidro, and points in between. The El Cajon line leaves from 12th Ave. and Imperial St.; the San Ysidro line leaves from the Old Town Transit Center (at Taylor St. and San Diego Ave.) and continues to the Mexican border. Although there are no turnstiles, the inspector does indeed check for tickets, and the fine is definitely *not* within reach of the budget traveler. (☎231-8549; www.sdcommute.com. Trolleys run daily 5am-1am. $1-2.50.)

SAN DIEGO

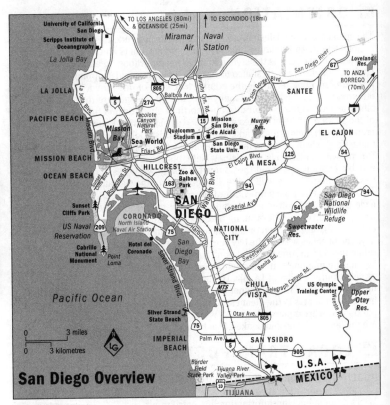

San Diego Overview

BY CAR. Southern California is the land of the automobile; renting a car will make your life easier and your trip more enjoyable. Most places will not rent to drivers under 21, but a letter from your insurer stating that you are covered for rental car crashes may go a long way toward getting you some wheels.

Bargain Auto, 3860 Rosecrans St. (☎299-0009). Used cars available to renters 18+. Cars from $19 per day with 150 mi. free, $99 per week with 500 mi. free. Ages 18-25 pay $6 per day surcharge, $35 per week. $27 per day for insurance if driving to Mexico. Credit card required. Open M-F 8am-6pm, Sa-Su 8am-4pm.

Dollar, 2499 Pacific Hwy. (☎234-3388; www.dollar.com), at the airport. Cars $28-54 per day with unlimited mileage. Must be 21+ with credit card; ages 21-25 pay $20 per day surcharge. Travel to Mexico $25 per day surcharge. Open daily 5:30am-midnight.

BICYCLES. San Diego has an extensive system of fairly easy **bike routes.** Some are separate from the road, while some are specially marked outer lanes. The flat, paved route along Mission and Pacific Beaches toward La Jolla affords ocean views and soothing sea breezes. Bikers beware: pedestrian traffic along the beaches rivals the automobiles on the boulevards. Buses with bike carriers make it possible to cart bikes almost anywhere in the city (call ☎233-3004 for info). For more bike info, contact the **City Bicycle Coordinator** (☎533-3110) or **CalTrans,** 4040 Taylor St., San Diego, CA 92110 (☎231-2453), in Old Town.

RENTALS: BIKES, BOARDS, & BLADES. Gear is available for rent throughout San Diego and the surrounding communities. Most rental stores are cheap enough for the budget traveler, and allow for a look at what makes San Diego an outdoor adventure paradise.

Action Sports, 4000 Coronado Bay Rd. (☎424-4466), at the Marina Dock of the Loews Coronado Bay Resort on **Coronado Island.** Beach cruisers and mountain bikes $10 per hr., $30 per 4hr. Open M-F 9am-6pm Sa-Su 8:30am-6:30pm.

Bike Tours, 509 5th Ave. (☎238-2444), in the **Gaslamp.** Well maintained mountain bikes $15 per day, $50 per week. Lock, protective gear maps, and roadside assistance are included. Open daily 7am-7pm.

Little Sam's, 1343 Orange Ave. (☎435-4058), near the Hotel Del Coronado on **Coronado Island.** Beach cruisers $6 per hr., half-day $14, full-day $20. Roller blades $5 per hr., half-day $14, full-day $20. Surfboards $15 per hr., full-day $25. All gear comes with safety equipment, locks, maps and advice. Open daily 8am-6pm.

Bikes and Beyond (☎435-7180), at the ferry landing on 1st St., on **Coronado Island.** Cruisers and mountain bikes $6 per hr., $18 per 4hr.; in-line skates $5 per hr., $15 per 4hr.; 4-peddler surry, $15 per 30min., $25 per hr. Locks, protective gear, and maps free. Open 8:30am-dusk.

South Coast Longboards, 5037 Newport Ave. (☎223-8808) in **Ocean Beach.** Soft surfboards $5 per hr., full-day $25 with $300 cash deposit or credit card. Open June-Aug. M-Sa 9am-7:30pm, Su 10am-6:30pm; Sept.-May daily 9am-6pm.

Cheap Rentals, 3221 Mission Blvd. (☎858-486-5533 or 800-941-7761. www.cheaprentals.com) in **Mission Beach.** Beach cruisers $6 per hr., full-day $15; skateboards $6 per hr., full-day $15. Open daily 8am-6pm.

Star Surfing Co., 4652 Mission Blvd. (☎858-273-7827) in **Pacific Beach.** Surfboards $5 per hr., full-day $2; bodyboards $3 per hr., full-day $12. Need driver's license or credit card for deposit. Open daily 10am-6pm.

Dana Landing Boat Rentals, 1710 W. Mission Bay Dr. (☎226-2929) on **Mission Bay.** 14-ft. Capri sailboats $20 per hr. Other water-sports equipment, such as jetskis and power boats, are also available. Open daily 6am-10pm.

Windsport, 844 W. Mission Bay Dr. (☎858-488-4642; www.windsport.net) in **Mission Beach.** Kayaks $15 per hr., full-day $75. 30min. and 2hr. kayak tours, including equipment rental, $60 per person. Open M-F 10am-6pm, Sa-Su 9am-6pm.

WALKING. Downtown, Balboa Park, and Old Town can easily be covered on foot, but beaches are less accessible because of the wide distances between them. **Walkabout International,** 835 5th Ave. #407, sponsors about 150 free walks each month, from downtown architectural strolls to 20 mi. La Jolla treks. (☎231-7463. Open M-F 9:30am-2:30pm.) Pedestrians almost always heed the walk signals, because jaywalking is actively prosecuted in San Diego.

◪ PRACTICAL INFORMATION

TOURIST & FINANCIAL SERVICES

Visitor Information:

International Visitor Information Center, 11 Horton Plaza (☎236-1212), downtown at 1st Ave. and F St. Helpful, multilingual staff dispenses publications, brochures, and discount coupons. 3hr. parking validation for lots with entrances on G St. and 4th Ave. Open June-Aug. M-Sa 8:30am-5pm, Su 11am-5pm; Sept.-May M-Sa 8:30am-5pm.

San Diego Convention and Visitors Bureau, 401 B St., #1400, Dept. 700, San Diego 92101 (☎236-1212; www.sandiego.org), also provides info.

Old Town and State Park Info, 4002 Wallace Ave. (☎220-5422), in Old Town Sq. Take the Taylor St. Exit off I-8 or bus #5. Free walking tours daily noon and 2pm. Open daily 10am-5pm.

Just Call (☎615-6111) is an information line operated by the city of San Diego.

Budget Travel: San Diego Council of American Youth Hostels, 521 Market St., San Diego, CA 92101 (☎338-9981; www.hostelweb.com/sandiego), in the Metropolitan Hostel at 5th St. Offers budget guides and info. Open daily 7am-11pm.

American Express, 7610 Hazard Center Dr. (☎297-8101). Open M-F 9:30am-6pm, Sa 10am-3pm. Call for other locations throughout the area.

LOCAL SERVICES

Library: San Diego Public Library, 820 E St. (☎236-5800), offers **Internet** access, foreign newspapers, borrowing privileges for visitors, a California information room, and an ongoing concert, film, and lecture series. Centrally located with an ultra-friendly staff. Open M-Th 10am-9pm, F-Sa 9:30am-5:30pm, Su 1-5pm.

Senior Citizens Services, 202 C St. (☎236-6905), in the City Hall Bldg. Provides senior ID cards and plans daytrips. Open M-F 8am-5pm.

The Access Center, 1295 University Ave., #10 (☎293-3500, TDD 293-7757), Hillcrest. Attendant referral, wheelchair repair and sales, emergency housing, motel/hotel accessibility referral. Open M-F 9am-5pm. **Accessible San Diego,** 2466 Bartel St. (☎858-279-0704), also has info. Open daily 10am-4pm.

The Center for Community Solutions, 4508 Mission Bay Dr. (☎233-8984, 24hr. hotline 272-1767), at Bunker Hill St. in Pacific Beach. Offers rape and domestic violence counseling, as well as legal services. Open M-F 8am-4:30pm.

Bi-Gay-Lesbian Organizations: Lesbian and Gay Men's Center, 3909 Centre St. (☎692-2077), provides counseling and info. Open daily 9am-10pm. The **Gay Youth Alliance** (☎233-9309) is a support and social group for people under 24. For a listing of queer events and establishments, check *Update* (☎299-0500), available at virtually all queer businesses, bookstores, and bars. The *Gay and Lesbian Times*, published every Th, provides event, bar, and club listings.

Ticket Agencies: Ticketmaster (☎220-TIXS/8497, concert info 581-1000). Beware of the high service charge. Get half-price tickets from **Times Arts Tix** (☎497-5000). Open Tu-Th 11am-6pm, F-Sa 10am-6pm.

Laundromat: Metro Wash and Dry, 724 4th Ave. (☎544-1284), between F and G St. Wash $1.25, dry $0.25 per 8min. Open daily 6am-7:30pm.

Weather Conditions: Weather Report (☎221-8824). Updated daily—as if the weather ever changes. The average daily temperature is 70°F, with nighttime lows around 60°F.

EMERGENCY & COMMUNICATIONS

Police: ☎531-2000.

Auto Repairs: AAA Emergency Road Service (☎800-400-4222).

Hospitals: Kaiser Foundation, 4647 Zion Ave. (☎528-5000); **Columbia Mission Bay,** 3030 Bunker Hill St. (☎858-274-7721), in Mission Bay.

24hr. Crisis Lines: Lesbian and Gay Men's Center Crisis Line (☎800-479-3339). **Women's Center Rape Hotline** (☎233-3088).

24hr. Pharmacy: Rite Aid, 535 Robinson Ave. (☎291-3705), in Hillcrest.

Radio: News/talk on KSDO (1130 AM), National Public Radio on KPBS (89.5 FM), popular top-40 on 103.5 FM.

Internet: San Diego Public Library (see above).

Post Offices: 2535 Midway Dr. (☎800-275-8777). Take bus #6, 9, or 35. Open M 7am-5pm, Tu-F 8am-5pm, Sa 8am-4pm. **Postal Code:** 92186. 2150 Comstock St. Open M-F 8am-5pm, Sa 8am-4:30pm. **Postal Code:** 92111.

>
> **AREA CODE** For most of San Diego, including downtown, Coronado, and Ocean Beach: **619.** Northern San Diego area codes (including Del Mar, La Jolla, parts of North County, and Pacific Beach): **858 and 760. Unless otherwise specified, the area code for the San Diego area is 619.**

⚑ ACCOMMODATIONS

Rates predictably rise on weekends and during the summer season. Reservations are recommended for all of the places listed below, particularly if you intend to stay during the busy summers. Beyond the hostel and residential hotel scene, San Diego is littered with generic chain motels, which are generally safe and clean, though a little more expensive. There is a popular cluster known as **Hotel Circle** (2-3 mi. east of I-5 along I-8), where summer prices begin at $60 for a single and $70 for a double during the week ($70 and $80, respectively, on weekends). If you choose to stay in a motel, be sure to pick up one of the traveler discount coupon books at a visitors center. Several beaches in North County, as well as one on Coronado, are state parks and allow camping.

DOWNTOWN

▨ **San Diego Downtown Hostel (HI-AYH),** 521 Market St. (☎525-1531 or 800-909-4776, ext. 43; www.hostelweb.com/sandiego/metro.html), at 5th Ave., in the heart of the Gaslamp, 5 blocks from the Convention Center. Quiet, impeccably clean hostel near San Diego's most popular attractions and clubs. Amenities include an airy common room with kitchen, pool table, and communal bathrooms. Smoking and drinking are not allowed. Free pancake breakfast. No curfew. Lockers (bring a lock) and laundry. Reception 7am-midnight. IBN reservations available. Groups welcome. 4-6 bed dorms $20, non-members $23; doubles $45-50. ❷

USA Hostels San Diego, 726 5th Ave. (☎232-3100 or 800-GET-TO-CA/438-8622; www.usahostels.com), between F and G St. in the Gaslamp. This Euro-style fun house hosts parties and organizes Tijuana tours ($10). Pancake breakfast included and dinner available for $4. Free linen and lockers. Coin-op laundry. Rooms are clean, and common areas are festive. **International passport required.** Dorms $19-20. The three private rooms are often booked, and go for $49 a night. $1 off for ISIC VIP and BUNAC cardholders. $3 off with brochures available at other USA hostels. ❷

J Street Inn, 222 J St. (☎696-6922), near the convention center and ritzy waterfront. All 221 fabulous studio rooms have cable TV, microwave, fridge, and bath. Gym and reading room. Enclosed parking $5 per day, $20 per week. Singles and doubles $50-70; each additional person $20. Weekly $179-249. ❹

La Pension Hotel, 606 W. Date St. (☎236-8000 or 800-232-4683) right in the heart of Little Italy. European-style hotel with small, comfortable rooms and modern furnishings. Covered parking available. Singles and doubles $60, $70 on weekends. ❹

Horton Grand Hotel, 311 Island Ave. (☎544-1886 or 800-542-1886) in the Gaslamp. This historic Victorian hotel offers distinctive rooms and lavish furnishings. All of the standard amenities, plus many extras. Rooms $159-289; may drop as low as $119 by booking in advance and during off-peak times. ❺

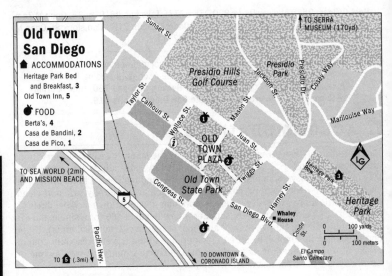

Old Town San Diego

🏠 ACCOMMODATIONS
Heritage Park Bed and Breakfast, **3**
Old Town Inn, **5**

🍴 FOOD
Berta's, **4**
Casa de Bandini, **2**
Casa de Pico, **1**

HILLCREST & OLD TOWN

Old Town Inn, 4444 Pacific Hwy. (☎260-8024 or 800-643-3025; www.oldtowninn.com). Clean rooms with standard amenities are a 10min. walk from Old Town Some rooms have kitchenettes. Pool. Large continental breakfast included. Singles $50-60; doubles $50-60; prices vary depending on the season. ❹

Heritage Park Bed and Breakfast Inn, 2470 Heritage Park Row (☎229-6832; www.heritageparkinn.com), near Old Town. This old Victorian mansion in Heritage Park now functions as a cozy B&B. Each of the 12 guest rooms is unique, but they all come with afternoon teas and nightly showings of vintage films. Rooms $120-250. Reservations at least 1 month in advance are strongly encouraged. ❺

The Hillcrest Inn, 3754 5th Ave. (☎293-7078 or 800-258-2280; www.bryx.com/hillcrestinn). 45 tastefully decorated studios. Each room has all the standard amenities, plus fridge and microwave. Sunning patio and jacuzzi. Very popular with gay visitors (though not exclusively catering to a gay clientele). All rooms are singles; standard bed $57, queen-sized $65, king-sized $79. Two-night min. stay on weekends. ❹

Studio 819, 819 University Ave. (☎542-0819; www.studio819.com). Tidy and compact studios with a range of amenities, including kitchenettes usually rented on a weekly or monthly basis, but also available for nightly rates. Underground parking ($2 per day) and laundry. Rooms for 1-2 people $50-58, slightly higher on weekends and holidays; weekly $329-385; monthly $630-710. ❹

COASTAL SAN DIEGO

🏚 **International House at the 2nd Floor,** 4502 Cass St. (☎858-274-4325) in Pacific Beach and 3204 Mission Bay Blvd. (☎858-539-0043) in Mission Beach. To reach PB via bus from downtown, take the #34 from Broadway to Mission and Garnet. Turn right onto Garnet and walk two blocks to Cass St. The hostel will be on the left. To reach MB, take via bus from downtown, take the #34 from Broadway to Mission Blvd and Mission Bay Dr. The hostel is located across the street. These two sister hostels are the newest additions to the San Diego scene. Both offer excellent service, clean and airy rooms, comfortable beds, Internet access, breakfast, and great locations. 28-day max. stay. Out-of-state ID or international passport required. Dorm rooms $20, students with ID $18; $110 per week. ❷

🎏 **Ocean Beach International (OBI),** 4961 Newport Ave. (☎223-7873 or 800-339-7263; www.oceanbeach.com/hostel), in **Ocean Beach.** Look for international flags. Free transport to and from airport, train, and bus terminals. If driving, Exit I-5 at 1-8 and head towards the beaches. Stay straight onto Sunset Cliffs Blvd. Take a right on Newport Ave. The hostel will be up a couple blocks on the left. The OBI features clean rooms, cable TV and kitchen near the beach. Pancake breakfast included. Beach gear rental. Laundry. Free BBQ and keg parties Tu and F night; free pasta Tu in winter. 29-day max. stay. **Proof of international travel in the last 6 months required.** 4-6 bed dorms $18-20; doubles (some with bath) $40-43. ❷

HI-Point Loma, 3790 Udall St. (☎223-4778), 1½ mi. from **Ocean Beach.** Take bus #35 from downtown to the 1st stop on Voltaire St. If driving, head west on Sea World Dr. from I-5 and bear right on Sunset Cliff Blvd. Take a left on Voltaire St., then a right on Worden St., and Udall St. is 1 block away—look for the hostel sign. Large kitchen, patio with ping pong, and common room with TV. Laundry. Bike rental $10 per day. Reception 8am-10pm. 14-night max. stay. Reserve 2 days in advance. Dorms $16-18; nonmembers $3 more. ❷

Inn at Mission Bay, 4545 Mission Bay Dr. (☎858-483-4222; www.innatmission-bay.com), near **Mission Bay.** Large motel with standard rooms and amenities. Singles and doubles $89-99 in summer; in winter from $54. $10 AAA discount. ❹

Shell Beach, 981 Coast Blvd. (☎858-459-4306 or 888-525-6552; www.lajolla-cove.com), in **La Jolla.** Considering its beachfront location, this is one of the most reasonably priced accommodations in the area. This otherwise expensive oceanfront property has a few tiny studios that make staying here possible even for budget travelers. Comfy, older rooms are mere steps from the beach. Non-oceanfront studio with queen-sized bed $65; lower Sept.-May. ❹

Tradewinds Motel, 4305 Mission Bay Dr. (☎858-273-4616) near **Mission Bay.** This pink and avocado green motel not only looks like a flash from times past, but its prices have come straight from the 50s. Clean, older rooms $40; on weekends $50. ❸

Silver Strand State Beach Campground (☎435-5184), along the 7 mi. strip connecting Coronado Island to the mainland. An endless ribbon of sand and rhythmic waves. Excellent surfing. The small and undeveloped camping areas set aside for RVs are first come, first camp. Sites $12. ❶

◻ FOOD

With its proximity to Mexico and large Hispanic population, San Diego is renowned for its exemplary Mexican cuisine. **Old Town** serves some of the best authentic Mexican food in the state. Beyond this, San Diego also offers a spectacular assortment of ethnic and more traditional eateries. Both the **Hillcrest** neighborhood and the historic **Gaslamp Quarter** provide visitors with a particularly satisfying selection.

DOWNTOWN

True budget food in the downtown area can be harder to come by than in nearby beach communities. However, for a few extra dollars, excellent eating is abundant, particularly in the **Gaslamp Quarter.** For super-quick bargain basement chow, try the food court at the **Horton Plaza,** a large shopping center between 1st and 4th Ave., and E and G St. It's cheap, but it still aspires to be more than simply fast food. Buy your own groceries downtown at **Ralph's,** 101 G St. (☎595-1581. Open 24hr.)

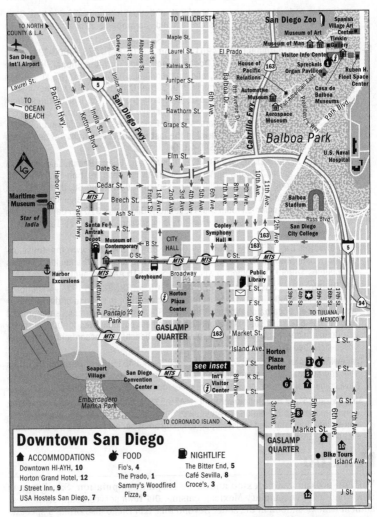

Downtown San Diego

🏠 ACCOMMODATIONS

Downtown HI-AYH, **10**
Horton Grand Hotel, **12**
J Street Inn, **9**
USA Hostels San Diego, **7**

🍴 FOOD

Fio's, **4**
The Prado, **1**
Sammy's Woodfired Pizza, **6**

🍸 NIGHTLIFE

The Bitter End, **5**
Café Sevilla, **8**
Croce's, **3**

Sushi Deli, 828 Broadway (☎231-9597). This small sushi place offers fresh sushi at amazingly low prices. Try their lunch special (teriyaki chicken, 4-piece California roll, edamame, rice, and salad for $6) or all you can eat sushi Monday for $15. Open Su 5-9pm, M-Th 11am-2pm and 5-9pm, F 11am-2pm and 5-10pm, Sa 5-10pm. ❷

Kansas City Barbecue, 610 W. Market St. (☎231-9680), near **Seaport Village.** The location of *Top Gun*'s sleazy bar scene and home of a very friendly bar staff. Giant lunches and dinners ($4-9) are adequate, and you gotta love the jukebox strains of "You've Lost that Lovin' Feeling." Open daily 11am-2am; kitchen closes at 1am. ❷

The Fish Market, 750 N. Harbor Drive (☎232-3474), within walking distance of **Seaport Village.** This local landmark serves up an amazing array of the freshest seafood. Ask for a patio table and enjoy your meal with an incomparable view of the bay. Entrees $12-28. Open daily 11am-10pm. The **Top of the Market** is the swankier version located directly upstairs. The linens, view, and ambience will cost you an extra $10 per plate for what is basically the same food. Open M-Sa 11am-10pm, Su 10am-2pm for brunch, 2-10pm for lunch and dinner. ❹

Fio's, 801 5th Ave. (☎ 234-3467), in the **Gaslamp.** For a very special evening, don your fancy clothing and head to the elegant finery of Fio's. Classic Italian food mixes with live music. Entrees start at $17. Open Su-Th 5-10pm, F-Sa 5-11pm. ❺

Trattoria Fantastica, 1735 India St. (☎ 234-1735; http://trattoriafantas.signonsandiego.com). In the heart of **Little Italy,** this family-owned restaurant serves heaping portions of scrumptious Italian food. Entrees and pastas from $10. Open daily 11:30am-3pm and 5-10pm. ❸

Sammy's California Woodfired Pizza, 770 4th Ave. (☎ 230-8888; www.sammyspizza.com). Upscale pizza joint offers 22 gourmet pizzas ($8-10) that have been called the best in SoCal. Huge salads $7-11. Open M-Th 11:30am-9:30pm, F 11:30am-10:30pm, Sa noon-10:30pm, Su noon-9:30pm. ❷

BALBOA PARK, HILLCREST, & UNIVERSITY HEIGHTS

The best food near Balboa Park is in nearby **Hillcrest** and **University Heights.** These trendy, youth-oriented neighborhoods are home to a diverse array of inexpensive restaurants. Health nuts will find many low-fat and vegetarian options. Shop for organic groceries in Hillcrest at **Whole Foods Market,** 711 University Ave. (☎ 294-2800. Open daily 8am-10pm.)

Extraordinary Desserts, 2929 5th Ave. (☎ 294-2001; www.extraordinarydesserts.com). Mounds of chocolate, cake, fruits, and other delectables can be savored at this desserts-only restaurant. The Asian-influenced decor and rich chocolate may lull you into a state of bliss. Whole cakes also available for carry-out (from $12). Open M-Th 8:30am-11pm, F 8:30am-midnight, Sa 11am-midnight, Su 8:30am-11pm. ❸

The Prado, 1549 El Prado (☎ 557-9441; www.pradobalboa.com), in **Balboa Park.** Since this restaurant opened 2 years ago, it's had nothing but rave reviews. The patio seating is beautiful any time of the year, and the calamari appetizer is big enough to be a meal ($9.50). Dinner entrees from $19. Open M-Sa 11am-9:30pm, Su 11am-8pm. ❺

City Delicatessen, 535 University Ave. (☎ 295-2747). Funky restaurant that emulates a New York-style deli. Breakfast specials ($7-10) are served all day. Open Su-Th 7am-midnight, F-Sa 7am-2am. ❷

OLD TOWN

Frequented by both locals and visitors, Old Town has the best Mexican food in San Diego. Don't be intimidated by the gigantic lines—Old Town's colorful and authentic restaurants have perfected the art of "move 'em in, move 'em out" without compromising quality. Many Old Town eats are in the **Bazaar del Mundo,** a cluster of restaurants and stores accessible only by foot.

◪ Casa de Bandini, 2754 Calhoun St. (☎ 297-8211). An Old Town institution and repeatedly voted best Mexican restaurant in San Diego. Set in a Spanish-style architectural landmark (built in 1829), Bandini dishes out superb food and boisterous Mariachi music. The colossal combo plates ($8) and heavyweight margaritas ($4-7) are the stuff of legend. Open M-Th 11am-9:30pm, F-Sa 11am-10pm, Su 10am-9:30pm. ❷

Casa de Pico (☎ 296-3267), just off Calhoun St. in the Bazaar. Gigantic plates overflowing with gooey cheese enchiladas ($7-8). Soup-bowl-sized margaritas are terrifically tasty ($5-7). Open M-F 10am-9pm, Sa-Su 10am-10pm. ❷

Berta's, 3928 Twiggs St. (☎ 295-2343). You may have to buy a copy of ◪ *Let's Go: Central America* to make your way through this menu. Dozens of Guatemalan, Honduran, and Costa Rican specialities $9-14. Open Tu-Su 11am-10pm. ❸

Old Town Cafe, 2489 San Diego Ave. (☎297-4330 or 888-234-9836; www.oldtown-mexcafe.com). A slightly cheaper, but no less tasty version of the restaurants in the Bazaar. 115 varieties of Tequila are served, and tortillas are made in the front window. Huge combo plates from $6. Open 7am-11pm daily. ❶

COASTAL SAN DIEGO

Mission Beach and **Pacific Beach** are crowded with youth-oriented bars and surfer dives. To rustle up your own meal, head to the supermarket **Ralph's,** 4315 Mission Blvd. (☎273-0778. Open 24hr.) Most of **Ocean Beach**'s inexpensive restaurants and bars are along the westernmost stretch of **Newport Avenue,** one of San Diego's trendiest drags and where shots for the movie *Almost Famous* were filmed.

🔳 **Kono's Surf Club,** 704 Garnet Ave. (☎483-1669), across from the Crystal Pier in **Pacific Beach.** Identifiable by the line stretching for a block out the door, Kono's is a surfer's shrine. Breakfast served all day ($3-4). Try the huge Egg Burrito #3, which includes bacon, cheese, potatoes, and sauce ($3.25). Open M-F 7am-3pm, Sa-Su 7am-4pm. ❶

World Curry, 1433 Garnet Ave. (☎689-2222; www.worldcurry.com), in **Pacific Beach,** further east than the main drag. The amazingly quick service delivers delicious curries from all over the world for $7. Open M-Sa 11am-10pm, Su 4-9pm. ❷

Eatopia, 5001 Newport Ave. (☎224-3237; www.eatopiaexpress.com), in **Ocean Beach.** Vegan fast-food with refreshing smoothies and excellent wraps. The Thai Delight wrap is especially delicious ($4.25). Open daily 10am-8pm. ❶

Rhinoceros Cafe and Grill, 1166 Orange Ave. (☎435-2121), on **Coronado Island.** Fresh pasta, salads and seafoods. Try their specialty: Penne a la vodka ($13.95 dinner, $8.95 lunch). Open daily 11am-2:30pm and 5-9pm. ❸

Cafe Crema, 1001 Garnet Ave. (☎858-273-3558), in **Pacific Beach.** A Euro-style coffeehouse stacked with pastries and sandwiches ($4-5). Internet ($1 per 10min.) and live music. Open Su 8am-1am, M-Th 7am-1am, F 7am-2am, Sa 8am-2am. ❶

LA JOLLA

Prospect Street, the main drag in La Jolla, is crammed with upscale shops and galleries, but tucked in between are a few excellent places to eat. **Girard Avenue** and its side streets also have a number of good places.

Rimel's, 1030 Torrey Pines Rd. (☎858-454-6045). With a number of spits right behind the counter, this restaurant and rotisserie sends wafts of delicious smells for blocks. And their selection will leave the taste buds and stomach, as well as the nose, satisfied. Half chicken $9, salads and sandwiches from $6. Open daily 11:30am-9:30pm. ❷

The Living Room, 1010 Prospect St. (858-454-8727). Home to mismatched sets of comfy chairs and amazingly large sandwiches ($5.50), this coffeehouse in the village is a local fave. Open daily 6:30am-midnight. ❷

The Pannikin, 7467 Girard Ave. (☎858-454-5453). This funky local chain specializes in coffee concoctions like the delicious white chocolate Frozen Iced Whitey ($3) and spicy Mexican hot chocolate ($2), and also serves great breakfasts and lunches. Open M-Th 5:30am-10pm, F 5:30am-11pm, Sa 6:30am-11pm, Su 6:30am-10pm. ❷

◎ SIGHTS

San Diego attractions are extremely varied, offering up plenty to any sort of traveler. Community events take place regularly, especially during the summer. Pick up a free copy of the weekly *Reader* at most stores for local event listings.

DOWNTOWN

San Diego's downtown attractions are concentrated in the corridor that includes its business, Gaslamp, and waterfront districts—all testaments to San Diego's continuing renaissance. Within this center of commerce and entertainment are the city's skyscrapers, its modern convention center, and its newest nexus of nightlife. Travelers should be careful outside of this corridor, the neighborhood to the southeast in particular is not as safe.

GASLAMP QUARTER. The Gaslamp houses antique shops, Victorian buildings, trendy restaurants and many nightclubs. Formerly the city's Red Light District and now home to Hustler, a three story adult-only store, the area's new bars and bistros have grown popular with upscale revelers (see **Nightlife,** p. 487). By day, the area's charm lies in its history. The **Gaslamp Quarter Foundation** offers guided walking tours as well as a small museum. *(William Heath Davis House, 410 Island Ave. ☎233-4692. Museum open Th-Su 11am-3pm. 2hr. tours Sa at 11am. $5; students, seniors, and ages 12-18 $3; under 12 free. Self-guided tour maps are available for $2.)* The **Horton Grand Hotel,** like most old buildings in San Diego, is supposedly haunted. Believers may catch a glimpse of Wyatt Earp or even Babe Ruth. *(311 Island Ave. ☎544-1886. Tours W at 3pm. Free. See **Accommodations,** p. 473.)*

SAN DIEGO MUSEUM OF CONTEMPORARY ART. This steel-and-glass structure encases 20th-century works of art from the museum's permanent collection and visiting works on a rotational basis. Artists represented in the permanent collection include John Baldessari, Philip Guston, and Ellsworth Kelly; works include a breathing wall. A La Jolla branch (see p. 485) shares the museum's collection. *(1001 Kettner Blvd. ☎234-1001. Open Th-Tu 11am-5pm. Free.)*

SAN DIEGO MARITIME MUSEUM. Displays at this museum showcase San Diego's rich maritime history. The museum also maintains three ships: the magnificently restored 1863 sailing vessel *Star of India* (the world's oldest active merchant ship), the ferryboat *Berkeley*, and the steam yacht *Medea*. *(1492 N. Harbor Dr. ☎234-9153; www.sdmaritime.com. Open daily 9am-8pm. $6; seniors, military, and ages 13-17 $4; ages 6-12 $3.)*

EMBARCADERO. Spanish for "dock," the Embarcadero has boardwalk shops and museums that face moored windjammers, cruise ships, and the occasional naval destroyer. Military and merchant marine vessels are anchored here, as well as the distantly visible North Island Naval Air Station, the Point Loma Submarine Base, and the South Bay's mothballed fleet; they serve as reminders of the US Navy's prominent presence in San Diego. *(Most afternoon tours of naval crafts free.)*

OTHER SIGHTS. The jewel of San Diego's redevelopment efforts is **Horton Plaza,** at Broadway and 4th. This pastel-hued urban creation is an open-air, multi-level shopping center covering seven blocks. Three blocks west of Horton Plaza, **Santa Fe Amtrak Depot,** 1050 Kettner Blvd., is a masterpiece of Mission Revival architecture. Its arches welcomed visitors to the 1915 Panama California Exposition. The kitschy **Seaport Village** houses over 75 shingled boutiques, ice cream shops, and a century-old carousel. *(649 W. Harbor Dr. ☎235-4014. Village open daily 10am-10pm; off-season 10am-9pm. Carousel rides $1. Free 2hr. parking, $1 per additional 30min.)*

BALBOA PARK & THE SAN DIEGO ZOO

Balboa Park was created from the baked dirt of an abandoned pueblo tract when pioneering horticulturists planted its first redwood seedlings in 1889. Today, the park nurtures these spectacular trees and a veritable profusion of flora. The centerpiece of the park is the world-famous San Diego Zoo, which houses a diverse array of animals in authentic and humane habitats. South of the zoo is a Spanish-style promenade lined with museums and other cultural attractions. You can reach the park by bus #7, and parking is free. Most museums offer free admission at least one Tuesday a month.

SAN DIEGO ZOO

2920 Zoo Dr., Balboa Park. From the north or south, take I-5 or I-15 to Rte. 163, get off at the Zoo/Museums Exit (Richmond St.), and follow signs. From the east, take I-8 to Rte. 163 south. Exit at Park Blvd. and turn left; zoo entrance is off Park Blvd. at Zoo Pl. ☎ 234-3153, Giant Panda viewing info 888-MY-PANDA/697-2632; www.sandiegozoo.org. Open late June to early Sept. daily 9am-10pm; early Sept. to late June 9am-dusk. Most of zoo is wheelchair-accessible and wheelchairs can be rented, but assistance may be necessary on the zoo's steep hills. $19.50 ($32 with 35min. bus tour and 2 tickets for the aerial tramway), ages 3-11 $11.75 ($19.75 with 35min. bus tour and aerial tramway; free in Oct.). Military in uniform free. Group rates available. Free on Founder's Day, the 1st M in Oct.

With over 100 acres of exquisite habitats, this zoo well deserves its reputation as one of the finest in the world. Its unique "bioclimatic" exhibits group animals and plants together by habitat. For example, the Polar Bear Plunge contains polar bears, Siberian reindeer, and Arctic foxes that fish and frolic tundra-style beside their own chilled, Olympic-size pool. The zoo currently showcases several **pandas** and invests over one million dollars a year on panda habitat preservation in China.

The most thorough way to tour the zoo is on foot. Alternatively, visitors can board the educational 35min. **double-decker bus tour** that races across about 80% of the zoo. Seats on the left provide a better vantage point to view the park. After-wards, the non-narrated express bus will take you to any of five stops throughout the park anytime during the day. *($8.50, ages 3-11 $6.50.)* The **Skyfari Aerial Tramway** rises 170 ft. above the park and lasts about two minutes but can save on walking time. *(One-way $2.)* If the bus and tramway appeal to you, purchase your tickets in advance when you buy your zoo admission.

BALBOA PARK & THE EL PRADO MUSEUMS

Most of the museums reside within the resplendent Spanish colonial-style build-ings that line **El Prado Street,** which runs west-to-east through the Park's central **Plaza de Panama.** These ornate structures—designed for the Panama California Exposition of 1915-16 and for the International Expositions of 1935-36—were orig-inally intended to last two years. Since many of the buildings are now going on 80, they are being renovated, this time with a more permanent construction.

BALBOA PARK VISITORS CENTER. The Visitors Center is in the House of Hospi-tality on El Prado St. at the Plaza de Panama. It sells park maps ($0.50) and the Passport to Balboa Park ($30), which allows admission into 13 of the park's muse-ums. Passports are also available at participating museums. The center also sells cold beverages, which are scarce within Balboa Park. *(1549 El Prado. ☎ 239-0512. www.balboapark.org. Open in summer daily 9am-4:30pm; in winter 9am-4pm.)*

MUSEUM OF MAN. Formerly a state building, the Museum of Man anchors the west end of the park. Its much-photographed tower and dome gleam with Spanish mosaic tiles. The museum traces human evolution with exhibits on primates and early man and often stages special exhibits, such as one ancient Mayan civiliza-tions. *(☎ 239-2001; www.museumofman.org. Open daily 10am-4:30pm. $6, seniors $5, ages 6-17 $3; free 3rd Tu of each month. Special exhibits require an additional ticket, usually $8.)*

NATURAL HISTORY MUSEUM. At the east end of Balboa Park, this museum was entirely redone in 2002. It now includes an IMAX theater which is free with admis-sion, as well as many exhibits on the natural wonders of Baja and Southern California. *(Near the intersection of Park Blvd. and Village Pl. at the east end of Balboa Park.* ☎ *232-3821; www.sdnhm.org. Open Memorial Day-Labor Day daily 9:30am-5:30pm; Labor Day-Memorial Day 9:30am-4:30pm. $7, seniors $6, children ages 6-17 $5; free 1st Tu of each month.)*

AEROSPACE MUSEUM. The museum displays 24 full-scale replicas and 44 original planes, as well as aviation history exhibits in the drum-shaped Ford Pavilion. The museum is one of 62 Star Station One sites nationwide that provide information on the International Space Station project. *(2001 Pan American Plaza.* ☎ *234-8291; www.aerospacemuseum.org. Open daily 10am-4:30pm. Extended summer hours. $8, seniors $6, ages 6-17 $3, under 6 and military in uniform free; free 4th Tu of each month.)*

REUBEN H. FLEET SPACE THEATER AND SCIENCE CENTER. The Fleet houses the world's very first Omnimax theater, complete with 153 speakers and a hemispheric planetarium. The science center has interactive exhibits, which change several times per year. *(1875 El Prado Way.* ☎ *238-1233; www.rhfleet.org. Open daily 9:30am-8pm. Exhibit entrance $6.75, seniors $6, ages 3-12 $5.50. 10-14 Omnimax shows per day with additional cost. Exhibit entrance free 1st Tu of each month.)*

CASA DE BALBOA MUSEUMS. The newly constructed **Museum of Photographic Arts (MOPA)** features contemporary photography in 8 to 10 exhibits per year. Its film program examines both the thematic and technical dimensions of serious cinematic works. *(*☎ *238-7559. Open daily 10am-5pm. $6, students $4; free 2nd Tu of each month. Theater admission $5, students $4.)* Recently relocated to the Federal Building, the **San Diego Hall of Champions** is a slick sports museum complete with Astroturf carpeting. Only an odor-proof glass pane separates you from jerseys and shoes worn by Ted Williams and Bill Walton. *(*☎ *234-2544. Open daily 10am-4:30pm. $4; seniors, military $3, ages 6-17 $2; free 2nd Tu of each month.)* The recently renovated 1915 Electricity Building houses the **Museum of San Diego History.** *(*☎ *232-6203. Open Tu-Su 10am-4:30pm. $5, seniors and military $4, children 5-12 $2; free 2nd Tu of each month.)* Also in the building are the **Research Archives.** *(Open Th-Sa 10am-4pm.)* Downstairs, hobbyists drool in the **San Diego Model Railroad Museum.** *(*☎ *696-0199. Open Tu-Fr 11am-4pm, Sa-Su 11am-5pm. $4; seniors $3; military and students $2.50; free 1st Tu of each month.)*

ART IN THE PLAZA DE PANAMA. The **San Diego Museum of Art** has a collection ranging from ancient Asian to contemporary Californian works. At the adjoining outdoor **Sculpture Garden Court,** a sensuous Henry Moore piece presides over other large abstract blocks. *(Museum* ☎ *232-7931, Sculpture Garden* ☎ *696-1990; www.sdmart.org. Open Tu-Su 10am-6pm Th 10am-9pm. $8, seniors and ages 18-24 $6, ages 6-17 $3; special exhibits $2-10 more.)* **Mingei International Museum,** one of the more interesting museums in Balboa Park, emphasizes unusual media and art from outside the US and Europe. *(Across from the Visitors Center.* ☎ *239-0003; www.mingei.org. Open Tu-Su 10am-4pm. $5, students and ages 6-17 $2. Free 3rd Tu of each month.)* Across the Plaza, the **Timken Art Gallery** houses a newly restored portrait by Rembrandt and a collection of Russian church icons. *(1500 El Prado Way.* ☎ *239-5548. Open Oct.-Aug. Tu-Sa 10am-4:30pm, Su 1:30-4:30pm. Free.)* **Spanish Village** is a colony of 300 artists at work in 36 studios. *(At the end of El Prado Way, which is closed to cars, take a left onto Village Pl.* ☎ *233-9050. Open 11am-4pm. Free.)*

BALBOA PARK GARDENS. The **Botanical Building** is a wooden structure filled with the scent of jasmine and the murmur of fountains. The **Desert Garden** and **Rose Garden** offer a striking contrast of flora. The Desert Garden is in full bloom from January to March, while the roses are best admired between April and December. Free ranger-led tours of the central part of Balboa Park leave Tuesday and Sunday at 1pm. Plant-lovers can meet on Saturdays at 10am for a free volunteer-led tour of the park. Each Saturday tour covers a different set of sights within the park. *(2200 Park Blvd.* ☎ *235-1100, tour info 235-1121. Botanical Building open F-W 10am-4pm. Free.)*

PERFORMANCE SPACES. Constructed in 1937, the **Old Globe Theater** is the oldest professional theater in California. Classical and contemporary plays are performed at the adjoining Lowell Davies Outdoor Theatre and the Cassius Carter Center Stage. Tickets for all three stages can be purchased at the box office. (☎ 239-2255; www.theglobetheatres.org. Call for listings, showtimes, and ticket prices.) At the Pan American Plaza, passing jets occasionally cause the actors in the **Starlight Musical Theater** theater to freeze mid-soliloquy and wait for the engine roar to subside before resuming. (☎ 544-7800.) Screaming turbines scarcely affect the action down the road at the **Spreckels Organ Pavilion,** as the racket created by the world's largest outdoor musical instrument can be heard for miles around. (☎ 226-0819. Free performance Su 2pm.)

OLD TOWN

In 1769, Father Serra, supported by a brigade of Spanish infantry, established the first of 21 missions that eventually would line the California coast in the area now known as Old Town. The remnants of this early settlement have become one of San Diego's tourist mainstays. Old Town is centered around the State Park, where 7 original buildings still stand, along with 21 reconstructed ones. While this setup might feel a bit contrived, it offers visitors a genuine glimpse into California history and stuffs them silly with the best Mexican food around (see **Food,** p. 477).

OLD TOWN STATE PARK. The most popular of the area's attractions, the park's early-19th-century buildings contain museums, shops, and restaurants. **Seely Stable** houses a huge museum of 19th-century transportation, namely of the horse and carriage. (☎ 220-5422. Open daily 9am-5pm. Tours every hr. 11am-2pm.) Take a tour of the **Whaley House,** which displays an authentic Lincoln life mask and the piano used in *Gone With the Wind.* The house stands on the site of San Diego's first gallows, which might explain why it is one of two **official haunted houses** recognized by the State of California. (2482 San Diego Ave. ☎ 298-2482, Old Town Historical Society tours 293-0117. Open daily 10am-4:30pm; entrance closes at 4pm. $4, seniors $3, ages 6-12 $2.) Across the street is **Heritage Park,** a group of seven 150-year-old Victorian buildings (six houses and a temple) collected from around the city. Four are open to the public, one of which you can stay in (see p. 474).

SERRA MUSEUM. Its stout adobe walls were raised at the site of the original fort and mission in 1929, and now beautiful Presidio Park surrounds what remains. Inside are exhibits documenting the settlement; outside is a really, really huge flagpole marking the former location of **Fort Stockton.** (In Presidio Park. ☎ 279-3258. Open in summer Tu-Su 10am-4:30pm; Sept.-May F-Su 10am-4:30pm. $5, seniors, students and military $4, ages 6-17 $2.)

COASTAL SAN DIEGO

Less than an hour from downtown, San Diego's superb beaches enrich what is already a wonderful city. Steady winds blow in off the ocean, guaranteeing mostly reliable surf and the perfect temperatures for which San Diego is renowned.

CORONADO ISLAND

Lovely Coronado Island is now in fact a peninsula. A slender 7 mi. strip of machine-hauled sand known as the "Silver Strand" tethers it to the mainland down near Imperial Beach. Famous for its elegant colonial Hotel Del Coronado, the island is perfect for strolling and browsing. Water babies love the frothy waves that break along the southern shore, and outdoor enthusiasts jog, roller-skate and bike along over 7 mi. of paved trails. Coronado has a huge military presence, and the entire northern chunk comprises the **North Island Naval Air Station,** the birthplace of American naval aviation. This area was in fact once an island, until diligent navy men used wheelbarrows full of sand to connect it to the rest of Coronado. Among the island's many naval enterprises is the training area of the famous Navy SEAL (sea, air, and land) commando teams.

The graceful **Coronado Bridge,** built in 1969, guides cars to Coronado from downtown San Diego along I-5. Bus #901 follows the same route, carrying passengers from the Hotel Del to San Diego and back ($2). Those who would rather skim the ocean than the asphalt can take the **Bay Ferry.** (Leaves for Coronado every hr. 9am-9pm, returns every hr. 9:30am-9:30pm. Tickets $2, bikes $0.50 extra, available at San Diego Harbor Excursion, 1050 N. Harbor Dr. ☎234-4111. Tickets also available at the Ferry Landing Marketplace on the Coronado side.) Once across, the **#904 Shuttle** carries passengers from the landing to the Hotel Del Coronado and back. (Leaves every 30min. 9:30am-5:30pm. $1.) Drivers who prefer the scenic route can take I-5 South to the Palm Ave. Exit and follow the signs to Silver Strand Blvd., which goes north into Coronado.

HOTEL DEL CORONADO. Coronado's most famed sight is its Victorian-style Hotel Del Coronado, one of America's largest wooden buildings. The long white verandas and the vermilion spires of the "Del" were built in 1898. It has since become one of the world's great hotels (rooms start at $250 per night), hosting 12 presidents and one blonde bombshell—Marilyn Monroe's 1959 classic *Some Like it Hot* was filmed here. *(1500 Orange Ave. ☎435-6611.)* **Coronado Touring** offers easy 90min. walking tours of the area around the hotel. *(Departs from the lobby of the Glorietta Bay Inn, 1630 Glorietta Bay Blvd. ☎435-5993. Tours Tu, Th, Sa 11am. $8 per person.)*

POINT LOMA

Although the US government owns the outer two-thirds of this peninsula, most of it remains open to citizens and visitors. The **Cabrillo National Monument,** at the tip of Point Loma, is dedicated to the Portuguese explorer Juan Rodríguez Cabrillo, the first European to land in California, but is best known for its views of San Diego and migrating whales. The Visitors Center offers hourly videos or slide presentations as well as information about the monument. *(☎557-5450; www.nps.gov/cabr/. Visitors Center open daily 9am-5pm, 7-day pass $5 per vehicle, $2 per person on foot or bike; Golden Eagle Passport accepted.)* **Whale-watching** season is mid-December to February. The 2 mi. **Bayside Trail** has stations that explain native vegetation and historic military installations and offer magnificent views of the bay and Coronado Island. Point Loma's oceanfront is rife with **tide pools;** turn right off Rte. 209 onto Cabrillo Rd. and drive down to the parking lot at the bottom of the hill. At the highest point of the peninsula sits the interesting museum at **Old Point Loma Lighthouse.** (Open daily 9am-5:15pm.)

OCEAN, MISSION, & PACIFIC BEACHES

Much of San Diego's younger population is drawn to these communities by the respectable surf and the hopping nightlife—noisy bars and grills crowd these shores (see **Food,** p. 478 and **Nightlife,** p. 487).

Ocean Beach (O.B.) caters to a more low-key crowd of surfers than the swanky set to the north. The relaxed atmosphere and gentle surf conditions make O.B. a great place to learn the art of wave-riding. Anglers can try their luck on the Western Hemisphere's longest fishing pier. **O.B. Pier Cafe and Baitshop,** on the pier itself, rents fishing poles and a bucket of bait. No license is required as long as you use no more than one pole. (☎226-3474. Open daily 8am-8pm. $10 per day.) From atop the majestic **Sunset Cliffs Park,** smoochy-smoochy romantics can sway together in the ocean breezes while watching the sun go down over the many surfers at the areas best waves. (Gates open 4am-11pm; quiet hours after 7pm. No camping.) Ocean Beach is also host to an awesome **Farmer's Market** that lasts throughout the year. (Open W 3-9pm.)

SAN DIEGO

**La Jolla,
Pacific Beach &
Mission Beach**

⬛ ACCOMMODATIONS

International House at the
2nd Floor:
    Pacific Beach, **11**
    Mission Beach, **8**
Shell Beach, **1**
Inn at Mission Bay, **10**

🍴 FOOD

Café Crema, **9**
The Pannikin, **4**
Kono's Surf Club, **6**
The Living Room, **2**
Rimel's, **3**

🎭 NIGHTLIFE

The Comedy Store, **5**
Pacific Beach Bar and Grill
and Club Tremors, **7**

In Mission Beach, at the corner of W. Mission Bay Dr. and Mission Blvd., is **Belmont Park,** a combination amusement park and shopping center that draws a youthful crowd from all over the city. Travel back in time on the bumpy **Giant Dipper** roller coaster. ($4. Free parking if you can find a spot.) The **Ocean Front Walk** through Pacific Beach toward La Jolla is always packed with joggers, walkers, cyclists, and the usual beachfront shops. Although both beaches accommodate those who limit their physical activity to shifting on their towels, beachside sports are very popular. Avoid swimming near surfers, and always don protective gear when skating.

SEA WORLD. Take Disneyland, subtract the rides, add a whole lot of fish and other marine life, and you've got Sea World. Though critics have long condemned the practice of training highly intelligent marine mammals to perform unnatural circus acts, most visitors find the playful goofballs irresistible. The A-list star here is the killer whale **Shamu,** whose signature move is a cannonball splash that soaks anyone in the first 20 rows (the original Shamu died long ago, but each of his successors has proudly borne the moniker). The precocious sea lions and intelligent dolphins are equally entertaining. In addition to the performers, there are habitats for sharks, penguins and other water-dwellers such as the endangered manatee, and shows featuring watersports and daredevil jet-ski riders.

Visitors receive a map and schedule upon entering the parking lot; even the most popular events occur only a few times daily, so a quick look at the schedule is a good idea. The park's newest attraction is **Pirates 4-D,** an interactive show geared mainly for the children. If Shamu's splash wasn't wet enough, head towards **Shipwreck Rapids,** Sea World's first-ever adventure ride. Those who feel they need a little cooling down without getting soaked should head to the **Anheuser-Busch Hospitality Tent,** which will give each guest (with 21+ ID) free beer and a short tour of the brewery. (☎226-3901; www.sea-world.com. Open daily in summer 9am-11pm. The park opens at 10am in winter, but closing hours vary. $43, ages 3-9 $33; Parking $7, RVs $9.)

LA JOLLA

The Spanish named the area *La Jolla* ("The Jewel") for its physical beauty. More recently, the craggy promontory developed as an exclusive hideaway for wealthy Easterners, and today it remains true to its tony roots. The gaudy pink hues of the opulent **La Valencia Hotel,** 1132 Prospect St., testify to an age of seaside luxury. While La Jolla is still an upscale enclave, it has evolved into a more inclusive area. From the brand-name shopping districts to the rugged beauty of La Jolla Cove, this eclectic community is a "must-see." To reach La Jolla, take the Ardath Exit west from I-5 or buses #30 or 34 from downtown.

BEACHES. La Jolla claims some of the finest beaches in the city. The **La Jolla Cove** is popular with scuba divers, snorkelers, and brilliantly colored Garibaldi goldfish. Wander south along the cliffs to a semi-circular inlet known as **The Children's Pool.** Established in 1931 by local philanthropist Ellen Browning Scripps as a wildlife preserve, the pool's inhabitants are a thriving community of sea lions who frolic and cavort in the sun. Don't feed the animals, and confine yourself to the established viewing areas lest you disrupt this fragile ecological enclave. Surfers are especially fond of the waves at **Tourmaline Beach** and **Windansea Beach,** which can be too strong for novices. **La Jolla Shores,** next to Scripps and UCSD, has gentle swells ideal for surfers, boogie boarders, and swimmers. **Black's Beach** is not officially a nude beach, but let's just say there are plenty of wieners and buns at *this* snack bar. The north end generally attracts gay patrons. **Torrey Pines Glider Port** is where hang gliders leap into the breeze for unadulterated views of the beaches below. To reach the Glider Port, take I-5 to Genesee Ave., go west, and turn left on N. Torrey Pines Rd. The beach is accessible by a steep staircase just south of the glider port and can be very popular with surfers.

MUSEUMS. The **San Diego Museum of Contemporary Art** houses a rotating exhibition of pop, minimalist, and conceptualist art (shared with the downtown branch; see p. 479). The museum is as visually stunning as the art it contains, with gorgeous ocean views and high-ceilinged, light-filled spaces. There are daily guided tours at various hours in both English and Spanish. (700 Prospect St. ☎858-454-3541; www.mcasd.org. Open June-Aug. M-Tu and Th-F 11am-8pm, Sa-Su 11am-5pm; Sept.-May Su-Tu and F-Sa 11am-5pm, Th 11am-8pm. $4; students, seniors, military, ages 12-18 $2.) The ▧**Birch Aquarium at the Scripps Institute of Oceanography** has great, educational exhibits, including a tank with a portly octopus and a large collection of seahorses. This isn't Sea World; revenues support actual oceanographic research. (2300 Expedition Way. ☎858-534-3474; http://aquarium.ucsd.edu. Open daily 9am-5pm. $9.50, students with ID $6.50, seniors $8, ages 3-17 $6. Parking $3.)

OTHER SIGHTS. The somewhat isolated **University of California at San Diego (UCSD)** sits above La Jolla. Buses #30 and 34 take you to campus, but cars or bikes are invaluable for getting to the campus's many residential and academic colleges. Be sure to check out the library, a space-age structure that was designed by Dr. Seuss. Kiosks on Gilman and Northview Dr. dispense maps and give information about campus tours. (☎858-534-2208. Open daily 7am-9pm.) At the foot of Girard Ave. in **La Jolla Village** is **Scripps Park,** where great waves shake the rocky shore, sending up plumes of silver sea spray. Ocean lovers, or lovers of any kind, can stroll here in the evenings and loll on the carefully manicured lawns.

ELSEWHERE IN SAN DIEGO

MISSION BASILICA SAN DIEGO DE ALCALÁ. Father Serra's group of soldiers were apparently a rough and unholy bunch, because in 1774 the padre moved his mission some 6 mi. away from their settlement to its current location. The mission is still an active parish church and contains a chapel, gardens, a small museum, and a reconstruction of Serra's living quarters. *(Take bus #43 or I-8 East to the Mission Gorge Rd. Exit. Turn left on Twain Ave. The mission will be 2 blocks ahead on the right side. ☎281-8449. Visitors Center open daily 9am-4:45pm. $3, students and seniors $2, under 12 $1, 45 min. tote-a-tape guided tours $2. Mass held daily at 7am and 5:30pm; visitors welcome.)*

QUALCOMM STADIUM. If you've been wondering about the lightning bolt stickers posted all over town, head out here on a fall Sunday and look at the helmets of the **San Diego Chargers,** the city's pro football team. The stadium also hosts baseball's **San Diego Padres,** at least until the new stadium is completed. *(West of the Mission near the junction of I-8 and I-15. Chargers tickets ☎280-2121, Padres tickets ☎881-6500.)*

IN THE NAVY. Freedom lovers can take a free tour of the gigantic **USS Constellation** (the vessel with the number "64" on its super-structure, visible from San Diego's downtown waterfront) and other aircraft carriers. *(Reservations ☎545-2427. Daily tours at 10am, 1, and 3pm. Reserve at least 48hr. in advance for weekend tours.)*

■ SEASONAL EVENTS

Gorgeous weather and strong community spirit make the San Diego area an ideal place for local festivals. The following is by no means a comprehensive list, so check the beach community weeklies for further festival information.

Penguin Day Ski Fest, De Anza Cove (☎858-276-0840), in Mission Bay. Jan. 1, 2003. This unique festival requires its participants to water-ski in the ocean and to lie on a block of ice without a wet suit. Those who do are honored with a "penguin patch," while those who fail get only a "chicken patch."

Ocean Beach Kite Festival, 4726 Santa Monica Ave. (☎531-1527), in Ocean Beach. 1st Sa in Mar. Kite-construction and flying competitions.

29th Annual San Diego Crew Classic, Crown Pt. Shores, (☎858-488-0700), in Mission Bay. First weekend in Apr. Crews from the US, Canada, and Europe compete at the only major collegiate regatta on the West Coast. $5.

San Diego Earthfair 2003, in Balboa Park (☎858-496-6666; www.earthdayweb.org). Mid-Apr.; 10am-5pm. Kids' activities, booths, exhibits, and dance festival. Free.

Summer Stargazing, at San Diego State University's Mt. Laguna Observatory (☎594-6182). June 1-Sept. 2 F 2-6pm, Sa 9am-6pm. Open to the public with free tickets available through the US Forest Service.

Summer Pops 2003 (☎235-0804), performed all summer by the San Diego Symphony. Late June-Sept. 2 on a stage in the harbor. Cheap tickets begin at $15.

Ocean Beach Street Fair and Chili Cook-Off (☎226-1936), Ocean Beach. Last weekend in June. Newport St. is lined with arts booths during this 2-day fest.

Pacific Beach Restaurant Walk (☎858-273-3303). End of June, noon-5pm. Free samples from more than 20 Pacific Beach restaurants.

Hillcrest Cityfest Street Fair (☎299-3330), on 5th Ave. between Ivy Ln. and University Ave., in the heart of San Diego's gay community. 2nd Su in Aug. Arts, crafts, food, live entertainment, and beer garden.

US Open Sand Castle Competition (☎424-6663), Imperial Beach pier. 3rd weekend in July. Sand-sculpting demigods exercise their craft in this largest and longest-running of American sand castle events. Parades, fireworks, and children's castle contest.

SummerFest La Jolla Chamber Music Festival (☎858-459-3724), La Jolla Museum of Contemporary Art. Late Aug.

La Jolla Rough Water Swim (☎858-456-2100), early Sept. Start and finish at the La Jolla Cove. Largest annual rough water competition in the US.

▩ ⛶ NIGHTLIFE & ENTERTAINMENT

Nightlife in San Diego isn't centered around any one strip, but scattered in several distinct pockets of action. Upscale locals and trend-seeking tourists flock to the **Gaslamp Quarter,** where numerous restaurants and bars feature live music nightly. The **Hillcrest** area, next to Balboa Park, draws a young, largely gay crowd to its clubs and dining spots. Away from downtown, the **beach areas** (especially Garnet Ave. in Pacific Beach) are loaded with clubs, bars, and cheap eateries that attract college-age revelers. The city's definitive source of entertainment info is the free *Reader,* found in shops, coffeehouses, and visitors centers. Listings can also be found in the *San Diego Union-Tribune*'s Thursday "Night and Day" section.

If cruisin' and boozin' isn't your idea of nightlife, you can spend a more sedate evening at one of San Diego's excellent theaters, such as the **Balboa Theatre,** 225 Broadway Ave. (☎544-1000), and the **Horton Grand Theatre,** 444 4th Ave. (☎234-9583), both downtown. Call for show information; ticket prices vary according to the show. The **La Jolla Playhouse,** 2910 La Jolla Village Dr., presents shows at the Mandell Weiss Theatre on the UC San Diego campus in La Jolla. To get there, turn onto Expedition from N. Torrey Pines Rd. (☎858-550-1010; www.lajollaplay-house.com.) On Coronado Island, sophisticates can take in a performance at the **Lamb's Players Theatre,** 1142 Orange Ave., San Diego's only year-round professional theater. (☎437-0600; www.lambsplayer.org.)

LATE-NIGHT RESTAURANTS

Although the restaurants below offer complete meals, they are better-known as night spots, be they bars, music clubs, or dance clubs.

Pacific Beach Bar and Grill and **Club Tremors,** 860 Garnet Ave. (☎858-272-1242 and 277-7228, respectively), in **Pacific Beach.** Live DJ packs the 2-level dance floor with a young and slinky crowd. The Bar and Grill has cheap, delicious food, more than 20 beers on tap, and live music on Sundays. Cover $5 if you enter through Club Tremors. Club open Th-Sa 9pm-1:30am; bar open 11am-1:30am; kitchen closes at midnight.

Cafe Lu Lu, 419 F. St. (☎858-238-0114), in the **Gaslamp.** Coffeehouse designed by local artists. See and be seen as you sip a raspberry-mocha ($3.75). Standing room only after midnight on the weekends. Open Su-Th 9am-1am, F-Sa 9am-3am.

Dick's Last Resort, 345 4th Ave. (☎858-231-9100), in the **Gaslamp.** Buckets of Southern grub attract a wildly hedonistic bunch. Dick's stocks beers from around the globe, from Africa to Trinidad, on top of native brews like the Dixieland Blackened Voodoo Lager. No cover for the nightly rock or blues, but you'd better be buyin'. Lunch burgers under $4, dinner entrees $10-18. Open daily 11am-1:30am.

CLUBS & BARS

▩ **Croce's Top Hat Bar and Grille** and **Croce's Jazz Bar,** 802 5th Ave. (☎233-4355), at F St. in the **Gaslamp.** Ingrid Croce, widow of singer Jim Croce, created this rock/blues bar and classy jazz bar side-by-side on the 1st floor of the historic Keating building. Live music nightly. Cover $5-10, includes 2 live shows. Open daily 7:30am-3pm and 5pm-midnight; bar open until 2am.

The Casbah, 2501 Kettner Blvd. (☎232-4355). This intimate nightspot is the best live music venue in the city. Cover varies, but it is always 21+. Call ahead for a schedule, as sometimes tickets sell out. Hours vary, usually 5pm-2am.

The Bitter End, 770 5th Ave. (☎338-9300), in the **Gaslamp.** This upscale, 3-level dance club is always packed with people dressed to impress. DJs spin on the upper floors, while live music pounds below. 21+. $5-10 cover after 9pm. Open daily 5am-2am.

The Comedy Store, 916 Pearl St. (☎858-454-9176), in **La Jolla.** One of the few joints around where you can be a part of the show. Clamber onstage Monday at 8pm for Pot-luck Night (call and sign up after 3pm). Better-known comedians other evenings. 21+. 2-drink minimum; drinks $3. Shows W-Th 9pm ($5), F-Sa 8 and 10:30pm ($15-20).

Cafe Sevilla, 555 4th Ave. (☎233-5979), in the **Gaslamp.** Downstairs, live bands lead patrons in Latin dances from salsa to flamenco every night. The Friday night flamenco dinner show includes a 3-course meal, the show and admission to the club afterwards for $40. Dress to impress. 21+ downstairs. Open Su-Th 5-11pm, F-Sa 5pm-1am.

GAY & LESBIAN NIGHTLIFE

Lesbian and gay clubs cluster in **University Heights** and **Hillcrest. The Flame,** 3780 Park Blvd., in Hillcrest, is a popular lesbian dance club. (☎295-4163. 21+. Open M-Th and Sa-Su 5pm-2am, F 4pm-2am.) **Bourbon Street,** 4612 Park Blvd., in University Heights, is a neighborhood bar with a gay following. (☎291-0173. 21+. Open M-F 2pm-2am, Sa-Su 11am-2pm.) **The Brass Rail,** 3796 5th Ave., in Hillcrest, feature dancing and drag on weekends. (☎298-2233. 21+. Cover Th-Sa after 9pm $5-7. Open daily noon-2am.)

SAN DIEGO'S NORTH COUNTY

San Diego's North County is a nearly unbroken beachland that stretches north from La Jolla toward Los Angeles. Sun and surf lovers alike come to enjoy this ocean playground. Several resort communities have arisen along the sand and crumbling cliffs. Large-scale attractions have also found their homes here: San Diego's Wild Animal Park and Legoland each provide a day's worth of entertainment. All of the North County towns are easily accessible along I-5 and historic U.S. 101 (the Pacific Coast Hwy.) by car, bike, or bus. Take North County Transit District bus #301 from La Jolla's University Towne Centre as far as Oceanside. (Daily every 30min. 5am-10pm; fare $1.50, free transfers.) The Coaster, a high-speed commuter train, also provides transportation from North County into downtown San Diego. (☎800-COASTER/262-7837; www.gonctd.com. 11 trains daily. 5am-7pm; fares $3.50-$4.75 depending on distance.) For more North County Transit info, call ☎800-266-6883.

Opportunities to sportfish off a pier or to book passage on a **deep-sea fishing** charter abound up and down the coast (see p. 493). The waters off the coast all the way down to Baja California teem with monstrous yellowfin tuna, giant grouper, and the ultimate trophy fish—the marlin. Imagine yourself bobbing in the foamy chop like "Papa" Hemingway himself, wrestling with a great beast, and then hauling your vanquished foe aboard.

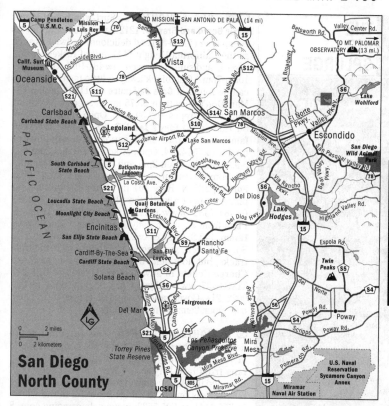

San Diego North County

DEL MAR   ☎858

North of La Jolla is the affluent suburb of Del Mar (pop. 5100), home to thorough-bred racehorses and famous fairgrounds. Lining either side of Camino Del Mar are many small boutiques and good eats. During June and the early July, Del Mar hosts the **San Diego County Fair,** one of the largest fairs in California. Solana Beach to the north boasts the Cedros Design District, full of warehouses turned artist studios.

7 PRACTICAL INFORMATION. The **Del Mar Chamber of Commerce and Visitor Center,** 1104 Camino Del Mar #214, has brochures and handouts. (☎ 755-4844; www.del-marchamber.org. Open Tu-Th 10am-4pm.) The **Amtrak** station, 105 Cedros Ave. (☎ 800-USA-RAIL/872-7245), in Solana Beach, is not only architecturally interesting, but also sends 11 **trains** per day to L.A. ($22 one-way). **Internet access** is available at the **Del Mar Public Library,** 1309 Camino Del Mar. Call ahead to reserve a one hour block of time, or drop in to use one of the computers for 15min. (☎ 755-1666. Open Tu 10am-6pm, W-Th 10am-8pm, F-Sa 10am-5pm, Su 1-5pm.)

THE BIG SPLURGE

COASTAL LUXURY

For complete indulgence, head up to **La Costa Resort and Spa,** in Carlsbad. This world-renowned tennis, golf, and spa resort is undergoing a 50 million dollar renovation, to be completed by spring of 2003. Set among rolling coastal hills at the edge of a lagoon teeming with wildlife, La Costa may be the perfect reward for having spent weeks sleeping in hostel bunks and on camping mats.

Golfers will find paradise at La Costa, home of two PGA championship courses. Those looking to improve their game can take lessons at The La Costa Golf School, which is ranked among the best in the country. For those who prefer racquets to clubs, La Costa offers 21 tennis courts with multiple clay, grass, and composite surfaces.

After a hard day on the green or the court, guests can head over to the brand-new 40,000 sq. ft. La Costa Spa. Mud wraps, shiatsu, aromatherapy, Roman pools, body scrubs, and Swiss showers will rejuvenate even the most world-weary traveler. (2100 Costa Del Mar Rd. ☎438-9111 or 800-854-5000; www.lacosta.com. Rooms start at $345, and level off at a cool $2400.)

FOOD & NIGHTLIFE. Surf-weathered locals favor **Board and Brew ❶,** 1212 Camino Del Mar, for its cheap beer ($1.50-$2) and delicious sandwiches such as the California Delight ($4), full of turkey, cream cheese, and sunflower seeds. (☎481-1021. Open daily 10am-7pm.) One block away, a little taste of Europe can be found at **Cafe de France ❷,** 1140 Camino Del Mar. Don't miss their $3.75 lunch specials including quiches or crepes. (☎350-1432. Open M-Sa 6am-6pm, Su 7am-6pm.) **Tony's Jacal ❶,** 621 Valley Ave., is a family-run establishment serving up zesty burritos for $4. (☎755-2274. Open M and W-F 11am-2pm and 5-9:30pm, Sa 11am-2pm and 5-10pm, Su 3-9:30pm.) For some awesome deep-dish pizza and "grog," **Pizza Port ❷,** 135 N. Hwy 101 in Solana Beach, is your place. Expect a wait, the place is usually packed. (☎481-7332; www.pizzaport.com. Pizzas from $6. Pints from $2. Open daily 11am-11pm.) The **Belly Up Tavern,** 143 S. Cedros Ave., off Lomas Santa Fe Dr. in Solana Beach, was once a warehouse near the train tracks, but now belts blues, rock, reggae, and jazz. Charge tickets in advance (☎481-8140 or 619-220-TIXS/8497; www.bellyup.com), or at the door. (☎481-9022. 21+. Cover varies with artist; expect $5-27. Open daily noon-2am; live music nightly.)

SIGHTS & BEACHES. The celebrity-studded **Del Mar Thoroughbred Club,** at the corner of Via de la Valle and Jimmy Durante Blvd., fills with racing fans from late July to the week after Labor Day. Founded in 1937 by Bing Crosby and Pat O'Brien, the racetrack is one of the most beautiful in the world. (☎755-1141 or 795-5533; www.delmarracing.com. 8 races per day M and W-F, 10 on Sa, 9 on Su. Post Time 2pm. Gates open M and W-F noon, Sa-Su 11:30am. $5 general admission, $8 clubhouse.) **Torrey Pines State Reserve and Beach,** along the coast just south of Del Mar, is one of only two native torrey pine groves on earth. (The other is on Santa Rosa Island in Channel Islands National Park; see p. 443.) Look for the entrance off Camino Del Mar about ½ mi. south of Del Mar Village. (☎755-2063; www.torreypine.org. Park open 7am-sunset. $2 per vehicle, pedestrians and bicyclists free.) The **Torrey Pines Lodge,** at the top of the hill on the entrance road, provides info on activities and hiking trails, as well as an exhibit on why the torrey pines are so unique. (Open daily 9am-sunset.) The park trails are wonderful for runners, cyclists, hikers and those who enjoy rules—there is no camping, no picnicking, no food, no smoking, no dogs (even if kept in cars), and no straying off the established trails. Try the beach trail down to flat rock for amazing views (1.5 mi. round trip) The 6 mi. of rocky beach are popular with hang gliders.

ENCINITAS, LEUCADIA, & CARLSBAD ☎760

North of Del Mar along the Pacific Coast Highway lie the towns of Encinitas and Leucadia, which betray traces of their hippie-mecca past through their hallucinogenic beauty and tie-dyed inhabitants. Farther up the coast is the charming lagoon hideaway of Carlsbad, where U.S. 101, here known as Carlsbad Blvd., winds past silky sands and shingled homes adorned with wild rosebushes.

▓ PRACTICAL INFORMATION. Orient yourself at the **Carlsbad Convention and Visitor's Center,** 400 Carlsbad Village Dr. (☎434-6093; www.carlsbadca.org. Open M-F 9am-5pm, Sa 10am-4pm, Su 10am-3pm.) **Internet access** is available at the **Georgina Cole Library,** 1250 Carlsbad Village Dr., near downtown (☎434-2870; open M-Th 9am-9pm, F-Sa 9am-5pm), or the **Carlsbad City Library,** 1775 Dove Ln. (☎602-2039. Open M-Th 9am-9pm, F-Sa 9am-5pm.)

▓▓ ACCOMMODATIONS & FOOD. Inexpensive lodging can be difficult to find in these resort communities. A great value can be found at the **Surf Motel ❸,** 3136 Carlsbad Blvd. Large, comfy rooms are located right across the street from the beach and a block from Carlsbad Village. (☎729-7961. Rooms $99-119; in winter $55-69.) A cheaper and more reliable alternative is **Motel 6 ❸,** 1006 Carlsbad Village Dr., just east of Carlsbad Village. (☎434-7135. Singles $50; doubles $56. Rates $6-8 higher on weekends.) Other locations are at 6117 Paseo del Norte, off I-5 at the Palomar Airport Rd. Exit (☎438-1242), and farther south, on Raintree Dr. (☎431-0745). The **Portofino Beach Inn ❹,** 186. N. Hwy. 101, in Encinitas, has nice rooms and a jacuzzi near the beach. (☎944-0301. Singles $70; doubles $88. Slightly lower rates in winter.)

Camping near the beach is allowed at **South Carlsbad State Park ❶** or at **San Elijo State Park ❶.** Both campgrounds are situated atop cliffs, and don't offer much in terms of privacy. However, the beaches below are beautiful. (South Carlsbad ☎438-3143. San Elijo ☎753-5091. Water, restrooms, showers, general stores, picnic tables, BBQ stands, and fire pits are all available. Reservations for both campgrounds can be made up to 7 months in advance by calling ☎800-444-7275 or logging on to www.parks.ca.gov. Reservations a must in summer. $12 a night for tents; $18 for RVs up to 35 ft.)

There are lots of good and varied beachfront restaurants along U.S. 101 (Pacific Coast Hwy.). Locals and tourists cram into the small and intimate dining area at ▓**Trattoria I Trulli ❸,** 830 S. Coast Hwy. 101, for good reason: the food is delicious. (☎943-6800. Dinner entrees from $10. Open Su-Th 11:30am-2:30pm and 5-10pm, F-Sa 11:30am-2:30pm and 5-10:30pm.) If the wait is too much, head one block away to **Rosanna's Italian Trattoria ❸,** 806 S. Coast Hwy. 101. Though the decor might not be as elegant, the food is just as excellent. (☎942-0738. Dinner entrees from $10. Open daily 10am-3pm and 5-10pm.) Life is sweet at **Honey's Bistro and Bakery ❶,** 623 S. Coast Hwy., in Encinitas, where they serve up large, fresh salads ($6), sandwiches ($5), and soups ($4), as well as mouth watering baked goods. (☎942-5433. Open daily 5:30am-3:30pm.) At the **Miracles Cafe ❷,** 1953 San Elijo Ave., in Encinitas, six dollars will get you banana Belgian waffles or a Supreme Scream sandwich. (☎943-7924. Open M-Th 6am-10pm, F-Sa 6am-11pm, Su 7am-9pm.)

◙ SIGHTS & SEASONAL EVENTS. In Encinitas, truth-seekers can partake of restorative contemplation at the new age ▓**Self-Realization Fellowship,** 215 K St. The lush and immaculate gardens furnish meditative serenity, especially when lit by a setting sun. (☎753-1811. Gardens open Tu-Sa 9am-5pm, Su 11am-5pm. Free.) To counter the asceticism of the Self-Realization Fellowship, you can indulge your materialistic appetites at the weekly **Seaside Bazaar,** along U.S. 101 at the north end of town, which peddles trinkets, jewelry, crafts, foods, and other odds and ends. (☎753-1611. Sa-Su 9am-4:30pm.) For floral fun, stroll through the **Quail Botanical Gardens,** 230 Quail Gardens Dr., where you will find one of the world's most diverse plant collections. Be sure to check out the huge bamboo groves and the beautiful waterfall. (☎436-3036; www.qbgardens.com. Open daily 9am-5pm. Free tours with admission Sa at 10am. $5, seniors $4, ages 5-12 $2.) **Legoland** is a goofball tribute to the interlocking kiddie blocks that have inspired countless junior architects. It can be a fun place, especially if you're a 12-and-under Legomaniac. Exit I-5 in Carlsbad at Cannon Rd., and continue to One Legoland Dr. (☎918-LEGO/5346. Open fall-spring M and Th-Su 10am-5pm, spring weekends open until 6pm; summer daily 10am-8pm. $40, ages 3-16 $34. Parking $7.) Shake, rattle, and roll at the extensive **Museum of Making Music,** 5790 Armada Dr., where over 450 vintage musical instruments highlight a survey of 20th-century American music. (☎438-5996 or 877-551-9976; www.museumofmakingmusic.org. Open Tu-Su 10am-5pm. $5; seniors, students, military, and ages 4-18 $3.)

The first Sunday in May and November, the famous **Carlsbad Village Street Faire,** the largest one-day fair in California, attracts over 900 vendors and 80,000 people. From early March to late April, the kaleidoscopic **Flower Fields** bloom with diverse wildflowers. The flowers cover a mile of hillside along I-5 north of Palomar Airport Rd. Take the Palomar Airport Exit off I-5, head east along Palomar Airport Rd. to the light at Paseo del Norte, and turn left. (☎431-0352. $4, ages 3-12 $2.) Upset that you can't pick the flowers? Try some fruit instead. **U-Pick Strawberries,** north of Cannon Rd. at Paseo del Norte, opens its farms up to the public for harvesting. (Open May to mid-July daily 8:30am-6:30pm. $4 small bucket, $8 large.)

◪ BEACHES. The California state park system maintains a number of beautiful beaches in the area. **Carlsbad State Beach** is long and attractive, despite the view of the mammoth Encinas Power Plant, which occupies the coast to the south. **Offshore Surf Shop,** 3179 Carlsbad Blvd., rents boogie boards and 6-8 ft. "soft" surfboards. (☎619-729-4934. Open daily 9am-7:30pm. Boogie boards $3 per hr., $10 per day. Surfboards $5 per hr., $25 per day. A $100 deposit for boogie boards and $300 deposit for surfboards or credit card is required for rentals.) The **Encinitas City Beach** has multiple access points. Try the **Stonesteps** at the end of South El Portal St. to get to over 3 mi. of public sands. Surfing neophytes can score a board at **Leucadia Surfboards,** 1354 N. Highway 101. Woody, the super-hip manager, is always psyched to help out. (☎632-9700. Open M-F 10am-5pm, Sa-Su 9am-5pm. Boards $5 per hr., $20 per day.) Cardiff-by-the-Sea is near **San Elijo Beach State Park** (☎753-5091) and **Cardiff State Beach** to the south. If you have a car, these beautiful beaches are worth the drive.

OCEANSIDE ☎760

Oceanside (pop. 146,230) is the largest and probably the least glamorous of San Diego's coastal resort towns. Home to Camp Pendleton, a Marine Corps base as well as one of the world's greatest surfing beaches at Oceanside Harbor, Oceanside suffers from a split-personality. The pier at Pierview Way attracts serious surfers year-round. Beaches are patrolled by lifeguards, and surfers stick to designated areas. The free parking in the lots off Mission Ave. fills up in summer, but metered curb spots can be found nearby.

◪ PRACTICAL INFORMATION. The **Oceanside Transit Center,** 235 S. Tremont, houses the local **Amtrak** (☎800-USA-RAIL/872-7245 or 722-4622) and **Greyhound** (☎722-1587) stations. The newly-renovated **California Welcome Center,** 928 N. Coast Hwy., has info about goings-on and a toll-free hotel reservation line. (☎721-1101 or

800-350-7873. Open daily 9am-5pm; closed holidays.) Thirty minute blocks of **internet access** are available at the **Oceanside Public Library,** 330 N. Coast Hwy. in the civic center. (☎435-5600. Open M-W 10am-8pm, Th-Sa 10am-5:30pm.) Access is also available at the **Oceanside Public Library Community Computer Center,** 321 North Nevada St. (☎435-5600. Open M-Th 10am-9pm, F-Sa 10am-5pm, Su noon-5pm. Call to reserve a computer.)

ⁿⁿ ACCOMMODATIONS & FOOD. Unlike its ritzier neighbors, Oceanside offers many inexpensive lodgings. Budget motels line Hwy. 101 both north and south of the main strip, though not all are reputable. A good choice is the dyslexic **Motel 9 ❸,** 822 N. Coast Hwy., which offers clean, simple rooms with cable TV and mini-fridges. (☎721-0300. Singles and doubles Su-Th $55, F-Sa $70.) Power up before hitting the waves at **The Longboarder ❶,** 228 N. Coast Hwy., which serves burgers ($5-6) and heaping omelettes ($5) to its surfer crowd. (☎721-6776. Open M-F 7am-2pm, Sa-Su 7am-3pm.)

ⁿⁿ SIGHTS & ACTIVITIES. The pier gets crowded during the **World Body Surfing Championships** in mid-August. Call the Oceanside Special Events Office (☎435-5540) for more info. With so much surfing history made along its shores, Oceanside is the perfect place for the ▩**California Surf Museum,** 223 N. Coast Hwy. (☎721-6876. Open Th-M 10am-4pm. Free.) You can catch your dinner by renting gear at **Helgren's Sportfishing Trips,** 315 Harbor Drive South. (☎722-2133. One-day license $7.25. Surface fishing rod $10, deep fishing rod $12. Half-day trips on the fishing boat $29, full-day $55. Non-fishing harbor cruise daily $10, ages 5-12 $5. Times vary with the seasons.) If you prefer good old-fashioned American mayhem, squeeze off a few rounds at **Iron Sights Public Indoor Shooting Range,** 618 Airport Rd. (☎721-4388. Prices vary but basic packages begin at $25, including ammo. Open daily 10am-10pm.) **Mission San Luis Rey de Francia,** 4050 Mission Ave., was founded in 1798, but the only original building still standing is the church built in 1807. Follow Mission Ave. east from N. Coast Hwy. for 4 mi., or take NCTD bus #303 at Rte. 21 and Mission Ave. (☎757-3651. Museum open daily 10am-4:30pm. $4, students and seniors $3, ages 8-14 $1. Cemetery free.)

ESCONDIDO ☎760

Thirty miles north of San Diego, amid rolling, semi-arid hills that blossom with wildflowers in the spring, lies Escondido (pop. 125,000), a good base from which to explore the surrounding countryside as well as home to several of its own attractions. The **San Diego North Convention and Visitors Bureau,** 360 N. Escondido Blvd., gives info on Escondido and the beach cities to the west. (☎745-4741, 24hr. hotline 800-848-3336. Open M-F 8:30am-5pm.) **Greyhound** (☎745-6522) stops at 700 W. Valley Pkwy., and sends 7 buses per day to San Diego ($9) and 12 to L.A. ($13).

Off Rte. 78, budget motels and fast food chains cluster to an extent that is astonishing even in Southern California. Exit at Center City Pkwy.; turn right on Mission Ave. **The Mt. Vernon ❷,** 501 W. Mission Ave., just before Washington on Center City Pkwy., offers unusually large, well-worn rooms with pool, jacuzzi, and a tennis court. (☎745-6100. Singles $40; doubles $44. Rates around $5 higher on weekends.)

A look at the free-roaming endangered species of the 2100-acre **San Diego Wild Animal Park** is an essential part of any trip to San Diego. From I-15, take the Via Rancho Pkwy. Exit (County Rte. S78) and follow the signs. While some of the exhibits are similar to any other zoo, the highlight of the park is the large enclosures where many species roam freely. The best way to see these enclosures is via the open-air **Wgasa Bush Line Railway,** a 55min. monorail safari included in park admission that travels through four created habitat areas. The park has typical shops, restaurants, and animal shows, but for adventure, try the 1 mi. Heart of Africa hike, meant to simulate a real African safari. For those willing to shell out some more dollars, the open-air **Photo Caravan** offers up-close and personal views of many animals. (☎619-718-3050. 1¾hr. safari $99, 3½hr. safari $145. Reservations required.) Or fall asleep to the sounds of an elephant snore at the **Roar and Snore overnight camping safari.** (☎619-718-3050. April-Oct. F-Su nights $126, includes park admission, all meals, camping, equipment, and special tours and programs.) Most of the park, including the monorail, is wheelchair accessible, but steep hills may require detours. (☎747-8702; www.wildanimalpark.org. Rail tours June-Aug. 9:30am-9pm; Sept.-May 9:30am-4pm; sit on the right if possible, unless you didn't get enough of the California chaparral on the drive in. Renting binoculars ($5-10) at the park entrance may enhance tour. Park open daily 9am, closing times vary with the season. $26.50, ages 3-11 $19.50. Parking $6. Discounts are often available at tourist bureaus and hotels.)

NORTH OF ESCONDIDO

Although the Hale telescope at Palomar Mountain's **Palomar Observatory** is over 40 years old, it remains one of the world's largest and greatest astronomical instruments. The observatory is accessible via S6. Diehard science buffs will find the sparse museum fascinating. (☎742-2119. Open daily 9am-4pm. Free.)

Cleveland National Forest contains the observatory and several excellent campgrounds, all of which are closed in the winter. S6 passes the wooded **Fry Creek ❶** and more airy and open **Observatory campgrounds ❶**, both of which provide water, toilets, and access to hiking trails (sites $12). A left onto S7 at the mountaintop store will bring you to **Palomar Mountain State Park ❶**. The park offers camping, showers, hiking trails, and fishing, but swimming is not allowed. (☎800-444-PARK/7275; www.parks.ca.gov. Reservations necessary on summer weekends well in advance. Sites $12; hiker/biker sites $3; vehicles $2.) All of these campgrounds are above 5000 ft., so warm clothing even in summer is a necessity.

One of California's still-operating missions is west of Mt. Palomar, on Rte. 76, 6 mi. east of I-15. The **Mission San Antonio de Pala**, on the Pala Indian Reservation, was an outpost of Oceanside's Mission San Luis Rey in 1816; it has since converted thousands of Native Americans. (☎742-3317. Open W-Su 10am-4pm. $2.)

BAJA CALIFORNIA

Peeled away from the mainland ages ago by earthquakes, the peninsula of Baja California claims a spectacular and diverse landscape: sparse expanses of desert give way to barren mountains that jut into Baja's azure sky at incredible angles, and bizarrely blue-green waters slap at Baja's miles of uninhabited shore. Called *el otro México* (the other Mexico), Baja is neither here nor there, not at all California yet nothing like mainland Mexico. A solid stream of tourists flows from California into Baja to surf, fish, and drink to their hearts' content. To explore the rest of Baja, pick up a trusty copy of 🖉*Let's Go: Mexico.*

The completion of the Transpeninsular Highway has made it quicker to travel the peninsula by **car,** but prepare to be cruising along at 60 mph and suddenly careen into a rutted curve that can only be taken at 30 mph. If you need roadside assistance, the *Ángeles Verdes* (Green Angels) pass along Hwy. 1 twice per day. Unleaded gas may be in short supply along this route, so don't pass a PEMEX station without filling your tank. All of Baja is in the *Zona Libre* (Free Zone), so strict vehicle permits are not required. If you will be driving in Baja for more than 72hr., you need to get a free permit at the border by showing the vehicle's title and proof of registration. You also need to pick up an US$18 tourist card from the border station if you plan to travel further south than Ensenada or for longer than three days. It is a good idea to get additional **car insurance** (around US$8.50 per day) in San Ysidro, at one of the many drive-thru insurance stores, or through AAA just before crossing the border. US insurance policies are not valid while driving in Mexico.

If your travels in Mexico will be limited to Tijuana and Rosarito, you will probably not need to exchange your dollars for pesos; the vast majority of shops and restaurants in these cities take greenbacks. If you plan to travel farther into Baja, prices will be quoted in pesos and some places will not accept dollars. Prices listed are in pesos or dollars. **If you have an emergency while in Baja California, dial ☎060.**

HIGHLIGHTS OF BAJA CALIFORNIA

CERVEZA. The drinking age in Mexico is 18.

THE BORDER. The border town of Tijuana (p. 497) thrives on transition—on those who cross the border from the California side to indulge in the benefits of less stringent Mexican laws, and those who await immigration into the US.

BAJA ESSENTIALS

DON'T DRINK THE WATER

Traveler's diarrhea, or *turista*, is one of the less cherished experiences encountered by many visitors to Mexico. *Turista* lasts two or three days, and its symptoms include cramps, nausea, vomiting, chills, and fever. To avoid *turista*, never drink unbottled water in Mexico; ask for *agua purificada* in restaurants and hotels. If you must purify your own water, bring it to a rolling boil (simmering isn't enough) and let it boil for 30min., or treat it with iodine drops or tablets. Don't even brush your teeth with tap water, and beware of impure ice cubes. Other sources for traveler's diarrhea include uncooked vegetables, shellfish, unpasteurized milk, and sauces that contain raw eggs. Imodium is a standard diarrhea-only treatment, but for all-out *turista*, take Lomotil, a drug sold over the counter in Mexican pharmacies. So don't drink the water—drink beer (did we mention that the drinking age is 18?).

TELEPHONES IN BAJA CALIFORNIA

To call Mexico direct from home, dial:

1. The international access code of your home country.
2. 052 (Mexico's country code).
3. The city code (see the city's **Practical Information** section) and local number.

CALLING ABROAD FROM MEXICO. The **LADATEL phones** that have popped up all over the country have revolutionized the way Mexico calls. To operate any LADA-TEL, you'll need to buy a colorful prepaid **phone card,** available at most *papelerías* (stationery stores) or *tiendas de abarrotes* (general stores)—look for the "De venta aquí LADATEL" signs posted in store windows. Cards come in 30-, 50-, and 100-peso increments. Once armed with your precious LADATEL phone card, calling using various methods can be a snap.

To call home with a calling card, contact the operator for your service provider in the US by dialing the appropriate toll-free access number: **AT&T** (☎800-288-2872 using LADATEL phones, or 800-462-4240); **Sprint** (☎800-877-8000); **MCI WorldPhone Direct** (☎800-021-8000 using Avantel phones, 800-674-7000 using Telmex phones).

CALLING WITHIN MEXICO. Telmex, the national phone company, has recently reconfigured the way local calls are made. In addition to the local number, you must dial the last digit of the area code. For example, if you are calling a hotel in Tijuana (area code 66) whose phone number is ☎12 34 56, dial ☎6 12 34 56. When making calls between cities, dial ☎0 before the area code and phone number.

GETTING HELP. The blue push-button phones do direct dial; the orange old-fashioned ones do not. To reach the English-speaking international operator on a plain old phone, dial ☎09 and wait until the operator answers (be prepared to wait 30min. or more). For direct calls, dial ☎01; for a national operator, 02; directory assistance, 04; bilingual emergency operators, 06.

 RUN FOR THE BORDER. At the world's largest border crossing, north-bound lanes often have backups of more than 150 cars. To minimize the wait, cross during a weekday morning, generally the slowest time. The southbound ride is generally smoother, but weekends can be rough in both directions. If you're crossing into Tijuana for a day or so, it's easier to leave your car in a lot on the US side and join the throngs of people walking across the border. You will still meet long lines returning to the US, even while walking. If you're in a hurry, rent a bike in Mexico, pass through the remarkably shorter bike line, and return it once across the border. Remember that you need a **tourist card** ($18) if you plan to travel farther south than Ensenada or San Felipe. Regardless of which way you are crossing, bring proper ID—ideally a driver's license or passport—and leave your bushels of fruit, truckloads of livestock, stashes of drugs, and armory of weapons behind.

TIJUANA ☎ 66

In the shadow of swollen, sulphur-spewing factories lies the most notorious specimen of a peculiar border subculture: Tijuana (pop. 2 million). By day, swarms of tourists cross the US border to haggle with street vendors, pour gallons of tequila down their throats, and get their picture taken with donkeys painted as zebras. By night, Revolución, the city's wide main drag, becomes a big, bad party with *mariachi* bands and exploding bottle rockets doing little to drown out the thumping dance beats blaring from the packed nightclubs. The three-ringed, duty-free extravaganza attracts more than 30 million tourists per year, most of them jaunting across the border for a couple of hours to unload wads of cash on everything from *jai alai* gambling to slimy strip shows. In recent years, the city has made a conscious effort to clean up its act, somewhat successfully eliminating sex shops and prostitution from the center of town. Still, rife with flashy sleaze and border intrigue, it's hard to say whether it's the city's strange charm, its cheap booze, or its sprawling, unapologetic hedonism that attracts tourists to Tijuana like flies.

▐ TRANSPORTATION

INTERCITY

From San Ysidro: Take the 10min. walk across the pedestrian footbridge, which continues as a walkway over the Río Tijuana and ends at the corner of Calle 1a and Revolución. Taxis on the Mexican side of the border charge US$5 for the same 6 blocks. You can leave your car in any of the secure parking lots off the last US Exit of I-5 for around US$7 a day. To avoid standing in long lines at the border, take the red Mexicoach **bus** (☎685 14 70, in the US 619-428-9517) from its terminal at Border Station Parking next to the Nike factory outlet. It stops right in the middle of all the Revolución madness. (Every 20-30min. 5:30am-9pm, US$1.50.)

From San Diego: Grab a trolley at Kettner and Broadway downtown (every 15min., US$4.50 round-trip) and take the 25min. ride all the way to the border. From there you can catch the southbound Mexicoach or walk into Tijuana.

By Bus: Tijuana has 2 bus stations. To get to the center of town from the **Central Camionera** (☎621 29 82), the more remote bus station, avoid the cab drivers' high rates (up to 80 pesos to downtown) by exiting the terminal, turning left, walking to the end of the building, and hopping on a local bus marked "Centro" (30min., every 5min. 5am-10pm, 4 pesos), which will let you off on Calle 3 and Constitución, 1 block west of Revolución. The **downtown station** is more conveniently located, at Calle 1A at Madero, 1 block east of Revolución. **Greyhound** (☎88 19 79) picks up passengers downtown before leaving the *Central* for **Los Angeles** (3hr., every hr. 5am-midnight, US$24), where it connects to other North American cities. **Suburbaja** (☎88 00 82), in the downtown terminal, sends buses to **Tecate** (every 20min. 5am-9pm, 29 pesos). The **Mexicoach** bus, leaving from the terminal on Revolución, can also take you to **Rosarito** (6 per day, 40 pesos) and **Ensenada** (4 per day, 75 pesos).

LOCAL

Traditional **yellow cabs,** which prey almost exclusively on tourists, charge absurd rates; make sure to set a price before getting in. **Communal cabs** are a popular option with many locals. Operating as miniature buses, they run circuits of the routes listed on the windshield, and are much cheaper than the yellow cabs—you can get almost anywhere in the city for 20-30 pesos. Most communal cabs originate on Madero between Calle 1 and Calle 5. Aside from the Central Camionera, colorful **station wagons** can take you to Parque Morelos (orange and grey; 5½ pesos), Rosarito (yellow and white; 10 pesos), or El Toreo (5 pesos), among other destinations. Tipping cabdrivers is not a common practice in Mexico, but drivers will often refuse to make change. It's a good idea to take cabs at night in the *centro*, and tourist officials recommend avoiding the *Zona Norte*, which is downhill from Calle 1a and filled with prostitution and drugs at all times.

✦ 🛈 ORIENTATION & PRACTICAL INFORMATION

Immediately south of the border, the area surrounding Revolución is known as the **Zona Centro,** aka the tourist hotspot. Most tourists never even leave Revolución, let alone venture into other areas of the city. East-west *calles*, which are both named and numbered, cross Revolución; perpendicular to the *calles*, *avenidas* run north-south, parallel to Revolución.

TOURIST, FINANCIAL, & LOCAL SERVICES

Tourist Office: Located in a small booth on the eastern side of Revolución between Calle 3 and Calle 4 (☎688 05 55). The English-speaking staff offers maps and advice for tourists. Open M-Sa 8am-5pm, Su 10am-5pm. **Customs Office:** (☎683 13 90) at the border on the Mexican side, after crossing the San Ysidro bridge. Open 24hr.

Consulates: Canada, German Gedovius 10411 (☎684 04 61, 800-706-2900 for after hours emergency assistance), in the Zona Río. Open M-F 9am-1pm. **UK,** Salinas 1500 (☎681 73 23, 686 53 20 for after-hours emergency assistance), in Col. Aviación, La Mesa. Open M-F 9am-3pm. **US,** Tapachula 96 (☎681 74 00), in Col. Hipódromo, adjacent to the racetrack southeast of town. In an emergency, call the San Diego office (☎619-692-2154) and leave a message. Open M-F 8am-4:30pm.

Currency Exchange: Banks along Constitución exchange money and traveler's checks at the same rates. **Banamex,** Constitución at Calle 4, has shorter lines (☎688 00 21; open M-F 9am-5pm) than more central **Bital,** Revolución at Calle 2 (☎685 00 06; open M-F 8am-7pm, Sa 8am-5:30pm). Both have **24hr. ATMs.** Located under large billboards with exchange rates, the many *casas de cambio* offer better rates but may charge commission and refuse to exchange traveler's checks.

Supermarket: Calimax, Calle 2 at Constitución (☎688 09 54). Open 6am-midnight.

Car Rental: Before driving into Mexico from the US, get **car insurance** for US$5 per day in San Ysidro. Many drive-through insurance companies have offices just before the border at Sycamore and Primero. **Budget,** Paseo de los Héroes 77, next to the Hotel Camino Real (☎634 33 03; open M-F 8am-7pm, Sa-Su 8am-4pm), and **Hertz,** 16 de Septiembre 213-B, in the Hotel Palacio Azteca, offer similar rates and a wide variety of vehicles. (☎686 12 22. Open M-F 8am-6:30pm, Sa 8am-4pm.)

Emergency: ☎060.

Police: Constitución at Calle 8 (☎638 51 68). English spoken. Specialized tourist assistance (☎688 05 55 or 078).

Red Cross: Gamboa at Silvestre (☎621 77 87, emergency 066). Some English spoken.

Pharmacy: Farmacia Vida, Calle 3 at Revolución (☎685 28 00). Open 24hr.

Hospital: Hospital General, Centenario 10851 (☎684 02 37 or 684 09 22), in the Zona Río. **IMSS** (☎629 63 42), Agua Caliente and Francisco Zarabia. Both open 24hr.

Fax: Telecomm (☎684 79 02; fax 684 77 50), to the right of the Post Office, in the same building. Open M-F 8am-5pm.

Internet: Cyber Tequila, Revolución 1200, just south of Calle 8. 20 pesos per hr. Open 24hr. Scanners and color printers available as well.

Post Office: (☎684 79 50). Located on Negrete at Calle 11. Open M-F 8am-5pm. **Postal Code:** 22000.

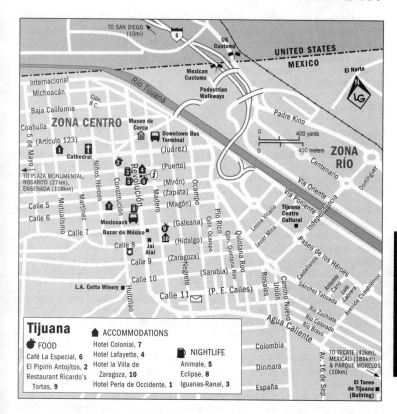

Tijuana

🍴 FOOD

Café La Especial, **6**
El Pipirín Antojitos, **2**
Restaurant Ricardo's
    Tortas, **9**

🏠 ACCOMMODATIONS

Hotel Colonial, **7**
Hotel Lafayette, **4**
Hotel la Villa de
    Zaragoza, **10**
Hotel Perla de Occidente, **1**

🍸 NIGHTLIFE

Animale, **5**
Eclipse, **8**
Iguanas-Ranal, **3**

ACCOMMODATIONS

Budget hotels concentrate on Calle 1, between Revolución and Mutualismo. As a general rule, hotels become sketchier the farther north you go. Avoid any in the area downhill from Calle 1 (the *Zona Norte*). Much of the *Zona Centro* teems with people during the day, but becomes something of a red-light district at night, especially between Revolución and Constitución close to the *Zona Norte*. Rooms at some motels may not fit the standards of cleanliness expected by US travelers— ask to see them before paying. **Exercise caution when walking home at night,** or take a cab (US$2) from anywhere on Revolución.

Hotel La Villa de Zaragoza, Madero 1120 (☎ 685 18 32), between Calles 7a and 8a. For those too squeamish to handle Tijuana's true budget offerings, rooms are a steal for those used to paying US hotel prices. Spacious rooms come with color TVs, enormous king-sized beds, and lots of good-smelling towels. Laundry, room service, and 24hr. security to keep you and your car safe. Singles 350 pesos; doubles 410 pesos. ❸

Hotel Lafayette, Revolución 325 (☎ 685 39 40 or 685 33 39), between Calles 3a and 4a. Remarkably quiet for being in the middle of the chaos that is Revolución. Large rooms have color TVs, phones, fans, and private baths, and the location is ideal for those want-ing a place to crash after a night on the town. Singles 200 pesos; doubles 260 pesos. ❷

Hotel Colonial, Calle 6a 1812 (☎688 16 20), between Constitución and Niños Héroes, in a quieter neighborhood away from Revolución. Large, comfortable rooms have A/C and private baths. Singles and doubles 260 pesos. ❷

Hotel Perla de Occidente, Mutualismo 758 (☎685 13 58), between Calles 1a and 2a, 4 blocks from the bedlam of Revolución. Though the rooms are run-down and sparse, the beds are comfy and the doors lock. Singles 140 pesos; doubles 280 pesos. ❶

FOOD

Like most things in Tijuana, restaurants tend to be loud and in-your-face; menu-waving promoters try to drag tourists—and their dollars—into the over-priced restaurants lining **Revolución.** Savvy travelers make tracks to **Constitución,** one block west of the mayhem, for better food, superior service, and a mellower environment. The ultra-cheap, ultra-fast food taco stands all over the *centro* hand over several tacos or a *torta* for 10 pesos.

▨ **Restaurant Ricardo's Tortas,** Madero and Calle 7 (☎685 40 31). A huge, sparkling restaurant, Ricardo's serves up the best *tortas* in town. Try the *super especial,* with ham, *carne asada,* cheese, avocado, tomato, and mayo (40 pesos). Open 24hr. ❶

Café La Especial, Revolucion 718 (☎685 66 54), down the alley next to the Hotel Lafayette. Like the hotel upstairs, La Especial is a refreshing respite from the noise of Revolución. Munch on a 2 enchilada and 1 taco special (49 pesos) amidst crooning *mariachis* and local families. Open daily 10am-10pm. ❶

El Pipirín Antojitos, Constitución 878 (☎688 16 02), between Calles 2 and 3, wows the weary tourist with exceptional food and service. Enjoy delicious burritos (35 pesos) under the gaudy orange arches. Open daily 8:30am-8:30pm. ❶

SIGHTS

Many of the most entertaining sights in town are right on Revolución, where zebra-striped donkeys and gaudily-costumed cowboys vie for your attention. Unfortunately, most tourists can't be bothered to move beyond the multi-tiered dance clubs and curio shops that line Revolución, but those who do are greeted with a wide array of beautiful parks and cultural attractions.

L.A. CETTO WINERY. Established in 1926 by Italian immigrants, this family-run winery maintains its vineyards in the Valle de Guadalupe, northeast of Ensenada. Visitors are welcome to tour the Tijuana-based production facilities and sample the products. Be sure to try the Nebbiolo; it's one of their specialties. Avoid removing anything from the storeroom—the staff still remembers the North American woman who pulled out the wrong bottle and caused a wine avalanche destroying more than 30 cases. *(Cañon Johnson 2108. Follow Constitución south to Calle 10a and turn right. ☎685 30 31. Tours M-Sa 10am-5pm. 18+, minors allowed if accompanied by parent or guardian. US$2 includes tasting; minors free.)*

MUSEO DE CERA. One of only three wax museums in Mexico, this Tijuana attraction is home to a motley crew of 86 eerie wax figures, including such strange bedfellows as Eddie Murphy, Gandhi, Gorbachev, and Tía Juana herself. The sculptures are split into four basic categories: history, cinema, politics, and terror. *(Calle 1A and Madero. ☎688 24 78. Open daily 10am-7pm. 15 pesos.)*

PARQUE TENIENTE GUERRERO. Dedicated in 1924 to the memory of Vicente Guerrero, the beautiful and shady park on Calle 3a and 5 de Mayo is a favorite gathering place for local families and an oasis from the noisy circus of Revolución.

CATÉDRAL DE NUESTRA SEÑORA DE GUADALUPE. Originally built in 1902 as a modest adobe chapel, modern expansions, and reinforcement have resulted in a huge stone cathedral checkered in adobe orange and grey and crowned with a giant image of the Virgin of Guadalupe. Check out the massive and magnificent central chandelier. *(At the intersection of Calle 2a and Niños Héroes.)*

PARQUE MORELOS. An assortment of exotic birds and picnic tables welcome families to this sprawling state-run park south of the *centro.* Attractions include rides, a miniature golf course, botanical gardens, and an open-air theater. *(Blvd. de los Insurgentes 26000. Take a green and white local bus (40min., 5½ pesos) from the corner of Calle 5a and Constitución or any of the orange and grey communal cabs (25min., 6½ pesos) on Madero south of Calle 2a. ☎625 24 69. Open M-F 9am-5pm, Sa-Su 9am-6pm. Adults and children over 11 5 pesos.)*

🎵 🍺 ENTERTAINMENT & NIGHTLIFE

In the 1920s, Prohibition drove US citizens south of the border to revel in the forbidden nectars of cacti, grapes, and hops, and the constant flow of American tourists eager to fill their stomachs with cheap and legal booze still remains strong. Stroll down Revolución after dusk and you'll be bombarded with thumping music and neon lights. This street doesn't know the meaning of the word quiet.

Animale, Revolución at Calle 4a, is the biggest, glitziest, and loudest hedonistic haven of them all. The huge dance floor and open balconies, as well as special drink deals (2 beers and a shot of tequila US$4, 2-for-1 mixed drinks US$6) attract kids and adults alike into the colorful lair. Open Su-Th 10am-4am, F-Sa 10am-6am.

Iguanas-Ranas, Revolución at Calle 3a (☎685 14 22). A sublimely wacky world of life-size plaster clowns, balloons, and various pieces of kitschy US pop culture items, Iguanas-Ranas is one of the most happening places in town. Where else do you get the opportunity to pound beers (US$2.50) in an authentic yellow school bus high above Revolución? On W guys pay US$1 per beer, girls drink free. Open M-Th 10am-2am, F-Su 10am-6am.

Eclipse, Revolución at Calle 6a. Brace yourself for this 3-tiered party palace. Miami-esque decor complete with platforms attracts masses of patrons eager to toss back some of the cheapest booze in town: 2 beers and a shot of tequila are a mere US$3. The 3rd floor doubles as a strip club, where drink prices (not to mention hemlines) are much higher. Open M-Th noon-2am, F-Su noon-4am.

CULTURAL EVENTS

The monumental **Tijuana Centro Cultural,** more popular with locals than tourists, is on Paseo de los Héroes at Mina. Inside the strikingly modern complex is the **Museo de las Californias,** a series of exhibits exploring the history and culture of Baja California. (☎687 96 50. Open daily 10am-8pm. 20 pesos, children 12 pesos.) The Centro Cultural also hosts a variety of other offerings, including a central gallery of temporary art exhibits. The enormous sphere in the plaza contains the **Cine Planetano,** a giant 180-degree screen that shows OmniMax films dubbed in Spanish. (Open daily 2-9pm. 45 pesos, children 23 pesos.) Another **theater** shows cycles of foreign films and children's movies. (Open Sa-Su 10am-8pm. 25 pesos, children's films free.) The **Sala de Ciencia** presents interactive exhibits about health and technology. Performances by visiting dance troupes, musicians, and theater groups take place in the **Jardín Caracol.** Ask at the information booth in the lobby for details on upcoming shows, and pick up a monthly calendar of events.

SPORTS

Completed in 1947 after 21 years of delays, the grandiose baroque **Frontón Palacio,** on Revolución at Calle 7a, hosts daily competitions of **jai alai.** (☎685 16 12. Games M-Sa 8pm. Free.) If you're in town on the right Sunday, you can watch the graceful and savage battle of man versus bull in one of Tijuana's two bullrings. **El Toreo de Tijuana,** southeast of town just off of Agua Caliente, hosts the first round of fights. (May-July, alternate Su.) To get to El Toreo, catch a bus on Calle 2a west of Revolución. The seaside **Plaza Monumental** hosts the second round (Aug.-Oct.). Tickets (95-400 pesos) to both rings go on sale at the gate the Wednesday before a fight (☎685 15 10 or 686 12 19) or at the Mexicoach office (☎685 14 70) on Revolución between Calles 6a and 7a. Mexicoach sends **buses** (round-trip US$4) to the Plaza Monumental on fight days. Alternatively, take the blue and white local buses (5 pesos) on Calle 3a at Constitución all the way down Calle 2a.

SHOPPING

As soon as tourists cross the footbridge from the US, they're bombarded with vendors peddling everything from brightly colored blankets to cheap shoes to pieces of rice with the tourist's name written on it. The crazy shopping scene continues most of the way up Revolución, ending near the intersection with Calle 7a. Other spots for assorted tourist-oriented wares are the **Mercado de Artesanía,** on Calle 1a right under the pedestrian footbridge, and the vendors on **Plaza Santa Cecilia** behind the tourist office. Bargaining is a must, as quoted prices can be more than twice the bottom line. For a good selection of higher-quality *artesanía*, visit the **Bazar de México** on Revolución at Calle 7a.

ROSARITO   ☎ 6

Blessed with a sandy beaches and placid seas unparalleled in northern Baja, Rosarito (pop. 120,000) offers Mexican charm without sacrificing much American convenience, comfort, or commercialism. Its proximity to the border and relative safety and cleanliness drew elite Hollywood stars to the landmark Rosarito Beach Hotel in this once little-known playground of the rich and famous. Today this young city is a hotspot for Mexican family outings and hordes of *gringos* in search of fun in the sun and cheap booze. Rosarito's scenic shores have remained popular with Hollywood types, now specifically filmmakers; the highest-grossing movie of all time, *Titanic*, was filmed just south of Rosarito.

⌐ TRANSPORTATION. To get to Rosarito from Tijuana, grab a yellow and white **taxi de ruta** (30min., 10 pesos) from Madero, between Calles 5A and 6A. To return to Tijuana, catch a *taxi de ruta* along Juárez or at its start in front of the Rosarito Beach hotel. **Mexicoach** (☎685 14 70) also makes the same trek six times daily (30min., 40 pesos). To go to Ensenada, take a "Primo Tapia" **taxi** from Festival Plaza, north of the Rosarito Beach Hotel, to the toll booth on Mex. 1 (4 pesos). From there, take a bus to Ensenada. (Runs every 30min. 6:30am-9:30pm, 30 pesos.)

⌐⌐ ORIENTATION & PRACTICAL INFORMATION. Rosarito lies 27km south of Tijuana. **Mex 1** runs straight through Rosarito, parallel to the city's main drag, **Boulevard Benito Juárez.** Coming from the toll road (Mex. 1), the first Rosarito Exit takes you to the north end of Juárez, which, with its non-sequential street numbers and almost universal lack of street signs, can be befuddling. Virtually all the businesses in town are on Juárez—mostly between the huge and very fluorescent Hotel Festival Plaza in the south and the pink Ortega's Restaurant in Oceana Plaza farther north. Police recommend staying in this area of town, and warn that the areas around Col. Constitucion and Col. Lucio Blanco are particularly unsafe.

The **Convention and Visitor's Center,** on the first floor of the gaudy pink and green Oceana Plaza, offers brochures, shopping coupons and a decent map. (☎612 02 00, Tourist info ☎800-962-BAJA/2252 or 662 30 78. Open M-F 10am-6pm, Sa 10am-1pm.) **Banamex,** on the western side of Juárez at Ortiz, exchanges cash and checks and has a **24hr. ATM** and a Western Union. (☎612 15 56. Open M-F 9am-4pm, Sa 10am-2pm.) For weekend pesos, visit a *casa de cambio* on Juárez and pay commission. For groceries, visit the busy **Calimax,** at the northern end of Juárez. (☎612 00 60. Open daily 7am-midnight.) Launder clothes at **Lavamática Moderna,** on the eastern side of Juárez at Acacias. (Wash 15 pesos, dry 4 pesos per 12min. Open daily 8:30am-8pm.) In an **emergency,** call ☎060. The **police** are on the eastern side of Juárez at Acacias (☎613 34 14). Some English is spoken. **Red Cross,** on Juárez at Ortíz, is around the corner from the police. English is spoken. (☎613 11 20, emergency 066.) Pharmacy services are at **Farmacia Roma,** on the eastern side of Juárez at Roble. (☎612 35 00. Open 24hr.) **El Tunel.com,** Juárez 208 (eastern side) near Cárdenas, upstairs from Gonzales Restaurant, offers **Internet access.** (☎ 613 12 97. Open M-F 9am-10pm, Sa-Su 10am-10pm. 24 pesos per hr.) The **Post Office** is on Juárez and Acacias, near the Police Station. (☎612 30 55. Open M-F 8am-3pm.) **Postal code:** 22710.

 ACCOMMODATIONS & FOOD. Most budget hotels in Rosarito are cramped or situated on the outskirts of town. Prices soar during spring break, holidays, and summer weekends. Exceptional **Hotel Palmas Quintero ❸** is tucked away on Privada Guadalupe Victoria 26, a quiet residential street. To get there from Juárez, turn onto Cárdenas, heading away from the ocean. Three blocks inland, take a left at the Oxxo store. The hotel will be three blocks ahead on the left. Its huge rooms have cable TV and clean baths. (☎612 13 59. Singles US$30; doubles US$60.) Right on Juárez is the brightly colored **Hotel El Portal de Rosarito ❷,** at Via de las Olas. The ceaseless din from Juárez may prevent rest, despite the spacious rooms with cable TV and A/C. (☎612 00 50. US$10 key deposit. Singles from US$27; doubles from US$60. Additional person at least US$15. Rates US$12 more on weekends.) To get away from it all, head 6 mi. south of Rosarito on Juárez to **Las Rocas Resort and Spa ❺.** This newer resort offers large rooms, all with oceanfront views and balconies, as well as two pools and three jacuzzis, a gym, two on-site restaurants, and a full-service spa. (☎614 03 54; www.lasrocas.com. Rooms from US$89, in off-season from US$74; suites from US$104.)

> **❗ SEEKING PETITE, DANGEROUS SCORPIO**
>
> "Scorpions?! But this isn't the jungle," you gasp. Tough break. These nasty little pests (*alacranes* in Spanish) frequent Baja, especially around the mid-peninsula. Unless you are allergic, you won't encounter a slow, painful death—these aren't the fatal black scorpions found in Asia and Africa, but beige, desert-and-beach-camouflaged scorpions. The critters like dark, warm, damp places, so shake your shoes and clothing before you put them on. Most bite victims experience intense pain for a day or two. Ice packs help alleviate the pain, while locals swear that garlic is the best relief. If you wake up in the middle of the night and a scorpion is crawling up your chest, don't try to flatten or squash it—it will get angry and sting your hand. Due to their hard protective armor, scorpions are hard to crush. Instead, give the intruder a hard flick from the side and watch it fly far, far away.

With tourists from around the world, Rosarito is full of international cuisine to suit their palates. Small taco stands abound downtown, but there are many creative sit-down options as well. For traditional Mexican fare, head to ⊠**La Flor de Michoacán ❷**, Juárez 291, at the north end of town, which is a carnivorous paradise. Huge *ordenes de carnitas* (60 pesos) come as either "solid" or "mixed" pork—solid comprises the parts of a pig usually eaten, while mixed includes tongues, stomachs, and all sorts of good stuff. Those with gargantuan appetites can order by the kilogram. (☎612 18 58. Burritos 30 pesos. Mixed pork 215 pesos per kg. Solid pork 225 pesos per kg. Open daily 9am-10pm.) Excellent Mediterranean cuisine in an elegant setting can be found at **Le Cousteu ❷**, Juárez 184, across the street from and slightly north of the Hotel Festival Plaza. Try their filling vegetarian crepes for 87 pesos. (☎612-2655. Open daily 1pm-11pm.) The bright interior of **Juice 'n Juice ❶** on Juarez near the police station offers a cheery respite from the busy street. This coffee shop uses natural ingredients in its delectable pastries and sandwiches. Try the flan. (Breakfast special US$3.60. Open daily 7am-3pm.)

⊙ 🎭 SIGHTS & ENTERTAINMENT. Rosarito entices with fancy resorts, beautiful shores, and wild nightlife. Spanning the coast two blocks west of Juárez, **Rosarito Beach** has soft sand and gently rolling surf. The **Museo de Historia Wa Kuatay,** on Juárez next to the Rosarito Beach Hotel, showcases local folk art and history. (☎613 06 87. Open W-Su 9am-5pm. Donations welcome.) The new **Foxploration** at **Fox Studios Baja,** 2km south of town on the free road, holds a number of exhibits on filmmaking in the area, including props from *Titanic,* an observation deck from which to watch new movies being filmed, and a large showcase of special effects. (☎614 94 44; www.foxploration.com. Open M and Th-F 9am-5:30pm, Sa-Su 10am-6:30pm. US$12.) Rosarito's nightlife centers around **Hotel Festival Plaza,** which hosts **Taco Rock 'n Roll,** a loud dance club. (Beers US$3. Live music on weekends. Open daily 10am-midnight.) The multitude of clubs on the streets behind the hotel are packed with drunken revelers on weekend and summer nights. Be wary that during spring break and Labor Day weekend, prices may increase exponentially. **Papas and Beer,** a multilevel party palace resembling the Swiss Family Robinson abode, includes a great beach volleyball court, as well as many cabanas, dance floors, a mechanical bull and access to the beach. (☎612 04 44; www.papasandbeer.com. 18+. Beer US$3. Cover Sa US$5-10. Open daily 11am-3am. Parking available.) **Club Iggys,** at **Iggy's Son of the Beach,** promises some of the craziest times in Rosarito. The complex has a pool, foam dancing, a mechanical bull and bungee jumping, and all-you-can-drink nights which includes transportation to and from local hotels for US$15. (☎612 05 37; www.iggysbaja.com. Open daily 11am-3am.)

THE DESERT

California's desert can be one of the most beautiful places in the world; it can also be among the loneliest. Roads cut through endless expanses of barren earth and landscapes seem untouched by human existence. Only a few hours from the complicated hustle of L.A., the wide open space of the Mojave can seem overwhelmingly simplistic. Exploration turns up elusive treasures: diverse flora and fauna, staggering topographical variation, and scattered relics of the American frontier. Throughout the year, the desert moves from a pleasantly warm refuge from colder climates to a blistering wasteland and back again; plan your trip accordingly.

ORIENTATION

California's desert divides roughly into the Low and High Deserts, names that indicate differences in both altitude and latitude. The **Sonoran,** or **Low Desert** (see p. 506) occupies southeastern California from the Mexican border north to Needles and west to the Borrego Desert. The **Mojave,** or **High Desert** (see p. 515) averages elevations of 2000 ft. and spans the southern central part of the state, bounded by the Sonoran Desert to the south, San Bernardino to the west, the Sierra Nevadas to the north, and Death Valley to the east. Four major east-west highways cross the desert. In the Low Desert, **I-8** hugs the California-Mexico border, while **I-10** passes Joshua Tree and Palm Springs. Cutting through the heart of the Mojave is **I-15.**

From Barstow, the Mojave's central pitstop, I-15 continues on to Las Vegas, while **I-40** cuts southeast through Needles and on to the Nevada desert.

All of the destinations in this chapter are on or near the major highways listed above. The Low Desert follows destinations along I-8 and I-10; the High Desert follows destinations along I-15. **Route 66** follows the old highway along I-40 through the Mojave Desert, continuing into Arizona as far as the Grand Canyon.

DESERT SURVIVAL

Here, **water** is life. The body loses at least a gallon of liquid per day in the desert (two gallons during strenuous activity), so *keep drinking.* Consuming huge quantities of water to quench your thirst after physical exertion is not as effective as drinking water before and during activity, even if you're just driving. Whatever you are doing, tote **two gallons of water per person per day.** Designate at least one container as an emergency supply. In the car, keep backup containers in a cooler. Drink the water you have. Avoid alcohol and coffee, which cause dehydration. Keep your strength up for long stays with a high-quality beverage with potassium compounds and glucose, such as **ERG** (an industrial-strength Gatorade).

Most people need a few days to adjust to the heat, especially before difficult hikes. Sunglasses with 100% UV protection, sunscreen, and a wide-brim hat are essential **sun protection,** but proper clothing is the most effective shield. Light-colored clothing helps reflect the sun's rays. Although it may be uncomfortable to wear a sweaty shirt, it prevents dehydration more effectively than going shirtless.

Heat is not the desert's only climatic extreme. At high elevations, temperatures during winter nights can drop well below freezing (a sweater is often necessary even in summer). Fall and spring **flash floods** can cause water to come down from rain-drenched higher elevations and wreak biblical devastation upon lands below, turning dry gulches into raging rivers. Don't walk in washes you can't scramble out of, beware of thunderstorms on the horizon, and never camp in washes or gullies.

For more thorough advice on managing potential hazards in the Mojave, consult the excellent *Desert Survival Handbook* (Primer; $7.95).

DRIVING IN THE DESERT. Conditions in the desert are as grueling on cars as they are on bodies; only recently serviced cars in good condition can take the heat. Bring at least five gallons of radiator water, extra coolant, a spare tire, proper tools to make minor repairs, and a few quarts of oil (car manuals recommend appropriate oil weights for varying temperatures). Avoid running out of gas by keeping your tank above half full; gas can be hard to find in the desert. Beware of gravel roads that turn to sand. A board and shovel may also be useful for sand-stuck cars.

Although towns are sometimes sparse, major roads usually have enough traffic to ensure that breakdowns are noticed. Still, isolated areas of the parks pose a threat, especially in summer, when few tourists visit. **Stay with your vehicle if it breaks down;** it is easier to spot than a person and provides crucial shade. Turn off **air-conditioning** immediately if the car's temperature gauge starts to climb. Air from open windows should be sufficiently comfortable at highway speeds. If your car overheats, pull off the road and turn the heater on full force. If radiator fluid is steaming or bubbling, turn off the car for 30min. If not, run the car in neutral at about 1500 RPM for a few minutes, allowing the coolant to circulate. Never pour water over the engine or try to lift a hot hood. **Desert water bags** ($5-10) are available at hardware or automotive stores. When strapped onto the front of the car and filled with water, these prevent overheating by speeding up evaporation.

It may be wise to pick up a manual or book with more specific desert driving tactics if you plan to be traveling extensively in the Mojave. The above-mentioned *Desert Survival Handbook* includes a comprehensive section on driving.

THE LOW DESERT

The Low Desert, home of Anza-Borrego Desert State Park and the Salton Sea, is flat, dry, and barren. Only a few resilient species have learned to flourish amidst the dust and broken rocks, but there is a simple and striking beauty to the fragility of life in the desert. Despite its arid climate, irrigation has brought abundant life both to the region's date groves and the posh resorts of Palm Springs.

ANZA-BORREGO DESERT STATE PARK ☎760

The largest state park in California, Anza-Borrego is layered with both natural and human history. A short drive from San Diego or Palm Springs, this harsh desert sprouts many plant species found nowhere else in California. Barbed cholla cacti, bruise-blossomed indigo bush, and thirsty tamarisk flourish in the withering heat. Beneath this scrub sprawls a diverse landscape of dunes, badlands, mountains, oases, and active faults. Hidden among these natural wonders are the abandoned relics of Native Americans, Spanish settlers, and oil pioneers. Though the Anza-Borrego Desert is just as beautiful as those at Death Valley or Joshua Tree, some things prevent it from reaching their popularity. First, the town of Borrego Springs (pop. 3000), mars the vast beauty of the desert valley. Secondly, without the funding of a national park, roads aren't well maintained, sights aren't always easy to find, and campgrounds are undeveloped. The beauty of Anza-Borrego can only be found by a true desert adventurer. Visit in the winter or early spring when the searing sun is off its warpath; high summer temperatures can make the desert deadly.

ORIENTATION & PRACTICAL INFORMATION. To reach the park from the west, take **State Route 78** east from I-15 in Escondido. From the south, take State Rte. 79 northbound from I-8 to Rte. 78. From the east, take **County Route S22** west from Rte. 86, which connects to I-10 in Indio. Once in the park, head to Borrego Springs, its only town, via **County Route S3** for info, lodging, and food.

The **Northeast Rural Bus System** serves the region. (☎767-4287. Info line open daily 7am-noon and 2-5pm.) **AAA Emergency Road Service** (☎800-222-4357) can refer troubled motorists to a towing company. For **Visitor Information,** stop by the **Anza-Borrego Desert State Park Visitors Center,** 200 Palm Canyon Dr., Borrego Springs. They have topo maps, books, exhibits, and slideshows. Rangers offer backcountry and safety info; stop here before hiking or camping. (☎767-4205. Open June-Sept. Sa-Su 9am-5pm; Oct.-May daily 9am-5pm.) For info in summer months, call the **Anza-Borrego State Park Headquarters.** (☎767-5311. Open M-F 8am-5pm.) Or stop by the **Borrego Springs Chamber of Commerce and Visitor Center,** 786 Palm Canyon Dr. (☎767-5555. For weather conditions, call ☎289-1212. Open M-F 10am-4pm.) The **Borrego Medical Center,** 4343 Yaqui Pass Rd., Borrego Springs, on Rams Hill, provides medical help. (☎767-5051. Open June-Sept. M-Tu and Th-F 9am-1pm, W 1-6pm; Oct.-May M-F 9am-5pm, Sa 9am-1pm.)

ACCOMMODATIONS, CAMPING, & FOOD. The small community of **Borrego Springs** provides adequate accommodations for park visitors. **Hacienda del Sol ❹,** 610 Palm Canyon Dr., offers comfy, old rooms. (☎767-5442. Singles and doubles June-Sept. $50; Oct.-May $60. Each additional person $15.) The prices at **Stanlunds ❹,** 2771 Borrego Springs Rd., are just as low. (☎767-5501. Breakfast included on weekends. Singles in summer $45; in winter $75. Doubles $10 more.) At higher prices, the western-themed **Palm Canyon Resort ❺,** 221 Palm Canyon Dr., offers a lot more. Two pools, fitness center, restaurant, saloon, and laundry are all avail-

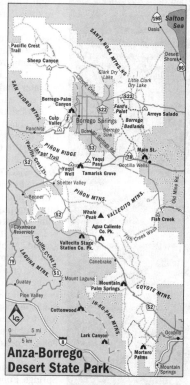

Anza-Borrego Desert State Park

THE DESERT

FROM THE ROAD

ANZA-BORREGO DESERT: A NOT SO SUBTLE BEAUTY

The average daily temperature while I was traveling in the desert was 106 degrees Farenheit. Before this trip, I don't think I even realized exactly how hot that was. It was the kind of heat that caused my chapstick to completely melt all over the dashboard of my car, never again to return to its pristine cylindrical shape. And it was the kind of heat that left sweat, plenty of sunscreen, and dirt caked on my legs (the "tan line" from my socks mercifully disappeared when I had the chance to shower).

I learned to accept that I had to forgo carrying my camera, a book, and my lunch in order to carry enough water when I hiked. I quickly grew bitter toward all the rangers in their wonderfully air-conditioned visitors centers, who told me to be patient in discovering the subtle beauty of the desert. And I learned first-hand why we urgently tell readers not to come to the California deserts in the summer. But certain events tend to make even the most difficult situations worthwhile.

The Desert Bighorn Sheep are notoriously elusive animals. During the cooler months, they hide out high in the desert mountains, usually far from the reaches of human populations and eyes. They camouflage perfectly with their mountain habitat and their balance and footing is impeccable, so they remain out of sight most of the time. Also, their numbers are incredibly small compared to the vastness of the desert. But as the summer heat drives most people

able. (☎800-242-0044. Singles and doubles during summer $70-85; in winter $95-130.)

Anza-Borrego is one of the few places left in the United States that still allows open **camping ❶**. Take advantage of this opportunity if at all possible; just remember that the chosen sites must be 100 ft. away from water and any road, and that fires are not permitted unless they're in your own metal container. The $2 daily park fee must be paid prior to camping. Beyond backcountry camping, Anza-Borrego hosts four developed campgrounds, as well as eight primitive campgrounds. **Borrego Palm Canyon ❶** has 122 developed sites for tents, RVs, and groups. (Flush toilets, water, showers, sun shades, fire rings, and picnic tables. Sites $10-18.) **Tamarisk Grove ❶** has 27 developed sites for tents and RVs. (Flush toilets, water, showers, sun shades, fire rings, and picnic tables. Sites $10.) For those who've wandered in without the aid of machines, **Horse Camp ❶** has 10 developed sites for horses and people only. (Flush toilets, water, showers, fire rings, and picnic tables. Sites $10.) **Bow Willow ❶** has 16 sites for tents or RVs. (Vault toilets, water, picnic tables, sunshades, and fire rings. Sites $7.) Reservations for all the sites can be made by calling ☎800-444-7275. Call ahead to check if all camps are open in the summer, some may be closed due to inadequate funding. The eight primitive campgrounds all have vault toilets (except for Yaqui Pass), but no distinct sites or other amenities.

Center Market, 590 Palm Canyon, Borrego Springs, sells groceries and supplies. (☎767-3311. Open M-Sa 8:30am-6:30pm, Su 8:30am-5pm.) Across the street is the local favorite, **Kendall's Cafe ❷,** 528 Palm Canyon Dr. Entrees ($6-10) include ½ lb. buffalo burgers. (☎767-3491. Open daily 6am-8pm.)

◉ 🔼 **SIGHTS & HIKES.** Hiking and desert exploration abound in Anza-Borrego for those willing. The 3 mi. round-trip **Palm Canyon Creek Trail** leads up to a huge fan palm oasis, where desert bighorn sheep come to water in the summer months. The trailhead is located in the back of the **Borrego Palm Campground.** Another short but rewarding hike can be found at **Slot Canyon.** Exit Rte. 78 east of Borrego Springs on a small dirt road labeled "Buttes Pass Rd." At the first fork, bear left. About 1 mi. down the road is a small parking area; Slot Canyon is below. The **Southern Emigrant Trail,** a 26 mi. self-guided auto-tour, follows a wagon trail used by Mormon settlers. Along the trail is a sod stage station built in 1852. **Font's Point,** accessible with a 4WD vehicle, looks down on the spectacular Borrego Badlands. Without 4WD, the badlands can be seen from S22 to the east of Borrego Springs. Follow this road east to reach the huge, salty lake known as the **Salton Sea.** The park's chief attraction is wildflower season, which turns barren waste-lands into blossoming wonderlands in spring. Call the **Wildflower Hotline** (☎767-4684) in the spring to learn if the unpredictable blooming has occurred. Rangers also offer special guided activities.

PALM SPRINGS ☎760

From its first known inhabitants, the Cahuilla Indians, to today's geriatric fun-lovers, the restorative oasis of Palm Springs (pop. 43,520) has attracted many. The medicinal waters of the city's natural hot springs ensure not only the vitality of its wealthy residents, but also its longevity as a resort town. With warm winter temperatures, celebrity residents, and more pink than a Miami Vice episode, this city is a sunny break from everyday life.

▐ TRANSPORTATION

Airport: Palm Springs Regional, 3400 E. Tahquitz-Canyon Rd. (☎318-3800). Only has State and limited national service.

Buses: Greyhound, 311 N. Indian Canyon Dr. (☎325-2053 or 800-231-2222.), near downtown. Open 8am-6pm. To: **L.A.** (9 per day; $17-19, round-trip $32-34); **San Diego** (9 per day, $25); **Las Vegas** (6 per day, $52.50).

Public Transportation: SunBus (☎343-3451). Local bus service connecting all Coachella Valley cities (Info office open daily 5am-10pm). Lines #23, 24, and 111 cover downtown and surrounding locales. The *SunBus Book,* available at info centers and in most hotel lobbies, includes schedules and a system map. Fare $1, transfers $0.50.

Taxis: Yellow Cab (☎345-8398) and **A Valley Cabousine** (☎340-5845) operate 24hr.

Trains: Amtrak, the corner of N. Indian Canyon Rd. and Amado Rd. (☎800-872-7245).

Car Rental: Starting at about $35 per day (excluding insurance); higher in winter. **Rent-A-Wreck,** 67555 Palm Canyon Dr. #A105, Cathedral City (☎324-1766 or 800-535-1391; www.rentawreck.com). Usually only rents to those 21 and older. $10 surcharge for those under 25. **Budget** (☎327-1404 or 800-221-1203), at Palm Springs Regional Airport. Must be 21 with major credit card; under 25 surcharge $20 per day.

Bike Rental: Bighorn Bicycles, 302 N. Palm Canyon Dr. (☎325-3367). Mountain bikes $8 per hr., $22 for 4hr., $29 per day. Tours available. Open Sept.-June Th-Tu 8am-4pm; closed July-Aug. **Tri-A-Bike,** 44841 San Pablo (☎340-2840), in Palm Desert. Mountain bikes $7 per hr., $19 per day, $65 per wk. Open M-Sa 10am-6pm, Su noon-5pm.

lack of water drives the sheep to scarce watering holes, such as the Palm Canyon Oasis in Anza-Borrego State Park.

In the searing heat, I ventured up the 3 mi. path, trying to avoid tripping as I kept my eyes on the canyon rims above. 1 reached the oasis and sat down to drink, disappointed not to have seen anything. Enjoying the cool shade of the fan palms, I stayed for an hour before setting out again, my eyes downcast. The cheerful (and comfortably cool) ranger had warned me that the sheep only come down to drink in the early morning, and retreat back into the mountains as the sun eats away at the available shade. But just as I became angry about how I had lost my chance, I heard a scuffle and looked up. About 10 ft. farther down the path, a huge ram had turned around to eye me. Two smaller females were retreating up the mountain. I cautiously reached around to my backpack for my camera, but felt only one thing: my half-empty gallon jug of water. So I just sat and watched, silently and singularly appreciating the not-so-subtle beauty of the desert.

–Sara Clark

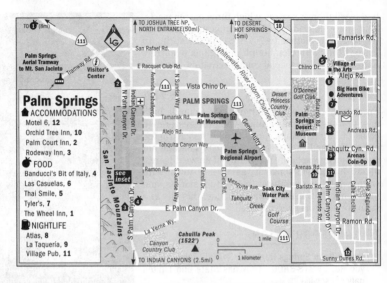

✦ ☑ ORIENTATION & PRACTICAL INFORMATION

Palm Springs is a two- to three-hour drive from L.A. along **I-10**. From the north on I-15, take I-215 East to Rte. 60 East to I-10 East. Exit at Indian Ave., which becomes **Indian Canyon Drive,** the major north-south thoroughfare. Indian Canyon Dr. and the North-South stretch of **Palm Canyon Drive,** the city's two main drags, connect to I-10. East Palm Canyon Dr. borders the southern edge of the city. There are two major east-west boulevards: **Tahquitz-Canyon Road** runs east to the airport, while **Ramon Road,** four blocks south, provides access to I-10.

Visitor Information: Visitors Center, 2781 N. Palm Canyon Dr. (☎778-8415 or 800-347-7746; www.palm-springs.org), 1 block beyond Tramway Rd. on the right. Free hotel reservations and friendly advice. Pick up *The Desert Guide* or *Play Palm Springs* for attractions and entertainment. Open daily 9am-5pm. **Chamber of Commerce,** 190 W. Amado Rd. (☎325-1577; www.pschamber.org). Grab the seasonal *Palm Springs Visitors Guide,* buy a map ($1), or make hotel reservations. Open M-F 8:30am-4:30pm.

Laundromat: Arenas Coin-Op, 220 E. Arenas Rd. (☎322-7717), ½ block east of Indian Canyon Dr. Wash $1.75, dry 10min. $0.25. Open daily 6:30am-9pm.

Road Conditions: ☎800-427-7623. **Weather Conditions:** ☎345-3711.

Police: 200 S. Civic Dr. (☎323-8116).

Rape Crisis Hotline: ☎568-9071.

Medical Services: Desert Regional Medical Center, 1150 N. Indian Canyon Dr. (☎323-6511).

Library and Internet Access: Palm Springs Public Library, 300 S. Sunrise Way (☎322-7323). Free access available in 30min. slots. Open M-Tu 9am-8pm, W-Th and Sa 9am-5:30pm, F 10am-5:30pm.

Post Office: 333 E. Amado Rd. (☎800-275-8777). Open M-F 9am-5pm, Sa 9am-1pm.

Postal Code: 92262; General Delivery 92263.

▟ ACCOMMODATIONS

Like most famous resort communities, Palm Springs caters mainly to those seeking a tax shelter, not a night's shelter. Nonetheless, affordable lodgings are surprisingly abundant. Motels cut prices 20-40% in the summer. Many offer discounts through the Visitors Center, and promotional publications often have terrific coupon deals, offering rooms for as little as $25. Reservations may be necessary in the winter. Prices listed don't include the county's **10% accommodation tax.**

Orchid Tree Inn, 251 S. Belardo Rd. (☎325-2791 or 800-733-3435). Large rooms with tasteful Spanish ambiance overlook a courtyard with lush gardens and pool. Tucked away off the main downtown strip, this quiet hotel is near good shopping. 1- or 2-person rooms start at $65 mid-week in July and Aug., but increase to $110-130 during the winter. Weekend rates $15-20 more. Studios, suites, and bungalows also available. ❺

Miracle Springs Resort and Spa, 10625 Palm Dr. (☎251-6000 or 800-400-4414; www.miraclesprings.com), in Desert Hot Springs. The newer and more luxurious of 2 hotels perched atop the famed hot springs of Palm Springs. 110 spacious units with bedrooms and living areas, some of which overlook the 8 pools of "miracle" water. Spa, casino, restaurants, and banquet facilities available within the complex. Standard rooms from $99 in the off-season; from $139 in winter. ❺

Rodeway Inn, 1277 S. Palm Canyon Dr. (☎325-5574 or 800-829-8099). Large rooms with refrigerators and phones. Laundry, continental breakfast, and a courtyard with pool and jacuzzi. Singles July-Aug. Su-Th from $44, F-Sa $60; Sept.-June $69-$125. ❹

Motel 6, 660 S. Palm Canyon Dr. (☎327-4200 or 800-466-8356), conveniently located south of the city center. Other locations at 595 E. Palm Canyon Dr. (☎325-6129) and 63950 20th Ave. (☎251-1425), near the I-10 off-ramp. Each has a pool and A/C. Singles $38; doubles $44; $4 higher on weekends. ❸

Palm Court Inn, 1983 N. Palm Canyon Dr. (☎416-2333 or 800-667-7918), between I-10 and downtown. Inside the melon-colored walls are 107 rooms as well as a pool and jacuzzi. June-Sept. singles $59; doubles $69. Oct.-May singles $69; doubles $79. All prices slightly higher on weekends. Look for discount coupons in visitors guides. ❹

▟ FOOD

Palm Springs offers a kaleidoscope of sumptuous food, from the classic greasy spoon to ultra-trendy fusions. However, prices are high. To cook for yourself, head to **Ralph's,** 451 S. Sunrise Way, for groceries. (☎323-9799. Open daily 6am-1am.)

▨ **Banducci's Bit of Italy,** 1260 S. Palm Canyon Dr. (☎325-2537). The promise of delicious Italian food draws crowds to this Palm Springs staple every night of the week. For a rich treat, try their fettucine alfredo, which comes with antipasto, minestrone soup, and buttery garlic bread ($13). Entrees from $8-15. Open daily 5-10pm. ❸

▨ **Thai Smile,** 651 N. Palm Canyon Dr. (☎320-5503). Just as friendly as the name implies, Thai Smile is authentic and inexpensive Thai cuisine. Vegetarian options (tofu pad thai $7). Don't miss the $5 lunch specials. Open daily 11:30am-10pm. ❷

Las Casuelas—The Original, 368 N. Palm Canyon Dr. (☎325-3213). Its immediate success made chainhood inevitable, but locals insist that The Original lives up to its name. Authentic Mexican dishes (from $6) and colorful decor give it that south-of-the-border feel. Open Su-Th 10am-10pm, F-Sa 10am-11pm. ❷

ZARDS LOSING GROUND

Northeast of the manicured lawns and perfect appearances of Palm Springs lies a small sliver of what Coachella Valley used to be like. Tall sand dunes, shimmering oases, and desert bluffs are home to various flora and fauna that can be found almost nowhere else in the world, including the projected fringe-toed lizard. The Coachella Valley Preserve was created in 1986 to help protect what is left of this unique species; it was the first act to create a protected area for lizards. In the early 90s, when the lizard population continued to decline, new dunes were created to protect it and to further its fragile ecosystem.

Nature's protectors now have another battle. Business in the Coachella Valley is booming, and instead of building sand dunes, developers are building offices and factories. Currently, developers want to create a 0,000-acre desert wonderland in the area north of the preserve that would be home to a university, 7,000 new homes, and 12 more golf courses. While land would not be taken from the preserve, many fear that the development would siphon water away from the oases, disrupting wildlife ranges in the preserve and in Joshua Tree National Park to the north. While new housing may provide the cushion for the rapidly expanding valley, it makes one wonder: in a valley with over 100 golf courses already, how many more do you really need?

Tyler's, 149 S. Indian Canyon Dr. (☎325-2990). The patio at this small cafe tucked in the middle of La Plaza is perfect for people-watching. Enjoy classic American fare, or treat yourself to a malt or root-beer float. Burgers $3-6. Soda-fountain drinks $2.50-4. Open M-F 11am-4pm, Sa 11am-5pm; in summer Tu-Sa 11am-4pm. ❶

The Wheel Inn, 50900 Seminole Dr. (☎909-849-7012), in Cabazon, directly off the stretch of I-10 west of Palm Springs. Legendary joint where Pee-Wee Herman met Simone. Daily specials ($6-7). Tasty pie ($2.50-3.75). Open 24hr. ❷

👁 🧗 SIGHTS & ACTIVITIES

Most people come to Palm Springs to drink, party, and schmooze with celebs, but the city also has its share of sights. Mt. San Jacinto State Park, Palm Springs's primary landmark, offers a variety of outdoor recreation. Hiking trails in the park are accessible year-round via the tram, and cross-country skiing is available in winter at higher elevations, though access is easier and cheaper from nearby Idyllwild. Despite its benign appearance, that Palm Springs is just a damp patch of otherwise ferocious desert. Summertime highs reach well into the hundreds.

DESERT HOT SPRINGS SPA. A trip to Palm Springs would not be complete without a visit to the town's namesake. This spa features eight naturally heated mineral pools of different temperatures, as well as saunas, professional massages, and body wraps. *(10805 Palm Dr. in Desert Hot Springs. ☎800-808-7727. Open daily 8am-10pm. M and W $5; Tu $3; Th men $3, women $5; F men $5, women $3; Sa-Su $6. After 3pm weekdays $3, weekends $4. Holidays $7. Rates include admission to pools, dry sauna, and locker rooms.)*

PALM SPRINGS DESERT MUSEUM. This remarkable museum features frequently changing exhibits centered on art, history, and culture. The museum sponsors performances in the 450-seat **Annenberg Theatre** (☎325-4490) as well as curator-led field trips into the canyons in winter. *(101 Museum Dr. Take SunBus #111. ☎322-4839. Open Tu-Sa 10am-5pm, Su noon-5pm. $8; seniors $6.50; students, ages 6-17, and military $3.50. Free 1st F of each month. Field trips $3.)*

UPRISING ROCKCLIMBING CENTER. Prep for nearby Joshua Tree at this gigantic outdoor climbing structure (the only one of its kind in the US). Whether you're a beginner or a seasoned climber, you'll find a fun challenge cranking on plastic rock beneath a canopy that wards off the sun. Expert instruction and supervision available; excursions on real rock by arrangement. *(1500 Gene Autry Trail. ☎888-254-6266; www.uprising.com. Open July-Aug. Tu-F. 4-8pm, Sa-Su. 10am-6pm; Sept.-June M-F 10am-8pm, Sa-Su 10am-6pm. Day pass $15, equipment rental $7. Lessons from $45 per day.)*

PALM SPRINGS AIR MUSEUM. Featuring an extensive collection of WWII aircraft and memorabilia, the museum is enjoyable for aviation buffs and novices alike. *(745 N. Gene Autry Trail, near the airport. ☎778-6262. Open Sept.-May daily 10am-5pm; June-Aug. daily 8am-3pm. $8, seniors $6.50, children $3.50.)*

PALM SPRINGS AERIAL TRAMWAY. If Mt. San Jacinto's 10,804 ft. escarpment is too much for your legs to take, this world-famous tram can whisk you to the top in 15min. At 8,516 ft. above the desert, the observation deck has great views of the Coachella Valley. *(On Tramway Rd. off North Palm Canyon Drive. ☎325-1449 or 325-1391; www.pstramway.com. Trams run at least every 30min.; M-F 10am-8pm, Sa-Su 8am-8pm. Last tram down at 9:45pm. Round-trip fare $21, seniors $19, ages 3-12 $14, ages 2 and under free.)*

INDIAN CANYONS. These four canyons offer the city's only naturally cool water, as well as remnants of the Cahuilla Indian communities. Ranger-led tours demonstrate how the Cahuilla people once utilized the area's flora and fauna, which includes the world's densest patch of naturally occurring palm trees. In the cooler months, these canyons are beautiful places to hike, picnic, or horseback ride. *(Three of the canyons are located 5 mi. south of town at the end of S. Palm Canyon Dr. ☎325-3400 or 800-790-3398. Open daily 8am-5pm. Tours M-Th 10am-1pm, F-Su 9am-3pm. Admission $6; students, seniors, and military $4.50; ages 6-12 $2; 5 and under free. Tours $6; children $2. Tahquitz Canyon is located at the west end of Mesquite Rd. ☎416-7044. It has a separate visitors center, as well as a spectacular 60 ft. waterfall during the winter. Tours $12.50, children $6.)*

TENNIS & GOLF. Palm Springs has several public tennis and golf facilities. There are 8 courts at **Ruth Hardy Park.** *(700 Tamarisk Dr., at Avenida Caballeros. Open dawn-dusk.)* **Tahquitz Creek Golf Resort,** managed by Arnold Palmer, claims to be one of the nation's top municipal golf courses. *(1885 Golf Club Dr. ☎328-1005. 18 holes M-F $28, Sa-Su $35; in winter M-F $60-90, Sa-Su $70-95. Discounts after 10pm. Fees include carts.)* The city's **Recreation Division** has more info on Palm Springs' many lawns and links. Many nicer hotels and resorts offer golf deals to their guests. *(☎323-8273.)*

KNOTT'S SOAK CITY WATER PARK. Immersed in the life-source of desert existence, fun-lovers of all ages surf, slide, and soak in the wave pool, inner tube river, and on 18 different waterslides and attractions. *(Off I-10 South on Gene Autry Trail between Ramon and E. Palm Canyon Dr. ☎327-0499. Open Mar.-Labor Day daily 11am-6pm; Labor Day-Oct. Sa-Su 11am-6pm. $22, children under 5 ft. and seniors $13, ages 2 and under free. $13 after 3pm. Parking $6.)*

CELEBRITY TOURS. Find further evidence that celebrities are wealthier and more glamorous than you—just don't expect to see an actual celebrity. Your closest brush with fame might be seeing Bob Hope's gardener weeding outside of Bob's high adobe wall. The 1hr. tour drives past 30-40 celebrity homes and includes guided narration. *(4751 E. Palm Canyon Dr., Ste. D. ☎770-2700. Open in winter daily 8am-5pm; summer Tu-Sa 7:30am-2:30pm. Guided tours from $17, seniors $15, under 17 $8.)*

WIND FARM TOURS. The unusual topography and outrageous temperatures of the Palm Springs region generate some of the world's strongest sustained winds. On the wind farm, about 3500 high-tech windmills harness this energy. Even if you forgo the tours, given by **Windmill Tours, Inc.,** drive down I-10 to see the oddly spectacular forest of whirling blades. *(Located 1¼ mi. west of Indian Canyon Drive on 20th Ave., just across I-10. ☎251-1997. 4 tours per day M-Sa 9, 11am, 1, 3pm. Reservations required. $23, seniors $20, students $15, ages 6-13 $10, under 6 free.)*

📢 NIGHTLIFE

The glitz of Palm Springs doesn't disappear with the setting sun—the city's nightlife is almost as heralded as its golf courses. Although a night of total indulgence here might cost a small fortune, several bars provide nightly drink specials and lively people-watching. **La Taquería,** 125 E. Tahquitz Way (☎778-5391), specializes in ultra-fresh and healthy Mexican cuisine; the mist-enshrouded tile patio is great for sipping Moonlight Margaritas ($6). Locals hang at the **Village Pub,** 266 S. Palm Canyon Dr., for easygoing beer-swilling and folksy live rock. The crowd is usually 25+, but it gets younger on the weekends. (☎323-3265. 21+. Open daily 11am-2am.) Those willing to open the wallet a little wider for a night on the town can head to **Atlas,** 210 S. Palm Canyon Dr. The hip, ultra-modern restaurant and dance club is in the heart of downtown. It's fusion specialties are just as modern. (☎325-8839. Entrees $15-25. Local DJs nightly. 21+ for dancing. Open daily 11am-2pm.)

Palm Springs is a major destination for gay and lesbian travelers. The gay scene sparkles with bars, spas, and clothing-optional resorts. The comprehensive *Gay Guide to Palm Springs*, available at the Visitors Center, provides a wealth of pertinent information about the area.

⬛ SEASONAL EVENTS

Village Fest (☎320-3781) takes over Palm Canyon Dr. downtown every Thursday night from 6-10pm (in summer 7-10pm). Vendors market food, jewelry, and crafts in a bargain bonanza, while townsfolk enjoy live entertainment. It's definitely a great place to bring kids.

Attempting to fulfill his campaign promise to heighten Palm Springs's glamour quotient, former mayor Sonny Bono instituted the annual **Nortel Networks Palm Springs International Film Festival** (☎778-8979. Jan. 9-20 in 2003). The **57th Annual National Date Festival,** Rte. 111 in Indio (☎863-8247; Feb. 14-23 in 2003), is not a hook-up scene but a bash for dried-fruit lovers. Palm Springs is also famous for its tennis tournaments and its professional golf tournaments, like the **44th Annual Bob Hope Chrysler Classic** (☎346-8184. Jan. 27-Feb. 2 in 2003) and the LPGA's **32nd Annual Kraft Nabisco Championship.** (☎324-4546.)

NEAR PALM SPRINGS

Living Desert Wildlife and Botanical Park, 47900 Portola Ave., Palm Desert, 1½ mi. south of Rte. 111, has Arabian oryx, camels, and meerkats. Wear sunscreen and bring water; there isn't much shade, though misters are available. (☎346-5694; www.livingdesert.org. Open Sept.-June daily 9am-5pm, last admission at 4pm; July-Aug. daily 8am-1:30pm, last admission at 1pm. Sept.-June $8.50, seniors and military $7.50, ages 3-12 $4.50; July-Aug. $6.50, ages 3-12 $3.50.)

Since the **Coachella Valley** is the self-proclaimed "Date Capital of the World," comb your hair, suck down a breath mint, and head to the **Shields Date Gardens,** 80225 Rte. 111, in nearby Indio. This palm grove sets itself apart from the rest by presenting an amusing, free film titled *The Romance and Sex Life of the Date.* (☎347-0996 or 800-414-2555. Open Sept.-May daily 8am-6pm; June-Aug. daily 9am-5pm.) If Palm Springs isn't enough of a zoo, you can observe wildlife at the **Big Morongo Canyon Preserve,** off Rte. 62, an animal and bird sanctuary. (☎363-7190. Open daily 7:30am-dusk. Free.) Northeast of Palm Springs in Thousand Palms, the **Coachella Valley Preserve** has a Visitors Center that can help you plan a hike through mesas, bluffs, or the **Thousand Palms Oasis,** which are homes to the protected fringe-toed lizard. (☎343-2733 or 343-4031. Open Sept.-June sunrise-sunset.)

THE HIGH DESERT

Scorching, silent, and barren, the High Desert is the picture of desolation. The Mojave, however, conceals unlikely treasures for those patient and brave enough to explore it. Genuine summer attractions are rare, but temperate winters allow one to trudge across drifting dunes and creep through spooky ghost towns.

JOSHUA TREE NATIONAL PARK   ☎760

When devout Mormon pioneers crossed this faith-testing desert in the 19th century, they named the enigmatic tree they encountered after the Biblical prophet Joshua. The tree's crooked limbs resembled the Hebrew general, who, with his arms upraised, seemed to beckon them to the Promised Land. Even today, Joshua Tree National Park inspires reverent awe in those who happen upon it. Piles of wind-sculpted boulders, flanked by seemingly jubilant Joshua trees, hearken to the magnificent devastation of Jericho. The park's five oases appear lushly Edenic against the desolate backdrop of the desert, forming unique reservoirs of life.

In recent years, climbers, campers, and daytrippers from Southern California have added to the mosaic. "Josh," as outdoor enthusiasts call it, has become a world-renowned mecca for both casual and elite climbers. History buffs will appreciate the vestiges of human occupation—ancient rock petroglyphs, 19th-century dams built to catch the meager rainfall for livestock, and gold mine ruins that dot the landscape. But the most attractive aspect of Joshua Tree is its remoteness and its freedom from the commercial mayhem that has infested many national parks, for its natural beauty is interrupted only by a few paved roads and signs.

At the north entrance to the park lies the town of **Twentynine Palms,** settled after World War I by veterans looking for a hot, dry climate to soothe their gas-seared lungs. Today, the town also hosts the world's largest US Marine Corps base, as well as lavish murals depicting personages and events from the town's past.

■✦🛈 ORIENTATION

About 160 mi. east of L.A., Joshua Tree National Park covers 558,000 acres northeast of Palm Springs. High and low desert ecologies subsist here. The park has over 4500 established rock climbing routes, and five oases. The most distinguishing features of Joshua Tree are the trees themselves. Visitors will be enchanted by the outline of their twisted limbs against the desert sky.

AT A GLANCE	
AREA: 558,000 acres.	**GATEWAYS:** Twentynine Palms.
CLIMATE: Arid and dry, high and low desert.	**CAMPING:** Reservations accepted at some sites, Oct.-May 14-day max stay. No RVs.
FEATURES: Joshua Trees, Cholla Cactus Garden, Oasis of Mara.	**FEES & RESERVATIONS:** $10 entrance fee per car; $5 if entering by foot or bike. No reservations necessary.
HIGHLIGHTS: Drive through Geology Tour Road, scramble through the Wonderland of Rocks.	

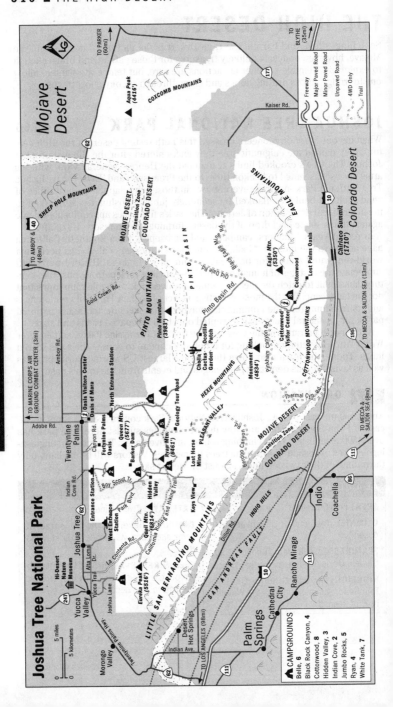

Joshua Tree National Park

Mojave Desert

Colorado Desert

TO PARKER (60mi)

TO BLYTHE (35mi)

TO AMBOY & 40 (48mi)

TO MARINE CORPS AIR GROUND COMBAT CENTER (3mi)

TO MECCA & SALTON SEA (13mi)

TO MECCA & SALTON SEA (8mi)

TO LOS ANGELES (98mi)

COXCOMB MOUNTAINS

Aqua Peak (4416')

SHEEP HOLE MOUNTAINS

Kaiser Rd.

MOJAVE DESERT TRANSITION ZONE COLORADO DESERT

PINTO BASIN

PINTO MOUNTAINS

Pinto Mtn. (3983')

Gold Crown Rd.

Old Dale Rd.

Black Eagle Rd.

EAGLE MOUNTAINS

Eagle Mtn. (5350')

Cottonwood

Lost Palms Oasis

Chiriaco Summit (1710')

Colorado Desert

Oasis Visitors Center

Oasis of Mara

North Entrance Station

Twentynine Palms

Adobe Rd.

Amboy Rd.

Canyon Rd.

Fortynine Palms Oasis

HEXIE MOUNTAINS

Cholla Cactus Garden

Ocotillo Patch

Pinto Basin Rd.

Monument Mtn. (4834')

Pinkham Canyon Rd.

COTTONWOOD MOUNTAINS

Cottonwood Visitor Center

Thermal Cyn. Rd.

Geology Tour Road

Queen Mtn. (5677')

Barker Dam

Ryan Mtn. (5461')

Lost Horse Mine

PLEASANT VALLEY

Berdoo Canyon

MOJAVE DESERT TRANSITION ZONE COLORADO DESERT

Entrance Station

West Entrance Station

Indian Cove Rd.

Boy Scout Tr.

Hidden Valley

Quail Mtn. (5814')

Keys View

California Riding and Hiking Trail

Joshua Tree

Hi-Desert Nature Museum

Alta Loma Dr.

La Contenta Rd.

Park Blvd.

Yucca Trail

Yucca Lane

Joshua Lane

Eureka Peak (5516')

LITTLE SAN BERNARDINO MOUNTAINS

SAN ANDREAS FAULT

Dillon Rd.

INDIO HILLS

Indio

Coachella

Rancho Mirage

Cathedral City

Palm Springs

Desert Hot Springs

Indian Ave.

Yucca Valley

Morongo Valley

Twentynine Palms Hwy.

Mojave Desert

CAMPGROUNDS
Belle, 6
Black Rock Canyon, 4
Cottonwood, 8
Hidden Valley, 3
Indian Cove, 2
Jumbo Rocks, 5
Ryan, 4
White Tank, 7

Freeway
Major Paved Road
Minor Paved Road
Unpaved Road
4WD Only
Trail

THE DESERT

5 miles
5 kilometers

🔍 PRACTICAL INFORMATION

 WHEN TO GO. The desert is very arid and dry. It is best to avoid visiting Joshua Tree from June-Sept. The park's most temperate weather is in late fall (Oct.-Dec.) and early spring (Mar.-Apr.); temperatures in other months often span uncomfortable extremes (summer highs 95-115ºF, winter lows 30º-40º). For more advice on beating the heat, see **Desert Survival,** p. 505.

The park is ringed by three highways: **I-10** to the south, **Route 62 (Twentynine Palms Highway)** to the west and north, and **Route 177** to the east. The northern entrances to the park are off Rte. 62 at the towns of **Joshua Tree** and **Twentynine Palms.** The south entrance is at **Cottonwood Spring,** off I-10 at **Route 195,** south of Palm Springs near the town of Indio. The **park entrance fee,** valid for seven days, is $5 per person or $10 per car.

Visitor Information:

Headquarters and Oasis Visitors Center, 74485 National Park Dr. (☎367-5500; www.joshua-tree.org), ¼ mi. off Rte. 62 in Twentynine Palms, is the best place to familiarize yourself with the park. Friendly rangers, plus displays, guidebooks, maps, and water. Open daily 8am-5pm.

Cottonwood Visitors Center, at the southern gateway of the park, 7 mi. north of I-10 and 25 mi. east of Indio. Information, water, and picnic areas are available here. Open daily 8am-4pm.

Indian Cove Ranger Station, 7295 Indian Cove Rd. (☎362-4367). Open Oct.-May daily 8am-4pm; summer hours vary.

Twentynine Palms Chamber of Commerce, 6455 Mesquite Ave., Ste. A (☎367-3445), provides info on murals, transportation, town accommodations, and food. Open M-F 9am-5pm; may close for lunch.

Rock Climbing Gear and Guiding: Nomad Ventures, 61795 Twentynine Palms Hwy., (☎366-4684) in the town of Joshua Tree, has a ton of gear, information and advice, especially for more experienced climbers. **Joshua Tree Climbing School** (☎800-890-4745; www.rockclimbing.com) will set you up with gear, guiding, and instruction, no matter what level of experience you have.

Emergency: 24hr. Dispatch (☎909-383-5651). Call collect.

Medical Services: Hi-Desert Medical Center, 6601 White Feather Rd. (☎ 366-3711), in Joshua Tree. Emergency care 24hr.

Internet Access: Tommy Paul's Beatnik Cafe (see **Food,** p. 518).

Post Office: 73839 Gorgonio Dr. (☎800-275-8777), in Twentynine Palms. Open M-F 8:30am-5pm. **Postal Code:** 92277.

🏠 ACCOMMODATIONS

Those who cannot stomach the thought of desert campgrounds can find inexpensive motels in **Twentynine Palms,** the self-proclaimed "Oasis of Murals." The **29 Palms Inn ❹,** 73950 Inn Dr., is an attraction in itself. Its 19 distinctly different rooms face the Mara Oasis, which has supported life for over 20,000 years. More recently, the life here has been of the celebrity genus, with guests like Michelle Pfeiffer and Nicolas Cage. Robert Plant composed his post-Zeppelin hit "29 Palms" here. (☎367-3505. Reservations required Feb.-Apr. Doubles June-Sept. Su-Th $50-80, F-Sa $65-105; Oct.-May $10-20 extra. Cottages for 4-8 people and air-stream trailers also available.) Clean, reliable **Motel 6 ❸,** 72562 Twentynine Palms Hwy., has a pool. (☎367-2833. Singles $40-44; doubles $46-50; each additional adult $3.) While creating the album *Joshua Tree* in 1987, U2 stayed in one of the 10 units at the **Harmony Motel ❹,** 71161 Twentynine Palms Hwy. (☎367-3351. Rooms recently refurbished. A/C. Singles and doubles $50-60, more for kitchen.)

🏕 CAMPING

Camping is an enjoyable and inexpensive way to experience the beauty of the park, except in the scorching heat of summer. Even then, when the sun goes down the temperatures drop to comfortable levels. Most campgrounds in the park operate on a first-come, first-camp basis and accept no reservations (campgrounds that require separate fees do take reservations). Spring weekends and holidays are the busiest times. Reservations can be made for group sites only at Cottonwood, Sheep Pass, Indian Cove, and Black Rock Canyon through DESTINET (☎800-436-7275). Experienced campers can register at the Visitors Center for a backcountry permit. All campsites have tables, firepits, and pit toilets. There are no hookups for RVs, and only those campgrounds that take reservations offer water or flush toilets—those who plan an extended stay should pack their own supplies. (Campgrounds Oct.-May 14-day max. stay; 30-day camping limit each year.)

■ **Indian Cove,** 3200 ft., on the north edge of Wonderland of Rocks. Enter at the north entrance on Indian Cove Rd. off of Twentynine Palms Hwy. Rains create dramatic waterfalls. Popular spot for rock climbers. 107 sites. Sites $10; 13 group sites $20-35. ❶

■ **Jumbo Rocks,** 4400 ft., near Skull Rock Trail on the eastern edge of Queen Valley. Take Quail Springs Rd. 15 mi. south of the Visitors Center. The highest and coolest campground in the park, featuring many sites surrounded by—imagine this—jumbo rocks. Front spots have shade and protection. Wheelchair accessible. 125 sites. Free. ❶

White Tank, 3800 ft. Few people, but watch for coyotes that may try to keep you company. 15 sites amid huge boulder towers. Free. ❶

Hidden Valley, 4200 ft., in the center of the park off Quail Springs Rd. Secluded alcoves are perfect for pitching tents, and enormous shade-providing boulders serve as perches for viewing the sun at dawn and dusk. Its proximity to Wonderland of Rocks and the Barker Dam Trail makes this a rock climber's dream. The 39 sites fill up quickly. Free. ❶

Sheep Pass, 4500 ft., in center of the park near the trail to Ryan Mountain. Huge boulders and lots of Joshua trees make this site fairly cool and secluded. 6 group spots only, which can be reserved up to 3 months in advance. Sites $20-35. ❷

Belle, 3800 ft., within view of the Pinto Mountains, is an ideal place to stare at the starry heavens. 18 sites, tucked away in the crevices of large boulders. Free. ❶

Ryan, 4300 ft., has fewer rocks, but also less privacy and less shade, than nearby Hidden Valley. The 3 mi. round-trip trail ascends to Ryan Mountain, which served as the headquarters and water storage for the Lost Horse gold mine. The sunrise is spectacular from nearby Key's View (see p. 519). 31 sites. Free. ❶

Black Rock Canyon, 4000 ft., at the end of Joshua Ln. off Rte. 62 near Yucca Valley. Good for those who haven't camped before, due to the proximity of Yucca Valley, water, and a ranger station. A great place to spot animals, and there are various hiking trails nearby. Wheelchair accessible. 100 sites. Reservations accepted. Sites $10. ❶

Cottonwood, 3000 ft., offers no shade from the open Colorado Desert portion of the park, but it's the first place where wildflowers appear after sufficient rain. (To find out when, see **Wildflower Hotline,** p. 520.) Flush toilets and running water. Wheelchair accessible. 62 sites, 30 in summer. Sites $8; 3 group sites for 10-70 people $25. ❶

🍴 FOOD

Although there are no food facilities within the park, Twentynine Palms offers groceries and grub. While the food is not exactly gourmet, it's certainly possible to eat well. If you are willing to cook, the **Stater Brothers** supermarket, 71727 Twentynine Palms Hwy., saves you a bundle and has a good selection. (☎367-6535. Open daily

6am-11pm.) The other option is fast food or its local equivalent. **The Finicky Coyote ❶**, 73511 Twentynine Palms Hwy., has sandwiches, coffee drinks, smoothies, and ice cream that will make you howl. (☎367-2429. Open M-Th 6am-6pm, F 6am-7pm, Sa-Su 7am-3pm.) **Rocky's New York Style Pizza ❸**, 73737 Twentynine Palms Hwy. is where all the locals go to satisfy their cravings. Pizzas and subs $7-15. (☎367-9525. Open 11am-10pm.) The friendly folks at **Tommy Paul's Beatnik Cafe ❶**, 61597 Twentynine Palms Hwy., in the town of Joshua Tree, serve hot coffee, but you may prefer to douse your heat-addled brain in frosty beer or ice cream while you search the Internet for heat stroke treatments. (☎366-9799. Open W 11am-midnight, Th and Su 11am-9pm, F-Sa 11am-11pm. Internet access $0.15 per min.)

◉ 🅝 SIGHTS & HIKING

Over 80% of Joshua Tree is designated as wilderness area, safeguarded against development, and thus lacks paved roads, toilets, and campfires. The park offers truly remote territory for back country desert hiking and camping. Hikers who seize the opportunity should pack plenty of water and keep alert for flash floods and changing weather conditions. Be sensitive to the extreme fragility of the desert and refrain from venturing off established trails. Do not enter abandoned mine shafts, as they are unstable and often filled with poisonous gases.

BY VEHICLE. The craggy mountains and boulders of Joshua Tree acquire a fresh poignancy at sunrise and sunset, when an earthy crimson washes across the desert. Daytrippers forgo these moments of quiet serenity for which the High Desert is justly renowned. A self-paced **driving tour** is an easy way to explore the park. All park roads are well marked, and signs labeled "Exhibit Ahead" point the way to information about unique floral and geological formations. One of these tours, a 34 mi. stretch across the center of the park from Twentynine Palms to the town of Joshua Tree, provides access to the park's most outstanding sights and hikes. An especially spectacular leg of the road is **Keys View** (5185 ft.), 6 mi. off the park road west of Ryan campground. On a clear day, you can see forever—or at least to Palm Springs and the Salton Sea. It's also a great spot for watching the sunrise. The longer drive through the park from Twentynine Palms to I-10 traverses High and Low Desert landscapes. The **Cholla Cactus Garden,** a grove of spiny succulents resembling deadly 3-D asterisks, lies in the Pinto Basin just off the road. A short hike through the garden is marked with numbers explaining the plant life.

Those with **four-wheel-drive** vehicles have even more options, including the 18 mi. **Geology Tour Road,** which climbs through striking rock formations and ends in the Little San Bernardino Mountains. In the spring and fall, **bikers** can enjoy these roads, especially the unpaved and relatively unpopulated 4WD-only roads through **Pinkham Canyon** and past the **Black Eagle Mines.** Both begin at the Cottonwood Visitors Center (see p. 517). Bikers should check the free park guide for more info.

BY FOOT. Despite the plethora of driving routes, **hiking** is perhaps the best way to experience Joshua Tree. The desert often appears monotonous through a car window, and it's only when walking that one begins to appreciate the subtler beauties of the park. On foot, visitors can tread through sand, scramble over boulders, and walk among the park's hardy namesakes. Twelve different interpretive trails, each easy to complete in under an hour, wind their way down well-marked paths. The 1 mi. **Hidden Valley Interpretive Trail** winds its way around boulders while signs point out the history of man in the park. Although the 1.1 mi. **Barker Dam Trail,** next to Hidden Valley, is often packed with tourists, its painted petroglyphs and eerie tranquility make it a worthwhile hike. In winter and spring, the dam holds back a pond of water, a rare sight in the dry desert. The **Arch Rock Interpretive Trail,** accessible

THE DESERT

FROM THE ROAD

DESERT DRIVING

've been driving in California for five years and thought I'd tackled it all: narrowing cliffs along Rte. 1 and San Francisco hills with a stick-shift. But 'd never driven in the desert. Flat and straight, what could be easier? But Death Valley threw a couple of unexpected tricks at me.

First, what appears flat in the Valley often isn't. Rising dunes seemed to stretch out horizontally in front of me, but my '86 Volvo station wagon, told another story. In third gear, I crawled along at 35 mph, wondering f my cell phone would work when my car quit. As the temperature gauge slowly rose, I angrily flipped off the A/C. Pressing my hand to the window told me it was still above 100°F outside. Shifting down to second brought me to the crest of the "flat," and I encountered the second danger of desert driving: the need for speed.

In the desert, it's very, very tempting to allow gravity to pull your car along well above the speed limit. Dips n the road become exhilarating roller-coaster rides and for a city girl, the oads in the desert made driving fun again. But all this fun can have a hefty price tag. To the west of Death Valley, the whoosh of air past the car was met with another sound: sirens. The $140 spent on a speeding ticket could have bought over 20 rides on Las Vegas's fastest roller coasters.

After spending some time successfully navigating in the desert, you begin to feel invincible. The trick is to not let this feeling take over, or you'll find yourself overheated, either because the air conditioning is off or because you're out $140.

–Sara Clark

behind site 9 at White Tank Campground, is a short jaunt through the geological history of Joshua Tree. The **Lost Horse Mine**, near Key's View, rests in peace at the end of a 1.5 mi. trail, commemorating the region's gold prospecting days with rusted machinery and abandoned mineshafts. From the top of **Ryan Mountain** (5461 ft.), the boulder formations in the encircling valley bear an unsettling resemblance to enormous beasts of burden toiling toward a distant destination. Bring plenty of water for the strenuous, unshaded 1.5 mi. climb to the summit. Or head to the northern edge of the park and hike the 1.5 mi. moderately strenuous climb to the pristine **49 Palms Oasis.** Again, be sure to bring plenty of water, as the oasis does not offer any potable water for hikers. The Visitors Center has info on the park's other hikes, which range from a 15min. stroll to the **Oasis of Mara** to a three-day trek along the **California Riding and Hiking Trail** (35 mi.). The ranger-led **Desert Queen Ranch Walking Tour** (Oct.-May daily 10am and 1pm; June-Aug. W and F 5:30pm; $5) covers the ranch of homesteader Bill Keys. Informative rangers lead the 1½hr. tour. Anticipate slow progress even on short walks; the oppressive heat and the scarcity of shade makes even the hardiest of hikers feel the strain and pain.

The tenacious wildflowers that struggle into colorful bloom each spring (mid-Mar. to mid-May) attract thousands of visitors. More robust plants like Joshua trees, cholla, and the spidery ocotillo have adapted to the severe climate in fascinating ways. To avoid the harsh social stigma that accompanies floral ignorance, get updates on the blooming status of yucca, verbena, cottonwood, mesquite, and other wildflowers by calling the **Wildflower Hotline** (☎818-768-3533).

The beds of wildflowers provide a habitat for Joshua Tree's many animal species, and the trees and reeds of the park's oases play host to ladybugs, bees, golden eagles, and bighorn sheep. Kangaroo rats, lizards, and stinkbugs scamper about at all times of day, while wily coyotes, bobcats, and the occasional rattlesnake stalk their prey (including people and unleashed pets) after dusk.

ROCK CLIMBING. The crack-split granite of Josh provides some of the best rock climbing and bouldering on the planet for experts and novices alike. The world-renowned boulders at **Wonderland of Rocks** and **Hidden Valley** are always swarming with hard-bodied climbers, making Josh the most climbed area in America. (For a local climbing instructor and guide, see **Practical Information,** p. 517.) Adventurous novices will thrill at the **Skull Rock Interpretive Walk,** which runs between Jumbo Rocks and Skull Rock. The walk not only offers info on local plants and animals, but also exciting yet non-technical scrambles to the tops of monstrous boulders.

DEATH VALLEY NATIONAL PARK ☎ 760

The devil owns a lot of real estate in Death Valley. Not only does he grow crops (at Devil's Cornfield) and hit the links (at Devil's Golf Course), but the park is also home to Hell's Gate itself. It's not surprising, then, that the area's astonishing variety of topographical and climatic extremes support just about anyone's idea of the Inferno. Visitors can stare into the abyss from the appropriately named Dante's View, one of several panoramic points approaching 6000 ft. in elevation, or gaze wistfully into the heavens from Badwater, which (at 282 ft. below sea level) is the lowest point in the Western Hemisphere. Winter temperatures dip well below freezing in the mountains, and summer readings in the Valley rival the hottest Hades. In fact, the second-highest temperature ever recorded in the world (134°F in the shade) was measured at the Valley's Furnace Creek Ranch on July 10, 1913.

Fortunately, the fatal threshold of 130°F is rarely crossed, and the region sustains an intricate web of life. Many threatened and endangered species, including the desert tortoise and the desert bighorn sheep, inhabit Death Valley. If you see something unusual, go to a visitors center and fill out a wildlife sighting card. Though much of the land seems desolate and barren, over 500 different species of plants grow in Death Valley.

Human inhabitants have a long history inside the Valley as well. The Shoshone Indians lived in the lower elevations during the winters and retreated into the cooler peaks during the summers. During the California gold rush, immigrants came into the Valley searching for a shortcut across the Sierras. They were unsuccessful, and left as soon as they could find a way out, though not before they lost a member. Looking back at the scene of their misery, someone exclaimed, "Goodbye, Death Valley!" thus naming the area for posterity. Later, miners looking for gold found borax (a type of salt used as a detergent and fire retardant) instead, and boom towns grew around the mines. But once the borax was gone, the prospectors left and often took much of their towns with them, though remains can be seen in places such as **Skidoo** and **Rhoylite.** By 1933, another industry began to grow: tourism. The US government set aside over 3 million acres as a **national park,** leaving the area desolate and beautiful today. The park entrance fee is $10 per vehicle, $5 for non-vehicles, and is collected at Furnace Creek Visitors Center, Grapevine, Stovepipe Wells, and the ranger station in Beatty.

AT A GLANCE	
AREA: 3.3 million acres.	**GATEWAYS:** Beatty, NV (p. 529), Lone Pine (p.295), Shoshone (p. 529).
CLIMATE: Very arid and dry.	
FEATURES: Badwater, Mosaic Canyons, Telescope Peak, Scotty's Castle.	**CAMPING:** 30-day max. stay, 14-day max. stay in Furnace Creek. Backcountry camping is free.
HIGHLIGHTS: Take Dante's View, drive to the bottom of Ubehebe Crater, photograph the Death Valley Sand Dunes.	**FEES & RESERVATIONS:** $10 entrance fee per vehicle, $5 for non-vehicles.

⚜ ORIENTATION

Death Valley is on the eastern edge of the state, next to Nevada and south of Inyo National Forest. Rte. 190 cuts east-west across the Valley. Many sites fall along Rte. 178, which runs north-south through the lower part of the park. Most of Death Valley is below sea-level. Wildflowers, snow-capped peaks, and some of the hottest, driest land in the world can all be found in Death Valley. It rains very infrequently in the park, and temperatures (like topography) fall into extremes.

THE DESERT

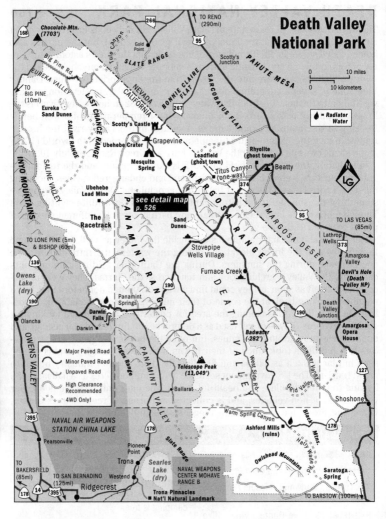

Death Valley National Park

THE DESERT

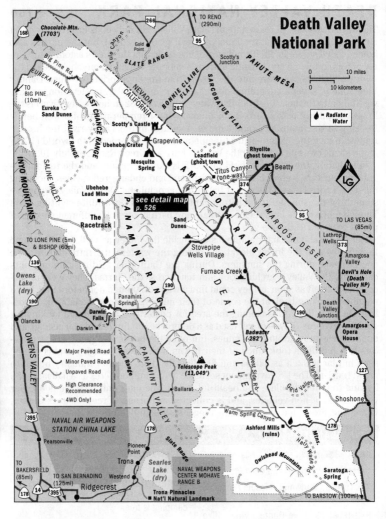

▐ TRANSPORTATION

BY CAR. Cars are the best way to get to and around Death Valley (3½hr. from Las Vegas; 5hr. from L.A.; 7hr. from Tahoe City; 10½hr. from San Francisco). If you are sharing gas costs, renting a car can be cheaper and more flexible than any bus tour. The nearest agencies are in Las Vegas (p. 530), Barstow, and Bishop.

Conditions in Death Valley are notoriously hard on cars. Radiator water (*not* for drinking) is available at critical points on Rtes. 178 and 190 and Nevada Rte. 374. There are only four **service stations** in the park (see **Gas Stations**, p. 523), and though prices are around $0.50 more per gallon than outside the Valley, be sure to keep the tank at least half full at all times. Check ahead with park rangers for road closings, and do not drive on wet and slippery backcountry roads.

Although **four-wheel-drive vehicles** and high-clearance trucks can be driven on narrow roads that lead to some of Death Valley's most spectacular scenery, these roads are intended for drivers with backcountry experience and are dangerous no matter what you're driving. In case of a breakdown, stay with your vehicle or find nearby shade. (For more tips, see **Driving in the Desert,** p. 506.)

Of the seven **park entrances,** most visitors choose Rte. 190 from the east. The road is well maintained, the pass is not too steep, and the visitors center is relatively close. But since most of the major sights adjoin the north-south road, the day-tripper with a trusty vehicle can see more of the park by entering from the southeast (Rte. 178 West from Rte. 127 at Shoshone) or the north (direct to Scotty's Castle via Nevada Rte. 267). Unskilled mountain drivers in passenger cars should not attempt to enter on the smaller Titus Canyon or Emigrant Canyon Dr.

BY OTHER FORMS OF TRANSPORTATION. No regularly scheduled public transportation runs in the Valley. **Guaranteed Tours,** with a depot at the World Trade Center on Desert Inn Rd. between Swensen and Maryland Pkwy. in Las Vegas, runs bus tours from Las Vegas to Death Valley. (☎ 702-369-1000. Open for reservations daily 6am-10:45pm. 9½hr. Tours depart Tu, Th, and Sa 8am. $130, includes lunch.) Those who **hitchhike** walk through the Valley of the Shadow of Death. Don't.

ⓘ PRACTICAL INFORMATION

Gas Stations: Get gas outside Death Valley at Lone Pine, Olancha, Shoshone, or Beatty, NV, or pay $0.50 more per gallon in Death Valley. For gas in the Valley: Furnace Creek Visitors Center (open 7am-7pm), Stovepipe Wells Village (open 7am-9pm), Panamint Springs (open 7am-5pm), or Scotty's Castle (open 9am-5:30pm). Don't play macho with the fuel gauge; fill up often. **AAA towing service, propane gas,** and **diesel fuel** available at the Furnace Creek Chevron.

Furnace Creek Visitors Center (☎ 786-3200; www.nps.gov/deva), on Rte. 190 in the Valley's east-central section. Write for info: Superintendent, Death Valley National Park, Death Valley, CA 92328. Guides and topographical hiking maps ($4-8), schedules of activities and guided hikes, and weather forecasts. A 12min. slide show, a short movie (every hr.), and nightly lectures in winter provide further orientation. Park entrance fee can be paid here. Open daily 8am-6pm.

Ranger Stations: Weather report, weekly naturalist program, and park info at each station. Emergency help provided. **Grapevine** (☎ 786-2313), at Rte. 190 and 267 near Scotty's Castle; **Stovepipe Wells** (☎ 786-2342), on Rte. 190; and **Shoshone** (☎ 832-4308), at Rte. 127 and 178 outside the valley's southeast border. Also in **Beatty, NV** (☎ 702-553-7200), on Nevada Rte. 374. All are technically open daily 8am-5pm, but rangers are often out of the office and in the park.

Death Valley Hikers' Association: Write for info c/o Darrell Tomer, P.O. Box 123, Arcata, CA 95521. The *Dustdevil* is their stellar publication.

Laundromat: (☎ 786-2345), on Roadrunner Ave. at Furnace Creek Ranch. $1 each for wash and dry. Open 24hr.

Showers: Stovepipe Wells Village (☎ 786-2387). Non-guests $2. Open daily 9am-9pm. Also, **Furnace Creek Ranch** (☎ 786-2345) $2. Open daily 9am-11pm.

24hr. Ranger Dispatch and Police: ☎ 786-2330.

Post Office: Furnace Creek Ranch (☎ 786-2223). Open M, W, F 8:30am-3pm, Tu and Th 8:30am-5pm. **Postal Code:** 92328.

THE DESERT

WHEN TO GO. Although the average high temperature in July is 115°F and the nighttime low 88°F, even summer visits can be enjoyable with wise planning. To this end, the Furnace Creek Visitors Center distributes the free pamphlet, *Hot Weather Hints.* There are summer days too hot to hike even with abundant water. Severe heat exhaustion strikes even the fittest people, so do not overestimate your tolerance. (See **Desert Survival,** p. 505.)

You can drive through and admire the beauty of the valley in July and August, but to enjoy the many hiking and camping options, visit between November and April. Winter is the coolest time (temperatures average 39-65°F in the Valley, with freezing temperatures and snow in the mountains) and also the wettest, with infrequent but violent rainstorms that can flood canyons and obliterate roads, trails, and ill-placed tract housing. Call ahead to find out which areas, if any, are washed out before exploring the park.

In March and April, desert wildflowers bloom everywhere, but the season is accompanied by tempestuous winds that whip sand and dust into a blinding frenzy for hours or even days. Traffic jams, congested trails and campsites, hour-long lines for gas, and 4hr. waits at Scotty's Castle plague the area over the winter holidays, during Easter, Thanksgiving, and many three-day winter weekends.

▮▯ ACCOMMODATIONS & FOOD

In Death Valley, affordable beds and inexpensive meals can be as elusive as the desert bighorn sheep. Motel rooms in surrounding towns are cheaper than those in Death Valley, but are over an hour away from top sights. Never assume that rooms will be available. In the winter, camping with a stock of groceries saves money and driving time, but camping can be uncomfortable (to say the least) in the summer, especially at lower elevations. (For more affordable accommodations outside the Valley, see **Life After Death Valley,** p. 529.) For those who wish to make their own meals, **Furnace Creek Ranch Store** is well stocked but expensive. (☎ 786-2381. Open daily 7am-9pm.) **Stovepipe Wells Village Store** is smaller and also expensive. (☎ 786-2578. Open daily 7am-9pm.) Both stores sell charcoal, firewood, and ice.

Stovepipe Wells Village (☎ 786-2387), 30 mi. northwest of Furnace Creek Visitor Center on Rte. 190, is a great in-park option when camping becomes too hot to handle. The village offers comfortable rooms, a mineral water swimming pool, and all the amenities one could ever need. The dining room offers plenty of food, but at stiff prices (breakfast buffet 7-10am, $8; dinner buffet 6-9pm, $17). Rooms for up to 2 people $50-92; each additional person $11. RV sites available. Full hookups $20. ❸

Panamint Springs Resort (☎ 775-482-7680; www.deathvalley.com), 23 mi. east of the park's western border on Rte. 190, is remote but comfortable. The complex includes a restaurant and bar, 18 rooms, RV hookups, campsites, and gas. None of the rooms include TV or phones, but a pay phone is available for public use. The only other tie to civilization is the thunderous roar of naval fighters as they loop and corkscrew overhead on maneuvers from China Lake Naval Weapons Station. Doubles from $65; RV sites $10-25; campsites $10. ❶

Amargosa Hotel (☎ 852-4441), at Death Valley Junction, Rte. 127 and 190, 29 mi. east of Furnace Creek. In a Spanish-style plaza developed by ballet dancer Marta Becket. 4 rooms feature Becket's murals; the other 10 are clean but mural-free. Though the hotel is a welcome retreat in the desert, visitors might be left feeling bored. Outside the opera (see **Southeast of Death Valley,** p. 529), the hotel is the *only* thing in Death Valley Junction. Reception open daily 10am-8pm. Singles from $49; doubles from $66. ❸

▶ CAMPING

The National Park Service maintains nine campgrounds in Death Valley, all of which can provide an inexpensive and comfortable way of seeing the park as long as time of year is taken into consideration. Some of the hottest are closed during the summer (Sunset, Texas Spring, and Stovepipe Wells), and Thordike and Mahogany Flat are closed due to snow and ice in the winter. Pay attention to elevation: the higher up you are, the more comfortable your visit will be when the temperature climbs into the triple digits. The Visitors Center (see **Practical Information,** p. 523) keeps records about site availability; be prepared to battle for a space if you come during peak periods (see **When to Visit,** p. 522). All campsites have toilets, but none have showers. Campers can't always count on water to be available, so always pack your own. The Visitors Center has unlimited free water, though it's as warm as bath water. Collecting wood is forbidden everywhere in the park, so pack your own firewood, and bring a stove and fuel to use where open fires are prohibited. Roadside camping is not permitted, but **backcountry camping** is free and legal, provided you check in at the Visitors Center and pitch tents at least 2 mi. from your car and any road, and ¼ mi. from any backcountry water source. All sites limit stays to 30 days except Furnace Creek, which has a 14-day limit.

Furnace Creek (☎800-365-2267), 196 ft. below sea level, north of the Visitors Center. Furnace Creek is particularly uncomfortable in summer, even though many of the 136 sites are shaded. Usually fills up first in winter, especially with RVs. Near Furnace Creek Ranch facilities ($2 shower access; laundry). 14-day limit. Reservations Oct.-Apr. Sites $16 in winter; $10 in summer. ❷

Sunset, 196 ft. below sea level, and **Texas Springs,** sea level, in the hills above the Furnace Creek Ranch Complex, These two sites are the best place for tents near Furnace Creek activities. Over 1000 sites available, some with shade. For wind protection, stick close to the base of the hills. Generators prohibited. Water and some tables. Open fires permitted. Flush toilets and dump station. Open Oct.-Apr. Sites $10-12. ❶

Stovepipe Wells, sea level. Near airstrip, 4WD trails, and sand dunes. Reminiscent of a drive-in movie lot. Tents compete with RVs for 190 gravel sites. Spots near the trees afford more protection from sandstorms. Close to hotel and general store. A few tables and fireplaces. (Don't confuse it with the trailer park.) Open Oct.-Apr. Sites $10. ❶

Mesquite Springs, 1800 ft., near Scotty's Castle, 2 mi. south of Grapevine Ranger Station. Located in a small valley, some of the 30 sites offer shade and protection from the wind. Listen for coyote and owls. Picnic tables, water, and flush toilets. Open fires permitted. Sites $10. ❶

Emigrant, 2100 ft., off Rte. 190, 9 mi. west of Stovepipe Wells Village across from the ranger station, on the way down from Towne Pass through Panamint Range. This is a tent-only site. Gorgeous view of Stovepipe Wells and the Valley, though sites are located directly next to Rte. 190. 10 sites can be comfortable even in the summer. Flush toilets and water. No fires. Free. ❶

Wildrose, 4100 ft., on the road to the Charcoal Kilns in Wildrose Canyon, at the end of Emigrant Canyon Rd. An old summer residence of the Shoshone Indians, this shady mountainside has the most comfortable temperatures in the park. Convenient base for trips to Skidoo, Aguereberry Point, and Telescope Peak. Water and pit toilets. Open fires permitted. 30 sites. Free. ❶

THE DESERT

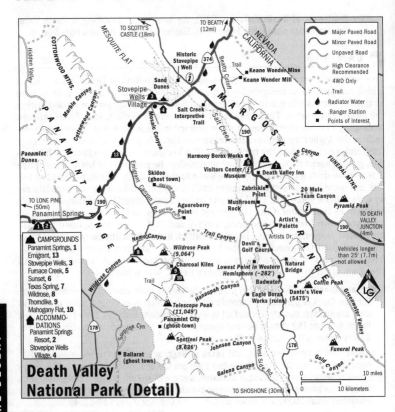

Death Valley National Park (Detail)

Map legend:
- ∼ Major Paved Road
- ∼ Minor Paved Road
- ∼ Unpaved Road
- ∼ High Clearance Recommended
- ---- 4WD Only
- .... Trail
- ◆ Radiator Water
- ▲ Ranger Station
- ■ Points of Interest

CAMPGROUNDS
1. Panamint Springs
2. Emigrant, 13
3. Stovepipe Wells, 3
4. Furnace Creek, 5
5. Sunset, 6
6. Texas Spring, 7
7. Wildrose, 8
8. Thorndike, 9
9. Mahogany Flat, 10

ACCOMMODATIONS
2. Panamint Springs Resort, 2
4. Stovepipe Wells Village, 4

SIGHTS & OUTDOOR ACTIVITIES

Plan your approach to Death Valley (see **Transportation,** p. 522, for a discussion of the various entrances). If exploring the Valley in a day, adopt a north-south or south-north route, rather than heading directly to Furnace Creek Visitors Center on Rte. 190, which connects east with west. Camera-toters should keep in mind that the best photo opportunities are at sunrise and sunset.

TOURS. Rangers and the handouts they dispense give the distances and times of recommended hikes. Ranger-led programs are generally unavailable in summer, but many popular programs, such as the **car caravan tours** and **interpretive talks,** are available in winter and spring. Astronomy buffs should speak to one of the rangers—they often set up telescopes at Zabriskie Point and offer freelance stargazing shows. During **wildflower season,** rangers offer tours of the blooming sites. Wildflower watching is best after a heavy rainfall, when the parched petals of Death Valley's flowers rouse themselves in gratitude. (See **Practical Information,** p. 523.)

DANTE'S VIEW. From atop this 5475 ft. summit, astonishing views along the Valley's floor are available. Temperatures here are around 20 degrees cooler than in the Valley and the area is perfect for a breakfast picnic, when the rising sun washes the entire valley in gold. *(From the Visitors Center, drive 14 mi. east along Rte. 190. Turn right at the Dante's View turn-off. The 13 mi. climb is especially steep at the top.)*

ZABRISKIE POINT. There is a reason Zabriskie Point is usually crawling with camera-toting tourists: it is a marvelous place from which to view Death Valley's corrugated badlands, especially at sunrise or sunset. For an intimate view of them, take the short detour along **20-Mule-Team Rd.** The well-maintained dirt road is named for the gigantic mule trains that used to haul borax 130 mi. south to the rail depot at Mojave. The view of the choppy orange rock formations is particularly stunning late in the day, when the dried lakebeds fill with auburn light. Before the sunset ends, scamper 2 mi. (and 900 ft.) down Gower Gulch to colorful **Golden Canyon,** where the setting sun makes the cliffs glitter like fool's gold. *(3 mi. south of Furnace Creek by car. Take the turn-off from Rte. 190, 1 mi. east of the museum.)*

BADWATER. A briny pool four times saltier than the ocean, this body of water is huge in the winter, but withers into nothing more than a large puddle in the summer. The surrounding salt flat dips to the lowest point in the Western Hemisphere—282 ft. below sea level. Note the sign bolted high on the canyon wall opposite the pool that indicates sea level. The pools shelter the extremely threatened Badwater snails, many of which are crushed by thoughtless waders. Stay out of the water to avoid injuring its fragile ecology. *(18 mi. south of the Visitors Center.)*

DEVIL'S GOLF COURSE. Cyclical flooding and evaporation nurtures the ongoing formation of these gnarled salt pillars. In the burning heat of summer, one can hear faint metallic tinklings as the salt crystals expand and shatter. Refrain from walking far into the saltpan to avoid hurting yourself on the jagged formations, and be careful not to damage the fragile crystals. *(15 mi. south of the Visitors Center.)*

ARTIST'S DRIVE. This one-way loop twists its way through brightly colored rock formations. The loop's early ochres and burnt siennas give way at **Artist's Palette** to sea green, lemon yellow, periwinkle blue, and salmon pink mineral deposits in the hillside. The effect is most intense in the late afternoon, when the setting sun causes rapid color changes of the deposits. The dizzying 9 mi. drive turns back on itself again and again, ending up on the main road only 4 mi. north of the drive's entrance. *(On Rte. 178, 10 mi. south of the Visitors Center.)*

DEATH VALLEY'S SAND DUNES. Although the soft sand can feel nice between the toes, be wary of tumbleweeds and mesquite spines, as well as scorching hot temperatures while clambering over these 150 ft. hills. Also be aware that perceived distances can be misleading; peaks that appear close may really be a 2hr. arduous climb. The most accessible dunes for day hikers lie 2¼ mi. east of Stovepipe Wells Village, where you can use the parking area and follow the 2 mi. trail.. If you want to try your hand at the shutter, ask for the handout on photographing in the setting or rising sun from the Visitors Center. *(22 mi. north of the Visitors Center.)*

MOSAIC CANYON. A half-mile-long corridor of eroded marble walls, this site stands out as a true natural wonder. A simple and relatively flat 2 mi. trail leads from the parking lot around the canyon to some awesome vistas. Occasional bighorn sheep sightings are a bonus. *(Take the turn-off from Rte. 190, 1 mi. west of Stovepipe Wells, to the 2½ mi. alluvial fan, accessible by foot, horseback, or car.)*

EMIGRANT CANYON ROAD. This winding road leads from the Emigrant Campground to Wildrose Canyon Dr. In between, there is a turn-off for the 4WD skedaddle to the ruins of **Skidoo,** a ghost town 5700 ft. up in the Panamint Range. Skidoo was the backdrop for the only full-length movie ever shot in Death Valley (Erich von Stroheim's *Greed*, 1923). A few miles down Emigrant Canyon Rd. is the turn-off for the dirt road to **Aguereberry Point** (may require 4WD), known for its fine sunset views. A left turn at Wildrose Canyon Dr. followed by a 10 mi. drive (last 2 mi. unpaved gravel) brings you to the 10 conical furnaces known as the **Charcoal Kilns,** huge ovens that once fired 45 cords of wood at a time to make charcoal for mines.

THE DESERT

HOMETOWN OF THE LIVING DEAD Authentic California ghost towns are hard to find. Darwin, which housed 5000 at its peak and allegedly produced 50% of the lead used by the U.S. in WWII, is probably the closest thing you'll find to a genuine, decaying-yet-walkable ghost town. Its mines and mills closed in the 1970s, leaving a population of 35-40 artists, writers, artisans, and retirees, plus a multitude of buried dead. The graveyard boasts poorly buried corpses, wooden markers, and the ostentatious tomb of Nancy Williams, Darwin's brothel keeper from better times. The only place in town where you're liable to find living people is the post office, which doubles as the business headquarters for "suspension eyewear," worn by the astronauts and Arctic explorers whose photos cover the walls. "The only thing you can buy in Darwin," they'll tell you, "is stamps." Take a look around anyway. If the abandoned tract housing, ramshackle homes, and RVs don't freak you out, the graveyard outside of town probably will. Spoooky.

TELESCOPE PEAK. A one-way, 14 mi. trail through the **Panamint Mountains** leads up to the 11,049 ft. summit of the park's highest peak. The strenuous hike begins at Mahogany Flat campground and winds 3000 ft. up past charcoal kilns and bristle cone pines, providing unique views of Badwater and Mt. Whitney. It is helpful to buy topographical maps of the area at a ranger station. The trek becomes a technical mountain climb in winter, requiring axes and crampons. Alert a ranger when you will be climbing and also tell him or her when you expect to return.

TITUS CANYON ROAD. This 27 mi. one-way road winds through rugged and colorful mountains and passes the Leadfield ghost town. The mouth of the canyon is available to all drivers by the 3 mi. gravel road to the west. The rest of the drive is advisable only for high-clearance vehicles, especially after winter rains. Those without such vehicles can hike in via either end. *(The entrance to the canyon is off Rte. 374, 21 mi. east of the junction with Rte. 190.)*

SCOTTY'S CASTLE. Remarkably out of place in the desert, this castle's imaginative exterior rises from the sands, complete with minaret and Arabian-style colored tile. The saga of the Castle's construction began with the friendship between Chicago insurance millionaire Albert Johnson and the infamous con artist Walter Scott (a.k.a. "Death Valley Scotty"). The museum and "living" tour guides offer a plethora of information on the rest of the story. *(From Rte. 190, look for sign near mile marker 93 and take road junction to Park Rte. 5; follow Rte. 5 for 33 mi. to castle. ☎ 786-2392. Open daily 9am-5pm. Tours every hr. May-Sept.; more frequently Oct.-Apr. $8, seniors $6, ages 6-15 $4. You can purchase tickets until 1hr. before closing, but there are often lines.)*

UBEHEBE CRATER. This blackened volcanic blast site is nearly 1 mi. wide and 462 ft. deep and boasts a spectacular view. The twisty gravel trail leading to the floor of the crater increases one's appreciation for the hole's dimensions, but not nearly as much as the grueling climb back out. A 4WD unpaved road continues 23 mi. south of the crater to the vast **Racetrack Playa**, a dried-up lake basin providing access into Hidden Valley and up White Top Mountain. See the trails left by mysterious **moving rocks** on this lake basin. For an outstanding view of the Racetrack, follow the **Ubehebe Peak Trail** (6 mi. round-trip) from the Grandstand parking area along a steep, twisting pathway. *(8 mi. west of Scotty's Castle.)*

LIFE AFTER DEATH VALLEY

NORTHEAST OF DEATH VALLEY: BEATTY ☎775

When approaching Death Valley from the north, consider kicking back briefly in the town of **Beatty**, NV. Situated 90 mi. northwest of Las Vegas on Rte. 95, Beatty offers weary travelers A/C and gambling facilities in an effort to make up for the desolation of the Valley. Compared to those in Reno and Las Vegas, Beatty's casinos are very relaxed. Wager as little as $1 at blackjack and jaw with the dealers, folks who play slow and seem genuinely sorry to take your money. All casinos are theoretically open 24hr., but by 2am the dealers start eyeing the clock.

Info can be found at **Beatty Visitor Information Center,** 119 E. Main St. (☎553-2424. Open M-F 10am-3pm.) There is public **Internet access** for a nominal fee at the **Beatty Public Library.** (☎553-2257. Open M, W, and Th 9am-3pm, Tu noon-7pm, Sa 9am-noon.) The **Beatty Ranger Station** is well stocked with books, maps, and safety info for desert-bound drivers. (☎553-2200. Open Tu-Sa 8am-4pm.) Sleep in peace at the **Stagecoach Hotel ❸,** on Rte. 95 ½mi. north of town. Amenities include a pool, jacuzzi, casino, and bar. The restaurant serves up diner favorites 24hr. a day, with dinners ranging from $6-10. (☎533-2419. Singles and doubles from $35.) Cheaper rooms can be found at the **El Portal Motel ❷,** on Rte. 374, one block from the junction with Rte. 95. (☎553-2912. Singles $30; doubles $33.) The **Happy Burro Inn ❸,** at Rte. 95 and 3rd St., has clean rooms and $15 RV hookups. The kitchen also serves up standard lunch counter fare. (☎553-2225, casino 553-2445. Kitchen open 24hr. Singles $35; doubles $40; prices $5 higher when they start to fill up.) Don't miss gas and water at the service station before leaving town.

WEST OF DEATH VALLEY

Ghost towns like **Darwin** and a few slightly more populated communities are the only developments that remain on Rte. 190 west of the park. In **Olancha,** the **Ranch Motel ❸** (☎764-2387), on U.S. 395, provides clean, homey rooms in cottage-type buildings. (Singles $49; doubles $59; cabins which sleep 4-8 $130. Rates may vary with the Lone Pine Film Festival or on other holiday weekends.)

Further north along U.S. 395 at the junction with Rte. 136 is the town of **Lone Pine.** Sitting at the base of Mt. Whitney, the shade of the high Sierra Nevadas can be a welcome refuge from the heat of the desert. (See **Lone Pine,** p. 295.)

SOUTHEAST OF DEATH VALLEY

In **Death Valley Junction,** at Rte. 127 and 190, 29 mi. from Furnace Creek, lives mime and ballet dancer Marta Becket, whose **Amargosa Opera House,** is the sole outpost of high culture in the desert. Becket incorporates parts of classical ballet, modern dance, and pantomime into a one-woman show with 47 different characters, drawing packed houses. (☎852-4441. Performances Oct., Dec.-Jan., and May Sa; Nov. and Feb.-Apr. M and Sa. Shows begin at 8:15pm. $15.)

The town of **Shoshone,** at Rte. 127 and 178, 56 mi. southeast of Furnace Creek, serves as a gateway to Death Valley and a base for outdoor adventures. The **Charles Brown General Store and Service Station** is a good place to stock up and fill up. (☎852-4242. Open daily 8am-9pm.) Next door is the brown **Shoshone Inn ❹,** which offers clean (but run-down) rooms and a swimming pool and cable TV. (☎852-4335. Singles $53; doubles $63.) The nearby **Shoshone Trailer Park ❶** has RV hookups, showers, a pool, and even some shade. (☎852-4569. Sites $10; hookups

$15.) Or stop by **Cafe Si Bon ❷,** an outpost of French cuisine in the middle of the desert. Crepes, coffee, and Internet access come at fair prices. (☎852-4224. Crepes $5-7. Internet $1 for 10min. Open M, Th, F 10am-4pm, Sa-Su 10am-6pm.)

South of Shoshone is the small town of **Tecopa,** which offers hot springs and a hostel for outdoor adventurers. Follow the signs to the **Desertaire Hostel HI-AYH ❶,** 2000 Old Spanish Trail Hwy., for knowledgeable owners and cheap sheets. (☎852-4580. Check-in 5-9pm. Open July-May. Dorms $12.)

LAS VEGAS ☎702

Rising out of the Nevada desert, Las Vegas is a shimmering tribute to excess. It is the actualization of a mirage, an oasis of vice and greed, and one very, very good time for those who embrace it. The modern incarnation of the city was founded on gambling, whoring, and mob muscle. And while the mob has more or less slunk away, the others remain indivisible features of this playground town. Nowhere else in America do so many shed their inhibitions and indulge otherwise dormant appetites. Vegas is about money and sex—but mostly money. The huge casinos that dominate the skyline are good at emptying wallets, but deals on entertainment can found if you look hard enough. The secret to enjoying this modern day Sodom is to know who you are. Walk into Vegas with a good idea of what you want to spend and walk away when you're done. There's a busted wallet and a broken heart for every garish neon light in the city.

The draw of Las Vegas lies south of downtown on the fabled Strip of casinos which line Las Vegas Blvd., beginning in earnest just south of the city limits. Here, corporations fall over themselves to one-up the competition and attract tourist dollars with progressively more expensive and over-the-top attractions. Promoters have exploited the themes of every culture, and giant hotels, casinos, minimalls, and amusement parks push the Strip's frontier ever southward, toward the booming housing development of Henderson. People come to this flashing, buzzing, jangling corner of the American dream to get married, then to celebrate anniversaries, and then to share with their kids the magic of Las Vegas.

✦ ORIENTATION

Driving to Vegas from Los Angeles is a straight 300 mi. shot on I-15 (5hr.). From Arizona, take I-40 to Kingman and then take U.S. 93.

Las Vegas has two major casino areas. The **downtown** area, around 2nd and Fremont St., has been converted into a pedestrian promenade. Casinos cluster close together beneath a shimmering space-frame structure spanning over five city blocks. The area is less spectacular than the Strip, but can offer relief from the burning heat and the high-roller lifestyle. However, the surrounding area can be unsafe—if you're not sure whether you belong somewhere, you probably don't. The other main area is the Strip, a collection of mammoth hotel-casinos along **Las Vegas Boulevard.** Parallel to the Strip and in its shadow is **Paradise Road,** also strewn with casinos. Both areas are very busy; traffic can be frustrating. For faster travel north or south, use one of the major roads further east, like Maryland Pkwy.

As in any city with a constant influx of money, many areas of Las Vegas are unsafe. Always stay on brightly lit pathways, and do not wander too far from the major casinos and hotels. **The neighborhoods just north and west of downtown can be especially dangerous.** Despite, or perhaps because of, its debauchery, Las Vegas has a **curfew.** Those under 18 aren't allowed unaccompanied in most public places Sunday through Thursday from 10pm to 5am and Friday and Saturday from midnight to 5am. Laws are even harsher on the Strip, where no one under 18 is allowed unaccompanied 9pm-5am, ever. **The drinking and gambling age is 21.** People under 21 may walk through the casinos, but loitering on casino floors is prohibited.

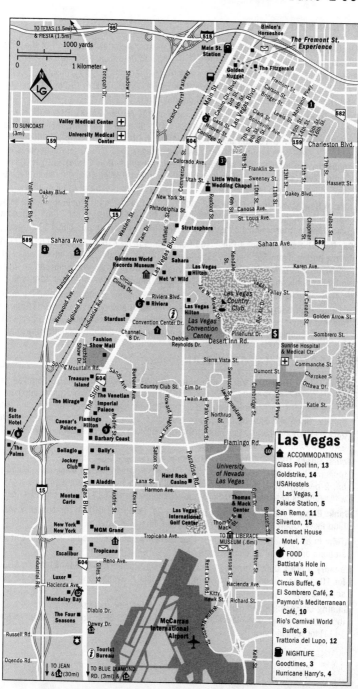

TO TEXAS (1.5mi) & FIESTA (1.5mi)

0   1000 yards

0   1 kilometer

N LG

TO SUNCOAST (3mi)

Binion's Horseshoe

The Fremont St. Experience

Main St. Station

Golden Nugget

The Fitzgerald

Fremont St.

Carson St.

Bridger St.

Clark St.

Lewis St.

Bonneville Ave.

Gass St.

Hoover St.

Coolidge St.

Valley Medical Center

University Medical Center

Charleston Blvd.

Colorado Ave.

Franklin St.

Utah St.

Sweeney St.

Little White Wedding Chapel

New York St.

Canosa Ave.

Philadelphia St.

St. Louis Ave.

Stratosphere

Oakey Blvd.

Hassett St.

Chapman

Talbot St.

Sahara Ave.

Karen Ave.

Guinness World Records Museum

Sahara

Las Vegas Hilton

Wet 'n' Wild

Riviera Blvd.

Las Vegas Country Club

Riviera

Las Vegas Hilton

Stardust

Convention Center Dr.

Las Vegas Convention Center

Golden Arrow St.

Sombrero St.

Channel 8 Dr.

Pinehurst Dr.

Desert Inn Rd.

Fashion Show Mall

Debbie Reynolds Dr.

Sierra Vista St.

Sunrise Hospital & Medical Ctr.

Commanche St.

Spring Mountain Rd.

Dumont St.

Cherokee S

Ottawa Dr.

Treasure Island

Country Club St.

Elm Dr.

Cambridge St.

Katie St.

The Venetian

Twain Ave.

Imperial Palace

The Mirage

Northup St.

Caesar's Palace

Flamingo Hilton

Barbary Coast

Rio Suite Hotel

The Palms

Bellagio

Bally's

Jockey Club

Paris

University of Nevada Las Vegas

Flamingo Rd.

Aladdin

Hard Rock Casino

Lana St.

Harmon Ave.

Monte Carlo

New York New York

Thomas & Mack Center

MGM Grand

Las Vegas International Golf Center

Tropicana Ave.

TO LIBERACE MUSEUM (.6mi)

Excalibur

Reno Ave.

Luxor

Hacienda Ave.

Hacienda Ave.

Mandalay Bay

Richard St.

The Four Seasons

Diablo Dr.

Russell Rd.

Dewey Dr.

McCarran International Airport

Oqendo Rd.

Tourist Bureau

TO JEAN & (30mi)

TO BLUE DIAMOND RD. (3mi) &

Las Vegas

🛏 ACCOMMODATIONS

Glass Pool Inn, **13**
Goldstrike, **14**
USAHostels
  Las Vegas, **1**
Palace Station, **5**
San Remo, **11**
Silverton, **15**
Somerset House
  Motel, **7**

🍴 FOOD

Battista's Hole in
  the Wall, **9**
Circus Buffet, **6**
El Sombrero Café, **2**
Paymon's Mediterranean
  Café, **10**
Rio's Carnival World
  Buffet, **8**
Trattoria del Lupo, **12**

🎭 NIGHTLIFE

Goodtimes, **3**
Hurricane Harry's, **4**

⌸ TRANSPORTATION

Airport: McCarran International (☎261-5743), at the southwestern end of the Strip. Main terminal on Paradise Rd. Vans to the Strip and downtown $3-5; taxi $12-14.

Buses: Greyhound, 200 S. Main St. (☎384-9561 or 800-231-2222), downtown at Carson Ave., near the Plaza Hotel/Casino. Tickets sold 24hr. To: **L.A.** (5-7hr., 22 per day, $33) and **San Francisco** (13-16hr., 6 per day, $63).

Public Transportation: Citizens Area Transit or **CAT** (☎228-7433). Bus #301 serves downtown and the Strip 24hr. Buses #108 and 109 serve the airport. All buses wheelchair accessible. Buses run daily 5:30am-1:30am (24hr. on the Strip). Routes on the Strip $2, residential routes $1.25, seniors and ages 6-17 $0.60. For schedules and maps, try the tourist office or the **Downtown Transportation Center**, 300 N. Casino Center Blvd. (☎228-7433). **Las Vegas Strip Trolleys** (☎382-1404) are not strip joints; they cruise the Strip every 20min. daily 9:30am-1:30am ($1.65 in exact change).

Taxis: Yellow, Checker, and **Star** (☎873-2000). All Las Vegas taxis operate on the same rate. Initial charge $2.30, each additional min. $1.80. For pickup, call 30min. ahead of time. Handicap accessible cabs available. McCarran Airport an additional $1.20 fee.

Car Rental: Sav-Mor Rent-A-Car, 5101 Rent-A-Car Rd. (☎736-1234 or 800-634-6779), at the airport. From $35 per day, $149 per week; 150 mi. per day included, each additional mi. $0.20. Must be 21+, under-25 surcharge $8 per day. Discounts can be found in tourist publications. Open daily 5:30am-1am, airport window opens at 7am.

Parking: Free parking is abundant in Las Vegas if you know where to look. All the major casinos offer both valet and self-park areas for anyone who wants to use it. Both are free, but remember to tip the valet. At some lots you need to validate your parking stub, but this is simply done by walking into the casino and finding the validation machine.

⏻ PRACTICAL INFORMATION

Visitor Information: Las Vegas Convention and Visitor Authority, 3150 Paradise Rd. (☎892-0711; fax 226-9011), 4 blocks from the Strip in the big pink convention center by the Hilton. Up-to-date info on headliners, conventions, shows, hotel bargains, and buffets. Open M-F 8am-5pm. To make reservations for tours, hotels, shows, or travel packages, try the **Las Vegas Tourist Bureau,** 5191 S. Las Vegas Blvd. (☎739-1482; www.lvtb.com). Open daily 7am-11pm.

Tours: Coach USA, 4020 E. Lone Mountain Rd. (☎384-1234 or 800-634-6579). City tours (3½hr., 3 per day, $39). Bus tours from Las Vegas to **Hoover Dam/Lake Mead** (4 hr., 2 per day, $39) and the **Grand Canyon's South Rim** (full-day, $149). Discounts with coupons in tourist publications and for children ages 3-11. Reserve in advance.

Bank: Bank of America, 1140 E. Desert Inn Rd. (☎654-1000), at the corner of Maryland Pkwy. Open M-Th 9am-5pm, F 9am-6pm. Phone assistance 24hr.

ATMs: In all major casinos, but there is at least a $2 charge for each use. Those at gas stations or banks often charge lower fees.

Laundry: Cora's Coin Laundry, 1099 E. Tropicana Rd. (☎736-6181). $1 wash, $0.25 for 10min. dry. Open daily 8am-8pm. Video poker is available while you wait for your socks to dry.

Gaming Lessons: Free at most major casinos in blackjack, roulette, craps, pai gow, Caribbean stud poker, and baccarat. Call **Aladdin** (☎785-5555) or **MGM Grand** (☎891-1111) for session times.

Library and Internet Access: Free Internet access is available at **Clark County Library,** 1401 E. Flamingo Rd. (☎733-7810), but lines are usually very long. Open M-Th 9am-9pm, F-Sa 9am-5pm, Su 1-5pm. A better bet may be **Kinko's,** 4440 Maryland Pkwy. (☎734-1515). $0.20 per min. Open 24hr.

Marriage: Marriage License Bureau, 200 S. 3rd St. (☎455-4415), in the courthouse. 18+ or at least 16 with parental consent. Licenses $50; cash only. No waiting period or blood test required. Open Su-Th 8am-midnight, F-Sa 24hr.

Divorce: Must be a Nevada resident for at least 6 weeks. $150 service fee. Permits available at the courthouse M-F 8am-5pm.

Road Conditions: ☎877-687-6237. **Weather Conditions:** ☎263-9744.

24-Hour Crisis Lines: Compulsive Gamblers Hotline (☎800-LOST-BET/567-8238). **Gamblers Anonymous** (☎385-7732). **Rape Crisis Center Hotline** (☎366-1640). **Suicide Prevention** (☎731-2990).

Police: Corner of Russell Rd. and S. Las Vegas Blvd. ☎795-3111.

Post Office: 301 E. Stewart Ave. (☎800-275-8777), downtown. Open M-F 8:30am-5pm. General Delivery pickup M-F 9am-2pm. Closer to the Strip: 4975 Swensen Ave. M-F 8:30am-5pm. **Postal Code:** 89101.

▟ ACCOMMODATIONS

Even though Vegas has over 100,000 rooms, most hotels fill up on weekend nights. If you get stuck, call the **Room Reservations Hotline** (☎800-332-5333), or go to one of the tourist offices. The earlier you reserve, the better chance you have of snagging a special rate. Room rates at most hotels in Vegas fluctuate all the time, and many hotels have different rate ranges for weeknights and weekend nights. The prices below are only a general guide; you can often get better deals during slow periods, but could be unpleasantly surprised if you try to reserve for a convention weekend. A room that costs $30 during a promotion can cost hundreds during conventions (two major conventions are in Jan. and Nov.). Check local, free, readily available publications such as *What's On In Las Vegas, Today in Las Vegas, 24/7, Vegas Visitor, Casino Player, Tour Guide Magazine, Best Read Guide,* and *Insider Viewpoint of Las Vegas* for discounts, coupons, general info, and several schedules of events.

Strip hotels are at the center of the action and within walking distance of each other, but their inexpensive rooms sell out quickly. Another cluster congregates around Sahara Rd. and S. Las Vegas Blvd. Motels also line **Fremont Street,** though this area is a little rougher; it is best to stay in one of the casinos in the **Fremont Street Experience** (see **Casinos,** p. 536) itself. There is another concentration of inexpensive motels along the southern stretch of the Strip, across from the ritzy **Mandalay Bay.**

Those under 21 may run into difficulty getting a room in Las Vegas. State law makes it illegal for any hotel/casino to rent a room to anyone under this age. However, most hotels are lenient, especially during slower periods. If you run into trouble, head to one of the smaller motels or hostels without casinos attached. **The 9% state hotel tax is not included in room rates listed below.**

▨ **Silverton,** 3333 Blue Diamond Rd. (☎800-588-7711; www.silvertoncasino.com). Cheaper because it's off the Strip, this spooky ghost town-themed gambling den has a re-creation every Su night of a great Wild West tradition—the luau. Free Las Vegas Blvd. shuttle for guests until 10pm. Singles start at $29 Su-Th; doubles $39. F-Sa singles $49; doubles $69. RV park is also available (hookups $27). ❸

THE HIDDEN DEAL

BOUNTIFUL BUFFET

Want to save some of that money for gambling? Haven't yet struck it rich at the black jack table? Though most buffets in Las Vegas are good deals, the **Circus Buffet**, at Circus Circus, is perhaps the best, and definitely the cheapest, buffet on the Strip.

Inside Circus Circus casino, which also holds a roller coaster, slot machines, card tables, a carnival mid-way, and seven other restaurants, Circus Buffet offers the most bang for your buck. The buffet was recently renovated and upgraded; its blue booths and warm wood interior give it a homey appeal. The sparkling service line and friendly chefs do little to dissuade your appetite.

But the best thing of all is that, unlike at other obesity-inducing Las Vegas buffets, you won't have to stuff yourself to feel like you got your money's worth. With breakfast at a reasonable $5.50 and dinner at a mere $8, Circus Buffet is by far the easiest way to keep yourself fueled for those future hot streaks, and comforted after those devastating losses. (2880 S. Las Vegas Blvd. ☎734-0410. Open daily 7am-1pm and 4:30-10pm.)

San Remo, 115 E. Tropicana Ave. (☎800-522-7366). Just off the Strip, this is a smaller, friendlier version of the major player casinos, without the gimmicks, crowds, and high prices. Live entertainment every night. Rooms may go as low as $29 during slow periods, but are usually Su-Th $42, F-Sa $70. ❸

Whiskey Pete's (☎800-248-8453), in Primm Valley, NV, 45 mi. south of Vegas on I-15, just before the California border. Whiskey Pete's is the cheapest of 3 Western-themed casinos right in the middle of the desert. Cheap as fool's gold and home to the wildest roller-coaster in Nevada ($6). Su-Th $19, F-Sa $50; prices vary with availability. ❸

USAHostels Las Vegas, 1322 Fremont St. (☎800-550-8958 or 385-1150; www.usahostels.com). A funky, fun place to stay, though it is far from the Strip and in an unattractive neighborhood. Rooms are clean, the international staff is friendly, and the atmosphere caters to students and international travelers. Private and dorm rooms are available, along with a pool, jacuzzi, laundry, kitchen and billiard room. Shared bathrooms. Offers free pickup from Greyhound station. Su-Th dorms $14-19; suites $40-42. F-Sa dorms $17-23; suites $49-51. **Must have international passport, proof of international travel or student ID.** ❷

Goldstrike, 1 Main St. (☎800-634-1359 or 472-5000), in Jean, NV, 30 mi. south of Vegas on I-15 (Exit 12). Vegas-style casino has various inexpensive restaurants (prime rib $7, dinner buffet $7.50). A genuine Vegas experience at cut-rate prices. Loose slots and low-limit tables. Rooms Su-Th $20-30; F $40, Sa $50; additional person $3. ❸

Somerset House Motel, 294 Convention Center Dr. (☎888-336-4280; www.somersethouse.com). A no-frills establishment within short walking distance of the major Strip casinos. Many rooms feature kitchens; all 104 units are large and impeccably clean. Dishes and cooking utensils provided upon request. Singles Su-Th $35; doubles $44. F-Sa singles $44; doubles $55. Additional person $5; rates lower for seniors. ❸

Palace Station, 2411 W. Sahara Ave. (☎800-634-3101). Free shuttles to Las Vegas Blvd. run from 8:45am-12:15am. The Palace Saloon has all the features of a Strip hotel. Home of the largest slot win in history—$25,000,000. Rooms Su-Th $40-80, F-Sa $100-130; additional person $10. ❺

Glass Pool Inn, 4611 S. Las Vegas Blvd. (☎800-527-7118 or 439-6800). Offers old but clean rooms south of the Strip. Its claim to fame: an above ground pool with windows that peer underwater. Singles and doubles Su-Th $29-39, F-Sa $59. ❸

CAMPING

Lake Mead National Recreation Area (☎293-8906), 25 mi. south of town on Rte. 93/95. Numerous campsites available throughout. Showers only at Calville and Overton Beach. Sites with flush toilets $10. ❶

Valley of Fire State Park (☎397-2088), 60 mi. north of Vegas, along Rte. 169. A splendid campground near the ancient petroglyph site of Atlas Rock. No electricity or hookups. Sites $13. ❶

Circusland RV Park, 500 Circus Circus Dr. (☎734-0410). Pool, jacuzzi, convenience store, showers. Open 6am-midnight. Hookups Su-Th $19, F-Sa $21. ❷

🖰 FOOD

Sloshed gamblers gorge themselves day and night at Vegas's gigantic buffets. For the bottomless gullet, there is no better value than the caloric intensity of these eateries. The trick to buffet enjoyment is finding those places that are more than glorified cafeterias. Beyond the buffets, Vegas has some of the best restaurants in the world, though there's little for the true budget adventurer.

▧ Carnival World Buffet at the Rio, 3700 W. Flamingo Rd. (☎252-7777). Hands down the greatest buffet in Vegas. Enjoy truly delicious food from any of the 11 stations, each reflecting a different theme. Breakfast $10 (served 7-11am), lunch $12 (11am-3:30pm), dinner $17 (3:30-10pm). ❹

El Sombrero Cafe, 807 S. Main St. (☎382-9234), is where the locals go for authentic Mexican food. The portions are huge and the staff is friendly. Their combination plates offer a lot of food for not much money ($8-11). Open M-Sa 11am-10pm. ❷

Benihana Village at the Las Vegas Hilton, 3000 Paradise Rd. (☎732-5755). Indoor village theme created with fish-filled pond, rain, and multi-level dining area. Sit down and watch your 5-course meal be flashingly prepared by charismatic hibachi chefs. A slight splurge, filling entrees are worth every penny of the $16-30 price tag. Open daily 5:30-10:30pm. ❹

Battista's Hole in the Wall, 4041 Audrie Ave. (☎732-1424), right behind the Flamingo. Adorning the walls are 28 years' worth of celebrity photos and novelties from area brothels, as well as the head of "Moosolini," the fascist moose. Though dinner at one of the Strip's best Italian restaurants is pricey, it is well worth it. Dinner $18-34, includes house wine. Open Su-Th 4:30-10:30pm, F-Sa 4:30-11pm. ❺

Saizan, 115 E. Tropicana Ave. (☎739-9000), in San Remo. The best sushi bar near the Strip offers only the freshest sushi and sashimi. The combo platters ($14-19) provide an excellent sampling. Open daily 5:30pm-midnight. ❹

Paymon's Mediterranean Cafe, 4147 S. Maryland Pkwy. (☎731-6030), serves up fresh, delicious Greek and Mediterranean specialties. Try the yummy combo plate with couscous, tabouli, and stuffed grape leaves ($10) or a big falafel and hummus pita bread sandwich ($6). Open M-Th 11am-1am, F-Sa 11am-3am, Su 11am-4pm. ❷

Trattoria del Lupo, 3590 S. Las Vegas Blvd. (☎740-5522), in Mandalay Bay. Celebrity chef Wolfgang Puck's first Italian restaurant, with lower-than-Spago prices. The pizzas ($9) and salads ($11) are big and delicious. Open M-Th 5:30-10pm, F 5:30-11pm, Sa-Su 11:30am-4pm and 5:30-10pm. ❸

THE DESERT

THE LOCAL STORY

CHEAP RENT, BIG TIPS

Ralph Griffo, a resident of Las Vegas, is a former blackjack dealer at the renowned Horseshoe Casino.

Q: Where do you come from?
A: New York City.

Q: So you're not a native Las Vegan. What made you move out West?
A: Well, basically it was because of housing; real estate was kind of high in New York, and we...we heard...real estate was cheap in Las Vegas. So, we came here on vacation—about 17 of us—and we decided we liked some houses here, and we left the deposits to move out here.

Q: Do you enjoy gambling in the casinos out here?
A: I like to gamble once in a while.

Q: Do you have any experience working at the casinos? I understand they employ a lot of people around here.
A: Yes, I dealt blackjack at Binion's Horseshoe, that's in downtown Vegas.

Q: Did you ever meet any famous people while dealing?
A: I remember once dealing to Dennis Rodman.

Q: What's the biggest payoff you had to deal out as a blackjack dealer?
A: Actually, I had a guy at the blackjack table playing two hands, $25,000 each hand. He'd win a few, and once he actually hit blackjack. On one of those hands, I had to pay him $37,500.

Q: Did he leave a big tip?
A: He tipped about $5000 altogether.

SIGHTS

Before the casinos inject you full of glitz and suck you dry of greenbacks, you might explore some of the simpler oddities of the city.

LIBERACE MUSEUM. Fans of classical music and kitsch will be delighted by this museum devoted to the flamboyant "Mr. Showmanship." Liberace's extravagant uses of fur, velvet, and rhinestone boggle the rational mind. *(1775 E. Tropicana Ave. ☎ 798-5595. Open M-Sa 10am-5pm, Su 1-5pm. $8, students and seniors $5, under 12 free.)*

GUINNESS WORLD RECORDS MUSEUM. Silly exhibits showcase repulsive and intriguing human oddities, as well as other bests and greatests. A compendium of the wacky. *(2780 S. Las Vegas Blvd. ☎ 792-3766. Open June-Aug. daily 9am-8pm; Sept.-May 9am-5:30pm. $5, students and seniors $4, ages 5-12 $3.)*

GUN STORE. It's been said that God made men, and Sam Colt made 'em equal. Experience Coltish justice—$10 plus ammo lets you try out an impressive array of pistols, including the enormous Magnum 44. And for $30, they'll even let you shoot real machine guns, Rambo. *(2900 E. Tropicana Ave. ☎ 454-1110. Open daily 9am-6:30pm.)*

DESPERADO ROLLERCOASTER. Way out in Primm Valley near the California border, this is the tallest and fastest bad-boy in the Vegas area, and one of the best coasters on the West Coast. *(Primm Valley, NV, along I-15 near the California border. ☎ 800-248-8453. Open Su-Th 10am-9pm, F-Sa 10am-midnight. $6.)*

LITTLE WHITE WEDDING CHAPEL. From 3min. drive-through whirlwinds to elaborate fantasy-themed extravaganzas, this Vegas wedding chapel is a mainstay of the city's matrimonial traditions. Vegas luminaries like Frank Sinatra and Liberace have been hitched here. The basic drive-through packages begin at a romantic $40 and expand with the imagination. Be sure to pick up your marriage license first—see **Practical Information,** p. 533. *(1301 Las Vegas Blvd. ☎ 382-5943; www.alittlewhitechapel.com. No reservations required for the drive-through services. Open 24hr.)*

CASINOS

Attracting tourist dollars with food, liquor, and fun has been taken to another level. Now casinos spend millions of dollars to fool guests into thinking they are somewhere else. Spittin' images of Venice, New York, Río, Paris (complete with Eiffel Tower), Cairo (complete with the Pyramids), and Monte Carlo already thrive on the Strip. Efforts to bring families to Sin City are evident with the surplus of shopping malls, arcades, amusement parks, and themed hotels.

Gambling is illegal for those under 21. If you are of age (or at least look it), look for casino "funbooks" that allow gamblers to buy $50 in chips for only $15. Cash goes in a blink when you're gambling, so it pays to have a budget. Be aware of your surroundings and guard your winnings: Vegas's seedy underbelly can slip through the Disney-like atmosphere at any point.

Casinos, nightclubs, and some wedding chapels are open 24hr. There are far more casinos and far more attractions within them than can be listed here; use the following as a compendium of the best, but explore the Strip for yourself. Check with the visitors center for more casino listings (see p. 532).

THE STRIP

The undisputed locus of Vegas's surging regeneration, the Strip is a seeming fantasy land of neon, teeming with people, casinos, and restaurants. The nation's 10 largest hotels line the legendary 3½ mi. stretch of Las Vegas Blvd. named an "All-American Road" and "National Scenic Byway." Despite the corporate facade, porn is still peddled in the shadow of family fun centers, and night denizens sporting open alcohol containers wander the street in search of elusive jackpots.

Aladdin, 3667 S. Las Vegas Blvd. (☎785-5555). More of a sight than a casino, the decor outshines its facilities. The Desert Passage shopping area is a mile-wide desert town complete with "weather patterns" and ambient noise.

Circus Circus, 2880 S. Las Vegas Blvd. (☎734-0410). While parents run to card tables and slot machines downstairs, their children spend *their* quarters upstairs on the souped-up carnival midway and in the titanic video game arcade. Within the hotel complex, Grand Slam Canyon is a Grand Canyon theme park with a roller coaster and other rides, all contained inside the bright pink "adventuredome." Open daily 24hr. Free daily shows, every ½hr. 11am-midnight.

Mirage, 3400 S. Las Vegas Blvd. (☎791-7111). Arguably the casino that began Vegas's reincarnation from decay in the early 90s. Among its attractions are a dolphin habitat, illusionists Siegfried and Roy's white tigers, and an equally flaming volcano that erupts in fountains and jets of fire every 15min.

MGM Grand, 3799 S. Las Vegas Blvd. (☎891-7979). A huge bronze lion guards this casino, and a couple of real live felines can be seen inside at the lion habitat. In addition to more than 5000 rooms, the MGM hosts world-class sporting events and concerts.

Caesar's Palace, 3570 S. Las Vegas Blvd. (☎731-7110). At Caesar's, busts abound: some are plaster, while others are barely concealed by the low-cut costumes worn by the cocktail waitresses. Neither is real. The pricey Forum Shops began the high-end shopping craze at Strip casinos and continue to lure consumers with fine eateries and 2 animatronic shows. Shops open M-F 10am-11pm, Sa-Su 10am-midnight.

New York, New York, 3790 S. Las Vegas Blvd. (☎740-6969). Towers mimic the Manhattan skyline, re-creating the glory of the Big Apple at this tacky casino. Traverse the sidewalk under a replica of the Brooklyn Bridge. Roller Coaster open daily 11am-11pm; $10, 2nd ride half-price.

Flamingo Las Vegas, 3555 S. Las Vegas Blvd. (☎800-732-2111). Mobster Bugsy Siegel bucked the cowboy casino trend with this resort-style Strip casino in 1946, thereby setting Vegas's trajectory for decades to come. Sprawling pool area plays home to penguins, flamingos, and fish.

Luxor, 3900 S. Las Vegas Blvd. (☎262-4000). This non-generic casino and architectural marvel recreates the majestic pyramids of ancient Egypt in opaque glass and steel. Wander into the depths of the desert at the **King Tut Tomb and Museum.** Museum daily Su-Th 9am-11pm; $5.

THE DESERT

FROM THE ROAD

CIRQUE CITY

came to Vegas with what seemed to be a mission impossible: find enough low-priced entertainment to keep me occupied for nine days. At first it was overwhelming—everything seemed to be outrageously overpriced. Riding an elevator to the top of the Stratosphere cost almost as much as hostels in other cities. But soon I learned the ropes. I knew that waiting until around 3pm to gorge myself on cheaper lunch buffets would save money on dinner later. If I played 5-cent slots slowly enough, I could usually get a drink before my dollar was gone. And I learned to appreciate the entertainment the Vegas spectacular itself could provide: people watching became my activity of choice.

A few days into my Vegas vacation something threw my newfound confidence. I waited patiently in line to buy tickets for one of Cirque de Soleil's spectacular performances, thinking I held an ace in the hole. Obstructed view tickets were discounted, and I was willing to put up with peeking out from behind a large pole. So I approached the counter, asked for an obstructed view ticket, and pulled out my wallet. The man behind the counter said "that'll be $74.50." I looked at him for a second. "No, I said *obstructed view* tickets," I replied. He gave me a look like I was crazy. "Ma'am, those are the obstructed view prices. Otherwise they're $80." I walked away stunned. And I realized that Vegas could always trick you. As a city built to take your money, there's only so much you can get for free.

–Sara Clark

Treasure Island, 3300 S. Las Vegas Blvd. (☎894-7111). At Treasure Island, throngs of pushy people squeeze together to see a campy send-up of pirate lore. In the Pirate Show, a British navy vessel engages a galleon of roguish sea criminals, resulting in one of the best free shows in Vegas. Crowded shows every 1½hr. The Kahunaville bartenders spin, toss, flip, and launch drinks against a flashy Hawaiian backdrop.

Stratosphere Casino Hotel and Tower, 2000 S. Las Vegas Blvd. (☎380-7777). The tallest structure west of the Mississippi River, the 1149 ft. free-standing tower can be seen from anywhere in the city and affords post-card-like photo opportunities. The world's two highest thrill rides rumble atop its observation deck, and another is slated to open. $7 to head up the tower. Rides open 10am-1am; $5-8.

Bellagio, 3600 S. Las Vegas Blvd. (☎888-987-6667). Boasts the distinction of being the world's largest five-star hotel. The classy Bellagio has a magnificent collection of art and carefully maintained botanical gardens that changes with the seasons. Muscle your way up for a view of the spectacular Water Show on its outdoor lake, where water jets elegantly propel streams of water several stories into the air during a musical aquatic ballet. Daily water shows every ¼hr. noon-11pm; free.

Paris, 3655 S. Las Vegas Blvd. (☎946-7000). This is the smallest and quietest of the "theme" casinos, with the attractions of the real Paris, including mimes and crepes. Almost to scale Eiffel Tower houses a restaurant and a beautiful view at its summit.

Venetian, 3355 S. Las Vegas Blvd. (☎733-5000). This huge casino features the upscale Grand Canal Shoppes, through which runs a 3 ft. deep chlorinated "canal." Singing gondoliers push tourists along in small boats while everyone else takes pictures. Architectural replicas of Venetian plazas, bridges, and towers adorn the Strip-side exterior.

DOWNTOWN & OFF-STRIP

The tourist frenzy that grips the Strip is slightly less noticeable in old Downtown Vegas. The Glitter Gulch offers tinier hotels, cheaper alcohol and food, and some serious gambling. The family atmosphere of the Strip is entirely lacking, however, and the downtown area cultivates a grittier feel. Years of decline were reversed with the 1995-opening of the Fremont Street Experience. The open desert sky above that thoroughfare is but a memory, and in its place a canopy of neon laser light plays throughout the night. The transformation of the neighborhood was furthered with the construction of a pedestrian promenade that now represents Fremont St. Despite the renewal, avoid Stewart and Main St. at night.

Northwest of the downtown area, tiny casinos cater to Vegas residents tired of crowds and lines. These "locals" often offer generous "comps" (free food, alcohol, and rooms) and hidden culinary gems. On Lake Mead Blvd., the **Texas Station,** North Rancho at Lake Mead Blvd. (☎631-1000), runs one of the busiest casinos in town. Across the street, the **Fiesta Casino Hotel,** 2400 N. Rancho Dr. (☎800-731-221 Rampart Blvd. (☎869-7777), pampers guest with luxury Mediterranean style accommodations and a world-class spa.

Las Vegas Hilton, 3000 Paradise Rd. (☎697-8700). Off-strip casino is a true "can't miss" stop thanks to its enormous free-standing "Las Vegas Hilton" sign. More than a mere ride, the $70 million Star Trek Experience immerses you in the Trekkie universe. Entrance to the "experience" also includes admission to the Star Trek Museum, which shows this cultural phenomenon with astonishing intricacy. Open daily 11am-11pm; $25.

Binion's Horseshoe Hotel and Casino, 128 E. Fremont St. (☎382-1600). The Binion family brought their love of high stakes gaming from Texas. Site of the World Series of Poker, this is a serious gambler's paradise. High craps odds, single-deck blackjack, and a willingness to honor almost any bet are Horseshoe hallmarks.

The Plaza Casino, 1 Main Street (☎386-2110). Majestically stands guard over the touristy Fremont St. Experience. Center Stage Restaurant furnishes a great view of the nightly light shows.

Golden Nugget, 129 E. Fremont St. (☎386-8121). Injecting a touch of Strip-like class into the downtown area, this perennial four-star hotel charms with marble floors, elegant chandeliers, and high-end gambling.

♫ ENTERTAINMENT

Entertainment abounds in Vegas, mostly revolving around the huge mega-casinos on the Strip. There are shows of all varieties, and wading through them can be quite a chore. To make your selection easier, pick up one of the free entertainment guides. These have showtimes, descriptions, prices and restrictions. Once you have a show picked out, be sure to check around for coupons or fliers. Often you can get $10 knocked off your ticket price, or receive freebies such as t-shirts, mugs, or drinks. Tickets to some of the most well received shows, such as **Cirque de Soleil's O** or **Mystere,** as well as the world famous **Siegfried and Roy,** can be well over $80. Others, such as **Catch a Rising Star** at the Excalibur, cost much less than an arm and a leg and still provide the glitz and glamour of a Las Vegas show.

The best deals, however, come from the free shows given by each of the major casinos. Most start after dark and repeat throughout the evening. Bellagio offers stunning **water fountains** which move to popular tunes every 15min., beginning when the sun goes down. The Mirage has a **giant volcano** that explodes every 15min. as well as the famous **white tigers** inside the casino. The **pirate show** at Treasure Island is a favorite with families; get there early because the walkways become very crowded. The Rio gives a free song and dance every hour with its 20min. **Masquerade in the Sky.** See **Indoor Thunderstorms** or a host of acrobatic acts without the cost of a Cirque de Soleil production at the Aladdin Desert Passage every hr. starting at 10am. Or just sit back and relax and enjoy the entertainment spectacular that is Vegas itself.

⚑ NIGHTLIFE

Nightlife in Vegas gets rolling around midnight and runs until everyone drops—or runs out of money. Cabs languish in line, waiting to take inebriated clubhoppers to the next happening joint. To save cash on covers and still see the hotspots, head out before midnight or on off-nights.

The Bars at the Hardrock Casino, 4455 Paradise Rd. (☎693-5000). Youthful crowd and electric atmosphere at this circular bar in the middle of the casino floor. Go late and gawk at whatever sweaty rock legend has wandered off stage at "The Joint" (a hot and intimate rock venue). Drinks $3-7. No cover. Open 24hr.

Ra, 3900 S. Las Vegas Blvd. (☎262-4000). Egyptian-themed night club at the Luxor, contains a sushi bar and state-of-the-art sound system. Arguably Vegas's hottest club with famous DJs, it's the place to see and be seen. Cover around $20, depending on the event and who you know. Open W-Sa 10pm-6am.

Club Río, 3700 W. Flamingo Rd. (☎247-7977). Another "in" place at which to gyrate all night long to grinding techno. Video walls radiate sultry and energizing images of the dance floor. If you don't look "in," you'll stand "out." Cover: men $10, women $5. Open W-Sa 10:30pm-dawn.

Club Paradise, 4416 Paradise Rd. (☎734-7990), across from Hard Rock Casino. Club Paradise Repeatedly voted best gentleman's cabaret (read: strip joint) in America. Classy, safe, and the g-strings stay on. Beer $6, cocktails $6-8. Cover: men $10. Open M-F 4pm-6am, Sa 6pm-6am.

Goodtimes, 1775 E. Tropicana Ave. (☎736-9494), is a gay bar/dance club in the renovated Liberace plaza with a M $10 all-you-can-drink special and bumping tunes that help it live up to its name. Open 24hr.

Hookah Lounge, 4147 S. Maryland Pkwy. (☎731-6030), features more than 20 flavored tobaccos (no opium, though) and a funky, intimate vibe that attracts pre-club crowds. Full bar and flavored teas. Open M-Th 5pm-1am, F-Sa 5pm-3am.

Hurricane Harry's, 3190 W. Sahara Blvd. (☎253-6013). There's a different special or theme every night at this dance club and bar. Frequent BBQ's, wet t-shirt nights, and radio station promotions. Retro Tu feature blasts from the past, and country W have a cowboy feel. Call ahead for cheap drink promotion. No cover. Open daily 24hr.

LEAVING LAS VEGAS

Away from Vegas, the mountains and waters in the surrounding desert offer wonderful opportunities for outdoor recreation. Roadtrippers stop to wonder at the engineering of the Hoover Dam, boaters enjoy the waters of Lake Mead, and hikers and climbers test the pristine stone at Red Rocks and Mt. Charleston. Near Lake Mead, the Valley of Fire sizzles with arid landscapes. The higher elevations around Las Vegas are cool. North of Vegas, Mt. Charleston (11,918 ft.) offers temperate alpine climates even when Vegas swelters in 110°F heat. Should the urge to strap on some hiking shoes hit you, head to Mt. Charleston and Kyle Canyon. In early spring, the Mary Jane and Big Falls trail reveals awesome vistas of sublime Kyle Canyon and cascading waterfalls. The trailhead can be reached via Hwy. 157 (Kyle Canyon Rd.), and welcomes hikers to the 1.5 mi. trek that climbs 1,000 ft. For more experienced hikers, try the 11 mi. north loop that ascends to the peak of the mountain. At Mummy Mountain, visitors are treated to a panoramic view of the Vegas Valley, with Lake Mead in the distance. (Take U.S. 95 N out of Las Vegas and watch for the left turn into the park about 18 mi. out of town.)

RED ROCKS

Just 20 mi. west of the Strip, the Red Rock Canyon National Conservation Area escarpment is a stupendous network of crimson sandstone bluffs and washes. From Vegas, take Hwy. 159 (Charleston Blvd.) west and continue for about 10min. until you reach the signs indicating the turn for the 197,000-acre park. You can either stick to the 13 mi. **scenic auto route** (open 6am-8pm; $5), or hike into the desert itself. Red Rocks is also one of America's premier **rock climbing** destinations, and hikers can watch the rock-jocks hang from the bluffs. An excellent **visitors center** introduces visitors to the wonders of this flourishing ecosystem with interactive exhibits and guided walking tours. (☎ 363-1921. Open daily 8am-4:30pm during off-season; in summer 8am-5pm.) The **campground ❶** is located off Rte. 159 near the visitors center, with picnic tables, grills, water, and toilets, but no hookups, for $10. For group site reservations call the visitors center. Backcountry **camping ❶** and overnight climbing require permits. (☎ 647-5050. Free.) The most popular hikes are those through the washes of the first and second pullouts along the scenic road. **Pine Creek Canyon** also has short easy hikes. At the base of Wilson Cliffs, **Spring Mountain Ranch State Park** houses a 520-acre historic ranch and scenic picnic sites. Each vehicle that enters the park is charged $5 and is granted access to the ranch (1-4pm daily) and the opportunity to follow guided tours (there are several throughout the day, call ☎ 875-4141 for more details.)

HOOVER DAM

Take U.S 93/95 south 18 mi. from Las Vegas. Head east 4 mi. on U.S. 93 until you get to the winding dam road. Visitors Center leads tours to the generators at the structure's bottom. (☎ 294-3510. Open daily 9am-5pm; exhibits close at 5pm. Self-guided tours with short presentations $10, seniors $8, ages 7-16 $4. More comprehensive "hardhat tours" are now a relic of the past, as heightened security has restricted visitor access to the dam. Parking in the garage on the Nevada side costs $5, but is free across the dam in Arizona.)

Built to subdue the flood-prone Colorado River after state leaders were given control over their stretch of the snaking waterway, this looming ivory monolith took 5000 men five years of seven-day weeks to construct. By the time of the dam's completion in 1935, 96 men had died during construction. When their sweat and blood finally dried, over 6.6 million tons of concrete had been crafted into a 726-ft. colossus that now shelters precious agricultural land, pumps big voltage to Vegas and L.A., and furnishes outdoor revelers with a watery playground amid the sagebrush and mountains. Though the dam has altered the local environment, it is a spectacular engineering feat, especially given the comparatively primitive state of heavy excavation equipment at the time of its construction. The nearby town of Boulder was created from nothing to house the enormous workforce. The scaled-down tours and interpretive center explore the dam's history, though in a self-congratulatory way. The dam exists as a lasting tribute America's "think-big" era of ambitious landscaping and culturally-transforming public works projects.

LAKE MEAD

When the rushing waters of the Colorado River met the stolid concrete of the Hoover Dam, the puddle that was created formed Lake Mead. This 100 mi.-long desert oasis thus became the unlikely location for the country's first national recreation area, hosting anglers, campers, hunters, beachgoers, and others eager to revel in its jarringly blue waters. To reach the lake, take Rte. 147 (Lake Mead Blvd.) east 14 mi. There is a $5 fee to enter the recreation area. Follow Rte. 147 to Rte. 167, which frames the western shore of the lake, shuttling visitors from Boulder Beach in the south to Overton in the north.

First-time visitors to the lake will benefit from a trip to the **Alan Bible Visitor Center**, 4 mi. east of Boulder City, and its brochures, maps, and plant garden. (☎ 293-8990. Open daily 8:30am-4:30pm.) For maps and info, pick up the *Desert Lake View* at one of the several ranger stations dotting Lake Mead's shores. Backcountry hiking and camping is permitted in most areas. Hunters can target deer and bighorn sheep in season, and should contact the **Nevada Division of Wildlife (NDOW)** (☎ 486-5121) for information on obtaining licences and firearm restrictions. Fishers can expect bites from large striped bass; the area around Boulder Beach often results in a few bites. Despite these other diversions, Lake Mead is really sustained by the multitude of Californians and weekend adventurers driving white pickup trucks with jetskis in tow. For those who come unprepared, watercraft can be rented. **Boulder Beach** is accessible by Lakeshore Dr., off U.S. 93. (☎800-752-9669. Jetskis $50 per hr., $270 per day; fishing boats $55 per 4hr., $100 per day.)

Alongside the Park Service **campsites ❶**, concessionaires usually operate RV parks (most of which have become mobile home villages), marinas, restaurants, and motels (sites $10). More remote concessionaires, including **Echo Bay Resort ❺**, also offer motel options. (☎800-752-9669. Singles $85; doubles $100; hookups $18.) Its restaurant, **Tale of the Whale ❷**, is decorated in nautical motifs, furnishes glimpses of Lake Mead, and cooks up $6 burgers. The resort rents jetskis ($50 per hr., $270 per day) and fishing boats ($30 for 2hr., $75 per day).

Northwest of Lake Mead, brilliantly colored rocks come alive in striking formations at the **Valley of Fire.** The robust crimson sandstone evokes landscapes usually associated with southwestern Utah. Rte. 169 bisects the park and leads to the extensive exhibits and short films on display at the **Visitors Center.** (☎397-2088. Open daily 8:30am-4:30pm.) Hiking areas are prevalent, and there are many sites with ancient petroglyphs. **Campgrounds ❶** at the western end of the park near Atlas Rock offer 51 semi-primitive sites. (Showers, water, and toilets; no hookups. Sites $13.) The most direct route to the park from Las Vegas carries you north along I-15 for 45 mi. Head east on Rte. 169 for 10 mi. and enter the park for a $5 fee.

Most distant from the bustle of nearby Las Vegas is **Overton Beach Resort ❷**, close to Overton, NV. The resort occupies a patch of green at the northern end of North Shore Scenic Dr. and has a mini mart, RV hookups ($18), gas, and a beach. Farther along Rte. 167 north., the tiny town of Overton welcomes beachgoers with food, cheap motels, a theater, and an ice cream shop. The **Overton Motel ❸**, 137 N. Moapa Valley Blvd., furnishes singles and doubles. (☎702-397-2463. Rooms from $32.)

ROUTE 66 & INTERSTATE 40

Route 66 was designated as such in November of 1926, replacing the National Trails Highway as the principal road for commerce and immigration between the Mississippi Valley and Southern California. Running from Chicago to Los Angeles and spanning seven states, the road was taken by Okies fleeing the Dust Bowl (see p. 12), by wide-eyed Easterners seeking to partake in the post-war boom around L.A., and later by tourists looking for the Grand Canyon and Disneyland.

If the Smithsonian Museum is America's attic, Rte. 66 is its junk drawer. Scattered along the heat-buckled asphalt—the remnants of an earlier tourist culture. Greasy-spoons, gaudy motels, and odd little towns—all without their former luster—testify to the American urge to bring fun and self-transformation to even the harshest places. The shift over the last generation toward the super-interstate, with its generic restaurants and chain motels, suggests a fundamental transformation in the lifestyle of Middle America.

Much of Rte. 66 has been swallowed up by the interstate or left to languish in the form of gravel or forlorn dirt. In other places, it trucks on as a patchwork of state and county roads (businesses along it sell $4 maps tracing its modern-day route). A good portion is not worth traveling, particularly the stretches through the vast emptiness of deserts and plains, where the only difference between Rte. 66 and I-40 is that the interstate is invariably faster and more convenient.

BARSTOW ☎760

Sitting midway between L.A. and Vegas on I-15, Barstow (pop. 23,056) is replete with cheap eats and sheets, not to mention the beauty of the California desert for those willing to explore the hot, desolate area.

🚺 PRACTICAL INFORMATION. The **Amtrak train** station, 685 N. 1st St. (☎800-USA-RAIL/872-7245), lacks ticket counters, so buy your tickets over the phone. One northbound and one southbound train leave the station per day. One train departs for L.A. (4am, $27). **Greyhound buses,** 681 N. 1st St. (☎256-8757 or 800-231-2222; open M-F 9am-2pm, Sa 3:30-6pm), go to L.A. (8 per day, $24) and Las Vegas (7 per day, $25). The **Barstow Chamber of Commerce,** 409 E. Fredrick, off Barstow Rd., has info on hotels, restaurants, and tourist attractions. (☎256-8617. Open M-F 10am-4pm.) Other services include: **police,** 220 E. Mountain View Rd. (☎256-2211); **Barstow Community Hospital,** 555 S. 7th St. (☎256-1761); and the **Post Office,** 425 S. 2nd Ave. (☎800-275-8777. Open M-F 9am-5pm, Sa 10am-1pm.) **Postal Code:** 92312.

🚹🛏 ACCOMMODATIONS & FOOD. East Main St. offers all the usual chains, but the best value is the **Best Motel ❸,** 1281 E. Main St., which is fairly clean, quite friendly, and has all the usual motel amenities. (☎256-6836. Singles $34; doubles $38. Weekly rates available.)

Every restaurant chain this side of the Pecos has a branch on Main St. You'll find a more inviting variety in Barstow's local offerings. **Rosita's Mexican American Food ❷,** 540 W. Main St., has a festive dining room filled with the odors of its tasty offerings. (☎256-9218. Lunch specials Tu-F under $5. Dinners $6-11. Open Tu-Sa 11am-9pm, Su 10am-9pm.) For some good, basic, hearty Italian food, head to **DiNapoli's Firehouse Italian Eatery ❸,** 1358 E. Main St. (☎256-1094. Dinner entrees $8-15. Open Su-Th 11am-9pm, F-Sa 11am-10pm.)

NEAR BARSTOW

RAINBOW BASIN NATURAL AREA & OWL CANYON CAMPGROUND. North of Barstow, these are beautiful areas for the adventurous explorer. Hikers can investigate the colorful canyon, and campers can stargaze at a sight unpolluted by city lights. The Bureau of Land Management has equipped the 31 **sites ❶** with fire rings, drinking water, and pit toilets, as well as created a short dirt loop for autos to explore the canyon. *(From N. 1st St. in Barstow, head north. Take a right onto Fort Irwin Rd. Drive 7 mi. and take a left on Fossil Bed Rd. Follow this dirt road for 3 mi. until you see signs directing you to the campsites and the scenic loop. Camping fee $6. For more information and a map contact the California Desert Information Center, 831 Barstow Rd. ☎256-8313.)*

BARSTOW TO NEEDLES ☎760

On the interstate after Barstow, small brown signs will direct you to "historic" Rte. 66. The old highway offers a smattering of very small towns and a long stretch of outright desolation. Dagget features only Marines and a factory, but railroad enthusiasts will be thrilled to know that the Union Pacific meets the Santa Fe in town. From I-40, hop back on Rte. 66 at Newberry Springs and head east to the **Bagdad Cafe ❷.** This slice of idiosyncratic outpost dishes out filling eats and friendly smiles. The sunny owner Andre presides over odd locals and foreign tourists who pay tribute to the cafe that inspired the 1987 movie of the same name (see p. 22), a Cannes Festival favorite. (☎257-3101. Chicken-fried steak $7, hamburgers $4-5, ostrich or buffalo burgers $7.50. Open M-Th 7am-7pm, F-Su 7am-9pm.) A beat-up, old-style gas station three doors down has appeared in countless movies and TV shows. In a pinch, you can get gas, eats, and a bed in Ludlow, which is nearly midway between Barstow and Needles.

After Ludlow comes the only stretch of Rte. 66 that diverges significantly from I-40. Here named the Old National Trail Hwy., it loops south to the fringes of military testing ranges. Save a few straggling motels and diners, this area has deteriorated considerably, although it's worth a trip for lovers of desolation and cinder cones. The **Mojave National Preserve** (see p. 545), however, is only accessible from I-40. If you take Rte. 66 instead of I-40 to Needles, bear left after Essex; going right will take you on a dead-end "1931 Alignment" of the old road.

NEEDLES ☎760

Back in the days when Needles (pop. 5202) was an important stop on the Santa Fe Railroad, the town drew Chinese, Mexicans, and Native Americans looking for work on section gangs. The railroad still passes through, but the visitors only stay to ski, splash, and sunburn on the Colorado River. Woven between the criss-crossing strands of the railroad, I-40, Rte. 95, and the old Rte. 66, Needles is convenient to Lake Havasu, Lake Mead, and the gambling halls in Laughlin, Nevada.

🚌 **PRACTICAL INFORMATION. Greyhound buses** run out of Needle Point Liquors, 1109 Broadway (☎326-5066), to: **Las Vegas** ($28); **L.A.** ($45); **Barstow** ($28). The **Chamber of Commerce**, 100 G St., is at the junction of Front and G St. (☎326-2050. Open M-F 9:30am-2:30pm.) **Bank of America**, 1001 W. Broadway, has a **24hr. ATM.** (☎800-338-6430. Open M-F 9am-5pm.) Other services include: **Colorado River Medical Center**, 1401 Bailey Ave. (☎326-4531; 24hr.); and the **Post Office**, 628 3rd St. (☎800-275-8777. Open M-F 9am-4:30pm.) **Postal Code:** 92363.

🏕️ **ACCOMMODATIONS, CAMPGROUNDS, & FOOD.** Like many sleepy desert hubs, Needles compensates for the lack of excitement with reasonable prices. A concentration of cheapies lies on the Needles Hwy. (use the J St. Exit off I-40). There is a similar concentration along E. Broadway "downtown" (follow the directions as above, take the Needles Hwy. to Broadway, and turn right). The **Econo Lodge ❷**, 1910 Needles Hwy., offers squeaky-clean rooms with fridges and microwaves, as well as a pool, at very reasonable prices. (☎326-3881 or 888-326-3888. Singles $25; doubles $29.) The **Traveler's Inn ❸**, 1195 3rd St. Hill, has spiffy rooms with access to a pool and, more importantly, a McDonald's. (☎326-4900. Singles and doubles $45.)

For campers looking to rough it, Needles doesn't have much to offer. However, it does have more RV parks per capita than any other town in the world. **Rainbow Beach**, 3520 River Rd., off Needles Hwy. 1 mi. north of town, has campsites with electricity, pool, and restrooms. Those who don't need hookups might try heading outside town to find a riverside spot. (☎326-3101. Sites from $25.)

The **California Pantry ❷**, 2411 Needles Hwy., is a friendly coffee shop with the most extensive menu in Needles. Try the chicken-fried steak with three eggs for $7. (☎326-5225. Open daily 5am-10:30pm.) **The Hungry Bear ❷**, 1906 W. Broadway, serves feasts to sate every appetite. "Bear's Favorite Burger" ($6) has all the fixings. (☎326-2988. Open daily 5:30am-9:30pm.)

🏃 **OUTDOOR ACTIVITIES.** The **Colorado River** offers a variety of recreational opportunities. Visitors can break the silence and explore galore on **jetskis.** The phonetically correct **Riverjetz Watercraft Rentalz,** 401 Needles Hwy., offerz rentalz. (☎326-4336 or 800-327-2386. From $35 per hr.) With rod in hand, outdoorsmen can find serenity at **Havasu National Wildlife Refuge,** a 4000-acre, marshy network of ponds, bays, and channels, frequented by fishermen from cock's crow on, where dove, quail, and beaver dwell. For info on wilderness hikes, call the **US Fish and Wildlife Service,** 317 Mesquite Ave. (☎236-3853), in Lake Havasu City. For an adventure, duck into the underpass where the Needles Hwy. bellies up to the railroad tracks. Its walls are painted by graffiti artists and Confederacy enthusiasts.

EASTERN MOJAVE DESERT ☎760

The rugged land between I-15 and I-40 is among the most isolated in California. There are few towns, and you can never assume that services will be available between Barstow and Baker along I-15 or Barstow and Needles along I-40. However, travelers who only use these towns as pit stops miss out on the Mojave's stunning natural attractions. Much of the region's attractions exist inside the Mojave National Preserve. 1.6 million acres of federally stewarded desert scenery boast dry lake beds, volcanic cinder cones, sweeping sand dunes, and the occasional splash of water. Dramatic geological formations rise from the seemingly infinite landscape, and resilient creatures crawl along the scorched terrain. Serene as the emptiness may be, it is still empty, and most drivers press onward, praying that their cars are up to the task (see **Driving in the Desert,** p. 506). Stop in Baker to visit the **Mojave National Preserve Desert Information Center,** which supplies suggestions about recreation spots, maps of the area, more detailed directions, and a modest exhibit on the area's geology. (☎733-4040. Open daily 9am-5pm.) Hunting and fishing are allowed in the preserve, but finding water may be an angler's toughest challenge. Deer and quail are popular targets in season, but only with a California State Fish and Game hunting license, available at local Wal-Marts.

Afton Canyon Natural Area (Baker Mojave Info Line ☎733-4040) lies 36 mi. northeast of Barstow en route to Las Vegas. Follow I-15 to Afton Rd. The flowing water you see in this "Grand Canyon of the Mojave" is no mirage, but a rare aboveground appearance of the Mojave River. Canyon walls tower 300 ft. above the rushing water and its willow-lined shores. Golden eagles, bighorn sheep, and desert tortoises reside around the canyon. **Hikers** may explore the caves and side canyons tucked along unmarked trails. Bring a flashlight. Visitors can stay in 22 developed **sites ❶** with water, fire pits, tables, and restrooms ($6 per person).

The **Kelso Dunes** in the Mojave National Preserve blanket a spectacular, barren landscape. Stretching lengths of 4 mi. and reaching heights of 700 ft., the dunes are off-limits to off-road vehicles. It takes 2-3hr. one-way to hike from the trailhead to the dune summit, and bear in mind that the formation acts as a giant oven in the summer—don't get baked. From the top you can hear the dunes sing on a windy day—the cascading sand thunders like the collapsing bulkheads of WWII submarine movies. The dunes are 30 mi. southeast of Baker via Kelbaker Rd. from Barstow; either take I-40 to the Kelbaker Rd. Exit (80 mi. to the east) or I-15 to Baker.

Providence Mountains State Recreation Area, P.O. Box 1, Essex 92332, is a popular, high-altitude (4000-5000 ft.) region with six primitive **campsites ❶** (☎928-2586; sites $8) and a **Visitors Center,** on Essex Rd., 17 mi. north of I-40. View the spectacular **Mitchell Caverns** on an informative 1.5 mi. tour through the stalactite-cluttered limestone chambers. (1½hr. tours June-Aug. Sa-Su 1:30pm; Sept.-May M-F 1:30pm; Sa-Su 10am, 1:30, 3pm. Tours $3, ages 16 and under free. Tour reservations may be made with a $1 surcharge by calling ☎928-2586.)

There are 61 primitive but beautiful sites in the Providence Mountains at the **Mid Hill** and **Hole-in-Wall campgrounds ❶** in the East Mojave National Scenic Area. Mid-Hill, at 5600 ft., is quite cool and surrounded by pinyon and juniper trees. Hole-in-Wall, at 4200 ft., is considerably warmer. The road into Mid Hill isn't paved and is not recommended for RVs. From Essex Rd., follow Black Canyon Rd. to Mid Hill or Wild Horse Canyon Rd. to Hole-in-Wall. Consult a park service newsletter for the location of other roadside and backcountry campsites. (Limited water and pit toilets, no hookups. Sites $12.)

Dune buggies and **jeeps** are still permitted at the **Dumont Dunes,** just off Rte. 127 about 33 mi. north of Baker. Look for the 3½ mi. road turning off 127 just after Harry Wade Rd. There is no sign, so keep your eyes peeled. The dunes are strewn with manmade striations—those from WWII training exercises are still visible in parts of the Mojave. Tracks persist in the sands for decades, so consider what legacy you want to leave behind.

ARIZONA

Arizona was the first state to begin a Historic Rte. 66 Association, and the old road is well marked and, in the west, easily accessible. After crossing the Colorado River on I-40, you can jet down Hwy. 95 South to the resort town of **Lake Havasu City** or head east toward the Grand Canyon (most often reached from the base town of Flagstaff, AZ). To go east, take the first exit for Topoc and Old Rte. 66 to **Oatman,** or continue on I-40 through great stretches of desert (and, believe it or not, through the front yard of a spherical house). Then pick up Rte. 66 at **Kingman,** a medium-sized, main-drag-dominated town of the type most commonly associated with the 66 mystique in popular American consciousness.

Rte. 66 splits off from Hwy. 95 in Golden Shores—bear right off the highway. The road meanders through undulating deserts before starting its climb through the Black Mountains. A sunset drive will silence anyone who's ever had snooty words for a painting of a western sunset. Be careful after dark, however; the road can be treacherous once it enters the rugged hills. For more on Arizona, see ▓ *Let's Go: Southwest USA 2003* or ▓ *Let's Go: USA 2003.*

LAKE HAVASU CITY   ☎ 520

Created by the 1938 damming of the Colorado River, Lake Havasu (pop. 50,000) embodies a new West, created by tourist dollars and an urge to kick back. Entrepreneur Robert McCulloch willed the city to life in 1963, as a place to test boat engines. He drew up a community plan, brought the London Bridge from Old England, and people arrived with boats in tow. Motorboats and jet skis endlessly churn the green waters into a roiling froth. Spring break is prime time in this party town, as high temperatures keep the adrenaline to a minimum in the summer.

◪ **ORIENTATION.** The lake is located on the California, Arizona, and Nevada borders, with the city lying in Arizona on Hwy 95, 21 mi. south of I-40. The small town of Parker lies 36 mi. to the south, and the gambling halls of Laughlin are a tempting 65 mi. north of town. Hwy. 95 runs north-south through the city, and is intersected downtown by the east-west thoroughfare **McCulloch Boulevard.** Just east of Hwy. 95 is Lake Havasu Ave., which shelters stucco installations of familiar fast-food spots. McCulloch runs west over a channel, spanned by the actual London Bridge, and connects to **The Island,** a prime locale for beach resorts.

7 PRACTICAL INFORMATION. Greyhound (☎800-231-2222) has daily **buses** to cities in Arizona and California, including **Las Vegas** (3½hr., 1 per day, $35) and **L.A.** (5½hr., 1 per day, $55). The **Chamber of Commerce** is in English Village, a mock British square with a brewery and food stands, at the corner of Hwy. 95 and London Bridge Rd. (☎855-4115. Open daily 9am-4pm.) **City Transit Services** is on call with curb-to-curb shuttle services throughout Lake Havasu City. (☎453-7600. Operates M-F 6am-9pm, Sa-Su 6am-6pm. $3, disabled $1.50, under 10 $2, under 5 free.) Other services include: **laundry** at **Busy "B"**, 3201 N. Hwy. 95 (☎764-2440; open daily 4:30am-11pm; $1.25 wash); and the **Post Office,** 1750 McCulloch Blvd. (☎855-2361. Open M-F 8:30am-5pm, Sa 10am-1pm). **Postal Code:** 86403.

ACCOMMODATIONS. There is an abundance of affordable motels along London Bridge Rd. Rates tend to be higher on summer weekends. The shiny **Windsor Inn ❸,** 451 London Bridge Rd., offers inexpensive rooms and all the desert amenities. Since you pay by the bed, two people can get single prices if they are willing to share or crash on the couch. (☎855-4135 or 800-245-4135. Singles Su-Th $39, F-Sa $59; doubles $45/$69.) The good-natured people at **Super 8 ❸,** 305 London Bridge Rd., offer predictable accommodations at predictable prices. (☎855-8844. Singles Su-Th $36, F-Sa $46; doubles $46/$56.) Campers should visit **Lake Havasu State Park ❶,** about 1 mi. up London Bridge Rd. off Rte. 95, where they will find a main campground. (☎855-2784. 34 sites. Showers, toilets, boat-launch. Sites $14.) Another camping option in the park is **Cattail Cove ❷.** (60 sites. Showers, toilets, RV hookups. Sites $17; hookups $19.)

FOOD & NIGHTLIFE. In addition to Lake Havasu Ave., there is also a tremendous concentration of fast food along Rte. 95, particularly where it intersects London Bridge Rd. For a less generic taste, try the Irish-inspired **Slainee's ❷,** 1519 Queens Bay Rd., which has hearty entrees (from $7), a slew of pool tables, and live tunes on weekends. (☎505-8900. Open daily 10am-1am.) At the **Barley Brothers Brewery and Grill ❷,** 1425 McCulloch Blvd. on the Island, knowledgeable bartenders serve inventive brews (locally brewed beer $4 per pint) as well as more refined cuisine. (☎505-7837. Sandwiches $8. Open Su-Th 11am-10pm, F-Sa 11am-11pm.) A short, but dark, walk over London Bridge from the Brewery, leads to the colossal **Kokomo's on the Channel,** at the London Bridge Resort, 1477 Queens Bay Rd. Shake your sunburned booty in the open-air superclub. Tiny mixed drinks are $4; hold out for the DJ-announced $1 specials. (☎855-0888. $5 cover on weekends. Open Su-Th 11am-11pm, F-Sa 11am-1am; things pick up at 11pm.)

SIGHTS & ACTIVITIES. The place to be in Lake Havasu is on the water. Any number of tourist publications can direct you to a reputable boat rental. Loungers should try **Windsor Beach,** 1 mi. up London Bridge Rd. off Rte. 95, in Lake Havasu State Park (day use $8). Free beaches line the eastern shore of the Island, but swimmers can avoid boat traffic by sticking to the southern end. Take Smoketree from Rte. 95 to get to **Rotary Beach,** where sand, volleyball, and picnic areas await. Take London Bridge Rd. north out of the city for 3 mi., and pass the Quail Ridge residential community to get to piers that look out over the spectacular **Havasu Game Preserve.** Lake Havasu's other and most unusual claim to fame is the **London Bridge.** Originally built in London, England in 1824, it was painstakingly dismantled and reconstructed under Robert McCulloch's sponsorship. The reconstructed bridge was dedicated in October 1971. See the bridge and associated tourist "attractions" at the intersection of Hwy. 95 and London Bridge Rd.

GRAND CANYON ☎928

Long before its designation as a national park in 1919, the Grand Canyon has captured the imagination of those who have strolled up to its edge and beheld its inconceivable span. Every summer, millions of visitors travel from across the globe to witness in person this natural wonder of the world, and validate the breathtaking images they've seen on countless postcards and screen-savers. Standing on the rim fills visitors with a variety of emotional responses. For some, viewing the gaping Canyon is a spiritual experience, proof of the work of some unseen hand. For others, the Canyon demonstrates the ancient history of our earth, extending the bounds of measured time to billions of years. Regardless of exactly how the Canyon provokes an individual, it never fails to elicit thought and reflection, which is sometimes as deep or as wide as the Canyon itself.

The Grand Canyon extends from Lee's Ferry, AZ to Lake Mead, NV, situated between two massive reservoirs. In the north, the Glen Canyon Dam backs up the Colorado into mammoth Lake Powell, a water-sports paradise. To the west, the Hoover Dam traps the remaining outflow from Glen Canyon to form Lake Mead, another haven for water enthusiasts, many from Las Vegas. Grand Canyon National Park proper divides neatly into three sections: the most frequently visited South Rim, the more remote North Rim, and the forbidding canyon gorge itself.

AT A GLANCE

AREA: 1,217,403 acres.

FEATURES: The Canyon, Colorado River, North Rim, South Rim, West Rim, Kaibab Plateau, Tonto Platform.

HIGHLIGHTS: Taking a mule ride to Phantom Ranch, rafting in luxury down the Canyon, backpacking from Rim to Rim on the South and North Kaibab Trails, standing in awe at the edge of either rim.

GATEWAY TOWNS: Flagstaff, Williams.

CAMPING: Mather Campground on the South Rim and the North Rim Campground require reservations. Backcountry camping requires a permit ($5 per person, $10 per group).

FEES: Weekly pass $20 per car, $10 for other modes of transportation; covers both South and North Rim.

SOUTH RIM

During the summer, everything on two legs or four wheels converges on this side of the Grand Canyon. If you plan to visit during the mobfest, make reservations well in advance for lodging, campsites, or mules, and prepare to battle the crowds. Still, it's much better than Disney World. A friendly Park Service staff, well-run facilities, and beautiful scenery help ease crowd anxiety. Fewer tourists brave the canyon's winter weather; many hotels and facilities close during the off season. Rte. 64 leading up to the Park entrance is surrounded by Kaibab National Forest.

▮ TRANSPORTATION

There are two park entrances: the main **south entrance** is about 6 mi. from the Visitors Center while the eastern **Desert View** entrance is 27 mi. away. Both are accessed via Rte. 64, which meets I-40 (to California) in Williams. From Las Vegas, the fastest route to the South Rim is U.S. 93 S to I-40 E, and then Rte. 64 N. From Flagstaff, head north on U.S. 180 to Rte. 64.

Trains: The **Grand Canyon Railway** (☎800-843-8724) runs an authentically restored train from Williams, AZ to the Grand Canyon (2¼hr.; leaves 10am, returns 3:30pm; $68, children $27). Guided tours of the rim area $25-35.

Public Transit: Free shuttle buses run the West Rim Loop (daily 1hr. before sunrise-sunset) and the Village Loop (daily 1hr. before sunrise-11pm) every 10-30min. A free **hiker's shuttle** runs every 30min. between the info center and the South Kaibab Trailhead, on the East Rim near Yaki Point. Early buses also run at 4, 5, and 6am.

Taxis: ☎ 638-2822.

Auto Repairs: Grand Canyon Garage (☎ 638-2631), east of the Visitors Center on the main road, just before the rim lodges. Open daily 8am-5pm. 24hr. emergency service.

▨ ORIENTATION

Maps and signs in the park make it easy to orient yourself. Lodges and services concentrate in **Grand Canyon Village,** at the end of Park Entrance Rd. The east half of the village contains the visitors center and the general store, while most of the rim lodges and the challenging **Bright Angel Trail** lie in the west section. The shorter but more difficult **South Kaibab Trail** is off **East Rim Drive,** east of the village. Free shuttle buses run along **West Rim Drive,** which is closed to private vehicles during the summer, stopping at eight rim overlooks. Avoid walking on the drive; the rim trails are safer and more scenic. For most services in the park, call the **main switchboard** (☎ 638-2631).

▨ PRACTICAL INFORMATION

Visitor Info: The first installment in the Park Service's plan to reshape visitor flow in the crowded park, the new **Canyon View Information Plaza,** across from Mather Point just after the entrance to the park, is the one-stop center for Grand Canyon info. The Plaza houses the Visitors Center (open daily 8am-6pm), a bookstore (open daily 8am-7pm), restrooms, and helpful kiosks answering frequently-asked questions. The Visitors Center stocks copies of *The Guide* (an essential), and assorted other pamphlets. To get there, park at Mather Pt., then get out and hoof it for ½ mi. to the info plaza. For those who want to be well-prepared in advance, the Park Service, through the Grand Canyon Association, sells a variety of informational books and packets (☎ 800-858-2808; www.grandcanyon.com, or www.nps.gov/grca). The **transportation info desks** in **Bright Angel Lodge** and **Maswik Lodge** (☎ 638-2631) handle reservations for mule rides, bus tours, plane tours, Phantom Ranch, taxis, and more. Open daily 6am-8pm.

Bank: Bank One (☎ 638-2437), in Market Plaza. Full-service branch with **ATM.** Currency exchange on traveler's checks, but not cash. Open M-Th 10am-3pm, F 10am-5pm.

Luggage Storage: In **Bright Angel Lodge.** Open 6:30am-9pm.

Equipment Rental: In the General Store. Comfy hiking boots, socks included ($8 first day, $5 per additional day); sleeping bags ($9 first day, $5 per additional day); tents ($15 first day for a two-person, $16 first day for four-person, $9 per additional day for both); day packs ($6 for a large, $4 for a small); and other camping gear (stoves $5). Deposits required; major credit cards accepted. Open daily 7am-8:30pm.

Groceries: Canyon Village Marketplace (☎ 638-2262), a general store at the Yavapai Lodge complex. Open daily in summer 7am-9pm. Near the east entrance, the **Desert View General Store** serves campers. Open daily 7am-8:30pm.

Showers and Laundry: Available at concession-run **Camper Services,** adjacent to the Mather Campground in Canyon Village. Showers $1 per 5min. Laundry open 6am-9:45pm; showers 6am-11pm.

Weather and Road Conditions: ☎ 638-7888.

Medical Services: Grand Canyon Clinic (☎ 638-2551), take a left at the first stoplight after the South Rim entrance. Open M-F 7am-7pm, Sa 10am-4pm. 24hr. emergency aid.

Post Office: 100 Mather Business Ctr. (☎ 638-2512), in Market Plaza, next to the General Store. Open M-F 9am-4:30pm, Sa 10am-5pm. **Postal Code:** 86023.

THE DESERT

WHEN TO GO. The South Rim, open year-round, is jam-packed in the spring, summer, and fall, and only the winter offers some measure of solitude, though services are closed and temperatures are chilly (lows in the 10s and 20s, highs in the 30s and 40s). Colder and less visited than its southern counterpart, the North Rim is open for day use only from October 15-December 1, and from December 1-May 15 the Rim closes entirely due to snow and ice. Summer temperatures rise with visitation figures, but are highly variable from rim to rim—average summer highs are about 85°F on the South Rim, 75°F on the North Rim (due to higher elevation), and 105°F in the Inner Canyon.

ACCOMMODATIONS

Compared to the six million years it took the Colorado River to carve the Grand Canyon, the year it will take you to get indoor lodging near the South Rim is nothing. **Summer rooms should be reserved 11 months in advance.** Even so, there are cancellations every day; you can check for vacancies or call the Grand Canyon operator (☎638-2631) and ask to be connected with the proper lodge. Reservations for **Bright Angel Lodge, Maswik Lodge, Trailer Village,** and **Phantom Ranch** can be made through **Xanterra Parks and Resorts,** 14001 E. Iliff, Ste. 600, Aurora, CO 80014 (☎303-297-2757). Most accommodations on the South Rim are very pricey.

Maswik Lodge (☎638-2631), in Grand Canyon Village near the rim and several restaurants. Small, clean cabins with showers but no heat are $66. Motel rooms with queen beds and ceiling fans are also available. Singles $79; doubles $121. Each additional person $7-9. ❹

Bright Angel Lodge (☎638-2631), in Grand Canyon Village. The cheapest indoor lodging in the park, in a historic building on the rim. Convenient to Bright Angel Trail and shuttles. "Rustic" lodge singles and doubles with shared bath $53, with private bath $71. "Historic" cabins available for 1 or 2 people $84-107. $7 per additional person. ❹

Phantom Ranch (☎638-2631), on the canyon floor, a day's hike down the Kaibab Trail or Bright Angel Trail. Breakfast $17. Box lunch $8.50. Stew dinner $20; steak dinner $29; vegetarian option $20. Don't show up without reservations, which can be made up to 23 months in advance. If you're dying to sleep on the canyon floor but don't have a reservation, show up at the Bright Angel transportation desk at 6am on the day prior to your planned stay, and take a shot on the waiting list. Male and female dorms $28; seldom-available cabins for 1 or 2 people $71.50. $10.50 per additional person.❹

CAMPING

Campsites usually fill up early in the day. In the **Kaibab National Forest,** along the park's southern border, you can pull off a dirt road and camp for free. No camping is allowed within ¼ mi. of U.S. 64. **Dispersed camping ❶** can be had along N. Long Jim Loop Rd.—make a right turn 1 mi. south of the entrance station. For more remote sites, follow signs for the Arizona Trail into the national forest between Mile 252 and 253 on U.S. 64. Sleeping in cars is not permitted in the park, but it is allowed in the Kaibab Forest. For more info, contact the **Tusayan Ranger Station,** Kaibab National Forest, P.O. Box 3088, Tusayan, AZ 86023 (☎638-2443). Reservations for some campgrounds can be made through **SPHERICS** (☎800-365-2267).

Mather Campground (call SPHERICS, ☎800-365-2267) in Grand Canyon Village, 1 mi. south of the Canyon Village Marketplace; follow signs from Yavapai Lodge. 320 shady, relatively isolated sites with no hookups. Check at the office even if the sign says the campground is full. 7-night max. stay. For Mar.-Nov., reserve up to 3 months in advance; Dec.-Feb. first-come, first-served. Sites Sept.-May $12; June-Aug. $15. ❶

Ten-X Campground (☎ 638-2443), in Kaibab National Forest, 10 mi. south of Grand Canyon Village off Rte. 64. Removed from the highway, with shady sites. Toilets, water, no hookups, no showers. First come, first served. Open May-Sept. Sites $10. ❶

Desert View Campground (☎ 638-7888), 25 mi. east of Grand Canyon Village. Short on shade and far from the hub of the South Rim, but a perfect place to avoid the crowd. 50 sites with phone and restroom access, but no hookups or campfires. No reservations; usually full by early afternoon. Open mid-May to Oct. Sites $10. ❶

Camper Village (☎ 638-2887), in Tusayan, 1 mi. south of the park entrance behind the general store. Showers and flush toilets. First-come, first-served tent sites; reservations required for RVs. 2-person tent sites and hookups $18-26; $2 per additional adult. ❷

Trailer Village (☎ 638-2631), next to Mather Campground. 84 sites designed for the RV. Showers, laundry, and groceries nearby. Office open daily 8am-noon and 1-5pm. Reserve 6-9 months in advance. 2-person hookups $24; $2 per additional person. ❷

☐ FOOD

Fast food has yet to sink its greasy talons into the South Rim (the closest McDonald's is 7 mi. south in Tusayan), but you can find meals at fast-food prices, and get a slightly better return for your money.

The **Canyon Village Market Place** ❶, at the Market Plaza 1 mi. west of Mather Point on the main road, has a deli counter with the cheapest eats in the park, a wide selection of groceries, a camping supplies department, and enough Grand Canyon apparel to clothe each member of your extended family with a commemorative gift. (☎ 638-2262. Sandwiches $2-4. Open daily in summer 7am-8:30pm; deli open 7am-6pm.) The well-stocked **Canyon Cafe** ❶, across from the General Store, offers a wider variety of food than the deli. (Hamburgers $3. Pizza $3.50-5. Dinners $5-7. Open daily 6:30am-9pm.) **Maswik Cafeteria** ❶, in Maswik Lodge, serves a variety of grill food, country favorites, Mexican specialties, and healthy alternatives in a wood-paneled cafeteria atmosphere. (Hot entrees $6-7. Sandwiches $3-5. Open daily 6am-10pm.) **Bright Angel Dining Room** ❷, in Bright Angel Lodge, serves hot sandwiches for $7-9. Breakfasts run $6-7 and pricey dinner entrees range $10-15. (☎ 638-2631. Open daily 6:30am-10pm.) Just out the door of the dining room, the **Soda Fountain** ❶ at Bright Angel Lodge chills eight flavors of ice cream and stocks a variety of snack-bar sandwiches. (1 scoop $2. Open daily 8am-8pm.)

From your first glimpse of the canyon, you may feel a compelling desire to see it from the inside, an enterprise harder than it looks. Even those young of heart and body should remember that an easy downhill hike can become a nightmarish 50° incline on the return journey: plan on taking twice as long to ascend than you took descending. Also keep in mind that the lower you go, the hotter it gets; when it's 85°F on the rim, it's around 100°F at Indian Gardens and around 110°F at Phantom Ranch. Heat stroke, the greatest threat to any hiker, is marked by a monstrous headache and red, sweatless skin. *For a day hike, you must take at least a gallon of water per person; drink at least a liter per hr. hiking upwards under the hot sun.* Apply sunscreen regularly. Hiking boots or sneakers with excellent tread are also necessary—the trails are steep, and every year several careless hikers take what locals morbidly call "the 12-second tour." Poor preparation and over-exertion greatly magnify the risks of Canyon hiking. A list of safety tips can be found in *The Guide.* Speak with a ranger before embarking on a hike—they may have important info about the trail. Hiking down to the river and back to the rim in the same day is discouraged by rangers. Resting at a campground is recommended, get a backcountry permit. Parents should think twice before bringing children more than 1 mi. down any trail both for the child's safety and to dwarf any motivation for later revenge.

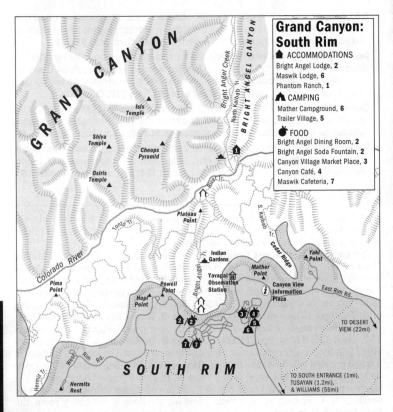

Grand Canyon: South Rim

🏠 ACCOMMODATIONS
Bright Angel Lodge, **2**
Maswik Lodge, **6**
Phantom Ranch, **1**

🏕 CAMPING
Mather Campground, **6**
Trailer Village, **5**

🍎 FOOD
Bright Angel Dining Room, **2**
Bright Angel Soda Fountain, **2**
Canyon Village Market Place, **3**
Canyon Café, **4**
Maswik Cafeteria, **7**

THE DESERT

🥾 HIKING & BACKPACKING

Although the Grand Canyon experience for the majority of park visitors involves stepping out of an air-conditioned tour bus, walking eagerly to the rim with camera in hand, enjoying the views, snapping a few keepsake shots, and then retreating to the bus before beads of sweat begin to form, there are many more invigorating and exciting ways to enjoy the Canyon's grandeur. Outdoor recreation in the park focuses mainly on hiking and backpacking, though commercial outfits provide services like mule rides, rafting, and flightseeing.

Hiking into the Grand Canyon reveals the individual beauty of the countless colorful cliffs, peaks, and mesas that together comprise the vast canyon-rim views. Most trails descend into the canyon, with disparate rates of descent and different levels of trail-maintenance. Rangers present a variety of free, informative **talks** and **guided hikes;** details are listed in *The Guide.* Said rangers will also gladly offer advice regarding trail guides and maps; the *Official Guide to Hiking the Grand Canyon* published by the Grand Canyon Association is the preferred choice.

For most backpackers, a multi-day trek through the Grand Canyon is an experience unlike any other. After combating stifling heat, scarce water, and drastic elevation changes, all under the weight of a heavy pack, many backpackers will never again face so grueling an outdoor experience. Despite these difficulties, applications for **backcountry permits** far outnumber availability, especially during the summer. If you get there late in the day, you can forget about getting a permit, and plan to start earlier the next day. Camping along such popular corridor routes is limited to **designated areas.** The Park Service divides the park into use areas, each with restrictions on camping and recreation. Much of the park remains inaccessible to trekkers because of cliffs and other impassable terrain. The footbridge spanning the Colorado River near Phantom Ranch is the only **river crossing,** making the ranch a necessary stop when traveling rim to rim. **Through-hiking** from the South to the North Rim generally connects either the Bright Angel or South Kaibab Trail with the North Kaibab Trail, covering 21-23 mi. with 10,000 ft. of elevation change. All overnight trips require a **backcountry permit** ($10 per group, $5 per person), obtainable at the Backcountry Information Center next to the Maswik Lodge (P.O. Box 129, Grand Canyon, AZ 86023; fax ☎928-638-2125; www.nps.gov/grca). Permits are available on the 1st of the month, four months before the proposed hike (e.g. July permits available March 1). Requests should include the proposed route, campsites, license plate numbers, group size, and contact info.

Rim Trail (11 mi. one-way, 4-6hr.). With only a mild elevation change (about 200 ft.) and the constant security of the nearby shuttle, the Rim Trail is excellent for hikers seeking a tame way to see the Canyon. The trail follows the shuttle bus routes along Hermit Rd. past the Grand Canyon Village to Mather Point. The Rim Trail covers both paved and unpaved ground, with 8 viewpoints along Hermit Rd. and 3 east of it. Bring plenty of water, as little is available along the trail.

Bright Angel Trail (up to 18 mi. round-trip, 1-2 days). Bright Angel's frequent switchbacks and refreshing water stations make it the into-the-canyon choice of moderate hikers. The trail departs from the Rim Trail near the western edge of the Grand Canyon Village, and the first 1-2 mi. of the trail generally attract droves of day hikers eager to try just a taste of canyon descent. Rest houses are strategically stationed 1.5 and 3 mi. from the rim, each with water between May and Sept. Indian Gardens, 4.5 mi. down, offers restrooms, picnic tables, 15 backcountry campsites open year-round, and blessed shade. From rim to river, the trail drops 4420 ft. Although spread over 9 mi., the round-trip is too strenuous for a day hike. The **River Trail** (1.7 mi.) runs along the river, connecting the Bright Angel Trail with the South Kaibab Trail.

South Kaibab Trail (7 mi. one-way to Phantom Ranch, 4-5 hr. descent). Those seeking a more challenging hike down might consider this route. Beginning at Yaki Pt. (7260 ft.), Kaibab is trickier, steeper, and lacks shade or water, but it rewards the intrepid with a better view of the canyon. Day hikes to Cedar Ridge (3 mi. round-trip; toilet facilities available) and Skeleton Point (6 mi. round-trip) are reasonable only for experienced, well-conditioned hikers, due to the trail's steep grade. Many hikers believe that the best route is to descend the South Kaibab Trail (4-5hr.) and come back up the Bright Angel (7-8hr.) the following day. The elevation change from trailhead to river is 4880 ft.

Grandview Trail (6.4 mi. round-trip to the Mesa). The costs of hauling ore up to Grandview Point (7400 ft.) from Horseshoe Mesa (4800 ft.) along the Hopi Indian-built Grandview Trail proved too great for turn-of-the-century miners. Hiking boots are a must. Backpackers can continue a steep 1.8 mi. to the Tonto Trail junction and follow the Tonto to typical canyon-floor destinations like Bright Angel Campground or Phantom Ranch. Expect a full day of hiking to Horseshoe Mesa and back.

Hermit Trail (9.3 mi. one-way to the river). Embarking from the Hermit Trailhead at Hermit's Rest (6640 ft.), this strenuous route descends the Supai cliffs. The Hermit Trail offers views of the West Rim. Going all the way to the Colorado is 9.3 mi.; hikers are advised to allow at least 7hr. to reach the overnight camping area, Hermit Creek (7.8 mi.). Day hikers should not go beyond Santa Maria Springs, 2.5 mi. down the trail.

THE DESERT

Tonto Trail (up to 95 mi.). Threading its way along the entire length of the Tonto Platform, the solid sandstone Tonto Trail travels a total of 95 mi. and connects all of the other rim-to-river. The trail is a rugged, wilderness path and requires route-finding. Most hikers use Tonto to connect other routes. There are 4.5 mi. of the trail between the Bright Angel and South Kaibab Trails, 21.3 mi between S. Kaibab and Grandview Trails. Several creeks cutting through the Tonto Platform provide year-round water.

◪ OTHER OUTDOOR ACTIVITIES

Beyond using your feet, there are other ways to conquer the canyon. **Mule trips** from the South Rim are expensive and booked up to one year in advance, although cancellations do occur. (☎303-297-2757. Day trip to Plateau Point 6 mi. down the Bright Angel Trail $127, overnight including lodging at Phantom Ranch and all meals $343 per person.) Mule trips from the North Rim are cheaper and more readily available. (☎435-679-8665. 8hr. day trip to Roaring Springs waterfall $95). Looking up at the Grand Canyon from a **whitewater raft** is also popular, yet pricey. Trips into the Grand Canyon proper vary in length from a week to 18 days; book far in advance. The *Trip Planner* lists several commercial guides; check the park website for info. If the views from the rim fail to astound you, see a doctor or try the higher vantages provided by the park's many **flightseeing** companies, all located at the Grand Canyon Airport outside of Tuyasan. **Grand Canyon Airlines** flies 45min. canyon tours hourly in summer. (☎866-235-9422. $75, children $45. Reservations recommended, but walk-ins generally available. Discount for lunchtime tours, 11am-2pm.) Flying smaller planes on a wider range of trips, **Air Grand Canyon** offers ½=1½hr. flights. (☎800-247-4726. $74-174.) Both airlines team up with Wilderness River Adventures to offer one-day combination flightseeing/rafting tours. For a rapid vertical thrill, check out the popular helicopter flights from **Papillon Grand Canyon Helicopters.** Tours of the Canyon depart as frequently as every 30min. between 8am and 5pm. (☎800-528-2418. 30min. tours $105, children $95. 50min. tours $175, kids $155.) Both **Scenic Airlines** (☎800-634-6801) and **Air Vegas Airlines** (☎800-255-7474) offer flight/hotel/canyon tour packages out of Las Vegas's northern airport. For a list of flight companies in the park, write the Grand Canyon Chamber of Commerce, Box 3007, Grand Canyon, AZ 86023.

THE DESERT

INDEX

WHO WE ARE

A NEW LET'S GO FOR 2003

With a sleeker look and innovative new content, we have revamped the entire series to reflect more than ever the needs and interests of the independent traveler. Here are just some of the improvements you will notice when traveling with the new *Let's Go*.

MORE PRICE OPTIONS

Still the best resource for budget travelers, *Let's Go* recognizes that everyone needs the occasional indulgence. Our "Big Splurges" indicate establishments that are actually worth those extra pennies (pulas, pesos, or pounds), and price-level symbols (❶ ❷ ❸ ❹ ❺) allow you to quickly determine whether an accommodation or restaurant will break the bank. We may have diversified, but we'll never lose our budget focus—"Hidden Deals" reveal the best-kept travel secrets.

BEYOND THE TOURIST EXPERIENCE

Our Alternatives to Touism chapter offers ideas on immersing yourself in a new community through study, work, or volunteering.

AN INSIDER'S PERSPECTIVE

As always, every item is written and researched by our on-site writers. This year we have highlighted more viewpoints to help you gain an even more thorough understanding of the places you are visiting.

IN RECENT NEWS. *Let's Go* correspondents around the globe report back on current regional issues that may affect you as a traveler.

CONTRIBUTING WRITERS. Respected scholars and former *Let's Go* writers discuss topics on society and culture, going into greater depth than the usual guidebook summary.

THE LOCAL STORY. From the Parisian monk toting a cell phone to the Russian *babushka* confronting capitalism, *Let's Go* shares its revealing conversations with local personalities—a unique glimpse of what matters to real people.

FROM THE ROAD. Always helpful and sometimes downright hilarious, our researchers share useful insights on the typical (and atypical) travel experience.

SLIMMER SIZE

Don't be fooled by our new, smaller size. *Let's Go* is still packed with invaluable travel advice, but now it's easier to carry with a more compact design.

FORTY-THREE YEARS OF WISDOM

For over four decades *Let's Go* has provided the most up-to-date information on the hippest cafes, the most pristine beaches, and the best routes from border to border. It all started in 1960 when a few well-traveled students at Harvard University handed out a 20-page mimeographed pamphlet of their tips on budget travel to passengers on student charter flights to Europe. From humble beginnings, *Let's Go* has grown to cover six continents and *Let's Go: Europe* still reigns as the world's best-selling travel guide. This year we've beefed up our coverage of Latin America with *Let's Go: Costa Rica* and *Let's Go: Chile;* on the other side of the globe, we've added *Let's Go: Thailand* and *Let's Go: Hawaii.* Our new guides bring the total number of titles to 61, each infused with the spirit of adventure that travelers around the world have come to count on.

MAP INDEX

MAP LEGEND

	Zoo		Amusement Park		Cave		
Hospital		Airport		Museum		Gate or Entrance	
Police		Bus Station		Hotel/Hostel		Golf Course	
Post Office		Train Station		Camping		Mission	
Tourist Office		SUBWAY STATION		Food & Drink		Ski Resort	
Bank		Ferry Landing		Beach		Trailhead	
Service		Church		Arts & Entertainment		Movie Studio	
Site or Point of Interest		Observatory		Nightlife		State Parks	
Boat Ramp		Picnic Ground		Mountain Pass		Parking	
Theater		Castle/Fort		Internet Café		Pedestrian Zone	
Library		Mountain		Winery		Stairs	
Waterfall		Ranger Station		Border Crossing		The Let's Go compass always points NORTH	